A PRACTICAL
CHINESE-ENGLISH DICTIONARY
FOR CSL LEARNERS

汉英双解对外汉语
常用重点难点词语
实用词典

朱丽云　林珍珍　钱　炜　■ 主编

復旦大學出版社

内容提要

《汉英双解对外汉语常用重点难点词语实用词典》根据《汉语国际教育用音节汉字词汇等级划分》(国家标准·应用解读本)及对外汉语教学的要求和实践经验,系统梳理对外汉语教学中的普及化等级即一、二、三级词汇及部分中级词汇,从中选取约1500个重点、难点词语,通过分析其语境语用条件、语意轻重、感情色彩、词语搭配,以及词义辨析、对错句比较等,指出词语在句子中的具体用法,助力汉语作为第二语言的学习者掌握这些词语,提高词语运用的准确性。

本词典从汉语词语运用的文化、思维入手,配以英语翻译,使外国学习者能更直接地理解汉语词语的文化背景和汉民族的思维习惯,从而能更快、更透彻地理解并掌握词语的意义和使用方法,有效提高学习汉语的效果,提升汉语的实际应用水平。

本词典收词精当,释义和分析简明扼要,例句充足实用,是汉语作为第二语言教学和学习的必备工具书。

Abstract

This dictionary selects some 1,500 basic and common Chinese words from the impossibly vast Chinese vocabulary for definition, description and illustration. The choice is based both on the *Chinese Proficiency Grading Standards for International Chinese Language Education* and on the practical demands and experiences the compilers have acquired in their past decades of teaching at home and abroad. The dictionary aims to enhance the accuracy of people in their efforts to learn Chinese as a second language and improve their fluency in the application of the included words through characterization and contextualization. To achieve these goals, enough attention is given to collocations of words as well as the fine differences between phonologically or orthographically similar words. The dictionary provides English translation, making it much easier for the intended users of this dictionary to understand precisely and effectively how native speakers of Chinese typically think and express themselves in real-life scenarios.

The thoughtful selection of every Chinese word, with their clear and concise definition and illustration, makes this dictionary an ideal tool in the study of Chinese as a second language.

编写人员

汉语主编	朱丽云
副主编	王明华　吴　坚　黄灵红
编写者	朱丽云　唐　莉　张　莹　胡彩敏　陈佳宏　王佳音　宋　玲 任　珊　万洁华　郑　颖　祁　青
英语主编	林珍珍　钱　炜
副主编	应娅舒　张　航
翻译者	宋　倩　赵　欣　龚庆华　王姗姗　葛黎妮　白丹娜　庄华萍

Editorial Team

Editor-in-Chief for Chinese: Zhu Liyun

Deputy Editors-in-Chief: Wang Minghua, Wu Jian, Huang Linghong

Editors: Zhu Liyun, Tang Li, Zhang Ying, Hu Caimin, Chen Jiahong, Wang Jiayin, Song Ling, Ren Shan, Wan Jiehua, Zheng Ying, Qi Qing

Editors-in-Chief for English: Lin Zhenzhen, Qian Wei

Deputy Editors-in-Chief: Ying Yashu, Zhang Hang

Translators: Song Qian, Zhao Xin, Gong Qinghua, Wang Shanshan, Lini Ge Polin, Dayna Bailey, Zhuang Huaping

目录 | Contents

凡例	Editorial Guide	1
编写说明	A Guide to the Use of the Dictionary	4
词条目录	Contents of Words	11
词条正文	The Dictionary A-Z	1—709
附录 量词的用法	Appendix：Quantifiers	710
主要参考文献	References	734

凡 例

词条选收

本词典共收录1500多个词条（包括量词100余条）。词条词语皆选自《汉语国际教育用音节汉字词汇等级划分》词汇大纲，涵盖全部普及化等级词汇和部分中级词汇中的重点、难点词语（多为常用副词、介词、连词、助词以及近义词实用辨析等）。该词汇大纲2010年10月由北京语言大学出版社出版，得到海内外100多位汉语教授、汉学家、学者的认可。

词条排列

词条词语按拼音字母次序排列，便于检索。

1. 相同汉字字形词条按拼音字母次序排列，如"着"有四个发音，按拼音次序分别排列四次。
2. "一"的词条发音根据《汉语国际教育用音节汉字词汇等级划分》词汇大纲按拼音及其四声（阴、阳、上、去）次序排列。
3. 发轻声的词语，拼音上不标音调。

词条释义

1. 词条词语按常用的不同词性用法列出。
2. 每一词条尽可能列出所选词语现在常用的义项，以利汉语学习者全面掌握词语用途。
3. 词语每一义项通常配有二至三个例句。除了个别词语，例句所用词语一般为普及化等级词汇全部和部分中级词汇，句子内容简单易懂，易为学习汉语的外国朋友接受、模仿。

"说明"部分

本词典的实用性着重体现在词条的"说明"部分。"说明"部分的内容着重阐述词条词语的词义、使用时的语用条件（包括语义选择、搭配和语体、感情色彩、语境要求）、近义词辨析异同等方面，重点突出词语应用的实际要求，以保证词语应用时的正确性。

部分词条结合外国人学习汉语时特别容易出现的错误，还列有少量常见的错句（错句前用星号"＊"标示），同时列出与其相对的正确句子。通过对比，让学习者感性、清楚地了解错在哪里，并知道怎么用才是对的。

"参见"

"参见"用"→"引出，指示本词条词语之近义词的页码。如果有两个以上的近义词，则这些近义词按拼音字母的次序排列。近义词辨析内容在后一个词语的"说明"里。

Editorial Guide

Words Chosen for Inclusion

This dictionary lists a total of over 1,500 words which are taken from the program of vocabulary in *The Classification of Syllabic Words of Chinese for the Use of International Education* (known as the National Standards), an academic work published in 2010 by Beijing Languages University Publishing House and acclaimed by over 100 Chinese and foreign professors, scholars, and Sinologists.

The Listing of Words

To facilitate the search, all the words are listed in accordance with the Chinese pin-yin system in an alphabetic order.

1. Chinese words of the same spelling are listed according to the alphabetic order. The word "着," for instance, has four different pronunciations, and so it is listed four times in line with the pin-yin system.
2. "一 (one)," as an entry, follows the pin-yin system with four tones, that is, level, rising, falling and entering.
3. Words that are pronounced softly follow the pin-yin system too, but not the tone system.

How Words Are Explained

1. Every word is classified in terms of their parts of speech.
2. Every effort is made to list the various meanings in common use for every word so that students of Chinese will have a comprehensive grasp of the listed word.
3. Every meaning of every word is illustrated by two or three examples. With the exception of a few words, words used for explanation belong either to the primary-level words for popularization or to the middle level. As a result, all the examples are easy to understand, internalize and model upon by foreign students learning the Chinese language.

Notes

"Notes," found at the end of every word, give full expression to the practical nature of this dictionary. They highlight the meaning of every word, the conditions under which the word in question is used, including the choice of its meaning, its collocation with other words, its style, emotional color, and its requirement of the language environment. The emphases are laid on the practical demands when a word is applied so as to ensure their accuracy.

Some entries list a few mistakes that foreign students are likely to make. So, side by side with the erroneous sentences (marked with an asterisk " * "), one will find their corresponding correct sentences. The comparisons will enable students to actually see a mistake while clearly knowing how to correct it, thus ensuring that they will use it correctly in the future.

References

"Reference" (→) shows the page number for a synonym. If there are two or more synonyms, they will be listed alphabetically in the pin-yin system. The content of the synonym analysis is found in the Notes for the latter word.

编写说明

编写缘起

　　1986 年,原杭州大学外办汉语教学中心学习汉语的德国留学生强烈希望有一本他们看得懂、能教给他们正确运用有关词语、具有实际指导作用的工具书。两年后,在他们离开学校时,给老师留下的期待是:等着看到老师写出一本学习汉语的外国人看得懂、有实用指导意义的书,帮助他们学习汉语。

　　改革开放以后,外国人学习汉语方兴未艾。从那时起,我们尽心尽力投入汉语作为第二语言的教学,对汉语作为第二语言教学的认识、方法、效果进行了积极的探索和研究。

　　2009 年,我们以对外汉语教师为对象,编写了《实用对外汉语重点难点词语教学词典》(以下简称《教学词典》),由北京大学出版社出版。《教学词典》不但得到了对外汉语教师,尤其是刚入行对外汉语教学的新老师的欢迎,而且也引起了学习汉语的外国留学生的注意。这是因为书市上虽然有世界各国语言与汉语对照的双语词典,但是指导汉语常用词汇实用的工具书所见不多。所以,我们在《教学词典》的前提下,又编写了这本《汉英双解对外汉语常用重点难点词语实用词典》(以下简称《实用词典》)。

词条选用

　　《实用词典》收集的词语遴选于北京语言大学出版社 2010 年 10 月出版的《汉语国际教育用音节汉字词汇等级划分(国家标准·应用解读本)》(以下简称《国家标准》)词汇大纲中普及化等级词汇全部和中级词汇部分重点、难点词语,多为动词、形容词、副词、介词、助词、连词等词性的词语,尤其是副词以及介词、助词、连词等虚词。这些词语在搭配其他词语构成一个完整的句子或片段时,起着关键的作用。

　　《国家标准》是根据国家汉办和孔子学院总部提出的"学得简单、学得容易、学得快"的国际汉语教育实用要求,经过海内外 100 多位汉语语言学教授、专家、汉学家参与后确定的。在词汇吸收和等级划分上,加强了实用性。

　　1. 有些在口语上常用的词语,原来是几个词组成,现在成为一个短语,如:"不得不、不一定、差不多、教学楼、就是说、老朋友",等等。对外国人来说,记住一个短语比记住几个词语或汉字再合成去记一个短语要简单容易得多。

　　2.《国际标准》突出了单音节汉字与其他汉字的搭配能力,很重视对单音节词的吸收。这样有利于国外学习汉语者发挥联想性,体现出词汇运用的实用性。因此,本词典也根据汉语语素构词的特点,注重单音节词的选入。选入的单音节词有 270 余条。这些单音节词后,跟出与其相同语素的双音节词语就有 400 多个。例如:

　　　　热——热烈、热门、热闹、热情、热线、热心

特——特别、特地、特点、特殊、特意、特征

汉语词汇中有很多单音节词又能作为语素,组成很多双音节词语。这个单音节词与由其组成的双音节词语,在词义上会有一定的联系,掌握这个规律,能提高学习汉语词汇的效率。

"说明"的价值

词典的"说明"部分体现的是本词典的实用价值。

1. 根据词条实际运用的需要,在词条的"说明"中,对有些词条词义和运用加以补充说明。例如,副词"再"一词,表示"又一次"的意思,但实际上,它的具体用法有八九种。每一种用法,"再"的词义有所增补,与其他词语的搭配也有所要求。因此,在该词条的"说明"中,举例解释补充了九种用法,以期给学习者较大的启发,并便于他们实际运用该词进行造句。

2. 为了能让学习者正确运用词语造句,"说明"部分对有些词语的造句条件进行分析。例如,"尤其"一词,一般使用时,应有前后两个分句,前一分句表示总体情况,"尤其"常用在后一分句句首,表示引出比前面句子提到的人或事物更进一步、更突出的人或事物的个体。如果只有一个句子,"尤其"用在谓语前面,句中含有与总体情况比较更进一步的语义。

3. "说明"还从词义轻重、词义褒贬、词语搭配、语体和感情色彩、词性及语法作用等方面为"参看"的近义词进行辨析,让学习者可以从不同角度、不同视觉区分近义词,从而正确运用所学的词语。

4. 词语教学实际是运用某个词语的过程。第二语言教学者认为在句子中学习词语的效果比单独记忆词语的效果好得多。因此,"说明"部分比较突出词语运用的语境条件和句子语义条件的分析内容。例如,"顺便"一词第二个义项:② 表示趁做第一件事的方便做第二件事。用"顺便"表示这个意思造句时,句子中要显性或隐性或半隐半显地体现出"方便"的语义。例如:

(1) 你去图书馆借书,顺便帮我还一本书。

"图书馆"是"借书""还书"的同一个地方,所以请别人代为还书还是比较方便的。"去图书馆"即是前后两个分句中明显体现"方便"的语义联系。

(2) 明天我去银行换钱,顺便去一下书店。

这两个分句之间"方便"的语义联系虽然是隐性的,但却是不言而喻的,因为从常识可以推知"银行"和"书店"都是在城里、在街上的。"去银行"就得"进城"或"上街"。这"进城"或"上街"就是前后两个分句"方便"语义的隐性联系。

模仿句型

学过汉语的外国人都觉得汉语的语法比较简单,不难学,但对汉语的句子意义却又不能一下子把握住,因为现实中的语言或者说言语是很复杂多变的。是否能给汉语初学者相对固定的句型,从进行模仿造句入手? 在第二语言教学中模仿造句不失为一个较有成效的教学方法。本书从实用性出发,以词语为视点,尽可能试着给所选词语的每一用法列出常用句式,供学习者参考模仿。

英语翻译

本书是汉英双解的词书，翻译成英语是为了便于懂英语的汉语学习者更好地掌握这本词典的功能，更直接、更容易明白怎么样使用某个词语，提高学习汉语的效率。

首先，对于英语翻译，在保证翻译准确性的前提下，我们尽可能选用高频词。例如，"大方"用作形容词，第三个词义是"表示衣服、装饰等的式样、颜色不俗气"。我们把"不俗气"翻译为"in good taste"，如此，既准确传达词义，又简单易懂。

其次，当汉语词文为了阐明词语的用法，涉及语法理论的长句时，为了便于学习者理解，我们尽可能采用短句或分句来翻译这些长句。

本书的编写思路全部来自对外汉语教学课堂实践。几十年的对外汉语教学，让我们对汉语作为第二语言教学，在词语教学思路、策略、重点和具体教学方法上都有了新的了解、认识和经验。但是，这些还远远不够。改革开放以来，汉语作为第二语言教学突飞猛进，世界各国越来越需要汉语教学，也越来越需要深入、开拓汉语作为语言教学的研究。限于水平，本书必定会有很多疏漏和不足。我们恳请广大读者多多提出宝贵意见，给予指正，对此我们不胜感激。

作为本书的编撰者，我们诚挚地感谢复旦大学出版社的大力支持。

《汉英双解对外汉语重点难点词语实用词典》编委

2023 年 11 月 28 日

A Guide to the Use of This Dictionary

Why This Dictionary

Back in 1986, some German students who were studying Chinese at the Chinese Learning Center operated by the Foreign Affairs Office of Hangzhou University expressed their strong desire to have a dictionary that they could easily understand and that taught them to use Chinese words correctly. Two years later, when they left for home, they again expressed their expectations for their teachers to produce such a dictionary.

When China entered the new era of reform and opening-up to the outside world in the 1980s, foreigners' passion for learning Chinese surged to new heights. It was then that we teachers of Chinese as a second language committed ourselves to searching for a new approach to the teaching of Chinese as a second language with more sophisticated methods and better results.

In 2009, targeting teachers of Chinese as a second language, we wrote *A Practical Dictionary for the Teaching of Important and Difficult Words to Foreign Chinese Learners* (hereinafter referred to as *The Teaching Dictionary*). It was published by the Peking University Press. To our pleasure, *The Teaching Dictionary* was not only embraced by teachers of Chinese as a second language, especially by those who newly joined the profession, but also caught the attention and aroused the interest of foreign students learning Chinese in China. This is understandable. Even though bilingual (between Chinese and another language) dictionaries are easily available in the book market, one can hardly find any dictionary that is actually aimed at guiding foreign students in Chinese learning. And so, basing ourselves on the *The Teaching Dictionary*, we began to work on this dictionary, namely, *A Practical Chinese-English Dictionary for CSL Learners* (hereinafter referred to as *The Practical Dictionary*).

Words Chosen for Inclusion

The Practical Dictionary takes its words from the program of vocabulary in the academic work of *The Classification of Syllabic Words in Teaching Chinese as a Second Language*, which was published by the Beijing Languages University Press in October, 2010. It came to be known as *The National Standards*, a version for application and explanation. The words in the dictionary fall into two types. The first type includes all the words that should be popularized at the primary level and the second type covers a fraction of important and difficult words to be learned at the intermediate level. Words included in this dictionary are mostly verbs, adjectives, and adverbs, but special attention is given to function words such as prepositions, auxiliary words and conjunctions. These words play a vital role in arranging all other words to make complete sentences and paragraphs.

The National Standards were established by the National Office for the Chinese language (NOCL). They meet the practical requirements for teaching Chinese in international education jointly put forward by NOCL and the headquarters of the Confucius Academy. Those requirements are: simple to learn, easy to learn, and learn fast. As is said already, over 100 Chinese and foreign professors, scholars, and Sinologists were involved in the job, which helped to ensure the practical nature of vocabulary absorption and classification.

1. Some expressions that are frequently used in our oral communication, made up of several characters, are listed in this dictionary as collocational phrases, such as "不得不 (cannot help but), 不一定 (not necessarily), 差不多 (almost, nearly), 教学楼 (the classroom building), 就是说 (that is to say), 老朋友 (old friend), etc." As we know, it is much easier for a foreign student to remember a phrase than the few characters separately that comprise the phrase.

2. *The National Standards* highlight the tendency of monosyllabic Chinese characters to collocate with other Chinese characters and call for attention to absorbing monosyllabic characters. While giving expression to the practical nature of word application, this will benefit foreign students in terms of the association of ideas. That is the reason why this dictionary pays a great deal of attention to including monosyllabic words while giving due attention to the fact that the Chinese language consists of morphemes. Over 270 monosyllabic words are found in this dictionary, and when combined with dissyllabic words of the same morpheme, they make more than 400 words. For example:

热 (hot) — 热烈 (enthusiastic), 热门 (popular), 热闹 (bustling), 热情 (zealous), 热线 (hot line), 热心 (warm-hearted)

特 (special) — 特别 (special), 特地 (specially), 特点 (special features), 特殊 (special), 特意 (specially), 特征 (characteristics)

In a Chinese vocabulary, one can find a lot of monosyllables serving as morphemes to form dual-syllable words. Naturally, such monosyllabic characters and dissyllabic phrases containing them are related. Grasping this rule will enhance the efficiency of learning Chinese words.

The Value of Notes

"Notes" in this dictionary show their practical value clearly.

1. To maximize the practical value of this dictionary, we attach to most word entries "Notes," which make supplementary explanations about the meaning and usage of these words. For instance, the word "再," which means "又一次 (again)." It has eight to nine

practical uses, and so we provide examples to illustrate all the nine uses. A foreign learner will be enlightened about how to use them in practice.

2. To help a learner to use a word in a context correctly, the "Notes" analyze the conditions for using the word to make sentences. Take "尤其 (especially)" for example. The phrase usually appears in a sentence that consists of two parts, the first part showing the general situation, and the second part with "尤其" at its beginning to single out one person, thing or situation over all others. But if a statement is just one sentence, "尤其" will appear before the predicate and serve to emphasize the meaning conveyed by the predicate.

3. In dealing with every word, the "Notes" elaborate on the word's denotation and connotation, its common collocation, and its stylistic or emotional overtones, along with its grammatical function and synonym analysis. Thus the learner will be able to approach a word from different perspectives and will learn to use it correctly.

4. Teaching words is actually a process of demonstrating how to apply words in context. Teachers of a second language share the belief that learning words through comparison is far more effective than just remembering single words one by one. That is why the "Notes" highlights the importance of contextualization so that the dictionary users will be clear about the conditions under which a word appears. Take "顺便 (by the way, in passing)" for example. The word has an interesting character: its exact meaning is either obvious, or hidden or in between, as in:

(1) When you go to the library, please "顺便" return a book for me.

As we all know, the library is a place where people borrow and return books. It is obviously convenient for someone going to a library to do a favor to someone else who needs to return a book.

(2) I am going to the bank to change currency tomorrow, and "顺便" I am going to visit a bookstore.

In this example, the convenience that exists between the two events is sort of hidden. But it goes without saying that the bank and the bookstore are in the same city, and doing two things together or "顺便" means saving the person a second trip to town.

Model Sentences

Foreigners learning the Chinese language all find its grammar pretty simple and not difficult to learn. But at the same time, they find it somewhat hard to grasp the exact meaning of a sentence because the language as they find it in real life is most complicated and changes a great deal. Is it possible for us to start by providing fairly fixed sentence patterns for them to model upon? Yes, it is. As a matter of fact, getting the students to make sentences after models has proved to be one of the most effective ways of teaching Chinese as a second language. Proceeding from the need to highlight practical use, this dictionary tries its best to supply the students with the commonly-used sentence patterns so that they can make their own sentences fast.

English Translation

As the name of this dictionary shows, it features both Chinese and English for every word that is included. This is done so that students who are familiar with English will find it easier to use the dictionary. And as a result, their learning efficiency will be enhanced.

In doing the English translation, we try our best to use English words that are most frequently used while ensuring the accuracy. Take "大方 (generous, open-minded)" for example. Its third meaning "不俗气" is about the color(s) of clothes and decorations not being vulgar. We translated it as "in good taste," which is not only accurate, but easily understood as well.

Moreover, in explaining the use of a word, there is often a need to use somewhat long sentences for explanation. In order for the learners to understand readily, we often cut them into short sentences when translating these sentences.

Overall, the ideas for compiling this dictionary all come from the practice of classroom teaching. Several dozen years of teaching Chinese to foreign students has enabled us to experience and develop new understandings of how to teach Chinese to foreign students, what methods or strategies to employ, and where to lay the focal points. Even more exciting is the fact that as China enters a new era of reform and opening up to the world, the teaching of Chinese as a second language has acquired a new status, that is, the status of being an essential skill for the advance of cultural and scientific exchange between China and other countries. Inevitably, intensive researches are being conducted about how to teach Chinese as a second language. This dictionary is simply an example testifying to the new trend. As for us, the editors of this dictionary, we are well aware that there are deficiencies and even mistakes in the dictionary. Every user of this dictionary is welcome to call our attention to them so that we could further improve the dictionary in the future. Such kind criticism from our dictionary users will always be embraced with our most sincere gratitude.

For the successful publication of this dictionary, we express our sincere appreciation and gratitude to Fudan University Press.

The Editorial Team
November 28, 2023

词条目录 | Contents of Words

A

āi 挨 ··· 1
ái 挨 ·· 1
àihào 爱好 ··· 2
àihù 爱护 →P2"爱惜" ························ 2
àixī 爱惜 →P2"爱护" ························ 2
āndìng 安定 →P492"稳定" ················ 3
ānjìng 安静 →P339"宁静"、P358"平静" ··· 3
ānpái 安排 →P4"安置" ······················ 4
ānzhì 安置 →P4"安排" ······················ 4
àn 按 →P5"按照"、P530"压"、P641"照" ··· 4
ànmó 按摩 ··· 5
ànzhào 按照 →P5"按"、P554"依照" ··· 5
ànshì 暗示 ··· 5

B

bǎ 把 ·· 6
bǎwò 把握 →P638"掌握" ··················· 9
bàle 罢了 ·· 9
bái 白 ··· 9
bǎi 摆 →P145"放" ······························ 11
bàn 办 ··· 11
bànfǎ 办法 →P78"措施" ··················· 11
bāng 帮 →P12"帮助" ························ 11
bāngmáng 帮忙 →P12"帮助" ············ 12
bāngzhù 帮助 →P11"帮"、P12"帮忙" ···· 12
bāo 包 ··· 13
bāohán 包含 →P13"包括" ················ 13
bāokuò 包括 →P13"包含" ················ 13
bāozhuāng 包装 ································ 14
bǎoguì 宝贵 →P646"珍贵" ··············· 14
bǎochí 保持 →P487"维持" ··············· 14
bǎohù 保护 →P15"保卫"、P487"维护" ··· 14
bǎoliú 保留 ······································· 14

bǎowèi 保卫 →P14"保护" ················· 15
bǎoxiǎn 保险 ···································· 15
bǎoyǎng 保养 ···································· 15
bǎozhèng 保证 ·································· 16
bàoqiàn 抱歉 →P100"道歉" ············· 16
bào 爆 ··· 16
bàofā 爆发 ·· 16
bēi 背 ·· 16
bēishāng 悲伤 →P17"悲痛" ·············· 17
bēitòng 悲痛 →P17"悲伤" ················ 17
běibiān 北边 →P17"北方" ················· 17
běifāng 北方 →P17"北边" ················· 17
bèi 背 ·· 18
bèijǐng 背景 ······································ 18
bèi 被 →P231"叫"、P389"让" ·········· 18
běn 本 →P21"本来" ·························· 21
běnlái 本来 →P21"本"、P610"原来" ··· 21
bǐ 比 →P25"比较" ···························· 22
bǐjiào 比较 →P22"比" ······················ 25
bìdìng 必定 →P26"必然"、P555"一定" ··· 26
bìrán 必然 →P26"必定" ··················· 26
bìxū 必须 →P27"必需" ····················· 27
bìxū 必需 →P27"必须" ····················· 27
bìjìng 毕竟 →P97"到底"、P248"究竟" ··· 28
biānzhì 编制 ····································· 28
biànchéng 变成 ································· 29
biàndòng 变动 →P29"变化" ············· 29
biànhuà 变化 →P29"变动"、P153"改变"
·· 29
biàn 便 →P250"就" ·························· 30
biànlùn 辩论 →P648"争论" ············· 31
biǎodá 表达 →P32"表明"、P32"表示" ··· 31
biǎomiàn 表面 ·································· 32
biǎomíng 表明 →P31"表达"、P32"表示"
·· 32
biǎoshì 表示 →P31"表达"、P32"表明" ··· 32
biǎoxiàn 表现 →P461"体现" ············ 33

bié 别 →P34"别的"	33
biéde 别的 →P33"别"	34
bìng 并 →P35"并且"	35
bìngqiě 并且 →P35"并"、P130"而且"、P621"再说"	35
bù 不 →P315"没/没有"	36
búbì 不必 →P489"未必"	40
búbiàn 不便	40
búcuò 不错 →P187"好"	40
búdàn 不但 →P48"不仅"	41
búduàn 不断	42
búgù 不顾	42
búguò 不过 →P90"但是"、P669"只是"	42
búliào 不料	44
búlùn 不论 →P47"不管"	44
búyàojǐn 不要紧	45
búzàihu 不在乎 →P495"无所谓"	45
bùchéng 不成	45
bùdébù 不得不 →P668"只得"、P668"只好"	46
bùdéliǎo 不得了 →P304"了不得"	46
bùgǎndāng 不敢当	46
bùguǎn 不管 →P44"不论"、P240"尽管"、P494"无论"	47
bùguāng 不光	48
bùjīn 不禁	48
bùjǐn 不仅 →P41"不但"	48
bùmiǎn 不免 →P334"难免"	49
bùrán 不然 →P150"否则"、P543"要不"	50
bùrú 不如 →P315"没/没有"	51
bùxíng 不行	52
bùyídìng 不一定	52
bùyóude 不由得	53
bùzěnmeyàng 不怎么样	53
bùzhí 不值	54
bùzú 不足	54

C

cái 才	55
cǎinà 采纳 →P56"采取"	56
cǎiqǔ 采取 →P56"采纳"、P56"采用"	56
cǎiyòng 采用 →P56"采取"	56
cǎisè 彩色 →P401"色彩"	57
cānguān 参观 →P144"访问"	57
cáng 藏 →P127"躲"	57
cāozòng 操纵 →P278"控制"	58
céng 曾 →P58"曾经"	58
céngjīng 曾经 →P58"曾"、P565"已经"	58
chà 差	59
chàbuduō 差不多	59
chà(yì)diǎnr 差(一)点儿 →P206"几乎"	60
cháng 常 →P61"常常"	60
chángcháng 常常 →P60"常"、P244"经常"、P415"时常"、P468"通常"、P483"往往"	61
chángnián 常年	61
chǎngdì 场地 →P63"场所"	62
chǎnghé 场合 →P62"场面"	62
chǎngmiàn 场面 →P62"场合"	62
chǎngsuǒ 场所 →P62"场地"	63
cháo 朝 →P483"往"、P512"向"	63
cháo 潮	63
chǎozuò 炒作	64
chéng 成 →P66"成为"	64
chéngjì 成绩 →P65"成就"	65
chéngjiù 成就 →P65"成绩"	65
chénglì 成立 →P224"建立"	65
chéngwéi 成为 →P64"成"	66
chéngxìn 诚信	66
chíxù 持续 →P217"继续"	66
chíyǒu 持有	66
chōng 冲	67
chōngtū 冲突 →P314"矛盾"	67
chōngdiàn 充电	67
chōngfèn 充分 →P68"充足"	68
chōngzú 充足 →P68"充分"	68
chóngfù 重复 →P139"反复"	68
chòng 冲	69
chūfā 出发 →P116"动身"	69
chūlù 出路 →P70"出息"	69
chūshǒu 出手	70
chūxi 出息 →P69"出路"	70
chū 初	70
chūbù 初步	71
chúfēi 除非 →P671"只有"	71
chúle 除了	72
chǔfèn 处分 →P72"处理"	72
chǔlǐ 处理 →P72"处分"	72
chǔyú 处于	73
chuàngbàn 创办 →P74"创立"	74

chuànglì 创立 →P74"创办"	74
chuàngzào 创造 →P134"发明"	74
chuī 吹	74
chúncuì 纯粹 →P75"纯洁"	74
chúnjié 纯洁 →P74"纯粹"	75
cóng 从 →P77"从来"、P594"由"、P688"自"	75
cóng'ér 从而 →P586"因而"	76
cónglái 从来 →P75"从"、P513"向来"	77
cóngqián 从前 →P182"过去"、P572"以前"	78
cóngshì 从事	78
cuòshī 措施 →P11"办法"	78

D

dādàng 搭档	79
dāyìng 答应	79
dádào 达到 →P97"到达"	79
dáfù 答复 →P202"回答"	79
dǎ 打	80
dǎbāo 打包	81
dǎchē 打车	82
dǎdī 打的	82
dǎfa 打发	82
dǎjiāodào 打交道	82
dǎrǎo 打扰 →P311"麻烦"	83
dǎsuàn 打算 →P214"计划"	83
dǎtīng 打听	83
dǎzào 打造	83
dǎzhāohu 打招呼	84
dàdà 大大	84
dàdū 大都 →P125"多半"	84
dàfāng 大方 →P269"慷慨"	84
dàgài 大概 →P86"大约"、P86"大致"	85
dàliàng 大量 →P85"大批"	85
dàpī 大批 →P85"大量"	85
dàyuē 大约 →P85"大概"、P86"大致"	86
dàzhì 大致 →P85"大概"、P86"大约"	86
dāi 呆	87
dài 代 →P88"代替"、P462"替"	87
dàitì 代替 →P87"代"、P462"替"	88
dānxīn 担心 →P88"担忧"、P641"着急"	88
dānyōu 担忧 →P88"担心"	88
dān 单 →P666"只"	88

dānchún 单纯 →P221"简单"	89
dāndú 单独 →P118"独自"	89
dàn 但 →P90"但是"	89
dànshì 但是 →P42"不过"、P89"但"、P273"可是"、P388"然而"	90
dāng 当 →P622"在"	91
dāngdì 当地	93
dāngnián 当年	93
dāngqián 当前	94
dāngrán 当然 →P693"自然"	94
dàng 当	94
dàngzuò 当作	95
dǎo 倒	96
dào 到	96
dàodá 到达 →P79"达到"	97
dàodǐ 到底 →P28"毕竟"、P248"究竟"、P677"终于"	97
dào 倒 →P385"却"	98
dàolǐ 道理 →P296"理由"	100
dàoqiàn 道歉 →P16"抱歉"	100
dé 得	101
déle 得了 →P441"算了"	101
déyì 得意	101
de 地 →P103"的"	102
de 的 →P102"地"、P106"得"、P654"之"	103
……dehuà ……的话	106
de 得 →P103"的"	106
……dehěn ……得很	108
děi 得	109
děng 等 →P110"等待"、P110"等候"	109
děngdài 等待 →P109"等"、P110"等候"	110
děnghòu 等候 →P109"等"、P110"等待"	110
díquè 的确 →P387"确实"	111
dǐkàng 抵抗 →P140"反抗"	111
diǎn 点	112
diào 掉 →P115"丢"	112
dǐng 顶 →P702"最"	113
dìng 订 →P114"定"	113
dìng 定 →P113"订"	114
diū 丢 →P112"掉"	115
dǒng 懂 →P324"明白"、P662"知道"	115
dòngjī 动机 →P328"目的"	115

dòngshēn 动身 →P69"出发" ·········	116
dōu 都 →P382"全"、P544"也" ·······	116
dútè 独特 →P457"特别" ············	118
dúzì 独自 →P89"单独" ·············	118
dùguò 度过 →P119"渡过" ············	119
dùguò 渡过 →P119"度过" ············	119
duì 对 →P121"对于" ···············	119
duìyú 对于 →P119"对"、P172"关于" ···	121
duō 多 →P126"多么" ···············	123
duōbàn 多半 →P84"大都" ············	125
duōme 多么 →P123"多" ·············	126
duōshao 多少 →P213"几" ···········	126
duǒ 躲 →P57"藏" ··················	127

E

ér 而 →P130"而且" ················	129
érqiě 而且 →P36"并且"、P129"而" ····	130
èr 二 →P303"两" ··················	131
èrshǒu 二手 ······················	132

F

fā 发 ····························	133
fādá 发达 →P137"发展" ············	134
fāhuī 发挥 →P136"发扬" ············	134
fājué 发觉 →P135"发现" ············	134
fāmíng 发明 →P74"创造"、P135"发现" ·········	134
fāxiàn 发现 →P134"发觉"、P134"发明" ·········	135
fāyáng 发扬 →P134"发挥" ···········	136
fāzhǎn 发展 →P134"发达" ···········	137
fánshì 凡是 ······················	137
fán 烦 ··························	138
fánhuá 繁华 →P138"繁荣" ···········	138
fánróng 繁荣 →P138"繁华" ···········	138
fǎn 反 ··························	139
fǎn'ér 反而 →P509"相反" ············	139
fǎnfù 反复 →P68"重复" ·············	139
fǎnkàng 反抗 →P111"抵抗" ···········	140
fǎnyìng 反应 →P141"反映" ···········	141
fǎnyìng 反映 →P141"反应" ···········	141
fǎnzhèng 反正 ····················	142
fāngfǎ 方法 →P143"方式" ···········	143
fāngshì 方式 →P143"方法" ···········	143
fǎngfú 仿佛 →P191"好像"、P439"似乎" ·········	144
fǎngwèn 访问 →P57"参观" ···········	144
fàng 放 →P11"摆" ·················	145
fēi…bù 非…不 ····················	146
fēicháng 非常 →P196"很"、P414"十分" ·········	147
fèi 费 ··························	147
fēnbié 分别 →P148"分离"、P381"区别" ·········	147
fēnlí 分离 →P147"分别" ·············	148
fēnmíng 分明 →P325"明明" ···········	148
fēnfù 吩咐 →P682"嘱咐" ·············	148
fēngguāng 风光 →P149"风景" ·········	149
fēngjǐng 风景 →P149"风光"、P246"景色" ·········	149
fēngxiǎn 风险 →P484"危险" ··········	149
fǒuzé 否则 →P50"不然" ·············	150
fú 服 ···························	150

G

gāi 该 →P588"应" ·················	152
gǎibiàn 改变 →P29"变化" ············	153
gǎigé 改革 →P155"改造" ·············	154
gǎijìn 改进 →P154"改善" ············	154
gǎishàn 改善 →P154"改进" ···········	154
gǎizào 改造 →P154"改革" ············	155
gǎizhèng 改正 →P247"纠正" ··········	155
gàikuò 概括 →P695"综合" ············	155
gān 干 ··························	155
gāncuì 干脆 ······················	156
gānrǎo 干扰 →P157"干涉" ············	156
gānshè 干涉 →P156"干扰"、P157"干预" ·········	157
gānyù 干预 →P157"干涉" ·············	157
gǎn 赶 ··························	157
gǎnjǐn 赶紧 →P158"赶快"、P158"赶忙" ·········	158
gǎnkuài 赶快 →P158"赶紧"、P158"赶忙" ·········	158
gǎnmáng 赶忙 →P158"赶紧"、P158"赶快" ·········	158
gǎndào 感到 →P159"感觉" ············	158

gǎndòng 感动 →P208"激动" ………… 159
gǎnjué 感觉 →P158"感到"、P159"感受"
　………………………………………… 159
gǎnshòu 感受 →P159"感觉" ……… 159
gǎnxìngqù 感兴趣 ………………… 160
gàn 干 →P706"做" ………………… 161
gànmá 干吗 ………………………… 161
gāng 刚 →P162"刚才"、P162"刚刚" …… 161
gāngcái 刚才 →P161"刚"、P162"刚刚"
　………………………………………… 162
gānggāng 刚刚 →P161"刚"、P162"刚才"
　………………………………………… 162
gǎo 搞 →P339"弄"、P706"做" …… 163
gè 各 →P318"每" …………………… 164
gègè 各个 …………………………… 164
gěi 给 ………………………………… 164
gēnběn 根本 →P207"基本" ………… 165
gēnjù 根据 →P257"据"、P552"依据" …… 166
gēn 跟 →P193"和"、P470"同"、P608"与"
　………………………………………… 166
gèng 更 →P168"更加" ……………… 167
gèngjiā 更加 →P167"更" …………… 168
gōngfu 工夫 →P169"功夫" ………… 169
gōngfu 功夫 →P169"工夫" ………… 169
gōngbù 公布 →P527"宣布" ………… 169
gōutōng 沟通 ……………………… 169
gòu 够 ……………………………… 169
guài 怪 →P366"奇怪"、P467"挺" … 170
guàibude 怪不得 →P333"难怪" …… 171
guān 关 …………………………… 171
guānhuái 关怀 →P172"关心"、P173"关注"
　………………………………………… 171
guānxīn 关心 →P171"关怀"、P173"关注"
　………………………………………… 172
guānyú 关于 →P121"对于"、P598"有关"、
　P674"至于" ………………………… 172
guānzhù 关注 →P171"关怀"、P172"关心"
　………………………………………… 173
guǎn 管 →P175"管理" …………… 174
guǎnlǐ 管理 →P174"管" …………… 175
guāng 光 →P666"只" ……………… 175
guǎngfàn 广泛 →P176"广阔" …… 176
guǎngkuò 广阔 →P176"广泛" …… 176
guī 归 →P201"回" ………………… 177

guīdìng 规定 →P177"规范"、P178"规则"
　………………………………………… 177
guīfàn 规范 →P177"规定" ………… 177
guīzé 规则 →P177"规定" ………… 178
guǒrán 果然 ……………………… 179
guò 过 ……………………………… 179
guòdù 过度 ………………………… 181
guòdù 过渡 ………………………… 181
guòmǐn 过敏 ……………………… 181
guòqù 过去 →P78"从前" ………… 182
guòyú 过于 ………………………… 183

H

hái 还 →P603"又" ………………… 184
háishì 还是 →P204"或者" ………… 185
hàipà 害怕 →P344"怕" …………… 186
hán 含 ……………………………… 186
hánhu 含糊 ………………………… 186
hánlěng 寒冷 →P295"冷" ………… 187
hánxuān 寒暄 ……………………… 187
hǎn 喊 →P187"喊叫"、P231"叫" … 187
hǎnjiào 喊叫 →P187"喊" ………… 187
hànyǔ 汉语 →P677"中文" ………… 187
hǎo 好 →P40"不错" ……………… 187
hǎobù 好不 ………………………… 190
hǎobùróngyì 好不容易 →P191"好容易"
　………………………………………… 190
hǎohāor 好好儿 …………………… 190
hǎoróngyì 好容易 →P190"好不容易" … 191
hǎoxiàng 好像 →P144"仿佛"、P439"似乎"
　………………………………………… 191
hé 合 ……………………………… 192
héshì 合适 →P424"适合" ………… 193
hé 和 →P166"跟"、P470"同"、P608"与"
　………………………………………… 193
héxié 和谐 →P517"协调" ………… 195
hěn 很 →P147"非常"、P209"极"、P467"挺"、
　P646"真" …………………………… 196
hěnnánshuō 很难说 ……………… 198
hòuguǒ 后果 →P236"结果" ……… 198
hòulái 后来 →P569"以后" ………… 198
hūlüè 忽略 →P199"忽视" ………… 199
hūrán 忽然 →P475"突然" ………… 199
hūshì 忽视 →P199"忽略" ………… 199

hútòngr 胡同儿 ⋯⋯⋯⋯⋯⋯⋯⋯⋯ 199	jiàqián 价钱 →P218"价格" ⋯⋯⋯⋯⋯ 218
hùxiāng 互相 →P510"相互" ⋯⋯⋯⋯ 199	jiàzhí 价值 ⋯⋯⋯⋯⋯⋯⋯⋯⋯⋯ 219
huā 花 ⋯⋯⋯⋯⋯⋯⋯⋯⋯⋯⋯⋯ 200	jiàzi 架子 ⋯⋯⋯⋯⋯⋯⋯⋯⋯⋯⋯ 219
huàjiě 化解 →P201"缓解" ⋯⋯⋯⋯⋯ 200	jiāndìng 坚定 →P220"坚决" ⋯⋯⋯⋯ 219
huānlè 欢乐 →P279"快乐" ⋯⋯⋯⋯⋯ 200	jiānjué 坚决 →P219"坚定" ⋯⋯⋯⋯ 220
huán 还 ⋯⋯⋯⋯⋯⋯⋯⋯⋯⋯⋯⋯ 200	jiānkǔ 艰苦 →P221"艰难" ⋯⋯⋯⋯ 220
huǎnjiě 缓解 →P200"化解" ⋯⋯⋯⋯ 201	jiānnán 艰难 →P220"艰苦" ⋯⋯⋯⋯ 221
huí 回 →P177"归" ⋯⋯⋯⋯⋯⋯⋯⋯ 201	jiǎndān 简单 →P89"单纯" ⋯⋯⋯⋯ 221
huídá 回答 →P79"答复" ⋯⋯⋯⋯⋯ 202	jiǎnzhí 简直 →P206"几乎" ⋯⋯⋯⋯ 222
huífù 回复 →P202"回应" ⋯⋯⋯⋯⋯ 202	jiàn 见 →P264"看"、P267"看见" ⋯⋯ 223
huíyìng 回应 →P202"回复" ⋯⋯⋯⋯ 202	jiànmiàn 见面 ⋯⋯⋯⋯⋯⋯⋯⋯⋯ 224
huì 会 →P335"能" ⋯⋯⋯⋯⋯⋯⋯⋯ 202	jiànlì 建立 →P65"成立" ⋯⋯⋯⋯⋯ 224
huó 活 ⋯⋯⋯⋯⋯⋯⋯⋯⋯⋯⋯⋯ 203	jiànshè 建设 →P225"建造"、P226"建筑"、
huòzhě 或者 →P185"还是" ⋯⋯⋯⋯ 204	P526"修建" ⋯⋯⋯⋯⋯⋯⋯⋯ 225
huòdé 获得 →P205"获取"、P382"取得"	jiànzào 建造 →P225"建设"、P226"建筑"、
⋯⋯⋯⋯⋯⋯⋯⋯⋯⋯⋯⋯⋯ 204	P526"修建" ⋯⋯⋯⋯⋯⋯⋯⋯ 225
huòqǔ 获取 →P204"获得" ⋯⋯⋯⋯ 205	jiànzhù 建筑 →P225"建设"、P225"建造"、
	P526"修建" ⋯⋯⋯⋯⋯⋯⋯⋯ 226

J

	jiànjiàn 渐渐 →P313"慢慢" ⋯⋯⋯⋯ 226
jīhū 几乎 →P60"差(一)点儿"、P222"简直"	jiāng 将 →P228"将要" ⋯⋯⋯⋯⋯⋯ 227
⋯⋯⋯⋯⋯⋯⋯⋯⋯⋯⋯⋯⋯ 206	jiāngyào 将要 →P227"将" ⋯⋯⋯⋯ 228
jīzhì 机制 ⋯⋯⋯⋯⋯⋯⋯⋯⋯⋯⋯ 207	jiānglái 将来 →P490"未来" ⋯⋯⋯⋯ 228
jīběn 基本 →P165"根本" ⋯⋯⋯⋯⋯ 207	jiǎnghuà 讲话 →P436"说话"、P455"谈话"
jīdòng 激动 →P159"感动" ⋯⋯⋯⋯ 208	⋯⋯⋯⋯⋯⋯⋯⋯⋯⋯⋯⋯⋯ 228
jíshí 及时 →P687"准时" ⋯⋯⋯⋯⋯ 209	jiǎngjiu 讲究 ⋯⋯⋯⋯⋯⋯⋯⋯⋯⋯ 229
jí 极 →P196"很"、P210"极其" ⋯⋯⋯ 209	jiāo 交 ⋯⋯⋯⋯⋯⋯⋯⋯⋯⋯⋯⋯ 229
jíduān 极端 ⋯⋯⋯⋯⋯⋯⋯⋯⋯⋯ 210	jiāohuàn 交换 →P230"交流" ⋯⋯⋯ 230
⋯⋯⋯ jíle ⋯⋯极了 ⋯⋯⋯⋯⋯⋯⋯ 210	jiāoliú 交流 →P230"交换" ⋯⋯⋯⋯ 230
jíqí 极其 →P209"极" ⋯⋯⋯⋯⋯⋯ 210	jiāowǎng 交往 ⋯⋯⋯⋯⋯⋯⋯⋯⋯ 231
jí 即 →P250"就" ⋯⋯⋯⋯⋯⋯⋯⋯ 211	jiào 叫 →P18"被"、P187"喊" ⋯⋯⋯ 231
jíjiāng 即将 ⋯⋯⋯⋯⋯⋯⋯⋯⋯⋯ 212	jiào 较 ⋯⋯⋯⋯⋯⋯⋯⋯⋯⋯⋯⋯ 232
jíshǐ 即使 →P240"尽管"、P330"哪怕"、	jiàoshī 教师 →P288"老师" ⋯⋯⋯⋯ 232
P398"如果" ⋯⋯⋯⋯⋯⋯⋯⋯ 212	jiàoxun 教训 ⋯⋯⋯⋯⋯⋯⋯⋯⋯⋯ 233
jímáng 急忙 →P300"连忙" ⋯⋯⋯⋯ 213	jiē 接 ⋯⋯⋯⋯⋯⋯⋯⋯⋯⋯⋯⋯ 233
jǐ 几 →P126"多少" ⋯⋯⋯⋯⋯⋯⋯ 213	jiēdài 接待 →P639"招待" ⋯⋯⋯⋯ 233
jìhuà 计划 →P83"打算" ⋯⋯⋯⋯⋯ 214	jiēlián 接连 →P301"连续" ⋯⋯⋯⋯ 233
jì 记 →P215"记得" ⋯⋯⋯⋯⋯⋯⋯ 215	jiēshōu 接收 →P234"接受" ⋯⋯⋯⋯ 234
jìde 记得 →P215"记"、P215"记忆" ⋯⋯ 215	jiēshòu 接受 →P234"接收" ⋯⋯⋯⋯ 234
jìyì 记忆 →P215"记得" ⋯⋯⋯⋯⋯ 215	jiēzhe 接着 →P388"然后" ⋯⋯⋯⋯ 235
jì 既 →P216"既然" ⋯⋯⋯⋯⋯⋯⋯ 216	jiéjiàrì 节假日 ⋯⋯⋯⋯⋯⋯⋯⋯⋯ 235
jìrán 既然 →P216"既" ⋯⋯⋯⋯⋯⋯ 216	jiénéng 节能 ⋯⋯⋯⋯⋯⋯⋯⋯⋯⋯ 236
jìxù 继续 →P66"持续"、P301"连续" ⋯ 217	jiéshěng 节省 →P236"节约" ⋯⋯⋯ 236
jiāyǐ 加以 ⋯⋯⋯⋯⋯⋯⋯⋯⋯⋯⋯ 217	jiéyuē 节约 →P236"节省" ⋯⋯⋯⋯ 236
jiàgé 价格 →P218"价钱" ⋯⋯⋯⋯⋯ 218	jiéguǒ 结果 →P198"后果" ⋯⋯⋯⋯ 236
	jiézhǐ 截止 →P237"截至" ⋯⋯⋯⋯ 237

jiézhì 截至 →P237"截止" ············ 237	
jiěshì 解释 →P238"解说" ············ 238	
jiěshuō 解说 →P238"解释" ············ 238	
jǐn 仅 →P239"仅仅" ··················· 238	
jǐnjǐn 仅仅 →P238"仅" ··············· 239	
jǐn 尽 ····································· 239	
jǐnguǎn 尽管 →P47"不管"、P212"即使" ································· 240	
jǐnkuài 尽快 ···························· 240	
jǐnliàng 尽量 →P241"尽力"、P242"尽量（jìnliàng）" ················· 241	
jìn 尽 ····································· 241	
jìnlì 尽力 →P241"尽量（jǐnliàng）" ··· 241	
jìnliàng 尽量 →P241"尽量（jǐnliàng）" ··· 242	
jìnxíng 进行 ···························· 242	
jīngcháng 经常 →P61"常常" ········· 244	
jīngguò 经过 →P468"通过" ·········· 244	
jīnglì 经历 →P245"经验" ············· 245	
jīngyàn 经验 →P245"经历" ·········· 245	
jīngshen 精神 ·························· 245	
jǐngsè 景色 →P149"风景"、P246"景象" ································· 246	
jǐngxiàng 景象 →P246"景色" ········ 246	
jìng 竟 →P247"竟然" ·················· 247	
jìngrán 竟然 →P247"竟"、P255"居然" ··· 247	
jiūzhèng 纠正 →P155"改正" ········· 247	
jiūjìng 究竟 →P28"毕竟"、P97"到底" ···· 248	
jiù 就 →P30"便"、P211"即" ········ 250	
jiùshì 就是 ····························· 252	
jiùshìshuō 就是说 →P643"这就是说" ··· 254	
jiùsuàn 就算 ··························· 254	
jūrán 居然 →P247"竟然" ············· 255	
jūzhù 居住 →P682"住" ··············· 255	
jǔbàn 举办 →P256"举行" ············ 255	
jǔdòng 举动 →P522"行动" ·········· 256	
jǔxíng 举行 →P255"举办" ··········· 256	
jùbèi 具备 →P257"具有" ············· 257	
jùyǒu 具有 →P257"具备"、P590"拥有" ································· 257	
jù 据 →P166"根据" ···················· 257	
jùshuō 据说 →P466"听说" ··········· 258	
juédìng 决定 →P258"决心" ·········· 258	
juéxīn 决心 →P258"决定" ··········· 258	
jué 绝 ····································· 259	
juéduì 绝对 ···························· 260	

K

kāi 开 ····································· 261	
kāifā 开发 ································ 262	
kāifàng 开放 ···························· 262	
kāishǐ 开始 →P703"最初" ············ 263	
kāitōng 开通 ··························· 263	
kāiyèchē 开夜车 ······················· 264	
kāizhǎn 开展 →P634"展开" ········· 264	
kàn 看 →P223"见"、P267"看见" ··· 264	
kànbuqǐ 看不起 ························ 266	
kànchéng 看成 ························· 266	
kànchū 看出 ···························· 266	
kàndào 看到 →P267"看见" ·········· 266	
kàndeqǐ 看得起 ························ 267	
kànhǎo 看好 ···························· 267	
kànjiàn 看见 →P223"见"、P266"看到" ··· 267	
kànlái 看来 →P268"看起来"、P268"看样子" ······························ 268	
kànqǐlái 看起来 →P268"看来"、P268"看样子" ······························ 268	
kànyàngzi 看样子 →P268"看来"、P268"看起来" ··························· 268	
kāngkǎi 慷慨 →P84"大方" ··········· 269	
kǎochá 考察 ···························· 269	
kào 靠 ···································· 269	
kě 可 ····································· 270	
kěbushì 可不是 ························ 272	
kějiàn 可见 ······························ 272	
kěnéng 可能 →P546"也许" ·········· 273	
kěshì 可是 →P90"但是" ·············· 273	
kěxī 可惜 →P564"遗憾" ·············· 274	
kěxiào 可笑 ···························· 275	
kěyǐ 可以 →P202"会"、P335"能" ··· 275	
kěn 肯 ···································· 276	
kěndìng 肯定 →P554"一定" ········· 277	
kōng 空 ·································· 277	
kǒngpà 恐怕 →P344"怕" ············ 277	
kòng 空 ·································· 278	
kòngzhì 控制 →P58"操纵"、P704"左右" ································· 278	
kù 酷 →P430"帅" ····················· 279	
kuài 快 ··································· 279	
kuàihuo 快活 →P279"快乐" ········· 279	

kuàilè 快乐 →P200"欢乐"、P279"快活" ………… 279
kuān 宽 →P281"阔" ………… 280
kùn 困 ………… 281
kuò 阔 →P280"宽" ………… 281

L

là 落 ………… 282
lái 来 →P570"以来" ………… 282
láibují 来不及 ………… 284
láidejí 来得及 ………… 285
láihuí 来回 →P285"来往" ………… 285
láiwǎng 来往 →P285"来回" ………… 285
láizì 来自 ………… 286
lài 赖 ………… 286
làn 烂 ………… 287
làngfèi 浪费 ………… 287
lǎo 老 →P696"总是" ………… 287
lǎoshī 老师 →P232"教师" ………… 288
lè 乐 ………… 289
le 了 →P179"过" ………… 289
lèisì 类似 →P510"相似" ………… 295
lěng 冷 →P186"寒冷"、P302"凉" ………… 295
lǐbài 礼拜 ………… 296
lǐjiě 理解 →P306"了解" ………… 296
lǐyóu 理由 →P100"道理"、P612"原因" ……… 296
lìhai 厉害 →P297"利害" ………… 296
lìjí 立即 →P297"立刻" ………… 297
lìkè 立刻 →P297"立即"、P311"马上" ……… 297
lìhài 利害 →P296"厉害" ………… 297
lìyòng 利用 ………… 297
lìwài 例外 ………… 298
lián 连 ………… 298
lián……dài…… 连……带…… 299
lián……dōu/yě…… 连……都/也…… ………… 299
liánmáng 连忙 →P213"急忙" ………… 300
liánxù 连续 →P217"继续"、P233"接连"、P308"陆续" ………… 301
liáng 凉 →P295"冷" ………… 302
liáng 量 ………… 302
liǎng 两 →P131"二" ………… 303
liǎng'àn 两岸 ………… 303
liǎo 了 ………… 304

liǎobudé 了不得 →P46"不得了" ………… 304
liǎobuqǐ 了不起 ………… 305
liǎojiě 了解 →P296"理解"、P662"知道" ………… 306
lièwéi 列为 ………… 307
línshí 临时 ………… 307
lìng 另 →P307"另外" ………… 307
lìngwài 另外 →P307"另" ………… 307
lùxù 陆续 →P301"连续" ………… 308
lù 露 ………… 309
lǚxíng 旅行 →P309"旅游"、P596"游览" ………… 309
lǚyóu 旅游 →P309"旅行"、P596"游览" ………… 309
luò 落 ………… 310

M

máfan 麻烦 →P83"打扰" ………… 311
mǎshàng 马上 →P297"立刻"、P536"眼看" ………… 311
mǎnyì 满意 →P312"满足" ………… 312
mǎnzú 满足 →P312"满意" ………… 312
màncháng 漫长 ………… 313
mànmàn 慢慢 →P226"渐渐" ………… 313
mànmànlái 慢慢来 ………… 314
máodùn 矛盾 →P67"冲突" ………… 314
méi/méiyǒu 没/没有 →P36"不"、→P51"不如" ………… 315
méishénme 没什么 →P318"没事儿" ………… 317
méishìr 没事儿 →P317"没什么" ………… 318
měi 每 →P164"各" ………… 318
ménlù 门路 ………… 319
mēng 蒙 ………… 320
méng 蒙 ………… 320
mí 迷 ………… 320
mìqiè 密切 ………… 321
miǎnde 免得 →P571"以免" ………… 321
miànduì 面对 →P322"面临" ………… 321
miànlín 面临 →P321"面对" ………… 322
miànqián 面前 →P329"目前"、P537"眼前" ………… 322
miànxiàng 面向 ………… 322
miànzi 面子 ………… 323
miáoshù 描述 →P323"描写" ………… 323

miáoxiě 描写 →P323"描述" ……… 323	niánjì 年纪 →P389"年龄" ……… 338
miào 妙 ……… 323	niánlíng 年龄 →P388"年纪" ……… 339
míngōng 民工 ……… 324	níngjìng 宁静 →P3"安静"、P358"平静" ……… 339
mínjǐng 民警 ……… 324	nòng 弄 →P163"搞" ……… 339
mǐngǎn 敏感 ……… 324	nuǎn 暖 →P341"暖和" ……… 340
míngyì 名义 ……… 324	nuǎnhuo 暖和 →P340"暖"、P490"温和" ……… 341
míngbai 明白 →P115"懂"、P379"清楚" ……… 324	
míngmíng 明明 →P148"分明" ……… 325	**O**
míngquè 明确 →P386"确定" ……… 326	ǒu'ěr 偶尔 →P342"偶然" ……… 342
míngxiǎn 明显 →P505"鲜明"、P507"显明"、P507"显著" ……… 326	ǒurán 偶然 →P342"偶尔" ……… 342
mìng 命 ……… 326	**P**
mócā 摩擦 ……… 327	pà 怕 →P186"害怕"、P277"恐怕" ……… 344
mò 末 ……… 327	pāishè 拍摄 →P346"拍照" ……… 345
mòmò 默默 →P373"悄悄" ……… 327	pāizhào 拍照 →P345"拍摄" ……… 346
mǒu 某 ……… 327	pái 排 →P347"排列" ……… 346
mù 木 ……… 328	páiliè 排列 →P346"排" ……… 347
mùbiāo 目标 →P328"目的" ……… 328	pài 派 ……… 347
mùdì 目的 →P328"目标"、P115"动机" ……… 328	pànwàng 盼望 →P498"希望" ……… 347
mùguāng 目光 →P536"眼光" ……… 329	páng 旁 →P348"旁边" ……… 347
mùqián 目前 →P222"面前"、P537"眼前" ……… 329	pángbiān 旁边 →P347"旁" ……… 348
	pǎo 跑 →P348"跑步" ……… 348
N	pǎobù 跑步 →P348"跑" ……… 348
ná……láishuō 拿……来说 ……… 330	péi 陪 →P350"陪同" ……… 349
nǎpà 哪怕 →P212"即使" ……… 330	péitóng 陪同 →P349"陪" ……… 350
nǎxiē 哪些 ……… 331	péiyǎng 培养 →P351"培育" ……… 350
nà 那 ……… 331	péiyù 培育 →P351"培养" ……… 351
nàxiē 那些 ……… 332	péi 赔 →P352"赔偿" ……… 352
nàixīn 耐心 ……… 332	péicháng 赔偿 →P352"赔" ……… 352
nándào 难道 ……… 332	pīpàn 批判 →P352"批评" ……… 352
nándé 难得 ……… 333	pīpíng 批评 →P352"批判" ……… 352
nánguài 难怪 →P171"怪不得" ……… 333	pīzhǔn 批准 →P472"同意" ……… 353
nánmiǎn 难免 →P49"不免" ……… 334	píqi 脾气 →P525"性格" ……… 353
nánshuō 难说 ……… 334	piān 偏 →P354"偏偏" ……… 354
nánwéi 难为 →P485"为难" ……… 334	piānpiān 偏偏 →P354"偏" ……… 354
nányǐ 难以 ……… 335	pīnmìng 拼命 ……… 355
nèizài 内在 ……… 335	pínkǔ 贫苦 →P355"贫穷" ……… 355
néng 能 →P202"会"、P275"可以"、P335"能够" ……… 335	pínqióng 贫穷 →P355"贫苦" ……… 355
néngfǒu 能否 ……… 337	pǐn 品 ……… 356
nénggòu 能够 →P335"能" ……… 338	pǐndé 品德 →P357"品质" ……… 356
niándù 年度 ……… 338	pǐnzhì 品质 →P356"品德" ……… 357

píngcháng 平常 →P357"平凡" ………… 357
píngfán 平凡 →P357"平常" …………… 357
píngjìng 平静 →P3"安静"、P339"宁静"
………………………………………… 358
pínggū 评估 →P359"评价" …………… 359
píngjià 评价 →P359"评估" …………… 359
píng 凭 ………………………………… 359
pòqiè 迫切 …………………………… 360
pǔbiàn 普遍 →P361"普通" …………… 360
pǔtōng 普通 →P360"普遍" …………… 361

Q

qīdài 期待 →P362"期望" …………… 362
qījiān 期间 →P418"时期" …………… 362
qīwàng 期望 →P362"期待" …………… 362
qí 齐 …………………………………… 363
qí 其 …………………………………… 363
qícì 其次 ……………………………… 364
qíshí 其实 …………………………… 364
qítā 其他 →P365"其余" ……………… 365
qíyú 其余 →P365"其他" ……………… 365
qízhōng 其中 ………………………… 365
qíguài 奇怪 →P170"怪" ……………… 366
qǐ 起 …………………………………… 366
qǐdào 起到 …………………………… 367
qǐlái 起来 …………………………… 367
qǐmǎ 起码 →P673"至少" …………… 368
qì 气 …………………………………… 368
qìhòu 气候 →P463"天气" …………… 369
qiàdàng 恰当 →P424"适当" ………… 369
qiàhǎo 恰好 →P370"恰恰" ………… 370
qiàqià 恰恰 →P370"恰好" ………… 370
qiānwàn 千万 →P481"万万" ………… 371
qiān 签 ………………………………… 371
qiánbian 前边 →P372"前面" ……… 371
qiánhòu 前后 →P504"先后" ……… 371
qiánlái 前来 ………………………… 372
qiánmiàn 前面 →P371"前边" ……… 372
qiǎn 浅 ………………………………… 372
qiáng 强 ……………………………… 373
qiāoqiāo 悄悄 →P327"默默" ……… 373
qiǎo 巧 ……………………………… 373
qiě 且 ………………………………… 374
qīnfàn 侵犯 →P375"侵略" ………… 374

qīnlüè 侵略 →P374"侵犯" ………… 375
qīnhélì 亲和力 ……………………… 375
qīnqiè 亲切 →P376"亲热" ………… 376
qīnrè 亲热 →P376"亲切" ………… 376
qīnshēn 亲身 ……………………… 376
qīnshǒu 亲手 →P377"亲眼" ……… 377
qīnyǎn 亲眼 →P377"亲手" ……… 377
qínfèn 勤奋 →P378"勤劳" ……… 378
qínláo 勤劳 →P378"勤奋" ……… 378
qīngyì 轻易 →P397"容易" ……… 378
qīng 清 ……………………………… 378
qīngchǔ 清楚 →P324"明白" ……… 379
qīnglǐ 清理 →P649"整理" ………… 379
qīngxǐng 清醒 ……………………… 380
qíngjǐng 情景 ……………………… 380
qíngkuàng 情况 →P381"情形" …… 380
qíngxing 情形 →P380"情况" …… 381
qíngxù 情绪 →P518"心情" ……… 381
qūbié 区别 →P147"分别" ………… 381
qǔdé 取得 →P204"获得" ………… 382
quán 全 →P116"都" ……………… 382
quánbù 全部 →P383"全体"、P480"完全"、
P560"一切" ……………………… 383
quántǐ 全体 →P383"全部" ……… 383
quē 缺 ……………………………… 384
quēfá 缺乏 →P384"缺少" ……… 384
quēshǎo 缺少 →P384"缺乏" …… 384
què 却 →P98"倒" ………………… 385
quèdìng 确定 →P326"明确"、P386"确认"
………………………………………… 386
quèqiè 确切 →P387"确实" ……… 386
quèrèn 确认 →P386"确定" ……… 386
quèshí 确实 →P111"的确"、P386"确切"
………………………………………… 387

R

rán'ér 然而 →P90"但是"、P273"可是" …… 388
ránhòu 然后 →P198"后来"、P235"接着"
………………………………………… 388
ràng 让 →P18"被"、P230"叫" …… 389
rè 热 ………………………………… 390
rèliè 热烈 →P391"热闹" ………… 391
rèmén 热门 ………………………… 391
rènao 热闹 →P391"热烈" ……… 391

rèqíng 热情 →P392"热心" ············ 392
rèxiàn 热线 ····················· 392
rèxīn 热心 →P392"热情" ············ 392
rénjiā 人家 ····················· 393
rénjia 人家 ····················· 393
rènwéi 认为 →P573"以为" ············ 393
rèn 任 ························ 394
rènxìng 任性 →P395"任意" ············ 395
rènyì 任意 →P395"任性" ············ 395
réng 仍 →P395"仍然" ··············· 395
réngjiù 仍旧 →P395"仍然"、P551"依旧"
··························· 395
réngrán 仍然 →P395"仍"、P552"依然"
··························· 395
rìyì 日益 →P615"越来越……" ········ 396
rìzi 日子 →P412"生活" ············· 396
róngxǔ 容许 →P616"允许" ············ 397
róngyì 容易 →P378"轻易" ············ 397
rú 如 →P398"如果" ················ 397
rúguǒ 如果 →P212"即使"、P397"如"、
P544"要是" ···················· 398

S

sǎn 散 ······················· 400
sàn 散 ······················· 400
sè 色 ························ 400
sècǎi 色彩 →P57"彩色"、P535"颜色" ···· 401
shāng 伤 ······················ 401
shānghài 伤害 →P448"损害" ·········· 401
shāngchǎng 商场 →P421"市场" ········· 401
shàng 上 ······················ 402
shàngdàng 上当 ··················· 403
shànglái 上来 ···················· 403
shàngqù 上去 ···················· 403
shàngshì 上市 ···················· 404
shàngwǎng 上网 ··················· 404
shang 上 ······················ 404
shāokǎo 烧烤 ···················· 405
shāo 稍 →P406"稍微" ··············· 405
shāowēi 稍微 →P405"稍" ············· 406
shěbudé 舍不得 ··················· 406
shéi 谁 ······················· 407
shēn 深 ······················· 407
shēnhuà 深化 →P408"深入" ··········· 408

shēnrù 深入 →P408"深化" ············ 408
shénme 什么 ···················· 409
shénmeyàng 什么样 ················· 410
shénmì 神秘 →P410"神奇" ············ 410
shénqí 神奇 →P410"神秘" ············ 410
shènzhì 甚至 ···················· 411
shēng 生 ······················ 411
shēnghuó 生活 →P396"日子" ·········· 412
shīfu 师父 →P413"师傅" ············· 413
shīfu 师傅 →P413"师父" ············· 413
shífēn 十分 →P147"非常" ············ 414
shízú 十足 ····················· 414
shí 时 ························ 415
shícháng 时常 →P61"常常" ··········· 415
shí'ér 时而 ····················· 416
shíhou 时候 →P416"时间"、P418"时刻"
··························· 416
shíjiān 时间 →P416"时候" ··········· 416
shíkè 时刻 →P416"时候" ············ 418
shíqī 时期 →P362"期间" ············ 418
shíjiàn 实践 →P419"实现"、P419"实行"
··························· 418
shíxiàn 实现 →P418"实践"、P419"实行"
··························· 419
shíxíng 实行 →P418"实践"、P419"实现"
··························· 419
shíyàn 实验 →P422"试验" ············ 420
shízài 实在 ····················· 420
shǐ 使 ························ 420
shǐde 使得 ····················· 420
shǐzhōng 始终 →P583"一直" ·········· 421
shìchǎng 市场 →P401"商场" ·········· 421
shìde 似的 ····················· 421
shìyàn 试验 →P420"实验" ············ 422
shì……de 是……的 ················ 423
shìfǒu 是否 ···················· 423
shìdàng 适当 →P369"恰当" ··········· 424
shìhé 适合 →P193"合适"、P424"适应"
··························· 424
shìyìng 适应 →P424"适合" ··········· 424
shìyòng 适用 ···················· 425
shōudào 收到 →P428"受到" ··········· 425
shōují 收集 →P440"搜集" ············ 426
shōushi 收拾 ···················· 426
shǒuduàn 手段 →P427"手法" ·········· 426

shǒufǎ 手法 →P426"手段" ………… 427
shòu 受 ………… 427
shòubuliǎo 受不了 ………… 427
shòudào 受到 →P425"收到" ………… 428
shūfu 舒服 →P428"舒适" ………… 428
shūshì 舒适 →P428"舒服" ………… 428
shú 熟 ………… 429
shǔ 属 ………… 429
shùmǎ 数码 ………… 430
shuài 帅 →P279"酷" ………… 430
shuàixiān 率先 ………… 431
shuìjiào 睡觉 →P432"睡眠" ………… 431
shuìmián 睡眠 →P431"睡觉" ………… 432
shùn 顺 →P534"沿" ………… 432
shùnbiàn 顺便 ………… 433
shùnshǒu 顺手 →P446"随手" ………… 434
shuōbudìng 说不定 ………… 434
shuōfǎ 说法 ………… 435
shuōhuà 说话 →P228"讲话"、P455"谈话"
  ………… 436
sīkǎo 思考 →P436"思索" ………… 436
sīsuǒ 思索 →P436"思考" ………… 436
sīwéi 思维 →P437"思想" ………… 437
sīxiǎng 思想 →P437"思维" ………… 437
sǐ 死 ………… 438
sìhū 似乎 →P144"仿佛"、P191"好像" … 439
sōng 松 ………… 439
sòng 送 →P440"送行" ………… 440
sòngxíng 送行 →P440"送" ………… 440
sōují 搜集 →P426"收集" ………… 440
suàn 算 →P442"算是" ………… 441
suànle 算了 →P101"得了" ………… 441
suànshì 算是 →P441"算" ………… 442
suī 虽 →P443"虽然" ………… 443
suīrán 虽然 →P443"虽" ………… 443
suí 随 →P447"随着" ………… 444
suíbiàn 随便 ………… 445
suíhòu 随后 ………… 445
suíshí 随时 ………… 446
suíshǒu 随手 →P434"顺手" ………… 446
suízhe 随着 →P444"随" ………… 447
sǔnhài 损害 →P401"伤害"、P448"损失"
  ………… 448
sǔnshī 损失 →P448"损害" ………… 448
suǒ 所 ………… 449

suǒwèi 所谓 ………… 451
suǒyǐ 所以 →P586"因此"、P586"因而"
  ………… 451
suǒyǒu 所有 →P560"一切" ………… 452
suǒzài 所在 ………… 452

T

tāshi 踏实 ………… 453
tái 台 ………… 453
táishang 台上 ………… 453
tài 太 ………… 454
tánhuà 谈话 →P228"讲话"、P436"说话"
  ………… 455
tánlùn 谈论 →P456"讨论"、P584"议论"
  ………… 456
tǎolùn 讨论 →P456"谈论"、P584"议论"
  ………… 456
tè 特 →P457"特别" ………… 456
tèbié 特别 →P118"独特"、P456"特"、
  P458"特殊"、P593"尤其" ………… 457
tèdì 特地 →P459"特意" ………… 458
tèdiǎn 特点 →P459"特征" ………… 458
tèshū 特殊 →P457"特别" ………… 458
tèyì 特意 →P458"特地"、P684"专门" … 459
tèzhēng 特征 →P458"特点" ………… 459
tí 提 ………… 460
tíshì 提示 →P460"提醒" ………… 460
tíxǐng 提醒 →P460"提示" ………… 460
tǐhuì 体会 →P462"体验" ………… 461
tǐxiàn 体现 →P33"表现" ………… 461
tǐyàn 体验 →P460"体会" ………… 462
tì 替 →P87"代"、P88"代替" ………… 462
tiānqì 天气 →P369"气候" ………… 463
tiānrán 天然 →P693"自然" ………… 463
tiānxià 天下 ………… 464
tiāo 挑 ………… 464
tiáojié 调节 →P465"调整" ………… 464
tiáozhěng 调整 →P464"调节" ………… 465
tiǎo 挑 ………… 465
tīngdào 听到 →P465"听见" ………… 465
tīngjiàn 听见 →P465"听到" ………… 465
tīngshuō 听说 →P258"据说" ………… 466
tíngliú 停留 →P466"停止" ………… 466
tíngzhǐ 停止 →P466"停留" ………… 466

tǐng 挺 →P170"怪"、P196"很"	467
tōng 通	468
tōngcháng 通常 →P61"常常"、P415"时常"	468
tōngguò 通过 →P244"经过"	469
tōnghuà 通话	470
tóng 同 →P166"跟"、P193"和"、P608"与"	470
tóngshí 同时	472
tóngyàng 同样 →P563"一样"	472
tóngyì 同意 →P353"批准"、P616"允许"、P626"赞成"	472
tòngkuài 痛快	473
tōu 偷 →P474"偷偷"	473
tōutōu 偷偷 →P473"偷"	474
tóu 投	474
tóurù 投入	475
tòu 透	475
tūchū 突出	476
tūrán 突然 →P199"忽然"	476
tǔ 吐	476
tù 吐	477
tuīdòng 推动 →P477"推进"	477
tuījìn 推进 →P477"推动"	477

W

wàibian 外边 →P478"外部"、P479"外界"、P479"外面"、P480"外头"	478
wàibù 外部 →P478"外边"、P479"外面"、P480"外头"	478
wàijiè 外界 →P478"外边"、P479"外面"、P480"外头"	479
wàilái 外来	479
wàimiàn 外面 →P478"外边"、P480"外头"	479
wàitou 外头 →P478"外边"、P479"外面"	480
wánměi 完美 →P480"完善"	480
wánquán 完全 →P383"全部"、P481"完整"	480
wánshàn 完善 →P480"完美"	480
wánzhěng 完整 →P480"完全"	481
wànwàn 万万 →P371"千万"	481
wànyī 万一 →P554"一旦"	482

wǎng 往 →P63"朝"	483
wǎngwǎng 往往 →P61"常常"	483
wēixiǎn 危险 →P149"风险"	484
wéi 为	485
wéinán 为难 →P334"难为"	485
wéibèi 违背 →P486"违反"	486
wéifǎn 违反 →P486"违背"	486
wéichí 维持 →P14"保持"	487
wéihù 维护 →P14"保护"	487
wèi 为	488
wèi 未	488
wèibì 未必 →P40"不必"	489
wèilái 未来 →P228"将来"	490
wēnhé 温和 →P341"暖和"、P491"温暖"	490
wēnnuǎn 温暖 →P490"温和"	491
wénhuà 文化 →P492"文明"	491
wénmíng 文明 →P491"文化"	492
wěndìng 稳定 →P3"安定"	492
wènhǎo 问好 →P493"问候"	493
wènhòu 问候 →P493"问好"	493
wúfǎ 无法	494
wúlùn 无论 →P47"不管"、P494"无论如何"	494
wúlùnrúhé 无论如何 →P494"无论"	495
wúsuǒwèi 无所谓 →P45"不在乎"、P317"没事儿"	495
wúyí 无疑	496
wùyè 物业	496
wù 误	496
wùhuì 误会 →P497"误解"	497
wùjiě 误解 →P497"误会"	497

X

xīwàng 希望 →P347"盼望"、P613"愿望"	498
xīshēng 牺牲	498
xǐ'ài 喜爱 →P499"喜欢"	499
xǐhuan 喜欢 →P499"喜爱"	499
xìxīn 细心 →P516"小心"、P688"仔细"	499
xià 下	499
xiàhǎi 下海	501
xiàlái 下来	501
xiàqù 下去	502

xiàzǎi 下载 ··· 503
xiān 先 ··· 503
xiānhòu 先后 →P371"前后" ··············· 504
xiānqián 先前 →P572"以前" ··············· 505
xiān 鲜 ··· 505
xiānmíng 鲜明 →P326"明显"、P506"显明"
 ··· 505
xiǎnchū 显出 ··· 506
xiǎnde 显得 ·· 506
xiǎnmíng 显明 →P326"明显"、P505"鲜明"
 ··· 506
xiǎnrán 显然 →P326"明显"、P507"显著"
 ··· 507
xiǎnzhù 显著 →P326"明显"、P507"显然"
 ··· 507
xiāngbǐ 相比 ·· 508
xiāngchǔ 相处 ······································· 508
xiāngdāng 相当 ···································· 509
xiāngfǎn 相反 →P139"反而" ··············· 509
xiānghù 相互 →P199"互相" ··············· 510
xiāngsì 相似 →P295"类似"、P511"相同"
 ··· 510
xiāngtóng 相同 →P510"相似" ············ 511
xiāngxìn 相信 →P520"信任" ············· 511
xiǎng 想 →P540"要" ··························· 511
xiàng 向 →P63"朝" ······························ 512
xiànglái 向来 →P77"从来"、P563"一向"、
 P583"一直" ·· 513
xiàngshàng 向上 ·································· 513
xiàng 像 ·· 513
xiāofèi 消费 →P514"消耗" ·················· 514
xiāohào 消耗 →P514"消费" ················ 514
xiāomiè 消灭 →P514"消失" ················ 514
xiāoshī 消失 →P514"消灭" ················· 514
xiāoxi 消息 →P519"新闻"、P521"信息"
 ··· 515
xiǎo 小 ·· 515
xiǎoqū 小区 ··· 515
xiǎoshí 小时 →P678"钟头" ················· 516
xiǎoxīn 小心 →P499"细心" ················· 516
xiàoguǒ 效果 →P516"效益" ················ 516
xiàoyì 效益 →P516"效果" ··················· 516
xiéshāng 协商 →P517"协调" ·············· 517
xiétiáo 协调 →P195"和谐"、P517"协商"
 ··· 517

xīnqíng 心情 →P381"情绪" ················ 518
xīnténg 心疼 ··· 518
xīnkǔ 辛苦 ··· 518
xīnrén 新人 ··· 519
xīnwén 新闻 →P515"消息" ················ 519
xìn 信 ·· 520
xìnrèn 信任 →P511"相信" ·················· 520
xìnxī 信息 →P515"消息" ····················· 521
xíng 行 ·· 521
xíngdòng 行动 →P256"举动"、P522"行为"
 ··· 522
xíngwéi 行为 →P522"行动" ··············· 522
xíngchéng 形成 →P701"组成" ··········· 523
xíngtài 形态 →P524"形状" ················· 523
xíngxiàng 形象 ····································· 523
xíngzhuàng 形状 →P523"形态" ········· 524
xìngkuī 幸亏 ··· 524
xìnggé 性格 →P353"脾气" ·················· 525
xiōng 凶 ··· 525
xiūxián 休闲 ··· 526
xiūjiàn 修建 →P225"建设"、P225"建造"、
 P226"建筑" ·· 526
xūqiú 需求 →P526"需要" ··················· 526
xūyào 需要 →P526"需求" ··················· 527
xuānbù 宣布 →P169"公布" ················ 527
xuǎn 选 →P528"选择" ························· 528
xuǎnzé 选择 →P528"选" ····················· 528
xuéwen 学问 →P663"知识" ················ 528
xúnqiú 寻求 →P529"寻找" ················· 528
xúnzhǎo 寻找 →P528"寻求" ·············· 529

Y

yā 压 →P4"按" ······································ 530
yālì 压力 ··· 530
yáncháng 延长 →P531"延期"、P531"延伸"、
 P531"延续" ·· 531
yánqī 延期 →P531"延长" ···················· 531
yánshēn 延伸 →P531"延长" ··············· 531
yánxù 延续 →P531"延长" ··················· 531
yán 严 →P532"严格" ···························· 532
yángé 严格 →P532"严"、P532"严厉"、
 P533"严肃" ·· 532
yánlì 严厉 →P532"严格"、P533"严肃" ····· 532
yánsù 严肃 →P532"严厉" ··················· 533

拼音词条	页码
yányǔ 言语 →P609"语言"	534
yányu 言语 →P609"语言"	534
yán 沿 →P432"顺"	534
yánfā 研发 →P535"研制"	535
yánzhì 研制 →P535"研发"	535
yánsè 颜色 →P401"色彩"	535
yǎnguāng 眼光 →P329"目光"	536
yǎnkàn 眼看 →P311"马上"	536
yǎnqián 眼前 →P322"面前"、P329"目前"	537
yǎnchū 演出	538
yáng 洋	538
yǎng 养	539
yàopǐn 药品 →P540"药物"	540
yàowù 药物 →P540"药品"	540
yào 要 →P511"想"	540
yàobù 要不 →P50"不然"、P543"要不然"	543
yàobùrán 要不然 →P543"要不"	543
yàohǎo 要好	544
yàoshi 要是 →P398"如果"	544
yàosù 要素	544
yě 也 →P116"都"	544
yěhǎo 也好	546
yěxǔ 也许 →P273"可能"	546
yèyú 业余	547
yèjiān 夜间 →P547"夜里"	547
yèlǐ 夜里 →P547"夜间"	547
yèshì 夜市	548
yèwǎn 夜晚	548
yī 一	548
yībǎshǒu 一把手	550
yī……jiù…… 一……就……	550
yīliú 一流	551
yījiù 依旧 →P395"仍旧"、P553"依然"	551
yījù 依据 →P166"根据"、P554"依照"	552
yīkào 依靠 →P553"依赖"	552
yīlài 依赖 →P552"依靠"	553
yīrán 依然 →P395"仍然"、P551"依旧"	553
yīzhào 依照 →P5"按照"、P552"依据"	554
yídài 一代	555
yídàn 一旦 →P482"万一"	555
yídào 一道 →P581"一同"	555
yídìng 一定 →P26"必定"、P277"肯定"	555
yígài 一概 →P559"一律"	557
yíhuìr 一会儿 →P561"一下"	557
yíkuàir 一块儿 →P580"一起"	558
yílù 一路	559
yílǜ 一律 →P557"一概"	559
yímiàn 一面 →P575"一边"、P577"一方面"	559
yíqiè 一切 →P383"全部"、P452"所有"	560
yíxià 一下 →P557"一会儿"、P562"一下子"	561
yíxiàzi 一下子 →P561"一下"	562
yíxiàng 一向 →P513"向来"、P583"一直"	563
yíyàng 一样 →P471"同样"、P575"一般"	563
yízài 一再 →P620"再三"	564
yíhàn 遗憾 →P274"可惜"	564
yǐ 已 →P565"已经"	565
yǐjīng 已经 →P58"曾经"、P565"已"	565
yǐ 以 →P568"以便"	567
yǐbiàn 以便 →P567"以"	568
yǐhòu 以后 →P198"后来"	569
yǐjí 以及	569
yǐlái 以来 →P282"来"、P568"以后"	570
yǐmiǎn 以免 →P321"免得"	571
yǐnèi 以内	572
yǐqián 以前 →P181"过去"、P504"先前"、P573"以往"	572
yǐwài 以外	573
yǐwǎng 以往 →P572"以前"	573
yǐwéi 以为 →P393"认为"	573
yìbān 一般 →P563"一样"	575
yìbānláishuō 一般来说	575
yìbiān 一边 →P559"一面"	576
yìdiǎnr 一点儿 →P582"一些"、P601"有(一)点儿"	577
yìfāngmiàn 一方面 →P559"一面"	577
yìkǒuqì 一口气 →P579"一连"	579
yìlián 一连 →P579"一口气"	579
yìqí 一齐 →P580"一起"	579
yìqǐ 一起 →P558"一块儿"、P579"一齐"、P581"一同"	580
yìshí 一时 →P625"暂时"	580
yìtóng 一同 →P555"一道"、P580"一起"	581
yìxiē 一些 →P577"一点儿"	582

| yìzhí 一直 →P421"始终"、P563"一向" …… 583
| yìlùn 议论 →P456"谈论"、P456"讨论" …… 584
| yìsi 意思 ………………………………… 584
| yìwài 意外 ……………………………… 585
| yìwèizhe 意味着 ……………………… 585
| yīn 因 …………………………………… 585
| yīncǐ 因此 →P451"所以"、P586"因而" … 586
| yīn'ér 因而 →P76"从而"、P586"因此" … 586
| yīnwèi 因为 →P595"由于" ………… 587
| yīn 阴 …………………………………… 588
| yīng 应 →P152"该"、P589"应当"、P589"应该" …………………………………… 588
| yīngdāng 应当 →P589"应该" ……… 589
| yīnggāi 应该 →P588"应"、P589"应当" …………………………………………… 589
| yìngyòng 应用 →P617"运用" ……… 590
| yìng 硬 ………………………………… 590
| yōngyǒu 拥有 →P257"具有" ……… 590
| yòng 用 ………………………………… 591
| yòngbuzháo 用不着 …………………… 591
| yòngchù 用处 →P592"用途" ……… 592
| yòngtú 用途 →P592"用处" ………… 592
| yōuliáng 优良 →P592"优秀" ……… 592
| yōuxiù 优秀 →P592"优良" ………… 592
| yóuqí 尤其 →P457"特别" …………… 593
| yóu 由 →P75"从"、P688"自" ……… 594
| yóuyú 由于 →P587"因为" ………… 595
| yóu 游 …………………………………… 596
| yóulǎn 游览 →P309"旅行"、P309"旅游" …………………………………………… 597
| yǒu 有 …………………………………… 597
| yǒudeshì 有的是 ……………………… 598
| yǒuguān 有关 →P172"关于" ……… 599
| yǒujìn 有劲 …………………………… 600
| yǒukòngr 有空儿 ……………………… 600
| yǒumíng 有名 →P683"著名" ……… 600
| yǒushí 有时 →P600"有时候" ……… 600
| yǒushíhou 有时候 →P600"有时" …… 600
| yǒu(yì)diǎnr 有(一)点儿 →P577"一点儿" …………………………………………… 601
| yǒuxiē 有些 …………………………… 603
| yǒuyìsi 有意思 ………………………… 603
| yòu 又 →P184"还"、P618"再" …… 603
| yú 于 →P622"在" ……………………… 605
| yúshì 于是 →P586"因此" …………… 607

yúkuài 愉快 →P279"快乐" …………… 608
yǔ 与 →P166"跟"、P193"和"、P470"同" …………………………………………… 608
yǔyán 语言 →P534"言语(yányǔ)"、P534"言语(yányu)" …………………… 609
yùbèi 预备 →P687"准备" …………… 609
yùdào 遇到 →P610"遇见" …………… 610
yùjiàn 遇见 →P610"遇到" …………… 610
yuán 原 ………………………………… 610
yuánlái 原来 →P21"本来"、P611"原先" …………………………………………… 610
yuánxiān 原先 →P610"原来" ……… 611
yuányīn 原因 →P296"理由"、P613"缘故" …………………………………………… 612
yuánfèn 缘分 ………………………… 612
yuángù 缘故 →P612"原因" ………… 613
yuànwàng 愿望 →P498"希望" …… 614
yuē 约 …………………………………… 614
yuēdìng 约定 →P615"约会" ……… 614
yuēhuì 约会 →P614"约定" ………… 615
yuè 越 …………………………………… 615
yuèláiyuè 越来越 →P396"日益" …… 615
yǔnxǔ 允许 →P397"容许"、P472"同意" …………………………………………… 616
yùnqi 运气 …………………………… 616
yùnyòng 运用 →P590"应用" ……… 617

Z

zāihài 灾害 →P618"灾难" …………… 618
zāinàn 灾难 →P618"灾害" …………… 618
zài 再 →P604"又" ……………………… 618
zàisān 再三 →P564"一再" ………… 620
zàishuō 再说 →P36"并且"、P130"而且" …………………………………………… 621
zài 在 →P91"当"、P605"于"、P650"正在" …………………………………………… 622
zàihu 在乎 …………………………… 624
zàiyú 在于 …………………………… 624
zànshí 暂时 →P580"一时" ………… 625
zànchéng 赞成 →P472"同意" …… 626
zànzhù 赞助 ………………………… 626
zāodào 遭到 →P626"遭受" ………… 626
zāoshòu 遭受 →P626"遭到" ……… 626

zāoyù 遭遇 ………………………………… 627	zhèngdāng 正当 →P651"正好" ………… 651
zāo 糟 …………………………………… 627	zhèngdàng 正当 ……………………… 651
zǎo 早 …………………………………… 627	zhènghǎo 正好 →P651"正当" ………… 651
zǎowǎn 早晚 …………………………… 628	zhèngzài 正在 →P622"在"、P650"正" … 652
zǎoyǐ 早已 ……………………………… 628	zhèngmíng 证明 →P653"证实" ……… 653
zé 则 …………………………………… 629	zhèngshí 证实 →P653"证明" ………… 653
zěnme 怎么 →P630"怎么样" …………… 629	zhī 之 →P103"的" ……………………… 654
zěnmeyàng 怎么样 →P629"怎么" ……… 630	zhījiān 之间 →P657"之内"、P658"之中"、
zēngjiā 增加 →P633"增进"、P633"增长"	P677"中间" ……………………… 656
………………………………… 632	zhīnèi 之内 →P656"之间"、P658"之中"
zēngjìn 增进 →P632"增加" ……………… 633	………………………………… 657
zēngzhǎng 增长 →P632"增加" ………… 633	zhīzhōng 之中 →P656"之间"、P657"之内"
zhǎnkāi 展开 →P264"开展" …………… 634	………………………………… 658
zhàn 占 ………………………………… 634	zhīqián 之前 →P661"之上" …………… 660
zhànlǐng 占领 →P635"占有" …………… 635	zhīshàng 之上 →P660"之前" ………… 661
zhànyǒu 占有 →P635"占领" …………… 635	zhīchí 支持 →P662"支援" …………… 661
zhàndòu 战斗 →P636"战争" …………… 636	zhīyuán 支援 →P661"支持" ………… 662
zhànzhēng 战争 →P636"战斗" ………… 636	zhīdào 知道 →P115"懂"、P306"了解" … 662
zhāng 张 ………………………………… 637	zhīshi 知识 →P528"学问" …………… 663
zhǎng 长 ………………………………… 637	zhí 直 …………………………………… 663
zhǎngdà 长大 …………………………… 638	zhí 值 →P665"值得" …………………… 665
zhǎngwò 掌握 →P9"把握"、P704"左右"	zhídé 值得 →P665"值" ………………… 665
………………………………… 638	zhǐ 只 →P175"光"、P88"单" ………… 666
zhāo 招 ………………………………… 638	zhǐbúguò 只不过 ……………………… 667
zhāodài 招待 →P233"接待" …………… 639	zhǐdé 只得 →P46"不得不"、P668"只好"
zhāohu 招呼 …………………………… 640	………………………………… 668
zhāoshǒu 招手 ………………………… 640	zhǐgù 只顾 →P668"只管" ……………… 668
zhāo 着 ………………………………… 640	zhǐguǎn 只管 →P668"只顾" …………… 668
zháo 着 ………………………………… 640	zhǐhǎo 只好 →P46"不得不"、P668"只得"
zháojí 着急 →P88"担心" ……………… 641	………………………………… 668
zhào 照 →P4"按" ……………………… 641	zhǐshì 只是 →P42"不过" ……………… 669
zhàocháng 照常 →P642"照样" ………… 642	zhǐyào 只要 →P671"只有" …………… 671
zhàoyàng 照样 →P642"照常" ………… 642	zhǐyǒu 只有 →P71"除非"、P668"只好"、
zhèjiùshìshuō 这就是说 →P254"就是说"	P671"只要" ……………………… 671
………………………………… 643	zhìshǎo 至少 →P368"起码" …………… 673
zhème 这么 →P645"这样" …………… 643	zhìyú 至于 →P172"关于" ……………… 674
zhèyàng 这样 →P643"这么" …………… 645	zhìdìng 制订 →P675"制定" …………… 674
zhe 着 …………………………………… 645	zhìdìng 制定 →P674"制订" …………… 675
zhēnguì 珍贵 →P14"宝贵" …………… 646	zhìzào 制造 →P675"制作" …………… 675
zhēn 真 →P196"很" …………………… 646	zhìzuò 制作 →P675"制造" …………… 675
zhēng 争 ……………………………… 648	zhōng 中 →P677"中间" ……………… 676
zhēnglùn 争论 →P31"辩论" …………… 648	zhōngjiān 中间 →P656"之间"、P676"中"
zhěng 整 →P649"整整" ………………… 648	………………………………… 677
zhěnglǐ 整理 →P379"清理" …………… 649	zhōngwén 中文 →P187"汉语" ………… 677
zhěngzhěng 整整 →P648"整" ………… 649	zhōngyú 终于 →P97"到底" …………… 677
zhèng 正 →P652"正在" ………………… 650	

zhōngtóu 钟头 →P516"小时" …… 678	zìcóng 自从 →P688"自" …… 690
zhòngdà 重大 →P679"重要" …… 678	zìdòng 自动 →P681"主动" …… 690
zhòngdiǎn 重点 …… 679	zìháo 自豪 …… 691
zhòngyào 重要 →P678"重大"、P681"主要" …… 679	zìjǐ 自己 →P694"自我" …… 691
zhōu 周 …… 679	zìjué 自觉 →P681"主动" …… 692
zhōudào 周到 →P680"周密" …… 680	zìrán 自然 →P94"当然"、→P463"天然" …… 693
zhōumì 周密 →P680"周到" …… 680	zìshēn 自身 …… 694
zhúbù 逐步 →P680"逐渐" …… 680	zìwǒ 自我 →P691"自己" …… 694
zhújiàn 逐渐 →P680"逐步" …… 680	zōnghé 综合 →P155"概括" …… 695
zhǔdòng 主动 →P690"自动"、P692"自觉" …… 681	zǒng 总 →P287"老"、P696"总是" …… 696
zhǔyào 主要 →P679"重要" …… 681	zǒngshì 总是 →P287"老"、P696"总" …… 696
zhǔfù 嘱咐 →P148"吩咐" …… 682	zǒngsuàn 总算 …… 697
zhù 住 →P255"居住" …… 682	zǒngzhī 总之 …… 698
zhùmíng 著名 →P600"有名" …… 683	zǒu 走 …… 698
zhuānmén 专门 →P459"特意" …… 684	zú 足 …… 700
zhuǎn 转 …… 684	zǔ'ài 阻碍 →P701"阻止" …… 700
zhuǎnbiàn 转变 →P685"转化" …… 684	zǔzhǐ 阻止 →P700"阻碍" …… 701
zhuǎnhuà 转化 →P684"转变" …… 685	zǔchéng 组成 →P522"形成" …… 701
zhuāng 装 …… 685	zuì 最 →P113"顶" …… 702
zhuàngkuàng 状况 →P686"状态" …… 686	zuìchū 最初 →P263"开始" …… 703
zhuàngtài 状态 →P686"状况" …… 686	zuìjìn 最近 …… 703
zhǔn 准 …… 686	zūnjìng 尊敬 →P704"尊重" …… 704
zhǔnbèi 准备 →P609"预备" …… 687	zūnzhòng 尊重 →P704"尊敬" …… 704
zhǔnshí 准时 →P209"及时" …… 687	zuǒyòu 左右 →、P278"控制"、P371"前后"、P638"掌握" …… 704
zhuó 着 …… 687	zuò 作 →P706"做" …… 706
zǐxì 仔细 →P499"细心" …… 688	zuòwéi 作为 …… 706
zì 自 →P76"从"、P593"由"、P690"自从" …… 688	zuò 做 →P161"干"、P163"搞"、P706"作" …… 706

Aa

āi 挨

用法 Usage:

动词 v.

靠近,紧接着。*To be close to; to get close to; to be next to.*

(1) 孩子们喜欢挨着妈妈。

(2) 我家房子右边紧挨着一条小河。

介词 prep.

顺着次序(做某件事)。*In the order of; one after another; in turn.*

(3) 请大家排好队,挨个儿上车。

(4) 今天村里开会,你一定要挨家挨户地通知。

说明 Notes:

1. "挨"作动词用,表示句子中的人或事物紧靠或者紧接着的是另一人或事物,是对两者在空间位置上的说明。句子中一定有表示空间的参照物,如例(1)和(2)中的"妈妈"和"小河"。*When used as a verb in a sentence, both "挨" and "挨着" indicate that what is close to the person or thing is also a person or thing. There must be something serving as a point of reference, such as "妈妈" and "小河" respectively in (1) and (2).*

2. "挨"作介词用,表示做某件事的顺序标准,是对时间先后上的说明,因此句子中一定要有表示顺序标准的词语,如例(3)和(4)中的"挨个儿"和"挨家挨户"。*When used as a preposition, it indicates the standard for order in terms of time. Therefore, there must be a word or expression to indicate that order, as "挨个儿" and "挨家挨户" respectively in (3) and (4).*

ái 挨

用法 Usage:

动词 v.

1. 遭受,忍受。*To endure; suffer from; be subject to something undesirable.*

(1) 他没做作业,挨老师批评了。

(2) 小时候,我没挨过父母的打骂。

2. 困难地度过(时光)。*To survive (difficult times); to experience with difficulty.*

(3) 挨过了这三天,你的病就好起来了。

(4) 紧张的三年高中学习总算挨过来了。

3. 拖延。*To drag out; dawdle.*

(5) 她想在家多待几天,一直挨到星期天晚上才回公司。

(6) 他挨到最后一个才交上考卷。

说明 Notes:

1. "挨"作第一义项动词时,常含有"被"字句的语意,如例(1)。*In the first usage, the sentence usually indicates the passive voice. For example, in (1) "挨" is similar to "被."*

2. "挨"作第二、第三义项动词用时,句子常带有时段性的语意,句子中常有表示时间意义的词语。*In the second and third usages, there is often a word or expression indicating a period of time.*

3. 用在第三义项中,"挨"表示时间的拖延,常与"才"合用。*In the third usage, "挨" indicates postponing an event/action until a later time. In this usage "挨" is usually used with "才."*

àihào 爱好

用法 Usage:

动词 v.

表示对某种事物有很大的兴趣。*To like, show strong interest in something.*

（1）我爱好旅行,他爱好音乐。
（2）我们都爱好打太极拳。

名词 n.

表示某种兴趣。*Hobby, interest.*

（3）我的爱好是足球,他的爱好是音乐。
（4）她有很多兴趣爱好。

说明 Notes:

1."爱好"做动词时,"爱好"的宾语可以是名词性词语,如:"爱好音乐"也可以是动词性词语"爱好听音乐";"爱好太极拳"也可以是"爱好打太极拳";等等。此外,句子中没有其他动词。*In the first usage, "爱好" is a verb. The object of "爱好" can be a noun or a verb phrase. In "爱好音乐," the object of the verb "爱好" is "音乐," which is a noun. In "爱好听音乐," the object of the verb "爱好" is a verb phrase "听音乐." And so, both "爱好太极拳" and "爱好打太极拳" are correct.*

2."爱好"做名词时,在句子中是主语或者宾语,句子中必须有其他动词,还常与"兴趣"一起连用,如例（4）。*"爱好," as a noun, functions in a sentence either as the subject or as the object. There must be some other verb functioning as the predicate. As a noun, "爱好" usually appears with "兴趣," as in (4).*

àihù 爱护 →P2"爱惜"

用法 Usage:

动词 v.

1.对人或集体,词义重在爱的感情或名誉、权益等的保护上。*To cherish and protect (people, or things highly valuable such as reputation, rights and interests).*

（1）你要好好爱护妹妹。
（2）我们要像爱护自己的眼睛一样爱护学校的名誉。

2.对事物,词义重在爱惜并保护,不随便破坏或滥用。*To care for; to protect (an object); not to allow damage or misuse.*

（3）他非常爱护自己的新车。
（4）这是姐姐送的书,你要好好爱护。

说明 Notes:

1.用在表示说话者怀有某种希望的句子里,常常和"要"搭配使用。*When used to express a certain hope that the speaker harbors, "爱护" often goes with "要."*

2.用在叙述句中,应写出"爱护"的宾语,或者在句子前指出,如例（3）（4）。*In a declarative sentence, it is necessary to have something as the object of the verb "爱护," as in (3) and (4), where it is made clear in an earlier part of the sentence.*

àixī 爱惜 →P2"爱护"

用法 Usage:

动词 v.

因重视而不糟蹋;爱护珍惜。*To treasure or value out of love or appreciation; not to allow something to go to waste.*

（1）爱惜时间要像爱惜生命一样。
（2）我们要爱惜粮食。

说明 Notes:

1."爱护"和"爱惜"都是动词,都有表示重视和保护的意思。"爱护"侧重保护,使不受到损害,对象多指容易受到伤害的人和事物。"爱惜"侧重"惜",有"舍不得"、不糟蹋乱用的意思,对象多是容易消耗的事物等。*Both "爱护" and "爱惜" are verbs, and both mean "to cherish and protect." "爱护" emphasizes "protecting from harm." Its object is mostly people or things that are easily hurt or damaged.* "爱惜" *focuses on* "惜," *with the meaning of* "*not wanting to part company with*" *or* "*not allowing something to go to waste.*" *Its objects are mostly things which are easy to be used up.*

2. 应用时容易用错"爱护""爱惜"后面的宾语。*The objects after* "爱护" *or* "爱惜" *are often misused.*

（3）＊每个国家的政府都爱惜自己的人民。
（4）每个国家的政府都爱护自己的人民。
（5）＊我要爱护在中国的时间，努力学习汉语。
（6）我要爱惜在中国的时间，努力学习汉语。

āndìng 安定 →P492"稳定"

用法 Usage:

形容词 *a.*

人的情绪、生活和社会形势的平静、正常和稳定，常做谓语和定语。*(Of emotions, life, society, etc.) calm, normal, stable. It's often used as a predicate or an attribute.*

（1）社会不安定，经济很难发展。
（2）我希望有一个安定的学习环境。

动词 *v.*

使达到或保持生活、人心平静的状态。*To stabilize (one's life, emotions, etc.).*

（3）一到中国，先要安定生活。
（4）你先安定妈妈的情绪，其他的事我来做。

说明 Notes:

1. "安定"做谓语，前面常有副词修饰，如例（1）。如果单独做谓语，为描述性句子，谓语分句一般要两个以上，表示语义、语气的完整。*When* "安定" *is used as a predicate, it is often modified by an adverb, as in (1). If it is used as a predicate on its own and the sentence is descriptive, it is usually followed by a similar phrase for the sentence to sound complete.*

（5）改革开放以来，中国社会安定、经济发展，人民生活水平提高了很多。

2. "安定"的动词用法，一般只做谓语，后面一定要有宾语，如"安定人心、安定情绪、安定生活"等。*When* "安定" *is used as a verb, it must be followed by an object, such as* "安定人心,安定情绪,安定生活."

ānjìng 安静 →P339"宁静"、P358"平静"

用法 Usage:

形容词 *a.*

1. 没有声音，没有吵闹和喧哗（的环境）。*(Of surroundings) quiet, peaceful.*

（1）教室里很安静，大家都在做练习。
（2）夜晚，这里安静极了。

2. 安稳平静，常形容人物的外部状态，或生活状态。*(Of a person's appearance or living conditions) stable and peaceful.*

（3）她回到家乡后，过了几年安静生活。

说明 Notes:

1. "安静"单独做谓语，常带程度副词或者程度补语，完整句子的语气。如例（1）和（2）。*When* "安静" *serves as a predicate, a degree adverb or a degree complement is often used to complete the meaning of the sentence, as in (1) and (2).*

2. "安静"做谓语，如果带趋向动词"下来"作补语，"安静下来"表示开始安静的意思。*When* "安静" *is used as a predicate and followed by the directional verb* "下来" *as its complement, it means* "*to start to become quiet.*"

（4）请同学们安静下来，老师要上课了。

3. "安静"形容人或环境的外部状态，一般不形容人的内心情绪。"安静" *is commonly used to describe a person's appearance or demeanor, not his inner emotions.*

（5）＊我心里很不安静。
（6）我心里很不平静。（因为什么事引起的激动和烦恼等 *Being excited by or annoyed for some reasons*）
（7）我很不放心。（因为担心什么事引起的

不安 Being unsettled because of some worries）

ānpái 安排 →P4"安置"

用法 Usage:

动词 v.

有条理、分先后地处理（事物）；安置（人员）。To arrange things based on the order of priority; to make certain arrangements for people.

（1）明天开会的事情，你安排好了吗？
（2）学院安排我当图书馆馆员。

名词 n.

指有条理、有顺序处理事物、安置人员的内容。Orderly arrangement of things; the logistical arrangement for people to settle down.

（3）这个周末的安排很好。
（4）这些工作安排，大家都已经知道了。

ānzhì 安置 →P4"安排"

用法 Usage:

动词 v.

1. 使人或事物有着落，得到适当的安放、安排。To make appropriate arrangements for things; to help people settle down.

（1）新来的留学生都安置好了吗？
（2）客人的行李安置好了。

2. "安置"也有名词用法。"安置" can also be used as a noun, which means arrangement.

（3）她的工作得到了适当的安置。

说明 Notes:

"安排"和"安置"都有把事物、人员处理好的意思，但两者有一些区别。Although "安排" and "安置" both carry the meaning of making appropriate arrangements for people or things, there are some differences between them.

1. "安排"着重于对事物有条理、有先后、有次序地处理，侧重处理的程序和过程。"安置"着重于使人或事物有着落。"安排" means the methodical arrangement of a thing, with a focus on the process of handling. By contrast, "安置" focuses on the location or destination about the arrangement that is made.

2. 在语体上，"安排"比较口语化；"安置"多用于书面体。"安排" is more of a colloquial expression whereas "安置" is often used in written language.

àn 按 →P5"按照"、P530"压"、P641"照"

用法 Usage:

动词 v.

1. 表示用手或者手指头用力压一下什么东西。To press or push down with a finger or hand.

（1）请按门铃！
（2）你用力按那个白圆点，伞就打开了。

2. 抑制、忍住某种情绪。To restrain one's emotions.

（3）他按下怒火，耐心地又说了一遍。
（4）她按不住心中的悲伤，大哭起来。

3. 用手压住事物不动。To press down on something to prevent its movement.

（5）你快按住那些纸，别让风吹走！
（6）按住她的手，不要让她动。

4. 压住，搁下事情。To put aside; shelve.

（7）他的申请报告我按下了，没交上去。
（8）先按下别的事情，你赶快去医院看病！

介词 prep.

表示依照某种规定、标准做某件事。According to (rules or plans).

（9）按学校制度的规定，学分不够不能毕业。
（10）按计划，明天我要去北京旅游。

说明 Notes:

1. "按"作介词用，与后面的名词组成介词短语，句子中一定还有别的动词做谓语，"按"字短语用在谓语前面，见例（9）和（10）。When "按" is combined with a noun to make a prepositional phrase, the sentence needs a verb phrase as the predicate, which follows the prepositional phrase as seen in (9) and (10).

2. "按"可以构成"按……说、按……规定"等相对固定的格式。"按" can be used in set phrases such as "按…说" and "按…规定."

（11）按道理说,他应该来参加你的生日晚会。

（12）按学校规定,你已经不能参加考试了。

ànmó 按摩

用法 Usage:

动词 v.

用手或器械在人身上推、按、捏、揉等,以促进血液循环,通经络,调整神经功能。*To massage; to knead, press, rub or pinch body parts with fingers, hands or an apparatus to promote blood circulation or to relax the muscles (for therapeutic purposes).*

（1）我给你按摩一下,你的头就不会痛了。

（2）每天晚上按摩脚部,对睡眠有帮助。

（3）妈妈,你的腰又痛了吗? 我给你按摩按摩。

说明 Notes:

"按摩"可以修饰有些名词,组成新的名词。如:"按摩器、按摩椅、头部按摩法、按摩技术"等。"按摩" *can combine with certain nouns to form noun phrases, such as "按摩器,按摩椅,头部按摩法,按摩技术."*

ànzhào 按照 →P5"按"、P554"依照"

用法 Usage:

介词 prep.

1. 根据,遵从。*According to; following (the rule, principle, etc.)*

（1）按照学校的规定,下个星期开始放假了。

（2）大家按照他说的做吧。

2. 表示遵从某种标准、时间次序或顺序做。*Following the standard, sequence, or order in doing things; in order of.*

（3）全班同学按照从矮到高排成一队。

（4）请按照从一班到六班的顺序坐。

3. 与"来说"搭配,可以组成"按照……来说"的短语,强调所根据的道理或理由。*Forming the expression "按照…来说" to stress the cause or reason that has to be followed.*

（5）按照辈分来说,你要叫我叔叔。

（6）按照汉字的笔画顺序来说,你这个字的笔画写错了。

说明 Notes:

"按"表示遵照、遵从的意思时,与"按照"的意思基本相同,强调按某种规定或者常理为依据,但是用的时候,"按"后面可以跟单音节词,"按照"后面不跟单音节词语。"按" *and* "按照" *are synonyms when they mean to follow or obey rules or conventions. They differ in that* "按照" *is not usually followed by monosyllabic words but* "按" *can be.*

（7）今天的作业,请大家按时完成。

（8）*今天的作业,请大家按照时完成。

（9）今天的作业请大家按照规定时间完成。

ànshì 暗示

用法 Usage:

动词 v.

不明说表示的意思,而用含蓄的言语或示意的眼神、举动使人领会。*To convey an idea without explicit statements; to give a hint with subtle verbal or non-verbal cues; to suggest, hint or imply.*

（1）他眨了一下眼睛暗示我,叫我别说。

（2）她碰了一下我的后背,暗示我不要答应他的要求。

名词 n.

一种心理影响。用言语、手势、表情的方式向对方示意。*In psychology it means to provide cues or stimuli with verbal language, gestures, facial expressions, etc.*

（3）在医生的暗示下,他睡着了。

（4）不要再给她心理暗示,她胆子本来就小。

说明 Notes:

作动词用,一般后面要有宾语或补语。*As a verb,* "暗示" *is usually followed by an object or a complement.*

Bb

bǎ 把

用法 Usage:

动词 *v.*

1. 用手握住。*To hold by hand; to take hold of.*

(1) 你把着方向盘,开车不要多讲话。

(2) 我来把住梯子,你爬上去。

2. 看守、把守。*To watch; to guard (against).*

(3) 你俩把住大门,不要让别人进来。

(4) 今天没有人把门,寺庙随便进。

介词 *prep.*

跟名词或名词短语构成介词短语,用在动词前面作状语。"把"字构成的介词短语在句子中主要有以下几种语义作用:"把" *is a particle marking a noun or noun phrase that follows as a direct object. The "把" structure functions as an adverbial modifier preceding the verb with the following semantic functions in sentences:*

1. 表示处置。*To indicate "to handle, or to deal with."*

"把"字后面的名词是这个句子动词的受事者,句子的动词只能是及物动词,通过具体的动作使确定的事物发生位置移动、形态转换等变化。*The noun that follows "把" in the sentence is the recipient of the action verb, which must be exclusively transitive. Position shift or transformation of fixed things occurs through specific actions.*

(5) 我把那本书放在书架上了。(位置移动 *Indicating a move of the position*)

(6) 姐姐把房间整理好了。(形态转换 *Indicating the transformation of the form or shape*)

"把"后接动词一般不带宾语,但有时也带。*The verb after "把" usually does not take an object, but sometimes it does.*

(7) 把这封信贴上邮票寄出去。

2. 表示致使。*To indicate "to cause, or to result in."*

后面的动词可以是及物动词,也可以是不及物动词,甚至可以是部分表示人可以控制的情感或者状态的形容词如"高兴、忙、累、急、气"等加上表示结果的补语。"把"字后面的名词一般是动作或情况所涉及的人,通过动作在这个确定的人身上产生一定的影响或结果。*The verb that follows the "把" structure can be either transitive or intransitive verb, or an adjective that indicates the emotion or circumstance that people can take control of, such as "高兴、忙、累、急、气, etc.," followed by a resultant complement. The noun after "把" is usually the person related to the action or condition, through which certain influence or result is generated.*

(8) 你再惹他,他能把你吃了。

(9) 吃慢点,别把你噎着了。

(10) 考了100分,把她高兴得跳了起来。

3. 表示动作的处所或范围。*To indicate the location or scope of the action.*

"把"字后面常常跟表示处所、范围的名词或名词短语。*Usually a noun or noun phrase follows "把" to indicate the location or scope of the action.*

(11) 这几天我把整个杭州都玩遍了。

(12) 你把昨天做的作业再检查一下。

4. 构成"把……当作",表示"当成、看成、看作、比作"的意思。*To form the "把...当作" structure, which means "to regard ... as," or "to compare ... as" (当成,看成,看作,比作).*

(13) 中国朋友把我当作她的妹妹,我非常高兴。

(14) 把我的家看作你的家一样,别客气。

说明 Notes:

"把"作介词用,特别要注意句子中"把"字和名词、动词的搭配问题。*To properly understand the "把" structure, it is critical to know how to collocate "把" with the subsequent nouns and verbs.*

主要有以下几点:*The key points are as follows:*

1. "把"字和名词的搭配。*How to match "把" with nouns.*

不确定的事物名词,不能与"把"搭配。"把"字后面的名词所指的事物是确定的,或者是上文已经提到过的,或者是说话双方都知道的,如例(5)和(7)。所以,与"把"搭配的名词前面常常带有"这""那"等限制性的词语。*"把" is not used together with indefinite nouns. The nouns that follow "把" are always determined ones, or those mentioned in the preceding context, or known to both the speaker and the listener, as in (5) and (7). Therefore, nouns following "把" usually have determiners such as "这" or "那."*

(15) *今天我把一本书看完了。

(16) 今天我把这本书看完了。

(17) *我把很多书买了。

(18) 我买了很多书。/我把那些书都买来了。

2. "把"字和动词的搭配。*How to match "把" with verbs.*

① 与"把"字搭配的动词一般都是及物动词,在语义上能够支配"把"字引进的名词。不能带宾语的离合动词一般不能充当"把"字句的谓语。*Verbs that can collocate with "把" are generally transitive verbs, which can semantically dominate the nouns introduced by "把." Separable verbs, which cannot be followed by an object, are not applied as the predicate in the "把" structure.*

(19) *老师把同学去吃饭了。

(20) 老师把同学请去吃饭了。

(21) *你把他洗澡干净一点。

(22) 你给他洗澡洗得干净一点。

② 某些表示判断、状态的动词,没有具体动作意义的动词不能与"把"字搭配使用,如"有、在、是、像、属于"等。*Certain verbs indicating an assertion or status do not match with the "把" structure, due to the fact that they do not have meanings that are related to specific actions, for example, "有,在,是,像,属于, etc."*

(23) *我把英汉词典有了。

(24) 我有英汉词典了。

③ 心理活动的动词一般不能与"把"字搭配使用,如"觉得、听见、认识、知道、以为、相信、同意、赞成"等。*Generally speaking, verbs indicating psychological activities, such as "觉得,听见,认识,知道,以为,相信,同意,赞成,etc.," are not used with the "把" structure.*

(25) *我们把他妹妹认识了。

(26) 我们认识了他的妹妹。

(27) *他们把下午要开会知道了。

(28) 他们知道了下午要开会。/下午要开会他们知道了。

④ 趋向并带处所宾语的动词除了在歌词、唱词等韵文中(夫妻双双把家还)以外,不能与"把"字搭配使用,如"进、出、上、下、来、回、到"

等。Verbs indicating direction or inclination and following objects of location, such as "进，出，上，下，来，回，到，" cannot be used in the "把" structure, unless in songs or rhymed texts.

(29) *下个星期我把西班牙回。
(30) 我下个星期回西班牙。
(31) *上午八点，把教室进的时候，我看见了她。
(32) 上午八点，进教室的时候，我看见了她。

⑤ 带可能式补语的动词不能与"把"字搭配使用。Verbs followed by a complement indicating probability cannot be used in the "把" structure.

(33) *明天我把这本书看得完。
(34) 明天我看得完这本书。
(35) *洗衣机把这件衣服洗不干净。
(36) 洗衣机洗不干净这件衣服。

⑥ 表示开始、结束、延续的动词，如"开始、结束、出发、到达、继续"等，不能与"把"字配合使用。Verbs indicating the start, completion or continuation of an action, such as "开始,结束,出发,到达,继续," are not used in the "把" structure.

(37) *我们上午八点钟把课开始。
(38) 我们上午八点钟开始上课。

⑦ 句子中，与"把"字搭配的动词后面一定要带有其他成分，一般不单独用，尤其是单音节动词。与"把"配合的动词要表达的语义是怎么样做、做得怎么样，所以动词前后会带上具有说明性的词语。Verbs, especially monosyllabic verbs, which collocate with "把," are usually followed by other components in sentences. Illustrative words or phrases are used in the sentence because verbs in the "把" structure are to express semantically how something is done and what is done.

"把"字句结构为："把"+名词+动词+补语。一般有以下几种句子: The "把 + n. + v. + complement" structure generally has the following categories:

(39) 她把汉字一个一个地都写对了。(带状语和补语 Followed by an adverbial and a complement)
(40) 快把我的手机充上电。(带宾语 Followed by an object)
(41) 你把黑板上的画儿擦了。(动词后面常常带"着、了"，不带"过"。The verb is often followed by "着" or "了," but not "过.")
(42) 明天早上你把课文朗读朗读。(没有附带成分，动词本身就重叠一下。There is no complement, just the repetition of the verb.)
(43) 星期天你们要把宿舍打扫一下。(带补语 Followed by a complement)

⑧ 动补结构的双音节动词可以与"把"字搭配使用，如"扩大、缩小、集中、解散、提高、降低、证明、说服"等，动词后面要带补语。Disyllabic verbs such as "扩大,缩小,集中,解散,提高,降低,证明,说服," which consist of a verb and a complementary component by themselves, can be used in the "把" structure, followed by a complement.

(44) 请你把写论文的资料集中起来。
(45) 妈妈叫你把那几门功课的成绩都提高一下！

3. 副词(尤其是否定词)、能愿动词与"把"字的配合。How to match adverbs (especially negative adverbs) and modal verbs with the "把" structure.

副词(尤其是否定词)、能愿动词一般只能放在"把"字前面，不能用在后面。Adverbs (especially negative adverbs) and modal verbs usually precede the "把" structure instead of following it.

(46) *把汉语不学好我不回国。
(47) 不把汉语学好我不回国。
(48) *下午你把作业能做完吗？
(49) 下午你能把作业做完吗？

bǎwò 把握 →P638"掌握"

用法 Usage:

动词 v.

掌握(多用于事物发展的方向、机会,事物本质等)。*To grasp; to seize; to hold (in most cases by taking control of the direction, the trend, the opportunity, or the essence of things, etc.).*

(1) 我们要把握住改革开放的机会,发展经济。

(2) 把握好经济发展方向,提高人民生活水平。

名词 n.

表示事情成功的可能性。*Chance, or certainty of success.*

(3) 三天内写完这篇文章,你有把握吗?

(4) 我有把握,他至少能得第二名。

bàle 罢了

用法 Usage:

助词 modal particle

用在陈述句后面,表示如此而已,对句子所表示的意义起着减轻的作用,含有无足轻重、关系不大的意思,相当于"而已"。句子前还常有"不过、只是、无非"等减轻句子原意的词语。*"罢了" is a modal particle used at the end of a declarative statement, indicating the meaning of "only," "inconsequential" or "nothing more," which is similar to "而已." There are usually words such as "不过, 只是, 无非," at the beginning of the sentence to soften the tone of the original sentence.*

(1) 他不过说说罢了,他不会真的打你。

(2) 你不用着急,她只是昨天晚上没睡好罢了。

动词 v.

对某些人或事,表示容忍,不再计较。相当于"算了"。*"罢了" is also used as a verb to express tolerance of something, or no more haggling over something, which is similar to "算了 (forget it)."*

(3) 说了几遍,她都不听。罢了,罢了,不跟他多说了。

(4) 虽然我不愿意给他,可他是我弟弟,我只得罢了。

说明 Notes:

1. "罢了"在句子中用作助词,一般只在句子最后。"罢了"作动词用,可在句子最后,也可以单独成为一个分句,如例(3)。*"罢了" as a modal word is generally put at the end of the sentence, while as a verb, it can be put at the end of the sentence as well as an independent structure, as in (3).*

2. "罢了,罢了"连用时,常常表示无奈,有点不满意。*When "罢了" is reduplicated in the sentence, the speaker is dissatisfied, but he/she can do nothing about it.*

bái 白

用法 Usage:

形容词 a.

1. 像雪一样的颜色,与"黑"相对。*As white as snow, opposite to "黑 (black)."*

(1) 她穿了一件白衬衣。

(2) 宿舍的墙很白。

2. 没加别的什么东西,空白。*Nothing added; blank; empty.*

(3) 她只吃了一碗白饭,没有吃菜。

(4) 他交给我的是一张白纸,上面一个字也没写。

3. 比喻丧事。*Figuratively referring to funeral affairs.*

(5) 村里人办红白事都要放鞭炮。

副词 ad.

1. 表示行为动作没有取得相应的效果,或者没有达到相应的目的,没有效果,徒然。*It is used with the action verb to indicate the meaning of "with no effect or result," or "achieving no results," or "in vain."*

(6) 他白跑了一趟，没买到那本书。

(7) 你真是白学了两年汉语，连这两个字都读不出来。

2. 表示无代价，无报偿。Cost free; free of charge.

(8) 今天我白看了一场电影，票是朋友买的。

(9) 她常常自己付钱，不白吃别人的东西。

动词 v.

1. 明白，弄明白（多用于某些成语）。To discover; to come to understand (used in idioms or proverbs).

(10) 十年后，事实经过终于天下大白。

2. 斜着眼睛看人，表示轻视或不满。To cast a glance (out of scorn or contempt).

(11) 他总是拿眼白人，很不礼貌。

名词 n.

指与古文相对的白话。Vernacular Chinese (vs. classical Chinese).

(12) 这篇古文有文白对照，看得懂。

(13) 文章的词语半文半白，不够通顺。

说明 Notes:

副词"白"用作第一义项时，可以重叠使用，成为"白白"，但在语气上以及句子结构、语用条件上有以下差别："白" when used as an adverb can be reduplicated (as "白白"), which indicates the meaning of "in vain." However, there exist the following differences in tone, structure and function between "白" and "白白":

1. 在语义上，"白"有不付出代价或钱就能得到好处的意思，"白白"没有这个意思。例如，例(8)和(9)不能说成："白白" has the meaning of "gaining benefit from something for free or without cost," but "白白" has no such meaning. For instance, (8) and (9) cannot be converted to the following sentences:

(14) *今天我白白看了一场电影，票子是朋友买的。

(15) *她常常自己付钱，不白白吃别人的东西。

2. 在语气上，"白白"比"白"强调的语气较重。"白白" is more emphatic than "白" in tone.

(16) 你没听我的话，我白说了那么多。

(17) 你没听我的话，我白白说了那么多。

3. 在句子前后的语用条件上，有以下不同："白" and "白白" have the following differences in pragmatic functions in sentences:

① "白"可以修饰单独的动词或单音节动词，而"白白"修饰的动词前后要有其他修饰词语或补充词语，不能修饰单音节动词。"白" is used to modify monosyllabic verbs, while "白白" is not. There must be other modifiers or complements before or after the verbs when "白白" is used.

(18) *不要再说了，你再说也是白白说。

(19) 不要再说了，你再说也是白说。

(20) *不要再说了，你再说也是白白费时间和精力。

(21) 不要再说了，你再说也是白白浪费时间和精力。

② "白白"后面可以加"地"，构成"白白地"作状语修饰动词，"白"后面不能加"地"。"白白" is used with "地" to form an adverbial structure, while "白" cannot be used this way.

(22) *他到国外根本没去学校学习。他妈妈白地花了那么多钱。

(23) 他到国外根本没去学校学习。他妈妈白白地花了那么多钱。

③ "白"前面可以有"不、没、不会、不能"等否定词语的修饰，并且有了强调语气。单音节"白"变成双音节"白白"，一般"白白"前面不用否定词语。"不, 没, 不会, 不能" can precede "白" in order to emphasize the negation. But "白白" is not generally used with negative words.

(24) *我们的太极拳表演得了第一名，我们的功夫没白白下。

(25) 我们的太极拳表演得了第一名，我们的功夫没白下。

(26) *这种药很有用。我没白白花钱。
(27) 这种药很有用。我没白花钱。

bǎi 摆 →P145"放"

用法 Usage:

动词 v.

1. 安放,排列。To put; to place; to array.
(1) 她家的窗台上摆了很多盆花。
(2) 把你桌子上的东西摆摆整齐。

2. 摇动、摇摆。To wave, to waggle.
(3) 她向我摆摆手,说了声再见,就走了。
(4) 远远地,我看见孩子们还在摆着双手。

3. 陈述,列举出来。To list; to enumerate.
(5) 你们要摆出理由来,我才会答应你们的要求。
(6) 你们有什么困难、问题,摆出来吧!

说明 Notes:

1. "摆"作动词用,后面可以带"着、了、过",可重叠用,如例(2)(3)(4)。"摆" as a verb can be followed by "着,了,过," and it can also be reduplicated, as in (2), (3) and (4).

2. 语意侧重于把东西有次序地排列出来,一般用"摆"。"摆" is generally used when things are arranged in good order.

bàn 办

用法 Usage:

动词 v.

1. 办理,处理。To conduct; to handle.
(1) 你首先要办一张银行卡,才能取钱。
(2) 办出国护照需要什么材料?

2. 创建,经营,举办。To set up; to manage; to hold.
(3) 我在学院办了一个绘画展览。
(4) 他在年轻时办了一所小学。
(5) 大学毕业后,他在网上办了一家商店。

3. 采购,置办。To place an order; to purchase.
(6) 我结婚时,你帮我办酒席好吗?

说明 Notes:

使用"办"第三义项时要注意:The following are things that you need to be careful about when using "办" in its third meaning:

"办"后面的宾语一般含有意思比较具体的名词,或者这个名词意思前文已有交代,或者有修饰语加以限定。如例(6)。The object of the verb "办" is usually nouns with a specific meaning, or it is something that has been mentioned previously in the context, or there is a modifier to specify it, as in (6).

又如:Other examples are as follows:
(7) *明天我要去上海办服装。
(8) 明天我要去上海办一批儿童服装。

bànfǎ 办法 →P78"措施"

用法 Usage:

名词 n.

处理事情或解决问题的方法。Method(s) used to deal with a problem.
(1) 这孩子哭起来就没完,我真没办法。
(2) 他是个很有办法的人。
(3) 这真是个好办法!

bāng 帮 →P12"帮助"

用法 Usage:

动词 v.

1. 帮助。To help.
(1) 你要我帮你吗?
(2) 我常常帮奶奶洗衣服。

2. 指从事雇佣劳动。To be employed as a laborer.
(3) 他是农民,现在城里帮人打工。
(4) 我在一家饭店帮厨。

名词 n.

1. 物体两旁或周围的部分,一般"帮"后面有"儿"。Both sides of a thing or all the parts around a thing, and the retroflex ending "儿(r)" is usually added.
(5) 这双鞋,帮儿是红的,底儿是白的,好看!

2. 有些蔬菜外面较老的叶子。The stem, or the outside part of a cabbage

(6) 这些菜帮太老了。

说明 Notes：

"帮"是单音节动词，在请求、希望的祈使句中一般重叠使用或在后面跟上表示小量、少量的副词"一下、一会儿"等，表示礼貌、客气的请求语气。"帮" as a monosyllabic word is usually reduplicated or followed by "一下" and "一会儿" in imperative sentences making a request or wish. It indicates humility or politeness of the speaker in making the request.

(7) *请你帮我。

(8) 请你帮我一下/请你帮帮我。

(9) *希望在汉语学习上你能帮我。

(10) 希望在汉语学习上你能帮帮我/你能帮我一下。

bāngmáng 帮忙 →P12"帮助"

用法 Usage：

动词 v.

帮助别人做事。To give a helping hand in doing something.

(1) 如果你有困难，他一定会帮忙。

(2) 请你帮一下忙，帮我拿一件行李。

说明 Notes：

"帮忙"是离合词，在动词和宾语之间可以插入名词性词语或数量词语，如例(2)，又如"帮个忙、帮帮忙"等，不能再带其他宾语。"帮忙" is a separable verb with the VO (verb+object) structure. So nouns or quantitative numerals can be inserted, as in (2). Other examples include "帮个忙，帮一下忙, etc." But no other objects could follow.

bāngzhù 帮助 →P11"帮"、P12"帮忙"

用法 Usage：

动词 v.

替人出力、出主意或给以物质上、精神上的支持。To lend a hand, or help or support materially, mentally, or spiritually.

(1) 这本书帮助我了解了中国的历史。

(2) 我们要互相帮助，互相学习。

名词 n.

"帮助"在某些场合可以用作名词。"帮助" can be used as a noun on certain occasions.

(3) 她有困难，我们应该给她点帮助。

(4) 这本书给我的帮助很大。

说明 Notes：

1. "帮"与"帮助"做动词，表示别人有困难给以支持时，意思相同。When used as a verb, "帮" and "帮助" both mean "to give support to someone in need."

它们的区别是：There are some differences between them:

① "帮"和"帮助"后面都可以带"过、了"。"帮"还可以带"着"，然后再带一个动词，但是"帮助"一般不能带"着"。Both "帮" and "帮助" can be followed with particles such as "了" or "过," but only "帮" can be used in the "帮 着 + v." structure. "帮助" cannot be used this way.

(5) *她正帮助着我洗衣服呢。

(6) 她正帮着我洗衣服呢。

② "帮助"有名词用法，而"帮"没有名词用法。"帮助" can be used as a noun, while "帮" cannot.

(7) *她很需要大家的帮。

(8) 她很需要大家的帮助。

2. "帮助"与"帮忙"的区别是："帮助" and "帮忙" are different in the following aspects:

① 在语义上，"帮助"着重于给以协助，可以是替人出力、办事情或给以物质的资助，也可以是替人出主意，解决思想上的问题，给以精神上的支持。施事者可以是人，也可以是事物，如"帮助"的例(1)和(4)，使用范围比较广。"帮忙"着重于帮助别人，使其繁忙状况或着急情绪有所缓解。"帮助" has a broader meaning and emphasizes semantically "providing assistance by making a contribution physically, or giving mental support by exerting oneself to contribute ideas or advice". The agent of the verb can be a person or a thing, as in (1) and (4) under "帮

助。" However, "帮忙" stresses helping others to get out of an overly busy or hectic situation.

②"帮助"做谓语可带宾语,还可以与"在……下"组成"在……的帮助下",做句子的状语。"帮忙"是离合词,做谓语不能带宾语,也不能组成"＊在……的帮忙下"。"帮助" can be followed by an object, while "帮忙" is a separable verb and cannot be followed by an object. "帮助" can be used in the adverbial structure "在... 的帮助下," but "帮忙" cannot be used this way.

(9) ＊她帮忙我买到了这本书。
(10) 她帮助我买到了这本书。

③"帮忙"没有名词用法。"帮忙" cannot be used as a noun.

(11) ＊我想请她给我一个帮忙。
(12) 我想请她给我一个帮助。

④"帮忙"中间可以插入其他成分,如"请你帮个忙",但"帮助"不行。Complements can be inserted between the two characters of "帮忙." For example, "请你帮个忙," but "帮助" cannot be used this way.

bāo 包

用法 Usage:
动词 v.

1. 用纸或布等把东西裹起来。To wrap something with paper, cloth or something else.
(1) 我们过春节,一定要包饺子。
(2) 请你把那几个蛋糕包起来。

2. 承担下任务,负责完成。To undertake a task and be responsible for its completion.
(3) 以前大学毕业生国家包分配。
(4) 这里所有的工作都包给我了。

3. 保证,担保。To guarantee; to assure.
(5) 这个宾馆的服务态度包你满意。
(6) 只要认真学习半年,包你会说汉语。

4. 付款承包,约定专用。To charter; to lease or pay for a temporary and exclusive use of something.

(7) 为了游览西湖,我们包了一条船。
(8) 明天我们包一辆车去上海。

5. 容纳在里面,总括在一起。常用于四字词语,如:"无所不包、包罗万象"。To include, contain or hold as a whole. It is frequently used in four-word idioms such as "无所不包" and "包罗万象."

名词 n.

1. 装东西的口袋。A bag.
(9) 带一个大包吧,我们要去超市买东西。
(10) 桌子上那个包是我的。

2. 包裹起来的东西。A package.
(11) 行李包已经打好了。
(12) 我要给妈妈寄个邮包。

3. 身体或物体上鼓起来的疙瘩。A lump on a body or an object.
(13) 不知为什么,我头上起了个大包。
(14) 这棵树的树干上长了很多包。

4. 毡制的圆顶帐篷。Dome-shaped tent made by felt; yurt.
(15) 草原上有很多蒙古包。

bāohán 包含 →P13"包括"

用法 Usage:
动词 v.

(指某种事物)里面含有。To contain; imply.
(1) 这句话包含了很多意思。
(2) 每件事情都包含着它的原因和结果。

bāokuò 包括 →P13"包含"

用法 Usage:
动词 v.

包含,容纳在内(列举各部分内容,或者指出其中一二项)。To include (listing every item or just one or two of them).
(1) 房租不包括水电费。
(2) 汉语课包括听、说、读、写四个方面。

说明 Notes:

"包含"和"包括"都指事物内部含有,如果指事物在数量或范围上的含有,两个词语常可以互用。例如,"包括"的例句(1)和(2)也可以用"包含"替代"包括"。"包含"and"包括"both mean containing something inside. The two words are interchangeable when used to indicate the inclusion of a certain amount or scope. For example, "包括" in (1) and (2) under "包括" can be replaced by "包含."

两者的区别是：Their differences are as follows:

1. 如果句子着重指事物内部的内在关系，用"包含"。例如，"包含"的例句(1)和(2)一般不能用"包括"替代"包含"。If the sentence stresses the internal relations between things, use "包含." For example, "包含" in (1) and (2) under "包含" cannot be replaced by "包括."

2. "包括"着重指出事物在数量上、范围上的各个部分或其中一部分。"包括" emphasizes all or a part of a certain amount or scope of something.

bāozhuāng 包装

用法 Usage:

动词 v.

1. 用专门的纸张把商品包裹起来，或者把商品装进盒子、瓶子等容器中。To pack goods with wrapping paper, or put goods into boxes, bottles or other containers.

(1) 请把这束花包装一下！

(2) 包装商品要讲究艺术。

2. 比喻对人或事物从形象上装扮、美化，使其更具吸引力或商品价值。(Figuratively) to dress up people or package things to make them more attractive or more commercially valuable.

(3) 这个明星是包装出来的。

名词 n.

指包装商品的纸、盒子、瓶子，或者人的衣着、服饰等。A reference to package such as wrapping paper, box or bottle; or people's dresses.

(4) 现在商品的包装越来越漂亮了。

(5) 年轻女孩很重视自身的包装。

bǎoguì 宝贵 →P646"珍贵"

用法 Usage:

形容词 a.

表示非常有价值、非常难得、很珍贵的意思。Highly valuable; quite rare and precious.

(1) 时间是很宝贵的。

(2) 北京有很多宝贵的文化遗产。

(3) 你的方法是非常宝贵的经验，我要向你学习。

说明 Notes:

"宝贵"多修饰表示抽象事物的名词，搭配的词语常有："生命、感情、青春、财富、经验、意见、精神、遗产、品质"等。"宝贵" is usually used to modify abstract nouns such as "生命,感情,青春,财富,经验,意见,精神,遗产,品质, etc."

bǎochí 保持 →P487"维持"

用法 Usage:

动词 v.

维持住原来的状况，使不消失或减弱。To maintain the original condition so that it does not vanish or weaken.

(1) 请大家保持教室干净。

(2) 回国以后我们要保持联系。

bǎohù 保护 →P15"保卫"、P487"维护"

用法 Usage:

动词 v.

尽力照顾、守护，使不受损害。To take care of; to protect from harm.

(1) 这些名胜古迹保护得很好。

(2) 为了保护眼睛，她从来不玩手机游戏。

bǎoliú 保留

用法 Usage:

动词 v.

1. 留着不去掉，保存不变。To keep something from any changes.

（1）这幅画保留着他年轻时候的绘画特点。

（2）家乡的老房子还保留着原来的样子。

2. 留着不拿出来。*To preserve, not sharing with others.*

（3）爷爷的画,他只保留了两幅,其他的都送给朋友了。

（4）有两张照片我要保留,别的你都可以拿去。

3. 暂时留着不处理(对象为对问题的看法、意见)。*To reserve someone's views or opinions.*

（5）不同的意见可以保留,我们明天再讨论。

4. 表示持否定意见或不同看法。*To express a negative opinion or a different view.*

（6）对学院的这个决定,我保留自己的看法。

bǎowèi 保卫 →P14"保护"

用法 Usage:

动词 *v.*

护卫,使不受侵犯。*To guard from encroachment.*

（1）他为了保卫国家去当兵了。

（2）全世界人民都要为保卫和平而努力。

说明 Notes:

"保卫"和"保护"的区别是：*The differences between "保卫" and "保护" are as follows:*

1. "保护"意思着重于照顾,使不受损害,对象多是人或事物。*"保护" emphasizes giving care and keeping from harm, the objects of which are mostly people or things.*

2. "保卫"意思着重于防卫,使不受侵犯,对象多是国家主权、生命安全等,如："保卫边疆、保卫和平、保卫下一代"。*"保卫" emphasizes guarding from invasion, the objects of which are mostly national sovereignty, life, or safety. For example, "保卫边疆,保卫和平,保卫下一代."*

bǎoxiǎn 保险

用法 Usage:

名词 *n.*

一种处理风险的方法。*Insurance, a way to deal with risk.*

（1）你得到的工资,已经扣除了社会保险的费用。

（2）一般旅游费中都含有一份人身保险。

形容词 *a.*

表示稳妥可靠的意思。*Reliable; trustworthy.*

（3）人们认为把钱存在银行里最保险。

（4）那件事这样做非常保险,我同意。

副词 *ad.*

表示确定,肯定的意思。*Definitely; of great certainty.*

（5）明天一早,你先生保险会来接你回去。

（6）我保险你能拿到奖学金。

bǎoyǎng 保养

用法 Usage:

动词 *v.*

1. 保护调养,使身体保持健康。*To take care of one's health so as to keep fit.*

（1）现在的老人很会保养身体。

（2）她保养得很好,看上去很年轻。

2. 通过经常性的检查、修理,使(机器、车辆)保持正常状况。*To maintain the normal condition of a vehicle or machine by regular maintenance*

（3）我的车每年都要保养一次。

（4）家用电器保养得好,使用期可以在十年以上。

说明 Notes:

"保养"的第一种用法,只限于人,不能用于动物。*The first usage of "保养" can only be applied to humans, not animals.*

bǎozhèng 保证

用法 Usage:
动词 v.

1. 确保既定的要求和标准,不打折扣。*To make sure that certain requirements or standards are fully met.*
(1) 中学生每天要保证有八个小时的睡眠时间。
(2) 最重要的是要保证产品质量。

2. 担保,担保做到。*To ensure; guarantee to accomplish.*
(3) 每个学期学生上课时间必须保证在三分之二以上。
(4) 我保证今天就完成作业。

名词 n.

起担保作用的事物或条件。*Things or conditions that are used as guarantee.*
(5) 社会和谐是改革开放成功的保证。
(6) 努力认真才是学习好的第一保证。

说明 Notes:

使用"保证"动词第二个义项时,后面的宾语多是动词或动词性词语,如例(3)和(4)。*When the second meaning of "保证" as a verb is used, the object is mostly a verb or a verb phrase as in (3) and (4).*

bàoqiàn 抱歉 →P100"道歉"

用法 Usage:
形容词 a.

形容因对不起别人而心里不安。可形容不安的心情,也可用于直接向别人表示歉意。*Feeling sorry and apologetic. It can express an uneasy feeling or a worry, and can also be used directly as an apology.*
(1) 她抱歉地说:"打扰你了,对不起!"
(2) 我很抱歉,昨天我不应该对你态度不好。

bào 爆

用法 Usage:
动词 v.

1. 猛然炸裂或迸出。*To explode; burst.*
(1) 汽车的轮子爆了。
(2) 玻璃杯爆了。

2. 突然出现或发生。*To happen or take place abruptly.*
(3) 我们学校爆出大新闻了。
(4) 昨天的足球赛爆冷门了。

3. 一种烹调方法,用旺火热油快速烹炒。*(As a way of cooking) to use hot cooking oil and big fire to quickly fry something for a dish.*
(5) 我今天中午请你吃爆鱿鱼卷。

bàofā 爆发

用法 Usage:
动词 v.

1. 火山内部岩浆冲破地壳向外喷发。*(Of volcano) to erupt.*
(1) 那座火山爆发了。

2. 突然发生,突然发作。*To take place or break out suddenly.*
(2) 昨天晚上他突然爆发了头痛病。
(3) 那年战争爆发,我的大学生活就结束了。

说明 Notes:

"爆发"一词使用的范围比较宽广。首先用于火山、大火、雷电等,同时也用于战争、革命、大举动、大声音等。*"爆发" is used widely. It describes the outbreak of a volcano, fire, lightning, etc. and also the outbreak of a war, revolution, big event and loud voice, etc.*
(4) 晚上十一点,邻居家突然爆发出一阵大笑。
(5) 1789年,法国大革命爆发。

bēi 背

用法 Usage:
动词 v.

1. 人用脊背驮东西。*To carry on the back.*

(1) 小时候爸爸常常背我。
(2) 孩子们高高兴兴地背着书包去学校。

2. 负担,承担。*To shoulder a responsibility; bear a burden.*
(3) 爸爸是背了债供我上学的。
(4) 这么大的责任我可背不起。

说明 Notes:
"背"在第一个义项中,宾语一般是"孩子、书包、背篓"等,通常不是太大或太重。*For the first usage, the objects of the verb "背" are usually not too big nor too heavy such as "孩子,书包,背篓."*

bēishāng 悲伤 →P17"悲痛"

用法 Usage:
形容词 *a.*
伤心,悲痛,难过。*Sad; mournful.*
(1) 姐姐的病很重,他很悲伤。
(2) 你别太悲伤了,钱丢了没关系,人没伤着就好。

bēitòng 悲痛 →P17"悲伤"

用法 Usage:
形容词 *a.*
极度伤心。*Grieved; being in extreme sadness.*
(1) 大火烧掉了森林,大家都非常悲痛。
(2) 我们要化悲痛为力量,重建家园。

说明 Notes:
"悲伤"跟"悲痛"的区别是:*The differences between "悲伤" and "悲痛" are as follows:*
1. "悲痛"是由重大的不幸事件引起的,难受到心痛,程度比"悲伤"深重。*"悲痛" is caused by a traumatic event that causes a most painful feeling. It is more profound than "悲伤."*
2. 可以说"化悲痛为力量",不能说"化悲伤为力量"。*We say "化悲痛为力量 (to turn sadness or sorrow into strength)," but we do not say "化悲伤为力量."*

běibiān 北边 →P17"北方"

用法 Usage:
名词 *n.*
1. 北,表示方向,常带儿化音为"北边儿"。*(Of direction) north; it is pronounced with a retroflex suffixation as "北边儿" in the northern dialect.*
(1) 教室在图书馆的北边儿。
(2) 图书馆北边儿是教室。

2. 指北部地区。在中国,指黄河流域及其以北的地区。*The northern region. In China, it refers to the Yellow River Basin and the region to its north.*
(3) 我刚到北边的时候,生活很不习惯。
(4) 北边的人长得高大。

běifāng 北方 →P17"北边"

用法 Usage:
名词 *n.*
1. 北,北面。*North; the north side.*
(1) 飞机向北方飞去了。
(2) 北方的天气比较干燥。

2. 指北部地区。在中国,指黄河流域及其以北的地区。*The northern region. In China, it refers to the Yellow River Basin and the region to its north.*
(3) 我刚到北方的时候,生活很不习惯。
(4) 北方人长得高大。

说明 Notes:
1. "北边儿"既可用于近距离,也可用于远距离,用"北方"的地方都可以换作"北边儿"。*"北边儿" can suggest both a short distance and a long distance, so "北方" can be replaced by "北边儿."*
2. "北方"一般只用于相对远的距离。*"北方" indicates a long distance only.*
(5) *教室北方的墙上挂着世界地图。
(6) 教室北边儿的墙上挂着世界地图。
(7) *图书馆的北方是食堂。

(8) 图书馆的北边儿是食堂。

bèi 背

用法 Usage:

名词 n.

1. 人体背部。Back of the body.

(1) 请你帮我擦擦背上的汗！

(2) 他的背很宽，看起来很有力量。

2. 某些物体的反面或后部，常读儿化音。Back or reverse side of a certain object; usually pronounced with a retroflex suffixation as "背儿" in the northern dialect.

(3) 手背上被虫子咬了一口，很痛。

(4) 椅子背儿上写着什么字？

动词 v.

1. 背部对着（跟"向"相对）。To back on(to); to sit, stand, move, etc. with the back towards (opposite to "向").

(5) 中国农村传统的房屋常常是背山面水。

(6) 背着光拍照，脸上光线比较暗。

2. 离开的意思。To go away; to leave.

(7) 不少农民背井离乡到城市打工。

3. 躲避，瞒。To conceal; to do something behind sb.'s back.

(8) 他背着大家，不知道在干什么事。

(9) 好话不背人，背人没好话。

4. 背诵。To recite; to learn by heart.

(10) 他每天早上都要背二十分钟课文。

5. 违背，违反。To violate; to act in violation of.

(11) 这是个背信弃义的人。

6. 朝着相反的方向。To turn away from.

(12) 她把脸背过去，装作没看见我。

bèijǐng 背景

用法 Usage:

名词 n.

1. 布景，即舞台上或电影、电视剧里衬托人物活动的四周的环境、景物等设施。Backdrop. It refers to the settings on stage, or in films or TV series.

(1) 这次演出，舞台背景很漂亮。

(2) 现在电影里的背景很多都是电脑制作的。

2. 图画、摄影里对主体事物起衬托作用的景物。Background against the main objects in a picture or photograph.

(3) 照片中的人还可以，背景不太清楚。

3. 对人物活动或事态发生、发展起重要作用的历史条件或现实环境。The historical or social context that plays an important role in the development of activities or events.

(4) 关于这个故事，我先介绍一些历史背景。

(5) 他们为什么分手，要了解一下背景原因。

4. 指人背后的靠山，即人背后依仗的力量。Powerful or influential connections as somebody's anchor.

(6) 她能进大公司，一定有背景。

bèi 被 →P231"叫"、P389"让"

用法 Usage:

介词 prep.

1. 用在句子动词前，引进动作的施事者，表示主语是动作的接受者。施事者放在"被"字后。By. It is used before a verb in the passive voice to introduce the performer of an action, and to indicate that the subject is the recipient of an action. The performer is placed after "被."

(1) 我买的香蕉被他们吃完了。

(2) 玛丽被老师叫去了。

2. "被"+动词+少数名词，构成名词性词语。如："被打者、被偷者、被雇用者"等。"被"+v.+n. forms a noun phrase, such as "被打者，被偷者，被雇用者, etc."

3. "被"+名词+"所"+单音节动词（+双音节动词时，"所"也可不写），构成带有文言色彩的词语，"被"可改为"为"字，多用于书面语。"被"+n.+"所"+monosyllabic verb forms a

phrase in the classical Chinese style (when the monosyllabic verb is replaced by a disyllabic verb, "所" can be omitted). It's often used in written language and "被" can be replaced by "为."

(3) 他们的旅行被风雨所阻,没能去成。

(4) 老师被他的学习态度所感动,特别安排时间给他上课。

助词 *aux. v.*

1. 用在动词前,表示这个动作是被动的,省略了施事者,构成被动结构。*It is used before the verb in the passive voice where the performer of the action is omitted.*

(5) 她被批评了。

(6) 他的自行车被偷了。

2. 口语里常常使用、相对固定的"被"字结构:"被……＋把＋动词、被……＋给＋动词"。*In colloquial language, the comparatively fixed pattern is either "被…＋把＋v." or "被…＋给＋v."*

(7) 这孩子太吵闹,被我把他拉出去了。

(8) 那块蛋糕太脏了,被我给丢了。

说明 Notes:

1. 汉语中被动句有两种,一种是有"被"字的被动句,如例(1)(2)。另一种是没有"被"字的被动句,被称为"意义上的被动句"。*There are two types of passive sentences in Chinese: one is the type with the word "被," as in (1) and (2). The other is the type without the word "被," which is called "the passive voice in meaning."*

① 无"被"字的被动句。*The passive sentence without the word "被."*

无"被"字的被动句,又称为意义上的被动句,常常是为了强调某事物受到某种动作的处置或影响后的结果、状况,并不需要指出施事者,所以不用"被/叫/让"字。无"被"字的被动句常用于口语。*A passive sentence without the word "被" is generally used to emphasize the result or condition of an object after being affected or influenced by a certain action, of which the performer is not necessarily mentioned. Therefore, the word "被/叫/让" is not used. Passive sentences without "被" are more common in spoken language.*

(9) 房间打扫得很干净!

(10) 你要的香蕉买来了。

② 有"被"字的被动句。*The passive sentence with the word "被."*

谓语动词前面有介词"被(叫、让)"的句子,叫有"被"字的被动句。有"被"字的被动句是为了避免歧义,清楚地表明动作的施事者或受事者,特别要强调施事者而用"被"字的被动句。有"被"字的被动句多用于书面语。*A sentence with the predicate verb preceded by preposition "被/叫/让" is called the passive sentence with "被." The word "被" is used to avoid ambiguity. It clearly shows the performer or the recipient of the action, and the emphasis is on the performer. Passive sentences with "被" are more common in written language.*

(11) 湖水被阳光照得金红金红的,非常美丽。

(12) 我们昨天晚上去跳舞的事儿被妈妈知道了。

有"被"字的被动句,使用"被"字时要注意与其他词语的搭配。否定副词和能愿动词要用在"被"字前面;表示时间状语的副词,如"刚才、已经、终于、突然"等,要用在"被"字前面;表示动作情况重复或不断交替的副词,如"又、常常、时常、再"等,要用在"被"字前面。*When "被" is used in the passive sentence, its collocation with other words should be noticed. Negative adverbs and modal verbs should be used before "被"; adverbs indicating a time such as "刚才, 已经, 终于" and "突然" should be used before "被"; adverbs indicating a repetitive or consecutive action or condition such as "又, 常*

常,时常,再" should be used before "被," too.

（13）这次考试,她没被学校录取。
（14）我们去上海的事可能被老师知道了。
（15）她刚才被她的同学叫去了。
（16）电脑又被你搞坏了。

2. 两类被动句在用词上的共同要求：
Common requirements of the two types of passive sentences in word usage:

① 句子中的名词一般是已知的、认定的。所以名词前面一定有修饰或限制的词语。The nouns in the sentences are usually known and defined. Therefore, there should be a modifier or qualifier before the noun.

（17）那本书被小王借走了。
（18）我的信写完了。你的信写完了吗？

② 被动句的谓语动词必须是及物动词。动词所带的宾语应是主语的一部分,是主语经过动作支配达到的结果,或者主语是处所名词等。The predicate verb in the passive sentences should be a transitive verb. The object of the verb should be part of the subject and it is the result of the subject influenced by an action; or the subject is a place noun.

（19）铅笔被小王借去了一支。
（20）她被全班同学选为代表去表演节目。
（21）墙上贴满了同学们的书画作品。

③ 如果是单个动词充当被动句的谓语动词,动词往往带有状语、补语、能愿动词或"了、过"等助词,如例(17)(19)(21)等。谓语动词只限于少数双音节动词,并且在"被"字前面一定要有助动词或表示时间的词语,且谓语动词常常位于句末,如例(13)(14)。If the predicate verb of the passive sentence is a monosyllabic verb, it is usually used with an adverb, complement, modal verb or an auxiliary word such as "了,过," as in (17), (19) and (21). The predicate verbs are limited to only a few disyllabic verbs, and there should be an auxiliary verb or a word indicating the time before "被." In this case, the predicate verb is often placed at the end of the sentence, as in (13) and (14).

（22）我的汉语不好,所以我说的话常常被中国朋友误会。
（23）我会跟你保持联系的。这点一定会被我给你的电话证明。

3. 使用"被"字时容易错的几种情况：
Common mistakes in using "被" in passive sentences:

① 不需要用"被"字,却用了"被"字。The unnecessary use of the word "被."

（24）＊电影《英雄》很早的时候就被看过了。
（25）＊《茶馆》是被老舍写的。

② 应该用"被"字却没有用。The incorrect omission of the word "被."

（26）＊她派到德国去教了两年汉语。
（27）＊最后留下来的几个旅客接走了。

③ 句子中,"被"字错位(或者说是其他词语错位)。The misplacement of the word "被" (or misplacement of some other word).

（28）＊她被她同学刚才叫去了。
（29）她刚才被她同学叫去了。
（30）＊这次考大学,她被学校没录取。
（31）这次考大学,她没被学校录取。
（32）＊我们去上海的事可能老师被知道了。
（33）我们去上海的事可能被老师知道了。

④ 没有谓语动词。The absence of the predicate verb.

（34）＊回家的路上突然下雨了。我的衣服被雨湿了。
（35）回家的路上突然下雨了。我的衣服被雨淋湿了。

⑤ 有"被"字的介宾词语放在了谓语动词后面。The word "被" and the object of the preposition misplaced after the predicate verb.

（36）＊我的词典搞丢了被小王。
（37）我的词典被小王搞丢了。

⑥ 谓语动词后面缺少补充词语,没有说明

动作的结果或影响。The absence of a supplemental word after the predicate verb, with no indication of the result or influence of the action.

(38) *今天上课的时候,我被老师问,三个问题都没有回答。

(39) 今天上课的时候,我被老师问了三个问题,(三个问题)都没回答对。

běn 本 →P21"本来"

用法 Usage:

名词 n.

1. 草木的茎和根。如:"水有源,木有本。" Stems and roots of vegetation. For example, "水有源,木有本."

2. 事物的根本,根源(与"末"相对)。The essence or origin of things, as opposed to "末."

(1) 现在生活富裕了,但也不能忘本。

(2) 一定要搞清楚事情是怎么开始的,千万别本末倒置。

3. 本钱,本金。Capital; principal.

(3) 这次生意没做好,连本儿都赔进去了。

(4) 祝你一本万利,财源滚滚!

4. 本子,本儿。如:"笔记本儿"。Notebook. For example, "笔记本儿."

代词 pron.

1. 用在名词前,说话人指自己或者自己所在的集体、机构、处所。如:"本人、本校、本地、本市"等。Used before a noun, it refers to the speaker or the community, institution or place where the speaker belongs. For example, "本人,本校,本地,本市, etc."

2. 相当于"这"。一般由"本+名词(表示事物的)"构成,以制作者或主管人身份措词时用。如:"本书共有三册。""本次航班由上海飞往北京。"等等。Similar to "这," it is usually composed of "本 + n. (of something)." It is used when the speaker is the maker or executive of something. For example, "本书共有三册." "本次航班由上海飞往北京."

3. 本+时间名词,指包括说话时间在内的一段时间。如:"本年度、本星期三、本世纪初"等。"本 + time noun", indicating a period including the time of speaking. For example, "本年度,本星期三,本世纪初, etc."

副词 ad.

本来。用在动词前面,多用于书面语。Originally. Appearing before a verb, it is often used in written language.

(5) 他本想不去,怕她不高兴才去的。

(6) 她本是南方人。后来全家搬到了北京。

形容词 a.

原来的。只用在单音节名词前面。如:"本意、本性"等。Original. It is only used before monosyllabic nouns. For example, "本意,本性."

说明 Notes:

使用"本+时间名词"这一词语结构时,容易出错。Learners often make mistakes when using the phrasal structure "本 + time noun."

(7) *本天下午三点,三班同学在教室上辅导课。

"本+时间名词"这一结构中的时间名词一般是表示一段时间的名词,不能用在表示现在、当天的"小时、天"等时间名词前面,如:不能说"本天、本小时"等。但是如果有介词"从",那么,"本"就可以用在"日"前,组成"从本日起……"的介词结构。Time nouns in this structure usually indicate a period. Therefore, relatively momentary time nouns such as "小时" and "天" cannot be used after "本," meaning "本天" or "本小时" is incorrect. But if there is a preposition "从," "本" can be used before "日" in the prepositional structure "从本日起...."

běnlái 本来 →P21"本"、P610"原来"

用法 Usage:

形容词 a.

原有的。修饰名词。Original. It is used

to modify nouns.

(1) 这件衬衣本来的颜色是黄的。

副词 ad.

1. 表示某种事实或道理原先就是如此；原先，先前。常常与"就"搭配使用，表示一直如此，修饰动词或形容词谓语。It indicates that a certain fact or reason is the same as the original, and it usually goes with "就," signifying a remaining unchanged state. It modifies the verb or the predicate adjective.

(2) 我本来就不胖，来中国以后更瘦了。

(3) 我本来就想到上海学汉语。

2. 表示事情理应如此、理所当然。It indicates what the matter should be like, and it's a matter of course.

(4) 他妈妈是中国人，汉语本来就应该说得比我们好。

(5) 本来嘛，学习汉语就是不容易的。

说明 Notes:

1. "本"和"本来"作副词用时都表示原先、先前或应该如此的意思。As adverbs, "本" and "本来" both indicate originally, previously or as it should be.

(6) 他本/本来是广州人。

(7) 他的作业没做好，本/本来不该去看电影。

2. "本"和"本来"的区别是：The differences between "本" and "本来" are as follows:

① 语体色彩不同。"本"多用于书面语，"本来"多用于口语。Difference in style: "本" is more common in written language; "本来" is more common in spoken language.

② 作形容词用时，"本"表示原来的意思，只能用在单音节名词前。"本来"表示原有的意思，只能修饰双音节名词。As an adjective, "本" means original, and it can only be used before monosyllabic words. "本来" means something that originally existed, and it can only modify disyllabic words.

(8) *我的本来意思是：我帮你学汉语，你帮我学英语。

(9) 我的本意是：我帮你学汉语，你帮我学英语。

(10) 我本来的意思是：我帮你学汉语，你帮我学英语。

③ "本"可以当指示代词用，"本来"不能。"本" can be used as a demonstrative pronoun, but "本来" cannot.

(11) *本来次列车8:00从杭州站始发。

(12) 本次列车8:00从杭州站始发。

bǐ 比 →P25"比较"

用法 Usage:

动词 v.

1. 比较，较量。可带"了、过"，可以重叠，可以带宾语。To compare, compete. It can be accompanied by "了" and "过." It can also be used in the reduplicative form, and it can take an object.

(1) 你比我高吗？我们比一下。

(2) 你跟她比比看，谁长得高？

2. 能够相比。可带名词、动词、代词作宾语，带出比较的对象，常用于否定句。肯定句只用在少数习惯语中。To be able to compare. It can take a noun, verb or pronoun as its object. They are the targets of a comparison. It is usually used in negative sentences, and only when used in a few idiomatic phrases can it be applied in affirmative sentences.

(3) 你去中国，不比在日本，一定要先学会汉语。

(4) 我不比你，你有个中国妈妈，一回家就跟你说汉语。

(5) 近邻比亲，邻居之间应该相互帮助，不用谢。

3. 比画（用手势帮助说话）。可带"了、着"，可重叠。To gesticulate (use gestures to help speak). It can be accompanied by "了" or "着," and can be used in the reduplicated form.

(6) 她又是说又是比,可我还是听不懂她的话。

(7) 他用手比了一个"吃"的动作,我明白了他的意思。

4. 比照,仿照。*To model after; to follow the example of.*

(8) 请你比着这件衣服的样子,给我做一件。

5. 比方,比喻。常跟"做、作"组合使用,用在"把"字句中。*Make an analogy; liken to. It is often combined with "做" or "作" in the "把" sentence structure.*

(9) 汉语里常常把姑娘比作花儿。

(10) 中国人常常把聪明的人比做诸葛亮。你知道诸葛亮吗?

6. 表示双方比赛得分的对比。*To indicate the contrast between scores in a game.*

(11) 这次足球赛,我们以三比二(3∶2)赢了他们。

介词 *prep.*

引进被比较的对象,用来比较性状或程度的差别,并得出结果(除了问句)。*It introduces the targets of a comparison to compare the differences in property, quality or degree, and then draws a conclusion (except in a question).*

用"比"的比较句,在用词上要注意以下几点:*Things to be noted about the word choices in comparative sentences with "比" are as follows:*

1. 两种事物比较,"比"的前后一般是同一种词类(名词、代词、动词、形容词等)或结构,可以有省略(一般省略后面的)。*In a comparison between two different subjects, the subjects before and after "比" are generally of the same word class (noun, pronoun, verb, adjective, etc.) or the same structure, sometimes the latter one can be omitted.*

(12) 他比你高三公分。

(13) 教室里的(电灯)比宿舍里的(电灯)亮。

2. 同一事物不同时间和不同空间相比较,"比"后面只带表示时间和空间的名词。*In a comparison of the same subject at different times or in different spaces, the nouns following "比" can only be time and space nouns.*

(14) 我们的生活水平比过去高多了。

(15) 杭州西湖的夜景比白天美得多。

3. "比"后面的谓语一般由形容词充当。为了把比较的差别说得更具体,形容词谓语的前后可加数量词或者表示程度的词语。*The predicate following "比" is generally an adjective. To specify the differences in a comparison, quantifiers and degree words can be placed before or after the predicate adjective.*

(16) 我二十一岁,比她大两岁。

(17) 她比我早来了二十分钟。

4. 谓语如果是动词,一般是表示愿望、爱好等心理动词,或者表示能力高低、增减的动词以及"有"和"没有"等动词。*If the predicate is a verb, it generally is a psychological verb that expresses one's desire or hobby, or a verb indicating competence, increase or decrease, and verbs like "有,没有."*

(18) 她的口语比刚来的时候好多了。

(19) 做饭我比她有经验。

(20) 比写汉字,我没有他写得好。

5. "比"后面如果是表示一般行为的动词,动词后面必须加"得",跟上补语,表示动词的结果。"比"可以在"动词+得"的前或后。*If the verb following "比" is one that expresses general behavior, it must be followed by "得" and a complement to indicate the result of the verb. "比" could be placed before or after the "verb+得" structure.*

(21) 小王比小李跑得快。/小王跑得比小李快。

(22) 小王比昨天来得早。/小王来得比昨天早。

6. "比"能组成相对固定的词语结构"一+量词+比+一+量词",表示程度的累进。*"比" can form the relatively fixed phrase "一+*

quantifier＋比＋一＋quantifier." It repeats itself before and after "比," indicating the progressive increase of degree.

(23) 我们的生活一年比一年好。

(24) 现在的孩子一个比一个聪明。

7. "比"的否定式"不比",表示"差不多"的意思。The negative form of "比" is "不比," meaning "差不多 (almost the same)."

(25) 她不比我胖。

(26) 我买的书不比你少。

说明 Notes:

用"比"造句容易出错的情况：Here are some common mistakes in the use of "比":

1. 混淆了"比"的动词用法和介词用法。Confusing the verb and preposition usages of "比."

(27) ＊我和你比一下,你写得好。

例(27)的"比"是动词用法。句子前部分意思是还没"比"过,后面却是"比"的结果。句子语义混乱。The "比" in (27) is used as a verb. The first half of the sentence indicates that the action of "比" hasn't taken place, and yet the latter half reveals the result of the action. The sentence is semantically confusing.

应改为：It should be corrected as:

(28) 我和你比一下,看谁写得好。(动词用法 As a verb)

(29) 你比我写得好。(介词用法 As a preposition)

2. 有"比"的比较句中本来就含有的否定语义指向不清楚。Being unclear about the inherent negative meaning in a comparative sentence with "比."

(30) ＊教室里的电灯比宿舍里的不亮。

用"比"的比较句,肯定和否定形式是体现在形容词谓语或者谓语的补语上的。In a comparative sentence with "比," the affirmative or negative meaning is reflected in the predicate adjective, or the complement of the predicate. Example (30) should be corrected as:

(31) 教室里的电灯比宿舍里的亮。(肯定教室里的电灯。The light in the classroom is in the affirmative.)

(32) 教室里的电灯比宿舍里的暗一点。(否定教室里的电灯。The light in the classroom is in the negative.)

3. 因为不明白要比什么,导致句子结构混乱。Being unclear about what to compare, resulting in disorder in the sentence structure.

(33) ＊他比我喝酒喝得多。

(34) ＊她比我买的书买得便宜。

例(33)要比"谁喝酒喝得多",例(34)要比"谁买的书便宜",所以应该把"喝酒"和"买的书"放在"比"前面。(33) compares who drank more; (34) compares who bought the cheaper book, so "喝酒" and "买的书" should be placed before "比." The two examples should be corrected as:

(35) 他喝酒比我喝得多。

(36) 她买的书比我买得便宜。

4. 量词补语位置混乱。Misplacing the complement to the quantifier.

(37) ＊妹妹比我一点儿胖。

(38) ＊小王比他妹妹两岁大。

数量词"一点儿"和"两岁"是补充说明谓语的补语,应在谓语后面。The quantifiers "一点儿" and "两岁" are the complements that explain and supplement the predicates and should be placed after the predicates. The two examples should be corrected as:

(39) 妹妹比我胖一点儿。

(40) 小王比他妹妹大两岁。

5. 动词的补语,缺少"得"字。The absence of "得" in the complement to the verb.

(41) ＊出租车比公共汽车开快。

(42) ＊他比小王跑快。

(43) 出租车比公共汽车开得快。

(44) 他比小王跑得快。

6. "比"字句,表示程度差别大小,是在谓语后面加"多、得多、一点儿、一些"等,不能用"很、太、十分、非常"等程度副词。When expressing the degree differences in a sentence with "比," words such as "多,得多,一点儿,一些" are placed after the predicate instead of the degree adverbs such as "很,太,十分,非常."

(45) *教室里的电灯比宿舍里的很亮。
(46) *我写汉字比他非常差。
(47) 教室里的电灯比宿舍里的亮得多。
(48) 我写汉字比他差多了。

7. "比"字句中,一般行为动作的动词做谓语时,表示时间先后、数量多少的"早、晚、多、少"等单音节形容词要放在动词谓语前。In sentences with "比," when the predicate is a verb about a general action, monosyllabic words that express chronological order or quantity, such as "早,晚,多,少," should be placed before the verb predicate.

(49) *他比我来中国早三个月。
(50) *我比他买书少一本。
(51) 他比我早来中国三个月。
(52) 我比他少买一本书。

bǐjiǎo 比较 →P22"比"

用法 Usage:

副词 ad.

表示具有一定的程度,有时含有"相当"的意思。It indicates a certain degree, and it sometimes implies the meaning of "相当."

1. 主要修饰形容词。It mainly modifies adjectives.

(1) 汉语拼音中,声调比较难。
(2) 大家都说杭州的夏天比较热。

2. 能修饰部分表示心理活动的动词、特殊的动词(有、助动词等)。It can modify some psychological verbs and special verbs (such as "有" and auxiliary verbs).

(3) 我比较喜欢古典音乐。
(4) 小王是个比较有办法的人。
(5) 他是个比较能喝酒的人。

3. 能修饰具有描写性质的短语,常常与"是"形成某种判断。It can modify phrases that describe the nature of things and is usually combined with "是" to form a certain judgment.

(6) 他是个比较热情又有耐心的老师。
(7) 杭州西湖是个自然山水与人文景观结合得比较好的世界遗产。

动词 v.

辨别两种、两种以上同类事物的异同或高下。To determine the difference or superiority between two or more subjects of the same type.

1. 做谓语。It serves as the predicate.

(8) 把两本词典比较一下,你就知道哪一本好了。
(9) 这两种方法比较比较,看哪种方法好。

2. 做定语或宾语。It serves as an attribute or object.

(10) 选修《比较文化学》这门课的学生很多。
(11) 用比较的方法上课,我们容易听懂。
(12) 任何事物有比较,就有区别。

介词 prep.

引出被比较的对象,用法跟介词"比"大致相同,带有文言色彩。It introduces the target(s) of a comparison. Its use is like that of the preposition "比," and has a tone of classical Chinese.

(13) 我们说汉语比较刚来的时候进步很大。
(14) 北方的风沙比较南方多多了。

说明 Notes:

1. "比较"的介词用法在现代汉语中已经很少使用,但仍可见于阅读材料中。The use of "比较" as a preposition is rare in modern Chinese, yet it can still be found in readings.

2. "比较"和"比"作动词用时,可以互换。When "比较" and "比" are used as verbs, they are interchangeable.

它们的区别是:"比"是介词,所以"比"的前后应该是名词。"比较"是副词,"比较"的后面直接是比较的结果,形容词或者动词。They differ as follows: "比" is a preposition, and nouns should go before and after it; "比较" is an adverb, and it is followed by the result of the comparison, which is presented by an adjective or a verb.

(15) *她比较我高。
(16) 她比我高。/她比较高。
(17) *这件衣服比较那件衣服贵。
(18) 这件衣服比那件衣服贵。/这件衣服比较贵。

bìdìng 必定 →P26"必然"、P555"一定"

用法 Usage:

副词 ad.

1. 表示判断的确凿或推论的必然,修饰形容词或动词性词语。It indicates an irrefutable judgment or inevitable inference, and modifies an adjective or a verbal phrase.

(1) 她必定是个韩国姑娘。
(2) 你妈妈知道你那么努力学习必定很高兴。

2. 表示坚定的意志和决心,强调主观意志,修饰动词性词语。It indicates a strong will or determination, and the emphasis is on the subjective will. It modifies verbal phrases.

(3) 这次足球赛,我们必定会赢。
(4) 明天我必定带你去看电影。

说明 Notes:

"必定"没有否定形式,前面不能加否定词"不",一般后面也不能用否定形式。"必定" has no negative form, and it cannot be preceded by "不," nor can it be followed by a negative structure.

(5) *你必定不要去那儿。
(6) 你一定不要去那儿。
(7) *你不必定去那儿。
(8) 你不必去那儿。

bìrán 必然 →P26"必定"

用法 Usage:

副词 ad.

强调所做出的判断一定会实现。It emphasizes that the judgment made is certain to be realized.

(1) 学外语,只要开口说话,必然学得好。
(2) 知道朋友来中国看她的消息,她必然会很高兴。

形容词 a.

一定的,表示事理上确定不移的。不能单独做谓语,能修饰名词或名词短语。单个名词前,"的"可有可无,名词短语前,一般都有"的"。Certain, inevitable. It indicates being firm about something. It cannot serve as a predicate alone. It modifies a noun or noun phrase. Before a single noun, "的" is dispensable, yet before a noun phrase, "的" is generally required.

(3) 她这次生气,跟你没给她礼物没有必然(的)联系。
(4) 中国经济越繁荣,学汉语的外国人越多。这是必然的结果。

名词 n.

哲学上指不以人们意志为转移的客观发展规律。Philosophically, it refers to the rules by which everything develops.

(5) 死亡是人生的必然。
(6) 旧词语消失,新词语产生,这是语言发展历史的必然。

说明 Notes:

"必定"与"必然"都表示"肯定是如此"的意思。"必定" and "必然" both mean "肯定是如此 (something is definitely so)."

它们的区别是:They differ as follows:

1. 肯定的角度不一样。"必定"着重于主观上肯定所作的判断或推论确凿无误,或事实上定然如此,多用于书面语。"必然"着重于从事物的客观规律、事理上判断、推论肯定会如此。不含主观色彩,常用于论证说理,语意比"必定"重,书面语色彩比"必定"浓。The perspective is different. "必定" focuses on the authenticity based on the subjective certainty of a judgment or deduction, or the inevitability of a fact; it is often used in written language. "必然" focuses on the certainty based on the objective law of things, and the judgment or deduction based on reasoning. There is no subjectivity in it, and it is usually used in argumentation, signifying stronger connotation than "必定" and it is more often used in written language than "必定."

2. "必定"是副词,只能修饰形容词和动词作状语。"必然"除了是副词,可以做状语以外,还是形容词和名词,可以做定语、谓语及主语,如"必然"的例(3)至(6)。"必定" is an adverb, which can only serve as an adverbial to modify an adjective or a verb. "必然" is not only an adverb serving as an adverbial, but also an adjective and a noun, which can function as an attribute, predicate or subject. See (3) to (6) under "必然."

3. "必定"有表示意志坚决的义项,一般用在第一人称讲话的祈使句,如"必定"的例(3)和(4)。"必定" also means a strong will and is generally used in an imperative sentence where the speaker uses the first person. See (3) and (4) under "必定."

"必然"没有表示意志坚决的义项,只是表示事理的客观必然性,不含主观色彩,强调客观性、客观规律,所以不太用于第一人称或第二人称的句子。"必然" doesn't imply a strong will. It just suggests the objective certainty of something without any touch of subjective flavor, and it focuses on objectivity and regularity. Therefore it is rarely used in first or second person sentences.

(7) *我到了中国,必然要去北京旅游。
(8) 我到了中国,必定要去北京旅游。

bìxū 必须 →P27"必需"

用法 Usage:
副词 ad.

1. 表示事理上和情理上的必要,一定要。修饰动词、形容词,或用于主语前。Indicating a necessity out of reason and sentiment, it modifies a verb or an adjective, and it can be placed before the subject.

(1) 要做好这件事,必须大家一起努力。
(2) 想上好每一节课,必须要先预习。

2. 用于祈使句,加强命令口气。It is used in an imperative sentence to strengthen the tone of a command.

(3) 你明天必须来!
(4) 你必须告诉我们,星期天你去哪儿玩了?

说明 Notes:

"必须"的否定形式是"无须、不须、不必"。The negative forms of "必须" are "无须,不须,不必."

(5) 这个问题我已经懂了,你无须再说了。
(6) 他已经回来了,你不必再去找他了。

bìxū 必需 →P27"必须"

用法 Usage:
动词 v.

一定要有,必不可少。对象一般是"物品、物资、原料、食品、药品、用品、人力、资金、条件"等,常常与"所"构成"(为)……所必需"的格式做谓语;与"是"连用做谓语时,后面不带宾语;"必需"做定语,与中心语之间一定要有助词"的"。It indicates what is essential and indispensable, the objects of which are generally "物品,物资,原料,食品,药品,用品,人力,资金,条件, etc." It is often combined with "所" in the pattern "(为)...所必需" to serve as the predicate. When it is combined with "是" to serve as the predicate, no object is allowed; when used as an attribute, the auxiliary word

"的" should be placed between "所" and the key noun.

（1）空气和水为每个人所必需。

（2）这本词典是你学习汉语所必需。

（3）这是妈妈给你准备旅行所必需的物品。

说明 Notes：

1. "必需"与"品"能构成名词。"必需" and "品" can be combined as a compound noun.

（4）词典是学习外语的必需品。

（5）蔬菜和水果是老人的必需品。

2. "必需"与"必须"的区别是：The differences between "必需" and "必须" are as follows:

① "必须"是副词，只能修饰谓语性成分。"必需"是动词，可以做谓语和定语，还可以构成"所"字结构。"必须" is an adverb, and it can only modify an element serving as the predicate. "必需," as a verb, can serve as the predicate or attribute, and it is also used in the "所" structure.

② 在词义上，"必须"强调非这样（"做"或者"呈某种状况"）不可。"必需"强调非有（这些东西）不可。In terms of word meaning, "必须" stresses that things must be done (or be present in a certain condition), while "必需" emphasizes that things must be obtained.

bìjìng 毕竟 →P97"到底"、P248"究竟"

用法 Usage：

副词 ad.

1. 表示不管怎么说，即使出现新情况，原来的状况还是不容否定。对事物的本质或特点表示确认或强调，相当于"到底、究竟"。可以构成"……毕竟是……"的格式，表示强调，多用于判断句。It indicates that the original situation cannot be denied whatever happens or even when a new situation emerges. The nature or characteristics of things are confirmed or emphasized. It is similar to "到底" and "究竟." It can appear in the pattern "……毕竟是……，" which has an emphatic meaning and is usually used in a judgmental sentence.

（1）他有不少缺点，但毕竟还是个孩子。

（2）机器人毕竟是机器人，最后还得由人操纵才行。

2. 强调某种情况或现象，到最后还是发生或者出现了。句中动词后常加助词"了"，表示完成时态，或句尾由表示新情况出现的语气助词"了"。It emphasizes that a situation or phenomenon happened or emerged eventually. The auxiliary word "了" is often placed after the verb in a sentence to indicate a perfect tense; or it is placed at the end of a sentence to indicate a new situation.

（3）虽然有不少错误，但他毕竟通过了汉语水平考试（HSK）六级。

（4）他的病毕竟好多了。

biānzhì 编制

用法 Usage：

动词 v.

1. 将细长物加以编织成器具。To weave thin and slender materials into artifacts as utensils.

（1）竹子可以编制成席子、篮子等很多用具。

（2）这些绳子可以编制一个网袋。

2. 编造，制订。To formulate and work out.

（3）这次旅游去的地方很多，应该先编制一个计划。

（4）装修房子应该编制装修方案。

名词 n.

单位、机构的人员定额和组织形式。The personnel quota and organizational structure of an institution.

（5）机关的编制要尽可能缩小。

（6）现在很多单位的工作人员是编制以外的。

biànchéng 变成

用法 Usage:

动词 *v.*

动词"变"带结果补语"成",组成动词性词语,表示变化成为的意思。To become. The verb "变" combined with the result complement "成" constitutes a verb phrase, which means changing to become.

(1) 一年不见,你就变成漂亮姑娘了。

(2) 没想到这座荒山十年后变成了一片果园。

说明 Notes:

动词"变"后面可以带上表示结果的"成、为、作"等动词做补语,表示"变化为……"的意思,并且后面一定带上宾语。The verb "变" can take a verb of result such as "成","为," or "作" as its complement to mean "变化为...," and an object is required in the sentence.

biàndòng 变动 →P29"变化"

用法 Usage:

动词 *v.*

1. 发生变化。多用于人事、组织机构等社会现象。(Of change) to take place. It often applies to social phenomena such as personnel and organizational affairs.

(1) 公司的人事虽然多次变动,但没有影响业务。

(2) 近几十年来,国际局势变动很大。

2. 改变。多用于计划、任务等事物。To change. It often applies to things such as plans and tasks.

(3) 大家注意,下个星期的课程表有所变动。

(4) 你变动了旅游计划,应该告诉我一下。

biànhuà 变化 →P29"变动"、P153"改变"

用法 Usage:

动词 *v.*

1. 事物在外形和本质上产生了新的状况,多做谓语,一般不带宾语。It indicates a new condition has occurred in the appearance or nature of a thing. It often serves as the predicate and generally takes no object.

(1) 这里的形势变化得很快。

(2) 生活环境变化了,生活习惯也要随着变化而改变。

2. 改变。To change.

(3) 老师的教学方法经常变化,我们很喜欢。

(4) 教育孩子的方法应该随着时代的变化而变化。

名词 *n.*

事物在形态上或本质上产生的新状况。The new condition in the appearance or nature of a thing.

(5) 这几年中国城市的变化很大。

(6) 到了国外,她的生活习惯有了很大的变化。

说明 Notes:

"变化"和"变动"都表示人或事物有所改变。"变化" and "变动" both indicate changes happening to people or things.

区别是:Their differences are as follows:

1. "变化"一般着重于人或事物本身产生了新情况,变化的原因可能是内在的,也可能是外在的。"变动"强调人或事物发生了改变,原因一般为外在、客观引起的。"变化" generally emphasizes that people or things generate some new situation by themselves, and the reason for the change may be internal or external. "变动," by contrast, emphasizes that the reason for the change is generally external or objective.

2. "变化"可用于人的思想、情感、性格、形体等抽象事物,也可用于自然、气候、形式等具体的事物。"变动"一般用于人事、机构、计划等社会现象。"变化" can apply to abstract things such as people's idea, sentiments, character or shape as well as concrete things such as nature, climate or form. "变动" generally applies to

social phenomena such as people, institutions or plans.

3. "变化"后面一般不带宾语。"变动"可以带宾语。"变化" generally cannot take any objects, but "变动" can.

(7) *他们变化了计划，没有通知我们。

(8) 他们变动了计划，没有通知我们。

biàn 便 →P250 "就"

用法 Usage:

副词 ad.

书面语，相当于"就"，有以下几种用法。Like "就," it is used in written language, and it has several usages.

1. 表示时间。Indicating time.

① 表示情况、行为出现或发生得早或快。所指的时间是在说话之前。在"便"之前常有表示时间的词语。It shows the earliness or rapidity of the occurrence of an action or the emergence of a situation. The time it refers to is earlier than the time when the talk is made, and before the word "便" there is generally a time expression.

(1) 一个星期前，我便来报到了。（早 Showing earliness）

(2) 她不到三分钟便跑完了八百米。（快 Showing rapidity）

② 表示前后两件事接着发生，中间几乎没有时间间隔。在"便"前常常有"刚、一"等词搭配。It indicates two things happening successively with no intervals. Before "便" there is often the word "刚" or "一."

(3) 我刚离开她便想她了。

(4) 她一回到房间便睡了。

③ 表示事情（或动作行为）立即或很快就会发生。It indicates that things (or actions and behaviors) will take place very soon.

(5) 你先去，我把这个句子写完便去。

2. 在表示因果、目的、条件、假设、选择、承接等关系的复句中，为了与前一小句的内容相呼应，"便"用在复句的正句中（一般为后一分句），表示相关的结论。In a complex sentence that expresses cause and result, purpose, condition, hypothesis, choice or an onward action, "便" is used in the main clause (generally the latter one) to indicate a related conclusion. It corresponds with the content of the preceding clause.

(6) 作业做完了，她便出去找朋友玩儿了。（因果 Cause and effect）

(7) 只要你看很多书，我便保证你会写作文。（条件 Condition）

(8) 为了提高口语水平，他便每天找一个中国人聊天。（目的 Purpose）

(9) 假如你找到那家咖啡店，我便在那家咖啡店里请你喝咖啡。（假设 Hypothesis）

(10) 不是你去，便是我去，我们俩一定要有个人去。（选择 Choice）

(11) 下了课，我们便去食堂吃饭了。（承接 Connection）

3. 表示语气。Expressing a specific tone.

① 表示确认、肯定的语气，常用在判断词"是"的前面。It expresses a confirming, affirmative tone, and is placed before the judgment word "是."

(12) 图书馆前那座建筑便是教学大楼。

② 表示勉强或被迫让步的语气。It expresses a reluctant or concessive tone.

(13) 他想买，便让他买吧。

连词 conj.

表示假设的让步，相当于"即使、即便"。"便"后常常带"是"，用在前一分句，后一分句常有"也"呼应使用。It indicates a hypothetical concession, equivalent to "即使" and "即便." "便" is followed by the word "是" and is used in the first clause; the word "也" is often used in the following clause.

(14) 那么晚了，便是你去，我也不去。

动词 v.

排泄屎或尿。To excrete feces or urine.

(15) 大夫,病人便血了。

形容词 *a.*

1. 方便,便利。*Convenient, favorable.*

(16) 出门在外,会有很多不便的时候。

(17) 社区有很多便民措施。

2. 方便的时候或顺便的机会。*Available (time) or convenient (opportunity).*

(18) 我是搭便车来的。

3. 非正式的,简单平常的。*Informal; simple and common.*

(19) 天晚了,吃了便饭再走吧。

(20) 她不在,你就写个便条吧!

名词 *n.*

屎或尿。排泄尿为"小便",排泄屎为"大便"。*Feces（大便）or urine（小便）.*

biànlùn 辩论 →P648"争论"

用法 Usage:

动词 *v.*

彼此用一定的理由来说明自己对事物或问题的看法,揭露对方的矛盾,以便最后得到正确的认识或共同的意见。*(Of both sides) to debate, using certain reasons to explain one's own view on an issue, and to expose the flaws in the opponent's opinion. The final purpose is to win the debate, and more importantly, arrive at a correct understanding and/or achieve a consensus.*

(1) 今天上午双方辩论得很激烈。

(2) 这个问题下午继续辩论。

名词 *n.*

申述理由、说明见解,揭露对方的矛盾,得到认识上的取胜或取得共识的过程。*A debate, arguing back and forth to illustrate one's own view on an issue and expose the flaws in the other side's view, the final purpose being to arrive at a correct understanding and achieve a consensus.*

(3) 这次辩论的题目是关于动物保护的。

(4) 通过这场辩论,大家都提高了认识。

说明 Notes:

1. "辩论"做动词时,可带名词宾语、动词宾语、形容词宾语和小句宾语。名词宾语一般指"某某问题",其他形式的宾语一般都指正反两种情况或选择某种手段、方法、方案等。*When "辩论" is a verb, it can be followed by a noun, a verb, an adjective or a clause as its object. The noun object generally refers to a certain issue, the choice of a method or plan, or views on an issue, pro and con.*

(5) 今天下午要辩论城市交通问题。请大家踊跃参加。

(6) 今天下午辩论如何缓解城市交通拥堵问题。请大家踊跃参加。

(7) 今天下午要辩论城市修建地铁的优劣。请大家积极参加。

2. "辩论"常与"激烈"搭配。*"辩论" usually goes with "激烈."*

(8) 大家对堵车问题辩论得非常激烈。

biǎodá 表达 →P32"表明"、P32"表示"

用法 Usage:

动词 *v.*

表示(思想、感情),用语言文字通过口头或书面形式,让别人知道自己的思想感情。可以做谓语、定语。做谓语时,宾语多为表示思想感情方面的名词或名词短语,如:"感激之情、希望、想念、热爱、爱、恨"等。做定语时,有语言能力的意思。*To express (thoughts, feelings); to use language, either written or spoken, to inform others of one's thoughts or feelings. It can serve as the predicate or attribute. When it is a predicate, the object is often a noun or noun phrase such as "感激之情,希望,想念,热爱,爱,恨." As an attribute, it means language capacity.*

(1) 他的话表达了我们大家的希望。

(2) 她的表达水平很高,大家都喜欢听她讲话。

biǎomiàn 表面

用法 Usage:
名词 n.

1. 物体表层与外界接触的部分。Surface, the outside or top layer of something exposed to the external world.

(1) 桌子的表面很干净。
(2) 蓝色的大气层包围着地球的表面。

2. 常与"上"组成词组"表面上",表示表现在外的意思。It often goes with "上" to form the phrase "表面上," meaning on the surface, or the external manifestation.

(3) 她表面上很高兴,实际上内心很难过。
(4) 他表面上说要帮助我,其实什么也没帮。

3. 事物的外在现象或非本质部分。The external appearance of things, or the non-essential part of things.

(5) 看事情要看本质,不要只看表面。
(6) 给你送花送礼物,这都是表面,你知道他的目的是什么?

biǎomíng 表明 →P31"表达"、P32"表示"

用法 Usage:
动词 v.

清楚地表示,表示清楚。To express or show clearly.

(1) 事实表明,你这样做是错误的。
(2) 今天每个人都要表明自己的看法,做出决定。

说明 Notes:

"表达"和"表明"都有通过言语或行为等手段,使自己的思想感情让别人知道的意思。"表达" and "表明" both mean to make one's thoughts and feelings known to others through language or action, etc.

它们的区别是:They differ as follows:

在语义上,"表达"重在说出来、讲出来这个动作本身,要表达的主要是人的思想和感情。"表明"语义重在"明",即"清楚"。不但要把自己的想法讲出来,而且要讲清楚。如果是对事物的看法,就要有明确的态度等。所以在强调对某事表态的句子中,就应用"表明",而不宜用"表达"。In terms of meaning, "表达" emphasizes the action of telling, and the things told are mainly about people's thoughts and feelings. "表明" focuses on the word "明," which means clearly. Often it concerns one's view on a matter, and one is expected to have a clear, unequivocal attitude. Hence when it comes to making a standpoint on a matter, it should be "表明" rather than "表达."

(3) *你表达一下自己的态度:去还是不去?
(4) 你表明一下自己的态度:去还是不去?

biǎoshì 表示 →P31"表达"、P32"表明"

用法 Usage:
动词 v.

1. 用言语行为显示思想、感情或态度、意见,使人知道、领会。To use words or actions to show one's thoughts, feelings, attitudes or opinions so that others can understand.

(1) 大家对他的建议都表示同意。
(2) 关于去哪儿实习,请大家表示一下自己的愿望。

2. 事物本身显示出某种意义或者凭借某种事物显示出某种意义。(Of things) to reveal a certain meaning or significance by these things or through something else.

(3) 这礼物表示我对你生日的祝贺。
(4) 这次考试你的成绩不错,这表示你最近的努力很有成效。

名词 n.

显示思想和感情的言语、行为动作或神情。Words, actions or expressions that reveal one's thoughts and feelings.

(5) 我考上了大学,可是爸爸妈妈一点表示都没有。
(6) 她帮了我那么大的忙,我总该有点表示吧。

说明 Notes:

"表示"与"表明""表达"的区别是：The differences between "表示" and "表明", and "表示" and "表达" are as follows:

1. "表示"不但可以用言语，而且还可以用行为动作或者神情来让大家知道人或者事物显示的是什么意思，传递信息的手段比"表达"和"表明"多。所以不但可以用于人，还可以用于事物。"表达"和"表明"一般不能用于事物。When "表示" is used, it includes multiple ways of message transmission such as words, actions, behaviors or facial expressions to suggest what someone or something means. It is more versatile than "表达" and "表明." Therefore, "表示" applies to both people and objects. But "表达" and "表明" cannot modify objects.

(7) *晚上建筑物上发光的红灯表达了这座建筑物的高度。

(8) *晚上建筑物上发光的红灯表明了这座建筑物的高度。

(9) 晚上建筑物上发光的红灯表示了这座建筑物的高度。

2. "表示"的使用范围比较广泛。"表达"使用范围侧重于思想、感情、心理的传递。"表明"使用范围侧重于态度、立场的明示。"表示" is used relatively more widely in range; "表达" focuses on expressing ideas, feelings and mentality; "表明" focuses on clarifying one's attitude or standpoint.

3. "表示"有名词用法。"表达"和"表明"没有名词用法，只有动词用法。"表示" can be used as a noun, but "表达" and "表明" can only be used as a verb.

biǎoxiàn 表现 →P461"体现"

用法 Usage:
动词 v.

1. 表示出来，显示出来，可带"了、过"。To display; demonstrate. It can be followed by "了" and "过."

(1) 孔子的教育思想表现在教学方法、内容及招收不同教学对象等很多方面。

(2) 她对中国的建筑艺术表现出很大的兴趣。

(3) 这位老师在教学中表现了高度的责任感。

2. 故意显示自己（有时含贬义），常用"表现＋自己"的格式。Show oneself off (sometimes derogatorily), usually in the pattern of "表现＋自己."

(4) 她非常喜欢表现自己。

(5) 她从来不喜欢表现自己。

名词 n.

通过行为和作风使情况或事实显现出来。常做主语、宾语。Performance; what is shown in one's action or manner. It usually serves as the subject or object.

(6) 一个人好不好，要看他实际行动的表现，光说是没用的。

(7) 小王最近在学习上的表现很好。

bié 别 →P34"别的"

用法 Usage:
副词 ad.

1. 表示禁止或劝阻，相当于"不要"。Had better not, used to prohibit or dissuade someone, like "不要."

(1) 别进去，她还在睡觉。

(2) 别走了，今晚住在这里吧!

2. 表示提醒（以免出现不应有的情况），常与"忘"搭配使用。Had better not, used to remind someone to avoid an undesirable situation. It often goes with "忘."

(3) 你走时，别忘了关门。

(4) 别忘了吃药!

3. 表示推测和担心。说的是希望不要发生的事，后面常常与"是、又、不是"连用，与"不是"连用组成的是反问句，表示"难道是、不会是"等意思。Hopefully not, used to show a speculation and worry. It expresses something

that is expected not to happen, usually going with "是, 又, 不是." When it is used with "不是" to form a rhetorical question, it is equivalent to "难道是" and "不会是."

(5) 他到现在还不来,别是生病了吧。

(6) 他到现在还不来,别又生病了吧。

(7) 他到现在还不来,别不是生病了吧?

4. 用在某些单音节动词前,相当于"另""另外"。这种用法较多地出现在成语里。When used before certain monosyllabic verbs, it is equivalent to "另," or "另外." This usage is more common in idioms.

(8) 南方的饺子跟北方的饺子相比,别有一种味道。

(9) 这种手机的设计别具一格。

动词 v.

1. 离开,分离,别离。带有抒情色彩,不用于一般的陈述。To leave; to separate; to depart. As it carries a lyrical color, it is not used in a general statement.

(10) 别了,我的母校!别了,我的同学们!

2. 用别针把某个东西固定或卡住。To have a certain object pinned or fixed.

(11) 开会的时候,请大家把代表证别在衣服上。

(12) 你把眼前的头发别住,那样眼睛就舒服多了。

3. 插上。To carry; to stick in.

(13) 那警察的腰上别着一支手枪。

4. 转动,转变。To turn; change.

(14) 她把头别了过去,流下了眼泪。

(15) 你很难把她那种脾气别过来。

代词 pron.

另外。Other.

(16) 那是别人的行李。

(17) 我们这里没有,你到别处去看看。

名词 n.

差别。单音节使用,只出现在成语或四字词组中,如:"天壤之别、内外有别"等。Discrepancy. It is used monosyllabically and is only present in idioms or four-character phrases such as "天壤之别,内外有别."

说明 Notes:

1. "别"的副词用法,在口语中,接着别人的话时,可以单用。When "别" is used as an adverb in oral language, one can use it monosyllabically as a response in a conversation.

(18) A：我也去帮你做饭吧。

　　B：别,别。你坐着看电视吧!饭一会儿就好。

2. "别"的副词用法,通常用于第二人称的句子,见例(1)(2)(3)(4)。用在第三人称,往往含有推测、担心的意思,见例(5)(6)(7)。一般不用于第一人称。Again when "别" is used as an adverb, it usually appears in second-person sentences. See (1), (2), (3) and (4). When it is used in third person sentences, it often expresses a speculation or some worry. See (5), (6) and (7). It is usually not used in first-person sentences.

(19) *我下午别去你的宿舍。

(20) 我下午不去你的宿舍。

3. "别"表示"推测和担心"的事,常常是自己所不愿意接受的事。一般要与"是"合用,如例(5)(6)(7)。What is speculated or worried about by using "别" is usually hard for oneself to accept. It often goes with "是," as seen in (5), (6) and (7).

4. "别"表示"转动、转变"意思的动词用法,带有方言色彩。When used as a verb meaning "to change" or "to turn," it carries some dialectal flavor.

5. "别"另有一个发音(biè),用在"别扭"。"别" has another pronunciation (biè), as in "别扭."

biéde 别的 →P33 "别"

用法 Usage:

代词 pron.

1. 指示代词。替代前面所说之外,同一范围之内的事物。在句子中做主语或宾语。*As a demonstrative pronoun, it is used to replace what is not said but within the same scope. It serves as the subject or object in a sentence.*

(1) 课外作业除了造句以外,还有别的吗?
(2) 我只记得前面两句诗,别的都忘了。

2. 一般代词。替代前面所说范围之外的任何事物。*As a general pronoun, it is used to replace anything apart from what is said.*

(3) 不说那件事了,说别的吧。
(4) 现在唯一要考虑的是决赛,别的都不重要。

说明 Notes:
"别的"只有代词用法,使用时一定要加上助词"的"。"别"不带"的"修饰名词,只限于"别人""别处""别家"。*"别的" can only be used as a pronoun, and the auxiliary word "的" is necessary. When "别" is used to modify a noun without the word "的," it is limited to "别人," "别处" and "别家."*

bìng 并 →P35"并且"

用法 Usage:
副词 *ad.*

1. 用在部分单音节动词、(成语中的)形容词前,表示两件以上的事同时进行,或对两件以上的事同等对待。常见的词语有:"并进、并举、并立、并列、并行、并论、并重、并存、声情并茂"等。*When used before a monosyllabic verb or adjective (in an idiom), it means two or more events happen at the same time, or two or more things are treated equally. Common words are: "并进,并举,并立,并列,并行,并论,并重,并存,声情并茂."*

(1) 我认为学好汉语要听、说、读、写并重。
(2) "一国两制"就是在一个国家中,两种不同的社会制度并存。

2. 用在否定词"不、没/没有、无、非、未"等前面,有加强否定语气、否定某种看法、说明真实情况、进行辩解的意思。*When used before a negative word such as "不,没/没有,无,非,未," it strengthens the negative tone, denies a certain view, explains a real condition and conducts a defense.*

(3) 情况并不是像你说的那样。
(4) 你猜错了。我并没去看电影。

连词 *conj.*

表示更进一层的关系,相当于"并且"。多连接并列的双音节动词、动词短语或分句。两分句若主语相同,后一小句主语承前省略。*It suggests a further connection. Equivalent to "并且," it usually connects parallel disyllabic verbs, verb phrases or clauses, and if the two clauses have the same subject, the subject in the latter clause can be omitted.*

(5) 我们要保持并发扬优秀的传统文化。
(6) 他是去年来到上海并在一个公司工作的。
(7) 今年夏天,她博士研究生毕业,并于九月回国,被一所大学聘为教授。

动词 *v.*

1. 合在一起。*Combine; put together.*
(8) 我们把三个小组并成两个大组。

2. 两种或两种以上的事物并排着。*Two or more things arranged side by side.*
(9) 他们三人手拉手、肩并肩地走了。

bìngqiě 并且 →P35"并"、P130"而且"、P621"再说"

用法 Usage:
连词 *conj.*

表示更进一层的意思。多用于书面。*And; also; as well as. It suggests a progressive increase and is found more common in written language.*

1. 连接动词、形容词或副词。也连接词性不相同的词语,但连接的词语都必须是双音节词。*It connects verbs, adjectives or adverbs. It also connects words that are not of the same*

part of speech, but those words should be disyllabic.

（1）我希望并且相信你一定会找到一个好工作。
（2）我们的教室漂亮并且干净。
（3）你必须把今天的作业马上并且全部做好，才能去看电影。

2.连接短语或小句。连接小句时，"并且"出现在后一小句前。It connects phrases or clauses. When it connects clauses, "并且" is placed before the latter clause.

（4）他已经订出旅游计划并且正在按照计划预订火车票和旅馆。
（5）我家里有英汉词典，并且有三本。

说明 Notes：

1.应用"并且"时要注意：When using "并且," one should note:

① "并且"后面常常与副词"还、也、更"等连用，表示递进的意思。"并且" is often followed by adverbs such as "还, 也, 更" to indicate progression.

（6）天黑了，并且肚子也饿了。我们就找了一家旅馆住了下来。
（7）这种辣白菜我们韩国很多，并且还更辣。

② 连接词语三项以上时，"并且"放在最后一项前。When connecting three or more items, "并且" is placed before the last one.

（8）我来中国以后，脸白了，人胖了，并且说话也比以前多了。

③ 后面的句子较长时，"并且"在后一句子前，可以单独停顿。When the sentence following "并且" is long, there will be a comma after "并且" so that the speaker can catch his/her breath before uttering the long sentence.

（9）参加汉语水平考试（HSK）能知道自己的汉语水平，并且，如果能通过HSK八级，找工作会更容易一点儿。

④ "并且"在连接句子时，可以与"不但"

"不仅"搭配使用。When used to connect sentences, "并且" collocates with "不但" or "不仅."

（10）他不但是韩国人，并且还是你的同乡。

2."并"与"并且"都有连词用法，但用法不完全相同。Both "并" and "并且" can serve as a conjunction, but their uses are not entirely the same.

① "并且"能连接句子，"并"不能连接句子。"并且"需要时可以停顿，"并"不能有停顿。连接小句时，"并且"连接的小句，句子的主语可以不同。而"并"连接的小句，主语则必须相同。"并且" can connect sentences, but "并" cannot. "并且" can be used separately when needed, but "并" cannot. When connecting clauses, the clauses connected by "并且" can have different subjects, but the clauses connected by "并" must have the same subject.

② "并且"常与"不但""不仅"等词搭配呼应，表示递进的意思，而"并"则不能。"并且" usually goes with words like "不但, 不仅" to imply progression. But "并" has no such usage.

③ "并"有表示并列的意思。"并且"只有递进意思，没有并列意思的用法。"并" can indicate coordination. "并且" can only express progression but not coordination.

3."并"有动词、副词用法。"并且"没有这两种词性的用法。"并" can be used as a verb or an adverb, but "并且" can only function as a conjunction.

bù 不 →P315"没/没有"

用法 Usage：

副词 ad.

一、用在动词（包括判断词、能愿动词、趋向动词）前，表示否定。It is used before verbs (including judging verbs, modal verbs, directional verbs) to express negation.

1. 常常用在动词或动词短语前面，如："不吃、不是、不想、不懂、不旅行、不上课"等。可以用在所有的能愿动词前。*It is usually used before a verb or verb phrase as in "不吃，不是，不想，不懂，不旅行，不上课, etc." It can be used before all modal verbs.*

（1）我不可以吃辣的东西。
（2）他不要去上海，要去西安。

2. "不"与趋向动词的否定形式有两种：一种是"不"在趋向动词前面，表示主观上的否定；一种是"不"嵌在趋向动词中间，表示客观上不可能的否定。*There are two kinds of negative forms involving "不" and directional verbs: 1) "不" precedes the directional verbs, suggesting subjective negation. 2) "不" is inserted in directional verbs, suggesting objective negation.*

不进来　　　　进不来
不回来　　　　回不来
不写下去　　　写不下去

3. "不"与动词可能补语的否定形式，表示不可能达到某种目的或不可能出现某种结果。*When "不" is used as a negative form of certain verb complements, it indicates impossibility to achieve a certain goal or result.*

跑不快　　吃不了　　看不懂
吃不饱　　去不了　　听不到

二、用在形容词或形容词短语前面，表示对事物性质、状态的否定。*When used before an adjective or adjective phrase, it means negation of the nature or state of things.*

（3）这件衣服不贵。
（4）他的房间不大。

三、用在部分程度副词前面，表示程度上的否定。*When used before certain degree adverbs, it suggests negation regarding degrees.*

（5）她的汉字写得不太清楚。
（6）那个饭店的服务态度我们不很满意。

"不"修饰副词，常常是副词与后面的形容词组成的形容词短语。"不"的位置可以有两种，一种是"不"在形容词与副词构成的短语前面，否定程度副词，表示否定的程度轻微；一种是"不"在副词与形容词中间，直接否定形容词，否定的语气比较重。*When "不" modifies an adverb, the adverb usually collocates with its following adjective to form an adjective phrase. There are two places for "不:" 1) "不" precedes the phrase formed by adjective and adverb to negate degree adverb, which shows a low degree of negation. 2) "不" is between an adverb and adjective to directly negate the adjective, which signifies a stronger tone of negation.*

不太清楚　　　　太不清楚
不很满意　　　　很不满意
不常常去他家　　常常不去他家

四、用在概数"几"和由"一"构成的数量词前，表示时间短或数量少。*When used before the approximate number "几" or quantifiers led by "一," it means a short duration or small quantity.*

（7）他不一会儿就吃下了两只香蕉。
（8）向前走不了几步就是一家书店。
（9）不几天就是春节了。时间过得真快！

五、单用，作否定的回答。有以下几种用法：*When used separately, it serves as a negative response, and there are several usages as follows:*

1. 在对话中，先用"不/不啦"否定回答别人的话，然后补充说明否定的原因。*In a conversation, first use "不/不啦" to give a negative response, and then explain the reason why.*

（10）A：明天还来玩儿吗？
　　　B：不，明天我没空儿了。

2. 用来更正自己说的话，或者引出更深刻、更全面的论述来补充前面说的话。*It is used to correct what one has already said, or to introduce a more profound and comprehensive statement to supplement what was said before.*

(11) 我买一本。不,买两本吧。一本送给朋友。

(12) "活到老,学到老"是你应该记住和做到的话。不,是每个人都要记住和做到的话。

六、用于正反并列形式,表示疑问。在北方话中,"不"用在句末,表示疑问(实际上是正反并列形式在句末的省略形式)。*When used before a positive or negative parallel structure, it indicates an interrogation. In northern dialect, "不" is used at the end of a sentence (actually it is an omission of positive and negative parallel pattern at the end of a sentence).*

(13) 今天你洗不洗衣服?/今天你洗衣服不?

(14) 你说这姑娘漂亮不漂亮?/你说这姑娘漂亮不?

(15) 还有牛奶,你喝不?

如果用于两个以上的音节,常常只重复第一个音节。*If used before a multisyllabic word, it usually repeats the first syllable only.*

(16) 下课以后,你打不打太极拳?

(17) 你们知不知道下个星期五我们要去旅游?

七、以"不"构成的几种相对固定的格式:*There are certain relatively fixed patterns formed by "不":*

1. 不……不……

① 用在意思相同或相近的单音节动词或文言词前面,表示"既不……也不……"的意思。*When used before semantically identical or similar monosyllabic verbs or classical Chinese words, it expresses the meaning of "既不…也不…."*

不说不笑　　不吃不喝
不言不语　　不声不响

② 用在意思相对的单音节形容词、方位词或文言词前面,表示适中、正好的意思。*When used before monosyllabic adjectives, localizers or classical Chinese words that have opposite meanings, it means being moderate or precise.*

不多不少　　不肥不瘦
不前不后　　不大不小

③ 用在意思相对的单音节动词、形容词、名词、方位词或文言词中间,表示既不像这,又不像那,而是一种让人不满意的中间状态。*When used between monosyllabic verbs, adjectives, nouns, localizers or classical Chinese words that have opposite meanings, it means being neither like this nor that, which is an unsatisfying in-between state.*

不死不活　　不男不女
不上不下　　不中不西

上面这种格式又可以说成:*The above structure can also be rendered as:*

死不死,活不活　　男不男,女不女
上不上,下不下　　中不中,西不西

④ 用在意义相对或相关的动词或短语中间,表示"如果不……就不……"。*When used between verbs or phrases that have opposite or relevant meanings, it indicates "如果不…就不…."*

不破不立　　不见不散
不去不行　　不说不明

⑤ 用在意思相同或相近的单音节形容词、动词中间,表示强调的语气。*When used between monosyllabic adjectives or verbs that have identical or similar meanings, it suggests an emphatic tone.*

不干不净　　不清不楚
不闻不问　　不慌不忙

⑥ 用在单音节的助动词、动词或形容词前面。表示双重否定的肯定,非如此不可。有时是强调语气,有时是委婉语气。*When used before monosyllabic auxiliary verbs, verbs or adjectives, it indicates affirmation through double negation, with no other alterative. It is sometimes emphatic, sometimes euphoric.*

不得不去　　不敢不吃
不写不行　　不可以不睡觉

2. 爱……不……

"爱"和"不"后面是同一个动词或动词短语,从形式上看可以选择,实际上是表示说话人决然作罢的情绪、语气。"爱" and "不" are followed by the same verb or verb phrase. Syntactically, choices are available, yet actually the angry tone and annoyed sentiment reveal that the speaker no longer cares whether or not a certain person would take the action as denoted by the verb.

爱吃不吃　　　　　爱来不来
爱做作业不做作业　爱参观不参观

3. 半……不……

用在意义相同或相对的单音节动词、形容词中间,表示一种让人不满意的中间状态。When used between monosyllabic verbs and adjectives that have the same or opposite meanings, it signifies an unsatisfying in-between state.

半懂不懂　　半生不熟
半醒不醒　　半死不活

4. 不……而……

用在单音节文言词前面,表示虽然不具有某种条件和原因,但也产生了某种结果,常用于成语。When used before monosyllabic classical Chinese words, it means a result is achieved despite an absence of certain condition and cause, commonly used in idioms.

不约而同　　不劳而获
不请而来　　不谋而合

如果用在短语或小句前面,表示否定前者,肯定后者,常与"而"连用。If used before a phrase or a clause, it negates the former phrase or clause and affirms the latter preceded by "而."

(18) 他不是英国人,(而)是法国人。
(19) 你为什么不去北京(而)去西安?

5. 不管(它)……不……

"不"用在相同的动词、形容词或名词中间,与前面的"不管"、后面句子中的"也、都"搭配使用,表示无论这样或不这样。When "不" is used between two identical verbs, adjectives or nouns, it collocates with "不管" preceding it, and "也,都" following it, which means whether this happens or not.

(20) 不管好不好,我都要买。
(21) 不管他来不来,我也要做这碗菜。
(22) 不管米饭不米饭,他都不吃。

6. 什么……不……

"不"用在相同的动词、形容词或名词中间,常常在后面带"的",与前面的"什么"配合使用,表示不在乎、无所谓。When "不" is used between two identical verbs, adjectives or nouns, it is usually followed by "的" that collocates with "什么" preceding "不," which indicates the speaker's indifference or lack of care.

(23) 什么难不难,只要下功夫就能学会。
(24) 什么贵不贵的,喜欢就买。

7. 不……就/才……

用在两个短语或两个句子之间,表示"不这样就会那样"的意思。It is used between two phrases or sentences, which means B would happen if you don't do A.

(25) 你不玩手机就能完成这些作业。
(26) 老年人不生病才是最有福气的呢!

8. 不(是)……就(是)……

用在短语或小句前面。表示二者必有其一的选择关系。It is used before two phrases or clauses, indicating either A or B holds true.

(27) 开学以来,他不是读就是写,学习非常努力。
(28) 不是今天去,就是明天去。我们一定要去一次。

9. 说……不……

用在两个相同的单音节形容词前,表示"说这样并不这样"的意思。It is used before two identical monosyllabic adjectives, meaning what is said is not the case.

(29) 我这几天说忙不忙,说空不空,还可以。
(30) 我们这城市说大不大,说小不小,住在这里是很舒服的。

说明 Notes：

1. "不"的声调，在书面上标调为第四声，在口语中，"不"在第一、第二、第三声调前读第四声；在第四声调以前读第二声。The tone of "不" is marked the fourth in written language, and takes the fourth tone before a first-, second- or third-tone word in oral language; but it assumes the second tone before a fourth-tone word.

2. 动词"有"的否定式，不是"不有"，是"没有"。The negative form of "有" is "没有" instead of "不有."

búbì 不必 →P489"未必"

用法 Usage：

副词 ad.

表示事理上或情理上不需要，用不着。是"需要""必要"的否定。Not necessarily; by no means. It indicates that there is no need for something either logically or emotionally. It is the opposite of "需要" and "必要." It is used in the following ways：

1. 不必＋动词。"不必"＋a verb.

(1) 不必去她家了，她去上海了。

(2) 词典不必买了，朋友送了我一本。

2. 不必＋形容词。一般形容词前面要有表示程度的修饰语。表示情绪、态度等的形容词，可直接受"不必"的修饰。"不必"＋an adjective. Usually an adjective needs a descriptive word before it to denote a degree. An adjective indicating an emotion or attitude may be modified by "不必" directly.

(3) 这画上，花的颜色不必那么红。

(4) 明天十点上课，你不必很早起床。

3. "不必"＋动词短语。"不必"＋a verb phrase.

(5) 明天的晚会，不必提前来，准时到达就好。

(6) 晚饭不必有鱼有肉，一碗蔬菜就可以。

4. "不必"后面的动词或形容词可以提前；在一定的语境条件下，"不必"后面的动词或形容词可以省略。A verb or adjective following "不必" may be moved forward. In certain contexts, a verb or adjective following "不必" may be omitted.

(7) 他打算重写一遍，我看不必了。

(8) A：我再打一次电话吧？

B：不必了，他的手机肯定关了。

búbiàn 不便

用法 Usage：

形容词 a.

不方便（与"方便、便利"相对）。Inconvenient (as opposed to "方便" and "便利").

(1) 这个小区很漂亮，就是交通不便。

(2) 爷爷的腿有病，行动不便了。

动词 v.

1. 不适宜（与"适宜"相对）。To be unsuitable (as opposed to "适宜").

(3) 她不多说，我也不便多问。

(4) 他们有困难，我就不便提要求了。

2. 缺钱用。To lack money.

(5) 你要是手头不便，我可以借你。

(6) 今天手头不便，我不上街了。

说明 Notes：

1. "不便"作动词第一种用法也说"不便于"，后面一定要带动词宾语，如例(3)和(4)。The first usage of "不便" as a verb can be rendered as "不便于," which should be followed by a verbal object, as in (3) and (4).

2. 跟动词第一种用法"不便"相对的肯定式是"便于"，不能用"便"。The positive form of the first usage of "不便" is "便于" instead of "便."

búcuò 不错 →P187"好"

用法 Usage：

形容词 a.

1. 不坏，好。常做谓语或补语。Not bad; good. It is used as a predicate or supplement.

(1) 王老师上课不错。

(2) 这种苹果味道不错。

2. "错"的一种否定形式。在这里不是形容词,常常单独使用,并在后面用逗号表示停顿。相当于"对"。*It serves as a negative form of "错." It is not an adjective and appears by itself. A comma follows it to serve as a pause, equivalent to "对."*

(3) 不错,我昨天晚上去看电影了。

(4) 你说得不错,这本书是我借来的。

3. 表示赞许、同意等语气。用在句子前面,单独使用,并在后面用逗号表示停顿。*Indicating an approval or agreement, it appears independently at the beginning of a sentence. It is followed by a comma to serve as a pause.*

(5) 不错,你说得很对!

(6) 不错,就照你说的去做。

说明 Notes:

"不错"是口头语,表示对人、对事或对事物等的肯定。具体的意思要看具体的句子才能正确体会。*"不错" is a colloquial expression indicating affirmation of people or things. Yet the exact meaning is decided by the specific context.*

búdàn 不但 →P48"不仅"

用法 Usage:

连词 conj.

用在表示递进关系复句的前一个分句中,指出并承认由"不但"引出的意思,同时表示除此以外,还有比这更进一层的意思。"不但"一般连接分句,有时也连接词或短语。*When used in the first clause of a progressive complex sentence, it introduces and acknowledges what follows "不但," and suggests that there is a further connotation apart from the previous one. "不但" generally connects clauses, and sometimes it connects words or phrases.*

1. 连接分句。*When connecting clauses.*

① 跟"而且、并且、同时、也、还、又"等连词搭配,连接分句。*It collocates with conjunctions such as "而且,并且,同时,也,还,又."*

(1) 她不但自己学习努力,而且还帮助别的同学努力学习。

(2) 妈妈不但给我买了练习本,同时给我的朋友也买了两本。

(3) 我们不但去北京、西安等大城市旅游了,还去了中国西部的农村。

② 跟"连……也/都……""甚至……也……"或"即使/就是……也……"等连词、副词搭配,表示进一层的意思,连接分句。*It collocates with conjunctions or adverbs such as "连…也/都…,""甚至…也…" or "即使/就是…也…," which brings a further connotation.*

(4) 那座山不但不长树,甚至连草也不长。

(5) 她不但汉语说得好,即使是阿拉伯语也说得很好。

③ 前一分句是否定句,后一分句是肯定句,后一分句前用"反而、相反、却"等表示转折的连词,与前面分句的"不但"呼应,表示进一层的意思。*When the former clause is negative and the latter is affirmative, transitional conjunctions such as "反而,相反,却" are used at the beginning of the latter clause to coordinate with "不但" in the former clause, which brings a further connotation.*

(6) 你这样不但安慰不了她,反而会让她更伤心。

(7) 这雨不但不停,相反越下越大了。

④ 如果两个分句的主语相同时,前一分句中的"不但"用在主语以后,主语不一样时,"不但"要放在主语前。*If a statement consists of two clauses, and the two clauses have the same subject, "不但" is placed after the subject; if the subjects are different, "不但" is placed before the first subject.*

(8) 小王不但学习好、善良,而且身体也好。

(9) 不但小王不去,而且她的朋友也不去。

⑤ 在复句中,一般"不但"可以省略,只用

后面分句中的"而且、又、还"等;但不能只用"不但",不用后面分句的"而且、又、还"等连词。*In complex sentences,"不但" can be omitted with the presence of"而且,又,还" in the latter clause; but not the other way round by keeping "不但" with the absence of"而且,又,还."*

（10）他学习进步了,而且身体也好多了。

（11）＊她不但学习进步了,身体好多了。

2."不但"可以在谓语前面,连接名词性成分或介词短语。*"不但" can be placed before the predicate to connect a nominal component or a prepositional phrase.*

（12）我们班不但日本同学,而且几乎所有的同学都参加了这次 HSK 考试。

（13）不但在这个书店,甚至在这个城市所有书店都买不到意大利文的词典。

búduàn 不断

用法 Usage:

动词 *v.*

连续不间断。*To go on uninterruptedly.*

（1）这家商店顾客不断,生意很好。

（2）这孩子大病没有,小病不断。

副词 *ad.*

连续地,不间断地,不停止地。*Continually, uninterruptedly, unceasingly.*

（3）历史在不断地前进,社会在不断地发展。

（4）我们要不断地建立各种规章制度。

说明 Notes:

1.副词"不断"与动词短语"不断"的形式完全相同,但是用法不同。副词"不断"只能用在动词前面做状语。动词短语"不断"是"断"的否定,"不"和"断"之间可以加入其他词语,常常做谓语。*The adverb "不断" and the verb phrase "不断" are identical in form, but different in usage. The adverb "不断" can only serve as an adverbial placed before a verb; the verb phrase "不断" is the negative form of "断," and other words can be added between "不" and "断," and it usually serves as predicate.*

（5）那座桥不会断,你放心走吧!

（6）只要那根绳子不断,就没有问题。

2.副词"不断"常常受"接连、连续"等词语的修饰,表示动作行为的连接状态。动词短语"不断"没有这种修饰。*The adverb "不断" is usually modified by words such as "接连,连续," indicating a continuing state of act or behavior; the verb phrase "不断" has no such modifications.*

búgù 不顾

用法 Usage:

动词 *v.*

"不顾"是"不管不顾"的缩略。*"不顾" is the abbreviated form of "不管不顾."*

1.不照顾。*Not to take care of.*

（1）你不要只顾自己,不顾别人。

（2）你怎么连弟弟也不顾,只顾自己玩。

2.不考虑,不顾忌。*Not to consider or not to care.*

（3）做事不能不顾后果。

（4）她不顾一切,大吵大闹起来。

búguò 不过 →P90"但是"、P669"只是"

用法 Usage:

连词 *conj.*

表示转折关系,连接分句或句子,有时也连接段落。一般用在后面分句开头。*It signifies a transition, connecting clauses or sentences and sometimes paragraphs; usually used at the beginning of the latter clause.*

1."不过"所在的句子是对上文内容修正性的补充,有时含有突出、强调的意味。这时,"不过"所表示的转折程度比较轻,相当于"只是"。如果"不过"后面还与"罢了、而已"呼应使用,则表示这种补充不但不削弱前面内容的意思,而且还起了加强作用。*Sentences beginning with "不过" are corrections and complements to the previous content, and sometimes with an* emphatic meaning. Here "不过" suggests a relatively minor transition, similar to "只是." If there are words such as "罢了,而已" collocating with "不过," they strengthen rather than undermine the meaning of the previous content.

(1) 他们两个人的建议是一样的,不过小王的更加详细而已。

(2) 你们要多吃一点是可以的,不过不容易消化罢了。

2. "不过"所在句子引出的意思与前一部分的意思不同甚至相反。这时,"不过"的转折程度较重,与"但是、可是"相近。前面的分句或句子里,有时用"虽然、尽管"等与"不过"相呼应。 The sentence using "不过" has a meaning different from or opposite to the meaning of the previous part. Here "不过" signifies a major transition, similar to "但是,可是." In its previous clause or sentence, sometimes words such as "虽然,尽管" are used to collocate with "不过."

(3) 虽然他心里非常不愿意去见她,不过他还是去了。

(4) 他的汉语发音尽管不太标准,不过说得很清楚。

副词 ad.

"不过"用作副词,表示"只、只是、仅仅"的意思。 Only; merely; solely.

1. 表示不超过一定的范围或限度,有往小里说的意思,有时含有轻视的意味。"不过"前面还可以加"只",表示限定的范围更加明显。 It indicates a limited scope or standard, and this limitation may sometimes signify contempt. "只" can be used before "不过," suggesting an even stronger limitation.

(5) 他的成绩没什么了不起,不过多了几分。

(6) 我没什么本领,只不过比你们多看了几本书。

2. "不过"常修饰判断词"是"。"不过"usually modifies judgment verb "是."

(7) 她不过是个孩子,犯错误是免不了的。

(8) 这不过是我个人的想法,供大家参考参考。

说明 Notes:

1. "不过"用作副词的第二种用法,一般都可以加"是",但因为"不过"后面有动词,这个"是"不是必须有的判断词,所以判断的意思比较虚。"不过"后面如还带有"而已、罢了、就是(了)"等词语呼应,轻视的语气就更重。 As an adverb, the second usage of "不过" is to collocate with "是," but because there are verbs following "不过," the word "是" here is not necessarily a judgment verb, therefore it is not a strong judgment. If there are words such as "而已,罢了,就是(了)" to collocate with "不过," the disrespect is stronger.

(9) 他不过是多了几个钱而已,没什么了不起。

(10) 我只不过是开个玩笑罢了,你生什么气呢?

2. 副词"不过"与动词"过"前面加否定词"不"组成的动词短语"不过",两者的用法不同。前者表示"只、只是、仅仅"的意思;后者是"不超过"的意思。 The adverb "不过" is different from the verb phrase "不 + 过 (v.)" (the negative form of the verb "过"). The previous one means "只,只是,仅仅," while the latter one means "不超过 (not to exceed)."

(11) 你不复习,考试的成绩一定不过八十分。

(12) 从学校到植物园不过一百米。

3. "不过"附在形容词或表示心理的动词后面,表示达到了最高限度。前面常有程度副词"再、最"等相呼应,后面常带助词"了"。如:"最喜欢不过了、再合适不过了、最爱喝咖啡不过了"等。 When "不过" is used after adjectives or verbs expressing psychological activities, it suggests a peak is reached. Words such as "再,最" are usually used before it, and

word "了" commonly follows it. For example, "最喜欢不过了,再合适不过了,最爱喝咖啡不过."

(13) 由他去执行这项任务,再合适不过了。

búliào 不料

用法 Usage:

连词 conj.

表示转折关系,含有"没想到、出乎意料"的意思。一般有两个小句组成。前一小句说明原先的情况或想法,后一小句表示转折,常用"却、竟、倒、还、仍"等副词呼应。Unexpectedly. It is an indication of a transition, with a sense of surprise and unexpectedness, and is usually used with two clauses: the former clause explains the original situation or thought; the latter clause indicates the transition, and adverbs such as "却,竟,倒,还,仍" are often used.

(1) 大家都以为他不来上课是身体不好,不料他却出去旅游了。

(2) 妈妈叫她起床,不料半个小时后,她还睡在床上。

(3) 大家都很喜欢她的书法,不料一见面才知道,她没有手,竟是用脚写的。

说明 Notes:

1. "不料"只能用在复句中,并用在后一小句句首,不能用在后一小句的主语后面。"不料" can only be used at the beginning of the second clause of a complex sentence, and it cannot be placed after the subject of the second clause.

(4) *我不料我妈妈参加旅行团来中国了。

(5) 我认为妈妈不会来看我,不料,妈妈竟参加旅行团来中国看我了。

2. 后一小句用"却、竟、还"等词语,比不用更加强调转折语气,如例(3)和(5)。If words such as "却,竟,还" are used in the second clause, the transitional tone is emphasized, as in (3) and (5).

búlùn 不论 →P47"不管"

用法 Usage:

连词 conj.

"不论",亦作"无论",与"不管"都是连词,用法基本相同,不再重复。请参见"不管"。"不论" is also written as "无论." Like "不管," it is a conjunction with basically an identical usage. Please refer to "不管."

说明 Notes:

1. "不管"常用于口语。"不论/无论"多用于书面。因此,"不论/无论"后面常用"是否、与否、如何、何"等文言色彩的词语。"不管"后面不常用。"不管" is often used in colloquial language. "不论/无论" is often used in written language. Therefore, "不论/无论" is often followed by words such as "是否,与否,如何,何" that are common in classical Chinese. But "不管" usually has no such usage.

(1) 不论你如何劝说,他都不听。

(2) 不论你买来的东西是否好吃,她都不尝一口。

2. "不管"有"不管+形+不+形"的句式,但是"不论/无论"后面一般不这样用,而是用形容词的反义词,中间加上"还是"才能使用。"不管+a.+不+a." is a sentence structure for "不管", but "不论/无论" has a different usage: what follows "不论/无论" is an adjective or its antonym with the word "还是" in between.

(3) 不管天气热不热,他都穿那么多。

(4) 不论天气热还是冷,他都穿那么多。

3. "不管"有"不管+名+不+名"的句式,"不论/无论"没有。"不管" has a sentence structure "不管+n.+不+n.," but "不论/无论" does not.

(5) 不管词典不词典,我都不买了。

(6) *不论词典不词典,我都不买了。

búyàojǐn 不要紧

用法 Usage:

1. 没有妨碍，不成问题，没有关系。常做谓语，有时可以单独插入，后面句子再说明什么问题不要紧。*Doesn't matter; not a problem; not serious; it is okay. It is often used as a predicate. Sometimes it can stand alone, and the following sentence will explain what is not serious.*

(1) 你的病不要紧，多喝开水，休息休息就好了。

(2) 不要紧，我会打电话告诉他的。

2. 表面上似乎事情本身没有问题，但是后面句子有转折，表示在某些方面还是有问题、有妨碍。"不要紧"用在前面分句中，一般不单独用。*It seems that the matter itself is not problematic, but a transition will appear in the latter sentence, indicating a problem or obstruction still exists.* "不要紧" *is used in the previous clause, and is generally not used alone.*

(3) 你重新做一遍不要紧，但是时间来不及了。

(4) 他这么一叫不要紧，可是邻居被他叫醒了。

búzàihu 不在乎 →P495"无所谓"

用法 Usage:

动词 v.

不把什么放在心上，怎么样都可以，自己自有主张。"不在乎"在句子中用法比较多。*Not to care; couldn't care less because one's mind is already made up.* "不在乎" *is used in several ways.*

1. 不在乎＋名词宾语。"不在乎"＋ *a noun object.*

(1) 她不在乎钱，只要对别人有帮助，她就给。

(2) 我不在乎这几件衣服。你要，你就拿去吧。

2. 不在乎＋动词短语。"不在乎"＋ *a verb phrase.*

(3) 只要能学到本领。他不在乎难学不难学。

(4) 我不在乎吃什么东西，能吃饱就好。

3. 不在乎＋小句宾语。"不在乎"＋ *an object clause.*

(5) 我不在乎你说什么。

(6) 他从来不在乎别人提意见。

4. "不在乎"可以做状语，也可以受程度副词的修饰。"不在乎" *can serve as an adverbial, and it can be modified by a degree adverb.*

(7) 他很不在乎地说："不让我去就不去。"

(8) 这点儿钱，他才不在乎呢。

5. 用在反问句中，"不在乎"前面一般要用能愿动词。*If it is used in a rhetorical question,* "不在乎" *is often preceded by a modal verb.*

(9) 他会不在乎考试的成绩？

(10) 你可以不在乎他说的那些话？

bùchéng 不成

用法 Usage:

动词 v.

不成功，无成效。*To be unsuccessful or unproductive.*

(1) 我是学歌不成，学舞也不成。

(2) 你不能什么都想学，什么都学不成。

形容词 a.

1. 不行，不可以，不允许。*Not possible; not allowed.*

(3) 不成，这里是医院，你们不能在这里唱歌跳舞。

(4) 损坏电脑不赔偿不成！

2. 不行，不中用。*Being out of the question; useless.*

(5) 玩扑克还行，下象棋我可不成。

(6) 不成，不成！喝一杯酒还可以，喝三杯绝对不成。

助词 aux. v.

用在句末，表示反问的语气，前面常有"莫非、难道"等词相呼应。*It is used at the end of a sentence to form a rhetorical question, and words* like "莫非" and "难道" usually collocate with it at the beginning of the sentence.

（7）老师一来,你就不说话。难道你怕老师不成?

（8）还不下课,莫非要让大家饿肚子不成?

bùdébù 不得不 →P668"只得"、P668"只好"

用法 Usage:

表示由于条件的限制或情况的变化,迫不得已只得如此,有"只能、只好、只得"的意思。做状语。Cannot but. One has no choice but to do so under certain restrictive conditions or changed circumstances, similar to "只能,只好,只得." It serves as an adverbial.

（1）爸爸要我到中国来学汉语,我不得不来。

（2）公共汽车没有了,她不得不坐出租车回去。

说明 Notes:

1."不得不"多用于口语。"不得不" is commonly used in colloquial language.

2."不得不"所在的句子一般有两个分句。前一分句表示条件的限制,表示原因;后一分句则表示在这样的情况下,只能这么做,表示结果。There are usually two clauses in a sentence using "不得不," with the former explaining the restrictive conditions or the reason, and the latter expressing what can be done under such circumstances.

bùdéliǎo 不得了 →P304"了不得"

用法 Usage:

形容词 a.

表示情况严重,没法收拾;也表示程度很深。(Of a situation or condition) being terrible and out of control; deep in degree.

1.表示情况严重,没法收拾。用在无主句,前面常用副词"可";如上下文中有说明情况的小句时,"不得了"前面常有副词"可、更、就、才"。It indicates that a certain situation is terrible and out of control. When used in a subject-less sentence, "不得了" is usually preceded by adverb "可"; when there are clauses for explanation in the context, it is usually preceded by adverbs such as "可,更,就,才."

（1）可不得了! 那边着火了!

（2）马路上有那么多车辆,如果被车碰一下,那就不得了了。

2.表示程度很深,用于程度补语。It indicates depth in degree and is used as a degree complement.

（3）他收到你的礼物后,高兴得不得了。

（4）今年夏天杭州热得不得了。

has no such modifications.

bùgǎndāng 不敢当

用法 Usage:

动词 v.

谦辞,表示承当不起(对方的招待、夸奖等)。Term of modesty. It is used as a modest word when hearing a compliment or attending a reception arranged by someone else.

1.对别人热情的招待如请客吃饭、送礼物或传递茶水等表示承受不起时,在口头上常用的谦辞。In response to others' warm hospitality presented in the form of a feast, gift, tea, and other services that one feels not well deserved. It is a modest term in colloquial language.

（1）你送我那么贵重的礼物,真不敢当!

（2）你那么客气,又是茶,又是点心,真不敢当!

2.对别人夸奖自己、说自己好话时,表示自己做得还不够,承受不了这样的奖励,在口头上常用的谦辞。In response to other people's praise or compliments, the phrase is used to show that one hasn't done well enough to deserve such an honor. It is used as a modest term orally.

（3）你们把我说得那么好,我真不敢当!

(4) 不敢当,不敢当! 那是我应该做的。

说明 Notes:

1. "不敢当"是口头习惯语。"不敢当" is an idiom used orally.

2. 特别要清楚地掌握使用"不敢当"时的文化背景。它只在一个人在物质上或精神上得到某种恩惠的情景或场合下才使用。见上列的例句。 It is important to understand the cultural background of using "不敢当." It is only used under the condition or circumstance that one has received certain favor materially or spiritually. See the above examples.

(5) A：谢谢你帮忙!
B：＊不敢当,不敢当!
B：不客气。

(6) A：对不起,请让一让!
B：＊不敢当!
B：没关系!

bùguǎn 不管 →P44"不论"、P240"尽管"、P494"无论"

用法 Usage:

连词 conj.

用在有疑问代词或并列短语的条件关系复句中,起排除条件的作用。表示在任何条件和情况下,结果都不会改变,有"不管怎样,都是如此"的意思。后边常与"都、也、总(是)、就、还(是)"等关系词呼应连用。 When used in conditional complex sentences where there are interrogative pronouns or parallel phrases, it excludes the condition mentioned. It means that the result would not change under any conditions or circumstances. It is similar to "不管怎样, 都是如此 (everything remains the same no matter what...)." It is usually followed by relative words such as "都, 也, 总(是), 就, 还(是)."

1. 排除一切条件。前面分句常带"怎(么)样、谁、什么"等疑问代词,表示非常广泛的周遍性。 Excluding all possible conditions. The previous clause, which is usually followed by interrogative pronouns such as "怎(么)样, 谁, 什么," indicates that everything is covered.

(1) 不管学什么,我们都要认真、努力。

(2) 不管是谁向他借照相机,他都借给别人。

2. 排除某个范围内的条件。"不管"的前后常常是表示范围的词语,前面分句常带疑问代词"怎样、哪儿、什么"等,表示周遍性。 Ruling out conditions within a certain range. Words expressing the range are often used before and after "不管," and interrogative pronouns such as "怎样, 哪儿, 什么" are frequently used in the former clause to show that everything is covered.

(3) 不管考什么,我都不怕,我全复习好了。

(4) 你不管到哪儿,都要给我打电话。

3. 排除两个以上范围内的条件。在"不管"后面是并列项,在各项之间常用连词"和、以及、还(是)、或、或者"等词连接。 Ruling out more than two conditions within the range. What follows "不管" is a parallel structure, where conjunctions such as "和, 以及, 还(是), 或, 或者" are commonly used to connect each component.

(5) 不管是下雨还是天晴,明天我们都要去苏州。

(6) 学习一门语言,不管你将来当翻译或者做老师,听说读写都很重要。

4. "不管"常见的句式还有："不管……,不管……,不管……,都/也……"; "不管……也好/也罢,不管……也好/也罢,都/也……"; "不管＋名/形＋不＋名/形,都/也……"; 等等。 Other common sentence patterns with "不管" include: "不管..., 不管..., 不管..., 都/也..."; "不管...也好/也罢,不管...也好/也罢,都/也..."; "不管＋n./a.＋不＋n./a., 都/也...;" etc.

(7) 不管你是东方人还是西方人,不管你来学汉语还是学文化,不管你学一年还是学两个月,我们都热情接待,认真教学,让你满意。

（8）不管你去北京也好，不管你去西安也好，你都能感受到中国古老的历史和文化。

（9）我不管欧美人不欧美人，学汉语的人都要写汉字。

（10）不管衣服脏不脏，只要穿过一次，他就要洗。

bùguāng 不光

用法 Usage:

副词 *ad.*

不只，不仅。后面常带"是"。*Not just; not limited to. It is usually followed by "是."*

（1）有这种想法的不光是我一个人。

（2）春节快到了，不光是高铁车票难买到，飞机票也很难买到。

连词 *conj.*

不但。*Not only.*

（3）他不光会俄语，还会德语、日语。

（4）南方的夏天不光闷热，而且还潮湿。

bùjīn 不禁

用法 Usage:

副词 *ad.*

抑制不住、禁不住（某种动作行为或感情、神情的产生），相当于"情不自禁、不由自主、不由得"。常做状语。*Unable to restrain, couldn't help but do (indicating the generation of an act, or a feeling, or a look), similar to "情不自禁, 不由自主, 不由得." It usually serves as an adverbial.*

（1）哥哥不让弟弟踢足球，弟弟不禁哭了起来。

（2）听说汉语写作不考试，大家高兴得不禁叫了起来。

说明 Notes:

1. "不禁"一般只能用在动词或动词性语前面，动词后面常常带有趋向动词"起来"，表示动作、行为或情绪不由自主地产生或出现。*Generally, "不禁" can only be used before a verb or verb phrase which is followed by the directional verb "起来" to indicate an involuntarily generated act, behavior or emotion.*

2. "不禁"的意思是禁不住产生或出现某种动作行为、情绪感受，有一个动作开始的过程，动词后面一般都有补充说明。所以只能用在多音节动词或动词短语前面。不能用在孤立的单音节动词前面。"不禁" *suggests that one cannot help but perform some action or behavior or generate certain emotion or feeling, and because it involves the beginning of an act, there are always explanations to indicate what the act is. Hence "不禁" is only used before a multisyllabic verb or verb phrase instead of a monosyllabic verb.*

（3）＊跟妈妈打了电话以后，她不禁想家。

（4）跟妈妈打了电话以后，她不禁想起家来了。

（5）＊桌子上有那么多蛋糕，她不禁先吃了。

（6）桌子上有那么多蛋糕，她不禁先吃了起来。

3. "不禁"不能用在否定形式前面。*"不禁" cannot be used before a negative form.*

（7）＊大家都笑了。她不禁不笑了。

（8）大家都笑了。她却没有笑。

bùjǐn 不仅 →P41"不但"

用法 Usage:

副词 *ad.*

表示超出某一数量或范围，不止。*Exceeding a certain quantity or range; not only.*

（1）想去西藏旅游的不仅是我一人。

（2）我要学习的语言不仅是汉语。

连词 *conj.*

连词"不仅"的用法跟"不但"基本相同（参看"不但"）。*The usage is basically similar to "不但" (cf. "不但").*

说明 Notes:

"不仅"作连词用，与"不但"的区别是：*As conjunctions, the differences between "不仅" and "不但" are as follows:*

1. 在语义上,"不仅"有比较明显的指定范围的意思。指出不仅是这一方面,而且还有其他方面。"不但"侧重内容本身客观递进的表述。*Semantically,"不仅" has a clearer reference to a designated scope, which indicates that there are more aspects instead of just one. However "不但" emphasizes an objective and progressive description.*

(3) 她不但自己努力学习,而且还帮助别的同学努力学习。

(4) 她不仅自己努力学习,而且还帮助别的同学努力学习。

2. 为了强调语气,书面上"不仅"可以写成"不仅仅",而"不但"不能。*To be emphatic,"不仅" can be rendered as "不仅仅," but "不但" cannot.*

(5) *学语言不但但是认真上课的问题,更重要的是实践。

(6) 学语言不仅仅是认真上课的问题,更重要的是实践。

3. 如果"不仅"的后一个分句中没有呼应的"还、也"等连词,后一分句的内容常常是总括性的。*If there are no conjunctions such as "还,也" to collocate with "不仅" in the latter clause, the latter clause is generally conclusive.*

(7) 这次口语比赛,不仅有两个同学得到了二等奖,而且参加比赛的同学都得到了优秀奖。

(8) 今年暑假,我不仅学完了第二册,而且学完了初级所有的课本。

bùmiǎn 不免 →P334"难免"

用法 Usage:
副词 ad.

表示由于某种原因而自然导致某种结果,或某种情况。这种结果或情况可以是已经出现的,也可以是可能出现的猜测。有"免不了""少不了"的意思。只修饰肯定形式的多音节动词短语或形容词短语,多用于两个分句的后一分句中。*Unavoidably; a certain cause naturally leads to a certain result or situation. This result or situation may already be present or, as a speculation, about to emerge. It is similar to "免不了" or "少不了." It only modifies affirmative polysyllabic verb phrases or adjective phrases, and usually appears in the second clause when the sentence contains two clauses.*

(1) 第一次拿到自己的工资,心里不免有些兴奋。

(2) 第一次来到中国,生活上不免有些不习惯。

(3) 公司刚刚成立,工作起来不免会有些困难。

说明 Notes:

1. "不免"的意思常常解释为"少不了""常常会出现"。常常会有以下错句。*"不免" is usually interpreted as "少不了 (cannot do without)" or "常常会出现 (often appear)." Mistakes may often appear when one tries to use "不免."*

(4) *因为要交学费,所以我回国不免打工。

(5) 因为要交学费,所以我回国少不了打工。

(6) *刚开始学汉语,不免有笑话。

(7) 刚开始学汉语,免不了会出现一些笑话。

2. "不免"后面出现的常常是不希望出现的结果或情况,见例(2)和(3)。*"不免" is often followed by an undesired result or situation. See (2) and (3).*

3. "不免"多用在复句中。前一分句表示某种原因,后一分句表示由此出现的某种结果或情况。"不免"用在后一分句中,表示比较委婉的语气。*"不免" is often used in a complex sentence. The former clause offers a certain reason, and the latter one indicates a certain result or situation. "不免" is used in the latter clause to convey a more euphemistic tone.*

(8) 公司刚刚成立,工作起来不免会有些困难。

(9) 公司刚刚成立,工作起来会有些困难。

例(9)句的语气比较肯定,一定会有些困难。例(8)句的语气比较留有余地,含有可能有困难也可能没有困难的意思,容易让人接受。The tone in (9) is fairly certain: it will certainly be somewhat difficult. The tone in (8) is less certain: the difficulty may occur or may not occur. This tone makes it easy for people to accept.

4."不免"一般不修饰单独的动词或形容词,更不能修饰单音节的动词或形容词。"不免" generally does not modify an independent verb or adjective, and does not modify monosyllabic verbs or adjectives.

(10) *小王考试一连得了三次一百分,不免骄傲。

(11) 小王考试一连得了三次一百分,不免骄傲起来。

(12) *小孩子打针,不免哭。

(13) 小孩子打针,不免要哭几声。

bùrán 不然 →P150"否则"、P543"要不"

用法 Usage:

连词 conj.

1. 表示对上文作假设性的否定,然后在下文指出假设后将会出现的情况。有"如果不这样"的意思,相当于"否则""要不"。连接分句或句子,后一句子常用"要、就、会"呼应。在"不然"后面可以加上"的话",以加强语气。Otherwise; if not. It indicates a negative hypothesis, and then points out what will happen in that hypothesis. It is similar to "如果不这样 (if not)", "否则 (otherwise)", "要不 (or)". It connects clauses or sentences; Words such as "要, 就, 会" are often used in the latter clause. "不然" can be followed by "的话" to strengthen the tone.

(1) 你赶快动身吧,不然上火车就来不及了。

(2) 她是不是有什么伤心事,不然的话,她为什么要哭?

(3) 你一定是少林寺的师父,不然的话,怎么有这样好的功夫?

2. 引出与上文交替的情况,表示选择。对上文的推测作假设性的否定,然后在下文作出另一选择。有"如果不这样,那就……"的意思。在"不然"前面可以加上"要、再",在后面可以带"的话",后面句子中常用"就、就是",以加强语气。It introduces a situation mentioned in the previous text, and expresses a choice. Or, it makes a hypothetical negation of the previous speculation, and then offers another choice in the upcoming text. It is similar to "如果不这样,那就... (If not so, then...)." Words such as "要, 再" can be added to "不然," and words such as "的话" can be used after it. In the latter part of the same sentence, "就" or "就是" can be used to intensify the tone.

(4) 她可能去桂林旅行了,要不然就是去广州了。

(5) 我们晚上不是复习就是预习,再不然就是做作业。

(6) 我们每天都吃白米饭或者吃汤面,再不然的话就是炒饭或炒面。

形容词 a.

1. "不是这样"的意思。做后一句子的谓语,可以受副词的修饰。It is similar to "不是这样 (not like this)." As the predicate of the latter clause, it can be modified by an adverb.

(7) 看上去他的身体很不好,其实不然。

(8) 别看现在这一片树林非常安静,刮起风来则不然,会吓死你。

2. 用在对话里,有"不是这样"的意思,用在表示否定对方说法的句子的开头。In a dialogue, it is similar to "不是这样 (not so)," used at the beginning of a sentence to indicate a negative statement.

(9) A:那么长时间没看到他,我想他是回国了。

B:不然。他回国的话,一定会来跟我告别的。

说明 Notes:

1."不然"作形容词用,有两个功能:一是做谓语;一是在句子前面表示否定对方的话,见例(9)。做谓语时,"不然"一般受"其实、则、并"等少数副词的修饰,见例(7)和(8)。*As an adjective,"不然" has two functions: one is to serve as the predicate; the other is to be used at the beginning of a sentence as a negation, as in (9). As a predicate,"不然" is generally modified by a few adverbs such as "其实,则,并," as in (7) and (8).*

2."不然"作连词用,也有两种用法:一种相当于"否则",起假设转折的作用;一种表示选择,引进与上文交替的情况,相当于"要不是这样,那就……"。"不然"前面常加"再、要",后面常用"就"。见例(4)(5)(6)。*As a conjunction,"不然" also has two functions: one is equivalent to "否则 (otherwise)," playing the role of a hypothetical turn of the event; the other is to introduce a choice, which is often something mentioned in the foregoing text, equivalent to "要不是这样,那就... (If this is not the case, then...)." "不然" is usually preceded by "再" or "要" and followed by "就." See (4), (5) and (6).*

bùrú 不如 →P315"没/没有"

用法 Usage:

动词 *v.*

表示前面提到的人和事物比不上后面所说的。用于比较,有"比不上"的意思。构成的比较句,句式较多。*To be not as good as. It indicates the above mentioned people or things are not as good as those mentioned later. It is used in comparison, similar to "比不上 (cannot compare with)." Its comparative sentence has many structures.*

1.常用于对话或前面已有语境说明的句子,句子并不说明具体比较的是什么。*It is usually used in a conversation or in a sentence already explained in the previous context, but the sentence does not indicate what exactly is compared.*

(1)路上人和车很多,坐公共汽车不如骑自行车。

(2)我们家的两个孩子,老大不如老二。

2.两种事物比较,有比较结果的说明。有时比较事项在前面出现,后面的比较项可以省略。*It is used in a comparison of two things, including the result of the comparison. Sometimes the items of comparison are in the front, and the subsequent comparison can be omitted.*

(3)我的汉语不如他的好。

(4)这间教室不如那间大。

3.同一事物不同时期的比较。*It is used in a comparison of the same thing at different times.*

(5)我现在的身体不如十年以前了。

(6)这个月来杭州的游客不如上个月的多。

4.用"连……都/也不如"的格式,把"不如"的宾语提前。"不如"用在句末。*If the structure "连...都/也不如" is used, the object of "不如" should be placed in advance while "不如" is placed at the end of the sentence.*

(7)这个道理你竟然不懂,真是连小孩都不如。

(8)现在你们的语言水平,连小学三年级的学生也不如。

连词 *conj.*

表示经过对比,进行取舍。前一小句常用"与其",说明舍弃的一项,后一小句则用"不如"表明选取的一项。*It indicates a decision being made after some comparison. "与其" is often used in the previous clause indicating the discarded choice, and "不如" is often used in the latter clause indicating the selected choice.*

(9)与其挤公共汽车,不如走路去。

(10)星期天,与其在宿舍里待着,不如去湖边散散步。

说明 Notes：

1. "不如"是"比不上"的意思。常见的格式是"A 不如 B+形容词"，在"不如"后面表示结果的形容词，一般应是表示积极意义的、褒义的词语。"不如" means "比不上" (not as good as). A common structure is "A 不如 B + a." The adjective following "不如" and indicating the result should generally be positive or commendatory words.

（11）*他写汉字不如我不好。

（12）我写汉字不如他好。

（13）*这个学校的留学生不如那个学校的少。

（14）那个学校的留学生不如这个学校的多。

2. 用"不如"进行比较，"不如"前后的名词、动词、小句等词类或结构要求相同，即比较项要相同。If "不如" is used to make a comparison, the nouns, verbs and clauses before and after "不如" should belong to the same category. That is, the comparison items should be the same.

（15）*我买的书不如他的便宜。

（16）我买的书不如他买的便宜。

例(15)是比较买的书的价格，后面的比较项应该是"他买的（书）"。Example (15) is to compare the prices of the books bought, and the comparison item after "不如" should be "他买的（书）."

bùxíng 不行

用法 Usage：

形容词 a.

1. 不好，水平不高。Not good. The level (of competency, skill, etc.) is not high (enough).

（1）她的英语发音不行。

（2）这件衣服的颜色不行。

2. 用在"得"字后做补语，表示程度很深；不得了。It is used after "得" as a complement to indicate a profound degree; very much.

（3）这几天工作太多，我累得不行了。

（4）窗外是个汽车站，整天吵得不行。

动词 v.

1. 不可以，不被允许。Not to be allowed, not to be permitted.

（5）不行！你不上课去旅游，一定要向老师请假。

（6）天气很冷。你只穿一件毛衣不行。

2. 后面带"了"，表示接近于死亡、垮台或某件事不成功。If followed by "了," it indicates approaching death or downfall, or something being unsuccessful.

（7）已经昏迷三四天，我看他不行了。

（8）这家商店不行了，要倒闭了。

bùyīdìng 不一定

用法 Usage：

"不一定"有两个不同的意思，一是"未必"，一是"不确定"。"不一定" has two different meanings: "未必" means "not necessarily" and "不确定" means "not certain."

（1）我的说法不一定对，仅供参考。（未必 Not necessarily）

（2）这部电影能否按期上映还不一定。（不确定 Not certain）

"不一定"是副词性词语。表示事实还没有确定，语气比较客观。在句子中可以做谓语、状语、宾语，也可以单独回答问题。"不一定 (Not necessarily; not certain)" is an adverbial phrase. It indicates that the fact hasn't been determined. The tone is relatively objective. It can serve as a predicate, adverbial, and object, and it can be used as an independent response to a question.

（3）看她那个样子，不一定会做饭。（状语 Adverbial）

（4）她来不来还不一定。（谓语 Predicate）

（5）你说她会来，我看不一定。（宾语 object）

（6）A：你妈妈会让你跟我一起去看电影吗？

B：不一定。（单独回答 Independent answer）

说明 Notes：

1. "不一定"的句子中常有表示任指的疑问代词。句后常与表示猜测语气的助词"呢"连用。*There is often a general-reference interrogative pronoun in a sentence using "不一定." At the end of the sentence, the particle "呢" often appears, carrying a tone of speculation.*

(7) 下个学期我在哪儿学还不一定呢。

(8) 她哪天回国还不一定呢。

2. "不一定"可以用在表示处所、时间的任指代词前后，但是其他任指代词只能在"不一定"后面。*"不一定" can be used either before or after a general-reference pronoun that indicates a location or time, but other such pronouns can only be placed after "不一定."*

(9) 下个学期我还不一定在哪儿学呢。

(10) 今天晚上的晚会还不一定谁去呢。

3. "不一定"做谓语，句子中如果有肯定否定正反并列式连用，表示客观的猜测。*When "不一定" serves as a predicate, and when there is a parallel usage of both a positive and a negative word, it suggests an objective speculation.*

(11) 她去不去那个学校学汉语还不一定。

(12) 是不是王老师带我们去教学实践还不一定呢。

bùyóude 不由得

用法 Usage：

副词 ad.

1. 表示由不得自己，不由自主地。*Can't help doing something; involuntarily.*

(1) 这孩子听到别的孩子哭，不由得也哭了起来。

(2) 妈妈看着我的成绩单，不由得笑着说："好！好！"

2. 有"不容"的意思，相当于"不得不"。后面接否定形式，用两个否定进行肯定，强调语气，组成兼语句式。*Similar to "不容" (not allowed) and equivalent to "不得不" (have to), it is usually followed by a negative idea. As a double negative makes a positive, the tone is emphasized, and a concurrent statement is made.*

(3) 夜市很有特色，不由得你不逛。

(4) 这本词典又好又便宜，不由得你不买。

(5) 她的邀请又真诚又热情，不由得你不答应。

bùzěnmeyàng 不怎么样

用法 Usage：

平平常常，不很好。"不怎么样"是任指疑问代词"怎么样"的否定式。用在否定句中，代替某种不说出来的动作或情况。语气比直接说出来委婉。常用在对话中，表示不太满意，但又不想直接说明自己的看法时常用的词语。在句子中常做谓语，并能单独回答问题。*Not very good; not up to much; so-so. "不怎么样" is the negative form of a general-reference interrogative pronoun "怎么样." If it appears in a negative sentence, it stands for a certain act or situation that is not expressed explicitly, and it is more euphemistic than straightforward speaking. It is often used in a dialogue to indicate dissatisfaction but an inclination not to directly express oneself. It can serve as a predicate in a sentence and can answer a question by itself.*

(1) A：这电影你看了怎么样？

B：不怎么样。

(2) 我看，这个教室也不怎么样。

(3) 我想，他的身体也不怎么样。

说明 Notes：

"不怎么样"的语境条件很重要：一是用在对话中，对话的语境比较清楚。二是用在叙述句子中，并要注意前后句子内容上对"不怎么样"的呼应。如例(2)，句子前后一定是在谈论教室的大小、是否干净等问题。*The context of "不怎么样" is important: one is in a dialogue, which has a relatively clear context; the other is in a narrative, where one has to pay close attention to the reaction to "不怎么样." In (2), the discussion must be about the size and the tidiness of the classroom.

bùzhí 不值

用法 Usage:

1. 也作"不值得",（指做某件事）没有价值和意义,相对于"值得"。Also written as "不值得," it means that something is not worth any value or meaning, as opposed to "值得."

（1）这点小事不值一提。

（2）这个问题根本不值一辩。

2. 指货物与价值不相当,是"值"的否定。The goods are not equal to the value; a negation of "值."

（3）我看,这件毛衣不值二百元。

（4）二十元才这么一小瓶苹果醋,真不值!

说明 Notes:

"不值"在句子中,多用作动词,有时能受程度副词修饰。In a sentence, "不值" often serves as a verb, and sometimes it can be modified by a degree adverb.

（5）跟他去商量很不值,因为他常常不同意别人的建议。

（6）这次去上海旅游非常不值。

bùzú 不足

用法 Usage:

形容词 a.

不充足。Insufficient.

（1）你买的蛋糕数量不足,生日晚会不够吃的。

（2）她的身体不好是因为营养不足。

动词 v.

1. 不满,不到,不够（某个数目）。To be less than (a certain number).

（3）这些年轻人看上去都不足三十岁。

（4）身边的钱不足两千,买手机、电脑已经不够了。

2. 不可以,不能。Not to be allowed; not to count.

（5）他的话不足为数。

（6）在法律上,亲戚朋友的话不足为证。

3. 不值得。多用于书面四字词组。Not to be worth it. It is often used in four-character phrases in written language.

（7）饭店挤满人,这种现象在我们这里不足为奇。

（8）这件小事不足一提。

cái 才

用法 Usage:

副词 ad.

1. 表示动作行为或事情发生不久。相当于"刚、刚刚"。用在单句或复句中。若用于复句,后一分句中常有"就"与之呼应。An action or something that has just happened; the equivalence of "刚, 刚刚." It can be used in simple sentences or complex sentences. When "才" is used in a complex sentence, "就" usually appears in the subsequent clause.

(1) 这是我才买的蛋糕。

(2) 上午才买的自行车,下午就丢了。

2. 表示动作行为或事情发生或结束得晚。"才"前面常有表示时间或为什么晚的疑问词语。An action or something happens or ends late. An interrogative word such as when or why usually appears before "才."

(3) 你怎么现在才来?

(4) 昨天晚上他两点才睡。

3. 表示数量少、程度低、范围小。相当于"只、只有、仅、不过"。"才"一般用在表示时间或地点词语的前面。Indicating a small quantity, a low degree or a small scope; the equivalence of "只,只有,仅,不过." "才" is always used before a time or place expression.

(5) 我到中国一年了,才去过上海和北京两个城市。

(6) 他才学了两个月汉语,还不太会说。

4. 表示只有在某种条件下或由于某种原因、为了某种目的,然后怎么样。一般用于表示条件、目的、因果等关系的复句中,起关联作用。Used to indicate that something happens only under certain conditions, for some reason or for some purpose in a parallel clause.

① 表示条件关系的复句中,"才"常用在后一分句,与前一分句中的"只有、必须、除非、非得"等词语呼应。In a compound sentence expressing a conditional relationship, "才" is always used in the main clause, echoing words such as "只有,必须,除非,非得" in the conditional clause.

(7) 只有多开口说话,才学得好汉语。

(8) 她不爱活动,非得别人叫她一起去,她才出门。

② 表示目的的句子中,常用"为了"与"才"相呼应。In a clause of purpose, "为了" usually coexists with "才."

(9) 我们都是为了学习汉语才来中国的。

(10) 我们是为了了解中国文化才去旅游的。

③ 表示因果关系的句子中,前一分句中常用"因为、由于"等词语,与主句中的"才"相呼应。In a clause of reason, words such as "因为" or "由于" are often used, echoing "才" in the main clause.

(11) 由于中国朋友的帮助,我的汉语水平才提高得很快。

(12) 因为她每天早上叫我起床,早上八点的课才没迟到。

5. 表示强调肯定的语气。常见的句式有:

才+形容词；才+动；才+不+动词。句末常用语气助词"呢"。Emphasizing the positive tone. The common sentence patterns are as follows: "才＋a."; "才＋v."; "才＋不＋v." The modal particle "呢" always appears at the end of the sentence.

（13）昨天的足球比赛那才精彩呢！
（14）她才是韩国人呢！
（15）我才不吃那种叫不出名字的东西呢。

名词 n.

1. 才能。Talent.
（16）她是个多才多艺的姑娘。
（17）他很有才，就是太骄傲。

2. 有才能的人。A capable person.
（18）他是我们单位的干才。（干才：有办事才能的人 A talented person）
（19）他是个天才。

说明 Notes：

1. "才"用在数量词前或后，语义不同。用在数量词前面，表示早或少。用在数量词后面，表示晚或多。"才" conveys different meanings when used before and after quantitative words. When used before a quantitative word, "才" means "early" or "a small amount of"; when used after a quantitative word, "才" means "late" or "a large amount of."

（20）现在才六点，你就起床干什么？
（21）他星期五才告诉我要去北京。

2. "才"是副词，要用在句子的主要动词前面。When "才" is used as an adverb, it should be placed before the main verb.

（22）*我们才到中国以后吃过一次西餐。
（23）我们到中国以后才吃过一次西餐。
（24）*这几个生词我才写了五遍记住。
（25）这几个生词我写了五遍才记住。

cǎinà 采纳 →P56"采取"

用法 Usage：

动词 v.

采取，接受（意见、建议或要求）。To take or accept (an opinion, a proposal, or a request).

（1）学院采纳了我们关于增加选修课的建议。
（2）老师采纳了我的意见，明天不进行听写测验。

cǎiqǔ 采取 →P56"采纳"、P56"采用"

用法 Usage：

动词 v.

表示选择并施行某种方针、政策、措施、手段、方案、形式、态度、意见、建议等。可带名词、动词做宾语。To adopt; to choose a kind of policy, measure, method, plan, form, manner, opinion, suggestion and so on and implement it. It can take a noun or verb as its object.

（1）你不能采取打骂的手段对待孩子。
（2）中国采取改革开放的政策以后，经济发展得非常快。

说明 Notes：

"采取"和"采纳"的区别是：The difference between "采取" and "采纳"：

"采纳"着重接纳别人提出的意见、建议和要求等。"采取"着重在选取施行，可以主动选择施行某种方针、政策、措施，也可以从别人的意见、建议、要求中选取施行。"采纳" emphasizes the acceptance of an opinion, a proposal or a request; while "采取" emphasizes choosing and implementing, which can either be the choice and implementation of a kind of policy, measure, and method or of others' idea, suggestion or request.

cǎiyòng 采用 →P56"采取"

用法 Usage：

动词 v.

表示对认为合适、值得或有利的事物进行利用。能带名词宾语，也能做定语。To adopt; to make use of what is considered appropriate, worthwhile, or beneficial. It can take a noun object, or can be used as an attribute.

(1) 数码照相机采用的技术是最新电子技术。

(2) 我采用了老师建议的练习方法，口语水平提高很快。

说明 Notes：

"采取"和"采用"的区别是：The differences between "采取" and "采用" are as follows:

1. 在词义上，"采取"侧重于选取。"采用"侧重于使用。In terms of semantic meaning, "采取" focuses on choosing something, while "采用" focuses on making use of something or acting upon something.

2. 在使用范围上，"采取"侧重用于抽象事物，它的宾语多为抽象名词，如"路线、方针、策略、政策、原则、方法、手段、措施、步骤、形式、立场"等。"采用"使用范围更广，可以用于抽象事物，也可以用于具体事物。它的宾语还可为"经验、技术、方法、方式"或"工具、材料、教材、稿件"等。In terms of use, "采取" usually refers to something abstract and its objects are always abstract nouns such as "路线, 方针, 策略, 原则, 方法, 手段, 措施, 步骤, 形式, 立场"; "采用" has a broader meaning and can refer to both abstract things and concrete things; words such as "经验, 技术, 方法, 方式" or "工具, 材料, 教材, 稿件" can serve as the object of "采用."

3. 在句法上，"采用"可以单独做谓语。"采取"不能。In terms of syntax, "采用" can be used as a predicate while "采取" cannot.

(3) A：这个办法我们采用吗？

B：采用。

cǎisè 彩色 →P401"色彩"

用法 Usage：

名词 n.

多种色彩组合在一起的颜色。常做定语。The combination of a variety of colors. It is usually used as an attribute.

(1) 我要买几张彩色纸。

(2) 彩色手机的光线对眼睛更不利。

说明 Notes：

"彩色"做定语时，常常省略"色"，单用"彩"，与被修饰名词中的一个词素组成缩略语，如"彩电(彩色电视)、彩照(彩色照片)、彩显(彩色显示)、彩车(经过装饰的汽车或彩色自行车)"等。When "彩色" is used as an attribute, the character "色" is usually omitted, and "彩" is used with a modified noun morpheme to form an abbreviation, for example, "彩电 (color TV), 彩照 (color photo), 彩显 (color display), 彩车 (decorated car or colored bicycle)," and so on.

cānguān 参观 →P144"访问"

用法 Usage：

动词 v.

到实地去观察工作成绩、设施、名胜古迹、博物馆等。To visit places of historical interest or museums, etc.; to pay a field visit to watch facilities or observe what has been accomplished.

(1) 在中国我参观了很多工厂和村庄。

(2) 明天我们要去参观博物馆。

cáng 藏 →P127"躲"

用法 Usage：

动词 v.

1. 躲藏，表示人和动物为了不被发现而隐藏起来。To hide; (Of people and animals) hide in order not to be found.

(1) 不知道他藏到哪儿去了，怎么也找不到他。

(2) 我把她的背包藏起来了。

2. 隐藏，收存。表示事物被隐蔽起来、收藏起来，不让人发现或看见。To conceal. It often refers to things that are collected and hidden from public view.

(3) 我家藏着两幅名画。

(4) 孩子们把小猫藏哪儿去了？

cāozòng 操纵 →P278"控制"

用法 Usage:

动词 v.

1. 控制或开动机器、仪器等。To control or operate a machine, instrument and so on.

(1) 那台电脑操纵着机器的开动和关闭。

(2) 医院里有不少手术都是医生操纵机器人进行的。

2. 用不正当的手段支配控制人、会议或某件事情。To use improper means to control somebody or something (even a conference or some other event).

(3) 这只股票走势诡异,背后一定有人在操纵。

(4) 他师傅操纵了他的一切活动。

céng 曾 →P58"曾经"

用法 Usage:

副词 ad.

表示动作、行为或情况发生在过去。Indicating an action, a behavior or a situation that happened in the past.

(1) 他年轻时曾在法国留过学。

(2) 去年夏天我们这里曾下了一次冰雹。

说明 Notes:

1. "曾"后面的动词常带"过、了"。Such characters as "过" and "了" are usually used with a verb after "曾."

2. "曾"的否定式为"未曾""不曾",常用于书面语。The negative form of "曾" is "未曾" or "不曾," which is usually used in written language.

(3) 他未曾尝过这种小吃。

(4) 他不曾见过他的叔叔。

céngjīng 曾经 →P58"曾"、P565"已经"

用法 Usage:

副词 ad.

表示从前有过某种行为或情况。意思与"曾"相同。Indicating something that happened in the past, it conveys the same meaning as "曾."

(1) 他曾经说过这件事。

(2) 我在留学的时候,曾经掉了两次钱包。

说明 Notes:

1. "曾经"的否定式,只能用"没、没有"。Only "没" or "没有" can be used for the negative form of "曾经."

2. "曾"与"曾经"的用法基本相同,都可以用在动词或形容词前面。在动词或形容词后面,一定带"过"或"了"。The usage of "曾" and "曾经" are almost the same. Both of them can be used before a verb or adjective. When they are so used, "过" or "了" should be added.

区别是:The differences are as follows:

① "曾"多用于单音节动词前面,多用于书面语。"曾经"多用于口语。"曾" always appears before a monosyllable verb in the written language, while "曾经" appears more in colloquial language.

② "曾"可受否定副词"不、未"修饰,表示否定。"曾经"只能用"没、没有"表示否定。In a negative sentence, "曾" can be modified by negative adverbs such as "不" or "未," while the negative form of "曾经" can only be "没" or "没有."

(3) *我没有曾经去过法国。

(4) 我没有去过法国。

③ "曾"可受"可、何、哪"的修饰,表示疑问或反问,常用于书面语。"曾经"不能。In interrogative sentences or rhetorical questions, "曾" can be modified by "可," "何," or "哪" and usually used in the written language, but "曾经" cannot.

(5) 老师可曾给你辅导过?

(6) 我何曾说过你一句坏话?

④ "曾"和"曾经"一般不修饰否定式。如果有,句子中要有时间限定,并且要说明原因。

In most cases, "曾" and "曾经" do not modify the negatives. If they do, there should be a time limit in the sentence, and a reason should be given at the same time.

（7）为了写好这本书,他曾/曾经三个月没出过门。

（8）为了减肥,他曾/曾经有两年不吃肉。

chà 差

用法 Usage:

动词 *v.*

1. 不相同,不相合。*To be different; not to be identical.*

（1）虽说她俩是姐妹,可她俩的脾气差远了。

（2）这两本书的内容完全一样,可价格差多了。

2. 不对,有差错。*To be wrong; to have a mistake.*

（3）查一查,两个数字差在哪儿?

（4）你差了,我的意思不是这样的。

3. 欠缺。*(Of somebody) to be absent; (Of something) to be lacking.*

（5）就差小王一个人没到了。

（6）我的成绩比你的差多了。

形容词 *a.*

（一般指质量)不好,不够标准。*Not good; not up to the standard.*

（7）这条公路修得真差。

（8）这个牌子的手机很差。

说明 Notes:

"差"是个多音字,不同的发音,词义不同,用法不同。*"差" is a polyphone. Different pronunciations bring different meanings and usages.*

1. "差"读 chā。*"差" pronounced as chā.*

① 作动词用,相同于"差 chà"的第一义项,表示不相同、不相合。*Used as a verb, it bears the same meaning as the first usage of "差 chà": it means being different; not identical.*

（9）他俩的成绩差多了。

② 作名词用。*Used as a noun.*

错误。*A mistake.*

（10）开车一定要集中精神,不然就会出差错。

（11）她是一念之差才做错了这件事。

③ 差数。*Subtraction difference.*

（12）七减二的差是五。

2. "差"读（chāi）。*"差" is pronounced as chāi.*

① 作动词用,指分派、打发、去做(某事)的意思。*Used as a verb, it means "to dispatch or send somebody on a mission."*

（13）我被她差去买咖啡了。

（14）我只是个被别人差来差去干活儿的人。

② 作名词用,指被派去做的公事。*Used as a noun, it means "the business that someone is sent to do."*

（15）明天我要出差去上海。

（16）她这几天出公差去了。

3. "差"读 cī。组成"参差 cēncī",表示长短、高低、大小不一致的意思。*"差" is pronounced as cī in the phrase "参差 (cēncī)," which means "different in length, height or size."*

（17）舞蹈演员的个子不能参差不齐。

（18）我们班同学的汉语水平参差不一。

chàbuduō 差不多

用法 Usage:

形容词 *a.*

1. (程度、时间、距离等方面)相近,相差有限。常做谓语或补语。*(Of degree, time or distance, etc.) similar, with limited difference. It is always used as a predicate or complement.*

（1）这两种颜色差不多。

（2）骑电动车和坐公交车时间差不多。

2. 表示一般、大多数、普通的意思,后面加"的",修饰名词。在前后语义清楚的情况下,可省略名词。Meaning "general, most, ordinary," it is always followed by "的" to modify a noun. The noun can be omitted when its semantics are clear.

(3) 差不多的汉字她都会写了。

(4) 不懂外语的同学,差不多的都没参加这次活动。

副词 ad.

表示相差很少,接近。可以用在动词、形容词、数量词前面。后面常常带有表示程度的词语。With little difference; close. It can be placed before a verb, adjective or numeral. Words of degree are usually used after it.

(5) 你才来。我差不多等了你两个小时了。

(6) 我的头发差不多全白了。

说明 Notes:

"差不多"用作副词时,不能用在形容词的否定式前面。When "差不多" serves as an adverb, it cannot be used before the negative form of an adjective.

(7) *他们俩买的衣服差不多不贵。

(8) 他们俩买的衣服差不多,都不贵。

chà(yì)diǎnr 差(一)点儿 →P206 "几乎"

用法 Usage:

副词 ad.

1. 表示不希望实现的事情几乎实现但没有实现,有庆幸的意思。动词用肯定式或否定式,意思一样,但多用肯定式。Often used to talk about a narrow escape, showing relief. The verb that is used may be in the affirmative form or the negative form, but the meaning is the same. In most cases, the affirmative form is used.

(1) 今天我在商店里差点儿(没)丢了皮包。

(2) 昨天他骑车差点儿(没)撞了人。

2. 表示希望实现的事情几乎不能实现但最终实现了,有庆幸的意思,动词用否定式。Used to talk about some accomplishment which was barely made, again showing relief. The verb is always in the negative form.

(3) 老师叫我回答问题,我差(一)点儿答不出来。

(4) 在飞机场她差点儿没接着妈妈。

3. 表示希望实现的事情几乎实现但最终没有实现,有惋惜的意思。动词用肯定式,后面常用"就"。Used to talk about something that was highly desirable but that was not realized, showing regret. The verb is always in the affirmative form and "就" often follows.

(5) 我这次汉语水平考试(HSK)差点儿就考出了8级。

(6) 这次100米比赛,她差点儿得第一。

说明 Notes:

1. "差(一)点儿"做副词时,要注意两种用法的区别是:区别希望和最后结果的不同;区别"差(一)点儿"动词后面是肯定式,还是否定式。When "差(一)点儿" is used as an adverb, pay attention to two differences: One is the difference between the hope and the final result, and the other is whether the verb following "差(一)点儿" is in the affirmative form or negative form.

2. "差(一)点儿"作为短语,表示稍次的意思。可以插入"了",如"差了点儿",常做谓语、补语。When "差(一)点儿" is used as a phrase, it has the meaning of "not as good as"; the word "了" can be inserted in between, such as "差了点儿;" it is always used as a predicate or complement.

(7) 我的成绩稍差点儿。

(8) 那个歌星唱得差了点儿。

cháng 常 →P61 "常常"

用法 Usage:

副词 ad.

1. 时常,常常。表示动作、行为或情况屡次发生,而且时间间隔较短。Often. To indicate an action, a behavior, or a situation that occurs repeatedly at short intervals.

(1) 她星期天最常去的地方是超市。
(2) 你有空常来玩儿。
2. 表示动作、行为或性状的长久性、一贯性。*To indicate the permanence and consistence of an action, behavior or trait.*
(3) 这是四季常青树。
(4) 她爸爸是常驻国外的大使。

名词 *n.*

伦常的意思。*Ethics, constant virtues.*
(5) 古代的"五常",一般指仁、义、礼、智、信。

形容词 *a.*

1. 表示一般、普通、平常的意思。*General; ordinary.*
(6) 我只是个常人,只懂得一些常识。
2. 不变的,经常的。*Constant; frequent.*
(7) 她父母每个月给她的生活费是个常数——八百元。

chángcháng 常常 →P60"常"、P244"经常"、P415"时常"、P468"通常"、P483"往往"

用法 Usage:

副词 *ad.*

词义和用法与"常"的第一义项相同。表示某种动作、行为或事情的发生不止一次,而且时间相隔不久。*The meaning and usage of "常常" are the same as the first meaning of "常." It is used to indicate an action, a behavior or a situation occurs repeatedly at short intervals.*
(1) 夏天我们常常在河里游泳。
(2) 他常常喝很多酒,对身体很不好。

说明 Notes:

1. "常常"的否定式是"不常"。*The negative form of "常常" is "不常."*
(3) 我不常开夜车。我喜欢早睡早起。
2. "常常"后面可以跟否定意义的动词或词语。*"常常" can be followed by a negative verb or word with a negative meaning.*
(4) 她常常不愿意跟我们一起吃饭。
(5) 他常常不让同学进他的房间。

3. "常"与"常常"用法基本相同。*The usages of "常" and "常常" are basically the same.*

区别是: *Their differences are as follows:*

① "常"后面多为单音节词动词。"常常"后面的词语音节数不等,语气比"常"重一点。*"常" is always followed by monosyllabic verbs. "常常" is a little bit heavier in tone, and the number of verb syllables may vary.*
(6) 我常去他家。
(7) 我常常去他家玩儿。

② "常"可以受程度副词"很、最"和否定副词"不"的修饰。"常常"一般不能这么用。*"常" can be modified by adverbs of degree such as "很" or "最" and the negative adverb 不 as well. However, "常常" cannot be used in this way.*
(8) *自行车是中国很常常见的交通工具。
(9) 自行车是中国很常见的交通工具。

③ "常常"可以出现在主语前,"常"不可以。*"常常" can be used before the subject, while "常" cannot.*
(10) *我们宿舍,常她先起床。
(11) 我们宿舍,常常她先起床。

chángnián 常年

用法 Usage:

副词 *ad.*

终年,长期。*All the year round; for a long time*
(1) 那个山头常年积雪。
(2) 她常年坚持洗冷水澡。

名词 *n.*

平常的年份(区别于特殊的年份)。*A normal year, which is different from a special year.*
(3) 医院住院部常年病床一千张。
(4) 我们村的粮食常年亩产八百斤。

chǎngdì 场地 →P63"场所"

用法 Usage:

名词 n.

空地。常指提供文娱体育活动或施工、实验等用的地方。*Vacant land. Often it refers to the land used for recreational and sports activities or for construction or experiment, etc.*

(1) 这次比赛的场地在留学生楼前面的运动场上。

(2) 演出场地的问题以后再讨论。

(3) 下雨天,学生就没有活动场地了。

chǎnghé 场合 →P62"场面"

用法 Usage:

名词 n.

一定的时间、地点、情况的综合环境及活动环境。*(At a certain time, place or in a certain situation) the comprehensive environment in which activities are conducted.*

(1) 她在人多的场合常常不说话。

(2) 在公共场合,一定要遵守公共秩序。

chǎngmiàn 场面 →P62"场合"

用法 Usage:

名词 n.

1. 戏剧、电影、电视剧中由布景、音乐或登场人物组合成的景况。*A scene which is formed by the combination of sets, music or characters in dramas, movies or TV series.*

(1) 舞台上就出现了闪电、雷雨、狂风大作的场面。

(2) 电视中常常有一群群游客登长城的场面。

2. 叙事性文学作品中,由人物在一定场合中相互发生关系而构成的生活情景。*In narrative literary works, the life scene composed of characters that are related to each other in a certain situation.*

(3)《红楼梦》这本小说,关于吃的场面描写得非常详细。

(4) 这个作者很善于描写夜市的场面。

3. 泛指一定场合下的情景。*The situation on a certain occasion.*

(5) 我们都喜欢除夕夜家人团圆的热烈场面。

(6) 奥运会开幕式的场面一定会让每个看过的人永远不忘。

4. 表面的排场。*A situation for ostentation and extravagance.*

(7) 她儿子结婚的场面真大,把全村人都请来喝喜酒了。

(8) 他家实际上并不富裕,为什么场面摆得这么大?

说明 Notes:

1. "场面"又指戏曲演出时伴奏的人员和乐器,管乐和弦乐是文场面,锣鼓是武场面,又称"文场、武场"。*"场面" also refers to accompanists and musical instruments in the opera performances. In traditional Chinese operas, the band music and stringed music constitute the string and wind section; gongs and drums form the percussion section. They are also called* "文场,武场."

2. "场面"跟"场合"的区别是: *The differences between "场面(scene)" and "场合 (occasion)" are as follows:*

"场面"着重于事物或事情的气势,着重于面的表现,让人观看,让人感觉。形成"场面"的因素繁多。"场合"虽然也是时间、地点、情况的总和,但其含义着重在对人的言行举止的要求或限制。*"场面" emphasizes the imposing manner of something and the manifestations on the surface, which induces the audience to observe and feel. Various factors contribute to the formation of a "场面." "场合" is also a combination of time, place and situation, but it emphasizes the requirements for or limitations on people's manners and behaviors.*

chángsuǒ 场所 →P62"场地"

用法 Usage:

名词 *n.*

活动的处所。*A place for activities.*

(1) 孩子们暑假活动的场所已经有了。

(2) 你们一定要遵守公共场所的秩序。

说明 Notes:

"场所"与"场地"的区别是：*The difference between "场所" and "场地" is as follows:*

在词义上，"场地"着重指露天的、较大的活动地方。"场所"着重指包括室内的、可大可小的活动地方。*Semantically speaking, "场地" puts emphasis on the open and large activity ground; while "场所" emphasizes places large or small for interior activities.*

cháo 朝 →P483"往"、P512"向"

用法 Usage:

介词 *prep.*

表示动作的方向。只用在动词前面，可以在后面加"着"，但跟单音节动词结合时不能加。*Indicating the direction of an action. It can only be placed before a verb, and the character "着" can be added to it. However, "着" cannot be added to "朝" when it is used with a monosyllabic verb.*

(1) 老师提出问题后，朝我们笑笑，等着我们回答。

(2) 小船朝着湖中心的小岛划去。

动词 *v.*

指人或物，面对某个方向；向。一定要带宾语。*To face. It must take an object.*

(3) 中国的房子常常是坐北朝南的。

(4) 你朝左，我朝右，看谁先到那里。

名词 *n.*

1. 朝代。如："唐朝、宋朝"。*Dynasty. For example, "唐朝,宋朝."*

2. 朝廷。与"野"相对。如："上朝、下朝，朝野上下"。*Imperial court which is opposite to "野." For example, "上朝,下朝；朝野上下."*

说明 Notes:

1. "朝"(cháo)跟单音节名词结合时，不能加"着"。*When "朝 (cháo)" is used with a monosyllabic noun, "着" cannot be added to it.*

(5) *飞机朝着东飞去。

(6) 飞机朝东飞去。/飞机朝着东面飞去。

2. "朝"是多音字。读 zhāo 时，有两个意思：一是"早晨"的意思，如："朝三暮四、朝令夕改"等。二是"日、天"的意思，如："今朝、明朝"。*"朝" is a polyphone. When it is pronounced as zhāo, it bears two meanings. The first meaning is "morning." For example, "朝三暮四,朝令夕改." The second meaning is "day." For example, "今朝,明朝."*

cháo 潮

用法 Usage:

名词 *n.*

1. 海水定时涨落的现象。*Tidal waves, a natural phenomenon of the rise and fall of tides at the mouth of a river.*

(1) 这里的海水什么时候涨潮？

(2) 这里是看潮最好的地方。

2. （思想、时尚、热情、行动等）像潮水一样起伏的态势，比喻有涨有落、有起有伏的社会现象。*The ups and downs of thoughts, fashions, passion, actions, etc., indicating the change of social trends.*

(3) 他穿的衣服都很新潮。

(4) 1978 年以后，中国的农村、城市掀起了经济改革的高潮。

形容词 *a.*

潮湿。在句子中常常做谓语。*Damp; humid; often used as a predicate in a sentence.*

(5) 今天早上的雾很大，地上也很潮。

(6) 饼干潮了，不好吃了。

说明 Notes:

1. "潮"的名词用法：在口语中，常常变成双音节的"潮水"，或者在前面加上修饰词语，如

"学潮、早潮"等。单音节的"潮"比较少用。*The noun usage of "潮": In colloquial language, it is usually used in the disyllabic word "潮水" or it takes a modifier before it, for example, "学潮," "早潮," and so on. The monosyllabic "潮" is rarely used.*

2."潮"的形容词用法：*The adjective use of "潮":*

① 可以加后缀，构成重叠形式，如"潮乎乎"。*The suffix can be added to it to form a reduplicated word. For example, "潮乎乎."*

② 修饰名词时，常常加"的"，构成双音节或重叠形式。*When it modifies a noun, "的" is always added to it to form a disyllabic or reduplicated word.*

(7) 潮的衣服穿在身上很不舒服。

(8) 潮乎乎的衣服穿在身上很不舒服。

chǎozuò 炒作

用法 Usage:

动词 v.

1. 指频繁买进卖出，制造声势，从中牟利（一般指房产、黄金、古董、土地等大宗财物）。*To buy and sell for profits frequently in real estate, gold, antiques, land, etc.*

(1) 他最近在炒作文物古董，赚了不少钱。

(2) 现在炒作房地产赚不了什么钱。

2. 为扩大人或事物的影响，通过媒体（报纸、广播、电视等）反复做夸大的宣传。*To engage in propaganda in media in order to expand the influence of somebody or something.*

(3) 这个三流演员通过媒体炒作，现在成了明星。

(4) 经过一番新闻炒作，这家成立仅一个月的公司名声大振。

chéng 成 →P66"成为"

用法 Usage:

动词 v.

1. 完成，成功。达到预期的效果，跟"败"相对。句子后面一定要加"了、过"。*To fulfil; to succeed. To achieve a desired result, which is opposite to "败." Characters such as "了" and "过" are always added to it.*

(1) 他们俩的婚事成了。

(2) 那件事情再有三年都成不了。

2. 成为，变成。用在句子里，要带"了"，后面一定要带名词宾语。*To become; to turn into. The character "了" is used after "成," and it's always followed by a noun object.*

(3) 那块冰已经化成水了。

(4) 我们后来成了好朋友。

3. 可以，行。可以带"了"。一般用在句首或句末。*To be alright; to be OK. It always appears at the beginning or the end of a sentence and can be followed by "了."*

(5) 成，我按照你的意见做。

(6) 送到这儿就成了，你们回去吧！

(7) 你不参加怎么成？

4. "成"与数量词构成短语，表示达到一定的量，后面常带集合量词，强调数量多或时间长，可以重叠。*To form a phrase with quantity words, which means reaching a certain amount. It is always followed by a collective quantifier to emphasize the large amount or the long time. It can also form reduplicative words.*

(8) 那个广场上，每年都有成千上万只鸽子。

(9) 她成日成夜地复习，会累出病来的。

5. 做补语。*Used as a complement.*

① 表示成功、完成、实现。可插入"得/不"变成可能补语短语。*To fulfil; to succeed in; to realize something. "得" or "不" can be inserted to form a complement phrase.*

(10) 他家的房子建成了。

(11) 因为大家都有课，这个会开不成了。

② 做动补结构的补语，表示成为、变为。不能插入"得/不"，后面一定要带宾语。*To change into; to turn into. It is used as a complement in the verb complement structure.*

It has to be followed by an object, and "得" or "不" cannot be inserted in.

(12) 教室里的桌子、椅子都换成新的了。
(13) 她变成了一个大姑娘。

chéngjì 成绩 →P65 "成就"

用法 Usage:
名词 n.

指工作、学习上的收获或成果。常常做主语、宾语。*The achievement or accomplishments in one's work or study. It is usually used as the subject or object in a sentence.*

(1) 她的学习成绩很好。
(2) 成绩的大小跟努力的程度是分不开的。

chéngjiù 成就 →P65 "成绩"

用法 Usage:
名词 n.

多指具有社会意义的事业或重大事情上的成绩。*The achievement of a career or an undertaking that has social significance.*

(1) 她在事业上取得了很大的成就。
(2) 改革开放以后,中国在经济建设上的成就是很大的。

动词 v.

表示使某事得以完成、成功。*To enable something to be accomplished or to be a success.*

(3) 他们俩结婚了。你成就了一件大好事。
(4) 你那么想看京剧,我成就你。送你一张京剧票吧。

说明 Notes:

"成绩"跟"成就"的区别是: *The differences between "成绩" and "成就" are as follows:*

1. 在词义上,"成绩"泛指一般的收获、成果,多用于日常工作、学习、体育运动方面,是中性词。"成就"着重指获得巨大的进展或突出、优异的成果,多用于具有社会意义的事业或重大的事情,如革命、建设、经济、学术研究、科技等方面。语意比"成绩"重,是褒义词。*"成绩" generally refers to results in daily work, study, sports and so on. It is a neutral word. "成就" refers to the tremendous progress or outstanding achievement in an undertaking of social significance or things of vital importance, such as revolution, construction, economy, academic research, science and technology. It is a commendatory word that carries much more weight than "成绩."*

2. 在词语搭配上,"成绩"表示学习、体育运动方面的成果时,多与"好、差、优秀、优良、优异、及格"等词语搭配表示程度。表示工作方面的成果时,多与"大、小、多、少"等词语搭配表示程度,常作"取得、公布、报告、评定、发扬、肯定、否定"等动词的宾语。"成就"常受"巨大、重大、伟大、光辉、突出、杰出、辉煌"等词的修饰,常与"取得、获得、汇报"等动词搭配使用。*In terms of word collocation, "成绩" indicates an achievement in learning, sports, and is always used with such words as "好,差,优秀,优良,优异,及格," indicating different degrees of success. When referring to accomplishments in work, it always goes with such words as "大,小,多,少" to show different degrees. It is usually used as the object of the verb such as "取得,公布,报告,评定,发扬,肯定,否定." "成就" is often modified by such words as "巨大,重大,伟大,光辉,突出,杰出,辉煌," and always collocates with verbs such as "取得,获得,汇报."*

chénglì 成立 →P224 "建立"

用法 Usage:
动词 v.

1. 指组织、机构等筹备成功。*To establish or organize an institution successfully.*

(1) 同学们,留学生足球队今天成立了。
(2) 中华人民共和国成立于1949年10月1日。

2. 指理论、意见有根据,站得住。*(Of a theory or an argument) to be able to stand (the*

test of time); to be tenable.

(3) 你的观点不能成立,因为理由不够充分。

(4) 这个论点要成立,必须从三个方面找根据才行。

chéngwéi 成为 →P64"成"

用法 Usage:

动词 v.

1. 变成。单独作谓语时,必须带宾语。To change into. When the predicate is used alone, it is followed by an object.

(1) 原来那儿是农田,现在已经成为居住区了。

(2) 这孩子会成为怎样的人呢?

2. 用在动词后面,表示目的、结果。一定要带宾语。To indicate the purpose or result of an action. It must be followed by an object.

(3) 他一定要把女儿培养成为外科医生。

(4) 我们一定要把杭州建设成为国际花园城市。

说明 Notes:

1. 用"成为"造句时要注意:Points to note about "成为" in the sentence:

① "成为"的主语一定是应该可以改变成所带的宾语的名词。如在例(1)和(2)中,"农田"可以改变为"居住区","孩子"可以改变为"怎样的人"。主语跟宾语在语义上必须是能够相呼应的。The subject of "成为" must be a noun that can be changed into its object. In (1) and (2), "农田" can be changed into "居住区" and "孩子" into "怎样的人." The subject and object must be semantically related.

(5) *他的学习非常努力成为好学生了。

(6) 经过非常努力的学习,他成为好学生了。

(7) *奖学金成为他的。

(8) 他得到了奖学金。

(9) 奖学金成为他捐给山区孩子的学费了。

② 在"成为"的第二种用法中,动词一般是含有动作行为过程的双音节动词,如:"教育、培养、塑造、改造、改变、建设"等。In the second use of "成为," verbs are usually disyllabic to indicate the process of an action such as "教育 (educate)," "培养 (train)," "塑造 (shape)," "改造 (transform)," "改变 (change)," "建设 (construct)," and so on.

2. "成"跟"成为"的区别是:The differences between "成" and "成为" are as follows:

"成"也有"成为"的意思,但与"成"搭配使用的动词一般是单音节动词,如:"弟弟把船画成大高楼了。"与"成为"搭配的动词一般是双音节动词,如例(3)和(4)。"成" can convey the meaning of "成为." However, verbs used with "成" are usually monosyllabic, for example, "弟弟把船画成大高楼了。" But verbs used with "成为" are usually disyllabic as seen in (3) and (4).

chéngxìn 诚信

用法 Usage:

形容词 a.

诚实,守信用。常做主语、谓语、定语等。Honest and trustworthy. It is often used as the subject, predicate, or attributive in a sentence.

(1) 诚信是做人的根本。

(2) 做生意一定要诚信。

(3) 诚信的品质是很宝贵的。

chíxù 持续 →P217"继续"

用法 Usage:

动词 v.

延续不断,继续。To continue; to last.

(1) 足球赛持续了两个小时才结束,没有输赢。

(2) 两国经济文化的交流持续了一千多年。

chíyǒu 持有

用法 Usage:

动词 v.

拿着,拥有。To hold; to be in the

possession of.

（1）参加今天的晚会，须持有入场券。

（2）在这个公司，他持有49%的股份。

chōng 冲

用法 Usage:

动词 v.

1. 用开水（或其他液体）浇。*To pour boiling water (or other liquid) into something.*

（1）给客人冲茶吧！

（2）孩子饿得哭了，快冲奶粉给他喝。

2. 冲洗，冲击。*To wash; to wash away.*

（3）全身是汗，让我先冲个澡。

（4）去年夏天发大水，冲走了我家的三间房。

3. 收支互相抵消。*To strike a balance.*

（5）公司的会议费冲好账了吗？

4. 很快地朝某一方向直闯，突破障碍。*To rush in a certain direction quickly and break through the barriers.*

（6）这孩子横冲直撞的，不好好走路。

（7）五号队员冲破了对方防线，终于踢进了一个球。

名词 n.

1. 通行的大道，重要的地方。*Thoroughfare; important place.*

（8）我老家在古代是交通要冲。

2. 山区里的平地，多用于方言。*Flat ground in the mountains, usually used in some dialect.*

（9）你去过韶山冲吗？

chōngtū 冲突 →P314"矛盾"

用法 Usage:

动词 v.

1. 矛盾表面化，发生争斗或争执。*To conflict; to fight or argue.*

（1）他们冲突起来了。

（2）我不想与她正面冲突。

2. 互相矛盾，不协调，甚至抵触。常用于时间、地点、言行等的对立与不一致。*To be contradictory; inconsistent. It usually refers to an inconsistency in time, place, words, deeds, etc.*

（3）两个班上课的教室冲突了。

（4）会上两种意见冲突起来了。

名词 n.

1. 矛盾，双方的争斗。*Conflict.*

（5）这是两种文化之间的冲突。

（6）应该用和平谈判的方式解决国与国之间的冲突。

2. 互相矛盾、不协调的事。常发生在时间、地点、言行等上的对立与不一致。常做宾语。*Contradiction; inconsistency. It usually refers to an inconsistency in time, place, words, deeds, etc. and is often used as an object.*

（7）如果我们的行程安排和你的计划发生冲突，请说一下。

（8）你说的和他说的内容有冲突。

说明 Notes:

1. "冲突"动词用作谓语时，不能带宾语，不能直接带动态助词"了、着、过"，如例（1）和（2）。*When "冲突" is used as a verb and functions as a predicate, it cannot take an object and it cannot be directly followed by dynamic auxiliaries such as "了，着，过" as seen in (1) and (2).*

2. "冲突"多用于书面语。*"冲突" is usually used in written language.*

chōngdiàn 充电

用法 Usage:

动词 v.

1. 把直流电源接到蓄电池的两极上，使蓄电池获得放电能力。也泛指用其他方法补充电源。*To recharge; to place the DC power supply to the two poles of the battery, so that the battery can get the discharge capacity. It can also refer to other ways of battery recharging.*

（1）手机没电了，赶快充电。
（2）电动车正在充电。

2. 比喻通过学习补充知识、提高技能等。It is used metaphorically, meaning to increase knowledge and improve skills through learning.

（3）每个人要不断地充电，才能赶上电子技术的发展。

3. 比喻用法。指人饥饿、劳累后通过休息、娱乐等补充能量。多用于口语。It is used metaphorically, meaning to recharge one's batteries; to replenish one's energy through rest, recreation, etc. when one feels hungry or tired. It is usually used in colloquial language.

（4）爬了三个小时山，又饿又累，该充电了。

chōngfèn 充分 →P68"充足"

用法 Usage:

形容词 a.

1. 表示足够。多用于抽象事物。可用作谓语、定语和补语。Enough; sufficient. Often referring to abstract things, it can be used as the predicate, attributive or complement in a sentence.

（1）你这样做的理由很充分。
（2）他考虑得很充分。

2. 表示尽量。多用于抽象动词前，充当状语。As much as possible. It is used as an adverbial modifier before an abstract verb.

（3）我们要充分发挥同学们的学习积极性。
（4）你应该充分认识到这件事的复杂性。

chōngzú 充足 →P68"充分"

用法 Usage:

形容词 a.

表示充分足够。多用于具体事务，可用作定语、谓语和补语。Sufficient, adequate. Often referring to specific transactions, it can be used as the attributive, predicate or complement in a sentence.

（1）这儿有充足的阳光。
（2）我们的活动经费很充足。
（3）他们准备得相当充足。

说明 Notes:

"充分"和"充足"都有相当多、足够的意思。都可形容"理由、证据"等少数表示抽象事物的词语。Both "充分" and "充足" convey the meaning of "sufficient" and "adequate." Both of them can describe words that indicate abstract things such as "理由" and "证据."

区别是：The differences are as follows:

1. "充分"侧重于程度上足够，尽可能达到最大限度，表示相当多。多用于比较抽象的事物，除以上例句的词语所列，还可修饰"信心、含义、民主、自由、说服力、根据、把握、事实、营养、思想准备"等。"充足"侧重于数量上的足够，多到能满足需要，多用于"人力、物力、金钱、阳光、水分、时间、粮食、工具"等。"充分" focuses on the degree of sufficiency. It means doing something to the maximum degree. It usually refers to abstract things. Besides what are mentioned in the above examples, "充分" can also modify such words as "信心,含义,民主,自由,说服力,根据,把握,事实,营养,思想准备." "充足," by contrast, emphasizes that the number or the amount of something is enough to meet one's needs, and always modifies such words as "人力,物力,金钱,阳光,水分,时间,粮食,工具."

2. "充分"可以做状语。"充足"不能。"充分" can be used as an adverbial, but "充足" cannot.

chóngfù 重复 →P139"反复"

用法 Usage:

动词 v.

1. 再次做（同样的事情）。To do something again, usu. the same thing.

（1）请把这几个动作重复几遍。

（2）请你把我的话重复一次。

2.（相同的东西）又一次出现。*(Of the same thing) to appear again.*

（3）这个句子跟前面的句子重复了。

（4）年纪老了，说话常常重复。

形容词 *a.*

表示同样的事物再次出现。做定语。*The repetition of the same thing. It is used as an attributive.*

（5）把重复的句子去掉吧。

（6）重复的话就别说了。

chòng 冲

用法 Usage：

介词 *prep.*

1. 表示动作的方向。*Indicating the direction of an action.*

（1）她转过脸来冲我笑了一下。

（2）孩子摇摇摆摆地冲着妈妈跑去。

2. 凭，根据。*According to.*

（3）冲你的态度，我就住在你们宾馆吧。

（4）就冲你说的话，我同意了。

动词 *v.*

正对某个方向。*To face a certain direction.*

（5）我的房间窗户冲南，望出去远远有座大山。

（6）你转过身来说话，别把背冲着我。

形容词 *a.*

1. 气味浓烈。*Smelling strong.*

（7）这房间酒味儿很冲。

（8）你身上的香味儿太冲了。

2. 力气大，劲儿足，说话声气高，不太平和。*With great strength; speaking in a loud voice and not being even-tempered.*

（9）年轻人干活儿有股冲劲儿。

（10）他这几句话说得太冲了。

chūfā 出发 →P116"动身"

用法 Usage：

动词 *v.*

1. 表示离开原来的地方到别的地方去。*To leave one place for another.*

（1）他们已经出发了。

（2）明天去动物园，什么时候出发？

2. 表示考虑或处理问题时以某一方面、某一角度为着眼点。常和介词"从"连用。*To consider or deal with a problem from a certain perspective. It is usually used with the preposition "从."*

（3）从同学们的身体健康出发，我们应该这样做。

（4）从你们学习的情况出发，语法课还可以上得快一些。

说明 Notes：

"出发"用在连动句中，常用"去……"或者"到……去"指出目的地。*In co-verbal sentences, "出发" is often used with "去…" or "到…去" to indicate the destination.*

（5）我们下午六点出发坐船去苏州。

（6）下午三点，我们出发到北京去。

chūlù 出路 →P70"出息"

用法 Usage：

名词 *n.*

1. 通向外面的道路。*The road to the outside.*

（1）他在森林里找了半天也没有找到出路。

（2）这座园林有三条出路，大家要走的是东边的一条出路。

2. 比喻生存或向前发展的途径，前途。*The way to survive or move forward; prospect.*

（3）在网上开电子商店是不错的创业出路。

（4）不知道我毕业以后的出路在哪儿？

3. 比喻货物的销路。*Sale of goods; market.*

（5）这种产品的出路在农村。

（6）那种商品在我们城市已经没有出路了。

chūshǒu 出手

用法 Usage:

动词 *v.*

1. 销售,卖出货物(多用于变卖)。*To sell; to sell off goods.*

(1) 昨天进的那批货要赶快出手。

(2) 那批货已经出手了。

2. 往外拿(钱财)。*To spend (money).*

(3) 我这朋友出手很大方。

(4) 她出手就给了我五千元。

3. 动手,开始行动。*To give a helping hand and start taking action.*

(5) 该出手时就出手,这才是朋友。

(6) 该我们出手了。

名词 *n.*

1. 指衣服袖子的长短。*Length of sleeve.*

(7) 你穿这件衣服,出手短了一点。

2. 开始做某件事,表现出来的本领。*Skills displayed in making opening moves.*

(8) 她一开始就出手不凡,我看她能完成这项任务。

(9) 出手不凡,他的武功有基础。

chūxi 出息 →P69"出路"

用法 Usage:

名词 *n.*

指人的发展前途或志气。*One's future development or ambition.*

(1) 这个人将来一定很有出息。

(2) 你这样下去是没出息的。

说明 Notes:

1. "出息"只能作"有、没有"的宾语。在有的方言中,"出息"有动词用法,表示长进、进步的意思。"出息" *can only be used as the object of "有" or "没有." In some dialects, "出息" can be used as a verb which means "making progress."*

(3) 这孩子比以前出息多了。

2. "出路"跟"出息"都有比喻义,都与前景有关。都可以与"有、没有"搭配使用。*Both "出路" and "出息" can be used metaphorically, which relates to one's prospects. Both of them collocate with "有" or "没有."*

区别是:*The differences are as follows:*

① "出路"着重于表示发展的途径、路子。可以用于人,也可以用于工作、事业等其他方面。*"出路" puts emphasis on ways of development. It can refer to people, one's work or career, etc.*

(4) 中国经济发展的出路在于改革。

"出息"着重于发展前途或志气,一般直接用于人。*"出息" emphasizes one's future or ambition. It usually refers to people.*

② "有"做谓语动词时,"有出息"的前面可以受程度副词的修饰,如:"很有出息"。"有出路"前不能受程度副词的修饰。*When "有" is used as a predicate verb, "有出息" can be modified by a degree adverb before it. For example, "很有出息." But "有出路" cannot be modified by any degree adverbs.*

③ "出息"有动词用法。"出路"没有动词用法。*"出息" has a verb usage while "出路" does not.*

④ "出路"还可以指商品买卖的去处。"出息"没有这个意义。*"出路" can refer to the market for the sale of goods while "出息" cannot.*

chū 初

用法 Usage:

形容词 *a.*

1. 开始的;原来的。如:"初冬、初夏、初心、初愿"等。*Initial; original. For example, "初冬,初夏,初心,初愿."*

2. (等级)最低的。如:"初级汉语、初级水平"等。*(Of level) primary. For example, "初级汉语,初级水平."*

副词 *ad.*

第一次;刚开始。如:"初恋、初试、初学"

等。For the first time. For example, "初恋,初试,初学."

名词 n.

开始的一段时间;原来的情况。如:"年初、学期初"等。The beginning of a period of time; the original situation. For example, "年初,学期初."

(1) 本年初/本学期初,我们举行了一次运动会。

(2) 你看,我把自行车完好如初地还给你了。

前缀 prefix

用在"一"至"十"的前面,表示农历一个月前十天的次序。如:"初一、初二、初三……"。Used before the number from "一" to "十", indicating the order of the first ten days in a lunar month. For example, "初一,初二,初三…."

chūbù 初步

用法 Usage:

形容词 a.

表示开始阶段的,不是最后的或完备的。可用作定语、状语。Preliminary; initial; rudimentary. It can be used as an attributive or adverbial in a sentence.

(1) 这是我的初步打算,还没有最后决定。

(2) 我们获得的成绩仅仅是初步的。

说明 Notes:

1. "初步"一般出现在名词前,如:"意见、想法、成绩、方案、工作"等。"初步" is always used before nouns such as "意见,想法,成绩,方案,工作, etc."

2. "初步"一般是非谓形容词,不能单独做谓语,不能受程度副词的修饰。In most cases "初步" is a non-predicate adjective; it cannot be used as the predicate separately and cannot be modified by adverbs of degree.

3. "初步"能修饰的动词很少,只限于有延续性的动词,如:"研究、调查、打算、计划、了解、考虑"等。Only a small number of verbs can be modified by "初步," those indicating a duration of time such as "研究,调查,打算,计划,了解,考虑."

chúfēi 除非 →P671"只有"

用法 Usage:

连词 conj.

只有。Unless; if not; only if; only when.

1. 表示唯一的条件,表示情况一定这样。相当于"只有",常跟"才、否则、不然"等配合着使用。Indicating the only condition that will make the case true. It is equivalent to "只有" and always collocates with such words as "才,否则,不然."

(1) 除非你吃,我才吃。

(2) 除非你吃,否则/不然我不吃。

2. 表示要想达到某种结果,一定要这样。常跟"要、如果"连用,常由两个分句组成。If someone wants to get a desired result, something must be done. It is usually used with "要" or "如果" and is composed of two clauses.

(3) 你明天考试想及格,除非今天晚上再开个夜车。

(4) 如果要让全家人都去,除非你答应妈妈的要求。

3. "除非"后面的动词一正一反叠用时,强调突出某种现象。"除非"所在的句子是处于陪衬地位的次要句子。In the subordinate clause, when "除非" is used with a negative adverb "不," the verb in the main clause is used affirmatively to emphasize a certain phenomenon.

(5) 他除非不请假,请起假来至少半个月以上。

(6) 他除非不看电影,看起电影来就是连着三场。

说明 Notes:

1. 如果两个分句的主语不相同,"除非"出现在主语前,如例(1)和例(2)。如果两个分句的主语相同,"除非"出现在主语后,如例(5)和例(6)。 If the subjects in the two clauses are different, "除非" should be put before the subject as in (1) and (2). However, if the two clauses share the same subject, "除非" is placed after the subject as in (5) and (6).

2."除非……才……"也可以从假设的另一角度说成"除非……不……"。 In the hypothetical adverbial clause, "除非…才…" can be replaced by "除非…不…."

(7)除非你去,我才去。/除非你去,我不去。

chúle 除了

用法 Usage:
介词 prep.

表示所说的不计算在内。"除了"常与"外、以外、之外"和"就是"连用,强调不同的意思。 Except (for). It means "what is said does not count." "除了" is always used with "外,""以外,""之外," or "就是," which emphasizes the difference.

句式有: Relevant sentence patterns are as follows:

1."除了……以外……",后面常用"都、全"呼应,表示排除特殊的,其他都一样,强调一致。如果后面用"不、没"呼应,强调唯一的事物或情况。"除了…以外…" echoes with such words as "都" and "全," indicating that "all are the same except the special ones", which emphasizes the sameness. However, if "除了…以外…" echoes with words such as "不" and "没," it emphasizes the only thing or situation that is being discussed.

(1)除了阿里以外,别的同学都/全去了。
(2)除了洗衣服以外,别的什么事都没干。

2."除了……以外……",后面常用"还、也"呼应,表示排除已经知道的,还要补充其他的。"除了…以外…" often echoes with such words as "还" and "也," meaning " in addition to those that are already known, other things should be supplemented."

(3)除了我们班去爬山以外,三班也去了。
(4)除了她是法国人以外,我也是法国人。

3."除了……就是……"。表示二者必居其一。"除了…就是…" means "either this or that."

(5)这几天他除了上课,就是做 HSK 练习题。

说明 Notes:

"除了"在主语前,前后两个分句的主语不相同,如例(1)和例(3)。在主语后,前后两个分句的主语相同,如例(5)。 When "除了" is placed before the subject, the two clauses have different subjects as in (1) and (3). When "除了" is placed after the subject, the two clauses share the same subject as in (5).

chǔfèn 处分 →P72"处理"

用法 Usage:
动词 v.

给犯错误或犯罪的人以处罚。 To punish those who commit a crime or do something wrong.

(1)他们刚刚处分了一个破坏考试纪律的学生。
(2)因为出了一个事故,不少领导人被处分了。

名词 n.

给犯错误或犯罪的人的处罚。 A punishment on somebody for having committed a crime or done something wrong.

(3)学校给了他一个很严重的处分。
(4)这样的处分不算重的。

chǔlǐ 处理 →P72"处分"

用法 Usage:
动词 v.

1.安排事务,办理事情,解决问题等。 To deal with something, attend to business, solve a problem.

（1）他到哪个班学习的事情你来处理。

（2）他们的宿舍安排问题请你处理一下。

2. 处分、惩治。主要是对人。To punish somebody.

（3）学院处理了两个经常不上课的学生。

（4）对犯错误的孩子，应该批评从严，处理从轻。

3. 减价出售（物品）。To sell something at a reduced price.

（5）这些苹果要处理了。

（6）商店正在处理夏季服装，很便宜，快去买啊。

名词 n.

指用特定的方法对工件或产品进行的加工，使其具有某种性能。前面常有定语。Referring to processing a workpiece or product in a particular way to make it perform in the desired way. The way of processing is always put before "处理" as a modifier.

（7）珍珠经过处理后会变得更亮。

（8）废水经过有效处理后才能排入江河湖海。

说明 Notes:

动词"处分"和"处理"都有"处罚"的意思。Both "处分" and "处理" have the same meaning as "to punish."

区别是：The differences are as follows:

1. "处分"除表示对犯罪者予以制裁外，一般还用于对在职人员或有军籍、党籍、团籍、学籍的人的纪律惩罚，如警告、记过、开除等。对象一定是人。"处理"着重于办理、料理、清理、治理、解决各种事务。对象可以是人，也可以是"文件、文稿"等具体事物或"问题、矛盾、关系、事件"等抽象事物。"处分"没有以上的意思。"处理"只有在表示处罚的意思时与"处分"相同，使用范围比"处分"大。Besides the punishment of a criminal, "处分" can also be used to refer to disciplinary action taken against such people as public employees, soldiers, party members, league members as well as students. The disciplinary practice might be a warning, demerit, firing, and so on. The object of "处分" should be a person. "处理" emphasizes arranging, sorting out or handling something. The object of "处理" can be a person or something concrete such as "文件，文稿," or something abstract such as "问题，矛盾，关系，事件". But "处分" doesn't convey this meaning. It is only when "处理" means "to punish" that it has the same meaning as "处分." Therefore, "处理" has more meanings than "处分."

2. "处分"和"处理"都表示惩治、处罚的意思时，"处分"的含义比较清楚，根据既有的法律或组织纪律处罚。"处理"的含义比较模糊、宽泛。When "处分" and "处理" are used to mean "to punish," "处分" carries a much clearer idea; it means "to punish somebody according to the law or the discipline." But the meaning of "处理" is vaguer and broader.

（9）他经常犯错误，学校处分了他。

（10）昨天学校处理了几个打架的学生。

chǔyú 处于

用法 Usage:

动词 v.

表示位于、处在（某种地位或境遇、状态）。To be in a certain status, position, or situation.

（1）美国在科技上处于全球领先地位。

（2）他现在处于领导地位，说话的声音也变了。

说明 Notes:

1. "处于"是强及物动词，后面必须出现宾语，而且宾语不能前置。"处于" is a transitive verb and it must take an object. Moreover, the object cannot be placed before the verb.

2. "处于"的宾语一般不能是表示地点的词语。Nouns denoting a location cannot be used as the object of "处于."

chuàngbàn 创办 →P74"创立"

用法 Usage:

动词 v.

开创,举办。To establish; to launch

(1) 20世纪初,中国就创办了女子大学。
(2) 去年我的家乡创办了山区茶叶展销会。

chuànglì 创立 →P74"创办"

用法 Usage:

动词 v.

初次建立。To launch; to establish

(1) 去年我们社区创立了青少年心理辅导站。
(2) 1979年,中国创立了经济特区。

说明 Notes:

1. "创立"和"创办"用于具体事业时,可以通用。When both "创立" and "创办" refer to a specific cause, they can be used interchangeably.

(3) 去年我们社区创立/创办了青少年心理辅导站。

2. "创立"的使用范围比"创办"广泛,可以是具体的事业,也可以是政党、国家和学说、理论等。"创立" has a broader meaning than "创办," which can refer to a specific cause, a party, a country, a doctrine, a theory, etc.

chuàngzào 创造 →P134"发明"

用法 Usage:

动词 v.

做出前人所没有做出的,初次做出或想出。做谓语,常带趋向补语"出"。To create something; to come up with (a new idea, product, etc.). When used as a predicate, it often takes "出" as a directional complement.

(1) 他创造了三次世界新纪录。
(2) 这个工厂创造出三种新产品。

名词 n.

指新方法、新成绩、新理论等创造的具体内容。What is invented or created through a new method, a new idea, a new theory, etc.

(3) 这是大学生的发明创造。
(4) 创造是年轻人的特点。

chuī 吹

用法 Usage:

动词 v.

1. 撮起嘴唇用力把嘴里的气吐出来。To blow by sending out a stream of air from one's mouth.

(1) 桌子上的灰,不要用嘴吹。
(2) 现在把蜡烛吹灭吧。

2. 吹奏(某种乐器)。To play (a kind of wind instruments).

(3) 我不会吹长笛,只会吹口琴。

3. 气流移动,冲击。(Air) to move; (wind) to blow.

(4) 窗户被风吹开了。

4. 说大话,夸口,也作为"吹牛、吹牛皮",多用于口语。To brag; to boast. It can also be expressed as "吹牛" or "吹牛皮" and is often used in the colloquial language.

(5) 你别吹,一口气怎么能喝下三十瓶啤酒?
(6) 事情是做出来的,不是吹出来的。

5. 吹捧。To flatter; to tout.

(7) 你别又吹又拉的,我没那么好。
(8) 你把她吹到天上去了,她有那么好吗?

6. 事情失败,关系破裂,常用于口语。(of something) to fail; (of relationship) to break up. It is usually used in the colloquial language.

(9) 我们和那公司签订合同的事儿吹了。
(10) 他跟女朋友早就吹了。

chúncuì 纯粹 →P75"纯洁"

用法 Usage:

形容词 a.

不掺杂别的成分的。Pure; not having any impurities.

(1) 这套睡衣是用纯粹的丝绸做成的。
(2) 这是用纯粹的黑巧克力加工成的。

副词 *ad.*

表示判断、结论的不容置疑。常跟"是"连用。Completely; purely; merely. "纯粹" is often used with "是" to indicate that something, such as a judgment or a conclusion, is certain and indisputable.

（3）他纯粹说谎，没有一句真话。

（4）她纯粹是为你好，没有别的意思。

chúnjié 纯洁 →P74"纯粹"

用法 Usage:

形容词 *a.*

纯正清白，没有污垢；没有杂念。Pure; stainless; not having any impurities or distractions.

（1）孩子们的心地都是天真纯洁的。

（2）她的品德优秀，思想纯洁，是个好姑娘。

动词 *v.*

让思想、组织等纯洁。To purify; to make something (such as one's thoughts or an organization) pure.

（3）为了纯洁绘画兴趣小组，没有绘画作品的同学不能再参加小组活动。

（4）要纯洁城市里所有河道的水质，保护水环境。

说明 Notes:

"纯洁"与"纯粹"的区别是：The differences between "纯洁" and "纯粹" are as follows:

1. 在词义上，"纯洁"侧重表示洁净、清白。"纯粹"侧重表示完全、真正，不掺杂其他成分。In terms of meaning, "纯洁" emphasizes purity while "纯粹" means truly or totally.

2. "纯洁"形容的对象多是水质、人的思想感情以及组织机构等。"纯粹"形容的对象多是物质、语言、品行以及味道等。"纯洁" is always used to describe things such as water, one's thoughts and feelings, and organizations. "纯粹", by contrast, is always used to describe such things as the quality of a substance, one's words and behaviors, one's taste and so on.

3. "纯洁"前面可以修饰"很、非常、十分"等程度副词。"纯粹"很少用。"纯洁" can be modified by adverbs of degree such as "很, 非常, 十分," but "纯粹" usually cannot.

4. "纯洁"有动词用法，"纯粹"没有动词用法。"纯洁" can be used as a verb while "纯粹" cannot.

cóng 从 →P77"从来"、P594"由"、P688"自"

用法 Usage:

介词 *prep.*

常与名词性词语构成介词短语，充当句子的状语，表示起点。From. "从" often goes with a noun to form a prepositional phrase which functions as an adverbial in the sentence to indicate the starting point.

1. 引进动作行为的时间、处所或范围的起点。常与"到、往、向"配合使用，相当于"自"。From, used to introduce the starting time, place or area of an action or a behavior. It is often used with words such as "到, 往, 向," bearing the same meaning as "自."

① 表示空间的起点或事物的来源。多与处所词语、方位词语结合使用。Indicating the origin of space or the source of things, it is often used with location words or position words.

（1）她刚从北方/北京回来。

（2）人类的知识都是从生活中来的。

② 表示时间的起点。多与时间短语、动词短语或小句组合使用。Indicating the starting time, it usually goes with a time phrase, a verb phrase or a clause.

（3）我们学院的短期班是从七月份开始的。

（4）从老师跟他讲了以后，他再也没有迟到过。

③ 表示动作行为的范围。多与名词、动词短语或小句组合使用。Indicating the range of actions or behaviors, it usually goes with a noun, a verb phrase or a clause.

(5) 请你从头到尾把课文读一遍。

(6) 上次我们从买礼物聊到了旅游,很有意思。

④ 表示实物发展、变化的起点。多与名词、动词、形容词、数量词组合。Indicating the starting point of a development or change of things, it usually goes with nouns, verbs, adjectives and quantity words.

(7) 她从一块布料裁剪到做成衣服,只要两个小时。

(8) 孩子从会爬到会走,用不了几个月时间。

2. 引进动作经过的路线、场所。多跟处所词语、方位词语组合。From, through, used to introduce the route or place of action. It often goes with position words and location words.

(9) 老师刚从教室门口经过。

(10) 从教室左边那条路走,就到食堂。

3. 引进动作行为的凭借、根据。多与名词组合。From, used to indicate the basis for judging. It's often used with nouns.

(11) 从今天的天气看,明天可能要下雨。

(12) 从你的汉语水平来说,你应该去高班。

动词 v.

1. 跟随。如:"愿从其后、年少从征"等。To follow. For example, "愿从其后,年少从征."

2. 依顺,听从。如:"力不从心、言听计从"等。To comply with. For example, "力不从心,言听计从."

3. 从事,参加。如:"从军、从政"等。To be engaged in; participate in. For example, "从军,从政."

4. 采取(某种原则或办法)。如:"待遇从优,批判从严,处理从宽"等。To adopt (some principles or measures). For example, "待遇从优,批判从严,处理从宽."

副词 ad.

从来。一般用在否定词前面,表示从过去到现在。Ever. It is usually placed before a negative word that means from the past to the present.

(13) 他在成绩面前从不骄傲。

(14) 我从没看到过这样漂亮的衣服。

说明 Notes:

"从"的动词用法,多用在书面语。When "从" is used as a verb, it is more often used in the written language.

cóng'ér 从而 →P586"因而"

用法 Usage:
连词 conj.

主要连接分句,连接的两个分句的主语是一致的。有时也连接短语。Thus; there by; as a result. "从而" is mainly used to link two clauses that share the same subject. Sometimes, "从而" can be used to link two phrases.

连接的两个分句或短语的关系有:The clauses and the phrases linked by "从而" can indicate the following relations:

1. 表示因果关系。连接的两个分句,前一分句表示原因,后一分句表示结果,这个结果一般是积极意义的。"从而"在后一分句前面,相当于"因此就、因而、于是"。Expressing a cause and effect relationship. When "从而" is used to link two clauses, the previous one expresses the cause while the latter one expresses the effect. The sentence often indicates a positive meaning. "从而" is put before the latter clause which functions the same as "因此就,因而,于是."

(1) 学校公布了奖学金制度,从而鼓励了大家更加努力地去学习。

(2) 他考了全班第一,从而改变了大家对他的看法。

2. 表示目的。连接的两个句子,前一分句是方法或条件,后一分句是通过这一方法或条件要达到的目的。"从而"相当于"以便"。一般用于将来时态。Expressing a purpose. When "从而" is used to link two clauses, the previous one expresses the method or the condition while the latter one expresses the purpose achieved through this method or condition. "从而"

functions the same as "以便" and is usually used in the future tense.

(3) 两个人在一起的时间应该长一点,从而使双方更加了解。

(4) 每天跟中国朋友聊天,从而提高自己的汉语口语水平。

cónglái 从来 →P75"从"、P513"向来"

用法 Usage:

副词 ad.

表示从过去到现在都是如此。Always; at all time; all along. It is used to indicate that someone or something has always been so from the past to the present.

1. 多用于否定句。Mainly used in negative sentences.

(1) 我从来不吸烟。

(2) 她从来没看过中国的电影。

2. 用于肯定句时,谓语一般用动词"是"或代词"这样、那样",一般修饰动词短语、形容词短语或小句,不修饰单个动词或形容词。When it is used in an affirmative sentence, the predicate is usually the verb "是" or the pronoun "这样" or "那样" to modify a verb phrase, an adjective phrase or a clause instead of separate verbs or adjectives.

(3) 她从来就喜欢这样穿衣服。

(4) 这个地方从来是女人养男人。

3. "从来+没/没有"修饰单音节动词、形容词,后面一般要带"过"。When "从来+没/没有" modifies a monosyllabic verb or adjective, the word "过" should be added to the end of the sentence.

(5) 那个地方我从来没去过。

(6) 我这颗牙齿有个洞,但从来没有疼过。

4. "从来+没/没有"修饰双音节动词和形容词,或由单音节动词和形容词组成的短语,不一定要带"过"。When "从来+没/没有" modifies a disyllabic verb or adjective, or a phrase composed of a monosyllabic verb and an adjective, the word "过" is dispensable.

(7) 即使遇到了很多挫折,我也从没后悔(过)。

(8) 他好像从来没有想清楚(过)自己要什么。

说明 Notes:

1. "从来+没/没有+形"的句式中,形容词前面加不加"这么、这样",意思完全相反。In the pattern "从来+没/没有+a.", when "这么" or "这样" is put before the adjective, the sentence meaning is completely opposite to that without "这么" or "这样."

(9) 他从来没有努力过。(现在仍然没努力 Still not working hard)

(10) 他从来没有这样努力过。(现在比以前努力 Working harder now than before)

2. "从来"与副词"从"的意思相同,但是用法有所区别。"从来" and the adverb "从" share the same meaning but their usages are somewhat different.

① "从"只用在否定词语"不、未、没/没有"等前面,多用于书面语。"从来"可以用在否定句,也可以用在肯定句,通用于口语、书面语。"从" can only be used before negative words such as "不, 未, 没/没有," which are more frequently used in the written language; while "从来" can be used both in negative sentences and affirmative sentences, both in the colloquial language and written language.

② 一般情况下,为了音节和谐,单音节动词前面总是用"从来",不用"从"。如:"从来不想/*从不想;从来不问/*从不问;从来不看/*从不看;从来不吃/*从不吃";等等。Generally, to achieve the syllabic balance, a monosyllabic verb is modified by "从来" instead of "从." For example, "从来不想/*从不想";"从来不问/*从不问";"从来不看/*从不看";"从来不吃/*从不吃."

③ "从"还有介词用法。"从来"没有介词用法。"从" can be used as a preposition while "从来" cannot.

cóngqián 从前 →P182"过去"、P572"以前"

用法 Usage:

名词 n.

过去的时候,以前。常用于句首、主语后、谓语前或者出现在名词前充当定语。A long time ago; some time ago. It is usually used at the beginning of a sentence, after the subject, before the predicate or as an attribute before a noun.

(1) 从前她常常迟到,现在不迟到了。
(2) 她从前周末都去上海,现在不太去了。
(3) 她已经忘了从前的事情了。

说明 Notes:

"从前"虽然是名词,但是一般不能单独做宾语。As a noun, "从前" cannot be used separately as the object by itself.

(1) *你不要忘了从前。
(2) 你不要忘了从前的事情。

cóngshì 从事

用法 Usage:

动词 v.

1. 投身到某种事业中去,进行某种活动。不能单独作谓语,必须带表示某种事业或活动的名词、动词、动词短语作的双音节以上的宾语。To devote oneself to; to be devoted to (a cause or an activity); to be engaged in an activity. It cannot be used separately as the predicate by itself. It is followed by a disyllabic or polysyllabic noun, verb or verb phrase that indicates a certain cause or activity.

(1) 王教授从事汉语教学工作已经三十年了。
(2) 他一生从事生命科学研究。

2. (按照某种方式或原则)对付,处理。仅出现在少数的几个固定搭配的短语中,如:"不要草率从事,要小心从事、谨慎从事、慎重从事"等。多用于祈使句。To deal with something (in accordance with a certain way or principle). It appears only in some fixed phrases such as "不要草率从事,要小心从事,谨慎从事,慎重从事." It mostly appears in an imperative sentence.

说明 Notes:

"从事"的宾语多是指某种工作或者某项事业,一般不能是具体的事。The object of "从事" is always some profession or a certain cause instead of the specific things.

(3) *他正在从事作业。
(4) 他正在做作业。
(5) *他从事厨师。
(6) 他从事烹调工作。

cuòshī 措施 →P11"办法"

用法 Usage:

名词 n.

一般指为解决某种重大问题所采取的办法。Measure. It usually refers to something done to solve a major problem.

(1) 实行这个规划的措施是什么?
(2) 为了发展经济,国家采取了不少措施。

说明 Notes:

1. "措施"多用于书面语,多用于较大事情。"措施" is mainly used in the written language, which refers to something important.

2. "措施"常作动词"制定、采取"的宾语。"措施" is often used as the object of such verbs as "制定,采取."

3. "措施"的量词多为"套、项"等内容含量较大的量词。"措施" is often modified by quantifiers that indicate large numbers, such as "套,项."

4. "措施"和"办法"都指解决问题的方法。区别是:"办法"侧重指具有直接操作的特点。"措施"多指解决某个重大问题比较完整、系统的手段和方法。Both "措施" and "方法" refer to problem-solving methods. The difference is that "办法" emphasizes the feature of using direct methods, while "措施" usually refers to complete and systematic methods for solving major problems.

dādàng 搭档

用法 Usage:

动词 v.

协作,合作。To cooperate; to work together.

(1) 这项工作你们俩搭档。

(2) 我和你搭档,这工作一定能完成得很好。

名词 n.

一起协作或合作的人。Partner.

(3) 他是我的搭档。

(4) 你们俩是搭档。

dāyìng 答应

用法 Usage:

动词 v.

1. 应声回答。To answer; to respond (to).

(1) 我叫你好长时间,你也不答应一声。我以为你不在呢。

(2) 我答应了,你没听见。

2. 表示同意。To agree; to promise.

(3) 爸爸答应我在中国学三年汉语。

(4) 管理员答应给我换房间了。

dádào 达到 →P97"到达"

用法 Usage:

动词 v.

1. 到,实现(某个目标或某种程度)。常做谓语。To reach; to achieve (a goal). It is usually used as a predicate.

(1) 这样做,你就可以达到目的。

(2) 他的汉语水平已经达到优秀。

2. "达到"中间可以插入"得/不",表示可能不可能。"得/不" can be inserted between "达" and "到," indicating possibility or impossibility.

(3) 他的要求太高,我们达不到。

(4) 他的要求不高,我们达得到。

3. 可以用肯定、否定形式提问。It can be used to ask a question with its affirmative form and negative form.

(5) 你的要求她达到没达到?

(6) 你的要求她达不达得到?

(7) 你的要求她达得到达不到?

dáfù 答复 →P202"回答"

用法 Usage:

动词 v.

回答别人提出的问题或要求。多做谓语。To give an answer to a question or to respond to a request. It is usually used as a predicate.

(1) 明天老师会答复我们的问题。

(2) 这些要求不高,你们应该立刻答复。

名词 n.

对别人提出的问题或要求的回答。An answer to a question; a response to a request.

(3) 她的答复我们不满意。

(4) 这就是他们的答复。

说明 Notes:

"答复"是书面语,比较正式,一般没有行为动作的方式,多用于书面语。"答复" is an expression in written Chinese. Usually, it does not have a specific way of behaviour.

dǎ 打

用法 Usage:
动词 v.

1. 敲打,打击,撞击。可带"了、着、过",可重叠。可带名词宾语。To knock; to strike; to hit. It can be followed by "了," "着," or "过," and can also be reduplicated as "打打." It can take a noun as its object.

(1) 你打打门,看看里面有没有人。
(2) 时钟打了十二下,又到半夜了。

2. 因撞击而破碎。可带"了、过"。可带名词宾语。To break; to smash. It can take a noun as its object and be followed by "了" or "过."

(3) 小心点儿,别把玻璃打了。
(4) 怎么办,我把她的花瓶打了。

3. 殴打,攻打。可带"了、着、过"。可带名词宾语。To beat up; to attack. It can take a noun as its object and be followed by "了," "着," or "过."

(5) 这两个小孩不知道为什么打了起来。
(6) 不能打人!

4. 发射,发出。可带"了、着、过"。可带名词宾语。To fire; to dispatch. It can take a noun as its object and be followed by "了," "着," or "过."

(7) 我从来没有打过枪。
(8) 你给他再打个电话。

5. 进行人与人之间的联系、交往、交涉。如:"打交道、打招呼、打官司"等。To make contact with somebody, such as "打交道,打招呼,打官司."

6. 制造。如:"打了一把刀、打了一套家具"等。To make. For example, "打了一把刀,打了一套家具."

7. 编织。如:"打件毛衣、打双手套、打辫子"等。To knit. For example, "打件毛衣,打双手套,打辫子."

8. 建造。如:"打地基、打了一堵墙"等。To build; to construct. For example, "打地基,打了一堵墙."

9. 捆绑。如:"明天回国,你行李打好了吗?" To pack up. For example, "明天回国,你行李打好了吗?"

10. 涂抹。如:"皮鞋要打打油了;化妆前,脸上要打个粉底"等。To polish. For example, "皮鞋要打打油了。""化妆前,脸上要打个粉底."

11. 写、画、印。如:"打草稿、打格子、打个图章"等。To draft; to draw; to print. For example, "打草稿,打格子,打个图章."

12. 揭开,凿,掀开。如:"打开盖子、打口井、打开被子、打开窗帘"等。To open; to unfold; to dig. For example, "打开盖子,打口井,打开被子,打开窗帘."

13. 举,提。如:"打伞、打灯笼"等。To hold up; to raise. For example, "打伞,打灯笼."

14. 开具,领取。如:"打个介绍信、打个证明"等。To issue, such as "打个介绍信,打个证明."

15. 除去,梳理。如:"打树枝、打树叶、打萝卜皮"等。To get rid of; to remove. For example, "打树枝,打树叶,打萝卜皮."

16. 舀取。如:"打饭、打一盆水、打开水"等。To ladle; to fetch. For example, "打饭,打一盆水,打开水."

17. 注入。如:"给自行车胎打气"等。To fill with air, such as "给自行车胎打气."

18. 零售,购买。如:"打酒、打油、打酱油、打汽车票、打火车票"等。To buy. For example, "打酒,打油,打酱油,打汽车票,打火车票."

19. 捕捉(禽兽)。如:"打鸟、打鱼、打兔子"等。To hunt for (birds, fish, rabbits, etc.). For example, "打鸟,打鱼,打兔子."

20. 收获农作物。如:"打麦子、打谷子"等。To reap. For example, "打麦子,打谷子."

21. 拨动,搬动。如:"打算盘、打方向盘"等。To calculate on an abacus; to steer. For

example,"打算盘,打方向盘."

22. 计算,预算。如:"又在打什么主意;打打成本看,要多少钱"等。*To think of a plan; to estimate the cost. For example,"又在打什么主意;打打成本看,要多少钱."*

23. 做,进行。如:"打工、打游击战、打埋伏"等。*To do. For example,"打工,打游击战,打埋伏."*

24. 进行体育运动,做游戏。如:"打篮球、打排球、打游戏、打牌、打麻将"等。*To play (games). For example,"打篮球,打排球,打游戏,打牌,打麻将."*

25. 表示做某种动作或某种状态。如:"打手势、打哈欠、打喷嚏"等。*To indicate a certain action or state. For example,"打手势,打哈欠,打喷嚏."*

26. 表示某种方法或方式。如:"打比方、打手势、打马虎眼"等。*To indicate a certain way. For example,"打比方,打手势,打马虎眼."*

27. 定为某种罪名。如:"打成右派、打成贪污分子"等。*To label somebody as. For example,"打成右派,打成贪污分子."*

介词 *prep.*

从。多用于北方话的口语。*Since; from (used in colloquial language). It is often used in northern dialects.*

(9) 打今儿起,每天早上朗读十五分钟课文。

(10) 打这儿往东走五百米,就是新华书店。

说明 Notes:

1. "打"表示买酒、买油等液体东西时,是指从大容器中舀取倒入小容器中,购买者常自带容器。买瓶装的,不用"打",用"买"。*When "打" means buying liquor, oil or other liquids, it means ladling liquids from a big container and then pouring it into a small container, in which case the buyer usually brings his/her own container. If he/she buys tinned or bottled liquids, he/she should say "买" instead of "打."*

2. "打"表示购买的意思时,除了"打票",还指购买吃的、喝的东西,如:在食堂"打三个菜、打两碗饭"。购买其他日用品或衣服不能用"打"。*When "打" means "to buy things," it can mean "打票." Besides, it can specially refer to buying food in a canteen such as "打三个菜,打两碗饭," but this use is not applied to clothes or other daily necessities.*

3. "打"可以带补语。*"打" can take a complement.*

① 带结果补语。如:"打破、打翻、打掉、打死"等。*Followed by a complement indicating a result such as "打破,打翻,打掉,打死, etc."*

② 带趋向补语。如:"打上去、打下去、打起来、打出"等。*Followed by a complement indicating a direction. For example,"打上去,打下去,打起来,打出."*

4. "打"作介词用并表示"从"的意思时,不能用在单音节词语前。单音节词语前必须用"从"。多用于口语。*When "打" is used as a preposition meaning "since," it cannot be placed before a monosyllabic word. In this case, "从" is used instead. It usually appears in colloquial language.*

(11) *打南到北,他几乎走遍了中国著名的风景地。

(12) 从南到北,他几乎走遍了中国著名的风景地。

5. "打"不时产生新的用法,如20世纪五六十年代有"打成右派"。现在又有"打车/出租"等。*New usages of "打" have come into being. For example,"打成右派" appeared in the 1950s and 1960s, and "打车/出租车" appeared later.*

dǎbāo 打包

用法 Usage:

动词 *v.*

1. 把物品包装起来。*To pack.*

(1) 行李可以打包了。

(2) 这些东西可以打成两个包。

2. 打开包装着的物品。*To unpack.*

（3）请稍等,您的行李要打包检查。
（4）她打开包,把里面的东西都拿了出来。
3. 在饭店吃饭后,把吃剩的食物包起来。*To put the leftovers in a doggy bag.*
（5）吃不完的就打包吧!
（6）服务员,请把这些菜和点心打两个包。

说明 Notes:

"打包"是离合动词,动词与名词之间可以插入其他成分,如例(2)(4)(6)。*"打包" is a separable verb, namely, other constituents can be inserted between the verb and the noun, as in (2), (4) and (6).*

dǎchē 打车

用法 Usage:

也称"打的",坐出租车。*It is also called "打的," which means taking a taxi.*
（1）末班车已经过去了。打车吧!
（2）路太远了,打个车吧。

说明 Notes:

"打车"只指租用或乘坐出租的小汽车。租用或乘坐大型、中型出租车,不能用"打车"。*"打车" only refers to taking a taxi or renting a car. It cannot be used when you take a large or medium-sized vehicle.*

dǎdī 打的

用法 Usage:

动词 *v.*

打车。"的",即"的士",taxi 的译音。用于口语。*It means taking a taxi. "的" or "的士" is the transliteration of a taxi. "打的" is colloquial.*
（1）公交车要换两次车,不方便,打的去吧。
（2）上下班高峰的时候,很难打的。

dǎfa 打发

用法 Usage:

动词 *v.*

1. 派（出去）。*To send.*
（1）我已经打发很多人去找他了。
（2）赶快打发人去请大夫,老人的病不能再拖了。
2. 让别人离开。*To send away; to dismiss.*
（3）同屋把他打发出去了。你们休息一会儿吧。
3. 消磨。*To kill time.*
（4）退休以后,他常常去公园散步,打发时间。
（5）她喜欢种草养花,打发业余时间。
4. 安排,照料。*To make an arrangement for; to take care of.*
（6）你不用操心,客人来了,他会打发得很周到。
（7）这次旅游,谁来打发我们的吃住问题?

dǎjiāodào 打交道

用法 Usage:

习惯语。表示人与人之间的交际、联系、来往和交涉。常用作谓语。*Idiom. It shows the communication, contact and negotiation between persons. It is often used as a predicate.*
（1）他不喜欢和别人打交道。
（2）你去跟他们打打交道,借两把椅子,好吗?

说明 Notes:

1. "打交道"是口语色彩很浓的词语。结构为动宾短语,后面不能再有宾语。*"打交道" is a highly colloquial expression. It is a verb-object construction, so it cannot take another object.*
2. 动词"打"和"交道"之间可以插入别的词语,如"打了几次交道"。*Other words can be inserted between "打" and "交道," and "打了几次交道" is an example.*
3. 动作涉及的对象可以用介词"和、跟、与"等引出,用在"打交道"前面。*The object of an action can be introduced by prepositions such as "和,跟,与." The objects are used before "打交道."*

(3) 我和他已经打了两次交道。

4. "打交道"的对象一般是人。但也可以引申用于牲口或物体。*Generally, the object of "打交道" is people, but the object can be extended to animals and inanimate things.*

(4) 他长年累月地和牲口打交道。

(5) 这个书呆子就知道与书本打交道。

dǎrǎo 打扰 →P311"麻烦"

用法 Usage:

动词 *v.*

1. 扰乱。*To disturb.*

(1) 姐姐正在做作业,你别去打扰她。

(2) 你别来打扰,我们在上班。

2. 请人帮助、感谢别人帮助或招待时的客套话。*A polite expression used to ask people for help or show gratitude to others' help or entertainment.*

(3) 我想坐到里面的位子去,打扰了。

(4) 多次打扰,真不好意思!

dǎsuàn 打算 →P214"计划"

用法 Usage:

动词 *v.*

表示考虑、计划。*To intend; to plan.*

(1) 他打算明天去北京。

(2) 我打算"五一"长假去旅游。

名词 *n.*

指想法、念头。*An idea; a plan.*

(3) 这个打算好。

(4) 我没有去北京的打算。

说明 Notes:

动词"打算"多用作谓语,可带宾语,但是宾语不能是名词性、形容词性的词语,而是动词性词语,如例(1)和(2)。*As a verb, "打算" is often used as a predicate, usually followed by an object. But its object can be verbal words rather than nouns or adjectives, as seen in (1) and (2).*

dǎtīng 打听

用法 Usage:

动词 *v.*

向有关的人探问消息、情况、意图等。常用作谓语。可以重叠为"打听打听"。*To ask somebody for information about a situation or whatever. Often used as a predicate, "打听" can be reduplicated as "打听打听."*

(1) 你去打听打听下个学期什么时候开学。

(2) 我已经打听过了,他们已经上到第八课。

说明 Notes:

"打听"的宾语大都与人或事的消息、情况有关。一般不直接带指人的宾语。如果要说明"打听"的对象,需用介词"向、跟"等引出。*Objects of "打听" are mostly information about somebody or something, yet it usually doesn't take an object about a person. If it is necessary to show the object of "打听," prepositions are used to introduce the person.*

(3) 他向我打听留学生楼怎么走。

(4) *我昨天打听了他。

(5) 我昨天向别人打听了他的情况。

(6) 我昨天打听了他的情况。

dǎzào 打造

用法 Usage:

动词 *v.*

1. 制造(多指金属器物)。*To make (esp. metal objects).*

(1) 他能打造出你会喜欢的金项链。

(2) 现在的汽车零件都是机器打造的。

2. 创造或造就。*To create; to train; to build up.*

(3) 公司用了十年时间才打造出这个优质品牌。

(4) 一百多年来,学院打造出了一批又一批优秀人才。

dǎzhāohu 打招呼

用法 Usage:

1. 见面时用语言、表情或动作向对方致意。*To greet somebody by language, expression or gesture.*

(1) 那边有个人在跟你打招呼。

(2) 他很有礼貌,看见老师就打招呼。

2. 就某件事或某个问题,事先予以通知、关照。*To give notice (of something) in advance.*

(3) 明天我们去他们学校参观,你跟他们打招呼了没有?

(4) 如果你们要去旅游,事先跟我打个招呼。

说明 Notes:

1. "打招呼"是动宾短语,后面不能再有宾语。*"打招呼" is a verb-object phrase, so it cannot be followed by another object.*

2. 动词"打"和"招呼"之间可以插入别的词语,如"打了个招呼"。*Other words can be inserted between "打" and "招呼," such as "打了个招呼."*

3. 动作涉及的对象可以用介词"和、跟、与"等引出。可以出现在动词前,也可以出现在主要动词后。*Objects of targets of "打招呼" can be introduced by a preposition such as "和," "跟" or "与." They can be used both before the verb and after the main verb.*

(5) 我跟他已经打了三次招呼。

(6) 我不愿意跟他打招呼。

dàdà 大大

用法 Usage:
副词 ad.

强调程度深、范围广、数量多、规模大等。表示超过一般的。常修饰动词。*Emphasizing high degree, wide scope, huge amount, etc., it indicates surpassing the average, and is often used to modify verbs.*

(1) 改革开放大大加快了农村的经济发展。

(2) 宿舍区建了小商店,大大方便了我们的生活。

说明 Notes:

副词"大大"要与形容词"大"的重叠式加以区别。形容词"大"重叠后可以用于名词前,如"大大的眼睛、大大的耳朵",而副词"大大"后面不能跟名词。*The adverb "大大" differs from the disyllabic word of the adjective "大." The disyllabic adjective "大大" can be used before a noun, such as "大大的眼睛,大大的耳朵," but the adverb "大大" cannot be followed by nouns.*

dàdū 大都 →P125"多半"

用法 Usage:
副词 ad.

口语中也读作"dàdōu"。大部分,大多数。常用作状语。*In spoken language, "大都" can also be pronounced as "dàdōu," which means the majority of something. It is often used as an adverbial.*

(1) 我们大都是学汉语的留学生。

(2) 他们大都从上海来。

说明 Notes:

"大都"是个范围副词。用在谓语前面可以限定谓语部分,包括宾语的范围。也可以在语义上限定主语的范围。*"大都" is a scope adverb. It is often placed before a predicate to limit its scope. It may also be used to limit the scope of the subject semantically.*

(3) 这些名胜古迹我大都游览过了。

dàfāng 大方 →P269"慷慨"

用法 Usage:
形容词 a.

1. 表示对金钱、财物不计较,不吝啬。*(In monetary matters) generous; not mean.*

(1) 他用钱很大方。

(2) 他很大方，什么东西都肯借给你。

2. 表示言谈举止自然、不拘束。(Of one's manners) natural; easy.

(3) 你见了人可要大方点，不要拘束。

(4) 她今天在那么多人面前，表现得很大方。

3. 表示衣服、装饰等的式样、颜色不俗气。(Of style, color of clothes, decoration, etc.) in good taste.

(5) 这件衣服样子很大方。

(6) 他今天穿得可大方了。

dàgài 大概 →P86"大约"、P86"大致"

用法 Usage:

形容词 a.

不十分详尽，不很准确，大致。可做定语、状语，一般不做谓语。Not exact; approximate; not detailed. It can be used as an attribute or an adverbial, but usually not as a predicate.

(1) 你们把那件事的大概情况讲一讲。

(2) 老师大概地给我们介绍了学校的情况。

副词 ad.

1. 表示对数量、时间不很精确的估计。An approximate estimate of a number or time.

(3) 学校大概离市中心三四公里路。

(4) 考试大概在下个星期进行。

2. 表示对情况的推测、估计，一般认为有较大的可能性。多用作状语，可以用在主语前面。An approximate estimate of a situation; probably. It is often used as an adverbial, and can precede the subject.

(5) 前边那幢大楼大概就是邮电局。

(6) 已经十一点了，他大概不会来了。

名词 n.

表示大致的内容或情况。一般只用作"知道、了解、听出、记得、看懂"等少数动词的宾语，不能用作主语。前面通常有量词"个"。The general idea; a broad outline. It is often used as the object of a few verbs such as "知道，了解，听出，记得，看懂," and there is always a measure word "个" preceding it. It cannot be used as a subject.

(7) 这件事我只知道个大概。

(8) 这篇文章有点难，我只看懂个大概。

说明 Notes:

"大概"作形容词用时，不能受程度副词的修饰，不能单独作谓语。When "大概" is used as an adjective, it can neither be modified by a degree adverbial nor be used as a predicate.

dàliàng 大量 →P85"大批"

用法 Usage:

形容词 a.

1. 表示数量大。只能做状语和定语，不能单独做谓语，不能受程度副词的修饰。A large number; a huge amount. It can only be used as an adverbial or an attribute, not as a predicate by itself. It cannot be modified by a degree adverbial.

(1) 周末有大量的作业要完成。

(2) 这种产品可以大量生产，市场上很需要。

2. 表示气量大、能宽容。Broad-minded; magnanimous.

(3) 你就宽宏大量地原谅他吧！

(4) 他很大量，不是个小气的人。

dàpī 大批 →P85"大量"

用法 Usage:

形容词 a.

表示同一个时期或同一次里数量多。多用作定语和状语。Indicating large quantities of something in a certain period of time or in a certain batch, it is mainly used as an attribute or an adverbial.

(1) 改革开放以后，大批农民开始进城打工。

(2) 那个公司去年引进了大批技术人才。

说明 Notes：

"大量"和"大批"都形容数量多。都只做定语或状语。区别是：Both "大量" and "大批" modify large quantities of something, and both can only be used as an attribute or adverbial. Yet, they are different in the following aspects:

1."大量"着重于一个个的个体很多,用于具体的人或事物,也用于抽象事物。前面不能加"一"字。"大量" emphasizes large numbers of individuals, modifying concrete persons, things or abstract concepts. It cannot take "一" before it.

（3）他在一年时间里写出了大量的文学作品。

（4）很多人的头脑里还存在大量的封建思想。

2."大批"着重于成批的数量大,比"大量"更有形象感。只用于人或事物,不能用于抽象事物。用作定语时,前面可以加"一"字。"大批" emphasizes large quantities of a group of persons or things. It cannot be used to modify abstract concepts. When it is used as an attribute, "一" can be put in front of it.

（5）这个工厂进了一大批农民工。

（6）春节时商店里每天卖出一大批一大批的烟花爆竹。

3."大量"还有表示人的气量大的意思。"大批"没有这个用法。"大量" can also be used to describe a broad-minded person, but "大批" does not have this usage.

dàyuē 大约 →P85"大概"、P86"大致"

用法 Usage：

副词 ad.

1. 表示对数量、时间等不很精确的、大致的估计。用作状语,后边常带数量词。Indicating the approximate estimate of quantity, time, etc., it is often used as an adverbial and followed by a quantifier.

（1）现在大约十二点。

（2）她大约有二十岁。

2. 表示对情况的推测,可能。用作状语。Indicating a speculation about something or possibility, it can be used as an adverbial.

（3）她大约已经去北京了。

（4）这么晚了,她大约不来了。

说明 Notes：

1."大约"一般不修饰形容词,如不能说"那些花大约很红"。Generally, "大约" cannot modify adjectives. For example, "那些花大约很红" is incorrect.

2."大约"和"大概"作副词用时,都能表示对时间、数量的不很精确的估计,都能表示对情况的推测。区别是：When "大约" and "大概" are used as an adverbial, both indicate the approximate estimate of time or quantity, and both show a speculation about a situation. Yet they are different in the following two points：

① "大约"侧重于对数量的推测。"大概"侧重于对情况的估计。"大约" focuses more on the speculation about quantity, while "大概" focuses more on the estimate of a situation.

② "大概"有名词、形容词用法。"大约"没有这两种用法。"大概" can also be used as a noun and an adjective, but "大约" cannot.

dàzhì 大致 →P85"大概"、P86"大约"

用法 Usage：

形容词 a.

大体上的,不详尽的,不精确的,概要。多用作定语和状语。Approximate; imprecise; general. It is often used as an attribute or an adverbial.

（1）我们只了解了大致的情况。

（2）我先大致地说一下。

副词 ad.

大体上,基本上,大概,大约。可以跟"上"连用,构成"大致上"的形式,在句子中做状语。Approximately; generally; about. It can take

"上" to form "大致上," which is used as an adverbial.

(3) 这首歌大致要唱三分钟。
(4) 这两本书的内容大致相同。
(5) 他每天大致上在七点半起床。

说明 Notes:

1. "大致"的词义着重于表示"就大多数情形来说"或"基本上来说"的意思。"大致" focuses on " in most cases " or " on the whole."

2. "大概""大约""大致"作副词、用于对数量、时间作不很精确的估计时,都要求后边带数量短语或时间词语,基本上可以通用。When "大概","大约" and "大致" are adverbials indicating the imprecise estimate of quantity or time, they must be followed by a quantitative phrase or time word. In that case, the three are interchangeable.

(6) 他大约/大概/大致二十岁。

区别是：The differences are as follows:

① "大概"作为副词,主要表示对某种有很大可能性的情况的推测、估计。"大约"能表示对情况的猜测,但是没有很大的可能性。"大致"没有这种用法。When used as an adverbial, "大概" indicates the most likely speculation or estimate about a situation. "大约" can indicate the speculation or estimate about a situation, but there isn't much probability. "大致" does not have this usage.

(7) *他大致是上海人。
(8) 他大概是上海人。
(9) 他大约是上海人。

② "大概"有名词用法,表示大致的内容或情况。"大致"和"大约"都没有这种用法。"大概" can be used as a noun, indicating the approximate content or situation, yet "大致" or "大约" does not have this usage.

③ "大概""大致"有形容词用法。"大约"没有这种用法。"大概" and "大致" can be used as an adjective, yet "大约" does not have this usage.

dāi 呆

用法 Usage:
形容词 a.

1. 形容呆滞,不灵活。Dull; dumb.
(1) 你看他那样子,呆头呆脑的。
(2) 别看他一副呆样子,可聪明呢。

2. 表情或动作死板,发愣。可以重叠。(Of an expression or action) rigid; blank. It can be used in its reduplicated form.
(3) 你看他那呆呆的样子,不知在想什么。
(4) 飞机失事的消息把她吓呆了。

动词 v.

也作"待"。表示停留、居留。多用作谓语,一般不带宾语,可带补语。不能重叠使用。To stay. Usually used as a predicate, it can be followed by a complement instead of an object, but it cannot be used in its reduplicated form.
(5) 他们在北京只呆/待了三天。
(6) 这两年,他一直呆/待在中国。

dài 代 →P88"代替"、P462"替"

用法 Usage:
动词 v.

1. 代替。可作连动式的第一个动词。To take the place of. It can be the first verb in a series of verbal expressions.
(1) 王老师给我代上过几节课。
(2) 你代我向你妈妈问好。

2. 代理。只能作定语,定语不加"的"。To act on behalf of somebody. It can only be used as an attribute, without "的."
(3) 他做了两年代市长。

名词 n.

1. 社会历史的分期。如:"古代、现代"等。Historical period, such as "古代,现代."
2. 朝代。如:"唐代、宋代"等。Dynasty, such as "唐代,宋代."

3. 辈分。如:"老一代、青年一代、下一代"等。Generation, such as "老一代,青年一代,下一代."

4. 地质年代分期的第一级。如:"新生代、古生代"等。Geological era, such as "新生代,古生代."

dàitì 代替 →P87"代"、P462"替"

用法 Usage:

动词 v.

用一事物替换另一事物,并起另一事物的作用;取代,替换。To substitute one thing for another and perform the function of the other thing; to take the place of; to replace.

(1) 今天我代替他姐姐来照顾他。
(2) 考试不能让别人代替。
(3) 可以用塑料板代替木板吗?

说明 Notes:

1. "代替"表示以甲换乙,所以参与动作的两个方面常出现在"代替"的前后,做主语或宾语。除了名词性词语以外,"代替"的前后还可以是动词性词语。如:"以争吵代替了商量、以谈判代替了战争"等。"代替" means " to substitute A for B," so the two sides involved in the action often appear before and after "代替," one serving as a subject and the other as an object. Apart from noun phrases, verbal phrases can precede or follow "代替," such as "以争吵代替了商量、以谈判代替了战争."

2. "代"动词用法的第一义项和"代替"的动词用法基本相同。区别是:The first usage of "代" as a verb basically equals the usage of "代替." Yet they are different in two aspects:

① "代替"没有动词"代"的第二义项的用法。"代替" does not have the second meaning of "代" as a verb.

② "代"有名词用法。"代替"没有名词用法。"代" can be used as a noun, yet "代替" cannot be used as a noun.

dānxīn 担心 →P88"担忧"、P641"着急"

用法 Usage:

动词 v.

有顾虑,放心不下。一般用作离合动词。To worry; to feel anxious (often used as a separable verb).

(1) 孩子都工作了,你还为他担什么心?
(2) 我很担心我妈妈的身体。

dānyōu 担忧 →P88"担心"

用法 Usage:

动词 v.

发愁,忧虑。To worry; to feel anxious.

(1) 不用担忧,路上不会有危险的。
(2) 老人常常为他们的身体健康担忧。

说明 Notes:

"担心"跟"担忧"的区别是:"担心" differs from "担忧" in the following aspects:

1. "担心"的词义较轻,只指放心不下。"担忧"的词义较重,不仅放心不下,而且还忧虑、发愁。"担心" is a general word that means to worry about something somewhat; "担忧," however, bears a strong meaning, not only worrying about something but also carrying a feeling of anxiety.

2. "担心"后面可以带宾语,"担忧"后面一般不带宾语。"担心" can be followed by an object while "担忧" normally cannot take an object.

3. "担心"是离合动词,中间可以插入其他成分,"担忧"不能。"担心" is a separable verb, so other constitutes can be inserted between "担" and "心," but "担忧" does not have this usage.

(3) *儿子外出几天,妈妈就为他担几天忧。
(4) 儿子外出几天,妈妈就为他担几天心。

dān 单 →P666"只"

用法 Usage:

形容词 a.

1. 单个,一个(跟"双"相对)。只能做定语,如:"单只鞋、单只手套、单扇门、单人床"等,不能加"的"。Single; odd [antonym: pair (双)]. It is used as an attribute and cannot be followed by "的," such as "单只鞋,单只手套,单扇门,单人床."

2. 奇数的(一、三、五、七、九等,跟"双"相对)。只作定语,不能加"的"。如"单号、单日、单数(与'偶数'相对)"等。Odd (odd numbers, such as one, three, five, seven, nine). It is used as an attribute and cannot be followed by "的," such as "单号,单日,单数 (antonym: even numbers)."

3. 单独。多用于固定词组。如"单身一人、单枪匹马"等。Solitary (often used in set phrases, such as "单身一人,单枪匹马").

4. 只有一层的。做定语,不能加"的",如"单衣、单裤"等。Unlined (used as an attribute and cannot be followed by "的," such as "单衣,单裤").

副词 ad.

表示限定范围。仅,只,光。常与"就"连用,构成"单……就……"的格式。(Indicating the limited scope) only; alone; merely. It is often used in the set phrase "单...就...."

(1) 学汉语单说不写,效果不是太好。
(2) 单说不做就等于没说。
(3) 我们家的书很多,单我的书就放了四个书架。

名词 n.

1. 登记人名或记事用的纸片儿。如:"名单、菜单、账单、包裹单"等。List of names or things, such as "名单,菜单,账单,包裹单, etc."

2. 单层的布或衣物。如:"床单、被单"等。Sheet, such as "床单,被单, etc."

dānchún 单纯 →P221"简单"

用法 Usage:

形容词 a.

1. 简单纯一,不复杂。Simple; unsophisticated.

(1) 小孩子都很单纯。
(2) 他的思想很单纯,不复杂。

2. 单一,单单。Alone; merely.

(3) 用单纯的分数观点来看一个人学习的好坏,是片面的。
(4) 最初,我单纯是为了我的爸爸妈妈来中国留学的。

dāndú 单独 →P118"独自"

用法 Usage:

副词 ad.

不跟别的合在一起,独自。常做状语、定语;做定语时,常带"的"。Alone; by oneself. It is often used as an adverbial or an attribute, and when used as an attribute, it is often followed by "的."

(1) 他单独住在校外的一套房子里。
(2) 我想跟他单独谈谈。
(3) 这是一次单独的采访。

dàn 但 →P90"但是"

用法 Usage:

副词 ad.

表示限制范围,相当于"只、只是、仅、仅仅",带有文言色彩。Only; just; merely. "但" as an adverb is used to limit the scope, equivalent to "只,只是,仅,仅仅." It often appears in classical Chinese.

(1) 但愿他的身体能好起来。
(2) 这次考试,我但求及格。

连词 conj.

在句子中表示转折关系。"但"所在的句子意义跟上文相对,或者是对上文意义的限制、补充,是句子意义的重点所在。But; yet; nevertheless. "但" as a conjunction indicates a transition, and its usage is similar to that of "但是." "但" introduces a sentence which contrasts with or limits or supplements the meaning of the previous sentence, and the sentence following "但" bears the focus of the meaning.

（3）这本书虽然很好，但我没有钱，所以没有买。

（4）他病了，但他还是坚持来上课。

说明 Notes:

"但"做连词，必须用在后一分句的前面，常常与前一分句的"虽然"相呼应（有时"虽然"也可以省略）。When "但" is used as a conjunction, it must be put at the beginning of the second clause, echoing with "虽然" in the first clause. Sometimes "虽然" can be omitted.

dànshì 但是 →P42"不过"、P89"但"、P273"可是"、P388"然而"

用法 Usage:

连词 conj.

表示转折关系，多连接分句或句子，有时也连接短语或段落。It shows a transition. It mainly connects clauses or sentences, and sometimes it also connects phrases or paragraphs.

1. 所连接的上下文意思互相排斥，"但是"所在的句子不是顺着上文的意思往下说，而是作了转折，引出跟上文相反或相对的意思，强调肯定的意思在"但是"所在的句子。Clauses connected by "但是" are mutually exclusive. "但是" is used to introduce a transition, indeed, a contrast, to the preceding clause and emphasize what is affirmed in the following clause.

（1）他学了两年英语，但是一句英语也不会说。

（2）我很喜欢中国古代白话文学，但是不懂古汉语。

2. "但是"前面有"虽然、尽管、固然"等表示让步的词语与之呼应，先认可上文所说的意思，然后在下文里说意思相反、相对或补充说明的另一层意思。"但是"连接的是分句。When "但是" is used together with a concessive conjunction, such as "虽然，尽管，固然，" it affirms what has been said and then puts forward an opposite with a relative or supplementary meaning. In this case, "但是" again joins clauses.

（3）我虽然认识他，但是叫不出他的名字。

（4）我尽管很想去北京、西安旅游，但是没有时间，也没有钱。

3. "但是"连接的上下文不是互相排斥的，而是在语气上转折，引起下文对上文作限制性或补充性的说明。在这种用法中，"但是"表示的转折程度比较轻，有时相当于"可是、不过"，甚至相当于"只是"。Clauses connected by "但是" are not mutually exclusive, but its use indicates a turn in the tone, and makes a restrictive or supplementary explanation. "但是" in this usage represents a small transition; its use is close to that of "可是，""不过，" or even "只是."

（5）她心里有话，但是又不好意思说出来。

（6）中国的经济有了很大发展，但是还比不上发达国家。

（7）他的汉语水平提高了，但是提高得不快。

说明 Notes:

1. 使用"但是"要注意：Pay attention to the following points when using "但是"：

① "但是"后面常与"却、也、还、仍然"等词语连用。"但是" is often followed by words such as "却，也，还，仍然."

（8）他要坐船，但是却不肯买船票。

（9）雨越下越大，但是他仍然坐在院子里，不肯进屋。

② "但是"与"虽然、尽管、固然"相呼应使用时，"但是"连接的是分句，如例（3）（4）。没有"虽然、尽管、固然"相呼应使用时，"但是"连接的是句子或段落。When "但是" goes with "虽然，""尽管，" or "固然，" it connects clauses as in （3） and （4）. It connects sentences or paragraphs when words like "虽然，""尽管，"

and "固然" are not used.

（10）这里还有一个展览馆可以参观，但是参观的时间只有半个小时了。

2."但是"跟"但"的意义和用法基本相同。它们的区别是："但是" and "但" have basically the same meanings and uses. Their differences are as follows:

① 在句子中，"但是"后面可以停顿，"但"后面一般不能停顿。*In a sentence, there might be a pause marked by a comma after "但是," but generally it is incorrect to pause after "但."*

（11）我们的要求已经说了，但还没有人答复我们。

（12）我们的要求已经说了，但是，还没有人答复我们。

② "但"还有副词用法，表示"只、只是、仅仅、仅"的意思。"但是"没有这个用法。*"但" can also be used as an adverbial, indicating "只，只是，仅仅，仅，" yet "但是" does not have this usage.*

3."但是"和"不过"的区别是：*The differences between "但是" and "不过" are as follows:*

① "不过"的转折程度，在一般情况下，都比"但是"轻，而且带有委婉语气。有时只表示说明、补充的意思，因此一般不能与"但是"替换。*Usually, "不过" indicates a smaller turn than "但是." Moreover, it often carries a euphemistic tone in making a supplementary statement. Therefore, "不过" often cannot be used to replace "但是."*

（13）我从来没有去过那座大山，不过听老一辈的人说，那座大山里有野人。

（14）＊我从来没有去过那座大山，但是听老一辈的人说，那座大山里有野人。

② "但是"多用于书面语。"不过"通用于口语和书面语。*"但是" mostly appears in written Chinese while "不过" is used in both oral and written Chinese.*

③ "但是"除了可以连接分句、句子和段落外，也可以连接短语或词。"不过"只连接分句、句子或段落。*In addition to linking clauses, sentences and paragraphs, "但是" can also be used to join words or phrases. "不过," by contrast, only joins clauses, sentences, or paragraphs.*

④ "不过"的第一义项中关于"补充"的用法，"但是"没有。*In its first meaning, "不过" may be used as a supplement. "但是" cannot be used in this way.*

dāng 当 →P622"在"

用法 Usage:

介词 prep.

1.表示事情发生的时间。一般有以下三种句型：*It indicates that something happens at a certain time, and basically there are three structures as follows:*

①"当"＋主谓词组/动词＋的时候/时。多用在主语前，有停顿。前面可以加"正"，

表示事情正在发生。*"当"＋subject-predicate word group/verb＋"的时候/时." In this structure, "当" appears before the subject, with a pause, and "正" can precede it, indicating something is happening.*

（1）当我第一次看到他时，他在上课。

（2）正当我要出门的时候，电话铃响了。

②"当"＋主谓词组/动词＋指示代词＋数量词＋时间名词。表示后一件事发生的时间背景。*"当"＋subject-predicate word group/verb＋demonstrative pronoun＋quantifier＋time noun. This structure is used to indicate the time background when the following event happens.*

（3）当你去云南旅游的这两个星期，我也去了广州和香港。

（4）当他回国的那天上午，我们在留学生楼门口进行了告别。

③"当"＋主谓词组/动词＋以前（或之

前)/以后(或之后),表示一件事发生在另一件事之前或之后。"当"+ subject-predicate word group/verb+"以前(or 之前)"/"以后(or 之后)." In this structure, one event happens before or after another event.

(5) 当他来中国之前,他已经学了半年汉语了。

(6) 当暑假开始以后,她就回国了。

2. 表示事情发生的处所。有以下几种用法: It indicates that something happens at a certain place. The usages are as follows:

① 与少数单音节名词组成介宾短语,表示事情或行动发生的方位、处所等意为"面对着、向着"。如:"当场表演、当众批评、当场昏倒"等。It forms preposition-object phrases with a few monosyllabic nouns, indicating the direction or place of an event or an action. It means "面对着" or "向着," such as "当场表演,当众批评,当场昏倒."

② 当(着)+名词或名词词组+面。表示面对面。"当"后面可以加"着",加"着"后,可以省略"面",但"当着"后面一般不能跟单音节词。"面"前面可以加修饰语。"当(着)"+noun/noun phrase + "面" means " in somebody's presence." When "当" is followed by "着," the following "面" can be omitted, but "当着" cannot be followed by monosyllabic words. Besides, there may be a modifier preceding "面."

(7) 我要当着大家(的面)把这件事说清楚。

(8) 这是三千元钱,请你当面点清。

动词 v.

1. 担任,充当。可重叠,常做谓语。To work as; to serve as. "当" can be used in a reduplicated form as "当当," and it is often used as a predicate.

(9) 她那么相信你,你就当当她的老师吧。

(10) 你这个哥哥当得不错。

2. 承当,承受。常做谓语。To deserve; to bear (often used as a predicate).

(11) 你把我说得那么好,我可当不起。

(12) "最好的学生",这个称号你当得起。

3. 掌管,主持。可重叠,多做谓语,常以"当家"的形式出现。To be in charge. As a predicate, "当" can be used in a reduplicated form as "当当" and it often appears as "当家."

(13) 你来当当这个家,看你怎么当。

(14) 我们这个大家庭,都是刚进门的新媳妇当家的。

助动词 aux. v.

应当,应该。Should; ought to.

(15) 我的孩子你当批评就批评,不用客气。

(16) 当奖就奖,当罚就罚。这个老师在学习上奖罚分明。

说明 Notes:

1. "当"作为介词用,学习时要注意: When "当" is a preposition, pay attention to the following points:

① "当"组成的介词短语一般用在句首或动词前作状语。A preposition-object phrase formed by "当" often appears at the beginning of a sentence or precedes a verb, serving as an adverbial.

② 用"当……时/的时候"表示时间,必定是在"当"分句内特有的某事情的发生,而叙述中一般时间的表达,只要直接将时间说出或者用"在"就可以。"当…时/的时候" indicates the time when a specific thing happens, yet when you express a common time in narration just say the time or use "在" instead.

(17) * 当我小的时候,常常去家乡的河边玩。

(18) 我小时候常常去家乡的河边玩。

(19) * 当1964年时,我家从纽约搬到了华盛顿。

(20) (在)1964年,我家从纽约搬到了华盛顿。

③ "当"表示发生事情的某一时刻,需要同表示时间的词语"时、时候"配合着用。"当"与"时"组合,不用"的";"当"与"时候"组合,要用"的"。Indicating a certain time when something happens. "当" should be used with time words "时" or "时候." When "当" is used with "时," do not use "的"; when "当" is used with "时候," there is a "的."

(21) *当听到上课铃声,我走进了教室。
(22) 当听到上课铃声时/当听到上课铃声的时候,我走进了教室。
(23) *当我考上大学时候,朋友们都向我祝贺。
(24) 当我考上大学的时候,朋友们都向我祝贺。
(25) *当她来我房间的时,我不在房间里。
(26) 当她来我房间时,我不在房间里。

2. "当"作动词用时,要注意：When "当" is used as a verb, pay attention to the following points:

① 表示人自然发育到某个时期的时候,不能用"当"。Do not use "当" when it indicates the time when a person grows naturally.

(27) *当她小孩子的时候,父亲就去世了。
(28) 她小时候/还是孩子的时候,父亲就去世了。

② "当"不含有动作继续或延续的过程。"当" does not include the process of a continuous action.

(29) *那次一起旅游以后,他当了我的好朋友。
(30) 那次一起旅游以后,他成了我的好朋友。

dāngdì 当地

用法 Usage:

名词 n.

人物所在的或者事情发生的那个地方,本地。与"外地"相对。The place where people stay or things happen; local (opposite to "外地").

(1) 当地盛产丝绸。
(2) 他下乡后,在当地找了个爱人。
(3) 他来杭州后,没向父母要钱,而是去当地的饭馆打工。

说明 Notes:

例(1)中的"当地"指这个地方。例(2)中的"当地"指"下乡的地方"。例(3)中的"当地"指"杭州"。所以,"当地"的确切语义,要根据具体的句子中的语境条件才能最后确定。"当地" in (1) refers to this place; "当地" in (2) refers to "下乡的地方"; "当地" in (3) refers to "杭州." Therefore, the exact meaning of "当地" is based on the context in which it appears.

dāngnián 当年

用法 Usage:

名词 n.

1. 指过去的某一时间,往往与"现在、如今"比较。It refers to a certain time in the past, often contrasting with "现在" and "如今."

(1) 想当年,我还是学校足球队的主要队员呢。
(2) 当年的小娃娃,如今已经长成了一个大姑娘了。

2. 指身体强壮、精力充沛的时期。做谓语、宾语。It refers to someone who is in the prime of life, often used as a predicate or an object.

(3) 他现在正当年,什么苦都能吃。
(4) 你们正在当年,这会儿不努力,什么时候努力呢?

说明 Notes:

1. "当年"表示"过去某一时间"的义项时,是时间名词,不受定语的修饰,做定语时,一般都带"的",如例(2)。In the first usage, "当年" is a noun for time, which cannot be modified by an attribute. When it serves as an attribute, it is often used with "的" as in (2).

2. "当年"表示"身强力壮时期"的义项时,一般要与"正"配合使用,使用面比较窄。如例(3)和(4)。In the second usage, "当年" is mainly used with "正" as in (3) and (4), but

this use is rather narrow in scope.

3. 当年（dàngnián），指事情发生的同一年。句中没有"现在、如今"等时间词语表示对比。"当年（dàngnián）" refers to something that happens in the same year. Words such as "现在" and "如今" are not used to make a comparison.

（5）这是年度电影票，当年就要用掉。

（6）那是当年的葡萄酒，很新鲜。

dāngqián 当前

用法 Usage：

名词 n.

现阶段，目前。Present; currentness.

（1）当前正是教育改革时期。

（2）一个人以后怎么发展，首先要看当前。

（3）当前的经济形势发展得很快。

动词 v.

表示在面前的意思。使用范围非常狭小，只能作"大敌、一事"等少数几个名词的谓语，形成比较固定的词组，书面色彩较浓。不能带宾语、补语。不能带"着、了、过"。It means "when facing something." Its scope of use is very narrow: Only a few nouns can go with it such as "大敌" and "一事." They form set phrases and often appear in the written language. They cannot be followed by an object or a complement, nor can they be followed by "着," "了," or "过."

（4）她这个人，一事当前，首先想到的是别人的利益。

说明 Notes：

"当前"作名词用时，不能受数量词、形容词的修饰。When "当前" is used as a noun, it cannot be modified by a quantifier or adjective.

dāngrán 当然 →P693"自然"

用法 Usage：

形容词 a.

应当如此。Sure.

（1）朋友之间有困难，相互帮助是当然的。

（2）我的病好了，多亏医生护士的治疗和护理，受到我全家人的谢意，理所当然。

副词 ad.

表示合乎事理和情理，没有疑问。Surely; of course. It means "it's rational," "it's reasonable," or "there is no doubt about it."

（3）他为群众着想，群众当然支持他。

（4）他爱她，她当然也爱他。

说明 Notes：

1. "当然"作形容词用时，前面不能再加"很、太"等程度副词。When "当然" is used as an adjective, it must not be preceded by degree adverbs such as "很，太."

2. "当然"可以单用或单独回答问题，常用于口语。"当然" can be used by itself or in answering a question. This use is common in oral Chinese.

（5）A：你明天一定会去祝贺他的生日吧？
　　B：当然！

（6）当然，我一定要去的。

dàng 当

用法 Usage：

动词 v.

1. 抵得上，等于。To match; to be equal to.

（1）他的劲儿大，干起活来一个人当两个人。

（2）他十元钱当两元用，一点不节约。

2. 作为，以为，认为。To regard as; to treat as; to think.

（3）昨天晚上你去跳舞了，你当我不知道？

（4）中国妈妈把我当女儿一样对待。

3. 表示在事情发生的时间。如："当天、当月、当年"。To indicate the time when something happens, such as "当天，当月，当年."

4. 抵押；用物品作为抵押品，向当铺借钱。To pawn (leaving an object to a pawnbroker in order to borrow money).

（5）这些东西现在不用，当了吧！

（6）家里没什么值钱的东西可以当。

名词 *n.*

表示欺骗人、作弄人的圈套。*A trap to deceive somebody or make a fool of somebody.*

(7) 在夜市上买东西很容易上当。

说明 Notes:

"当"做动词时要注意：*When* "当" *is used as a verb, pay attention to the following points:*

1. 词义是"等于、抵得上"时，句子中的主语和宾语都不能缺少。*When* "当" *means* "等于(match)" *and* "抵得上(be equal to)," *both the subject and the object are indispensable in a sentence.*

2. 词义是"当作、算作"时，必须带宾语。*When* "当" *means* "当作" *and* "算作," *an object is indispensable.*

3. 词义是"以为、认为"时，句子必须有主语，有"当"的分句后面常跟一个表示转折语义的分句。如例(3)。*When* "当" *means* "以为" *and* "认为," *a subject is indispensable. The clause following* "当" *often indicates a transition in meaning, as in (3).*

dàngzuò 当作

用法 Usage:

动词 *v.*

认为(是)，作为，看成。做谓语，必带名词宾语。有时可带"了"。不能带补语。常用于"把"字句或"被"字句。*To regard as; to treat as; to look upon as. It is used as a predicate and followed by a noun as its object. Sometimes there is a* "了" *following it. It cannot be followed by a complement, however. It is often used in sentences with* "把" *or* "被."

(1) 他把学校当作了自己的家。

(2) 这支笔被当作一件珍贵的礼物送到了我的手里。

(3) 不要把老师的批评当作耳旁风。

说明 Notes:

1. "当作"也常作为"当成"。"当作" *is commonly used as* "当成."

2. "当"与"当作"很容易误用，需注意。"当" *and* "当作" *are often misused. Therefore, be careful.*

① "当作"的词意是"看成"时，有的句子中"当作"可以替换为"当"。"当"与宾语组合后，一般都作为状语修饰后面的谓语动词。所以后面还应该有动词，否则句子语义显得不完整。如：例(5)很容易写成例(4)。*When* "当作" *means* "看成," "当作" *can be substituted by* "当" *in some sentences. The structure* "当＋object" *serves as an adverbial to modify the following predicate, so there should be a verb following, otherwise the meaning of the sentence is incomplete. For example, (5) is likely to be written as (4).*

(4) *他一直把我当亲儿子。

(5) 他一直把我当亲儿子对待。

(6) *他三步当两步，很快就到了家。

(7) 他三步当两步走，很快就到了家。

② "当作"词义为"作为"时，不可替换为"当"。如：例(2)不能写成例(8)。*When* "当作" *means* "作为," *it cannot be substituted by* "当." *For example, (2) cannot be written as (8).*

(8) *这支笔被当一件珍贵的礼物送到了我的手里。

③ "当"表示"充当，担任……工作"的意思时，宾语常常是表示人的名词，不能用"当作"。*When* "当" *indicates* "充当" *and* "担任...工作," *the object is often a person or a group of people. In this meaning,* "当" *cannot be substituted by* "当作."

(9) *他愿意当作我的汉语辅导老师。

(10) 他愿意当我的汉语辅导老师。

④ "当"表示加入某种工作、活动时，宾语常常是表示人的名词，不能用"当作"。*When* "当" *means to take part in a job or an activity, the following object is often a person or a group of people. The use of* "当作" *in this meaning is incorrect.*

(11) *你同意我当作体育老师吗？

(12) 你同意我做/当体育老师吗？

dǎo 倒

用法 Usage:

动词 v.

1. 人或竖立的东西横躺下来。(Of a person or an erect thing) to fall over.

① 做谓语,宾语常为施事宾语。Used as a predicate, when the object is usually an agentive object.

(1) 那边倒了两间房。
(2) 他进屋就倒在床上。

② 做补语。Used as a complement.

(3) 路上太滑,好几个人都摔倒在地上。
(4) 太累了,他病倒在工作岗位上。

2. 表示转移,转换,腾挪。可重叠,常作谓语。多用于口语。To change; to shift; to move around. It can be used as a disyllable word "倒倒." It is often used as a predicate, especially in spoken language.

(5) 到那里得倒两趟车呢。
(6) 地方太小,倒不开身。
(7) 那个醉汉歪歪倒倒地沿街走去。

dào 到

用法 Usage:

动词 v.

1. 表示到达,达到的意思。可带表示处所或数量的宾语。To arrive; to reach. It can be followed by an object indicating a place or an amount.

(1) 我妈妈今天到上海。
(2) 这小孩儿还不到五岁。

2. 去,往的意思。后面一定要带表示处所的宾语。宾语后面还可以加上"来、去",表示朝着说话人所在地来,或者离开说话人所在地。To go to; to leave for. It must be followed by an object showing a place and the object can take words like "来" or "去" to indicate the direction of the movement. "来" means coming to the place where the speaker is, and "去" indicates going away from the speaker.

(3) 他们要到上海旅游。
(4) 你到那儿去,他到这儿来。

3. 用在动词后面作补语,表示动作达到了目的或有了结果。可以在动词与"到"之间插入"得/不",表示可能性。句式为:动+到+名(受事)。Following a verb, it is used as a complement to indicate the goal or the result of an action. "得/不" can be inserted between the verb and "到" to show possibility. The structure is "v.+到+n. (the object of an action)."

(5) 我今天收到了朋友给我的信。
(6) 你要说到做到,不要说到做不到。
(7) 我说的话你听得到吗?

4. 用在动词后面,表示人或事物随动作到达某地。宾语后面还可以加"来、去",表示动作是朝说话人所在地来,还是离说话人所在地去。句式为:动+到+名(处所)。Following a verb, it indicates somebody or something reaches a certain place along with an action. There can be "来" or "去" after the object to show the direction towards or away from the speaker. The structure is "v.+到+n. (a certain place)."

(8) 他把她送到火车站去了。
(9) 她三十分钟赶得到飞机场来吗?

5. 用在动词后面,表示动作继续到什么时间。句式为:动+到+名(时间)。Following a verb, it indicates that an action continues to a certain time. The structure is "v.+到+n. (time)."

(10) 我在中国要学到明年九月。
(11) 今天的雨下到下午四点才停。

6. 用在动词、形容词后面,表示动作或性质状态达到某种程度。名词多为数量短语或者表示程度的词语。在肯定句中,前面常有"已经"与之配合。句式为:动/形+到+名/表示程度的词语或短语。Following a verb or an adjective, it indicates an action or state

reaching a certain degree. The noun is mostly a quantitative phrase or a word showing a degree. In an affirmative sentence, "到" is often used together with a preceding "已经." The structure is " v./a. ＋到＋n./word or phrase showing degree."

(12) 这里的夏天能热到摄氏三十八度。

(13) 她的病情已经发展到很严重的地步了。

(14) 他的汉字已经写到每分钟二十个的水平了。

7. 用在形容词后面,表示状态达到的程度。"到"的作用相当于引进情态结果补语的结构助词"得"。多数"到"都可以改用"得"。句式为:形 ＋ 到 ＋ 短语/小句。*Following an adjective, it indicates that a state reaches a certain degree. In this case, "到" functions as the structural auxiliary word "得," which introduces a modal complement of result. Most "到" can be changed to "得." The structure is "a. ＋到＋phrase/clause."*

(15) 录音机的声音高到不能再高了。

(16) 老师的字写得很小,小到坐在前面的同学也看不清楚。

说明 Notes:

注意用法1和用法4有所不同。用法1,句子中"到"前面没有其他动词。用法4,句子中"到"前面有其他动词,"到"是这个动词的补语。*Usage 1 is different from Usage 4. In Usage 1, there is not a verb preceding "到" while in Usage 4, there is another verb preceding "到," in which case "到" is a complement of the other verb.*

dàodá 到达 →P79"达到"

用法 Usage:

动词 *v.*

抵达,到了(某一地点、某一阶段)。*To arrive; to get to (a certain place or stage).*

(1) 下午三点,火车到达了北京。

(2) 人类到达信息化时代后,生活发生了很大变化。

说明 Notes:

"到达"和"达到"的区别是:*Here are the differences between "到达" and "达到":*

1. 词义稍有侧重。"到达"侧重陈述已有的客观情况,"达到"蕴含着某种选择的目标,是经过一定的努力才达到的事实。*"到达" focuses on expressing the existing and objective condition, while "达到" indicates a certain goal set some time ago has been achieved through efforts.*

2. 词语搭配有所侧重。"达到"多与表示抽象事物或程度的名词搭配;"到达"多与表示处所、地点的词语搭配。*"达到" often collocates with words indicating an abstract object or a degree; while "到达" often collocates with words indicating a place.*

(3) 经过努力,我们达到了目的。

(4) 经过努力,我们到达了目的地。

dàodǐ 到底 →P28"毕竟"、P248"究竟"、P677"终于"

用法 Usage:

副词 *ad.*

1. 用于疑问句中(常用于选择问句),表示进一步追究的语气,相当于"究竟"。位置通常在动词或形容词前。主语如果由疑问代词充当,"到底"只能用在主语之前,做状语。*It is used in interrogative sentences, especially in alternative questions, to pursue an answer to a question. In this meaning, it is equals to "究竟." It is usually put before a verb or an adjective. If an interrogative pronoun serves as the subject, "到底" must be used before the subject, serving as an adverbial.*

(1) 你明天到底去不去上课?

(2) 到底哪里是我的宿舍楼?

2. 用于陈述句,表示经过一定的时间或过程,最后出现某种结果,相当于"终于、最终"。

出现在动词、形容词前,受它修饰的动词或形容词常常带"了"或其他表示完成的词语。It is used in declarative sentences to indicate that a certain result is reached through a period of time or process. In this meaning, it is equal to "终于" or "最终." When it appears before a verb or an adjective, the verb or the adjective is often followed by "了" or some other word showing completion.

(3) 研究了几天几夜,问题到底解决了。

(4) 在医生和护士的抢救下,小王到底活过来了。

3. 用陈述句,表示强调事物本质、某种原因、特点不因其他因素而改变,或对某一状况的肯定,相当于"毕竟"。可用在动词、形容词或主语前,作状语。"到底"前后的词或词语可以重复,构成"……到底是……"的格式,表示强调。It is used in declarative sentences to indicate an emphasis on the essence of things, reasons, changeless features or certainty of a condition. In this meaning, it is equal to "毕竟." It can appear before a verb, an adjective or a subject as an adverbial. The words before and after "到底" may be the same, forming the structure "...到底是..." for emphasis.

(5) 他到底是专家,一下子就把机器修好了。

(6) 到底是玻璃做的,一打就碎了。

(7) 飞机到底是飞机,上午在北京,下午就到海南了。

动词 v.

短语词。表示到尽头,到终点的意思。可带动态助词"了"。It is a phrasal word which means "to the end," and can be followed by the auxiliary word "了."

1. 做谓语,不带宾语。Used as a predicate, without an object.

(8) 这条路已经到底了。

(9) 这辆公共汽车坐到底,那儿就是图书馆。

2. 做补语。用在动词后面,不用"得"。Used as a complement following a verb. It cannot be used with "得."

(10) 你一定要坚持到底,我也陪你到底。

(11) 这个学期我学到底,下个学期我不学了。

说明 Notes:

"毕竟"和"到底"的区别是:The differences between "毕竟" and "到底" are as follows:

1. "毕竟"和"到底"都可以表示强调事物的本质或特点,但是"毕竟"表示的程度比"到底"高,而忽略其他方面消极的因素。Both can be used to emphasize the essence or characteristics of a thing, but "毕竟" indicates a higher degree, ignoring the negative factors in other fields.

2. "到底"能用于疑问句,表示追究。"毕竟"没有这个用法。"到底" can be used by a superior to pursue a question. "毕竟" cannot be used in this way.

3. "毕竟"多用于书面语。"到底"多用于口语。"毕竟" appears more in written Chinese while "到底" appears more in oral Chinese.

dào 倒 →P385 "却"

用法 Usage:

动词 v.

1. 反转或倾斜容器,使里面的东西出来,倾倒。它的搭配对象可以是具体事物,也可以是抽象事物。可用于"把"字句和"被"字句中。To reverse or tilt a container to make the substance inside flow out. It can collocate with both concrete and abstract objects. It can be used in structures beginning with "把" or "被."

① 做谓语,可带宾语、补语。When used as a predicate, it can be followed by an object or a complement.

(1) 你把冷水倒了吧,我给你倒热水。

(2) 把心里的难受和不满全都倒出来吧!

② 做定语,要带"的"。When used as an attribute, it is followed by the word "的."

(3) 在大城市里,每天人们倒的垃圾无法计算。

倒 dào

(4) 倒的时候要把包里的东西都倒干净！

2. 向相反的方向移动，后退。常与表示车辆、时间意义的词语搭配，可重叠，常做谓语，可带宾语、补语。*To move towards the opposite direction; move backwards. It often collocates with words indicating vehicles or time; it may be used in a reduplicated form as "倒倒." Also it often serves as a predicate followed by an object or a complement.*

(5) 把车倒到车库里。

(6) 真希望我的年纪能倒回去三十年。

3. 上下或前后的位置、顺序颠倒。*To turn upside down; to reverse.*

① 做谓语，常带趋向补语。*When used as a predicate, it is often followed by a directional complement.*

(7) 小心！啤酒箱不能倒过来。

(8) 这张照片倒过来看，很有意思。

② 做补语。*Used as a complement.*

(9) 他很激动，把照片也拿倒了。

(10) 信封上收信人和寄信人的地址写倒了。

③ 做状语。*Used as an adverbial.*

(11) 他是倒数第一名。

(12) 这个字左右两个部分写倒了。

副词 *ad.*

1. 表示跟一般情理相反，或跟意料的情况相反，常与"反"连用。相反的意思较明显时，可以换用"反而"。用在动词、形容词前面，做状语。*Contrary to common sense or expectations. It is often used together with "反." If the contrary meaning is obvious, "反" can be replaced by "反而." Also it is placed before a verb or an adjective to serve as an adverbial.*

(13) 吃了药不但没好，咳嗽反倒更厉害了。

(14) 衣服旧了一些，洗得倒很干净。

2. 表示事实不是那样，有责怪的意思和反说的语气。通常用在主语是第二、第三人称的句子里，做状语。动词限于"说、想、看"等，形容词限于"容易、简单、轻巧、好、美"等。*Contrary to the fact. Implying blame or irony, it often appears in sentences with a second-person or third-person subject, serving as an adverbial; verbs are limited to words such as "说," "想," "看," and adjectives are limited to words such as "容易,简单,好,轻巧, etc."*

(15) 你说得倒轻巧，要不你来试试。

(16) 他想得倒美，哪有这么好的事？

3. 表示催促或追问，含有祈使或不耐烦的语气。用在动词性词语前作状语。*Used when one urges someone to do something or inquires about something. It is spoken in an imperative or impatient tone. It appears before a verbal phrase to be an adverbial.*

(17) 你倒说句话呀！你不说，我们怎么知道？

(18) 你倒去不去啊？

4. 用在复句中。*Used in compound sentences.*

① 表示转折。前一分句可用"虽、虽然"，"倒"后用表示积极意义的词语。*Indicating a transition. The first clause may contain the word "虽" or "虽然," while in the second clause, words with a positive meaning are used after "倒."*

(19) 她的房间不大，布置倒很讲究。

(20) 文章写得不长，词语倒用得很正确。

② 表示让步。"倒"在前一分句做状语，后一分句中常有"可是、但是、不过、就是"等词呼应。*Indicating concession. "倒" is an adverbial in the first clause, and there is often a word like "可是," "但是," "不过," or "就是" in the second clause.*

(21) 这件衣服好倒好，就是太贵了。

(22) 她倒很想做这个翻译，但是她的汉语水平还不太高。

5. 用在谓语前面表示舒缓语气。*Used before a predicate to soften the tone.*

① 用在肯定句中，后面常用表示积极意义词语。*When it is used in a declarative sentence, it is often followed by words with a* positive meaning.

(23) 一个人住倒也挺自由自在。

(24) 退休了,钓钓鱼,打打拳,倒很轻松。

② 在否定句,若"倒"用在后一分句,则前一分句常为一个疑问句。若"倒"用在前一分句,则后一分句中常有"只是"等词语呼应。多用作状语。In a negative sentence, if "倒" appears in the latter clause, then the previous clause is interrogative; if "倒" appears in the previous clause, then there is a word like "只是" in the latter clause. "倒" is mostly used as an adverbial in both cases.

(25) 你说她不会来?这倒不一定。

(26) 我倒不反对你去旅游,只是你的课怎么办?

说明 Notes:

副词"倒",也可说成"倒是"。副词"倒是"用在动词前面,中间不能插入其他成分,不能分开用,要与副词"倒"与由"是"组成的动词短语合用区别开来。The adverb "倒" can also be "倒是." When the adverb "倒是" appears before a verb, other words cannot be inserted between "倒" and "是." The adverb "倒是" differs from the verbal phrase formed by adverb "倒" and "是."

(27) 这儿倒还是个好地方。("倒"与"是"的短语合用 The verbal phrase formed by "倒" and "是")

(28) 她倒是想去,可是没有时间。

dàolǐ 道理 →P296"理由"

用法 Usage:

名词 n.

1. 表示事情、论点是非得失的根据,理由,情理。常与"有、讲、懂、明白、清楚"等动词搭配使用,可受"大、小"等形容词的修饰。Reason; argument. It often collocates with verbs such as "有、讲、懂、明白、清楚," and can be modified by adjectives such as "大" or "小."

① 做主语。一般不单独做主语,常有定语"的"修饰。Used as a subject (often with an attribute "的" to modify).

(1) 为什么要努力学习的道理谁都明白。

(2) 你所说的道理我也知道。

② 做宾语。可以单用,一般不用定语修饰。Used as an object. It may be used alone, without an attribute.

(3) 父母给我讲了很多道理,可我一点也听不进。

(4) 他那么做,当然有道理。

2. 指事物的规律、正确的事理。句中常带上定语做主语、宾语。Law; principle. It is often modified by an attribute, and together they serve as the subject or object in a sentence.

(5) 水为什么能结冰的道理你懂吗?

(6) 他从这次比赛失败中懂得了很多道理。

dàoqiàn 道歉 →P16"抱歉"

用法 Usage:

动词 v.

"道歉"是离合动词,表示致以歉意,认错。To apologize (a separable verb).

(1) 那件事我错了,我向你道歉。

(2) 他已经诚恳地道过歉,你别说他了。

说明 Notes:

"抱歉"与"道歉"的区别是: There are differences between "抱歉" and "道歉:"

1. "抱歉"是形容词,形容觉得对不起别人、心里不安的意思。"道歉"是离合动词,指因自己的过失而向别人承认错误,表示歉意的行为。"抱歉" is an adjective; it means acknowledging a debt of apology to somebody. "道歉" is a separable verb, making an apology to somebody for a mistake.

(3) 给你添麻烦了,我很抱歉。

2. "抱歉"常做谓语或状语。"道歉"是离合词,常做谓语,后面不能再带宾语,其道歉语义的对象,常常由介词"向、对"等引出,且因是离合词,可以插入其他词语。"抱歉" is often used as a predicate or an adverbial. "道歉," a separable verb, is often used as a predicate, which cannot be followed by an object. Prepositions such as "向" and "对" are often used to introduce the object to whom somebody apologizes. Since "道歉" is a separable verb, other words can be inserted between "道" and "歉."

(4) 他已经向你道了三次歉了,你就原谅他吧。

dé 得

用法 Usage:

动词 *v.*

1. 表示得到、获得,与"失"相对。*To get; to obtain (the opposite of "失").*

(1) 这次比赛,我得了第一名。

(2) 我们班有三个同学得了奖学金。

2. "得"常用在口语中表示完成、同意或禁止、无可奈何等意思。*To be ready; to approve or prohibit; to show helplessness. It is often used in spoken language.*

(3) 饭菜一会儿就得,大家先喝茶吧。(表示完成 *To be ready*)

(4) 得了,你不必说了。(表示禁止 *To prohibit*)

(5) 得,就按照你的方法做。(表示同意 *To approve*)

(6) 得,一件衣服就这样被你搞丢了。(表示无可奈何 *To show helplessness*)

3. 用在动词前,表示许可、可以(多用于法令和公文)。*To permit. It often appears in legal or official documents.*

(7) 参加艺术团的同学得在今天下午报名。

(8) 阅览室的杂志不得带出室外。

4. 计数得到结果。*(Of a calculation) to result in.*

(9) 二二得四,三三得九。

(10) 七减五得二。

5. 表示适合。*To suit.*

(11) 这件衣服,你穿很得体。

(12) 她教我的方法很得用。

déle 得了 →P441"算了"

用法 Usage:

动词 *v.*

"得了"是动补结构。常用于口语。*It appears in the verb-complement structure, especially in spoken language.*

1. 做句中的独立成分。在口语中用于结束谈话的时候,表示禁止或同意,算了,行了。*That's enough. As an absolute construction, it appears at the end of a conversation to express approval or prohibition.*

(1) 得了,就这么办吧。

(2) 得了,别再说了。

2. 做助词,用于陈述句,表示肯定的语气。常用于动词后面,用于句末。*As an auxiliary in declarative sentences to indicate affirmation, it often appears after a verb at the end of a sentence.*

(3) 干脆扔了得了。

(4) 还是去得了,别再犹豫了。

3. 做谓语。在口语中,常为"(你)得了吧"的形式,表示不满或否定。*As a predicate, it often appears in "(你)得了吧" to indicate dissatisfaction or disapproval.*

(5) 你得了吧,走开!越帮越忙。

(6) (你们)得了吧,想出的办法那么复杂。

déyì 得意

用法 Usage:

形容词 *a.*

表示称心如意,在大多数情况下,指因成功而沾沾自喜、骄傲自满的意思。可做定语(常带"的")、状语(要带"地")、谓语(可带补语)等。*Being proud. It indicates that somebody is pleased or conceited with his own success or achievement. It can be used as an attribute (often with "的"), an adverbial (often with "地") or a predicate (followed by a complement).*

(1) 看他那得意的神情,我真想打他一拳。

(2) 他觉得自己的文章很不错,便暗暗得意起来。

(3) 他得意地欣赏着自己的作品。

说明 Notes:

1. "得意"能构成固定词组,如"自鸣得意、洋洋得意、得意洋洋、得意忘形"等。"得意" can form set phrases such as "自鸣得意,洋洋得意,得意洋洋,得意忘形."

2. "得意"是形容词,做谓语时,不能带宾语,只能带补语。"得意" is an adjective. When it is used as a predicate, it can only be followed by a complement instead of an object.

(4) *他今天得意考试了第一名。

(5) 因为考了第一名,他得意得一连喝了两瓶啤酒。

de 地 →P103"的"

用法 Usage:

助词 aux.

用在动词或形容词前面,表示它前面的词或词组是状语,"地"是状语的标志,用在谓语前面。Preceding a verb or an adjective, "地," which is a sign for an adverbial, indicates that the word or phrase before it is an adverbial, and is used before a predicate.

(1) 他笑嘻嘻地跑进来。

(2) 有个东西"嘭"地从上面掉了下来。

说明 Notes:

状语后面带不带"地",情况比较复杂,大致的规律如下:Complicated as it is, there are some general principles of whether "地" is used after an adverbial:

1. 要用"地"。When "地" is used.

① 双音节形容词做状语一般要用"地",但跟动词经常组合的,可用可不用。Usually there is a "地" when a disyllabic adjective serves as an adverbial. When it is used together with another verb, "地" is optional.

(3) 那个中国大学生友好地告诉我留学生楼怎么走。

(4) 我们在农村详细(地)调查了留守儿童的现状。

(5) 老师要求我们认真(地)讨论。

② 如果形容词前有程度副词,做状语要用"地",但个别单音节形容词例外。If there is a degree adverb preceding an adjective, there must be a "地." A few monosyllabic adjectives are exceptions to this rule.

(6) 妈妈非常热情地招待了我的同学。

(7) 他的困难很快(地)就解决了。

③ 名词、单音节拟声词、各种词组做状语时,一般要带"地",如例(2)(6)。When nouns, monosyllabic onomatopoetic words or phrases are adverbials, generally there is a "地," as in (2) and (6).

2. 可用可不用"地"。When "地" is optional.

① 形容词重叠式做状语时,"地"可用可不用。"地" is optional when disyllabic adjectives are adverbials.

(8) 你要好好(地)工作。

(9) 他高高兴兴(地)在我家玩儿了一天。

② 数量词名词短语的重叠式和少数几个动词做动词、形容词的状语时,"地"字可用可不用。"地" is optional when noun phrases formed by reduplicated quantifiers and a few verbs are used as adverbials modifying a verb or adjective.

(10) 他一个字一个字(地)写,写得很认真。

(11) 三天以后,他胜利(地)完成了任务。

③ 四字词语或其他词语做动词、形容词的状语时,"地"可用可不用。动词、形容词后面不带别的词语时,一般都可不用。"地" is optional when four-character idioms or other words function as adverbials modifying a verb or adjective. "地" is often omitted when verbs and adjectives are not followed by any other words.

(12) 她自言自语(地)说：这点困难我不怕。
(13) 风一吹，树叶就哗啦啦(地)响了。

3. 以下情况一般不用"地"："地" is generally not used in the following cases:

① 当单音节形容词做动词的状语时。When monosyllabic adjectives are adverbials modifying a verb.

(14) 这幅画近看就看出问题来了。
(15) 老人平躺在床上，一动也不动。

② 当副词做动词、形容词的状语时。When adverbs are adverbials modifying a verb or adjective.

(16) 长城确实非常(地)雄伟。
(17) 她渐渐(地)走远了。

de 的 →P102"地"、P106"得"、P654"之"

用法 Usage:

助词 aux.

一、"的"做结构助词，表示它前面的词语是定语。As a structural auxiliary word, "的" is used to indicate that the word preceding it is an attribute.

1. 附在前面的词或词语后面，一起充当中心语的定语，起修饰或限制的作用。"的"后面是代词或名词、名词性短语，"的"是定语的标志。Used after a word or phrase to form an attribute, modifying or limiting the head word. "的" is a sign of an attribute, and it is followed by a pronoun, noun, or nominal phrase.

① 表示定语与中心语之间是修饰或限制关系。Indicating a modifying or modified relationship between an attribute and a head phrase.

(1) 蓝蓝的天上飘着白云。
(2) 他们过着幸福的生活。

② 表示定语与中心语之间是领属关系。名词做定语表示领属关系时，后面要加结构助词"的"；人称代词做定语，而中心语是亲属称谓或表示集体、单位等名词时定语可以不用结构助词"的"。Indicating a possessive relationship between an attribute and a head phrase. A noun, which serves as an attribute to indicate a possessive relationship, must be followed by "的." If a personal pronoun serves as an attribute, and the head word is a kinship term or a noun for a group or an organization, "的" is optional.

(3) 小王的姐姐是电脑公司的职员。
(4) 我们(的)学校非常大。
(5) 他(的)妈妈是我阿姨。

2. "的"用在主谓短语之间，使主谓结构变成名词性偏正结构，起强调作用。Used between a subject-predicate phrase to form a nominal structure of modification, "的" is used for emphasis.

(6) 汉语水平的考试是对一个人汉语能力的测试。
(7) 她的出现使男同学的学习积极性有了很大提高。

3. "的"用在动词或动词短语后面，表示人或事物名称的作用，组成"的"字结构，相当于一个名词，"的"字结构后面虽不出现中心词，但一般可以理解。有的则需要上下文的帮助获得明确的含义。一般可以充当名词所能充当的句子成分，表示某人或某事物。Used after a verb or verb phrase to form a noun phrase without a head word, this "的" structure generally indicates somebody or something, which can function as a noun.

(8) 教室里有许多同学，有看书的，有写汉字的，还有听录音的。
(9) 家里吃的、穿的、用的，都是你爸挣来的。

4. "的"可以组成"动词＋的＋动词""形容词＋的＋形容词"的形式，表示不同的施事者发出不同的行为动作，或者不同的人或事物情况、状态的不同。Used to form the "v.＋的＋v." structure or the "a.＋的＋a." structure, indicating different actions from different doers, or different states or situations of different people

or things.

（10）在汉语晚会上，同学们说的说、唱的唱，表演得都很出色。

（11）我们包了很多汤圆，甜的甜，咸的咸，味道好极了。

5. "的"用在谓语动词后面（可以带宾语，也可以不带宾语），强调动作、行为的发出、接受，或者强调已经发生、已经完成的动作、行为的时间、地点和方式。这个用法只限于已经过去的事情。Used after the predicate verb, with or without an object, to emphasize the doing or receiving of an action, or the time, place, method of an action that has already happened or come to an end.

（12）我昨天上午去的（图书馆）。图书馆没开门。

（13）她用自己的零钱买的礼物，你收下吧。

（14）她在商店门口等的你，你没看见她吗？

6. "的"加在指人的名词或代词后面，插入某些动宾短语中，表示这些人是所说的动作、行为的接受者。Used after a noun or pronoun indicating people. It can be inserted between predicate-object phrases, meaning these people are the receivers of the action.

（15）你别开她的玩笑，她是刚来的新同学。

（16）他总说小王的错，他自己呢？

7. "的"用在跟主语相同的人称代词后面，做宾语，表示这些人跟别的事情没有关系。After a pronoun, which is the same as the subject, to serve as an object, indicating that these people have nothing to do with other things.

（17）他吃他的，我们吃我们的。

（18）你旅游你的，我们干什么，我们自己决定。

8. "的"用在两个同类的词或短语后面，表示"等等、之类"的意思。有时用"什么的"，也表示"等等、之类"的意思。Used after two words or phrases of the same kind to indicate "and so on" or "and the like"; sometimes "什么的" is used to indicate the same meaning.

（19）宿舍的墙上，照片、画儿的贴了一大片。

（20）这箱子里就是书、词典、练习本什么的，没有其他东西。

9. "的"用在首句的某些词语后面，强调原因、条件、情况、状态等。这种用法多见于口语。Used after some words which appear at the beginning of a sentence to emphasize a reason, condition, or situation. This use is common in spoken language.

（21）好好的，吃什么药？

（22）大白天的，开灯干什么？

（23）爬啊爬的，爬了两个多小时才爬到山顶。

二、"的"做语气助词，强调句子表达的语气。Used as a modal auxiliary word to emphasize the tone of a sentence.

1. "的"用在陈述句末尾，表示肯定、强调的语气。Used at the end of a declarative sentence to indicate a definite and emphatic tone.

（24）他一会儿就回来的。

（25）这件事我知道的。

2. "的"用在动词谓语的句子末尾，表示已然的语气。Used at the end of a sentence with a predicate to indicate that something has happened.

（26）他昨天去上海的。

（27）你们什么时候结婚的？

3. "的"与"是"构成"是……的"格式，既表示对时间、地点、方式等内容肯定、强调的语气，又表示已然的语气。"是"常常可以省略。Used to form the "是…的" structure, indicating an affirmation of what is said about a time, place, or method. Also, its emphatic tone indicates that something has happened. "是" is often omitted.

(28) 我是一个人走的。
(29) 他是在北京出生的。
(30) 我们是今天上午八点坐飞机来的。

4. "的"用在陈述句的形容词重叠式、带附加成分的形容词、拟声词、一些四字词语和谓语的补语后面,除了表示一般的陈述语气外,还表示某种情形或状态。Used at the end of a declarative sentence to indicate not only a declarative tone but also a certain situation or state. It's collocated with an adjective reduplication, an adjective or onomatopoetic word with an adjunct, a four-character word or a complement.

(31) 他的房间里干干净净的。
(32) 马路旁的草地绿油油的。草地那边的小河流水哗啦啦的。
(33) 这次活动大家都兴高采烈的。

5. "的"用在疑问句后,表示加强疑问语气。Used at the end of an interrogative sentence to emphasize the interrogative tone.

(34) 你怎么搞的?那么长时间还没做好作业。
(35) 这衣服是谁的?掉在这里两三天了。

说明 Notes:

一、"的"的用法比较复杂,主要是什么时候必须用"的",什么时候可以不用"的"的问题,就句解句。是否用"的",常见有以下几种使用原则,可供参考。The usages of "的" are complicated. This complexity lies in when to use "的" and when not to use "的." Here are some principles for reference.

1. 词语意义已经专门化的,不用"的"。Do not use "的" when the meaning of the words has been specialized.

(36) 我们是法国(的)留学生。
(37) 这是装配(的)车间,那是包装(的)车间。

2. 除了加强语气以外,一般单音节形容词后面不用"的"。Apart from an emphasis on the tone, "的" is generally not used when it follows a monosyllabic adjective.

(38) 他想卖掉旧(的)房子,再买一套新(的)房子。
(39) 红(的)花、绿(的)草、蓝(的)天、白(的)云,春天真美啊!

3. 修饰语和中心语经常组合的,"的"字可用可不用,如例(38)(39)。但是,修饰语和中心语不常组合的,常表示一种特别的情况或含有比喻义的修饰,要用"的",如例(40)(41)。If the modifier and the head word come together, "的" is optional, as in (38) and (39). But when the modifier does not collocate frequently with the head word, there is a "的" to indicate a special situation or a modification of a figurative meaning, as in (40) and (41).

(40) 这支军队有铁的纪律。(表示纪律严明 Indicating good discipline)
(41) 这老人常说他的艺术的春天已经过去了。

4. 当形容词以重叠、前加或后附等形式修饰名词时,形容词和名词之间必须用"的"。There must be a "的" between an adjective and a noun if the adjective is reduplicated or appears before or after the noun it modifies.

(42) *他做了一件很好事情。
(43) 他做了一件很好的事情。
(44) *我很喜欢这个安安静静教室。
(45) 我很喜欢这个安安静静的教室。

5. 两个或者三个以上的"的"字短语修饰一个名词时,"的"重复使用会造成句子语音节律上的不协调,甚至句子语义也会不清楚。限制"的"的重复出现,一般有以下两种方法:Two or more "的" phrases modifying a noun will lead to disharmony in phonetic rhythm and confusion in meaning. There are two ways to limit the recurrence of "的."

① 减少"的"字短语修饰名词的层次,改为修饰语与中心语直接组合的名词结构。Reduce the number of nouns modified by a "的" phrase, and turn them into a nominal structure that combines the modifier and a head word directly.

(46) 他们的汉语学习的计划很好。→他们的汉语学习计划很好。

(47) 海南岛的海边的沙滩的环境很不错。→海南岛海边沙滩的环境很不错。

② 变换句式,减少"的"字。Change the syntactic structure in order to reduce the number of "的."

(48) 留学生楼的前面的超市的东西很便宜。→留学生楼前面的超市,东西很便宜。

(49) 他妈妈坐今天下午三点的日本航班的飞机来杭州。→他妈妈今天下午三点,坐日本航班的飞机来杭州。

6. 语气助词"的",表示事情已经发生,必须用"的"。As a modal auxiliary, "的" indicates something has happened, and so "的" is compulsory.

(50) 他什么时候回国?(表示还没有回国,想知道什么时候回国。He is not yet back in the country, and the speaker wants to know when he will be back.)

(51) 他什么时候回国的?(表示已经回国,但不知道是什么时候回国的。He is already back in the country, and the speaker doesn't know when he came back.)

二、"的"和"地"的区别如下:"的" differs from "地" as follows:

1. 结构助词"的"和"地"在普通话中都读轻声 de。以前"的""地"不分,20 世纪初开始,人为地规定"的"用作定语的标志,"地"用作状语的标志。As structural auxiliary words, both "的" and "地" are pronounced as "de" in Mandarin. There used to be no differences between the two in the past. But from the beginning of the twentieth century, "的" has been prescribed to be a sign of an attribute and "地" a sign of an adverbial.

2. 定语标志"的"用在名词或名词性词语前面,在句子中一般用在主语、宾语前面。状语标志"地"用在动词、形容词谓语前面。"的," a sign of an attribute, is used before a noun or nominal phrase and often appears before a subject or an object. As a sign of an adverbial, "地" appears in front of a verb or an adjective predicate.

……dehuà ……的话

用法 Usage:
助词 aux.

1. 常与连词"如果、假如、要是、只要"等或副词"万一"等呼应,表示假设或条件。一般用在前一分句句末,有时也可以把这一分句移到后面。It often echoes with conjunctions such as "如果,假如,要是,只要," or adverbs like "万一," to indicate an assumption or condition. It can occur at the end of the first clause, but this clause is sometimes put at the end of the whole sentence.

(1) 假如昨天上火车的话,今天下午就可以到了。

(2) 任务一定能完成,如果大家合作好的话。

2. 同"否则、不然、要不然"等连词或副词"不"连用,表示转折语气,引出一个假设分句。"……的话"的前后都有一个停顿,书面上用逗号隔开。It often goes with conjunctions such as "否则,不然,要不然," or adverbs like "不," to indicate a transition and introduce a hypothetical clause. There are pauses before and after "...的话," which in written language is separated by a comma.

(3) 学外语一定要开口说话,否则的话,口语提高不快。

(4) 你必须在八点以前赶到,要不的话,就迟到了。

de 得 →P103"的"

用法 Usage:
助词 aux.

1. 表示可能、可以、允许。Indicating possibility or permission.

① "得"用在动词后面。在表示肯定的句子中,动词限于单音节;表示否定,在"得"前面加"不",动词不限于单音节。*Used after a verb. In an affirmative sentence, the verb must be a monosyllabic word; in a negative sentence, the verb does not have to be a monosyllabic word. The negative form is to place "不" before "得."*

(1) 你看得,那我也看得。
(2) 篮子里的鸡蛋压不得。
(3) 他的话相信不得。

② "得"用在动词与补语之间,表示可能;"得"换成"不",表示不可能。*Used between a verb and its complement to indicate possibility. If it indicates impossibility, "得" must be substituted by "不."*

(4) 黑板上的字我看得见。
(5) 黑板上的字你看得见看不见?

2. 用在动词或形容词后面,连接表示程度和结果的补语。所连接的补语可以是单个的词也可以是短语。基本句型是"动/形+得+补"。表示否定结果补语,在"得"后面加"不"。"得"是补语的标志。*Used after a verb or an adjective to link its complement, indicating a result or degree. Its complement may be a single word or a phrase. The basic structure is "v./a. + 得 + complement." The negative form of the complement is to add "不" to "得." "得" is a sign of a complement.*

(6) 这件衣服洗得干净吗?——这件衣服洗得不干净!
(7) 他跑得真快!
(8) 他忙得饭都没时间吃。

① 如果"得"用在动词带宾语的短语后,要重复动词。*Repeat the verb if "得" is used in the phrase of verb plus object.*

(9) 她跳舞跳得好极了。
(10) 我做作业做得累死了。

② 有时"得"后面的补语不说出来,有无法形容的意思。常用于口语。*Sometimes the complement after "得" is not stated, indicating a meaning difficult to put to words. This is often used in spoken language.*

(11) 看把你美得!
(12) 你说的话把她气得!

说明 Notes:

1. 助词"得"做可能补语和做程度补语的区别是:*The potential complement "得" is different from the degree complement "得":*

比较项目 Items	可能补语 Potential complement	程度补语 Degree complement
句型 Sentence pattern	这件衣服洗得干净。	这件衣服洗得干净。那件衣服洗得不干净。
能否加程度副词 Degree adverb modification	不能	可以
否定形式 Negative form	这件衣服洗不干净。	这件衣服洗得很不干净。

2. "的"和"得"的区别是:*The differences between "的" and "得" are as follows:*

"得"是补语的标志,"的"是定语的标志。*"得" is a sign of a complement, while "的" is a sign of an attribute.*

(13) 他说的/得很有道理。
(14) 他想的/得很复杂。

上面的句子中,可以用"的"也可以用"得"。如用"的","他说的""他想的"是主语,"很有道理""很复杂"是谓语。如用"得","他"是主语,"说得很有道理""想得很复杂"是谓语,"得"后面是补语。*In the two sentences above, "的" and "得" are interchangeable, but with different meanings. If "的" is used, the subject is "他说的" or "他想的," and the predicate is "很有道理" or "很复杂." If "得" is used, "他" is the subject, and "说得很有道理" or*

"想得很复杂" is the predicate, and the part following "得" is the complement.

3. "记得""认得""懂得"中的"得"是动词的后缀还是结构助词,要看具体的语言环境。在"我们都记得你""我认得你""连小动物都懂得报恩"中,"得"是动词后缀,后面部分是宾语。而在"我记得很清楚""我认得很多""他懂得多,我懂得少"中,"得"是结构助词,后面部分是补语。Whether "得" in "记得,认得,懂得" is the suffix of the verb or the structural auxiliary word, it depends on the context. "得" is the suffix of the verb in "我们都记得你,""我认得你,""连小动物都懂得报恩," and followed by an object. "得" is a structural auxiliary word in "我记得很清楚,""我认得很多,""他懂得多,我懂得少," and followed by a complement.

……dehěn ……得很

用法 Usage:

"……得很"是补语结构,与表示程度相当高"很……"的格式意思相同。口语性很强。"…得很" is a complement structure, which bears the same meaning as the "很…" structure. It is very colloquial. 一般有以下几种格式:The usual structures are as follows:

1. 可直接接在形容词后,作形容词的补语。Used directly after an adjective to serve as its complement.

(1) 这本书好得很!(意为"很好"。It means "很好".)

(2) 这件事麻烦得很。(意为"很麻烦"。It means "很麻烦".)

2. 用在形容词短语结构后,作形容词短语的补语。Used after an adjective phrase to serve as its complement.

(3) 这样的事让人头疼得很。(意为"这样的事让人很头疼"。It means "这样的事让人很头疼".)

(4) 这几天他心烦得很。(意为"他心里很烦"。It means "他心里很烦".)

3. 可接在某些心理动词后,一般此时的心理动词不加宾语,并且为双音节词语。Used after some disyllabic verbs indicating mental activities, and followed by no objects.

(5) 他这个人,讨厌得很。

(6) 小明对那些动物呀,喜欢得很!

4. 可表示某些动词短语的程度。Indicating degree of verbal phrases.

(7) 他呀,有钱得很。

(8) 他对这件事情有把握得很,你不用操心。

说明 Notes:

1. "……得很"与"很+形容词"表示肯定意思时,可以互换。When "…得很" and "很+a." express an affirmative meaning, they are changeable.

(9) 今天他高兴得很。

(10) 今天他很高兴。

区别是:They differ in the following aspects:

① "很……"可带否定结构,而"……得很"一般用于肯定句,不用于否定句。"很…" may be followed by a negative structure, but "…得很" is often used in affirmative sentences, not negative sentences.

(11) *最近他不开心得很。

(12) 最近他很不开心。

(13) *这样的做法他不喜欢得很。

(14) 这样的做法他很不喜欢。

② "很+心理动词"可以带宾语,而"……得很"一般不这样用。"很 + verb denoting mental activity" may be followed by an object, but "…得很" does not have this usage.

(15) *我爱他得很。

(16) 我很爱他。

(17) *老师希望大家都能得到奖学金得很。

(18) 老师很希望大家都能得到奖学金。

③ 有的"很……"修饰动宾结构,不能用"……得很"替代。Some sentences where "很…" is used to modify the predicate-object structure cannot be replaced by "…得很."

(19) *他干这个,有一套得很。

（20）他干这个，很有一套。
（21）*对付这种人，他有一手得很。
（22）对付这种人，他很有一手。
（23）*他这个人啊，没有主意得很。
（24）他这个人啊，很没有主意。

④"很……"的结构可充当定语，而"……得很"则不能。The structure with "很..." can serve as an attribute, but not the structure with "...得很."

（25）*他是个有头脑得很的人。
（26）他是个有头脑的人。

2. 使用了"……得很"后，在被修饰语前一般不再使用其他表示程度的副词。When "...得很" is used, other degree adverbs are not used before the modified word.

（27）*妈妈听到我说的话非常高兴得很。
（28）妈妈听到我说的话，高兴得很。

děi 得

用法 Usage:
助动词 aux. v.

1. 表示情理上、事实上或意志上的需要，相当于"应该、必须"。不能单独回答问题。表示否定用"无须、不用、用不着"等，不能用"不得"。常用于口语。Indicating need, similar to "应该," or "必须." It cannot be used alone to answer questions. When indicating a negative meaning, "无须," "不用," or "用不着" is used. This use often appears in spoken language.

（1）你得快点儿了，还有二十分钟火车就要开了。
（2）你有点发烧，得去医院看看。

2. 表示估计、猜测必然如此，相当于"会"。不能单独使用。没有否定形式。Indicating an estimation or assumption that is certain, the same as "会." It cannot be used alone, nor can it be used in the negative form.

（3）你的生日晚会，她准得来。
（4）音乐放得那么响，又得挨邻居的骂了。
（5）要下雨了，快走，要不得淋雨了。

3. "得"后面可以跟数量词，表示对时间的估计。常用于对话中。"得" can be followed by a quantifier to show an estimate of time. This is common in a conversation.

（6）从上海去北京坐高铁最快得四个多小时。
（7）A：修筑这条高速公路要多长时间？
　　B：得三年。

děng 等 →P110"等待"、P110"等候"

用法 Usage:
动词 v.

1. 等同。To equate.
（1）这些苹果大小不等，但都很好吃。
（2）跳舞的女孩们高矮、胖瘦相等，真漂亮！

2. 等候，等待。To wait for; to await.
（3）我们到校门口去等他们。
（4）九点了还没来，我们不等了。

介词 prep.

等到。引进某种时机或情况，这种时机或情况对某种事物、情况的发生、发展或变化具有一定的意义或影响。形成连动词组作谓语。By the time when. It is used to introduce an opportunity or a situation, which has an impact on the development or change of a thing or situation. It serves as a predicate by forming a linked-verb phrase.

（5）他要等做完作业再去吃晚饭。
（6）等我买到电影票再给你打电话。

助词 aux.

1. 用在人称代词或指人的名词后面，表示复数。通常只用于书面语。It appears after a personal pronoun such as "你等，我等" to indicate the plural form. It is often used in written language.

（7）你等在这里休息一下，我先去看看前面的路。
（8）我等年轻人都是喜欢流行歌曲的。

2. 用在一个词语或几个并列词语后面，表示列举未尽。可以重叠。It appears after a

word or several parallel words to indicate an unfinished list, in which case it can be used in a reduplicated form as "等等."

（9）中国古代小说有《西游记》《红楼梦》《三国演义》等等。

（10）我知道的中国文学家有鲁迅、巴金、郁达夫等。

3. 用在全数列举以后，表示列举已完，做个结尾。后面常带前面列举各项的总数。*It is used to signal an ending when all the examples have been listed, often followed by the total number of the examples listed.*

（11）他喜欢的运动项目有游泳、滑雪、网球、乒乓球等四种。

（12）我买的水果有葡萄、橘子、草莓、梨、苹果等五种，够吗？

说明 Notes:

"等"做列举未尽用时，可以重叠，但是要注意：*When used to indicate an unfinished list, "等" may be repeated. But take note of the following aspects:*

1. 为表示尊重，"等等"一般不用于专有名词后面，如不说"鲁迅、巴金等等"。*To show respect, "等等" is not used after proper nouns. We don't say, for instance, "鲁迅，巴金等等."*

2. "等等"后面一般不再有其他词语。*No other words will follow "等等."*

3. "等等"还可以重复，如："家电商店的商品有电视机、电冰箱、洗衣机、吸尘器等等，等等。" *Even "等等" may be repeated. Here is an example:* "家电商店的商品有电视机，电冰箱，洗衣机，吸尘器等等，等等。" *(The shop for selling domestic appliances sells TVs, refrigerators, washing machines, dusters, etc., etc.)*

děngdài 等待 →P109"等"、P110"等候"

用法 Usage:

动词 *v.*

等着所期望的人、事物或情况出现。*To wait for [expected person(s), thing(s) or situation(s) to appear].*

（1）你和你家里人商量一下，明天我等待你的回音。

（2）他自己不写，就等待着朋友先给他写信。

（3）她等待了十多年，但是她的丈夫一直没回来。

说明 Notes:

"等"和"等待"的对象都可以是具体的，也可以是抽象的。*The objects of "等" and "等待" can be both concrete and abstract.*

区别是：*Their differences are as follows:*

1. "等"多用于具体的对象。"等待"的对象更多的是抽象的事物或事件。*The objects of "等" are often concrete objects. The objects of "等待," however, are mostly abstract things or events.*

（4）小鸟们都等待着春天的来临。

（5）我们在学校门口等你。

2. "等"多用于口语。"等待"多用于书面语。*"等" is often used in spoken language and "等待" in written language.*

děnghòu 等候 →P109"等"、P110"等待"

用法 Usage:

动词 *v.*

等，等待。*To wait for; to await.*

（1）有什么消息，我会打电话给你，你不用在这里等候。

（2）他们已经在饭店等候多时了，我们快去吧。

说明 Notes:

1. "等候"和"等"的区别是：*There are differences between "等候" and "等":*

① "等"的对象更多的是比较具体的人、事物或事件。*The objects of "等" are mostly concrete people, things or events.*

（3）*你要和歌星见面的事，再等候别的机会吧。

（4）你要和歌星见面的事，再等别的机

会吧。

②"等候"是具有郑重色彩的书面语。"等"是口语词。"等候" is a solemn written word while "等" is a spoken word.

2."等候"和"等待"的区别是："等候" differs from "等待" in the following aspects:

①"等候"表示一直等在某个地方或保持某种状态不变,直到所期望的人出现;"等待"表示不采取行动,直到所期望的人、事物或情况出现,着重于等着到来。"等候" indicates waiting all the time at a place or remaining in a state steadily till the expected person appears; "等待" indicates not taking any action until the expected person, thing or situation has appeared.

②"等候"的对象可以是人,也可以是事物。一般不用于抽象事物。"等待"的对象除了可以是人、动物及其活动,或者是事物或情况的出现,还可以是时机、机会等抽象事物。The objects of "等候" may be persons or things but not abstract things. The objects of "等待" may be the emergence of persons, animals, other activities or situations. Besides, its objects can also be abstract things such as opportunities.

(5)＊他每天下午五点都去码头等待轮船,希望他的妻子从船上走下来。

(6)他每天下午五点都去码头等候轮船,希望他的妻子从船上走下来。

(7)＊你想找一个好工作得等候时机啊。

(8)你想找一个好工作得等待时机啊。

3."等"与"等待""等候"的区别是："等" differs from "等待" and "等候"as follows:

①"等"有助词用法。"等待"和"等候"没有这种用法。"等" can be used as an auxiliary, but "等待" and "等候" cannot.

②"等"的动词用法中,有"等同""等到"的用法。"等待"和"等候"没有这个意思的用法。When "等" is used as a verb, it can mean "等同" or "等到," while "等待" and "等候" do not have this meaning.

díquè 的确 →P387"确实"

用法 Usage:

副词 ad.

表示所说的客观情况完全符合实际,十分肯定的意思。用在动词、形容词前面做状语,也可以用在句首,但要有停顿,表示加强语气。可以重叠使用,表示加强语气。*Indeed; really; as a matter of fact. It means certainty, showing that what is said is in full accord with the reality. It is placed before a verb or an adjective as an adverbial. When it appears at the beginning of a sentence, a pause is needed to reinforce the tone. The overlapped use "的的确确" can reinforce the tone.*

(1)电子技术发展的速度的确很快。

(2)我的的确确这样想过。

(3)的确,这是汉代的文物。

说明 Notes:

"的确"修饰的成分除了形容词可以是单音节以外,一般要求两个音节以上的词语(个别动词,如"有、是、去"可以受"的确"修饰)。*Generally, "的确" modifies words with two or more syllables. Exceptions include 1) monosyllabic adjectives; 2) a few monosyllabic verbs such as "有,是,去."*

(4)这种颜色的确好。

(5)这种颜色的确漂亮。

(6)星期天的确有朋友来我家。

dǐkàng 抵抗 →P140"反抗"

用法 Usage:

动词 v.

表示用力量制止、抗拒对方的进攻或某种力量的侵入。可用作句子的主要语法成分。*To resist an attack or withstand the invasion of a certain power. It can be used as a main grammatical constituent in a sentence.*

(1)我们要坚持锻炼身体,增强对疾病的抵抗力。

(2)小镇老百姓顽强地抵抗敌人的入侵。

说明 Notes:

1. "抵抗"经常做"进行、予以、开始、坚持、停止、组织、主张、反对、遭到、受到"等动词的宾语。"抵抗" is often used as an object of verbs like "进行,予以,开始,坚持,停止,组织,主张,反对,遭到 and 受到."

(3) 面对敌人的进攻,他们进行了三天三夜的抵抗。

2. "抵抗"也能做主语、宾语,但常要带定语。When "抵抗" is used as a subject or an object, there is often an attribute before it, as is shown in (4).

(4) 他们很快就打败了敌人的抵抗。

diǎn 点

用法 Usage:

动词 v.

1. 用笔加上点。To put a dot to something.

(1) "大"字左下方点上一个点,就成了"太"。

(2) 有个成语叫"画龙点睛"。

2. 触到物体立刻离开。To touch something lightly.

(3) 在他手背上轻轻一点,他就叫了起来。

(4) 他只轻轻一点,窗户纸上就破了一个洞。

3. 使液体一点点向下落。To allow liquid to go to a place, drop by drop.

(5) 每天早上他都要点眼药水。

4. (头或手)向下稍微动一动,立刻恢复原位。(Head or hand) to drop a little but return to the original position immediately.

(6) 他点了点头,表示同意了。

5. 一个个地查对。To check one by one.

(7) 每个老师上课时都要点名。

(8) 到月底我们就要清点商店的货物。

6. 在许多人或事物中指定。To designate... out of many people or things.

(9) 你先到饭店点菜,我们很快就去。

(10) 卡拉 OK 时,先点歌,再唱。

7. 指点,启发。To enlighten; to inspire.

(11) 他是聪明人,一点就明白了。

(12) 那件事你不用多讲,点一下就可以了。

8. 引着火。To light a fire.

(13) 你别给他在这里点烟,让他到外面去抽。

(14) 春节时,我们村家家门口都点着红灯笼。

名词 n.

1. 液体的小滴。如:"雨点、水点、油点"等。Tiny liquid drops, such as "雨点,水点,油点."

2. 规定的钟点。A specified point of time.

(15) 下午一点就开始上课。

(16) 火车误点了。晚了三十分钟。

3. 事物的方面或部分。Part of a thing such as a speech or an article.

(17) 这篇文章讲了三点。

4. 点心。Snack(s).

(18) 这个食堂的早点品种丰富,且价格便宜。

diào 掉 →P115 "丢"

用法 Usage:

动词 v.

1. 往下落。To fall; to drop.

(1) 苹果掉在地上了。

(2) 她已经掉眼泪了。

2. 遗失,遗漏。To lose.

(3) 他的钱包掉了。

(4) 他很细心,没掉过东西。

3. 减少,降低。常用于口语。To reduce; to decrease. It is often used in spoken language.

(5) 今年夏天空调的价格掉了很多。

(6) 考大学复习了一个月,他的体重掉了不少。

4. 回,转。可重叠。To turn round. It can be used in a reduplicated form as "掉掉."

(7) 他掉头就走。

(8) 车子要在这里掉掉头。

5. 互换。可重叠。*To exchange. It can be used in a reduplicated form as* "掉掉."

(9) 咱们掉掉位置,怎么样?

(10) 咱们俩掉件衣服穿穿,好吗?

6. 用在某些动词后面,表示动作的完成,作补语。"掉" *can follow some verbs to indicate the completion of an action, serving as a complement.*

(11) 你把这些垃圾扔掉。

(12) 随便吐痰的习惯一定要改掉。

dǐng 顶 →P702"最"

用法 Usage:

名词 n.

人体或物体上最高的部分。常用做语素构成合成词"顶端、顶峰、顶上"等。*The top of something. It is often used to form compound words such as* "顶端,顶峰,顶上."

(1) 山顶上有一间屋子。

(2) 他的头顶上已经没有头发了。

动词 v.

1. 用头支撑。可重叠。*To carry on the head. It can be used in a reduplicated form as* "顶顶."

(3) 你说不重,那你来顶顶这一盆水。

(4) 脑袋上顶着一个大箱子。

2. 从下面拱起。*To push up from below.*

(5) 泥土被种子顶起来了。

(6) 热气顶起了锅盖。

3. 用头撞击。可重叠。*To gore; to head (a ball). It can be used in a reduplicated form as* "顶顶."

(7) 这只山羊能把人顶翻。

(8) 他用头顶顶球,球就进去了。

4. 支撑,抵住。*To hold out against; to stand up to.*

(9) 这孩子用桌子顶住了门,不让人进去。

(10) 屋顶只用了四根柱子顶着。

5. 相当,抵。可构成兼语词组作谓语。*To be equivalent to. It can be used to form a modest term, serving as a predicate.*

(11) 三个臭皮匠,顶个诸葛亮。

(12) 他一个人干的活顶得上我们三个人干的。

6. 顶替。可重叠。*To substitute. It can be used in a reduplicated form as* "顶顶."

(13) 父亲退休,儿子顶了他的职。

(14) 他没来上班,今天你顶顶他的班吧。

7. 指转让或取得企业经营权、房屋租赁权。*To transfer or acquire the right to operate a business or lease a house.*

(15) 我们三人顶了一个乡镇企业。

(16) 这房子已经顶出去了。

副词 ad.

1. 表示程度最高。多用于口语。可重叠。*Indicating the highest extent. It often appears in spoken language and can be used in a reduplicated form as* "顶顶."

(17) 这是顶顶好的办法了。

(18) 这个节目顶受大家的欢迎。

2. 表示最大限度。含有让步语气。常用在"多、少、快、慢、大、小、长、短、厚、薄、好、坏、麻烦、复杂"等形容词前面。*To the fullest extent, indicating a concessive mood. It often appears before an adjective such as* "多,少,快,慢,大,小,长,短,厚,薄,好,坏,麻烦,复杂."

(19) 签证,顶快也要一周后才能拿到。

(20) 这屋子顶大也不过二十平方米。

3. 跟方位词组合,表示方位的极端。*Used together with a location word to indicate the extreme of a location.*

(21) 她每次跑步跑在顶前面。

(22) 他总是在顶后边坐着。

dìng 订 →P114"定"

用法 Usage:

动词 v.

1. 经过研究或商议后立下(条约、契约、计划、章程等)。*To draw up (a treaty, contract, plan or agreement).*

(1) 我订了一个学习计划。
(2) 他的租房合同还没订好。
2. 预先约定。To order.
(3) 我们已经订了去北京的飞机票。
(4) 我的朋友在西安给我订好一个房间。
3. 把零散的书页或纸张装订成册。To staple together.
(5) 他把他们俩来往的信件订在一起,订了好几本。
(6) 这本书破了,什么地方可以装订?
4. 表示订正、校订的意思。常用作词素。To revise; correct. It is often used as a morpheme.
(7) 请大家订正一下作业上的错句。
(8) 这篇文章已经校订了三遍,还是有错字。

dìng 定 →P113"订"

用法 Usage:

动词 v.

1. 决定,使确定。可重叠。可做谓语、补语。To decide; to fix. It can be used as a predicate or a complement.

(1) 请你赶快把出发的时间定下来。
(2) 明天我们几点在哪儿见面,定下了吗?

2. 使平静,使稳定。多用于心理、情绪方面。可重叠。可带动态助词"了"。常做谓语,宾语限于"心、神、魂"等少数几个词。To calm down; to stabilize. It is often used to express some emotion or mental activity. Sometimes it appears in a reduplicated form as "定定." It can be followed by the dynamic auxiliary "了." And it is often used as a predicate, with a few words like "心,神,魂" as its object.

(3) 她心神不定,一定发生了什么事。
(4) 他先坐下定了定神,然后才告诉我们发生了什么事。

3. 表示固定、使固定的意思。To fix.

① 用作词素构成合成词,如"定睛、定影"等。Used as a morpheme to form compound words such as "定睛,定影。"

② 做谓语,一般都带有补语。Used as a predicate, often followed by a complement.

(5) 我的两脚好像被定住了。
(6) 他的眼睛定在书本上,一动也不动。

4. 表示约定。To order; to make an appointment.

(7) 飞机票已经定好了。
(8) 他们俩见面的时间定好了吗?

形容词 a.

1. 表示平静,稳定。可做谓语(常用在固定词组中)、补语。Calm; stable. It can be used in set phrases as a predicate or a complement.

(9) 她平心定气,一点也不慌。
(10) 大家坐定了,系上安全带。飞机就要起飞了。

2. 已经确定的,不可改变的。常做补语。Fixed; decided. It is often used as a complement.

(11) 我和你说定了,明天一起上街。
(12) 我学汉语,学定了。

副词 ad.

表示必定、一定的意思。多用于书面语。Definitely; surely. It is often used in written language.

(13) 你的目标定能达到。
(14) 他不去上海定有什么原因。

说明 Notes:

"定"和"订"的区别是:"定" differs from "订" in the three aspects that follow:

1. "定"和"订"在表示"预先约定"的意思时,互相通用,如"订购/定购、订婚/定婚、订货/定货"等。They are interchangeable when they mean "预先约定" such as "订购/定购,""订婚/定婚," and "订货/定货."

2. "定"有决定、确定的意思。"订"没有这个意思。"定" can mean "to decide" and "to fix", while "订" does not have this meaning.

3. "订"有装订、校订、修订的意思。"定"没有这些意思。"订" can mean "to staple together" and "to revise," while "定" does not have this meaning.

diū 丢 →P112"掉"

用法 Usage:
动词 v.

1. 遗失。否定式一般用"没"。用"不"否定,"不"后一般有能愿动词,或"不"前有"从来、向来"等表示习惯性的副词。常做谓语,也可做补语。*To lose. The negative form of "丢" is usually "没丢." When "不" is used, there is often a modal verb following it or there is a habitual adverb before it like "从来" and "向来." It can be used as a predicate or a complement.*

(1) 昨天他丢了钱包。
(2) 所有的东西都被他们弄丢了。
(3) 我长这么大,没丢过东西。
(4) 他这么努力,不会丢工作的。

2. 扔。常做谓语,带宾语或补语,补语常由介宾词组"给……""在……"充当。*To throw away. It is often used as a predicate, followed by an object or a complement, which is often a prepositional phrase such as "给…" and "在…."*

(5) 麻烦你把我的钥匙丢下来。
(6) 别把肉骨头丢给小狗吃。
(7) 别把垃圾丢在地上。

3. 搁置,放。*To put aside; to set aside.*

(8) 他丢下手中的活儿就走了。
(9) 这两年他为了赚钱,把自己的专业也丢了。

说明 Notes:

1. 在词义上,"掉"和"丢"只有一个相同的义项,即表示"遗失"的意思,其他义项完全不同。*Semantically, "掉" and "丢" are identical when they mean "to lose," yet they are totally different for other meanings.*

2. "掉"和"丢"都可以做补语。"丢"做补语时,前面的动词一般是"弄、搞",在口语中可以是具体进行的某个动作,如"看孩子看丢了""小狗在我身后跑,可跑着跑着就跑丢了"等,不能用在具有"完成"意义或造成最后物体消失的动词后面,如"扔、甩、消灭、改、删、划、抹、勾、掉"等。但"掉"可以跟在以上动词的后面,因此,只有"丢掉"而没有"掉丢"。*Both "掉" and "丢" can be used as a complement. When "丢" serves as a complement, the preceding verb is usually "弄" or "搞," and in oral language it can be a specific ongoing action as in "看孩子看丢了" and "小狗一直跟在我身后跑,可跑着跑着就跑丢了," but it cannot be a verb with a meaning of having done something or that of leading to the disappearance of an object such as "扔,甩,消灭,改,删,划,抹,勾,掉." However, "掉" can follow all those words, so there is only "丢掉," but not "掉丢."*

dǒng 懂 →P324"明白"、P662"知道"

用法 Usage:
动词 v.

1. 知道,了解。常做谓语,后面可带具体名词或抽象名词。如:"懂电脑、懂汉语、懂技术、懂你的意思、懂法律"等。*To know; to understand. It is often used as a predicate, followed by a specific or abstract noun such as "懂电脑,懂汉语,懂技术,懂你的意思,懂法律."*

2. 能受程度副词修饰,可在动词后作补语。*"懂" can be modified by adverbs of extent. It can also be used as a complement following a verb.*

(1) 这孩子很懂礼貌,也懂规矩。
(2) 这本书你看懂了吗?
(3) 刚到中国时,汉语我一句也听不懂。

dòngjī 动机 →P328"目的"

用法 Usage:
名词 n.

推动人从事某种行为的因素、念头。可做主语、宾语,或构成介词短语做状语。*Motive; a factor or an idea that pushes one to do something. It can serve as a subject, an object, or as an adverbial by forming a prepositional phrase.*

(1) 动机好，办法不对，事情也就做不好。
(2) 做事不能只强调动机，而不看效果。
(3) 做一件事情不能把动机和效果对立起来。

dòngshēn 动身 →P69"出发"

用法 Usage:

动词 *v.*

出发，启程。*To set out; to start a journey.*

(1) 我明天动身去上海。
(2) 你明天早上几点动身？

说明 Notes:

"动身"和"出发"都有表示离开所在地去某处的意思。*Both "动身" and "出发" mean that one leaves A for B.*

它们的区别是：*They differ in the following aspects:*

1. "动身"着重于起身离开，有形象色彩。一般用于人，不用于车船等交通工具。多用于口语。"出发"着重于离开所在地向目的地进发。有郑重的听命令的态度色彩。多用于人的集体行动。也可用于人乘坐的交通工具。通用于口语和书面语。*"动身" emphasizes leaving, carrying with it a vivid image. It is applied to people, but not vehicles, and it appears mostly in spoken language. "出发" emphasizes leaving for a destination. Often it shows a serious attitude of obeying an order. And it often refers to the collective action of a group of people. Besides, "出发" can also be used for vehicles and appear in both spoken and written language.*

2. "动身"是离合动词，中间可插入其他词语。*"动身" is a separable verb, so other words can be inserted between "动" and "身."*

(3) 明天动不/得了身。

3. "出发"有表示考虑和处理问题时以某一方面为依据的意思。"动身"没有。*"出发" can indicate the basis (like the point of departure "出发点") from which you consider or handle matters, but "动身" does not have this meaning.*

(4) 从你的身体情况出发，明天你不能去爬山。

4. 在祈使句中，常常用"出发"，而不用"动身"。*In imperative sentences, "出发" instead of "动身" is often used.*

(5) 你们明天早上五点必须出发！

dōu 都 →P382"全"、P544"也"

用法 Usage:

副词 *ad.*

1. 表示总括全部。除疑问句以外，所总括的内容对象必须放在"都"前面。后面常跟动词和形容词。*Indicating all. All the objects included must be put before "都" except in interrogative sentences. "都" is often followed by a verb or an adjective.*

(1) 我们都游泳了。
(2) 孩子们在学校里都很努力。

在句子中，"都"常与以下词语配合使用："都" *often collocates with the following words in a sentence:*

① "都"前面常常与"一切、所有、任何、全、凡、每、各、到处"等全指性的词语合用，更明显地表示总括的意思。*"都" often collocates with preceding all-inclusive words such as "一切, 所有, 任何, 全, 凡, 每, 各, 到处," showing obviously all of something.*

(3) 一切有生命的东西都离不开空气和水。
(4) 我们班的同学全都来了。

② "都"前面可以与表示任指的疑问代词合用，含有多数的意思。*"都" collocates with preceding interrogative pronouns to mean the majority of something.*

(5) 他骑自行车比谁都快。
(6) 你们有问题什么时候都可以来办公室问我。

③ 在表示条件的复句中，"都"可以与在所总括对象前的"无论、不论、不管"等连词相呼应使用。*In conditional sentences, "都" can echo* with conjunctions such as "无论,不论,不管," which precede all the objects included.

(7) 无论下雨还是晴天,他都要去跑步。

(8) 不管难不难,我都会学下去的。

2. 在疑问句中,总括的对象(疑问代词)可以放在"都"前面,也可以放在"都"后面。 In interrogative sentences, all the objects included (interrogative pronouns) can be put either before or after "都."

(9) 你们家都有谁(哪些人)啊?

(10) 他们说的话,你们什么都听不懂吗?

3. "都"与"是"字连用,说明原因、理由,有责备的意思。"都" and "是" are lumped together to explain a cause or a reason, indicating blame.

(11) 都是昨天这场大雨不好,我的衬衣被风吹到楼下不见了。

(12) 昨天晚会上她没唱歌,都是因为你说了她一句。

4. 表示强调的语气,有"甚至"的意思。在这种句子中,"都"和"也"可以互换,并且"都"和"也"要轻读。 Indicating emphasis, it means "甚至 (even)." In such sentences, "都" and "也" are interchangeable and they must not be read with a stress.

① "都"前后用同一个动词,常是前一个肯定,后一个否定。 The same verb is used before or after "都," usually the first affirmative and the second negative.

(13) 他一动都/也不动。

② "都"前面用"一+量词",后面带动词的否定。 When "一 + quantifier" is used before "都," the negative form of a verb follows "都."

(14) 他一点儿都/也不吃。

③ "都"前面常用"连""就是"等词搭配,加重强调的语气。 Words like "连" and "就是" are often placed before "都" for emphasis.

(15) 他连饭都/也没吃就走了。

(16) 他一睡着,就是把他扔到河里都/也不会醒来。

④ "都"用在让步复句的偏句里,举出突出的事例,表示甲尚且如此,乙就更不例外了。 When used in the subordinate clause of a concessive complex sentence, "都" highlights an outstanding example to show that A is impossible, to say nothing of B.

(17) 他喉咙痛得话都/也说不出来,怎么还能去唱歌呢?

5. 表示"已经"的意思,可直接出现在数量词、名词前面,句子后面常带"了/啦",形成"都……了"的格式。 Meaning "已经 (already)," it can be placed before a quantifier or a noun and the sentence ends with "了/啦," thus forming the pattern of "都...了."

(18) 饭都凉了,快吃吧。

(19) 都十二点了,他还没回来。

(20) 都大学生了,应该自觉地学习了。

说明 Notes:

1. 用"都"造句,要注意所总括的对象应放在"都"字前面。如果总括的对象是动词的宾语,也要把这部分内容提到"都"前面。"都"后面基本都跟动词或形容词,而不是名词。 When "都" is used in a sentence, all the targeted objects should be put before "都." Even if all the objects serve as the object of the verb, they must be put before "都." Anyway, words following "都" are mainly verbs or adjectives, not nouns.

(21) *我做完都作业了。

(22) 作业我都做完了。

(23) *都中国的大城市我去过。

(24) 中国的大城市我都去过。

2. 否定词用在"都"后,表示否定全部;用在"都"前,表示否定其中一部分。 When a negative word appears after "都," it indicates a total negation; when a negative word appears before "都," it indicates a partial negation.

(25) 我们都不是留学生。

(26) 我们不都是留学生。

(27) 他们都没去。

(28) 他们没都去。

3. 和其他副词如"也、就"等,一起在句中做状语时,要注意先后顺序,一般"都"在"也、就"之后。When "都" joins other adverbs such as "也" and "就" to form an adverbial, "都" is often put after "也" or "就."

(29) *坐在前面的是韩国留学生,坐在后面的都也是韩国留学生。

(30) 坐在前面的是韩国留学生,坐在后面的也都是韩国留学生。

(31) *上完课后,我们都就去食堂吃饭了。

(32) 上完课后,我们就都去食堂吃饭了。

4. 用"都是"来说明理由,有抱怨的语气,所以后面的句子描写的常常是消极的客观事实。When "都是" is used to explain a cause or a reason, indicating blame, the second clause often describes a negative fact.

(33) *都是因为我喜欢看电影,所以我天天看电影。

(34) 我喜欢看电影,所以我天天看电影。

(35) 都是因为我天天看电影,所以很多作业没有做。

5. 用"连……都/也……"的格式中,被强调的人或事物放在"连"的后面,而不是"都"的后面。In the pattern of "连…都/也…," the emphasized person or the thing should be used after "连" instead of "都."

(36) 连我都不知道这件事,更不用说他了。

(37) 我连这件事都不知道,更不用说那件事了。

(38) *都老师们参加运动会,你这么年轻为什么不参加?

(39) 连老师们都参加运动会,你为什么不参加?

dútè 独特 →P457"特别"

用法 Usage:
形容词 a.

独有的,特别的。多表示积极的意义。常用作谓语、定语,能用在"是……的"格式中。Unique; special. Carrying a positive meaning almost all the time, it is often used as a predicate or an attribute, and can be used in the pattern of "是…的."

(1) 他的生活习惯是很独特的。

(2) 四川菜有独特的麻辣味。

(3) 故宫建筑体现了中国古代建筑艺术的独特风格。

dúzì 独自 →P89"单独"

用法 Usage:
副词 ad.

自己一个人。常和"一人"连用,能做状语、定语。Alone. It is often used with "一人" and can serve as an adverb or an attribute.

(1) 中秋夜,他独自一人在湖边赏月。

(2) 在国外我只能独自生活了。

说明 Notes:

"独自"和"单独"都形容不跟别的人或事物合在一起的意思。Both "独自" and "单独" describe you are not with any other people or things.

它们的区别是:They are different in the following aspects:

1. "独自"着重于自身一个,强调自己一个,没有别人。"单独"侧重一个人(或一个群体),不和他人共同行动。"独自" emphasizes an individual, without any other people. "单独" emphasizes an individual (or a group), without the joint action of other people.

(3) 他独自一个人走了,不会有问题吧?

(4) 只有我们这个班单独去上海。

2. "独自"不能作定语,而"单独"既可作状语也可作定语。"独自" cannot be used as an attribute, while "单独" can be used both as an adverbial and as an attribute.

(5) *我们给他准备了一个独自的教室。

(6) 我们给他准备了一个单独的教室。

3. 一般"独自"修饰人比较多。而"单独"可以修饰一个人,也可修饰一个群体、一个单位,还可以修饰事物。Generally speaking, "独自" is mostly used to modify people, yet "单独" may go with a person, a group, a unit or a thing.

(7) *这种化学产品应该独自存放,不要跟其他产品混放。

(8) 这种化学产品应该单独存放,不要跟其他产品混合。

(9) *学院让我们班独自进行教学实习。

(10) 学院让我们班单独进行教学实习。

dùguò 度过 →P119 "渡过"

用法 Usage:

动词 v.

过(日子)。多用于书面语,能带动态助词"了"。常作谓语,能带处所状语用在"是……的"格式中。To spend (time); (of time) to pass. It is often used in written language, and can be followed by the dynamic auxiliary "了." It is often used as a predicate, and also can be used in the pattern of "是...的," where it collocates with an adverbial of place.

(1) 谢谢你让我度过了一个美好的夜晚。

(2) 他的童年是在福利院度过的。

dùguò 渡过 →P119 "度过"

用法 Usage:

动词 v.

1. 从江河湖海的这一岸到那一岸,通过。能带动态助词"了"。常做谓语。To cross a river/lake/ocean; pass through. It can be followed by the dynamic auxiliary "了." Often it serves as a predicate.

(1) 等到我们渡过了河,他们不知走到哪儿了呢。

(2) 我们就用这只小船渡过了这条大河。

2. 比喻经历了艰辛、困难的阶段。To go through a difficult period of time.

(3) 他们互相帮助渡过了地震之灾。

(4) 我们团结一致,共同渡过了公司的困难岁月。

说明 Notes:

1. "度过"和"渡过"都是动词,是"度"和"渡",加上结果补语"过"构成的,都有经历过、通过的意思,且读音相同。但是"度""渡"的基本意义不同。"度"的基本意义是"过、经过"(指时间),"渡"的基本意义是从此岸到彼岸。Both "度过" and "渡过" are formed by the verb "度" or "渡" plus "过," which indicates a result as a complement. Both can mean getting through and passing through, and they have the same pronunciation. But their basic meanings are different. The basic meaning of "度" is to spend a period of time, while "渡" refers to pass through a river, from one bank to the other bank.

2. "度过"和"渡过"适用范围不同。"渡过"常用于过江河湖海,从这一岸到那一岸,同时也用于经历了难关、灾荒等困难、艰难的阶段。如:"横渡长江""渡过难关",不能用"度"。"度过"专用于时间的转移,多用于生活了一段时间,常与"时代、季节、节日、光阴、岁月、节日"等词语搭配使用,如"欢度春节""度假"只能用"度"。"度过" and "渡过" apply to different scopes. "渡过" is often used when crossing a river/lake/ocean, from one bank to the other bank. It can also mean to get through a hard period of time such as "横渡长江" and "渡过难关." "度过," however, is especially reserved for the passage of time, and so it often collocates with words like "时代,季节,节日,光阴,岁月,节日." We say, for example, "欢度春节" and "度假."

(5) *他在大西北渡过了一生。

(6) 他在大西北度过了一生。

duì 对 →P121 "对于"

用法 Usage:

介词 prep.

1. 引进动作行为的对象。相当于"向、

跟",常构成介词短语作状语。*Introducing the object of an action. It is equivalent to "向" and "跟," and often used as an adverbial by forming a prepositional phrase.*

(1) 你有什么要求对我提出来吧。

(2) 好像所有的人都对钱感兴趣。

2. 引进对待的对象,相当于"对于"。*Introducing the object of a treatment, it is equivalent to "对于."*

(3) 这些书对他有用,对我没有用。

(4) 对这个词语的用法,大家还有什么不懂的地方吗?

动词 v.

1. 对待,对付,对抗。做谓语,必带宾语。*To treat; to cope with; to counter. It is used as a predicate and must be followed by an object.*

(5) 这次足球比赛是留学生队对中国学生队。

(6) 他对我就像父亲对儿子一样。

2. 朝,向,面对。做谓语。*To face. It is used as a predicate.*

(7) 楼外楼饭店正对着西湖。

(8) 他背对着我一句话也不说。

3. 投合,适合。做谓语。*To fit; to agree with. It is used as a predicate.*

(9) 这些菜都很对我的胃口。

(10) 这孩子的脾气很对我的脾气。

4. 把两个东西放在一起互相比较,看是否符合。能重叠,做谓语。*To put two things together and compare; to identify; to check (answer). It can serve as a predicate and appear in a reduplicated form as "对对."*

(11) 你用照片对对,看看是不是他。

(12) 考完后,我跟老师对了答案。我都做对了。

5. 调整使符合一定标准。能重叠,做谓语。*To adjust so as to meet a criterion. It can serve as a predicate and appear in a reduplicated form as "对对."*

(13) 他跟我对了对表。

(14) 闹钟已经对过了。

6. 掺和(多指液体)。可重叠,做谓语。*To mix (mainly referring to liquids). It can serve as a predicate and appear in a reduplicated form as "对对."*

(15) 这牛奶对了水,不好喝。

(16) 咖啡太苦,我要对点牛奶和糖。

7. 使两个东西配合或接触。做谓语。*To bring two things into cooperation or contact. It is used as a predicate.*

(17) 劳驾,请对个火!

(18) 用钥匙卡对着门上的电子感应锁,门就开了。

形容词 a.

正确,正常,相合。可受程度副词修饰。做谓语(可用在"是……的"格式中)、补语,可以单独回答问题。*Right; normal; proper. It can be modified by an adverb of degree; can be used as a predicate (used in the pattern of "是…的") or a complement, and can be used alone to answer a question.*

(19) 这些答案都不对。

(20) 对,你说的都对,但我们不可能这么做。

说明 Notes:

1. 介词"对"在句子中的语义作用一般有以下几种:*When "对" is a preposition, there are four semantic meanings:*

① 引进动作行为的对象;朝,向。*Introducing the object of an action; to; towards.*

(21) 你要对他说一声"谢谢"。

(22) 那个小女孩对我笑了一笑。

② 表示人与人之间的关系。*Indicating a relationship among people.*

(23) 大家对他都很热情。

(24) 同学们对我的帮助太大了。

③ 表示对事物的态度。*Indicating an attitude toward things.*

(25) 有些同学对写汉字总是不感兴趣。

(26) 我们对去哪儿旅游都很关心。

④ "对……"与"来说/说来"搭配使用,组成"对……来说/说来",有把要谈论的对象单独提出来并加以强调的意义。"对…" collocates with "来说/说来" to form "对…来说/说来," highlighting the object of a conversation.

(27) 写汉字,对日本人来说很容易,对美国人来说有点难。

(28) 一台电视机 3 000 元,对富人来说很便宜,对穷人说来比较贵。

2. "对"做动词用,第一种用法,必须带宾语。第二种用法,"对"后面常带"着"。When "对" is a verb, it must be followed by an object as in Usage 1, and followed by "着" as in Usage 2.

duìyú 对于 →P119"对"、P172"关于"

用法 Usage:

介词 prep.

表示人、事物、行为之间的对待关系,用来介绍出有关系的人或事物。Indicating the relationship between things, behaviors, and people, that is, how they treat or relate to each other. It is used to introduce related person(s) or things.

在句子中的用法有:In a sentence, it serves as:

一、构成介词短语,做句子的状语。Forming a prepositional phrase to serve as an adverbial.

1. 作用是引进动作行为的对象。有以下几种句式:Introducing the object of an action in the following sentence structures:

① "对于"所引进的词语是句子谓语动词的受事宾语。The words introduced by "对于" is the recipient object of the predicate verb.

(1) 对于油画,我一无所知。

(2) 对于这件事,我不想再说什么了。

② 如果句子的谓语是"加以、进行"一类的形式动词,它们的宾语一般也是动词或者名物化的动词。这时"对于"引进的对象是句子中宾语的受事。If the predicate of a sentence is a dummy verb like "加以" or "进行," its object is often a verb or a nominalized verb. In this case, the object introduced by "对于" is the recipient of the action denoted by the nominalized verb in the sentence.

(3) 对于同学们的意见,老师进行了认真的研究。

(4) 医生对于妹妹的病,加以特别的关注。

③ 如果"对于"这个句子后面有"是……的"的结构,而且这个结构中又带有表示动作意义的词语,则"对于"引进的对象就是这个词语的受事宾语。If the "是…的" structure appears in the clause following "对于," where there is a word indicating an action, the object introduced by "对于" is the recipient object of the word.

(5) 对于同学们的意见,老师是很重视的。

(6) 对于老师提出的建议,我们全班同学是很赞成的。

2. "对于"的作用是引进动作行为的关系者。"对于"引进的词语不是后面动作行为的支配对象,而是表示有关的人或事物。Introducing the relevant people of an action. The words introduced by "对于" is not the dominating object of the following action but relevant people or things.

有以下四种句式:There are four sentence structures as follows:

① 当"对于"的介词短语做后面的动词或动词短语的状语时,"对于"引进的是某种动作行为所关涉到的人或事物。When the prepositional phrase formed by "对于" serves as an adverbial of the following verb or verbal phrase, the words introduced by "对于" are the people or things involved in an action.

(7) 虽然他已经工作了,但是他对于学习仍然很抓紧。

(8) 打太极拳,对于一些老人很有好处。

② 当"对于"的介词短语做后面形容词谓语的状语时,"对于"引进的是某种性质和状态

所关涉到的人或事物。When the prepositional phrase formed by "对于" serves as an adverbial of the following adjective predicate, words introduced by "对于" are the people or things that are relevant to a certain quality or state.

(9) 别人说,我们班的同学对于旅游最积极。

(10) 对于工作,他一直很努力。

③ "对于"的介词短语用在判断词"是"前面,"对于"引进与这种判断有关系的人或事物。When the prepositional phrase formed by "对于" is placed in front of the linking verb "是," "对于" is used to introduce the people or things that are related to a judgment.

(11) 每天读课文,对于提高汉语口语是很有帮助的。

(12) 学书法,对于一个失去双手的人是很不容易的。

④ "对于"的介词短语与"来说(说来)"配合使用,仍然表示与判断相关的人或事物,但有强调作用,强调所提出来的论断、看法与"对于"引进的人或事物的关系。有的句子里的"对于……来说/说来",有引进并强调主动者的作用,这时句子中的主语一般在句子的前边,而在语义上则成了意念中的受事。When the prepositional phrase formed by "对于" collocates with "来说(说来)," it still indicates the people or things relevant to a judgment, but it emphasizes the relationship between the judgment or opinion and the people or things introduced by "对于." In some sentences, "对于…来说/说来" introduces and emphasizes an agent, in which case the subject is often put at the beginning of the sentence and semantically becomes the object in terms of concept.

(13) 对于妈妈来说,孩子就是她的生命。

(14) 去北京旅游,对于她来说,是这次来中国最重要的活动。

二、组成介词短语,做定语。须加"的",修饰名词或动名词。Forming a prepositional phrase to serve as an attribute. In that case, "的" must be used to modify the noun or the gerund.

(15) 大家可以谈谈对于这个问题的看法。

(16) 对于同学们的帮助,他是很感激的。

说明 Notes:

1. "对于"的介词短语做状语,都有把所引进的词语提到谓语前面加以处置的作用。这种用法的原因有的是为了突出和强调处置的对象,如例(1)(2)(5)(6);有的是句式的需要,如例(3)(4);有的是因为宾语比较长,把宾语提前处置,如例(14);还有的是出于修辞的需要。When a prepositional phrase serves as an adverbial, the introduced words are often placed before the predicate. This is done to highlight and emphasize the object of treatment as in (1), (2), (5), and (6). Some serve a structural need as in (3) and (4). Some move a long object to the front as in (14), and still others are for rhetoric purposes.

(17) 对于那些一心想学好汉语的同学,对于那些想了解中国文化的同学,对于那些想旅游中国名胜古迹的同学,我们都会给以最大的帮助。(排比句 Parallelism)

2. "对"和"对于"都能用作介词,都能引进动作的对象或与动作有关的人或事物,组成介词短语作状语和定语。Both "对" and "对于" can serve as a preposition to introduce the object of an action or the relevant people or things of an action. And both can be used to form a prepositional phrase to serve as an adverbial or attribute.

它们的区别是:They are different in the following aspects:

① 词性不完全相同。"对于"只有介词用法。"对"还有动词、形容词、量词的用法。They are not completely identical in terms of parts of speech. "对于" can only be used as a preposition, while "对" can be used as a

② 作介词时,"对"和"对于"的意义范围不完全相同。"对于"只表示对待关系。"对"除表示对待关系外,还可指示动作的对象,表示"向、朝"等的意思。因此只有表示对待关系时,凡是用"对于"的地方,都能用"对"(介词)换用。但语体色彩略有不同。"对于"比较正式,更适合用于书面语;"对"比较通俗,更适合口语。When used as a preposition, the semantic ranges of "对" and "对于" are not completely identical. "对于" only indicates a treatment relationship. Besides a treatment relationship, "对" can also indicate the object of an action, meaning "向" and "朝." Therefore, "对于" and "对"(preposition) are interchangeable when they indicate a treatment relationship. Still, their stylistic features are slightly different. "对于" is quite formal, more suitable for written language; "对" is colloquial, more suitable for oral language.

(18) 对/对于妈妈来说,孩子是最宝贵的财产。

③ "对"比"对于"的动作性强,所以当"对"引进动作的对象、表示人与人之间的关系时,只能用"对",不能用"对于";表示"向、朝"等意义时,也不能换成"对于"。"对" indicates a more dynamic action than "对于." And so, "对," not "对于," is to be used when introducing the target of an action and dealing with human relationship. It is not to be replaced by "对于" when meaning "向" or "朝."

(19) *他对于我笑了笑说:"请坐。"
(20) 他对我笑了笑说:"请坐。"

④ 用"对"构成的介词短语,做状语可以用在主语前(要有停顿),也可以用在主语后,意思相同;可用在动词、形容词、主谓词组、助动词或副词前,也可用在助动词、副词后,意思相同。由"对于"构成的介词短语不能用在助动词或副词之后。一般都用在主语后,助动词、副词、谓语前。A prepositional phrase formed by "对," serving as an adverbial, can be put either before a subject (there must be a pause) or after a subject, indicating the same meaning. It can be put either before a verb, an adjective, a subject-predicate phrase, an auxiliary, an adverb or after an auxiliary, an adverb, meaning all the same. A prepositional phrase formed by "对于" cannot be used after an auxiliary or an adverb, but it is usually put after a subject or before an auxiliary, an adverb or a predicate.

(21) 对你的问题,明天他们会讨论。
(22) 对于你的问题,明天他们会讨论。
(23) *今天他们会对于你的问题进行讨论。
(24) 今天他们对你的问题会进行讨论。
(25) 今天他们对于你的问题会进行讨论。
(26) 今天他们会对你的问题进行讨论。

duō 多 →P126"多么"

用法 Usage:

形容词 a.

1. 表示数量大(跟"少、寡"相对)。可做谓语、定语。Many or much (be opposite to "少," "寡"). It can be used as a predicate or an attribute.

(1) 我们学校有很多国家的留学生。
(2) 他的中国朋友多,我的外国朋友多。

2. 用在动词前后作状语或补语,表示在数量上有所增加、有所超出。An increase in quantity. It is used before or after a verb as an adverbial or a complement.

(3) 我今天多喝了几杯,头有点儿晕了。
(4) 话说多了,别人会讨厌的。

3. 表示相差的程度大,多用在形容词后面作补语。A big difference. It mainly follows an adjective as a complement.

(5) 杭州比上海热多了。
(6) 你的汉语比我好多了。

动词 v.

1. 表示超出了原有的或应有的数量或限

度。做谓语，一般得带宾语。*To be greater in quantity or degree than the original or expected. Serving as a predicate, it is generally followed by an object.*

(7) 你不要多心,我们不是在说你。

(8) 北京的春天多风沙。

2. 表示超过,剩余。*To exceed.*

(9) 他们教室里多了几张桌子。

(10) 怎么会多了十块钱?

数词 num.

1. 用在数量词(数词为个位整数或带个位整数的多位数,量词主要是标准量词或时间量词)后面,表示个位数以下的不确定数。*Following a quantifier to indicate an uncertain single digit (The numeral is a single digit number or a multiple digit number with an integer. The numerals refer mainly to standard numerals or temporal quantifiers.).*

(11) 他在上海住了三年多。

(12) 我们买了四斤多苹果。

2. 用在数词(数词是十位以上的整数)后,表示整位数以下的不确定数。*Following a numeral (the number is a single digit number or a multiple digit number with an integer), it indicates an indefinite number smaller than a single digit number.*

(13) 他家门口停着二十多辆车。

(14) 这件衣服要一百多块钱。

副词 ad.

1. 用在疑问句里,询问程度或数量。相当于"多少",做谓语。前面常与"有"连用,句末还可用"吗、呢"。*Inquiring about degree or quantity. It is equivalent to "多少" and used as a predicate. "有" is often placed before it, and "吗" or "呢" can appear at the end of a sentence.*

(15) 他多大岁数?

(16) 这座楼有多高呢?

2. 用在感叹句里,表示程度很高,带有夸张语气和强烈的感情色彩。相当于"多么"。句末常带"啊"等感叹词。*Indicating a high degree in exclamations. Spoken in an exaggerated tone, it often carries a powerful emotion. It is equivalent to "多么," and the sentence often ends with an exclamatory word such as "啊."*

(17) 西湖多美啊!

(18) 这小孩儿多不简单啊!

3. 用在陈述句里,表示程度很高。有以下两种句式: *Indicating a high degree in declarative sentences. There are two sentence structures as follows:*

① "动+不(+了)+多+形"或"没+多+形"。*"v. +不(+了)+多+a." or "没+多+a."*

(19) 他在这里学不了多长时间的。

(20) 去那儿没多远,用不了十分钟。

② 跟连词"无论、不管"、副词"都"配合使用,表示任何一种程度的意思。相当于"多么"。*It can be used together with conjunctions like "无论" and "不管" or the adverb "都," indicating any degree. It is similar to "多么."*

(21) 无论/不管多累,每天晚上他都要看电视新闻。

(22) 多难的语法问题,他都能用最简单的说明让你很快就懂。

4. 在句子中,重复连用"多",表示强调某种程度或数量。*When used repeatedly and successively, "多" indicates emphasis for a certain degree or quantity.*

(23) 我妈很好,我要多(少)钱就给我多(少)钱。

(24) 那种药,你能多买就多买点儿。

说明 Notes:

1. "多"不能单独作定语用,须在前面加"很",组成偏正词组才可以。这里的"很",表示程度高的语义已经弱化。*"多" cannot be used alone as an attribute: "很" must be placed before it. Originally meaning "a very high degree," "很" has been softened in this use.*

(25) *学习汉语我有多困难。

(26) 学习汉语我有很多困难。

2. "多"用在数量词前时,量词常常是:度量词、容量词、时间量词或"倍"。When "多" is used before a quantifier, numerals are often measure words, capacity words, temporal quantifiers, or "倍(fold)."

主要有以下五种情况。There are mainly five situations.

① 标准量词常见的是"个"。The common standard quantifier is "个."

(27) 他只吃了一个多馒头就不想吃了。

② "多"如果用于时间,"多"前面是数量词,后面必须直接带时间名词。"多"与时间名词之间不能插入其他词语。When "多" refers to time and the word before it is a quantifier, there must be a temporal noun directly following it. Other words cannot be inserted between "多" and the temporal noun.

(28) *他做了三个多的钟头作业。

(29) 他做了三个多钟头作业。

(30) 她在北京住了五个多月。

③ 如果时间名词是"年、天","多"用在"年、天"后面,如:"一年多、三天多"不能是"一多年、三多天",因为"年、天"前面不用量词,表示完整的整数必须是"一年、三天"。If the temporal noun is "年" or "天," "多" must be put after "年" or "天" such as "一年多" and "三天多." As "年" or "天" cannot be placed after a quantifier, the integer must be "一年" or "三天" indicating a whole number.

④ "十"是一个特殊的整位数,当"十"与标准量词合用时,"多"在量前、量词后,意思完全不同。"十" is a special whole number. When it is used with a standard quantifier, its meaning is totally different before or after the quantifier.

(31) 我们买了十多斤鱼。(比十斤多,不到二十斤 More than 10 jin but less than 20 jin)

(32) 我们买了十斤多的鱼。(比十斤多,不到十一斤 More than 10 jin but less than 11 jin)

⑤ "多"用在量词后面,量词前面的数词不能是十位以上的整位数,如:不能说"*五十斤多米、*三十里多路"等(除"十"以外)。If "多" appears after a quantifier, the number before the quantifier must not be a whole digit number larger than 10. For example, we cannot say "五十斤多米" or "三十里多路." The only exception is "十."

3. 副词用法中,"多"修饰的形容词一般是单音节的,而且形容词一般都是表示积极意义的,如:"高、远、长、宽、大、重"等。When "多" is an adverb, the adjectives modified by "多" are mostly monosyllabic words, and these adjectives basically have positive meanings such as "高,远,长,宽,大,重."

duōbàn 多半 →P84"大都"

用法 Usage:

副词 ad.

1. 表示某一数量内的半数以上,大部分。可儿化。More than half; most. The suffix "儿" can be added to it.

(1) 游览杭州西湖的多半儿是外地人。

(2) 我的书多半是自己买的。

2. 通常。Usually.

(3) 星期天,我们多半儿去父母家看望他们。

(4) 他多半在十二点半去食堂吃饭。

3. 表示对情况的估计,很有可能。在句子中一般有其他词语配合表示估计的语义。Most probably. Indicating an estimate of a situation. Generally, there are other words to collocate with it.

(5) 如果宿舍里找不到,他多半去图书馆看书了。

(6) 他多半儿不会来,我们不用等他了。

数量词 quantifier

表示一大半,超过半数。The greater part;

more than half.

(7) 这次运动会,我们班多半同学都参加比赛。

(8) 去西安旅游的占一多半。

说明 Notes:

1. "多半"又说为"一多半"。"多半" is interchangeable with "一多半."

2. "多半"和"大都"的区别是:"多半"有数量词用法。"大都"只有副词用法,只能用在谓语前面。"多半" differs from "大都" in that while "多半" can be a quantifier, "大都" can only be used as an adverb, and it appears only before a predicate.

(9) 我们班多半同学今天去上海了。

(10) *我们班大都同学今天去上海了。

(11) 我们班同学今天大都去上海了。

duōme 多么 →P123"多"

用法 Usage:

副词 ad.

1. 用在感叹句里,表示程度很高。含夸张的语气和强烈的感情色彩,多用于书面语,做状语。Indicating a high degree in exclamations. Spoken in an exaggerated tone, it expresses a powerful emotion. It is often used in written language and can be used as an adverbial.

有以下两种句式:There are two syntactic structures:

① "多么+形容词/动词"。句末常带"啊(呀、哪、哇)"。"多么+a./v." This structure often ends with words such as "啊、呀、哪、哇。"

(1) 秋天的树叶多么美丽啊!

(2) 大家多么盼望快放假啊!

② "多么+不+形容词/动词"。"多么+不+a./v."

(3) 她多么不容易呀!

(4) 大家多么不愿意离开这儿啊!

2. 用在陈述句里,表示任何很深的程度。多用在"无论/不管……多么……"等格式中,常用于书面语,作状语。Indicating a high degree in declarative sentences. It is often used in the pattern of "无论/不管…多么…" in written language, and it serves as an adverbial.

(5) 不管学汉语有多么难,我们都要学。

(6) 无论山多么高,路多么远,他总是走在最前面。

3. 用在疑问句里,询问程度。Inquiring about degree in questions.

(7) 杭州离上海有多么远?

(8) 你知道那只大象有多么重吗?

说明 Notes:

1. 副词"多么"多表示程度,分别用在三种句型,表示三种程度方面的义项。其中,疑问句的用法不常见,主要用于感叹句。Though "多么", as an adverb, can be used in three sentence structures, i.e., declarative, exclamatory, and inquisitive, it is rather uncommon in questions. It is primarily used in exclamations.

2. "多么"的用法基本上与"多"的副词用法相同。但是没有"动+不+多+形"或"没+多+形"的用法。The usage of "多么" is basically similar to the adverb usage of "多," but "v.+不+多+a." and "没+多+a." do not exist.

(9) *他在这里学不多么长时间的。

(10) 他在这里学不多长时间的。

(11) *去那儿没多么远,走去用不了十分钟。

(12) 去那儿没多远,走去用不了十分钟。

duōshao 多少 →P213"几"

用法 Usage:

代词 pron.

1. 用作询问数量。Used in a question, it asks about "How many/much?"

(1) 你们班有多少泰国人?

2. 用在客观的陈述句,表示不定的数量。Used in an objective statement to indicate an uncertain amount.

(2) 你会写多少汉字就写多少。

3. 用在否定句,表示数量少。Used in a negative sentence to mean small in amount.

(3) 我口袋里没多少钱。

4. 用在肯定句,表示数量多。Used in a positive sentence to mean a large amount.

(4) 天气一天热一天冷的,多少人都感冒了。

副词 ad.

"多少"作副词用时,发音为 duōshǎo,可以重叠为"多多少少"。"多少" is pronounced as "duōshǎo." It can be reduplicated as. "多多少少."

用法有：It is used in the following ways:

1. 表示或多或少,具有一定的程度。Meaning "more or less."

(5) 你多少吃一点吧。

(6) 来中国半年了,我多少也有了几个中国朋友。

2. 表示稍微的意思,常与"一点儿、一些、有点儿"等词语合用。Meaning "just a little." It often goes with "一点儿,一些,有点儿."

(7) 他和我比,他比我多少学得好一些。

(8) 都十一月了,天气多少有点儿冷了。

3. 指数量的大小,作状语,修饰动词。Indicating an indefinite amount, it serves as an adverb modifying the verb.

(9) 每个班的人数多少不等,有的十五个,有的二十四个。

说明 Notes:

一、"多少"用作代词时,要注意以下两点。Take care when using "多少" as a pronoun.

1. 表示不定的数量,用在客观的陈述句时,在句子中常常出现两次,前后呼应,如例(2)。It often appears twice in a sentence, one echoing the other when it indicates an indefinite amount in making an objective statement as in (2).

2. "多少"不能和不定量词"些、点儿"等合用提问。It cannot be used with indefinite measuring words such as "些,点儿" in an interrogative sentence.

(10) *你喝了多少点儿啤酒?

(11) 你喝了多少啤酒?

二、"多少"作副词用时,要注意以下两点。Take care when using "多少" as an adverb.

1. 表示"稍微"的意思,修饰形容词,只能用于已经发生的情况。It can only be used to describe a situation that has happened when it means "稍微."

(12) *后天你多少早点儿来。

(13) 后天你稍微早点儿来。

2. "多少"修饰形容词,不能用于祈使句。If it serves to modify an adjective, it cannot be used in an imperative sentence.

(14) *山路很窄,多少不小心,就会掉下山!

(15) 山路很窄,稍微不小心,就会掉下山!

(16) *请你多少再大声点儿!

(17) 请你稍微再大声点儿!

duǒ 躲 →P57"藏"

用法 Usage:

动词 v.

躲避,躲藏。表示故意离开或隐蔽起来,不让人发现,看见。多用作谓语。To hide; to conceal. It indicates leaving or hiding on purpose in order not to be easily found or seen. It is often used as a predicate.

(1) 你家这条小狗,老是躲着人。

(2) 听说有人要找他,他就躲起来了。

(3) 他正躲在家里复习功课呢。

说明 Notes:

"躲"和"藏"都有隐藏起来、不暴露的意思。Both "躲" and "藏" can mean hiding, not to be exposed.

两者的区别有以下四点。They differ from each other in the following four aspects.

1. "藏"可以是施事者的主动行为,也可以是受事者的被动行为。"躲"只是施事者的主动行为,没有被动行为,一般不用于被动句、把字句。"藏" can be both the active behavior of a doer and the passive behavior of an object. "躲," however, can only be the active behavior of a doer, so it cannot appear in passive sentences and the sentence structure with "把."

(4) 不知道她躲/藏到哪儿去了?

(5) *他们把小猫躲起来了。

(6) 他们把小猫藏起来了。

(7) 小猫被孩子们藏了起来。

2. "藏"的施事者和受事者除了人、动物或事物外,还可以是抽象事物。并且可受"深、深深地;严、严严地"等词语的修饰。"躲"不能这样用。Apart from people, animals or things, the doer and object of "藏" can also be abstract things. "藏" can also be modified by words like "深, 深深地, 严, 严严地." But "躲" does not have this usage.

(8) 她把自己的痛苦深深地/深藏在心底。

(9) 这些话不能讲给她听,只能严藏在心里。

3. "躲"有表示避开不愿接触对自己不利的人或事物的意思。"藏"没有。"躲" can indicate avoiding something or someone that is disadvantageous to oneself or that one is unwilling to come into contact. But "藏" does not have this usage.

(10) 雨下得那么大,到那儿去躲一躲吧。

(11) 刚才差一点儿撞到车了,辛亏她躲得快。

4. 在相对固定的词组中,"躲"与"藏"不能换用。如:在"躲得了初一,躲不了十五"和"躲得了今天,躲不了明天"等句子中,都不能用"藏"。"躲" and "藏" are not interchangeable in some set phrases such as "躲得了初一,躲不了十五," and "躲得了今天,躲不了明天."

ér 而 →P130"而且"

用法 Usage:

连词 conj.

"而"是从古汉语沿用下来的连词,多用于书面语。常连接形容词、形容词短语和动词、动词短语,也连接分句和句子,有时还连接段落,表示转折、并列、承接等关系。"而" is a conjunction from classical Chinese that is still in use, especially in written Chinese. It is often used to connect adjectives, adjectival phrases, verbs, or verb phrases, and can also be used to connect clauses and sentences. Sometimes it can be used to connect paragraphs, and can indicate a transition, juxtaposition, continuation, etc.

1. 表示转折关系。Indicating a transition.

"而"既可以表示轻度的转折,又可以表示重度的转折。其意思和作用相当于"可、可是、但、但是、然而、却、倒"等词语,但有时这些词语不能替代"而"。"而" can indicate a minor or major transition. Its meaning and usage are equivalent to words such as "可,可是,但,但是,然而,却,倒," but sometimes these words cannot be used in place of "而."

① 连接并列的动词、形容词,"而"前后两部分意思相反,或后一部分修正补充前一部分。Connecting juxtaposed verbs or adjectives. The words preceding and following "而" have opposite meanings, or the following section is used to revise or supplement the preceding section.

(1) 他的足球队常常胜而不骄。

(2) 杭州的东坡肉肥而不腻。

② 连接分句,表示相对或相反的两件事,"而"只能用在后面分句的开头。Connecting clauses to indicate two opposing situations, "而" can only be used at the beginning of the second clause.

(3) 上午他还在北京,而下午他已经到杭州了。

(4) 杭州已经是桃红柳绿,而哈尔滨还是冰天雪地。

③ 用于主语和谓语之间,表示假设,同时又含有转折意味,有"如果、但是"的意思,后面还要有表示结论的另一分句。常用于反问句。Used between the subject and the predicate, indicating a presumption and simultaneously implying a transition, with the same meaning as "如果,但是." It should be followed by another clause indicating a conclusion. It is often used in rhetorical questions.

(5) 你是个学生而不认真学习,能算学生吗?

(6) 做一个妈妈而不照顾孩子,能是个好妈妈?

2. 表示互相补充、承接关系。Indicating mutual supplementation, continuation.

① 连接并列的形容词。Connecting juxtaposed adjectives.

(7) 西藏美丽而神秘,吸引了很多中外游客。

(8) 王老师的课紧张而生动,同学们都很喜欢。

② 连接动词短语或句子,两部分内容有承接或递进的关系。连接的动词短语结构常常比较固定,如"取而代之、学而时习之"等。连接分句时,"而"常用于后一分句的开头。Connecting verb phrases or sentences where both parts have a continued or progressive relationship. The structure of the connected verb phrases is often fixed, as seen in "取而代之,学而时习之, etc." When connecting clauses, "而" is often placed at the beginning of the second clause.

(9) 你们的口语学得不错,而与中国朋友的交流进步也很大。

(10) 阿里将来要做汉语翻译,而玛丽还想当中国通呢。

3. 把表示目的、原因、依据、方式、状态等的状语连接到谓语动词上。Connecting adverbial modifiers to a verb predicate, indicating purpose, reasoning, foundation, manner, condition, etc.

① 前面用"为、为了、为着、因为、由于、通过、向、随着"等词语组成介词短语作状语,连接动词谓语。"而" can be preceded by "为,为了,为着,因为,由于,通过,向,随着, etc." to make prepositional phrases into adverbial modifiers or to connect verb predicates.

(11) 他为了减肥而拼命运动。

(12) 她的病随着气温升高而逐渐好转。

② 前面用"依、因、就、对、随、从"等介词,"而"后面常用单音节动词。When preceded by words such as "依,因,就,对,随,从,""而" is often followed by a monosyllabic verb.

(13) 这栋房子依山而建,风格独特。

(14) 树叶的颜色依季节而变。

③ 与介词"由、自、从"等组成"由/自/从……而……"等的格式,表示"从……到……"的意思,多连接在意义上可分阶段的名词性词语,表示从一个阶段(或状态)过渡到另一个阶段(或状态)。When used with the prepositions "由,自,从," etc., "而" can compose patterns such as "由/自/从…而…" to indicate the same meaning as "从…到…" (from … to …). These patterns often create noun-type phrases with semantically linked meanings that cover multiple stages or conditions, indicating that one stage (or condition) is transitioning to another stage (or condition).

(15) 每年的十一月,中国自北而南进入冬天。

(16) 黄河、长江由西而东,流入大海。

4. 用"而"衬托构成四个字的成语或短语,"而"起协调音节的作用。如:"不得而知、推而广之、无往而不胜"等。Using "而" to form a four-character idiom or phrase: "而" plays the role of balancing the syllables, as seen in "不得而知,推而广之,无往而不胜, etc."

érqiě 而且 →P36"并且"、P129"而"

用法 Usage:

连词 conj.

1. 表示意思更进一层,连接动词、形容词、副词、短语、分句或句子。Indicating that the meaning is advancing to another layer, linking verbs, adjectives, adverbs, phrases, clauses, or sentences.

① "而且"连接分句时,后面常有副词"还、也、又、更"配合使用,强调更进一层的意思。When connecting clauses, "而且" is often followed by adverbs "还,也,又,更," emphasizing advancement to a further layer of meaning.

(1) 我们班有很多韩国人,而且有的还是我高中的同学。

(2) 这几天的蔬菜不贵,而且农贸市场的更便宜。

② "而且"前面常常有"不但、不仅、不只、不光"等连词搭配使用,更加突出前后两句的

递进关系。"而且" is often preceded by conjunctions such as "不但,不仅,不只,不光." Arranged in pairs, it further highlights the progressive relationship of the two clauses.

(3) 这种手机不仅漂亮,而且特别实用。

(4) 用微信联系朋友。不但免费,而且更快更直接。

③ "而且"连接句子,如果句子较长,"而且"可以单独停顿。When "而且" is used to connect clauses, "而且" can stand alone with a pause if the clause is found relatively long.

(5) 我的中国朋友不但在学习上帮助我,而且,他还在生活上照顾我。

2. "而且"连接词语,表示并列关系。When used to connect words and expressions, "而且" expresses a parallel relationship.

(6) 你可以而且一定能学好汉语。

(7) 这篇文章的语言简单而且优美。

说明 Notes:

1. "而"和"而且"连接并列的形容词时,用法基本相同。如:"少而/而且精,简洁而/而且生动". When connecting juxtaposed adjectives, "而" and "而且" have a similar usage. For example, "少而/而且精,简洁而/而且生动."

它们的区别是:连接动词词语,表示递进或承接关系时,"而且"不能替代"而"。如:"取而代之"不能成为 *"取而且代之";"兼而有之"不能成为 *"兼而且有之"。Their difference is as follows: When connecting verbs and indicating a progressive or continual relationship, "而且" cannot be used in place of "而." For example, "取而代之" cannot be replaced by "取而且代之." "兼而有之" cannot be replaced by "兼而且有之."

2. "而且"和"并且"都能连接词、词组、分句和句子,表示后一部分有进一层的意思。前面有"不但、不仅"等连词搭配使用时,所表示的进一层的意思更加突出。"而且" and "并且" can both connect words, phrases, clauses, and sentences, indicating that the following section has advanced to a further layer of meaning. If preceded by "不但,不仅" or other similar conjunctions, the advancement of the layer of meaning is more prominent.

它们的区别是:The differences between them are as follows:

① "而且"可以连接动词,还可以连接单音节、双音节形容词。"并且"多连接动词和双音节形容词,一般不连接单音节形容词。"而且" can connect verbs, and can also connect monosyllabic or disyllabic adjectives. "并且" mostly connects verbs and disyllabic adjectives, and typically does not connect monosyllabic adjectives.

② "而且"可以表示并列关系,"并且"一般不能,只表示更进一层的意思。"而且" can express juxtaposed relationships, while "并且" typically cannot, as it only indicates advancement in layers of meaning.

èr 二 →P303 "两"

用法 Usage:

数词 num.

1. 一加一后所得数目。The sum arrived at when one is added to one.

二乘二等于四。

2. 序词。如:"第二、二哥、二月、二等品"等。Ordinal number, as in "第二,二哥,二月,二等品."

3. 两样。如:"货不二价、心不二用"等。Two different (things), as in "货不二价,心不二用."

4. 不专一。如:"三心二意、誓死不二"等。Not devoted, as in "三心二意,誓死不二."

说明 Notes:

注意,"二"主要用在:Note that "二" is primarily used in:

1. 读数目字。Reading numerals.

一、二、三、四

三分之二

零点二

2. 序数。如:"二班、二组、二叔"等。An ordinal number as in "二班,二组,二叔."

èrshǒu 二手

用法 Usage:

形容词 a.

指间接的,经人转手得来的或已经使用过再出售的(事物)。Secondhand, referring to things that have been passed on by another person or that have been previously used and now offered for resale.

(1) 这辆车不是新的,是二手车。

(2) 虽然这是二手的资料,但是也很有价值。

说明 Notes:

"二手"常与单音节的名词搭配,组成新的名词,如"二手车、二手房、二手烟"等。"二手" is often paired with monosyllabic nouns to compose a new noun. For example, "二手车,二手房,二手烟."

fā 发

用法 Usage:

动词 v.

1. 送出,交付(跟"收"相对)。后面可以带"了、过"等助词。*To send out; to deliver (the opposite of "收"). It can be followed by particles such as "了,过."*

(1) 他每星期给妈妈发电子邮件。

(2) 奖学金已经开始发了。

2. 发生,发作。后面多带名词。*To put forth; to flare up. It is often followed by a noun.*

(3) 春天来了,柳树已经发芽了。

(4) 妈妈发脾气了。

3. 表达,发布。*To publish; to express; to convey.*

(5) 她在报上发了一篇小说。

(6) 他对所有的事都要发发议论。

4. 感到(多指不舒服、不愉快的感觉、情况)。后面多带单音节、形容词性的词做宾语。*To feel, often referring to uncomfortable or unpleasant feelings or situations. It is often followed by monosyllabic adjective-type words functioning as a predicate.*

(7) 我的手和脚都发麻了。

(8) 吃得多了一点儿,胃开始发胀了。

5. 流露、呈现(多指不愉快的感情和不愉快的情况)。后面多带单音节、动词性词语做宾语。*To display; to show. It often indicates unpleasant feelings or situations, and is often followed by monosyllabic verb-type words functioning as a predicate.*

(9) 那人气得全身发抖了。

(10) 第一次上台演讲,我紧张到声音发颤。

6. 兴旺,发达。*To prosper; to flourish.*

(11) 他的公司这几年发了。

(12) 为了发家致富,他外出做生意了。

7. 发酵或因吸水而膨胀。*To ferment; to swell or expand as a result of absorbing water.*

(13) 做馒头先要发发面。

(14) 干木耳要用水先发一下才能做菜吃。

8. 起程。常用在四字词组,如"朝发夕至、整装待发"。*To set off on a journey. It is often used in four-character phrases such as "朝发夕至,整装待发."*

(15) 早上六点发车。

说明 Notes:

"发"这个动作有自主和不自主两种。动作由人直接控制、自主发出时,句子中的"发"可以重叠,如例(6)(16)。*The action "发" has both volitional and non-volitional types. If the action is performed by a person, when done volitionally, "发" can be reduplicated in a sentence, as seen in (6) and (16).*

(16) 大家都想发发财,把日子过得好一点儿。

动作不能自主,如描述人体各部分的感觉、自然的变化或在固定词组中时,句子中的"发"不能重叠,如例(7)(8)。*If the action is not volitional, such as describing feelings in parts of the body, natural changes, or when it is used in* set phrases, "发" cannot be reduplicated, as seen in (7) and (8).

fādá 发达 →P137"发展"
用法 Usage:
形容词 *a.*
表示事物发展的水平高（跟"落后"相对）。*Highly developed (the opposite of "落后").*
（1）这个城市的交通很发达。
（2）美国是发达国家，中国还是发展中国家。
（3）不能成为一个四肢发达、头脑简单的人。
动词 *v.*
发迹，显达。*Causing something to develop or move forward.*
（4）你今后发达了，可别忘了老同学啊。
说明 Notes:
1. 用"发达"造句，主语一般指的是事物、事业。常见主语有"经济、交通，工业、科技、事业、语言、文化"等，具有正面、积极的意义。一般不用于工作和学习。*When "发达" is used in a sentence, the subject is typically a professional or social undertaking or institution. Commonly used subjects include "经济，交通，工业，科技，事业，语言，文化，etc." that have a positive meaning. This word is typically not used to describe work or study.*
2. 用于人时，一般指人的身体的某一部位，特别指四肢、肌肉这些与精神相对的物质主体。如例（3）。*When used to describe people, it is typically used to refer to a specific part of the body, especially the arms and legs, muscles, or similar physical body parts not related to energy. See (3).*

fāhuī 发挥 →P136"发扬"
用法 Usage:
动词 *v.*
1. 把内在的性质或能力表现出来，产生（作用）。*To set forth an internal quality or ability; bring about (an effect or function).*
（1）孩子们发挥了自己的想象力，画出很多有意思的画儿。
（2）她的能力发挥得很出色，工作很不错。
2. 把意思或道理充分表达出来。*To express an idea or the truth clearly; to explain something fully.*
（3）事实就是这样，请不要借题发挥。
（4）他的文章把题意发挥得很完整。

fājué 发觉 →P135"发现"
用法 Usage:
动词 *v.*
开始察觉、发现（隐秘的或以前没有注意到的东西或行为）。宾语一般为动词短语或小句。*To begin to perceive; to discover (hidden or concealed objects or activities, or those which one has not previously paid attention to). The object is often a verb phrase or short sentence.*
（1）他回到家，才发觉自己把钥匙忘在办公室了。
（2）他一直低头玩游戏，没发觉有人偷走了他的包。

fāmíng 发明 →P74"创造"、P135"发现"
用法 Usage:
动词 *v.*
创造（前所未有的事物或方法）。动词"发明"只能带名词性宾语。*To invent; to create an object or methodology that is entirely new. This word can only be accompanied by noun-type objects.*
（1）他发明了一辆会飞的汽车。
（2）他发明了把废水变成新能源的方法。
名词 *n.*
创造出的新事物或新方法。*Newly-created objects or methods.*
（3）他的父亲全力支持他搞科学发明。
（4）这些发明让他成了发明大王。
说明 Notes:
"发明"和"创造"都表示造出前所未有的事物或方法。*"发明" and "创造" both indicate the*

creation of an object or a methodology that didn't exist before.

区别是：The differences are as follows:

1. "发明"着重于研制出原来没有的东西或方法。"创造"除了研制出新东西、想出新方法，还有建立新理论、做出新成绩等。使用范围比"发明"大。"发明" indicates the development of a previously unknown or nonexistent thing or methodology. "创造," aside from developing a new object or coming up with a new methodology, can also include establishing new theories and making new achievements. "创造" thus has a wider scope of application than "发明."

2. "发明"的对象一般是具体的东西或方法。"创造"的对象可以是"人类、世界、财富、语言、文字"等具体事物，也可以是"文化、历史、未来、条件、典型、人物、风格、理论、经验、奇迹、成绩、记录"等抽象事物，词语搭配范围比"发明"广得多。The object paired with "发明" is usually a physical object or methodology. The object paired with "创造" can be physical such as "人类,世界,财富,语言,文字," or can be intangible things such as "文化,历史,未来,条件,典型,人物,风格,理论,经验,奇迹,成绩,记录, etc.," and it can be paired with a much wider range of words than "发明."

3. "发明"可构成"发明家、发明者、发明人"等多指人的词语。"创造"可构成"创造性、创造力"等多指能力的词语，构词范围各有侧重。"发明" and "创造" are somewhat different in the way they form word combinations. "发明" often forms terms to refer to people, such as "发明家,发明者,发明人." "创造," by contrast, forms words such as "创造性" and "创造力," both of which indicate capability.

4. "发明"有名词用法，可以说"一项发明、新发明"。"创造"不能这样说。"发明" can be used as a noun, and can be used in phrases such as "一项发明,新发明." "创造" cannot be used in this way.

fāxiàn 发现 →P134"发觉"、P134"发明"

用法 Usage:

动词 v.

1. 经过研究、探索等，看到或找到本来存在但前人未知的事物或规律。To observe or find previously unobserved things or laws through research, exploration, etc.

（1）科学家发现鸟类与恐龙有紧密的关系。

（2）医学家发现通过拳击运动可以预防老年痴呆。

2. 发觉。To find.

（3）如果你坚持学习汉语，你会发现汉语很精美。

（4）他一出门就发现自己忘了带手机。

说明 Notes:

1. "发现"和"发觉"都有"觉察"的意思，在这个意义上，"发现"和"发觉"可以互换。如："我发现/发觉她已经走了。"Both "发现" and "发觉" have the meaning of "觉察" (to detect); when indicating this meaning, they are interchangeable. For example,"我发现/发觉她已经走了."

区别是：The differences are as follows:

① "发觉"着重于通过人的感官而觉察到，相当于"觉得"，是一种感觉或粗浅的认识。"发现"着重于借助一定的物质手段和思维方式认识到，是一种认识。在科学研究上，"发现"的结果具有较高的可靠度。"发觉"的事情不具有完全的可靠性，有时是一种心理感觉，一般用于日常生活。"发觉" emphasizes that something is detected through a person's senses (i.e. sight, touch, etc.), and like "觉得," it is a type of shallow recognition based on feeling. "发现" emphasizes that something is recognized through the aid of some technique or through reasoning. It is a higher level of recognition. In scientific research, the results of "发现" hold a relatively high degree of dependability. Things that use the verb "发觉" do not have complete dependability, and are sometimes a type of mental feeling, used more commonly in daily life.

② "发现"一般指经过探索或努力后而得到的结果,侧重于新的、奇怪的、与众不同的现象和事物,不同于一般看到的现象,所以日常具体的事物名词一般不能做"发现"的宾语。"发现" typically indicates a result that is obtained through exploration or effort, emphasizing a new, unusual, or uncommon phenomenon or object. So nouns referring to objects for daily use typically cannot be used as the object of "发现."

(5) *在街上,他发现了许多自行车。
(6) 在街上,他看到了许多自行车。
(7) *他发现桌子上有一只茶杯。
(8) 他看到桌子上有一只茶杯。

③ 除了表示"觉察"的意思以外,"发现"都不能换用"发觉"。"发现"的宾语大多是名词性宾语。"发觉"的宾语大多是非名词性宾语,不指事物或东西,所以不能用在如例(9)这种情况中。Aside from indicating the meaning of "觉察 (detect)," "发现" cannot be replaced by "发觉." "发现" almost always takes noun-type objects while "发觉" typically takes objects that are not nouns and cannot be used to refer to things, and as such cannot be used in (9).

(9) *天文学家发觉了一颗小行星。
(10) 天文学家发现了一颗小行星。

④ "发现"还有名词用法;"发觉"不能作名词用。"发现" also has a noun usage; "发觉" cannot be used as a noun.

2. "发现"和"发明"都指发觉了新事物。"发现" and "发明" both indicate the object of a discovery.

它们的区别是:Their differences are as follows:

① "发现"所指的不知道的事物或规律是已经存在的,只是到目前为止没有被看到,是人们经过研究探索把它揭示出来,"首先看到或找到"的。"发明"所指的不知道的事物、方法是原来并不存在的,人们通过创造活动,使它出现了,是"首次创造出"来的。"发现" indicates that the unknown objects or laws (i.e. of nature) previously existed but had not been observed until the present moment, something revealed through exploration or research, something "首先看到或找到的 (first observed or found)." "发明" indicates that unknown objects, methodology, etc. originally did not exist, and appeared through the creative action of people; they are "首次创造出来的 (first created by)."

② "发现"既可以用于事物,也可以用于事情、情况、问题等。"发明"只用于事物和方法,所以只能带名词性宾语。"发现" can also be used to describe objects as well as events, conditions, issues, etc. "发明" can only be used for objects or methods, and therefore can only go with noun-type objects.

fāyáng 发扬 →P134 "发挥"

用法 Usage:

动词 v.

发展和提倡,宣扬。To develop and advocate; to publicize.

(1) 我们在学习上要发扬不怕困难的精神。
(2) 一个人要善于发扬优点,改正缺点。

说明 Notes:

"发扬"和"发挥"都指把性能表现出来。"发扬" and "发挥" both indicate displaying a natural ability.

区别是:The differences are as follows:

1. "发挥"着重于把事物内在的潜力、性质、能力等充分表现出来,对象一般是隐藏在内部的事物,如"才能、作用、特长、力量、积极性、主动性、创造力、想象力、聪明才智"等,是中性词。"发扬"是着重在原有的基础上进一步扩展、加强或提高,对象一般都是已经存在的好的事物,如"优点、传统、作风、精神、成绩、风格"等,是褒义词。"发挥" emphasizes fully displaying something's inherent potential, nature, capability, etc. and its object is typically something hidden inside something else, for example, "才能,作用,特长,力量,积极性,主性,创造力,想象,聪明才智, etc." It is a neutral term. "发扬" indicates expansion on an already-existing foundation, strengthening or improving, and the object is typically a positive thing that already exists, for example, "优点,传统,作风,精神,成绩,风格, etc." It is a commendatory term.

2. "发扬"没有"发挥"的第二个义项和用法。"发扬" does not have the same usage as "发挥" in the second usage.

fāzhǎn 发展 →P134"发达"

用法 Usage:

动词 v.

1. 事物由小到大、由简单到复杂、由低级到高级地变化,使上升。(Of something) to change from small to large, simple to complex, or from a low to a high level; to be made to improve.

(1) 我们大学要大力发展研究生学位教育。

(2) 发展农业现代化是中国四个现代化的内容之一。

2. 扩大,扩充(规模、组织)。To expand and strengthen (scale or organization).

(3) 汉语角人越来越多,发展得很快。

(4) 他的公司很快地发展到了全国各地。

说明 Notes:

"发展"和"发达"两个词的区别是:The differences between "发展" and "发达" are as follows:

1. "发达"是形容词。"发展"是动词。"发达" is an adjective while "发展" is a verb.

2. "发展"侧重于表示由小到大、由简单到复杂、由低级到高级上升的过程,强调一种上升式的不停止变化,可受"不、欠、较"等表示不同阶段的副词修饰。"发达"侧重于表示充分发展后达到的较高状态,具有一种完成的持续状态的色彩。因此,"发达"不能与"继续"等表示非完成意义的词搭配,"发展"则可以。"发展" emphasizes change from small to large, simple to complex, or the process of elevation from a low level to a high level. It focuses on the unceasing change of a type of improvement. It can be modified by adverbs such as "不,""欠," and "较," to indicate different levels. The emphasis of "发达" is on the fact that with full development, something has reached a better condition and an already completed, lasting state. Thus, "发达" cannot be paired with words such as "继续" to indicate that something is incomplete, while "发展" can be used in this way.

fánshì 凡是

用法 Usage:

副词 ad.

总括某个范围内的一切,表示在某一范围内无一例外,有"只要是"的意思。Including everything within a certain scope; indicating that there is no exception in a certain range. It has the same meaning as "只要是."

(1) 凡是鲁迅先生写的小说我都看过了。

(2) 凡是这个公司的职员都参加了昨天的晚会。

说明 Notes:

1. "凡是"也可以单用"凡",一般用在句首。"凡是" can also be written simply as "凡." It is typically used at the beginning of a sentence.

(3) *我凡是想要的东西都有了。

(4) 凡是/凡我想要的东西都有了。

2. "凡是"后面常跟有"都、没有不、总、尽、无不、无一、一律"等词语,其基本句型为"凡是……都/就/没有不"。"凡是" is often

followed by words such as "都, 没有不, 总, 尽, 无不, 无一, 一律" and its basic sentence pattern is "凡是...都/就/没有不."

3. "凡是"后面一般是有定语修饰的名词或名词短语，而这些名词或名词性短语常常是句子的主语。"凡是" is often followed by words or phrases with attributive qualities, and these nouns or noun phrases are often the subject of the sentence.

fán 烦

用法 Usage:

形容词 *a.*

1. 烦闷, 烦躁。 *Unhappy; moody; agitated.*

(1) 最近要解决的问题太多了, 我烦得很。

(2) 和女朋友分手, 他心里很烦, 每天都喝酒。

2. 又多又乱。 *Chaotic and confused; disorderly.*

(3) 他说话怎么那么烦。

(4) 出国的手续太烦了, 你得耐心去办。

动词 *v.*

1. 使人讨厌, 厌倦。 *To trouble or frustrate someone.*

(5) 最近我正为找工作发愁呢, 别烦我。

(6) 别唱了, 你的声音烦得我什么书也看不了。

2. 请, 托。敬辞。 *(Politely) to ask or plead with someone to do something as a favor.*

(7) 烦您给他捎个信, 我明天不去找他了。

(8) 这个房间刚打扫干净, 烦您换鞋再进。谢谢!

说明 Notes:

多与单音节词, 配合使用, 如"别烦我、烦你了"等。"烦" *often pairs with monosyllabic words. For example, "别烦我, 烦你了."*

fánhuá 繁华 →P138"繁荣"

用法 Usage:

形容词 *a.*

形容城镇、街市繁荣热闹。 *Flourishing and busy; prosperous. It is used to describe cities, towns, or downtown areas.*

(1) 这一带是城里最繁华的地区。

(2) 南京路是上海最繁华的一条商业街。

fánróng 繁荣 →P138"繁华"

用法 Usage:

形容词 *a.*

形容经济或事物蓬勃发展、兴旺昌盛。做谓语, 可带宾语表示使动用法。 *Fast and flourishing development of an economy or of a thing; thriving and prosperous. When used as a predicate, it can take an object and indicate a causative action.*

(1) 这个城市经济发达, 市场繁荣。

动词 *v.*

使繁荣。 *To cause something to flourish.*

(2) 我们要努力繁荣经济, 提高人民生活水平。

说明 Notes:

"繁华"和"繁荣"都形容兴旺的景象, 都是褒义词。 *Both being commendatory terms, "繁华" and "繁荣" are used to describe a flourishing scene.*

它们的区别是： *They differ as follows:*

1. "繁华"侧重于兴旺热闹的具体景象。多形容街道、城镇、市场等地方的热闹, 如人群众多、商业发达、物品丰盛等景象。"繁荣"侧重指经济或各项事业的蓬勃发展、欣欣向荣。常形容"经济、工业、商业、科学、文化、艺术、国家、社会"等比较抽象的重大事物, 也形容"城镇、市场"等具体地方, 使用范围比"繁华"广一些。 *"繁华" emphasizes the description of a physical place that is flourishing and bustling. It is often used to describe streets, cities, markets, and other such places with large crowds of people, developed businesses, and an abundant supply of products. "繁荣" describes the flourishing development of a thriving economy or business. It is often used to describe "economy, industry, commerce, science, culture, art, country, society" or other concepts that are abstract but important. It can also be used to describe cities*

and towns, markets, and other physical locations; its scope of usage is wider than that of "繁华."

2. "繁荣"除有形容词词性外,还有动词词性,表示"使……繁荣"的意思。如"繁荣"例(2)。"繁华"只作形容词。 Aside from having an adjectival usage, "繁荣" can also be used as a verb to indicate "使…繁荣," as seen in Example (2) under "繁荣." "繁华" can only be used as an adjective.

fǎn 反

用法 Usage:

形容词 a.

颠倒的,方向相背的(跟"正"相对)。 Upside down, inside out or backwards [the opposite of "正 (straight, properly oriented)"].

(1) 你把毛衣穿反了。
(2) 这个汉字的偏旁写反了。

动词 v.

1. 反抗,反对。如:"反侵略、反法西斯、反腐败"等。 To oppose; to fight. For example, "反侵略,反法西斯,反腐败."

2. 翻转。常用于四字词组,如:"反败为胜、反客为主、易如反掌"等。 To flip over. Often used in four-character phrases. For example, "反败为胜,反客为主,易如反掌."

3. 类推。如:"举一反三"。 To reason by analogy. For example, "举一反三."

4. 背叛。 To betray.

(3) 你想反我?

副词 ad.

反而,相反地。 Conversely; on the contrary.

(4) 他自己不明白,反说别人糊涂。
(5) 她不但不感谢,反把好心当坏意。

fǎn'ér 反而 →P509"相反"

用法 Usage:

副词 ad.

表示后面的句子跟前面说的意思相反,或出乎预料和常情之外,在句中起转折作用。 On the contrary; instead, indicating the clause that follows has the opposite meaning of what has just been said or goes against what is expected or normal. Typically appearing in the middle of a sentence, it functions as a turning point.

(1) 风不但没停,反而更大了。
(2) 老师没有批评他,反而表扬了他。

说明 Notes:

1. "反而"常用在复句中,常与"不但不/没有""不仅不/没有"等词搭配使用,形成"不但不/没有……,反而……""不仅不/没有……,反而……"的格式,表示不但没有出现符合常理常情或预期的情况,还出现了相反的结果。如例(1)(2)。 "反而" is often used in complex or compound sentences, and is often paired with phrases such as "不但不/没有," "不仅不/没有" to form patterns "不但不/没有...,反而..." or "不仅不/没有...,反而...." Such patterns indicate that nothing conventional, reasonable or expectable has happened, but that the result was the very opposite of what is expected, as seen in (1) and (2).

2. 如果前后两个句子,不是同一主语,"反而"应在后一主语之后。 If the two clauses do not have the same subject, "反而" should be placed behind the second subject.

(3) 到了考试的时候,他反而玩得更起劲了。
(4) 这个学期他看课外书看得更多,学习成绩反而比以前好了。

fǎnfù 反复 →P68"重复"

用法 Usage:

副词 ad.

表示重复多次,一次又一次地。 Repeatedly; again and again; over and over again.

(1) 汉语的声调一定要反复练习才能掌握。
(2) 他反复考虑,最后决定去中国留学。

动词 v.

1. 前面的过程又重复出现。做谓语。(Of a process that is previously mentioned) to occur again. It is used as a predicate.

(3) 如果你不好好休息,你的病情还会反复。

(4) 要注意这个语法错误,你已经反复了好几次。

2. 表示颠来倒去；推翻前面的决定。To reverse or overturn a previous decision, indicating "over and again."

(5) 他是个反复无常人。他的话不能随便相信。

(6) 那件事已经决定,不能再反复了。

名词 n.

表示重复的情况。(Of a condition) appearing again; (Of a disease) having a relapse.

(7) 他的病可能还会有反复。

说明 Notes:

"反复"和"重复"的动词用法,表示同一言行或现象等再次或多次出现。When used as a verb, both "反复" and "重复" indicate the same thing has happened more than once or the same statement has been made more than once.

它们的区别是：They differ as follows:

1. "反复"着重于一次又一次地多次出现,不一定照原来的样子。一般只能修饰表示有持续动作的动词,如"讨论、研究、考虑、思考"等。"重复"着重于已出现的言行或现象等再重新出现一次或多次,强调照原样、无变化的出现。"反复" emphasizes that something has happened over and over again, but not necessarily in conformity with the original state. It can typically only modify verbs or actions that express continuity, such as "讨论,研究,考虑,思考." "重复," by contrast, emphasizes statements, actions or phenomena that have reoccurred once or multiple times but are consistently the same each time and do not change with each occurrence.

2. "反复"做谓语,一般不能用于"把"字句。"重复"作谓语,可用于"把"字句。When used as a predicate, "反复" typically cannot be used in conjunction with "把." When "重复" is used as a predicate, it can be used with "把."

(8) *你把这句话反复一遍。

(9) 你把这句话重复一遍。

3. "反复"重叠为"反反复复",表示事物、情况的来回变化、不确定。动词"重复"重叠为"重复重复"；形容词"重复"重叠为"重重复复"。"反复" can be reduplicated as "反反复复" to indicate repeated change and uncertainty. The verb "重复" is reduplicated as "重复重复" while the adjective "重复" is reduplicated to become "重重复复."

(10) 他的感冒已经反反复复好几次了。

(11) 我就怕事情反反复复。

(12) 奶奶重重复复地只唠叨一句话。

(13) 老师跟你说的话你再重复重复。

4. "反复"有表示翻悔、颠来倒去的意思。"重复"没有这个意思。"反复" can mean backing out of a commitment or promise or reconsidering one's original decision. "重复" does not have this meaning.

(14) *说一是一,说二是二,决不重复。

(15) 说一是一,说二是二,决不反复。

fǎnkàng 反抗 →P111"抵抗"

用法 Usage:

动词 v.

表示用行动反对、抵抗。To actively oppose something; to resist or revolt against.

(1) 中国人民坚决反抗外来武力的侵略。

(2) 青春期的孩子常常会激烈反抗爸妈对他的要求。

说明 Notes:

"抵抗"和"反抗"都是动词,都可表示用力量制止别人的进攻。"抵抗" and "反抗" are

both verbs, and both express using force to stop another person's attack.

它们的区别是：They differ as follows:

1. "抵抗"强调用力量制止某种进攻,可以有直接的行动,也可以没有具体的行为动作,如:"抵抗病菌的侵入"。"反抗"强调用明显的行为动作回击外力的侵略或者某种势力的压制。如例(1)(2)。 "抵抗" emphasizes using force to stop some type of attack. It may or may not involve direct or concrete action, as in "抵抗病菌的侵入." "反抗" emphasizes taking visible action to counterattack the aggression of an invader or the oppression of an outsider, as seen in (1) and (2).

2. 对象有所不同,搭配的词语不同。"抵抗"的对象一般是敌对的武力,搭配的词语,如"侵略、进攻、屠杀"等。"反抗"的对象与搭配的词语,除敌对武力的"侵略、进攻"等以外,还常常是"压迫、剥削、统治"等。The objects are somewhat different, and words that can be paired with each are different. The object of "抵抗" is a hostile force and can be paired with words such as "侵略,进攻,屠杀." "反抗" not only can be paired with words describing hostile forces such as "侵略" and "进攻," but is also used with words such as "压迫,剥削,统治."

3. "抵抗"的对象一般是群体力量,不是单个的人,"反抗"的对象还可以是个人。The object of "抵抗" is typically a collective force, not a single person. But the object of "反抗" can be an individual.

fǎnyìng 反应 →P141"反映"

用法 Usage:

动词 *v.*

表示有机体受到外界刺激后引起相应的活动,也可以指物质发生化学或物理的变化。To respond, meaning that the effect of external stimuli on an organism has given rise to a certain reaction; (Of a substance) to go through chemical or physical change.

（1）他讲了一个笑话,但大家一时没反应过来,都没笑。

（2）吃了药以后,她的反应很大。

名词 *n.*

1. 表示由于受到某些刺激而引起的相应的情况和现象。A phenomenon or condition that has occurred because of an outside stimulus; response; reaction.

（3）老师教你回答问题,你的反应太慢了。

（4）这件事在学生中引起了不小的反应。

2. 由某种情况引起的看法、评价、态度等。An attitude, evaluation, or opinion resulting from exposure to some type of condition.

（5）对他的工作,大家的反应很好。

（6）朋友给他介绍了三个女朋友,但他没有任何反应。

3. 表示因打针、吃药或其他物质对身体引起的异常症状。Abnormal symptoms or bodily reactions brought on by injections, medications, or other substances.

（7）他吃鱼,皮肤就有过敏反应。

（8）她对花粉有过敏反应。

fǎnyìng 反映 →P141"反应"

用法 Usage:

动词 *v.*

1. 通过水或镜子把物体返照出来。To reflect the image of some object in water, a mirror, etc.

（1）西湖水把保俶塔的倒影反映得非常清楚。

（2）两岸楼房和大树的倒影,反映在清清的运河水面上。

2. 比喻把客观事物或现象的实质显示出来。To metaphorically display the essence of an objective thing or phenomenon.

（3）这篇小说反映了中国改革开放的社会现实。

(4) 同学们的歌声反映了他们对中国的友好感情。

3. 把客观情况或别人的意见告诉上级或有关部门。To make the objective conditions or the opinions of others known to the upper levels in an organization or a relevant department.

(5) 学生们把他们的要求向老师反映了。
(6) 请你向上级反映反映我们这里的情况。

名词 n.

指反映的意见（多是批评的）。Ideas (often criticisms) that are brought to the attention of related people or department.

(7) 多听听学生的反映，可以提高教学水平。
(8) 你听到学生对食堂的反映没有？

说明 Notes:

1. "反映"的本义是镜子中的映像或反照，又经常引申使用于人脑、人的思想，如："一部音乐作品是音乐人自己思想、情感的反映。""反映"还是哲学上和心理学上的专有名词。The original meaning of "反映" is the reflection of an image seen in a mirror, and this meaning is often extended to include people's minds and thoughts, for example "一部音乐作品,是音乐人自己思想,情感的反映." In the realms of philosophy and psychology, "反映" is a noun with its proper meaning.

2. "反应"和"反映"都有显示事物的作用。但语义上不同。Both "反应" and "反映" carry the meaning of displaying something, but they are semantically different.

区别是：Their differences are as follows:

① "反应"着重于受到外界刺激后,生命体相应的活动,不同的生命体,其活动的程度是不一样的,因此对相同的外界事物或刺激,会有各种各样的反应,反应的内容具有较强的主观性。"反映"的本义是镜子中的映像或反照,被反映出来时是客观的,不做什么改变。因此,两个词不能替换。"反应" emphasizes the reaction of a living organism to some stimulus from the outside world. Different substances or living organisms have different levels and types of reaction, and therefore may have different reactions to the same external stimuli. The content of the reaction has a relatively strong subjectivity. The original meaning of "反映" is the image of a reflection in a mirror, water, etc. The reflected thing is seen objectively and does not change. Thus, these two words are not interchangeable.

② "反应"作动词用时,不能重叠,后边不能带宾语,不能带"了、着、过",只能带补语"过来"。"反映"可以带宾语,可以重叠使用,如例(6)。When used as a verb, "反应" cannot be reduplicated, and it cannot take an object. It also cannot be used with "了,着,过", and can only be used with the complement "过来." By contrast, "反映" can take an object and can be reduplicated, as seen in Example (6).

fǎnzhèng 反正

用法 Usage:

副词 ad.

1. 强调在任何情况下结果都一样。前面句子中常有"无论、不管",或表示正反两种情况的词语。多用在主语前。Indicating that the results will be the same under any type of conditions. The first clause often contains the word "无论" or "不管," or indicates or describes two opposing (proper and improper) conditions. It usually appears before the subject of the second clause.

(1) 不管你同意不同意,反正我一定要去。
(2) 无论钱多钱少,反正我不干了。
(3) 他来不来还没决定,反正我一定来。

2. 表示坚决肯定的语气。一般用在句子开头。Carrying a firmly definite tone, it is typically placed at the beginning of a sentence.

(4) 你不用着急,反正钱我一定会给你的。
(5) 大家尽量喝吧,反正我们家有的是酒。

(6) 慢慢来，反正我们有的是时间。

3. 指明情况或原因，意思与"既然"相近，但语气更强。多用在动词、形容词或主语前。*Pointing out a condition or reason, it has a similar meaning to "既然" but with a more emphatic tone. It is often placed before a verb, adjective, or the subject of a sentence.*

(7) 路反正不远，我们就走着去吧。

(8) 他反正要去食堂，给你把饭带回来，不麻烦。

说明 Notes：

运用"反正"的三种用法时一定要注意：*Be sure to pay attention to the three usages of "反正":*

1. 强调任何情况下结果都一样的语义时，与"无论……都/也……""不管……都/也……"句式的用法基本相同。一般情况下，后一分句用了"反正"，常常与"一定"配合使用，语气非常强烈，"都、也"一般不再使用，如例(1)(3)。"反正"可用在主语前，也可用在主语后。但用在主语前，语气更强烈。*When used to stress that the results will be the same regardless of the conditions, it is used the same way as "无论…都/也…" or "不管…都/也…." Under normal circumstances, the second clause starting with "反正" often goes with "一定" and carries a more emphatic tone. "都" and "也" are typically not used, as seen in (1) and (3). "反正" can be placed before or after the subject of the sentence, but it has a stronger semantic emphasis when placed before the subject.*

2. 表示肯定语气的用法时，一般有两个分句组成。前一分句表示对别人的要求，后一分句表示这一要求的原因或理由。"反正"一般用在表示原因或理由那个句子的开头。*There are usually two clauses when expressing an affirmation. The first clause indicates the request of someone else while the second one expresses the cause or reason of that request. "反正" usually appears at the beginning of the second clause.*

3. 指明情况或原因的用法与第二种用法有点相像，都有一种因果关系。两个分句前后次序可以互换。区别是：第三种用法强调原因，"反正"用在前面的表示原因的分句中，要求后面一定是动词、形容词或小句，如例(7)(8)。*The third usage of indicating a condition or reason is like that of the second usage: both represent a cause-and-effect relationship, and the sequence of the two clauses can be exchanged. The difference is that the third usage stresses reasoning. When "反正" is used in the first clause indicating a cause or reason, what follows must be a verb or adjectival phrase or a clause, as in (7) and (8).*

fāngfǎ 方法 →P143"方式"

用法 Usage：

名词 *n.*

解决问题并达到某种目的的门路、措施、程序等。*Method, way or procedure for solving a problem or reaching a goal.*

(1) 学习汉语有许多好方法。

(2) 他们采用了一种新的研究方法。

fāngshì 方式 →P143"方法"

用法 Usage：

名词 *n.*

说话做事所采取的方法和形式。*Way or method of saying or doing something.*

(1) 批评别人要注意方式。

(2) 东西方人的生活方式有很大的不同。

说明 Notes：

"方法"和"方式"都是指工作、学习的手段。可以并用。如："批评人要注意方式方法"。*Both "方法" and "方式" refer to the way or method of doing something, including study. They can be juxtaposed to express an idea, as in: "批评人要注意方式方法."*

区别是：The differences are as follows:

1. "方法"侧重表示解决问题的具体做法，常与"思想、工作、学习、创作"等词搭配。"方式"侧重表示办事、说话所采取的办法和形式，更为具体，有一种外在的客观性，常与"生活、生产、经营"等词搭配使用。"方法" emphasizes the concrete method(s) of solving a problem; it often goes with words such as "思想,工作,学习,创作." "方式," by contrast, emphasizes the way or method of doing something or saying something. It tends to be more specific and objective, and therefore it often goes with words such as "生活,生产,经营."

2. "方式"常用于生活、工作、生产等方面，形成固定搭配"生活方式、居住方式、行为方式、生产方式"等。"方法"可构成"想方设法、方法论"等固定结构。Often applied to our daily life, work, and production, "方式" is found in fixed expressions as "生活方式,居住方式,行为方式,生产方式." By contrast, "方法" appears in fixed expressions such as "想方设法,方法论."

fǎngfú 仿佛 →P191"好像"、P439"似乎"

用法 Usage:
副词 ad.

1. 表示不十分确定的感觉和判断，似乎，好像。Seemingly; as if. It is used to indicate an uncertain judgment.

(1) 这个人我仿佛在哪儿见过。
(2) 看样子，仿佛他很痛苦。

2. 表示某一情况或事物表面如此或某人这样认为，后面常有"实际上、事实上、其实"等词语开头的分句，进一步说明真实情况。Looking as if; indicating a judgment made on the basis of seeing what appears on the surface. It is often followed by "实际上,""事实上," or "其实," which is placed at the beginning of another sentence and will clarify the situation.

(3) 他看起来仿佛很傻，其实很聪明。
(4) 他的字表面上仿佛不漂亮，实际上这是很难学的孩儿体。

动词 v.

像，差不多。表示两个人或事物相类似。多用于书面语。(Of two people or things) to be similar; to look more or less the same. It usually appears in the written language.

(5) 这两座楼房的外观相仿佛。
(6) 这个孩子的年龄跟我儿子的年龄相仿佛。

说明 Notes:

1. "仿佛"作动词表示两个人或两个事物相类似时，一般在前面加副词"相"，构成"相仿佛"的短语。"仿佛," as a verb, often goes with "相" to form "相仿佛," which is used to indicate the similarity between two people or two things.

2. "仿佛"用作动词时，一般不能带宾语、补语，也不能带时态助词"着、了、过"。"仿佛," as a verb, cannot take an object or complement, nor can it be placed with any aspect markers like "着,了,过."

fǎngwèn 访问 →P57"参观"

用法 Usage:
动词 v.

有目的地去看并了解情况。可以是对人，也可以是对某个工厂、农村、家庭等地方。To visit; to go and see first-hand so that one can understand something. It can be applied to people or to a factory, a farm or a family, etc.

(1) 这个周末我访问了几个农民工的家庭。
(2) 他就要出国访问，可能半个月以后才能回来。

说明 Notes:

"参观"和"访问"都能去有关处所，可以带表示处所的宾语。Both "参观" and "访问" can take the name of a place as its object.

(3) 我们参观/访问了丝绸博物馆。

区别是：Their differences are as follows:

1. 词义侧重点不同。"参观"重在"看"，实地观察。"访问"的原意是有目的地去看一个人并与他谈话，词义重在"问"，重在通过谈话了解。因此两个动词可以带的宾语有所不同。"参观"的宾语多为"工厂、农村、展览馆、博物馆"等，或者是表示名胜古迹的名词，如"故宫、颐和园"等。"参观"不能带表示人的宾语。"访问"可以带表示处所的宾语，但必定含有谈话了解的内容，并多带有表示人的宾语。"参观" emphasizes "看," that is, seeing with one's own eyes; it is a kind of on-the-spot inspection. "访问," by contrast, carries the original meaning of purposefully visiting a place to talk with someone. So it emphasizes "问" — to understand through a talk. As a result, "参观" and "访问" take different objects. The former goes with "工厂, 农村, 展览馆, 博物馆, etc.," or a noun indicating a scenic spot or a place of historical interest, such as "故宫" and "颐和园." "参观," by contrast, cannot take a person as its object. And while "访问" may take the name of a place as its object, it has to contain some information about what is learned through a talk (or talks). "访问" often takes a person as its object.

（4）＊下个星期老师要带我们去参观一个农民工。

（5）下个星期老师要带我们去访问一个农民工。

（6）＊昨天我们访问了他新买的房子。

（7）昨天我们参观了他新买的房子。

2. "访问"的词义在使用中有所演变。范围由访问人扩大到了访问地区、国家。词义从有目的地去看一个人并谈话，参合了"参观、拜访"的意思。因此"访问"还可以带表示国家的宾语。"参观"不能。The meaning of "访问" has undergone some changes through many years of use. One can now "访问" a country or a region. It does not just mean visiting some place to talk with someone, but calling on someone. As a result, "访问" can now take the name of a country as its object.

（8）＊他明天就要出国参观。
（9）他明天就要出国访问。
（10）＊她成功地参观了英国、法国。
（11）她成功地访问了英国、法国。

fàng 放 →P11"摆"

用法 Usage:
动词 v.

1. 解除约束，使自由。To remove the restrictions on; to free.

（1）我们把小鸟放了吧。
（2）你们放了我吧，我要回家做作业了。

2. 在一定的时间停止（工作或学习）。To stop working or studying at a certain time.

（3）快放暑假了，你们打算去哪儿旅游？
（4）这几天太累了，我要给自己放放假，休息休息。

3. 放牧，把牲畜或家禽赶到屋子外面去找东西吃或活动。To allow animals or poultry to go outside the house and look for food by themselves.

（5）我在农村的时候，每天早上要把羊放到山上去。
（6）你们放过牛吗？

4. 发出、发射。To let off; to shoot.

（7）西湖博览会的时候，西湖边放礼花，可好看了。
（8）你听，这好像是放枪的声音。

5. 点燃。To ignite.

（9）春节的时候，差不多家家都要放鞭炮。
（10）他们俩的婚礼上还放了很多烟花。

6. 扩展、扩大。To enlarge; to extend.

（11）这张照片你要放大吗？
（12）放眼看看，这里的变化多大呀！

7. 搁置，使停留在原来的地方或状态。To put aside; to lay aside.

（13）今天的作业放一放，把昨天的作业先做起来。

(14) 东西在冰箱里不能放得太久。

8. 安置,安放,使(人或事物)处于一定的位置。*To place something at a certain place; to make a person stay at a certain spot.*

(15) 把行李放到车后座去,前面坐人。

(16) 书架里应该放书,为什么放那么多糖果?

9. 加进去。*To add something into.*

(17) 锅里炒的青菜还没放过盐。

(18) 我喜欢在咖啡里放点儿糖、放点儿牛奶。

10. 放送,放映。*To show; to play; to project.*

(19) 今天晚上学校大礼堂放电影《西游记》。

(20) 我给你放 CD,好吗?

11. 使物体随气流上升或随水移动。*To allow something to fly with the air flow or with water.*

(21) 每到春天,许多孩子都到广场上来放风筝。

(22) 我们把小纸船放到水里,让它漂到大海去好吗?

12. 控制速度、声音、态度等,使达到某种状态。*To control the speed, sound, or attitude, making them reach a certain state.*

(23) 车开得太快了,放慢点儿。

(24) 你把声音放小一点儿,人家都休息了。

13. 花朵开放,常用于四字词语中。如:"百花齐放、心花怒放"等。*(Of flowers) to bloom, often used in four-character words, such as "百花齐放,心花怒放."*

说明 Notes:

"放"是个多义项动词,其中只是"安置、安放,使处于一定的位置"这一义项与"摆"的第一义项有相同之处。在这个义项上,"摆"和"放"的用法是一样的。*"放" is a verb that has many different meanings. Only when it means "to place something at a certain place; to make a person stay at a certain spot" does it have the*

same meaning as the first meaning of "摆." That is where "摆" and "放" are used in the same way.

区别是: *The differences are as follows:*

1. "放"的语义重在东西安置在什么地方,安置的地方可以是让人看得见这东西或者也可以是人看不见这东西的地方。要把东西安置在人一眼看不见的地方时一般用"放",不用"摆"。*"放" emphasizes placing something in a place where people can see it readily or cannot see it at all. "放," not "摆," is used when the thing is put in a place not readily seen by anyone.*

(25) *那张照片我摆进照相本里了。

(26) 那张照片我放进照相本里了。

2. 语义侧重在陈列出来、有次序地排列出来让人看时,一般用"摆",不用"放"。*"摆," not "放," is used when we emphasize displaying something, arranging it in an orderly way.*

(27) *把那套我从中国带回来的瓷器放出来,让大家看看。

(28) 把那套我从中国带回来的瓷器摆出来,让大家看看。

3. 如果"摆""放"后面有处所宾语时,在语法意义上是相同的,在语义上都侧重于东西搁置在什么地方,强调处所。*If "摆" or "放" is followed by an object indicating the place where something is kept, then both are correct; both emphasize the place where something is kept.*

(29) 把那套我从中国带回来的瓷器摆在餐桌上,让大家看看。

(30) 把那套我从中国带回来的瓷器放在餐桌上,让大家看看。

fēi……bù 非……不

用法 Usage:

副词"非"与"不"组成固定结构,表示一定要这样,必须,必定。"非"后面多为动词或动词短语,也可以用小句或指人的名词。"非"后面有时加"得"。句子后一部分常用"不行、不可、不成"等。"非" and "不," both adverbs, are combined into a fixed expression meaning "have to be like this; it is required that …; necessarily." Words that follow are usually a verb, a verb phrase or a clause or a noun indicating a person. In the second part of the sentence one can often find "不行,不可,不成."

(1) 要学好芭蕾舞非得下苦功夫不可。
(2) 要开这辆车非李师傅不行。

说明 Notes:

"非……不"是双重否定,表示一定要这样。在口语中,句子后面也可以不用"不可"等词语,常用于承接上文或反问句中。"非...不" constitute a double negative meaning "It is absolutely necessary that…." In oral Chinese, the second part may not contain the word "不可" or a similar expression. This usage is quite common in a rhetorical question or a context that allows it naturally.

(3) 为什么非要他写,我写不可以吗?
(4) 学习写汉字非得有耐心。

fēicháng 非常 →P196"很"、P414"十分"

用法 Usage:

副词 ad.

表示程度极高,极,十分。可以重叠。Very much, exceedingly, indicating a very high degree. It can be reduplicated as "非常非常."

(1) 这几天,杭州的天气非常舒服。
(2) 我非常喜欢看电影。

形容词 a.

不同寻常的,不一般的,特殊的。多与名词结合,类似一个复合词语,也可以构成"的"字短语再修饰名词。有时用作补语。Unusual; out of the ordinary; special. Often it is combined with a noun to form a complex expression. Also it can be a phrase with "的" to modify a noun. Sometimes, it is just used as a complement.

(3) 现在是非常时期,请多保重!
(4) 大热天突然一场冰雹,真是非常的现象。
(5) 这儿人来人往,热闹非常。

fèi 费

用法 Usage:

动词 v.

1. 花费,耗费。To consume; to spend.
(1) 我费了半天时间,才写完这篇作文。
(2) 孩子留学的事要你费心费力了。

2. 用的过多,消耗过多(跟"省"相对)。To overspend; to over-consume (the opposite of "省").
(3) 妈妈说我这个月用钱太费了。
(4) 这种空调很费电。

名词 n.

费用。The amount of money.
(5) 在法国上大学要多少学费?
(6) 夏天和冬天的电费一定比春秋天高。

fēnbié 分别 →P148"分离"、P381"区别"

用法 Usage:

动词 v.

1. 分开,离别。To say good-bye to; to be separated.
(1) 我们高中毕业分别已经有二十年了。
(2) 他和女朋友刚见面又要分别,真遗憾!

2. 区分,辨别。To distinguish; to tell A from B.
(3) 我分别不出这两个包有什么不同。
(4) 这场电影里很难分别出谁好谁坏。

副词 ad.

表示分头,各自。Separately; respectively.
(5) 明天七点出发,现在我们分别去通知学生吧。
(6) 这几个问题我明天会分别解释一下。

名词 n.

表示不同。Being different.
(7) "未"和"末"两个字笔画的分别一定要看清楚。

说明 Notes：

副词"分别"表示的"分头、各自"意义的用法有三种。"分别," as an adverb, has three different uses when it means "separately" or "respectively."

1. 一个主体对几个对象。One subject vs. several objects.

（8）老师分别给每个同学一个口语题。

2. 几个主体对一个对象。Several subjects vs. one object.

（9）口语老师和阅读老师分别给我们布置了很多作业。

3. 数目相同的主体和对象一个对一个。Equal in number, the subject vs. the object.

（10）我们班的玛丽和阿里分别获得了奖学金一等奖和二等奖。

fēnlí 分离 →P147"分别"

用法 Usage：

动词 v.

1. 把连在一起的事物分开来，分开。To separate people or things that formerly stayed together; to set apart.

（1）他从小跟父母分离，和奶奶生活在一起。

（2）请把这筐苹果按大小分离成两堆。

2. 别离，离散。To be separated; to be unable to be together.

（3）没想到我们分离了十年，竟在中国见面了。

（4）战争分离了多少家庭的亲人啊！

说明 Notes：

"分别"和"分离"都有动词用法，表示有关系的两个人较长久地分开，离别。Both "分别" and "分离" can be used as a verb, indicating that two closely related people are separated for a pretty long period of time.

它们的区别是：They differ as follows:

1. "分别"指一般地分开，离别。可以是主动的行为，也可以是客观原因造成的分开。分开的时间可长可短。"分离"着重于客观原因造成的,分开的时间一般较长。"分别" generally means to be separated or kept away from each other. It may be the result of an initiative taken by people, or it may be the result of something done by others. The time for separation may be long or it may be short. But "分离" emphasizes the separation as a result of some objective condition, and the time of separation is usually quite long.

2. "分离"有把东西"分开"的意思，如例（2）。"分别"没有。"分离" may have the meaning of setting things apart, as in (2); "分别" doesn't have this meaning.

fēnmíng 分明 →P325"明明"

用法 Usage：

副词 ad.

显然，明白无误。Obviously; undoubtedly.

（1）他这样说分明是不同意我们的计划。

（2）我分明看见他进来了，怎么又不见了呢？

形容词 a.

清楚，不含糊。使用时常为四字短语。Clearly; without any ambiguity. It often appears in four-character expressions.

（3）做任何事情都要是非分明。

（4）孩子的眼睛黑白分明，非常明亮。

说明 Notes：

"分明"作形容词用时，句子中常常含有两种事物对比的语义，如：例（3）是"是非"的对比；例（4）是"眼白"跟"眼珠"的对比。"分明," as an adjective, is often used for a comparison between two things. In (3) it is a comparison between "是" and "非" while in (4) it is one between "眼白 (white of the eye)" and "眼珠 (eyeball; apple of the eye)."

fēnfù 吩咐 →P682"嘱咐"

用法 Usage：

动词 v.

口头指派、命令或叮嘱。To tell; to instruct;

to order — all done orally.

（1）老师吩咐学生做完作业再回家。

（2）我来中国前,妈妈吩咐了又吩咐,要我每个星期给她打一次电话。

名词 n.

口头的指派、命令或叮嘱。*Oral instruction, order, or admonishment.*

（3）你的吩咐他怎么会不听。

（4）我随时听候您的吩咐。

说明 Notes:

名词"吩咐",常做"听、照、依、按、听候"等动词的宾语,前面常常有定语。*As a noun, "吩咐" often follows "听，照，依，按，听候" as their object, and an adjectival usually appears before it.*

fēngguāng 风光 →P149"风景"

用法 Usage:

名词 n.

风景,景色,景象。*Scenes; sights.*

（1）我最喜欢北国风光。

（2）这里真是山清水秀好风光啊!

形容词 a.

荣耀,光荣;体面,面子上好看。方言,多用于口语。*(A dialect) glorious; honorable; bringing dignity to. It often appears in oral Chinese.*

（3）儿子考上了大学,今天她好风光啊!

（4）今天她穿得真风光。

fēngjǐng 风景 →P149"风光"、P246"景色"

用法 Usage:

名词 n.

一个地区内由山川、花草、树木、建筑物以及某些自然条件（如雨、雪）所形成的足以供人观赏的景观。*An attractive scenic spot or sight in an area that is composed of mountains, rivers, trees, flowers, buildings and natural conditions created by rain, snow, etc.*

（1）西藏的风景是特有的。

（2）千岛湖的风景是国家级的。

说明 Notes:

1. "风景"可组成词语"煞风景",又作"杀风景"。表示损坏美好的景色。比喻在兴高采烈的时候,某人做了不合适的行为动作,使人扫兴。*"风景" can be used to form derogatory expressions like "煞风景" or "杀风景," meaning damaging the beautiful sights or, figuratively, doing something improper to dampen the high spirits shown by others.*

（3）真是煞风景,那么漂亮的湖边,堆了那么多垃圾。

（4）大家都高高兴兴的,你说这些话真是煞风景。

2. "风景"和"风光"的区别是：*The differences between "风景" and "风光" are as follows:*

① "风光"所指的范围比较广,包括大自然的景色,也包括积极的、欣欣向荣的社会现象和状况；"风景"主要指可观赏的景色、景观,范围相对小些。*"风光" covers a large range of things including natural scenic spots and a flourishing society. By contrast, "风景" refers largely to attractive scenic sights.*

② "风光"有比喻用法,如例（3）（4）。"风景"没有这种用法。*"风光" can be used figuratively as in Examples (3) and (4). "风景" cannot be used in this way.*

fēngxiǎn 风险 →P484"危险"

用法 Usage:

名词 n.

可能发生的危险。*Potential danger; possible risk.*

（1）炒股票是有一定风险的。

（2）这个试验会有风险,你一定要考虑再考虑。

fǒuzé 否则 →P50"不然"

用法 Usage:

连词 *conj.*

如果不是这样。*Otherwise; if not.*

有以下用法：*The usages are as follows:*

1. "否则"相当于"不然"。用法与"不然"基本相同。连接句子或分句,多用于书面语。与"否则"呼应的常常有"就、将、会、便、要"等词。"否则" is similar to "不然." and it is used more or less in the same way. It appears mostly in written Chinese when it is used to connect sentences or clauses. Corresponding to "否则" are words such as "就,将,会,便,要."

(1) 我们必须在七点出发,否则就上不了飞机。

(2) 你一定要学会用手机,否则便落在时代后面了。

2. 在"否则"后面可以带"的话",写在书面上,必须有停顿。"否则" may be followed by "的话." But when it is written down, there has to be a pause.

(3) 今天大概不上课吧,否则的话,教室里怎么没有人?

3. "否则"后面可以带反问句。"否则" can be followed by a rhetorical question.

(4) 你一定要到中国来。否则你怎么能了解中国呢?

说明 Notes:

"否则"与"不然"连词的第一种用法基本相同。"否则," as a conjunction, is used the same way as "不然."

它们的区别是：*Their differences are as follows:*

1. "不然"的假设性比较强,前一分句的语意常常暗示着后面有假设性否定的结果或情况。用"否则"的句子,前一分句一般是平叙,没有暗示作用。"不然" implies a highly possible supposition. The first clause tends to hint that the second one contains a presumably negative result or situation. However, a clause using "否则" is just a statement, hinting at nothing.

(5) 还好我跟你一起去了,不然这么多东西你一个人是拿不回来的。

(6) 做作业不要马虎,否则会出现不应该错的问题。

例(5)后一分句是假设句,因为实际上东西已经拿回来了,并且用"还好"暗示:"如果我不去,那么多东西,你一个人是拿不回来的。"例(6)用"会"表示将来可能出现的情况,并不是假设。*The second clause in (5) is a supposition because the actual situation is already there. Furthermore, "还好" is used to give a hint: "如果我不去,那么多东西,你一个人是拿不回来的." As for (6), "会" is used to indicate a situation that may appear in the future; it is not a supposition.*

2. "不然"前面可以加用"再、要"等词。"否则"前面不能加用这些词。"不然" can be preceded by "再,要" or similar words. "否则," by contrast, cannot be preceded by those words.

3. "否则"没有形容词用法。"不然"有形容词用法。"否则" cannot be used as an adjective, but "不然" can.

fú 服

用法 Usage:

动词 *v.*

1. 服从,信服。*To obey; to believe.*

(1) 他这样处理问题公平合理,我心服口服。

(2) 事实证明我就是比你强,你服不服?

2. 使人信服。*To convince.*

(3) 你说的道理不能服人。

(4) 他的话以理服人,我们不能不听。

3. 承当(义务、刑罚等)。一般只带单音节形容词或动词。*To take on; to take up; to bear (obligations, punishment, etc.). Usually it goes only with mono-syllable adjectives or verbs.*

(5) 他在军队已经服役三年了。

(6) 在事实面前,他终于服罪了。

4. 适应,习惯。多用于否定结构。*To adapt to; to be accustomed to. Mostly it appears in a negative sentence.*

(7) 他有点儿水土不服,出国后老是拉肚子。

(8) 你老是吃不下饭,可能是不服这里的水土吧。

5. 吃(药)。书面语。*To take (medicine).* *It is usually used in written Chinese.*

(9) 医生说你一天要服三次药。

(10) 不但要按时服药,而且还要按量服,病才好得快。

说明 Notes:

"服"有时有强制的含义,如:"你服不服?" "我不得不服。" *Sometimes, "服" has a compulsory connotation, as in:* "你服不服?" "我不得不服。"

gāi 该 →P588"应"

用法 Usage:

助动词 aux. v.

1. 表示理应如此,应该。可以单独回答问题。否定用"不该"。Should; supposed to be. This single word may serve to answer a question. The negative form is "不该."

(1) 你累了,该休息一下了。

(2) 今天上课的内容很重要,你不该迟到。

2. 表示估计、推测情况应该如此。不能单独回答问题。没有否定形式。有时后面可带"会"。句末常有"吧",加强估计、推测的语气。To infer from an estimate or speculation. It cannot serve to answer a question without any modifiers. Sometimes it comes together with "会." "吧" often appears at the end of a sentence to intensify the estimative or speculative tone.

(3) 这孩子今年该上小学了吧。

(4) 妈妈知道该会生气吧。

3. 用于感叹句,表示推测并加强语气,用在表示将来的句子里。后面如果是名词短语,"该"后面多带"有＋多……",如果是形容词短语时,"有"可带可不带。When used in an exclamatory sentence, it serves to carry an estimative and emphatic tone, and predict the future. When followed by a noun phrase, "该" often appears with "有＋多...." When followed by an adjective phrase, "有" may either appear or disappear.

(5) 要是你也能来,该(有)多好啊!

(6) 再过十年,这里该有多么大的变化啊!

动词 v.

1. 应该是。Should be.

(7) 八个苹果四个人分,每人该两个。

2. 轮到。To be one's turn.

(8) 星期三该你值班了。

3. 理应如此,活该。表示没委屈某人,是他应得的结果(多指不好的结果)。It goes without saying; to deserve (usually punishment, etc.).

(9) 挨批评了吧? 该! 谁让你不听妈妈的话!

指示代词 demonstrative pron.

指代上文说过的人或事物,多用于上对下的公文函件。书面语。"该" refers to people or things mentioned above. It appears in written language, especially in official documents from the superior to the subordinate.

(10) 该生认真好学,多次得到学校奖学金。

(11) 该公司已经提前一个月完成了全年的任务。

说明 Notes:

短语"该不是"表示估计和推测,多用于不如意的事情。The phrase "该不是" indicates an estimate, often describing an unsatisfactory situation.

(12) 他好几天没来上课了,该不是生病了吧。

gǎibiàn 改变 →P29"变化"

用法 Usage:

动词 *v.*

1. (事物)发生明显的变化。在句子中一般用在句末,多做谓语,不带宾语。这种句子实际上是没有"被"字的被动句。*(Of something) to change apparently. It often appears at the end of a sentence as a predicate without an object following it. This kind of sentence is in the passive voice without "被."*

(1) 他的想法改变了,要学汉语了。
(2) 人的性格是很难改变的。

2. 改换,更动。谁使什么发生变化。主动句,可带宾语,宾语一般是双音节词语。*To change, alter. Someone changes something. The sentence is in active voice and "改变" takes an object, which is usually a disyllabic word.*

(3) 我决定改变原来的计划,提前到中国去。
(4) 我想改变一下发型。

3. 用在"开始、加以、进行"等形式动词后面做宾语,表示变动的过程。*To serve as an object after dummy verbs such as "开始,加以,进行" to suggest the process of a change.*

(5) 她睡懒觉的习惯开始改变了。
(6) 她的旅游计划必须进行改变,不然,实现不了。

说明 Notes:

"改变"和"变化"都表示人或事物有所变动。*Both "改变" and "变化" suggest changes in someone or something.*

它们的区别是:*They differ as follows:*

1. "改变"词义着重于变化、更动,人或事物与原来的状况有了明显的差别,相对地说,过程比较迅速,且多是人为的、主动的。"变化"着重于人或事物本身产生了新情况。变化的原因可以是主观的,也可以是客观的,但强调事物本身的变动。*"改变" stresses changes, because of which things are obviously different from what they used to be. The process of change is relatively quick, the result of someone pushing it actively. "变化" stresses new things that take place in someone or something. The causes can be either subjective or objective.*

2. "改变"可用于具体事物,如"声音、相貌、形状、位置、姿势、状态、景色、环境"等,也可用于抽象事物,如"思想、立场、观点、作风、形式、局面、性质、关系、计划、策略、习惯、命运"等。"变化"可用于人,如人的"思想、感情、性格、形体"等,也可用于事物,如"大自然、气候、形式、情况"等。*"改变" can describe specific things like "声音,相貌,形状,位置,姿势,状态,景色,环境." It can also modify abstract things such as "思想,立场,观点,作风,形式,局面,性质,关系,计划,策略,习惯,命运." "变化" can refer to humans, such as their "思想,感情,性格,形体." It can also refer to things, such as "大自然,气候,形式,情况."*

3. "改变"后面一般可以带宾语。"变化"一般后面不带宾语。*Generally, an object can follow "改变" but not "变化."*

(7) 小张改变了想法,不去杭州旅游,要到昆明旅游。
(8) 我们可以感觉到这个城市每天都在变化着。

4. "改变"和"变化"都可用做名词。"改变"着重强调事物发生变化的动作过程或动作本身。"变化"主要说明事物产生的新状况,强调结果。*Both "改变" and "变化" can serve as a noun. "改变" stresses the process of change or the movement, while "变化" stresses new things that happen to someone or something with an emphasis on the result.*

(9) 小张的行为有了彻底的改变。
(10) 这件事使我现在的生活有了很大的变化。

5. 特别要注意"改变"和"变化"在句子中的词语搭配。*Pay special attention to the collocation of "改变" and "变化" in sentences.*

(11) *他改变了缺点。

(12) 他改正了缺点。

"改变"不与"错误、缺点、毛病、过失"等词语搭配。Remember that "改变" does not go with words such as "错误,缺点,毛病,过失."

(13) *来中国后,我要变化我的生活方式。

(14) 来中国后,我要改变我的生活方式。

"变化"一般不带宾语。"变化" generally takes no objects.

gǎigé 改革 →P155"改造"

用法 Usage:

动词 v.

把事物中,旧的、不合理的部分变成新的,能适应客观情况。To transform; to change the obsolete and irrational parts in an old thing into new ones that fit the objective circumstances.

(1) 改革管理体制,使中国经济面貌发生了巨大的变化。

(2) 改革教育体制,会使科学创新得到巨大发展。

名词 n.

改进革新的举动。Actions to transform.

(3) 中国的经济体制改革已经有了很大的成就。

(4) 简化字是中国文字改革的一个重要内容。

gǎijìn 改进 →P154"改善"

用法 Usage:

动词 v.

改变旧的情况,使其有所进步。To improve; to make changes in the old situation for advancement.

(1) 老师改进了教学方法,记生词方便多了。

(2) 我们厂改进了落后的工艺和技术,大大提高了生产力。

gǎishàn 改善 →P154"改进"

用法 Usage:

动词 v.

1. 改变原有的情况,使之更好一些。可以重叠使用。To improve; to make or become better. It can be reduplicated as "改善改善."

(1) 今年我家要盖新房子,改善改善居住条件。

(2) 为了改善两国关系,两国政府做了很大努力。

2. 用在口语中,表示某一天或某一餐要吃得好一点儿。(In daily conversation) to suggest having better food on a certain day or for a certain meal.

(3) 星期天的中餐,一定给大家改善改善。

说明 Notes:

"改进"和"改善"都有改变原来的情况,使之更好的意思。Both "改进" and "改善" mean to improve or to change for the better.

它们的区别是:Their differences are as follows:

1. "改进"着重在原有的基础上有所进步和提高,改进的结果是使总体有进步、有好转。"改善"着重在原有的基础上进一步完善,尽如人意,使好的程度更高。"改进" stresses progress and improvement from the original level. The result is advancement in the overall situation. "改善" stresses improvement from the original level for satisfactory results. It suggests improvement to a higher level.

2. "改进"的对象多为"工具、设备、装备、工艺、教学、管理、作风、技术、工作、方法"等,常常受"不断、努力、继续"等状语的修饰,后面可以带补语"改进了许多、改进了不少、改进不了"等。"改善"的对象多为抽象事物,如"生活、环境、条件、待遇、关系"等。"改进" often serves to modify things such as "工具,设备,装备,工艺,教学,管理,作风,技术,工作,方法." It often goes with adverbials like "不断,努力,继续" and comes after a complement, forming phrases such as "改进了许多,改进了不少,改进得了,改进不了." The object of "改善" is often abstract things such as "生活,环境,条件,待遇,关系."

gǎizào 改造 →P154"改革"

用法 Usage:

动词 v.

1. 对原有的事物进行修改或变更,使适合需要。To alter or revise the original thing to meet demands better.

（1）改造旧城区是一项非常复杂的工程。

（2）房子要定期进行安全检查,并及时维修、改造。

2. 从根本上改变旧的、建立新的,使适应新的形势和需要。To fundamentally change old things and establish new ones to suit new trends and needs.

（3）劳动能改造世界。

（4）由于人类要改造社会、发展社会,便产生了科学。

说明 Notes:

"改造"和"改革"都是指把原有的事物加以变更以适应需要。Both "改造" and "改革" mean changing the original thing to serve needs better.

它们的区别是：They differ as follows:

"改造"是从根本上改变,把原来旧的改换成新的。"改革"是改掉不合理的部分,保留合理的部分。如"改造思想"是把原来的旧思想全都改变成新思想。"改革文字"是把不适合需要的部分内容简化或改变形状,不是用新的一套文字符号代替原来的。因此不能说"改造文字"或"文字改造"。"改造" means to make fundamental changes by replacing old things with new ones. "改革" means to remove the irrational parts and retain the rational ones. For example, "改造思想" means to transform old thinking into new thinking. "改革文字" means to simplify the outdated parts or change their shapes. It does not mean to replace the original version with a completely new set of writing symbols. Therefore, we could not say "改造文字" or "文字改造."

gǎizhèng 改正 →P247"纠正"

用法 Usage:

动词 v.

把错误的改为正确的。To rectify; to correct what is wrong.

（1）请把这几个写错的字改正过来。

（2）一个人不怕有错误,就怕不改正错误。

gàikuò 概括 →P695"综合"

用法 Usage:

动词 v.

把事物的共同特点归结在一起,总括。To generalize; to sum up (e.g. the common features of a thing).

（1）请你概括一下这篇文章的意思。

（2）以上内容可以概括为三点。

形容词 a.

表示简明扼要的意思。Brief and to the point.

（3）他把电影故事向大家概括地说了一遍。

（4）老师讲话很概括,从不啰唆。

gān 干

用法 Usage:

形容词 a.

1. 没有水分或水分很少（和"湿"相对）。可做谓语、定语。Having little or no water, opposite to "湿 (wet)." It can serve as a predicate or attribute.

（1）我口干得很,哪儿有水喝?

（2）这件衣服只能干洗。

2. 净尽,空无。做谓语、补语,后面不能有宾语。*Empty; bottom up. It can only serve as a predicate or complement, and can take no objects.*

（3）酒和可乐都喝干了。

（4）那么长时间没下雨,河水都干了。

3. 加工制成的没有水分的食品。如:"葡萄干,萝卜干,豆腐干,饼干"等。*Processed and dried (food), such as "葡萄干,萝卜干,豆腐干,饼干."*

4. 结义,拜认（亲属）。*Sworn or adopted (relative) without religious or legal obligations.*

（5）这是我孩子的干妈。

（6）她是我的干姐姐。

副词 *ad.*

1. 只具有形式的,不真实。只做状语。*Hollowly; falsely. It only serves as an adverbial modifier.*

（7）他干笑了几声就离开了。

（8）见别人都在哭,他也干叫起来。

2. 白白地,徒然。做状语。*In vain; helplessly. It is an adverbial modifier.*

（9）看着外边的大雨,我们只能干着急。

（10）我们先走着去,也比坐着干等好。

动词 *v.*

牵连,涉及。*To implicate; to involve.*

（11）那件事与我无干。

（12）我睡懒觉,干你何事?

名词 *n.*

1. 岸,水边。书面语。如:"江干""河之干、山之巅"。*Riverbank, waterside. It appears in written language such as "江干,""河之干、山之巅."*

2. 天干。天干地支是古代用来表示年、月、日时间的序号。天干一共有"甲乙丙丁戊己庚辛壬癸"等十个。*Heavenly stems. Heavenly stems and earthly branches are sequences used to suggest the year, month, and day in ancient China. Heavenly stems are composed of 10 items, namely, "甲乙丙丁戊己庚辛壬癸."*

gāncuì 干脆

用法 Usage:

形容词 *a.*

（言语行动）直截了当;爽快,利落。*(Of words and action) direct and straightforward.*

（1）我们的口语老师说话非常干脆。

（2）你们干脆一点,快点决定,到底买不买?

副词 *ad.*

索性。*Simply; might/just as well.*

（3）天气那么好,干脆多玩几天吧。

（4）既然来留学了,干脆学个本科专业吧。

说明 Notes:

1. "干脆"无论做形容词还是做副词都是用来修饰人的活动、性格。*"干脆," whether used as an adjective or adverb, modifies people's activity or character.*

2. "干脆"可以重叠成"干干脆脆",表示程度加深。*"干脆" can appear in the reduplicated form "干干脆脆" for stress.*

（5）他干干脆脆地回答说:"我愿意。"

gānrǎo 干扰 →P157 "干涉"

用法 Usage:

动词 *v.*

1. 扰乱,打扰。因无关事物影响、妨碍了某种活动的正常进行。*To interfere; to disturb or disrupt a normal activity because of irrelevance.*

（1）一只蜜蜂在我眼前飞来飞去,干扰我做作业。

（2）轻一点,不要干扰别人休息。

2. 某些电磁振荡对妨碍无线电设备正常接收信号造成妨碍。*(Of electromagnetic oscillation) to prevent wireless facilities from receiving signals normally.*

（3）什么信号干扰了,电视机画面很不清楚。

名词 *n.*

指干扰信号。*Disturbing signals.*

（4）有干扰。电视画面看不清楚了。
（5）干扰来了，快来看，是什么干扰。

gānshè 干涉 →P156"干扰"、P157"干预"

用法 Usage:

动词 v.

过问或制止，多指对别人的事情强行制止。*To interfere or meddle in. It often suggests using force to stop the business of someone else.*

（1）父母不应该干涉儿女的婚姻。
（2）这是我的私事，你不能干涉。

说明 Notes:

"干涉"和"干扰"都表示扰乱别人。区别是：*Both "干涉" and "干扰" suggest disturbing others. Their differences are as follows:*

1."干涉"着重于强行过问，要求别人怎么样去做某件事，是人为的干预，语意较重。"干扰"着重于在形式上妨碍或者打扰别人做某件事，可以是人为的，也可能是非人为的。*"干涉" stresses being bossy, ordering others to do something in a certain way. It is intentional intervention. "干扰" stresses obstructing or disturbing others. It can suggest both intentional and unintentional intervention.*

（3）你也看书去，别干扰姐姐做作业。（着重外在形式上的影响 *Focusing on external and formal influences*）
（4）让你姐姐自己决定，你不要干涉姐姐恋爱。（着重实质内容上的干预 *Focusing on substantive impact*）

2."干扰"有名词用法，"干涉"没有。"干扰" *can serve as a noun, but "干涉" cannot.*

gānyù 干预 →P157"干涉"

用法 Usage:

动词 v.

干涉，参与，过问。又作"干与"。*To intervene; to be involved in; to bother about. It is also written as "干与".*

（1）这是他们家的事，你不要去干预。
（2）不要干预那件事，不然你也要承担责任。

说明 Notes:

"干预"和"干涉"的区别是："干预"不但过问、干涉别人的事情，而且还参与其中。"干涉"没有参与的意思。*The differences between "干预" and "干涉" are as follows: "干预" not only suggests obstructing or intervening in other people's affairs, but also suggests getting involved. However, "干涉" does not carry the meaning of involvement.*

gǎn 赶

用法 Usage:

动词 v.

1. 追。*To pursue; to follow up; to catch up with.*
（1）她是个赶时髦的人。
（2）运动场上，小学生正在你追我赶地进行跑步比赛。

2. 加快行动，使得不耽误时间。*To quicken the pace to prevent delay.*
（3）天已经晚了，我们要快点儿赶路。
（4）他骑着自行车，飞快地往学校赶。

3. 驾驭（车马）。*To drive; to herd.*
（5）大叔赶着马车走了。
（6）清早，我就赶着羊群到山坡上吃草。

4. 遇到（某种情况），碰上（某种机会）。*To come across; to encounter (a certain situation or opportunity).*
（7）我到他家时，正赶上他吃晚饭。
（8）去年他们公司招工，我就赶上了。

5. 驱逐。*To expel; to drive away.*
（9）把那只苍蝇赶出去！
（10）大家都去赶野猪了。

6. 去，到（某处）。*To go (somewhere for an activity).*
（11）今天大家都去赶集了。
（12）你怎么没去赶庙会？

介词 prep.

等到(以后某个时候)。多用于口语,句子前面。*Waiting until (a certain time in the near future). It often appears at the beginning of a sentence in oral Chinese.*

(13) 赶明儿我也要做老师。

(14) 赶放了暑假我就去山区做志愿者。

gǎnjǐn 赶紧 →P158"赶快"、P158"赶忙"

用法 Usage:

副词 ad.

表示抓紧时机,尽快行动。多用于表示事情、时间紧急的语义。*Seizing the time and acting quickly. It often points to an urgent situation.*

(1) 赶紧做作业,我们还要去看电影。

(2) 要下雨了,赶紧把衣服拿进来。

gǎnkuài 赶快 →P158"赶紧"、P158"赶忙"

用法 Usage:

副词 ad.

指抓住时机,加快速度。*Seizing the time; speeding up.*

(1) 天要黑了,我们赶快离开这里吧。

(2) 赶快起床,你要迟到了。

gǎnmáng 赶忙 →P158"赶紧"、P158"赶快"

用法 Usage:

副词 ad.

连忙,表示行为动作的迅速或急迫。*In a hurry; promptly. It is used to indicate that the action has to be swift and quick.*

(1) 他赶忙道歉道:"对不起,我不是故意的。"

(2) 听到喊声,小张赶忙跑出来。

说明 Notes:

"赶紧""赶快""赶忙"都表示时间快,立即行动。*"赶紧,赶快,赶忙" all carry the meaning of taking immediate action.*

它们的区别是:*They differ as follows:*

1. "赶紧"和"赶快"都多用于祈使句,都表示催促。"赶紧"着重于抓紧时机,不拖延,在时间上毫不延误。可以表示还未做的事情赶快做,也可以表示已经在做的事情催促赶紧做完。"赶快"着重于加快速度,尽快行动,不拖拉,使用频率比"赶紧"高,多用于未做的事情。*"赶紧" and "赶快" often appear in an imperative sentence to urge someone to do something immediately. "赶紧" stresses seizing the time to prevent any delay. It can also suggest quickening the pace to do things that are not done yet, or urging someone to finish things that have already begun. "赶快" stresses quickening the pace and allowing no delay. It is more frequently used than "赶紧" and it often modifies things not done yet.*

(3) 你赶紧吃完饭就去教室。

(4) 你赶紧吃饭,吃完就去教室。

(5) 你赶快点,吃完就去教室。

2. "赶忙"一般只用于陈述句,陈述已经做的,或者正在做的事情。相对比,"赶紧""赶快"是请别人或要求别人抓紧时间去做某件事。*Generally, "赶忙" just appears in declarative sentences to describe something that has been done or is being done; while "赶紧" and "赶快" stress asking or urging someone to quicken the pace to finish something at hand.*

(6) 你赶紧/赶快打个电话,问问他明天火车是几点开。

(7) 他赶忙打了个电话,问了他明天是几点的火车。

gǎndào 感到 →P159"感觉"

用法 Usage:

动词 v.

1. 通过感觉器官感觉到,觉得。所带的宾语一般是动词、动词短语、形容词和句子,不能是单个名词。不带宾语时常带时态助词"了、过"。*To feel (with one's sense organs); to*

become aware of. The object that follows it is often a verb, a verb phrase, an adjective or a sentence, but not a single noun. When not followed by an object, it often goes with a tense auxiliary like "了,过."

（1）秋天到了,大家都感到很舒服。
（2）我感到老师对我们很关心。
（3）A：昨天夜里不知哪儿地震了,你感到了吗?
　　B：我感到了。

2.表示有某种想法,接近"认为",但比"认为"的语意轻。To have some idea. Close to "认为(think)," it carries a less strong meaning.
（4）大家都感到这个建议不错。
（5）同学们都感到这个老师的教学水平很高。

说明 Notes：
"感到"常带表示身心感受的形容词宾语。如例（1）（2）。"感到" often comes before an adjective that describes psychological and physiological feelings as in (1) and (2).

gǎndòng 感动 →P208"激动"

用法 Usage：
动词 v.
思想感情因受外界事物影响而激动。To be moved; (of one's emotions and feelings) to be stirred by external factors.
（1）很多观众看这个电影时,都感动得流下了眼泪。
（2）他那么热情地帮助我,我非常感动。
（3）他讲的故事太感动人了。

gǎnjué 感觉 →P158"感到"、P159"感受"

用法 Usage：
动词 v.
1.产生某种感觉,感到,觉得。To feel (like); to have a certain feeling coming over.
（1）我感觉有点儿冷。
（2）他们感觉饿了,想知道哪儿能买点吃的。
2.认为(语气不是很肯定)。To believe

(but not so sure); to be afraid (that-clause).
（3）我感觉这个句子有些问题。
（4）我感觉这里的条件不错。

名词 n.
客观事物的个别特性在人脑中引起的反应。Feeling; a reaction sparked in one's mind by the specific characteristics of something that exists in the outside world.
（5）跟中国的老师和同学在一起,我有在自己家的感觉。
（6）站在美丽的湖边,我心中有一种特别的感觉。

说明 Notes：
1.动词"感觉"后面常常带形容词、动词短语或句子做宾语。如果带名词性宾语,必须加"到"或者"有"。The verb "感觉" often comes before an adjective, a verb phrase or a sentence. If a noun follows it as its object, the use of "到" or "有" is necessary.
（7）*我感觉一个声音。
（8）我感觉到一个声音。
（9）*我感觉一种香味。
（10）我感觉有一种香味。

2."感觉"跟"感到"的区别是：The differences between "感觉" and "感到" are as follows:
① "感觉"有名词用法,"感到"没有名词用法。"感觉" can serve as a noun, but "感到" cannot.
② "感觉"和"感到"的动词用法基本相同,但是"感觉"后面宾语是名词,名词前面必须加"到",或者"有"。"感觉" and "感到" have similar usage when serving as a verb. However, when the object that follows "感觉" is a noun, it has to go with "到" or "有."

gǎnshòu 感受 →P159"感觉"

用法 Usage：
动词 v.
受到(影响),接受。To experience; to

receive; to be subject to (an influence).

（1）我强烈地感受到了她对我的爱。

（2）阿里在生病时,深深地感受到同学们对自己的关心。

名词 n.

生活实践中得到的体会。Experiences acquired from life and practice; feelings.

（3）来中国时间虽然不长,但我已经有了很多感受。

（4）我很想体会一下做父亲的感受。

说明 Notes:

1. 动词"感受",作谓语一般要与"到"连用,如例(1)(2)。When serving as a predicate, the verb "感受" must go together with "到," as is shown in (1) and (2).

2. "感觉"和"感受"的区别是：The differences between "感觉" and "感受" are as follows:

① "感觉"着重于客观事物的个别属性在人脑中的直接反映。这种反映是具体的,如"冷、热、饿、痛、舒服、快乐"等。"感受"着重于客观事物对人的精神、情绪的影响,侧重人的心理感受或体会,因此"感受"的多是抽象事物,如："温暖、友谊、幸福、苦难、艰辛、关怀、自豪"等。"感觉" stresses one's sensory response sparked by objective things. This response is as specific as "冷,热,饿,痛,舒服,快乐." By contrast, "感受" stresses the influence of objective things on someone's emotions with the emphasis on internal feelings. So the objects of "感受" are often abstract things such as "温暖,友谊,幸福,苦难,艰辛,关怀,自豪."

② "感觉"词义作为"认为"用时,"感觉"表示的是抽象的感受,后面常常是动词短语或句子做宾语,如"感觉大家对我很好,感觉不应该这样做,感觉他是不对的,感觉到是红的"等。"感受"没有这样的用法。When conveying the meaning of "认为,""感觉" describes abstract feelings and often appears before a verb phrase or a sentence as in "感觉大家对我很好,感觉不应该这样做,感觉他是不对的,感觉到不对头." "感受" does not have such uses.

③ "感觉"和"感受"都可用作名词,但是语义侧重不同。"感觉"侧重感官的具体感受或者是对客观事物的认识、看法。"感受"侧重内心的体会和感触。Both "感觉" and "感受" can serve as a noun, but the stresses are different. "感觉" stresses specific sensory feelings, or the views and understanding of something objective. "感受" stresses internal feelings.

（5）我的感觉是这里比城里凉快多了。

（6）参观农村小学以后,我的感受很深。

gǎnxìngqù 感兴趣

用法 Usage:

动宾词组。表示对人或事物产生喜好或关切的情绪。A verb-object phrase that means "to be or feel interested in something." It relates to one's feelings of care or love for someone or something.

（1）他对中国的历史文化很感兴趣。

（2）阿里对学汉语不太感兴趣,对北京烤鸭很感兴趣。

说明 Notes:

使用"感兴趣"时要注意：Watch out for the use of "感兴趣":

1. "感兴趣"的对象,只能通过介词"对"引进,组成"对……（不）感兴趣"的句式。Only the preposition "对" can introduce the object of "感兴趣." It appears in the structure "对…(不)感兴趣."

（3）杰克对写汉字不感兴趣,对口语很感兴趣。

（4）没想到她对电脑游戏也很感兴趣。

2. "感兴趣"作定语,一定要加"的"。When serving as an attribute, "感兴趣" must go with "的."

（5）在中餐中,麻辣豆腐是留学生最感兴趣的一道菜。

（6）张老师最感兴趣的东西是书。

gàn 干 →P706"做"

用法 Usage:

动词 *v.*

1. 做。*To do.*

(1) 你真懒,什么事都不肯干。

(2) 你下午干什么?

2. 担任(某种职务),从事。*To assume (a certain post or position); to work as; to do as a profession.*

(3) 他干过班长。

(4) 这种服务员工作我不想干了。

3. 争吵,打架,斗争。*To argue; to fight with each other.*

(5) 他俩又干起来了。

(6) 我们要和他们干到底。

说明 Notes:

"干"使用时要注意以下两点。*Watch out for the use of* "干."

① "干"是个多音字,做动词用是第四声,在学习的时候要注意其读音。"干" *is a polyphone, and it is of a falling tone as a verb. Pay attention to its pronunciation when learning the word.*

② 表示"担任、从事"的词义时,多做谓语,带名词作宾语时,常常与"过"连用,表示过去担任过什么、做过什么工作,如例(3)。一般不直接带名词作宾语。因此,一般不用于将来句式。*It often serves as a predicate when it carries the meaning of "担任,从事." When the object is a noun, it often goes with "过" to suggest that someone has assumed a certain post or position. The word does not go directly with a noun. Therefore, it does not appear in the future tense.*

(7) *将来我想干汉语教师。

(8) 将来我想做/当汉语教师。

gànmá 干吗

用法 Usage:

"干吗"也可以说成"干嘛",是"干什么"的口语形式,带有中国北部地区的地方色彩。可以单独使用。"干吗" *also comes as* "干嘛." *Both are informal expressions for* "干什么." *They are typical expressions in China's northern areas, and can stand alone.*

1. 表示"为什么""做什么"的意思,相当于疑问代词。用来询问目的和原因。可以放在句子最后,也可以放在谓语的前面。*Meaning* "为什么,做什么," "干吗" *serves as an interrogative pronoun to ask for purpose and reason. It may appear at the end of a sentence or before the predicate.*

(1) 王老师找我干吗?

(2) 今天是周末,干吗还去上课?

2. 为什么(问原因)。*Why (used to ask for reasons).*

(3) 八点半才上课,你干吗起这么早?

(4) 今天这么热,你干吗还穿那么多衣服?

3. "干吗"可以单独使用。"干吗" *may appear by itself.*

(5) A:小张,你过来一下。

B:干吗?

说明 Notes:

1. "干吗"一般情况下多用于口语。如:"干吗不吃饭?" "干吗" *often appears in oral language. For example,* "干吗不吃饭?"

2. 如果询问客观的道理则不能用"干吗",而要用"为什么"。*When one asks for objective reasons, one should use* "为什么" *instead of* "干吗."

(6) *人干吗不能离开空气而生存?

(7) 人为什么不能离开空气而生存?

gāng 刚 →P162"刚才"、P162"刚刚"

用法 Usage:

副词 *ad.*

1. 表示动作、情况或状态在说话前不久发生。*(Of an action, situation or state) happening only a short while ago.*

(1) 我刚来中国,所以汉语说得不太好。

(2) 我刚吃完饭。

2. 表示事物(时间、空间、程度、数量)正好达到某一点,恰好、正好(不大不小、不多不少、不早不晚、不前不后)等,刚好。Exactly; just (neither too big nor too small; neither too much nor too little; neither too early nor too late; neither too far in the front nor too far at the back, etc.)

(3) 这双鞋我穿不大不小,刚合适。

(4) 行李刚二十公斤,没有超过标准。

3. 表示勉强达到某种程度,相当于"仅仅"。Barely reaching a certain degree or extent, it is equal to "only" and "just."

(5) 她的声音很小,我刚能听见。

(6) 他的病好了一点儿,现在刚能坐起来喝水。

4. 常和"就、又"连用,表示两个动作或情况接连发生。有时也说"刚一"。Paired with "就" or "又," it means two actions or two situations happening one after another. Sometimes we also say "刚一."

(7) 我刚进教室,上课铃就响了。

(8) 他刚一出门,就碰见王老师了。

形容词 a.

硬,坚强(跟"柔"相对)。Hard; firm. It is opposite to "柔 (soft)."

(9) 太极拳的动作是柔中带刚,刚中带柔。

(10) 她的脾气很刚,不像女孩子。

gāngcái 刚才 →P161"刚"、P162"刚刚"

用法 Usage:

名词 n.

时间词,指说话以前不久的时间。用在动词、形容词或者主语前面作状语,也可作定语。Just now, just. It means a short while ago. It appears as an adverbial to modify a verb, an adjective, or the subject. In addition, it can serve as an attribute.

(1) 刚才有一个人来找你。

(2) 刚才的话你都记住了吗?

(3) 刚才很痛,现在不痛了。

gānggāng 刚刚 →P161"刚"、P162"刚才"

用法 Usage:

副词 ad.

"刚刚"和副词"刚"的用法基本相同。"刚刚" is similar to the adverb "刚."

说明 Notes:

1. 实际上,"刚刚"是"刚"的重叠,表示动作、事情发生在不久以前。修饰动词或少数能表示变化的形容词,如"好、安静"等。"刚刚" is the reduplicated form of "刚." It means something happened just now. It modifies verbs or a few adjectives that represent a change such as "好,安静."

"刚刚"和"刚"的区别是:Here are the differences between "刚刚" and "刚":

① 用于表示时间时,"刚刚"比"刚"表示的时间更短,语气比较重。用于表示程度时,"刚刚"比"刚"表示的程度更深。When it represents a time, "刚刚" indicates an even shorter time than "刚" and carries a heavier tone. When it represents a degree, "刚刚" implies a deeper extent.

(1) 我刚刚回到学校。

(2) 我刚回到学校。

(3) 字写得太小了,刚刚能看到。

(4) 字写得太小了,刚能看到。

② "刚"常常和"一"连用,表示前后两个动作间隔的时间比较短,"刚刚"没有这个用法。When used with "一," "刚" means that the time between two actions is quite short. "刚刚" does not have this usage.

(5) *他刚刚一出门,就碰到王老师了。

(6) 他刚一出门,就碰到王老师了。

③ "刚"和"刚刚"都可以用在数量词的前面。"刚"侧重说明数量比较少,"刚刚"表示数量正好、恰好。Both "刚" and "刚刚" may come before a quantifier. "刚" focuses on the small number while "刚刚" emphasizes that the number is just right.

(7) 李老师的孩子刚七岁,还没有上学。(说明年龄小 Indicating that the child is too young)

(8) 李老师的孩子刚刚七岁,今年可以上小学了。(说明正好到了上学的年龄 Indicating that the child has reached school age)

2. "刚""刚刚""刚才"都表示动作情况发生不久以前。"刚,""刚刚"and"刚才"all mean something happened just now.

区别是:Here are their differences:

① "刚"和"刚刚"是副词,只能在动词前做状语。"刚才"是时间名词,可以做状语、定语。"刚"and"刚刚"are adverbs and can only appear in front of a verb. "刚才"is a time noun, and can serve as an adverbial or an attribute.

② "刚"和"刚刚"做状语时只能放在主语后面,"刚才"放在主语前、后都可以。When "刚"and"刚刚"serve as an adverbial, they can only appear behind the subject, while "刚才"can be placed either in front of or behind the subject.

(9) 你刚刚去哪里了?

(10) 你刚去哪里了?

(11) 刚才你去哪里了?

③ 有时"刚"和"刚刚"时间很短,实际上是说话人与时间长相比较的感觉而已。"刚"和"刚刚"前面可以有表示时间的词语。"刚才"前面不能出现表示时间的词语。While both "刚"and"刚刚"mean only a short time, they just express a feeling of the speaker. The time expression can appear before "刚"or"刚刚." However,"刚才" does not have this use.

(12) *我是昨天早晨刚才到的。

(13) 我是昨天早晨刚/刚刚到的。

④ 如果动词后面有时量补语,只能用"刚/刚刚"做状语,而不能用"刚才"。If the verb is followed by a quantifier complement, the adverb must be "刚/刚刚" rather than "刚才."

(14) *我刚才来中国一个月。

(15) 我刚来中国一个月。

(16) *他刚才来一会儿。

(17) 他刚刚来一会儿。

⑤ "刚才"后面可以用否定词,"刚"和"刚刚"后面不能用。"刚才" can go with negative words while "刚" and "刚刚" cannot.

(18) *你刚/你刚刚不买,现在到哪儿去买?

(19) 你刚才不买,现在到哪儿去买?

gǎo 搞 →P339"弄"、P706"做"

用法 Usage:

动词 v.

1. 做,干,从事。可带"了、着、过"。可重叠。可带名词宾语。To do; to engage in. It can go with "了,着,过." It allows a reduplicated form and can take a noun as its object.

(1) 他搞服装设计,我搞室内装修设计。

(2) 她搞了一辈子英语翻译。

2. 设法获得,弄。所带名词宾语常常表示具体事物,前面常有数量词。To get; to find. The noun object often refers to something specific, with a quantifier before it.

(3) 我给你搞到一张足球票。

(4) 去哪儿搞点儿酒来!

3. 整治人,让人有麻烦、做事不顺利。To put somebody in trouble.

(5) 不要背后搞人,有什么意见向他提出就可以了。

说明 Notes:

"搞"常常用在口语中,代替各种不同的动词,随着不同的宾语而有不同的意义。"搞"can replace different verbs in spoken Chinese, and has different meanings with different objects.

(6) 这个语法一定要搞清楚。(学习、理解、研究的意思 To learn, understand or study)

(7) 小王正在跟小李搞对象呢。(恋爱、找结婚对象的意思 To find someone to marry)

(8) 你们快搞一个方案出来。(制订方案的意思 To work out a plan)

gè 各 →P318"每"

用法 Usage:

代词 *pron.*

指某个范围内的每个个体(表示不止一个),相当于"每个"。常用在名词或量词前面做定语。*Every individual in a certain category, including everyone. It equals "每个," serving as an attribute before a noun or particle.*

(1) 我们是来自世界各国的留学生。
(2) 各位同学,你们好!

副词 *ad.*

指分别做某事或分别有某种属性(表示不止一人做某事或不止一物有某种属性)。常用在动词、动词短语或数量词短语前作状语。*Doing something respectively or having some attributes respectively, indicating that it is not just one person who does the job, or it is not just one thing that has a certain attribute. It often serves as an adverbial before a verb, a verb phrase or a quantifier phrase.*

(3) 他们一人一本,你我各三本。
(4) 大家别讲话,各做各的作业。

gègè 各个

用法 Usage:

代词 *pron.*

每个,所有的那些个别(人或事物)。*Everyone; all.*

(1) 他的计划很详细,各个方面都考虑到了。
(2) 苏州的园林,各个都有什么特点?

副词 *ad.*

逐个,表示依次(解决或处理)。*One by one, taking turns in doing or resolving something.*

(3) 这些问题要各个解决。
(4) 你们提出的要求,学校会各个考虑,并作出回答。

说明 Notes:

1. 代词"各个"做主语时,所指代的具体对象或范围,常常在前文出现过。*When "各个" serves as a subject, it usually refers to something that has appeared earlier.*

(5) 去哪儿、什么时候去、怎么去,各个问题都会在明天决定。

2. 代词"各个"作定语,直接修饰名词,一般不加"的"。*When "各个" serves as an attribute, it can directly modify a noun without "的."*

(6) *各个的问题都要在明天决定。
(7) 各个问题都要在明天决定。

gěi 给

用法 Usage:

动词 *v.*

1. 使对方得到某些东西。可带"了、过"。可带双宾语。可在"给"后面再带动词。*To give; to grant. In this usage, "给" can appear with "了" or "过." It can have two objects (indirect object + direct object), and the direct object can be followed by another verb.*

(1) 他给了我一张电影票。
(2) 姐姐给你钱是让你买书的。

2. 使对方受到某种遭遇。可带"了、过"。一般都要带双宾语,有时可以只带直接宾语,但不能只带间接宾语。直接宾语前面常加数量词。*To make someone suffer. In this sense, "给" can appear with "了" or "过." Usually, "给" should go with two objects. Sometimes the direct object alone will do, but it will not do just to have the indirect object. A particle usually appears before the direct object.*

(3) 这次车祸给了他一个沉重的教训。
(4) 他买了两斤苹果,只给了五元钱。

3. "给"可以替代某些具体动作的动词。*It can replace some action verbs.*

(5) 她一生气,就给了他两脚。("踢"的意思 *To kick*)
(6) 给他几句,让他好好想想。("批评"的意思 *To criticize*)

4. 相当于"叫、让"。*It is similar to "叫"*

or "让," meaning "to make or allow."

(7) 这么重的箱子,给我累死了。

(8) 看着他,别给他跑了。

5. 表示容许对方做某种行为动作。*To allow someone to do something.*

(9) 妈妈的信给看,妹妹的信不给看。

介词 *prep.*

1. 引进交付、传递等动作行为的接受者。可以用在动词前,也可以用在动词后。*Like "deliver to" or "pass to," it introduces the object of an action. It can be used before or after a verb.*

(10) 到了北京,请你给我来个电话。

(11) 妈妈寄给我圣诞礼物了。

2. 引进动作的受益者。*Introducing the beneficiary of an action.*

(12) 我给他当翻译。

(13) 王大夫正在给病人治病。

3. 引进动作的受害者。*Introducing the victim of an action.*

(14) 对不起,这件衣服给你弄脏了。

(15) 你怎么把书桌给我搞得这样乱?

4. "给我"加动词,起加强语气的作用。用于祈使句,根据上下文语境,有两种可能的意思。*Forming the phrase "给我" to strengthen the imperative tone. It has two different meanings in different contexts.*

① 同"为我、替我"。*Similar to "为我" or "替我."*

(16) 出去的时候给我把门关好。

(17) 我的手机不见了,你给我找一找。

② 加强命令语气,表示说话人的意志。*Strengthening the imperative tone to indicate the speaker's will.*

(18) 你给我走开!

(19) 你给我睡觉去!别在这里捣乱!

5. 引进动作的对象,相当于"朝、对、向"等。*Introducing the object of an action, equal to "朝," "对," or "向."*

(20) 我给小朋友们讲了一个故事。

(21) 你错了,快给她道个歉。

6. 引进动作行为的主动者,表示被动。"给"后面必定出现施事者。相当于"被"。*"给," similar to "被," must appear before an agent to introduce the doer of the action, indicating the passive voice.*

(22) 门给风吹开了。

(23) 衣服给雨淋湿了。

助词 *aux. v.*

直接用在动词前。多用于"把"字句或被动句,加强处置语气。多用于口语。*Mostly used in sentences with "把" or passive sentences, it comes before a verb and often appears in colloquial language.*

(24) 大家把教室给布置好了。

(25) 玻璃杯,我给打破了一个,怎么办?

说明 Notes:

1. 介词"给"用在动词前,有时会出现歧义,要根据上下文来判断。*Ambiguity may arise when "给" comes before a verb. The context will tell.*

(26) 你给他打个电话,说他过一会儿就去。(替他打电话通知别人 *Making a call on his behalf to inform someone else*)

(27) 你给他打个电话,叫他马上到这儿来。(打电话通知他本人 *Giving him a call to inform him*)

2. "给"在"供给""给养""给予"等词中读 jǐ。*"给" is pronounced as "jǐ" in phrases like "供给,给养,给予."*

gēnběn 根本 →P207"基本"

用法 Usage:

名词 *n.*

事物的根源或最重要的部分。*The source or the most essential part of a thing.*

(1) 水、土是农业的根本。

(2) 解决问题的根本是要他说老实话。

形容词 *a.*

最重要的,起决定作用的。"根本"只做定

语,前面可以加副词"最"。*Most important, decisive. Used as an attribute only, it can take the adverbial "最" as a modifier.*

(3) 汉语学不好,其中最根本的原因是信心问题。

(4) 当前中国最根本的问题是要把经济搞上去。

副词 *ad.*

1. 彻底。用在动词前面做状语。*Meaning "radically," it modifies a verb after it.*

(5) 问题已经根本解决了。

(6) 要根本改造自然环境,还需要相当长的时间。

2. 从头至尾,始终,完全。多用于否定句。谓语中常有副词"就"连用。*From beginning to end; totally. It appears mostly in negative sentences where "就" goes with the predicate.*

(7) 我根本不认识他,怎么会跟他一起看电影呢?

(8) 这件事我根本就不知道。

说明 Notes:

为了强调语气,"根本"有时可提前到句子前面。*A sentence can begin with "根本" to strengthen the tone.*

(9) 根本我就没同意。

(10) 根本你就不对嘛!

gēnjù 根据 →P257"据"、P552"依据"

用法 Usage:

动词 *v.*

"以……为根据",即把某事作为结论的前提或语言行为的基础。必带宾语。*To base a conclusion, speech or action upon something. An object always follows it.*

(1) 水、电等能源的使用要根据节约的原则。

(2) 你根据什么作出这个结论?

介词 *prep.*

表示以某种事物、动作为前提或基础。*The premise or base of something or some action.*

1. "根据"后面带名词。用在主语前面时,有停顿。*It comes before a noun. When it comes before the subject, there may be a pause in the sentence.*

(3) 他根据小说拍了一部电影。

(4) 根据现有的材料,我们还不能做出最后的决定。

2. "根据"后面带动词。一般用在主语前,有停顿。"根据"后面的动词不能再带宾语,如果动词有施事者,一般动词前面加"的",带有名词性。*It is followed by a verb preceding the subject with a pause. The verb cannot take any object. If there is an agent for the verb, usually there is "的" before the verb. The external function of the verb is nominal.*

(5) 根据调查,现在有不少留学生希望在中国工作。

(6) 根据大家反复讨论,这次旅行先去西安。

名词 *n.*

作为论断前提或言行基础的事物。*The premise for judging or the basis for words and deeds.*

(7) 你说这事是他干的,有什么根据吗?

(8) 一点儿根据也没有,你不能这样说别人。

说明 Notes:

"根据"通用于口语和书面语。强调不容置疑的事实前提和出发点。*Used both in colloquial and written language, "根据" emphasizes the premise of a fact or a point of departure that allows no doubt.*

gēn 跟 →P193"和"、P470"同"、P608"与"

用法 Usage:

介词 *prep.*

1. 表示共同,协同。只跟表示人的名词组合,该名词常常在动作过程中起主导作用。"跟"后面有"一起、一道、一同、一块"等词语搭配时,表示动作是双方共同发出的。句子表示否定意义时,"不"用在"跟"前或后的语义不一样:"不跟"表示主观意愿,"跟……不"表示客观事实。"没"用在"跟"的前后意思一样。 Indicating involvement or relationship with somebody. The noun (somebody) before "跟" usually predominates the action. Together with phrases like "一起，一道，一同，一块, etc." it signifies the action being made by both sides. In negative sentences, "不" expresses different meanings: "不跟" indicates the subjective will while "跟...不" indicates some objective fact. However, there is no difference in meaning regardless of the relative position between "没" and "跟."

(1) 我跟你一起去。
(2) 我不跟他去看电影。
(3) 我跟她不住在一起。
(4) 我没跟这个人见面。(我跟这个人没见面。I didn't meet him.)

2. 指示与动作有关的对方。只跟表示人的名词组合。有时候意思与"对、从……那里、向"等相近。Indicating the other person or people involved in the action. It goes only with a noun denoting a person or persons. Sometimes it is similar to words like "对，从...那里，向, etc."

(5) 把你的想法跟大家谈谈。
(6) 这本书我跟王老师借来的。
(7) 我跟你打听一件事。

3. 表示与某事物、某人有无联系。相当于介词"和、与"。Indicating connection to something or somebody, it is an equivalent to the preposition "和" or "与."

(8) 他跟这件事没有关系。
(9) 我去不去跟你没有关系。

4. 引进用来比较或比拟的对象。后面常用"比、相同、不同、一样、差不多、相像、相反、似的"等词或词语。Introducing subjects for comparison. "跟" is usually followed by words like "比，相同，不同，一样，差不多，相像，相反，似的, etc."

(10) 我的爱好跟你的一样。
(11) 她的衣服跟你的比，当然是你的好。

连词 conj.

表示平等的联合关系，"和"。一般连接名词、代词或名词短语。多用于口语。And. It indicates a relationship of equality or union. It serves to join two words (nouns, prepositions, or noun phrases), mostly used in colloquial language.

(12) 你跟他都是韩国人吗？
(13) 护照跟钱包我都拿了。

动词 v.

表示在后面紧接着向同一方向行动。不能单用，必须加趋向动词或在前面加介词短语。To follow the same direction. It cannot be used by itself. It must be followed by a directional verb or be preceded by a prepositional phrase.

(14) 你走慢一点，走快了，老太太跟不上。
(15) 爸爸在前面走，小华在后面跟着。

名词 n.

表示脚的后部或鞋袜的后部。如："脚后跟、高跟鞋"。Heel (of the foot, a shoe, a sock, etc.) as in "脚后跟，高跟鞋."

说明 Notes:

有时候，"跟"是介词用法还是连词用法，要看前后语境条件才能决定。In some cases, whether "跟" functions as a preposition or a conjunction depends on the context.

(16) 不能让她一个人去，你跟她一起去。(和，连词用法 And; conjunction)
(17) 不是跟我去上海，是跟她一起去上海。(表示随同，介词用法 Together with; preposition)

gèng 更 →P168 "更加"

用法 Usage:

副词 ad.

1. 表示在原来的基础上程度的加深或数量的增减。常用于比较。To have a greater degree than usual; to become larger or smaller in number or amount. It is usually used to compare.

(1) 他比你吃得更多。

(2) 经过学习,大家的汉语说得更好、更流利了。

2. 表示强调,相当于"尤其"。前面常用"不仅、不光"呼应。To emphasize. Synonymous with "尤其," it often has "不仅" or "不光" before it.

(3) 我不喜欢打扑克,更不喜欢搓麻将。

(4) 我不仅要听他怎么说,更重要的是要看他怎么做。

3. 相当于"再、又、还"等。多用于书面语。It is synonymous with "再,又,还." It appears in written language more.

(5) 欲穷千里目,更上一层楼。

(6) 他在地上写了字,更画起画来了。

说明 Notes:

1. "更"后面可以带形容词、动词。如果动词后面用"得"引进补语,"更"可以在动词前面,也可以在补语中间,以在补语中为常见。"更" usually appears before an adjective or a verb. If it is necessary to introduce a complement by "得" after a verb, "更" can appear either in front of the verb or between "得" and the complement. The latter choice is more common.

(7) 我让他别唱了,可他更唱得来劲儿了。

(8) 我让他别唱了,可他唱得更来劲儿了。

2. 在否定句中,"更"在否定词前边。In negative sentences, "更" comes before the negative word.

(9) 她比我姐姐更不爱说话。

3. "更"有时不含"原来也有一定程度"的意思,而只是和相反的一面比较,常与"反而、相反"等词语连用。In some cases, "更" does not mean a greater degree. Instead, it just brings out an opposite situation where words like "反而,相反" will appear.

(10) 我让他开得慢一点儿,他反而开得更快了。

(11) 你这一改,文章反而更有说服力了。

4. "更"后面可以带可能补语,"得/不"后常用趋向动词和"了(liǎo)、住、着(zháo)"等词。但多用否定形式。A potential complement can follow "更," where one will find "得/不" followed by a directional verb and words like "了(liǎo),住,着(zháo)." This usage usually appears in negative sentences.

(12) 他比以前更沉得住气了。

(13) 连你兄弟都来了,我就更帮不着你的忙了。

(14) 快十二点了,我就更回不去了。

gèngjiā 更加 →P167"更"

用法 Usage:

副词 ad.

表示程度上又深一层或者数量上进一步增加或减少。与"更"的第一种用法相同。To have a greater degree than usual, to become larger or smaller in number or amount. It is synonymous with the first meaning of "更."

(1) 她显得更加漂亮、更加年轻了。

(2) 你这么说,我更加不明白了。

说明 Notes:

"更加"的意思和用法同"更"的第一种用法基本相同,常在形容词和动词前作状语。"更加" is synonymous with the first meaning of "更," often serving as an adverbial before an adjective or a verb.

它们的区别是:Their differences are as follows:

1. "更加"多修饰双音节词语。用在句末时,一般后面带双音节词语结束,语气比"更"重一些。如例(1)(2)。"更加" often modifies disyllabic words. When it appears at the end of a sentence, the sentence usually ends with a disyllabic word and indicates a heavier tone, as in (1) and (2).

2. "更加"多用于书面语,没有"更"的第二、三种用法。"更加" does not have the second meaning and the third meaning of "更." "更加" often appears in written language.

gōngfu 工夫 →P169"功夫"

用法 Usage:

名词 n.

1. 所用的时间(也包括所花的精力、心思等)。Time that one spends (in) doing something (using both physical energy and mental energy).

(1) 他三天工夫就学会了游泳。
(2) 我准备用三年工夫学习汉语。

2. 表示空闲的时间。Spare time.

(3) 明天有工夫再来玩吧。
(4) 这几天我们要考试了,没工夫陪你逛街。

3. 表示本领、造诣、功力。Talent, skill, capability.

(5) 他写毛笔字的工夫很深。
(6) 他在中国文学研究方面很有工夫。

gōngfu 功夫 →P169"工夫"

用法 Usage:

名词 n.

1. 做事所要的时间、本领、技艺、造诣等。Time, skill, capability, etc. that one needs in doing something.

(1) 他的山水画功夫很深。
(2) 功夫不负有心人。

2. 指中国武术。Chinese martial arts.

(3) 我们都很喜欢中国功夫。
(4) 他很爱看功夫片。

说明 Notes:

"功夫"和"工夫"的区别是：The differences between "功夫" and "工夫" are as follows:

1. 指动作、行为所花的时间,空闲的时间,花费的时间时,多用"工夫"。"工夫" means time spent in doing something, or just one's spare time.

2. 指本领、造诣的意思时,多用"功夫"。"功夫片"就不能说"工夫片"。"功夫" usually involves skill, ability, or capability. For example, we can say "功夫片," but not "工夫片."

gōngbù 公布 →P527"宣布"

用法 Usage:

动词 v.

公开发布法令、文告、注意事项,让大家知道。To announce; to make something (such as a decree, statement, notice, etc.) known to the public.

(1) 航空公司已经把飞机失事的原因向全世界公布了。
(2) 这次考试的成绩什么时候公布?

说明 Notes:

"公布"常与"法令、消息、结果、成绩、牌价、数字"等词语搭配。"公布" usually goes with words like "法令,消息,结果,成绩,牌价,数字," etc.

gōutōng 沟通

用法 Usage:

动词 v.

使两方能通连。To communicate; to link up; to join two parties or two parts.

(1) 我要学好汉语,做沟通中西文化的使者。
(2) 长江大桥沟通了南北交通,促进了经济发展。
(3) 朋友间要加深了解,就必须多加沟通。

说明 Notes:

"沟通"多用于抽象事物的通连,如"人际沟通、亲子沟通、文化沟通、心灵沟通、信息沟通、语言沟通、沟通古今、沟通感情"等。"沟通" usually refers to the connection or communication between abstract things, such as "人际沟通,亲子沟通,文化沟通,心灵沟通,信息沟通,语言沟通,沟通古今,沟通感情."

gòu 够

用法 Usage:

动词 v.

1. 满足需要的数量。To be enough for; to

have enough to meet somebody's needs or wants.

（1）你带的钱够不够？
（2）两个面包够吃了。

2. 达到某种标准、水平、程度或要求。*To meet certain standards or requirements.*

（3）他的学术水平已经够当个教授了。
（4）我现在当翻译还不够条件。

3. 用手或工具伸向不易达到的地方去触摸或拿取。*To reach for; to stretch one's hand or some tool toward something (usually hard to reach) in order to touch it, or to fetch it.*

（5）那么高的书架，我可能够不着。
（6）药物要放在孩子够不着的地方。

副词 *ad.*

1. 修饰形容词，表示程度很高（形容词可以是积极意义的，也可以是消极意义的）。*Reaching a very high degree. It modifies an adjective (either positive or negative in meaning).*

（7）别再麻烦他们，他们已经够忙了。
（8）那人够凶恶的。

2. 修饰形容词，表示已经达到了一定的标准（形容词可以是积极意义的，也可以是相应的反义词）。*Meeting certain standards. It modifies an adjective (either positive or negative).*

（9）教室里的灯光够亮了。
（10）电视机的声音开得够小了。

说明 Notes:

1. "够"可以用在动词后面，有时中间可插入"不"，多含不耐烦的语气。*"够" can follow a verb, and "不" can come between the verb and "够." In this sense, "够" usually implies impatience.*

（11）你们笑够了没有？有什么好笑的？
（12）他这些话你还听不够？我早听够了。
（13）这菜我吃够了，再也不想吃了。

2. "够"作副词用，句子后面常有"了、的"，表示强调或肯定语气。如例（7）（8）（9）（10）。*"够" may serve as an adverb, usually followed by "了" or "的" to stress or affirm something, such as in (7), (8), (9) and (10).*

guài 怪 →P366"奇怪"、P467"挺"

用法 Usage:

动词 *v.*

责备、埋怨。可带"过"，必须带名词宾语或兼语。*To put the blame on someone or complain about him or her. "过" can follow "怪," which must be followed by a noun object or what is called a complex object in English, that is, the noun object of a verb followed by an infinitive phrase.*

（1）我从来没有怪过你。
（2）这事不能怪他，怪我没让他去。

形容词 *a.*

奇怪，不常见。在句子中可做谓语、定语、补语。*Strange; unusual; uncommon. It may serve as a predicate, attribute, or complement.*

（3）这个人很怪，谁也不知道他在说什么。
（4）这座新图书馆什么都好，就是形状有点怪。

副词 *ad.*

表示有相当高的程度。用于口语，后面必须用"的"。*Very; quite; rather. Indicating a high degree, it often appears with "的" in spoken language.*

（5）这孩子长得怪可爱的。
（6）几天不见，怪想他的。
（7）他这样说，我心里怪不高兴的。

名词 *n.*

怪异的人或事物，怪物，妖怪。常与别的名词组合一起用。*A weird person or thing; a monster. It usually appears with some other noun.*

（8）他是我们这个小镇一怪。
（9）他又在给孩子们讲鬼怪的故事了。

说明 Notes:

1. "怪"作副词用时，前面不能用否定词。*When "怪" serves as an adverbial, no negative words should appear before it.*

（10）＊这套衣服，不怪好看的。
（11）这套衣服，怪不好看的。

2."怪"带形容词、动词时,动词常常是表示心理状态的,后面必须加"的",构成"怪……的"结构,在句子中做状语、定语或补语,如例(6)(7)。 When "怪" appears with an adjective or a verb, the verb usually indicates a mental state. In this case, the use of "的" is necessary, forming the phrase "怪...的." The phrase usually serves as an adverbial, an attribute, or a complement in a sentence. See (6) and (7).

guàibude 怪不得 →P333"难怪"

用法 Usage:

动词 v.

不能责备,别见怪(某人)。必带名词宾语。 Not to blame (someone for something). It must take a noun object.

(1) 这事是我弄错了,怪不得他。

(2) 这场比赛输了,怪不得天气,只怪咱们自己水平还不够高。

副词 ad.

表示明白了原因,对某种情况就不觉得奇怪。前后常有表明原因的语句。 No wonder. Words or sentences indicating the reason appear before or after "怪不得."

(3) 下雪了,怪不得这么冷!

(4) 怪不得他汉语说得那么好,原来他爸爸是中国人。

说明 Notes:

"怪不得"常用于口语。"怪不得" is often used colloquially.

guān 关

用法 Usage:

动词 v.

1.关闭,闭合。 To turn off; to shut.

(1) 现在开始上课,大家把手机关了。

(2) 下大雨了,快关上窗户。

2.禁闭,待在里面不让出来。 To lock in; to bar; to prevent something or someone from going out.

(3) 他偷了很多电动车,先把他关起来。

(4) 这鸟儿被关在笼子里好多年,飞不高了。

3.倒闭或歇业。 (Of a business) to close; to shut down.

(5) 最近好几家工厂关了。

(6) 今天起,商店关了,大家好好儿休息休息。

4.牵连。 To have something to do with.

(7) 弟弟自己摔跤的,不关我事。

(8) 事关重要,大家都要想想办法解决。

名词 n.

1.边界或交通要道重要的通道口。 A pass at the borders or a guarded passage.

(9) 中国越南两国边界的关口叫友谊关。

(10) 中国有山海关、嘉峪关、雁门关等九大名关。

2.进出口检查或收税的地方,常与另一个名词组合使用。 A place where inspection is done for imports and exports and tariffs are imposed; customhouse.

(11) 现在我们要排队过海关了。

(12) 这批货物的进口关税增加了5%。

3.城门外附近的地区。 A neighborhood just outside the city gate.

(13) 我不住在城里,住在城关。

4.比喻严格的标准。 Rigorous standards (fig.).

(14) 在质量上你要把关,不合格的产品不能出厂。

(15) 祝贺你,你做的衣服已经过了质量关。

5.比喻重要阶段或转折点。 An important phase; a turning point.

(16) 今年我们公司的利润突破了五亿大关。

(17) 让我们团结起来,共渡难关!

guānhuái 关怀 →P172"关心"、P173"关注"

用法 Usage:

动词 v.

关心(包含爱护、照顾之意)。多用于上对

下、老对小、集体对个人。*To show care for (subordinates, juniors or any individuals).*

（1）谢谢老师关怀！我的病已经好了。

（2）现在各级政府都很关怀老人的生活。

名词 *n.*

对人关心的言语或举动。前面必须用介词"对"引出关怀的对象。*Words or behaviors showing care. Usually "对" is used to introduce the target of care.*

（3）谢谢老师对我的关怀！

guānxīn 关心 →P171"关怀"、P173"关注"

用法 Usage:
动词 *v.*

把人或事物常放在心上；重视和爱护。*To care for; to cherish and value (a person or an object).*

（1）人们非常关心灾区孩子的学习和生活。

（2）我们班的留学生互相关心、互相帮助，就像一家人。

名词 *n.*

对人关心的言语或举动。前面必须用介词"对"引出关心的对象。*Words or behavior showing care for people. Usually "对" introduces the target of care.*

（3）我永远不会忘记姐姐对我的帮助和关心。

guānyú 关于 →P121"对于"、P598"有关"、P674"至于"

用法 Usage:
介词 *prep.*

1."关于"组成介词短语做状语，引进跟某种动作行为有关的人或事物。"关于"构成的介词短语一般在主语前面，在书面上要用逗号分开。*The prepositional phrase starting with "关于" serves as an adverbial to introduce related people or objects. It usually appears before the subject of the main clause. A comma serves to separate the subject and the adverbial in the written form.*

（1）关于他的旷课问题，我们明天再讨论决定。

（2）关于交男女朋友，每个人都会有很多话要说。

2."关于"组成介词短语，做定语或与"是"字构成判断句式，表示某种事物涉及的范围或包括的内容。做定语时，"关于"组成的介词短语与中心词之间一定要用"的"。*The phrase starting with "关于" can be an attributive, or a defining clause with "是" to state what is included in or impacted by the subject. When used as an attribute, it must go with "的" to echo with the headword.*

（3）我想买一本关于中国文化的书。

（4）我想了解的是关于留学生学习本科专业的问题。

3."关于"有提示作用，所以"关于"组成的介词短语常常做文章的题目。如："关于社会养老问题""关于文化选修课"。*The phrase starting with "关于" often appears as part of the title of an article such as "关于社会养老问题,""关于文化选修课." It functions as a lingual cue.*

说明 Notes:

"关于"和"对于"都是介词，引进所涉及的对象范围，都能构成介词短语作状语、定语。*"关于" and "对于" are similar in that they both are prepositions to introduce what is covered in the field and they both can form phrases to serve as an adverbial or attributive.*

区别是：*Their differences are as follows:*

1."关于"多用来表示动作所关涉的事物或事物所涉及的范围，"关于"后面的名词在语义上是被后面句子陈述的对象。"对于"多用来指出对象，表示对待关系，"对于"后面的名词在语义上是后面句子里动词的宾语。因此，表示关联、涉及的事物，用"关于"；单纯指出动作行为对象时，用"对于"。*"关于" usually introduces the thing or its field impacted by a* certain action. Semantically the object after "关于" is most often the object of the main clause. "对于" implies a mutual relationship, which means the object of "对于" is also that of the verb in the main clause. Therefore, "关于" shows relevance while "对于" simply indicates the target of the action.

(5) 关于孙悟空,民间还有很多有趣的传说。

(6) 对于大熊猫,我们要尽力采取保护。

兼有两种情况的,可以用"关于",也可以用"对于"。They are interchangeable if both choices are possible.

(7) 对于/关于五一节去苏州旅游的建议,大家都很赞同。

2. "关于"构成的介词短语做状语时,它的位置一般在句子开头,并且有停顿。"对于"构成的介词短语做状语时,其位置可以在句子开头,也可在句子主语后面,可以有停顿,也可以没有停顿。The phrase with "关于" often comes at the beginning of the sentence with a pause if it serves as an adverbial. As for the phrase with "对于," it is flexible in its position and pause if it serves as an adverbial.

(8) *大家关于去博物馆参观的事项还有什么意见?

(9) 关于去博物馆参观的事项,大家还有什么意见?

(10) 对于去博物馆参观的时间,我们还没确定。

(11) 我们对于去博物馆参观的时间还没确定。

3. "关于"组成的介词短语,可以单独做文章的题目。"对于"只有跟名词组成偏正词组后(其中一定要加"的"),表示对某个问题的看法、认识的意思时,才能做题目。如:"对于教学实习时间的安排""关于教学实习时间安排"。The prepositional phrase starting with "关于" can be the title of an article while the one starting with "对于" cannot. Only by forming a subordinate phrase with "的" and a noun can a prepositional phrase starting with "对于" be a title, such as "对于教学实习时间的安排,""关于教学实习时间安排."

guānzhù 关注 →P171 "关怀"、P172 "关心"

用法 Usage:

动词 v.

关心,重视。可以涉及人或者事物。To care for or attach importance to (a person or an object).

(1) 我发现那个男孩一直关注着你。

(2) 全世界的医学界都在关注这个小女孩的疾病。

名词 n.

The act of caring for or attaching importance to (a person or an object).

(3) 教育改革引起了社会上各界人士的关注。

说明 Notes:

"关怀""关心""关注"都是动词,都可用作名词。"关怀,""关心," and "关注" all can be verbs and nouns.

它们的区别是:They differ as follows:

1. 词义侧重点不同。"关怀"重在关爱之情,常记在心怀。"关心"重在惦记爱护,常放在心上。"关注"重在格外注意、重视。They differ in emphasis. "关怀" highlights loving care, "关心" emphasizes care and concern, and "关注" focuses on particular attention.

2. 涉及的对象有所不同。They appear with different objects.

① "关怀"涉及的对象一般是人,用在上对下,也可以是对国家民族的大事。"关怀" generally applies to a person, usually to subordinates. It can also apply to things like national affairs.

(4) 全国人民时刻关怀着灾区人民的生活。

② "关心"涉及的对象范围较广,可以是人,也可以是事物。可以用在上对下、长辈和小

辈之间,也可以用在同事之间、同学之间等。"关心" is a general word that can apply to both people and objects. It may show care by a superior for the subordinates, a senior for the children or grandchildren, or simply care for each other among colleagues and peers.

③"关注"涉及的对象可以是人,也可以是事物,一般不分上下、长幼。"关注" can also apply to people or objects regardless of social status or birth order.

3. "关怀"和"关注"多用于书面语。"关心"多用于口语。"关怀" and "关注" are more formal while "关心" is more colloquial.

guǎn 管 →P175"管理"

用法 Usage:

动词 v.

1. 管理,担任、负责某项工作或事务。To manage; to be responsible for a task or a mission.

(1) 她是管留学生生活的。

(2) 在病房里,一个医生管三个病人。

2. 管教,照料。To discipline or take care of someone or something.

(3) 管好你的狗,别让它到处拉屎。

(4) 管孩子可得有耐心。

3. 过问,干预。To intervene or meddle with others' affairs.

(5) 他就喜欢管别人的事。

(6) 孩子大了,你不用多管他的事。

4. 保证,负责。To ensure something; to take care of; to handle.

(7) 如果一年内洗衣机坏了,我们商店管修。

(8) 来中国留学,我的父母管飞机票、管学费。

名词 n.

1. 中间空的棍状物体。常与名词组合使用。如:"竹管、煤气管、水管、管子"等。Tube; hollowing club-like objects. It usually appears with a noun, such as "竹管,煤气管,水管,管子."

2. 吹奏的乐器。常与名词组合使用。如:"管弦乐、黑管、铜管乐"等。Tubular wind instruments. It usually appears with a noun, such as "管弦乐,黑管,铜管乐."

3. 形状像管子的电器。常与名词组合使用,如:"电子管、显像管"等。Electric or electronic appliance in the shape of a tube, such as "电子管,显像管."

介词 prep.

1. 作用相当于"把",与"叫"构成"管……叫……"的格式,用来称说人或事物。只用于口语。It has the same usage as "把," and it can appear in the form of "管…叫…," which usually refers to someone or something in colloquial language.

(9) 他们管我叫"韩辣椒"。

(10) 古代人管眼睛叫"目"。

2. 相当于"向",引进动作行为的对象。It is the same as "向," used to introduce the object of an action.

(11) 她为什么不给你电影票,你管她要去。

(12) 小时候我总是管妈妈要钱,不敢向爸爸要钱。

连词 conj.

用在方言中,表示行为动作不受所举条件的限制,相当于"不管"。"管"后面的小句主语必定是"你"或"他"(有时"他"是虚指的),谓语或者是肯定和否定连用,或者有疑问代词。后一分句中,常用"都、也、就"呼应。No matter (what, how, etc.), mainly used in dialects. It shows that the behavior defies any restrictions (the same as "不管"). The subject of the clause after "管" must be "你" or "他" ("他" actually does not refer to a specific person), and the predicate is a combination of both affirmative and negative, or go with an interrogative pronoun. The latter clause commonly uses "都,也,就" to echo with it.

(13) 管你有空没空,这个星期天你一定要陪我看电影。

(14) 管他同意不同意,我都要去爬山。

guǎnlǐ 管理 →P174"管"

用法 Usage:

动词 v.

1. 负责某项工作,使具有秩序、正常运行。To manage or administer a business; to conduct the normal day-to-day operation.

(1) 别看他那么年轻,他管理着两个饭店呢。

(2) 现在他管理留学生的生活。

2. 保管和料理。一般指比较单一的工作或事物。To take care of something or to be in charge of something.

(3) 他在工厂管理仓库。

(4) 退休以后,他到一个中学管理图书资料去了。

3. 照管,管束。To look after or to have control over.

(5) 管理住校中学生的生活是很复杂的工作。

(6) 在家里每个人管理好自己的事,妈妈的家务劳动就轻松多了。

名词 n.

"管理"用作名词,可有修饰语。如:"经济管理、旅游管理、饭店管理"等。"管理," as a noun, can have a modifier with it, such as "经济管理,旅游管理,饭店管理."

说明 Notes:

1. "管理"做谓语时,后面的宾语多为双音节以上的词语。When used as a predicate, "管理" often goes with disyllabic or polysyllabic words.

2. "管"和"管理"的区别是:The differences between "管" and "管理" are as follows:

① 在词义上,"管"的词义范围比"管理"广泛。"管理"的三个词义,"管"都可以替用。"管理"没有"管"的关于"管教、照料""过问、干预""保证、负责"的词义。在这三种用法中,"管理"不能替换"管"。"管" carries a wider meaning than "管理." All the three meanings of "管理" can be replaced by "管," but "管理" does not mean "管教,照料," "过问,干预," or "保证,负责," all of which come within the sphere of "管." "管理" cannot take the place of "管."

② "管"有介词和连词的用法。"管理"没有。"管" can serve as a preposition or a conjunction; however, "管理" cannot.

guāng 光 →P666"只"

用法 Usage:

名词 n.

1. 光芒,光亮,指照在物体上,使人能看见物体的那种物质。Light; ray, a substance that shines on an object and makes it visible.

(1) 屋子里一点光也没有,什么也看不见。

(2) 光的传播速度每秒大约30万公里。

2. 光彩,荣誉。Splendor; honor; glory.

(3) 孩子没考上大学,他觉得脸上无光,心里很不高兴。

(4) 他得了奥运会的金牌,为父母争了光,也为祖国争了光。

3. 比喻好处。Benefit; advantage (fig.).

(5) 他爸爸是总经理,但是他没沾过他爸爸的光。

(6) 今天我们沾了他的光,受到了那么好的招待。

4. 景物,光景。一般与其他词组合,如:"春光、光景、风光"等。A scene or scenery. It often joins with other words to make sense as in "春光,光景,风光."

5. 敬语,指对方来临。如:"欢迎光临、敬请光顾、谢谢赏光"等。Polite expressions to show appreciation of the arrival of someone, such as "欢迎光临,敬请光顾,谢谢赏光."

形容词 a.

1. 滑,光溜。Slippery; smooth.

(7) 桌面、地板都很光。这木工师傅的技术不错。

(8) 这苹果又大又红又光,真想吃一个。

2. 一点也不剩,全没有了,完了。多用作前一动词的补语。To be used up; to be finished off; all gone. It often serves as a complement to the verb before it.

(9) 我的钱都用光了。

(10) 你把饺子吃光了?

3. 加上后缀,可以构成形容词的生动形式。如:"光亮亮、光灿灿、光闪闪"等。With suffixes, "光" can constitute a vivid form of adjectives, such as "光亮亮,光灿灿,光闪闪."

动词 v.

1. 赤,露出。To be bare; to be naked.

(11) 秋天了,光着脚,要受凉的。

(12) 小孩儿光着身子从床上爬了下来。

2. 光大,荣光。多用于固定词组中。如:"光宗耀祖、光前裕后"等。To add glory to. It appears in fixed phrases such as "光宗耀祖,光前裕后."

副词 ad.

限定范围,表示"只、单"的意思,后面常与"就"搭配使用。多用于口语。可用在动词、形容词前,也可用在句首。Merely; only. It has a similar meaning to "只" or "单." Often followed by "就," it often appears before a verb or an adjective, or at the beginning of a sentence in spoken language.

(13) 我们班的同学光通过HSK八级的就有六个。

(14) 她光红毛衣就有十件。

(15) 光你一个人去不够,你得叫上几个人一起去。

说明 Notes:

"光"在做形容词和副词时,可以重叠为"光光"。When "光" serves as an adverb or an adjective, it can repeat itself to become "光光."

(16) 他那光光的头上一根头发都没有。

(17) 别光光想着自己,也要想想别人。

guǎngfàn 广泛 →P176 "广阔"

用法 Usage:

形容词 a.

(事物涉及的)方面广、范围大,普遍。Extensive; wide-ranging; large-scale; general.

(1) 在农村,手机的使用范围也非常广泛了。

(2) 这些科学成果都广泛地应用到了人们的日常生活中。

说明 Notes:

"广泛"着重形容人们活动涉及的方面多、范围广。做状语时常修饰"使用、征求、开展、应用、建立、流行"等动词,常与"内容、体裁、兴趣、影响、知识、作用、联系、用途"等词语搭配。"广泛" stresses the wide range of things people are involved in. It usually modifies verbs such as "使用,征求,开展,应用,建立,流行" when used as an adverbial. It often collocates with words such as "内容,体裁,兴趣,影响,知识,作用,联系,用途."

guǎngkuò 广阔 →P176 "广泛"

用法 Usage:

形容词 a.

形容广大宽阔。Vast; wide; broad.

(1) 中国农村是一个广阔的市场。

(2) 广阔的草原上牛马成群。

(3) 他的理想远大,胸怀广阔。

说明 Notes:

1. "广阔"着重于空间上的宽阔。可以修饰具体名词,如"田野、土地、草原、道路、天空、海洋"等,也可以描写抽象名词,如"境界、胸怀、前景、眼界、思想、视野"等。"广阔" emphasizes the vastness in space. It can modify concrete nouns such as "田野,土地,草原,道路,天空,海洋," or abstract nouns such as "境界,胸怀,前景,眼界,思想,视野."

2. "广泛"和"广阔"都形容大而广。区别是,两者使用范围有所不同,词语搭配不同(见各自的"说明")。"广泛" and "广阔" both

express the meanings of wide and broad, yet they apply to different areas and have different collocations. (Refer to their respective notes).

guī 归 →P201 "回"

用法 Usage:

动词 v.

1. 返回。To return; to get back to.
(1) 他是归国华侨。
(2) 可怜的流浪狗无家可归。

2. 还给,归还。To give back to.
(3) 地上捡的一万元,今天终于物归原主了。

3. 趋向或集中于一个地方。To collect; to merge into.
(4) 千条河流归大海。
(5) 请把大家的钱归到一起。

4. 属于（谁所有）。必须带宾语。To belong to. It must appear before an object.
(6) 土地归国家所有。
(7) 哥哥走了,他的自行车就归你了。

5. 用在相同的动词之间,表示动作并未引起相应的结果。Sandwiched between two verbs using the same word or expression, it shows no corresponding results were reached by the action.
(8) 批评归批评,奖金一分也没少给。
(9) 吵归吵,闹归闹,这么多年他们俩也没分手。

介词 prep.

由（谁负责),用于兼语句,主语是兼语后面动词的受事者。In charge of. It appears in a sentence with a concurrent phrase or expression. The recipient following the object is the subject.
(10) 学生报到的事情都归他们管。
(11) 其他工作归第三小组负责完成。

guīdìng 规定 →P177 "规范"、P178 "规则"

用法 Usage:

动词 v.

事先对某一事物在数量、质量、方式、方法等方面定出要求。To stipulate; to place advance requirements on a thing in terms of quantity, quality, manner, methods and other aspects.
(1) 学校规定国庆节放七天假。
(2) 父母规定她每天晚上十点前必须回家。

名词 n.

事先对某一事物在数量、质量、方式、方法等方面做出规定的内容。Stipulation; rules and regulations; advance requirements on a thing in terms of quantity, quality, manner, methods and other aspects.
(3) 我们应该遵守学校的规定。
(4) 请你看一下这几条规定。

说明 Notes:

1. "规定"可以是书面的,也可以是口头宣布的。"规定" can appear in both written and colloquial language.

2. "规定"名词用法,多与"有、是、遵守、违反、合乎、实行、执行、符合"等动词搭配,通用于口语和书面语。"规定," as a noun, often goes with verbs like "有,是,遵守,违反,合乎,实行,执行,符合" in both written and colloquial language.

guīfàn 规范 →P177 "规定"

用法 Usage:

动词 v.

使合乎规范,规定共同遵守的模式。To make someone conform to a rule or standard; to make rules and regulations; to regulate; to standardize.
(1) 每个人必须用新的社会道德来规范自己的行为。
(2) 制定考试管理规定的目的就是要规范每个学生的考试行为。

形容词 a.

合乎标准的。Standard.
(3) 你的太极拳打得还不够规范。
(4) 这个句子的语法很规范。

名词 n.

约定俗成或明文规定的标准。*Conventional or explicitly issued regulations.*

（5）汉语拼音方案是学习汉语普通话的语音规范。

说明 Notes:

"规定"和"规范"的区别是：*The differences between "规定" and "规范" are as follows:*

1. 用作名词时，"规定"使用范围比较广泛，可以是机关、学校等单位制定，也可以是个人制定。"规范"是一种比较正规的、大家共同承认并遵守的标准，一般不适用于个人制定。*"规定," as a noun, covers a wide range of things. Not only organizations such as government bodies or schools, but also individuals can make "规定." By contrast, "规范" is more formal and commonly agreed on; it usually does not apply to the conduct of individuals.*

（6）*进来要先敲门，这是我的规范。

（7）进来要先敲门，这是我的规定。

2. "规范"可以用作形容词。"规定"不可以。*"规范" can serve as an adjective, but "规定" cannot.*

（8）*这个词的用法很规定。

（9）这个词的用法很规范。

3. 用作动词时，"规定"的宾语一般是句子，表示规定什么人怎么做，或者什么事怎么样。"规范"的宾语一般是带有修饰语的名词。*As a verb, "规定" usually has a noun clause as its object. "规范," by contrast, usually takes as its object a noun with an adjective modifying it.*

（10）学校规定学生不能在上课时吃东西。

（11）学校要规范学生在教室里上课时的行为。

guīzé 规则 →P177"规定"

用法 Usage:

名词 n.

共同遵守的某一方面的具体规定。*Specific rules that people commonly abide by in a certain field.*

（1）为了您和家人的幸福，请遵守交通规则。

（2）老师按学校规则处理了这件事。

形容词 a.

指形状、结构等整齐、对称，合乎一定的方式。*Regular or symmetrical in shape and structure, both of which follow a certain rule.*

（3）这张图画得很规则。

（4）这是规则的平行四边形。

说明 Notes:

"规定"和"规则"的区别是：*The differences between "规定" and "规则" are as follows:*

1. 用作名词时，"规定"着重指所指定的关于事物的数量、质量的标准，或处理事物的方式、方法。"规则"着重指制定出来的供大家共同遵守的制度、章程。*When used as a noun in a sentence, "规定" emphasizes the standards of quality and quantity or the way of dealing with a situation. "规则," by contrast, indicates the official rules and regulations people have to follow.*

2. 在形式上，"规定"可以是成文的，也可以是口头宣布的。"规则"一般是成文的，如"比赛规则、交通规则、考试规则、借书规则"等。*In form, "规定" could be written or verbal, while "规则" is usually written, such as "比赛规则,交通规则,考试规则,借书规则."*

3. "规定"多与"实行、执行、符合"等动词搭配。"规则"常与"制定、执行"等动词搭配，通用于口语和书面语。*When used as a noun, "规定" is often used with verbs like "实行,执行,符合," while "规则" often appears with verbs like "制定,执行," both of which appear in oral or written language.*

4. "规则"有形容词用法。"规定"没有形容词用法。*While "规则" can serve as an adjective, "规定" cannot.*

guǒrán 果然

用法 Usage:

副词 ad.

1. 表示事实与所说或所料相符,有"真的、确实"的意思,只作状语,可用在句首,也可用在句中。"果然"用在分句、句子、段落的开头,往往兼有承上启下的作用,在"果然"的后面常常加逗号。Really, used to indicate that the fact accords with the prediction or expectation. In this sense, it serves only as an adverbial in a sentence. It may appear both at the beginning of a sentence or in its middle. When used at the beginning of a clause, a sentence or a paragraph, it plays the role of a conjunction to join ideas before and after it. There is usually a comma following it.

(1) 他说下午要下雪,现在果然下雪了。

(2) 果然,她没有来,你估计得没错。

2. "果然"用于疑问句时,兼有加强语气的作用。When used in interrogative sentences, it intensifies the tone of the speaker.

(3) 你刚才说的话果然是真的吗?

(4) 情况果然像他所说的那样简单吗?

3. "果然"与"不出……所料"构成"果然不出……所料",是一种常用的格式。"不出"后面一般是双音节词语。"果然" plus "不出…所料" forms "果然不出…所料" structure. It means that the result turned out to be exactly what one had expected. "不出" usually takes disyllabic words.

(5) 果然不出他们所料,辽宁队赢了!

(6) 果然不出你所料,今天他又没有来上课。

4. "果然"可通过添加副词"不"和语气助词"其",构成四字成语"果不其然",强调不出所料。也说"果不然"。"果然" can form a four-character idiom "果不其然" by adding the adverb "不" and the modal particle "其" to emphasize that what happens is not unexpected. It can also be used as "果不然."

(7) 我早说要下雪,果不其然,下了吧!

(8) 果不其然,同学们都在图书馆看书呢。

连词 conj.

表示假设关系。连接分句,有"如果真的、如果确实"的意思。用在偏句里,在正句里常有"就"与之呼应。有时"果然"后面带助词"的话",加强假设语气。Suppose/supposing, which can serve to join two clauses, meaning "if so." When used in a subordinate clause, it often appears with "就" in the main clause. Sometimes it pairs with "的话" to intensify the subjunctive mood.

(9) 你果然爱他的话,明天就应该对他说。

(10) 果然像你说的那样,这事情就好办了。

guò 过

用法 Usage:

动词 v.

1. 渡过,经过(处所)。To cross (a river); to pass (a place).

(1) 去那个村子要过一条河。

(2) 婚礼的车队正好从我家门前过。

2. 经历,经过(时间)。To spend/pass (time).

(3) 今年你回家过春节吗?

(4) 再过半个月,你就可以出院了。

3. 使经过,做某种处理。可重叠。(As a method of processing something) to go through; to go over. It can be reduplicated.

(5) 你脑子里再过过今天发生的这件事。

(6) 这几件衣服已经在水里过了好几遍了。

4. 超过某种范围或限度。To surpass; to exceed; to go beyond.

(7) 过了今天,牛奶就过期了。

(8) 他虽然年过八十,但体力还是跟年轻人一样。

5. 从甲方转移到乙方。如:"过户、过账"等。To transfer something (e.g. money or

ownership) from A to B, as in "过户,过账".

6. 用在动词后面,做趋向补语。*Used as a directional complement after a verb.*

① 用在动词后,表示经过,或从一处到另一处。动词的动作要求有方向感。*It can be used after a directional verb to indicate passing by or moving from one place to another.*

(9) 他走过食堂,向图书馆走去。

(10) 上课的时候,他传过一张纸条来。

② 用在动词后,表示物体随动作改变方向。*It can be used after a verb to indicate the change of direction.*

(11) 他转过脸去看了她半天。

(12) 汽车掉过头往东开去了。

③ 用在动词后,表示超过一定的界限。*It can be used after a verb to indicate exceeding a certain limit.*

(13) 明天早晨六点钟的火车,你别睡过了。

(14) 你别把话说过头,不然别人会生气的。

④ 用在动词后,表示胜过,可以加"得、不",表示可能性。*It can be used after a verb, meaning doing better than others, followed by "得" or "不" to show a possibility.*

(15) 他汉语说得很好,谁也说不过他。

(16) 你跑步能跑得过他? 我不相信。

⑤ 用在动词后,表示动作经过某处。*It can be used after a verb, meaning to cross or pass by.*

(17) 汽车开过了我家门口。

(18) 我游不过这条河。

⑥ 用在动词后,表示超过了合适的处所、地方。*It can be used after a verb, meaning missing the right place such as a bus stop.*

(19) 快下车,我们已经坐过站了。

(20) 他们光顾说话,已经走过中国银行了。

⑦ 用在动词、形容词后,表示超过。*It can be used after a verb or an adjective, meaning to outstrip or surpass.*

(21) 向日葵已经长得超过人头了。

(22) 他的电脑技术比我强过很多。

副词 *ad.*

1. 表示"过分、过于"的意思。只用于修饰单音节形容词。*Meaning "more than enough" or "more than is good for," it is used only to modify a monosyllabic adjective.*

(23) 他的胃病刚好,东西不能吃得过多。

(24) 房子够住就好,不用买得过大。

2. 表示"十分、非常"的意思。如:"过细的工作、过长的报告"。*Very; much too. For example, "过细的工作,过长的报告."*

助词 *aux.*

1. 用在动词后,表示动作已经完毕。这种"动词+过"的动补短语,比较特殊,中间不能插入"得、不",也不能有否定用法,后面可带"了",相当于表示动作完成的"了"。*It can appear after a verb, meaning the action has been finished. A phrase like "v.+过" cannot have "得" or "不" inserted in between, and there is no negative use. It means the action has been finished when followed by "了."*

(25) 你吃过了饭再去吧。

(26) 等我问过了他,再告诉你。

2. 用在动词后,表示动作行为曾经发生过,或某一事物曾经存在过,但没有延续到现在,只是一种经历或历史。在动词前常有表示确定时间的名词、副词或其他词语。否定时,前面加"没有、未曾、不必"等。*Coming after a verb, "过" means something happened or existed before, as an experience or part of history. The verb often appears with a noun, adverb or some other word that indicates a certain time. To make it negative, one uses "没有,未曾,不必" before it.*

(27) 高中时,我看过这本书。

(28) 我们走过不少地方,但未曾去过桂林。

3. 表示某种性质或状态曾经存在过,但没有延续到现在。句中一般需要说明是过去的某个时间,有同现在相比的意思。前面加"没、没有"表示否定。*To indicate that something happened in the past but did not last to the*

present. To make that explicit, a past time is mentioned to present a contrast with the present. It forms a negative when it takes "没,没有" before it.

(29) 他小时候胖过。

(30) 这孩子从来没这么安静过。

名词 n.

错误,过失。如:"改过自新、记过一次、过错"等。Mistake or blunder, as in "改过自新,记过一次,过错."

说明 Notes:

1. "过"作动词用时,后面可加"着、了"。When "过" serves as a verb in a sentence, it can go with "着,了."

2. "过"不能用在动作性不强的动词后面作趋向补语。如:"知道、以为、认为、觉得、免得、属于、使得、可以、必须、能、肯、敢、在"等动词不能带"过"。"过" cannot serve as a directional complement following a verb without an obvious directional meaning. Because of this, verbs such as "知道,以为,认为,觉得,免得,属于,使得,可以,必须,能,肯,敢,在" should not be followed by "过."

3. 动作行为不能重复的动词如"牺牲、死"等不能带"过"。When verbs denote actions that cannot be repeated, they should not appear with "过," such as "牺牲,死."

4. "过"做助词时,一般读轻声。If "过" serves as an auxiliary word, people usually pronounce it in a light tone.

5. "过"作助词时,在动词、形容词后面表示的动作、行为、状态、变化等可以是预计、推断、假设发生过的,也可以是不肯定的。If "过" serves as an auxiliary word, the action, behavior, state or change that follows a verb or an adjective may be certain (as predicted, deduced or supposed) or uncertain.

(31) 如果提前预习过,听课就容易多了。

(32) 看起来,他已经来过了。

(33) 到底是什么味道,你等一下自己尝过就知道了。

guòdù 过度

用法 Usage:

形容词 a.

超过适当的限度。多修饰表示心理或情感的双音节形容词。Excessive; beyond the proper limit. Very often it modifies disyllabic adjectives about sentiments or emotions.

(1) 喝酒不能过度。

(2) 我喝了三杯咖啡,过度兴奋了,一个晚上没睡好觉。

(3) 因为过度伤心,她病倒了。

说明 Notes:

"过度"可以用在形容词前面作状语,也可以用在形容词后面作补语。"过度" can serve as an adverb or complement in a sentence to modify an adjective.

guòdù 过渡

用法 Usage:

动词 v.

1. 乘船过河。To cross a river in a boat.

(1) 河上没桥,只好借船过渡了。

2. 事物由一个阶段或一种状态逐渐发展变化而转入另一个阶段或另一种状态。To transit gradually from one phase or one stage to another.

(2) 工业生产正在向现代化过渡,不学电子技术是不行的。

(3) 大家先在旧房子过渡一下,两个月后就让大家住新房子。

guòmǐn 过敏

用法 Usage:

动词 v.

机体对某些药物或外界刺激的感受性不正常地增高的现象。To be allergic, sensitive or irritable to a certain medicine or abnormal external stimulus.

（1）他对酒精过敏，所以不能喝酒。
（2）春天很多人会花粉过敏。

形容词 a.

过于敏感。多指心理感受。Too sensitive; allergic. It often serves to describe physical or mental reactions.

（3）她属于过敏体质。
（4）你不要太过敏，没人议论你。

guòqù 过去 →P78"从前"

用法 Usage：

名词 n.

表示现在以前的时间（区别于"现在、将来"）。The past, indicating a time before now (different from "现在，""将来").

（1）过去的成绩是过去的，现在还是得从头开始。
（2）过去，我妈妈是个一字不识的农民。

动词 v.

1. 人或物离开或经过说话人所在位置向另一地点运动。(Of a person or thing) to move away from or past a place where the speaker is to another place.

（3）我要过去看看，你过去吗？
（4）刚刚过去一辆出租车，现在又得等了。

2. 表示经历完了一段时间。To pass, indicating the experience of passing a period of time.

（5）一年又过去了，日子过得真快！
（6）好几个月过去了，他一直没来信。

3. 表示某种情况、状态已经结束或消失。To be over, showing that a certain state or situation has disappeared or come to an end.

（7）病人的危险期已经过去了。
（8）紧张的高考总算过去了，同学们玩儿去吧！

4. 委婉语，指人死亡。(Euphemism) to pass away.

（9）邻居家的爷爷昨天晚上过去了。

5. "过去"用在动词后面作趋向动词补语。"过去" is placed after a verb to serve as a complement.

① 表示人或物随着动作向另一处所运动。To indicate a person or thing moving toward another place.

（10）他一边叫着，一边跑过去。
（11）无人机已经飞过去了。

② 表示背向说话人。To indicate turning the back (of somebody or something) to the speaker.

（12）他把头转过去不理我了。
（13）他把信纸反过去放在桌子上，不让我看。

③ 表示失去原来的、正常的状态，多用于不好的意思。常用的动词不多。To indicate the loss of the original, normal state. It is applied mostly to something undesirable. Not many verbs are used this way.

（14）爷爷气得昏过去了。
（15）他是个已经死过去一回的人了。

④ 表示事情或动作结束，多用于否定句。To indicate a thing or an action coming to an end. This use appears mostly in negative sentences.

（16）这一次，他骗我们骗不过去了。
（17）年纪大的人，有的话说过去就忘了。

⑤ 表示人和事物随动作从某处经过，处所名词要插入"过去"中间（常跟"得"或"不"连用）。To indicate that a person or thing passes a certain place. The name of the place is inserted between "过" and "去" (often used in connection with "得"或"不").

（18）这辆车开得过这座木桥去吗？
（19）我以为孩子们游不过河去，你看现在他们已经站在对岸了。

6. 用在形容词后面，表示超过（多与"得"或"不"连用）。Placed after an adjective, it means "to surpass." (Often used in connection with "得"或"不").

（20）杭州冬天再冷也冷不过哈尔滨去。

(21) 你的拳头再硬也硬不过石头去。

7. "说得/不+过去"组成习惯语"说得过去/说不过去",表示比较合理,勉强可以交代或不合情理,无法交代。常用于表示反问、揣测的句子。*"说得/不+过去" forms the idiomatic expression "说得过去/说不过去," indicating fairly reasonable or passable or not reasonable or not passable. It often appears in rhetorical questions or guesses.*

(22) 你一个人占两个座位说得过去吗?

(23) 大家都在做作业,你把音乐放得那么响,有点说不过去吧?

8. "看得/不+过去"组成习惯语"看得过去/看不过去",表示比较合意或者不能容忍、不忍心。*"看得/不+过去" forms the idiomatic expression "看得过去/看不过去," indicating something is or is not suitable or to one's liking, or even unbearable.*

(24) 这件衣服还看得过去,买一件吧。

(25) 那孩子太没礼貌了,实在看不过去,我就批评了他。

说明 Notes:

"从前"和"过去"都指现在之前的时期。*Both "从前" and "过去" refer to the period of time before now.*

它们的区别是: *Their differences are as follows:*

1. "从前"常常用于一个故事的开头。"过去"一般不这样用。*"从前" often appears at the very beginning of a story, but "过去" doesn't.*

2. "从前"可以指过去,也可以指遥远的过去。相对来说,"过去"指离说话时间不太远,不指遥远的过去。*"从前" may refer to the past, even to the remote past. In comparison, "过去" refers to a past not too far from now; it doesn't refer to the remote past.*

3. "过去"常常与"现在、将来"并提,区别不同的时段。"从前"一般不与"现在""将来"并提。*"过去" is often mentioned at the same time as "现在" and "将来," thus distinguishing different periods of time. "从前," by contrast, is usually not mentioned at the same time as "现在" or "将来."*

4. "过去"前面可以有名词性成分的修饰,如"他的过去","中国的过去"等。"从前"前面,一般不接受别的词语的修饰。*"过去" may be preceded by an element with the nature of a noun such as "他的过去" and "中国的过去." However, "从前" is usually not modified by other words.*

guòyú 过于

用法 Usage:

副词 ad.

表示程度或数量超过一定的限度。不能出现在主语前。后面应带双音节形容词或动词。*Exceeding a certain degree or limit. It cannot appear before a subject. Adjectives or verbs following "过于" should be disyllables.*

(1) 你的身体不好,不能过于劳累。

(2) 别把问题想得过于简单。

(3) 这件事不能都怪你一个人,不必过于担心。

hái 还 →P603"又"

用法 Usage:

副词 ad.

1. 表示动作、状态持续进行，或情况维持不变；仍然，仍旧。*Still, indicating that an action or a behavior goes on as before — without any change.*

(1) 他还在教室里。

(2) 雨还下着呢。

2. 表示程度的加深，更加。常用在比较句。*More, indicating a higher degree. It often appears in comparative sentences.*

(3) 他比我还高。

(4) 上海怎么比北京还冷？

3. 表示进一层的意思，而且，常跟"不但、不光、不仅"等呼应。*Also; Moreover. It often echoes with "不但，不光，不仅，" etc.*

(5) 他有哥哥，还有姐姐。

(6) 他不但去了上海，还去了北京。

4. 表示情况早已发生或存在，常跟"就"连用。*Indicating that the situation happened or existed long ago. Often it appears with "就."*

(7) 还在上小学的时候，我就学汉语了。

(8) 我还在三岁时就学游泳了。

5. 表示范围的扩大或数量的增加。*Indicating the scope has extended and the amount increased.*

(9) 我还要一杯茶。

(10) 你要带飞机票，还要带护照才能上飞机。

6. 表示情况比较让人满意，含有评价的意味。*As an evaluation, it shows that the situation is satisfying.*

(11) 你这次考试的成绩还不错。

(12) 商店就在旁边，买东西还很方便。

7. 表示应该怎样，而不怎样，名不副实，含有讽刺的语气。句子前常用"亏你"开始，句末常用"呢"。*Meaning that the actual situation does not conform to the reputation. It carries an ironical tone. The sentence often starts with "亏你" and ends with "呢."*

(13) 亏你还是医生呢，吃饭前都不洗手。

(14) 亏你还学过四年汉语呢，这个字也不认识。

8. 表示出乎意料。*Expressing the idea of being unexpected.*

(15) 你写得还真好！

(16) 她还真感冒了。

9. 表示反问的语气。*Speaking with a counter-question.*

(17) 都十二点了，你以为还早吗？

(18) 这还少吗？

10. 表示限于某种范围。*Meaning "to be limited to a certain scope."*

(19) 生那场病的时候，她还只有五岁。

(20) 大家安静一下，还有三分钟就下课了。

11. 尚且;都。用在前面句子表示陪衬,后面句子作出推论,说明情况不可能发生。*Still. It appears in the first clause as an accompanying word: the second clause makes the conclusion, showing that the situation cannot happen.*

(21) 这个地方你还不认识,我就更不认识了。

(22) 我连汉字还不会写,别说写文章了。

hái shì 还是 →P204"或者"

用法 Usage:

副词 ad.

1. 仍然,仍旧。表示行为动作、状态保持不变,或不因为上文所说而改变。*Still, indicating that a behavior or action continues as before, without any change in spite of what is said in the foregoing context.*

(1) 好久不见,你还是那么漂亮。

(2) 你的病好了一些,但药还是要吃。

2. 表示经过比较、考虑,做出选择。用"还是"引出所选择的一项。*Expressing a choice made after some consideration and comparison. "还是" is used to introduce the choice.*

(3) 想快点儿的话,还是坐地铁去吧。

(4) 还是去苏州吧,西安太远了。

3. 没想到如此,而居然如此。表示行为动作或状态有点出乎意料。*Indicating that the action, behavior or state is somewhat unexpected.*

(5) 没想到汉字还是很难写。

(6) 想不到,最后他还是没去参加比赛。

4. 用在表示时间的词语前面,强调时间早,常与"就"搭配;用在做状语的"第一次、头一回"的词语前面,强调次数少。*Placed before an expression indicating time, it emphasizes that something happened some time ago. It often echoes with "就." When it appears before an adverbial such as "第一次" or "头一回," it emphasizes the scanty times.*

(7) 还是在2008年的时候,他就来过一次北京。

(8) 我在中国住了那么长时间,还是第一次吃北京烤鸭。

连词 conj.

1. 连接可供选择的若干事项,表示在两种或两种以上的事物、情况中进行选择。可连接词、短语、分句或句子。有"……还是……、是……还是……、还是……还是……"等格式。多用于疑问句,也可用于陈述句。*Joining two or more alternatives, it serves to connect words, phrases, clauses, or sentences. It appears as "…还是…,是…还是…,还是…还是…." It appears more in questions than in statements.*

(9) 今天去还是明天去,你说吧。

(10) 去上海,还是去北京,还是去广州?你决定吧。

2. 连接无须选择的一些事项,跟"无论、不管、不论"等连用,表示不受所说的条件影响。*Joining some items that call for no choices, it goes with "无论,不管,不论," indicating that things are not to be influenced by the listed condition(s).*

(11) 无论平时还是周末,西湖边总是有很多人。

(12) 不管刮风还是下雪,他都坚持来上课。

说明 Notes:

1. 副词"还是"用在动词、形容词前面时,可以省作"还"。用在主语前,不能省略。*When "还是" appears before a verb or an adjective, it can be reduced to just one word, that is, "还." But this omitting cannot happen if it appears before the subject of the sentence.*

(13) 多年不见,她还/还是那么年轻漂亮。

(14) *星期天,还你来我家好。

(15) 星期天,还是你来我家好。

2. 连词"还是"除用在疑问句外,在其他句式中都可以换成"或者",意思不变。Except for questions, "还是" as a conjuction can be replaced by "或者" in all other types of sentences.

(16) 无论双休日还是/或者寒暑假,他都在旅游。

3. "还是"后可以带"的",说成"还是的",表示认可,常用在对话中。"还是" plus "的" forms "还是的," indicating one's consent in day-to-day conversation.

(17) A:叫你快一点,你不听,迟到了吧。
　　 B:还是的,早五分钟出发就好了。

hàipà 害怕 →P344"怕"

用法 Usage:
动词 v.

心理动词。在困难或危险面前,心里发慌,情绪不安,感到恐惧。可做谓语、定语、宾语和状语等。To fear; to be afraid. As a verb indicating one's mentality, it means being afraid in face of difficulty or danger. It serves as the predicate, attribute, object or adverbial.

(1) 她很害怕一个人在家。
(2) 他害怕地看着山脚下的那片黑森林。
(3) 深夜一个人在马路上走,我感到很害怕。

hán 含

用法 Usage:
动词 v.

1. 东西放在嘴里,不吞下,也不吐出。To keep something in one's mouth, neither swallowing it nor spitting it out.

(1) 他嘴里含着一块糖。
(2) 嘴里含了一口水。

2. 包括在内,藏在里面,容纳。To include; to hide; to contain.

(3) 他的眼里含着泪水。
(4) 报考硕士研究生的条件是学历在本科以上(含本科)。

3. (指思想感情等)怀而不露。To harbor but not disclose (ideas, feelings, etc.).

(5) 她的话中含着满满的幸福感。
(6) 这本书含有很深刻的哲学道理。

说明 Notes:

"含"常常被用在四字短语里,如"含泪不语、含苞欲放、含情脉脉"等。"含" often appears in four-character idioms, such as "含泪不语,含苞欲放,含情脉脉."

hánhu 含糊

用法 Usage:
形容词 a.

1. 模糊,不明确,不清楚。Vague; ambiguous; not clear.

(1) 他的话含糊不清,听不清楚是什么意思。
(2) 这封信写得很含糊,到底什么意思不明白。

2. 敷衍马虎,漫不经心,不认真。Careless; fooling around; not devoted to what one is doing.

(3) 这件事很重要,你一点都不能含糊。
(4) 老师对我们作业上的错误从不含糊。

3. (指态度)暧昧,不鲜明。可重叠使用。(Of an attitude) vague; ambiguous. It can appear in its reduplicated form.

(5) 你的态度那么含糊,问题怎么解决?
(6) 要做决定了,他不能再含含糊糊的。

4. "含糊"前面加上"不",组成"不含糊",表示"有能耐、真行"的意思,常用在肯定、赞扬的话中。"不" plus "含糊" forms "不含糊," meaning "truly capable" or "really wonderful." It often appears as part of a sincere praise.

(7) 他干起活来一点儿也不含糊。
(8) 她真不含糊,那么长的课文一个小时就背出来了。

hánlěng 寒冷 →P295"冷"

用法 Usage:
形容词 a.

表示温度很低,冷。Cold, indicating the temperature is very low.

(1) 这个地方一年到头都很寒冷。
(2) 我最不喜欢寒冷的冬天。
(3) 谁喜欢她脸上那种让人感到寒冷的表情?

说明 Notes:

"寒冷"能做表示心理活动动词的宾语,如例(3)。As is shown by (3),"寒冷" can serve as the object of a verb indicating mental activity.

hánxuān 寒暄

用法 Usage:
动词 v.

见面时谈天气冷暖之类的话,用于见面打招呼或应酬。To make small talk about such things as weather when meeting someone. It is commonly used in greeting or entertaining.

(1) 他们俩寒暄了几句,就开始谈论正事。
(2) 他很热情,自我介绍后,就跟我寒暄起来。

hǎn 喊 →P187"喊叫"、P231"叫"

用法 Usage:
动词 v.

1. 大声地叫。To shout.
(1) 大家一起喊"加油!加油!"
(2) 喊什么?别人都睡觉了。

2. 叫(人),打招呼。To ask somebody to do something; to greet.
(3) 见到老人要喊爷爷、奶奶。这是礼貌。
(4) 他被邻居喊去帮忙了。

hǎnjiào 喊叫 →P187"喊"

用法 Usage:
动词 v.

大声地叫。To shout.

(1) 我喊叫了大半天,没人理我。
(2) 突然隔壁传来大声喊叫:"快来人啊!"

说明 Notes:

"喊"和"喊叫"的区别是: The differences between "喊" and "喊叫" are as follows:

1. 如果宾语是表示人的名词或代词,只能用"喊",不能用"喊叫"。If the object is a noun or pronoun indicating a person, only "喊" can be used, not "喊叫."
(3) *过来,喊叫一声"奶奶!"
(4) 过来,喊一声"奶奶!"

2. "喊叫"只有"大声地喊"这一个词意,没有"喊"称呼人、招呼人的词义。"喊叫" just means "大声地喊." It does not mean greeting a person, as "喊" does.

hànyǔ 汉语 →P677"中文"

用法 Usage:
名词 n.

中国汉族的语言,中国的通用语言,是世界上使用人数最多的一种语言。普通话是现代汉语的标准语。The language of the Han nationality of China, also the lingua franca of the country. It is used by more people in the world than any other language. Mandarin is the standard language in modern Chinese.

(1) 我们正在学汉语。
(2) 汉语是一种很有意思的语言。

hǎo 好 →P40"不错"

用法 Usage:
形容词 a.

1. 优秀的,优点多的,使人满意的(与"坏"相对),可以重叠。Outstanding; excellent; satisfying (the opposite of "坏"). It can appear in its reduplicated form.

(1) 她唱得很好。
(2) 好好儿的一件衣服,为什么不要了?

2. 用在动词前,表示令人满意的性质在哪个方面(与"难"相对),只限于少数几个动词如

"吃、看、听、闻、使"等，并且结合得很紧。Appearing before a verb, it indicates where the satisfying quality lies (the opposite of "难"). This use is limited to only a few verbs like "吃，看，听，闻，使，" but they are all knit closely.

（3）昨天的音乐会很好听。
（4）中国菜太好吃了。

3. 表示容易（与"难"相对）。Meaning "easy" (the opposite of "难").

（5）这个问题很好回答。
（6）今天的作业好做。

4. 友爱,关系亲密。Friendly, kind, used to indicate a close and intimate relationship.

（7）他俩是好朋友。
（8）老师跟我很好。

5. 用在动词后做补语,表示完成。有时动词可以省略。Serving as a complement to a verb, it means that some action is already finished. The verb may be omitted sometimes.

（9）作业已经做好了。
（10）我已经（准备）好了,走吧。

6. (身体)健康,(疾病)痊愈。Healthy; fully recovered from a disease.

（11）他的病好了。
（12）他常常锻炼,身体越来越好了。

7. 表示赞许、同意或结束等语气。Spoken with a tone of consent, approval or conclusion.

（13）好,同意你明天请假。
（14）好,今天的课就上到这里。

8. 用疑问形式或感叹形式表示问候。Expressing a greeting with a question or exclamation.

（15）身体好吗？
（16）您好！

9. 用疑问形式表示征求意见,带有商量或不耐烦的语气。Using a question to ask for ideas. It shows either one's readiness for a discussion or just impatience.

（17）我们这个星期天去爬山好吗？
（18）我们去中国学生食堂吃饭,好不好啊？

10. 反语。表示不满意、蔑视、讽刺或幸灾乐祸。Irony, indicating dissatisfaction, contempt, irony or gloating over someone else's misfortune.

（19）好啊,吃不完了吧,谁叫你买那么多？
（20）好,这下你的计划全完了。

11. 合适,妥当。Being suitable or appropriate.

（21）初次见面,不知说点什么话好。
（22）今天要参加舞会,不知穿哪件衣服好。

副词 ad.

1. 用在形容词、动词前,表示程度深,多含感叹语气。Placed before an adjective or a verb, it indicates a profound degree. Often it carries the feeling of an exclamation.

（23）今天好冷啊！
（24）你让我好找啊！

2. "好"跟"不"与部分双音节形容词构成"好＋不＋形"的结构,表示肯定的意思,带有感叹语气。"好"＋"不"＋a. (usually disyllabic) — this structure is both affirmative and exclamatory.

（25）公园里好不热闹啊！
（26）她哭得好不伤心啊！

3. 用在形容词(多、久)、数量词(限一、几)或时间词前面,表示多或久。Appearing before 1) the adjective "多" or "久" or 2) the quantifier "一" or "几" or 3) a time expression, it means many/much or long.

（27）好久不见！
（28）我过了好一会儿才想起这个字怎么写。

代词 pron.

疑问代词。在方言里,用在形容词前面问数量或程度,相当于"多、多么"。An interrogative pronoun equivalent to "多,多么," it appears before an adjective in some dialects to ask about quantity or degree.

（29）杭州到上海好远？
（30）这位老大爷好大年纪？

动词 v.

1. 让（别人）有利，后面必带宾语。*To benefit (someone else). It must be followed by an object.*

（31）这样做就好了你了。

（32）只要能好了大家，我麻烦点儿没关系。

2. 助动词，表示"便于、以便"的意思。*As an auxiliary, it means "so that," indicating a purpose. Also it means "to make it easy to do something."*

（33）你把电话号码告诉我，我们好联系。

（34）带一本词典，上课好用。

3. 方言里表示"可以、应该"的意思。*It means "may" or "should" in some dialects.*

（35）我好进去吗？

（36）太晚了，你好回去了。

名词 n.

表示表扬、喝彩声，或者问好。用时常儿化。*Indicating a praise or greeting or "Hurrah!" In practical use, it often appears with "儿."*

（37）请代我向你父母问个好。

（38）观众们连声叫好儿。

说明 Notes：

1. "好"用在动词前，只限于少数几个动词，如："吃、看、听、闻、使、受、玩"等，并且结合得很紧，如："好吃、好看、好听、好闻、好使、好受、好玩"等。"好"的反义词是"难"，所以也可以组成"难吃、难看、难听、难闻、难使、难受"等词语。但是"好玩儿"的否定式是"不好玩儿"。"难玩儿"的意思是"不容易玩儿"。*"好" appears only before a limited number of verbs. These verbs include "吃,看,听,闻,使,受,玩," and they are knit together closely, as in "好吃, 好看, 好听, 好闻, 好使, 好受, 好玩." The antonym of "好" is "难" and naturally, it is okay to say "难吃, 难看, 难听, 难闻, 难使, 难受." However, the negative form of "好玩儿" is "不好玩儿." As for "难玩儿," it means "不容易玩儿."*

2. "好"用作形容词时有些义项与"不错"相同。一般在肯定某一点的陈述句中，"好"都能换成"不错"。但如果做谓语，"好"前面要加上"很"。*"好," when used as an adjective, is the same as "不错" in some uses. Generally, "好" can be replaced by "不错" in a statement affirming something. But if it serves as a predicate, "很" has to appear before "好."*

（39）这家面店的拉面不错。

（40）这家面店的拉面很好。

3. "好"与"不错"的区别是：*"好" and "不错" differ as follows:*

① 表示"优秀"意思的"好"替换成"不错"，"不错"只能用在句末，不能用在句首或句中，如例（39）。*If "好" is replaced by "不错" to mean "outstanding" or "excellent," "不错" must appear at the end of a sentence, not anywhere else, as in (39).*

② 在表示抽象意思时，"好"与"不错"可以互用，但在表示具体意思时要慎用。*"好" and "不错" are exchangeable when the meaning is abstract, but one has to be careful when the meaning is concrete.*

（41）看上去你的身体很好。

（42）看上去你的身体不错。

（43）看上去你的伤好了。

（44）＊看上去你的伤不错了。

例（43）中的"好"意思是"痊愈"，"不错"没有这个意思，不能用。*"好" means "痊愈" in (43), but "不错" does not have that meaning, therefore it is wrong to use it.*

③ "好"与"不错"互用时要注意与句子词语搭配时的语意变化。*Watch out for the difference in different meanings resulting from different collocations when using "不错" and "好."*

（45）她长得不错。

（46）她长得很好。

"不错"与"长（zhǎng）"搭配，句子内容侧重在对人外貌的肯定。用"好"时，句子的内容可以指外貌好看,也可以指孩子被抚养、成长得很好。When "不错" goes with "长(zhǎng)," it means a praise for one's appearance. When "好" is used, it may mean appearance, but it may also mean a child having been well taken care of and so growing well.

④ "不错"没有副词、动词、名词的用法。"不错" cannot be used as an adverb, a verb, or a noun.

hǎobù 好不

用法 Usage:

副词 ad.

用在少数双音节形容词前表示评价(带有感叹语气),"好不"相当于"很、多么"的意思,都可以用"好"替代,表示肯定。An equivalent to "很, 多么," "好不" appears before a few disyllabic words to serve both as an evaluation and an exclamation. They can all be replaced by "好" to show an affirmation.

(1) 考试得了第一名,他好不/好高兴啊!
(2) 新年到了,大街上好不/好热闹啊!

说明 Notes:

用在形容词"容易"前面,无论是"好不"还是"好",只表示对"容易"的否定,表示"不容易"的意思。When placed before the adjective "容易," both "好不" and "好" carry a negative meaning, not a positive one, equivalent to "不容易."

(3) 商店都关门了,我好容易/好不容易才买到几个面包。

虽然面包买到了,但是否定"容易",表示买到面包很不容易。The bread was bought, but "容易" is negated by "好不," so it simply means that it was not easy to buy the bread.

hǎobùróngyì 好不容易 →P191"好容易"

用法 Usage:

1. 副词性固定短语。一般结构分析为"好不＋容易"表示很不容易的意思。后面常用副词"才"搭配。用在动词前面做状语。有时为了强调,用在动词后面,用逗号分开。A fixed phrase serving as an adverbial, "好不容易" is generally considered to be formed by "好不＋容易," indicating "far from being easy." Often, another adverb "才" comes after it. Both appear before a verb as an adverbial. Sometimes they appear after a verb to intensify the tone, and there is a comma to separate them.

(1) 我好不容易才买到回家的火车票。
(2) 今天作业太多了,我好不容易才做完。
(3) 下周末总决赛,我买到这两张票,好不容易啊!

2. 前面用"好不容易",后面常常跟有转折内容的句子。When "好不容易" appears somewhat early, it is often followed by an abrupt turn in the event.

(4) 好不容易买到的新手机,一下子就被你摔破了。
(5) 我好不容易才擦干净,又被你弄脏了。

hǎohāor 好好儿

用法 Usage:

形容词 a.

情况正常,完好。常做句子的谓语、定语、补语。Indicating the situation is normal or perfect, "好好儿" often serves as the predicate, attribute or complement in a sentence.

(1) 那幢老房子至今还保存得好好儿的。
(2) 好好儿的一本书,就被他这么撕破了。
(3) 你刚才还好好儿的,这会儿怎么肚子疼了?

副词 ad.

尽力地、尽情地、耐心地。在动词前做状语。Meaning "doing one's best," "enjoying doing something," or "patiently," it appears before a verb as its adverbial.

(4) 这个假期,你好好儿休息休息。
(5) 这件事能成功,多亏了他,得好好儿感谢他。

说明 Notes:

1."好好儿"用作形容词时,常与"的"组成"好好儿的"。As an adjective,"好好儿" often goes with "的" to form "好好儿的."

2."好好儿"作副词时,用在动词前,中间一般不加"地",如例(4)(5)。As an adverb, "好好儿" usually appears before a verb without "地" as in (4) and (5).

hǎoróngyì 好容易 →P190"好不容易"

用法 Usage:

副词 ad.

1. 表示很不容易。用在动词前面,表示事情经过周折、困难才完成。多与"才"连用。Meaning "not easily done," it appears before a verb to signify that one went through setbacks or difficulties to get something done. Often it goes with "才."

(1) 这篇文章有很多生词,我好容易才看完。

(2) 找了半天,好容易才找到这支笔。

2. 前面用"好容易",后面常跟表示转折的内容。An early appearance of "好容易" is usually followed by an abrupt turn in the event.

(3) 好容易让他睡着了,你们又把他吵醒了。

(4) 好容易积了一点钱,却被大火烧掉了。

说明 Notes:

"好容易"是一个特殊结构的副词。它与"好不容易"的意思和用法基本相同,都表示不容易的意思。"好容易" is an adverb of a special structure. Its meaning and use are basically the same as "好不容易." Both mean "far from easy getting something done."

它们的区别是:They differ as follows:

1. 在词性上,"好容易"是副词,只能用在动词前面。"好不容易"是副词性短语,可以用在动词后面。"好容易," as an adverb, can only appear before a verb. However, "好不容易" is an adverbial phrase, and as such, it may appear after an adverb.

(5) 好容易才找到你的家!

(6) 总算找到你家了,好不容易啊。

2. "好容易"又可以是"好+容易"短语的语言形式,"好"是"很"的意思,表示很容易,常表示感叹语气。在句子中可以做谓语、补语等。"好容易" may be considered as a phrase of "好+容易." Here "好" means "很," so it serves as an exclamatory expression meaning "it is very easy to...." It serves as a predicate or complement in a sentence.

(7) 这场比赛二十分钟就结束了,我们赢得好容易啊。

(8) 这次考试的题目好容易啊!

"好不容易"不能拆分,只能作为固定的副词短语。"好不容易" is not separable and it can only serve as a fixed adverbial phrase.

hǎoxiàng 好像 →P144"仿佛"、P439"似乎"

用法 Usage:

动词 v.

如同,有些像,类似。表示比拟,必须带宾语,常与"一样、似的"搭配使用。To seem; to look like. Indicating a sort of matching, it has to take an object. Often it goes with "一样" or "似的."

(1) 他好像我哥哥一样,很照顾我。

(2) 这里的风景好像一幅画似的。

副词 ad.

1. 仿佛,似乎。表示不十分确定的推测、判断或感觉的意思。可以与"一样、似的"搭配使用。As if. It shows an estimate, a judgment, or a feeling that is not so sure or certain. It can be used together with "一样" or "似的."

(3) 我好像听说过这件事。

(4) 这件事好像就他一个人知道一样。

2. 表示某一情况或事物,表面如此或某人这样认为,但实际情况或说话人看来并不是这样。可以与"一样、似的"搭配使用。Indicating that something looks like ... or someone thinks

so, but the actual situation is not, or the speaker does not think so. Again it can be used together with "一样" or "似的."

（5）这件事看起来好像很复杂一样。

（6）这箱子好像很重似的，实际上很轻。

说明 Notes：

1. "好像"用作动词时，几乎所有的句子都可以和"一样、似的"搭配使用，句子意思不变，如例（2）。When "好像" serves as a verb, almost all sentences can go with "一样" or "似的," and the meaning of the sentence will remain the same as in (2).

"好像"用作副词时，如果后面的动词是"知道、了解、理解、懂、明白"等，是否与"一样、似的"搭配使用，句子意思有所不同。When "好像" serves as an adverb, and when the verb following it is "知道," "了解," "理解," "懂" or "明白," the meaning of the sentence may be different whether "一样" or "似的" is used.

（7）这件事好像就他一个人知道一样。（意思是：不只有他一个人知道这件事，别的人也知道这件事。It is not just he alone, but also some other people, that know this.）

（8）这件事好像就他一个人知道。（意思是：这件事只有他一个人知道，但有点不确定。He alone knows this, but I am not sure about it.）

2. "好像"与"仿佛"用作副词时，用法基本相同。When serving as an adverb, both "好像" and "仿佛" are used in the same way.

它们的区别是：They differ as follows：

① "好像"常用于书面语、口语。"仿佛"多用于书面语。"好像" appears both in written and oral language while "仿佛" is used more in written language.

② 在词语搭配上，"仿佛"多与"一般、样、似的"搭配。"好像"多与"一样、似的"搭配，很少与"一般"搭配。"仿佛" goes more with "一般，一样，似的," while "好像" usually goes

with "一样" and "似的." It seldom goes with "一般."

③ "仿佛"有"相仿佛"的动词用法。"好像"不能这样用。"仿佛" may serve as a verb, meaning "相仿佛." "好像" cannot be used this way.

hé 合

用法 Usage：

动词 v.

1. 闭上，合拢（跟"开"相对）。To close (the opposite of "开").

（1）请合上书。

（2）他笑得都合不上嘴了。

2. 结合到一起，凑到一起，共同（跟"分"相对）。To come together; to pull efforts to do something (the opposite of "分").

（3）这个学校是两个公司合起来办的。

（4）我们要同心合力完成这项工作。

3. 符合，合乎。To conform (to the rule or convention); to agree.

（5）你做的菜很合我的口味。

（6）你这么做合情合理，做得很好。

4. 投合，融洽。To be harmonious; to match.

（7）他俩情投意合，很快就结了婚。

（8）他俩一拍即合，很快就成好朋友了。

5. 配合。To cooperate.

（9）只有里应外合，军队才能进得了这座城堡。

6. 折合，等于。To be equal to.

（10）一公里合两市里。

7. 总计，全。To total; to come to the sum of.

（11）这个宾馆连吃带住，合多少钱一天？

说明 Notes：

1. "合"的第一义项使用时，一般不搭配"门、窗、灯"等有机械制作过程的器具的名词，常常搭配"书、嘴、眼"等名词。When "合" is used in its first meaning, it usually doesn't go with "门、窗、灯," all of which involve devices for

mechanical processing. But it does go with such nouns as "书,嘴,眼."

2. 在祝愿词语中,"合"用在名词前面,为形容词性使用。Expressing a wish, "合" appears as an adjective before a noun.

(12) 祝你新年快乐,合家安康!

héshì 合适 →P424"适合"

用法 Usage:

形容词 a.

符合实际情况或客观要求,适宜。Suitable; in conformity with the actual situation or objective requirements.

(1) 这件衣服我穿正合适。
(2) 你能不能给他介绍一个合适的女朋友?
(3) 这个词用在这里不合适。

hé 和 →P166"跟"、P470"同"、P608"与"

用法 Usage:

介词 prep.

"和"的介词用法与"跟"的介词用法基本相同。As a preposition, "和" is used the same way as "跟."

1. 引进另一施事者(这一施事在动作过程中不起主导作用,起主导作用的是"和"前面的主语所代表的人或事物),有时"和……"后面有"一起、一块、一道"等词语搭配,表示动作行为由双方共同发出。Introducing another doer (but this doer does not play a dominant role in the action: it is the person or thing that comes before "和" that is dominant). Other times, "和..." goes with "一起,""一块," or "一道" to signify that the action is jointly done by the two parties.

(1) 我和你一块去买菜。
(2) 他和奶奶生活在一起,对奶奶的生活习惯非常了解。

2. 引进动作行为涉及的对象,含有"对、向"的意思。Introducing the target of the action, it carries the meaning of "对" or "向."

(3) 老师和大家讲了这次考试的范围。
(4) 售货员和顾客解释了这种新产品的使用方法。

3. 引进与某一事物有关联的另一事物。有时引进的词语可以修饰、限制名词,做定语,要加"的"。Introducing something related. Sometimes, the introduced word may serve as an attribute and modify or restrict a noun. In this case, the addition of "的" is required.

(5) 风的产生和运动有关系。
(6) 每个同学都要搞好和其他同学的关系。

4. 引进比较的对象,后面常有"一样、一般、相同、相反"等词语,说明事物的异同。Introducing the target for comparison. Often, words such as "一样, 一般, 相同, 相反" will appear to show the similarities or dissimilarities between things.

(7) 动物、植物和人一样,时刻都需要呼吸。
(8) 中国的领土差不多和欧洲的面积相等。

连词 conj.

1. 连接名词、代词、动词、形容词、名词短语或形容词短语等,表示并列关系。And, used to join nouns, pronouns, verbs, adjectives, noun phrases or adjective phrases, showing they are parallel.

(9) 造纸术、印刷术、指南针和火药是中国古代的四大发明。
(10) 参加网球比赛的有你和我。
(11) 今天晚上要复习和预习,没有时间看电影。

2. 连接词或短语,表示选择关系。意思和用法相当于"还是"或"或者"。Or, used to join words or phrases to indicate a relationship of choices. Its meaning and use are similar to those of "还是" and "或者."

(12) 不管是书法和绘画,我都喜欢。
(13) 去北京和去西安,你自己决定。

说明 Notes:

一、"和"作并列连词的形式和作用。As a parallel conjunction, "和" appears in the following forms and plays the following roles.

1. "和"一般相当于顿号。连接三个以上的并列项时，"和"一般用在最后一项的前面，如例(9)。"和" is a slight-pause mark to join words together. It appears before the last item when there are three or more items as in (9).

2. 如果连接的短语较长，短语之间需要停顿，可以在"和"前面加逗号。A comma may appear before "和" if the phrases are fairly long and call for a pause.

(14) 她今天穿了一件白底蓝星点的衬衣，和一条浅蓝色的牛仔裤。

3. 有时候"和"的作用小于顿号。Sometimes, "和" plays a smaller role than a slight-pause mark in the sentence.

(15) 大和小、长和短、热和冷都是相对的反义词。

4. "和"起连接作用的同时，有时还兼起分类作用。如果"和"用的位置不恰当，句子读起来就很别扭。"和" does not just join words or phrases together, it also serves to classify. And that is why the sentence will sound awkward if "和" is placed at the wrong position.

"和"的分类情况有：Here are some cases where "和" classifies:

① 列举的各项可以分成类的话，"和"用在类与类之间。If the listed items may be classified, "和" is sandwiched between items of different classes.

(16) 他把苹果、香蕉、葡萄和鲜花、彩纸、年画放在桌子上后又跑了出去。

② 如果一类接一类(或一组接一组)地列举事物，"和"用在每类(或每组)事物的中间，表示"和"所连接的两个部分是属于同一类(或同一组)的。If several groups of items are listed, "和" is placed between every different group. That means the two parts joined by "和" belong to the same class or group.

(17) 鸡蛋和牛肉，米饭和面条，蔬菜和水果，这些都是人所必需的营养。

③ 连接的几个部分之间有轻重、主次之分时，"和"放在主要部分与次要部分之间。If the different parts joined by "和" may be divided into the primary and the secondary, "和" will be positioned between the primary and the secondary.

(18) 在老师的辅导、自己的努力和同学的帮助下，他才取得了比赛的好成绩。

二、"和"与"跟"的介词用法基本相同。用作连词时，"和"通用于口语、书面语，使用得很广泛。"跟"在北方话中，多用于口语。As a preposition, "和" and "跟" are used in the same way. When serving as a conjunction, "和" is used widely both in oral and written language, while "跟" appears more in oral language in north China.

三、使用"和"要注意以下几个方面：Notes special to the use of "和" are as follows:

1. "和"连接动词或形容词，这种并列结构一般不能单独做谓语。如果做谓语，前面必定有共同的修饰成分，或者后面有共同的宾语。When "和" joins verbs and adjectives, the resulting parallel structure usually cannot serve as the predicate by itself. If it serves as the predicate, there must be a shared modifying element before it, or a shared object after it.

(19) ＊她漂亮和聪明。
(20) 她更加漂亮和聪明了。

2. 并列结构的前后如果带补语，或者本身做补语，各并列成分之间一般不用"和"，尤其是单音节之间更不能用"和"。If a complement comes before or after the parallel structure, or if the structure serves as a complement itself, "和" cannot be inserted into the various elements, especially among monosyllabic words.

(21) ＊他的汉字写得清楚和整齐，非常好看。
(22) 他的汉字写得清楚整齐，非常好看。
(23) ＊她说得轻和快，我们听不清楚。
(24) 她说得又轻又快，我们听不清楚。

3. 如果要连接的形容词意思相近、相似，或虽相反却互为衬托补充，而且句子的意思是提出一种要求或者客观的叙述时，一般不用"和"连接，而是用"而"或"又"连接。如："少而精／＊少和精；紧张而有秩序／＊紧张和有秩序；汽车开得又快又稳／＊汽车开得快和稳"。但是当这种并列结构作为议论的话题或者比较的对象时，又可以用"和"连接。Instead of "和," we use "而" or "又" if the joined adjectives are close or similar in meaning, or if they complement each other by being opposites but serving to highlight each other, and if the meaning of the sentence requires that a request be raised or an objective statement be made, as in "少而精／＊少和精，""紧张而有秩序／＊紧张和有秩序，""汽车开得又快又稳／＊汽车开得快和稳." However, if this kind of parallel structure is presented as a topic for discussion or a target for comparison, the use of "和" for joining is legitimate.

（25）把车开得快和稳，是每个驾驶员的心愿。

4. 用"和"连接的词或短语，一般必须是相同的词类或结构。不能一个是名词，一个是动词，也不能一个是单音节词，一个是短语。Words or phrases joined by "和" usually belong to the same category or structure. They should not be a noun going with a verb, or a monosyllabic word going with a phrase.

（26）＊大家都很高兴和累。

（27）＊为了了解中国文化，我们要进行社会实践和看书。

5. 为了避免重复和混乱，一般在一个句子中不宜用两个或两个以上的"和"，介词"和"与连词"和"也不宜在一个句子中同时出现。To avoid repetition and confusion, do not use two or more than two "和" in one sentence. And do not use a preposition "和" and a conjunction "和" together in one and the same sentence.

（28）＊山上，三班的同学正穿过茶树田和松树林，争取尽早和四班同学会面。

（29）山上，三班的同学正穿过茶树田和松树林，争取尽早跟四班同学会面。

6. "和"所连接的词或短语前后颠倒后，虽然基本意思一般不变，但是如果原来的顺序是说话人按照时间的先后、空间的方位顺序、程度的深浅、主宾的地位、内容的主次轻重、内在的逻辑关系或说话的习惯等有意安排，则不能随便颠倒。Words and phrases joined by "和" may retain the same meaning when their order of appearance is inverted. But if the arrangement of word order is made by the speaker intentionally — like in the order of time, of space, of degree, of importance, of logic, of habit of speaking, etc. — then the order must not be changed at will.

（30）在现代化建设中，我们必须相信和依靠知识分子。

（31）树上的叶子从绿到黄和红，最后都飘落在地，只剩下光光的树干。

7. "和"不能连接分句和句子。"和" cannot be used to join clauses or sentences.

（32）＊他们两人结婚了和他们两人感情很好。

（33）＊他得了奖学金和大家选他做班长。

以上两句中的"和"都应该改为"而且"。"和" in the above two sentences should be changed into "而且."

héxié 和谐 →P517 "协调"

用法 Usage:
形容词 a.

1. 配合得很适当。*Coordinating properly.*

（1）这两种颜色放在一起很和谐。

（2）他俩的声音配合得很和谐。

2. 气氛良好。*Having a good atmosphere.*

（3）讨论的气氛显得很和谐。

3. 比喻感情融洽。*Showing harmonious feelings toward each other.*

（4）他们两人的关系比以前和谐多了。

说明 Notes:

"和谐"着重于事物之间的融洽,相互之间没有矛盾,可用在音调、颜色、线条、建筑、摆设的布局以及人的生活、行为举止等。常与"旋律、声音、色彩、节奏、情调、关系、气氛"等词语搭配。
"和谐" emphasizes the harmony between things with no contradiction. It may apply to tone, color, lines, architecture and layout as well as people's life, actions and behaviors. Often it goes with words such as "旋律,声音,色彩,节奏,情调,关系,气氛."

hěn 很 → P147 "非常"、P209 "极"、P467 "挺"、P646 "真"

用法 Usage:

副词 ad.

表示程度高。Very much, indicating a high degree.

有各种用法:It has various uses:

1. 用在形容词前,表示程度高。能做状语、补语。Placed before an adjective to indicate a high degree. It can serve as an adverbial or a complement.

(1) 他开车很快。
(2) 他生活得很幸福。

2. 用在表示心理、态度、理解、评价、状态并能体现程度的动词前,表示程度高。Placed before a degree-indicating verb to show one's attitude, mentality, understanding, evaluation and state, all indicating a high degree.

(3) 他奶奶很喜欢我。
(4) 中国朋友很愿意帮助我。

3. 用在助动词或动词短语前,表示程度高。Placed before an auxiliary verb or a verbal phrase, again to indicate a high degree.

(5) 多回家看看父母亲,这是很应该的。
(6) 他的双手很有劲儿。

4. 用在"得"后面做补语,表示程度高。但能用在"得很"前面的形容词不是很多。Placed after "得" as its complement, showing a high degree. But there are not many adjectives that can be placed before "得很" to indicate a degree.

(7) 春天,来杭州旅游的人多得很。
(8) 他的宿舍里每天晚上都热闹得很。

5. 用在一部分描写性的和表示态度、心理、评价的四字短语前,表示程度高。Placed before a number of four-character descriptive idioms to indicate an attitude, mentality or evaluation.

(9) 这个老师很平易近人。
(10) 手机上的游戏很引人入迷。

说明 Notes:

1. "很"修饰形容词时要注意以下五点。Watch out when using "很" to modify an adjective.

① 本身已体现出某种程度之意的形容词前面不能用"很",如"永久、真正、广大"等。"很" cannot be placed before an adjective that indicates some sort of degree itself, such as "永久,真正,广大."

② 没有程度可言的形容词前面不能用"很",如"错、温、灰"等。"很" cannot be placed before an adjective that has no degree to talk of, such as "错,温,灰."

③ 一般描述性(包括单音节形容词重叠)的形容词前面不能用"很",如"鲜红、雪白、绿油油、红红的"等。Generally descriptive adjectives (including reduplicated monosyllabic adjectives) such as "鲜红,雪白,绿油油,红红的" cannot be preceded by "很."

④ 除了"很多"可以直接修饰名词以外,"很+形"修饰名词时,一定要加"的",如"很热的水、很努力的同学、很普通的汉字、很深的感情"等。While "很多" may be used to modify a noun directly, "的" has to be added to the structure "很+a." to modify a noun, such as "很热的水 (very hot water),很努力的同学 (a very diligent student),很普通的汉字 (a very common Chinese character),很深的感情 (very deep feelings), etc."

⑤ 单音节形容词做谓语,常用在对比的句子中,通常有两个分句来完成整个句子的语气。所以,当单音节形容词在单句中做谓语时,要用"很"来完成句子的语气作用。这时,"很"完成句子的语法意义大于"很"本身表示程度的词语意义。When a monosyllabic adjective serves as the predicate of a sentence,"很" is often placed before it. This is because monosyllable adjectives serving as the predicate of a sentence often appear in a sentence with two clauses. "很" is used more for its grammatical function than for its meaning of a high degree.

(11) 这个图书馆大,那个图书馆小。

(12) 这个图书馆很大。

2. "很"修饰助动词和动词要注意以下四点。Watch out when using "很" to modify an auxiliary verb or a verb.

① 除了"应该、应当、可能"能单独受"很"的修饰外,"敢、会、能、肯、能够、可以"等助动词必须与后面的动词构成动词短语后,才能受"很"的修饰。如:"很会唱、很肯学、很能讲、很可以试试"等。助动词"得",无论是单独还是组成动词短语,都不能受"很"的修饰。While "应该,应当,可能" may be modified by "很" alone, auxiliary verbs such as "敢,会,能,肯,能够,可以" must combine with a following verb to form a verb phrase before it can be modified by "很," as in "很会唱,很肯学,很能讲,很可以试试," etc. "得," as an auxiliary verb, cannot be modified by "很" whether it is used alone or appearing in a verb phrase.

② 有些动词单独不能受"很"的修饰,但是带宾语后就可以。如:"很有礼貌、很讲道理、很占地方、很受欢迎、很使人高兴、很叫人喜欢、很说明情况、很掌握情况"等。Some verbs cannot be modified by "很" when they are used alone, but they can if they are followed by an object. Examples include "很有礼貌,很讲道理,很占地方,很受欢迎,很使人高兴,很叫人喜欢,很说明情况,很掌握情况."

③ "很"可以修饰可能补语,但是只限于少数表示态度、心理、感受、评价等能体现程度的动词词语组成的可能补语。如:"很看得起,很看不起;很靠得住,很靠不住;很过意得去,很过意不去;很合得来,很合不来;很沉得住气,很沉不住气"等。"很" may be used to modify a complement indicating a possibility, but this use is limited to a small number of verb phrases that act as a complement indicating a possibility: they show an attitude, mentality, evaluation and feeling. For example,"很看得起,很看不起;很靠得住,很沉不住;很过意得去,很过意不去;很合得来,很合不来;很沉得住气,很沉不住气."

④ "很"修饰带数量词的动词短语时,动词后面常常带"了、过",数词只限于"一、两、几"。如:"很花了一些钱、很有两下子、很认识几个人"等。When "很" modifies a verb phrase with a numeral, the verb is often followed by "了" or "过," and the numerals are confined to "一、两、几" as in "很花了一些钱,很有两下子,很认识几个人."

3. "很"与"不"的修饰关系如下:The descriptive relationship between "很" and "不" are as follows:

① 用在"不"前面,表示程度高。When placed before "不," it means a high degree.

(13) 你这样说很不好。

(14) 你的想法我很不赞成。

② 用在"不"后面,与"很不……"相比,表示程度减弱。When placed after "不," it indicates a weakened degree as compared with "很不……"

(15) 你这样说不很好。

(16) 你的想法我不很赞成。

应该注意:首先,"很不"后面的形容词或动词也是有所选择的。除了个别的词语如"不好、不坏"以外,其他形容词或动词,能受"很不"修饰的,一般是褒义词。中性词、贬义词一般不能受"很不"的修饰。如:"很不简单(*很不复杂)、很不仔细(*很不粗心)、很不认真(*很不马虎)、很不赞成(*很不反对)、很不大方(*很不小气)"等。Be careful: Firstly, adjectives and verbs following "很不" have to be carefully chosen. Except for "不好, 不坏," adjectives and verbs that can be modified by "很不" are usually commendatory terms. Terms that are neutral or derogatory cannot be modified by "很不." Examples: 很不简单(*很不复杂), 很不仔细(*很不粗心), 很不认真(*很不马虎), 很不赞成(*很不反对), 很不大方(*很不小气).

(17) 他的汉字写得那么好,真是很不容易。

(18) *他的水平很高,完成这件工作是很不困难的。

其次,要注意形容词或动词受"很不"的修饰后,绝大部分是表示消极意义的。表示态度、心理、状态时,大部分是表示否定的程度,如"很不客气、很不礼貌、很不同意、很不赞成、很不喜欢、很不愿意、很不整齐、很不健康"等。表示评价时,有的是表示肯定的程度,如"很不简单、很不容易"等。Secondly, remember that the majority of adjectives and verbs modified by "很不" express something negative. When used to indicate an attitude, mentality or state, "很不" usually shows a negative degree, as in "很不客气,很不礼貌,很不同意,很不赞成,很不喜欢,很不愿意,很不整齐,很不健康." When indicating an evaluation, it may convey a positive degree, as in "很不简单,很不容易."

4. "非常"和"很"的区别是:"非常"and "很" have the following differences:

① "非常"的程度比"很"高。"非常" indicates an even higher degree than "很."

② "很"前面可以用"不"表示程度低。"非常"不能。"很" may be preceded by "不" to indicate a low degree, but "非常" cannot.

③ "很"可用在"得"后,表示程度高,如:"好得很"。"非常"不能。"很" may follow "得" to show a high degree, as in "好得很," but "非常" cannot.

④ "非常"可以和"之""地"连用,语意更突出,如:"风景非常之美""天气非常地冷"。"很"不能这样连用。"非常" may go with "之" or "地" to project the meaning, as in "风景非常之美" and "天气非常地冷," but "很" cannot be used this way.

⑤ "非常"有形容词用法。"很"没有。"非常" may be used as an adjective, but not "很."

hěnnánshuō 很难说

用法 Usage:

不容易说,不好说,表示不容易推断。Difficult to say; not easy to say. It is used to indicate the difficulty in inferring.

(1) 这件事还很难说。

(2) 雨下得这么大,很难说他会不会来。

(3) 很难说有没有危险,因为病情还不稳定。

hòuguǒ 后果 →P236 "结果"

用法 Usage:

名词 n.

最后的结果。Consequences; the final result.

(1) 吃错了药,后果很严重。

(2) 检查不仔细,会造成很坏的后果。

说明 Notes:

"后果"多用在表示坏的方面。"后果" is more often used to describe something undesirable.

hòulái 后来 →P569 "以后"

用法 Usage:

名词 n.

指某一时间之后的时间。Later on; thereafter.

(1) 他是去年毕业的,后来我就没见过他。

(2) 他们开始互相不认识,后来成了好朋友。

说明 Notes:

1."后来"不能用在表示某一时间点或某一件事情的词语后面。如：不能说"春天后来、三个星期后来、吃饭后来、见面后来、上课后来"等。"后来" cannot be used after a certain specified point of time or following a certain specified event. We cannot say, for instance, "春天后来,三个星期后来,吃饭后来,见面后来,上课后来."

2."后来"只能指过去的时间,不能指将来的时间。"后来" refers only to sometime in the past, not in the future.

(3) 这次旅游我们去南京,以后再去上海吧。

(4) *这次旅游我们去南京,后来再去上海吧。

hūlüè 忽略 →P199"忽视"

用法 Usage:

动词 v.

1. 没有注意到,疏忽。To overlook; ignore; neglect.

(1) 只要求数量,忽略了质量可不行。

(2) 你这样讲,完全忽略了别人的感受。

2. "忽略"还有"略而不计"的意思。To regard something as being unworthy of consideration.

(3) 这么少的一点钱,可以忽略掉。

hūrán 忽然 →P475"突然"

用法 Usage:

副词 ad.

突然,表示情况发生得迅速而又出乎意料。Suddenly, indicating something happened all of a sudden.

(1) 我正要去超市买东西,忽然小张推门进来了。

(2) 我忽然想起来今天的作业还没有做完。

说明 Notes:

1."忽然"只能作状语。它可以放在主语前,也可以放在主语后。"忽然" can only serve as an adverbial. It may be placed either before or after the subject of a sentence.

2."忽然"也作"忽然间""忽然之间",用法一样。"忽然" is also written as "忽然间" or "忽然之间." They are used the same way.

hūshì 忽视 →P199"忽略"

用法 Usage:

动词 v.

不注意,不重视。To ignore; not to value something or pay attention to it.

(1) 他只知道学习,忽视了身体健康。

(2) 不要忽视普通老百姓的生活困难。

说明 Notes:

"忽略"多用于无意地疏忽。"忽视"多用于有意地漠视。"忽略" means to neglect while "忽视" means to ignore.

hútòngr 胡同儿

用法 Usage:

名词 n.

巷,小街道。Lane; side street.

(1) 北京的胡同儿吸引着各方游客。

(2) 那家饭店在一条胡同里。

说明 Notes:

"胡同儿"多用于北方区域,"巷""小巷"或者"弄"多用于南方区域。"胡同儿" is often used in North China, while "巷," "小巷," or "弄" is often used in South China.

hùxiāng 互相 →P510"相互"

用法 Usage:

副词 ad.

表示彼此对待的关系,你这样对待我,我也这样对待你。Mutually. It suggests a relationship between people.

(1) 我们刚认识,互相还不了解。

(2) 同学之间要互相帮助、互相关心。

huā 花

用法 Usage:

名词 n.

1. 可供观赏的植物。Flowers.
   (1) 你过生日,我送你一束花。
   (2) 很多老人爱种花。

2. 形状像花朵的东西。Flower-shaped objects.
   (3) 窗户上有一片片雪花。

3. 烟火的一种,在夜间燃放,能喷出许多火花,供人观赏。A kind of firework that shoots off into the evening sky, releasing sparks and attracting people.
   (4) 夜空升起了无数礼花。
   (5) 小孩子不要一个人玩烟花。

4. 花纹。Patterns.
   (6) 这被套花儿太密。
   (7) 这件衣服上的蓝白花儿真漂亮。

5. 比喻年轻漂亮的女子。Young and pretty girls — a metaphor.
   (8) 她是我们学校的校花。

6. 棉花。Cotton.
   (9) 这村里的妇女每天弹花。

7. 某些小的像花的东西。Tiny flower-shaped objects.
   (10) 汤里放点儿葱花儿。
   (11) 他的脸上还挂着泪花。

形容词 a.

1. 颜色或种类错杂的。Of mixed colors or varieties.
   (12) 这是一只花猫。
   (13) 每次看到她的花白头发,都让我心酸。

2. (眼睛)模糊。(Of eyes) blurry.
   (14) 年纪大了,眼睛花了。

3. 用来迷惑人的,不真实的或不真诚的。Unreal or insincere. It is used to confuse and impress others.
   (15) 她打的花拳很好看。
   (16) 不要被他的花言巧语骗了。

动词 v.

用,耗费。To consume; to cost.
   (17) 这个月他花了很多钱。
   (18) 这项工作太花时间了。

说明 Notes:

"花"作动词用时,常与"时间、钱、精力、力气、心思"等词搭配。When used as a verb, "花" often goes with words such as "时间,钱,精力,力气,心思."

huàjiě 化解 →P201"缓解"

用法 Usage:

动词 v.

解除,消除。To make something disappear; to resolve; to dissolve.
   (1) 我们要想办法化解他们的矛盾。
   (2) 我们要及时化解风险。

说明 Notes:

"化解"常与"矛盾、风险、恩怨"等词搭配。"化解" is often used with words such as "矛盾,风险,恩怨."

huānlè 欢乐 →P279"快乐"

用法 Usage:

形容词 a.

快乐(多指集体的)。可做状语、定语,可重叠为"欢欢乐乐"。Happy; joyous. It often refers to group activities and can serve as an adverbial or an attribute. It can be reduplicated as "欢欢乐乐."
   (1) 教室里响起了欢乐的歌声。
   (2) 春节快到了,人们都欢欢乐乐地准备着过年。

huán 还

用法 Usage:

动词 v.

1. 返回原来的地方或恢复原来的状态。To return to the original place or to restore to the original status.

(1) 在外打工的人大都还乡过春节来了。
(2) 很多山地已经退耕还林了。

2. 归还，与"借"相对。*To return; to give back (opposite to "借").*

(3) 欠你的钱，我下个月还你。
(4) 今天我要去图书馆还书。

3. 回报别人对自己的行动。*To respond to the action of someone else.*

(5) 去市场买东西可以讨价还价。
(6) 你打吧，我不还手。

huǎnjiě 缓解 →P200"化解"

用法 Usage:

动词 *v.*

1. 剧烈、紧张的程度有所减轻，缓和。*To ease or alleviate (a tense situation).*

(1) 地铁开通以后，缓解了交通堵塞的现象。
(2) 住院一个星期后，爷爷的病情缓解了。

2. 表示目的时，前面可以有能愿动词"能、要、会"等。*Verbs such as "能，要，会" can precede it to indicate a purpose.*

(3) 今年我们的目标是要缓解交通拥堵的问题。
(4) 这种药能缓解你的头痛。

说明 Notes:

"缓解"与"化解"的区别是：*The differences between "缓解" and "化解" are as follows:*

"缓解"是使剧烈、紧张的程度有所减轻，缓和，但是并没有完全解决。多用于某种现象、状态。"化解"是使矛盾、风险、危急等彻底解除、消除。*"缓解" means to ease or alleviate a tense situation without completely solving the problem. It usually applies to a certain phenomenon or state. "化解" means to completely resolve a conflict, risk and danger. Often it is applied to a problem that exists between two parties.*

huí 回 →P177"归"

用法 Usage:

动词 *v.*

1. 从别的地方到原来的地方，还。*To come back, to return.*

(1) 我每年都要回家过年。
(2) 他准备8月回国。

2. 掉转。*To turn around.*

(3) 他回头看了看我。
(4) 他走了，突然又回过身来。

3. 答复，回应。*To reply, to answer.*

(5) 我一直等着他的回信。

4. 谢绝（邀请）、退掉（预订的酒席等）、辞去（伙计、佣工）。*To refuse (an invitation); to decline a gift; to cancel (a booked seat); to fire (a servant, an employee).*

(6) 他们的礼物不能收，我都回掉了。
(7) 这人不认真工作，老板打算回了他。

5. 趋向动词。表示人或事物随动作从别的地方到原来的地方，用在动词后面。*A directional verb that carries the meaning of somebody or something going back to the original place by taking an action. It is used after a verb.*

(8) 杂志看完后，请放回原处。
(9) 同学们已经把小王送回宿舍了。

说明 Notes:

"回"和"归"的区别是：*The differences between "回" and "归" are as follows:*

1. "回"和"归"都有动词用法，除表示从别处到原来的地方，这个意思及用法相同以外，两个词的其他动词意思及用法都不一样。*Both "回" and "归" can serve as a verb. In the meaning of "returning to the original place," the two words mean the same thing and are used in the same way. Otherwise, they mean differently and are used in different ways.*

2. "归"可以做介词用。"回"没有。*"归" can be used as a preposition, but "回" cannot.*

huídá 回答 →P79"答复"

用法 Usage:

动词 v.

对提问或要求给以必要的反应。To respond to a question or a request.

(1) 老师的许多问题我都回答不出来。
(2) 玛丽,请你回答我的问题。

名词 n.

对提问或要求所做出的反应。A response to a question or a request.

(3) 我的回答对吗?
(4) 老师很满意同学们的回答。

说明 Notes:

"回答"和"答复"都表示对问题、对要求给以回复或表示意见,都有动词、名词用法。Both "回答" and "答复" carry the meaning of responding to a question or a request, and both can serve as a verb and a noun.

它们的区别如下:Their differences are as follows:

1. "回答"的方式可以有口头、书面,也可以是某种行为动作。"答复"一般不用动作行为的方式。"回答" may take the oral form or the written form; it may be an action or a behaviour. "答复," however, usually does not take the form of an action or a behaviour.

(5) *他用实际行动答复了你的问题。
(6) 他用实际行动回答了你的问题。

2. "答复"是书面语,比较正式,多指用书面回答。"回答"书面语和口语都用,多用于口头。"答复" appears mostly in written Chinese; it is more formal. So we often have "书面答复 (a written response)." "回答" is used in both oral and written Chinese, though more in oral Chinese.

3. "回答问题"在课堂教学上是个专用术语,指考试或做练习的一种方式。"答复"没有这种固定的搭配或含义。"回答问题" is a special term in classroom teaching: it means a form of examination or exercise. "答复" can't be used in this way.

huífù 回复 →P202"回应"

用法 Usage:

动词 v.

1. 回答,答复(多指用书信)。To reply; to answer. It is often used in letter-writing.

(1) 我会很快回复你的请求。
(2) 回复邮件时要看清楚收件人地址。

2. 恢复(原状)。To be restored to (the original status).

(3) 酒醒之后,他回复了常态。

huíyìng 回应 →P202"回复"

用法 Usage:

动词 v.

回答,答应。To reply; to answer; to respond to.

(1) 经理回应了我们的建议。
(2) 敲了半天门,没有人回应。

说明 Notes:

1. 有时"回应"也有名词用法。Sometimes "回应" also serves as a noun.

(3) 你的问题,我后天给你回应。
(4) 我问过三个同学,但是一个回应都没有。

2. "回应"与"回复"都有名词用法,区别是:"回复"一般用书面的形式回答或答复别人。"回应"较多用于口头,也可以是书面形式。Both "回应" and "回复" can be used as a noun. Their difference is that "回复" often means to answer in writing while "回应" is used in both oral and written Chinese, more often in oral Chinese.

huì 会 →P335"能"

用法 Usage:

动词 v.

1. 聚合,合在一起。To gather together.

(1) 三天以后,他们要在香港会合。

(2) 昨天很多医生给妈妈会诊了。

2. 见面,会见。可重叠。To meet; to see. It can be used in reduplicated form.

(3) 我明天下午要会朋友,没有空。

(4) 小张,出来会会客人吧!

3. 理解,懂得。To understand; to comprehend.

(5) 老师一讲,我就会了。

(6) 那种感觉只可意会,不可言传。

4. 熟习,通晓。To be proficient in.

(7) 他会英语,我会法语。你会什么?

助动词 aux. v.

1. 表示懂得怎样做或有能力做(多指需要学习的事情)。用在动词前面。Indicating that one knows how to do something or has the ability to do it. Often it refers to things that require learning. It is used before a verb.

(8) 他的孩子刚会走路,还不会说话。

(9) 我会滑雪,不会滑冰。

2. 表示擅长。Indicating that one is skillful at doing something.

(10) 他是一个能说会道的人。

(11) 他会唱会弹,很有音乐才能。

3. 表示有可能实现。Suggesting a probability.

(12) 他会来的,你不要担心。

(13) 明天不会下雨。

名词 n.

1. 有一定目的的集会。A purposeful gathering.

(14) 今天下午老师要开会。

(15) 明天有一个欢迎会。

2. 某些团体、组织。A certain institution or organization.

(16) 他们是红十字会的。

(17) 这次旅游是学校工会组织的。

3. 主要的城市。如:"都会、省会"。Major cities, as in "都会" and "省会."

4. 时机,机会。Opportunity; chance.

(18) 来中国学习汉语的机会很难得。

说明 Notes:

1. "会"作助动词第一义项,可以单独回答问题,否定用"不会"。As an auxiliary in Usage 1, the single word "会" can be used to answer a question, and its negative form is "不会."

2. "会"作助动词第二义项,前面常加"很、真、最"等词,不能单独回答问题;否定用"不会"。As an auxiliary in Usage 2, "会" often follows such words as "很,真,最," but the single word cannot be used to answer a question. The negative reply is "不会."

3. "会"作助动词第三义项,一般表示将来的可能性,可以单独回答问题,"会"或者"不会",可以用"会不会"表示疑问。As an auxiliary in Usage 3, "会" suggests a future probability. Here the single word "会" can be used to answer a question and the negative form is "不会." "会不会" can be used to show doubt.

(19) 他到底会不会来?

huó 活

用法 Usage:
形容词 a.

1. 活动,灵活。Flowing; living.

(1) 西湖的水是活水。

2. 生动活泼,不死板。Vivid and lively; not rigid.

(2) 同学们脑子很活,都很聪明。

(3) 这一段文字写得很活、很形象。

动词 v.

1. 生存,有生命(跟"死"相对)。To live; to survive (opposite to "死").

(4) 活着就要学习,这就是终身学习。

(5) 鱼在水里才能活。

2. 在活的状态下。To be alive.

(6) 我们要活捉这只老虎。

3. 维持生命,救活。To sustain a life; to make a living.

(7) 别打死,让它活着。

(8) 我要努力工作，养家活口。

说明 Notes:

1. "活"作形容词的第一个义项，只修饰名词。When "活" is used as an adjective in Usage 1, it only modifies a noun.

2. "活"作动词的第一个义项，可带"了、着"。Again when "活" is used as a verb in Usage 1, it can be followed by "了" and "着."

3. 否定式一般用"没活""不是活的"。"不活了"等于"不想活了"。"没活" and "不是活的" are often used as the negative form; "不活了" means "不想活了."

huòzhě 或者 →P185"还是"

用法 Usage:

连词 conj.

连接词、短语、分句或句子构成并列结构，表示选择、并列或等同关系。It serves to connect words, phrases, clauses and parallel structures, indicating a relationship of choices, juxtaposition, or being equal to each other.

1. 表示选择关系。连接多项时，"或者"可以用在各项前面，也可以用在最后一项前面。有时连用两个或两个以上的"或者"，表示提出两种以上的可能性供选择，选择项具有周遍性，"或者"相当于"要么"。Indicating a relationship of choices. "或者" can appear before each item or just before the last item. Sometimes, two or more "或者" are used to indicate two or more choices. In that case, "或者" is equal to "要么."

(1) 我打算明天或者后天动身回国。

(2) 你买或者我买都可以。

(3) 或者去上海，或者去苏州，反正时间只有两天。

2. 表示并列关系。有时相当于"有时、有的"；有时跟"无论/不论、不管"相配合，表示并列，具有周遍性；有时跟"不是……就是……"搭配，表示列举. Indicating a parallel relationship. Sometimes it means "有时，有的." Sometimes it pairs with "无论/不论，不管" to indicate parallelness. It may also pair with "不是……就是" to list a number of items.

(4) 最近几天他或者复习数学，或者复习英语，已经不玩手机了。

(5) 每天他不是吃面包，就是吃三明治，或者吃比萨，就是不吃米饭。

3. 表示等同关系。连接的两部分意义大致相同，后一部分对前一部分有解释、说明的作用，相当于"即、就是"。"或者"的后面有时带"说"。Indicating a relationship of equality. The two parts mean more or less the same, the second one offering a further explanation or interpretation. In that case, "或者" is equal to "即，就是." "或者" is sometimes followed by "说."

(6) 现在她在学线条画，或者说是速写，别的都不画。

说明 Notes:

"还是"和"或者"都可以用来表示选择。区别是，"还是"可以用在选择疑问句。"或者"不能，只能用在陈述句中。Both "还是" and "或者" can be used in making a choice. Their difference is that "还是" can also be used in selective questions, but "或者" cannot.

(7) *今天下午的课，是一点开始或者两点？

(8) 今天下午的课，是一点开始还是两点？

huòdé 获得 →P205"获取"、P382"取得"

用法 Usage:

动词 v.

表示经过努力取得或得到的，一般得到的是好的结果或令人满意的事物。To get a result or achieve an object — often through hard work — that is often satisfactory.

(1) 他帮助老人的事情获得了学校的表扬。

(2) 经过半年的努力，他获得了奖学金。

说明 Notes:

"获得"是褒义词，得到的对象多为有积极

意义的抽象事物,如"知识、成绩、经验、表扬、奖励、荣誉、称赞、好评、独立自由、解放、新生"等。可以构成名词"获得者",多为书面语。*"获得" is a positive word, and it usually modifies positive and abstract objects such as "知识,成绩,经验,表扬,奖励,荣誉,称赞,好评,独立自由,解放,新生." Its derivative noun "获得者" is often used in written language.*

huòqǔ 获取 →P204"获得"

用法 Usage:

动词 *v.*

取得,猎取。*To acquire; to get.*

(1) 他从老师的讲话中获取了很多信息。
(2) 这本书让他获取了大量的知识。

说明 Notes:

"获取"与"获得"的区别是:*The differences between "获取" and "获得" are as follows:*

"获取"常与"信息、情报、利润、知识、教训"等名词搭配。"获得"的宾语常常表示令人满意的事物,多为抽象名词,范围比较小。*"获取" often goes with nouns such as "信息,情报,利润,知识,教训." "获得," by contrast, is often followed by things that bring satisfaction: they tend to be abstract nouns, and the range of meaning is quite limited.*

jīhū 几乎 →P60"差(一)点儿"、P222"简直"

用法 Usage：

副词 ad.

1. 表示十分接近某种程度、范围、数量或性质状态，相当于"差不多""接近于"。可以带动词、形容词（含有数量词）、名词、动词短语或者形容词短语。Being an equivalent to "差不多" and "接近于"; indicating being very close to a certain degree, extent, quantity or state. It can be used with a verb, an adjective (including a quantifier), a noun, a verb phrase, or an adjective phrase.

（1）我们分别几乎有十年了。

（2）她的眼睛几乎全瞎了。

2. 相当于"差一点""差点儿"。Nearly; almost. It is an equivalent to "差一点" and "差点儿."

① 句子所说的事情或现象是说话人不希望发生的，"几乎"后面常带肯定形式。句子的意思是好像就要发生，实际上没有发生，表示否定。一般用在意义不积极的动词前面。The result or situation in the sentence is what the speaker did not expect. "几乎" is often followed by an affirmative form. The sentence means that it looked as if something was about to happen but it did not. So this sentence carries an affirmative meaning. "几乎" is usually used before a verb which does not have a positive meaning.

（3）今天我几乎迟到。

（4）你不拉住，他几乎就摔倒了。

② 句子的意思是说话人不希望发生的事情或现象。后面接带有"没、没有"的否定形式，意思与肯定形式一样。The speaker is talking about something that he/she didn't want to see happen. "几乎" is followed by "没" or "没有", which is equivalent to an affirmative form.

（5）回家晚了，她几乎没赶上吃晚饭的时间。

（6）她走路看手机，几乎没有发现对面走过来的人。

③ 句子所说的事情或现象是说话人希望发生的，句子意思是积极的、肯定的。后面常常接带否定形式的动词短语。句子意思表示事情已经发生，并含有庆幸的意思。The speaker is talking about something that he/she would like to see happen. The sentence is affirmative and carries a positive meaning. In a sentence like this, "几乎" is often followed by the negative form of a verbal phrase, meaning that fortunately the thing the speaker would like to see happen did happen.

（7）没有你的帮助，我今天几乎回不到学校。

（8）公交车太挤了，几乎没坐上。

3. 句子有表示所接近的程度、性质、状态带有比喻、夸张或强调的色彩，意思与"简直"相同。Being an equivalent to "简直," "几乎" indicates being close to a certain degree, quality

or state. The sentence is spoken in a figurative, exaggerated or emphatic tone.

(9) 他饿得几乎连路也走不动了。

(10) 她非常生气,几乎鼻子都气歪了。

说明 Notes:

"几乎"相当于"差(一)点儿"的用法。The usage of "几乎" is similar to that of "差(一)点儿."

它们的区别是：Their difference is as follows:

"差(一)点儿"多用于口语,"几乎"多用于书面语。"差(一)点儿" is often used in spoken language, whereas "几乎" is usually used in written language.

jīzhì 机制

用法 Usage:

名词 n.

1. 机器的构造和工作原理。The construction and working principle of a machine.

(1) 首先要清楚计算机的机制,才能修好这台计算机。

(2) 作为一名资深工程师,他非常熟悉发动机的机制。

2. 指有机体的构造、功能及相互关系。An organism's mechanism, function and their relationship.

(3) 不明白人体的机制,怎么做医生？

(4) 萤火虫的光可以作为一种防御机制,让天敌昆虫大倒胃口,食欲不振。

3. 指一个工作系统的组织或部分之间相互作用的过程和方式。The process and way of interaction among parts of a system.

(5) 公司的管理机制必须科学化、现代化。

(6) 公司的经营机制一定要根据市场情况的变化而调整。

形容词 a.

用机器制造的（区别于手工制造）。Machine-made (different from hand-made).

(7) 这些是机制水饺,那些是手工水饺。

(8) 这把机制紫砂壶看似精美,却没有手工壶的质感。

jīběn 基本 →P165"根本"

用法 Usage:

名词 n.

根本。Foundation.

(1) 经济是国家发展的基本。

(2) 发音是学习语言的基本。

形容词 a.

根本的,主要的。Basic; main; fundamental.

(3) 各国语言的基本词汇都是差不多的。

(4) 衣食住行是人们最基本的生活条件。

副词 ad.

大体上。用在形容词、动词前作状语。Basically. It is used before an adjective or a verb as an adverbial.

(5) 这批商品的质量基本合格。

(6) 这篇论文基本没有问题。

说明 Notes:

"基本"和"根本"都有形容词用法,一般做定语,不做谓语。都能修饰"矛盾、问题、任务、条件、方针、原则、方法、措施、原因、利益、保证"等抽象词语,都只受程度副词"最"的修饰。Both "基本" and "根本" can be adjectives and are usually used as attributes instead of predicates. Both can modify abstract words like "矛盾,问题,任务,条件,方针,原则,方法,措施,原因,利益,保证," and both can only be modified by the degree adverb "最."

它们的区别是：Their differences are as follows:

1. "根本"着重于最重要的、关键性的、起决定作用的。"基本"着重于最基础的、重要的、起主要作用的、不可缺少的,词义比"根本"轻。"根本" emphasizes the most important and critical, which plays a decisive role, while "基本" emphasizes the most basic and important, which plays a main role and is indispensable. The meaning of "基本" is lighter than that of "根本."

2. 除了共同搭配的词语以外,"根本"还可以跟"分歧、途径、出路、变化"等抽象词语搭配。"基本"跟"对象、队伍、群众、概念、事实、建设、力量、要求、原理、内容、状况、精神、规律"等词语搭配。Besides some shared collocations, "根本" can be used with abstract words such as "分歧,途径,出路,变化," while "基本" collocates with words like "对象,队伍,群众,概念,事实,建设,力量,要求,原理,内容,状况,精神,规律."

3. "根本"做状语,一般用于否定句,可以用在前面,修饰整个句子,谓语部分常有"就"呼应。"基本"没有这样的用法。"根本," serving as an adverbial, is usually used in negative sentences and can be put at the beginning to modify the whole sentence, with no pause in between, and there is often a coordinating "就" in the predicate. "基本," however, does not have this usage.

(7) 根本我就没同意。
(8) 你的想法根本就不对。

4. "基本"做状语,表示"大体上"的意思,"根本"不能表示这个意思。"基本", serving as an adverbial, indicates "大体上 (basically)," but "根本" does not have this meaning.

(9) *你的观点,我根本同意。
(10) 你的观点,我基本同意。

5. 当修饰事物最基础的组成部分"概念、提纲、内容、事实"等词,一般用"基本"。"根本"不能替换。"基本" is usually used to modify the basic components of something, such as "概念,提纲,内容,事实." In this meaning, "根本" cannot be used to replace it.

(11) *这本书介绍了电子科学的根本概念。
(12) 这本书介绍了电子科学的基本概念。

jīdòng 激动 →P159"感动"

用法 Usage:
动词 v.

感情因受刺激而冲动。To get excited because of a particular feeling, emotion or reaction.

(1) 听了他的故事,你激动吗?
(2) 他非常激动,甚至流下了眼泪。

形容词 a.

形容情绪激扬冲动。Being excited while feeling very happy and enthusiastic; exciting.

(3) 看球赛时,他总是激动地叫着、喊着。
(4) 毕业五十年后的聚会,那个激动的场面你是想象不到的。

说明 Notes:

"感动"和"激动"都表示受外界影响而感情冲动。Both "感动" and "激动" indicate excitement because of external stimuli.

它们的区别是: They differ follows:

1. 使人"感动"的一般都是具有正面意义、积极的事物。使人"激动"的可以是正面、积极的事物,也可以是反面、消极的事物。What makes you "感动" is usually a positive thing, while what makes you "激动" can be a positive thing or a negative one.

(5) *他很感动,因为钱包掉了。
(6) 他很激动,因为钱包掉了。

2. 在词义上,"感动"着重于产生强烈的感受而动感情。施事者一般不主动施加影响,而是受事者不自觉地受了影响,引起感情上的共鸣、同情或敬佩。"激动"着重于因受刺激而感情冲动。Semantically, "感动" emphasizes becoming emotional due to a strong feeling. The doer of the action does not exert influence actively, but the object of the action is affected unconsciously, leading to an emotional resonance, sympathy or admiration. "激动," by contrast, emphasizes becoming emotional due to stimulation.

3. "激动"的主语或宾语可以是人,也可以是和人的思想感情有关的词语。"感动"的主语或宾语一般只能是人。如:"心情激动、情绪激动、激动人心"中的"激动"都不能用"感动"替代。The subject or object of "激动" can be both people and words relevant to personal

feelings, while the subject or object of "感动" can only be people. For example, "感动" cannot be used to substitute "激动" in "心情激动,情绪激动,激动人心."

4. "感动"常常做"受"的宾语。"激动"不能。"感动" instead of "激动" is often used as the object of "受."

(7) *大家听了这个孩子的故事,很受激动。

(8) 大家听了这个孩子的故事,很受感动。

5. "感动"后面可以带表示人的宾语。"激动"不能。"感动" can be followed by an object indicating people, but "激动" cannot.

(9) *他的故事深深地激动了我。

(10) 他的故事深深地感动了我。

jíshí 及时 →P687"准时"

用法 Usage:
形容词 a.

正赶上需要的时候;正合适的时候。可以做谓语、补语、定语等;受程度副词修饰,表示对动作行为的评价。*Just in time; timely. It can be used as a predicate, a complement or an attribute. It can be modified by an adverb of degree, indicating an estimate of an action.*

(1) 你来得很及时,我正要出门呢。

(2) 这真是一场及时雨,菜地正需要浇水。

副词 ad.

不拖延,马上,立刻。用在动词前面,做状语。*Without delay; immediately. It is used before a verb, serving as an adverbial.*

(3) 谢谢你把这个消息及时告诉了我。

(4) 作业要及时做、及时交给老师。

jí 极 →P196"很"、P210"极其"

用法 Usage:
名词 n.

1. 顶端,尽头。常用于"登峰造极、无所不用其极"等词语。*The utmost point; extreme. It is often used in phrases like "登峰造极,无所不用其极."*

2. 地球的南北两端或磁体、电路的正负两端。如:"南极、北极、阳极、阴极、正极、负极"等。*Pole. For example,* "南极,北极,阳极,阴极,正极,负极."

动词 v.

努力去达到最大限度。后面常带有名词或形容词,表示状态或方式方法,如:"极目远望、极乐世界、极力争取"等。*To try to reach the extreme. It is often followed by a noun or an adjective, indicating a state or method such as* "极目远望,极乐世界,极力争取."

形容词 a.

最终的,最高的。*Utmost; extreme.*

(1) 他真的是极度疲劳了,一连睡了两天才醒。

(2) 他说话太极端了。

副词 ad.

用在一些形容词(单音节较多)、动词短语前,表示达到最高程度。*Extremely, used before some adjectives (mainly monosyllabic words) and verbal phrases, indicating reaching the extreme.*

(3) 他极能吃,但不胖。

(4) 这件衣服极便宜。

说明 Notes:

1. 运用"极"要注意: *When "极" is used, pay attention to the following points:*

① "极"不能修饰状态形容词,如不能说"极亲爱、极绿绿的、极清清楚楚的"等。"极" *cannot be used to modify descriptive adjectives. For example, you cannot say* "极亲爱," "极绿绿的," *or* "极清清楚楚的."

② "极"带形容词修饰名词时,名词前面一般要加"的",如"极热的夏天、极漂亮的女孩"等。*When "极" is followed by an adjective to modify a noun, there is often a* "的" *in front of the noun, such as* "极热的夏天,极漂亮的女孩."

③ 用在可能补语前,表示程度最高,但只应用在表示态度、感觉等范围的可能补语前,如

"极靠不住、极过意不去、极不好意思"等。When used before a potential complement, "极" indicates the highest degree. But it can only be used before potential complements showing attitudes, feelings and the like, for example, "极靠不住,极过意不去,极不好意思."

④ 用在"不"前,表示最高的程度。"不"后的形容词、动词限于积极意义的双音节词语,以及"好、稳、准"等少数单音节形容词。When "极" is used before "不," it indicates the highest degree. Adjectives or verbs following "不" are limited to disyllabic words with a positive meaning and a few monosyllabic adjectives like "好,稳,准".

(5) 那个地方极不安全。
(6) 他目前的身体状况极不好。

2. "极"与"很"的用法基本相同。Basically, the usage of "极" is similar to that of "很."

它们的区别是：They differ as follows:

① "极"修饰动词的范围比"很"小。动词后面要有宾语。The scope of "极" modifying verbs is smaller than "很."

② "极"用于可能补语的范围也比"很"小。The scope of "极" used in potential complements is smaller than that of "很."

③ "很"可以用在"不"后面,表示程度稍有减弱。"极"不能用在"不"后面。"很" can be used after "不," indicating a degree has been weakened, but "极" cannot.

jíduān 极端

用法 Usage:
名词 n.
表示事物顺着某个发展方向达到的顶点。Extreme. It is used to indicate things developing to the highest or furthest point, or simply to the extreme.

(1) 他的学习成绩在我们班里是个极端。
(2) 看事情要客观、全面,不要极端。

形容词 a.
绝对的,偏激的,不受任何限制的。Extreme; excessive; without limitations.

(3) 你的观点太极端了,千万别再产生极端行为。
(4) 哪个国家都没有极端的民主自由。

副词 ad.
表示程度极深。Extremely, indicating a very great degree.

(5) 在加拿大北部,你就可以看到极端漂亮的北极光。
(6) 这个山区经济不发达,老百姓极端贫困。

说明 Notes:
"极端"搭配的词语多为双音节词语。Words that can be used with "极端" are mainly disyllabic.

……jíle …… 极了

用法 Usage:
"极"可以做补语,但前面不能用"得",后面一般带"了",表示达到最高程度。"极" can be used as a complement, and "得" cannot be used before it. There is often "了" following "极," indicating reaching the highest degree.

(1) 这里的风景美极了。
(2) 早饭没吃,我现在饿极了。

说明 Notes:
"极了"前面一般搭配形容词或部分心理动词,后面不能带宾语。Words preceding "极了" are usually adjectives or some verbs depicting personal preferences, and it cannot be followed by an object.

(3) 我对这个宾馆的服务态度满意极了。
(4) *我喜欢极了这道菜。
(5) 这道菜我喜欢极了。

jíqí 极其 →P209"极"

用法 Usage:
副词 ad.
"极其"的用法相同于"极",表示非常,语气比"极"重。The usage of "极其" is similar to that of "极." It means reaching the extreme, yet its tone is more serious than "极."

说明 Notes:

"极"与"极其"的区别如下:"极" differs from "极其" in the following points:

1. "极"可以修饰双音节词和单音节词。"极其"只能修饰多音节形容词或动词。"极" can be used to modify both disyllabic words and monosyllabic words, while "极其" can only be used to modify multisyllabic adjectives or verbs.

2. "极"可以带"了",用在动词、形容词后面做补语,表示程度极高。"极其"不能。"极" can be followed by "了" and can be used after a verb or an adjective as a complement, indicating a very high degree. "极其" does not have this usage.

(1) *他的汉语口语好极其了。

(2) 他的汉语口语好极了。

3. "极"有名词、动词、形容词用法。"极其"只有副词用法。"极" can be used as a noun, a verb or an adjective. "极其" can only be used as an adverb.

4. "极"通用于口语、书面语。"极其"多用于书面语。"极" can be used in both spoken and written language; "极其" is mainly used in written language.

jí 即 →P250"就"

用法 Usage:

动词 v.

1. 表示判断,相当于"就是、等于",常用于书面。在句子中常用在名词之间。To be. It has the same meaning as "就是" or "等于." Often it appears between two nouns in written language.

(1) 孙逸仙即孙中山。

(2) 我的家乡即苏州,是个很美丽的地方。

2. 靠近,接触。多用于书面语、四字词语,如:"不即不离、若即若离、可望而不可即"等。To approach; to be near. It often appears in written language as part of four-character idioms or phrases such as "不即不离,若即若离,可望而不可即."

3. 到,开始从事,登上。To assume; to undertake.

(3) 古代皇帝第一天坐上皇位叫即位。

连词 conj.

1. 连接同位语,后一成分解释或说明前一个成分,相当于"就是、也就是",在句子中作为插入语。It combines appositives with the latter explaining the former. An equivalent to "就是" and "也就是," it serves as a parenthesis.

(4) 改革开放那年,即1978年,我才八岁。

(5) 李老师,即口语老师,已经有两个孩子,看上去真年轻。

2. 用在让步复句的偏句中,表示让步,相当于"即使、就是",正句中常有"也"与之呼应。Used in a subordinate clause of a concessive complex sentence, it indicates concession and is equivalent to "即使" and "就是." In the main clause one will find "也."

(6) 你即去过上海,这次也仍然要去。

(7) 你们即吃了晚饭,也一定要尝尝我做的菜。

3. 与"非"组成"非……即……",常用于四字词语,相当于"不是……就是……",表示选择。It is used to form "非...即...," a four-character phrase, which means "不是...就是...," indicating two alternatives.

(8) 他从小非写即画,现在成了很有名的书画家。

(9) 现在的爸妈对孩子不像以前的父母那样非打即骂了。

副词 ad.

表示时间。Indicating time.

1. 表示动作在很短时间内或某种条件下很快发生,相当于"立即、就"。Indicating that an action will happen in a short time or under

certain circumstance, it is an equivalent to "立即," or "就."

（10）这种药吃下去半个小时即有效果。
（11）我们的房东很好,租房合同一谈即成。

2. 用在时间名词后面,表示动作行为发生得早或结束得早。相当于"就"。 Used after a temporal noun to indicate that an action happens early or ends early, it is an equivalent to "就."

（12）他早上七点即到了教室。
（13）我们去年即通过了HSK六级。

3. 表示一个动作行为紧接着另一个动作行为发生。相当于"立即、马上、就"。 Indicating that an action happens immediately after another action, "即" means "立即," "马上," or "就."

（14）别急,手机过两分钟即可使用。
（15）你打完电话即去通知大家。

说明 Notes:
组成"非……即……"短语时,其中嵌入的是单音节词或文言词。如例(8)(9),还有"非此即彼、非唱即跳"等。When "即" is used to form the "非…即…" pattern, words inserted are monosyllabic words or classical Chinese words as seen in (8) and (9), and "非此即彼," "非唱即跳," etc.

jíjiāng 即将

用法 Usage:
副词 ad.
表示要出现的事物、现象或情况在说话后不久就要发生。相当于"将要、就要、很快就要"。 It indicates that the coming things, phenomena or situations will happen soon. It is an equivalent to "将要," "就要," or "很快就要."

（1）比赛即将开始,请运动员们开始准备!
（2）这部电影即将上映,你想看吗?

说明 Notes:
1. "即将"常用于书面语,一般不修饰单音节动词。"即将" is often used in written language, and usually cannot modify monosyllabic verbs.
（3）*我们即将吃中饭,你别走了。
（4）我们马上吃中饭,你别走了。
（5）*你别说了,给妈妈的电话,我即将打。
（6）你别说了,给妈妈的电话,我马上打。

2. "即将"后面一般不带表示具体时间的名词。Generally, "即将" cannot be followed by a noun with a specific time.
（7）*秋季运动会即将于9月20日开幕。
（8）秋季运动会将于9月20日开幕。

jíshǐ 即使 → P240"尽管"、P330"哪怕"、P398"如果"

用法 Usage:
连词 conj.
表示让步关系。"即使"用于偏句的句首,表示正句的意思不因为偏句的意思而改变。相当于"就是、就算"。在正句中用"也、还(是)、仍然"等词语呼应。It indicates a concession. When "即使" appears at the beginning of a subordinate clause, the meaning of the main clause will remain the same: it will not be affected by the meaning of the subordinate clause. It is equivalent to "就是," or "就算." It collocates with words like "也," "还(是)," or "仍然" in the main clause.

1. 带有假设性的让步。"即使"后面说的是没有实现或不能实现的事实或情况。Serving as a conditional concession. What follows "即使" is a fact or situation that did not materialize or cannot be accomplished.
（1）即使你给再多的钱,她也不会卖这张画。
（2）如果不道歉,即使等到明天天亮,他也不会开门让你进去。

2. 不带有假设性的让步。"即使"后面说的是已经实现或存在的事实或情况。Serving

as a concession made without any conditions. What follows "即使" is a fact or situation that has materialized or come into existence.

(3) 她即使发烧,也去上课的。
(4) 即使全家人反对,他还是要跟她结婚。

3. "即使……也……"句子前后两部分指同一件事,后面部分表示退一步的估计。*The two parts before and after "也" in "即使…也…" refer to the same thing; the latter part indicates an estimate of a concession.*

(5) 明天即使下雨也不会很大。
(6) 即使你现在去也来不及了。

4. "即使(是)……也(都)……"表示一种极端的情况。"即使"后面常常是一种极限的状况。前一部分是名词或介词短语(介词只限于"在、跟")。*In "即使(是)…也(都)…," what follows "即使" is often an extreme situation. Only two prepositions ("在" and "跟") can be used here.*

(7) 即使在冬天,他都坚持每天在湖里游泳。
(8) 即使是只蜘蛛,他也会吓得大叫起来。
(9) 即使跟男朋友一起去,她也不愿意。

说明 Notes:
"即使"所在的分句一般用在前面,有时为了突出正句,"即使"所在的偏句也可以放到后面去。*Generally, the clause with "即使" is used at the beginning of a sentence, but sometimes it is used after the main clause to highlight it.*

(10) 读课文对提高口语水平有很大帮助,即使每天只读十分钟。

jímáng 急忙 →P300"连忙"

用法 Usage:
副词 ad.
因为着急而行动急速匆忙。可以重叠。*To act in a hurry because of anxiety. It can be repeated.*

(1) 接了医院给他的电话后,他急忙开车走了。
(2) 看到动车进站了,旅客们急急忙忙拿起行李上车。

jǐ 几 →P126"多少"

用法 Usage:
数词 num.

1. 询问数目。"几"所指的数目限于二至九,但"几"又可以用在"十、百、千、万、亿"等大数目前或后发问。*Inquiring numbers. "几" refers to numbers from 2 to 9, and it can also be used before or after large numbers like "十,百,千,万,亿."*

(1) 你孩子几岁啦?
(2) 三加三等于几?
(3) 今年我们学院有几千个留学生?
(4) 这次你吃饭花了三百几?

2. 表示不定数量,用法与上面相同,但是"几"后面要带量词。*Indicating an indefinite number, it is similar to Usage 1, but "几" is followed by a quantifier.*

① "好几、几十、几百、几千、几万……"强调数量多。*"好几,几十,几百,千,几万…" emphasize a large quantity.*

(5) 这些汉字我已经写了几十遍了,还是听写不出来。
(6) 我们好几年不见了。

② 没(有)/不+几+量,表示数量不多,"几"前面不能有别的数词。*"没(有)/不+几+quantifier" indicates the quantity is not large and no other numerals can be used before "几."*

(7) 过不了几天他就回来了。
(8) 啤酒没几个人喝,少买几瓶。

3. 在一定的语境中,"几"可以表示确定的数目。*In some contexts, "几" can indicate a definite number.*

(9) 只有阿里、玛丽、大卫,我们几个人去看京剧。
(10) 墙上写着"请勿吸烟"几个字。

说明 Notes：

1."几"和"多少"在询问数目与表示不定数目时，常常通用。When used to inquire numbers and indicate indefinite numbers, "几" and "多少" are often interchangeable.

(11) 中国人口有几/多少个亿？

(12) 她来了没几/多少天。

2."几"和"多少"的区别是：The differences between "几" and "多少" are as follows:

① "多少"可以表示较小的数目，也可以表示较大的数目，而"几"除了能用于位数"十"的前后及用于"百、千、万、亿"等位数前之外，一般用于询问十以内的数目。所以询问数目时，估计数目不大用"几"，数目大则用"多少"。"多少" can indicate both small numbers and large numbers, while "几" often indicates numbers smaller than ten except when collocated with some classifiers such as "十、百、千、万、亿." Therefore, "几" is used when the number is not large, while "多少" is used when it is large.

② "几"除了"人、岁"以外，后面一般只带量词，不直接带名词。Apart from "人、岁," "几" is usually followed by a quantifier, and it cannot be followed directly by a noun.

(13) 有几人去云南旅行？

(14) * 你有几中国朋友？

(15) 你有几个中国朋友？

③ 对序数词的提问，无论数目多大，指称的只是其中的一个对象，一般都应用"几"提问。When you inquire about an ordinal number, no matter how large it is, the referent is only one object, so "几" is often used.

(16) 这场篮球比赛，阿里得了几分？

(17) 他考了第几名？

④ 问具体的时间，一般用"几"提问。"几" is usually used to inquire about a specific time.

(18) 你的生日是几月几号？

(19) 现在几点？

⑤ 号码表示序数时，其指称对象仍然只是一个事物，因此用"几"提问。When numbers indicate an ordinal, "几" is used because its referent is still one object.

(20) 你住几号房间？

⑥ 在常用的"……号码是……?"问句中，号码不是序数排列，也没有相应的名词或量词，提问时不用"几"。In the common question "...号码是...?", the number is neither an ordinal nor a corresponding noun or quantifier, "几" cannot be used.

(21) * 你的电话号码是几？

(22) 你的电话号码是多少？

(23) 你的房间号码是多少？

jìhuà 计划 →P83"打算"

用法 Usage：

名词 n.

想法，念头，预先拟定的工作内容和行动步骤。Plan; idea; work or action that is planned in advance.

(1) 寒假计划你订好了没有？

(2) 这是本学期的教学计划，大家看看有什么意见。

动词 v.

打算，做出计划。To plan; to intend.

(3) 学院领导计划这个学期要举办一次运动会。

(4) 你计划计划这个周末怎么过。

说明 Notes：

"计划"和"打算"都指事先的考虑。Both "计划" and "打算" refer to considerations that are made before work is done and action taken.

它们的区别是：They differ as follows:

"打算"着重于设想，比较随便，大事、小事都可以用，多用于口语。"计划"着重于有所安排，语气比较郑重，讲究一定的步骤和目的，一般用于比较正经的、重要的或比较大的事情、安排或活动。多用于书面语。"打算" focuses on planning in advance; it is rather casual, applicable to both important things and trifles.

Often it appears in oral Chinese. "计划" *focuses on arrangements made in advance with specific steps and targets. It applies to formal and important things, events and people. It mostly appears in written Chinese.*

jì 记 →P215"记得"

用法 Usage:

动词 *v.*

1. 在脑子里保持着印象,不忘。*To keep in mind, not to forget.*

(1) 十八课的生词我已经记住了。
(2) 请你做的那件事你要记在心上。

2. 用笔写下来。*To write down.*

(3) 黑板上的生词你记下来了没有?
(4) 我要把你家的地址记在本子上。

jìde 记得 →P215"记"、P215"记忆"

用法 Usage:

动词 *v.*

以前进行过的、说过的事情想得起来,没有忘记。*To remember what has been done and said; not forgetting.*

(1) 她的名字我记得。
(2) 我已经不记得在哪儿见过他了。
(3) 我记得名字,不记得样子了。
(4) 我记得他,他不记得我了。

说明 Notes:

"记"的第一义项与"记得"的区别是:*The differences between the first usage of* "记" *and the structure of* "记得" *are as follows:*

1. "记"是单纯的动词,"记得"是动补结构的动词。"记" *is a pure verb while* "记得" *is a verb-complement structure.*

2. 在词义上,"记"只是表示一个动作过程。"记得"不但表示动作过程,而且还表示动作以后有积极的结果。*Semantically,* "记" *only indicates a behavioral process, while* "记得" *indicates not only a behavioral process but also the positive result of that behavior.*

3. 除了固定词组,"记"后面必定带有补语成分。"记得"可以用在句子的最后,让宾语提前。如例(1)。"记得"的宾语常常为短语或小句子,如例(2)。单个名词、代词也可以做"记得"的宾语,如例(3)(4)。*Except in set phrases,* "记" *must be followed by a complement.* "记得" *can be used at the end of a sentence, moving the object forward such as in (1). The object of* "记得" *is often a phrase or a clause such as in (2). Monosyllabic nouns or pronouns can also be used as the objects of* "记得," *such as in (3) and (4).*

jìyì 记忆 →P215"记得"

用法 Usage:

动词 *v.*

记住或想起以前的事情。一般后面需带补语。*To remember or recall what happened before. It is often followed by a complement.*

(1) 幼儿园的事情我记忆不起来了。
(2) 小学里的事情我能够记忆起来。

名词 *n.*

保持在脑子里的过去事物的印象。*Impression of something from the past.*

(3) 发高烧以后,他的记忆消失了。
(4) 这种中药能够帮助恢复记忆。

说明 Notes:

"记得"与"记忆"的区别是:"记得" *differs from* "记忆" *in the following aspects:*

1. "记得"表示记住了某件事。动词"记忆"一般用于表示能够想起某件事情,或者想不起来某件事的动作过程。"记得" *indicates that you have learned something by heart. The verbal usage of* "记忆" *usually indicates that you remember something or you fail to remember the behavioral process of something.*

(5) *那件事我记得不起来了。
(6) 那件事我记忆不起来了。
(7) *那件事我记忆。
(8) 那件事我记得。/我记得那件事。

2."记得"与动词"记忆"的否定形式不同。"记得"的否定形式是"不记得""记不得"。"记忆"的否定形式是"记忆不起来"。"记得" and "记忆," both as a verb, are different in their negative form. The negative form of "记得" is "不记得" or "记不得," while the negative form of "记忆" is "记忆不起来."

(9) *我不记忆那件事了。
(10) 我不记得那件事了。
(11) *那件事我记得不起来。
(12) 那件事我记忆不起来了。

3."记忆"后面不能带宾语。"记得"可以带宾语。如例(10)。"记忆" cannot be followed by an object, while "记得" can be followed by an object as seen in (9) and (10).

jì 既 →P216"既然"

用法 Usage:

连词 conj.

用在因果复句的偏句里,提出已经肯定的原因或理由,作为正句推论出结果或疑问的依据。相当于"既然"。正句里常常用"就、便、也、还、又、总、则、那么"等词相呼应。一般情况下,偏句在前,正句在后。但为了突出正句,也可以把正句放在前面。It is used in the subordinate clause of a cause-effect complex sentence, setting forth the reason or cause for affirmation and serving as the basis on which the effect or question is inferred. It is equivalent to "既然." In the main clause, there are words like "就、便、也、还、又、总、则、那么" echoing with it. Generally, the subordinate clause appears before the main clause. But the main clause can also be put forward for emphasis.

(1) 他既答应借给你,就一定会把词典送来。
(2) 她既来学汉语,总该来上课吧。
(3) 你既/既然希望她与你同去,为什么你不叫她呢?

副词 ad.

表示"已经"的意思,书面语,一般用于固定格式。如:"既成事实、既得利益"等。Meaning "already" in written language, it often appears in set phrases such as "既成事实,既得利益."

jìrán 既然 →P216"既"

用法 Usage:

连词 conj.

用法与"既"基本相同。用于前一分句,提出已经成为事实或已经肯定的前提,后一分句根据这一前提推出结论,常用"就、也、还、那/那么"等词相呼应,有时"那么"也可以不出现,后一分句的推断或结论用问句或反问句表示。Its usage is basically similar to that of "既." When the subordinate clause comes first, "既然" sets forth a premise which has become a fact or has been affirmed. The main clause draws a conclusion from that premise, and there are words like "就,也,还,那/那么" echoing with "既然." Sometimes, instead of using "那么," a question or a rhetorical question is used to express an inference or conclusion.

(1) 你父母既然都同意了,那你就去吧。
(2) 大家既然都希望你去,你也一起去吧。
(3) 既然你知道错了,为什么不改正呢?

说明 Notes:

1. 一般情况下,前后分句主语相同时,"既然"用在主语前面,如例(3);前后主语不同时,"既然"用于主语后面,如例(1)(2)。Generally, when the subjects of the former clause and main clause are the same, "既然" is used before the subject as in (3). When the two subjects are different, "既然" is used after the subject as in (1) and (2).

2."既"跟"既然"的区别是:"既" differs from "既然" in the following three aspects:

① "既"只能用在主语后,不能用在主语前。"既然"可以用在主语前,也可以用在主语

后。"既" can only be used after a subject while "既然" can be used either before or after a subject.

（4）＊既你要去上课，我就回去了。
（5）你既要去上课，我就回去了。
（6）你既然要去上课，我就回去了。
（7）既然你要去上课，我就回去了。

② "既"的书面色彩比"既然"重。"既然"通用于口语和书面语。While "既" is by far a more literary expression, "既然" can be used in both spoken and written language.

③ "既然"没有"既"的副词用法。"既然" does not have the adverbial usage of "既."

jìxù 继续 →P66"持续"、P301"连续"

用法 Usage:

动词 v.

指（活动）连下去，延长下去，不间断。(Of an action or activity) to go on; to endure; to extend without stop.

（1）我想回国以后继续学习汉语。
（2）大雨继续了三昼夜。
（3）大家要继续努力。

说明 Notes:

1. "继续"做动词，要求带非名词性宾语，如"继续工作、继续学习、继续进行"等等，后面常带"下去"作为补语，但也可以不带宾语，如例（3）。When "继续" serves as a verb, it requires a non-noun object, as in "继续工作，继续学习，继续进行," etc. Often "下去" follows it as a complement, but it may be followed by no object, as in (3).

2. "继续"还有名词用法，表示跟某一事有连续关系的另一事。"继续" can also serve as a noun, indicating something that is related to a certain thing.

（4）他觉得这件事是上一次好运的继续。
（5）读博士学位是我学习生活的继续。

3. "继续"跟"持续"都有表示动作行为延长下去、接连下去的语义。它们的区别是：

Both "继续" and "持续" express the semantic meaning of the extension and succession of an action. Their differences are as follows:

① "继续"侧重动作行为的不间断，即使有简短的停顿也是暂时的。"持续"侧重动作行为的持久性，一般是对行为动作所花费时间全部的判断和陈述。"继续" emphasizes that the action or behavior extends uninterruptedly or with a short pause temporally. "持续," by contrast, focuses on the continuity of an action or behavior, and it is judgmental and declarative about the time taken by the action or behavior.

（6）足球赛持续了两个半小时才结束。
（7）足球赛又继续了半个小时才结束。

例句（6）侧重陈述足球赛一共用了两个半小时。例句（7）陈述的语义是足球赛比赛了两个小时后，又加时了半个小时才结束。Example (6) emphasizes that the football match last alltogether two hours and a half. Example (7) indicates that the football match went into an extra half an hour overtime.

② "继续"可以带宾语，"持续"不能。"继续" can take an object, yet "持续" cannot.

（8）＊下面我们持续上课。
（9）下面我们继续上课。

③ "继续"有名词用法。"持续"没有。"继续" can serve as a noun, yet "持续" cannot.

jiāyǐ 加以

用法 Usage:

动词 v.

用在多音节动词前，表示如何对待和处理前面所提到的事物，即对前面的事物施加某种动作。"加以"是个形式动词，真正的动词在"加以"后面。动词的承受者常常在前面。It is often used before a multisyllabic verb or a noun which is transformed from a verb, indicating the way to deal with the thing mentioned previously, namely, exerting an action on it. "加以" is a verb only in name, and the real verb appears after "加以." The object of the real verb is often used in the front.

一般有以下几种句式：The structures are as follows:

1. 介＋名＋"加以"＋动。prep. ＋ n. ＋ "加以"＋v.

（1）对于他们吵架的情况要加以分析,才能知道谁对谁错。

（2）对同学们提出的要求,老师们要加以讨论才能决定。

2. 动＋名＋"加以"＋动。v. ＋ n. ＋"加以"＋v.

（3）写汉字,必须对汉字结构加以了解。

（4）知道别人的困难并加以帮助,这是应该的。

3. 名＋助动/副＋"加以"＋动。n. ＋ aux. v./ad. ＋"加以"＋v.

（5）你手上的伤必须加以治疗！

连词 conj.

表示进一步的原因或条件,承接前面所说的,引出另外的原因或条件,含有"加上""再加上"的意思,连接分句。It introduces a further cause or condition. It joins what has just been mentioned with the other cause or condition to be explained. It means "加上" or "再加上."

（6）她原来就喜欢吃肉,加以东坡肉那么好吃,就一连吃了三大块。

（7）他学过一年汉语,再加以妈妈是中国人,所以学得特别好。

说明 Notes:

1. "加以"一般用于书面语。用作动词时,前面的主语一般是名词或名词性短语,"加以"实际上只是个形式动词,后面还要加上动词。"加以"后面的动词一般都是抽象意义的动词,如"研究、重视、分析、改革、表扬、批评"等。"加以＋动词"后面不出现宾语。"加以" is usually used in written language. When used as a verb, the subject is often a noun or nominal phrase. In fact, "加以" is a verb in name and must be followed by another verb, usually with an abstract meaning such as "研究,重视,分析,改革,表扬,批评." "加以 ＋ v." does not take object.

（8）＊会议应加以讨论明年的工作计划。

（9）会议应对明年的工作计划加以讨论。

2. "加以"做动词的第三种用法,如果"加以"前面是副词,副词必须是双音节。单音节副词后面只能用"加"。About the third usage of "加以" as a verb, if there is an adverb before "加以," it must be disyllabic. If it is a monosyllabic adverb, "加" is used instead.

（10）＊学习那么忙,身体要多加以注意。

（11）学习那么忙,身体要多加注意。

（12）学习那么忙,身体要多多加以注意。

3. "加以"用作连词,一般有三个分句。第一个分句是原来就有的原因,第二个分句是后来加上去的原因,第三个分句是前两个原因后的结果。见例(6)(7)。When "加以" is used as a conjunction, there are usually three clauses. The first clause is the original cause, the second is the one that has been added, and the third is the effect resulting from them as in (6) and (7).

jiàgé 价格 →P218"价钱"

用法 Usage:

名词 n.

商品价值的货币表现,一般指某一具体商品所卖的钱数。Price; the value of a commodity expressed in currency. Usually it refers to the price at which a specific commodity is sold.

（1）这台电视机的价格很贵。

（2）在不同的饭店,麻辣豆腐价格不同。

jiàqián 价钱 →P218"价格"

用法 Usage:

名词 n.

1. 价格,着重指东西卖出的钱数。多用于口语。Price. Emphatically it refers to the

amount of money at which the commodity is sold. It is used mostly in oral Chinese.

（1）这件衣服的价钱太高了。
（2）很多人认为价钱越贵,质量越好。

2.指做事的报酬、条件。The reward or condition for doing something.

（3）给您办事是应该的,谈什么价钱？
（4）他做任何事情都不讲价钱。

说明 Notes:

1."价格"跟"价钱"都表示商品的钱数,用于口语时,可以互换。Both "价格" and "价钱" stand for the amount of money for a commodity. They are interchangeable in oral Chinese.

（5）这件衣服价格/价钱不贵。

2."价格"可用于口语,也可用于书面语；"价钱"主要用于口语。"价格" may be applied to both oral and written Chinese, but "价钱" is primarily applied to oral Chinese.

3.询问或商店标志货物多少钱时,多用"价格"。When customers ask about the prices of merchandises, and stores show prices, the word "价格" is usually used.

jiàzhí 价值

用法 Usage:

名词 n.

1.体现在商品里的社会必要劳动。价值量的大小决定于生产这一商品所需的社会必要劳动时间的多少。不经过人类劳动加工的东西,如空气,即使对人类有使用价值,也不具有价值。(Of a commodity) Value; the necessary social labor embodied in a commodity. The amount of the value depends on the number of hours that is required for the commodity in terms of the necessary social labor. Anything, such as air, which doesn't come into being or exist by virtue of human labor but is of great use to human beings, doesn't have the value discussed here.

（1）商品的价值是经常变动的。
（2）房地产商的竞争提高了土地的价值。

2.用途或积极作用。Use or a positive role.

（3）你的论文很有价值。
（4）这些资料很有参考价值。

jiàzi 架子

用法 Usage:

名词 n.

1.由某些材料纵横交叉构成的器具,用来放置器物,支撑物体或安装工具等。Shelf; a piece of furniture that is made by crisscrossing certain materials; it is used for keeping various appliances, supporting something heavy, or assembling tools.

（1）那个葡萄架子很漂亮。
（2）那个木头架子是爸爸的工具柜。

2.比喻事物的组织、结构。(Figuratively) the structure or/and organization of things.

（3）那座房子的架子还没搭起来呢。
（4）你写的这篇文章,架子很好。

3.比喻自高自大,不理睬人或装腔作势的样子。多用于口语。A proud and egoistic air; haughty manner. It is used to refer to a person who is inclined to brag and boast or lord it over others. It is used mostly in oral Chinese.

（5）那个老师架子很大,我叫了他三声,他都没有理我。
（6）他虽然当了官,但是没有官架子。

4.比喻做事情的样子、架势或状态。(Figuratively) the way one does things, the stance one takes towards others.

（7）你看这小孩儿写毛笔字的架子,还真像个小书法家。
（8）他那炒菜的架子,好像是个大厨师。

jiāndìng 坚定 →P220"坚决"

用法 Usage:

形容词 a.

指立场、主张、意志等不受外力影响,坚持

不变,不动摇。可做定语、状语或谓语。 Having a stand or opinion or showing a strong will on things — something no outside forces can change or influence. It is used as an attribute, adverbial or predicate.

(1) 他坚定地相信他这样做是对的。
(2) 她的态度很坚定,没有人能说服她。
(3) 他有坚定的意志,这件事一定会成功。

动词 v.

使人的信心、意志、立场坚定。用作谓语,常带宾语。 To enable a person to have a firm confidence, a strong will or stand. Usually it is used as the predicate with an object in a sentence.

(4) 你要坚定信心,我相信你一定会考上大学。
(5) 一个人坚定了自己的信念,就什么事都能成功。

说明 Notes:

1. "坚定"与"动摇"相对。做定语时,后面的名词或名词性短语前,一般都要用"的",用以区别"坚定"的动词用法。"坚定 (firm)" is just the opposite of "动摇 (shaky)." When it is used as an attribute, the noun or noun phrase following it has to go with "的," which differentiates it from "坚定" as a verb.

(6) *他以坚定信心,开始了创业。
(7) 他以坚定的信心,开始了创业。

2. "坚定"做动词时,后面常带宾语。宾语常常是"立场、信念、意志、志向、目标、决心"等抽象意义的名词。When "坚定" is used as a verb, it is often followed by an abstract noun as its object, such as "立场, 信念, 意志, 志向, 目标, 决心."

jiānjué 坚决 →P219"坚定"

用法 Usage:

形容词 a.

表示态度、主张、行动确定不移,不犹豫。词义与"犹豫"相对。多做状语,也做谓语。 Firm; having a firm attitude and opinion accompanied by resolute action. It is the opposite of "犹豫." Mostly it is used as an adverbial although it can serve as a predicate, too.

(1) 他态度很坚决。
(2) 他坚决要去国外留学。

说明 Notes:

"坚定"与"坚决"的区别如下: The differences between "坚定" and "坚决" are as follows:

1. 在词义上,"坚定"着重于坚强、稳定,不可动摇。多用于思想、立场方面,带有褒义色彩。"坚决"着重于下定决心、不可改变,多用于态度、行动方面,不带褒义色彩。 A commendatory term, "坚定" emphasizes high stability arising from a firm stand or a strong belief. By contrast, "坚决" focuses on one's unshakable determination. It doesn't carry a commendatory sense.

2. 在修饰词语上,"坚定"作形容词用时,一般修饰"立场、信念、意志、志向、目标、目光、语调、语气"等抽象名词。"坚决"比"坚定"更常做状语,并且可以直接做状语,一般修饰"支持、拥护、反对、执行、贯彻、打击、取缔、改正、服从、斗争"等动词。 As an adjective, "坚定" is often used to modify abstract nouns such as "立场, 信念, 意志, 志向, 目标, 目光, 语调, 语气." "坚决," by contrast, is more often used as an adverbial, modifying verbs such as "支持, 拥护, 反对, 执行, 贯彻, 打击, 取缔, 改正, 服从, 斗争."

3. "坚定"可做定语。"坚决"一般不做定语。 "坚定" can be used as an attribute, but "坚决" cannot.

jiānkǔ 艰苦 →P221"艰难"

用法 Usage:

形容词 a.

艰难困苦,形容条件差、困难多。多做谓

语、定语。作定语一般要带"的"。*Full of difficulty and hardship. It is often used to describe the difficult condition one finds oneself in. Mostly it serves as the predicate or attribute. As an attribute, it usually takes "的."*

（1）山区学校的条件很艰苦。

（2）他在极其艰苦的环境下生活了三年。

jiānnán 艰难 →P220"艰苦"

用法 Usage:

形容词 a.

形容困难很大，程度较深。多做谓语、定语和状语。*(Of condition) very difficult; (Of a difficulty) deep in degree. Usually, it serves as the predicate, attribute or adverbial in a sentence.*

（1）他很艰难地维持着这家公司。

（2）我爷爷那时候的生活很艰难。

（3）艰难的生活能锻炼一个人坚定的意志。

说明 Notes:

"艰苦"与"艰难"的区别如下：*The differences between "艰苦" and "艰难" are as follows:*

1. 语义侧重点不同。"艰苦"着重于外界条件困难，使人难受、痛苦。"艰难"着重于困难大，程度深，不易排除。*"艰苦" emphasizes the huge difficulty found in the outside condition: it makes one suffer. By contrast, "艰难" focuses on the difficulty being so deep in degree that it is hard to remove it.*

2. 词语搭配侧重点不同。"艰苦"常与"生活、工作、条件、岁月、斗争、作风、精神"等词语搭配。"艰难"常与"处境、生活、世事、世道、岁月、年代、步伐、道路"等词语搭配，形容行为动作的状态。*In word collocation, "艰苦" often goes with "生活,工作,条件,岁月,斗争,作风,精神." By contrast, "艰难" often goes with "处境,生活,世事,世道,岁月,年代,步伐,道路," describing the way of an action or behavior.*

搭配的词语有所相同，但用在句子中，语义侧重点是不同的。*Even if they may go with the same words, each has its own focus.*

（4）他的日子过得非常艰苦。（着重于生活很苦。*Life is difficult.*）

（5）他的日子过得非常艰难。（着重于生活难以维持。*Life can hardly go on.*）

（6）他的工作非常艰苦。（着重形容工作进行的环境、条件很艰辛。*The condition of his work is very tough.*）

（7）他的工作非常艰难。（着重形容工作本身难度很大。*His work is very difficult to do.*）

3. 用法上，"艰苦"常做谓语、定语，一般不能形容行动和具体的动作，不做状语。"艰难"可以做谓语、定语，还可以做状语，形容动作行为的状态。*"艰苦" often serves as the predicate or attribute, not as an adverbial. And usually it cannot be used to modify a behavior or a specific action. "艰难," by contrast, can serve not only as a predicate or attribute, but also as an adverbial modifying the way of a behavior.*

（8）＊她艰苦地走着。

（9）她艰难地走着。

（10）＊他的学习非常艰难。

（11）他学习得非常艰难。

（12）＊他的学习非常艰苦。

（13）他的学习条件非常艰苦。

jiǎndān 简单 →P89"单纯"

用法 Usage:

形容词 a.

1. 形容事物结构、道理单纯，头绪少，容易理解、使用或处理。*Simple; uncomplicated in structure; easy to understand, use or deal with.*

（1）这种机器结构很简单，很容易学会。

（2）那么简单的道理，你还不懂吗？

2. 草率，不认真，不仔细。*Rash; careless; not serious.*

（3）他真是个头脑简单的人。
（4）你这张画儿画得太简单了。

3.（经历、能力等）平常、平凡。多用于否定句,但句子意思表示肯定。(Of a person's experience, ability, etc.) ordinary; common. It often appears in negative sentences, but their meaning is positive.

（5）那个人骑摩托车的技术真不简单!
（6）你汉字写得这么好,真不简单!

说明 Notes:

"简单"和"单纯"都有简单不复杂的意思。Both "简单" and "单纯" carry the meaning of being uncomplicated.

它们的区别是：They differ as follows:

1."单纯"着重于"纯",无杂质,含有"纯粹、纯洁"的意思。形容人时,多含褒义。"简单"着重于"简",表示不复杂、幼稚的意思,形容人时不予肯定,甚至含有贬义。"单纯" focuses on being pure with no impurities. It carries the meaning of being pure and clean. When used to describe a person, it is a complimentary word. "简单," by contrast, emphasizes being simple. It carries the meaning of being uncomplicated and childlike. When used to describe a person, it is not positive: it may even carry a derogatory meaning.

（7）这些孩子多单纯、可爱呀!
（8）他把问题想得太简单了。

2."单纯"和"简单"除了都可形容思想(但褒贬不同)以外,形容的对象有所侧重。"单纯"多形容为人、心地、感情等。"简单"多形容结构、机械、言语和思想等。While both "简单" and "单纯" may be used to describe things related to ideology (but different in terms of compliments or criticisms), their targets are somewhat different: "单纯" is mostly used to describe a person's character or behaviour while "简单" often describe a structure, machine or words.

3."单纯"有单一、只顾的意义。"简单"没有。"单纯" may mean simply; caring only about. "简单" does not carry that meaning.

4."简单"有简易、方便、不复杂的意义。"单纯"没有。"简单" may mean simple and easy, convenient, uncomplicated, but "单纯" does not have those meanings.

jiǎnzhí 简直 →P206"几乎"

用法 Usage:
副词 ad.

强调完全如此或差不多如此,带有夸张的语气。表示事物或状态达到的程度非常高。Simply, used to emphasize a state or situation with an exaggeration: it has reached a very high degree, if not the extreme.

1."简直"后面带有比喻或比较,表示接近或达到某一程度。常与"像……一样""连……也(都)……""是"等词语配合使用。相当于"几乎"。"简直" is often followed by a metaphor or comparison, indicating the degree reached or almost reached. It goes with expressions such as "像…一样,""连…也(都)…," and "是." It is equivalent to "几乎."

（1）这个馒头简直硬得像石头一样。
（2）她高兴得简直连话也说不出来了。
（3）他简直是个孩子。

2.带有强调语气,表示程度很高,含有"实在、真是、完全"的意思。Carrying the tone of an emphasis to indicate a very high degree. It means "实在,真是,完全."

（4）这个菜简直太辣了。
（5）他简直太无理了。

3."简直"可以与"是"配合,单独使用。形式上像是话没有说完,实际上是表示一种慨叹的语气。"简直" may go with "是"; together they can stand as a sentence. It looks as if the sentence were incomplete; it just expresses a sigh.

（6）你怎么又忘了,简直是!

说明 Notes：

1. 使用"简直"时，要注意以下四点：Pay attention to the following points when using "简直"：

① "简直"与"是"搭配使用时，后面可以是动词、形容词，也可以是名词，如例(3)。When "简直" goes with "是," what follows can be a verb, an adjective or a noun as in (3).

(7) 哪儿是蓝色的？简直是黑的嘛。

② 在带"得"的补语句中，"简直"可以在"得"的前面，也可以在"得"的后面。"简直" can be placed either before or after "得" if it appears in a sentence with a complement with "得."

(8) 他简直忙得连睡觉的时间也没有。

(9) 他忙得简直连睡觉的时间也没有。

③ 带有"很、挺、非常、比较"等表示程度词语的句子，不能再用"简直"修饰，因为这些程度副词是修饰比较客观的事实，不含有夸张的语气。"简直" cannot be used if the sentence already has a degree adverb such as "很，挺，非常，" or "比较." This is because those degree adverbs are used as an objective modifier of some fact that bears no exaggeration.

(10) *火车来了，走在铁路线上的孩子简直很危险。

(11) 火车来了，走在铁路线上的孩子简直危险极了。

(12) 火车来了，走在铁路线上的孩子很/挺/非常/比较危险。

④ "简直"后面的词语，不能是单音节词或一个双音节词。一般都是多音节词语，并含有表示夸张或强调的语气。What follows "简直" should not be a monosyllabic expression or merely a disyllabic expression. Instead, it should be a multi-syllabic expression showing exaggeration or emphasis.

(13) *下课的时候，我简直饿。

(14) 下课的时候，我简直饿极了。

(15) *那个姑娘简直漂亮。

(16) 那个姑娘简直太漂亮了。

2. "简直"与"几乎"的区别是：The differences between "简直" and "几乎" are as follows:

① "简直"指完全如此，又带有夸张语气。"几乎"指接近于，重在事实描述。只有"几乎"表示接近于某种程度、性质或状态，而这种程度、性质或状态又带有比喻、夸张或强调性质时，"几乎"才与"简直"的意思相同。"简直" means "completely so" and conveys the tone of an exaggeration. "几乎" means "close to" and focuses on the description of a fact. "几乎" and "简直" share the same meaning only when "几乎" means "close to a certain degree, quality or state" and when the speaker uses a figurative, exaggerating, or emphatic tone.

(17) 这个面包不知道多长时间了，简直/几乎跟石头一样硬。

② "几乎"使用的范围大。"简直"使用的范围小。"简直"没有"几乎"的"差一点(差点儿)"的意思，也不能表示接近某种范围或数量，没有"差不多"的意思。"几乎" is applied in a wider range of situations than "简直." "简直" doesn't have the meaning of "差一点/差点儿," which "几乎" carries. "简直" cannot be used to mean "close to a certain scope or amount," nor does it mean "差不多."

(18) *她七点五十分才起床，上课简直迟到。

(19) 她七点五十分才起床，上课几乎迟到。

(20) *她看上去很老，简直有八十多岁了。

(21) 她看上去很老，几乎有八十多岁了。

jiàn 见 →P264"看"、P267"看见"

用法 Usage：

动词 v.

1. 看到，看见。一般不单独做谓语，不单独用在句末。To see. Usually it does not serve as the predicate in a sentence, nor is it placed at the end of a sentence by itself.

(1) 我还没见过他。
(2) 我刚才还见了你爸爸。

2. 接触，遇到。只能带名词宾语，常常与"就"配合使用。To meet; to contact. It can take only a noun as its object, and it is often used together with "就."

(3) 这种动物怕见光。
(4) 冰淇淋见热就化。

3. 看得出，显现出。只能带名词、形容词做宾语。多用于书面语。To be apparent; to be obvious. It can only take a noun or an adjective as its object. This use is common in written Chinese.

(5) 这种药一吃就见效。
(6) 她工作以后，家里的生活水平日见提高。

4. 会见，会面。可以重叠，一般用于人。To meet, to be face-to-face with. It can be reduplicated, and its object is usually a person.

(7) 我明天去公司见他。
(8) 我的朋友想见见你。

5. 指文字、材料等出现在某处，可以参看。一定要带名词宾语。多用于书面语。(Of some written material) to appear. It has to take a noun as its object. This use is common in written Chinese.

(9) 这个词语的用法请见课本第56页。
(10) "守株待兔"的故事请见第三册第四课。

6. 做动词的结果补语，表示感觉到。多与听觉、嗅觉等感觉有关。To serve as a verb complement to indicate a result. This use is mostly related to one's sense of hearing or smelling.

(11) 我看见黑板上还有练习题。
(12) 走过食堂就闻见饭菜的香味。

jiànmiàn 见面

用法 Usage:
动词 v.

彼此对面相见。To meet face to face.

(1) 我明天要跟朋友见面。
(2) 我们明天见面，怎么样?
(3) 昨天下午我跟他见了一次面。

说明 Notes:

1. "见面"是离合动词，中间可以增加其他词语，如例(3)。"见面" is a separable verb, and so one can insert some other word in between, as in (3).

2. "见面"后面不能带宾语，"见面"的对象由"与、跟、和、同"等词引出，用在"见面"前面。"见面" cannot take an object. Its object, or target, is introduced by words such as "与、跟、和、同，" and placed before "见面."

(4) *今天下午我要见面她。
(5) 今天下午我要跟她见面。

jiànlì 建立 →P65"成立"

用法 Usage:
动词 v.

1. 表示某种组织、机构开始成立。To establish (an organization or other institution).

(1) 打工三年，他为山区的家乡建立了一所小学。
(2) 他的电子商务网建立得很早。

2. 表示事物之间某种东西、关系开始产生，开始形成。(Of a relationship or something else) to begin to take shape or to form.

(3) 中国和美国在1979年建立了正式外交关系。
(4) 我非常珍惜我们之间建立起来的友谊。

说明 Notes:

"建立"跟"成立"都有组织机构开始出现、开始工作的意思。Both "建立" and "成立" mean the establishment of an organization.

区别是：Their differences are as follows:

1. "建立"的语意重在创建和刚刚开始，重在组织机构自身的创建，含有创建过程的意思。"成立"重在一个组织机构的出现、对外公开某组织已经开始工作。"建立" emphasizes the

launching of a new organization and the process of creating something new while "成立" emphasizes the appearance of an organization and its beginning to operate.

2. 在使用范围上,"建立"的对象除了具体的组织机构以外,还可以是抽象的事物,它可以带"友谊、关系、威信、权威、感情、联系、规章制度、体系、功绩、功勋、风格、秩序"等抽象名词做宾语。但是"建立"没有"成立"的第二种义项的用法。"成立"只用于专有的组织机构的专用名词,一般不能用于抽象事物名词。In the field of application, the target of "建立" can be something abstract in addition to the specific organization that has been established. It can take abstract nouns as its object such as "友谊,关系,威信,权威,感情,联系,规章制度,体系,功绩,功勋,风格,秩序." But "建立" cannot be used in the second meaning of "成立." Moreover, "成立" may be applied only to proper nouns of specially set-up organizations, not abstract nouns.

(5) *老师跟学生成立了感情。
(6) 老师跟学生建立了感情。

3. 两个词在语意表达中,时间段长短不同。"建立"一般从准备的时间就开始,可以说"正在建立"。"成立"没有准备过程的语意,不能说"正在成立"。Now the time factor. Usually, "建立" is a process that begins when preparations get under way, and so we can say "正在建立." But we cannot say "正在成立" because "成立" doesn't include preparations.

(7) 我们的学校正在建立之中。
(8) *我们的学校正在成立之中。

jiànshè 建设 →P225"建造"、P226"建筑"、P526"修建"

用法 Usage:

动词 v.

表示创立新事业,增加新设备的意思。"建设"后面做宾语的名词可以分为两大类:一类是比较具体的房屋、道路、桥梁、厂房、水电站等名词。另一类是词义比较抽象的国家、社会、家乡、农村、基地、军队、精神文明、物质文明等名词。To launch a new undertaking including increasing new equipment. Nouns following "建设" as its object fall into two categories. One is concrete nouns such as houses, roads, bridges, buildings, and hydraulic stations. The other is fairly abstract nouns such as the country, society, hometown, village, base, army, spiritual civilization and material civilization.

(1) 杭州要建设成一个花园城市。
(2) 今年我们山区要建设一条高速公路。
(3) 为了建设现代化新农村,去年我回到了家乡。

名词 n.

表示新创立的事业,新增加的设备。A newly launched undertaking along with newly added equipment.

(4) 改革开放以后,城市建设的效果非常明显。
(5) 最近几年国家很重视贫困地区的基本建设。

jiànzào 建造 →P225"建设"、P226"建筑"、P526"修建"

用法 Usage:

动词 v.

建筑,修建的意思。宾语多为具体可见、可触摸的物体名词,如房子、道路、桥梁、机器、船舶、防护林、绿化带等。句子中常做谓语、定语。To build; to construct. Nouns that "建造" takes are tangible: one can see them with one's eyes and touch them with one's hands, such as houses, roads, bridges, machines, ships, protective forests, or a green-belt. It often serves as the predicate or attribute in a sentence.

(1) 明年将在这个城市建造一个国际机场。

（2）他出外打工五年，自己家的房子就建造起来了。

说明 Notes：

1. "建设"和"建造"都有修建的意思。但是修建的对象有所不同。"建设"的对象范围最广。词义比较抽象的国家、社会、家乡、农村、基地、军队、精神文明、物质文明等一类名词，不能作"建造"的宾语。"建造"的对象除了土木建筑物以外，还可以是机器、船舶、飞机等。Both "建设" and "建造" carry the meaning of building, but their targets are different. "建设" covers a very wide range of objects. Included are fairly abstract nouns such as country, society, hometown, village, base, army, spiritual civilization and material civilization, none of which can serve as the object of "建造." As for the object of "建造," they range from civil constructions to machines, ships, airplanes.

2. "建设"可以构成名词"建设性"，"建造"一般不能构成名词。"建设" can combine with "性" to make a noun "建设性," but "建造" cannot.

jiànzhù 建筑 →P225"建设"、P225"建造"、P526"修建"

用法 Usage：

动词 v.

1. 表示修建（房屋、道路、桥梁）等。宾语一般限于土木工程类的建筑物名词。在句子中多做谓语、定语。To build (houses, roads, bridges, etc.). Its objects are limited to the buildings in civil engineering. And it usually serves as the predicate or attribute of a sentence.

（1）这里要建筑一座大型游乐园。

（2）我们在海面上已经建筑了两座大桥。

2. 比喻用法，表示建立的意思。(Figurative use) to build.

（3）不要把自己的幸福建筑在别人的痛苦上。

（4）朋友应该建筑在互相信任、互相帮助的基础上。

3. 可以构成"建筑家、建筑学、建筑物"等名词。It can be used to form nouns such as "建筑家,""建筑学," and "建筑物."

名词 n.

表示建筑物的意思。Building(s).

（5）这个城市保留的古老建筑不多了。

（6）那座建筑是全市最高的。

说明 Notes：

1. "建设""建造""建筑"都有修建的意思，但是修建的对象有所不同。"建筑"的对象一般只指土木工程的建筑物，不能说"建筑机器、建筑船舶"。"建设，""建造" and "建筑" all carry the meaning of building something, but their targets are different. The object of "建筑" is restricted to buildings in civil engineering. One cannot say "建筑机器" or "建筑船舶."

2. "建筑"有比喻用法，"建设"和"建造"不能这样用。"建筑" can be used figuratively, but "建设" and "建造" cannot.

3. "建筑"可以构成"建筑家、建筑学、建筑物"等名词。"建筑" may be used to make nouns such as "建筑家,建筑学,建筑物."

jiànjiàn 渐渐 →P313"慢慢"

用法 Usage：

副词 ad.

表示程度或数量逐步增加或减少。多做句子的状语。Gradually, often indicating a degree or amount increasing or decreasing slowly but steadily.

（1）天气渐渐地冷了。

（2）学汉语的外国人渐渐地多起来了。

说明 Notes：

"渐渐"可以单用为"渐"，都是副词，修饰动词，表示变化的缓慢，都用于书面语。"渐渐" and the single "渐" are both adverbs modifying a verb, indicating a slow but steady change. Both are used in written Chinese.

它们的区别是：*They differ as follows:*

1. "渐"后面带的一般是单音节动词、形容词，可以带补语，也可以不带补语。"渐" *is usually followed by a monosyllabic verb or attribute; it can be followed further by a complement. Or no complement.*

（3）天色渐变，可能要下雨，你快回家吧！

（4）路上行人渐少，时候不早了。

"渐渐"修饰动词、形容词时，后面带的动词、形容词可以是多音节的，也可以是单音节的，但若是单音节的，一定要带补语。*When "渐渐" modifies a verb or an adjective, they may be multi-syllabic or monosyllabic words. But if it is a monosyllabic word, it has to be followed by a complement.*

（5）我渐渐地认识和结交了很多中国朋友。

（6）*天气渐渐冷。

（7）天气渐渐冷了。

2. "渐渐"带结构助词"地"，有停顿，可以用在句首。"渐"后面不能带结构助词"地"，"渐"不能用在句首。*"渐渐" with a structural auxiliary "地" may be placed at the beginning of a sentence with a pause. But "渐" cannot be used in this way.*

（8）渐渐地，我们就不来往了。

（9）*渐地，我就喜欢上汉语了。

（10）渐渐地，我就喜欢上汉语了。

jiāng 将 →P228 "将要"

用法 Usage:

介词 *prep.*

1. 引进动作、行为所处置的对象，相当于"把"。多用于书面语。*Like "把," it is used to introduce the target of an action or behavior. This appears mostly in written Chinese.*

（1）他将这件事告诉了老师。

（2）谁将这本书放在我的床上了？

2. 引进动作行为所凭借的工具或事物，相当于"拿""用"。多用于成语或方言，如："将心比心、将功补过"等。*Like "拿" or "用," it introduces the tool or some other thing with which the action or behavior is done. It appears mostly in dialects or idioms such as "将心比心,将功补过."*

（3）大家将酒杯在桌子上敲了几下，就算是碰杯了。

3. 引进动作、行为赖以产生的条件或凭借，有"顺（着）、就（着）、接（着）"的意思。多用于成语，如："将错就错、将计就计"等。*Carrying the meaning of "顺（着）,就（着）,接（着）," it introduces the condition under which an action or behavior emerges or becomes possible. Again, it appears often in idioms such as "将错就错,将计就计."*

副词 *ad.*

1. 表示接近某一个时间。*Indicating closeness to a time.*

（4）从毕业到现在将有十年了。

（5）将开车的前五分钟，他才赶到了火车站。

2. 表示动作、行为不久就要发生或某种情况、事物不久就要出现。相当于"将要、快要、就要"。句末一定有"了"与"将"配合使用，表示情况就要变化。*Indicating that an action or behavior is going to happen soon or something will happen soon. It means more or less the same as "将要,快要,就要." At the end of the sentence, "了" is used to correlate with "将" and indicate that things are going to change.*

（6）再过五分钟，飞机将起飞了。

（7）晚会将开始了。

3. 表示对未来情况的判断。意思与"会、一定"相近。*To indicate a judgment of a future situation. Its meaning is similar to that of "会" and "一定."*

（8）看样子，雨将下一个晚上。

（9）做任何事情，你花下多大努力，就将得到多大收获。

4. 表示勉强达到某个数量或某种程度，相当于"刚、刚刚"，可以重叠使用。*Like "刚,刚刚," it means barely reaching a certain amount*

or degree. It can be reduplicated for use.

（10）我们俩的工资加起来将近八千块。

（11）你这次考得不好，将将及格。

5. 表示关联，相当于"又"。*An equivalent of "又," it indicates an association of ideas.*

（12）听了他的话，我将信将疑。

动词 *v.*

1. 下象棋时表示攻击对方的"将"或"帅"，也比喻出难题为难别人。*To checkmate in playing chess; (figuratively) to put a difficult and embarrassing question to someone.*

（13）我将你的"帅"了。

（14）他昨天提的问题将了老师一军。

2. 表示用言语刺激，相当于"激将"。*To stimulate with strong words, being equivalent to "激将."*

（15）你不要拿那种话来将我。

jiāngyào 将要 →P227"将"

用法 Usage:

副词 *ad.*

表示动作或情况不久就会发生，相当于副词"将"的第二个义项。*Similar to "将" in its second usage as an adverb, it means that an action or situation will happen soon.*

（1）他将要出国留学了。

（2）今天晚上在大剧场将要举办我的演唱会。

说明 Notes:

"将要"跟"将"的区别如下：*The differences between "将要" and "将" are as follows:*

1. "将"常修饰单音节动词。"将要"多修饰双音节动词。*"将" often modifies a monosyllabic verb while "将要" usually modifies a multi-syllabic verb.*

2. "将"跟"将要"都是书面语，但是"将"的书面色彩更浓。*Both "将" and "将要" are used in written Chinese, but "将" is even more so.*

3. "将要"着重于事情很快就会发生，时间上比"将"紧迫。"将要"没有"将"的其他用法。*"将要" means that something is going to happen very soon; it carries a higher urgency than "将." And it doesn't have the other uses of "将."*

jiānglái 将来 →P490"未来"

用法 Usage:

名词 *n.*

指今后的时间，一般指距离现在比较远的时间，区别"过去、现在"。*Future. Usually it refers to a future time pretty far from now. It is different from both "过去" and "现在," the three terms forming a continuance of time.*

（1）将来的世界是你们年轻人的。

（2）不远的将来，这里就是一片树林。

（3）将来再说这件事吧！

jiǎnghuà 讲话 →P436"说话"、P455"谈话"

用法 Usage:

动词 *v.*

1. 用语言表达意见，发言。*To speak; to use words to express oneself; to make a speech.*

（1）今天的会，每个人都要讲话。

（2）经理正在讲话，你先等一下儿。

2. 表示说好话，说情的意思。*To speak something nice for someone; to speak on one's behalf.*

（3）这是他的错，你不用替他讲话。

（4）你能不能为我在领导面前讲几句话？

3. 表示指责、非议的意思。*To scold, or to disparage someone for doing something wrong.*

（5）你不等红灯过马路，会有人讲话的。

（6）你放的音乐这么吵，邻居会讲话的。

名词 *n.*

1. 表示讲演的话。*Speech.*

（7）今天领导发表了重要的讲话。

（8）他的讲话，我觉得很有意思。

2. 表示一种普及性的著作体裁，常用于书名。*A genre of writing for popularizing some special knowledge, often seen in the title of a book.*

(9) 我买了一本《现代汉语语法讲话》。

说明 Notes:

1. "讲话"作为动词用时,是离合动词,中间可以插入其他词,如例(4)。"讲话" is a separable verb, and one can insert some other word(s) into it, as in (4).

(10) 他激动得讲不出话来。

2. "讲话"可以是说话单方的行为,也可以是说话双方的行为。"讲话" can be the behavior of just one person or that of two people.

(11) 上课的时候,他们俩常常讲话。

jiǎngjiu 讲究

用法 Usage:

动词 v.

表示讲求、重视的意思。着重要求达到完美、高水平的境界。多做谓语,一般要带宾语。To pay attention to; to set store by. It seeks to reach perfection, a high degree of achievement. Mostly it serves as the predicate, and generally it requires an object.

(1) 中国菜讲究色香味俱全。

(2) 她吃饭很讲究环境。

形容词 a.

表示精美、漂亮,精致美观的意思。多做谓语、补语。做谓语时,一般不带宾语。Perfect; beautiful; truly attractive. It usually serves as the predicate or complement in a sentence. When serving as a predicate, it doesn't take an object.

(3) 她做菜很讲究。

(4) 他买的衣服颜色都很讲究。

说明 Notes:

1. "讲究"还有名词的用法,表示一定的方法或道理。"讲究" can also be used as a noun, meaning certain method(s) or reason(s).

(5) 做这道菜有很多讲究。

2. "讲究"用作动词时,除了表示"重视"的意思以外,还有一层在主观上对某一方面追求完美、高水平,自己对自己提出高要求的意思。

不能与"重视"替换使用。When used as a verb, "讲究" not only means paying attention to something, but also indicates that the person sets high demand on himself and seeks perfection in doing things. So it cannot be replaced by "重视."

(6) *老师很讲究我们作业上的错误。

(7) 老师很重视我们作业上的错误。

(8) 她很讲究自己的衣着,懂得穿衣打扮。

jiāo 交

用法 Usage:

动词 v.

1. 把事物转移给有关方面,付给。可带名词宾语、双宾语。To pass something onto someone else or a certain department; to give. It can take a noun as its object or a double object.

(1) 这件事交给我做吧。

(2) 你去办公室交学费了没有?

2. 连接,交叉。后面常跟"于"一起用,前面有时加"相"。(Of two routes) meet; to cross. It is often followed by "于" and sometimes preceded by "相."

(3) 两条路相交于浙江大学门口。

(4) 这条路跟那条路不相交。

3. 结交,交往。"交"后面可以带趋向补语,再带宾语。To make friends (with) "交" may be followed by a complement showing inclination plus an object.

(5) 听说他最近交了一个女朋友。

(6) 这次他交上了好几个中国朋友。

4. 到(某一时辰或季节)。(Of a certain time or season) to arrive.

(7) 气候已交立春,春天来啦!

(8) 时间已交子时,过年啦,吃饺子吧!

名词 n.

1. 相连接的时间或地方。The time or place for a meeting or connection.

(9) 现在正是春夏之交。

(10) 这座山位于两省之交。

2. 友谊、交情,关系。*Friendship; relationship.*

(11) 我跟他只有一面之交。

(12) 早在新中国成立时,两国就建交了。

说明 Notes:

1. "交"后面加"给"时,常带双宾语。可以只带指人宾语,不能只带指物宾语。"交" plus "给" is often followed by two objects. If it is followed by one object, it must be the indirect object, but not the direct object.

(13) 昨天他交给我一份文件。

(14) 那份文件我交给他了。

(15) *我交给一份文件。

2. "交"还有副词用法。多用于四言词组。如:"百感交集、贫病交迫、内外交困、心力交瘁"等。"交" may be used as an adverb, mostly seen in four-character idioms such as "百感交集,贫病交迫,内外交困,心力交瘁."

jiāohuàn 交换 →P230"交流"

用法 Usage:

动词 *v.*

1. 双方各自拿出自己的给对方。*To exchange. It means that each side gives something of its own to the other.*

(1) 圣诞节我们互相交换了礼物。

(2) 毕业的时候,同学们互相交换照片作留念。

2. 互相调换。*To exchange.*

(3) 双方交换了场地,继续比赛。

(4) 我跟他交换了一下座位。

3. 以物易物,买卖商品。*To trade goods, which is a way of selling and buying commodities.*

(5) 孩子用巧克力交换了同学的玩具。

(6) 以前可以用动物的皮毛交换大米。

jiāoliú 交流 →P230"交换"

用法 Usage:

动词 *v.*

1. 彼此把自己所有的提供给对方,互相沟通。*To communicate: each side offers what it has to the other side.*

(1) 我跟他交流了意见,觉得还是按照老办法做比较好。

(2) 两所大学的老师互相交流了各自的教学经验。

2. 同时流出,表示交错流淌的意思。*To converge; to flow simultaneously from the same place or source, showing prosperity or mixed feelings.*

(3) 这里是三江交流的交通中心,所以经济很发达。

(4) 他哭得涕泪交流。

名词 *n.*

指交流本身的过程。*The process of exchange itself.*

(5) 两国之间应该增加文化交流。

(6) 高校与高校之间应该多作学术交流。

说明 Notes:

"交流"跟"交换"的区别是:*The differences between "交流" and "交换" are as follows:*

1. "交换"和"交流"的动词用法表示彼此把自己有的给对方。但是"交换"侧重于互换,"交流"侧重于互相沟通。*When used as a verb, both "交换" and "交流" carry the meaning of giving the other side what one has. But "交换" focuses on the mutual exchange while "交流" emphasizes communication.*

2. "交换"和"交流"搭配的词语有所不同。"交换"搭配的词语多为"礼品、纪念物、资料"等具体的事物,此外还有"眼色、眼光",或"意见、印象、情况"等抽象事物。"交流"搭配的词语多为"经验、知识、思想、感情、信息、心得、经济、文化、人才、学术观点"等抽象事物。此外有时也可以与"物资、产品"等词搭配。*"交换" and "交流" have different collocations. "交换" usually goes with concrete things such as "礼品,纪念物,资料," and abstract things such as "眼色、眼光," or "意见,印象,情况." By contrast, "交流" mostly goes with abstract

things such as "经验,知识,思想,感情,信息,心得,经济,文化,人才,学术观点." In addition, it can go with "物资,产品" and other such words.

jiāowǎng 交往

用法 Usage:

动词 v.

(人们)互相来往。(Of people) to make contact; to connect.

(1) 我跟她没有交往。

(2) 他不大习惯和别人交往。

说明 Notes:

"交往"后面不能带宾语。"交往" cannot take an object.

(3) *我交往过他。

(4) 我跟他交往过。

jiào 叫 →P18"被"、P187"喊"

用法 Usage:

动词 v.

1. 人、动物或物体发出较大的声音,表示某种情绪、感觉、欲望和信息,喊叫,吼叫,鸣叫。可带"了、着、过"。To shout; people, animals or things give out a loud voice or sound to express a certain sentiment, feeling, desire or message; to roar, to howl, to hoot, etc. They can be followed by "了,着,过."

(1) 他大声地叫了起来。

(2) 上船的汽笛已经叫过两遍了。

(3) 有一只猫在叫。

2. 呼唤,召唤,招呼。可带"了、着、过",可重叠。可带名词宾语。宾语可以是所叫的人,也可以是要求提供的事物。To call; to call on; greet. Again, they can be followed by "了,着,过," and reduplicated. They can also take a noun as their object: the object may be the person who is called or something that he is called to provide.

(4) 我叫你好几遍了,你怎么都没听见?

(5) 请你帮我叫叫出租车。

3. 致使,使,命令。一定带兼语,组成兼语短语。To ask or request or order (someone to do something). It is always followed by a complex object to form a complex phrase.

(6) 老师叫你去他办公室。

(7) 他叫我星期天去他家吃饭。

4. 称呼,称为,名字是。一定带名词宾语。To be called; to be named, meaning "one's name is..." It has to be followed by a noun as its object.

(8) 他叫王小明。

5. 称呼。带双宾语。To call; to address. It is followed by a double object.

(9) 你叫他叔叔。

(10) 大家都叫她李大姐。

介词 prep.

相当于"被"的介词用法。一般用于口语。It is used in the same way as "被." It appears mostly in oral Chinese.

(11) 手机叫弟弟拿走了。

(12) 花瓶叫小明打破了。

说明 Notes:

1. 动词"叫、喊、嗥、吼、嘶、鸣、吠"等都指人或动物发出声音,但"叫"的概括性最高,泛指一切动物(包括人)发出声音。Verbs like "叫,喊,嗥,吼,嘶,鸣,吠" all refer to people or animals making sounds. Of all these verbs, "叫" is the most representative: it refers to all creatures (including humans) making sounds.

2. "叫"与"喊"的区别是：The differences between "叫" and "喊" are as follows:

① "喊"只用于人。"叫"还可以用于动物的鸣叫、吼叫。"喊" is applied only to humans. "叫" can also be applied to animals making sounds, like "tweet (鸣叫)" or "roar (吼叫)."

② "喊"只作动词用,"叫"除了动词以外,还可以做介词。"喊" can serve only as a verb, but "叫" can also be used as a preposition.

3. "叫"与"被"的区别是：The differences

between "叫" and "被" are as follows:

① 语体色彩不同。"被"用于比较正式场合,书面语。"叫"用于口语。用"叫"的被动句,其动词的特性、所带宾语的要求等语用条件基本与带"被"的被动句一样,不再重复。"被" is used in written Chinese for fairly formal occasions while "叫" is used in oral Chinese. When "叫" appears in a sentence in the passive voice, it is treated the same as "被" in terms of the characteristics of a verb and the requirements for its object, something discussed earlier and not to be repeated here.

② 用"被"的被动句,有时"被"可以不带施事者。用"叫"的被动句,"叫"后面,一般要带表示施事者的名词。In a sentence of the passive voice, "被" may sometimes go without the person who takes the action, but if "叫" is used, the person who takes the action has to be mentioned.

(13) 他的自行车被借走了。
(14) 他的自行车叫人借走了。

4. 用"叫"的被动句还有以下两种相对固定的短语结构。When "叫" is used in a sentence in the passive voice, it appears in two fixed phrasal structures.

① "叫…＋给＋动词",有时"给"也可以不用。"叫…＋给＋v.," sometimes, "给" can be omitted.

(15) 那些旧衣服叫我给送人了。
(16) 那些旧衣服叫我送人了。

② "叫……把……＋动词""叫……把……＋给＋动词"。"叫…把…＋v." or "叫…把…＋给＋v."

(17) 照相机叫我把快门弄坏了。
(18) 照相机叫我把快门给弄坏了。

jiào 较

用法 Usage:
副词 ad.

表示具有一定程度。相当于"比较"的意思。Fairly, indicating a certain degree. It means the same as "比较."

(1) 最近的气温较低。
(2) 用较少的钱,买较多的东西。

介词 prep.

用于比较性状、程度。引出比较的对象,相当于"比",后面常常用"为"配合使用,不能用于否定式。It is used for comparison in nature, degree, amount, etc. introducing the target of comparison. It is used more or less like "比." It is often followed by "为," but it cannot be used in a negative sentence.

(3) 今年的留学生人数较去年增加了300名。
(4) 这里的风景较为漂亮。

动词 v.

表示比、相比的意思。To compare; to be compared with.

(5) 你别跟他较劲儿,他的脾气不好。
(6) 两支足球队较量了五年,实力还是不分上下。

说明 Notes:

1. "较"多修饰单音节形容词,有时修饰某些动词或动词短语。"较" is often used to modify monosyllabic adjectives. When it is used as an adverb, it can modify some verbs and verb phrases.

2. 不能用于否定式。It cannot appear in a negative form.

(7) *这种面包较不便宜。
(8) 这种面包较贵。

3. 只用于书面语。It is limited to written Chinese.

jiàoshī 教师 →P288"老师"

用法 Usage:
名词 n.

履行教育、教学职责的专业人员。Teacher; a professional whose job is to teach and educate.

(1) 这所中学的教师队伍水平很高。

(2) 教师是值得尊敬的人。

jiàoxùn 教训

用法 Usage:
动词 v.

1. 表示教育和训诫的意思。*To educate and to admonish.*

(1) 老师正在教训上课迟到的同学。
(2) 你不做作业玩手机,当心妈妈教训你。

2. 打、揍,多用于口语。*To give someone a beating, mostly in oral Chinese.*

(3) 你骂人！你再骂人我就教训你。
(4) 你还玩游戏,还要爸爸教训你一顿吗?

名词 n.

从错误和失败中取得的经验。*Experience acquired from mistakes and failures.*

(5) 只要我们吸取教训,继续努力,一定会成功。
(6) 这是一个沉痛的教训。

jiē 接

用法 Usage:
动词 v.

1. 迎接。可重叠。*To meet. It can be reduplicated.*

(1) 你帮我去车站接接朋友,好吗?
(2) 老师每天都要去幼儿园接女儿回家。

2. 收取,接受。*To receive; to accept.*

(3) 请等一下,我接一个电话。
(4) 他今天接到了三个快递。

3. 托住,承受。*To take; to support.*

(5) 不知道怎么回事,我今天连球也接不住。
(6) 箱子有点儿重,你要接住啊!

4. 继续。*To continue.*

(7) 你接着说。
(8) 虽然他辞职了,但是我们的工作还得接下去做。

5. 接替。*To replace.*

(9) 一个小时以后,小王来接你的班。
(10) 今天我来接小王的工作,小王生病了。

6. 连接。*To join; to connect.*

(11) 你把这两根绳子接起来。
(12) 中间需要再加一个词,这两个句子才能接起来。

7. 挨近,接触。*To get close to; to contact.*

(13) 这个人越接近越觉得他好。
(14) 我要跟经理接个头,告诉他我们的安排。

说明 Notes:

"接"和"收"都表示把递送的东西拿过来。*Both "接" and "收" mean taking something from someone else.*

它们的区别是:*Their differences are as follows:*

"接"侧重把东西从别人手里拿过来,不一定是接受,有可能要转交给别人。"收"一般表示接受了。*"接" focuses on taking something from someone else, but it doesn't necessarily mean accepting it, maybe for a transfer to someone else. "收" usually means accepting it.*

(15) 他接下了这封辞职信,打算明天交给总经理。
(16) 他收下了她送的礼物,心里很高兴。

jiēdài 接待 →P639"招待"

用法 Usage:
动词 v.

与来访人见面并办理与来访有关的事宜。*To meet a visitor and do something for which the visitor has come.*

(1) 九月一号,我们要接待新生。
(2) 宿舍服务员很耐心地接待了我们。

说明 Notes:

"接待"可以组成"接待室、接待站"等词语。*"接待" can be used to form expressions such as "接待室,接待站。"*

jiēlián 接连 →P301"连续"

用法 Usage:
副词 ad.

一次跟着一次,一个跟着一个。*Time and*

time again; one after another.

（1）最近接连下了好几天雨，衣服都晾不干。

（2）找他的电话接连不断。

说明 Notes:

"接连"表示某种情况一次一次地出现，没有强调动作不间断的意思。"接连" indicates the repeated occurrence of a certain situation; it doesn't, however, mean the action being continuous without any stops.

jiēshōu 接收 →P234"接受"

用法 Usage:

动词 v.

1. 收受（有关信息等）。To receive (information, etc.).

（1）今天我接收了几十条微信。

（2）这里是山区，接收不到网络信号。

2. 根据法令接管机构、财产、人员等。To take over an organization, property and personnel in accordance with the law or regulations.

（3）1945年8月，我们在这里接收了日军投降后的医院。

（4）慈善机构接收了志愿者募捐来的钱款。

3. 接纳（人员）。To take in (personnel); to enroll.

（5）小学今年接收了许多农民工的孩子。

（6）歌唱团九月开始接收新团员。

jiēshòu 接受 →P234"接收"

用法 Usage:

动词 v.

1. 收取（给予的东西）。To accept (what is given).

（1）有很多贫困大学生接受了企业的资助。

（2）他说礼物太贵重了，不能接受。

2. 领受，容纳而不拒绝。一般宾语为抽象名词。To receive; to accept; not to refuse. Usually its object is an abstract noun.

（3）每个孩子都要接受国家九年制义务教育。

（4）他接受了同学们的意见。

说明 Notes:

"接受"和"接收"的区别是："接受" and "接收" have the following differences:

1. 词义侧重有所不同。"接收"重在收下的动作上。"接受"重在随着收下的动作，内心的领受。"接收" focuses on the action of accepting something while "接受" implies that one is happy to accept what is offered.

2. "接收"的对象一般是具体的人员、机关、企业、公司或者电视、信息、广播等。"接受"的对象可以是具体的，如礼物、名誉称号等，也可以是抽象的，如接受"教育、教训、批评、考验"等。"接收" has its usual target of "personnel, organization, business, company or TV, information and broadcasting, etc." As for "接受," its target may be something concrete such as a gift or an honorary title; but it can also be something abstract such as "教育，教训，批评，考验."

① 如果是具体的对象，"接受"和"接收"可以换用，但是语义有所不同。If the target is concrete, "接受" and "接收" can be used, but each has its own emphasis.

（5）他接受了朋友赠送给他的手提电脑。（重在内心的领受。The emphasis is on one's being happy in accepting the gift.）

（6）他接收了朋友赠送给他的手提电脑。（重在收下这个动作。The emphasis is on the action of accepting the gift.）

② 如果是抽象的对象，"接受"和"接收"不能互换。If the target is abstract, "接受" and "接收" are not interchangeable.

（7）*他没有在国内接收高中教育。

（8）他没有在国内接受高中教育。

3. "接受"能带动词性宾语。"接收"不能。

"接受" can be followed by an object carrying the features of a verb, but "接收" cannot.

（9）这位老先生接受访问。

（10）＊这位老先生接收访问。

jiēzhe 接着 →P388"然后"

用法 Usage:

副词 ad.

表示某一动作、行为或情况紧接着另一动作、行为或情况发生。相当于"紧跟着"的意思。后面常带"就、便、又"等副词。*Indicating one action, behavior or situation happens right after another. Very much the same as "紧跟着" in meaning, it is followed by adverbs such as "就,便,又."*

（1）他们的节目表演完,接着就是我们班表演。

（2）他先去了银行,接着便去了书店。

动词 v.

1. 用手或其他东西承受落下的物体。*To receive; to use one's hand to support a falling object.*

（3）你发球吧,我接着呢。

（4）你倒酒,我拿杯子接着。

2. 表示连着,紧跟着（前面的话或做的事情）。*To follow, to follow closely (what has just been said or done).*

（5）他接着前面同学的建议,说了自己的意见。

（6）他接了一个电话后,接着做作业。

3. 表示收下。*To take; to accept.*

（7）这是爷爷给你的礼物,你接着吧。

（8）你接着吧,这是姐姐给你买的衣服。

说明 Notes:

"接着"动词用法第二项,在使用时,要求有两个分句,"接着"后面多带动词性宾语,如例（5）（6）。*About the second use of "接着" as a verb, it requires the use of two clauses, and "接着" is followed by an object that carries the features of a verb, as in (5) and (6).*

jiéjiàrì 节假日

用法 Usage:

名词 n.

节日和假日的合称。一般用于口语。*The combination of a festival and a holiday. It is usually used in oral Chinese.*

（1）中国的节假日你是怎么过的?

（2）他节假日从来不出去玩。

说明 Notes:

1. 节日是指：*A festival means:*

① 有纪念意义的日子,如五一节、国庆节、儿童节等。*Memorable days such as May Day, the National Day and the Children's Day.*

② 传统的庆祝或祭祀的日子,如春节、清明节、端午节、中秋节等。*Traditional occasions for celebration or offering sacrifices such as the Spring Festival, the Bright and Clear Day, the Dragon Boat Festival, the Mid-Autumn Festival.*

2. 假日是指：放假或休息的日子,如学校的寒假、暑假、周末双休日等。*A holiday means a vacation or just a day for rest, such as the winter vacation, the summer vacation, and the weekend.*

3. "节日"和"假日"两个词语各自使用时要注意：*Use "节日" and "假日" properly, paying attention to their collocations:*

"节日"可以和很多词搭配,如"欢度节日、庆祝节日、纪念这个节日、欢乐的节日、祥和的节日、节日的气氛、节日的问候、节日的晚宴"等,也常说"节日快乐",或"节日期间商店里到处都是购物的人群"。*"节日" goes with a lot of words as in "欢度节日,庆祝节日,纪念这个节日,欢乐的节日,祥和的节日,节日的气氛,节日的问候,节日的晚宴." Also we often say, "节日快乐," or "节日期间商店里到处都是购物的人群."*

"假日"搭配的词语不多。除了"祝你假日快乐""欢快的假日"等以外,一般不受"庆祝、纪念、欢乐、祥和"等词语的修饰,一般也不修饰其他名词。"假日" doesn't have a lot of words to go with it. Except for "祝你假日快乐," "欢快的假日," it is not modified by words such as "庆祝,纪念,欢乐,祥和." Nor is it used to modify other nouns.

jiénéng 节能

用法 Usage:

动词 v.

节约能源。To save energy.

（1）不但工厂要节能,家庭也要节能。
（2）地球的能源正在减少,每个人都要节能。

名词 n.

节约能源（的）。多做定语。Energy-saving. It is usually used as an attribute.

（3）今年的节能计划已经订好了。
（4）节能是地球上每个人的责任。

jiéshěng 节省 →P236"节约"

用法 Usage:

动词 v.

把可以不耗费的省下来或减少耗费。To save; reduce consumption.

（1）他买了一本旧书,节省了五十元钱。
（2）他把零花钱节省下来,给孩子们买了练习本和铅笔。

形容词 a.

俭省,不浪费。Thrifty; not wasteful.

（3）他很节省,从来不浪费一分钱。
（4）他节省的钱都用来买书了。

jiéyuē 节约 →P236"节省"

用法 Usage:

动词 v.

节省（跟"浪费"相对）。To save, the opposite of "浪费 (to waste)."

（1）节约用水、节约用电,人人有责。

形容词 a.

节省的。Thrifty.

（2）他虽然很有钱,但用钱节约得很。

说明 Notes:

"节省"和"节约"都表示使可能被耗费掉的不被耗费掉或少耗费。两个词的意思比较接近,动词用法时都只带名词性宾语。Both "节省" and "节约" mean to reduce consumption and not to consume what doesn't have to be consumed. The two terms are close in meaning, and both are followed by a noun as its object.

它们的区别是：Their differences are as follows:

"节省"强调当用的也尽量少用或不用,以减少消耗。常用于人力、财物、语言、文字、时间等,用于一般场合,在口语中较为多见。"节省" emphasizes not consuming or using as little as possible of what should be consumed. It focuses on reducing consumption, and it applies to human and financial resources, language, text, time, etc. It is used in ordinary situations, especially in oral Chinese.

"节约"强调当用的用,不当用的不用,以避免浪费。通用于口语和书面语,常用于较大的场合,如"提倡节约、厉行节约、节约能源、节约模范"等。By contrast, "节约" emphasizes spending what has to be spent and not spending what should not be spent so as to avoid waste. It is applied to both written and oral Chinese. In particular, it suits formal occasions, such as "提倡节约,厉行节约,节约能源,节约运动,节约模范."

jiéguǒ 结果 →P198"后果"

用法 Usage:

名词 n.

在一定阶段,事物发展所达到的最后状态。Result, the final state that things will reach at a certain stage of development.

（1）你的成绩好,是你学习努力的结果。
（2）比赛的结果现在还没有出来。

连词 conj.

1. 表示顺承关系,在某种条件或情况下产生某种结局。用在后一分句句首。(In a relationship of continuation) indicating the result reached under certain conditions. It usually appears at the beginning of the second clause.

(3) 问了他好几遍,结果他还是没有告诉我。

(4) 昨天晚上的比赛我没看完,结果谁赢了?

2. 表示转折关系,出现在后一分句,后面有"是、还是、却"等词语相呼应。如果前后主语不同,后一分句主语应该在"结果"之后。表示转折关系的复句用了"结果",句中常常不再出现"虽然……但是……"等关联词语。(In a relationship of transition) it appears in the second clause and is followed by "是,""还是," or "却." If the two clauses don't have the same subject, the subject should appear after "结果." And when "结果" is used to indicate a transition in a complex sentence, conjunctions like "虽然…但是…" will not be used.

(5) 他说今天要到我家来,结果他却没有来。

(6) 我第二次去了北京,结果长城还是没去成。

动词 v.

1. 表示把人处死。多用于书面语或早期白话文。To have someone killed. This use is common in written Chinese or early vernacular.

(7) 黑社会的人结果了他。

2. 作为离合动词,表示长出果实的意思。To serve as a separable verb meaning to bear fruit.

(8) 苹果树开花结果了。

(9) 花盆里的草莓才结了三个果。

说明 Notes:

"结果"和"后果"的区别如下：The differences between "结果" and "后果" are as follows:

1. "结果"是名词,又有连词、动词用法。"后果"只是名词,没有连词用法。"结果" is a noun, but it can also serve as a conjunction and a verb. "后果" can only be used as a noun, and cannot serve as a conjunction.

2. "结果"用作名词时,表示最后的结果,好坏都有。"后果"是贬义词,多指坏的结果。When "结果" serves as a verb, the final result can be either good or bad. "后果," by contrast, is a derogatory term: it usually means bad results.

(10) *他喝酒骑电动车,撞了人,结果很严重。

(11) 他喝酒骑电动车,撞了人,后果很严重。

jiézhǐ 截止 →P237"截至"

用法 Usage:

动词 v.

到一定期限停止。To set a deadline for something.

(1) 这次报名昨天已经截止了。

(2) 这次展览会一个星期,将于本月15日截止。

jiézhì 截至 →P237"截止"

用法 Usage:

动词 v.

1. 截止到(某个时候)。(Of a certain time) to be set as the deadline.

(1) 这次报名截至本月30日。

2. 截止到(某个时候)。多用于事情发展的情况叙述。(Of a certain time) to be set as the deadline. It is often used to describe the development of something.

(2) 截至昨天,已经有两百多人参加了这次比赛。

说明 Notes:

"截止"和"截至"都跟结束的时间有关。Both "截止" and "截至" carry a meaning related to the deadline.

它们的区别是：They differ as follows:

1. "截止"强调活动、比赛、报名等等事件停止的时间。"截至"指到某个时间为止,带有从什么时候到什么时候的语义,强调活动、事件限定的某一时间范围。"截止" refers to the deadline for an activity, a game or registration. "截至" focuses on the range of time, from time A to time B, when an activity or event will be held.

2. "截止"后面不能直接带时间名词做宾语,时间名词一般放在"截止"前面,如果时间名词要放在"截止"后面,"截止"后面要加补语"到"。"截至"后面必须直接带时间名词。"截止" cannot take a time noun as its object: the time noun is usually placed before "截止." If the time noun is placed after "截止," the supplement "到" has to be added. "截至," by contrast, must be followed directly by a time noun.

（3）*选修课报名截止星期五。
（4）选修课报名星期五截止。
（5）选修课报名今天开始,截至星期五。

3. "截至"有指出到某个时间为止,事情的发展情况如何,而且事情可能还在发展的语义。"截止"一般没有这个意思。"截至" may mean that by a certain time, things have developed to a certain stage, and further development is possible. "截止" does not have this meaning.

（7）截至昨天,这次飞机失事已有七人死亡。

jiěshì 解释 →P238"解说"

用法 Usage:
动词 v.

1. 对含义、原因、理由等加以阐明。To explain the meaning, cause or reason.

（1）老师把这个语法点又解释了一遍。
（2）你不用解释了,大家都知道你的情况。

2. （对事物的深层内涵）分析说明。To make an in-depth analysis of something.

（3）北极光为什么那么漂亮的原因,他解释得很清楚了。

（4）3D摄影的原理,如果解释不清楚是很难理解的。

jiěshuō 解说 →P238"解释"

用法 Usage:
动词 v.

（对事物）讲解说明。To explain something.

（1）听,导游开始解说旅游路线了。
（2）展览馆的讲解员解说得很不错。

说明 Notes:

1. "解释"和"解说"都有名词用法。Both "解释" and "解说" can be used as a noun.

（3）导游对每个景点的解说很有意思。
（4）你的解释让我知道了他为什么每天都要迟到。

2. "解释"和"解说"都是把事物说清楚。Both "解释" and "解说" mean to give a clear explanation of something.

它们的区别是:"解说"重在把别人不知道的情况加以说明,使知其然。"解释"重在对事物的知其所以然。Their difference is as follows: "解说" emphasizes explaining something that others don't know. "解释," by contrast, focuses on explaining "why."

下面的句子中,就不用"解说"。"解说" cannot be used in the following two sentences:

（5）为什么"见面"后面不能有宾语,老师解释得真清楚!
（6）你能解释一下地球为什么有吸引力吗?

jǐn 仅 →P239"仅仅"

用法 Usage:
副词 ad.

范围副词,限定动作、行为或事物的范围。有文言色彩,书面语色彩。As a scope adverb, "仅" is used to set a limit to some action, behavior or thing. It's more often used in classical and written Chinese.

1. 用在动词或动词短语前，限定动作、行为所涉及的范围，以限制动作的对象，有排他性。相当于"只"。Placed before a verb or a verb phrase, it limits the scope of an action or behavior. Since it sets limits, it is more or less exclusive, with a meaning similar to "只."

（1）这次去北京，我仅去了故宫。
（2）他仅学过英语，没学过别的外语。

2. 表示数量少、时间短。Indicating a small amount and a short time.

① 直接用在数量短语前。It appears directly before a phrase indicating an amount.

（3）出国留学时他仅十六岁。
（4）参加这次比赛的仅十人。

② 用在带有数量短语的动词或动词短语前，限定跟动作、行为有关的数量，表示时间短、数量少。相当于"只"。Placed before a verb or a verb phrase with another phrase indicating an amount, it sets a limit to the amount related to the action and behavior, indicating a short time and a small amount. Again, its meaning is similar to "只."

（5）他来过几次中国，我因为太忙，仅见过他一次。
（6）他仅用了十分钟，就把手机修好了。

3. 用在名词或名词性短语前，带有举例性质，举出例证，借以说明整体情况，相当于"光（是）……"的意思，后面多用"就"呼应。Placed before a noun or a noun phrase, it introduces an example to illustrate the whole situation. Its meaning is similar to "光（是）…" and often one will find "就" to echo with it.

（7）今天买了很多书，仅小说就买了三本。
（8）这家饭店生意很好，仅昨天晚上就接待了两千多位顾客。

jǐnjǐn 仅仅 →P238"仅"

用法 Usage:

副词 ad.

意义、用法与"仅"基本相同。只是语气比较重一些。It has basically the same meaning as "仅," and it is used more or less the same way. The only thing to remember about "仅仅" is that it carries a more serious tone.

（1）这个星期，他仅仅上了三节课。
（2）我仅仅和他通过一次电话，没见过面。

说明 Notes:

"仅"和"仅仅"的区别如下：The differences between "仅" and "仅仅" are as follows:

1. "仅仅"既可用于书面语，也可用于口语。"仅"多用于书面语。"仅仅" is applied to both oral and written Chinese while "仅" appears mostly in written Chinese.

2. 在书面语中，由于音节关系，常用"仅"修饰单音节词，很少用"仅仅"。In written Chinese, "仅" is often used to modify monosyllabic words. "仅仅" is rarely used.

（3）＊以上意见，仅仅供参考。
（4）以上意见，仅供参考。
（5）＊超市在本地仅仅此一家。
（6）超市在本地仅此一家。

jìn 尽

用法 Usage:

动词 v.

1. 达到力所能及的限度。To reach the limit by doing one's best.

（1）我会尽最大的努力学好汉语。
（2）他一定会尽最大的可能去做好这件事。

2. 达到极限，表示以某个范围为极限。To reach the extreme, indicating the limit to a certain scope.

（3）你喜欢吃什么就吃什么，尽着这二百元吃吧。
（4）尽这三个小时，你去西湖边看看就回来。

3. 表示放在最先。常与"先"连用。北方人多用这种句式。To give top priority to, often used together with "先." Northerners use

it frequently.

（5）这本书先尽着你们看吧,你们看完我再看。

（6）先尽着客人上车,我们等第二辆车再上。

副词 ad.

1. 老是,总是。Always.

（7）最近一段日子尽下雨。

（8）这一个月我尽感冒。

2. 最,用在表示方位的词语前面。The utmost. It is placed before a word indicating location or position.

（9）尽前头那个就是阿里。

（10）尽后面那座是我们的教学楼。

说明 Notes:

动词"尽"不能单独做谓语,不能单独成句,如例（1）（2）。"尽," as a verb, cannot serve as the predicate in a sentence. Nor can it be used as a sentence by itself, as in (1) and (2). It has to take an object.

jǐnguǎn 尽管 →P47"不管"、P212"即使"

用法 Usage:

副词 ad.

表示没有条件限制,可以随意去做。Meaning "unconditionally" and so one can feel free to do something.

（1）你有什么问题尽管来问我。

（2）你尽管来吧,我随时欢迎你。

连词 conj.

表示让步,虽然,即使。Though; even if. It indicates a concession.

（3）他尽管身体不好,还是坚持来上课。

（4）尽管父母反对,但是他还想出国。

说明 Notes:

1. 使用"尽管"要注意：Watch out the following points when using "尽管"：

① "尽管"做副词时,后面的动词一般不能用否定式,也不能带"着、了、过"。When "尽管" serves as an adverb, the verb cannot appear in the negative, nor can it go with "着","了," or "过."

② "尽管"做连词时,后一小句常用"但是、可是、然而、可、还是、仍然、却"等呼应。因为"尽管"是表示一种事实,所以"尽管"后面不能用表示任指的词语。When "尽管" serves as a conjunction, one is likely to find "但是,可是,然而,可,还是,仍然,却," each of which echoes with it. By contrast, "尽管" is not to be followed by any term meaning anything and everything because what "尽管" expresses is always a fact.

（5）*尽管雨下得多么大,我还是要去。

（6）尽管雨下得很大,我还是要去。

③ 连词"尽管"可以用于后一分句,前面的分句不用"但是、可是、然而"等词语。"尽管" can be used in the second clause, but one must not use "但是,可是,然而" in the first clause.

（7）大家仍在外面唱着、跳着,尽管天已经开始下雨了。

（8）他没有来,尽管我叫了他两次。

2. "尽管"和"不管"的区别如下："尽管"表示一种事实,"不管"表示一种假设。The difference between "尽管" and "不管" is as follows: "尽管" indicates a fact while "不管" indicates an assumption.

（9）尽管你不来,我还是会想念你的。

（10）不管你来不来,我都会等你的。

3. "尽管"和"即使"都有连词用法,表示让步的意思。区别是,"尽管"的句子是表示一种事实,"即使"的句子是表示一种假设的事实。Both "尽管" and "即使" can be used as a conjunction to express a concession. Their difference is that the clause starting with "尽管" indicates a fact while "即使" indicates a hypothesis.

jǐnkuài 尽快

用法 Usage:

副词 ad.

尽量加快。As soon as possible.

（1）我会尽快把茶叶给你寄去。
（2）我要尽快把论文写出来。

说明 Notes：

"尽快"修饰动词或动词短语。常见搭配有"尽快完成、尽快处理、尽快答复、尽快离开、尽快弄清、尽快做完、尽快修好"等等。这些短语前面不能再加程度副词。"尽快" is often used to modify a verb or a verb phrase. Common collocations include "尽快完成，尽快处理，尽快答复，尽快离开，尽快弄清，尽快做完，尽快修好，" etc. Remember not to precede any of these phrases with a degree adverb.

jìnliàng 尽量 →P241"尽力"、P242"尽量（jǐnliàng）"

用法 Usage：

副词 ad.

力求在一定范围内达到最大限度。可以修饰动词或形容词。Trying to reach the highest degree within a certain scope. It can be used to modify a verb or an adjective.

（1）我尽量早一点儿来。
（2）只要我能帮你的，我尽量帮。
（3）说话要尽量准确、简洁。

jìn 尽

用法 Usage：

动词 v.

1. 完，毕。To end; to come to an end.

（1）我已经把话说尽了，他还是不肯吃药。
（2）我们家乡的大山就像是一座取之不尽的宝山。

2. 全部使出。To do one's best.

（3）医生对他的病已经尽了力了。
（4）我尽了最大的努力，作业还是没有完成。

3. 用力完成。To try one's best to accomplish.

（5）对孩子要尽到做父母的责任。
（6）对老人要尽到做儿女的义务。

副词 ad.

都，全，完全。后面常带"是"。All; completely; having no exception. It is often followed by "是."

（7）他衣服上尽是画画的颜色。
（8）孩子不能为自己的行为做解释，这种做法不尽合理。

说明 Notes：

1. 表示"完、毕"的动词"尽"常位于动词后作补语，如"用尽、说尽、吃尽、想尽、消灭尽"等。Verbs meaning "come to an end" are usually placed after the verb as a complement such as "用尽，说尽，吃尽，想尽，消灭尽."

2. 表示"全部使出"的意思时，常见的搭配为"尽了力、尽最大的努力、尽自己的力量"等。When meaning "do one's best," it often appears in expressions such as "尽了力,尽最大的努力,尽自己的力量."

3. 表示"用力完成"时，"尽"常带"责任、义务"等作宾语。When meaning "trying one's best to accomplish," "尽" often takes "责任，义务" as its object.

4. 副词"尽"所修饰的动宾词组，总是一个"是＋名词"的句式。As an adverb, the verb object structure modified by "尽" is always "是＋n."

（9）这个旅游团的成员尽是老年人。
（10）桌子上尽是鲜花水果。

在口语中，有时"是"可以省去，"尽"直接出现在名词前面。如："桌上尽鲜花水果。""是" is sometimes omitted in oral Chinese. As a result, "尽" appears directly before a noun, for example, "桌上尽鲜花水果."

jìnlì 尽力 →P241"尽量（jǐnliàng）"

用法 Usage：

副词 ad.

用一切力量。Doing one's best; doing one's utmost.

（1）你别担心，我一定尽力帮助你。
（2）每个人都应该尽力做好自己的工作。

jìn 尽

动词 v.

表示用尽力量。多用作谓语。To do one's best; to do one's utmost. It serves as the predicate in a sentence.

(3) 你的事,我会尽力的。

(4) 为了这张飞机票,他尽了很大的力。

(5) A：你能不能在三天内完成这些作业？
　　 B：我尽力吧。

说明 Notes:

"尽力"和"尽量"都有做出最大努力,用一切力量的意思,都可以做状语,有时可以互换。Both "尽力" and "尽量" mean doing one's best or doing one's utmost. Both may serve as an adverbial. They are often interchangeable.

(6) 我们一定尽量/尽力满足你的要求。

(7) 他会尽量/尽力帮助你。

它们的区别是：They differ as follows:

1. 副词"尽量"着重表示在一定范围内达到最大限度,重点在"量"上。副词"尽力"着重指用尽一切力量或力气,重点在"力"上。所以有些句子两个词不能互换。As an adverb, "尽量" focuses on reaching the highest degree within a certain scope: its emphasis is on the "amount." However, "尽力" as an adverb emphasizes devoting all one's energy or strength to something one is doing. Therefore, the two terms are not always interchangeable.

(8) *我会尽力抽时间给你打电话。

(9) 我会尽量抽时间给你打电话。

(10) *我会尽量给你买到龙井茶叶。

(11) 我会尽力给你买到龙井茶叶。

2. "尽力"是离合动词,中间可以插入其他词语,可以做谓语。"尽量"不能。"尽力" is a separable verb and some other word can be inserted in between and serve as the predicate. "尽量" cannot be used this way.

(12) *他已经尽了量了。

(13) 他已经尽了力了。

jìnliàng 尽量 →P241"尽量(jǐnliàng)"

用法 Usage:

动词 v.

达到(数量上的)极限。To reach the extreme.

(1) 他吃了两碗饭还没尽量,还要添一碗。

(2) 别劝他再喝了。今天喝酒,他已经尽量了。

说明 Notes:

"尽量(jìnliàng)"和"尽量(jǐnliàng)"的区别如下：The differences between "尽量(jìnliàng)" and "尽量(jǐnliàng)" are as follows:

动词"尽量"(jìnliàng)是指达到数量上的最大限度,多指酒量、饭量,适用的范围小,如例(1)(2)。"尽量(jǐnliàng)"多指各种事物在一定范围内达到最大限度,适用范围大。As a verb, "尽量(jìnliàng)" means to reach the highest degree. Very often it refers to the highest degree when one eats or drinks as in (1) and (2). The range of its usage is limited. By contrast, the use of "尽量(jǐnliàng)" is wider. It often refers to the highest degree of things within a certain range.

jìnxíng 进行

用法 Usage:

动词 v.

从事持续性的活动。可带"了",一般不带"着、过"。To carry on; to conduct. If it is a continuous activity, it can be followed by "了," but usually it cannot be followed by "着" or "过."

(1) 我们对你的问题进行了讨论。

(2) 试验进行得很顺利。

(3) 你的作业自己要好好儿地进行检查。

说明 Notes:

1. "进行"的宾语一般是动词性的,而且这个动词是双音节的,它的动作具有持续性的特点,如"讨论、帮助、比赛、改革、研究、生产、服务、创新、分析、调查"等双音节动词,组成"进行调查、进行帮助、进行比较"等动词短语。在这样的句子中,"进行"实际上是个形式动词,真正具有句子语义上意义的动词是"进行"的动词宾语,如例(1)(3)中的"讨论"和"检查"。The object of "进行" is usually a kind of verb, and a disyllabic verb at that. All these verbs indicate an action that can continue for a long or pretty long time, such as "讨论,帮助,比赛,改革,研究,生产,服务,创新,分析,调查." And they can form verb phrases such as "进行调查,进行帮助,进行比较." In these sentences, "进行" is actually just a verb in form: the true verb is the object to the verb "进行," as "讨论" and "检查" in (1) and (3).

2. "进行"后面不能带单音节动词。"＊进行查、＊进行帮、＊进行比、＊进行吃"都是错的。应该为:"进行检查、进行帮助、进行比赛、正在吃饭"。"进行" cannot be followed by monosyllabic verbs. "＊进行查,＊进行帮,＊进行比,＊进行吃" are all wrong. The correct versions are:"进行检查,进行帮助,进行比赛,正在吃饭."

3. "进行"的宾语动词不能再带宾语,如果动词在语义上要求带出对象,可以用"对、将、把"引进。The object-verb with the meaning of "进行" cannot take any objects. If it is necessary to indicate the target of the verb, "对,将,把" are used to introduce them.

(4) ＊请进行比较这两种 DNA。
(5) 请把这两种 DNA 进行比较。
(6) ＊警察进行了调查这起交通事故。
(7) 警察对这起交通事故进行了调查。

4. "进行"只用于比较正式、庄重的活动,不用于短暂、具体的操作性动作行为。所以,可以说"进行谈判、进行讨论",不能说"进行说话、进行叫喊、进行做饭"等。"进行" is applied to fairly formal and solemn activities, not temporary or concrete operational behavior. So we can say "进行谈判,进行讨论," but not "进行说话,进行叫喊,进行做饭," etc.

(8) ＊现在开始,我在中国进行学习汉语了。

(9) 现在开始,我在中国学习汉语了。

例(8),"学习"虽然是个表示持续性动作的动词,但是后面带上"汉语",组成"学习汉语"的词组,就变成个有很具体的动作、行为的动词词语;而且在这个句子中,不用"进行",语义本身已经很清楚。In (8), "学习" is a verb indicating an action that can go on for a long time, but it is followed by "汉语" to form a phrase "学习汉语." Thus it becomes a verb phrase indicating a concrete action. Moreover, the meaning of the sentence is quite clear without using "进行."

5. "进行"一般多与一些行为显现的、持续的动词搭配,不跟具有对待关系意义的表心理活动的动词搭配,所以不能说"进行关心、进行相信、进行注意、进行体贴"等。"进行" is usually used in combination with verbs whose action is apparent and continuous, not with verbs indicating a mental activity about dealing with something, and so we cannot say "进行关心,进行相信,进行注意,进行体贴," etc.

6. "进行"作为句子的唯一动词时,后面常常带程度补语或趋向补语,如"顺利、下去、到"等。一般"进行"后面不直接带名词性宾语,受事名词一般在"进行"前面做主语。When "进行" serves as the only verb in a sentence, it is often followed by a complement showing a degree or inclination, such as "顺利,下去,到." "进行" usually does not take a noun as its object: the noun as the receiver of an action appears before "进行" as the subject of the sentence.

(10) 按现在的速度进行下去,地铁二号线下个月就能完成。

(11) 实验进行到这一步了,怎么能停下来?

jīngcháng 经常 →P61 "常常"

用法 Usage:

副词 *ad.*

表示动作、行为或情况屡次发生，而且具有一贯性。Often; frequently. It is used to indicate the repeated occurrence of an action, behavior or situation, all of which is marked by consistency.

(1) 他经常吃面条，不喜欢吃米饭。
(2) 他们经常去卡拉 OK。

形容词 *a.*

表示"平常的、日常的"意思。常与别的词语一起，用作定语。可受程度副词修饰。Ordinary; daily. It often goes with some other word to serve as an attribute. It may be modified by a degree adverb.

(3) 学习语言说错句子是很经常的事情。
(4) 可口可乐是不能经常喝的饮料。

说明 Notes:

"经常"和"常常"使用时，要注意在句子中的位置。句子中多状语时，"常常（经常）"排列在什么地方，可以根据语义的需要决定。但必须在谓语的前面。Pay attention to where to position "经常" and "常常" when they are used. It depends on the requirement of the meaning when more than one adverbial appears in the sentence, but definitely it has to appear before the predicate.

(5) *他们在十二点常常/经常睡觉。
(6) 他们常常/经常在十二点睡觉。（强调时间 Emphasizing the time）
(7) *半夜里，他们去常常/经常吃夜宵。
(8) 半夜里，他们常常/经常去吃夜宵。（强调动作 Emphasizing the action）
(9) *她给我写信常常/经常用微信。
(10) 她常常/经常用微信给我写信。（强调方式方法 Emphasizing the means）

"经常"和"常常"的区别如下：The differences between "经常" and "常常" are as follows:

1. 在词义上，"经常"着重于一贯性，有经久常行的意思，动作频率比"常常"更高。"常常"重在指动作行为的重复。Semantically, "经常" focuses on consistency: it carries the meaning of something being done again and again and its frequency is higher than "常常." However, "常常" lays more emphasis on the repetition of a certain action.

(11) 他们经常去饭店吃饭。
(12) 他们常常去饭店吃饭。

2. "经常"还可以用作形容词。"常常"不能。"经常" may serve as an adjective, but "常常" cannot.

(13) *学习语言说错句子是常常的事情。
(14) 学习语言，说错句子是经常的事。

jīngguò 经过 →P468 "通过"

用法 Usage:

名词 *n.*

过程，经历。Process; experience.

(1) 他把事情的经过都告诉我了。
(2) 这次车祸的经过我还不太清楚。

动词 *v.*

1. 从某处通过。To pass.

(3) 这辆公共汽车经过学校。
(4) 从北京坐火车到上海要经过南京、苏州。

2. 延续。可带"了"。"经过"后面必须带时间名词做宾语。To last; to continue. It may be followed by "了." "经过" has to be followed by a noun as its object indicating time.

(5) 经过五个小时，他们就到了北京。
(6) 经过了两个星期，他们才拿到法国的签证。

介词 *prep.*

经历（活动、事件）。必带名词、动词、小句做宾语。Going through; past (an activity or event). It has to be followed by a noun, a verb or a clause as its object.

(7) 经过这次旅游，我们都积累了很多经验。

(8) 经过仔细考虑之后,我做出了决定。

jīnglì 经历 →P245"经验"

用法 Usage:

名词 n.

亲身见过、做过或遭遇过的事。*Experience, things one has seen, done or encountered.*

(1) 我对他在黄山的经历很感兴趣。
(2) 我爷爷经常给我讲他年轻时的经历。

动词 v.

亲身见过、做过或遭遇过。*To see, do, or encounter something (in one's life).*

(3) 他在国外到底经历过什么,没有人知道。
(4) 这几年我经历了很多事情。

说明 Notes:

"经历"表示人的阅历、经过的事情。强调亲身见过、做过或遭遇过的事情。不包括从实践中得来的知识和技能。*"经历" means things one has seen or encountered in one's life. It emphasizes one's personal experience, but it doesn't include knowledge and skills one acquires through the experience.*

jīngyàn 经验 →P245"经历"

用法 Usage:

名词 n.

由实践得来的知识和技能。*Knowledge and skills acquired through practice.*

(1) 他在公司十年了,工作经验很丰富。
(2) 同学们经常交流学习经验。

说明 Notes:

1. "经验"作名词用时,有比较广泛的搭配,如"生活经验、工作经验、社会经验、实践经验、宝贵的经验、丰富的经验、个人的经验、经验不足、经验丰富、介绍经验、传授经验、缺乏经验"等。另外,还可以说"很有经验、有很丰富的经验、没有经验、很缺乏经验"等。*As a noun, "经验" goes with many nouns, such as "生活经验,工作经验,社会经验,实践经验,宝贵的经*

验,丰富的经验,个人的经验,经验不足,经验丰富,介绍经验,传授经验,缺乏经验." In addition, one can also say "很有经验,有很丰富的经验,没有经验,很缺乏经验."

2. 在有些词典里,"经验"还列有动词用法。但是在当代汉语中,"经验"的动词用法已经淡化,一般只做名词用。*In some dictionaries, "经验" is also entered as a verb. But in contemporary Chinese, the use of "经验" as a verb has been weakened; it is generally used only as a noun.*

3. "经验"和"经历"的区别如下:*The differences between "经验" and "经历" are as follows:*

① 作名词用时,"经验"表示从实践中得来的知识、技能,"经历"表示人的阅历、经过的事情。*As a noun, "经验" means knowledge and skills acquired through practice while "经历," also as a noun, means things a person has seen, done, or gone through in his life.*

② "经历"有动词的用法,"经验"一般不作动词用。*"经历" can be used as a verb, while "经验" normally cannot.*

(3) 他是一个经验丰富的教师。
(4) 他在年轻时经历过战争。

jīngshen 精神

用法 Usage:

名词 n.

表现出来的活力。*Energy that is displayed.*

(1) 昨天睡得太晚,今天我一点儿精神也没有。
(2) 他工作起来特别有精神。

形容词 a.

形容人活跃或有生气。*Energetic; full of life.*

(3) 虽然他已经七十岁了,但是看上去还很精神。
(4) 你今天打扮得真精神。

说明 Notes:

1. "精神"做名词时,常与"振作、抖擞、焕发、打(不)起、提(不)起、饱满、旺盛、振奋、好、坏、有、没有"等词语搭配。As a noun, "精神" goes with many words, such as "振作,抖擞,焕发,打(不)起,提(不)起,饱满,旺盛,振奋,好,坏,有,没有."

2. "精神"做名词时又读 jīngshén,意思是: "精神," as a noun, is sometimes pronounced as jīngshén, It means:

① 指人的意识、思维活动和一般的心理状态,如"精神面貌、精神上的负担"等。A person's consciousness, thoughts, and ordinary mental state, and so we have "精神面貌,精神上的负担," etc.

(5) 她最近精神压力很大。

② 指宗旨,主要的意义。Main idea; gist.

(6) 我们应该明白这篇文章的精神。

(7) 院长讲话的主要精神是什么?

jǐngsè 景色 →P149"风景"、P246"景象"

用法 Usage:

名词 n.

风景,有色彩的自然现象。多做主语、宾语。Natural scenery; scenes and sights. Usually it serves as the subject or object of a sentence.

(1) 这边的景色很漂亮。

(2) 我没见过这么漂亮的景色。

说明 Notes:

"景色"和"风景"都指一个地区内包括山川、花草、树木、建筑物等在内的、能让人赏心悦目的自然和人文景观。通用于口语和书面语。Both "景色" and "风景" refer to the natural scenery and human landscape in an area, including rivers and mountains, trees and flowers, buildings and other things that are pleasing to the eye. Both are used in written and oral Chinese.

它们的区别是: They differ as follows:

1. 在词义上,"风景"所指的范围比"景色"所指的大,包含的内容多。"景色"更侧重自然风光。Semantically, "风景" covers a wider scope than "景色" which focuses on natural attractions.

2. "风景"可以做定语,"景色"不能。如:"风景画、风景区"。"风景" can serve as an attribute such as "风景画,风景区," but "景色" cannot.

3. "风景"有比喻用法,如"煞风景",比喻在美好的事物中出现了令人扫兴的事情。"风景" is occasionally used as a figure of speech like "煞风景," which means something unpleasant has erupted in a generally nice and happy environment.

jǐngxiàng 景象 →P246"景色"

用法 Usage:

名词 n.

现象,状况。Scene; situation.

(1) 城市里到处都是一片繁忙的景象。

(2) 秋天的田野上,到处是一片丰收的景象。

说明 Notes:

"景色"和"景象"的区别如下: The differences between "景色" and "景象" are as follows:

1. 在语义上,"景象"是指自然景物或人们活动所构成的图景,侧重于外观的情景和现象。它也可以指工厂、农村、集体、社会等一些较大场面中呈现出来的现象。它的特点是场面大,并具有"呈现出来的"动态的特点。"景色"是指可观赏的风景,泛指山水、花草、树木等构成的大自然色彩,并能表现出季节特点或地方特色的风景。"景象" means a scene presented by natural scenery and related human activities: its focus is a scene or situation that one sees. It may also describe some "fairly big scenes" one sees in a factory, village, collective, or society. It covers a wide view, which tends to "present itself" to those who watch. By contrast, "景色" usually refers to rivers and mountains, trees and flowers — all part of what is called

nature. It is marked by seasonal or local characteristics.

2. "景象"的意思相对抽象,修饰语多为"欣欣向荣、神奇、欢腾、热闹、庄严、丰收、繁荣"等。常用于书面语。"景色"的修饰语多为"优美、美丽、赏心悦目"等形容词。通用于口语、书面语。The meaning of "景象" is rather abstract. And so it often goes with "欣欣向荣,神奇,欢腾,热闹,庄严,丰收,繁荣," etc. It appears mostly in written Chinese. By contrast, words that are used to modify "景色" are adjectives such as "优美,美丽,赏心悦目." It appears in both written and oral Chinese.

jìng 竟 →P247"竟然"

用法 Usage:
副词 ad.

表示违背一般规律或常情,或者出乎意料的语气,相当于"居然、竟然"。Doing something in violation of ordinary rules and common sense. It is usually spoken in a tone showing unexpectedness. It is similar to "居然" and "竟然."

(1) 我竟忘了带钥匙出门了。
(2) 原来他竟会做中国菜。

动词 v.

表示完整、全部,完毕,完成。To finish; to complete; to succeed in doing something.

(3) 我哥哥学业未竟,在大学三年级就结了婚。

说明 Notes:

1. "竟"做副词时,修饰形容词常有"竟这么便宜、竟贵成这样、竟比他还聪明"等表示对比、比较的词语和语义。"竟," as an adverb, is often found in expressions such as "竟这么便宜,竟贵成这样,竟比他还聪明." It always implies a comparison or contrast.

2. "竟"做动词时,带有文言色彩。如例(3)。As a verb, "竟" appears often in classic Chinese, as in (3).

jìngrán 竟然 →P247"竟"、P255"居然"

用法 Usage:
副词 ad.

出乎意料地。用在动词谓语前,做状语。Unexpectedly. It usually appears before a verb which serves as the predicate of the sentence, and modifies the verb as an adverbial.

(1) 她竟然一个人去北京了。
(2) 他平时成绩很一般,这次考试竟然得了第一名。

说明 Notes:

1. "竟然"是副词,在句子中只能做状语,不能做句子的其他成分。"竟然"前面也不能再受程度副词的修饰。As an adverb, "竟然" can only serve as an adverbial in a sentence, not as anything else. And "竟然" cannot be modified by a degree adverb.

(3) *他说要出国留学,大家都觉得很竟然。
(4) 他说要出国留学,大家都觉得很突然。

2. "竟"跟"竟然"的区别是:The differences between "竟" and "竟然" are as follows:

"竟"用于书面语,"竟然"用于书面语和口语。"竟"有动词的用法,而"竟然"没有动词用法。The differences between "竟" and "竟然" are that "竟" is used in written Chinese while "竟然" is used both in written and oral Chinese and that "竟" can serve as a verb but "竟然" cannot.

jiūzhèng 纠正 →P155"改正"

用法 Usage:
动词 v.

把错误改正为正确的,把有偏向或偏差的事情加以改正。To correct a mistake; to rectify something that has gone wrong or deviated from the right path.

(1) 现在不纠正语音错误,以后要改就比较难了。

（2）他这种观点纠正起来不容易。

说明 Notes：

"纠正"和"改正"都指把错误改成正确的，都要带双音节以上词语的宾语，一般不带单音节宾语。Both "纠正" and "改正" mean correcting a mistake. Both should be followed by a disyllabic or multisyllabic object and they cannot be followed by a monosyllabic word.

它们的区别是：They differ as follows:

1."纠正"的对象既可以是较严重、较重大的政治、思想、行为方法上的重大错误，也可以是一般语言文字、语音、语法方面的字面错误。"改正"的对象一般是谈话或文章中有关内容、字句上的错误，也可以是行为举止上的缺点、毛病、不良习惯，也可以是一般性的冤假错案等，应用范围比较广泛。The target of "纠正" can be major political, ideological or behavioral mistakes; it can also be language mistakes, whether it is the use or pronunciation of a word or grammatical mistakes. The target of "改正," by contrast, can be language or content mistakes found in an article or speech, or shortcomings or drawbacks in one's behavior or one's involvement in a case of false accusation. Anyway, it covers a wider scope.

2."纠正"的语义比较重，含有外在力量的强迫意味，"改正"的语义比较轻，一般指靠自己的力量改错为正。"纠正" is a serious term, often involving some outside force, and so it implies pressure from other people. "改正," by contrast, is not that serious: usually it means correcting a mistake through one's own effort.

jiūjìng 究竟 →P28"毕竟"、P97"到底"

用法 Usage:

副词 ad.

1.用在问句中，表示进一步追究，有加强语气的作用。意义相当于"到底"。与副词"到底"的第一、第三义项用法相同。多用于书面语，做状语。Like "到底," it is used in a question to pursue an answer. As a matter of fact, it is similar to the first and third use of "到底." It appears as an adverbial and mostly in written Chinese.

① 用在动词、形容词前，也可以用在主语前。Placed before a verb or adjective or before the subject of a sentence.

（1）你究竟还买不买那本书了？

（2）那面条究竟辣不辣？

② 针对主语提问。主语是疑问代词，"究竟"只能在主语前面。When the question is asked about the subject, or the subject is a pronoun, "究竟" can only be placed before the subject.

（3）究竟哪本书是你的？

（4）究竟你去还是他去？

③ "究竟"不能用在带"吗"的问句中。"究竟" cannot be used in a question ending with "吗。"

（5）*你究竟是日本人吗？

（6）你究竟是哪国人？

2.表示毕竟、归根到底的意思。多用于含有评价意义的陈述句，加强语气，做状语。Meaning "finally" or "in the end," it appears often in a statement indicating an assessment and it serves to show emphasis. Anyway, it is an adverbial.

① 常用在动词、形容词前。一般都有两个分句，"究竟"用在前一分句，后一分句是前一分句动词或形容词产生的建议或结果。Placed before a verb or an adjective. In this case, there are usually two clauses. "究竟" appears in the first clause, and the second clause expresses the suggestion or result produced by the verb or adjective in the first clause.

（7）爸爸的年纪究竟大了，别让他再上班了。

（8）她究竟是个有经验的老师，什么问题都讲得很清楚。

② 用于"是"字句,强调事物的特征。可以同两个相同的名词或名词短语构成"……究竟是……"的格式。Placed in a sentence with the word "是" to emphasize the characteristics of a thing. It can join two nouns or noun phrases to form the "...究竟是..." if the two nouns or noun phrases are the same.

(9) 颜色究竟是绿色的让人心情愉快。
(10) 孩子究竟是孩子,什么都不懂。

说明 Notes:

1. "究竟"还有名词用法。表示事情开始和结果的全过程。常做宾语。"究竟" can be used as a noun, meaning the whole process of a thing from beginning to end. It serves as an object in the sentence.

(11) 你快说吧,大家都想知道个究竟。
(12) 他真的生病了? 我得回宿舍去看个究竟。

2. "究竟"修饰形容词(常常是积极意义的形容词)时,一般形容词前面不再加"很、非常、十分"等表示程度的副词。When "究竟" modifies an adjective (an adjective with a positive meaning), the adjective is usually not preceded by degree adverbs such as "很,非常,十分."

(13) *他究竟很努力。
(14) 他究竟是努力,每次考试都不低于九十分。

3. "究竟"与"到底"相同的地方如下:The similarities between "究竟" and "到底" are as follows:

① 都表示追究或强调事物本质、特点的意思。Both are used to pursue an answer to a question and often to find out the essence and special characteristics of a thing.

② 都能用于疑问句,可用的疑问句式有:Both can be used in questions. Here are the different question forms:

(15) 他究竟/到底是谁?
(16) 事情到底/究竟怎么样了?

(17) 你究竟/到底去不去?
(18) 你究竟/到底去还是不去?
(19) 你究竟/到底有没有去?
(20) 你究竟/到底想去上海还是想去北京?

③ 主语如果由疑问代词充当,"究竟"和"到底"都只能用在主语之前。"到底" and "究竟" can only be placed before the subject if the subject is an inquisitive pronoun.

(21) 究竟/到底谁去上海?
(22) 究竟/到底哪间是多媒体教室?

④ 都不能用于句末有"吗"的疑问句。Neither can be used in a question ending with the word "吗."

(23) *你究竟/到底是日本人吗?
(24) 你究竟/到底是不是日本人?

4. "究竟"与"到底"的区别是:The differences between "究竟" and "到底" are as follows:

① "究竟"多用于书面语。"到底"多用于口语。"究竟" is more used in written language, while "到底" is more used orally.

② "究竟"没有表示某种情况或结果经过一定的时间和过程,最后终于出现的意思,没有"终于、最终"的意思。"到底"有这个意思。"究竟" does not carry the meaning of the final situation or result appearing after a certain time or process, of which you find in "终于,最终." But "到底" does carry the above mentioned meaning.

(25) *经过两年自学,我究竟获得了 HSK 六级的证书。
(26) 经过两年自学,我到底获得了 HSK 六级的证书。

5. "究竟"和"毕竟"在表示强调事物本质或特点上,在判断句中,用法相同。"究竟" and "毕竟" are used the same way in a judgmental sentence if both are used to emphasize the essence or special features of a thing.

(27) 她究竟/毕竟是我们的老师,怎么会不给我们辅导呢?

6. "究竟"和"毕竟"的区别是：The differences between "究竟" and "毕竟" are as follows:

① "究竟"可以用于疑问句、陈述句。"毕竟"只能用于陈述句。"究竟" can be used in both an interrogation and a statement, but "毕竟" can be used only in a statement.

(28) 你究竟同意不同意？

(29) *你毕竟同意不同意？

② "究竟"有名词用法，"毕竟"不能作为名词用。"究竟" may be used as a noun, but "毕竟" may not.

jiù 就 →P30"便"、P211"即"

用法 Usage:

副词 ad.

1. 表示在很短的时间内。"就"前面常常有表示时间很快的副词"马上、立刻"或表示时间很短的词语"等一下"等。Meaning "in a very short time," it is often preceded by adverbs "马上" and "立刻," both of which mean in a very short time, or by "等一下," which is an expression meaning "just a moment."

(1) 他马上就到了。

(2) 等一下，我就去。

2. 表示动作行为发生得早或结束得早。"就"前面必须有时间词语或其他表示时间早的词语。Indicating that an action or behavior happens or ends early. In this case, "就" must be preceded by a time phrase or some other phrases indicating early time.

(3) 他今天六点就起床了。

(4) 这件事我很早就知道了。

3. 表示前后两件事紧接着发生。句子中一般都有两个动作、行为。Indicating that two things happen fast, one close upon the heels of the other. In this case, the sentence usually contains two actions or behaviors.

(5) 我一毕业就工作了。

(6) 他一回到家就吃饭。

4. 表示在某种条件或可能情况下自然出现某种结果。多用于条件复句或假设复句。前一分句常有"只要、要是、既然"等词语呼应。Indicating the natural emergence or result when a certain condition or situation appears. This use is common in conditional or assumptive complex sentences. The first clause usually contains "只要, 要是, 既然" to echo with "就."

(7) 只要你说一声，我马上就去买。

(8) 既然明天是晴天，我们就去爬山吧。

5. 表示对比起来数目大、次数多、能力强。Indicating, in a comparison, a big amount, a greater capability or many times.

(9) 我一个人就吃了五十个饺子。

(10) 他一个人就干了三个人的活儿。

6. 放在两个相同成分的词语之间，表示容忍、让步。Showing tolerance or concession when placed between two similar components.

(11) 房间小点儿就小点儿吧，安静就行。

(12) 坏了就坏了吧，再买一个，反正也不贵。

7. 表示原来或早已这样。常与"本来、原来、开始"等词语连用。Used in combination with "本来, 原来, 开始," it means "That's what I thought" or "That's what it was."

(13) 我本来就不想去。

(14) 他原来就想这样做了。

8. 表示只，只有。"就"可以直接出现在名词或数量词前面。Meaning "只，只有." In this sense, "就" may be placed directly before a noun or a measure word.

(15) 我们班就我一个俄罗斯人。

(16) 我现在身边就一百块钱。

9. 表示坚决，不容易改变。Indicating one's resolution: one is unlikely to change one's mind.

(17) 他就不给你，你能怎么样！

(18) 我就不去！

10. 表示事实正是如此。Meaning "That

is the fact."

(19) 他就是我要找的人。

(20) 这种围巾就是我想要的。

11. 承接上文,得出结论。*Taking over what is said in a conversation and drawing a conclusion.*

① 承接对方的话,表示同意。*Taking over what is said in a conversation and expressing approval.*

(21) 好,你就这样去做吧。

(22) 我们就在这家饭店吃饭吧,我没有意见。

② 如果/只要/既然/因为/为了……就……。*Drawing a conclusion in the structure "如果/只要/既然/因为/为了...就...."*

(23) 为了你的健康,你就少抽一点儿烟吧。

(24) 你既然不想去,那就别去了。

③ 不……就不……。表示"如果不……就一定不……"。*"不...就不..." means "如果不...就一定不..."*

(25) 他说不要就不要,你给他再多的钱,他也不会要。

连词 *conj.*

表示假设的让步,相当于"即使",用于口语。*An equivalent to "即使," it is an assumptive concession. It is used in oral Chinese.*

(26) 他就(是)送给我,我也不要。

(27) 就(是)三天三夜不睡觉也做不完这工作啊。

介词 *prep.*

引进动作的对象、范围或行为的凭据。*Introducing the target of an action or scope or the basis of a certain behavior.*

(28) 就房子来说,你家比我家大。

(29) 大家就去哪儿旅游这个问题提了很多建议。

动词 *v.*

1. 凑近,靠近。后面要加"着"。*To get close to; to approach. It has to be followed by "着."*

(30) 他就着路灯看了一下手机。

(31) 停电了,他就着窗外的月光继续看书。

2. 趁着,借着。后面要加"着"。*To take advantage of; to make use of. It has to be followed by "着."*

(32) 阿里就着在中国留学的机会,旅游了很多地方。

(33) 就着这场雨,我们快把树种下去。

3. 表示搭配,"着"可加可不加。*To match. "着" following it may be omitted.*

(34) 绿衣服就着白裙子穿,特别好看。

(35) 辣椒酱就白米饭,他能吃两大碗。

4. 表示开始从事,参加到。*To start doing something; to participate in.*

(36) 他在电视上作了就职演说。

(37) 现在的大学都很关心学生的就业情况。

说明 Notes:

1. 使用"就"要注意:*When using "就," pay attention to the following points:*

① 强调在很久之前已经发生时,"就"前一定要有时间词或其他副词。见例(4)。*"就" has to be preceded by a time word or some other adverb if one is emphasizing something that happened long ago, as in (4).*

(38) 通知昨天就贴出来了。

② 表示两件事情紧接着发生时,两件事情有时属于同一主语,有时属于不同的主语。注意分辨。*When two things happened one close upon the heels of the other, they might belong to one and the same subject, but sometimes they don't.*

(39) 我听完就明白了。(同一主语,我听完我就明白了。*The same subject: I understand after I hear it.*)

(40) 他讲完就明白了。(不同的主语,他讲完我就明白了。*Different subjects: I understand after he explained it.*)

③ "就＋动＋数量"，"就"重读，说话人认为数量少，动词有时可以省略。"就"轻读，前面的词语重读，说话人认为数量多，动词也可以省略。When "就" in the structure "就 + v. + quantifier" is read with a stress, the speaker thinks it is a small number. The verb may be omitted. If "就" is read without a stress, then the speaker thinks it is a large number. And the verb can be omitted, too.

(41) 今天就学了一个小时。("就"重读，表示数量少。"就" is stressed to indicate a small number.)

(42) 老王就(是)买了五张票。("就"轻读，前面的"老王"重读，表示数量多。"就" is weakened after the stressed "老王" to indicate a large number.)

④ "就"用于复句,当前后分句的主语不同时，"就"应在主语后。When "就" appears in a complex sentence, it should be placed after the subject if the two clauses have two different subjects.

(43) *如果明天不下雨,就我去爬山。

(44) 如果明天不下雨,我就去爬山。

⑤ "就"作为连词表示假设让步关系时，多用于口语，"就"只用在前一分句的主语后、动词或形容词之前，后一分句常有"也"与之呼应。"就" often appears in oral Chinese when it is a conjunction to indicate an assumptive concession. In this case, "就" just appears behind the subject and before the verb in the first clause. "也" appears in the second clause to echo with it.

(45) *就你不去,也没关系。

(46) 你就不去,也没关系。

2. "就"和"即"都有副词用法，区别是，在表示时间的义项上，"就"都可以替代"即"，除此以外，"就"的其他用法，"即"都不能替代"就"。Both "就" and "即" can be used as an adverb. Their difference is that in a meaning related to time, "就" can be used to replace "即," but otherwise it cannot be replaced by "即."

3. "便"和"就"都有副词、连词、动词用法，一般用"便"的地方都可以换成"就"。但"就"的地方不一定能换成"便"。Both "便" and "就" can serve as an adverb, a conjunction, or a verb. Usually, "就" can be used where "便" is used. But where "就" is used, one may not necessarily use "便."

"便"和"就"的区别是：Their differences are as follows:

① "便"用于早期白话文，现代书面语。"就"通用于现代口语和书面语，使用范围比较广。"便" is used in early-stage vernacular Chinese and modern written Chinese. "就" is commonly used in both modern oral and written Chinese. Its scope of application is pretty wide.

② 当"就"表示"只、仅"或者强调语气的意思时，"就"不能换成"便"。"就" cannot be replaced by "便" when it means "only, merely" or when it is used for emphasis.

(47) *别人都不去,便我一人去。

(48) 别人都不去,就我一人去。

(49) *她说："我不去,便不去！"

(50) 她说："我不去,就不去！"

③ "就"可以表示规定或限制动作、行为的时间、范围，"便"不能。"就" may be used to specify or limit the time and scope of an action or behaviour. "便" does not have this use.

(51) 一切都准备好了,就等明天去机场了。

(52) 大家都来了,就等你一个人了。

jiùshì 就是

用法 Usage:
副词 ad.

1. 单独使用，表示同意，赞同，对。Used by itself, it means approval: "Right!" Or, "Agree! Agree!"

(1) 就是,就是,你说得完全对。

(2) 就是呀,这样做不是很好吗?

2. 表示坚决,不可更改。Indicating resoluteness. "It is unlikely to change."

(3) 他就是要那样做,我没办法。

(4) 我就是要出国,我已经决定了。

3. 强调某种性质和状态,含有反驳的意味。Emphasizing a certain quality or state. It is often used in refuting something.

(5) 他画的画就是好看,我喜欢他的画。

(6) 我做的饭就是比他做的好吃。

4. 强调动作迅速果断,快。"就是"后面带动量词。Emphasizing an action being fast, resolute and decisive. It is often followed by a dynamic measure word.

(7) 他抬腿就是一脚,把门踢开,把孩子抱了出来。

(8) 他伸手就是一拳,把玻璃窗砸碎了。

5. 指说话人认为数量多。"就是"直接带数量词。Indicating that the speaker thinks it is a large number. "就是" is followed directly by a measure word.

(9) 他一走就是好几个月。

(10) 我跟她一聊就是半天。

6. 表示很单纯,没有别的情况。后面的句子是对前面"这样、那样"的注释。Indicating it is as simple as that; nothing else. The second sentence is a footnote to "这样" or "那样" in the first sentence.

(11) 就是那样,他不喜欢喝咖啡。

(12) 就是这样,他去北京了。

连词 conj.

1. 表示让步关系,相当于"即使"。前面常用"不但/不仅,只要、别说"等呼应,后面要用"也"搭配。An equivalent to "即使," it indicates a concession. "不但/不仅,""只要,"or "别说" will appear in the first clause, and "也" will be present in concert in the second.

"就是"表示让步关系有两种情况:But be careful "就是" indicating a concession falls into two categories:

① "就是"后面涉及的是没有出现或不可能出现的情况,是一种假设性让步。The situation following "就是" is one that didn't appear or one that is unlikely to appear. This is an assumptive concession.

(13) 明天就是下雨,我也要去爬山。

(14) 别说是三百块,就是六百块,我也会买。

② "就是"后面涉及的是已经出现或存在的事实情况,"就是"只表示让步,不表示假设。The situation following "就是" is one that has already appeared or one that is an actual existence. In this case, "就是" indicates a concession, but it is not an assumption.

(15) 别说是稀饭,就是牛奶,他也喝不下。

(16) 只要是那个歌手开演唱会,别说是上海,就是北京,她也要去看。

2. 表示轻度转折关系。Indicating a light transition.

有两种情况:Again, it falls into two categories:

① 含有"不过"的意思,对前面句子所说的内容起限制、补充的作用。It means "不过," restricting or supplementing what is said in the first clause.

(17) 这种苹果很好吃,就是太贵了。

(18) 她排球打得很好,就是个子矮了一点儿。

② 含有"都是因为"的意思,解释动作、事件没有完成或没有做好的原因。It means "都是因为," explaining why the action was not completed or not done well.

(19) 我早就想请你吃饭了,就是最近工作太忙,实在没时间。

(20) 你这次考得那么差,就是平时不努力。

3. 与"不是"组成固定格式"不是……就是……",表示选择关系或列举。To form the structure "不是...就是..." with "不是." It shows alternatives.

(21) 你每天不是在公司,就是在家里,你的生活真没意思。

(22) 球赛好像不是今天,就是明天。

4. 连接两个部分,后一部分是对前一部分的解释或说明。Serving to join two parts, the second part being an explanation of the first.

有两种情况：Again, it falls into two categories:

① 相当于"即",连接的两部分是同位关系。An equivalent to "即," it joins two parts that are appositives.

(23) 国庆节假期,就是十月一日到七日。

② 连接的两部分不是同位关系。The two parts that are joined are not appositives.

(24) 写汉字还要注意的一点就是笔画一定要按顺序写。

说明 Notes:

1."就是"还有助词用法。用在句末,表示语气。"就是"后面多加"了"。"就是" may serve as an auxiliary. It appears at the end of a sentence, and it is often followed by "了."

有三种情况：There are three situations:

① 表示同意、答应,有顺从的意味。Indicating approval, it means the speaker is going along with someone.

(25) 你不要着急,我给你买就是了。

② 表示不用顾虑,不用担心的意味。Telling someone not to worry.

(26) 我不会跟别人说的,你放心就是了。

③ 与"罢了""而已"相似。Similar to "罢了,""而已."

(27) 你以为别人没意见吗? 别人只是不想说就是了。

2."就是"和"就"可以通用的义项：Situations where "就是" and "就" are the same and are interchangeable:

① 表示坚决、不容改变的意思时,可以通用。When it means resoluteness; or "it is unlikely to change."

(28) 我就/就是要去法国,我已经下定决心了。

② 表示"如果不……就不……"的意思,可以通用。When it means "如果不……就不…."

(29) 你不上课就/就是不上课,为什么要哭呢?

③ 指说话人认为数量多的意思时,可以通用。When the speaker thinks it is a large number.

(30) 他一买就/就是三件。

④ 表示确定范围,排除其他的意思时,可以通用。Indicating a designated scope, excluding all other possibilities.

(31) 别人都不能干,就/就是你能干!

⑤ 表示没有别的情况的意思时,可以通用。When the speaker means "That's all. (Nothing else.)"

(32) 就/就是这样,我来到中国了。

jiùshìshuō 就是说 →P643"这就是说"

用法 Usage:

位于一个句子后,表示解释说明,一般看成是插说。That is to say. When "就是说" appears at the end of a sentence, it stands for an explanation or some sort of parenthesis.

(1) 他不在了,就是说,他去世了。

(2) 我不打算买那套房子,就是说,我不喜欢那套房子。

说明 Notes:

"就是说"后面有停顿,也可以说成"这就是说"。There is a pause after "就是说." One can also say, "这就是说."

jiùsuàn 就算

用法 Usage:
连词 conj.

表示假设的让步,相当于"即使、即便",多用于口语。An equivalent to "即使,即便," it expresses an assumptive concession. This use is common in oral Chinese.

1."就算"与"也、还、总"等呼应,"就算"引出的分句表示假设的情况,后一分句表示不受这一假设情况的影响。"就算" is used to echo with "也，还，总." The clause introduced by "就算" indicates a hypothetical situation, while the latter clause indicates not being affected by the hypothetical situation.

（1）就算说错了，也没关系。
（2）就算大家都不相信你，我还是相信你。

2."就算"与"但是、难道、可是"等配合，后一分句表示强调以让步为前提的转折，后面的分句多为反问句。"就算" is used to echo with "但是，难道，可是." The second clause indicates that the turn is possible on the condition that the concession is made. The second clause is often written as a counter-question.

（3）就算你昨天没来，但是你为什么不打电话问一下呢？
（4）就算他做错了，难道你一点责任也没有吗？

jūrán 居然 →P247"竟然"

用法 Usage:
副词 ad.
表示出乎意料。"居然" always indicates unexpectedness.

有三种情况：There are three possible situations:

1.表示本来不应该发生的事竟然发生了。Indicating that something shouldn't have happened.

（1）他居然把时间看错了。
（2）我们都以为他俩不会好，他们居然结婚了。

2.表示本来不可能发生的事竟然发生了。Indicating that something impossible happened.

（3）医生说他的病治不好了，但是他居然好了。
（4）外面的音乐声那么大，你居然没听见？

3.表示本来不容易做到的事情竟然做到了。Indicating that something very difficult to do was done.

（5）他们的语言完全不通，居然成了好朋友。
（6）那么高的山，他居然爬上去了。

说明 Notes:
"居然"和"竟然"都表示出乎意料。Both "居然" and "竟然" indicate unexpectedness.

它们的区别是：Their differences are as follows:

1."居然"表示超出一般的常情常理，有转折意味。比"竟然"语义要重。"居然" is about something that exceeds common sense. It involves some turn in the development of a thing. It carries a more serious meaning than "竟然."

2."居然"可以位于主语前，也可以位于主语后。"竟然"只能用于主语后。"居然" may be placed either before or after the subject, but "竟然" can only appear before the subject.

（7）大家居然都通过了这次考试。
（8）居然大家都通过了这次考试。
（9）*竟然大家都通过了这次考试。
（10）大家竟然都通过了这次考试。

jūzhù 居住 →P682"住"

用法 Usage:
动词 v.
较长时间住在一个地方。To live in a place for a long time.

（1）在美国时，我一直居住在旧金山。

说明 Notes:
"居住"只能带数量词宾语，不能带名词宾语。"居住" can take a measure word as its object, but not a noun.

（2）必须居住一个月以上，才能领取居住证。

jǔbàn 举办 →P256"举行"

用法 Usage:
动词 v.
进行（活动），办理（事务）。To host (an event or activity); to handle (an affair, etc.).

(1) 这次运动会由两个大学共同举办。
(2) 他们正在为举办新年晚会做准备。

jǔdòng 举动 →P522"行动"

用法 Usage:
名词 n.

1. 表示人的动作，行动。Human action.
(1) 他的举动有点奇怪，快去看看他怎么啦。
(2) 你要考虑轻率的举动会带来什么后果。

2. 情况，状况。Situation; condition.
(3) 工作找不到，他下面会有什么举动呢？
(4) 这是个意外事件，接下来要注意他会发生什么异常举动。

说明 Notes:
"举动"的第二种用法，是对将来的一种预测。The second meaning of "举动" is just a forecast of what may happen in future.

jǔxíng 举行 →P255"举办"

用法 Usage:
动词 v.

进行（某种仪式、集会、比赛等）。To conduct (a ceremony, assembly, game, etc.).
(1) 下个月在我们学校要举行汉语研讨会。
(2) 这次网球比赛将在上海举行。

说明 Notes:
"举行"和"举办"都有"发起、兴办"的意思。Both "举行" and "举办" carry the meaning of hosting or conducting an activity.
它们的区别是：Their differences are as follows:

1. 在词义上，"举行"侧重于活动的实行、进行，多为时间和地点。"举办"重在办理、筹备、组织等工作。"举行" emphasizes conducting an activity, and often it is related to its time and place. "举办," by contrast, focuses on the organization and preparations of the event.
(3) 学校运动会什么时候举行？
(4) 学校运动会举办得怎么样？

2. "举行"的宾语常常是"集会、仪式、典礼、球赛"等，"举行"还可以带动词性宾语，如"会谈、谈判、游行、起义、比赛"等。"举办"不能带动词性宾语。"举行" takes as its object words such as "集会, 仪式, 典礼, 球赛." It may also be followed by an object carrying the features of a verb, such as "会谈, 谈判, 游行, 起义, 比赛." "举办," by contrast, cannot be followed by a verbal object.
(5) *两国政府将于下月举办会谈。
(6) 两国政府将于下月举行会谈。

3. "举办"大多带名词性宾语，常见有"讲座、学习班、报告会、展览、晚会"等，如果宾语是名词性短语，"举行"不能替代。"举办" is primarily followed by a noun as its object, such as "讲座, 学习班, 报告会, 展览, 晚会." If the object is a noun phrase, "举行" cannot be used to replace it.
(7) *下个月学院要举行京剧培训班。
(8) 下个月学院要举办京剧培训班。

4. "举行"重在进行，主语可以是"举行"的受事，当主语是"举行"的受事时，举办单位或举办者一般不出现，但是比较强调举行的场所、时间、情况等。"举行" emphasizes the on-going of an event, and its subject may be the object of "举行." And when that happens, the institution or the person who hosts the event usually is usually not mentioned. What is mentioned is often the time, place of the event and related things.
(9) 这次比赛在学校的体育馆举行。
(10) 演讲比赛于今天下午两点在礼堂举行。

5. "举办"重在办理，一般离不开举办的单位或举办者。所以主语常常是举办者单位或者举办人的名词。如果"举办"的宾语提前，位于主语前，举办单位或举办者则由介词"由"引进，或者谓语只是描述性内容。"举办" emphasizes handling various things, which cannot be done without the sponsor. And so, the subject of the sentence tends to be the name of the institution or person(s) hosting the event. If the object is placed before the subject, the institution or person(s) hosting the event will be introduced by the preposition "由," or the predicate will be simply something describing the event.

(11) 留学生自己举办了足球比赛。

(12) 这次的展览会由市政府举办。

(13) 新年晚会举办得很成功。

jùbèi 具备 →P257"具有"

用法 Usage:

动词 v.

具有,齐备。To be qualified for; to be well equipped.

(1) 这个大学已经具备举办大型国际会议的条件。

(2) 舞蹈演员必须具备良好的身体。

jùyǒu 具有 →P257"具备"、P590"拥有"

用法 Usage:

动词 v.

有。To have; to possess.

(1) 他对中国历史具有很大的兴趣。

(2) 这些建筑具有中国古典传统风格。

说明 Notes:

1. "具有"和"有"的区别如下：The differences between "具有" and "有" are as follows:

"具有"的意思是"有",只用于书面语,多带抽象的宾语。"有"的宾语既可以是具体的,也可以是抽象的。"具有" means "有." It appears only in written Chinese and usually takes abstract objects. As for "有," its objects may be either concrete or abstract.

(3) 他是一个具有乐观精神的人。

(4) 他是一个有乐观精神的人。

(5) 他有英文词典。

(6) *他具有英文词典。

2. "具备"和"具有"的区别如下：The differences between "具备" and "具有" are as follows:

① "具备"有"齐备"的意义,多用于较为具体的技能、条件、本领等,适用范围较小。在使用时,句子中常常会有表示条件的词语。"具有"没有这个意义。"具备" carries the meaning of "齐备." It applies mostly to concrete skills, conditions or capabilities, but its scope of application is rather limited. When it is used, the sentence often contains words indicating the necessary conditions. "具有" doesn't have this meaning.

(7) *一切条件都已具有,就等领导通知了。

(8) 一切条件都已具备,就等领导通知了。

② "具有"表示存在,除用于具体事物外,还可以用于意义、价值、作用等抽象概念,使用范围较广。如"具有浓厚兴趣、具有特殊风味、具有较高水平"等。"具备"不能替代其中的"具有"。"具有" is used in a wider scope. In addition to concrete things, it may also apply to abstract ideas such as meaning, value, and role, such as "具有浓厚兴趣,具有特殊风味,具有较高水平." "具备" cannot be used to replace "具有" in those expressions.

jù 据 →P166"根据"

用法 Usage:

动词 v.

1. 占据,占有。To occupy; to possess.

(1) 看到山顶上的红旗吗？爬到山上,据红旗者为胜。

(2) 这是大家用的词典,你不能据为己有！

2. 依靠,凭借。To depend on; to rely on.

(3) 这个仓库据山而建,比较坚固。

介词 prep.

依照,按照。On the basis of; according to.

(4) 这个电视剧据我所知是由小说改编的。

(5) 双方正在据理力争，都想得到这条河流的管理权。

名词 n.

可以用作证明的事物。可组成如"有据可证、言必有据、查无实据"等。Something that can serve as evidence. It can be used to form expressions such as "有据可证,言必有据,查无实据."

说明 Notes:

"据"和"根据"的区别是：The differences between "据" and "根据" are as follows:

1. "据"多用于书面语、四言词组。"根据"多用于口语。"据" appears mostly in written Chinese and 4-character expressions while "根据" appears mostly in oral Chinese.

2. 可以与单音节词组成双音节词，如"据说、据传"等。"根据"不能。"据" can pair with a monosyllabic word to form a dissyllabic word such as "据说,据传." But "根据" cannot.

3. "据"可以直接与"某人说、某人传、某人看来"等小句组合成"据某人说、据某人传、据某人看来"等短语。"根据"则常常先要把这些小句，改为名词性短语，才能组合成短语，如"根据某人说的、根据某人的看法、根据他的看法"等。"据" can pair directly with clauses such as "某人说,某人传,某人看来" to form phrases such as "据某人说,据某人传,据某人看来." As for "根据," we need to turn those clauses into noun phrases before forming phrases such as "根据某人说的,根据某人的看法,根据他的看法."

jùshuō 据说 →P466"听说"

用法 Usage:

据别人说，根据别人说（有时是有出处而不愿意说明）。常用于句首，作插入语。It is said; according to someone (the speaker doesn't want to disclose the sources). It usually appears as a parenthesis at the beginning of a sentence.

(1) 据说，她是我们班的老师。

(2) 据小王说，这个人武功很好。

juédìng 决定 →P258"决心"

用法 Usage:

动词 v.

1. 对如何行动定下主张。带宾语、补语。宾语往往是非名词性词语，带宾语时一般不带动态助词。To decide (e.g. what to do next). It is followed by an object or a complement. The object is usually a word, which is not a noun. And when followed by an object, it doesn't take a dynamic auxiliary.

(1) 我决定去北京工作。

(2) 到底去不去，你怎么还没决定啊？

2. 某一事物成为另一事物的先决条件。可带动态助词。(Of one thing) to become the prerequisite for another. It can take a dynamic auxiliary.

(3) 一个人的性格往往决定了一个人的命运。

(4) 成绩的好坏决定于一个人努力的多少。

名词 n.

1. 决定的事项。常带上定语一起充当句子相应的成分。A decision. It often takes an attribute along to play some role in a sentence.

(5) 下午就可以知道公司的决定。

(6) 经过三天时间的考虑，他才做了这个决定。

2. 做定语，表示某一事物的性质。To serve as an attribute and indicate the nature of a thing.

(7) 大自然对我们的生活环境最终起着决定的作用。

(8) 这场比赛对中国队来说具有决定意义。

juéxīn 决心 →P258"决定"

用法 Usage:

动词 v.

下决心。宾语常常是动词性短语或小句。To make up one's mind. Its object is often a verb phrase or a clause.

(1) 我决心从今天开始戒烟。
(2) 他决心一定要跟她做朋友。

名词 n.

坚定不移的意志。常做主语,或组成动词短语做状语。Determination; an unshakable will. Often it serves as the subject of a sentence or to form a verb phrase to be used as an adverbial.

(3) 我的决心是不会变的。
(4) 我相信你下决心一定能成功。

说明 Notes:

"决心"和"决定"都表示对某件事的决断。Both "决心" and "决定" indicate a decision made about something.

它们的区别是：Their differences are as follows:

1. 在词义上,"决定"着重在几种情况中,选择出自己的主张。"决心"着重于在犹豫的情况下,最后做出的决断。Semantically, "决定" focuses on making one's choice from a number of alternatives. "决心" emphasizes making the final decision although one is bothered by a great deal of hesitation.

(5) 他决定来中国留学。(可能曾经还有去别国留学的想法。He may have considered going to other countries.)
(6) 他决心来中国留学。(不再犹豫不定。He does not have any hesitation.)

2. 用作名词时,"决心"常见的搭配有"下决心、有决心、没有决心、表决心",也可以说"决心很大、决心不大、决心不足"等；用作动词时,"决心"必须带宾语,所带的宾语必须是谓语性的,如"决心学好汉语、决心不让父母失望、决心打赢这场比赛"等。"决定"可以不带宾语。As a noun, "决心" often goes with "下决心, 有决心, 没有决心, 表决心." One can also say "决心很大, 决心不大, 决心不足," etc. As a verb, "决心" must be followed by an object, which bears the nature of a predicate. For example, we say, "决心学好汉语,决心不让父母失望,决心打赢这场比赛." "决定," by contrast, doesn't have to have an object.

(7) *去哪儿你决心吧。
(8) 去哪儿你决定吧。

jué 绝

用法 Usage:

形容词 a.

1. 独一无二的,高超的,没人能赶上的。Unique; superlative; being over and above everyone else.

(1) 他的表演简直是绝技。
(2) 大家都说他切菜的功夫真绝。

2. 走不通的,没有出路的。Desperate; hopeless.

(3) 昨天爬山遇到危险,好在我们绝处逢生。
(4) 生活几乎把他推到了绝境。

副词 ad.

1. 绝对。用在否定词"不、无、非"等前面,表示完全否定,排除任何例外。做状语。Absolutely; by any means. It is placed before "不, 无, 非" to mean a complete negation. Usually it serves as an adverbial.

(5) 你说我也想吃？不,我绝无此意。
(6) 你这个决定,我绝不同意。

2. 极,最。限用于某些形容词的前面,表示程度深,但不能用在和这些形容词意义相反的词语前面。做状语。Extremely; utmost. It is limited to being placed before a few adjectives, indicating a deep degree. But it cannot be placed before words whose meanings are just the opposite of those adjectives. It serves as an adverbial.

(7) 他绝少参加这种晚会。
(8) 绝大部分同学都参加了这次活动。

动词 v.

1. 断绝。To block; to sever relations.

(9) 你不要绝了别人的生路。
(10) 听说他们两人绝交了。

2. 完全没有了,穷尽。*To be exhausted; to run out of.*

(11) 办法都想绝了,他的病就是好不起来。

(12) 战争时代,弹尽粮绝是常有的情况。

juéduì 绝对

用法 Usage:

形容词 *a.*

1. 没有任何条件的,不受任何限制的(跟"相对"相对),完全。*Absolutely; completely; unconditionally. It is the opposite of "相对 (comparatively)."*

在句子中可以做以下成分:*It can play the following roles in a sentence:*

① 在名词前,做定语。*As an attribute before a noun.*

(1) 这个世界上,没有绝对的事情。

(2) 对任何人都不能作绝对的否定。

② 做谓语。"绝对"前常加"太、很"等程度副词。*As the predicate. Used this way, "绝对" is often preceded by degree adverbs such as "太" and "很."*

(3) 你这么说太绝对了。

(4) 看一个人不能很绝对,要客观。

③ 做补语。*As the complement.*

(5) 这件事你说得太绝对了。

(6) 话说得太绝对,不太好。

④ 可用于"是……的"格式中。*To appear in the structure "是…的."*

(7) 运动不是绝对的,静止也不是绝对的。

(8) 每个人的看法不一样,所以美也不是绝对的。

副词 *ad.*

表示完全、一定。*Completely; certainly.*

1. 用于肯定句,常和助动词配合使用,做状语。*In a positive sentence, it often goes with an auxiliary verb to serve as an adverbial.*

(9) 他既然说了会去,就绝对会去。

(10) 这绝对是个错误。

2. 用在动词、形容词前,做状语。*Placed before a verb or an adjective to serve as an adverbial.*

(11) 绝对禁止贩卖人口。

(12) 那家饭店的菜绝对好吃。

3. 排除任何可能性。用于否定词前,加强否定,做状语。*Excluding all possibilities. It is placed before a negative word to highlight a negation. It serves as an adverbial.*

(13) 我绝对不会做这种事。

(14) 考试的时候,绝对不能作弊。

K k

kāi 开

用法 Usage:

动词 *v.*

1. 把关闭着的东西打开。可以重叠,可以在别的动词后做补语。*To open; turn on; switch on. It is often followed by such words as "着" or "了," and it can be used in its reduplicated form and act as a complement to another verb.*

(1) 妈妈,请开开门,我回来了。

(2) 天黑了,开灯吧!

2. 打通,开辟。*To open; to open up.*

(3) 我们山区的公路开通了。

(4) 村民开山造林,绿化了两座山。

3. (合拢的东西)舒张,(连接的东西)分离。*(Of closed things) to open up; (of connected things) to separate.*

(5) 前几天还是花苞,太阳一出来全开了。

(6) 你的衣服扣儿开了。

4. 解除(封锁、禁令、限制等)。*To lift (a blockade, ban, restriction, etc.).*

(7) 伊斯兰教的同学今天开斋了。

(8) 他戒烟戒了两个月,昨天又开戒了。

5. 发动或操纵(枪、炮、飞机、车船、机器、机械等)。*To start to operate; to set in motion (a gun, aircraft, vehicle, ship, machines, etc.).*

(9) 现在开车的人越来越多了。

(10) 谁想开飞机,可以到航空俱乐部去。

6. 开办,建立(工厂、商店、医院等)。*To set up (a factory, shop, hospital, etc.).*

(11) 如果找不到工作,我就开一家商店。

(12) 我们小区开了一家老人福利院。

7. 开始。*To begin; to start.*

(13) 工厂元宵节后开工。

(14) 中小学生都在九月一日开学。

8. 举行(会议、座谈会、展览会等)。*To hold or sponsor (a meeting, discussion, exhibition, etc.).*

(15) 明天学院开会欢迎新生。

(16) 阿里在活动室开了一个摄影展览会。

9. (液体)受热而沸腾。*(Of liquid) to boil.*

(17) 水开了,可以放饺子了。

10. (饭菜等)摆出来(让人吃)。*To get the food ready.*

(18) 现在食堂还没到开饭时间呢。

11. 开除,革除。*To dismiss or expel somebody.*

(19) 他被老板开了。

12. 写出(单据、发票等),说出(价钱)。*To write out (a document, invoice, prescription, etc.); to offer (a price).*

(20) 医生给我开了两张药方。

(21) 这件衣服开价不高。

13. 指按十分之几的比例分开(多用于分配或评价)。*(Often used in distribution or evaluation) to divide by percentage.*

(22) 根据合同,每年利润我们跟他们四六开。

14. 开设，设置。*To offer; to establish*

(23) 这个学期学院新开了两门选修课。

(24) 我家附近新开了一家便利店。

15. 趋向动词，用在别的动词后面做趋向补语，表示各种意思。*(As a directional verb) to serve as a complement to another verb, indicating the direction or expressing a different idea.*

① 表示离开或分开。*Indicating the direction of movement.*

(25) 大家在这里等一下，不要走开。

(26) 把窗打开，让阳光进来！

② 表示展开或扩大。*Spreading or expanding.*

(27) 玛丽得了奖学金的消息一下子就传开了。

(28) 这把雨伞打不开了。

③ 比喻（思想）开阔或（把事情搞）清楚。*(Of mind) to be optimistic; (of a matter) to remove a misunderstanding.*

(29) 找个女朋友不难，你一定要想开点。

(30) 我们俩还是把误会说开了吧？

④ 表示开始并继续下去。*(Of an action) to begin or continue.*

(31) 他还没说完话，大家就笑开了。

(32) 望着她的背影，我就想开了我们的将来。

说明 Notes:

1. "开开"是动词重叠，如："你开开窗吧！" "开开"也可以是动补结构，如："他把门锁开开了。" *The expression "开开" can be a reduplicated verb. For example, "你开开窗吧！" "开开" can also be used as a verb-complement construction. For example, "他把门锁开开了。"*

2. "开"与不同的词语按照不同的语法要求组成句子，表示不同的意思，是个多义词。使用时必须注意前后搭配的词语的意思，确定"开"的意思。*"开" is a polysemous word which bears different meanings when used with different words to form a sentence in accordance with different grammatical requirements. In that case, the meaning of "开" must be decided by the context.*

kāifā 开发

用法 Usage:

动词 *v.*

1. 开采，发掘（土地、矿山等自然资源等）。*To exploit; to open up (natural resources such as land, mines, etc.).*

(1) 农村要大力开发风力发电。

(2) 我们已经在东海开发石油了。

2. 发现、发掘并利用（人才、技术等）。*To develop and utilize (talent, technology, etc.)*

(3) 小王的工作是开发人才。

(4) 华为公司不断开发出新手机。

3. 开辟，发现（使发挥作用）。*To discover; to open up (new resources, new products, etc. in order to allow them to play their roles).*

(5) 近年来，我的家乡开发了三个旅游景点。

(6) 公司要发展，就要不断开发新产品。

说明 Notes:

"开发"的宾语范围较广。第一义项中，"开发"的宾语常是"荒山、矿藏、森林、水利"等。第二义项中，"开发"的宾语常是"人才、技术、能源"等。第三个义项中"开发"的宾语常是"新景点、新旅游点、新产品"等。*The objects of "开发" cover a wide range of fields. In its first meaning, the objects of "开发" are almost always natural resources as "荒山,矿藏,森林,水利." In the second meaning, "开发" is often followed by objects such as "人才,技术,能源." In the third meaning, "开发" is used with words that indicate new things such as "新景点,新旅游点,新产品."*

kāifàng 开放

用法 Usage:

动词 *v.*

1. （指花朵）展开，跟"凋谢"相对。*(Of*

flowers) to bloom. It is opposite to "凋谢 (wither)."

（1）院子里的玫瑰花开放了。

2. 解除封锁、禁令、限制等，跟"封锁"相对。To lift a blockade, ban, or restriction. It is opposite to "封锁 (blockade)."

（2）农村经济要发展，必须改革开放农贸市场。

（3）机场只关闭了半天，很快就开放了。

3.（指公共场所，如博物馆、图书馆等公共场所）接待游人、读者等，跟"关闭"相对。(Of public places, such as museums, libraries) to receive visitors, readers. It is opposite to "关闭 (close up)."

（4）杭州西湖景区向游客免费开放。

（5）图书馆上午9点开放。

形容词 *a.*

形容性格开朗，思想开通，不受拘束。Showing a cheerful disposition; an open and unrestricted mind.

（6）我们班老师的思想很开放。

（7）这姑娘长得很漂亮，性格也很开放。

kāishǐ 开始 →P703"最初"

用法 Usage:

动词 *v.*

1. 以某一点作为起始（跟"结束"相对）。To start at a certain point (opposite to "结束").

（1）快进去吧，电影开始了。

（2）我们从汉语语音开始学。

2. 着手进行（跟"结束"相对）。To start to do something (opposite to "结束").

（3）我准备好了，可以开始考试了吗？

（4）生日晚会现在开始！

3. 着手做某事。To set out to do something.

（5）孩子开始学英语了。

（6）他开始做饭了。

名词 *n.*

开头的阶段，开初（跟"最后、最终"相对）。The beginning stage (opposite to "最后" and "最终").

（7）这是一个很好的开始。

（8）开始我不认识他，现在我们是好朋友了。

说明 Notes:

"开始"着重从头起或从某一点起，可带宾语，一般带谓词性宾语。通用于口语和书面语。"开始" emphasizes starting from the beginning or from a certain point, which can be followed by an object, usually a predicate object. It can be used in both spoken and written language.

kāitōng 开通

用法 Usage:

动词 *v.*

1. 使线路畅通，多指电讯、网络等线路开始使用。To open lines, usually referring to lines for telecommunications and network.

（1）手机还没开通，现在不能打电话。

（2）我的信用卡刚刚开通了网上银行。

2. 开掘，使通畅（与"堵塞"相对）。多指交通、河道等。To open; to keep clear (usually refers to the traffic or river, etc.). It is opposite to "堵塞 (block)."

（3）山区到城里的公路去年开通了。

（4）河道开通了，可以坐船去外婆家。

3. 开导，使转变（与"闭塞"相对）。多指原来闭塞的思想、风气等。To enlighten; to change It usually refers to the narrow-minded and the general mood of society, and is opposite to "闭塞."

（5）要开通山里人的风气，开放他们的思想。

（6）让她到外面走走看看，开通开通思想。

形容词 *a.*

1. 指思想开明、通达（与"保守、守旧"相对）。Open-minded. It is opposite to "保守 (conservative)" or "守旧 (old-fashioned)."

（7）他母亲是个思想开通的女性。

2. 做事大方,不拘谨。Generous.

(8) 她很开通,见到不认识的人很大方。
(9) 在钱的问题上,他是个很开通的人。

kāiyèchē 开夜车

用法 Usage:

1. 在夜间开车。To drive at night.
(1) 开夜车的司机白天一定要休息好。
(2) 你开了两天夜车,今天不能再开了。
2. 比喻为了赶时间在夜间继续工作或学习。To indicate working late into the night; to burn the midnight oil.
(3) 小张在学习上,从来不开夜车。
(4) 为了这次考试,他已经开了好几天夜车了。

说明 Notes:

"开夜车"的比喻用法,只运用于工作和学习方面。不用于娱乐等其他方面。The figurative usage of "开夜车" can only be used when you stay up late for work or study. It cannot be used for recreation or other fun activities.

kāizhǎn 开展 →P634"展开"

用法 Usage:
动词 v.

1. 使某件事、某项工作从小向大,由浅到深地发展。To carry on; to conduct (a job or something), expanding it in size or depth.
(1) 我们学院与国外五十多所大学开展了交流。
(2) 开展话题讨论,提高了学生的口语水平。
2. 某件事、某项工作从小向大,由浅到深地发展。(Of a job or something) to develop in size or depth.
(3) 环境保护的活动已经开展起来了。
(4) 写汉字比赛的活动开展得很好。
3. 是"开始展出"的缩略语,多指某某展览会开始展出。As a contraction of "开始展出" (launch the exhibition), it means that an exhibition has just started.
(5) 留学生的摄影展览明天开展。
(6) 我们的书法展今天开展了。

kàn 看 →P223"见"、P267"看见"

用法 Usage:
动词 v.

1. 使视线接触人或物。观看,阅读。可带名词、动词、小句等宾语。To look at; to watch; to read. It can take a noun, verb or a clause as its object.
(1) 昨天晚上我看电影了。
(2) 我看过他们俩的乒乓球比赛。
2. 观察。可重叠,宾语多为抽象名词或问句形式的小句。To observe. It can be used in the reduplicated form and take as its object an abstract noun or clause that is in the form of a question.
(3) 每个人看问题都有自己的角度。
(4) 你去看看他们在干什么。
3. 诊治(病人接受医生的治疗,医生给病人诊治),可重叠。To diagnose, meaning that a patient receives a doctor's treatment or a doctor treats a patient. It can be reduplicated.
(5) 你的病要去医院看看。
(6) 医生看好了他的病。
4. 访问,探望。可以重叠。必定带名词宾语。To visit somebody. It can be used in the reduplicated form and it must take a noun as its object.
(7) 星期天我要去看看黄老师。
(8) 如果她来中国,就会来看我。
5. 观察后,做出判断,相当于"以为、认为"。常带动词、小句作的宾语。"看"后面可以停顿。主语是第一人称时,句子为陈述句。主语是第二人称时,句子为问句。一般不用于第三人称。To observe and judge. It bears the same meaning as "以为 (think)" or "认为 (consider)." It usually takes a verb or clause as

its object. There might be a pause after "看." When the subject is the first person, the sentence is in the declarative form. When the subject is the second person, the sentence is in the interrogative form. The third person is generally not used as the subject.

(9) 我看今年不会下雪。你看今年会下雪吗？

(10) 我看，她的主意不错。你看怎么样？

6. 小心，注意。用于祈使句，提醒对方。可带名词、动词做宾语。动词做宾语，不再带名词宾语时，必定带"着"。To take care; watch out. Used in the imperative form to remind somebody of something, it takes a noun or a verb as its object. However, when the object is a verb instead of a noun, it should be followed by "着."

(11) 过马路时，要看两边的车辆！

(12) 别跑那么快，看摔着！

7. 对待，看待。常用在"把"字句的句末，或者用在有疑问代词的问句。To treat; regard. It is usually used at the end of a sentence in the "把" structure, or in an interrogative sentence with a pronoun.

(13) 我一直把你当妹妹看。

(14) 她已经这样做了。你怎么看？

8. 决定于，取决于。句子常分为两个部分，或两个分句。前一部分讲某一件事，后一部分讲实现这一件事，决定于怎么样，或决定于什么、决定于谁。To depend on. The sentence is often divided into two parts or two clauses. The first part talks about one thing, and the second part tells the dependent condition of the following question word, such as: how, what and who.

(15) 学习得好不好，就看你努力不努力。

(16) 你是不是第一名，就看最后的比赛了。

说明 Notes:

一、"看"的其他用法如下：Other usages of "看" are as follows:

1. 看(kàn)。"看" pronounced as "kàn."

① 照顾，照料，守护。To take care of; to tend to.

(17) 妈妈又要看老人，又要看孩子，真的很忙。

(18) 他找了一个看停车场的工作。

② 看管，看押，监视。To keep someone under surveillance; to keep an eye on.

(19) 看着这个小偷，别让他跑了。

2. "看"还有助词用法，用在动词(动词重叠、动词带动量词、时量词)后面，表示尝试的意思，多用于第一人称、第二人称。Auxiliary usage of "看": It is used after the verb (reduplicated verb, verb with a quantifier or temporal quantifier), which means "try." The subject is usually the first person or the second person.

(20) 你尝尝看，饺子好不好吃？

(21) 这十个词语你再读一下看！

3. 在句子中做插入语，对果然不出所料的事，表示感叹。Used as a parenthesis to express exclamation for expected things.

(22) 我说他不在家，看，屋里没人吧！

二、"看"和"见"的区别是：The differences between "看" and "见" are as follows:

在词义上，与人见面的情况下，"见"是"会见、接见"的意思，一般用在外交关系等比较正式的人际关系场合，有主客、大小或者上下级之分。"看"是"访问、探望"的意思。带有关怀、友好的情感色彩，多用在友情、亲情等的人际关系。Semantically, when people meet, "见" means "会见，接见." It is generally used for formal interpersonal relations such as on diplomatic occasions, where there are clear divisions of hosts and guests; seniors and juniors; superiors and subordinates. When "看" means "访问，探望," it carries an emotional tone of care or closeness. It is usually used to show kinship or friendship.

(23) *我姐姐常常来见我。

(24) 我姐姐常常来看我。
(25) *听说学院领导要看我们新来的留学生。
(26) 听说学院领导要见我们新来的留学生。

kànbuqǐ 看不起

用法 Usage:
动词 v.
表示轻视、小看别人的意思(与"看得起"相对),常用于口语。To show contempt for someone or something; underestimate someone or something (opposite to "看得起"). It is commonly used in spoken language.
(1) 你不要看不起这种工作。
(2) 城里人不要看不起农民工。
(3) 别看不起这本小词典,学汉语它很有用。
说明 Notes:
1. "看不起"常用于口语,表示程度很深时,前面可以加"很、非常、十分"等副词。"看不起" is often used in colloquial language. Such adverbs as "很,非常,十分" can be put in front of it to intensify the degree.
2. "看不起"作为一个词语用。"看不起"的对象可以是人,也可以是职业,甚至物品,如例(1)(3)。When "看不起" is used as a phrasal verb, its object can be a person, an occupation, or even an article, as in (1) and (3).

kànchéng 看成

用法 Usage:
1. 视……为,把……看作(具有某种特性或身份)。To take a person or thing for another; to see someone or something as having some characteristics or identity.
(1) 你把我看成傻瓜了。
(2) 我把你送的生日礼物看成是最宝贵的。
2. 把……看作(看错了)。To mistake a person or thing for another.
(3) 玛丽把"夫"字看成"天"字了。
(4) 我把那个人看成是我弟弟了。

说明 Notes:
"成"是"看"的补语,表示成功、完成、实现。否定形式,前面加"没/没有"。"成" is the complement of "看," which means succeeding in doing, completing or realizing something. The negative form of it is to put "没/没有" in front of it.
(5) 昨天的京剧你有没有看成?
(6) 昨天我有事,没看成。

kànchū 看出

用法 Usage:
通过观察感觉到,察觉,发现。To perceive through observation; to be conscious of; to discover.
(1) 从他脸上的表情,我看出他有些生气了。
(2) 王经理一下子就看出了问题。
说明 Notes:
"看出"的否定形式是"没看出"或"看不出"。The negative form of "看出" is "没看出" or "看不出."
(3) 我没看出他心里不高兴。
(4) 从他的习惯,看不出他是个很随便的人。

kàndào 看到 →P267"看见"

用法 Usage:
动词 v.
1. 视线接触到,看见。To see; to catch sight of.
(1) 前面左拐就能看到百货大楼。
(2) 他的眼睛现在什么也看不到了。
2. 看出,觉察到。To perceive; to be aware of.
(3) 困难的时候要看到自己的力量,看到希望。
(4) 我看到他的健康状况正在好起来。
说明 Notes:
"看到"是动补结构的离合动词,中间可以插进其他词语,如"看得到、看不到"。"看到"

is a verb complement structure and it can have other words inserted into it, such as "看得到,看不到."

kàndeqǐ 看得起

用法 Usage:

动词 v.

重视,看重,(与"看不起""轻视"相对),常用于口语。To value someone or something. It is the opposite of "看不起" and often used in oral Chinese.

(1) 你要是看得起我,今天就到我家吃饭。
(2) 你首先要看得起别人,别人才会看得起你。

说明 Notes:

"看得起"作为一个词语用,有固定的词义,跟可能补语形式"我有钱,看得起病"中的"看得起(动补结构的可能补语)"意思完全不同,不能混淆。因为词语形式一样,它们的具体意义通过它们前后的语境、语用条件进行区别。When used as a phrase, "看得起" has a fixed meaning, which is completely different from the complement form of "看得起" in the sentence of "我有钱,看得起病." Because of the same form and structure, the exact meaning has to be differentiated from the contextual or pragmatic conditions.

kànhǎo 看好

用法 Usage:

动词 v.

1.(事物)将要出现好的势头。否定形式为"不看好"。(Of something) to show a favorable tendency. The negative form is "不看好."

(1) 未来两年股市仍然看好。
(2) 今年雨水充足,粮食收成看好。

2. 认为(人或事物)将要向好的方向发展。否定形式为"不看好"。To believe that (someone or something) will develop in the right direction. The negative form is "不看好."

(3) 我们公司对海南旅游市场的前景十分看好。
(4) 这场比赛,人们看好上海队。

3. 辨认清楚。否定形式为"看不好"。To identify clearly. Its negative form is "看不好."

(5) 东西看好了再买,买了以后不能退换!
(6) 那东西是真是假,我一时还看不好。

kànjiàn 看见 →P223"见"、P266"看到"

用法 Usage:

动词 v.

看到。可带名词、代词、小句做的宾语。To see. It can take a noun, pronoun or clause as its object.

(1) 我没看见过大海。
(2) 一出车站,他就看见我了。
(3) 我看见她和朋友出去了。

说明 Notes:

1. 使用"看见"时要注意：Attention should be paid to the following aspects while using "看见":

① "看见"是离合动词,中间可以加"得"或"不",如"看得见、看不见"。"看见" is a separable verb and "得" or "不" can be inserted between the two characters, such as "看得见,看不见."

② "看见"的否定式是"没看见",一般不用"不看见"。The negative form of "看见" is "没看见" instead of "不看见."

2. "看"和"看见"的区别是：The differences between "看" and "看见" are as follows:

① "看"表示动作本身。"看见"主要表示动作结果。"看" indicates the action, while "看见" emphasizes the result.

② "看"是持续性动词,可以重叠,前面可以加"正、正在",表示动作进行状态,"看"后面可以带时间量词。"看见"不是持续性动词,没有以上的用法。"看" is a continuous verb that can be reduplicated; words such as "正, 正在" can be put before "看" to indicate a sustaining action. Temporal quantifiers can be used after "看." But "看见" is not a continuous verb and doesn't have the above usages.

（4）你的手机让我看看好吗？
（5）那本杂志他正看着呢。
（6）这本书你借我看一天，好吗？

以上三个句子中的"看"都不能用"看见"替代。 In the three sentences above, "看" cannot be replaced by "看见."

3. "看见"与"看到"的区别是： The differences between "看见" and "看到" are as follows:

① "看见"与"看到"词义基本相同。但"看见"多用于看见具体的事物。"看到"的事物可以是具体的，也可以是抽象的。 The meanings of "看见" and "看到" are similar. However, "看见" always refers to the sight of concrete things; while the objects of "看到" can either be concrete or abstract things.

（7）她看见/看到你们在饭店喝啤酒。
（8）*你应该看见她的进步。
（9）你应该看到她的进步。

② "看见"中的"见"，可以单独使用，意思一样。"看到"中的"到"，不能单独使用。 The character "见" in "看见" can be used separately, which has the same meaning as "看见；" while the character "到" in "看到" cannot be used separately.

（10）我看见过她。
（11）我见过她。
（12）我看到过她。
（13）*我到过她。

kànlái 看来 →P268"看起来"、P268"看样子"

用法 Usage：

根据经验或已知情况作出大概的推断。用作插入语，可以在主语前面，也可以在主语后面。用逗号点开，插入句子使用。 To make a speculation according to an understanding of the situation. As a parenthesis, it can be used before or after the subject and can be separated by a comma when inserted in the sentence.

（1）已经十一点了，这些作业看来今天做不完了。
（2）看来，她还没有做出决定。
（3）她看来还没做出决定。

kànqǐlái 看起来 →P268"看来"、P268"看样子"

用法 Usage：

意思和用法相当于"看来"，用作插入语。"看起来"在句中多用逗号点开。 To figure out; to estimate. It is equivalent to "看来" both in meaning and usage. As a parenthesis, it is often separated with a comma when used in a sentence.

（1）风刮得很厉害，看起来天要下雨了。
（2）看起来，你对中国书法很有研究。
（3）已经这么晚了，看起来，他今天不来了。

说明 Notes：

"看起来"和"看来"这两个词语基本可以互换使用，尤其是在用"看起来"的句子中，都可以用"看来"代替。 "看起来" and "看来" are usually interchangeable. "看起来" can always be replaced by "看来" in the sentence.

kànyàngzi 看样子 →P268"看来"、P268"看起来"

用法 Usage：

根据某种外表现象，做出某种预测或猜测。用作插入语，多用逗号点开。 To make a prediction or guess on the basis of a certain outward appearance. As a parenthesis, it is often separated with a comma when used in a sentence.

（1）看样子，你今天考得很好。
（2）她今天脸色不太好。看样子，昨天晚上没睡好。

说明 Notes:

"看来""看起来""看样子"都是插入语,都有表示猜测、估计的意思,但是猜测、估计的事实根据有所侧重。"看来,看起来,看样子" are all used as parenthesis. All of them can mean "to make a prediction or estimate." However, the emphasis might be slightly different.

1. "看来""看起来"侧重某种情况、因素的分析后产生推断、猜测和估计。"看来" and "看起来" emphasize "making a speculation or estimate after the analysis of a certain situation or factor."

2. "看样子"侧重对外表现象的分析后产生猜测或估计。"看样子" emphasizes "making a prediction or guess on the basis of a certain outward appearance."

kāngkǎi 慷慨 →P84"大方"

用法 Usage:
形容词 a.

1. 多形容经济方面不吝;大方(与"吝啬"相对)。Generous in giving and spending; not stingy. It is the opposite of "吝啬 (miserly)."

(1) 他今天很慷慨啊,在那么贵的饭店请客。

(2) 她是个慷慨大方的姑娘。

2. 形容情绪激动,意气昂扬。多用于固定词组、书面语。如:"慷慨陈词、慷慨激昂"等。Excited; in high spirits. It often appears in fixed expressions and written language such as "为人慷慨 (be generous),慷慨陈词 (express oneself excitedly),慷慨激昂 (be excited)."

说明 Notes:

"大方""慷慨"都表示不小气、不吝啬的意思。Both "大方" and "慷慨" mean not stingy or miserly.

它们的区别是:Their differences are as follows:

1. "大方"一般用于口语。"慷慨"一般用于书面语。"大方" is used in oral Chinese while "慷慨" appears in written Chinese.

2. "大方"可以按形容词重叠方式重叠为"大大方方"。"慷慨"不能重叠。"大方" may be repeated as an adjective and so we have "大大方方," but "慷慨" cannot be repeated.

3. "大方"和"慷慨"各自都有别的词义和用法。Each has its own different meanings and usages.

kǎochá 考察

用法 Usage:
动词 v.

1. 实地观察调查。To do an on-the-spot observation and investigation.

(1) 张经理上个星期去法国考察了。

(2) 他去考察南极的地形去了。

2. 反复检验、考研和观察。可以重叠使用。To inspect, examine or observe repeatedly. It can be reduplicated as "考察考察."

(3) 这个项目还需要再考察考察。

(4) 老师考察了很长时间,觉得他真是个学习语言的天才。

名词 n.

实地观察调查或细致深刻观察的过程。The process of field observation and investigation, or the process of careful and thorough observation.

(5) 这次考察,他得到了很多第一手材料。

(6) 他花了几个晚上整理出了南极考察的资料。

kào 靠

用法 Usage:
动词 v.

1. 人或者事物凭借别的人或事物支持着。(Of a person or a thing) to be supported by another person or thing; to lean against.

(1) 他的头靠在沙发上睡着了。

(2)把那堆书靠在墙上,不会倒下。

2.接近,挨近。指动态的移动的动作。To approach. It is used to refer to a dynamic movement.

(3)你往我这边靠一靠,让他走过去。

(4)有一排自行车倒了,杂乱地靠在人行道上。

3.(指位置)临近,邻近。(Of a place) to be close to.

(5)书店靠着邮局,你走过去就看到了。

(6)我们老家的房子,前靠河,后靠山,环境好极了。

4.依靠,依赖。To depend on; to rely on.

(7)父亲去世后,我家的生活就靠妈妈一个人工作。

(8)在国外留学,生活都要靠自己,不能总是靠朋友。

5.可信任,信赖。To be reliable.

(9)小刘很靠得住,他办事你就放心吧。

(10)小王这人有时候靠不住,做事马马虎虎的。

介词 prep.

组成介词短语,用在动词前,表示动作行为所凭借的手段、工具或依据。Used to form a prepositional phrase, it appears before a verb as a means, a tool, or a basis for an action.

(11)任何事情只有靠自己的努力才能成功。

(12)有的农民工就靠双手打工赚钱,回家盖起了楼房。

说明 Notes:

注意"靠"的动词用法和介词用法。"靠"作动词用,后面一般是名词或名词性短语,如例(7)(8)。"靠"作介词用,名词或名词性短语后面还要有动词或动词性短语,如例(11)(12)。When "靠" is used as a verb, it is generally followed by a noun or noun phrase, as in (7) and (8). When "靠" is used as a preposition, the noun and noun phrase should be followed by a verb or verb phrase, as in (11) and (12).

kě 可

用法 Usage:

副词 ad.

用在陈述句、疑问句、感叹句、祈使句中,起强调各种语气的作用,多用于口语。It may appear in a declarative, interrogative, exclamatory or imperative sentence to strengthen the tone. It is usually used in oral Chinese.

1.用于陈述句,表示加强肯定、强调的语气,有时含有申辩或声明的语气。与"好"配合使用,有时表示否定的语气。When used in a declarative sentence, it indicates a tone of affirmation or emphasis, and sometimes, a tone of argument or a statement. When used with "好," it can indicate a negative tone.

①"可+动/形""可+动/形短语"。如果谓语是单独的动/形,句末常带"了"。"可+v./a."; "可+v.-phrase/a.-phrase." If the predicate is a separate verb or adjective, the sentence often ends with "了."

(1)她可会吃了。一次能吃四个肉包子。

(2)他们俩可好了,每天都在一起。

(3)我可知道他为什么不喜欢你的原因。

②"可+不+形"。后面形容词一般有消极的评判意味。"可+不+a." The adjective generally bears the meaning of a negative judgment.

(4)星期天要洗的衣服可不少。

(5)这种话可不是随便能说的。

③"可+好"(在有表示否定语义的分句中)构成反语,表示否定语气。"可+好" (in clauses with a negative meaning). It forms an irony, indicating a negative tone.

(6)你这么一说可好啦,老师给我们的作业更多了。

(7)这下可好,连电灯也不亮了。

④ 表示申辩或声明的语气. Indicate the tone of an argument or statement.

(8)你再不说,我可要生气了。

(9) 那些话可不是我说的。

2. 用在疑问句里,表示或加强疑问的语气。When used in a question, it expresses or reinforces the interrogative mood.

① 用在一般的疑问句中,句子里可有表示疑问的助词或代词。如果句子里没有疑问助词或代词,"可"含有"是否"的意思。In a general question, there may be an interrogative particle or pronoun indicating the question. If there are no interrogative particles or pronouns, "可" bears the meaning of "是否."

(10) 这么重的箱子,我一个人可怎么拿呀?

(11) 你来中国后,可去过别的城市?

② 用在反问句里表示或加强反问的语气。In a rhetorical question, it indicates or reinforces the tone.

(12) 大家都说他生病了,可谁去宿舍看过他了?

(13) 你总说去买衣服,可什么时候你去买过了?

3. 用在感叹句里,表示或加强各种感叹的语气。When used in an exclamatory sentence, it expresses or enhances various kinds of an exclamation tone.

① 表示加强,有时还带有夸张的意思。"可"后面带的多是形容词或形容词短语,有时也可带动宾短语,句子末尾,常带有"啊、了、啦、呢"等语气助词。Used to strengthen the tone, sometimes with an exaggerated meaning. "可" is often followed by an adjective, adjective phrase, or sometimes by a verb-object phrase. Modal particles such as "啊,了,啦,呢" are always used at the end of the sentence.

(14) 杭州可美了!

(15) 他唱歌可有名啦!

② 用在表示赞叹希望得以实现的句子,加强赞叹语气,句子中必有语气助词或动态助词配合使用。这时,"可"含有"总算、终于"的意思。When used in a sentence that hails the achievement of a wish or wishes, it enhances the tone of exclamation. In this case, a modal particle or dynamic auxiliary should be used. Here, "可" bears the meaning of "总算" or "终于."

(16) 今天可看到埃菲尔铁塔啦!

(17) 我可吃过北京烤鸭了!

③ "可+真",用于表示埋怨、厌恶或赞叹语气的感叹句,加强埋怨、厌恶或赞叹的语气。"可"+"真" is used in an exclamatory sentence to emphasize the tone of complaint, disgust or admiration.

(18) 这个公园可真漂亮!

(19) 汉字可真难写!

4. 用在祈使句里,加强祈使语气,有"一定、无论如何、千万"的意思,后面常带助动词"要、得"。在表示规劝、警告、提醒的祈使句子里,"可"表示委婉的语气,但态度是很坚决的,"可"后面带否定副词时,尤其如此。When used in an imperative sentence, "可" carries the meaning of "一定,""无论如何," or "千万" to strengthen the imperative mood. It is often followed by an auxiliary verb such as "要" or "得." In an imperative sentence of persuasion, warning, or reminding, "可" expresses a euphemistic tone in a firm attitude, especially when "可" is followed by a negative adverb.

(20) 到了中国,你可得常常给我打电话!

(21) 暑假里,我可要多旅游几个城市。

(22) 这件衣服你可不能丢了。

连词 conj.

连接分句或句子,表示转折关系。表示的转折程度有两种: It is used to connect clauses or sentences to indicate a transitional relationship. There are two different degrees of transition:

1. 所连接的前后两句子的内容是互相矛盾的,"可"的转折程度就比较重。When the two clauses express contradictory ideas, "可" bears a stronger degree of transition.

(23) 很多事情都是说说容易，可实际上做起来不那么容易。

(24) 我知道龙井茶，可从来没看到过真正的龙井茶。

2. 所连接的前后两句子的内容并不互相矛盾，只是用"可"形成语气上的转折，引出下文，对前面的内容做出限制性、补充性的说明，"可"所表示的转折程度比较轻。When the two clauses do not express contradictory ideas, "可" is used just to make a transitional tone leading to the second clause. It is used to make a restrictive and complementary description of the preceding ideas. In this case, "可" bears a weaker degree of transition.

(25) 她跳舞的样子很美，可没有力量。

(26) 我可以陪你去办公室找老师，可问题得你自己说。

说明 Notes：

1. "可"还有动词用法，表示同意、可以的意思。多用于比较固定的词组里，如"模棱两可、不置可否、无可无不可"等。"可，" as a verb, means agreement or "Go ahead." It is often used in a few fixed phrases such as "模棱两可, 不置可否, 无可无不可".

2. "可"作前缀，与单音节的心理动词组合，构成形容词，表示意愿或感情，如"可喜、可恨、可恼、可悲、可爱、可憎、可怜"等。"可，" as a prefix, goes with monosyllabic psychological verbs to form adjectives indicating desires or feelings such as "可喜, 可恨, 可恼, 可悲, 可爱, 可憎, 可怜."

3. "可"作前缀，与单音节名词组合，构成形容词，表示适合，如"可口、可身、可脚、可心"等。"可，" again as a prefix, may go with a monosyllabic noun to form an adjective to indicate appropriateness such as "可口, 可身, 可脚, 可心."

kěbushì 可不是

用法 Usage：

也说"可不、可不是吗"。表示"怎么不是呢""哪能不是"的意思，形成反问语气，表示附和或赞同对方的话。习惯语。多用于对话之中。An idiomatic expression, it can also be expressed as "可不" or "可不是吗，" both of which mean "怎么不是呢" or "哪能不是，" expressing a rhetorical tone that shows the approval of the other side. It is usually used in a conversation.

(1) A：今天的雾真大！
B：可不是，十米之外都看不见了。

(2) A：这老人身体真好！
B：可不是，那么高的山都爬上来了。

说明 Notes：

"可不是"要与副词"可＋不是"的用法区别开来。"可不是" should be distinguished from the adverbial structure "可＋不是."

(3) 你喜欢吃饺子。我可不是。

(4) 星期六你去上海，她可不是。

在例(3)(4)中，"可不是"的意思是"我可不喜欢吃饺子""她可不是去上海"。"可不是" in (3) and (4) means "我可不喜欢吃饺子" and "她可不是去上海" respectively.

kějiàn 可见

用法 Usage：

连词 conj.

连接上下句，承接上文，表示可以推出结论。It can be seen that .... It is used to connect the context for a reasonable conclusion.

(1) 她不告诉你她的电话号码，可见她还不想跟你有联系。

(2) 那么便宜都没人买，可见，这种橘子不好吃。

说明 Notes：

1. 连接长句或段落时，常用"由此可见"替代"可见"。When it connects long sentences or paragraphs, "由此可见" is often used instead of "可见."

2. "可见"连接句子或段落，要用于句子前面。When it is used to connect sentences or

paragraphs, "可见" should be placed at the beginning.

(3) *那么慢的速度,我还听不懂。我的听力水平可见不高。

(4) 那么慢的速度,我还听不懂。可见我的听力水平不高。

3. "可见"还可用作形容词,如"可见度、可见光、清晰可见"等。"可见" can also be used as an adjective, such as "可见度,可见光,清晰可见."

kěnéng 可能 →P546 "也许"
用法 Usage:
助动词 aux. v.

表示对可能性的估计和推测。用在动词或动词性谓语前。May; can. Indicating an estimate and conjecture of the possibility, it is used before a verb or verb predicate.

(1) 她可能不知道你要去英国留学的消息。

(2) 你的朋友可能已经到上海了。

名词 n.

表示能成为事实的属性。一般用在句末,多作"有"的宾语。Possibility; probability; likelihood. It is usually used at the end of a sentence as the object of the verb "有."

(3) 这个故事的结果有三种可能。

(4) 我觉得这次比赛她有获得第一名的可能。

(5) 他不来的原因有一种可能是他的身体又不好了。

形容词 a.

表示"能成为事实的、可以实现的"意思。多用作定语或谓语。Possible; probable; likely. Indicating the expression of something that can become true or that can be realized, it is usually used as an attribute or predicate.

1. 做定语,限于修饰表示"情况、机会、事情、结果、事"等少数名词。如果"可能"前面有数量词修饰,则"可能"修饰的名词就比较多。When used as an attribute, it can only modify such nouns as "情况,机会,事情,事." If "可能" is preceded by a quantifier, it can modify more nouns.

(6) 他会打毛衣,这是根本不可能的事。

(7) 妈妈说要想尽一切可能的办法治好我的病。

(8) 你做这件事,有两种可能的结果。

2. "可能"修饰"范围、条件"这两个名词,只能用于肯定形式。When "可能" modifies "范围" or "条件," it can only be used in an affirmative sentence.

(9) 请你在可能的范围内,给我找一套公寓房。

(10) 你要换专业,可能的条件只有一个。

3. 做谓语时,"可能"前面多带有"很、不大、完全"等副词修饰。When used as the predicate, "可能" is usually modified by such adverbs as "很,不大,完全."

(11) 你想一个人做成这件事不大可能。

(12) 他说不去,这完全可能。

说明 Notes:

"可能"作助动词用时,可以在主语前,也可以在主语后,并且"可能"前面也可以有"很、不大、完全"等副词修饰。Being an auxiliary verb, "可能" can be used before or after the subject, and it can take such adverbs as "很,不大,完全" as its modifiers.

(13) 很可能她还不知道姐姐已经到上海的消息。

(14) 她完全可能在上海买到那张飞机票。

kěshì 可是 →P90 "但是"
用法 Usage:
连词 conj.

表示转折或限制;但是。一般连接句子或分句,有时也连接段落。后面常带"却、也、还、仍然"等。But; however. Indicating a transition or restriction, it usually connects sentences or clauses, and sometimes paragraphs. "可是" is often followed by such words as "却, 也, 还, 仍然."

1. 所连接的前后两部分意思互相矛盾。在这种情况下,"可是"的转折程度较重,与"但是"的第一种用法相同。The meanings of the two parts connected by "可是" are contradictory. In this case, "可是" carries the degree of transition in a stronger sense. It bears the same meaning of the first usage of "但是."

(1) 放寒假回家过年了,可是如果不抓紧订机票就赶不上年夜饭。

(2) 今天的风很大,可是天气不怎么冷。

2. 所连接的两部分在意义上并不矛盾,"可是"只是起语气上的转折,下文对上文的意思作限制、补充性的说明。这时,"可是"的转折程度较轻。The meanings of the two parts connected by "可是" are not contradictory. "可是" only carries a transitional tone, where the content that follows it functions as an explanation of restriction and supplement. In this case, "可是" carries the degree of transition in a relatively weaker sense.

(3) 老人头发白是自然现象,可是为什么有些青年人的头发也会白呢?

(4) 他一学就会,可是我比他努力多了,还是学不好。

副词 ad.

真是,实在是。Indeed; really.

(5) 这次HSK考到了八级,我可是太高兴了。

(6) 你帮我买到了足球比赛的票,可是不容易呀!

说明 Notes:

1. "可是"作连词用时,一般放在主语前面,但有时也可以放在主语后面。When "可是" is used as a conjunction, it is usually put in front of the subject. However, "可是" sometimes can also be placed behind the subject.

(7) 三个孩子都长大了,他可是没抱过一个,没抱过一次。

2. "可是"和"但是"都表示转折意思。Both "可是" and "但是" carry the transitional meaning.

它们的区别是:Their differences are as follows:

① "但是"表示的转折程度比"可是"重。The degree of transition of "但是" is stronger than that of "可是."

② "可是"多用于口语。"但是"通用于口语和书面语。"可是" is often used in spoken language. However, "但是" is usually used in both spoken and written language.

③ "但是"可以连接短语。"可是"不能。"但是" can be used to connect phrases, yet "可是" cannot.

(8) *他是个聪明可是懒惰的男孩。

(9) 他是个聪明但是懒惰的男孩。

kěxī 可惜 →P564"遗憾"

用法 Usage:

形容词 a.

值得惋惜。多用作谓语和定语。Feeling regretful. Deserving pity. It is usually used as the predicate and attribute.

1. 做谓语时,主语多为动词短语或小句。When used as the predicate, its subject is always the verbal phrases or clauses.

(1) 那件衣服丢了太可惜。我很喜欢的。

(2) 你没看这电影真可惜。

2. 做定语时,"可惜"修饰的名词不多,常见有"事情、事"等。"可惜"前面常带程度副词,后面常带"的"。When used as the attribute, it can only modify a few nouns such as "事情" or "事." In this case, "可惜" often takes an adverb of degree before it and "的" after it.

(3) 考上了大学而不能读大学,这是十分可惜的事情。

动词 v.

表示感到惋惜的意思。To feel regretful for.

(4) 我不小心把蛋糕掉到了地上,他可惜得哭了起来。

(5) 就差三分没考上大学,我真为你可惜。

副词 *ad.*

表示只能惋惜的意思。只用在主语前面,后面带的句子一般多为消极意义。*Expressing the feeling of regret. In this case, it can only be used before the subject and the sentence after it often bears a negative meaning.*

(6) 今天来的人,有很多是她的同学,可惜她没来。

(7) 她很喜欢那件衣服,可惜(她)丢了。

kěxiào 可笑

用法 Usage:

形容词 *a.*

1. 令人耻笑,(人的言行)使得别人非常不满,甚至轻蔑。*Being ridiculous; (of words and deeds) making others feel very unhappy, and even feel scorn.*

(1) 他太可笑了,想用一个星期就学会汉语。

(2) 他真可笑,想用一件衬衣换我的一辆电动车。

2. 引人发笑,(因为言语或动作)让人觉得幽默、有意思而高兴。*Being funny; (of words or actions) making others feel humorous, interesting and happy.*

(3) 你们笑什么,他讲的故事一点儿都不可笑。

(4) 他的动作真可笑,大家看了都笑得合不上嘴。

说明 Notes:

使用"可笑"一词时,注意不要混淆褒贬两种义项的词义。*While using the word "可笑," do not mix up the commendatory meaning with the derogatory meaning.*

(5) *她是个可笑的人。她讲话,大家就要笑。

(6) 她是个很有意思的人。她讲话,大家就要笑。

(7) *他每次走进教室都伸一下舌头,大家看了都可笑。

(8) 他每次走进教室都伸一下舌头,这个动作很可笑。

(6)和(8)两个句子要表达的是人的动作或言语令人发笑的意思,没有贬义。如果"可笑"的主语直接指人本身,一般表示贬义。如例(1)。*(6) and (8) mean that one's actions or words make people laugh ("令人发笑"), which does not bear a derogatory meaning. However, if the subject of "可笑" is somebody, it often bears a derogatory meaning as in (1).*

kěyǐ 可以 →P202"会"、P335"能"

用法 Usage:

助动词 *aux. v.*

1. 表示可能或能够,相当于"能"。"可以"能用在主语前后。否定形式为"不能",而不是"不可以",因为"不可以"主观因素比较强。*Indicating possibility or capability. It bears the same meaning as "能." "可以" can be used before or after the subject. The negative form is "不能" rather than "不可以," because "不可以" has a relatively stronger sense of subjectivity.*

(1) 那双皮鞋可以你穿,也可以你哥哥穿。

(2) 这次比赛你可以去参加,他不能参加。

2. 表示有某种用途。能单独回答问题。*Indicating a certain function or purpose. It can be used to answer a question by itself.*

(3) 竹子可以做桌子、椅子,也可以做衣服、毛巾。

(4) A:这种药可以治咳嗽吗?
B:可以。

3. 表示同意、许可。可以单独回答问题。否定可以用"不可以",也可以用"不能"。但是单独回答问题常常说"不行、不成",主观色彩更重些。*Indicating agreement or permission. It can be used to answer a question by itself. Its*

negative form is either "不可以" or "不能." However, when it is used to answer a question by itself, "不行" or "不成" is often adopted, which has a stronger sense of subjectivity.

(5) A：我可以喝酒吗?
　　B：不行,你还是孩子。
(6) 现在你长大了,可以喝酒了。

4. 表示值得的意思。不能单独回答问题。"可以"前面常用"很、倒"进行修饰,后面的动词常常重叠或带有动量词。表示否定时,不说"不可以",而说"不值得"。 Indicating that something is worth doing. In this case, "可以" cannot be used to answer a question by itself, but it can often take "很" or "倒" as a pre-modifier. The verbs after it are often reduplicated or followed by verbal measure words. When it is used to express a negative meaning, "不值得" is always used instead of "不可以."

(7) 这本书不错,很可以买一本看看。
(8) 你觉得可以买,我觉得不值得。

形容词 a.

1. 表示还好、不坏、过得去的意思。只能做谓语或补语,前面常有"还"修饰。 Being passable; not bad; so-so. It is often modified by "还," and can only be used as the predicate or complement in a sentence.

(9) 他的汉字写得还可以。
(10) 最近他的身体还可以。

2. 表示程度很高,过分。前面不能加"很",可以加"真"。 Indicating a high degree; excessive. The pre-modifier is "真" instead of "可以."

(11) 他一个人喝完了那么多啤酒,真可以!
(12) 这里的夏天热得可以啊!

说明 Notes:

1. "可以"的两种形容词用法都没有否定形式。 The two adjective usages of "可以" do not have negative forms.

2. "可以"与"会"都有表示可能和能够的意思。 Both "可以" and "会" can be used to express the meaning of possibility or capability.

它们的区别是：They differ as follows:

① "可以"侧重表示有能力、有水平去做某一件事了。"会"侧重经过学习、练习后学会了某种技能。一般句子后面都带有"了",表示一种变化。"可以" implies that someone has the ability to do something. However, "会" emphasizes the acquisition of some skills after study or practice. Usually, "了" is used at the end of the sentence to indicate the change of the ability.

(13) 他可以说汉语了。
(14) 他会说汉语了。

② "会"还有表示善于做某种事情的意思。前面常常有"很"进行修饰,后面不带"了"。"可以"不能这样用。"会" bears the meaning of being good at doing something. In this case, "很" can be used as a pre-modifier, yet "了" cannot be placed after it. "可以" does not have this usage.

(15) *他很可以唱歌。
(16) 他很会唱歌。

③ "会"可以表示情理上或客观上的可能性。"可以"不能。"会" indicates a reasonable or objective possibility, while "可以" does not have this meaning.

(17) *那么晚了,他还可以来吗?
(18) 那么晚了,他还会来吗?

④ 否定式不同。"会"的否定式是"不会"或"不能"。 They have different negative forms. The negative form of "会" is "不会" or "不能."

---

kěn 肯

用法 Usage:

动词 v.

表示同意。 To agree; to indicate agreement.

(1) 你去借,他一定肯。
(2) 他肯唱歌,但是不肯跳舞。

助动词 aux. v.

表示主观上愿意或乐意（怎么做），用在动词前。*Be willing to do something. It is placed before a verb.*

（3）他肯帮助你的，你放心吧！

（4）他怎么也不肯到你家吃饭。

说明 Notes:

1. "肯"作动词单独用时，"肯"前面不能加"很"。*When "肯" is used as a verb independently, "很" cannot be put before it.*

（5）*请他唱歌，他很肯的。

2. 助动词"肯"可以组成"不肯不……"，表示一定要、十分坚决（怎么样）。*The adverb "肯" can form the phrase "不肯不…" A double negative, it expresses a strong determination to do something.*

（6）他如果知道我们去看电影，是不肯不去的。

kěndìng 肯定 →P554 "一定"

用法 Usage:

动词 v.

1. 承认事物的存在或事物的真实性，与"否定"相对。*To acknowledge the existence or the truth of something, the opposite of "否定."*

（1）做父母的一定要肯定孩子的成绩。

（2）肯定一切或者否定一切都是不客观的。

2. 做出判断，确定。*To make a judgment; to affirm.*

（3）他来不来参加晚会，我不能肯定。

（4）现在可以肯定，他不会来了。

形容词 a.

1. 表示承认的、正面的，与"否定"相对。*Affirmative; positive. Indicating acknowledgement or something positive, it is the opposite of "否定."*

（5）我们要不要帮助他呢？答案当然是肯定的。

2. 确定，明确，与"含糊"相对。*Definite;*

sure. *It is opposite to "含糊."*

（6）你给我一个肯定的回答，来还是不来？

（7）他一点也不含糊，说得很肯定。

副词 ad.

一定，必定，无疑问（与"未必"相对）。*Certainly; inevitably; undoubtedly. It is opposite to "未必"）.*

（8）他肯定会来祝贺你的生日。

（9）上海是我肯定要去的城市。

kōng 空

用法 Usage:

形容词 a.

1. 里面没有东西。可以重叠。*Being empty. It can be used in the reduplicated form.*

（1）教室里空空的，一个人也没有。

（2）不好意思，我没带礼物，空手来了。

2. 里面缺乏内容，不切实际的。*Lacking content; unrealistic.*

（3）文章里写的都是空话，没有实际的内容。

（4）他一句话也不说，你这不是空谈吗？

名词 n.

天空，空间。一般与其他词组合使用，如："天空、长空、晴空、真空、星空、太空"等。*Sky, space, usually used in combination with another word such as "天空、长空、晴空、真空、星空、太空."*

副词 ad.

没有效果，白白地。*Ineffectively; in vain.*

（5）妈妈不来中国了，我空喜欢一场。

（6）你为什么不参加比赛？真是空有一身武功。

kǒngpà 恐怕 →P344 "怕"

用法 Usage:

副词 ad.

1. 表示估计，相当于"大概、也许"。*Indicating an estimate. It equals "大概," or "也许."*

(1) 今年暑假恐怕有两个半月的时间吧。
(2) 这一课学完恐怕要考试了。
2. 表示估计兼担心。Making an estimate that implies some worry; supposedly.
(3) 这么远的路,两个小时恐怕回不来。
(4) 这孩子老是哭,恐怕有什么地方不舒服吧。

kòng 空

用法 Usage:

动词 v.

腾出来,使地方空(kōng)出来。To leave a space blank; to make way for; to empty a place.

(1) 每段文章开始要空两格。
(2) 教室后面一排座位先空出来。

形容词 a.

没有被利用的或里面缺少东西的。Being vacant; not occupied.

(3) 那个车厢空得很,我们去那边坐吧。
(4) 我的书架还很空,你的书可以放我这里。

名词 n.

1. 还没利用的空间,空隙地儿。Vacancy; unoccupied space.

(5) 箱子里塞得满满的,一点空儿都没了。

2. 还没占用的时间,空隙时间。Spare time; time available for something else.

(6) 有空儿就来我家玩吧!
(7) 下个星期一点空儿都没有。

kòngzhì 控制 →P58"操纵"、P704"左右"

用法 Usage:

动词 v.

1. 掌握住,不使任意活动或越出范围,操纵。To control; not to allow to do something or go beyond the limits.

(1) 这个开关控制着整个车间的电路系统。
(2) 每个人都应该学会控制自己的感情。

2. 使处于自己的占有、管理或影响之下。常用于被动句。To subject somebody or something to one's possession, management, or influence. It is often used in the passive voice.

(3) 这些人已经被控制在警察的监视之中。
(4) 孩子一上初中,我就控制不住他了。

3. 限制、节制。To limit; to restrain.

(5) 你想减肥,首先要控制甜食。
(6) 控制人口是保护地球环境的重要措施。

说明 Notes:

"操纵"和"控制"在开动支配机器仪表的意义上是相同的,可以互用。"操纵" and "控制" share the meaning of setting in motion and controlling the meters and instruments in a machine, and they are replaceable with each other in that meaning.

(7) 整个工厂的机器都是用电脑操纵/控制的。

它们的区别是:Their differences lie in:

1. "操纵"的第二义项,着重于用不正当的手段去控制与支配,多指幕后的阴谋活动,对象可以是政权、某种社会活动、市场、会议,也可以是人或组织。在这个用法上"操纵"是贬义词。"控制"一般不带褒贬色彩。In its second usage, "操纵" emphasizes using improper means to control and dominate. Often it hints at behind-the-scenes activities, the object of which can be a political power, a social activity, the market or a conference. It can also be people or organizations. In this sense, "操纵" is a derogatory term. "控制," by contrast, is neutral.

2. "控制"着重于用力量、权势、意志等去掌握、限制,对象可以是国家、政权、局势、会议、地区、速度、感情等。被"控制"的对象可以是他人,也可以是自己。使用范围比"操纵"广泛,是中性词。"控制" focuses on using force, power and will to control and influence the target, which ranges from a country, a political power,

a situation, a conference, a region to a speed or feelings. The target of "控制" may be someone else or oneself. It is applied to a wider scope than "操纵." It is neutral.

3. "控制"有"限制、节制"的义项。"操纵"没有。"控制" may carry the meaning of "限制（limiting）" or "节制（restraining）." "操纵" doesn't have this meaning.

kù 酷 →P430"帅"

用法 Usage:

形容词 a.

1. 残酷。如："酷刑、酷吏、酷法"等。Cruel. For example, "酷刑,酷吏,酷法."

2. 程度深的,炽烈的。如："酷热、酷暑、酷寒"等。Extreme; severe; intense. For example, "酷热,酷暑,酷寒."

3. 形容人的外表英俊潇洒,表情冷峻坚毅,有个性。一般形容男人。(Usually used to describe a man's appearance) handsome; cool.

(1) 这男人真酷！
(2) 那人长得真酷！

副词 ad.

极,很。Very much; extremely.

(3) 他酷爱京剧,所以来到了中国。
(4) 这孩子长得酷似其父。

kuài 快

用法 Usage:

形容词 a.

1. 做事情花的时间比平常短、少（跟"慢"相对）。Being quick in doing something. It is the opposite of "慢."

(1) 他跑步跑得很快。
(2) 我看书很快,一本书两天就看完了。

2. 赶快,表示催促。常用在祈使句。Hurrying up; making haste. It is used in an imperative sentence.

(3) 他们已经出发十分钟了,你快点儿。
(4) 快点过来吃饭,大家都在等你。

3. 灵敏、敏捷。Being quick in response.

(5) 他的脑子快,一听就懂。
(6) 年轻人聪明、手快,一下子就完成了任务。

4. 直爽,爽快。Being straightforward; frank and outspoken.

(7) 这是个心直口快的人。

5. 愉快,畅快,多用于书面语。Being pleasant; happy. It is usually used in written language.

(8) 那件事情做得真是大快人心！
(9) 这几天他心中不快,话也说得很少。

6. （刀、剪刀、斧子等工具）锋利（跟"钝"相对）。(Of tools like a knife, an axe or scissors) being sharp. It is the opposite of "钝 (blunt)."

(10) 剪刀不快,该磨一磨了。

副词 ad.

表示时间上接近,即将出现某种情况,快要。(Of time) approaching; (of something) about to happen; soon; before long.

(11) 上海站快到了。
(12) 快走吧,妈妈在等我们呢。

kuàihuo 快活 →P279"快乐"

用法 Usage:

形容词 a.

因称心如意、身心舒适而感到快乐、欢畅。Feeling pleasant and cheerful, a result of satisfaction and comfort.

(1) 他每天都很快活。
(2) 小学生今天春游,玩得都很快活。

kuàilè 快乐 →P200"欢乐"、P279"快活"

用法 Usage:

形容词 a.

感到幸福或满意,愉快、高兴的样子（跟"痛苦"相对）。Feeling happy, satisfied and pleasant. It is opposite to "痛苦."

(1) 祝你俩生日快乐！
(2) 和他在一起,大家感到非常快乐。

名词 n.

指愉快欢乐的心情。Pleasure; being in a pleasant mood.

（3）他觉得学习是生活中最大的快乐。

（4）能帮助你是我最大的快乐。

说明 Notes:

1. "快活"和"快乐"都形容人由于对生活感到幸福、对事情感到满意,心情愉快而欢乐。Both "快活" and "快乐" refer to a pleasant mood resulting from happiness or satisfaction.

它们的区别是：The differences are as follows:

① "快乐"着重于因称心如意而愉快欢乐,带有幸福满意的感觉色彩。多形容人的心情,通用于口语和书面语。"快活"着重于因称心如意而舒畅欢快,是在"快乐"的基础上,又增添有轻松、活跃的感觉。可形容心情,还可形容表情、性格、气氛等。多用于口语。"快乐" emphasizes a pleasant mood because of satisfaction, which carries the feeling of happiness. It is often used to describe one's mood and appears in both spoken and written language. "快活," by contrast, means somewhat more than "快乐." Besides referring to a pleasant mood, "快活" can also indicate a relaxing and brisk mood, which can be used to describe one's expressions, characters and the atmosphere as well. It is often used in spoken language.

② 在形容表情、气氛时,两个词语不能替换。When used to describe one's facial expressions or the atmosphere, they can't be used interchangeably.

（5）*他说的话使原来会议室里沉闷的气氛变得快乐起来了。

（6）他说的话使原来会议室里沉闷的气氛变得快活起来了。

2. "快乐"和"欢乐"都能表示心情愉快和高兴。区别是："快乐"侧重描述人的心情。"欢乐"还能描述人们聚会的场面、气氛。"快乐" and "欢乐" both mean "happy and high-spirited." Their difference lies in the fact that "快乐" is primarily used to describe a person's state of mind while "欢乐" deals with the atmosphere and the environment.

（7）*老朋友见面,场面非常快乐。

（8）老朋友见面,场面非常欢乐。

kuān 宽 →P281"阔"

用法 Usage:

形容词 a.

1. 横向距离大（与"窄"相对）,表示面积或范围广。(Of width and breadth) being wide and broad, which is the opposite of "窄." It refers to a large area or a wide range.

（1）我们这里的马路都这样宽。

（2）他的知识面很宽。

2. 宽容,不严格。(Of requirements, rules and regulations) being loose; not strict.

（3）这个公司的管理制度太宽了。

（4）那个老师对学生的要求很宽。

3. 宽大。Being flexible or moderate.

（5）他认识了自己的错误,得到了从宽处理。

4. 富裕。Being well-off.

（6）这几年手头儿一宽,就买了房子。

动词 v.

1. 表示放松、使宽松的意思。可以重叠使用。To make one feel relaxed. "宽" can be reduplicated.

（7）你去劝劝老人家,让他宽宽心。

（8）她是个心宽体胖,不会着急的人。

2. 表示延长、延缓时间的意思。多用于口语。To extend a time limit; to make more time available for something to be done. It is often used in spoken language.

（9）欠你的钱能不能再宽几天还?

（10）你们要的东西得宽限几天才能送到。

名词 n.

表示宽度。*Width; breadth.*

(11) 这只箱子有一米宽。

kùn 困

用法 Usage:

形容词 a.

1. 疲倦想睡。*Feeling tired and sleepy.*

(1) 孩子困得都闭上眼睛了,让他去睡吧。

(2) 我很困了,你还不困吗?

2.（因劳累）疲乏,精力不济。*Feeling exhausted (because of tiredness).*

(3) 这几天很困,想好好休息休息。

动词 v.

1. 陷入艰难痛苦之中,无法摆脱。*To be trapped in a difficult situation.*

(4) 他家好几个病人要照顾,简直把他困住了。

2. 控制在一定的范围里,围困。*To besiege; to keep ... within a limited area or range.*

(5) 我们已经把敌人困在小山沟里了。

kuò 阔 →P280"宽"

用法 Usage:

形容词 a.

1. 面积宽广,距离大。多用于比较固定的词语中。*Referring to a wide area or a long distance, it is often used in some fixed phrases.*

(1) 海阔天空,你愿意到哪儿就到哪儿。

(2) 波澜壮阔的大海养育了我。

2. 比喻时间长。多用于书面语。*Referring to a long time, it is often used in written language.*

(3) 我与她阔别多年,今天见面几乎都认不出来了。

3. 富裕,奢侈,讲排场。*Being well-off; being luxurious and extravagant.*

(4) 你看她结婚的场面多阔!

(5) 这几年,他阔起来了。

4. 不切实际。*Being unrealistic, impractical.*

(6) 他就会高谈阔论,办不了实事。

说明 Notes:

"宽"与"阔"都形容面积大,都有表示富裕的意思。*Both "宽" and "阔" can refer to a wide area or a rich and wealthy state.*

区别是：*The differences are as follows:*

1. 表示面积,"宽"侧重横向性意义。"阔"带有伸展性意义。*When it refers to a wide area, "宽" refers to the lateral side while "阔" refers to the horizontal side.*

2. 表示富裕,"宽"没有奢侈、讲排场的意思。*When it refers to a rich state, "宽" does not bear the meanings of luxury and extravagance.*

3. "宽"有名词"宽度"的用法,"阔"没有这个用法。*"宽" has the noun usage of "宽度," while "阔" cannot be used in this way.*

4. "阔"没有宽松、宽大的用法。*"阔" does not carry the meaning of being loose or spacious.*

L l

là 落

用法 Usage:

动词 v.

1. 遗漏。*To miss.*

(1) 这里落了两个字,应该加上。

(2) 对不起,把你的名字落掉了。

2. 把东西放在一个地方,忘记拿走。*To leave something behind; to forget to take something along.*

(3) 我急着出来,把书落在教室里了。

(4) 大家仔细检查自己的行李,别落下什么了。

3. 跟不上,被丢在后面。*To fail to keep up with; to be left behind.*

(5) 大家都努力学习,谁也不愿意落在后面。

(6) 他很胖,爬山时总落在最后。

说明 Notes:

1. 在第二义项用法中,"落"后面常有表示地方的补语,如例(3)。*In its second use, "落" is often followed by a complement, which is usually the name of a place, as seen in (3).*

(7) 糟糕,我把手机落在出租车上了。

2. 在第三义项用法中,"落"后面一般加"在后面、在最后面"。*In its third use, "落" is usually followed by "在后面、在最后面."*

lái 来 →P570"以来"

用法 Usage:

动词 v.

1. 从别的地方到说话人的地方(跟"去、往"相对)。*To come; to go from another place to where the speaker is (the opposite of "去,往").*

(1) 你到我这里来一下。

(2) 昨天家里来客人了。

这一用法主要有下面这些句式：*This usage is applied to the following sentence patterns:*

① "名词(表示地方或时间)+来+施事者"。后面的名词前常带数量词。"*n. (indicating a time or place) + 来 + the actor.*" *The noun that follows is often followed by a numerical.*

(3) 那边来了一辆出租车。

(4) 昨天来过两个人。

② "名词(施事者)+来+名(受事者)"。后面的名词前常带数量词。"*n. (indicating the actor) + 来 + n. (indicating the recipient).*" *The noun that follows is often followed by a numerical.*

(5) 他来过两个电话。

(6) 初级班可以来四个同学。

③ "名词(施事者)+来+名(处所)"。"*n. (indicating the actor) + 来 + n. (indicating the place).*"

(7) 你妈妈明天要来中国。

(8) 她要来你这儿看看。

④ "来+名词(人或东西)"。常用于祈使句,表示命令、请求。"*来 + n. (a person or a thing).*" *It is usually used to indicate an order* or a request.

(9) 请来一碗炒面,再来一碗西红柿蛋汤!

(10) 来人啊! 有人摔倒了。

2. 表示(问题、事情)发生,来到。(Of a problem or something) to happen; to arrive.

(11) 问题来了,就得解决。

(12) 工作来了,你就走开,这样好吗?

3. 做某个动作(代替有具体意义的动词)。很少带"了、过"。To take an action (instead of using a verb with a certain specific meaning). It seldom goes with "了,过."

(13) 你帮我拿背包,这个箱子我自己来。

(14) 我们来一场足球比赛,怎么样?

4. 用在另一个动词前面,表示要做什么事。To be placed before another verb, indicating an intention to do something.

(15) 我来做饭,你去洗衣服。

(16) 大家一起来唱个歌!

5. 用在另一个动词或动词短语(或介词短语)后面,表示前者为做什么事(表示目的)而来。To be placed after another verb or verb structure, indicating the reason why the former has come.

(17) 我们给你过生日来了。

(18) 她到学校看老师来了。

6. 跟"得"或"不"连用。To be used together with "得" or "不."

① 表示融洽或不融洽的意思。只限于"谈、合、处"等少数几个具有要求双方配合意义的动词。To indicate the idea of getting along or not getting along with each other. It is used only with a few verbs such as "谈、合、处," each of which requires both sides to get along well.

(19) 她们俩很谈得来。

(20) 她跟她的男朋友合不来,去年就分手了。

② 表示有(或者没有)能力去完成某件事情。To indicate that one has or does not have the ability to do something.

(21) 这个汉字我写不来。

(22) 她汉语歌也唱得来,请她唱吧!

③ 表示习惯(或者不习惯)某件事情。多用于吃东西的口味或欣赏趣味。To indicate that one is or is not used to doing something. This usage is applied mostly to tastes or what one appreciates in art and literature.

(23) 他是四川人,当然吃得来辣的。

(24) 现在年纪大的人,多数都听不来摇滚音乐。

7. 用在某些动词(能非常明显地表示动作方向的)后面,表示动作朝着说话人所在的地方进行。一般作为趋向动词用法。To follow a few direction-showing verbs to indicate that the action is going in the direction of the speaker. This use is in accord with that of a verb indicating the direction.

(25) 那边走来了一个人。

(26) 你把报纸拿到我这里来。

8. 用在某些动词后面,表示动作的结果,相当于"过来"。To follow some verbs to express the result of an action. It is equivalent to "过来."

(27) 一觉醒来,发现同屋已经不在了。

(28) 一路走来,确实看到不少书店。

9. 用在动词"看、说、想、算、听"后面,表示估计或限于某个方面,可替换成"起来"。To be placed after "看,说,想,算,听" to indicate an estimate or some sort of limit. It can be replaced by "起来."

(29) 看来/起来她今天不会来了。

(30) 算来/起来他已经回国两个多星期了。

10. 用在动词短语(或介词短语)与动词(或动词短语)之间,表示前者是方式、方向或行为,后者是目的。To be used between verbal phrases (or prepositional phrases) and verbs (or verbal phrases) to mean that the former is the manner, direction or action, while the latter is the purpose.

(31) 他们到苏州来了解中国的园林艺术。
(32) 你能用什么理由来说服他呢?

助词 aux.

1. 表示大概的数目。一般指不到那个数目,有时也指比那个数稍大或稍小。*About; around. Normally it means up to a certain number, or slightly greater or less than the number.*

有以下几种情况: *It is used in the following ways:*

① 用在数词后量词前,数词限于十或末位为十的多位数。一般不用在个数后面。*It is used after a numeral word or before a measure word. The numeral word is limited to "十" or multi-digit number ending with "十." It's not used after a single digit.*

(33) 看上去,他有六十来岁。
(34) 寒假只有二十来天时间,我不回国了。

② 用在度量衡量词后(一般是单音节量词),数词可以是个位数或多位数。后面一般要有相关的形容词或名词。*It is used after weights and measures (normally monosyllabic). In this case, the number can either be a single digit or a multi-digit, and "来" should be followed by a related adjective or noun.*

(35) 这条鱼有八斤来重。
(36) 从这儿到那儿,二里来地,走走就到了。

2. 用在"一、二、三"等数词后,表示列举理由或原因。*It is used after numerals such as "一,二,三" to give a list of causes or reasons.*

(37) 我到中国留学,一来是为了学汉语,二来是想看看我父母的故乡。
(38) 他的汉语说得那么好,一来他妈妈是中国人,二来他自己学得很努力。

3. 用在时间词后,表示从过去某个时间到现在。*It is used after time words to mean "ever since."*

(39) 三天来,他什么东西也没吃。真急死人了!
(40) 几十年来,母亲就这样为我们一家人辛勤地劳动着。

4. 用在诗歌、戏词、熟语、叫卖声中,起舒缓语音的修饰作用。*It is used in poems, drama lines, idioms or peddler's cries to function in a modified slow voice.*

(41) 正月里来呀,闹新春,家家户户挂红灯。
(42) 卖青菜来——大萝卜!

说明 Notes:

1. "来"用在表示时间的单音节名词前,表示"未来的"意思。如:"来年、来日方长、来生报答、来世还做朋友"等。*When "来" is placed before a monosyllabic word indicating a time, it always means a time in the future, as in "来年,来日方长,来生报答,来世还做朋友," etc.*

2. "十来斤重"跟"十斤来重"的意思不同。前者可以比十斤多或少一二斤。后者只能比十斤多或少一二两。又如:"十来尺长、十尺来长、十来里路、十里来路"等。"十来斤重" *is different from* "十斤来重" *in meaning. The former could be one or two jin heavier or lighter while the latter can be one or two liang heavier or lighter. Similarly we have* "十来尺长,十尺来长;十来里路,十里来路," *etc.*

láibují 来不及

用法 Usage:

动词 v.

1. 因为时间短促,无法顾到或赶上。后面只能带动词性的宾语。*To be unable to keep up or catch up with because of a shortage of time. It can be followed only by a verbal phrase as its object.*

(1) 他六点就走了,来不及告诉他。
(2) 火车就要开了,来不及买东西了。

2. 前后可以重复同一个动词,但是要跟"都、也"一起使用。*Before and after "来不及," the same verb is repeated, but it collocates with "都" or "也."*

(3) 这盒巧克力我看也来不及看一下,就被同屋吃了。
(4) 菜上得太快,都来不及吃了。

láidejí 来得及

用法 Usage:

动词 *v.*

表示时间还有,能够顾到或赶上。前面常用"还、也、都",后面只能带动词性词语。*To indicate that there is enough time to do something or to catch up with.* "还、也"或"都" *often appears before it.*

(1) 车开慢点,时间还来得及。

(2) 去飞机场还有两个小时,来得及去超市买点东西吗?

说明 Notes:

1. "来得及"的否定式有两种:"来不及"和"没来得及"。前者表示当前的情况,后者表示过去的情况。*The negative form of* "来得及" *could be either* "来不及" *or* "没来得及." *The former is about a current situation while the latter is about a past situation.*

(3) 飞机快起飞了,来不及打电话了。

(4) 没来得及打电话,飞机就起飞了。

2. 在客观的连续的叙述中,有时也可以用"来不及"。"来不及" *can be used when giving an objective account of things that happened one soon after another.*

(5) 今天起床晚了,来不及/没来得及吃早饭就来上课了。

láihuí 来回 →P285"来往"

用法 Usage:

副词 *ad.*

1. 表示来来去去地,常重叠使用。*To come and go. It is often used in a reduplicated form as* "来来回回."

(1) 那只苍蝇在房间里来回地飞,真讨厌!

(2) 孩子们在他身边来来回回地跑,他不感到吵闹。

2. 表示反反复复地。*To do something repeatedly.*

(3) 他来来回回地就说那么一句话:我要出国留学。

(4) 这些汉字他来来回回地不知道写了多少遍了。

láiwǎng 来往 →P285"来回"

用法 Usage:

动词 *v.*

1. 来去,往返。可以重叠。*To come and go. It can be reduplicated as* "来来往往."

(1) 前面在建造地铁,禁止车辆来往。

(2) 游船在湖面上来来往往,非常好看。

2. 互相走动,互相交际。可重叠。*To exchange visits; to exchange information. It can be used reduplicated as* "来往来往."

(3) 我们和邻居经常来往。

(4) 同学之间应该常常来往来往。

说明 Notes:

1. 动词"来往"如果着重于动作状态的描述,带有形容词性质,可以重叠为AABB,如例(2)。"来往," *as a verb, can be reduplicated in the form of AABB if it is used to describe the state of an action and carries the nature of an adjective, as seen in (2).*

2. "来回"与"来往"的区别是:*The differences between* "来回" *and* "来往" *are as follows:*

① 副词"来回"侧重描述动作一来一回全过程的状态,"来"与"回"的动作一般为同一个施事者发出。动词"来往"侧重指来的来去的去,描述事物整体的动态,"来"与"往"可以由不同的施事者发出,如例(1)。"来回," *as an adverb, describes the whole process of coming and going; both actions are taken by the same person.* "来往," *as a verb, emphasizes one party coming and the other party going. Obviously, the two actions are taken by two different persons (or parties), as seen in (1).*

② 两个词都有名词的用法,但是意思不一样。"来往"表示"来来去去"。"来回"表示一个往返的时间或距离。*Both expressions can be used as a noun, their meaning being different:*

"来往" means coming and going while "来回" means the time or distance involved in a trip.

③ 副词"来回"有"来来去去"的意思,"来往"中的"往"也有"去"的意思,所以使用时要注意两个词语的语义区别。"来回,"as an adverb, means coming and going, while the "往" in "来往" also carries the meaning of going. So, we must be careful about their different meanings when using them.

(5) *马路上来回的车辆很多。
(6) 马路上来往的车辆很多。
(7) *她在房间里来往地走。
(8) 她在房间里来回地走。

④ "来往"没有副词用法。"来往" is never used as an adverb.

láizì 来自

用法 Usage:
动词 v.

这是介词"自"用在某些动词后组成的词语。表示动作的来由,相当于"从……＋动＋(的)"结构的意思。To come from. This verb phrase is formed by combining a verb with the preposition "自" after it. It explains the reason for an action and is equivalent to the meaning of the structure of "从...＋v.＋的."

(1) 今年有二十多个学生来自北欧四国。
(2) 展览会的古画都来自北京故宫博物院。
(3) 这些散文来自中国近现代的著名散文大家。

说明 Notes:

1. "自"前面的动词一般要求是单音节动词,而且这个动词一般要含有从什么地方来或汇集到这儿的趋向意义的动词。如:"来、借、选、买"等。The verb before "自" is usually a monosyllable that carries the meaning of where it has come from and explains the purpose of converging at the place. The verbs are therefore often "来,借,选,买," etc.

2. 多用于书面语。This expression is mostly used in written language.

lài 赖

用法 Usage:
动词 v.

1. 表示留在某处不肯走开。后面的补语常指某个地方。To refuse to leave a place. The complement that follows is usually the name of a place.

(1) 孩子看到好吃的好玩的就赖着不走了。
(2) 别赖在教室里,出去活动活动吧!

2. 不承认自己的错误或责任,抵赖。To refuse to admit one's mistake or responsibility; to disclaim or deny.

(3) 这笔账你是赖不掉的。
(4) 明明是你先动手打人,难道你还想赖吗?

3. 硬说别人有错误,诬赖。宾语多指人。To claim that someone else made the mistake; to falsely accuse. Its object is usually a person or persons.

(5) 他自己错了总是赖别人。
(6) 这是你的责任,怎么赖在我的身上。

4. 表示责怪。宾语多指人、物。To accuse; to put the blame on. Its object usually refers to people or things.

(7) 你要是失败了,可别赖我。
(8) 睡不着,你别赖这床不好。

5. 依赖,依靠。To rely on; to depend on.

(9) 能取得这么好的成绩,全赖大家的努力。

形容词 a.

1. 指无赖。Shameless; brazen.

(10) 他说话不算数,真赖!
(11) 你输了常常不请客,你很赖哦!

2. 形容不好,坏。一般用于口语。Not good; bad. It is mostly used in oral Chinese.

(12) 这部手机常常卡住,真赖!

(13) 不管好的赖的都只能接受了。

làn 烂

用法 Usage:

形容词 a.

1. 表示某些固体物质组织被破坏或水分增加后变得松软。常做谓语和补语。(Of a solid matter) being destroyed or turning soft or loose as a result of submerging in water. It is usually used as the predicate or complement.

(1) 车祸很严重,车头都撞烂了。

(2) 肉已经煮得很烂了。

2. 腐烂。Rotting.

(3) 香蕉很容易烂。

(4) 千万别吃烂水果,对身体不好。

3. 破碎,破烂。常做补语、定语和谓语。Being broken or worn out because of frequent use. It usually serves as the complement, attribute or predicate.

(5) 为了学习汉语,他把词典都翻烂了。

(6) 这真是部烂手机,一摔就烂。

4. 表示程度深。Being very deep in degree.

(7) 每一课课文,他都读得烂熟。

(8) 昨晚他喝酒喝得烂醉。

làngfèi 浪费

用法 Usage:

动词 v.

指对人力、财物、时间等用得不恰当或没有节制地乱用。To squander; to waste; to put human, financial or time resources into irrational and unrestrained use.

(1) 年轻时要努力学习,不要浪费青春。

(2) 出门就关灯吧,别浪费电。

说明 Notes:

"浪费"是动词,但有描述行为的一种状态,所以前面可以加"很、非常"等表示程度的副词,后面可以加"极了、得很、得不得了"等表示程度的补语。Although used as a verb, "浪费" describes a state or situation, and so it can be preceded by "很,非常" or other such adverbs indicating a degree and can be followed by "极了,得很,得不得了," also indicating a degree.

(3) 每天上班要花一个半小时在路上,很浪费时间。

(4) 他每次吃饭都要剩很多饭菜,浪费得不得了。

lǎo 老 →P696"总是"

用法 Usage:

形容词 a.

1. 表示年纪大,年长,跟"少、幼"相对。Old in age or elderly. It is the opposite of "少,幼."

(1) 现在的老人都是人老心不老。

2. 形容很有经验。Rich in experience.

(2) 要说玩手机游戏,他可是老手了。

3. 表示陈旧、过时或沿袭至今,跟"新"相对。Outdated; former; passed down from the old times. It is the opposite of "新."

(3) 工厂里的机器都老了。

(4) 按老规矩清明节得扫墓。

4. 表示原来的意思。Remaining the same as before.

(5) 明天老地方见。

(6) 十年了,你还是老样子,那么年轻漂亮!

5. 表示很久以前就存在的,就有的。Existing long, long ago.

(7) 永久牌自行车是老牌子。

(8) 昨天遇到了多年不见的老同学。

6. 形容经历长。Having a long duration.

(9) 他做老师已经八年,是个老教师了。

7. 形容菜做得不嫩,跟"嫩"相对。Describing a dish that is overdone. It is the opposite of "嫩."

(10) 牛肉不要烤得太老了。

8. 形容衰老。Aging, looking old.

(11) 这两年照顾生病的孩子,她老了很多。

9. 形容不感到难为情,脸皮厚。Not feeling ashamed; brazen-faced.

(12) 尿床了还笑,老脸皮!

10. 表示时间的持续,相当于"很久"。Extending over a long period of time. It is equivalent to "很久."

(13) 最近老见不着你,去哪儿了?

(14) 我在这里等你老半天了。

11. 表示排序在最后的意思,多用于北方地区。Indicating the last of several children, it is usually used in northern dialects.

(15) 他是爸妈的老儿子,特别受宠爱。

(16) 我有三个妹子,这是老妹子。

副词 ad.

修饰动词或动词短语,表示动作行为在一段较长的时间内一直持续或不断反复。有时为了强调,也说成"老是"。Modifying a verb or a verb phrase, it signifies that the action is repeated over a long period of time. It is replaced by "老是" when one wishes to emphasize the idea.

主要用法有:It is used in the following ways:

1. 相当于"总、总是、常常"。Meaning the same as "总,总是,常常."

(17) 刚学汉语的时候,我老/老是担心说错而不敢说。

(18) 我妈老/老是打电话来,问我在国外过得好不好。

2. 只表示时间持续,不表示重复,相当于"很久"。Indicating just the extension of the time, not repetition. It is equivalent to "很久."

(19) 你最近忙什么,怎么老/老是不来我家玩儿?

(20) 他老/老是穿蓝衣服,好像没别的衣服似的。

3. 修饰形容词或形容词短语,表示程度高,相当于"很"。可以和形容词一起重叠使用。Modifying an adjective or adjectival phrase and indicating a high degree. It is the same as "很." And it can be reduplicated with an adjective.

(21) 那座山离我家老远老远呢!

(22) 为了不堵车,每天我老早就从家里出来了。

说明 Notes:

1. 作为委婉语,"老"还有动词用法,表示老人去世,并且只限于老人去世才用。"老"前面常常有时间名词,后面必须带"了"。As a euphemism, "老" can be used to mean an old person passing away. This use is limited only to old people, and one often finds a noun indicating a time before it and "了" following it.

(23) 邻居张奶奶昨天晚上老了。

2. 做前缀,用于称人、排行次序,用在姓或者数字前面。As a prefix, it describes the rank in a series of people or things. It appears before a Chinese surname or a numerical.

(24) 老王,好久不见!

(25) 姥姥有五个孩子,我妈是老三。

3. 做副词时,"老"与"很"都表示程度高。区别是:"老"一般只修饰单音节、词义积极的形容词。如"高、大、长、深、早、宽、远、红、香"等。When used as an adverb, both "老" and "很" indicate a high degree. Their difference is that "老" is applied only to monosyllables with a positive meaning, such as "高,大,长,深,早,宽,远,红,香."

4. 用作形容词时,要注意"老"与"旧"的区别。当表示物品经过长时间或经过使用而变色或变形的时候用"旧",不能用"老"。When used as an adjective, "老" is different from "旧." When talking about something having changed its color or shape as a result of wear and tear, we should use "旧," not "老."

(26) *这件衣服老了,孩子不喜欢穿。

(27) 这件衣服旧了,孩子不喜欢穿。

lǎoshī 老师 →P232"教师"

用法 Usage:

名词 n.

1. 对教师的尊称。A respectful way of

addressing a teacher

（1）王老师对我们很关心。

（2）毕业以后,我要做教师。

2. 泛称传授文化、技艺的人或在某方面值得学习的人。*A general term used of a person who teaches culture or skills or who has something worth learning from.*

（3）我要向你学习做中国菜,拜你为老师。

（4）口语学习上,你是我的老师。

3. 尊称中年以上的人。*A respectful way of addressing anyone who is middle-aged or above.*

说明 Notes:

"老师"和"教师"都指在学校或从事教学工作的人员。*Both "老师" and "教师" refer to someone who is teaching at school or who is engaged in teaching anything.*

它们的区别是：*Their differences lie in:*

1. "教师"带有工作职业性质,是对从事教学工作人员的总称,不能用于对个人的称呼。如不能叫"王教师、李教师"。"老师"除了指在学校从事教学工作的人员以外,还可以尊称在某一方面值得学习的人,一般用于对个人的尊称。*"教师" is a general term that is related to one's career whose job is to teach. It cannot be used as a way of addressing an individual: we cannot say "王教师" or "李教师." "老师," by contrast, may be used as a respectful way of addressing someone who teaches something worth learning, in addition to those who teach at school.*

2. "教师"是职业总称,可以用"人民、光荣的、优秀的"等词语修饰,还可以组成"教师节、教师队伍、教师宿舍"等词语。"老师"不能。*A general term for a career, "教师" can be modified by "人民, 光荣的, 优秀的" and can form expressions such as "教师节, 教师队伍, 教师宿舍.""老师" cannot be used this way.*

3. "老师"还有别的意思。"教师"没有。所以"老师"的使用范围比"教师"广泛。*"老师" has some other meanings that "教师" does not have. Therefore, "老师" is applied to a wider scope than "教师."*

lè 乐

用法 Usage:

形容词 *a.*

表示快乐、愉快。*Happy; full of joy.*

（1）妈妈收到孩子送的礼物,心里乐得像开了花。

（2）他是一个助人为乐的好人。

动词 *v.*

1. 乐于。*To take delight in; to enjoy.*

（3）我们很多农民工已经在这个城市安居乐业了。

（4）我最喜欢那些老百姓喜闻乐见的民歌。

2. （快乐地）笑。*To laugh (happily).*

（5）听了他的话大家都乐了。

（6）小王,最近有什么高兴的事,看你每天都乐呵呵的。

le 了 →P179"过"

用法 Usage:

助词 *modal particle*

一、用作动态助词。*As an aspect particle.*

用在句中动词后面,表示动作的完成。句式有以下六种。*Placed after a verb to mean that the action has been completed, it appears in the following six sentence patterns.*

1. 在单句中,常常表示动作完成,"了"在动词和宾语或补语之间,如果是结果补语,"了"要在结果补语后面。*In an independent, complete sentence, it often means the action has been completed. In this case, "了" is placed between the verb and its object or complement. By contrast, if it serves as a result complement, it must appear after that complement.*

（1）我已经喝掉了两杯牛奶。

(2) 他已经做完所有的作业了。

2. 在单句中,如果动词是由几个动词组成的动词短语,"了"可以在动词短语后面,也可以在任何一个动词后面。Again in an independent, complete sentence, if it is a verb phrase composed of several verbs, "了" can be placed after the verb phrase or after any of the verbs.

(3) 浙江大学发起并组织了这次活动。

(4) 浙江大学发起了并组织了这次活动。

3. "了"在动词重叠式中(一般用在单音节动词重叠中),除了表示动作完成以外,还表示动作持续的短暂,有"做一做就停"的意思。Used as part of a reduplicated verb — usually the verb is a monosyllable — "了" not only indicates the completion of the action, but also its short duration. Thus, it carries the meaning of "做一做就停."

重叠形式有:The forms of duplication can be:

① "A 了(一)A"强调动作时间短暂,后面可以带宾语。"A 了(一)A" emphasizes the shortness of the action. It can be followed by an object.

(5) 他看了(一)看我没说什么就走了。

(6) 他擦了(一)擦头上的汗,喝了一口水又跑了。

② "A 了又 A"。表示动作的完成,还表示动作的多次重复。"A 了又 A" means that the action of the verb is completed and that it is repeated several times.

(7) 我把今天的生词写了又写,终于记住了。

(8) 妈妈把姐姐写给她的信看了又看,高兴极了。

4. 连动句和兼语句中,"了"一般用在后一个动词后面。但是要强调第一个动作的完成时,"了"也可以在第一个动词后。In a successive-verb sentence or a sentence with a complex object, i.e. "v. + object + infinitive," "了" usually appears after the first verb. But it can also be placed after the first verb if one wishes to emphasize the completion of the first action.

(9) 我坐飞机去了北京。

(10) 他找了朋友帮他修电脑。

5. 有些动词后面的"了",表示动作有了结果,相当于动词后面的"掉",这样的动词有"忘、丢、关、喝、吃、泼、洒、扔、放、抹、擦、碰、撞、踩、卖、还、伤、摔"等。这个意义的"了",还可以用于命令句和"把"字句。动词前还可以加助动词。"了" indicates that the action has already produced a result, like "掉," if it follows such verbs as "忘,丢,关,喝,吃,泼,洒,扔,放,抹,擦,碰,撞,踩,卖,还,伤,摔." In this meaning, "了" can be used in a sentence expressing an order or request or in a sentence with "把." An auxiliary verb may appear before the verb.

(11) 你把她忘了吧。

(12) 你能关了电视吗?

6. "了"可以用在已经动词化的形容词后面,形容词后面还可以带表示数量、状态的词语做补语。"了" may follow an adjective that has been turned into a verb. Following this adjective, there may appear a complement of words expressing a number or a state.

(13) 教室里安静了几分钟。

(14) 他的脸红了起来。

二、用作语气助词。As a modal particle.

用在句子末尾,表示肯定事态出现了变化或即将出现变化。When "了" appears at the end of a sentence, it is a confirmation that some change has appeared or is likely to appear.

用法有以下四种:It is used in the following four situations:

1. 用在句末动词后面。动词如果带宾语,"了"用在宾语后面。To appear after a verb at the end of a sentence. "了" is placed behind the object if the verb has an object.

(15) 每天一到十点他就吃苹果了。

(16) 学期结束了,该回国了。

2. 用在形容词后面,一般情况下,"了"既表示新情况的出现,又表示变化的完成。*To appear after an adjective. Usually "了" does not just show that a new situation has appeared, but that the change has been completed.*

(17) 爷爷的头发全白了。

(18) 你越来越瘦了。

3. 如果着眼于当前,"了"只是肯定已经出现的情况或即将出现的情况。句子中常有表示近指的"这"配合使用或表示将要变化的"就要、快要、快、要"等词语配合使用。*If the emphasis is on the present, "了" is used to confirm a situation has appeared or is going to appear soon. In the sentence, one is likely to find "这" referring to something close by or words such as "就要,快要,快,要" to indicate changes that will happen soon.*

(19) 这本书我看完了。

(20) 春节快要到了。

4. 用在句末名词或数量词后面常常是告诉一种新情况。*To appear after a noun or numerical at the end of a sentence to indicate a new situation.*

(21) 冬天了。

(22) 三十岁了,不小了。

三、动词、形容词后面加"了"和句末加"了"连用,一般前面的"了"是动态助词,后面的"了"是语气助词。*"了" appears behind a verb or adjective and then appears again at the end of a sentence. The first "了" is a dynamic auxiliary while the second one is a modal particle.*

句式有:*Here are the sentence patterns:*

1. "动词+了+宾语+了"。"v.+了+object+了."

句中的"了"表示动作完成,句末的"了"表示事情的变化。*The first "了" indicates that the action is already completed while the second one means that some change has happened.*

(23) 我弟弟已经考上(了)大学了。

(24) 他们都做完(了)作业了。

2. "动词+了+数量短语+了"。"v.+了+a numerical phrase+了."

整个句子表示动作从开始到目前经过的时间和情况,不表示动作的完成。动作或行为是否继续,要看句子的上下文意思决定。*This sentence shows the time it takes for the action to move from the beginning to the present as well as things involved. It does not indicate the action has been completed, but the context will show whether the action or behavior is continuing.*

(25) 我学会了两千五百个汉字了。

(26) 北京他去了五次了。

3. "形容词+了+数量短语+了"。"a.+了+a numerical phrase+了."

前面的"了"表示变化完成,后面的"了"表示新情况出现,数量短语表示变化的程度。*In this sentence pattern, the first "了" indicates that the action has been completed and the second one shows the new situation that has appeared. The numerical phrase is used to show the degree of the change.*

(27) 衣服改了以后又小了。

(28) 孩子病了以后体重轻三斤了。

四、句子中只有一个"了",这个"了"用在不带宾语的动词或形容词后面,又处于句末,既表示动作或变化的完成,又肯定事态的变化。这个"了"既是动态助词又是语气助词。*Only one "了" appears in the sentence: it follows a verb that does not have an object and it appears at the very end of the sentence. In that case, "了" means not only the action or change has been completed but confirms the change of the situation. "了" in this sentence is both a dynamic verb and a modal particle.*

(29) 飞机起飞了。

(30) 他的脸红了。

说明 Notes:

一、动词后面都可以带动态助词"了"。但

下面几类动词不能带"了"：Not all verbs can be followed by "了" as a dynamic auxiliary. Usually the following types of verbs belong to this group:

1. 不表示变化词义的动词,如"是、姓、好像、认为、希望、属于、需要、作为、觉得"等。Verbs that don't indicate any changes, such as "是,姓,好像,认为,希望,属于,需要,作为,觉得."

2. 句子中的动词表示经常性的动作,动词后面不带"了"。"了" is not used when the verb in a sentence indicates an action that happens regularly.

(31) *我每天上课了。

(32) 我每天上课。

3. 句子中的第一个动词(除形式动词以外,如"进行"等)带动词宾语时,一般第一个动词不能带"了"。The first verb in a sentence (except for a verb just in form such as "进行") can't go with "了" if it has got an object.

(33) *学校宣布了放假。

(34) 学校宣布放假了。

二、"了"的否定句式有下面几种：The negative of "了" takes the following forms:

1. 用"没"的否定句式。动词后面一般不能再用"了"。Negative sentences using "没." In such sentences, the verb cannot be followed by "了."

主要有以下几种情况：Pay attention to the following points:

① 否定动词后面的"了",在动词前面用"没"。To negate "了" after a verb, you should place "没" before the verb.

(35) 我们吃饭了。——我们没吃饭。

(36) 我们去上课了。——我们没去上课。

② 否定句末表示已经出现新情况的"了",用"还没……(呢)"。To negate "了" at the end of a sentence indicating the emergence of a new situation, you should use "还没…(呢)."

(37) 玛丽已经看电影去了。——玛丽还没去看电影呢。

(38) 他们已经来了。——他们还没来。

③ 否定句末表示将出现新情况的"了",用"还没……(呢)"或"还不……(呢)"。To negate "了" at the end of a sentence indicating an upcoming new situation, you should use "还没…(呢)" or "还不…(呢)."

(39) 快放寒假了。——还没放寒假呢。

(40) 他快回家了。——他还不想回家呢。

④ 有数量词表示动作的结果时,否定整个动作,用"一……也/都没……"。"一…也/都没…" is used to negate the whole action if there is a measure word to indicate the result of an action.

(41) 他已经做完八个练习了。——他一个练习也没做。

(42) 她看完两本书了。——她一本书也没看。

⑤ 只否定数量,可以用"没"或其他词语。"没" or some other expression is used to negate only the numerical.

(43) 三个月没下雨了。

(44) 丝绸衬衣,她没买两件,只买了一件。

⑥ 否定与"掉"词义相似的"了",动词前面加"没",动词后面的"了"可以不用。"没" is placed before a verb if one wants to negate "了" meaning like "掉." There is no need to use "了" after the verb.

(45) 你还没忘(了)那件事吗？

(46) 还好这双鞋子没扔(了),不然奶奶会骂死我的。

⑦ 有的句子既有"没",又有"了",前面是"没+动",后面是句末的"了",不是动词后面的"了"。Some sentences have both "没" and "了." First there is "没+v.," and then there is "了" at the end of the sentence. This "了" is not the "了" behind the verb.

(47) 好几天没见到你了。

(48) 他两天没来上课了。

⑧ 否定连动句、兼语句后的"了","没"用

在第一个动词前面。"没" is placed before the first verb if one wants to negate "了" after a successive-verb sentence or a pivotal sentence.

（49）他没去南京旅游。

（50）我没请中国朋友吃饭。

2. 用"不"的否定句式。有的句子否定用"不"，但又有"了"，形成"不……了"的格式，一般表示两种语义。Negative sentences using "不" may have both "不" and "了," resulting in the pattern of "不…了." This structure usually has two different meanings.

① 先有"不＋动"，后面是语气助词"了"。表示改变原来的计划或倾向，因而出现了新情况。"不＋v." appears first, followed by the modal particle "了." This indicates the emergence of a new situation as a result of a change in the original plan or tendency.

（51）这本书我不看了，还给你吧。

（52）他不跟你去北京了，他朋友来看他了。

② 用"不"否定，动词后面的"了（动态助词）"，但不是真正的否定，只是假设性的否定，相当于"如果不……"的意思。动词后面的"了"也可以不用。"不" is used to negate "了 (aspect particle)" that follows the verb. It is not a true negation, however, just a hypothetical negation, which is equivalent to "如果不 (if not) …." The "了" may be omitted.

（53）到了超市里，不买了他要的玩具他是不会离开的。

（54）不吃完（了）这些蔬菜，妈妈是不会给你吃肉的。

3. 用"别"的否定句式里，又用"了"。"了" is used in a negative sentence using "别."

句式有：The following sentence structures may apply:

① "别"＋动＋句末的"了"，意思是叫对方停止他正在进行的动作或行为。句子中常有表示时间的名词。"别"＋v.＋"了" (at the end of a sentence)." This structure is used when asking the listener to stop the action or behavior he is engaged in. A time expression is usually found in such a sentence.

（55）你听音乐听了那么长时间，别听了。

（56）我们已经一个星期没上课了，别再旅游了，回校吧！

② "别"＋动＋动词后的"了"，这个"了"的词义相当于"掉"的意思。表示叫对方别做某种动作行为。"别"＋v.＋"了 (following a verb)." This "了" means exactly the same as "掉": it asks the listener to refrain from a certain action or behavior.

（57）这两个香蕉是留给妹妹的，你别吃了/别吃掉。

（58）桌子上的报纸我要用，你别扔了/别扔掉。

4. 否定形容词后面的"了"，可以用"没"，也可以用"不"。一般用在对话中。One may use either "没" or "不" to negate "了" following an adjective. This use is usually found in a conversation.

（59）A：这件衣服，我穿太大了。

B：我觉得没太大/不太大。

三、用"了"句子的疑问形式。把有"了"的句子改成疑问句，一般是在原句后面加"没有"。原句中"了"的数量或位置有些改变。How to make an interrogative sentence that has "了"? Usually, one adds "没有" to the end of the original sentence. There is some change in the number or position of "了."

有下面几种情况：It takes the following forms:

1. 如果原句有两个"了"，一般只留一个，或者是动词后面的"了"，或者是句末的"了"。If there are two "了," only one will be retained, either the one following the verb or the one at the end of the sentence.

（60）他读了课文没有？

（61）他读课文了没有？

2. 如果原句中只有一个"了"，"了"的位置也可以改变。If there is only one "了" in the

original sentence, the position of "了" may change.

（62）昨天你听讲座了没有？
（63）昨天的讲座你听了没有？
3. 动词不带别的成分，"了"的位置不变。"了" remains where it is if the verb goes with no other elements.

（64）他开始学习了没有？
（65）你吃了没有？

四、用"了"要特别注意：Pay special attention to the usage of "了" as follows:

1. 经常性的客观情况描述，动词后面不用"了"。The description of an objective situation that happens frequently does not go with "了."

（66）* 我在中国学习了很努力。
（67）我在中国学习很努力。

2. 一般否定句不用"了"。General negative sentences usually don't go with "了."

（68）* 星期天我没有去上海了。
（69）星期天我没有去上海。

3. 动词后面如果有介词或介词短语做补语，"了"在补语后面。If a verb is followed by a preposition or a prepositional phrase as its complement, "了" is placed after the complement.

（70）* 他们把篮球打了在我的头上。
（71）他们把篮球打在了我的头上。

4. 已经完成动作或改变情况的动词后面要用"了"。"了" has to be used when an action has been completed or a change has been made in the situation.

（72）* 他终于去她的宿舍。
（73）他终于去了她的宿舍。

五、"了"与"过"的区别如下：The differences between "了" and "过" are as follows:

1. 在词义上，"了"表示动作的完成或变化，与时间没有必然的联系，可以用于过去、现在或将来。"过"表示经历，与过去的时间总是连在一起。与现在、将来没有联系。"了" means the completion of an action or its change. It is not necessarily connected with time: it may be used of the past, the present, or the future. "过," by contrast, involves an experience; it is always connected with something in the past and has nothing to do with the present or the future.

（74）三年以前我来过中国。
（75）明天我们参观了博物馆以后再去爬山。

2. 在词义上，带"了"的动词，其动作可以延续到现在。带"过"的动词，其动作不能延续到现在。The action of a verb with "了" may extend to the present while that of a verb with "过" cannot extend to the present.

（76）他当了兵。（现在可能还在当兵。He is probably still in the army.）
（77）他当过兵。（现在不当兵了。He is demobilized.）

3. 在词义上，带"了"的动词，表示有一定的结果。带"过"的动词不一定有结果。The action of a verb that goes with "了" has produced some result, but the action of a verb that goes with "过" may have produced no result.

（78）他学了汉语。（有会汉语的意思。It implies that he can speak Chinese.）
（79）他学过汉语。（不一定学会。It doesn't necessarily mean he can speak Chinese.）

4. 在结构上，"了"可以用于动词重叠形式，表示"做一下就停"或"尝试"的意思。"过"不能这样用。如："看了看/* 看过看"。Structurally speaking, "了" may apply to a verb in its repeated form, meaning "to stop or pause after doing" or "to try to do something." But "过" cannot be used in this way, as in "看了看/* 看过看."

5. 否定句式都用"没(有)"，但是"了"在否定式里，一般不再保留。"过"仍然保留。Both their negative forms use "没(有)." While "了" is not retained in the negative sentence, "过" may be kept.

(80) 我没去过上海。
(81) 我没去上海。

lèisì 类似 →P510"相似"

用法 Usage:

动词 v.

表示大致相像。做谓语,后面加宾语时可以说成"类似于"。To indicate two things being or looking more or less the same; to be alike. It serves as the predicate, and when followed by an object, we may have "类似于."

(1) "杯具"的意思是"悲剧",类似这样的网络词语还有很多。
(2) 韩国语中有不少发音类似于浙江方言的词语。

形容词 a.

形容大致相像。Looking more or less the same.

(3) 天文学家发现了八颗新星球,其中两颗与地球非常类似。
(4) 历史常常会有很多类似的地方。

说明 Notes:

1. "类似"做形容词时可以用"非常"修饰,一般不用单音节"很"修饰。"类似," as an adjective, can be modified by "非常," but not the monosyllable "很."

2. "类似"做动词时后面不带表示程度的补语。"类似," as a verb phrase, is not to be followed by a complement indicating a degree.

(5) *我们俩的情况类似得很。
(6) 我们俩的情况非常类似。

lěng 冷 →P186"寒冷"、P302"凉"

用法 Usage:

形容词 a.

1. 温度低,感觉温度低。Feeling cold; low in temperature.

(1) 天气越来越冷了。
(2) 穿这么少,你冷不冷?

2. 对人的态度不热情,不温和。Not enthusiastic toward others; cold.

(3) 他对人总是不冷不热的。
(4) 你不要总是摆出一副冷冷的面孔。

3. 比喻失望或灰心。Being disappointed or frustrated.

(5) 他对她那么好,她还是不理他,他的心冷了。
(6) 他们都不同意我的建议,我的热情也就冷下来了。

说明 Notes:

"冷"与"寒冷"都表示天气温度低的意思。"冷" and "寒冷" both mean the low temperature.

它们的区别是：Their differences lie in:

1. "寒冷"是双音节词,一般不受程度副词"很"的修饰。"寒冷" is a disyllabic word and it is not modified by the degree adverb "很."

(7) *虽然外面天气很寒冷,但屋内是暖暖的。
(8) 虽然外面天气非常寒冷,但屋内是暖暖的。
(9) 虽然外面天气很冷,但屋内是暖暖的。

2. "寒冷"的词义比较狭隘,只用来表示温度很低。"冷"除了表示温度低,还形容人的态度不热情,形容人失望、灰心等心理状态等,义项较多。"寒冷" is rather narrow in its meaning, merely indicating the temperature is very low. "冷," by contrast, does not just mean low temperature; it may also signify a person's attitude, which is not warm or enthusiastic. It may, indeed, indicate disappointment or even lost confidence. It carries many psychological connotations.

3. "冷"是单音节词,作为词素能组成很多其他结构的词语,表达的方式也很多,如"冷淡、冷清、冷落、冷僻、冷箭、冷枪、冷言冷语、冷冰冰、冷森森"等。"寒冷"不能。As a monosyllabic word, "冷" may be used to form many expressions and its way of expression varies a lot, such as "冷淡,冷清,冷落,冷僻,冷箭,冷枪,冷言冷语,冷冰冰,冷森森。" "寒冷" cannot be used in these ways.

4. "冷"可以重叠成"冷冷"。"寒冷"不能重叠使用。"冷" can be reduplicated as "冷冷," but "寒冷" cannot.

lǐbài 礼拜

用法 Usage:

名词 *n.*

表示星期。*Week.*

(1) 开学已经三个礼拜了。

(2) 明天又是礼拜一了。

动词 *v.*

宗教徒向信奉的神行礼。*(Of religious people) to bow to God they believe in.*

(3) 麦克每周六都去教堂礼拜。

(4) 基督教徒虔诚地礼拜上帝。

说明 Notes:

"礼拜"的名词用法常用于口语。*"礼拜," serving as a noun, often appears in oral Chinese.*

lǐjiě 理解 →P306"了解"

用法 Usage:

动词 *v.*

表示懂，很深地了解。对象是道理、这样做的理由、内容和人的想法、看法、心情等。可以重叠。*To understand something fully and thoroughly. Its object is the reason for doing something, content of something, or other people's thoughts, ideas, and moods. It can be reduplicated as "理解理解."*

(1) 人们互相理解理解，就不会产生很多矛盾。

(2) 我理解你的心情，但是现在不能进去，里面正在动手术。

(3) 老师又讲了一遍词语的意思，可我还是不太理解。

lǐyóu 理由 →P100"道理"、P612"原因"

用法 Usage:

名词 *n.*

指发生某件事情或产生某种结果的根据或基础。*The reason or basis for something to happen or for a result to appear.*

(1) 你明天要请假的理由是什么？

(2) 我们是好朋友，我没有任何理由不帮他。

说明 Notes:

"道理"与"理由"都指事情或结果（论点）是非得失的根据或基础。区别是："道理"一般指正确的事理、事物中客观存在的规律，指人们做事应该遵循的规矩。"理由"不一定是正确的事理或客观规律。有时"理由"具有个性特征，有时甚至是错误的。*Both "道理" and "理由" refer to the basis upon which stands a point of view about right or wrong, plus or minus. Their difference is that while "道理" means a law that exists in the objective world and people have to follow it if they hope to achieve some desired result, "理由" may not be an objective law: it may, indeed, carry personal characteristics and may be wrong even.*

(3) *天为什么下雪的理由你知道吗？

(4) 天为什么下雪的道理你知道吗？

(5) 你去上海的理由是什么？

(6) 你年龄最小，好东西就要给你吃。这个理由对吗？

lìhai 厉害 →P297"利害"

用法 Usage:

形容词 *a.*

1. 表示某种行为动作非常剧烈。*(Of a behavior) very harsh or severe.*

(1) 你最近踢球踢得太厉害了，人都瘦了许多。

(2) 听到别人吵架的声音，她的心就跳得很厉害。

2. 表示某种程度很高、了不起，或很严重。*(Of a degree) very high or severe.*

(3) 他病得很厉害。我们去看看他。

(4) 他的汉语很厉害。

3. 表示态度严肃或性情凶猛。*(Of an attitude) solemn and serious; (of temper or temperament) vicious.*

(5) 这个老师很厉害。我们都有点怕他。

(6) 老虎和狮子谁更厉害？

4. 表示对某种情况难以忍受或对付。*Indicating that one finds it difficult to put up*

with or deal with a certain situation.

（7）天气热得真厉害！
（8）她的嘴太厉害了，谁也说不过她。

lìjí 立即 →P297"立刻"

用法 Usage:
副词 ad.

表示情况、动作很快发生，或很快出现新情况，或两种情况、两种动作先后紧接着发生。*Immediately; right after. It is used to show that things or actions happen very fast, that a new situation emerges pretty quickly, or that two situations or actions follow closely.*

（1）接到电话他立即就出门了。
（2）奶奶说想吃西瓜，姐姐立即给她买了一个。

说明 Notes:

1."立即"一般用于书面语。后面一般加多音节词，不加单音节词。*"立即" usually appears in written language, to be followed by a multi-syllable word, not a monosyllable one.*

（3）*吃了饭我们立即去。
（4）吃了饭我们立即就去。

2."立即"表示动作进行得快，中间间隔的时间很短。如果时间间隔不是很短，一般不用"立即"。*"立即" means that two actions happen fast with a short pause in between. It cannot be used if the two actions do not take place one immediately after another.*

（5）*我们立即毕业了。
（6）我们马上毕业了。
（7）*新年立即就要来临了。
（8）新年很快就要来临了。

lìkè 立刻 →P297"立即"、P311"马上"

用法 Usage:
副词 ad.

马上，表示事情或动作出现得快，常常紧接在某个时刻后面。修饰动词、形容词作状语。常用于口语和书面语。*Immediately, showing that things or actions appear fast, one right after another. It is used to modify verbs and adjectives, and it often appears both in written and in oral language.*

（1）她见了陌生人，脸立刻红了起来。
（2）明天飞机一到就给我打电话，我立刻开车去机场接你。

说明 Notes:

用于书面语的"立即"，其用法与"立刻"基本相同。*The use of "立即" in written language is basically the same as that of "立刻."*

lìhài 利害 →P296"厉害"

用法 Usage:
名词 n.

利益和损害。*Interests and damage(s).*

（1）你知道做这件事情的利害得失吗？
（2）交朋友不能计较利害关系。

说明 Notes:

1."利害"有两个发音，是形容词时，发音为 lìhai。*"利害" has two pronunciations. When used as an adjective, it's pronounced as "lìhai."*

2."利害(lìhai)"作形容词用时，与"厉害"同音同义，两词可以交换使用，意思不变。*When used as an adjective, "利害 (lìhai)" is pronounced the same as "厉害." Their meanings are the same, too, and so they are interchangeable.*

（3）她俩的武功很厉害/利害。
（4）今年冬天冷得太厉害/利害了。

3."厉害"没有名词用法。*"厉害" cannot be used as a noun.*

（5）*我跟他没有厉害关系。
（6）我跟他没有利害关系。

lìyòng 利用

用法 Usage:
动词 v.

1.使人或事物发挥效能。*To make use of; to allow someone or something to give play to their usefulness.*

(1) 我要利用学习汉语的机会,在中国好好旅游一下。

(2) 玛丽经常利用双休日的时间做家教。

2. 用手段使人或事物为自己服务。常含有贬义。 *To use certain means to make someone or something serve oneself. This use carries a derogatory meaning.*

(3) 利用父亲的关系,他得到了这份工作。

(4) 他利用人们的善良和信任,骗取他们的钱财。

3. 凭借,依靠。 *To take advantage of; to rely on.*

(5) 他利用权力,获取了不少钱财。

(6) 山区的人们利用高山的泉水,办起了矿泉水工厂。

lìwài 例外

用法 Usage:

动词 *v.*

表示在一般的规定或通常的规律之外。 *To do something not in accordance with a rule or regulation.*

(1) 每个人都要遵守法律,谁也不能例外。

(2) 我一般不喝酒,但是今天例外。

名词 *n.*

表示在一般的规律、规定之外的情况。 *A person or thing that is not included in a general statement; a thing that doesn't follow a rule; exception.*

(3) 在法律面前没有例外。

(4) 我的家人都爱好体育,只有我是一个例外。

说明 Notes:

"例外"用作动词时,后面不能加宾语。 *When used as a verb,* "例外" *cannot be followed by an object.*

lián 连

用法 Usage:

动词 *v.*

1. 表示连接,贯穿在一起。 *To connect; to join.*

(1) 前后两个句子意思连不起来。

(2) 毕竟母子连心,孩子心情不好,妈妈很快就感觉到了。

2. 连带,牵连,连累。 *To involve; to get involved in.*

(3) 这是他的问题,为什么把你也连上了?

副词 *ad.*

表示连续发生同一个动作行为或同一种情况,一个接着一个。 *Showing that the same action or behavior happens repeatedly, one after another.*

(4) 我连发了三封邮件给他,他都没回。

(5) 这部电影太好看了,我连看了两遍。

介词 *prep.*

1. 表示包括在内,算上。 *Including; counting someone or something in.*

① 句子中一定带有数量短语。 *There must be a numerical phrase in the sentence.*

(6) 这件行李连箱子共重三十公斤。

(7) 我们班连我有七个韩国人。

② "连……"可以在主语前面,有停顿。 "连…" *may appear before the subject of a sentence. A pause is taken.*

(8) 连这一次,这部电影我一共看了四遍。

(9) 他吃了五个肉包子了,连这个。

2. 表示不排除另一有关事物。 *Not excluding what is related.*

(10) 苹果可以连皮吃。

(11) 你要连他妈妈一起请来。

说明 Notes:

1. "连"用作副词时,一般用来修饰单音节词。如果用来修饰双音节词,则应该用"一连""接连"或"连连"。 *When* "连" *serves as an adverb, it usually modifies a monosyllabic word; if it is used to modify a disyllabic word,* "一连," "接连" *or* "连连" *is used.*

(12) *为了参加舞蹈比赛,我们连准备了两个月。

(13) 为了参加舞蹈比赛,我们一连准备了两个月。

2. "连"和"连连"之间的区别是：*The differences between "连" and "连连" are as follows:*

① "连"作副词用时一般修饰单音节词。"连连"则用于修饰双音节动词或动词短语。两者不能混用。*"连," as an adverb, is usually used to modify a verb with only one syllable. "连连," by contrast, is usually used to modify a verb with two syllables or a verb phrase. They are not to be exchanged.*

（14）*他妈妈连连发了三个邮件，叫他回去。

（15）他妈妈连发了三个邮件，叫他回去。

（16）*他连向大家说：谢谢，谢谢。

（17）他连连向大家说：谢谢，谢谢。

② "连"可以接上表示数字的短语。"连连"不能。*"连" may be followed by a phrase indicating a number, but "连连" cannot be used this way.*

（18）*这孩子连连摔三次都没哭。

（19）这孩子连摔三次都没哭。

lián……dài…… 连……带……

用法 Usage：

1. 表示包括前后两项。与名词或动词（常为离合动词或动词短语）组合，表示两个事物或两件事。可在主语前，可停顿。*Indicating two things or two events, "连…带…" is often used to link two nouns or two verbs — separable verbs or verb phrases. It can be placed before the subject, with a pause.*

（1）他们连车带人都掉到了河里。

（2）连吃饭带看电影，我今天一共花了八十块钱。

2. 表示两个动作同时发生，不分先后。如果跟两个单音节动词组合，这两个动词的性质相近。类似于"又……又……"。*Indicating that two actions happen simultaneously. If the two verbs are monosyllabic, they are similar in nature. It is akin to "又…又…" in usage.*

（3）新年联欢会上，留学生连唱带跳地表演了很多节目。

（4）孩子们连呼带叫地跑向公园的草地。

说明 Notes：

用于表示包括前后两项格式中的两件事物，关系往往很密切。如：例（1）中的"车"和"人"是紧紧连在一起的；例（2）"吃饭"和"看电影"是同一天进行的事情。*"连…带…" is used when talking about two closely related events or things that happen, as in (1), where the vehicle and the person are closely related; and in (2), where having lunch and watching a movie are done on the same day.*

lián……dōu/yě…… 连……都/也……

用法 Usage：

"连"作介词用时，用来强调句子中的某一部分，含有"甚至"的意思。有时"甚至"可以用在"连"的前面。常跟"都、也、还"等搭配使用，组成"连……都/也……"的短语格式，举出突出的事例，强调程度很深。*"连," as a preposition, is used to emphasize a certain part of a sentence. It carries the meaning of "even." Sometimes, "甚至" can be placed before "连." It is often combined with "都, 也, 还," etc. to form a prepositional phrase "连…都/也…." In this way, some outstanding example is given to show the high degree of something that has happened.*

从强调的内容来看，句式有：*Here are the sentence patterns related to this use:*

1. "连＋名＋都/也……"。"连＋n.＋都/也…."

① 强调动作行为的对象（即受事者）。*Emphasizing the target of the action, that is, the receiver of the action.*

（1）她连饭也没吃就去了。

（2）我们连他的名字都不知道。

② 强调动作行为的主体（即施事者）。*Emphasizing the person who takes the action.*

（3）这个句子是什么意思，连她自己也说

不清楚。

(4) 写汉字写得连手都痛了。

③ 强调处所、方式。Emphasizing the place or the manner.

(5) 我连床下都找了，还是没找到。

(6) 连开着车去他家请，他也不肯来。

2. "连＋动＋都/也＋否定式"。"连"强调某一动作、行为，再在"都/也"之后对这一动作、行为加以否定，有时都/也前后动词相同。In "连＋v.＋都/也＋negative," "连" is used to emphasize a certain action or behavior. Then this action or behavior is negated following "都/也." Sometimes the same verb is used before and after "都/也."

(7) 她连看都没看就答应了。

(8) 他连打篮球也不会。

3. "连＋数量词＋都/也……"。"连"后面的数词限于"一"，如果表示时间，数词可以在表示整体的"一"以下。谓语限于否定式。"连＋numerical＋都/也...." The numerical after "连" is limited only to "一." If this expression is used to express a time, the numerical may be less than "一." The predicate for this kind of sentence must be a negative.

(9) 学了两个星期了，连一句话也不会说。

(10) 他到现在连半分钟都没休息过。

4. "连＋动词小句＋都/也……"。动词短语或小句限于由疑问代词或不定数词构成。"连＋a mini-sentence featuring a verb＋都/也...." Here the verb phrase or a clause featuring a verb is limited to something formed by an interrogative pronoun or an indefinite numerical.

(11) 我连他叫什么名字也不知道。

(12) 他连这件衣服多少钱也忘了。

liánmáng 连忙 →P213 "急忙"

用法 Usage:

副词 ad.

表示动作行为很快，相当于"赶紧、急忙"。只用于陈述句和描述句。Showing the action happens very fast, it is equivalent to "赶紧," or "急忙." It is used only in a statement or a descriptive sentence.

(1) 发现护照丢了，我连忙去补办了一个。

(2) 接到爸爸的电话，他连忙打的去了机场。

说明 Notes:

"连忙"与"急忙"的区别是：The differences between "连忙" and "急忙" are as follows:

1. 在词义上，它们都表示动作、行为迅速，用法基本相同。但"急忙"着重于心里着急的意思，侧重描述动作者神情状态。"连忙"强调动作本身在时间上的迅速，往往着重表示某一动作、行为或情况在时间上是紧接着上一动作、行为或情况产生、出现。Both indicating the action or behavior happens fast, they are used more or less in the same way. But "急忙" emphasizes the psychological state of the person: he or she is full of worry. "连忙," by contrast, emphasizes the speedy happening of the action. Most likely the action, behavior or situation happens close upon the heels of the former action, behavior or situation.

(3) 听说家里来了客人，她急忙赶回家了。

(4) 听说家里来了客人，她连忙赶回家了。

2. 在使用范围上，"急忙"跟"连忙"一样，只能用于陈述句和描述句。被修饰的行为、动作已经发生或正在发生。不能用于祈使句。Both "急忙" and "连忙" are limited to the use in a statement or a descriptive sentence. The described behavior or action has already happened or is happening right now. It cannot be used in an imperative sentence.

(5) ＊你妈妈叫你急忙/连忙回家。

(6) 你妈妈叫你马上回家。

3. "急忙"作为形容词可以重叠使用。"连忙"不可以。"急忙," as an adjective, can be reduplicated, but "连忙" cannot be used this way.

liánxù 连续 →P217"继续"、P233"接连"、P308"陆续"

用法 Usage:

动词 v.

表示一个接一个、一次接一次、相继不断、前后没有间断的意思。后面多有表示时间或次数的词语配合使用，常做谓语，或与名词构成动词短语充当状语或定语。做谓语可以带宾语、时量补语和趋向补语。To continue without pause or interruption; to happen one right after another. Following this expression are often words indicating time or the number of times. It often serves as the predicate in the sentence, or it can go with a noun to form a verb phrase, serving as an adverbial or attribute. When it serves as the predicate, it can be followed by an object, a time-amount complement or a complement indicating the tendency.

（1）大雨连续下了一个多星期了。

（2）马克连续六天没来上课。

说明 Notes:

1. "连续"和"继续"都是动词，都有连接不断的意思。Both "连续" and "继续" are verbs, meaning to continue without interruption.

它们的区别是：Their differences are as follows:

① "连续"强调动作或活动整体在时间上不能间断、在动作上一个接着一个。"继续"强调前后相继，强调动作与前面有关系的动作或活动的连接，中间可以有间隔，也可以没有间隔，动作或活动可以停顿，中断后又接着原来的动作行为进行。虽然有时在句子中，"连续"和"继续"可以替换，但是句子意思不同。"连续" focuses on an action or activity going on one after another without any interruption. "继续," by contrast, emphasizes the actions are following one upon the heels of another. But there might be an interruption or no interruption. A pause might follow an action or activity, but the original action or activity will resume and go on as before. Although "连续" and "继续" may replace each other, their meanings are somewhat different.

（3）他连续看了三个小时书。

（4）他继续看了三个小时书。

② "连续"可以用于否定句。"继续"不能。"连续" can appear in negative sentences, but "继续" cannot.

（5）*他继续两天没吃饭了。

（6）他连续两天没吃饭了。

2. "连续"和"接连"都有副词用法，表示"一个接一个、一次接一次"的情况。Both "连续" and "接连" can serve as an adverb, indicating a situation where one follows another, or simply "time and again."

它们的区别是：Their differences are as follows:

① "接连"是副词。"连续"虽有副词用法，但它是动词，表示紧密联系，中间不中断，如："这场雨已经连续二十天了。""接连" is an adverb. "连续" is a verb although it can also serve as an adverb. It means close relationship without any interruptions, as in "这场雨已经连续二十天了."

② "连续"有强调动作"不停息"的意思，常与表示时间或次数的词语配合使用。"接连"表示某种情况一次一次地出现，并不强调动作的不间断。"连续" puts an emphasis on the action being uninterrupted. Often it goes with words indicating: 1) a time; 2) the number of times. "接连" indicates a situation being repeated time and again without any interruptions.

（7）*这个实验应该接连进行，不能中断，直到有了结果才能结束。

（8）这个实验应该连续进行，不能中断，直到有了结果才能结束。

③ "连续"可以组成"连续性、连续剧"等名词性词语。"接连"不能。"连续" can be used

to form nominal expressions such as "连续性，连续剧.""接连" cannot.

liáng 凉 →P295"冷"

用法 Usage:
形容词 a.
1. 温度低，微冷。Low in temperature; mildly cold.
（1）东北的夏天，一早一晚还是很凉的。
（2）饭有点凉了，要不要再热一下？
2. 表示失望灰心。Showing disappointment or frustration.
（3）考了几次都没通过，我的心都凉了。
（4）听说喜欢的人已经结了婚，他的心顿时凉了。

说明 Notes:
"凉"跟"冷"都表示温度低。"凉"和"冷"后面都可以加后缀，如："凉飕飕、凉丝丝、凉津津；冷飕飕、冷清清、冷森森"；等等。"冷"和"凉"表示灰心失望时用法一样。Both "凉" and "冷" are related to the low temperature. Both can be followed by some affixes as in "凉飕飕, 凉丝丝, 凉津津; 冷飕飕, 冷清清, 冷森森; etc." And both can mean disappointment or frustration.
（5）你这样对我，我的心都凉/冷了。
它们的区别是：Their differences are as follows:
1. "凉"的温度比"冷"要高一点。表示温度的一系列形容词从低到高依次是：冷，凉，暖，热。一般来说，冬天的"冷"相对的是"暖"，夏天的"热"相对的是"凉"。"凉" indicates a temperature somewhat higher than "冷." Words expressing temperature are ranked from low to high as: 冷, 凉, 暖, 热. Generally speaking, the opposite of "冷" in the winter is "暖" while the opposite of "热" in the summer is "凉."
（6）*夏天外面很热，但是屋子里却很冷。
（7）夏天外面很热，但是屋子里很凉。
2. "凉"也可以作动词，读"liàng"。表示把热的东西放一会儿，使温度降低。这个用法和"冷"的动词用法一样。"凉," used as a verb, is pronounced as "liàng." It means to allow something hot to cool down. This use is the same as "冷," which can also be used as a verb.
（8）水太烫，凉一凉/冷一冷再喝。

liáng 量

用法 Usage:
动词 v.
用尺、容器或其他作为标准的器具来确定事物的长短、大小、多少或其他性质。To use a ruler, container or something else to measure the length, size, amount or other properties.
（1）体检时一般要量身高和体重。
（2）孩子发烧了，妈妈不停地给他量体温。
（3）我量了一下，这件衣服比那件长了两厘米。

说明 Notes:
1. 作为衡量标准的东西一般是有高低或长短刻度的工具。能通过高低长短来表示的事物性质可以用"量"，不能用高低长短来表示的事物性质一般不用"量"，比如重量除了"体重"，别的一般不能用"量"。Usually a device with graduation is used to measure the height or length of something. "量" is used if the nature of a thing can be expressed as a height or length; otherwise, "量" cannot be used. Except for "体重," "量" is not used.
（4）*请帮我量一下这些苹果有多重。
（5）请帮我称一下这些苹果有多重。
2. "量"还有名词用法，读"liàng"。"量" is also used as a noun, pronounced as "liàng."
① 表示数量、数目。一般用在词尾。Indicating quantity and number, it usually appears at the end of a word.
（6）要通过HSK六级，我还需要扩大我的词汇量。
（7）每年中秋节月饼的消费量都很大。
② 表示能容纳或经受的最大限度，多用在词尾。Indicating the upper limit that can be

contained or sustained, it often appears at the end of a word.

(8) 我的胆量很小。

(9) 他的酒量比我大多了。

liǎng 两 →P131"二"

用法 Usage:

数词 num.

1. 一个加一个后的数量词——两。一般后面都要有量词。 One plus one is two. It is usually followed by a measure word.

(1) 这两栋楼是留学生宿舍。

(2) 我来中国已经两年了。

2. 表示双方。多用于书面或固定格式。如:"两全其美、两相情愿"。 Indicating both sides, applied primarily to written Chinese or some fixed form, as in "两全其美 (satisfying to both sides),""两相情愿" (both are willing)."

(3) 你去银行,我去书店,然后再一起吃饭。你我两便,挺好的安排。

3. 表示不定的数目,相当于"几"。 Indicating an indefinite number, it is equivalent to "几 (several)."

(4) 关于参观博物馆的事,我来说两句。

(5) 别以为看了两本书,就什么都懂了。

4. 指称有些本来成双或被认为成双的亲属或事物。如:"两夫妻、两姐妹、两兄弟、两极分化、两耳不闻窗外事"等。 Referring to people and things that usually appear in two, as in "两夫妻,两姐妹,两兄弟,两极分化,两耳不闻窗外事, etc."

5. 重量单位。如:"一市斤等于十市两、此地无银三百两"。 A unit for the weight, as in "一市斤等于十市两,""此地无银三百两."

说明 Notes:

"二"和"两"都是数字,都可以用在"百、千、万、亿"前面。 Both "二" and "两" are numerals. Both can be placed before "百,千,万,亿."

它们的区别是: Their differences are as follows:

1. "十"前面只能用"二",不能用"两"。 "十" is preceded only by "二," not "两."

2. "二"可以单说,如"一、二、三、四"。"两"不能。 "二" can stand by itself, as in "一,二,三,四," but "两" cannot.

3. 多位数中的个位数用"二",如"十二、一百零二、百分之二"等。"两"不能这样用。 A single digit in a multi — digit numeral uses "二," as in "十二,一百零二,百分之二.""两" is not to be used.

4. "二"可以用在亲属称呼前面,如"二弟、二伯、二姨"。"两"不能。 "二" can be applied when addressing relatives, as in "二弟,二伯,二姨.""两" cannot.

5. "两"可以用在所有度量衡单位之前,但作为度量衡单位的"两"前面只能用"二"。"二"只能用在度量衡单位之前,如:可以说"二斤、二两、二尺"等,不能说"二个、二只、二条"。"两" can be applied to all measuring units, but we can say "二斤,二两,二尺," (not "二个,二只,二条") because "二" can appear before a measuring unit. When "两" serves as a unit of measurement, however, it is preceded only by "二."

6. "两"可以直接用在某些名词或临时量词之前,如"两国、两家、两校、两手、两脚、两杯、两碗、两瓶"等。"二"除了偶尔只说"二手(车)"以外,一般不能直接用在名词前。"两" can appear before certain nouns or temporary units of measuring as in "两国,两军,两校,两手,两脚,两碗,两瓶," etc. By contrast, "二" usually cannot be placed directly before a noun except for "二手(车)."

liǎng'àn 两岸

用法 Usage:

名词 n.

1. 指江河、海峡等两边的地方。 Both sides of a river or strait.

(1) 河两岸种满了柳树。

2. 特别指台湾海峡两岸,也就是中国大陆和台湾省。*Referring especially to both sides of the Taiwan Straits, that is, China's mainland and Taiwan Province.*

(2) 统一中国是两岸同胞的共同愿望。

liǎo 了

用法 Usage:

动词 *v.*

1. 表示完毕、结束。可与"事情、事儿、心事、活儿、工作、差事、案子"等少数名词搭配,可带"了(le)"。否定式在"了"前面加"没"。*To come to an end; to be over. It can be used with a few nouns such as "事情,事儿,心事,活儿,工作,差事,案子." "了" is pronounced as (le). "没" is placed before "了" as a negative form.*

(1) 儿子结婚了(le),妈妈的心事才了了(liǎo le)。

(2) 那个工作还没了(liǎo),新的任务又来了(le)。

2. 用在动词后,跟"得、不"连用,表示对行为实现的可能与否做出估计。*To indicate an estimate of whether the behavior is practicable or not, "了" is placed behind a verb along with "得" or "不."*

(3) 两瓶葡萄酒不多,他喝得了。

(4) 报纸上的文章我读不了,因为生词太多。

3. "了"用在形容词后,有两种句式。*There are two sentence structures where "了" follows an adjective.*

① 跟"得、不"连用,表示对事物状态的变化做出估计。肯定、否定都可以用。*Indicating an estimate of a change in the state or condition of something, it is used together with "得,不." This use is applicable to both positive and negative sentences.*

(5) 他的病好得了。

(6) 他的病好不了。

② 表示对事物性状的程度做出估计。一般用于否定式。用在肯定式,句子为问句或回答问句。*Indicating an estimate of how things are. This use is usually applicable to negative sentences. When it appears in a positive sentence, the sentence is either a question or the answer to a question.*

(7) 飞机票便宜不了,还是坐火车吧。

(8) 他们俩好得了吗?

(9) 他们俩好得/不了。

说明 Notes:

1. "了"也用"不"表示否定,但用于固定格式中,如"不了了之"等。*"了" also goes with "不" to indicate a negative, but this use is limited to some fixed form or pattern. For instance, "不了了之."*

2. "了"还表示"清楚、明白"的意思。一般用于书面语。如"了如指掌、一目了然"等。*"了" may mean "清楚" or "明白," usually in written language, as in "了如指掌,一目了然."*

liǎobudé 了不得 →P46"不得了"

用法 Usage:

形容词 *a.*

1. 表示超出平常,非常突出。*Outstanding; over and above the ordinary.*

(1) 他很了不得,已经拿到博士学位了。

(2) 你真了不得,学了一年汉语,就考出了HSK五级。

2. 表示程度很深,常常用在形容词后做程度补语。*Indicating a very profound degree, it often follows an adjective as a degree complement.*

(3) 马克认识的汉字多得了不得。

(4) 今年冬天,北京冷的了不得。

3. 表示情况严重,没法收拾。*Indicating that the situation is so serious that it is beyond control or repair.*

(5) 这没有什么了不得的问题,不要着急,能够解决。

(6) 了不得了,你们看,那座大楼起火了!

说明 Notes：

"了不得"和"不得了"都是形容词,表示情况严重、无法收拾,程度很深的意思。*Both "了不得" and "不得了" are adjectives indicating a situation is so serious that it is beyond control or repair.*

它们的区别是：*Their differences are as follows:*

1. "了不得"有超过寻常,非常突出的意思。"不得了"没有这个意思。*"了不得" may mean outstanding or over and above the ordinary. But "不得了" doesn't carry that meaning.*

2. 做形容词的程度补语时,虽然意思差不多,但多用"不得了"。"了不得"不常用。*"不得了," usually not "了不得," is used to indicate a very profound degree and follow an adjective as a degree complement.*

3. 用"了不得"常常有代词、名词性主语,如例(1)(2)(3)。"不得了"一般没有。*"了不得" is often used with a noun or pronoun subject as in (1), (2) and (3). "不得了" is not used in this way.*

4. "了不得"可以做定语。"不得了"不能做定语。*"了不得" may serve as an attribute, but "不得了" cannot.*

5. "了不得"可以用在"有/没有"后面表示否定时,前面常有疑问代词"什么",如例(5)。"不得了"不能。*When "了不得" is used after "有" or "没有" to indicate a negation, it is preceded by "什么" as in (5). "不得了" cannot be used in this way.*

liǎobuqǐ 了不起

用法 Usage：

形容词 *a.*

1. 用于积极方面,常形容值得称道的人、事和行为,表示突出、不平凡的意思。用法与"了不得"第一义项相同,有称赞的语气。*Outstanding; wonderful. As a positive expression, it is used to describe highly praise-worthy people, things and behaviors. It is used the same way as Usage 1 for "了不得" in a praising tone.*

用法有：*The usages are as follows:*

① 修饰名词必须带"的"。*It must be followed by "的" when it is used to describe a noun.*

(1) 历史上有许多了不起的人物。

(2) 网络是一种了不起的科技发明。

② 可在"以为、觉得"后面做宾语。*It can follow "以为" and "觉得" as their object.*

(3) 他以为自己很了不起。

(4) 我觉得他能这样做真了不起！

③ 做谓语时,前面常用"真"。*"真" often appears before it when it serves as the predicate in the sentence.*

(5) 这个人真了不起！

④ 可做补语。*It can serve as a complement.*

(6) 四十年前,出国留学的事被看得很了不起。

2. 用于消极方面,表示严重的意思。常形容困难、过错以及其他对人不利的事和行为。多用于反问句或否定句,"有/没/没有/不是＋什么/啥＋了不起(的)",表示不必看得很严重。*It means serious or harsh when it is used with a negative sense. It refers to behaviors that are difficult, wrong, or harmful to others. It often appears in a rhetorical question or a negative sentence. The pattern "有/没/没有/不是＋什么/啥＋了不起(的)" means there is no need to look upon it as very serious.*

(7) 只是破了一点皮,不是啥了不起的伤。

(8) 现在大家的生活都还不错,出国旅游没有什么了不起。

说明 Notes：

1. "了不起"多用于口语。*"了不起" is mostly used in oral Chinese.*

2. 可以单独回答问题。*It can be used to answer a question by itself.*

(9) A：我博士学位拿到了。

　　B：了不起啊！

liǎojiě 了解 →P296"理解"、P662"知道"

用法 Usage:

动词 v.

1. 表示知道得很清楚,很明白。可受程度副词修饰。可重叠为ABAB式。可带"了",一般不带"着"。*To know well, to be aware of. It can be modified by adverbs of degree, and it can be reduplicated in the form of ABAB. "了" can follow it, but usually it doesn't go with "着."*

可用作：*It can serve as:*

① 谓语,宾语常常是主谓短语。*The predicate. The object tends to be a subject-predicate phrase.*

(1) 我非常了解他是个怎么样的人。

(2) 到了中国,你可以了解了解中国的佛教文化。

② 定语,或构成短语作定语,常带"的"。*The attribute. It is used to form a phrase and serve as an attribute. It is often followed by "的."*

(3) 我对他了解的情况很少。

(4) 了解她的人都愿意跟她做朋友。

③ 带上定语可用作名词,做句子动词的宾语。*The noun. When it goes with an attribute, it plays the part of the object of a corresponding verb.*

(5) 到中国各地去旅游,可以加深对中国的了解。

(6) 这里的风景很美,但是我只有大概的了解。

2. 表示打听、调查的意思。可重叠为ABAB式。*To find out; to investigate. It can be reduplicated in the form of ABAB.*

常用作：*It often serves as:*

① 谓语,宾语常常是主谓短语。*The predicate. The object is often a subject-predicate phrase.*

(7) 你先要去了解一下那个大学有哪些专业。

(8) 明天我们去工厂了解了解他们的环保情况。

② "进行、开始、加紧"等动词的宾语。*The object to verbs such as "进行,开始,加紧."*

(9) 你说的情况,我们会很快进行了解。

③ 带上定语可以作为名词做主语。*The subject where "了解" is a noun with an attribute.*

(10) 对中国的了解一年两年是不够的。

说明 Notes:

"理解"和"了解"的区别是：*The differences between "理解" and "了解" are as follows:*

1. "理解"和"了解"的对象不一样,"理解"是明白道理、这样做的理由、内容和人的想法、看法、心情等,是更深层次的认识。多用于书面语。"了解"是通过调查接触对人或事物的情况、历史、变化等知道得很清楚。词意比"理解"的层面浅。口语书面语都用。两个词语在句子里不能互换。"理解"and"了解"*take different things as their objects. "理解" refers to understanding truth, the reason for doing something, people's thoughts, ideas, and mood. It represents an understanding on a deeper level. Therefore, it mostly appears in written language. "了解," by contrast, is to have a very good understanding of things, their history of development and changes through investigation and contacts. It represents an understanding on a level less deep. It is used both in written and oral language. "理解" and "了解" are not interchangeable in a sentence.*

(11) 我理解他。(意思是我知道他是怎么想的,明白他这么做的理由。*I know how he looks at the matter and why he did it.*)

(12) 我了解他。(意思是我知道他是什么样的人。*I know what kind of a person he is.*)

2. "了解"还有打听、调查的意思,"理解"没有这个意思。*A second meaning of "了解" is to investigate and try to find out. "理解" doesn't have that meaning.*

lièwéi 列为

用法 Usage:

意思是安排到某类事物中。*To list things in a certain category; to place in a particular class or group.*

(1) 2011年,"杭州西湖文化景观"被列为世界文化遗产。

(2) 据报道,不少欧美国家把汉语列为外语考试科目。

说明 Notes:

"列为"使用的语法结构一般是:"……被列为……",或者"把……列为……"。*Pay attention to the grammatical structure when using "列为." It is either "... 被列为..." or "把...列为...."*

línshí 临时

用法 Usage:

形容词 *a.*

表示短时期的,暂时的,非正式的。*Temporary; informal; short in terms of time duration.*

(1) 他暂时在这家单位当临时工。

(2) 全国运动会时,这里建了很多临时建筑。

副词 *ad.*

表示到事情发生的时候。做状语。*Used as an adverb, it indicates that something didn't happen until....*

(3) 原来我打算今天去西湖玩,但是临时有事,去不了了。

(4) 小王突然生病不能出差,经理临时派我去了。

lìng 另 →P307"另外"

用法 Usage:

代词 *pron.*

指上文中所说的范围之外,另外的,别的。"另"后面一定带数量词语。*Outside the scope indicated by the context; something else.* "另" is always followed by a word indicating a number or quantity.

(1) 他们走了另一条路。

(2) 除了这个艺术馆,我还去过另两个画廊。

副词 *ad.*

表示在上文所说的范围之外。多用在单音节动词前面作状语。*Outside the scope indicated by the context. It is usually used as an adverbial before a monosyllabic word.*

(3) 今天我很忙,我们另找时间见面吧。

(4) 除了汉语以外,我还想另选一门课。

lìngwài 另外 →P307"另"

用法 Usage:

代词 *pron.*

指上文所说范围之外的人或事。后面带的是名词性词语,或者加"的",构成"的"字结构。*People or things outside the scope of the context. Typically, it is followed by a nominal word or expression. Sometimes it is followed by "的."*

(1) 我还要跟你谈另外一件事。

(2) 这个字还有另外的意思。

副词 *ad.*

表示在上文所说范围之外,用在动词或动词词语前做状语。常与"还、又、再"连用。*Referring to something beyond what is said in the context, it usually appears as an adverbial before a verb or verb phrase. Often it goes with "还,又,再."*

(3) 关于这个问题,我们另外再找时间讨论。

(4) 这个礼物是妹妹的,你的我另外买给你。

连词 *conj.*

表示除了前面说过的以外,还有其他内容。用在后面分句、句子或段落开头,表示连接作用。多用于口语。*Indicating that there is something else in addition to what is already* said earlier. Serving as an expression to join things together, it appears at the beginning of a clause, a sentence, or a paragraph that follows. This use is common in oral Chinese.

（5）你到中国除了学汉语，另外还要学英语。

（6）这些作业做完后，另外再写一张毛笔字。

说明 Notes：

"另"和"另外"都有代词的用法，意思相同。区别是：Both "另" and "另外" can be used as a pronoun. Their meaning is the same, but they do have some differences as follows:

1. 语言色彩有所不同。"另"书面色彩重。"另外"多用于口语。"另" carries the mark of a written language while "另外" appears mostly in oral Chinese.

2. 词语搭配有所不同。"另"后面一定要带数量词，不能加"的"。"另外"后面也可以跟数量词，后面是名词时，可以加"的"。Their collocations differ. "另" is always followed by a word indicating a number or amount; and it cannot be followed by "的." As for "另外," it can be followed by a word indicating a number or amount. And it can go with "的" when it is followed by a noun.

（7）*你们两个住在这个楼，另的同学跟我来。

（8）你们两个住在这个楼，另外的同学跟我来。

3. "另"和"另外"做副词时，一般"另"用在单音节动词前。"另外"可用在单音节前，也可用在多音节动词前。Both "另" and "另外" may serve as an adverb and both can appear before a monosyllabic word, but "另外" can also appear before a multisyllabic word.

4. "另"和"另外"做副词时，"另"一般用在副词"还、又、再"后面。"另外"一般用在副词"还、又、再"的前面。When serving as an adverb, "另" is usually placed after adverbs such as "还、又、再" while "另外" is placed before those words.

（9）她的手机坏了，昨天又另买了一个。

（10）她的手机坏了，昨天另外又买了一个。

5. "另外"有加"的"形容词用法。"另"没有这种用法。如："另外的一本书、另外的一件事情"；"*另的一本书、*另的一件事情"；等等。"的" may be added to "另外" to make it an adjective, but "另" cannot be used in this way, as in "另外的一本书，另外的一件事情." It would be wrong to say "*另的一本书，*另的一件事情."

lùxù 陆续 →P301 "连续"

用法 Usage：

副词 ad.

表示动作行为前后相继，时断时续。常用于表述客观状态的句子，可以重叠为"陆陆续续"，加强语气，只能用作状语。One after another; in succession. It indicates that the action or behavior goes on continually with short pauses in between. Typically, it appears in a statement that gives an objective account of things that happen. To emphasize, it can be reduplicated as "陆陆续续," which can only be used as an adverbial.

（1）华为公司陆续推出了一系列手机新产品。

（2）上课时间到了，同学们陆陆续续走进了教室。

说明 Notes：

"陆续"和"连续"都有副词用法，表示事物或动作接连出现或进行，可做状语。Both "陆续" and "连续" can be used as an adverb meaning things or actions happen in succession. Both are used as an adverbial in that case.

它们的区别是：Their differences are as follows:

1. 词性不一样。"连续"是动词，可以带宾语、补语，可以做状语、定语。"陆续"是副词，只能做状语。In terms of parts of speech, "连续"

is a verb that can be followed by an object or a complement while "陆续" is an adverb and is used only as an adverbial.

2. 在词义上，"陆续"着重于先后相继，时断时续。"连续"没有间断。*In terms of their meanings,* "陆续" *emphasizes following each other, and there are possible pauses.* "连续," *by contrast, doesn't allow any pauses.*

3. "陆续"可以重叠，"连续"不能。"陆续" *can be reduplicated while* "连续" *cannot.*

4. "陆续"前常有动词短语，表示状态的出现。*A verb phrase often appears before* "陆续," *indicating the appearance of a state or condition.*

（3）上课了，操场上玩儿的同学陆陆续续回到了教室。

5. "连续"可构成"连续性、连续化"等名词短语。"陆续"不能。"连续" *can be used to form noun phrases such as* "连续性、连续化," *but* "陆续" *cannot.*

lù 露

用法 Usage:

动词 *v.*

1. 显现，暴露。*To appear; to be exposed.*

（1）他笑了起来，露出一口雪白的牙齿。

（2）袜子破了，脚趾头露在外面了。

2. 在房屋、帐篷等的外面，表示没有遮盖。*To be outside a house, a tent, etc. with nothing to block the view.*

（3）为了看日出，我们打算在山上露宿。

名词 *n.*

1. 露水的通称。如："朝露、露水"等。*The general term for dew, as in* "朝露，露水."

2. 用花、叶、果子等制成的饮料。如："橘子露、玫瑰露"等。*A drink made of flowers, leaves or fruits, such as* "橘子露，玫瑰露."

说明 Notes:

1. 动词"露"还常用于四言词组，如"藏头露尾、不露声色、风餐露宿"等。"露," *as a verb,* also appears in four-character word groups such as "藏头露尾，不露声色，风餐露宿."

2. 动词"露"，在口语中也可以读成 lòu，如"露一手、露脸、露馅儿"等。"露，" *as a verb, can also be pronounced as* lòu. *For instance,* "露一手，露脸，露馅儿."

3. "露"的名词用法，前面常有定语修饰，或者用于固定词语，如"雨露滋润、阳光雨露"等。*As a noun,* "露" *is often preceded by an attribute or a fixed expression such as* "雨露滋润，阳光雨露."

lǚxíng 旅行 →P309"旅游"、P596"游览"

用法 Usage:

动词 *v.*

为了办事或游览，从一个地方到另一个地方，多指去比较远的地方。*To travel; to go from one place to another in order to do something or see sights. It usually refers to a place pretty far away.*

（1）在中国你旅行了没有？

（2）他去北京旅行了。

说明 Notes:

1. "旅行"一般不带宾语。"旅行" *usually does not carry an object.*

（3）*我旅行了上海。

（4）我去上海旅行了。

2. "旅行"还有名词用法。"旅行" *can be used as a noun.*

（5）长时间的旅行是很辛苦的。

（6）年轻人很喜欢旅行。

lǚyóu 旅游 →P309"旅行"、P596"游览"

用法 Usage:

动词 *v.*

表示外出游览风景名胜。*To travel in order to see scenic spots and places of historical interest.*

（1）他妈妈到中国旅游来了。

（2）很多外国人到中国旅游，只去北京、上海、西安。

说明 Notes:

1."旅游"后面不可以带宾语。"旅游" cannot take an object.

(3) *我旅游了上海。

(4) 我去上海旅游了。

2."旅游"可以做主语和宾语。"旅游" may be used as the subject or predicate.

(5) 旅游是很多人的爱好。

(6) 很多人都爱好旅游。

luò 落

用法 Usage:

动词 v.

1. 掉下,脱落。 *To fall; to drop.*

(1) 大家都感动得落泪了。

(2) 秋风一起,树叶就黄了,落了。

2. 下降,降低。 *To go down; to set.*

(3) 太阳落山了。

(4) 水落石出,潮水退下了。

3. 遗留在后面。 *To lag behind; to fall behind.*

(5) 比赛开始后,大家你追我赶,谁也不想落后。

(6) 阿里在这次演讲比赛中名落孙山。

4. 停留,留下,住下。 *To stay; to settle down.*

(7) 今天晚上我们就在这里落脚。

(8) 不少青年人在农村安家落户了。

5. 归属。 *To fall onto; to rest with.*

(9) 照顾妹妹的责任就落到了他的肩上。

(10) 最后,那幅画落到了他的手里。

6. 用笔写或画。 *To write or draw with a pen.*

(11) 请你从这里开始落笔。

máfan 麻烦 →P83"打扰"

用法 Usage:

形容词 a.

烦琐,费事。形容事情做起来不方便,要花很多时间和精力。Troublesome; tricky. It means not easy to do things. It usually takes a lot of time and energy.

(1) 出国旅行时,护照丢了很麻烦。
(2) 这里的服务员不怕麻烦,态度很好。

动词 v.

让人费事或增加负担。表示给别人带去不方便。常用在请求别人帮助或表示感谢别人帮助自己后。使用时,常常直接带上表示人物的称呼或代词做宾语。To bring trouble to or add burden to somebody. It indicates causing inconvenience to others. It is often used when asking someone for help or expressing gratitude for help. When in use, it is directly followed by one's name or a personal pronoun as the object.

(3) 麻烦您帮我写一下学校的地址。
(4) 麻烦你了,这么热的天给我送外卖。

名词 n.

指烦琐难办的事情。常用在"有、添、找、遇到"等动词后作宾语。Bother; trouble. It usually serves as the object of verbs such as "有,添,找,遇到."

(5) 如果遇到了麻烦,就给我打电话。
(6) 到杭州旅游,要给你们添麻烦了。

说明 Notes:

"麻烦"和"打扰"都是动词,都可以用在给别人带去不方便时,用在请求别人帮助或表示感谢别人帮助自己后。Both "麻烦" and "打扰" are verbs we use when creating inconvenience for someone else or expressing gratitude for his or her help.

区别是:Their differences are as follows:

1. "麻烦"有形容词、名词用法。"打扰"没有。"麻烦" can be used as an adjective or a noun, but "打扰" cannot.

2. "打扰"有搅乱别人正常工作、学习或生活的意思。"麻烦"没有这个意思。"打扰" may carry the meaning of interrupting someone's normal work, studies, or life. "麻烦" does not carry this meaning.

mǎshàng 马上 →P297"立刻"、P536"眼看"

用法 Usage:

副词 ad.

1. 表示(某件事)即将发生。常和"就、就要、就是"等词语配合使用。句子后面一般带"了"。Immediately. It indicates that something is about to happen soon, and it often goes with "就,就要,就是." The sentence often ends with "了."

(1) 马上就是春节了。
(2) 她马上就来,你等一会儿吧。

2. 表示某件事紧接着一件事发生。相当于"立即、即时"。Shortly. Similar to "立即,即时," it indicates one thing happens right after

another.

（3）一见有老人上车，他马上站起来让座。
（4）老师走进教室，同学们马上就安静下来了。

说明 Notes：

"马上"和"立刻"都是副词。都表示事情、动作立即发生或者紧接着某一件事、某一动作发生。"马上" and "立刻" are both adverbs. They both indicate that something will occur immediately or shortly after a certain thing or action takes place.

它们的区别是：They differ as follows:

1."立刻"着重于即刻发生、即刻行动。时间确定，刻不容缓，有紧迫的感情色彩。通用于口语和书面语。"立刻" emphasizes instant occurrence or immediate action within a certain time: it allows no delay. It signifies an urgency and is commonly used both in spoken and written language.

（5）接到通知，你们要立刻出发。
（6）发现有人看她，她立刻低下了头。

2."立刻"的使用条件，一般是在前面的动作或命令、通知等的影响下，第二个动作即刻发生，如例（5）（6）。"马上"不一定需要这样的条件。"立刻" is generally used when a second action will soon happen because of the previous action, or some order or notice, such as（5）and（6）. "马上" has no such limitation.

3."马上"着重于在很短的时间内发生或行动，但时间幅度伸缩性比较大，时间不一定很短，可以表示在几个月或一年内发生的事情，有时是说话人的主观感觉。紧迫的感情色彩没有"立刻"强烈。"马上" focuses on the occurrence of an action happening in a short time, the scale of which is relatively flexible. The time doesn't have to be quite short: it may last several months to a year. This is sometimes a feeling of the speaker, and it is less urgent than "立刻."

（7）马上就要开学了，你还要出去旅游。
例（7）句子中的"马上"不能换成"立刻"。

In Example (7), "马上" cannot be replaced by "立刻."

mǎnyì 满意 →P312"满足"

用法 Usage：

动词 v.

表示心里感到满足，符合心意。To be satisfied; to be pleased with something; to feel content.

（1）换了三个房间，他才满意了。
（2）你这样做，爸爸不会满意的。

"满意"是个心理动词，也有形容词用法。"满意" is a verb indicating mental state or activity. It can also be used as an adjective.

（3）妈妈的脸上露出满意的笑容。
（4）大学刚毕业时很难找到满意的工作。

说明 Notes：

1."满意"有个常用结构"对……（很/不）满意"，中间内容一般是（很/不）满意的宾语。In the structure "对…（很/不）满意，" what the subject is satisfied or dissatisfied with is inserted into the structure.

（5）老师对同学们上课迟到很不满意。

2."满意"有时可以带宾语，如例（6）。"满意" can sometimes take an object as in (6).

（6）孩子们很满意妈妈买的礼物。

mǎnzú 满足 →P312"满意"

用法 Usage：

动词 v.

1.感到满意，感到已经够了。如果带宾语，宾语前常有介词"于"。To feel contented and fulfilled. If it takes an object, the preposition "于" is usually placed before the object.

（1）现在我有车有房，还结了婚，很满足了。
（2）他很努力，不会满足于现在的成绩。

2.使要求、需要实现，达到某个条件。To meet a need or demand; to come up to a certain requirement.

（3）他满足了我的要求。

(4) 为满足同学们的愿望,学院开设了许多选修课。

说明 Notes:

1. 关于"满足"的用法说明：Notes about how to use "满足":

① "满足"前常与"很""十分"等连用,表示程度较高。"满足" is often modified by "很" and "十分," both of which mean a high degree.

② "满足"的第二种用法,后面常带"希望、要求、愿望、需要"等宾语。In its second usage, "满足" is usually followed by objects such as "希望,要求,愿望,需要."

2. "满足"跟"满意"都是心理动词,表示符合意愿而感到高兴,都能受程度副词的修饰。"满足" and "满意" are both psychological verbs. Both mean feeling happy for something that provides satisfaction, and both can be modified by a degree adverb.

它们的区别是：Their differences are as follows:

① "满意"着重从心愿的角度感到如愿,合乎心意。多用于自己对别人或别人对自己的感受。"满足"着重从需求的角度来说,表示感到足够,别无他求。多用于自身的感受。"满意" emphasizes the fulfillment of one's desire and a satisfaction from the heart. It is more often used as a feeling of oneself toward others or others toward oneself. The focus of "满足" is one's demands. Its use indicates that one feels there is enough and asks no more than that.

② "满意"可以带宾语。"满足"的第一用法,如带宾语,宾语前有介词"于",如例(2)。"满意" can take an object. In the first usage of "满足," if it takes an object, the preposition "于" is placed before the object, as in (2).

màncháng 漫长

用法 Usage:

形容词 a.

1. 长得看不到尽头的(指空间的距离)。Endless (indicating the distance in space).

(1) 中国东南面是漫长的海岸线。

(2) 到我家只能走那条漫长而狭小的山路。

2. (指时间的延续)很长。Very long (indicating the duration of time).

(3) 经过十二个小时漫长的飞行,我们终于到达了北京。

(4) 中国有漫长的五千年历史。

3. (指经历的时间和空间)让人感觉很长。(Of the passage of time and space) making one feel very long.

(5) 这就是她在深圳漫长而艰难的打工经历。

(6) 一个人从小学到大学毕业,道路漫长,有辛苦,也有快乐。

mànmàn 慢慢 →P226"渐渐"

用法 Usage:

副词 ad.

"慢慢"是形容词"慢"在句子中作状语时的重叠形式,第二个音节要读第一声。"慢慢"在句子中作状语。"慢慢" is the reduplicated form of the adjective "慢" which is used as an adverbial in the sentence. The second syllable is read in the first tone. "慢慢" is used as an adverbial in the sentence.

1. 用在动词、形容词前面,描述变化本身的状态,后面不带补语。用在祈使语气的句子可以带"地",也可以不带。Appearing before a verb or an adjective, it describes the state of a change itself, followed by no complement. When it appears in an imperative sentence, it can be followed by "地."

(1) 这些CD片你拿去慢慢听吧。

(2) 我吃完了。你们慢慢地吃!

2. 用在动词、形容词前面,描述变化发展过程的缓慢。与"渐渐"词义相同,常带有补语。Appearing before a verb or adjective, it describes the slow process of a change — with a meaning similar to that of "渐渐" and followed

by a complement.

（3）天气慢慢地暖和起来了。

（4）爷爷的身体慢慢地好了起来。

说明 Notes：

"慢慢"和"渐渐"都是副词。Both "慢慢" and "渐渐" are adverbs.

它们的区别是：Their differences are as follows:

1. "慢慢"只有用在带有补语的动词、形容词前面时，词义才与"渐渐"相同。"慢慢" has the same meaning as "渐渐" only when it appears before a verb or an adjective followed by a complement.

2. "慢慢"是单音节"慢"表示缓慢意思的形容词重叠用法，有强调作用。"渐渐"不强调缓慢的意思。"慢慢" is the reduplication of the monosyllabic word "慢" meaning "slow." It plays the role of emphasizing that meaning. "渐渐," however, does not emphasize that.

（5）*学语言，不能着急，得渐渐地一个生词、一个句子地学。

（6）学语言，不能着急，得慢慢地一个生词、一个句子地学。

mànmànlái 慢慢来

用法 Usage：

1. 表示有些事情不能很快达到目的。It suggests that things cannot be achieved quickly.

（1）教育孩子要慢慢来，不能着急。

（2）中药治病，尤其是慢性病只能慢慢来。

2. 让听话人不要着急，慢慢地做某件事。多为礼貌、客气语。(To the listener) to take things easy; to take your time; not to hurry. It is more used as a polite platitude.

（3）我们会等你的，你慢慢来！

（4）请你做的那件事，你慢慢来，我们不着急。

说明 Notes：

"慢慢来"第二种用法是"慢慢＋动词"的短语形式，多用于祈使语气的句子，表示礼貌或客气。后面的动词，就看对方当时的行为动作而定。The second usage of "慢慢来" is a structure of "慢慢＋v.", usually used in an imperative sentence to show politeness. The verb after it depends on the act of the listener.

（5）我吃完了，你们慢慢吃！

（6）你走啦？慢慢走！

（7）我先走了，你们慢慢聊！

máodùn 矛盾 →P67 "冲突"

用法 Usage：

名词 n.

矛是古代用来攻击的武器，盾是古代用来抵御的武器。有人同时卖矛和盾，说他的矛最锋利，什么都能刺破；又说他的盾最牢固，什么都刺不破。旁人问他：那用你的矛刺你的盾，怎么样？那人回答不了。后来"矛盾"连用，比喻言语或行为自相抵触的现象。Here is the folk story that tells the birth of this word. The spear（矛）was an ancient weapon for launching offensives while the shield（盾）was a defensive weapon. Long, long ago, there was a man who was selling both the spear and the shield at the market. He bragged that his spear was the sharpest of all and could pierce every shield in the world and that his shield was the strongest of all shields and could resist, or rather, defy any spears and suffer no damage. A passenger asked the man: "What if one uses your spear to pierce your shield?" The man was tongue-tied and made no answer. Later the combination of "矛" and "盾" is used as an analogy of contradicting acts or words.

1. 因认识不同或言行冲突而造成的隔阂、嫌隙。Gaps or rifts caused by different understandings or conflicts of words or actions.

（1）他说的话前后有很多矛盾。

（2）婆婆和媳妇一起生活，很容易产生矛盾。

(3) 他俩吵过几次，矛盾很深。

2. 哲学上指一切事物中所包含的既相互排斥又相互依存的两个侧面。*Philosophically it refers to the two facets of everything that are mutually exclusive but interdependent.*

(4) 一切事物都有矛盾的两个方面。

(5) 要抓住矛盾的主要方面，才能解决问题。

形容词 *a.*

形容自相抵触、有冲突的感觉。*Conflicting, contradictory.*

(6) 她想在家照顾孩子，又想去公司工作，心里很矛盾。

说明 Notes:

1. "矛盾"的名词用法常与"存在、处理、解决、正视、揭露、克服"等动词搭配，受数量或指量短语的限制，如"一对/一组矛盾"。*As a noun,* "矛盾" *often goes with verbs such as* "存在，处理，解决，正视，揭露，克服." *It may be limited by numerals as in* "一对/一组矛盾."

2. "矛盾"用作形容词时，前面常用"很、非常、十分"等程度副词修饰。*As an adjective,* "矛盾" *often goes with degree adverbs such as* "很,非常,十分."

3. "矛盾"有时可以做动词，能带动态助词"着、了"，但不能带宾语。*Sometimes* "矛盾" *can serve as a verb, to be followed by* "着,了," *but it cannot take any objects.*

(7) 要不要去旅游，她内心一直矛盾着。

4. "矛盾"和"冲突"都表示互相抵触、互不兼容。*Both* "矛盾" *and* "冲突" *indicate mutually conflicting or exclusive.*

它们的区别是：*Their differences are as follows:*

① "矛盾"着重指互相抵触、互不兼容的两种事物、言行及其情状。"冲突"着重表示矛盾已表面化，双方发生了激烈争斗。"矛盾" *emphasizes two things, behaviors or situations that are mutually conflicting and exclusive.* "冲突," *however, indicates that the conflicts have intensified to involve a sharp or even violent struggle.*

(8) 在这个问题上，她俩发生了矛盾。

(9) 在这个问题上，她俩发生了冲突。

② "冲突"表示两种客观事物互相对立，常用于表示时间、地点、言行等的对立、不一致。"矛盾"一般不用于时间、地点这类事物上，而用于言行，特别表示事物本身、主观心理方面。"冲突" *means two things that exist objectively are mutually contradictory. It is often applied to time, place, words or behaviors.* "矛盾," *by contrast, is usually not applied to time and place. But it can be applied to words and behaviors, especially things themselves or subjective mentality.*

(10) *因时间矛盾，他不得不取消了这次会议。

(11) 因时间冲突，他不得不取消了这次会议。

(12) *他的内心一直充满了冲突。

(13) 他的内心一直充满了矛盾。

③ "矛盾"是一个哲学名词，它所具有的哲学上的意义，"冲突"没有。"矛盾" *is a philosophical term carrying with it a philosophical meaning. But* "冲突" *carries no philosophical sense.*

(14) 矛盾的对立双方可以相互转化。（不能用"冲突"。"冲突" *cannot be used.*）

④ "矛盾"有形容词用法。"冲突"没有。"矛盾" *can be used as an adjective, but* "冲突" *cannot.*

(15) *他心里非常冲突。

(16) 他心里非常矛盾。

méi/méiyǒu 没/没有 →P37"不"、→P51 "不如"

用法 Usage:

动词 *v.*

1. 表示对"有""具有"的否定。*The negative form of* "有(have)" *or* "具有(own)."

(1) 我没/没有汽车，只有一辆自行车。

(2) 他没/没有时间来看我。
2. 表示对"存在"的否定。The negative form of "存在(exist)."
(3) 房间里没/没有人。
(4) 学校旁边没/没有酒吧。
3. 用在"谁、哪个"等词前边,表示"全都不"的意思。When used before "谁, 哪个, etc.," it means "全都不(none)."
(5) 没/没有谁像你这样努力学习了。
(6) 大雪天的晚上,没/没有哪个会出门。
4. 用于比较,表示"不如""不及"等否定的意思。When used in comparison, it suggests a negative meaning such as "不如,不及."
(7) 堵车那么厉害,坐车没/没有自行车快。
(8) 你没/没有他说得好。
5. 用在数量词等前边,表示"不够、不到、不足"的意思。When used before a measure word, it suggests inadequacy, meaning "不够, 不到, 不足."
(9) 生活不习惯,去了没/没有两个月就回国了。
(10) 她跑了没/没有几步就停下来了。

副词 ad.

1. 用在动词前,对行为动作的发生或完成表示否定。When used before a verb, it negates the occurrence or completion of an act.
(11) 我没/没有学过汉语。
(12) 今天起床晚了,他还没/没有吃过早饭。
2. 用在形容词前边,对形状转变的发生或完成表示否定。When used before an adjective, it negates the occurrence or completion of a change of state.
(13) 你没/没有老,还那么年轻。
(14) 天气还没/没有转暖,你就脱下棉衣,要受凉的。
3. "没有"用在句末,表示客观地询问(不做主观猜测)。When used at the end of a sentence, it indicates an objective inquiry (making no assumptions).
(15) 双休日你们去上海了没有?

(16) 你给妈妈打电话了没有?
说明 Notes:
1. "没"和"没有"用法基本相同。Both "没" and "没有" basically share the same usage.
① "没/没有"做副词时,一般不跟"了"一起用。When "没" or "没有" serves as an adverb, they don't go with "了."
(17) *我没/没有学过法语了。
② 表示对"曾经"的否定,常与"过"一起用,如例(11)。As a negation of "曾经," it usually goes with "过," as in (11).
③ "没/没有"做动词的肯定形式是"有",如:"没/没有词典——有词典"。做副词的肯定形式是去掉"没/没有",并在句末加"了",如:"没/没有吃饭——吃了/吃饭了"。不能说"*有吃饭"。The affirmative form of "没/没有" as a verb is "有," as in "没/没有词典—有词典." Its affirmative form is to remove "没/没有" and add "了" at the end of the sentence, as in "没/没有吃饭—吃了/吃饭了." It's not correct to say "*有吃饭."
④ "还+没/没有+动词+呢"表示行为动作到现在为止没有发生,但以后会发生。The structure "还 + 没/没有 + v. + 呢" suggests that an act or behavior hasn't occurred yet, but is going to in the future.
(18) 我还没吃饭呢。
(19) 他还没回家呢。

它们的区别是:Their differences are as follows:
① 在句子(包括陈述句和疑问句)的末尾,一般都用"没有"。"没有" is commonly used at the end of a sentence (including declarative and interrogative sentences).
(20) 宿舍里一个人也没有。
(21) 他们去了没有?
② 用于回答问题时,"没有"可以单独回答,"没"一般与询问的动词或形容词一起回答。When used as the answer to a question, "没有"

can be used independently, but "没" is generally used along with a verb or adjective in the answer.

(22) 他们去上海了没有？——没有/没去。

2. "没/没有"与"不"都是否定副词,区别是: "没/没有" and "不" are negative adverbs, but there are differences between them:

① "没/没有"用于对现象的客观叙述。"不"用于主观意愿。"没/没有" is used in an objective narration; "不" expresses a subjective will.

(23) 昨天晚上我没/没有去跳舞。
(24) 今天晚上我不去跳舞。

② "没/没有"一般指过去和现在,不指将来,"不"可以指过去、现在和将来。"没/没有" generally refers to the past and the present instead of the future; "不" can refer to all.

(25) *明天你的生日晚会她没/没有去。
(26) 明天你的生日晚会她不去。

③ "没/没有"只能用在少数能愿动词,如"能、能够、要、肯、敢"等前面。"不"可用在所有的助动词前面。"没/没有" can only be used before a few modal verbs such as "能,能够,要,肯,敢." "不" can be used before all of them.

(27) *现在我没/没有愿意看书。
(28) 现在我不愿意看书。

3. "没有"与"不如"都能用于比较句。有时可以互相替换。Both "没有" and "不如" can be used in comparative sentences. Sometimes they can replace each other.

(29) 今年冬天不如/没有去年冬天暖和。
(30) 这本词典不如/没有那本词典好。

它们的区别是: Their differences are as follows:

① "没有"后面的形容词可以是消极的,贬义的。形容词前常加用"这么、那么"。"不如"后面的比较结果,意思一般是积极的。Adjectives following "没有" may be negative and derogatory, and "这么" or "那么" often appears before the adjective(s). In contrast, "不如" is often followed by the result of a contrast, which is usually positive.

(31) 在找女朋友的问题上,他没有他哥哥那么笨。
(32) 在找女朋友的问题上,哥哥不如他聪明。
(33) 去年冬天没有今年冬天这么冷。
(34) 今年冬天不如去年冬天暖和。

② "没有"后面一定要出现比较事项和结果。"不如"可以不用。"没有" must be followed by the items for and the results of a comparison. But not "不如."

(35) 在个儿上,哥哥不如弟弟。
(36) 在个儿上,哥哥没有弟弟高。

③ "不如"可以跟"与其"搭配,构成"与其……不如……"的格式,表示对比取舍的关系。"没有"不能。"不如" can pair with "与其" to make the pattern "与其...不如...," indicating a comparison and a preferred choice. "没有" cannot be used in this way.

(37) 与其坐公交车,不如骑自行车。

méishénme 没什么 →P318"没事儿"

用法 Usage:

1. 习惯语。没关系,别在意。An idiom. It means "Never mind" or "Don't take it seriously."

(1) 麻烦你了,真不好意思！——没什么。
(2) 谢谢你的帮助！——没什么。

2. 不要紧,不用担心。Nothing serious; don't worry.

(3) 摔痛了没有？——没什么。
(4) 只要你高兴,我辛苦一点没什么。

3. 指没有特定的人或事物时,是表示强调的否定短语。An emphatic negative phrase, meaning that no particular person or thing is mentioned.

(5) 你们在谈什么？——没什么。
(6) 我最近没什么时间。
(7) 这本书没什么好看的。

méishìr 没事儿 →P317"没什么"

用法 Usage:

1. 表示没有事情做，有空闲时间。常做谓语、定语。There is nothing to do, having free time. It usually serves as a predicate or attributive.

（1）今晚没事儿，我们看电影去。

（2）没事儿的时候我喜欢找朋友聊天。

2. 没有职业。Having no occupation.

（3）他最近没事儿，在家闲着。

3. 没有事故或意外。Without accidents; being all right.

（4）医生说没事儿，只破了一点皮。

（5）你不用担心，我只是感冒，没事儿的。

4. 不要紧，不用担心或没有责任。It doesn't matter; don't worry; No one is to take responsibility.

（6）你把情况说清楚就没事儿了。

（7）只要大家高兴，我辛苦一点没事儿。

5. 没关系，别在意。Never mind; don't take it seriously.

（8）对不起！——没事儿。

（9）谢谢你的帮助！——没事儿。

说明 Notes:

1."没什么"和"没事儿"只有在表示"不要紧、不碍事、不必顾虑"这个意思上可以通用。"没事（儿）"有一种轻松、乐观的语气，年轻人用得较多。"没什么"有时语气较为低调，有时甚至比较含蓄。"没什么" and "没事儿" are interchangeable only when they express the meaning of "Never mind" like "不要紧，不碍事，不必顾虑." "没事（儿）" has a relaxed and optimistic tone, which is more often used among young people. "没什么" sometimes carries a tone of being low-key or implicit.

2."没事儿"有"没有事情干"和"没有出什么事故"的意思。"没什么"没有。"没事儿" may mean "having nothing to do（没有事情干）" or "having no accident（没有出什么事故）." But "没什么" doesn't have such meanings.

měi 每 →P164"各"

用法 Usage:

代词 pron.

指全体中的任何一个。It refers to any one of the whole.

（1）他每年都来上海看朋友。

（2）每个大学生都会一点儿英语。

副词 ad.

表示同一个动作反复的有规律的出现。It refers to the regular occurrence of an event or a repeated action.

（3）世界杯每隔四年就举行一次。

（4）我每读一本书都感到自己又有了进步。

说明 Notes:

1."每"做代词，常与数量词组合或分别与数词、量词结合做定语、状语，后面常用副词"都"，表示"全都是这样"，如例（1）（2）。As a pronoun,"每" often goes with a numeral-classifier compound or with a numeral and measure word to serve as an attributive or adverbial. It is usually followed by the adverb "都," and suggests "It's all this（全都是这样）." See (1) and (2).

2."每"可以做时间名词的前置修饰语，如："天/日、年、周/星期、分钟、秒、小时"等。"每" can be a premodifier of nouns that denote time, such as "天/日，年，周/星期，分钟，秒，小时."

3."每"做副词，用在动词、介词前作状语，后面常与副词"就、都、总、便"等连用，如例（3）（4）。As an adverb,"每" serves as an adverbial before a verb and preposition, which is often followed by words such as "就，都，总，便，" as in (3) and (4).

4."每"和"常"不能同时出现在一个句子里。"每" and "常" cannot be used in one and the same sentence simultaneously.

(5) *每天下午他常去散步。
(6) 每天下午他都去散步。

5. "每"和"各"都指总体中的所有的个体。只有在"每家每户/各家各户都换上新春联"这些客观描述的句子中,"每"和"各"可以替换,其他一般都不能替换。Both "每" and "各" refer to all the individuals in a totality. But only in objective descriptions such as "每家每户/各家各户都换上新春联" can they be used to replace each other.

它们的区别是:Their differences are as follows:

① "每"着重于逐个指出总体中无一例外的所有个体,句子后面用"都"又强调个体之间的共性。"各"着重于分指总体中情况不同的个体,强调个体之间的差异。"每" focuses on all the individuals in a totality — without any exceptions. "各" appears later in a sentence to further highlight this common character. "各," by contrast, emphasizes the different features of the individuals: it focuses on their differences.

(7) 每个同学每天早上都要读15分钟课文。
(8) 各个同学根据各人的兴趣,可以报名参加选修课。

② "每"一般要跟量词或数量词结合才能加在名词前。可用于表示人、事物或动作单位的各种量词如"每+位、个、尺、升、斤、只、条、种、次、遍、场、下儿"等之前。可直接用于具有量词性质的普通名词或时间名词,如:"每+人、家、队、村、年、月、日、天、星期、周"等。与量词或名词之间可用数词,如"每+一种、一回、一家、一年"等。"每" has to take a numeral or a measure word before it can be placed before a noun. This applies to measure words in indicating a unit for people, things and actions such as "每+位,个,尺,升,斤,只,条,种,次,遍,场,下儿." It can also be applied to common nouns or temporal nouns that carry the nature of a measure word such as "每+人,家,队,村,年,月,日,天,星期,周." A numeral may appear before a measure word or a noun as in "每+一种,一回,一家,一年."

③ "各"可以直接用在名词前。只能用于部分表示人或事物单位的量词之前,常用的有:"各+个、位、种、类、式、样、条、门、路、届"等,使用的范围比"每"狭窄。可用于部分表示人、机关、单位、组织、党团、阶级、国家的普通名词之前,常用的有:"各+人、家、队、村、省、地、工厂、学校、企业、部队、单位、车间、办公室、民族"等,使用范围比"每"宽,但不能用于时间名词之前,与量词或名词之间一般不能用数词。"各" may appear directly before a noun. But this use is possible only before some measure words indicating a unit of people or things such as "各+个,位,种,类,式,样,条,门,路,届." The scope of use is more limited than "每." It may appear before common nouns indicating people, government offices, organizations, parties, classes and nations. Often we say "各+人,家,队,村,省,地,工厂,学校,企业,部队,单位,车间,办公室,民族." Its scope of use is broader than that of "每." But it cannot appear before a temporal noun. And no numerals can be used before a measure word or a noun.

④ 副词"每"表示重复出现。副词"各"表示分别具有。"每" as an adverb, indicates repeated appearances. "各" as an adverb, means every individual is in possession of something.

(9) 各人有各人的长处。
(10) 每四小时吃一次药。

ménlù 门路

用法 Usage:
名词 n.

1. 做事的诀窍,解决问题的途径。The knack of doing something; the way to solve a problem.

(1) 大家都在找赚钱的门路。
(2) 节约用水的门路很多，就看大家做不做。
2. 特指能达到个人目的的方法、途径；后门。Special reference to a method or approach to achieving some personal purpose through what is known as the "back door."
(3) 我不托人找门路也找到了一个好工作。
(4) 音乐会的票子他是走门路才得到的。

mēng 蒙

用法 Usage：
动词 v.
1. 蒙骗，欺骗。To deceive; to cheat.
(1) 今天不上课？你蒙我吧。
(2) 一会儿说来，一会儿说不来。他是不是在蒙人呢？
2. (没有根据地)胡乱猜测。To make wild guesses.
(3) 这次考试太难了，很多题目我都是蒙的。
(4) 我不知道应该怎么选择，只好蒙了一个。
3. 昏迷，神志不清。To be in a coma; to be unconscious.
(5) 出了车祸，大家都蒙了，连电话也忘了打。
(6) 她被篮球打蒙了。

méng 蒙

用法 Usage：
动词 v.
1. 遮，盖，捂。To cover; to hide; to block.
(1) 外面风沙很大，出去头上要蒙一块纱巾。
(2) 把病人的眼睛蒙上，手术开始了。
2. 遭，受，承。To suffer from; to meet with; to bear.
(3) 去年有不少乘客因飞机出事而蒙难。
(4) 我在中国承蒙关照，谢谢你！

形容词 a.
1. 形容雨点很细小，可以重叠使用。如："细雨蒙蒙"。Drizzling of the rain. It can be used in the reduplicated form as in "细雨蒙蒙."
(5) 蒙蒙春雨让人感到很浪漫。
2. 形容愚昧无知。如："启蒙教育"。Ignorant and illiterate as in "启蒙教育."
(6) 现在小孩的启蒙教育年龄越来越小了。
说明 Notes：
因为"濛"(形容雨点等很小的意思)简化为"蒙"，"矇"(眼睛失明的意思)也简化为"蒙"，所以"蒙"有形容词用法。"濛，" which describes the tiny drops of rain, is simplified as "蒙，" and "矇，" which means being blind, is also simplified as "蒙." Therefore, "蒙" can function as an adjective.

mí 迷

用法 Usage：
动词 v.
1. 分辨不清，失去判断能力。To be unable to identify things; to lose one's ability to judge.
(1) 刚来这个城市，我常常迷路。
(2) 在沙漠开车很容易迷了方向。
2. 因对某人或某事物产生特殊爱好而沉醉。"迷"后常加"上"。To be crazy about someone or indulge in something. "迷" is usually followed by "上."
(3) 他迷上了网上游戏。
(4) 妈妈迷上了广场舞，每天晚上都去跳。
3. (因为什么事物)让人沉醉、迷恋，常用于四字词组。To have someone intoxicated or infatuated with something, often used in four-word phrases.
(5) 今晚月色迷人，我们散步去。
(6) 他是个财迷心窍的人。
说明 Notes：
"迷"常用作语缀。口语中常用"迷"表示沉醉、迷恋于某个人或某种事物的人，如"足球迷、篮球迷、影迷、歌迷"等。"迷"本身不能单用。"迷" is often used as an affix. In spoken language, "…迷" refers to a person who is intoxicated or infatuated with someone or something. For example, "足球迷,篮球迷,影迷,歌迷," and so on. "迷" cannot be used independently.

(7) *他是个电脑游戏的迷。
(8) 他是个电脑游戏迷。

mìqiè 密切

用法 Usage:
形容词 a.
1.（关系）亲近。*(Of relationship) close; intimate.*
(1) 网络跟每个人的生活关系已经很密切了。
(2) 他们俩来往十分密切。

2.（对某事、某问题等）重视,考虑仔细周到。*Attaching importance to something; being considerate.*
(3) 我们要跟二班的同学密切配合,搞好这次活动。
(4) 医生说要密切注意他的体温。

动词 v.
让关系亲近,常带有宾语。*To bring a relationship close, often with an object.*
(5) 我们要进一步密切两国人民的友好关系。
(6) 旅行能密切人与人之间的关系。

miǎnde 免得 →P571"以免"

用法 Usage:
连词 conj.
避免出现（某种不希望发生的情况）,省得。*Lest; so as not to create (an undesirable situation).*
(1) 天阴了,带把雨伞去,免得淋雨。
(2) 到了北京就给我们打电话,免得我们担心。

说明 Notes:
"免得"和"避免"都有"不让某种情况发生"的意思。"免得" and "避免" both mean "not to have something happen（不让某种情况发生）."

它们的区别是：*Their differences are as follows:*

1. "免得"是连词,连接两个分句,常用于后面表示目的分句的开头,如例(1)(2)。"免得" is a conjunction which connects two clauses. It is often used at the beginning of the second clause to indicate a purpose as in (1) and (2).

2. "避免"是动词,可直接带宾语,如"避免错误、避免损失、避免迟到"等。"避免" is a verb that can take an object as in "避免错误,避免损失,避免迟到."

3. "避免"可以用于表示事情已经发生的句子。"免得"只能用于表示事情还没发生的句子。"避免" can be applied to a sentence expressing an event that has already happened. "免得," by contrast, can be applied to something that hasn't happened.

(3) *幸亏司机及时停了车,免得了一场交通事故。
(4) 幸亏司机及时停了车,避免了一场交通事故。

miànduì 面对 →P322"面临"

用法 Usage:
动词 v.
1. 当面对着（人或物）。*To face (someone or something).*
(1) 她面对着老师一句话也讲不出来。
(2) 阿里天天面对墙上的地图思考问题。

2. 面前对着（问题、情况等）。*To be face to face with; to encounter (a problem, situation, etc.).*
(3) 面对困难,不同的人有不同的做法。
(4) 面对突然来的灾难,他一点儿也不害怕。

miànlín 面临 →P321"面对"

用法 Usage:
动词 v.

1. 面对,靠近(某事物)。To be faced with; to be up against (certain things).

(1) 小山村背靠青山,面临大河,环境很美。
(2) 面临着大海,她想起了远方的妈妈。

2. 面前遇到(问题、困难、矛盾、挑战等)。To encounter (a problem, difficulty, contradiction, challenge, etc.).

(3) 发展工业生产,就会面临环境污染的问题。
(4) 中学生面临高考时压力很大。

说明 Notes:

"面临"和"面对"的区别是:The differences between "面临" and "面对" are as follows:

1. "面对"的对象可以是人。"面临"的对象只能是事物。The object of "面对" may be a person; yet the object of "面临" can only be something.

(5) *面临着衰老的父母,他流下了眼泪。
(6) 面对着衰老的父母,他流下了眼泪。

2. 从时间和空间的距离上说,"面临"的时空比"面对"的宽泛。如例(3)。In terms of the distance of time and space, "面临" covers a wider range than "面对." See (3).

miànqián 面前 →P329"目前"、P537"眼前"

用法 Usage:
名词 n.

指面对着的、距离近的地方。常用在指人的名词或指事物的名词后面。It refers to a place close by that one is facing. It often appears after a noun representing a person or a thing.

(1) 面前是一大片沙漠。
(2) 那只狗一下子就跑到了我面前。
(3) 你面前的书都是她送你的。

说明 Notes:

1. 句子语意表示主语行为动作的处所、方位时,事物的名词后面不能用"面前"。When the sentence suggests the location or position of the subject's action or behavior, "面前" cannot be used after a noun which gives the name of the thing.

(4) *她一回家就坐在录音机面前练习英语。
(5) 她一回家就坐在录音机前面练习英语。
(6) *我们约好在学校南门面前见面。
(7) 我们约好在学校南门前见面。

2. "面前"在句子中常以"在……面前"的格式出现,中间是指人的名词或者是指事物的名词。"面前" often appears in the structure "在…面前," in the middle of which is often a noun representing a person or thing.

(8) 在我们面前没有做不好的事情。
(9) 在集体力量面前,任何困难都能解决。

3. "面前"也可以用在"法律、胜利、命运、自然、真理"等抽象名词后面。"面前" can also be used after abstract nouns such as "法律,胜利,命运,自然,真理."

(10) 法律面前人人平等。
(11) 人在命运面前常常感到无助。

miànxiàng 面向

用法 Usage:
动词 v.

面对着(某个方向、某些人或某些事物)。动词用法。To face; to turn in the direction of (a person or thing). It serves as a verb.

(1) 面向东方,她祝愿爸爸妈妈身体健康。
(2) 我们的技术服务要面向农村。
(3) 国家公务员的工作首先要面向群众。

说明 Notes:

1. "面向"后面一般跟着表示方位的名词。"面向" is often followed by a noun indicating a direction or position.

2. 如果"面向"后面是表示人或物的名词,这些人或物,常常是一种层面或群体,并且含有社会地位的语义。如：在例(2)(3)中，"农村"与"城市"相对，"群众"与"干部"相对。If "面向" is followed by the name of a person or thing, it often indicates a class or group that signals the social status. In (2) and (3), one sees "农村" versus "城市," and "群众" versus "干部."

miànzi 面子

用法 Usage:

名词 n.

1. 指物体的表面。The surface or the outer part of an object.

(1) 这件衣服的面子是丝绸的。

(2) 这个手提包面子上的花样很好看。

2. 指人的表面形象，脸面，体面。常组成"有面子、丢面子、要面子"等词语。The image of a person; one's face and decency. Common collocations include "有面子, 丢面子, 要面子," etc.

(3) 上名校，看起来很有面子。

(4) 你说的话伤着她的面子了。

3. 情面，情分，人和人之间的私人感情。常组成"卖面子、看在(谁的)面子上、给面子、伤面子"等词语。Feelings; affection; personal feelings between people. Common collocations include "卖面子, 看在(谁的)面子上, 给面子, 伤面子, etc."

(5) 要不是看在我朋友的面子上，这茶叶能那么便宜卖给你？

(6) 这件事你给个面子吧，帮帮我。

miáoshù 描述 →P323"描写"

用法 Usage:

动词 v.

(用语言文字)形象地叙述。To describe; to narrate vividly.

(1) 病人要把自己不舒服的状况描述给医生听。

(2) 小说生动地描述了农民的生活。

miáoxiě 描写 →P323"描述"

用法 Usage:

动词 v.

用语言文字把人物、时间、环境等形象具体地表现出来。To describe people, time and environment, etc. in a concrete way.

(1) 中国有很多描写月亮的诗句。

(2) 她最善于描写儿童的内心活动。

说明 Notes:

"描述"和"描写"的区别是："描述"侧重于用语言文字说出来；"描写"侧重于用语言文字写出来。The difference between "描述" and "描写" is that "描述" focuses on words being uttered while "描写" focuses on words being written down.

(3) 她生动形象地对我描述了她那奇妙的旅行经历。

(4) 她在小说里生动形象地描写了她那奇妙的旅行经历。

miào 妙

用法 Usage:

形容词 a.

1. 好，美妙。Fine; wonderful.

(1) 你的办法妙极了。

(2) 游览黄山真是妙不可言。

(3) 房价下跌，很多房地产公司的情况不妙。

2. 神奇，巧妙。Exquisite; ingenious.

(4) 你用了什么妙计，让妈妈同意我们办公司了？

(5) 这个魔术师的手法真妙！

说明 Notes:

"妙"可以组成不少成语。如："妙语连珠(指不停说出有意思、有趣的话)、妙手回春(指大夫治病技术高明)、妙不可言(指好得很难用语言来说)"。There are many idioms with the word "妙," such as "妙语连珠" (which means frequent flashes of wit in a speech), "妙手回春" (which indicates a highly skillful doctor bringing a very sick patient back to youth and vigor), and "妙不可言" (which means being wonderful beyond words).

míngōng 民工
用法 Usage:
名词 n.

1. 指临时组合起来从事修筑公路、水坝或运输等工作的人。Laborers who are temporarily summoned to work on public projects such as the buildings of roads, dams, or transportation.

(1) 那时先后组织了两万民工修筑了这个水库。
(2) 我们山村的公路都是民工自愿参加建成的。

2. 指到城市打工的农民。Farmer-turned workers.

(3) 有很多民工在城市里买了房子。
(4) 到了春节,民工都要回老家过年。

mínjǐng 民警
用法 Usage:
名词 n.

1. "人民警察"的简称。The short form for "人民警察 (People's Police)."

(1) 在中国你有什么困难,找民警就行。

2. 特指办理百姓日常警务的警察。中国每个居民社区都有。It refers specifically to the police who perform the daily police duties. They can be found in every community in China.

(2) 我们社区的民警工作很负责。

说明 Notes:
按照管理的警务分有:"刑警"(刑事警察)、"交警"(交通警察)、民警(社区警察)等。Policemen in China are divided according to the different affairs they handle, such as "刑警" (criminal police), "交警" (traffic police), "民警" (community police).

mǐngǎn 敏感
用法 Usage:
形容词 a.

1. 生理上或心理上,对客观事物的存在或变化反映很快。常形成"对……(很/十分)敏感"的短语。Physiologically or psychologically sensitive to the existence or change of things in the outside world. It's often used in the phrase of "对…(很/十分)敏感."

(1) 他对味道十分敏感,一尝就尝出食物新鲜不新鲜。
(2) 很多艺术家的性格都很敏感。

2. 十分关注的、易于敏锐感觉并迅速做出强烈反映的。Very concerned, fast to spot and quick to react — often strongly.

(3) 对女士来说,年龄是个敏感话题。
(4) 很多家长认为儿童性教育是个敏感话题。

míngyì 名义
用法 Usage:
名词 n.

1. 身份,资格,名分。指做某事时用来作为依据的名称。常形成"以……名义"的短语。Identity; qualification; name. People use it as a basis for doing things. It often appears in the phrase of "以…名义" (in the name of…).

(1) 他以个人的名义捐给医院一百万人民币。
(2) 公务员不能接收各种名义的礼物。

2. 形式,外表,常与"上"字连用。Form; appearance. It often goes with "上," meaning "nominally."

(3) 他名义上是这家公司的经理,其实他什么也不管。
(4) 名义上每个班二十五人,实际上都只多不少。

míngbai 明白 →P115"懂"、P379"清楚"
用法 Usage:
动词 v.

了解,知道,懂得。To understand; to

realize; to know.

(1) 大家都不明白他说的意思。
(2) 我明白你为什么这样做。

形容词 a.

1. 内容、思想清楚明确,容易让人理解。*(Of content or idea) clear and easy to understand.*

(3) 他说的意思明白极了,他喜欢你。
(4) 谁都明白的问题,你为什么就不懂?

2. 公开的,明确的。常用在动词前。*Open; explicit. It often goes before a verb.*

(5) 他已经明白地告诉你,他不去跳舞。
(6) 我明明白白地对你说,再不起床要迟到了。

3. 聪明,懂得道理。*Intelligent; sensible.*

(7) 他是个明白人,知道该怎么做。
(8) 大家都是明白人,还要多说什么?

说明 Notes:

1. "明白"做动词,重叠形式是 ABAB,做形容词时,重叠形式是 AABB。*As a verb, the reduplicated form of "明白" is ABAB; and as an adjective, the reduplicated form is AABB.*

2. "明白"做形容词,常在"想、弄、搞、看、听"等动词后面作补语。*As an adjective, "明白" often serves as a complement following verbs such as "想,弄,搞,看,听."*

(9) 我搞不明白他俩为什么又吵架了。
(10) 这篇文章,我终于看明白了。

3. "明白"和"懂"的区别是：*The differences between "明白" and "懂" are as follows:*

① 做动词时,所搭配的宾语名词范围不同。"明白"可以带"道理、事理、意思"或其他一些带有在理的短语或小句,但不能带"汉语、礼貌、规矩、技术"等类的名词。"懂"常常带"英语、汉语、日语"或者"礼貌、道理、技术、规矩、事"等名词。*When they serve as a verb, the noun that they take as an object varies in scope. "明白" can go with "道理,事理,意思" or some other phrases or clauses related to something reasonable. But it cannot go with* "汉语,礼貌,规矩,技术" *or other such nouns.* "懂," *by contrast, usually goes with* "英语,汉语,日语," *or nouns such as* "礼貌,道理,技术,规矩,事."

② 做动词时带的补语不同。"明白"可以带"过来"。"懂"不能。*Again, when they serve as a verb, the complement that follows is different.* "明白" *can go with* "过来," *but* "懂" *cannot.*

(11) *听了他的话,我一下子懂过来了。
(12) 听了他的话,我一下子明白过来了。

③ 两者都能做"看、听"的补语,"明白"还可以做某些动词的补语,"懂"不能。*Both can serve as the complement of* "看" *and* "听." *But some verbs can take* "明白" *as their complement but not* "懂."

(13) *我终于想懂了。
(14) 我终于想明白了。

míngmíng 明明 →P148"分明"

用法 Usage:

副词 ad.

表示显然如此、清清楚楚、确确实实。*Obviously and undoubtedly.*

(1) 我姐姐明明很瘦,但她还要减肥。
(2) 明明用红色好看,她就是不用。

说明 Notes:

1. 常用于表示转折的句子或带有反问的句子。用"明明"的分句表示一种客观事实,但是后一分句出现和前一分句矛盾的情况,如例(1)(2)。*It is often used in transitional or rhetorical sentences. The clause with* "明明" *indicates an objective fact, but it is followed by another clause where something contradictory happens as in (1) and (2).*

2. 用在反问的单句中,表示肯定的,显然如此,无可怀疑。*When used in a simple sentence with a rhetorical question, it suggests affirmation, meaning absolutely certain and without doubt.*

(3) 你这不是明明要我难受吗?

3. "明明"和"分明"做副词,用法基本相同。"明明" and "分明," as adverbs, are used basically in the same way.

它们的区别是:Their differences lie in:

① "分明"有形容词用法。"明明"没有。 "分明" can be used as an adjective, while "明明" cannot.

② "明明"可以修饰动词、形容词及其短语。"分明"一般修饰动词。"明明" may modify a verb, an adjective, or a phrase. "分明," by contrast, usually modifies a verb.

míngquè 明确 →P386"确定"

用法 Usage:

动词 v.

使(目标、动机、任务、分工、关系等)明白而确定。To make clear and certain (an objective, motive, task, division of labor, relationship, etc.).

(1) 我们应该先明确分工,再开始工作。

(2) 大家都明确这个学期的学习任务了吗?

形容词 a.

明白而确定。Clear and certain.

(3) 学校明确规定:缺课超过三分之一的学生不能参加考试。

(4) 她来中国的目的非常明确。

说明 Notes:

在句子中使用"明确"的条件。When using "明确," be careful about three things.

① "明确"做定语,后面一定要带"的"。如"明确的目标、明确的态度"等。When used as an attribute, it has to be followed by "的," such as "明确的目标、明确的态度."

② "明确"做补语,前面一定要有"得"。如"说得很明确、规定得很明确"等。When used as a complement, it has to be preceded by "得," such as "说得很明确、规定得很明确."

③ "明确"做谓语,主语常常是抽象名词,如"态度、观点、方向、目标"等。When used as a predicate, its subject is often an abstract noun such as "态度,观点,方向,目标."

míngxiǎn 明显 →P505"鲜明"、P507"显明"、P507"显著"

用法 Usage:

形容词 a.

明白,显著,清晰。表示清楚地显露出来,容易让人看出或感觉到。Clear; obvious; prominent. It is used to indicate the revelation is clear and easily seen or felt.

(1) 最近几年,来华留学生人数明显增加。

(2) 汉语和英语不同的语法点非常明显。

mìng 命

用法 Usage:

名词 n.

1. 生命,性命。Life.

(1) 车开得那么快,不要命了吗?

(2) 你听,有人在叫救命。

2. 寿命。Lifespan.

(3) 长命百岁。

3. 命运,人的遭遇或机遇。Fate; one's experience or opportunity.

(4) 不愁吃,不愁穿,你的命真好!

(5) 有人说,她命中注定会有三个孩子。

4. 指示,命令。常用在短语中,如:"恭敬不如从命、俯首听命"等。Order; instruction. It is often used in phrases as in "恭敬不如从命,俯首听命."

(6) 我是奉命前来请你们参加舞会的。

动词 v.

1. 差遣,指派。后面常与单音节词组合使用。To send; to assign. It usually goes with a monosyllabic word.

(7) 公司命你速回上海。

(8) 班长命你现在就把作业交给他。

2. 取定,给予(名称等)。To assign and give (a name, title, etc.) to.

(9) 今天是玛丽的命名日。

(10) 我们练习的文章一般是命题作文。

mócā 摩擦

用法 Usage:

动词 v.

两个物体互相接触并来回相对移动。To conflict; (of two objects) to touch each other and move back and forth relatively.

(1) 轮胎在地面上摩擦出长长的一道黑印。

(2) 别拖箱子, 会把地板摩擦坏的。

名词 n.

比喻个人之间、单位之间或各派社会力量之间因存在矛盾而发生的冲突, 也作"磨擦"。Friction; the conflict between individuals, institutions or social forces due to contradictions. It is also called "磨擦."

(3) 中美之间有贸易摩擦, 也有很多共同利益。

(4) 两个人一起生活, 总会产生一些摩擦。

mò 末

用法 Usage:

名词 n.

1. 最后, 终了(多对时间来说)。如:"期末(学期的最后一段时间)、春末(春季最后一段时间)、周末(一周最后两天)、明末清初、世纪末(一个世纪的最后一段时间)"。The last; the end (often referring to time). For example, "期末 (the end of the semester)," "春末 (late spring)," "周末 (the weekend)," "明末清初 (the late Ming and early Qing Dynasties)," "世纪末 (the end of a century)."

(1) 期末考试 6 月 10 号开始。

(2) 20 世纪末网络已经在中国流行开了。

(3) 谁说世界末日就要到了?

2. 次要的、非根本的事物, 事物次要的一面, 跟"本"相对, 常用在四字词组中。Nonessentials; minor details. It is opposed to "本," and usually used in four-word phrases.

(4) 做事情不要本末倒置、舍本求末。

3. 碎屑, 粉末。Dust; powder.

(5) 茶叶没有, 只有茶叶末。

(6) 你买点肉末回来, 我要做饺子。

mòmò 默默 →P373"悄悄"

用法 Usage:

副词 ad.

不说话, 不发出声音。Silently; without any sound.

(1) 他们俩默默无语, 坐了两个小时。

(2) 他默默地低着头, 听老师批评。

mǒu 某

用法 Usage:

代词 pron.

1. 指一定的人或事物(知道而不说时用)。A certain person or thing (known but unsaid).

(1) 去年十二月, 我在那家商店看到过王某。

(2) 你在外面干了某事, 你以为我们不知道吗?

2. 指不定的人或事物。后面常跟序列词、数词(限于"一、几"等)、量词。An indefinite person or thing. It is usually followed by ordinal words, numerals (but limited to "一、几"), and particles.

(3) 你某时某地做了某事, 都要说清楚。

(4) 今天某几个同学上课迟到了, 以后请注意。

说明 Notes:

1. "某"用在姓氏后, 代替别人的名字, 有时表示随意或不客气的意思。The use of "某" to replace the real name of a person indicates casualness or impoliteness.

(5) 李某, 我吃了一个你的苹果。

(6) 王某, 你如果再骂人, 就对你不客气了。

2. 可以叠用。如:"某某人、某某学校"等。"某" can be used in the reduplicated form as in "某某人, 某某学校."

mù 木

用法 Usage:

名词 *n.*

1. 树木（木本植物的通称）。如："果木、独木不成林"等。Tree (a general term for woody plants) as in "果木,独木不成林."

2. 木材,木质的。如："红木、松木；木门、木地板"等。Wood; wooden material as in "红木,松木；木门,木地板."

形容词 *a.*

1. 形容反应迟钝,不灵活。Unresponsive and inflexible.

（1）这孩子真木,讲了三遍还不懂。
（2）你看起来很聪明,怎么做起事情来,脑袋这么木。

2. （肢体）发僵,感觉麻木。可以重叠。(Of limbs) numb; feeling stiff. It can be used in the reduplicated form.

（3）太冷了,我的脚都冻木了。
（4）抱着孩子睡觉,一动也不能动,手臂都木木的了。

mùbiāo 目标 →P328"目的"

用法 Usage:

名词 *n.*

1. 标的,射击、攻击或寻求的对象。Target; object of shooting, attack or search.

（1）警察已经发现了目标。
（2）那只野兔就是你射击的目标。

2. 目的,做事情想要达到的标准。Goal; standards for doing things.

（3）今年我有一个目标,就是通过 HSK 六级考试。
（4）每个人都有生活目标。

mùdì 目的 →P328"目标"、P115"动机"

用法 Usage:

名词 *n.*

1. 想要达到的地点或境地。Destination or purpose one wants to reach.

（1）这次我旅游的目的地是云南。
（2）我了解情况的目的是想知道他做了什么事。

2. 想要达到的结果或效果。Result or effect one wants to achieve.

（3）讲故事的目的是为了提高大家的口语水平。
（4）到西安旅游的目的是为了让大家了解中国唐朝的历史文化。

3. 企图,图谋。Attempt; plot.

（5）他这样做一定有他的目的。
（6）为什么不说出来,难道有不可告人的目的吗？

说明 Notes:

1. "目标"和"目的"都指想要达到的境地,想要得到的结果。"目标" and "目的" both refer to the objective or the result one wants to achieve.

它们的区别是：Their differences are as follows:

① "目标"着重指出努力的方向和攻击或寻求的对象。"目的"着重指出行为的意图,追求的结果。"目标" emphasizes the direction of efforts and the target of attack or pursuit. "目的," by contrast, focuses on the intention of a behavior and the result of a pursuit.

（7）＊注意,目的发现了。
（8）注意,目标发现了。

② "目标"一般可以与表示肯定意义的词语搭配。如可受"远大、伟大、宏伟"等词语的修饰,不能与表示否定意义的词语搭配。如不受"卑鄙、可耻、罪恶、不可告人"等词语的修饰。"目的"可以与表示肯定意义的词语搭配,也可以与表示否定意义的词语搭配。"目标" can usually go with words with a positive meaning. It can be modified by words such as "远大,伟大,宏伟." It cannot go with derogatory words. For example, it cannot be modified by words such as "卑鄙,可耻,罪恶,不可告人." "目的"

can go with both affirmative and negative words.

(9) *这个目标太卑鄙了。

(10) 这个目的太卑鄙了。

③"目标"还有尺度、标准、攻击对象的意思。"目的"仅指人们想要达到的地点、境地或想要得到的结果、效果。"目标" also has the meaning of a scale, standard and target of attack. "目的" only refers to the destination or the purpose people want to reach, or the desired result or effect.

(11) *跳远的成绩,我的目的要达到4米。

(12) 跳远的成绩,我的目标要达到4米。

④"目标"常与介词"向着、朝着"搭配使用。"目的"常与介词"为了"搭配使用。"目标" often goes with prepositions such as "向着,朝着." "目的" usually goes with the preposition "为了."

⑤"目的"可以构成"目的地、目的性"等词语。"目标"不能。"目的" can form nominal expressions such as "目的地,目的性." But "目标" cannot.

2. "目的"和"动机"在词义上都是中性词,但使用时有以下区别:Both "目的" and "动机" are neutral in terms of meaning, but their usages differ in the following aspects:

①"动机"多带有贬义色彩,能构成"动机不良、动机不纯"等短语。"动机" tends to be derogatory and forms expressions such as "动机不良" and "动机不纯." They mean "ulterior motives" and "impure motives" respectively.

② 两个词在句子中表示的语义不同。"动机"多为做事情的起点、出发点,做事前的想法。"目的"则为做事希望达到的最后目标。"动机" means the point of departure or one's idea or view when doing a thing. "目的," by contrast, refers to the target one hopes to reach in the end.

③"目的"可与"性"组成名词"目的性"。"动机"没有这种组合。"目的" can join "性" to form "目的性," which is a noun. "动机" cannot be used in this way.

mùguāng 目光 →P536"眼光"

用法 Usage:

名词 n.

1. 指视线。Line of vision; line of sight.

(1) 大家的目光都转向了最后进来的那位同学。

2. 眼睛的神采。Expression in the eyes.

(2) 她用热烈的充满爱护的目光看着他。

3. 眼光,见识。比喻观察事物、预见事物的能力。Foresight; insight; vision.

(3) 目光短浅的人不能办大事。

(4) 我们要有远大的目光。

说明 Notes:

1. 在第三个用法中,"目光"是引申义,常与"短浅、远大、敏锐"等形容词搭配使用。In its third usage, "目光" is used as an extension of its original meaning. It often goes with adjectives such as "短浅,远大,敏锐."

2. "目光",多用于书面语。"目光" appears mostly in written language.

mùqián 目前 →P222"面前"、P537"眼前"

用法 Usage:

名词 n.

眼前,现在说话的时候(有别于"先前""以后")。Right now; at the moment (different from "先前,""以后").

(1) 目前还不知道有多少人参加这次旅游。

(2) 目前的问题是他们开口不说汉语而说英语。

说明 Notes:

"目前"和"面前"的区别是:"目前"表示时间的名词;"面前"是表示空间方位名词。The difference between "目前" and "面前" is that "目前" is a noun expressing a time while "面前" is a noun expressing a direction in space.

ná……láishuō 拿……来说

用法 Usage：

习惯语。表示以某人或某事作为例子,来说明某个情况或道理。*Idiomatic expression, meaning to take someone or something as an example (to illustrate a particular situation or a theory).*

(1) 她的学习成绩很好,拿期中考试来说,三门课都得了优。

(2) 我们班很厉害,拿这次运动会来说,我们班得了三个第一名。

说明 Notes：

1. "拿……来说"常用于口语,书面语是"以……为例"。*"拿...来说" is commonly used in colloquial language, and "以...为例" is frequently used in written language.*

2. 用"拿……来说"造句,句子前面常常有一分句表示某个现象或情况的整体性程度,"拿……来说"是举个例子说明,所举的例子一定要放在"拿"和"来说"之间,常常是名词、名词性短语或动词性短语。*When "拿...来说" appears in a sentence, there is always a clause before it, indicating the general picture of a certain phenomenon or situation. "拿...来说" is to give an example, and the example given must be put between "拿" and "来说," which is often a noun, a noun phrase or a verbal phrase.*

3. "拿……来说"也可以说成"就拿……来说、(就)拿……来说吧"。*"拿...来说" can also be rendered as "就拿...来说" or "(就)拿...来说吧."*

nǎpà 哪怕 →P212"即使"

用法 Usage：

连词 conj.

表示就算承认某种事实。一般用在句子前面。*Even if (acknowledging a certain fact). It is generally used at the beginning of a sentence.*

(1) 哪怕明天下雨,我们也要去游玩。

(2) 哪怕你再道歉,你也已经把他的电脑摔坏了。

说明 Notes：

1. 用"哪怕"这个词语的句子一般有两个分句,后面常有"也、都"等副词一起使用,强调即使在这样的情况下,也改变不了原来的打算、结论或已有的事实。*In a sentence, "哪怕" is generally used in the first clause, and in the following clause, adverbs like "也" and "都" are frequently used to emphasize that no change could be done to the original intention or conclusion even under the presumed circumstance.*

2. "哪怕"多用于口语,带有夸张的意味。*"哪怕" is usually used in colloquial language with a tone of exaggeration.*

3. "哪怕"和"即使"的用法基本相同。*"哪怕" and "即使" basically share the same usage.* 它们的区别是：*Their differences are as follows:*

① "哪怕"多用于口语,"即使"多用于书面

语。"哪怕" is more colloquial whereas "即使" is more of a written language.

② 在语气上,"哪怕"表示就算承认某种事实,也不能改变原来的决定和结果,语气比较肯定。"即使"表示退一步说,语气比较缓和。In terms of tone, "哪怕" suggests that even if a certain fact is acknowledged, no change could be done to the previous decision or the consequence, and the tone is quite certain; "即使" indicates that a concession is already made, and the tone is relatively softened.

nǎxiē 哪些

用法 Usage:

代词 prep.

哪一些。后面一般是名词。Which (followed by a plural noun).

(1) 我们班哪些同学是法国人?
(2) 你们今天有哪些问题要问?

说明 Notes:

"哪些"用在问时间上,可以说:"哪些天? 哪些年? 哪些月份? 哪些日子? 哪些时候?"不能说:"哪些日? 哪些月? 哪些星期?"等等。Using "哪些" to inquire about time, one could say, "哪些天?哪些年?哪些月份?哪些日子?哪些时候?" but not "哪些日？哪些月？哪些星期?"

nà 那

用法 Usage:

代词 pron.

离说话人比较远的人、时间、地方或事物。A person, time, location, or thing that is farther away from the speaker.

1. 单用,一般只用在动词前面。指代人时,只用在动词"是"的句子里,做主语。指代事物时,没有这个限定。Used independently, it usually appears before a verb. When referring to a person, it serves as the subject only in sentences with the verb of "是"; when referring to a matter or a thing, there is no such restriction.

(1) 那是我的口语老师。
(2) 那属于你的。

2. 用在名词、量词、数量词前,对人和事物起确指作用。跟"这"相对。Used before a noun, quantifier or numeral, it refers to a certain person or thing. It is opposite to "这."

(3) 带这本词典就可以了,那本不用带了。
(4) 那毛衣是姐姐的。

3. 泛指事物、处所,一般与"这"对用。A general reference to a matter or a location, it usually goes with its opposite "这."

(5) 这也要,那也要,你什么都要啊!
(6) 这也不吃,那也不吃,什么东西你才吃呢?

4. 用在句子或小句前面,复指前文。Used before a sentence or a clause, it refers to an earlier statement.

(7) 八点就上课,那太早了一点。
(8) 要是能把她请来,那真的要谢谢你了。

5. 在口语里,有时用在动词或形容词前面,表示夸张的作用(与"那个"相同)。In colloquial language, it sometimes appears before a verb or an adjective for the effect of exaggeration (same as "那个").

(9) 她哥哥长得那高呀,你伸手都碰不到他的肩膀。
(10) 老虎那叫啊,十里外都听得到。

6. 在口语里,"那"还能构成"那+一+动/形"的格式,起加强语气的作用。Again in colloquial language, the structure of "那+一+v./a." emphasizes the message.

(11) 他那一跳,就跳过了小河。
(12) 她那一高兴,就让我去买一箱啤酒来喝。

连词 conj.

顺着上文的语意,引出下文应有的判断和结果,与"那么"用法相似。Following a previous statement, it expresses a consequent judgment or result. The usage is similar to "那么."

(13) 要是咳嗽、头痛,那可能感冒了。

(14) 如果你买,那我也买。

说明 Notes:

1. "那"用在量词或数量词前,在口语中,常常读作"nèi"。When "那" appears before a quantifier or numeral, it is pronounced as "nèi" in colloquial speech.

(15) 那两个苹果留给你吃。

2. "那"用作连词时,主要连接两个分句,常常与"如果、假如、要是"等词语连用,见例(13)(14)。As a conjunction, "那" connects two clauses, and is usually used with "如果,假如,要是, etc." See (13) and (14).

nàxiē 那些

用法 Usage:

代词 pron.

指示离说话者比较远的两个以上的人或事物。Those; a reference to two or more persons or things that are farther away from the speaker.

(1) 那些留学生都是英国来的。

(2) 那些东西是我送给你的。

说明 Notes:

1. "那些"在问句中,只指物,不指人。When "那些" appears in an interrogative sentence, it refers to things instead of persons.

(3) *那些是谁?

(4) 那些是谁的东西?

2. 如果问人,一般应该在"那些"后面加上"人"。If the question is about persons, "那些人" is generally used.

(5) 那些人是谁?

3. 如果在句子中,前面用"那些",后面与"东西"或"家伙"连用,"那些"就是指讨厌、憎恶的人。If "那些" is followed by "东西" or "家伙" in a sentence, it refers to some disgusting and detestable people.

(6) 你们知道那些家伙是哪儿来的吗?

(7) 那些东西真不是人!

nàixīn 耐心

用法 Usage:

形容词 a.

心里不怕麻烦,不急躁。Patient; least concerned about troubles; not in haste.

(1) 妈妈对孩子总是非常耐心。

(2) 老师很耐心地给我们讲语法。

名词 n.

指不厌烦、不急躁、什么烦恼都能受得住的心理状态。Patience, a state of mind that is forbearing, patient and able to endure any troubles.

(3) 好老师首先要有耐心。

(4) 山本做事的耐心值得我学习。

nándào 难道

用法 Usage:

副词 ad.

1. 用在反问句中,加强反问的语气。句子末尾常带"吗、不成"。Used to reinforce a rhetorical question. At the end of such a sentence, "吗" or "不成" is often used.

(1) 这个道理你难道还不明白吗?

(2) 你这么发脾气,难道孩子就听你话了不成?

2. 表示自己对某事揣测的语气。Expressing one's own speculation.

(3) 那么晚了,灯还亮着,难道女儿还在做作业吗?

(4) 现在还没回家,难道他出了什么事不成?

说明 Notes:

1. "难道"也常用作"难道说",可以放在主语之前,也可以放在主语之后。"难道" is often replaced by "难道说," which can be placed before or after the subject of a sentence.

2. 当句子末尾有"不成"一起使用时,前面常常表示一种猜想，并且是不希望出现的动作行为。When "不成" is placed at the end of a sentence using "难道," it often indicates a speculation of an undesired act or behavior.

nándé 难得

用法 Usage:

形容词 a.

1. 不容易得到或做到（含有宝贵、可贵的意思）。Not easily achievable; not readily available. It is used to suggest something valuable and precious.

(1) 这次出国学习的机会很难得。

(2) 蓝色的玫瑰花很难得看到。

2. 表示不经常发生。Happening only occasionally.

(3) 爸爸难得做一次饭。

(4) 毕业以后，全班同学很难得聚在一起。

说明 Notes:

要注意"难得"与"难+得"的不同用法。Please pay attention to the different usages of "难得" and "难+得."

(5) 这样的数学题难得有几个。

(6) 这个数学题难得连老师也做不出来。

nánguài 难怪 →P171"怪不得"

用法 Usage:

副词 ad.

表示明白了原因，对所怀疑的事情顿然醒悟，不再觉得奇怪，怪不得。No wonder; no longer feeling strange about something previously suspected.

(1) 这次汉语水平考试她考得很好，难怪她那么高兴。

(2) 难怪他没来上课，原来他生病了。

动词 v.

不应该责怪（含有谅解的意思）。Not to be blamed for .... It is used to indicate forgiveness.

(3) 他刚刚开始学习汉语，说得不好也难怪。

(4) 这也难怪，他第一次写毛笔字，怎么写得好呢！

说明 Notes:

1. "难怪"做副词时，经常用在表示因果关系的结果分句前面，表示原因的分句常常有"原来"等词语配合使用，如例(2)。When "难怪" serves as an adverb, it usually appears at the beginning of a result clause in a conditional sentence. "原来" is often used if it is a clause indicating a reason, as in (2).

2. "难怪"做动词时，是"难+怪"的组合，表示很难责怪的意思，句子中常常有不要责怪的原因，如例(3)(4)。When "难怪" serves as a verb, it is a combination of "难" and "怪," indicating that it's hard to blame someone for something. In the sentence one will find a reason about why not to blame, as in (3) and (4).

3. "难怪"和"怪不得"都有副词、动词用法。Both "难怪" and "怪不得" can serve as an adverb or a verb.

它们的区别是：Their differences are as follows:

① 在语义上，"难怪"着重于过去觉得奇怪是有道理的、理所当然的。"怪不得"着重于说话之前不能不感到奇怪。"难怪" emphasizes the fact that it was reasonable in the past to find something strange. "怪不得," by contrast, focuses on that feeling shortly before speaking.

② "怪不得"做动词时，一般都带宾语。宾语可以是名词性的，也可以是动词性的。"难怪"可以不带宾语。"怪不得," as a verb, usually takes an object, which may be nominal or verbal. However, "难怪" doesn't have to take an object.

(5) 他刚从国外回来，不知道这里的情况，难怪！

(6) 他刚从国外回来，不知道这里的情况，怪不得他说错话了。

③"难怪"通用于口语、书面语。"怪不得"多用于口语。"难怪" is found in both written and oral Chinese while "怪不得" appears mostly in oral Chinese.

nánmiǎn 难免 →P49"不免"

用法 Usage:
形容词 a.
不容易避免。Hard to avoid or avert.
（1）老年人记忆力不好是难免的。
（2）第一次来中国，难免会遇到各种各样的困难。
说明 Notes:
1."难免"所表达的内容往往是说话者不希望发生的事情或行为。"难免"主要用在动词前，后面常跟"要""会"等动词。"难免" is usually used to talk about something or behavior that the speaker does not hope to see. "难免" is mainly used before a verb, and it often pairs with verbs like "要" and "会."
2."难免"后的动词前有否定词，句子意思并不改变，但语气加强了。The meaning of a sentence remains unchanged when the verb following "难免" is made negative, but the tone of the sentence is strengthened.
（3）人的一生中难免犯错误。
（4）人的一生中难免不犯错误。
3."难免"与"不免"都能用在动词前面。Both "难免" and "不免" can be place before verbs.
它们的区别是：Their differences are as follows:
①"难免"是形容词，还可以用在动词后面。"不免"没有形容词用法，不能用在动词后面。"难免" and "不免" could both be used before a verb, but "难免" is an adjective that could also be used after a verb. "不免" is not an adjective and therefore could not be used after a verb.
（5）*写汉字，写错是不免的。

（6）写汉字，写错是难免的。
②"难免"后面可以是肯定形式，也可以是否定形式，如例（3）（4）。"不免"后面一般是肯定形式。Verbs after "难免" could be either positive or negative as seen in（3）and（4）. Verbs after "不免" are usually positive.

nánshuō 难说

用法 Usage:
动词 v.
1.不容易说，不好说，不能确切地说。It's hard to say; it's not easy to make comments; it's unable to say in an exact way; you can never tell.
（1）玛丽什么时候回国还很难说。
（2）这场足球赛谁赢很难说。
2.难以说出口。It's hard to speak out.
（3）你就根据事实说，没有什么难说的。
（4）错就是错，有什么难说的。
说明 Notes:
注意"难说"与"难＋说"结构的区别。Note the difference between "难说" and the structure of "难＋说."
（5）这个人很难说（话）。（指这个人不容易打交道 Meaning this person is difficult to deal with）
（6）这个人来不来参加活动很难说。（指这个人参加不参加活动，说不准。It is not certain whether this person will attend this activity.）

nánwéi 难为 →P485"为难"

用法 Usage:
动词 v.
1.让人为难，作弄，与"为难"同义。To put someone in an embarrassed situation; to tease. It is the same as "为难."
（1）她不会喝酒，你就不要难为她了。
（2）这件事很不好意思，我真的不是要难为你。
2.多亏，幸亏，多用在某人做了不容易做

的事情时。To thank somebody for help. It is often used when someone has made remarkable efforts.

（3）难为你了，不然我的护照就丢了。

（4）这次去上海旅游，真是难为玛丽了。

3. 感谢话，用以表达感谢别人为自己做事。Words of gratitude. They are used to express gratitude for someone doing things for the speaker.

（5）难为你了，把我的行李送到了楼上。

（6）难为你，帮我带两个馒头来。

说明 Notes:

"难为"表示感谢意思时，可以用"谢谢"替代。When "难为" is used to express gratitude, it can be replaced by "谢谢."

nányǐ 难以

用法 Usage:

动词 v.

表示不容易，难于。To be not easy to do; to be difficult to do.

（1）她说的情况让人难以相信。

（2）我的心情难以平静。

说明 Notes:

"难以"一般用在双音节的动词或形容词前面，如"难以忘记、难以回答、难以接受、难以拒绝、难以相信、难以安静"等。"难以" is generally used before disyllabic verbs or adjectives, such as "难以忘记，难以回答，难以接受，难以拒绝，难以相信，难以安静，难以平静."

nèizài 内在

用法 Usage:

形容词 a.

1. 人或事物本身所固有的（跟"外在"相对）。Inherent; being part of the basic nature of someone or something. It's opposite to "外在 (external)."

（1）他没做好这事儿，有他内在的原因。

（2）大自然有它的内在规律。

2. 存在于内心，不表现出来。Existing inside; not shown outside.

（3）她的内在美很有魅力。

说明 Notes:

"内在"一般只做修饰语，不做谓语。Generally, "内在" serves only as a modifier rather than a predicate.

néng 能 →P202"会"、P275"可以"、P335"能够"

用法 Usage:

助动词 aux. v.

跟句子的主要动词紧密连用。It stays close to the main verb in a sentence.

1. 表示具备某种能力。与"会"同义。Having power, means or skill to do something. It is the same as "会."

（1）他能开飞机。

（2）马丁能做面包。

2. 表示有能力或有条件做某事。否定还没发生的行为或情况，用"不能"，否定过去的行为或情况还可以用"没能"。Having the ability or means to do something. "不能" is used when denying an action or situation that hasn't happened. "没能" is used when denying an action or situation that has already happened.

（3）玛丽说星期五晚上我们能/不能去看电影。

（4）过去我不/没能拍出这样的照片，现在可以了。

3. 表示情理上同意、许可。多用于疑问句或否定句。表示肯定的一般用"可以"。Being able to do something for a certain reason or out of personal feeling. It is usually used in an interrogative or negative sentence. To express a positive meaning, "可以" is generally used.

（5）我们星期天能去你家玩吗？

（6）他感冒了，不能再去麻烦他了。

4. 表示环境上许可，多用于疑问或否定，表示肯定时一般用"可以"。Being permitted in a certain environment. It usually appears in an

interrogative or negative sentence. To express a positive meaning, "可以" is generally used.

（7）这儿能抽烟吗？

（8）听老师上课的时候不能大声说话。

5. 表示有某种用途。可以单独回答问题，否定用"不能"。Having a particular use. It can be used independently to answer a question. Its negative form is "不能."

（9）这种笔能写出不同颜色的字。

（10）A：那种药能治这种病吗？

B：不能。

6. 表示善于做某事，可以受程度副词的修饰。一般不能单独回答问题。否定用"不"。Being good at doing something. It can be modified by an adverb of degree. It is generally not used independently to answer a question. Its negative form is "不."

（11）马克很能弹吉他。

（12）A：听说你很能做中国菜。

B：不，不。

7. 表示有可能。Being possible.

① 常与"得"连用。Used together with "得."

（13）只要坚持学下去，就能学得会。

（14）多洗几遍，一定能洗得干净。

② 可以用在"应该"后面，可以用在"愿意"前面。Used after "应该" or before "愿意."

（15）这个问题你应该能回答。

（16）那么贵的书，他们能愿意买吗？

8. 跟"不"组成"不能不"，表示必须、应该。不等于"能"或"不能"。Used with "不" to form "不能不," indicating something must or should be done. It is different from "能" or "不能."

（17）她可以不去，你不能不去。

（18）放假时间延迟了，我不能不改变旅游计划。

形容词 a.

表示有能力的，能干的。常做谓语、定语。Being capable, competent. It is usually used as a predicate or attribute.

（19）他一下子就修好了自行车，真能！

（20）老王是个大能人。

名词 n.

1. 能力、才干。常做宾语、定语。Capacity; talent. Usually it is used as an object or an attribute.

（21）她长得很漂亮，可惜是个低能儿。

（22）社会上不喜欢高分低能的学生。

2. 能量。常和表示能源的一些名词组成新词，如："太阳能、电能、水能、核能"等。常做主语、宾语。Energy. It is usually used with a noun to indicate a certain type of energy such as "太阳能，电能，水能，核能." It serves as the subject or object in a sentence.

（23）核能可以用来发电。

（24）人类应该充分利用太阳能。

说明 Notes：

1. "能"与"会"的区别是：The differences between "能" and "会" are as follows:

① 指刚学会的某种动作或技术，可以用"能"，也可以用"会"，但用"会"比较多。而指恢复某种能力，只能用"能"，不能用"会"。When referring to a newly acquired ability or a skill, either "能" or "会" could be used, but "会" is used more often. As for the recovery of a certain ability or skill, however, only "能" could be used, not "会."

（25）学了三个月后，她就能/会说汉语了。

（26）*老师的病好了，又会给我们上课了。

（27）老师的病好了，又能给我们上课了。

② 表示具备某种能力可以用"能"，也可以用"会"。但是表示达到某种效率、程度，只能用"能"，不能用"会"。When talking about having a certain ability, either "能" or "会" could be used. But when indicating a certain efficiency or level of development that has been newly acquired, only "能," not "会," can be used.

（28）她能/会用英语给我们翻译。

（29）*她一分钟会写二十个汉字。

（30）她一分钟能写二十个汉字。

③ 表示有可能语义的句子,可以用"能",也可以用"会"。这类句子在北方口语中多用"能",在南方口语中多用"会"。When indicating something is likely to take place, either "能" or "会" could be used. In such sentences, "能" is more often used in the northern dialect while "会" is often used in the southern dialect.

(31) 今天太阳能出来吗?

(32) 今天太阳会出来吗?

④ 组成双重否定时,"不能不"表示"必须","不会不"表示"一定"。When expressing a double negation, "不能不" means "必须," and "不会不" means "一定."

(33) 这次旅游我不能不去。(表示客观情况要求我必须去 Indicating that certain conditions compelled me to go travelling)

(34) 这次旅游我不会不去。(表示个人的主观愿望,所以一定去 Indicating that my own intention leads me to travelling)

⑤ "会"有助动词用法,也有动词用法,可以单独作为句子谓语。"能"只有助动词用法,不能单独作为句子谓语。"会" could be used as an auxiliary verb or a verb, and can also be used independently as a predicate; "能," as an auxiliary verb, cannot be used this way.

(35) *他能英语、法语。

(36) 他会英语、法语。

2. "能"与"可以"都有表示可能和能够的意思。Both "可以" and "能" can be used to mean "可能" and "能够."

它们的区别是: The differences are as follows:

① "可以"侧重表示条件上有可能去做某一件事了。"能"侧重表示有能力去做某一件事。"可以" is used to mean that one can do something under certain conditions while "能" is more used to mean that one has the ability to do something.

(37) 他可以写汉字了。

(38) 他能写汉字。

② "能"有表示善于做某事的意思。前面常有"很"等程度副词修饰。"可以"不能。"能" has the meaning of being good at doing something. Usually it has an adverbial of degree modifier before it. "可以" cannot be used in this way.

(39) *他很可以说,一说就说上两三个小时。

(40) 他很能说,一说就说上两三个小时。

③ "能"可以表示情理上或客观上的可能性。"可以"不能。"能" can mean a possibility in terms of logic or objective conditions, but "可以" cannot be used to mean the same.

(41) *那么晚了,他还可以来吗?

(42) 那么晚了,他还能来吗?

④ "能"可以和"愿意"连用。"可以"不行。"能" can be used with "愿意," while "可以" cannot be used in the same way.

(43) *你不让他去,他可以愿意吗?

(44) 你不让他去,他能愿意吗?

⑤ "能"常常用"不能不"的形式表示必须、必定等强调的意思。"可以"一般不能用"不可以不"的形式表示。"能" is often used in the form of "不能不" to mean "必须" or "必定" for emphasis, but "可以" normally cannot be used in the form of "不可以不" for emphasis.

⑥ "可以"做谓语时,主语可以是动词短语或小句。"能"不行。When "可以" is used as a predicate, the subject can either be a verbal phrase or a clause. The same cannot be applied to "能."

(45) *这本词典送给她也能。

(46) 这本词典送给她也可以。

néngfǒu 能否

用法 Usage:

动词 v.

能不能。Can or cannot.

(1) 你能否告诉我，到底是怎么回事？
(2) 这里能否进去参观？

说明 Notes：

"能否"具书面色彩，"能不能"具口语色彩。"能否" appears more in written language, and "能不能" appears more colloquially.

nénggòu 能够 →P335"能"

用法 Usage：

助动词 aux. v.

1. 表示具备某种能力，或可以起到某种作用。To be able (or to have certain abilities or means) to accomplish something.

(1) 他能够到高班学习。
(2) 她能够把情况跟同学们讲清楚。

2. 表示条件或情理上的许可。To be permitted to do something (according to logic or condition).

(3) 这个教室能够坐28个人。
(4) 这次活动能够带朋友参加。

说明 Notes：

"能够"和"能"做助动词的用法基本相同。As auxiliary verbs, "能够" and "能" are basically used in the same way.

它们的区别是：Their differences are as follows：

1. "能够"多用于书面语，"能"通用于书面语和口语。"能够" is more often used in written language, while "能" is used in both written and spoken languages.

2. "能"可以用肯定否定重叠的形式（即"能不能"）表示提问。"能够"一般不这样用。"能" can be used with positive and negative forms combined together, which is "能不能，" to raise a question; "能够" cannot be used in this way.

3. 用"能够"的地方，一般都可以用"能"替换。用"能"的地方不一定能用"能够"替换。如修饰单音节动词时，一般不能用"能够"。在表示条件、情理上许可时，常常用"能"，不用"能够"。"能够" could be replaced by "能" in most cases, but not vice versa. For example, when modifying a monosyllabic verb, generally "能够" should not be used. When indicating a permission resulting from logic or condition, "能" instead of "能够" is often used.

(5) *他很能够喝。
(6) 他很能喝。
(7) *这个餐厅里能够不能够抽烟？
(8) 这个餐厅里能不能抽烟？

niándù 年度

用法 Usage：

名词 n.

根据业务性质和需要制定的，有一定起讫日期的十二个月。A period of time spanning 12 months. It is decided by the nature of business or its needs.

(1) 年底到了，公司在进行年度工作总结。
(2) 每年开始，我都要制订一份年度学习计划。

niánjì 年纪 →P389"年龄"

用法 Usage：

名词 n.

指人的年龄、岁数。One's age.

(1) 他不懂事，因为年纪还小。
(2) 我不知道马丁的年纪。

说明 Notes：

1. "年纪"用来指人的岁数。可与"大、小、老、轻"等形容词组成"年纪大、年纪小、年纪老、年纪轻"等词语。"年纪" refers to the age of a person. It can be used with adjectives such as "大，""小，""老，" and "轻" to form phrases as "年纪大，""年纪小，""年纪老，" and "年纪轻."

2. 可与动词"有、上"组成"有点年纪了、上了年纪了"等词语，通用于口语和书面语。It can be used with verbs such as "有" and "上"

to form phrases as "有点年纪了" and "上了年纪了," both of which are common in written and spoken languages.

3. 问成年人年纪,常用"多大年纪";问孩子年纪,一般说:"你多大了？" When asking about the age of an adult, the expression is "多大年纪"; when asking about the age of a child, the expression is, "你多大了？"

niánlíng 年龄 →P388"年纪"

用法 Usage:

名词 n.

指人或动植物已经生存的年数。The number of years a human, an animal or a plant has lived or survived.

（1）我不知道她的年龄。

（2）这棵树的年龄已经有两千多年了。

说明 Notes:

1. "年龄"比"年纪"使用范围大,既可指人,也可以指动植物的生存时间。"年龄" is more broadly applied than "年纪," as it can refer to the time when a human, an animal or a plant lives in the world.

2. 用于动植物及其他事物时,常用一个"龄"字搭配,如"树龄、狗龄"等。When referring to the age of an animal, a plant or the duration of a certain matter, "龄" is usually used, such as "树龄" and "狗龄."

3. 在词语搭配上,"年龄"可受"虚、实足、实际、入学、结婚、退休"等词语的修饰,不能与"有、上"等动词搭配。"年纪"一般不与上面的词语搭配。In collocation, "年龄" can be modified by words such as "虚足,实足,实际,入学,结婚,退休," but cannot be modified by verbs like "有" or "上.""年纪" usually cannot be used in collocation with the above words.

4. "年龄"语言色彩郑重,多用于书面语、正式场合。填表格时,常有"年龄"一栏。"年龄" has a solemn tone color, and is often used in written language and on official occasions. For example, when filling a form, there is a column called "年龄."

níngjìng 宁静 →P3"安静"、P358"平静"

用法 Usage:

形容词 a.

表示人的心情或者环境静态的安静。(Of a person's state of mind) showing calmness; (of the environment) showing quietness.

（1）夜晚,校园里十分宁静。

（2）她那宁静的内心被打乱了。

说明 Notes:

"宁静"和"安静"的区别是：The differences between "宁静" and "安静" are as follows:

1. "安静"可以描述人的性格、情状,而"宁静"不可以。"安静" can be used to describe a person's personality or his/her emotional state. "宁静" has no such usage.

（3）*她这个人很宁静。

（4）她这个人很安静。

2. "宁静"强调安宁,在程度上比"平静"要深,在感觉上,先有动感的"平静",然后达到相对静态的"宁静",所以"宁静"后面一般不带有趋向补语"下来"。"宁静" emphasizes tranquility which is deeper in degree than "平静." And in the sense one's feeling, dynamic "平静" often comes before relatively static "宁静." In this case, "宁静" does not take directional complement "下来" after it.

（5）*他的心宁静下来了。

（6）他的心平静下来了。

nòng 弄 →P163"搞"

用法 Usage:

动词 v.

1. 能代替部分动词的动作,随着宾语的不同而具有不同的意思。可带"了、着、过",可重叠,可带名词宾语。"弄" is often used to replace some verbs indicating an action. Its meanings vary, depending on the object. It can be used with "了,""着," or "过," and it could be used as "弄弄."

（1）今天晚上你弄饭,好不好?（表示做饭 Meaning cooking）

（2）你把房间弄得干净一点儿。（表示打扫 Meaning cleaning）

（3）你别把孩子弄哭了。（表示逗孩子玩;玩耍 Meaning playing with a kid; playing）

2. 表示想办法得到。可带"了、过",后面常带数量词语。To acquire something through some action. It can be used with "了" or "过," and usually with numeral words following it.

（4）他弄到了两张音乐会的票。

（5）你去弄点儿酒吧。

说明 Notes:

"弄"和"搞"的区别如下：The differences between "弄" and "搞" are as follows:

1. 都可代替一些具体动作的动词。其词义随着宾语的不同而不同,宾语常常是表示具体事物的名词。Both can replace certain verbs indicating a specific action. The meanings vary according to different objects, which are often nouns indicating specific things or matters.

（6）到哪儿去搞/弄瓶矿泉水来?

（7）这电脑不知道哪儿出了问题,你帮我搞搞/弄弄。

2. 都有表示设法取得的意思。They both share the meaning of acquiring something through some action.

3. 都可以带结果补语、可能补语和趋向补语。如:"弄/搞错、弄/搞明白、弄/搞好、弄/搞成、弄/搞起来、弄/搞得了、弄/搞不了"等,对象多为"事、事情、问题";"弄/搞到、弄/搞来"等,对象多为东西、物体。此外,还有"弄/搞下去、弄/搞上、弄/搞出来、弄/搞上去"等。They both can be followed by a result complement, a potential complement or a directional complement. For example, "弄/搞错,弄/搞明白,弄/搞好,弄/搞成,弄/搞起来,弄/搞得了,弄/搞不了, etc." The objects are mostly "事,事情,问题." As for "弄/搞到,弄/搞来, etc.," the objects are usually things and items. There are other usages such as "弄/搞下去,弄/搞上,弄/搞出来,弄/搞上去."

4. 表示抽象意义的名词,一般只能做"搞"的宾语,不能做"弄"的宾语,如"搞革命、搞建设、搞工作、搞工业、搞翻译、搞调查、搞承包、搞活动"等。Abstract nouns could only serve as objects of "搞," not "弄." For example, "搞革命,搞建设,搞工作,搞工业,搞翻译,搞调查,搞承包,搞活动."

5. "搞"可以指担任的职务、做具体的工作,如"搞IT的,搞医的,搞教学的,搞研究的"。"弄"不能。"搞" could refer to an occupation or line of work. For example, "搞IT的,搞医的,搞教学的,搞研究的." "弄" has no such usage.

6. "搞"通用于口语、书面语。"弄"比"搞"更多地使用于口语。"搞" is used both in written and spoken languages. "弄" is more frequently used in colloquial language than "搞."

nuǎn 暖 →P341 "暖和"

用法 Usage:

形容词 a.

和暖,温暖,暖和。与"暖和"同义。可以重叠。Warm; balmy. It is the same as "暖和." It can be reduplicated.

（1）春天来了,天气变暖了。

（2）外边很冷,房间里暖暖的。

动词 v.

使变得温暖。可以重叠使用,后面要带宾语。To warm something up. It can be reduplicated as "暖暖" and it is followed by an object.

（3）天气太冷了,快进屋暖暖身子。

（4）她说的话真是暖人心哪。

nuǎnhuo 暖和 →P340"暖"、P490"温和"

用法 Usage:
形容词 *a.*

指气候、环境、衣服、阳光、身子等不冷也不热。常做谓语、补语，重叠形式为 AABB。*(Climate, environment, clothes, sunshine or body, etc.) being neither too cold nor too hot. It usually serves as a predicate or a complement; the reduplicated form is AABB.*

（1）这件棉衣暖暖和和的，快穿上！
（2）这房间朝南，太阳照得很暖和。

动词 *v.*

表示让你暖和起来。重叠形式为 ABAB。*To enable someone to feel warm. The reduplicated form is ABAB.*

（3）外面太冷了，快到屋里暖和暖和。
（4）天真冷，喝杯热茶暖和暖和！

说明 Notes:

"暖"和"暖和"，词义和用法基本相同。*The usages and meanings of "暖" and "暖和" are basically the same.*

它们的区别是：*Their differences are as follows:*

1."暖"是单音节词，"暖和"是双音节词，与其他词语搭配上，常常是单音节与单音节搭配，双音节与双音节搭配。*In terms of collocation, the monosyllabic "暖" usually goes with monosyllabic words, and the disyllabic "暖和" generally goes with disyllabic words.*

2."暖和"做动词，可以重叠为"暖和暖和"，一般后面不带宾语，如例（3）（4）。"暖"做动词，重叠后一般必带宾语。*When "暖和" serves as a verb, it appears as "暖和暖和," and is usually not followed by an object, such as in (3) and (4). When "暖暖" is used as a verb, it is usually followed by an object.*

（5）*给你个热水袋暖暖。
（6）给你个热水袋暖暖手。

ǒu'ěr 偶尔 →P342"偶然"

用法 Usage:

副词 ad.

表示有时候,不常发生(与"常常""经常"相对)。Occasionally; not happening often. It is opposite to "常常" and "经常."

(1) 他住在学校里,偶尔回一趟家。

(2) 回国后我们很久没见面了,只是偶尔打个电话。

说明 Notes:

"偶尔"有时也用作形容词,表示不常发生的、很少发生的。"偶尔" can sometimes be used as an adjective, showing that something seldom happens.

(3) 我们已经好几年没来往了,只靠偶尔的电话联系一下。

(4) 去卡拉OK唱歌,对我来说只是偶尔的事。

ǒurán 偶然 →P342"偶尔"

用法 Usage:

副词 ad.

表示不经常,偶尔。Not often; occasionally.

(1) 有一天,我偶然发现了他的秘密。

(2) 迟到情况偶然发生一两次问题不大。

形容词 a.

表示超出一般规律和常情而出现的(跟"必然"相对)。做定语、补语等。Happening by chance (opposite to "必然"). It is used as an attribute or a complement.

(3) 这件事发生得很偶然。

(4) 这只是一个偶然事件。

说明 Notes:

1. "偶尔"和"偶然"都表示不经常发生的,都多用于书面语。Both "偶尔" and "偶然" mean that something happens occasionally. Both are more used in written language.

它们的区别是:Their differences are as follows:

① "偶尔"着重于偶发,次数和数量极少。"偶然"着重于意外,不是必然的、经常的,表示事情发生超出一般事理和规律。"偶尔" emphasizes occasional happening, with very low frequency and occurrence, while "偶然" emphasizes happening by chance, not often, not following the routine, the rule or law.

② "偶尔"在句子中只做状语。如果做定语,与中心语之间一般要用"的"。不能受程度副词的修饰。"偶然"能受程度副词的修饰,在句子中可做谓语、主语、定语、状语、宾语等。与中心语之间的"的"可用可不用,使用范围比"偶尔"广。"偶尔" can only be used as an adverbial. If it is used as an attribute, there is often a "的" in between. It cannot be modified by an adverb of degree. "偶然" can be modified by an adverb of degree, and can be used as a predicate, a subject, an attribute, an adverbial or an object. What's more, it is optional to use "的" between "偶然" and the head of the phrase. "偶然" is used in a wider range than "偶尔."

③ "偶然"可构成"偶然间、偶然之间"作状语,还可构成"偶然性"。"偶尔"不能。"偶然" can be used to form phrases like "偶然间,偶然之间", serving as an adverbial. It can also be used to form "偶然性.""偶尔" does not have this usage.

④ 一般说,"偶然"是副词,又是形容词。"偶尔"通常只用作副词。Generally speaking, "偶然" can be either an adverb or an adjective, but "偶尔" is usually used as an adverb.

2. 注意"偶尔"和"偶然"误用。Pay attention to the following incorrect usages of "偶尔" and "偶然."

(5) *他偶然去图书馆看书。
(6) 他偶尔去图书馆看书。
(7) *我是偶尔认识她的。
(8) 我是偶然认识她的。
(9) *这种事太偶尔了。
(10) 这种事太偶然了。

pà 怕 →P186"害怕"、P277"恐怕"

用法 Usage:

动词 *v.*

1. 害怕，畏惧，感到胆怯。可带名词、动词、小句做宾语。可受程度副词修饰。To be afraid; to fear; to feel nervous. It can be followed by a noun, a verb or a clause as an object, and it can be modified by an adverb of degree.

(1) 他很怕一个人在家。

(2) 她怕蛇怕极了。

2. 表示疑虑，担心（某事发生或某种情况出现），恐怕。必带动词、形容词、小句做宾语。To indicate doubt; worry about (things that might happen); to be afraid of. It must be followed by a verb, an adjective or a clause as its object.

(3) 我怕上课迟到，所以每天七点就起床了。

(4) 妈妈就怕孩子生病。

3. 表示担心。"怕"的后面多是否定形式。To show worry. "怕" is often followed by something that is negative.

(5) 这么大的雪，路上怕不好走了。

(6) 我还没复习完，明天考试怕考不好了。

4. 表示不能承受，经受不住。必带动词宾语。To be unable to endure or withstand. It must be followed by an object.

(7) 玻璃杯怕摔，我这人马马虎虎，不敢用。

(8) 这孩子最怕打针，一到医院就要哭。

副词 *ad.*

表示推测、估计，相当于"恐怕、大概、也许"的意思。句尾常带有语气助词"吧"。"怕"有时也说成"怕是"。Making a guess or an estimation, equivalent to "恐怕, 大概, 也许." The modal particle "吧" is often used at the end of the sentence. Sometimes "怕" is interchangeable with "怕是."

(9) 这么大的西瓜，怕有十几斤重吧。

(10) 这座山有点高，爷爷怕是爬不上去吧。

(11) 现在不走，他怕要上不了飞机了。

说明 Notes:

1. "怕"用作副词时，要注意：When "怕" serves as an adverb, pay attention to the following aspects:

① "怕"只能出现在动词性短语前做状语，在句中不能做谓语。动词性短语中多出现"会、要、能、得"等能愿动词，如例(11)。As an adverb, "怕" can only be used before a verbal phrase as an adverbial, and it cannot serve as a predicate. There is often a modal verb such as "会、要、能、得" in the verbal phrase, as in (11).

② 多用于口语，在句末常有语气词"吧"，以加强推测时的委婉语气。"怕" is often used colloquially. The Chinese modal particle "吧" often appears at the end of the sentence to show moderation in making a speculation.

③ "怕"做副词表示"推测、估计"，主语只能是被推测、估计的人或事，而不能是估计者本身。When "怕", as an adverb, indicates a guess or an estimation, the subject of the sentence can only be the person or thing that is speculated about or estimated.

(12) 这么大的雨，他怕是不会来了。(副词"怕"as an adverb)

(13) 这么大的雨，我怕他不来了。(动词"怕"as a verb)

④ 为了避免动词"怕"与副词"怕"的混淆，副词"怕"常用"怕是"代替，如例(10)(12)。In order to avoid confusion between the verb "怕" and the adverb "怕," the adverb "怕" is often substituted by "怕是," as in (10) and (12).

2. "怕"与"害怕"都有表示恐惧的意思，都可以受程度副词的修饰。它们的区别是：Both "怕" and "害怕" can indicate fear and be modified by an adverb of degree. Their differences are as follows:

① "怕"有"经受不住，表示疑惑、担心，表示估计"的意思。"害怕"没有这些意思，词义没有"怕"广泛。"怕" can mean "经受不住；表示疑惑，担心；表示估计," which "害怕" does not cover. The range of meanings covered by "害怕" is not as wide as "怕."

② "怕"是单音节词，多作为词素组成双音节词语，如："可怕、害怕、惊怕、生怕、惧怕、哪怕、恐怕"等。"害怕"是双音节词，没有这个功能。"怕" is a monosyllabic word, so it is often used as a morpheme to form disyllabic words such as "可怕，惊怕，生怕，惧怕，哪怕，恐怕." "害怕," a disyllabic word, does not have this function.

3. "恐怕"和"怕"都有表示疑惑、担心和猜测、估计的意思。它们的区别是：Both "恐怕" and "怕" express the meaning of doubt or worry, and guess or estimate. Their differences are as follows:

① "恐怕"是副词，总是用在谓语前面。"怕"是动词，只有表示"估计、疑虑和担心"的词义时，用法与副词一样，用在动词前面。"恐怕" is an adverb that always appears before the predicate. By contrast, "怕" is a verb. Only when it is used to express the meaning of "estimate, doubt, and worry," will it appear before a verb like an adverb.

② 表示"疑虑、担心"的意思时，"恐怕"带有"估计"的意思，并且多用在主语前，着重表示担心的事情。"怕"可用在主语前后，除了担心什么事情以外，还突出表示是谁在担心。"恐怕" carries the meaning of "estimate" when it expresses "doubt" or "worry." In this meaning, it often appears before the subject, focusing on one's worry about something. "怕" may appear before or after the subject. In addition to showing one's worry, it highlights who is worrying.

(14) 恐怕妈妈迷路了。

(15) 哥哥怕妈妈迷路了。

③ 表示"估计"的意思时，"恐怕"也常常带有表示对估计的情况所产生结果的担心。"怕"一般是对事物数量多少或情况发生可能性的估计。When expressing an estimate, "恐怕" often carries a feeling of worry for the result of the estimated situation. By contrast, "怕" generally refers to the estimation on the quantity of things or the possibility of the occurrence of a situation.

(16) 恐怕末班车一过，我就回不去了。

(17) 这条鱼怕有三四斤重。

④ "怕"有表示"害怕、恐惧和禁受不住"的意思。"恐怕"没有。"怕" may carry the meaning of "fear, dread, and being unable to endure." "恐怕" doesn't have this meaning.

pāishè 拍摄 →P346"拍照"

用法 Usage:
动词 v.

用照相机或摄像机把人、景物的形象记录在底片、录像带或者其他存储介质上。To use a camera to record the image of someone or something on a film, video tape or other storage devices.

(1) 明天要拍摄外景，请大家做好准备。
(2) 我们要把手术的过程拍摄下来。

说明 Notes：

"拍摄"可以用在形式动词"进行、开始"等后面作宾语。"拍摄" may serve as an object to a dummy verb such as "进行" or "开始."

(3) 电视剧明天进行拍摄。
(4) 那个电视剧开始拍摄了没有？

pāizhào 拍照 →P345"拍摄"

用法 Usage：

动词 v.

照相，摄影。离合动词，可以插入其他成分。To take a picture; to photograph. It is a separable verb, so other constituents can be inserted.

(1) 大家不要走，我们还要拍照。
(2) 我要回国了，请大家跟我拍个照吧！

说明 Notes：

"拍摄"和"拍照"的区别是："拍摄" differs from "拍照" as follows：

1. "拍摄"着重指"拍照、摄影、录像"时拍的动作。动作涉及的范围比较广泛。"拍照"只指照相机把人、景物的形象记录在底片上。"拍摄" emphasizes the action of "拍" in "拍照,摄影,录像," and the scope of action concerned is fairly wide. "拍照" only means to record the image of someone or something by using a camera that has a film sensitive to light inside it.

2. "拍照"是离合动词，"拍摄"不是。"拍照" is a separable verb, but "拍摄" is not.

pái 排 →P347"排列"

用法 Usage：

动词 v.

1. 一个挨一个地按着次序摆。在句子中做谓语，可带宾语，可带状语，可带补语。To put in order. It is used as a predicate in a sentence and can be followed by an object, and there might be an adverbial before it and a complement after it.

(1) 教室里的桌子椅子排得整整齐齐。
(2) 人行道上排着十几辆共享单车。

2. 排演，演练。常和戏剧、节目等方面的词搭配。To rehearse. It often goes with words about drama and program.

(3) 这是最近新排的话剧《日出》。
(4) 我们正在为春节晚会排节目。

3. 用力除去。To remove; to discharge.

(5) 下了几天大雨，马路上的水排不出去了。
(6) 赶快把船里的水排出去。

名词 n.

1. 表示行列，常和序数词、方位词组合。如："前排、后排、旁边一排、第五排、上面第七排"等。组合后表示方位，具有方位词的语法特征，可以做主语、宾语和定语。Row; line. It often goes with an ordinal or a word indicating a location, which can be used as a subject, an object or attribute. For example, "前排，后排，旁边一排，第五排，上面第七排."

(7) 大家都喜欢坐在教室的前几排。
(8) 坐在第一排的男学生是英国人。

2. 一种水上交通工具，用竹子或者木头并排地连在一起做成。也作为一种运输工具，把竹子或木头扎成排，在水上运输。An aquatic vehicle made of pieces of bamboo or wood, named as a bamboo or wooden raft; a mode of water transport by tying pieces of bamboo or wood together.

(9) 他们坐木排过河了。
(10) 水面上有许多竹排和木排。

3. 一种西式食品，用大而厚的肉片煎成。如："牛排、猪排"等。A kind of Western food made from large, thick slices of meat, such as "牛排 (beefsteak), 猪排 (pork chop)."

(11) 今天中午我吃了一份法国牛排。

说明 Notes：

作为动词，"排"多用于口语。As a verb, "排" is often used in spoken language.

páiliè 排列 →P346"排"

用法 Usage:

动词 v.

按照行列次序放,或者站。在句子中做谓语,常带状语,有时带宾语和补语。*To put in order or stand in line. It is used as a predicate in a sentence, often followed by an adverbial, sometimes followed by an object and a complement.*

(1) 请把四个句子的顺序排列一下。
(2) 展览大厅里排列着世界各国的小汽车。

说明 Notes:

1. 短语"按……排列"是常用固定搭配,如"按时间排列、按字母顺序排列、按日期排列、按人数排列、按类别排列、按姓氏笔画排列"等。*"按...排列" is a set phrase as seen in "按时间排列,按字母顺序排列,按日期排列,按人数排列,按类别排列,按姓氏笔画排列."*

2. "排"跟"排列"的区别是:*"排" differs from "排列" in the following two ways:*

① 动词"排"比"排列"口语性更强。*The verb "排" is more colloquial than "排列".*

② 跟"排"搭配的词语,可以是单音节,也可以是两个以上更多的音节,如"排课、排座位、排名次、排桌椅、排日程表、排第一名"等。与"排列"搭配的词语,一般不能是单音节。如:不能说"排列课、排列名、排列序"等,可以说"排列座位、排列桌椅"等。*Words going with "排" may be monosyllabic, disyllabic or multisyllabic such as "排课,排座位,排名次,排桌椅,排日程表,排第一名." Generally speaking, words going with "排列" cannot be monosyllabic, so it is incorrect to say "排列课,排列名,排列序," but it is correct to say "排列座位,排列桌椅."*

pài 派

用法 Usage:

动词 v.

1. 分派,派遣,委派。*To assign; to send; to appoint.*

(1) 他被公司派到上海分公司去了。
(2) 学院派王老师去法国教汉语了。

2. 摊派,分配。*To apportion; to allocate.*

(3) 国家派到农民头上的农业税早就取消了。
(4) 中学生出国留学,常常会被派到老外家里吃住。

名词 n.

1. 指立场、见解或作风习气相同的一群人。*A group of people with a similar standpoint, viewpoint or style.*

(5) 他俩是不同党派的人。
(6) 不同学派的人得出的结论是不同的。

2. 气派或风度。*Style; manner.*

(7) 旗袍有京派和海派两大类。
(8) 那个帅哥很有派!

3. 一种带馅儿的西式点心。如:"苹果派、巧克力派"等。*A type of Western snack with fillings, such as "苹果派,巧克力派."*

pànwàng 盼望 →P498"希望"

用法 Usage:

动词 v.

殷切地期望。宾语常常为动词性词组。*To look forward to something eagerly. Its objects are often verbal phrases.*

(1) 我盼望快点儿放假,可以去西藏旅游。
(2) 我特别盼望过生日。

páng 旁 →P348"旁边"

用法 Usage:

名词 n.

1. "旁"作为方位名词,表示旁边,附近的意思。*A noun indicating a direction or position, which means next to or near.*

(1) 路旁有个卖鲜花的小姑娘。
(2) 你没看见车旁有个老人吗?

2. 汉字的偏旁。如:"木字旁、双人旁、言字旁"等。*Lateral radical of a Chinese character, such as "木字旁,双人旁,言字旁."*

代词 *pron.*

其他，另外。*Other(s); something or someone else.*

(3) 先把作文做完，再做旁的作业。

(4) 这是我跟他的事情，旁人不要多管。

说明 Notes:

"旁"作为方位名词，不能单独使用。只有在成语或习惯语中，作为特例，如"旁若无人、从旁观测"等。*As a noun indicating a direction or position, "旁" cannot be used by itself except in some idioms or set phrases such as "旁若无人, 从旁观测."*

pángbiān 旁边 →P347"旁"

用法 Usage:

名词 *n.*

左右两侧，附近的地方。*Side; adjacent place.*

(1) 马路旁边停着很多小车和自行车。

(2) 坐在你旁边的同学叫什么名字？

说明 Notes:

"旁"和"旁边"都可做方位名词，但是用法有所区别。*Both "旁" and "旁边" can be used as a noun indicating a direction or position, yet they are different in the following aspects.*

1. "旁边"可以单独使用，"旁"不能。*"旁边" can be used by itself, but "旁" cannot.*

(3) *旁有棵大树。

(4) 旁边有棵大树。

2. 用在名词后，"旁边"前可以加"的"也可以不加。"旁"不能加。*When "旁边" is used after a noun, there might be a "的" preceding it; but there is no "的" preceding "旁."*

(5) *马路的旁有一间小屋。

(6) 马路的旁边有一间小屋。

(7) 马路旁有一间小屋。

3. "旁边"一般与双音节词配合使用，如"旁边的房间、房间旁边"。"旁"一般与单音节词，配合使用，如"身旁、旁人"等。*"旁边" often goes with disyllabic words such as "旁边的房间, 房间旁边." Also, "旁" often goes with monosyllabic words such as "身旁, 旁人."*

pǎo 跑 →P348"跑步"

用法 Usage:

动词 *v.*

1. 指人或动物用腿迅速前进，也指车船等迅速前进。*(Of people or animals) to move quickly by using legs; (of vehicles) to move quickly; to run.*

(1) 明天我们跑八百米，请大家准备好。

(2) 火车比汽车跑得快。

2. 逃走。*To escape.*

(3) 抓住那个骗子，别让他跑了！

(4) 到了警察手里，他就跑不了了。

3. 为某种事情奔走。常见的搭配有："跑买卖、跑业务、跑销售、跑材料、跑码头"等。也可带地名做宾语，意指为某事在某地奔走。*To run about doing something. It is often used in collocations such as "跑买卖, 跑业务, 跑销售, 跑材料, 跑码头." It can also be followed by the name of a place as an object, indicating running about doing something in that place.*

(5) 我全年在外面跑买卖，回家的机会很少。

(6) 我最近为了业务跑了好几次上海。

4. 物体离开了原来的位置。*(Of things) to leave the original place; to escape.*

(7) 衣服被风刮跑了。

(8) 自行车轮胎的气跑了。

5. 液体因挥发而损耗；泄，漏。*(Of liquids) to evaporate; to leak.*

(9) 酒精倒在杯子里，一会儿就跑光。

(10) 茶叶的香味都跑光了。

pǎobù 跑步 →P348"跑"

用法 Usage:

动词 *v.*

按照规定的姿势向前跑。可做主语、谓语。

"跑步"为离合动词，不能带宾语。*To run forward according to a required posture. It can be used as a subject or a predicate.* "跑步," *a separable verb, cannot be followed by an object.*

（1）跑步对身体有好处。
（2）每天早上他都会跑十分钟步，打十五分钟太极拳。

说明 Notes:

1. 运用"跑步"要注意：*When* "跑步" *is used, pay attention to the following aspects:*

① "跑步"是离合动词，不能直接带补语，带补语须重复动词。*As a separable verb,* "跑步" *cannot be followed directly by a complement. The verb must be repeated when there is a complement.*

（3）*他跑步得很快。
（4）他跑步跑得很快。

② 离合动词后面的时量补语、动量补语、结果补语以及"着、了、过"等助词的正确位置，应该在动宾结构之间。*The right position for a time-measure complement, an action-measure complement, or a result-measure complement or an auxiliary like* "着，了，过" *is in between the verb and its object.*

（5）*他跑步了半个小时。
（6）他跑步跑了半个小时。
（7）*跑步完应该喝点儿水。
（8）跑完步应该喝点儿水。

2. "跑"和"跑步"的区别是：*The differences between* "跑" *and* "跑步" *are as follows:*

① "跑"和"跑步"的意义不完全一致。两个动作行为的目的不完全一致。"跑"是一般意义的快速前进。"跑步"是一种运动方式，目的是健身。*The meanings of* "跑" *and* "跑步" *are not completely the same. The two actions do not have the same purpose.* "跑" *means moving fast, while* "跑步" *is a form of physical exercise, which aims to keep a person fit.*

② 两者的用法不同。"跑"具有一般动词的特点，可带宾语、补语、状语等，还可以作为语素与别的语素组合成词，如："快跑、慢跑；跑供销、跑上海"等。而"跑步"是离合词，可有分离形式，不能带宾语，如例（2）。*Their usages are different.* "跑" *has the features of a common verb, which can be followed by an object, a complement, an adverbial, and so on. It can also be used as a morpheme to form words like* "快跑，慢跑；跑供销，跑上海." "跑步" *is a separable verb, but cannot be followed by an object as in (2).*

péi 陪 →P350"陪同"

用法 Usage:
动词 *v.*

随同、伴随。做谓语，后面常带主谓词组，与"陪"一起组成兼语词组，表示陪同某人做某件事情，构成"陪某人做某件事"句式。*To accompany; to keep sb. company. It is used as a predicate and often followed by a subject-predicate phrase to form a concurrent phrase,* "陪某人做某件事," *indicating doing something with somebody.*

（1）明天我要陪妈妈去医院。
（2）他心情不好，我想陪他聊聊天。

说明 Notes:

1. "陪"为可持续性动词，可带时间名词做时量补语，表示动作延续时间的长短。"陪" *is a durative verb and can be followed by a complement indicating the duration of the action.*

（3）我在医院里陪了她一整天。
（4）每天他都陪爷爷散一会儿步，陪他说一会儿话。

2. "陪"的对象与"陪"的施事（一般是主语）有主次之分。一般说来，"陪"的对象是从事该事情的主要一方，"陪"的施事只是伴随者。*The object of* "陪" *is the primary person of doing an action, while the doer (subject) of* "陪" *is the person who goes with the primary person.*

(5) 今晚我一个人在家，你能来陪陪我吗？
(6) 你要看电影，我陪你去吧。

3. "陪"必须有对象，所以大都有表示动作主体的名词、代词做"陪"的宾语，但有时可直接带动词或事物名词做宾语，这时省略了"陪"的对象。There must be an object for "陪," mostly a noun or pronoun doing the action and serving as the object of "陪." But sometimes the object of "陪" is omitted and "陪" is directly followed by a verb or a noun.

(7) 她每晚都在健身房陪练。
(8) 他的工作就是陪吃、陪喝、陪玩。

péitóng 陪同 →P349"陪"

用法 Usage:

动词 v.

陪伴着一同进行某种活动。做谓语，"陪同"的对象一般做宾语，后面可带动词表示从事某种活动，构成"陪同某人做某事"的句式。To accompany somebody in doing something. When used as a predicate, the object of "陪同" usually serves as the grammatical object in the sentence and can be followed by a verb indicating doing a certain activity. Thus, we have the structure "陪同某人做某事."

(1) 王经理陪同客人参观了公司和工厂。
(2) 校长陪同我们一起度过了中国的春节。

名词 n.

陪伴活动的人。A guide; an escort.

(3) 旅行社的全程陪同是一位可爱的姑娘。
(4) 请帮我们找一位当地的陪同。

说明 Notes:

"陪"与"陪同"都表示陪伴在一起。Both "陪" and "陪同" indicate accompanying.

它们的区别是：Their differences are as follows:

1. "陪"多用于一般场合，常用于口语。"陪同"多用于领导、外宾、贵宾等参观、出访、接见、外交等正式场合，常用于书面语。"陪" is often used in common situations and more common in spoken language. "陪同" is mostly used in formal situations and more common in written language, for example, to accompany leaders, friends or distinguished guests on inspections, visits to a foreign country, and diplomatic occasions.

2. "陪"着重于随同，做伴。施事多是人，也可以是动物或事物。做谓语，常带动态助词"着"，"陪同"着重于伴随着一同进行某种活动，施事者只有人。"陪" emphasizes keeping somebody company. The doer is usually a person, but sometimes it can be an animal or a thing. It serves as a predicate, often followed by a dynamic auxiliary "着." "陪同" emphasizes accompanying somebody in doing certain activity and the doer can only be a person.

(5) 这只狗陪我过了三年了。

3. "陪"的陪同者可以用介词"由"引进，组成介词短语，做状语。"陪同"的陪同者常用"在……的陪同下"的格式引入。The accompanying person of "陪" can be introduced by the preposition "由" to form a prepositional phrase, which serves as an adverbial, while the accompanying person of "陪同" is often introduced by the structure "在...的陪同下."

(6) 王教授由校长陪着参观了我们校园。
(7) 在校长的陪同下，王教授参观了我们校园。

4. "陪"后面可直接带宾语。"陪同"后面一般不直接带宾语。"陪" can be followed directly by an object, yet generally "陪同" cannot be followed directly by an object.

(8) *这几天我陪同妈妈去了上海。
(9) 这几天我陪妈妈去了上海。

péiyǎng 培养 →P351"培育"

用法 Usage:

动词 v.

1. 以适宜的条件使生物繁殖。To provide

favorable conditions for the multiplication of animals or plants.

（1）经过努力，科技人员终于培养出了水稻的新品种。

（2）他们在实验室里培养细菌。

2. 按一定的目标进行长期的管理教育或训练，使其产生或成长、发展。*To train people through long-term management, education and training so that they will flourish.*

（3）这个大学培养了很多科学家。

（4）父母应该从小就培养孩子的责任心。

péiyù 培育 →P351"培养"

用法 Usage:

动词 v.

1. 培养幼小的生物，使其发育成长。*To cultivate young living things.*

（1）他们又培育出了草莓的新品种。

（2）三年来，他培育了山上所有的树苗。

2. 培养教育（人）。*To nurture and educate (people).*

（3）努力培育青少年是全社会的责任。

（4）父母亲是培育孩子最重要的老师。

说明 Notes:

"培养"跟"培育"的区别是："培养" differs from "培育" in the following aspects:

1."培养"词义使用范围广，可用于生物，对象如"花草、树苗、水稻新品种、幼畜、细菌"等；用于人，着重于有目的地教育、训练，使具有某种素质、情感、习惯、兴趣等，或使增长才智和知识、掌握技能等。"培育"的词义着重于让生物或人从幼小稚嫩的状态下发育成长，词义范围比较狭窄。"培养" *covers a wider range of usage. When "培养" refers to the cultivation of living creatures, it emphasizes the multiplication of "花草，树苗，水稻新品种，幼畜，细菌，etc.," under favorable conditions. When referring to people, it emphasizes the development of qualities, emotions, habits and interests through education and practice, or the cultivation of intelligence, knowledge and skills. However, "培育" emphasizes the physical development of living creatures. The range of usage is narrower.*

2."培育"的宾语局限于"孩子、学生、青少年、一代新人"等表示幼小稚嫩状态的人的名词，数量比较少。不能带"技术人员、科学人才、优秀教师"等等非幼小稚嫩状态的人的名词。"培养"则没有这种限制，可以"培养孩子"，也可以"培养技术人员、干部、科学人才"等。*The grammatical objects of "培育" are limited to a few nouns referring to young people such as "孩子，学生，青少年，一代新人." It cannot be followed by nouns referring to people who are not young, such as "技术人员，科学人才，优秀教师." There are no such limitations on "培养," so it is correct to say "培养孩子," and "培养" can also be followed by words like "技术人员，干部，科学人才."*

3. 有时两个动词可以互换，但是语义有所区别。*The two verbs are sometimes interchangeable, but their meanings are different.*

（5）老师和父母培养我长大成人。

（6）老师和父母培育我长大成人。

例（5）着重于知识、才能、品德等方面的培植。例（6）着重于身体的养育。*Example (5) emphasizes the development of knowledge, attitude, quality and so on. Example (6) emphasizes the physical development.*

4."培育"的对象一般是具体的生物或人。"培养"的对象可以是具体的生物或人，也可以是抽象的事物，如："培养接班人、培养下一代、培养高科技人才、培养优秀演员；培养好习惯、培养感情、培养毅力、培养动手能力"；等等。*Generally speaking, objects of "培育" are concrete living creatures or people; objects of "培养" can not only be concrete creatures or people but also abstract things such as, "培养接班人，培养下一代，培养高科技人才，培养优秀演员；培养好习惯，培养感情，培养毅力，培养动手能力."*

péi 赔 →P352"赔偿"

用法 Usage:

动词 v.

1. 赔偿。To compensate.

（1）损坏了东西就要赔。

（2）你说我要赔你多少钱？

2. 向受损害、受伤害的人道歉或认错。To apologize or say sorry to somebody who has been hurt.

（3）你碰痛了她，向她赔礼道歉吧！

3. 做买卖损失了本钱（与"赚"相对）。To lose money in business. It is opposite to "赚 (to make a profit)."

（4）去年我买卖西瓜赔钱了。

（5）今天你的生意是赔了还是赚了？

péicháng 赔偿 →P352"赔"

用法 Usage:

动词 v.

因给对方造成损失而给予补偿。To make compensation for somebody's losses.

（1）这次车祸，他要给对方赔偿五千元。

（2）手机是他丢掉的，为什么要我赔偿？

名词 n.

赔偿的钱或财物。Compensation (in the form of money or otherwise).

（3）这是他们给你的赔偿，请你收下。

（4）你觉得他给你的赔偿太少了吗？

说明 Notes:

"赔偿"和"赔"都有使他人或集体受到损失而给以补偿的意思。Both "赔偿" and "赔" can mean making compensation for the losses of an individual or of a group.

它们的区别是：They differ as follows:

1. 做动词时，"赔偿"只有一个意思，"赔"还有道歉和亏本的意思。When used as a verb, "赔偿" has only one meaning, i.e., to compensate, yet "赔" can also mean apologizing and losing money in businesses.

2. "赔偿"有名词用法，"赔"没有名词用法。"赔偿" can be used as a noun while "赔" cannot.

pīpàn 批判 →P352"批评"

用法 Usage:

动词 v.

1. 对错误的思想、言论或行为做系统的分析，并且予以坚决的否定。在句中可做谓语、状语等。To systematically analyze an erroneous idea, speech or behavior, and furthermore, reject them firmly. It can be used as a predicate, an adverbial and so on.

（1）错误的思想应该批判。

（2）我们要批判地吸收他人的观点和经验。

2. 批评。比较少用。To criticize. This meaning is seldom used.

（3）做错了事，他常常自己批判自己。

（4）你们在批判他什么事情？

pīpíng 批评 →P352"批判"

用法 Usage:

动词 v.

1. 指出优点和缺点，评论好坏。To point out merits and demerits; to comment on advantages and disadvantages.

（1）学术批评是学者的治学之道，是促进学术进步的重要手段。

（2）他是搞文艺批评的。

2. 专指对错误和缺点提出意见。可带批评的对象或批评的内容作宾语。To give advice on faults or shortcomings. The target or content of criticism can follow "批评" as its grammatical object.

（3）必须对网络小说的滥写和抄袭现象进行批评！

（4）小张上班老是迟到，经理批评了他。

（5）妈妈批评我对人不礼貌的行为。

说明 Notes:

"批判"和"批评"都指出错误并作评判。它们的区别是：Both "批判" and "批评" point out and criticize faults. They differ in the following aspects:

1. 从对象来说，"批判"针对的是思想、言论或行为。"批评"的对象是人或某种不好的思想行为。About objects, "批判" aims at ideas, speeches or behaviors; "批评" aims at people or certain thoughts and behaviors which are considered not good or proper.

2. 从语体色彩上看，"批判"常用于书面语。"批评"常用于口语。About stylistic features, "批判" is often used in written language while "批评" is used more colloquially.

3. 从语义轻重上看，"批判"比"批评"重得多。Semantically, "批判" is more severe than "批评."

4. 从两个动词的内涵来看，"批判"必须是对某种思想行为进行系统的深刻的分析以后，加以否定。"批评"则指出缺点，指出做得不够的地方，可以随时随地自由地进行。About the connotation of the two verbs, "批判" means analyzing a thought and behavior systematically in depth before disapproving it, while "批评" can happen anytime and anyplace when an error or underperformance occurs.

5. 从充当句子成分上看，"批判"与"批评"都可以做谓语。"批判"还可以做状语，因为"批判"含有"分清正确和错误或有用和无用（而分别对待）"的意义。"批评"不能。While both "批判" and "批评" can be used as the predicate, "批判" can also be used as an adverbial to indicate discrimination between right and wrong, or between usefulness and uselessness, but "批评" does not have this usage.

（5）*我们要批评地继承文学艺术遗产。

（6）我们要批判地继承文学艺术遗产。

pīzhǔn 批准 →P472"同意"

用法 Usage:

动词 v.

上级对下级的意见、建议或请求表示同意。多做谓语，可带宾语（表示"批准"的内容），也可带状语、补语；可做宾语。(Of people in a higher position) to approve an idea, a suggestion or a request that is submitted by people in a lower position. It is often used as a predicate with an object (the contents of "批准"), an adverbial or a complement. It can also be used as an object.

（1）学院领导批准了我们去西安实习的计划。

（2）经理还没有批准我的请假申请。

说明 Notes:

1. "批准"可以带小句作宾语。"批准" can be followed by a clause as its object.

（3）学校已经批准李教授出国讲学。

2. "批准"有时可以用作名词。"批准" can be used as a noun sometimes.

（4）没有老师的批准，我还不能去买回国的机票。

píqi 脾气 →P525"性格"

用法 Usage:

名词 n.

1. 性情，性格。Disposition; character.

（1）他爸爸的脾气很好，很耐心。

（2）你了解他的脾气吗？

2. 指易怒的性情，急躁的情绪。Bad temper; short temper.

（3）他常常对孩子发脾气。

（4）没说几句话，他就发脾气了。

说明 Notes:

在口语中常有这种句子："昨天跟他打球，我输得一点儿脾气都没有。"常出现在否定句中，"一点儿脾气都没有"指毫无办法和输得口服心服。In oral language, you can say, "昨天跟他打球,我输得一点儿脾气都没有." Often used in negative sentences, "一点儿脾气都没有" indicates "have no choice but" or "admit defeat from the bottom of one's heart."

piān 偏 →P354"偏偏"

用法 Usage:

副词 ad.

1. 表示故意跟要求或客观情况相反,常与"要、不"合用,用在动词(动词短语)前,语气比"倒、反、却"更加坚决。Being the very opposite of external demands or objective conditions, it often goes with "要, 不." When it is used before a verb or verbal phrase, it shows a more determined tone than "倒,反,却."

(1) 你不让我吃,我偏吃。
(2) 孩子偏要买玩具,父母怎么办?

2. 表示跟主观愿望相反,体现出主语的不满意,用在动词(动词短语)前。Being the opposite of subjective wishes; showing dissatisfaction of the subject. It is used before a verb or verbal phrase.

(3) 我没带雨伞,天偏下起雨来,真倒霉!
(4) 我今天很忙,孩子偏在今天发烧。

3. 表示限定范围,有"只、只有、仅仅、单单、就"等的意思。Setting a limit to a scope, meaning "只,只有,仅仅,单单,就."

(5) 有那么多饮料可以喝,为什么你偏要喝水?
(6) 别人都同意,为什么偏你不同意?

形容词 a.

1. 表示不正,倾斜(跟"正"相对)。Inclined (opposite to "正").

(7) 那张画挂偏了。
(8) 太阳偏西了,我们下山吧。

2. 仅注意一方面或对人对事不公正。Partial; prejudiced.

(9) 偏听偏信会对人不公平的。
(10) 在家里,父母会偏爱你弟弟妹妹吗?

说明 Notes:

1. 副词"偏"常常运用于由两个分句组成的句子。一个分句表示客观、外界的情况或要求,"偏"用在另一个表示主观意愿故意与之相反的分句的动词前面,如例(1)(2)。The adverb "偏" is often used in sentences with two clauses. One clause indicates objective and external conditions or demands, while the other clause with "偏" preceding the verb shows that subjective wishes are deliberately contrary to objective and external conditions or demands, as seen in (1) and (2).

2. "偏"做形容词,一般修饰单音节词,中间不加"的",如"偏心、偏甜、偏听、偏西"等。"偏," as an adjective, often modifies monosyllabic words without "的" in between, such as "偏心,偏甜,偏听,偏西."

3. "偏"的否定形式有两种,"偏不"或"偏没"。There are two negative forms for "偏", namely, "偏不" or "偏没."

(11) 我很喜欢她穿红裙子,可是她偏没穿。(强调客观事实结果 Emphasizing objective results)
(12) 我很喜欢她穿红裙子,可是她偏不穿。(强调主观意愿 Emphasizing subjective wishes)

piānpiān 偏偏 →P354"偏"

用法 Usage:

副词 ad.

1. 表示主观上故意与客观要求或实际情况不同或相违反。Deliberately contrary to objective demands or conditions.

(1) 明明是姐姐不让我去,你偏偏说是妈妈。
(2) 大家都说没问题了,他偏偏还要提起那个老问题。

2. 表示事实恰恰跟主观愿望或常理相反。Contrary to subjective wishes or conventions.

(3) 我真不想回国,可偏偏家里出事,非要我回去不可。
(4) 家里要我快点回去,却偏偏买不到飞机票。

3. 表示限定范围,有"只、只有、仅仅、单单、就"等的意思。Setting a limit to a scope,

meaning "只,只有,仅仅,单单,就."

（5）大家都同意了,偏偏你还有意见。

（6）什么人都可以看电影,为什么偏偏我不可以？

说明 Notes:

"偏偏"和"偏"的区别是："偏偏" differs from "偏" in the following aspects:

1. "偏偏"和"偏"的用法基本相同,因为"偏偏"是叠音词,所以,在语气上比"偏"更重一些。Basically, the usage of "偏偏" is similar to that of "偏." "偏偏," as a reduplication, is stronger in tone than "偏."

（7）你不要我去,我偏要去。

（8）你不要我去,我偏偏要去。

2. 表示故意与客观要求或实际情况不同或相违反的意思时,以单用"偏"为多。表示事实恰恰跟主观愿望或常理相反的意思时,以用"偏偏"为多,如例（3）（4）。"偏" is more often used to indicate being deliberately contrary to objective demands or conditions, while "偏偏" is more often used to indicate being contrary to subjective wishes or conventions as seen in (3) and (4).

3. 用在动词前的"偏偏"也可以用"偏",但是用在主语前的"偏偏"不能换成"偏"。When used before a verb, "偏偏" can be substituted by "偏," but when used before a subject, "偏偏" cannot be replaced by "偏."

（9）原想去春游的,谁知偏偏/偏碰上天下雨。

（10）*我昨天找你去看电影,偏你不在。

（11）我昨天找你去看电影,偏偏你不在。

4. "偏"有形容词用法。"偏偏"没有形容词用法。"偏" can be used as an adjective, yet "偏偏" cannot.

pīnmìng 拼命

用法 Usage:

动词 v.

1. 不顾自己生命地去搏斗,豁出生命。做谓语。To risk one's life to fight. It is used as a predicate.

（1）为了保护公司的财产,他跟一群小偷拼命了。

（2）他们俩打在一起,拼起命来了。

2. 形容努力去完成某事。一般用在动词前作状语,表示程度。To do something with all one's might. It is used before a verb as an adverbial, indicating degree.

（3）他拼命往山上爬,很快爬到了山顶。

（4）他拼命地学习,希望考上这所大学。

说明 Notes:

"拼命"是离合词,中间可以插入其他成分。"拼命" is a separable verb, so other constituents can be inserted.

（5）他拼了命也要把这项工作完成。

（6）为了多挣些钱,大家拼着命地干活。

pínkǔ 贫苦 →P355"贫穷"

用法 Usage:

形容词 a.

贫穷,生活困苦。Poor; poverty-stricken.

（1）小时候,家里生活贫苦,所以他懂事很早。

（2）这样贫苦的家庭却培养出了三个博士生。

pínqióng 贫穷 →P355"贫苦"

用法 Usage:

形容词 a.

贫困穷苦,缺乏钱财或物资。Poor; being short of financial or material resources.

（1）这个小山村曾经很贫穷。

（2）科学技术改变了家乡贫穷的面貌。

说明 Notes:

"贫穷"与"贫苦"区别是："贫穷" differs from "贫苦" in the following aspects:

1. "贫穷"是指没有钱,经济落后,着重于生活贫困、不富裕,是从客观上进行描述。"贫苦"除了指没有钱、经济落后、条件差,还突出了"苦"的成分,表现出人的感受。"贫穷" indicates having

no money and being backward in economy, emphasizing that life is poor and badly off, which is an objective description. Apart from having no money, being backward in economy and in bad conditions, "贫苦" also emphasizes the feelings of "苦."

2. 在词语搭配上,"贫穷"可以形容"人、家庭、家境、家乡、国家、地区、乡镇"等,常与"落后"并用。"贫苦"可形容"家境、生活、出身、人家、老百姓、学生"等。两者比较,"贫穷"多形容区域名词,"贫苦"多形容个体性名词。Regarding collocation, "贫穷" can describe words like "人,家庭,家境,家乡,国家,地区,乡镇," and often used with "落后." "贫苦" can describe "家境,生活,出身,人家,老百姓,学生." "贫穷" is more used to modify nouns referring to regions, while "贫苦" is more used to modify nouns referring to individuals.

3. "贫穷"和"贫苦"同时形容"家庭、生活、家境"等,但在语义上有细微的差别,前者是客观的描述,后者兼带人的感受。如果是纯粹的客观描述,一般用"贫穷"。When they are used to describe "家庭,生活,家境," there is a tiny difference semantically. "贫穷" is an objective description, yet "贫苦" can also show people's feelings. For a purely objective description, "贫穷" is generally used.

(3) 贫穷的生活养成了他节约的好习惯。
(4) *我们要改变山村的贫苦面貌。
(5) 我们要改变山村的贫穷面貌。

pǐn 品

用法 Usage:
动词 v.
1. 仔细辨(味道),品尝,品评。如:"品茶、品酒"等。To taste something with discrimination; to sample; to appraise, For example, "品茶,品酒."
2. 琢磨意思,评论人物,体察好坏。To think hard; to comment; to savor.
(1) 这首诗的意思要好好品味。
(2) 你们不要对人评头品足,那是不礼貌的。

名词 n.
1. 物品。如:"商品、产品、精品"等。Article; commodity; product, as in "商品,产品,精品."
2. 等级。如:"上品、下品"等。Rank; class, as in "上品,下品."
3. 种类。如:"品种、品类"等。Variety, as in "品种,品类."
4. 品行,品质。Character; quality.
(3) 这是个品学兼优的学生。
(4) 看一个人,首先要看他的人品。

说明 Notes:
"品"有做后缀的用法。"品" can be used as a suffix.

1. 跟在某些动词或名词后面,构成名词。表示按质量、规格或等级分类的物品,如"精品、正品、次品、废品、成品、半成品"等。Following some verbs or nouns, it is used to form nouns indicating articles classified by quality, standard or rank, such as "精品,正品,次品,废品,成品,半成品."

2. 跟在某些动词或名词后面,构成名词。表示按原料、性能、用途、制作方法分类的物品,如"商品、产品、食品、药品、毒品、豆制品、奶制品、印刷品、宣传品"等。Following some verbs or nouns, it is used to form nouns indicating articles classified by raw material, function, purpose, manufacturing method, such as "商品,产品,食品,药品,毒品,豆制品,奶制品,印刷品,宣传品."

3. 跟在某些名词后面,构成名词。表示人的品格、风格,如"人品、画品、文品、酒品"等。Following some nouns, it is used to form nouns indicating character and style such as "人品,画品,文品,酒品."

pǐndé 品德 →P357"品质"

用法 Usage:
名词 n.
人品,德行。Moral character.

(1) 这个学生的优秀品德受到了大家的赞扬。
(2) 这位医生品德高尚。

pǐnzhì 品质 →P356"品德"

用法 Usage:

名词 n.

1. 一个人在行为作风上所表现出来的思想、认识、品性等方面的本质属性。Intrinsic characteristics of one's thoughts, knowledge and quality in behavior and style.

(1) 良好的品质应该从小就培养。
(2) 教师应该具备良好的师德品质。

2. 产品的质量。Quality of products.

(3) 产品的品质是企业的生命。
(4) 没有稳定可靠的品质,就没有企业的发展。

说明 Notes:

"品质"和"品德"的区别是:"品质" differs from "品德" in the following aspects:

1. "品德"着重指人的品质和道德。"品质"除指人的品性本质以外,还指产品的质量,而且进一步扩大范围,指一些非产品的抽象事物的质量,如"文化品质、生活品质、教育品质"等。"品德" emphasizes quality and moral character of people. As for "品质," while it describes people's moral character, it can also refer to quality of products, which include both concrete products and abstract products such as "文化品质,生活品质" and "教育品质."

(5) 江西景德镇的瓷器品质优良。
(6) 人们越来越关注自己的生活品质。

2. 在词语搭配上,"品德"常与"崇高、高尚、优良、高贵"等词语搭配。"品质"除了以上"品德"的搭配词语搭配外,还可以与"可贵、宝贵、美好、优秀、低劣"等词语搭配,还可以受"道德、政治、革命、英雄"等词语的修饰。多用于书面语。Both "品德" and "品质" can go with words like "崇高,高尚,优良,高贵." Yet, "品质" can also be used with words such as "可贵,宝贵,美好,优秀,低劣." What's more, "品质" can be modified by words like "道德,政治,革命,英雄." It is often used in written language.

(7) 他那可贵的英雄品质值得大家学习。
(8) 品质的优劣直接影响商品的使用价值。

píngcháng 平常 →P357"平凡"

用法 Usage:

名词 n.

平时的意思。时间名词,多做状语。A noun for time, meaning "平时 (in ordinary time)." It is often used as an adverbial.

(1) 他平常都是准时上班,今天怎么还没来?
(2) 平常这个超市不热闹,周末非常热闹。

形容词 a.

一般,普通,不特别。常做定语、谓语和状语。可以重叠。Ordinary, common. It is often used as an attribute, a predicate or an adverbial. It can be used in a reduplicated form as "平平常常."

(3) 我是一个很平常的人。
(4) 他平平常常吃饭,平平常常睡觉,和一般人没什么两样。

píngfán 平凡 →P357"平常"

用法 Usage:

形容词 a.

平常的,不稀奇的。Ordinary; common; undistinguished.

(1) 我们都是平凡的人,过着平凡的生活。
(2) 她是售货员,工作很平凡。

说明 Notes:

"平常"与"平凡"的区别是:"平常" differs from "平凡" in the following aspects:

1. 在词义上,"平常"侧重于"一般的、不特别"的意思,"平凡"侧重于"一般的、没有特别成就或高人一筹"的意思。Semantically, "平常" emphasizes being average or not special, while "平凡" focuses on being average, with no outstanding achievement, not considering oneself superior to others.

（3）我们都是平常人。

（4）我们都是平凡的人。

2."平凡"多修饰人和事，一般不修饰物品，搭配的词语常常是"人、生活、工作、人生、事迹、贡献"等。"平常"可以修饰物品。"平凡" often modifies people and things, but not articles. Collocations include words like "人,生活,工作,人生,事迹,贡献.""平常" can modify articles.

（5）*她的手表太平凡了。

（6）她的手表太平常了。

3."平常"的否定形式"不平常"可能是好的意思，也可能是坏的意思，具体哪种含义取决于上下文。"不平常," the negative form of "平常," can imply both good quality and undesirable quality. It depends on the context.

（7）他短短一年时间就发表了几篇重要的论文，真是一个不平常的人。

（8）他走后门，拍马屁，真是一个不平常的人。

píngjìng 平静 →P3"安静"、P339"宁静"

用法 Usage:

形容词 a.

强调人的心情和环境平稳安定，没有不安和动荡。Emphasizing calmness and peace in feelings and surroundings; without turbulence.

（1）听到儿子回家的开门声，她的心平静下来了。

（2）湖水多么平静啊！

说明 Notes:

1."平静"形容环境或人的心情、情绪没有不安或动荡，有时带有动感的描述，后面常带趋向补语"下来"或者表示程度的"多"等词语。使用"平静"做句子，前后常常有词语或者句子说明"平静"前后的情况。"平静" indicates that there is no turbulence in the surroundings and feelings, and sometimes it shows a dynamic description. It is often followed by a complement "下来," showing tendency, or "多," showing degree. When "平静" is used, there are words or sentences showing the conditions before and after "平静."

（3）太湖上的风浪平静下来了。（说明刚才水面上有风浪 Showing there were stormy waves a while ago）

（4）哭了一场以后，她平静多了。（说明哭前她的情绪很不平静 Showing she was not calm a while ago: she was crying）

2."平静"跟"安静"的区别是："平静" is different from "安静" in the following aspects:

① 描写环境时，"平静"重在没有动乱，"安静"重在没有声响。When describing surroundings, "平静" emphasizes that there is no disturbance, but "安静" indicates quietness.

（5）太湖水面上平静极了。

（6）太湖上的风浪安静下来了。（把"风浪"拟人化了。"风浪" is personified.）

（7）*哭了一场以后，她安静多了。（用"安静"不妥，因为句子意思主要指人的内心情绪。It is inappropriate to use "安静" because the meaning of the sentence emphasizes a person's inner feelings.）

② 描写人物时，多用"平静"。"平静" is often used to describe people.

（8）哭了一场以后，她平静多了。

3."宁静"和"平静"的区别是：The difference between "宁静" and "平静" lies in:

"宁静"多指心境、环境的安宁。在程度上比"平静"要深，在感觉上先有动态的"平静"，然后达到相对静态的"宁静"。因此，"宁静"后面不适合带趋向补语"下来"，也不能用在祈使句中。"宁静" often refers to a peaceful psychological state or a tranquil environment. It is deeper than "平静," because "平静" is a dynamic state that is felt at first, and then the relatively static "宁静" arrives. Therefore, "宁

静" is usually not followed by directional complement "下来," and should not be used in imperative sentences.

（9）*她的心宁静下来了。
（10）她的心平静下来了。
（11）*上课了,请大家宁静!
（12）上课了,请大家安静!

pínggū 评估 →P359"评价"

用法 Usage:
动词 v.
根据标准评议,估计,评价。*To appraise; to evaluate; to assess according to standards.*
（1）这套房子的价值应该请人评估一下。
（2）教育机构每年要评估学校的教学研究水平。
名词 n.
评估的结果、情况。*Result of assessment.*
（3）我们学校的评估结果怎么样?
（4）企业的资产评估报告已经收到了。

píngjià 评价 →P359"评估"

用法 Usage:
动词 v.
评定人或事物的价值高低。*To judge and assess the value of people or things.*
（1）评价历史人物不能离开当时的历史年代。
（2）大家对你评价很不错。
名词 n.
通过评定得出的有关事物价值的结论。*Judgment and assessment of the value of people or things.*
（3）老师对我们班同学的评价很高。
（4）观众给这部电影艺术很高的评价。
说明 Notes:
"评估"和"评价"都是对事物的评判。*Both "评估" and "评价" refer to judgment of things.*
它们的区别是：*They are different in the following aspects:*

1."评估"的"估",有估计的意思,对事物的评判确定性比较弱。"评价"的"价",突出是对事物价值的评判。词语的词义侧重点不同。*"估" in "评估" means estimation, which is weak in judgment; "价" in "评价" highlights judgment of the value of things. Their semantic emphasis is different.*

2."评估"的对象一般与具体的钱财、物质、技术含量等水平有关,如"评估资产、评估管理水平、教学评估、风险评估"等。"评价"的对象范围比较广泛,除了评判以上物质方面的价值以外,还包括对事物社会价值、意识形态价值的评判,如"人物评价、艺术评价、电影评价"等。*Objects of "评估" are often relevant to the level of concrete property, substance, technology, such as "评估资产,评估管理水平, 评估教学水平,风险评估." Objects of "评价" cover a wider range, which includes not only judgment of value of mentioned materials but also judgment of social and ideological values such as "人物评价,艺术评价,电影评价."*

píng 凭

用法 Usage:
动词 v.
1.身体靠着。必定带宾语,宾语常为单音节名词,用于书面语。*To lean on/against. It must be followed by an object, which is often a monosyllabic noun used in written language.*
（1）他凭窗远望,望着远处的山峰。
（2）她最喜欢在湖边凭栏而坐。
2.依靠,倚仗。必定带宾语。*To rely on; to depend on. It must be followed by an object.*
（3）公司能有今天,全凭着大家的努力。
（4）他是个打工者,全凭自己两只手赚钱。
介词 prep.
凭借,依靠,依据。有"依仗、依据、根据、借着、靠着"等意思。*By virtue of, indicating "依仗,依据,根据,借着,靠着."*

1. 一般跟名词或名词性短语组合，构成介词短语做状语，可在主语前，有停顿。与"凭"搭配的对象是行为、动作所依据的事物、条件、理由等。*It is generally followed by a noun or a nominal phrase to form a preposition-object structure, serving as an adverbial, which can be put before the subject with a pause in between. Objects going with "凭" are things, conditions, reasons on which actions depend.*

（5）单凭一点事实，不能得出这个结论。
（6）光凭热情是做不好工作的。

2. 有时后面也可以跟动词或动词性词组。*It is sometimes followed by a verb or a verbal phrase.*

（7）他凭打工过日子。
（8）就凭你做家教能挣多少钱？

连词 conj.

表示无论在什么条件下都是如此。有"无论、不管、任凭、不论"的意思。在"凭"后面常带人称代词和表示任指的词语。口语色彩较浓。*No matter how, what, where, when, etc., meaning "无论, 不管, 任凭, 不论." A typical colloquial expression, it is often followed by a personal pronoun or a demonstrative pronoun.*

（9）凭你怎么说，他也不吃饭。
（10）凭你打多少电话，她都不接。

说明 Notes：

1. 介词"凭"后面的名词性短语比较长时，可带助词"着"，但后面就不能跟单音节词语。*When the nominal structure after the preposition "凭" is long, "凭" can be followed by the auxiliary "着" and there will be no monosyllabic words.*

（11）凭着儿时的记忆，我找到了那间老屋。
（12）凭着以前学的技术干活，现在不行了。

2. "凭什么"和"凭啥"是固定格式，表示质问。*"凭什么" and "凭啥" are set expressions indicating a question.*

（13）你凭什么不让我去？
（14）他们凭啥要检查我的行李？

pòqiè 迫切

用法 Usage：

形容词 a.

（对某种）需要，到了难以等待的程度，十分急切。*(Of a certain need) pressing; very urgent.*

（1）那个公司迫切需要开发对外贸易。
（2）他去中国留学的心情越来越迫切。

说明 Notes：

1. "迫切"是指某一事情（包括心情、要求、愿望、问题、任务等）急需解决，已经到了不能等待的程度。在语义上，既可以指人的愿望、要求、期待等，也可指事情本身的解决。"迫切"既可修饰人的要求、愿望等心理反应，又可描述事情本身。*"迫切" refers to something, such as mood, request, desire, problem, or task that needs to be dealt with immediately. Semantically, "迫切" can describe psychological reactions such as desire, request, hope and the solution of a problem itself.*

（3）买房已经成为他最迫切的要求。
（4）你迫切的心情我理解。

2. 主体"人"不能单独做主语，成为"迫切"描述的对象。*"人" alone cannot serve as the subject of "迫切."*

（5）＊他很迫切，因为他没钱了。
（6）他最近打工的愿望很迫切，因为他没有钱了。

3. "迫切"的意思是急需去解决的某一事物，所以，没有这个语义的词语如"说、话语"等，均不能成为"迫切"修饰、说明的对象。*"迫切" refers to an urgent thing, so words without such a meaning as "说，话语" cannot be modified by "迫切."*

（7）＊他说得很迫切。
（8）他说得很急。

pǔbiàn 普遍 →P361"普通"

用法 Usage：

形容词 a.

普及的，遍及各方面的，存在的面很广泛的，具有共同性的(与"个别、特殊"相对)。*Universal; widespread; in general existence; common; not special. It is opposite to "个别" and "特殊."*

(1) 乒乓球运动在中国十分普遍。
(2) 这个地区的老人普遍长寿。

pǔtōng 普通 →P360"普遍"

用法 Usage:
形容词 *a.*

平常的,一般的。可以重叠使用。*Ordinary; average. It can be used in a reduplicated form as "普普通通."*

(1) 这个办法很普通,大家都想得到。
(2) 他是一个普普通通的人。

说明 Notes:

"普遍"和"普通"都包含广泛存在的意思。*Both "普遍" and "普通" can mean being in general existence.*

它们的区别是：*They are different in the following aspects:*

1. 在词义上"普遍"侧重指存在的面很广、范围大。"普通"侧重指事物"性质一般"。*Semantically, "普遍" emphasizes the ubiquity of something while "普通" emphasizes the normal or common character of something.*

(3) 这是很普遍的现象。(范围很广 *Covering a large scope*)
(4) 这是很普通的现象。(情况一般,不突出 *Normal, ordinary*)

2. 在修饰对象上,"普遍"修饰的对象主要是抽象名词,不是具体的人或事物,如"普遍真理、普遍现象、普遍情况、普遍的认识、普遍反映"等。"普通"修饰的对象可以是人或事物,如"普通话、普通人、普通邮票、普通朋友、普通的东西、普通的现象、普通的打扮"等。*Objects modified by "普遍" are mostly abstract nouns, as in, "普遍真理,普遍现象,普遍情况,普遍的认识,普遍反映." Objects modified by "普通" can be either people or things, as in "普通话,普通人,普通邮票,普通朋友,普通的东西,普通的现象,普通的打扮."*

3. "普遍"可以在动词前面做状语。"普通"只修饰名词性词语,能做谓语或补语。*"普遍" can be used before a verb as an adverbial; "普通" can only modify nominal words, and be used as a predicate or a complement.*

(5) *顾客普通反映这种空调省电。
(6) 顾客普遍反映这种空调省电。

4. "普通"可以重叠为"普普通通";"普遍"不能重叠。*"普通" can be reduplicated as "普普通通," while "普遍" does not have this usage.*

(7) 这是一只普普通通的手机。

qīdài 期待 →P362"期望"

用法 Usage:

动词 *v.*

期望，等待。To expect; to hope and wait for.

(1) 父母都期待出国的孩子能早点回来。
(2) 大家都在期待着春节的到来。

qījiān 期间 →P418"时期"

用法 Usage:

名词 *n.*

在某一段时间内。常和其他词语构成偏正短语或介词短语，在句中做状语。Within a certain time frame. Often used with other words to form modifier + modified phrases or prepositional phrases, or as an adverbial adjunct in a sentence.

(1) 我在中国留学期间认识了小李。
(2) 五一长假期间，图书馆照常开放。

说明 Notes:

1. "期间"表示具体的某一段时间。修饰"期间"的词语有的是明确的时间名词，有的不是明确的时间名词，但它指代的事情是在某一段时间内发生的，如"在上海工作期间、上大学期间"等。"期间" expresses a specific time frame, and the words modifying "期间" can be nouns describing either definite or indefinite time periods, but the events referred to always occur within a specified time frame, for example, "在上海工作期间，上大学期间."

2. "期间"所代表的时间可长可短，但是一般不指操作性很强的具体动作的完成时间。如：我们一般不说"吃饭期间、上课期间、睡觉期间"等，而说成"吃饭的时候、上课的时候、睡觉的时候"，或"吃饭时、上课时、睡觉时"等。"期间" can describe either long or short time frames, but is usually not used to refer to the completion time of verbs with a strong operative nature. For example, "吃饭期间，上课期间，睡觉期间" are generally not said, but rather are phrased as "吃饭的时候，上课的时候，睡觉的时候，" or "吃饭时，上课时，睡觉时."

qīwàng 期望 →P362"期待"

用法 Usage:

动词 *v.*

表示对人或事情未来的前途有所希望和等待。做谓语。To have something to hope for about the future of a person or a thing. It can serve as a predicate.

(1) 村民期望着这个山村能早点通高铁。

名词 *n.*

表示对人和事所抱的期待和希望。Expectation and hope on a person or thing.

(2) 我们应该努力学习，不辜负老师的期望。

说明 Notes:

"期望"和"期待"都表示对人或事物将来的希望。"期望" and "期待" both express some

hope for the future of a person or thing.

它们的区别是：The differences between them are as follows:

1. "期望"的对象一般是尚未发生的将来，比较抽象、未知。"期待"的对象也可以是抽象的，但一般比较具体，只是时间上的等待。The target of "期望" is typically a future event that has not yet occurred: it is rather abstract or unknown. By contrast, the target of "期待" can also be abstract but it is typically concrete and time-based.

（3）我期待着你早日学成归来。
（4）我期望着你有个美好的未来。

2. "期望"可以做宾语，如例（2）。"期待"一般不做宾语。"期望" can be used as the object of a sentence, as in (2). "期待" typically cannot serve as an object.

qí 齐

用法 Usage:
形容词 a.

1. 整齐。Neat; tidy.
（1）我们班的健美操做得最齐。
（2）书架上的书放得很齐。

2. 一致,同样。Unanimous; equal.
（3）心齐,力量大。
（4）我们全班同学齐心协力,运动会一定能得集体第一名。

3. 全,完备。多做补语。Whole; complete. It is often used as a complement.
（5）旅行用的物品都已经准备齐了。
（6）今天去爬山的同学都来齐了没有？

动词 v.
表示达到相同的高度。To reach a similar degree or height.
（7）头发很长,都齐肩了。
（8）这湖水最深也只是齐腰,没有危险。

副词 ad.
一起,共同。Together; jointly.
（9）全家人齐动手,一会儿就打扫完了房间。

（10）春天一到,百花齐放,我的家乡可美了。

qí 其

用法 Usage:
代词 pron.

1. 人称代词,相当于"他/她/它＋的、他们/她们/它们＋的"。多做定语。Personal pronoun, equivalent to "他/她/它＋的,他们/她们/它们＋的," often used as an attribute.
（1）听其言、观其行,才能真正了解一个人。
（2）他说话自相矛盾,很难自圆其说。

2. 人称代词,相当于"他/她/它、他们/她们/它们"。多做宾语。Personal pronoun, equivalent to "他/她/它,他们/她们/它们." It is often used as an object.
（3）大家都祝其早生贵子。
（4）我们对孩子的兴趣爱好是顺其自然的。

3. 指示代词,相当于"那个、那样、这个、这样"。Demonstrative pronoun, equivalent to "那个,那样。"
（5）经过两个多月的调查,最后的结论是查无其事。
（6）退休老人越来越多,发展老人健康产业正当其时。

4. 虚指。Indefinite denotation.
（7）人在玩儿的时候,不要忘其所以,否则会乐极生悲的。

说明 Notes:

1. "其"有较浓的书面色彩,常出现在固定词组中,如"各得其所、自圆其说、若无其事、忘其所以"等。"其" has a strong literary characteristic, and is often seen in fixed phrases such as "各得其所,自圆其说,若无其事,忘其所以。"

2. 与"他"不同的是,"其"相当于"他/她/它、他们/她们/它们"或"他/她/它＋的、他们/她们/它们＋的"时,可以任指人、物、事,而现代汉语中的"他"只指人。*Different from "他", when "其" is used as "他/她/它, 他们/她们/它们" or as "他/她/它＋的, 他们/她们/它们＋的," it can be used to refer to people, things, or events, while in modern Chinese "他" can only be used to refer to a person.*

qícì 其次

用法 Usage:

代词 *pron.*

1. 指次序较后的,次要的。可在句中做谓语或定语,修饰名词要带"的"。前面常有"第一、首先、先"等词与其呼应,具有排列次序的作用。*Next; secondly; then. Indicating something towards the end of a sequence, it can be used as a predicate or an attributive, and takes "的" when modifying a noun. It is often preceded by words such as "第一,首先,先," and is used for listing objects in an orderly way.*

(1) 明天的节目首先是小明唱歌,其次就是你表演舞蹈。

(2) 在中国,房价最高的城市是北京,其次是上海。

2. 表示次要的地位。*Indicating a secondary position or status.*

(3) 对学生来说,最重要的事情是学习,其次才是休闲娱乐。

(4) 找男朋友,人品是主要的,收入其次。

说明 Notes:

1. "其次"用在列举事项时,在序列上与"第二"比较相近。*When "其次" is used to refer to objects in order, it is similar to "第二".*

2. "其次"不能在一个句子中单独使用,前面一定要有个句子,且句子中有"首先、最重要"等词语相呼应。"其次"一般用在第二个分句的开头。*"其次" cannot be used alone in a sentence; it must be preceded by a full sentence including a phrase such as "首要" or "最重要"; "其次" is typically used at the beginning of the second clause.*

3. "其次"前面可以受"再"的修饰。如"再其次"。*"其次" can be preceded by the modifier "再", as in "再其次."*

qíshí 其实

用法 Usage:

副词 *ad.*

表示所说的是实际情况。*Actually; in fact; as a matter of fact. It is used to indicate that what is to be said is the actual situation.*

1. "其实"承接上文,引出和上文相反意思的下文,有更正上文的作用,表示下文所说的才是事实真相,含有转折意味。*Continued from a preceding paragraph or sentence or clause, "其实" is used to mark a transition to a contrary idea in the following statement. It can be used to make corrections to the preceding statement or to indicate that the following statement is the actual truth. It implies a transition or turnaround.*

(1) 这件事说起来很简单,其实做起来不容易。

(2) 我以为他三十几岁,其实他已经五十多岁了。

2. 用"其实"对上文所描述的情况进行补充或修正。不含转折意味,相当于"实际上、其实质"的意思。*"其实" is used to indicate a supplement or revision to the fact or event described in the preceding statement. It does not indicate a transition, but rather is similar to "实际上,其实质."*

(3) 我们只知道他会说汉语,其实他还会说日语。

(4) 他说自己会英语,其实只会说一些日常用语。

说明 Notes:

1. "其实"使用时,前后要有两个以上的分句,"其实"一般用在后一分句的句首,在主语或动词前。如果用在主语前,常用逗号或语气词"呢"与主语隔开。In actual use, "其实" must be both preceded by and followed by a clause. "其实" typically appears at the beginning of the second clause preceding the subject or verb. If preceding the subject, it is often followed by a comma or is followed by the modal particle "呢."

（5）父母都觉得他不喜欢讲话,其实呢,在朋友面前他挺爱说话。

2. "其实"不但可以用于句首,也可以用于段落的开头,表示对前一段话的补充或修正。"其实" can be used not only at the beginning of a sentence, but also at the beginning of a paragraph to indicate a supplement or revision to the previous paragraph.

qítā 其他 →P365"其余"

用法 Usage:

代词 pron.

指示代词,表示别的人（或事物）。A demonstrative pronoun that indicates some other person(s) or thing(s).

（1）今天的晚餐,除了东坡肉,其他还有红烧鱼、蔬菜等。

（2）你只要做好自己的事情,其他（的事情）就不用管了。

qíyú 其余 →P365"其他"

用法 Usage:

代词 pron.

指示代词,表示剩下的人（或事物）。A demonstrative pronoun that indicates the remaining person(s) or thing(s).

（1）除了玛丽,其余的同学都已经到了。

（2）这四本书留下,其余的都送给你。

说明 Notes:

"其余"和"其他"都是指示代词,都指示除此以外留下来的人或事物。"其余" and "其他" are both demonstrative pronouns indicating the remaining or unmentioned person(s) or thing(s).

它们的区别是：The differences between them are as follows:

1. "其余"多用作确指,如例（1）（2）。"其他"多用做范围不太明确的泛指。"其余" is often used to refer to something specific, as seen in (1) and (2) under "其余.""其他" is often used to make a general reference to things not explicitly defined.

（3）你来了就好,其他人不来没关系。

2. "其余"修饰名词时一定要加上"的",如"其余的任务,其余的钱"等。"其他"可以直接修饰名词,不一定加上"的",如"其他人、其他收入、其他任务"等。When "其余" is used to modify a noun, it must be accompanied by "的," as in "其余的任务,其余的钱," while "其他" can directly modify a noun without the addition of "的," as in "其他人,其他收入,其他任务."

qízhōng 其中

用法 Usage:

名词 n.

方位名词,表示那里面（指处所、范围）。A directional noun indicating the inside of something (location, limits, range, etc.).

（1）高级汉语班共十五个学生,其中八个学生是韩国人。

（2）我一星期上五天课,其中两天在经济系上课。

说明 Notes:

1. "其中"做定语时,一般要有两个句子,前面分句表示全部范围,后面句子由"其中"引出这个范围中的部分人、部分事物、部分时间或空间是怎么样的。When "其中" is used as the attributive in a sentence, there are typically two clauses: the preceding clause describes the complete scope or limits of something, while the following clause with "其中" in it points out

and describes a portion of people, things, times, places, etc. within the previously expressed limits.

2. "其中"必定用在后面分句句首。"其中" must be used at the beginning of the second clause.

qíguài 奇怪 →P170"怪"

用法 Usage:
形容词 a.

1. 跟平常不一样。Strange; not the same as usual.

(1) 今天小狗很奇怪,看到我不跑过来了。
(2) 你今天干吗穿得那么奇怪?

2. 出乎意料,难以理解。Unexpected; hard to understand.

(3) 真奇怪,床上的手机忽然不见了。
(4) 我很奇怪,他们怎么到现在还不来。

说明 Notes:

"怪"和"奇怪"都有形容词用法,表示不同于寻常。Both "怪" and "奇怪" can serve as an adjective, meaning "not the same as usual."

它们的区别是:Their differences are as follows:

1. "怪"和"奇怪"在使用时都要注意音节的和谐。"奇怪"做定语时,一般要加"的"。如果"怪"前面受程度副词的修饰,后面就应加"的"。Both have to be used with close attention paid to the harmony of syllables. Usually, when "奇怪" serves as an adjective, it has to be followed by "的." If "怪" is preceded by a modifying degree adverb, it should be followed by "的," too.

(5) *这是个奇怪人。
(6) 这是个怪人。
(7) 这是个奇怪的人。
(8) *这是个很怪人。
(9) 这是个很怪的人/这是个怪人。

2. "奇怪"一般只作形容词用。"怪"除了形容词用法,还有名词、动词和副词用法。"奇怪" usually serves as an adjective. "怪," however, can also serve as a noun, verb, or adverb.

qǐ 起

用法 Usage:
动词 v.

1. 表示由坐、躺、卧而站立的动作。To move from a sitting or reclining position to a standing position.

(1) 快起,让老人坐下。
(2) 冬天老人就该早睡晚起养身体。

2. 离开原处。必带名词或动词做宾语。To leave one's original location. It must be accompanied by a noun or verb object.

(3) 他起跑慢了一点,没能拿第一。
(4) 她起身离开座位,走出了教室。

3. 发动,发生。可带"着、了、过",可带名词宾语。To start; to launch; to happen; to occur. It can take "着,了,过" and can also take a noun as its object.

(5) 这几年我们农村起了很大变化。
(6) 这种药,开始吃的时候起过作用,现在不起作用了。

4. 拟定。可带"了",可带名词宾语。To draft; to draw up; to work out. It can be accompanied by "了," and can take a noun object.

(7) 我还没出生,爷爷就给我起了名字。

5. 创,建立。To create; to build; to establish.

(8) 去年我家起了三层楼房。
(9) 万丈高楼平地起。

6. 开始。To begin.

(10) 从这儿起,就是杭州西湖世界遗产的区域。
(11) 我明天起,早上6点就起床。

7. 用在动作有延续性的动词后面,表示这个动作开始,常与"从……"连用。When used after a verb describing a continuing action, it

indicates the beginning of the action, and is often used together with "从…."

（12）这件事情要从哪儿说起呢？

（13）外国人学汉语，一般从汉语拼音学起。

8. 用在动作有方向性的动词后面，表示向上，做趋向补语。When used after a verb describing the direction of an action, it acts as a directional complement to indicate an upward direction.

（14）他背起书包就走了。

（15）请你帮我把箱子抬起一点，好吗？

9. 用在动词后面，与"得/不"连用，构成可能补语，表示某种可能性。When used after a verb and used with "得/不", it can form a potential complement to describe some possibility.

（16）这个房价还可以，我买得起。

（17）这个学校学费太贵，我付不起。

10. 表示动作关涉到某事。动词限于"说、谈、讲、问、提、想、回忆"等少数有言语意义的及物动词。Indicating that the action denoted by a verb is related to a certain event; the verbs used in this way are limited to a small number of transitive verbs with meanings related to speech, such as "说,谈,讲,问,提,想,回忆."

（18）我常常想起我教过的那些外国学生。

（19）小王在电话里提起你，还问起你的病好了没有。

qǐdào 起到

用法 Usage:

这个词语由动词"起"（表示发生、产生的意思）带补语"到"组成，表示动作有结果。This expression is composed of the verb "起" (meaning " to happen, occur, produce, emerge," etc.) and the complement "到," which indicates that the action has a result.

（1）这种中草药起到了预防感冒的作用。

（2）多表扬孩子，能起到很好的教育作用。

说明 Notes:

1. "起到"是"到"在动词"起"后面做补语，组成动补性词语。"起到"中间可加"得、不"，组成词语"起得到、起不到"，在句子中表示一种可能性，如例（3）。"起到" is formed by the verb "起" followed by "到" as its complement. "起到" can be combined with "得" or "不" to make a phrase "起得到" or "起不到," and is used to express a type of possibility as in (3).

（3）孩子做错了事，你不讲道理，总是骂他，起得到作用吗？

（4）这些措施恐怕起不到什么作用。

2. "起到"需要在后面带上宾语，才能成句。一般与"作用、效果、影响"等词语搭配使用。"起到" must be followed by an object in order to form a sentence. It is often used with words such as "作用,效果,影响."

qǐlái 起来

用法 Usage:

1. 动词"起"＋简单趋向补语"来"，做谓语。The verb "起"＋ the simple directional complement "来" forms a predicate.

① 由坐卧而站立，或由躺着而坐起来，在句中做谓语，可带"了、过"。To stand up from a sitting or lying-down position, or to sit up from a lying-down position. When used as a predicate, it can take "了,过."

（1）有好几个年轻人起来给老人让座。

（2）一个上午他都在电脑前坐着，没见他起来过。

② 由静止状态而积极行动，泛指兴起、奋起、升起等。可以带"了"。To go from a static condition to an active condition, indicating excitement, exertion, etc. It can take "了."

（3）看到一桌子的玩具，孩子们的兴趣都起来了。

（4）他拉了几下绳子，风筝就起来了。

2. "起来"用在动词后面做趋向动词。When following a verb, "起来" can be used as

a directional verb.

① 表示人或事物随动作由下而上，形式为：动词＋起来。否定形式为："没＋动词＋起来"（表示过去的），或"动词＋不＋起来"（意思是不能动起来）。Indicating that a person or object is moving from a lower to higher position in accordance with a specified verb. It is used in the pattern "v.＋起来," or in the negated form "没＋v.＋起来" (to indicate something that has not happened), or "v.＋不＋起来" meaning that something cannot move upward.

（5）太阳升起来了。
（6）桌子太重了，他们没抬起来。
（7）桌子太重了，他们抬不起来。

② 表示动作完成，有聚拢或达到一定的目的、结果的意思。Indicating that the action of a verb has been completed and a goal or result has been achieved.

（8）他把礼物藏了起来，准备生日那天再给孩子。
（9）他的名字我终于想起来了。

③ 表示动作或状态开始并有继续下去的意思。动作和"起来"之间一般不能加"得、不"。形式为："动词＋起来""形容词＋起来"。Indicating that an action or state of affairs has begun and will continue. "起来" and the related action typically cannot be separated by "得" or "不." The pattern is: "v.＋起来," "a.＋起来."

（10）他的脸红了起来。
（11）听说明天去苏州旅游，大家都欢呼起来。

④ "动词＋起来"在句中做插入语，有估计或着眼于某一方面的意思。不能加"得、不"。"v.＋起来" can be used as a parenthesis in a sentence indicating an estimation or focus on a specific aspect. This form cannot be used with "得" or "不."

（12）这个计划听起来很诱人。
（13）算起来，我到中国已经两年了。

说明 Notes：

与"起来"搭配的动词如果带有宾语，或该动词是离合动词，则名词应在"起"和"来"之间。句式为："动词＋起＋名词＋来"。If the verb before "起来" takes an object, or if it is a separable verb, the noun should fall between "起" and "来" in the pattern "v.＋起＋n.＋来."

（14）一做完作业他就看起电视来了。
（15）他手也没洗就吃起饭来了。

这是外国人学趋向补语很容易做错句子的地方。Foreign students tend to make mistakes when learning to use directional complements.

（16）＊他练书法起来非常认真。
（17）他练起书法来非常认真。
（18）＊他一听到音乐就跳舞起来。
（19）他一听到音乐就跳起舞来。

qǐmǎ 起码 →P673 "至少"

用法 Usage：
形容词 a.

表示最低限度，至少。多用做定语和状语。At the least. Indicating the lowest limit, it is often used as an attribute or adverbial.

（1）作为一名学生，上课认真听讲是最起码的要求。
（2）这个工程起码要三年时间才能完成。

说明 Notes：

1. "起码"多用于口语。"起码" is frequently used in colloquial speech.

2. "起码"前可以受程度副词"最"修饰。如例（1）。"起码" can be modified by the degree adjective "最," as seen in (1).

qì 气

用法 Usage：
名词 n.

1. 表示气体。Gaseous material.
（1）厨房里都是水蒸气，快开窗！
（2）天然气是一种比较清洁的能源。

2. 专指空气。Specifically referring to air or atmosphere.

（3）你感觉房间里气闷吗？
（4）请打开车窗透透气吧。

3.（呼吸时出入的）气息。Breath.

（5）那么高的山，爬得我上气不接下气，累死了。
（6）老人家吐出了最后一口气，闭上了眼睛。

4.（鼻子可以闻到的）气味。Smell; odor.

（7）我很喜欢兰花的香气。
（8）垃圾都发出臭气来了，快去扔掉！

5. 人的精神状态。An individual's state of mind.

（9）他说话气儿很足，精神很好啊！
（10）你怎么有气无力的，生病了吗？

6. 人的作风习气。An individual's style and habits.

（11）这个女孩太傲气，让人不喜欢。
（12）二十多岁的人了，还那么孩子气。

7. 中医指人的活力、生命力。(In Chinese Medicine) an individual's life force or vitality.

（13）老人说：元气是父母遗传给的，是人体最基本的气。

8. 指自然界冷热雨晴等现象。Weather phenomena such as temperature, precipitation, etc.

（14）北方将有一股寒冷气流到达，明天本市降温八度。

动词 v.

生气，发怒。To be angry.

（15）他气得说不出话来。
（16）妈妈不气别的，就气你们事先没通知她。

说明 Notes:

名词的"气"经常跟其他语素组合在一起构成一个词语，如："空气、煤气、天然气；受气、生气、叹气；和气、暖气、福气"，等等。As a noun, "气" is typically used with other morphemes to construct an expression, for example, "空气、煤气、天然气；受气、生气、叹气；和气、暖气、福气; etc."

qìhòu 气候 →P463"天气"

用法 Usage:

名词 n.

1. 表示一定地区里经过多年观察所得到的概括性的气象情况，它与气流、纬度、海拔、地形有关。Expressing the general atmosphere, state, and conditions of a specific location as observed over a period of several years; including air current, latitude, height above sea level, and other aspects related to topography.

（1）云南的昆明四季如春，气候宜人，很适合居住。
（2）温带海洋性气候冬暖夏凉，很舒服。

2. 比喻动向或情势。(Metaphorically) a trend of events, situations, or circumstances.

（3）大家觉得现在全球的政治气候怎么样啊？

3. 结果或成就。A result or achievement.

（4）他们的科学研究刚开始，还成不了气候。

说明 Notes:

"气候"表示结果或成就时，多用为否定式，如"不成气候、未成气候、成不了气候"等。When "气候" is used to express a result or achievement, it is often used in a negated form such as "不成气候,未成气候,成不了气候."

qiàdàng 恰当 →P424"适当"

用法 Usage:

形容词 a.

表示合适，妥当。Suitable and appropriate.

（1）这个词语用在这个句子里不恰当。
（2）这件事公司处理得很恰当。

说明 Notes:

"恰当"做谓语时，主语多半是小句、动词性短语。如果是名词，也常常是名词性短语。如果没有上下文的语境，"恰当"在单句里，句子意思一定要完整，如例（1）（2）。When "恰当" is used as a predicate, the subject is typically a clause or a verb phrase. If used with a noun, it's typically a noun phrase. If there is no context surrounding "恰当" in a simple sentence, the sentence must contain a complete thought as in (1) and (2).

qiàhǎo 恰好 →P370"恰恰"

用法 Usage:

副词 ad.

正好在那个点上(表示时间不早不晚、空间不大不小、数量不多不少、机会不迟不早、条件正好的意思),正合时宜。一般在句中做状语。 Just right and exactly appropriate in a certain aspect (indicating that timing is neither late nor early, space is neither too small nor too large, volume is neither too much nor too little, opportunities are neither too late nor too early, and conditions are just right). It is typically an adverbial modifier.

(1) 我要买的书,书店里恰好有一本。

(2) 你想上街,恰好我也要上街,一块儿去吧!

说明 Notes:

1. "恰好"可以用在主语后面,也可以用在主语前面。"恰好" can be used either preceding or following the subject in a sentence.

(3) 恰好星期六是你的生日,我请你看电影。

(4) 你的生日恰好是星期六,我请你看电影。

2. 注意,"恰好"不能理解成"刚好、刚刚好"的意思。Take note that "恰好" cannot be interpreted as equal to "刚好,刚刚好."

(5) *她昨天买的背包和那件衣服颜色很恰好。

(6) 她昨天买的包的颜色跟她的衣服恰好相配。

(7) 她昨天买的包的颜色配她的衣服刚/刚刚好。

qiàqià 恰恰 →P370"恰好"

用法 Usage:

副词 ad.

1. 表示刚好,正好的意思。常常做状语。Exactly; just so; coincidentally. It is often used as an adverbial modifier.

(1) 他的意见恰恰也是我的想法。

(2) 十月一日恰恰是我的生日。

2. 用在正反对比的句子里,表示十分肯定的语气。When used in a sentence expressing positives/negatives or pros/cons, it expresses a tone of absolute certainty.

(3) 姐姐回国恰恰是他出国的时候。

(4) 指出别人缺点,不是对他不好,恰恰是为了他好。

说明 Notes:

1. "恰恰"前后相连的两个意思可能是一致,也可能是相反以加强句子前后内容的对比。格式是:"恰恰＋(就/也)是",如例(1)(2)(3)(4)。 Two ideas connected by "恰恰" can be in agreement or in contrast, in which case the contrasting composition of the sentence is intensified; the pattern is: "恰恰＋(就/也)是," as seen in (1), (2), (3) and (4).

2. "恰恰"经常与"相反"搭配,加强转折的意味。"恰恰" is often used in conjunction with "相反" to strengthen the opposite meaning.

(5) 与你的想法恰恰相反,我认为这么做完全是错的。

(6) 你以为她会笑,恰恰相反,她更加生气了。

3. "恰恰"与"恰好"的区别是:The differences between "恰恰" and "恰好" are as follows:

① "恰好"着重表示希望发生,而实际上也发生了的事。"恰恰"重在对客观事实的描述,如例(3)(4)(5)(6)。"恰好" emphasizes the realization of a wish or desire, while "恰恰" emphasizes the description of an objective fact, as seen in (3), (4), (5) and (6).

② "恰恰"还可以用在为了加强前后成分的对比，或引出与前一分句不同或相反的意见，可用于肯定句，也可用于否定句。语气比"恰好"强烈。"恰好"没有这种用法，一般只用在前后意思一致的句子里。"恰恰" can also be used to reinforce the contrast between two clauses or to introduce an idea or opinion contrary to or different from the previously stated clause. It can be used in an affirmative or negative sentence, and has a stronger semantic tone than "恰好." "恰好" does not have this usage, and is typically only used in sentences expressing two ideas in agreement with one another.

③ "恰恰"只能做状语。"恰好"可以做状语，也可以做补语。"恰恰" can only be used as an adverbial, while "恰好" can be used as either an adverbial or a complement.

(7) *你来得恰恰，我正要去找你呢。

(8) 你来得恰好，我正要去找你呢。

qiānwàn 千万 →P481"万万"

用法 Usage:

副词 ad.

务必，必须。表示叮咛、嘱咐，可重叠为"千万千万"。Must; be sure to. It is used to express careful or earnest instructions. It can be reduplicated as "千万千万."

(1) 一个人出门在外，千万要注意自己的身体。

(2) 千万千万不要忘了下周有HSK考试。

数词 num.

表示数量非常多。可重叠为"千千万万"。Indicating that there is a large quantity of something. It can be reduplicated as "千千万万."

(3) 现在大城市都有千千万万个来自外地的打工者。

qiān 签

用法 Usage:

动词 v.

1. 表示为了负责而在文件、单据上亲自写上姓名或画上记号。To sign one's name or make other insignia on a document, receipt, etc. to show that one is responsible.

(1) 请你在上面签名。

(2) 这两个公司刚刚签了一份合同，准备合作开发一个项目。

2. 用比较简单的文字写出（想法或意见）。To write out (thoughts or ideas) in relatively simple language.

(3) 学院领导已经签好意见了。

(4) 老师在学生的申请书上签了"同意"两个字。

说明 Notes:

"签"经常与"名字、合同、协议、意见"等词语搭配使用，构成动宾短语。"签" is often used with words such as "名字，合同，协议，意见" to make a verb-object phrase.

qiánbian 前边 →P372"前面"

用法 Usage:

名词 n.

前面。一般表示空间。The front. It generally refers to a space or an area.

(1) 房子的后边是座山，房子的前边是条河。

(2) 前边的同学，请你们快点走！

qiánhòu 前后 →P504"先后"

用法 Usage:

名词 n.

1. 表示在某一时间稍早或稍晚的一段时间。Around the time of. It indicates a time a little earlier or later than the specific point of time.

(1) 我春节前后回国。

(2) 我父母中秋节前后要来中国旅行。

2. 表示从开始到结束的整个时间。可以重叠。Indicating all the time from beginning to end. It can be reduplicated as "前前后后."

（3）大山里的高铁前前后后用了两年时间就建好了。

（4）做这道菜,他前后只用了六分钟时间。

3. 前面和后面（表示空间）。可以重叠。(In space) either in the front or in the rear. It can be reduplicated as "前前后后."

（5）房子的前前后后都有草坪和树林。

（6）你朋友好像就住在我家前后,我看到过他。

qiánlái 前来

用法 Usage:
动词 v.

表示到这里来,上前来,向这个方向来。To come to a place; to move forward in the speaker's direction.

（1）公司派小张经理前来商谈业务。

（2）这事儿需要你亲自前来办理。

说明 Notes:

1. "前来"不能单独做谓语,必须在后面带上表示"干什么"的动词性宾语才能成句。"前来" cannot be used alone as a predicate; it must be followed by a verb-type object expressing an action in order to form a complete sentence.

（3）*请你前来。

（4）请你前来老师办公室报名。

2. "前来"常用于书面语。It's usually used in written language.

qiánmiàn 前面 →P371"前边"

用法 Usage:
名词 n.

1. 空间或位置靠前的部分,前边。The front-facing part of an object or location; the front.

（1）食堂前面有一块空地可以打太极拳。

（2）坐在后面的同学请坐到前面来。

2. 次序靠前的部分,文章或讲话中先于现在所叙述的部分。The beginning or foremost part of a sequence; in essays or conversation, the portion of a story that is currently being told.

（3）前面我们讲了两个问题,现在讲第三个问题。

（4）现在复习一下前面学过的十个生词。

说明 Notes:

"前边"和"前面"着重于"边"和"面"的单向空间,在表示空间方位的意义上,用法基本相同,都可以受副词"最"的修饰,都可以儿化,如"前边儿、前面儿"。区别是,"前面"可以表示次序前后。"前边"一般不这样用。"前边" and "前面" emphasize "边" and "面" in unidirectional space. In terms of meaning, the usage is fundamentally the same; they can both accept the modifier "最"; both can take an 儿 suffix, for example, "前边儿,前面儿." The difference between them is that "前面" can be used to describe the order in a sequence, while "前边" typically does not have this usage.

（5）前面我们学了结果补语,今天我们学可能补语。

（6）*前边我们学了结果补语,今天我们要学可能补语。

qiǎn 浅

用法 Usage:
形容词 a.

1. 表示从上到下、从前到后或从外到里的距离少（跟"深"相对）。Shallow, indicating that a space from top to bottom, front to back, or outside to inside in which the distance is small. It is the opposite of "深."

（1）这口井水很浅。

（2）这个山洞不浅,禁止小孩进内！

2. 颜色淡。Pale in color.

（3）她穿了一条浅蓝色的裙子,很漂亮。

（4）窗帘的颜色浅一点更好看。

3.（内容）浅显,（理解）不难,容易懂。 Easy to understand; simple.

（5）这些儿童读物文字少、内容浅,孩子们喜欢看。

4.浅薄,肤浅。Superficial; shallow.

（6）他对自己的错误认识太浅。

5.感情不深厚。Not profound in emotion or sentiment.

（7）我认识他已经十年了,但交情很浅。

6.（程度）轻,不严重。(In degree) light; not serious.

（8）网络上的骗子真是害人不浅。

qiáng 强

用法 Usage:

形容词 a.

1.强壮,力量大(跟"弱"相对)。Strong; the opposite of "弱."

（1）他从小身强力壮,很健康。

（2）公司需要业务水平很强的人。

2.（感情和意志所要求达到的）程度高,坚强。Staunch; emotionally strong in determination and willpower.

（3）她是个很要强的女孩子。

（4）一个人责任心强,工作就能做得好。

3.优越,好(用于比较)。Good, superior (used in comparisons).

（5）现在的日子比以前强多了。

（6）他的能力比我们这几个人强多了。

qiāoqiāo 悄悄 →P327"默默"

用法 Usage:

副词 ad.

表示没有声音或声音很低,行动不让别人知道。Quietly or silently; acting in a way so as to not let others find out.

（1）妈妈悄悄地走出了孩子的房间。

（2）你悄悄儿地告诉我,到底发生了什么事情？

说明 Notes:

1."悄悄"可以修饰名词性成分,如"悄悄话"。"悄悄" can modify noun components such as in "悄悄话."

2."悄悄"常常儿化,如例（2）。"悄悄" often takes the suffix "儿," as seen in (2).

3."悄悄"和"默默"都是副词,表示没有声音的意思。区别是,"悄悄"多用于行为动作没有发出声音或声音很小,不让人听见。"默默"多用于人本身不说话,安静无声的样子。Both "悄悄" and "默默" are adverbs meaning "silently." Their difference is that "悄悄" is mostly applied to an action or behavior making little or no noise so that nobody can hear it while "默默" is mostly applied to people being quiet and saying nothing.

（3）妈妈睡着了,你悄悄儿地走吧。

（4）他默默地坐在一边听朋友们谈天。

qiǎo 巧

用法 Usage:

形容词 a.

1.技艺高超,精巧。Advanced in skill or artistry; exquisite; ingenious.

（1）红木家具的收藏标准是："材质好、设计巧、工艺高。"

（2）这些根雕的构思真巧。

2.（手、口）灵巧。(Of the hand or mouth) dexterous; nimble; skillful.

（3）他嘴巧,学什么叫像什么叫。

（4）妈妈的手很巧,一会儿就剪出了各种漂亮的窗花。

3.恰好,正好。正遇到某种机会。Just right; just in time (of an opportunity, etc.).

（5）巧了,玛丽跟我在一个班学习汉语。

（6）来得早不如来得巧。我又赶上好吃的了。

4.虚浮不实、强词夺理的（话）。(Of words) superficial and unrealistic; with fallacious reasoning.

(7) 我不喜欢嘴巧手笨的人。

(8) 他真会巧辩,错的能说成对的。

qiě 且

用法 Usage:

副词 ad.

1. 表示暂且、暂时先进行(或停止),别的事暂时不管。*Doing (or refraining from doing) something for the time being, leaving other things unattended.*

(1) 你且安心养病,工作的事儿先不用操心。

(2) 这本词典你且用着,我要用词典会有办法的。

2. 有时单纯表示时间不会太长,相当于"暂时、暂且"。*Sometimes, it refers to a short period of time, and is equivalent to "暂时,暂且."*

(3) 他马上就到,你且等一下。

(4) 你且闭上眼睛,我说好了,你再张开。

连词 conj.

1. 尚且,表示让步。常与"不说、不谈"等构成固定形式"且不说、且不谈",表示暂且不说某些事,先列举另外的事实或理由,加强论述。*Even; yet; still. It indicates yielding or giving in. Often it is used to go with "不说,不谈" to form "且不说,且不谈," expressing a situation in which one raises several examples or reasons to strengthen the reasoning before referring to a certain matter.*

(5) 死且不怕,流点血,算什么事?

(6) 且不说我不知道,就是知道也不能对你说。

2. 并且,而且。表示并列或递进关系,连接分句或句子,有时也连接并列的词或词语,意思相当于"而且"。*Moreover; furthermore. It indicates side-by-side or progressive connections and connects clauses or sentences. It can sometimes connect juxtaposed words or phrases with a meaning equivalent to that of "而且."*

(7) 他很聪明,且十分努力,当然会取得好成绩。

(8) 这次数学考试的题目多且难度大。

(9) 教学实习计划已定,且已被学院批准。

3. 用在两个形容词之间,相当于"又",并与"既"构成"既……且……"的格式,表示两种状态都存在。相当于口语中的"又……又……"。*When used between two adjectives, it is equivalent to "又," and can be used with "既" to form the pattern "既…且…," which means that two types of conditions exist simultaneously, equivalent to the colloquial pattern "又…又…."*

(10) 他写汉字既快且好。

(11) 那孩子长得既高且壮,很健康。

4. 构成"且……且……"的格式,多连接两个单音节动词,表示两种动作、行为同时进行,相当于口语中的"边……边……",多用于叙述的书面语。*When forming the pattern "且…且…," it commonly connects two monosyllabic verbs to indicate that two actions are simultaneously occurring, equivalent to the colloquial pattern "边…边…." This usage is commonly seen in narrative literary language.*

(12) 她一进门就且歌且舞地要我看看她跳得好不好。

(13) 老师在黑板前且写且说,很认真地教我们。

qīnfàn 侵犯 →P375"侵略"

用法 Usage:

动词 v.

1. 表示非法干涉别人,损害对方的权利。*To interfere or intervene in an illegal or unlawful manner; to infringe on the rights of another individual.*

(1) 你要注意创作时不要侵犯别人的著作权。

(2) 侵犯别人的利益是不道德的行为。

2. 用武力或非法手段干涉、入侵别国的领域。*To use armed force or other illegal methods to interfere with or invade the territory*

of another country.

（3）国家主权不允许任何人侵犯。

（4）每个国家都不许外国军用飞机侵犯自己国家的领空。

qīnlüè 侵略 →P374"侵犯"

用法 Usage:

动词 *v.*

表示一个国家或几个国家联合起来,非法侵占别国的领土（包括领海、领空）、主权,掠夺别国财富并奴役别国的人民。*(Of one or more countries joining together) to unlawfully seize the territory (including territorial waters or airspace) or sovereign rights of another country, or to pillage the riches and enslave the people of another country.*

（1）历史上的中国被许多外国军队侵略过。

（2）外国势力不但在军事上,而且还在文化上进行侵略。

说明 Notes:

"侵犯"和"侵略"都有表示入侵、危害他国主权、利益的意思,都是贬义词。*"侵犯" and "侵略" both indicate invading and harming another country's interests or sovereign rights, and are both derogatory terms.*

它们的区别是：*The differences between them are as follows:*

1. "侵犯"表示一般的武力入侵或触犯、损害等。"侵略"一般表现为大规模的有组织有计划的武力入侵或掠夺,以及对别国的政治干涉、经济文化渗透等。因此,"侵略政策、侵略战争、经济侵略"等不能说成"侵犯政策、侵犯战争、经济侵犯";而"侵犯我国领空,凛然不可侵犯"也不能说成"侵略我国领空、凛然不可侵略"。*"侵犯" indicates invasion or harm through armed forces, while "侵略" typically expresses large-scale military invasion as well as political interference and economic and cultural interference in another country. Therefore, "侵略政策,侵略战争,经济侵略" cannot be expressed as "侵犯政策,侵犯战争,经济侵犯." "侵犯我国领空,凛然不可侵犯" cannot be expressed as "侵略我国领空,凛然不可侵略."*

2. "侵犯"还表示非法干涉别人,损害别人利益的意思。如："侵犯肖像权、侵犯个人隐私、侵犯消费者权益、侵犯人身自由、侵犯人身安全、侵犯著作权、侵犯专利权、侵犯宗教信仰自由权"等。"侵略"没有这个义项。*"侵犯" can also describe illegally interfering in other people's affairs and damaging their rights and interests, for example, "侵犯肖像权,侵犯个人隐私,侵犯消费者权益,侵犯人身自由,侵犯人身安全,侵犯著作权,侵犯专利权,侵犯宗教信仰自由权." "侵略" does not have this meaning.*

qīnhélì 亲和力

用法 Usage:

名词 *n.*

1. 两种或两种以上的物质结合成化合物时互相作用的力。*The interactive force of two or more substances when they are combined to form a chemical compound.*

（1）水泥和水之间的亲和力非常强。

2. 表示使人亲近、愿意接触的一种力量。*A type of intimate or genial force that causes individuals to be willing to engage with one another.*

（2）这位老师特别有亲和力,同学们都很喜欢他。

（3）张阿姨平易近人,很有亲和力,大家都愿意找她谈心。

说明 Notes:

"亲和力"主要用来形容一个人身上具有亲切和蔼的一种吸引人的力量,褒义词。*"亲和力" is mainly used to describe the genial and amiable force that appeals to others. It is a commendatory term.*

qīnqiè 亲切 →P376"亲热"

用法 Usage:

形容词 *a.*

1. 亲近，亲密。多做谓语、宾语。*Intimate; close. It is often used as a predicate or object.*

(1) 他待人亲切和蔼，大家都喜欢他。

(2) 服务员的微笑很亲切。

2. 热情、真挚恳切。*Warm-hearted and genuinely sincere.*

(3) 老师露出亲切的笑容看着我们。

(4) 每次见到她，她都会亲切地跟我打招呼。

说明 Notes:

"亲切"是一方对另一方的态度或感觉，做谓语时，它的主语不会是双方的。*"亲切" is a feeling or attitude one party has towards another. When used as a predicate, the subject cannot include both parties.*

(5) *她和他的关系很亲切。

(6) 她和他的关系很亲密。

(7) 她对他很亲切。

qīnrè 亲热 →P376"亲切"

用法 Usage:

形容词 *a.*

亲密而热情。可以重叠为"亲亲热热"。*Intimate and warm-hearted. It can be reduplicated as "亲亲热热."*

(1) 孩子们和阿姨亲热得很。

(2) 他们一见面就亲亲热热地聊起了家常。

动词 *v.*

用动作表示亲密和喜爱。可以重叠为"亲热亲热"。*To use actions to express affection and love. It can be reduplicated as "亲热亲热."*

(3) 外婆奶奶带大的孩子，常跟爸妈亲热不起来。

(4) 外婆，我要跟你亲热亲热！

说明 Notes:

"亲热"和"亲切"都形容关系亲近，态度热情、关切。*"亲热" and "亲切" both describe intimate relationships with a warm attitude.*

它们的区别是：*The differences between them are as follows:*

1. "亲切"着重于感情的亲密恳切（与"冷漠"相对）。多形容人的音容笑貌、言谈举止，也形容人在感受某些熟悉的事物时，产生的亲近心情。"亲切"常做"觉得、感到、变得、显得"等词的宾语。*"亲切" emphasizes the sincerity of an emotion (the opposite of "冷漠"). It's often used to describe an individual's voice, speech, expression, and behavior. It can also describe the intimate sense of familiarity brought on by familiar objects. "亲切" is often used as the object of words such as "觉得, 感到, 变得, 显得."*

(5) 服务员对客人的态度显得非常亲切。

(6) 我觉得他对任何人都很亲切。

"亲热"着重于态度的亲近、关切、热情（与"冷淡"相对）。多形容人的谈吐、表情、行动。有时也用于动物。*"亲热" emphasizes an intimate, considerate, and warm attitude (the opposite of "冷淡"). It is often used to describe an individual's expressions and actions. It can also be used to describe animals.*

(7) 夫妻俩亲亲热热地说着话。

(8) 小狗亲热地摇着尾巴，迎接主人进门。

2. "亲热"做形容词时，可以重叠为"亲亲热热"，做动词时，可以重叠为"亲热亲热"。"亲切"不能重叠。*When "亲热" is used as an adjective, it can be reduplicated as "亲亲热热." When used as a verb, it can be reduplicated as "亲热亲热." "亲切" cannot be reduplicated.*

qīnshēn 亲身

用法 Usage:

形容词 *a.*

本身，自身。表示自己直接的感受（或经历

等）。Self; by oneself; personally, not vicariously.

（1）这是我亲身的体会，一辈子都不会忘记。

（2）考察队员亲身经历了这一场生死考验。

说明 Notes:

"亲身"是强调自己直接感受到、体验到并获得客观事实或信息。像这样结构的词语还有"亲眼、亲耳、亲口、亲手"等，表示自己直接看到、直接听到，或是自己说、自己做的意思。"亲身" emphasizes that one has personally felt or experienced something or obtained an objective fact or information. More phrases with such structure are "亲眼，亲耳，亲口，亲手，" indicating that one has personally seen, heard, said, or done something.

qīnshǒu 亲手 →P377"亲眼"

用法 Usage:

副词 ad.

表示用自己的手（做）。多做状语。Done by oneself. It expresses that an action is done by one's own hand. It is often used as an adverbial.

（1）这件衣服是我亲手做的。

（2）孩子亲手制作了一张新年贺卡送给妈妈。

说明 Notes:

1. "亲手"强调用自己的手完成某一动作，所以"亲手"后面的动词是有明显的由手来完成的特征，如"包、指、织、做、擦、写、放、摆、抓"等。"亲手" emphasizes that one has completed an action by one's own hand; the verbs following "亲手" must have obvious characteristics of involving the use of one's hand, such as "包，指，织，做，擦，写，放，摆，抓."

2. "亲手"带有积极主动的语义，在表示不好的事情上要慎用。"亲手" has an implication of positive initiative, and should be used with caution when expressing an undesirable situation.

（3）*我亲手丢了护照。

（4）我把护照弄丢了。

qīnyǎn 亲眼 →P377"亲手"

用法 Usage:

副词 ad.

表示用自己的眼睛（看）。多做状语。Seeing something with one's own eyes. It is often used as an adverbial.

（1）亲眼所见的事情也未必是真实的。

（2）我亲眼看到父亲钓了一条十多斤重的鱼。

说明 Notes:

"亲手"和"亲眼"都有亲自、直接的意思，都有强调直接参与的语义。"亲手" and "亲眼" both involve a personal and direct action and imply direct participation.

它们的区别是：The differences between them are as follows:

1. "亲手"强调为了重视某事，或某事不便、不可能由别人代做，而由自己直接来做，而且用手完成。"亲眼"强调信息的获得是自己的眼睛直接看到的。一般用于对过去事情进行陈述的句子，或者表示对某事的愿望，基本不用于正在发生的事情。"亲手" emphasizes that due to an individual placing high importance on a matter, or due to a matter being inconvenient or impossible to be done by another person, he must do it personally by means of his own hand. "亲眼" emphasizes that an individual has gained information by personally witnessing it. It is typically used in sentences declaring events that have already occurred, or to express a desire related to a specific event; and is typically not used in reference to events that are still currently occurring.

2. 与"亲眼"搭配的一般是双音节词，如"看到、看见、瞧见、所见"等；或者是动词带"过、着"，如"亲眼见过这种动物、亲眼看着他长大"等；或者是动词重叠，如"亲眼见见她、亲眼看看长城"等。"亲手"与后面搭配词语的要求比较自由，在时间上也没有限制。Words paired

with "亲眼" are typically a) disyllabic verbs such as "看到, 看见, 瞧见, 所见," b) verbs carrying "过" or "着," such as "亲眼见过这种动物, 亲眼看着他长大," or c) reduplicated verbs such as "亲眼见见她, 亲眼看看长城." "亲手" has far fewer restrictions on word pairings, and has no restrictions regarding the time frame.

qínfèn 勤奋 →P378"勤劳"

用法 Usage:

形容词 a.

表示振作精神、鼓足劲头努力工作或学习。(Working or studying) diligently and vigorously.

(1) 阿里在学习上非常勤奋。

(2) 他勤奋地工作了两年就当上了经理。

qínláo 勤劳 →P378"勤奋"

用法 Usage:

形容词 a.

表示不断努力地劳动, 不怕辛苦。Hardworking; working with diligence and no fear of hardship.

(1) 山区的农民很勤劳, 天一亮, 就上山干活了。

(2) 这两口子靠勤劳致富, 现在盖起了房, 买上了车。

说明 Notes:

"勤劳"和"勤奋"的区别是: The differences between "勤劳" and "勤奋" are as follows:

1. "勤奋"的对象多指工作或学习。"勤劳"的对象多指体力劳动。The object of "勤奋" is typically related to work or study, while the object of "勤劳" is typically related to manual labor.

2. "勤奋"词义重在对劳动者振作的精神上、劲头上的描述。"勤劳"重在对劳动者认真肯干, 不怕辛苦状态上的描述。"勤奋" is used to describe the laborer's energy and strength, while "勤劳" emphasizes the laborer's attitude of willingness to work without fear of hardship.

qīngyì 轻易 →P397"容易"

用法 Usage:

形容词 a.

表示不费力, 轻松容易。Not strenuous; simple and easy.

(1) 成功不是能轻易得到的。

(2) 他轻易地取得了800米跑步第一名。

副词 ad.

表示随随便便, 轻率。Being careless or reckless.

(3) 他从不轻易开口求人。

(4) 不了解情况就别轻易下结论。

qīng 清

用法 Usage:

形容词 a.

1. 表示(液体或气体)纯净, 没有混杂的东西(跟"浊"相对)。(Of liquids or gases) pure; not mixed with other substances (the opposite of "浊").

(1) 虎跑泉的泉水很清很清。

(2) 天朗气清, 今天应该去湖边走走。

2. 干净, 纯洁。Clean; pure.

(3) 请保持教室的清洁。

(4) 这是一束清一色的白玫瑰花。

3. 寂静。多形容环境。(Typically of an environment) silent.

(5) 山谷特别清静。

(6) 大多数人都去外面打工了, 村里显得很冷清。

4. 清楚。多形容事情、道理。(Typically of situations or principles) clear; distinct; without ambiguity.

(7) 这件事我一两句话说不清, 请原谅。

(8) 你先分清对错, 再批评。

5. 公正廉洁。Honest and impartial.

(9) 他是个清官。

(10) 父母希望他为官清正,替民做主。

6. 单纯,不掺杂别的东西。*Pure; unmixed with any other substances.*

(11) 只喝一杯清茶,别的什么都不吃。

(12) 他的京剧清唱很有名。

7. 尽,完。*Used up; finished.*

(13) 欠他的钱,今天我还清了。

动词 *v.*

1.(账目)还清,结清,清理。*(Of an account) to pay off; to settle up.*

(14) 这笔账,我总算清了。

(15) 这几天超市清仓打折,东西很便宜。

2. 表示一个一个点验。多用于口语。*To examine one by one, often used in colloquial speech.*

(16) 你今天清一清货物的数量。

(17) 刚才清了一下人数,总共32人。

qīngchǔ 清楚 →P324"明白"

用法 Usage:

形容词 *a.*

1. 事物容易让人了解、辨认。*Easy for people to understand or identify.*

(1) 他写的汉字很清楚。

(2) 老师说的话很清楚,我们一听就懂了。

2. 不糊涂,能明辨事理。对事物了解很透彻。*Not muddled or confused; able to clearly discern logic; with a thorough understanding of things.*

(3) 他虽然九十多岁了,但是头脑很清楚。

(4) 我们非常清楚谁对谁错。

动词 *v.*

知道,了解。*To know; to understand.*

(5) 我不清楚他为什么不来上课。

(6) 电影院、银行在哪里,他清楚得很。

说明 Notes:

"清楚"和"明白"的形容词、动词用法基本相似。*The usages of "清楚" and "明白" as adjectives and verbs are both fundamentally similar.*

它们的区别是:*The differences are as follows:*

1. 在词义上,"清楚"有表示事物外形清晰可辨的意思。"明白"重在对事物内容、思想清楚明确,使人容易了解的意思。*Semantically, "清楚" expresses that an object's exterior is distinct and recognizable, while "明白" emphasizes that something's content or ideology is clear and easy to understand.*

2. 做形容词时,如果主语是很具体的事物,后面不能用"明白"。如:例(1)中,主语是"汉字",谓语不能用"明白";例(3)中,主语是"头脑",谓语不能用"明白"。"明白" *is sometimes used as an adjective, but if the subject is a concrete or specific object, the subject cannot be followed by "明白." In (1), since the subject is "汉字," the predicate cannot be "明白." In (3), where the subject is "头脑," the predicate also cannot be "明白."*

3. "清楚"没有"明白"做形容词时表示"聪明、懂道理的"意思。*"清楚" doesn't have the adjectival meaning of "聪明,懂道理的" like "明白" does.*

(7) *他是清楚人。

(8) 他是明白人。

qīnglǐ 清理 →P649"整理"

用法 Usage:

动词 *v.*

表示彻底整理或处理。*To put things in order; to straighten out; to handle thoroughly.*

(1) 我们应该经常清理电脑垃圾。

(2) 星期天,我要把房间清理一下。

说明 Notes:

"清理"表示彻底整理或处理,留下有用的、需要的东西,丢掉没用的、不需要的东西。*"清理" expresses arranging or dealing with things thoroughly: What is useful and necessary is kept while what is useless or unnecessary is discarded.*

qīngxǐng 清醒

用法 Usage:

形容词 a.

表示(头脑)清楚,明白,不糊涂。Sober-minded; (of the mind) clear, sensible, not confused.

(1) 早晨,头脑最清醒。
(2) 对国际形势,要有清醒的认识。

动词 v.

表示(神志)脱离昏迷状态到恢复正常。To be out of a confused, disoriented or comatose state and return to normal.

(3) 他总算清醒过来了。
(4) 手术后需要一些时间,人才能清醒过来。

说明 Notes:

"清醒"一词常常修饰人的头脑,所以一般只用于人。The word "清醒" is typically used to describe one's mental faculties, and as such is typically used to refer to people.

qíngjǐng 情景

用法 Usage:

名词 n.

1. 表示具体场合中的情况和景象。Conditions, scenes, or sights of a situation.

(1) 哈尔滨和海南岛的冬天,是两个完全不同的情景。
(2) 看到这张照片,就想起我们在高中的学习情景。

2. 感情和景物(专指文学作品中,景物描写和环境渲染同人物感情抒发紧密结合,融为一体的境界)。Emotion and scenery (especially vivid descriptions of scenery and environment closely knitted with dramatized human emotions).

(3) 这篇作文写得情景交融,很感动人。
(4) 这首歌曲的音乐跟画面配合,情景结合得更紧密了。

说明 Notes:

"情景"重在借助于视觉,内心感知的景象,多指某一个让人感动的具体场合的景象。"情景" emphasizes scenes relying heavily on visual and emotional perception, typically referring to a type of situation or scene that moves or touches the observer.

qíngkuàng 情况 →P381"情形"

用法 Usage:

名词 n.

1. 表示事物的情形、状况。The circumstances or conditions of something.

(1) 你爸爸的身体情况怎么样?
(2) 明天去不去春游,得看天气情况再定。

2. 表示事情的变化和发展动向。有时专指军事状况的变化。The change or developmental tendency of something; sometimes referring to changes in military conditions.

(3) 这两天股市没有新情况。
(4) 注意!有情况,大家做好战斗准备!

说明 Notes:

1. "情况"泛指事物发生、存在、变化的各种状态。形成这种状态的时间可长可短,所指的事物可以是具体的事情,也可以是抽象的事情。前者如"天气情况、考试情况、生活情况";后者如"思想情况、经济情况、政治情况"。"情况" generally refers to various conditions related to an occurrence, existence, or change. The time taken for this status to occur can be short or long, and the object or thing referred to can be concrete as in phrases such as "天气情况,考试情况,生活情况" or can be abstract, as in "思想情况,经济情况,政治情况."

2. "情况"的第二种用法,表示事情的变化和发展动向。常常表述为"有/没有情况"。The second usage of "情况" refers to the changes and developmental tendency in something, and is typically expressed as "有/没有情况."

qíngxíng 情形 →P380"情况"

用法 Usage:

名词 n.

事物表现在外的状态和样子。An object's external condition, form, or appearance.

(1) 永远忘不了我们去意大利旅游的情形。
(2) 当时具体的情形怎么样,我记不清了。

说明 Notes:

"情形"和"情况"都是表现事物的样子。"情形" and "情况" both describe the appearance of an object.

它们的区别是:The differences are as follows:

1."情况"可以指具体的事情,也可以指抽象的事情。"情形"一般只指具体的事情。如:"思想情况、经济情况、政治情况"不能说成"思想情形、经济情形、政治情形"。"情况" can refer to concrete objects and can also refer to abstract concepts, while "情形" can typically only refer to concrete objects. For example, "思想情况,经济情况,政治情况" cannot be expressed as "思想情形,经济情形,政治情形."

2."情况"可以和"紧急、危急、严重、调查、反映、发生"等词搭配。"情形"不能。"情况" can be used with words such as "紧急,危急,严重,调查,反映,发生," but "情形" cannot.

3."情况"还指事情的发生、变化,军事情势的发生、变化。"情形"没有这个用法。"情况" also refers to occurrences or changes of trends in military situations; "情形" does not have this usage.

4."情况"可受形容词"新、旧"的修饰。"情形"不能。"情况" can be modified by adjectives such as "新,旧," but "情形" cannot.

qíngxù 情绪 →P518"心情"

用法 Usage:

名词 n.

1.表示一个人在从事某种活动时产生的兴奋心理状态。An excited state of mind brought about by engaging in a certain activity.

(1) 妈妈最近的情绪特别好,做饭都唱着歌。
(2) 听说五一节放假三天,大家情绪很高。

2.特指有不愉快的情感。前面常有动词"闹、有"等。When specifically referring to an unhappy emotion, it is often preceded by verbs such as "闹," or "有."

(3) 这个孩子脾气不好,经常闹情绪。
(4) 不让他参加活动,他有情绪呢。

qūbié 区别 →P147"分别"

用法 Usage:

名词 n.

彼此不一样、有不同的地方。Differences between two things or people.

(1) 这对双胞胎姐妹,外表看不出什么区别。
(2) 他们家的生活,十年前后的区别很大。

动词 v.

表示把两个或两个以上的对象进行比较,认识他们的差异、不同的地方。To compare two or more objects and identify the differences between them.

(3) 学习汉语词汇一定要注意区别近义词的用法。
(4) 孩子小,还不会区别真假和善恶。

说明 Notes:

"区别"和"分别"都表示把不同的事物或人划分开来。它们的区别是:"区别" and "分别" both express differences between two objects. Their differences are as follows:

1."区别"着重于比较分辨,划分出事物或人之间的差异。这些差异是经过比较后才得出的。"分别"着重于分开,多用于差别比较明显的事物和人。"区别" emphasizes comparison and separating objects or people by their differences. These differences are only determined after comparisons are made. "分别" emphasizes separation, especially of objects or people that have obvious differences.

2."区别"做名词时,前面可修饰"根本、原则、本质"等抽象名词,而且常与"有、无、没有、存在"等动词搭配。"分别"前面不常带这些修饰成分,一般不做"有、无、没有、存在"等动词的宾语。When "区别" is used as a noun, it can be preceded by intangible noun modifiers such as "根本, 原则, 本质." Furthermore, it is often used with "有, 无, 没有, 存在." "分别" is usually not preceded by a modifying component, and is typically not the object of verbs such as "有, 无, 没有, 存在."

3."分别"有"离别、分离"的意思。"区别"没有。"分别" has the meanings of "离别, 分离," while "区别" does not.

4."分别"有副词用法。"区别"没有。"分别" has an adverb usage, while "区别" does not.

qǔdé 取得 →P204"获得"

用法 Usage:
动词 v.

表示通过努力,经过争取而获得。To achieve or obtain something through great effort; to strive, fight, or compete for something in order to obtain it.

(1)要想取得成功,必须不断地努力。
(2)经过几十次的试验,终于取得了成功。

说明 Notes:

"取得"和"获得"的区别是: Differences between "取得" and "获得" are as follows:

1."获得"着重于经过努力而有所得。"取得"则强调是经过争取才得到的结果。"获得" emphasizes undergoing effort to earn something, while "取得" emphasizes results, which are achieved only through a fight or competition.

2."获得"的对象多为有积极意义的抽象事物,是褒义词。"取得"是中性词。The object of "获得" is frequently an abstract thing with a positive connotation; it is a commendatory term. "取得" is a neutral term.

quán 全 →P116"都"

用法 Usage:
形容词 a.

1.表示齐全,完备。Complete; perfect.
(1)这套书一共有四本,但现在已经不全了。
(2)所有的礼物都买全了。

2.表示整个、全部的意思。常与"都"配合使用。Whole; complete; total. It is often used together with "都."
(3)今年夏天我们全家都去哈尔滨旅游。
(4)这次,全班同学都参加了运动会。

副词 ad.

表示完全,都。概括的对象(句子的主语)一般在"全"前面,常与"都"连用。Completely; all. A generalized object (the subject of the sentence) typically precedes "全," and is often connected to the following phrase with "都."

(5)高级班的学生不全是新同学,还有几位老生。
(6)我把老师讲课的内容全都记下来了。

说明 Notes:

1.形容词"全"表示"整个、全部"意义时,修饰名词不用带"的",如"全国、全家、全校、全世界、全班"等。这些名词的共同点是表示集体名词。When "全," as an adjective, expresses the meaning of "整个" or "全部," the modifying noun doesn't necessarily need to be used with "的," for example, "全国, 全家, 全校, 全世界, 全班." These are all collective nouns.

2."全"和"都"做副词都有表示总括的意思,总括的对象一般都在"全""都"前面。它们的区别是:"全" and "都" are both adverbs used to express something all-inclusive, and "全" or "都" is used following the object of the sentence. The differences are as follows:

①"全"着重于人和物数量方面的总括。"都"使用的范围比"全"广泛,还包括时间、空间、地方等等许多范围。"全" emphasizes inclusiveness of people or objects on the basis of numerical quantity. "都" has a wider range of usages than "全," and can also be used to describe time, space, location, etc.

② "全"一般不跟疑问代词配合使用。"都"可以。"全" is typically not used with interrogative pronouns.

（7）*他吃饭比谁全快。
（8）他吃饭比谁都快。
（9）*她哪儿全会跟他去。
（10）她哪儿都会跟他去。

③ 在含有让步状语的复句中，前面有"无论、不论、不管"等词语合用时，一般用"都"，不用"全"。 In compound sentences that have concessive adverbial clauses, when the sentence begins with words such as "无论,不论,不管," "都" is typically used, but "全" is not.

（11）*不管汉语难不难，我全要学。
（12）不管汉语难不难，我都要学。

④ "都"有"甚至"的意思，表示程度深，强调的语气。"全"没有这个用法。"都" has the meaning of "甚至," which expresses a deep degree and has an emphatic tone; "全" does not have this usage.

（13）*他一点儿全不害怕。
（14）他一点儿都不害怕。

⑤ "都"有"已经"的意思，"全"没有。"都" has the meaning of "已经 (already)," while "全" does not.

（15）*他全来了，你才想起要打电话叫他。
（16）他都来了，你才想起要打电话叫他。

⑥ "全"不能组成"连……都/也……"格式。"全" cannot be used to form the "连...都/也..." pattern.

⑦ "都"没有形容词用法，"全"有。"都" cannot be used as an adjective, while "全" can.

quánbù 全部 →P383"全体"、P480"完全"、P560"一切"

用法 Usage:
名词 n.

1. 各个部分的总和，整个。 The sum of various parts; whole; entire.

（1）你们的问题已经全部解决了。
（2）大家的课本全部拿来了。

2. 用在"是"后面，意思是"所有的"。 Used after "是," it means "所有的."

（3）这个女儿是他的全部。
（4）我说的是事情的全部。

副词 ad.

表示所有部分都包括在内。做状语，后面常带范围副词"都"。 Used as an adverbial modifier to express that all parts are included, it is often followed by the scope adverb "都."

（5）同学们全部都到了，我们上课吧。
（6）我们家的粮食全部是自己种的。

说明 Notes:

"全部"的用法中，名词用法比较多，"全部"作副词用，常常去掉"部"，只用"全"。"全部" is most frequently used as a noun. When used as an adverb, "部" is commonly omitted, leaving only "全."

quántǐ 全体 →P383"全部"

用法 Usage:
名词 n.

各个个体或部分的总和，一般只用于指人（所有人员的总和）。 The sum of all individuals or parts. It is typically used to refer to people.

（1）今天下午召开全体留学生大会。
（2）这个建议得到了全体老师的支持。

说明 Notes:

"全部"和"全体"都有整体、各个部分总和的意思，被修饰的词语一般都是双音节。"全部" and "全体" both express the sum of all individuals or parts, and typically modify disyllabic words.

它们的区别是：They differ as follows:

1. "全部"多用于事物，较少用于人。"全体"多用于人，较少用于事物。"全部" is often

used to describe objects, and is not typically used to refer to people. "全体" is often used to describe people, but is not typically used to refer to objects.

2. "全部"有副词用法。"全体"没有副词用法。"全部" has an adverb usage while "全体" does not.

3. "全部"做定语时,修饰单音节词语,前面要用"的",如"全部的爱、全部的情"等;修饰名词性短语,要用"的",如"妈妈对儿女全部的付出、对他全部的爱"等;修饰双音节词语时,可以不用"的",如"全部财产、全部粮食"等。"全体"做定语修饰名词一般不用"的",如"全体留学生、全体老师"。When "全部" is used as a modifier for single-syllable words, it should be preceded by "的," as in "全部的爱,全部的情." When modifying noun phrases, it should also be preceded by "的," as in "妈妈对我的全部的培养,对他的全部的爱." When modifying disyllabic words, "的" may be omitted, as in "全部财产,全部粮食." When "全体" is used as an attributive, it typically is not used with "的," such as "全体留学生,全体老师."

quē 缺

用法 Usage:
动词 v.

1. 表示缺乏,短少。To lack; to be short of.
(1) 三班还缺个口语老师。
(2) 这份报告还缺很多事实材料。

2. 表示残破,残缺。To be broken and incomplete.
(3) 这本杂志缺了一页。
(4) 这部手机缺一张 SIM 卡。

3. 该到而未到。To be absent from an event one should have attended.
(5) 玛丽这周缺课两天。
(6) 二十个同学没有一个缺席。

quēfá 缺乏 →P384"缺少"

用法 Usage:
动词 v.

表示没有或不够(所需要的,想要的或一般应有的事物)。To be lacking in (something one needs, desires, or should have).
(1) 他刚参加工作,还缺乏经验。
(2) 这个贫穷的山区缺乏生产资源。

说明 Notes:
"缺乏"的宾语一般是抽象名词,宾语前面一般不能有数量词语。The object of "缺乏" is typically an abstract noun that generally is not preceded by a number or a measure word.
(3) *我们班还缺乏三本口语书。
(4) 我们班还缺/少三本口语书。

quēshǎo 缺少 →P384"缺乏"

用法 Usage:
动词 v.

表示缺乏(多指人或物数量不够)。To lack or be short of, typically referring to people or objects.
(1) 这个句子缺少一个动词。
(2) 打麻将要四个人,缺少一个人就打不成。

说明 Notes:
"缺少"和"缺乏"都表示应该有、需要有而没有或不够。Both "缺少" and "缺乏" refer to the situations in which something required or desired is lacking or insufficient in quantity.

它们的区别是:The differences are as follows:

1. "缺少"着重于在数量上不足或没有。对象多指人或能够计数的具体事物,可用数量词做宾语,指出缺少的具体数量,如例(1)。"缺少" emphasizes that the quantity of something is insufficient, or that there is none. Its object is typically people or concrete objects that can be counted. It can be followed by an object with a

quantifier and measure word which indicates the concrete amount that is lacking, as seen in (1).

2. "缺乏"着重于应该具备但极少或没有,语义比"缺少"重。对象多是抽象事物,如:"精神、能力、信心、决心、勇气、经验、感情、积极性、组织性、纪律性"等名词都可以做宾语;还可以有"了解、调查、研究、锻炼、教育、准备"等动词做宾语;统指的具体事物名词,如"工具、原料、资金、药品"等也可以,但是一般不带数量词。"缺乏" emphasizes that there is little or none of something that one should possess; it has a stronger semantic tone than "缺少." Its object is typically an abstract noun or the generic reference of an abstract noun. For example, "精神,能力,信心,决心,勇气,经验,感情,积极性,组织性,纪律性" and other such nouns can all be used as the object. Verbs such as "了解,调查,研究,锻炼,教育,准备" can also be used. Collective concrete nouns such as "工具,原料,资金,药品," can also be used, but typically do not take measure words.

(3) ＊我缺乏三元钱。
(4) 我缺少三元钱。
(5) 我缺乏资金。

3. "缺少"一般不受程度副词的修饰。"缺乏"可以。"缺少" typically cannot be modified by adverbs that express a degree, while "缺乏" can.

què 却 →P98"倒"

用法 Usage:
副词 ad.

表示转折,但词义比"但、但是"轻,相当于"倒、可"。Indicates a transition, but with a tone softer than "但,但是;" similar to "倒,可."

(1) 刚才还有很多话想说,一见到你却什么都说不出来了。
(2) 他说的话不多,道理却很深刻。

说明 Notes:

1. "却"一般用在偏正复句的正句中,提出跟偏句意思相反或不一致的动作、行为或状况等。在句子中一般用在主语后面。"却" is typically used in the modified clause (or the main clause) of a complex modifier-modified sentence; it indicates that the meaning of the modifier clause (or the subordinate clause) is contrary to or in disagreement with the action, behavior, condition, etc. It is typically used after the subject of a sentence.

2. "却"和"倒"都有副词用法,表示转折语气。Both "却" and "倒" may serve to show a turn in the development of events.

它们的区别是: Their differences are as follows:

① "却"表示的转折语气比较轻。"却" indicates a smaller turn of events than "倒."

(3) 国际学院校区不大,环境倒很优美。
(4) 国际学院校区不大,环境却很优美。

② "倒"后面多用意义积极的词语。"却"后面的词语,意义积极与否没有限制。"倒" is mostly followed by words with a positive meaning. "却," by contrast, does not have any limits in this regard: it may be followed by words either with a positive meaning or with a negative one.

(5) 他汉语口语学得很好,汉字却写得不好。
(6) ＊他汉语口语学得很好,汉字倒写得不好。

③ "倒"有表示让步、责怪、追问或催促、舒缓语气的用法。"却"没有。"倒" may be used to make a concession, a blame, an urging, or a question pursuing an answer. Also, it may help to make a statement less severe or painful.

(7) ＊你却好,到现在还不起床。
(8) 你倒好,到现在还不起床。

quèdìng 确定 →P326"明确"、P386"确认"

用法 Usage:

动词 v.

制定,决定,规定,表示明确而肯定。To determine, decide or establish. It means that something is clear-cut and thus is decided upon.

（1）参加口语比赛的同学已经确定了。

（2）读什么专业,我已经确定,但是考哪个大学还没确定。

形容词 a.

明确而肯定。Clear-cut and confirmed.

（3）你最好给我一个确定的答复。

（4）在学习上,他每年都有一个确定的目标。

说明 Notes:

1. 动词"确定"着重于把某事物从没有正式确立、不稳定或不明确的状态中,明确地固定下来或肯定下来,因此是动态的。所以一般不做状语或补语。As a verb, "确定" emphasizes that something that has not been formally established, is not stable, or is in an unclear situation has now been clearly defined or confirmed. It is thus dynamic. It typically cannot be used as an adverbial modifier or a complement.

（5）*他确定地说："我不去上海。"

（6）他明确地说："我不去上海。"

（7）*他说得很确定："我不去上海。"

（8）他说得很明确："我不去上海。"

2. "确定"和"明确"的区别: The differences between "确定" and "明确" are as follows:

① "明确"着重于清晰、明白而确定。"确定"着重于把某事物从没有正式确立、不稳定或不明确的状态中明确地固定下来或肯定下来。"明确" focuses on being clear, evident, and established. "确定," by contrast, emphasizes the process of bringing something from a state of being unclear and uncertain to that of being clear and certain.

② "明确"在句子中可以做谓语、定语和状语。"确定"一般不做状语和补语。"明确" can appear in a sentence as a predicate, attribute or adverbial. But "确定" usually does not serve as an adverbial or complement.

（9）*他说得很确定,他明天不来。

（10）他说得很明确,他明天不来。

quèqiè 确切 →P387"确实"

用法 Usage:

形容词 a.

1. 准确,恰当。Precise, exact, accurate, fitting.

（1）告诉我确切的航班时间,我去机场接你。

（2）这篇文章逻辑清楚,用词确切,写得很好。

2. 确实。True, reliable.

（3）你说的消息确切吗？

（4）你要确切地告诉我,他到底几岁。

quèrèn 确认 →P386"确定"

用法 Usage:

动词 v.

表示明确承认,确定认可（事实、原则等）。To clearly recognize or admit, to definitively confirm (a fact, principle, etc.).

（1）这事需要进一步确认,现在作出结论还太早。

（2）护照的信息已经确认,你可以走了。

说明 Notes:

"确认"和"确定"都有表示明确肯定的意思。"确认" and "确定" both express the confirmation of something.

它们的区别是: The differences are as follows:

1. "确认"着重于对方对事实的承认、认可。"确定"着重于对事实本身的肯定。"确认" emphasizes that the other party is recognizing or acknowledging a fact. "确定" emphasizes that the fact itself is definite and

certain.

(3) 你的机票要去确认一下日期和航班。
(4) 机票的日期和航班确定了吗？

2. "确定"有形容词用法。"确认"没有。"确定" has an adjectival usage, while "确认" does not.

quèshí 确实 →P111"的确"、P386"确切"

用法 Usage:

形容词 a.

表示准确，真实可靠。可以重叠。Accurate, true, and reliable. This term can be reduplicated.

(1) 这是确确实实的消息，你应该相信。
(2) 我认为这些数字不确实，需要再核查一遍。

副词 ad.

表示对客观情况真实性的肯定。可以重叠使用。Affirming the truthfulness of an objective situation. This term can be reduplicated.

(3) 我确确实实不知道他去哪儿了。
(4) 最近，他的口语确实有很大的进步。

说明 Notes:

1. "确实"和"确切"的区别是：The differences between "确实" and "确切" are as follows:

① "确实"着重于实实在在，没有虚假。"确切"着重指切合实际，没有差错。"确实" emphasizes that something is dependable and not false; "确切" emphasizes that something corresponds to reality without error.

② "确实"可以重叠为"确确实实"，还有副词用法。"确切"不能重叠，没有副词用法。"确实" can be reduplicated as "确确实实," and also has an adverbial usage; "确切" cannot be reduplicated, and does not have an adverbial usage.

2. "确实"和"的确"都可以做副词用，表示所说的客观情况完全符合实际，其真实性肯定无疑。在句中做状语，可以换用。Both "确实" and "的确" can serve as an adverb to confirm something that has been said. And they can be used interchangeably.

它们的区别是：Their differences are as follows:

① 在语义上各有侧重："确实"侧重客观情况的属实性，强调有根有据的意思。"的确"侧重强调事物的性质、行为动作的绝对真实准确，带有不可置疑的肯定意思。Semantically, "确实" focuses on the fact that what is said is based on fact, not fiction. By contrast, "的确" emphasizes that what is said about the nature of a thing or about an action or behavior is absolutely reliable: it admits of no room for doubt.

② "确实"有形容词用法。"的确"没有形容词的用法。"确实" can be used as an adjective, but "的确" cannot.

(5) *我已经得到了的确的消息。
(6) 我已经得到了确实的消息。

rán'ér 然而 →P90"但是"、P273"可是"

用法 Usage:
连词 conj.

表示转折关系。"然而"引出跟上文相对立的意思,或限制,或补充上文。主要连接分句或句子,也连接短语或段落。相当于"但是、可是"。 Indicating a turn in relationship, "然而" introduces a new meaning that is opposite to, limits, or complements the meaning expressed in the previous text. Mainly used to connect clauses or sentences, it connects phrases or paragraphs as well. The usage is similar to that of "但是" or "可是."

（1）大家都积极地参加讨论,然而他却在一旁一句话也不说。

（2）他的脚受伤了,然而他走起路来比我们还快。

说明 Notes:

"然而"和"但是""可是"的区别是：The differences between "然而" and "但是,可是" are as follows:

1. "然而"多用于书面语。"然而" is mostly used in written language.

2. "然而"很少与"虽然"等词语呼应使用。如例(1)(2)。"然而" is rarely used together with conjunctions such as "虽然," as seen in (1) and (2).

ránhòu 然后 →P198"后来"、P235"接着"

用法 Usage:
连词 conj.

1. 表示某种动作或情况发生以后,接着会怎么样。后一句有时用"才、才能"等词,表示有前一行为,才有后一行为的出现。To show what might happen following an action or a situation. "才" or "才能" is sometimes used in the second clause to indicate that the action or situation in the first clause is essential for the action or situation in the second clause to happen.

（1）你吃了,然后才能知道好吃不好吃。

（2）你们学了,然后就知道是容易还是难了。

2. 表示一件事情以后,接着又发生另一件事情。前一句有时用"先、首先"等词,后一句常用"再、又、还"呼应。表示承接关系。To show that one thing happens after another. "先" or "首先" is sometimes used in the first clause, which often corresponds with "再," "又," or "还" in the second clause for continuation.

（3）我们先商量一下,然后再做决定。

（4）他首先去看了住院的爸爸,然后又去看了女朋友的父母。

3. "然后"与"呢"组成"然后呢"。可以独立成句,表示对接下来将发生事情的追问。Used with "呢" to form "然后呢," which can be a stand-alone question inquiring what may

happen in the future

（5）A:"毕业后你打算干什么？"
B:"找工作。"
A:"然后呢？"
B:"工作两年以后,再考研究生。"

说明 Notes:

1. "然后"与"后来"都可以用在复句中,但是语意和用法不同。"然后" and "后来" can both be used in compound sentences, but the meaning and the usage vary.

① "然后"是连词,主要连接句子。它常跟"先、首先"呼应,表示两个动作或两件事件的先后顺序,"然后"带出后一个动作或事件。"后来"是时间名词,主要用来表示时间。As a conjunction, "然后" is mostly used to connect sentences. Often it corresponds with "先" or "首先" to indicate a sequential relationship of two actions or events. "然后" introduces the second action or event. As a time-related noun, "后来" is mostly used to indicate time.

② "然后"因为表示的是动作或事件的先后顺序,所以它连接的两个动作或事件是接连发生的。"后来"所表示的时间具有到某时为止的持续意义,所以两个动作或事件的发生可以相隔一段时间。Since "然后" indicates a sequential relationship, the two actions or events connected by "然后" happen in succession. The time introduced by "后来" may continue up to a certain point. Therefore, there may be an interval of time between the two actions or events connected by "后来."

（6）首先请阿里提出一个问题,然后我们再讨论他提出的问题。

（7）开始他还给我发微信,后来一点儿消息也没有了。

③ "然后"既可用于过去,也可用于将来。"后来"只跟过去的时间相联系。"然后" can be used for past or future time references, whereas "后来" can only be used with a past reference.

（8）我们先参观了美术博物馆,然后去饭店吃了饭。（过去 In the past）

（9）暑假里我准备先去北京,然后再去哈尔滨。（将来 In the future）

（10）听说,后来她结了婚,有了两个孩子。（过去 In the past）

2. "接着"和"然后"都有表示一个动作发生以后,接着又发生了另一个动作的意思。"接着" and "然后" can both indicate the occurrence of one action after another, but the semantic meanings have different emphases.

它们的区别是：Their differences are as follows:

① "接着"强调一个动作紧跟着另一个动作,在时间上两个动作连接得很紧。"然后"虽然也是一个动作在前,一个动作在后,但强调的是这个动作之后再发生了什么,不强调时间的长短,不强调动作之间是否连接得很紧密。"接着" emphasizes that one action immediately follows another and that there is little time between the two actions. Although "然后" also indicates sequential relationship, the emphasis is on what happens after the first action or event, rather than the time between the two actions or events, or whether the two are closely connected in time.

（11）他们从故宫出来,接着就去吃午饭了。

（12）他们从故宫出来,然后去吃午饭了。

② "接着"有动词用法。"然后"没有动词用法。"接着" can be used as a verb. but "然后" cannot be used as a verb.

（13）奶奶给的压岁钱,你接着吧。快谢谢奶奶！

ràng 让 →P18"被"、P230"叫"

用法 Usage:

动词 v.

1. 把方便、好处和有利的条件给别人。To sacrifice one's own convenience, benefits, or favorable conditions for those of others.

(1) 他把大苹果让给妹妹吃了。
(2) 把方便让给别人,把困难留给自己。

2. 谦让,请人接受招待。*To yield; to entertain guests.*

(3) 她一边让客人坐,一边端茶请客人喝。
(4) 在公共汽车上,年轻人应该给老人让座。

3. 有代价地转移所有权或使用权。*To transfer ownership or right to use with compensation.*

(5) 这种词典我有两本,我可以让一本给你。
(6) 他让给我一张电影票,晚上我要去看电影。

4. 表示致使、愿望、容许或听任,必带兼语,构成兼语短语。*To cause, wish, allow or indulge.* "让" *has to be used with a pivotal phrase here.*

(7) 我不清楚她喜欢什么颜色,让她自己去挑吧。
(8) 妈妈让我一到中国就给她打电话。

5. 避开,躲闪,离开原来的地方。可以带"了",可带名词宾语,可重叠。*To avoid; to dodge; to leave a space for;* "让" *can be used with* "了" *or a noun object. It can also be reduplicated.*

(9) 请大家让一让,车开过来了。
(10) 对不起,请让让道,让我过去!

介词 *prep.*

与"叫"一样,相当于"被"的介词用法。同时,"让"的介词用法与"叫"一样,也有相对固定的词语结构:"让……给+动词"和"让……把……+动词、让……把……给+动词"。*Similar to the prepositional usage of* "叫" *and* "被." *Similar to* "叫," *the prepositional usage of* "让" *follows fixed structures:* "让…给＋verb," "让…把…+v.," *and* "让…把…给+v."

(11) 爬山的时候,她让树枝给划了一下。
(12) 爬山的时候,她让树枝把脸划了一下。
(13) 爬山的时候,她让树枝把脸给划了一下。

说明 Notes:

"叫""被"与"让"的区别是:"叫,""被"and "让" differ as follows:

1. "让"和"叫"一样,常用于口语。*Like* "叫," "让" *is often used colloquially.*

2. 介词"让"和"叫"后面,如果跟指人的名词或代词,可能会与"让""叫"的动词语义义项用法相混淆,产生句子的歧义。"被"字没有这种问题。*When a noun or pronoun referring to people follows the preposition* "让" *or* "叫," *the usage of the preposition may be confused with the usage as a verb, which can lead to ambiguity. By contrast,* "被" *does not cause such ambiguity.*

(14) 我让朋友说了几句。

如果没有上下文,例(14)的句义就可以理解成三种意思:*Isolated from the context, the sentence (14) may be interpreted in three ways:*

我请朋友说了几句。*I invited my friend to say a few sentences.* ("让"的动词"谦让"义项"让" *used as a verb meaning "to request"*)

我允许朋友说了几句。*I allowed my friend to say a few sentences.* ("让"的动词"致使、容许"义项"让" *used as a verb meaning "to cause, to allow"*)

我被朋友说了几句。*I was lectured by my friend.* ("让"的介词用法"让" *used as a preposition*)

3. "被"经常直接用在动词前,作为被动的助词用法。"叫"很少用,"让"则没有这种用法。"被" *is often used as a passive auxiliary word directly before the verb.* "叫" *is rarely used like this, while.* "让" *has no such usage.*

(15) *马路上出了车祸,人让撞了。
(16) 马路上出了车祸,人被撞了。
(17) 马路上出了车祸,人叫撞了。

rè 热

用法 Usage:

形容词 *a.*

1. 热能多,温度高,感觉温度高(跟"冷"相对)。*With high thermal energy or high*

temperature (the opposite of "冷").

(1) 杭州夏天很热。

(2) 走路以后热起来了。

2. 形容非常羡慕或急切想得到。Jealous; yearning for something.

(3) 她很眼热你的连衣裙。

3. 吸引很多人的,受欢迎的。Attractive to or welcomed by many people.

(4) 如何养老成了社会上热议的话题。

(5) 近几年对外汉语教学成了热门专业。

4. 情意深厚,热烈,热情。如:"热心肠儿、热爱、热诚"等。Having profound enthusiasm; passionate, as in "热心肠儿,热爱,热诚."

5. 表示气氛浓烈,兴旺,红火。如:"热闹、热火朝天"等。Thriving, flourishing, as in "热闹,热火朝天."

6. 加在名词、动词或词组后面表示形成的某种热潮。如:"出国旅游热、足球热、自学考试热、健身热、瑜伽热"等。Used after a noun, verb or a phrase to indicate a certain trend, as in "出国旅游热,足球热,自学考试热,健身热,瑜伽热."

名词 n.

生病引起的高体温。High body temperature due to sickness.

(6) 昨天晚上他发热了。

(7) 吃药两个小时后就退热了。

动词 v.

多指给食物加热。可以重叠。To heat up food ("热" can be reduplicated).

(8) 饭菜热热再吃。

(9) 请把汤热一下!

rèliè 热烈 →P391"热闹"

用法 Usage:

形容词 a.

形容气氛活跃,情绪高昂,兴奋激动。Enthusiastic. It is used to describe an active atmosphere where people are excited.

(1) 热烈欢迎新同学!

(2) 我们班里的口语课,每次都上得很热烈。

rèmén 热门

用法 Usage:

名词 n.

指吸引很多人的事物。Things that are popular among a lot of people.

(1) 最近开网店成了大学毕业生的热门话题。

(2) 这种运动鞋是今年的热门货。

说明 Notes:

"热门"也可以用作形容词。"热门" can be used as an adjective too.

(3) 今年夏天这种运动鞋很热门。

rènao 热闹 →P391"热烈"

用法 Usage:

形容词 a.

形容景象繁盛、兴旺、活跃。可以重叠为"热热闹闹"。Describing a bustling scene. It can be reduplicated as "热热闹闹."

(1) 晚上,那个广场是个很热闹的地方。

(2) 他热热闹闹地为自己举办了婚礼。

动词 v.

使场面活跃,精神兴奋,气氛热烈。可以重叠为"热闹热闹"。To enliven the atmosphere or to lift up the mood. It can be reduplicated as "热闹热闹."

(3) 周末我们开个舞会,热闹热闹怎么样?

(4) 每到星期六,妈妈就要想办法让大家回到家里热闹一番。

说明 Notes:

1. "热闹"还有名词用法,指繁盛活跃的景象。When used as a noun, "热闹" refers to a bustling scene.

(5) 他就喜欢看热闹,我不喜欢热闹。

(6) 你在这儿凑什么热闹,快回家。

2. "热烈"和"热闹"都可以形容气氛活跃,不冷清。可以形容"场面、交谈、景象"等。Describing an active, not cheerless atmosphere, both "热烈" and "热闹" can be used with

words such as "场面,交谈,景象."

它们的区别是：Their differences are as follows:

① "热烈"着重于情绪兴奋、激动,气氛强烈、火热。词意比"热闹"严肃,可以形容"感情、心情、爱情、口号声、掌声"等。常做状语,修饰"响应、拥护、支持、欢迎、讨论、追求、握手"等词语。"热闹"着重于情景、场面的繁盛、活跃。词意比"热烈"活泼,可以形容"市场、商店、集市、街道、地方、人群、婚礼"等。"热烈" describes an enthusiastic atmosphere where people are excited and the word carries a more serious meaning than "热闹." It can be used with words such as "感情,心情,爱情,口号声,掌声." It is often used as an adverb to describe words such as "响应,拥护,支持,欢迎,讨论,追求,握手." By contrast, "热闹" describes a bustling scene and carries a livelier tone. It can also be used to describe "市场,商店,集市,街道,地方,人群,婚礼, etc."

② "热闹"有动词、名词用法,还可以重叠,动词为"热闹热闹",形容词为"热热闹闹"。"热烈"只有形容词用法,不能重叠。"热闹" can be used as a verb or a noun. When reduplicated, the verb form is "热闹热闹," whereas the adjective form is "热热闹闹." "热烈" can only be used as an adjective and cannot be reduplicated.

rèqíng 热情 →P392"热心"

用法 Usage:

形容词 a.

形容感情热烈。Enthusiastic. It is used to describe a person's high enthusiasm or passion.

（1）这个服务员态度很热情。
（2）他热情地跟我打招呼。

名词 n.

热烈的感情。High enthusiasm or passion.

（3）这个老师教学热情很高。
（4）他的热情感染了大家。

rèxiàn 热线

用法 Usage:

名词 n.

1. 为了便于马上联系而经常准备着的直通电话或媒体线路。Hot line; a direct telephone or media line ready for immediate contact.

（1）12345是各地市人民政府设立的政务服务便民热线。
（2）广播台有个音乐热线点播,你想听什么音乐打个电话就可以。

2. 指运输繁忙,客流量、货流量大的交通线路。Transportation routes with busy traffic and large passenger or cargo flow.

（3）杭州到西安、杭州到北京的高铁都是旅游热线。
（4）国外旅游热线最近又多了好几条。

rèxīn 热心 →P392"热情"

用法 Usage:

形容词 a.

有热情,有兴趣,肯尽心竭力。Showing passion and interest; willing to devote efforts to helping others.

（1）他对朋友非常热心。
（2）你热心地帮助了他,他很感激你。

动词 v.

表示做事非常积极。一定要带宾语。To be actively engaged in something. It must be followed by an object.

（3）这个公司热心慈善事业,受到了人们的好评。
（4）王阿姨热心服务,同学们都很喜欢她。

说明 Notes:

1. "热心"作为动词,意思是对某些事情很有热情,主动提供各方面的帮助,它的对象应该是事情（或事业）而不是具体的人,宾语不能是"人",如例（3）（4）。When used as a verb, "热心" means to be passionate about certain things and to actively provide help with materials or

service. The recipient must be a thing rather than a person. Therefore, the object cannot be a person as seen in (3) and (4).

2. "热心"与"热情"都可作形容词用,形容感情热烈。"热心" and "热情" can both be used as an adjective to describe high enthusiasm or passion.

它们的区别是: The differences are as follows:

① "热情"着重于感情热烈、洋溢,用于对人对事,一般流露于待人接物的言谈举止之中,通用于口语和书面语。"热心"着重于态度积极,主动关心,有兴趣,肯尽力。常用于对事。"热情" describes high enthusiasm or passion toward things or people, which is often exhibited in one's words and behaviors toward others. It can be used in both colloquial and written language. "热心" emphasizes an active attitude, interest and devotion. The recipient is usually a thing rather than a person.

(5) 他对人很热情。
(6) 他对这件事很热心。

② "热情"有名词用法,"热心"没有。"热心"有动词用法,"热情"没有。"热情" can be used as a noun but not as a verb. "热心" can be used as a verb but not as a noun.

rénjiā 人家

用法 Usage:
名词 n.

1. 住户。Household.
(1) 住在山上的人家不多了。
(2) 我们山村没几户人家,都搬下山了。

2. 指家庭,家世。前面一般都要有修饰语。Family; family background (normally preceded by an attributive).
(3) 她出身于贫穷人家,从小很会吃苦。
(4) 他是书香人家子弟,对人有礼貌,很懂道理。

3. 指婆家。一般指女孩子找婆家。The husband's family (often in the case of a woman seeking a spouse).

(5) 女儿大了,该找人家了。
(6) 你别想了,那女孩子已有人家了。

rénjia 人家

用法 Usage:
代词 pron.

1. 指别人。Others.
(1) 人家能做到的,我为什么不能做到?
(2) 我听人家说,春节有七天假期。

2. 指某个人或某些人。A specific individual or certain people.
(3) 快把CD片给人家送回去。
(4) 快谢谢人家!

3. 指"我",说话的本人(有亲热或俏皮的意味)。One's self or the person who is talking (sometimes in an intimate or witty tone).
(5) 人家不爱吃的东西你偏买,你自己吃吧!
(6) 现在才来,人家都等你半天了。

说明 Notes:

关于代词"人家"的第三种用法理解比较难。这种用法常常是对事态、情况有所不满或不便但又不愿意直接表示自己态度、意见的一种间接表示方法。使用时,句子中必须清楚地表示有所不满或不便的事由,同时必定有第二人称代词"你"与隐性的说话者、第一人称"我"(即句子中的"人家")相映衬。The third usage of "人家" as a pronoun may sometimes cause confusion. It is often used to insinuate one's negative attitude or opinion toward the situation. The sentence must clearly indicate the reason for one's discontent or inconvenience. Also, the second-person pronoun "你" is always used in the sentence to correspond with "人家," which represents the first-person pronoun "我."

rènwéi 认为 →P573 "以为"

用法 Usage:
动词 v.

对人或事做出某种判断,表示确定的看法。在句子中做谓语,可以带动词、形容词、小句宾语。用于被动句,采用"被/让……认为"的格式。*To think; to consider. It makes a judgment about people or things and expresses one's views in clear-cut terms. Used as a predicate, it can take a verb, an adjective, or a clause as its object. When used in a passive-voice sentence, it takes the form of "被/让…认为."*

(1) 我认为绿色象征生命、自然、宁静。

(2) 大家都认为散步是一种很适合老人的运动。

(3) 李老师被留学生认为是最好的老师。

说明 Notes:

"认为"着重于经过认真思考后,对事物表明确定的看法、判断,常常是在分析、理解、认识的基础上得出的,因此"认为"的语气较为肯定。*"认为" focuses on showing clear views after careful consideration. The judgment made is often based on analysis and understanding. Therefore, the tone of "认为" is usually quite certain.*

rèn 任

用法 Usage:

动词 *v.*

1. 委派,使用。常与"为"配合使用。*To appoint (often used with "为").*

(1) 他一到那个公司,就被任为经理。

(2) 他被校长任为中文系系主任。

2. 担当,担负。*To undertake; to be charged with a certain responsibility.*

(3) 他在中学任教四十年了。

(4) 老王任职以来一直跟大家一起干活。

3. 表示不管不问,听其自然,或听其自便。相当于"任凭、听凭、随、由"等。多带人称代词做宾语或兼语。*To allow things to take their own course, not to interfere. Similar to the usage of "任凭,听凭,随,由," it is often followed by a personal pronoun as an object or a subjective-object.*

(5) 学院的选修课很多,任你挑选。

(6) 这是老毛病了,任其自然吧。

有时"任"后面还可以带"着",表示一种随意的情态,一般"任着"后面不跟单音节词。*Sometimes "任" is followed by "着," which indicates a casual mood. "任着" is usually not followed by a monosyllabic word.*

(7) 你不能任着孩子喝甜饮料,那样对身体不好。

(8) *他上课时总是吃东西,我们不能任着他。

(9) 我们不能任着他上课时总是吃东西的行为。

连词 *conj.*

1. 表示条件关系中的无条件,即表示在任何条件下都这样,相当于"无论、不管",后面常带疑问代词"什么、怎么、谁"等表示普遍性,在后一个句子里,常用"都、也"呼应。*No matter what/who/how. It is used to indicate an unconditional state, which stays the same regardless of conditions. Similar to the use of "无论,不管," it is often followed by an inquisitive pronoun such as "什么,怎么,谁" to indicate universality, which usually corresponds with "都" or "也" in the following clause.*

(10) 任我们怎么劝说,他都不吃。

(11) 任你是谁,都要遵守交通规则。

2. 表示不管情况如何,也是如此,相当于"即使、就是",在后一句子中,常用"也"呼应。*Even though; even if. It is used to indicate that the result stays the same however much the situation may change. It usually corresponds with "也" in the following clause.*

(12) 任你们怎么反对,我也要跟她好。

(13) 任他逃到天边,我也要把他追回来。

说明 Notes:

"任"还有量词用法。用于任职的次数。*"任" can also be used as a measure word to indicate the number of terms at a position.*

(14) 他当厂长已经是第二任了。

rènxìng 任性 →P395"任意"

用法 Usage:

形容词 a.

放任自己的性子,不加约束,指性格的特征。Indulging oneself without restrictions; self-willed; unruly. It refers to one's character, that is, one's personality features.

(1) 在同学面前你别太任性!

(2) 任性的毛病对别人不好,对自己也不利。

rènyì 任意 →P395"任性"

用法 Usage:

副词 ad.

没有限制,没有约束,爱怎么样就怎么样。Having no restriction or limitation; doing things as one wishes.

(1) 希望有一天我能任意购买我喜欢的东西。

(2) 这几个题目中,你可以任意选一个。

形容词 a.

表示没有任何条件的。Unconditional.

(3) 电脑键盘上有一个任意键。

(4) 快看,要罚任意球了。

说明 Notes:

"任性"和"任意"都表示没有约束,没有限制。"任性" and "任意" both indicate the lack of restriction or limitation.

它们的区别是:They differ as follows:

1. "任性"着重于性情的放任。"任意"着重于随个人的意愿行事,比"任性"稍有点理性因素。"任性" emphasizes indulging oneself. "任意" emphasizes doing things as one wishes. It is slightly more rational than "任性."

2. "任性"是形容词,可以做谓语。"任意"是副词,只能修饰动词做状语。"任意"也有形容词用法,但是只能修饰名词,不能做谓语。"任性" is an adjective and can be used as a predicate. When used as an adverb, "任意" can only describe a verb. When used as an adjective, "任意" can only describe a noun and cannot serve as a predicate.

(5) *这孩子太任意了。

(6) 这孩子太任性了。

3. "任意"是书面语,口语中用得不多。"任意" is mostly used in written language and seldom used colloquially.

réng 仍 →P395"仍然"

用法 Usage:

副词 ad.

意义和用法跟"仍然"基本相同(详见"仍然")。多修饰单音节词,多用于书面语。The meaning and usage of "仍" are quite similar to those of "仍然" (see "仍然" for more detailed explanations). It is mostly used in written language to describe monosyllabic words.

(1) 他已经吃了两个星期的药,咳嗽仍不见好。

(2) 尽管我成绩很好,但爸妈总是对我说"仍要努力"。

réngjiù 仍旧 →P395"仍然"、P551"依旧"

用法 Usage:

副词 ad.

意义和用法跟"仍然"相同(详见"仍然")。The meaning and usage are the same as those of "仍然." (See "仍然" for more detailed explanations).

réngrán 仍然 →P395"仍"、P552"依然"

用法 Usage:

副词 ad.

1. 表示某种情况持续不变,有"继续、还是"的意思。"仍然"多用于表示转折的后一小句中,常常有"可是、但是、却"相呼应。Still. It is used to indicate the continuation of a situation. Similar to the meaning of "继续,还是," "仍然" is often used to signal a turn in the second clause, which usually corresponds with "可是,但是,却."

(1) 大家都睡了,只有他仍然开着灯在看书。

(2) 他虽然退休了,但仍然在公司当顾问。

2. 表示事情或情况曾一度中断或发生了变化,后来又恢复了原状。有"照样、照旧"的意思。*All the same; as before. It is used to indicate that an event or a situation returns to normal after an interruption or a change. It is similar to the meaning of* "照样,照旧."

(3) 他从美国回来后,仍然在研究所工作。

(4) 两年以后,他仍然来到中国学习历史。

说明 Notes:

"仍""仍旧""仍然"的意义和用法基本相同。*The meaning and usage of* "仍,""仍旧," *and* "仍然" *are quite similar.*

它们的区别是:*The differences are as follows:*

1. "仍"的书面色彩比"仍旧"和"仍然"浓一点。三个词多见于书面语,"仍旧"口语和书面语都用。*All three expressions are mostly used in written language.* "仍" *is slightly more literary than* "仍旧" *and* "仍然." "仍旧" *can be used in both colloquial and written language.*

2. "仍"多与单音节词结合使用,并且表示将来的情况时,跟有些单音节词连用,结合得很紧密,书面色彩较浓。这时"仍旧"和"仍然"不能替换。"仍" *is mostly used with monosyllabic words. When referring to a future situation,* "仍" *is closely connected to certain monosyllabic words. Such usage has a strong literary sense and* "仍" *cannot be replaced by* "仍旧" *or* "仍然."

(5) 聚会以后,我们的友谊仍当保持下去。

(6) 虽然已经通过了汉语水平考试六级,但我的汉语水平仍需继续提高。

rìyì 日益 →P615"越来越……"

用法 Usage:

副词 ad.

表示程度一天比一天(加深或提高),用于书面语。*Increasingly, indicating an increasing extent of change. It is used in written language.*

(1) 通过努力,大家的汉语水平正在日益提高。

(2) 住院后,爷爷的身体状况日益转好。

说明 Notes:

1. "日益"一般用于客观的叙述,在句子中常表示结果性的语义,所以常常有上下句的语境表示。上句常常表示下句有这个结果的原因,如:例(1)的上句"通过努力"是原因,"汉语水平正在日益提高"是结果。例(2)的上句"住院后",可以推测出是原因,"爷爷的身体状况日益转好"是结果。因为是客观情况的叙述,所以在句子末尾,一般不加"了"。*Normally used for objective statements,* "日益" *often indicates the result in a sentence with two clauses. The first clause explains the reason and the second clause shows the result. In Example (1),* "通过努力" *is the reason and* "汉语水平正在日益提高" *is the result. In Example (2), the inferred reason of* "住院后" *is the treatment at the hospital, and* "爷爷的身体状况日益转好" *is the result.* "了" *is normally not used at the end of the sentence because the sentence is an objective statement.*

2. "日益"修饰的动词或形容词多为双音节词语或短语,如"增加、改善、增多、繁荣、壮大、成熟、激烈和尖锐、完善和提高"等,一般不修饰单音节词。"日益" *normally describes disyllabic verbs or adjectives such as* "增加,改善,增多,繁荣,壮大,成熟,激烈和尖锐,完善和提高." *It is usually not used to describe monosyllabic words.*

rìzi 日子 →P412"生活"

用法 Usage:

名词 n.

1. 日期,表示这一天或那一天。*A day (this day or that day).*

(1) 发奖学金的日子最让人高兴了。

(2) 今天是你结婚的大喜日子,祝你新婚快乐!

2. 时间,指天数(这些天或那些天)。*The number of days (these days or those days).*

(3) 我常常想起暑假在海边度过的那些日子。

(4) 我住院的这些日子,妈妈每天都给我打电话。

3. 指生活。*Life.*

(5) 现在我们家的日子比以前好多了。

(6) 结婚后他们过着幸福的日子。

róngxǔ 容许 →P616"允许"

用法 Usage:

动词 *v.*

表示许可,允许。*To permit; to allow.*

(1) 在讨论的时候,要容许别人说跟你不同的意见。

(2) 上中学的时候,妈妈不容许我晚上十点以后回家。

róngyì 容易 →P378"轻易"

用法 Usage:

形容词 *a.*

1. 做起来不费事的,不难,简便。*Easy to do; convenient.*

(1) 很多事情是说说容易做起来难。

(2) 这本小说很容易读。

2. 发生或出现某种情况的可能性大。*Having high probability of occurrence.*

(3) 秋冬是容易感冒的季节。

(4) "未"和"末"这两个字很容易看错。

说明 Notes:

"容易"跟"轻易"都有简便、不费力的意思。"容易" and "轻易" can both mean "convenient" or "doing something with little effort."

它们的区别是: *The differences are as follows:*

1. "容易"的语义重在表示某件事本身实践过程中难度的大小。"轻易"则重在表示行动者做某件事能力的大小。"容易" emphasizes the level of difficulty in the execution of an action. "轻易," however, emphasizes the ability of the person who carries out the action.

(5) 跳过一米五十的高度很容易。

(6) 他轻易地跳过了二米的高度。

2. "容易"是形容词,可以做谓语;"轻易"一般不做谓语。*As an adjective,* "容易" *can serve as a predicate, while* "轻易" *cannot serve as a predicate.*

3. "轻易"有随随便便、轻率的意思。"容易"没有。"轻易" *can mean* "careless" *or* "hasty." "容易" *has no such meaning.*

4. "轻易"书面语色彩较重。"容易"多用在口语。"轻易" *is normally used in written language.* "容易" *is often used in colloquial language.*

rú 如 →P398"如果"

用法 Usage:

动词 *v.*

1. 表示顺从(某种心愿)的意思,可带"了",一定要带宾语,宾语只限于"愿、意"等词语。*To fulfill one's wish. It may be used with* "了" *and has to be followed by an object such as* "愿,意."

(1) 今年能来中国学汉语,是如他的愿了。

(2) 万事如意,实际上是不太可能的。

2. 像,如同。一定要带宾语: *To be similar to. It has to be followed by an object.*

① 常常用于熟语。*Often used in fixed expressions.*

(3) 他数十年如一日地学习外语,已经学会七门外语了。

(4) 湖水平静如镜。

② 如+……的+那样/那么+形。前面可用"不"否定。用"那样"时,后面形容词可以省略。*In the pattern,* "如+...的+那样/那么+a." *It can be negated with* "不." *When used with* "那样," *the adjective may be omitted.*

(5) 他的身体并不如你们所说的那么差。

(6) 情况并不如我们所想的那样。

③ 书面语中还可组成"如……所……"等格式,常用于公文、文件等。*The pattern of "如... 所..." is often used in official documents.*

(7) 如上所述,我们的进步是很大的。

3. 表示及、比得上的意思,只用于比较句的否定句: *To be equal to, only used in negative comparative sentences.*

① 两种事物比较,后面不说明比较的事项(如性质、数量等)。*Comparison of two things with no details of the comparison (e.g. quality, quantity).*

(8) 他们家的狗不如我们家的。

(9) 坐公共汽车去不如走路去。

② 两种事物比较,后面说出比较的项目。有时比较项目也可以说在前面。*Comparison of two things with details of the comparison at the beginning or the end of the sentence.*

(10) 这个教室不如那个教室大。

(11) 说到聪明,姐姐不如妹妹。

③ 同一事物,不同时期的比较。*Comparison of the same thing at different times.*

(12) 现在他的身体不如以前了。

(13) 平时旅游的人不如周末旅游的人多。

④ 在程度补语句中,"不如"可以用在前面,也可以用在后面。*In a sentence with the complement of degree, "不如" can be used before or after the verb.*

(14) 这张照片不如那张照得好。

(15) 这张照片照得不如那张好。

⑤ 与"连"配合,把"不如"后面的宾语提前。*The object after "不如" may be placed in front of it when used with "连."*

(16) 我的成绩连他的都不如。

(17) 我妈妈说,我小时候走路连他那样都不如。

4. 用于举例,相当于"例如"。*Used to provide an example. It is the same as "例如."*

(18) 中国有很多旅游城市,如北京、陕西西安、云南丽江、广西桂林、安徽黄山等。

介词 *prep.*

1. 适合,按,依照。与其他的词或词语构成介词短语,用在动词前作状语。如:"如约、如期、如愿、如数"等。*According to; in according with. It can form a prepositional phrase with other words or phrases, and is used as an adverbial before a verb. For example,* "如约、如期、如愿、如数."

(19) 工程将如期完成。

2. 常在单音节形容词后面,用于比较,表示超过。*Often used after monosyllabic adjectives to make a comparison, indicating that something becomes better or stronger with the passage of time.*

(20) 我的口语一天好如一天。

连词 *conj.*

相当于如果。*If, same as* "如果."

(21) 你如不去,就让别人去了。

(22) 如再迟到,老师要批评你了。

rúguǒ 如果 →P212"即使"、P397"如"、P544"要是"

用法 Usage:

连词 *conj.*

表示假设。*If. It is used to indicate a hypothesis.*

1. 用于表示假设复句中的偏句,引出假设性的前提、条件或情况。正句是根据这一假设推断出的结论、结果、情况或提出的问题。在正句中常有"就、那、那么、则、便"等词语与之呼应。"如果"的末尾可以带助词"……的话",组成"如果……的话",加强假设语气。"如果"也可以省略。*It is used to introduce a hypothetical premise, condition or situation in a subordinate clause of a complex sentence. The main clause is the conclusion, result, situation or question deduced from the hypothesis. It often corresponds with* "就, 那, 那么, 则, 便" *in the main clause. It can be used with* "…的话" *(*"如果…的话"*) to enhance the hypothetical*

tone. "如果" may be omitted.

(1) 如果你学,那么我也学。
(2) 如果天下雨的话,我们就不去你家了。
(3) 她不同意的话,那我们怎么办?

2. 偏句引出假设,正句对假设的内容给以评论或判断。正句里常用"这、那"复指偏句中所说的内容。The subordinate clause introduces the hypothesis, the content of which is judged or evaluated in the main clause. "这" or "那" is often used in the main clause to refer back to what is mentioned in the subordinate clause.

(4) 如果你看了这本书很高兴,那就是说,这是一本让人快乐的书。
(5) 如果认为天下雨他就不运动,那你就错了。

3. "如果"说明一种事实或做出一种判断,或引出一种比喻、对比或衬托,作为对正句进行论证的依据,加强正句的说服力。偏句常常用"如果说、如果……的话"的格式,正句常用"那么"相呼应。有"如果"的偏句不能在后面。"如果" can illustrate a fact or make a judgment. It can also introduce a metaphor, a comparison or contrast as the basis of a more convincing argument in the main clause. The subordinate clause often takes the form of "如果说,如果...的话," which corresponds with "那么" in the main clause. The subordinate clause with "如果" should be placed in front of the main clause.

(6) 如果说不是你每天陪我走路,那么我的脚不会好得这样快。
(7) 如果只在教室里学汉语的话,那么他对中国的了解就不会这么多。

说明 Notes:

1. 为了突出或强调正句,正句可以放在偏句前面。偏句在前,"如果"可以省略。偏句在后,"如果"就不能省略。The main clause can be placed in front of the subordinate clause for emphasis. "如果" may be omitted if the subordinate clause goes first. Otherwise it cannot be omitted.

(8) 没有空气、阳光和水,生命就不能存在。
(9) 生命不能存在,如果没有空气、阳光和水。

2. "如果"和"如"表示假设时,用法相同。When introducing a hypothesis, "如果" and "如" have similar usage.

它们的区别是：Their differences are as follows:

① "如果"没有"如"的动词用法。"如" can be used as a verb, but "如果" cannot be used as a verb.

② "如"没有"如果"的第二种用法。"如" does not have the second usage of "如果".

3. "如果"和"即使"都是连词,都有表示假设的意思。Both "如果" and "即使" are conjunctions indicating a supposition.

它们的区别是：Their differences are as follows:

① "即使"更加强调、证实正句的意思。"如果"则表示一般的可能性的假设。"即使" emphasizes and confirms what is said. "如果," by contrast, indicates an ordinary possibility.

(10) 即使下雨,我们也要去黄山。
(11) 如果不下雨,我们就去黄山。

② 带"即使"的句子与正句之间显示出转折的语义。带"如果"的句子则没有。The use of "即使" indicates an apparent turn from what is said. But the use of "如果" doesn't.

sǎn 散

用法 Usage:

动词 v.

松散，分散。*To loosen or scatter.*

(1) 刚才跑得太快，鞋带都散了。

(2) 公司快要倒闭了，人心都散了。

形容词 a.

零碎的，不集中的。*Fragmentary; loose or scattered.*

(3) 这种糖，袋装的比较贵，散装的便宜些。

(4) 有的少数民族集中居住在一个地区，有的少数民族则散居各地。

sàn 散

用法 Usage:

动词 v.

1. 指聚集在一起的人或物分开（跟"聚"相对）。*To separate people or objects; to disperse. It is opposite to "聚."*

(1) 太阳出来，白雾就散开了。

(2) 孩子们跑着、跑着，就散到操场的各个角落去了。

2. 分发，分给，散发。*To distribute; to send out.*

(3) 你听说过"天女散花"的故事吗？

(4) 我要去中国朋友那里散发调查表，写论文要用到。

3. 排遣，排除。常说"散散心"，指排除烦闷，使心情舒畅。可以重叠。*To dispel; to relieve; to get rid of. It can be used in a reduplicated form as "散散," as in "散散心," which means "to relieve one's boredom" or "to free one from anxiety."*

(5) 出去散散心吧，不要在家里想那些不高兴的事儿。

(6) 这几天你老是不讲话。走！到外边去散散闷儿吧。

sè 色

用法 Usage:

名词 n.

1. 颜色，色彩。*Color.*

(1) 她喜欢穿白色的毛衣。

(2) 春天到了，植物园里的花儿五颜六色的，漂亮极了。

2. 脸上表现出的神情，样子。*Countenance, the expression on the face.*

(3) 他的脸色很不好，生病了吧？

(4) 小女孩的脸上露出了害怕的神色。

3. 情景，景象，景色。*Scene; landscape; view.*

(5) 今晚夜色这么美，我们出去散散步吧。

(6) 湖面上的水色太美了！

4. 种类，品种。*Kind; sort; description.*

(7) 街上有各色点心，都很好吃。

5. 指妇女美貌。*Women's good looks.*

(8) 女模特色艺双绝，表演很有精神。

6. 情欲。*Sexual passion; lust.*

(9) 这些黄色书刊要赶快处理。

(10) 因为贪色，他的身体越来越差了。

sècǎi 色彩 →P57"彩色"、P535"颜色"

用法 Usage:

名词 n.

1. 颜色。Color.

(1) 你为什么不穿色彩漂亮点儿的衣服?

(2) 这幅画的色彩明亮,令人赏心悦目。

2. 比喻人的某种思想倾向或事物的某种情调,如:"感情色彩、时代色彩、地方色彩、政治色彩"等。A figure of speech about a person's ideological tendency and a thing's taste or appeal as in "感情色彩(emotional taste),时代色彩(a taste of the times),地方色彩(local color),政治色彩(political color)."

说明 Notes:

"色彩"和"彩色"都表示颜色的名词。Both "色彩" and "彩色" are nouns with the meaning of color.

它们的区别是:Their differences are as follows:

1. "色彩"可以指各种颜色,也可以指一种颜色,"彩色"只指多种颜色。"色彩" may refer to different kinds of color or just one color. "彩色," however, refers only to different kinds of color.

(3) *这种蓝,彩色鲜亮。

(4) 这种蓝,色彩鲜亮。

2. "色彩"有比喻用法。"彩色"不能这样用。"色彩" can be used figuratively, but "彩色" cannot.

(5) *小说的语言很有地方彩色,你看着、看着就觉得自己在北京。

(6) 小说的语言很有地方色彩,你看着、看着就觉得自己在北京。

shāng 伤

用法 Usage:

动词 v.

1. 损害,伤害。多用于人体或其他物体、人的精神或感情。To hurt, harm or damage, usually to human body or other objects, also to one's spirit or emotions.

(1) 他的脚伤了。

(2) 朋友之间千万别伤了感情。

2. 因过度而感到厌烦(多指饮食)。To be sick of something because of overeating (usually referring to food and drink).

(3) 我吃蛋糕吃伤过,现在看到蛋糕就想吐。

3. 悲哀,悲伤。To grieve; to feel sad or grievous.

(4) 你这样做会伤了妈妈的心。

(5) 小狗死了,弟弟伤心了好几天。

名词 n.

人体或其他物体受到的损害、损伤。The injury or damage to the body or other objects.

(6) 手上的伤已经好了。

(7) 在战争中,他受过很多次伤。

shānghài 伤害 →P448"损害"

用法 Usage:

动词 v.

使身体或思想感情受到损伤。To injure one's body or hurt one's feelings.

(1) 不要伤害那些流浪猫。

(2) 你可以不喜欢他,但不要伤害他的感情。

shāngchǎng 商场 →P421"市场"

用法 Usage:

名词 n.

1. 指商品比较齐全的大型综合商店。A large comprehensive store with a full range of goods.

(1) 百货商场的商品又多又好又便宜。

(2) 这家商场的服务是一流的。

2. 由一个或相连的几个建筑物内的各种商店、摊位所组成的市场。A market consisting of various shops and stalls in one or several connected buildings.

(3) 城西有一个文化用品商场,那里的书很便宜。

(4) 你能说说电子商场跟电子商店有什么不同吗？

shàng 上

用法 Usage:

动词 v.

1. 到，去(某个地方)，常以"上＋地名＋(去)"的形式出现。To go to (a place); to leave for, usually used in the form of "上＋地名＋(去)."

(1) 姐姐上超市去了。

(2) 你们打算上哪儿去？

2. 登上，爬上，由低处到高处。To ascend or climb up (from a lower position to a higher one); to board (a plane, a bus, etc.).

(3) 王老师，请您上四楼。

(4) 这会儿他已经上飞机了。

3. 按规定时间开始工作或学习等。To start work or study at a fixed time.

(5) 你白天上班，晚上还去上英语课，累吗？

(6) 你儿子每天几点上学？

4. 向上，向前进。To advance; to move upward.

(7) 五星红旗在国歌声中慢慢地上升。

(8) 他是个见困难就上的人。

5. 把食物端上桌子。To serve (food and drink); to bring the food onto the table.

(9) 客人到齐了吗？可以上菜了吗？

(10) 先上茶吧，大家都口渴了。

6. 出场。To come on the stage; to enter the court (for a game).

(11) 快看，演员上场了。

(12) 你看，5号运动员上了。

7. 登载。To publish (in newspapers or magazines); to be carried in a publication.

(13) 看，我们的照片上报了。

(14) 你设计的服装式样上广告了。

8. (趋向动词)用在动词后面，表示由低处向高处。To move upward (as a directional verb following a verb).

(15) 他爬上十楼，累得话都说不出来了。

(16) 他们二十分钟就登上了山顶。

9. (趋向动词)用在动词后面，表示达到目的。To achieve a goal (as a directional verb following a verb).

(17) 菜包子卖完了，我没吃上。

(18) 你们先走吧，我关上空调，锁上门就去。

10. (趋向动词)用在动词后面，表示开始并继续。To start doing something (as a directional verb following a verb).

(19) 你快坐下吧，大家已经喝上酒了。

(20) 他爱上了中国，就留在了北京工作。

名词 n.

1. (方位名词)位于高处的，常跟"下"相对配合一起用。(Position noun) a higher place or position. It usually coordinates with "下."

(21) 中年人上有父母，下有子女，要工作，要管家，很累。

(22) 她老是做上不着天、下不着地的美梦。

2. (方位名词)指等级高或质量好的。(Position noun) a higher grade, level or quality.

(23) 她的汉语在中上水平。

(24) 龙井茶叶是绿茶中的上品。

3. 表示时间或次序在前面的。(Of time or order) preceding; first.

(25) 上星期我们已经学完了第三课。

(26) 这套书有上、中、下三册。

说明 Notes:

1. "上"用在动词后面作趋向补语时，一般读轻声。When "上" is used as the directional complement after a verb, it is usually read without a stress.

2. 作为名词使用时的第三义项，要注意"时间名词"前的量词使用。时间名词是单音词，一般前面不加量词"个"，如："上周"，不说"上个周"。时间名词是双音节词，前面的量词"个"可加可不加，如："上(个)星期、上(个)季度"。As is shown in the third item where "上" is used as a noun, attention should be paid to the use of quantifiers before the temporal nouns. When the temporal nouns are

monosyllabic, the quantifier "个" is not supposed to be added. For example, "上周" should be used instead of "上个周." However, when the temporal noun is disyllabic, the quantifier "个" can either be added before the noun or be omitted. For instance, both "上星期" and "上个星期," "上季度" and "上个季度" are acceptable.

shàngdàng 上当

用法 Usage:

动词 v.

因受骗而吃亏。 To suffer a loss as a result of being deceived.

（1）今天我上当了，买来的西瓜不甜。
（2）他很容易相信别人，所以常常上当。

说明 Notes:

"上当"是离合动词。 "上当" is a separable verb.

1. "上当"后边不能再接宾语。 No objects should be used after "上当."

（3）＊我又上当他。
（4）我又上了他的当。

2. "上当"是离合动词，中间可以插入其他词语，如："上了当、上过当；上了一次当、上过坏人的当"等。 As "上当" is a separable verb, other words can be inserted into it. For example, "上了当, 上过当；上了一次当，上过坏人的当."

3. "上当"不能用在被字句和把字句，因为在被动句中，主语是受事者，是受骗的人。 "上当" cannot appear in a sentence where "被" or "把" is used because the subject of the sentence is the affected entity, namely, someone who is acted upon.

（5）＊我被他上当了。
（6）我上了他的当。
（7）我被他骗了。
（8）＊骗子没把我上当。
（9）我没上骗子的当。

（10）我没被骗子骗。

shànglái 上来

用法 Usage:

动词 v.

1. 开始，起头。 To begin; to start.

（1）老师一上来就让我们自我介绍。
（2）他一上来就很热情地帮我拿行李。

2. 表示动作朝着说话人所在的地方，由低处到高处，由一处到另一处。 To move towards the place where the speaker is located (from the lower place to the higher place or from one place to the other).

（3）电梯从二楼上来了。
（4）我看到她从楼下上来了。

3. 表示出现，必带施事宾语。 To appear (followed by an agent object).

（5）楼下上来了三个人。
（6）从乡下上来的弟弟很少说话。

4.（趋向动词）用在动词后，表示动作朝着说话人所在地，由低处到高处，由远处到近处。 (As a directional verb) used after the verb, it indicates an action that moves from a lower place to a higher place or from a place far away to where the speaker is located.

（7）我的早餐怎么还没送上来？
（8）饭可以端上来了。

5.（趋向动词）用在动词后，表示成功地完成某些动作。 (As a directional verb) used after the verb, it indicates that the action has been successfully done.

（9）这几句话我怎么也说不上来。
（10）那个行李袋很重，但我还是拿上来了。

shàngqù 上去

用法 Usage:

动词 v.

1. 表示动作离开说话人所在地，由低处向高处，或由近处向远处。 To move away from the place where the speaker is located (from the

lower place to the higher place or from the near to the far).

（1）那么高，没有电梯我怎么上去？

（2）大家都上去迎接他们了！

2. 带施事宾语，表示出现。To appear (followed by an agent object).

（3）后来上去了几个人帮着推车，车终于开走了。

（4）小狗上去了几步，但又跑了回来。

3. 中间嵌入处所名词，表示去向。To indicate a direction (with a location noun inserted between "上" and "去").

（5）师父上山去了。

（6）你们上哪儿去？

4.（趋向动词）用在动词后面，表示动作离开说话人所在地，由低处向高处，或由近处向远处，或由主体向对象。(As a directional verb) to indicate an action moving away from the speaker, from a lower place to ta higher place, from nearby to a place far away, or from the subject to the object.

（7）老人都爬上去了，你还爬不上去？

（8）我们把所有的力量都用上去了。

5.（趋向动词）用在动词后面，表示人或事物随动作由低层到高层。(As a directional verb) to indicate the direction of the movement of a person or a thing.

（9）同学们的意见已经反映上去了。

（10）你昨天的作业交上去了吗？

6.（趋向动词）用在动词后面，表示增添或合拢。(As a directional verb after the verb) to indicate addition or adhesion.

（11）明天要把画儿贴上去。

（12）书架上放满了书，这些书放不上去。

shàngshì 上市

用法 Usage:

动词 v.

1.（货物）开始在市场上出现并出售。(Goods) to begin to appear and sell on the market.

（1）今年的苹果上市了。

（2）这种手机，刚上市就卖完了。

2. 股票、债券、基金等金融产品经批准后，在证券交易所挂牌交易。(Stocks, bonds, funds and other financial products) to trade on the stock exchange after being reviewed for approval.

（3）今天又有三个新股上市。

（4）公司要上市，不是那么简单的事情。

shàngwǎng 上网

用法 Usage:

动词 v.

用手机或计算机进入互联网，在网络上进行信息查询、娱乐、社交等活动。To use a mobile phone or computer to surf the Internet to conduct information inquiries, entertainment, and social activities on a network.

（1）我现在可用手机上网了。

（2）我最喜欢上网购物。

说明 Notes:

1. "上网"与"下网"相对。"上网" is opposite to "下网."

2. "上网"和"网上"意思不一样。"上网"是"进入"网络的意思，是"动词＋名词"的离合动词。"网上"中的"上"是方位名词，由"(在)＋处所名词＋方位名词"构成，一般不独立使用。运用时注意区分。"上网" is different from "网上." "上网" is a separable verb in the structure of "v. ＋ n.," which means going online and becoming part of the Internet. However, "上" in "网上" is a directional noun used in the structure of "(在)＋ location noun ＋ direction noun." It cannot be used separately.

（3）我喜欢上网购物。

（4）我喜欢(在)网上购物。

（5）*我喜欢网上。

（6）我喜欢上网。

shang 上

用法 Usage:

名词 n.

作为方位名词的"上"，发音是轻声。When

"上" is used as a direction noun, it should be pronounced without a stress.

1. 用在名词后,以"名词+上"的结构出现,表示在物体的顶部或表面(与"下"相对)。When "上" follows a noun, as in the "n. +上" pattern, it indicates the surface or the top of an object, which is opposite to "下."

(1) 桌子上放着几本汉语书。
(2) 楼上住了一对老夫妻。

2. 用在名词后,以"名词+上"结构出现,表示在某个范围。When "上" follows a noun, as in the "n. +上" pattern, it indicates a certain field.

(3) 报纸上有什么新消息?
(4) 他在课堂上发言很积极。

3. 用在名词后,以"名词+上"的结构出现,表示某个方面。Again, when "上" follows a noun, as in the "n. +上" pattern, it may indicate a certain aspect.

(5) 他在学习上很愿意帮助别人。
(6) 在工作上,她的态度很认真。

4. 和某些表示人体部分的名词组合,表示某个部位,意思比较虚。When "上" goes with a noun that is part of a human body, it conveys a rather weak or abstract sense.

(7) 她嘴上说去,实际上不会去的。
(8) 你的事我一定放心上。

说明 Notes:

"名词+上"结构中,第一个义项和第二个义项要注意区分,应根据具体语境和上下文判断语义。In the "n. +上" pattern, the first item and the second item should be differentiated according to the semantic context.

(9) 报纸上放着一杯咖啡。(表示位置,与"下"相对 Indicating the location which is opposite to "下")
(10) 报纸上的娱乐新闻我一般都不看。(表示消息刊登的范围 Indicating the column where the news is carried)

shāokǎo 烧烤

用法 Usage:

动词 v.

用炭火烧或烤肉食品等。*To grill or roast meat with charcoal; to barbecue.*

(1) 羊肉,烧烤一下很好吃。
(2) 周末我们去烧烤,怎么样?

名词 n.

1. 用炭火烧制或烤制的肉食品。*The meat grilled or roasted on charcoal; barbecued meat.*

(3) 多吃烧烤对身体不利。
(4) 我不喜欢吃烧烤。

2. 指卖烤羊肉串等食品的摊贩。*A street peddler who sells mutton shashlik and other food.*

(5) 我们学校门口的烧烤,今天没来。
(6) 一到夏天,路边的烧烤就多了起来。

shāo 稍 →P406"稍微"

用法 Usage:

副词 ad.

表示程度轻微、数量不多或时间短暂。多修饰单音节词,主要用于书面语。*Slightly. It indicates a slight degree, a small amount or a short time. It often modifies monosyllabic words and is mainly used in written language.*

(1) 请稍候!
(2) 我的分数只是比你稍多了几分。

说明 Notes:

使用"稍"时要注意:*Attention should be paid to the following aspects while using "稍"*:

1. "稍"所修饰的动词和形容词后面,常常带有"一点儿、一些、一下、几"等,表述数量不多。*Verbs and adjectives modified by "稍" are often followed by words such as "一点儿,一些,一下,几" to indicate a small amount.*

(3) 你们先走,我稍晚几分钟再去。
(4) 那张画贴得稍高一点,更好看。

2. "稍"在否定句中,用在"不"或"没"前面。*In negative sentences,"稍" is used before "不" or"没."*

（5）这孩子真难带，稍没注意他就跑出去了。

（6）大雾天开车，稍不注意就会碰到前面的车子。

3. 在肯定句中，"稍"常与"有、作、见"等单音节词连用，再修饰双音节词语，或者"稍"重叠，并且常与"一点儿、一些、一下、几"等表示数量少的词语搭配使用。*In a positive sentence, "稍" is often used with monosyllabic words such as "有, 作, 见" to modify a disyllabic word. It is reduplicated as "稍稍" to go with words that indicate the small amount, such as "一点儿, 一些, 一下, 几."*

（7）最近房价稍降了一些。

（8）他的病情稍稍好了一点。

（9）＊这学期我的口语比上学期稍提高了。

（10）这学期我的口语比上学期稍有提高。

shāowēi 稍微 →P405"稍"

用法 Usage:

副词 ad.

表示程度不深、数量不多或时间不长。也作"稍为"，多用在口语中。*Slightly. Indicating a slight degree, a small amount or a short time, it can also be expressed as "稍为" in oral language.*

常见句式有："稍微" *is often used in the followings structures:*

1. "稍微＋动词"。动词常常重叠，或前面有副词"一"，或后面有"一点儿、一些、一下、一会儿"等。"稍微＋v." *The verb is often reduplicated; it is preceded by the adverb "一" or followed by words such as "一点儿, 一些, 一下, 一会儿."*

（1）这孩子睡觉不踏实，稍微一动就醒了。

（2）他稍微喝一点儿酒，脸就红。

2. "稍微＋形容词＋一点／一些／一下"。"稍微＋a.＋一点／一些／一下."

（3）你说得稍微快了一些，我听不大懂。

（4）这件衣服比那件稍微贵了一些。

3. "稍微＋不＋形容词／动词（短语）"。常与"注意、留神、小心"等词连用。"稍微＋不＋a./v. (phrase)." *It is always used with words such as "注意, 留神, 小心."*

（5）空调机挂得稍微不正就会影响功能。

（6）汉字稍微不注意就会写错。

说明 Notes:

"稍微"与"稍""稍稍"的意义一样。*"稍微" expresses the same meaning as "稍" or "稍稍."*

它们的区别是："稍"是书面语，主要跟单音节词搭配。"稍微""稍稍"用于口语，常与双音节词语搭配。*They differ as follows: "稍" is used in written language and mainly collocates with monosyllabic words, while "稍微" and "稍稍" are used in colloquial language and often collocate with disyllabic words.*

shěbudé 舍不得

用法 Usage:

动词 v.

1. 不忍离开。在句中作谓语，后面常带名词、动词（短语）做宾语。*To hate to part with. It is always used as the predicate in a sentence with a noun or a verb (phrase) as its object.*

（1）在这里学习生活了三年，真舍不得离开。

（2）分别时，说了很多话，就是舍不得说再见。

2. 不忍放弃或使用。*To hate to give up or use something because of an attachment one has developed for it.*

（3）这件衣服是她送我的，我一直舍不得穿。

（4）那些书是奶奶给我的，我舍不得给你。

3. 不忍批评、责罚。*To be unwilling to criticize or punish; can't bear doing something.*

（5）他是老师的宝贝学生，老师舍不得批评他。

(6)妈妈舍不得骂我,更舍不得打我。

说明 Notes:

1."舍不得"后面可以带名词做宾语,但带动词做宾语也很常见。"舍不得" can be followed by a noun as its object. However, it is more common to take a verb.

(7)我舍不得(离开)你们。

(8)小时候很舍不得花钱买东西。

2."舍不得"的肯定式是"舍得","舍得"没有"舍不得"用得多。"舍得"常用于问句或者对比句中。The positive form of "舍不得" is "舍得." "舍得" often appears in interrogative or contrastive sentences and is less frequently used as "舍不得."

(9)你舍得把这本书送给他吗?

(10)你舍得,我可舍不得。

(11)这条围巾给我,你舍不舍得?

shéi 谁

用法 Usage:

代词 pron.

1.用在一般疑问句里,表示问人。可以指一个人,也可以不止一个人。做主语、宾语。修饰名词多带"的"。Who. It is used in an interrogative sentence to ask about a person. It can either refer to one or more than one. It can be used as a subject or an object. When "谁" modifies a noun, "的" is used after it.

(1)谁是我们的汉语老师?

(2)这是谁的书?

2.用在反问句里,表示没有一个人,后面常与否定词"不、没有"搭配使用,表示句子肯定的意思。Who. It is used in a rhetorical question to indicate no one. It often goes with the negative word "不" or "没有" to express a positive meaning.

(3)谁不说他好?

(4)现在的年轻人,谁没有手机?

3.虚指某人。表示不能肯定的人,包括不知道的人,或者无须或无法说出姓名的人。Indicating someone the speaker is not certain about or doesn't know. Sometimes it is simply unnecessary or unable to give the name.

(5)今天没有谁给你买饭,你自己去食堂吃吧。

(6)有谁去书店?帮我买一本词典。

4.任指。表示任何人。有以下用法:It is used to refer to anybody. The usages are as follows:

① 用在"也、都"前面,表示所说的范围之内没有例外。It can be used before "也" or "都" to indicate no exception within a certain scope.

(7)他出国的消息谁也不知道。

(8)谁都说不出他叫什么名字,是哪国人。

② 主语和宾语都用谁,指不同的人,表示彼此一样。多用于否定句。It is used both as the subject and the object in the same sentence, indicating that they behave the same though they are different people. It appears in a negative sentence more frequently.

(9)两辆车谁也不肯让谁先走。

(10)他们夫妻俩谁也不用谁的钱。

③ 两个"谁"前后照应,同指任何一个人。It is used to refer to anybody. The two "谁" are used correlatively in the sentence to indicate the same person.

(11)谁先到谁就买票。

(12)谁做好了练习题谁就说。

说明 Notes:

"谁"还有一个读音是"shúi"。"谁" can also be pronounced as "shúi."

shēn 深

用法 Usage:

形容词 a.

1.与"浅"相对。表示从上到下的距离大,或从外到里的距离大。Deep, the opposite of "浅." It indicates the long distance from the surface to the bottom, or from the outside to the inside.

(1) 这个山洞有点儿深。
(2) 深海中的鱼类漂亮极了。

2. 与"浅"相对，表示颜色浓。*Deep or dark, the opposite of "浅." It indicates the strong degree of a color.*

(3) 深蓝色是我最喜欢的颜色。
(4) 这件衣服颜色有点儿深，我想要浅一点的。

3. 感情、情谊、关系、印象等深刻。*(Of feelings or impressions) deep; (of friendship or relationship) profound.*

(5) 只见了一面，她就给我留下了很深的印象。
(6) 他们的感情那么深，不会分手的。

4. 深奥，高深（跟"浅"相对）。*Profound or difficult, being opposite to "浅."*

(7) 这篇文章的内容太深，看不懂。

5. 深厚，密切。*(Of relationship) deep or close.*

(8) 他们的关系很深。

6. 离开始的时间很久。*Late; in the small hours.*

(9) 深夜了，你们还吵什么？

副词 *ad.*

很，非常。如："深得人心、深信不疑"等。*Very much; deeply; greatly. For example, "深得人心，深信不疑."*

说明 Notes：

1. "深"可以重叠为"深深"，强调距离大，程度强烈。*"深" can be reduplicated as "深深" to emphasize a long distance or strong degree.*

(10) 他陷入了深深的痛苦中。
(11) 他深深地吸了一口气，又深深地叹出一口气。

2. "深"和"高""长"容易用错。注意词义的区别是："深"的原义表示从地表面向下的垂直空间距离大，或者从外向内的距离大，隐喻义可表示颜色、时间、情感等。"高"原义表示从地表面向上的垂直空间距离大。"长"则表示横向的长度，强调两端的距离。*It is easy to confuse "深" with "高" and "长." Attention should be paid to the differences between their meanings. The original meaning of "深" is the vertical distance from the surface to the bottom, or the distance from the outside to the inside. It can be used metaphorically to refer to the degree of color, the length of time or the depth of emotion. The original meaning of "高" is the vertical distance from the ground up to the top. "长" refers to the lateral length, emphasizing the distance between the two ends.*

(12) 树高是因为根深啊。
(13) 这棵柳树真高啊。
(14) 柳枝好长啊。

shēnhuà 深化 →P408"深入"

用法 Usage：
动词 *v.*

程度不断加深，向更高、更新的阶段发展。*To deepen; to go deeper; to develop into a higher or newer stage.*

(1) 他们的矛盾深化了。
(2) 我们国家正在深化改革，扩大开放。

说明 Notes：

"深化"表示程度的加深，搭配的词语一般是"改革、矛盾、认识、主题"等可以扩大范围程度的抽象名词。这些抽象名词可以做主语，如例(1)，也可以做宾语，如例(2)。*"深化" means going deeper. It generally collocates with abstract nouns that show the expansion of the scope, such as "改革，矛盾，认识，主题." These abstract nouns can either act as the subject as in (1), or act as the object as in (2).*

shēnrù 深入 →P408"深化"

用法 Usage：
动词 *v.*

透过外部，进入事物内部或中心。很少单独做谓语，常带宾语。*To go deep into, to enter somewhere from the outside to the interior or center of it. It seldom acts as a predicate by* itself, but it often takes an object.

(1) 深入实际，才能了解真实情况。

(2) 只有深入群众，才能很好服务群众。

形容词 a.

深刻,透彻。Profound and thorough.

(3) 我们要对这些材料进行深入的分析、研究。

(4) 经过深入的调查，终于清楚了事情的真相。

(5) 做一个好老师，首先要深入了解学生的需求。

说明 Notes:

"深化"和"深入"都有深一步的意思。Both "深化" and "深入" carry the idea of "going deeper".

它们的区别是：Their differences are as follows:

1."深化"侧重事物发展的程度、范围。"深入"侧重发展到事物的内部或中心。"深化" emphasizes the degree or scope of the development, while "深入" emphasizes entering somewhere from the outside to the interior or center — sometimes figuratively.

2."深化"搭配的词语一般是可以扩大范围程度的抽象名词，如："改革、矛盾、认识、主题"等。"深入"搭配的词语一般是词义比较具体的实体名词或动词，如："人心、基层、群众"等名词，"调查、研究、分析"等动词。"深化" always collocates with abstract nouns that show the expansion of the scope, such as "改革,矛盾,认识,主题." "深入," by contrast, collocates with concrete nouns such as "人心,基层,群众," or verbs such as "调查,研究,分析," all with a more specific meaning.

3."深入"有形容词用法。"深化"没有。"深入" can be used as an adjective while "深入" cannot.

shénme 什么

用法 Usage:

代词 pron.

1.表示疑问。What. It is used to ask a question.

句式有：The sentence patterns are as follows:

① 单用,问事物。Used alone to ask about something.

(1) 这是什么？

(2) 什么叫小说？

② 用在名词前面,问人或事物。Used before a noun to ask about somebody or something.

(3) 他是什么人？

(4) 什么动物能生活在陆地,又能生活在水里？

2.虚指,表示不确定的事物,一般用在肯定句。Something. It is used as an indefinite denotation, referring to an indeterminate thing, usually used in an affirmative sentence.

(5) 和我一起去商店吧,我想买点儿什么。

(6) 他好像在写什么。

3.用在名词前,表示否定。Nothing. It is used before a noun to express a negative meaning.

(7) 他是什么东西！

(8) 今天就要交练习本,你还有什么时间做作业？

4.表示任指。Anything. It is used to refer to something arbitrarily.

句式有：The sentence patterns are as follows:

① 用在"也、都"前面,表示所说的范围之内没有例外。Used before "也,都" to mean that there is no exception within the field mentioned.

(9) 他什么也不会。

(10) 只要认真学,什么都能学会。

② 两个"什么"前后照应,表示由前者决定后者。The two "什么" used correlatively to indicate that the former determines the latter.

(11) 你吃什么我也吃什么。

(12) 你想说什么就说什么吧。

5.引述别人的话,前面加"什么",表示不同意。"什么" is placed before what someone else has just said to show disagreement or disapproval.

（13）什么学不会，就是不想努力嘛。

（14）什么做不好菜，只是懒得不想做。

6. "什么"前加"有"，后面带形容词，表示并不如此。With "有" before "什么" and an adjective after it to show that it is not the case.

（15）她有什么漂亮，比她漂亮的女孩多着呢。

（16）想多赚钱有什么不好，只要不损害别人的利益。

7. 用在几个并列成分前，表示列举不尽。Used before several juxtaposed constituents to indicate that the enumeration is not limited to those listed.

（17）什么唱唱跳跳啊，写写画画啊，都是老人喜欢的活动。

（18）什么桌子啦，椅子啦，都是他出钱买的。

8. 单独使用，表示惊讶。What, used separately to express a surprise.

（19）什么！他不愿意！

（20）什么！你到现在还没吃饭！

说明 Notes：

1. "他是什么人？"和"他是谁？"语气不一样。前句是不客气的问话，后者是一般问话，不带感情色彩。"他是什么人？" and "他是谁？" are different in tone. The former is an impolite question, while the latter is a general interrogation without any emotional color.

2. "他是什么东西？"句中"什么东西"是骂人，不是指事物。"什么东西" in the sentence "他是什么东西？" doesn't refer to something. Instead, it's a curse.

shénmeyàng 什么样

用法 Usage：

代词 pron.

疑问代词。表示什么模样的，什么样子的。Used as an interrogative pronoun to inquire about what it looks like.

（1）他到底是个什么样的人，这么神秘？

（2）未来二十年，手机会是什么样的状况？

说明 Notes：

1. "什么样"做疑问代词时，一般以"什么样＋的＋名词"形式出现，如："什么样的人、什么样的城市、什么样的教育、什么样的工作"等。也有单独做谓语的情况，但出现频率不高，如"未来世界究竟什么样"等。When "什么样" is used as an interrogative pronoun, it is generally used in the pattern of "什么样＋的＋n." such as "什么样的人，什么样的城市，什么样的教育，什么样的工作." Meanwhile, it can occasionally be used as a predicate by itself, such as "未来世界究竟什么样."

2. "什么样"的用法一般有以下几种："什么样" can be used in the following ways:

① 最常见的是表示一般疑问。The most common usage is to raise a general question.

（3）你到底要找什么样的工作？

② 表示非疑问的任指。Used as a non-interrogative reference.

（4）你这么聪明，什么样的工作都能找到。

③ 表示非疑问的虚指。Used as a non-interrogative indefinite denotation.

（5）今天我们吃什么样的点心呢？

④ 表示否定。Used as a negation.

（6）像他这么懒的人能找到什么样的工作？

shénmì 神秘 →P410"神奇"

用法 Usage：

形容词 a.

难以捉摸的，高深莫测的。Mysterious, too profound to be understood.

（1）我终于进入了神秘的金字塔内部。

（2）听说飞碟又神秘地出现了。

shénqí 神奇 →P410"神秘"

用法 Usage：

形容词 a.

不寻常的，不普通的，奇特的。Unusual;

uncommon; extraordinary.

（1）这个魔术太神奇了！
（2）北极光是一种神奇的自然现象。

说明 Notes:

"神秘"和"神奇"有共同的语素"神"，表示不可思议的，神妙的。Both "神秘" and "神奇" have the morpheme "神," which indicates something uncommon and miraculous.

它们的区别是："神秘"的"秘"即"秘密"，强调不为人知的，不可捉摸的。"神奇"的"奇"则强调奇特的，不寻常的。Their differences are as follows: "秘" in "神秘" refers to the secret which emphasizes something unknown and subtle, while "奇" in "神奇" refers to something uncommon and extraordinary.

（3）她真是个神奇的女人！（强调这个女人不同寻常 Emphasizing that the woman is uncommon）

（4）她真是个神秘的女人！（强调这个女人很难了解、琢磨 Emphasizing that the woman is inscrutable）

shènzhì 甚至

用法 Usage:

副词 ad.

表示强调，后面常用"也、都"或"连……也/都……"呼应。Even; so much so that. It is used to emphasize something and is always followed by "也, 都" or "连…也/都…."

（1）这种语法现象甚至连我的中国朋友也讲不清楚。
（2）露天音乐会的人太多了，甚至连站的地方都没有。

连词 conj.

1. 用在并列的名词、形容词、动词、介词短语最后一项的前面，表示后面所提出的是进一步的，更突出的事例。可与"都"或"也"搭配使用。Placed before the last of a string of nouns, adjectives, verbs, and prepositional phrases to highlight it as a further, or more prominent example. It can collocate with "都" or "也."

（3）这支歌太流行了，年轻人、孩子，甚至老年人都会唱。
（4）为了一点儿小事俩人争了起来、吵了起来，甚至打了起来。

2. 连接分句时，如果后一分句有主语，"甚至"可以用在主语前，也可以用在主语后。有时前一分句可以用"不但、不仅"，与后一分句的"甚至"呼应，表示明显的递进关系。When used to connect clauses, "甚至" can be placed either before or after the subject if the latter clause has a subject. Sometimes "不但" or "不仅" can be used in the former clause to echo with "甚至" in the latter clause, which indicates a clear progressive relationship.

（5）冬天，他不但在南方的湖里游泳，甚至也去北方的湖里游泳。
（6）他的听力很好，新闻广播甚至也能听懂。
（7）他的听力很好，甚至新闻广播也能听懂。

说明 Notes:

1. "甚至"也可以说成"甚而、甚至于"等。"甚至" can also be expressed as "甚而, 甚至于."

2. "甚至"用作连词时，常以"A, 甚至B"的格式出现。可以是单句，如例（3）（4）；也可以是复句，如例（5）（6）。不论单句还是复句，前后句子里所描述的事物的性质是同一层面的，"甚至"则强调更进一步、更突出的情况。如例（7）。When "甚至" is used as a conjunction, it is often used in the structure of "A, 甚至B." It can be used in simple sentences, as is shown in (3) and (4). It can also be used in clauses as in (5) and (6). In both cases, the things described are of the same nature. "甚至" emphasizes a further and more prominent situation as in (7).

shēng 生

用法 Usage:

动词 v.

1. 生育。To give birth to.

(1) 我姐姐生了个小女孩儿。

2. 出生。To be born (usually followed by a word indicating a place or time).

(2) 他生于1970年。

(3) 我生在一个海边的小城市。

3. 产生,发生。To produce, generate or develop.

(4) 她生病住院了。

(5) 护照从三月一日开始生效。

4. 生长。To grow.

(6) 种子生根发芽了。

5. 生存,活着(与"死"相对)。To live or to be alive, opposite to "死."

(7) 经过九死一生,现在他很珍惜生命了。

(8) 他俩同生死、共患难,是一对永不分离的好朋友。

6. 使柴、煤、天然气等燃烧。To make a fire (by using wood, coal, natural gas, etc.)

(9) 快生火做饭!

形容词 *a.*

1. 没长成熟的水果(与"熟"相对)。(Of fruits) unripe opposite to "熟 (ripe)."

(10) 这西瓜还生,不能吃。

(11) 香蕉生的时候就摘下来了。

2. 没煮熟,没经过烹饪的(与"熟"相对)。Raw; uncooked or undercooked, opposite to "熟 (cooked)."

(12) 你能区分出生鸡蛋和熟鸡蛋吗?

(13) 我特别喜欢吃生鱼片。

3. 生疏的,陌生的(与"熟、熟悉"相对)。Unfamiliar or unacquainted, opposite to "熟 (familiar)" or "熟悉 (acquainted)."

(14) 我刚到这儿,人生地不熟的,请大家多多关照。

(15) 都说"一回生,二回熟"嘛!

4. 生疏的,不熟悉的。Unfamiliar or new.

(16) 这课文生词太多了。

名词 *n.*

1. 学习的人,如:"学生、师生、毕业生、博士生"等。A student, for example, "学生,师生,毕业生,博士生."

2. 生平。One's Life.

(17) 他的前半生是在农村度过的。

(18) 老师的教育,我终生受用。

3. 传统戏剧中扮演男性人物的角色称呼之一,如:"老生、小生、武生"等。One of the male roles in traditional Chinese opera, for example, "老生,小生,武生."

4. 某些指身份的称呼,如:"医生、实习生"等。An identifying word for certain professions, for example, "医生,实习生."

---

shēnghuó 生活 →P396"日子"

用法 Usage:

名词 *n.*

1 人在衣食住行等方面的境况。One's livelihood in terms of food, clothing, shelters and other necessities.

(1) 我的家人都很关心我在国外的生活。

(2) 山区人民的生活水平有了很大的提高。

2. 人或生物为了生存和发展而进行的活动。Activities that people or creatures engage in to survive and develop.

(3) 生活的道路上总会有各种各样的困难。

(4) 在中国留学的生活怎么样?

动词 *v.*

为生存、发展而进行各种活动,生存,活着。To perform all kinds of activities for survival and development.

(5) 我们生活在一个高科技时代。

(6) 谁脱离了社会都无法生活下去。

说明 Notes:

"生活"和"日子"做名词,都表示人的衣食住行等生计的意思。"生活" and "日子" are both used as a noun to mean a person's livelihood in terms of food, clothing, shelter and other necessities.

它们的区别是:They differ as follows:

1."生活"有动词用法。"日子"只有名词用法。"生活" can also be used as a verb while

"日子" can only be used as a noun.

2."日子"一般只作句子的主语和宾语,只与动词"过"搭配使用。"生活"能做主语、定语和宾语,词语搭配范围比较广,可以受"享受、热爱、观察、深入、接触、体验、物质、精神、个人、家庭、集体、快乐的、幸福的、简单的"等词语的支配或修饰,同时也能修饰"质量、习惯、方式、水平"等词语,做它们的定语。"日子" can only be used as the subject or the object of a sentence and can only collocate with the verb "过," while "生活" can be used as a subject, an attributive and an object and it covers a wider range in collocation. For example, it can be modified by such words as "享受,热爱,观察,深入,接触,体验;物质,精神,个人,家庭,集体;快乐的,幸福的,简单的." In addition, "生活" can be used as an attributive to modify words such as "质量,习惯,方式,水平."

shīfu 师父 →P413"师傅"

用法 Usage:

名词 n.

1.以前泛指从事教学工作的老师,现在一般是武术、戏剧等传统领域内对老师的尊称。Formerly it refers to any teacher engaged in teaching and now it is generally a respectful form of address for a master in the traditional fields of martial arts, drama, etc.

(1)要想学京剧,先得拜师父。

(2)这个师父的功夫很厉害。

2.用于对僧侣、道士、尼姑等出家人的尊称。A respectful form of address for a monk, a Taoist or a nun.

(3)《西游记》讲的是唐僧师父带着三个徒弟上西天取经的故事。

shīfu 师傅 →P413"师父"

用法 Usage:

名词 n.

1.对从事某些行业的人的尊称(包括女性)。A respectful form of address for a person, both male and female, engaged in a certain profession.

① 从事修理、安装或其他具有技术特长行业的技工,习惯上被称为师傅。A mechanic who is engaged in the maintenance and installation of equipment or other related jobs is traditionally called a "师傅."

(1)师傅,我们家的空调又坏了,麻烦您给看看。

(2)师傅,麻烦给我的自行车修一修。

② 厨师、司机等,习惯上也被称为师傅(包括女性)。Chefs, drivers, etc. both males or females, are traditionally known as "师傅."

(3)师傅(司机),我要去杭州大剧院。

(4)师傅(厨师),你做的菜味道真不错!

2.徒弟对传授技艺的老师的尊称(包括女性)。The respectful address of an apprentice for a teacher, both male and female, who teaches skills.

(5)她是我师傅,对我要求很严格。

(6)师傅教了我十年手艺,对我像对自己的孩子一样。

3.对一般人,特别是中年以上男人的称呼。A name for anyone, especially a man above a middle age.

(7)师傅,请问一下,前边有超市吗?

说明 Notes:

"师傅"和"师父"的含义基本相同,但在使用过程中,用法逐渐发生了变化。"师傅" and "师父" have basically the same meaning. However, the usage has changed gradually in the process of use.

1."师父"可用于对僧侣、道士、尼姑等出家人的尊称。"师傅"一般不能用。"师父" can be used as a respectful form of address for a monk, a Taoist, or a nun, but "师傅" can't.

2."师傅"的以下义项,一般不能用"师父"替换: In the following sentences, "师傅" cannot be replaced by "师父":

① 对从事某些行业的人的尊称(包括女性)：从事修理、安装或其他具有技术特长行业的技工,或者厨师、司机等"师傅"的称呼。When "师傅" means a mechanic, who is engaged in the maintenance and installation of equipment or other related jobs, or a chef in a kitchen, or a driver.

② 对一般人,特别是中年以上男人等"师傅"的称呼。When "师傅" means anyone, especially a male above the middle age.

3. 表示从事教学、传授技艺的老师时,"师傅""师父"二者有混用情况,但"师父"更常在戏曲、武术等领域中使用。When it refers to a teacher or someone engaged in teaching skills, "师傅" and "师父" can be used interchangeably, but "师父" is more frequently used in the fields of drama, martial arts, etc.

shífēn 十分 →P147"非常"

用法 Usage:
副词 ad.

相似于"非常、很、极其"等程度副词。一般用来修饰形容词或心理动词,强调状态或程度高、强烈。Very much. Like degree adverbs such as "非常,很,极其," "十分" is generally used to modify adjectives or verbs indicating a mental attitude, emphasizing a high or strong state or degree.

(1) 十分感谢您的帮助!
(2) 我十分热爱教师这个职业。

说明 Notes:

1. 从文化含义上说,"十分"表示"多"和"满"的意思,象征"完美"和"圆满"。因此,"十分"表示很高的程度。In terms of cultural connotation, "十分" implies "多" and "满," which symbolizes "完美" and "圆满." Therefore, "十分" indicates a very high degree.

2. "十分"和"非常"都是副词,常修饰形容词或表示心理活动的动词,说明状态、程度不同寻常。"十分" and "非常" are both adverbs, which are often used to modify adjectives or verbs indicating a mental attitude, showing an unusual state or degree.

它们的区别是：Their differences are as follows:

① "非常"着重于程度之高,非寻常可比。"十分"着重于到了充分的程度。"非常" emphasizes a high and extraordinary degree while "十分" focuses on the full extent.

② "非常"可以重叠起来用,如："非常非常美"。"十分"不能。"非常" can be reduplicated as "非常非常" as in "非常非常美," while "十分" can't.

③ "十分"前面可以用"不"修饰,如"不十分好",表示程度不高。"非常"不能用"不"修饰,其否定形式只能是"非常不好"。"十分" can be modified by "不" such as "不十分好," which indicates that the degree is not high. However, "非常" can't be modified by "不" and its negative form can only be "非常不好."

④ "非常"后面可以带"之、地"。"十分"不能。"非常" can be followed by such words as "之" and "地," while "十分" can't.

(3) 他的品德非常之高贵,谁也比不了。

shízú 十足

用法 Usage:
形容词 a.

1. 达到充分的、充足的程度,达到完全的地步。常与"信心、神气、傲气、人气、干劲"等词语搭配,或与表明某种身份的词语如"小气鬼、懒鬼、酒鬼、好人、坏人、书呆子"等搭配。Reaching a sufficient degree or a complete level. It often collocates with such words as "信心,神气,傲气,人气,干劲," or words which show one's identity, such as "小气鬼,懒鬼,酒鬼,好人,坏人,书呆子," etc.

(1) 你看他神气十足的样子。
(2) 这部电视剧很受欢迎,演员们最近也人气十足。

(3) 他是个十足的酒鬼,每天都要喝酒。

2. 成分纯粹的。(Of ingredients) pure.

(4) 这可是十足的黄金。

说明 Notes:

1. "十足"第一个义项在使用时,若单独作为谓语,一般主语不能单独为人,应具体到人的某方面,如"信心、神气、傲气、人气、干劲儿"等。When "十足" is used in its first meaning as the predicate of a sentence, its subject cannot be a person. Instead, it should be something specific about the person, such as "信心,神气,傲气,人气,干劲儿."

(5) *他十足。

(6) 他信心十足。

2. "十足"第二个义项在使用时,可以作为定语修饰中心语,如例(4)。单独作为谓语时,主语一般是含有成色或质量程度物质的名词。In its second meaning, "十足" can be used as an attributive to modify the central word, as is shown in (4). When used as the predicate, the subject is a material noun indicating its degree of purity or quality.

(7) *这块黄金十足。

(8) 这块黄金成色十足。

shí 时

用法 Usage:

名词 n.

1. "……的时候"的简化。The short form for "...的时候."

(1) 他们三个是我高中时最好的朋友。

(2) 上课时别说话,认真听课。

2. "有时候"的简化,和反义词一起组成词组,后边一般接单音节词。Short for "有时候," it forms a phrase with two contradictory words, both of which should be monosyllabic.

(3) 她对我时冷时热。

(4) 这手表时快时慢,该修了。

3. 钟点,类似于"点",有书面语色彩。Hour, like "点," which carries the tone of the written language.

(5) 明天上午十时二十分,飞机准时起飞。

(6) 今晚八时,篮球赛开幕式准时开始。

4. 规定的、确定的时间,常以"按时、准时"等形式出现。A specified, determined time which is always used in the form of "按时,""准时," etc.

(7) 八点准时上课,不许迟到。

(8) 请按时交纳房租。

5. 时代,较长的一段时间。The time, a longer period.

(9) 古时,这里是皇城的中心。

(10) 旧时旗袍曾在上海流行一时。

6. 季节。Season.

(11) 要多吃应时水果、蔬菜。

(12) 种水稻,绝对不能误了农时。

7. 时机。Opportunity.

(13) 有什么消息,请你及时通知我。

(14) 机不可失,时不再来。

shícháng 时常 →P61"常常"

用法 Usage:

副词 ad.

表示动作、行为和情况的发生、出现的次数多,相当于"常常"的用法(与"偶然、偶尔"相对)。书面语色彩。Often; frequently. Indicating the repeated occurrence of an action, behavior or situation, it has a similar usage as "常常" (which is opposite to "偶然" and "偶尔") and carries the tone of the written language.

(1) 他时常想念在老家生活的奶奶。

(2) 最近他时常说起小时候的事儿。

说明 Notes:

"时常"和"常常"区别是:The differences between "时常" and "常常" are as follows:

1. "时常"侧重表示次数多,"常常"侧重表示动作的重复。"时常" emphasizes the number of occurrences, while "常常" emphasizes the repetition of an action.

2. "常常"前面可以用否定词"不"。"时常"前面不能有否定词。*The negative word "不" can be used before "常常," but not before "时常."*

3. "常常"后面可以带否定动词。"时常"后面一般不带否定动词。*A negative verb can follow "常常," but not "时常."*

（3）他常常不来上课。

（4）＊他时常不来上课。

shí'ér 时而

用法 Usage:

副词 *ad.*

1. 表示动作或情况不定时重复发生。*Sometimes; from time to time. It indicates that an action or situation occurs repeatedly at an intermittent time.*

（1）清晨,时而传来几声鸟叫。

（2）他坐在那儿写着什么,时而停下来抽一支烟。

2. 不同的几种现象,在一定的时间内,交替重复发生。*"时而…时而…" is used to indicate the alternative repetition of some different phenomena within a certain period.*

（3）教室里传来孩子们朗读的声音,时而高,时而低。

（4）他的手时而举起,时而放下,显得十分不安。

说明 Notes:

"时而……时而……"也可简化为"时……时……"。与之相应,后边一般也跟单音节词。*"时而…时而…" can be simplified as "时…时…," which is followed by monosyllabic words.*

（5）声音时高时低。

shíhou 时候 →P416"时间"、P418"时刻"

用法 Usage:

名词 *n.*

1. 表示时间的某一点。*A point of time.*

（1）你打算什么时候回国？

（2）在我吃饭的时候,不要谈论工作。

2. 指长时间里的某一段时间。用法有：*A span of time in a longer duration. It has following usages:*

① 经常受主谓短语、动词短语的修饰,构成名词性的偏正短语,表示时间,在句子中做状语。*It is often modified by a subject-predicate structure or a verb phrase to form a noun phrase that represents time. It is used as the adverbial in a sentence.*

（3）心情不好的时候,我喜欢听音乐或者看电影。

（4）做作业的时候,别玩手机。

② 经常受疑问代词"什么"、指示代词"这、那、这个、那个"的修饰。*It is often modified by the interrogative pronoun "什么" or demonstrative pronouns such as "这,那,这个,那个."*

（5）你什么时候来我家？

（6）那时候我还在读小学。

3. 指代某些特殊的时间点,句中常常流露出不满的语义,常与"都"配合使用。*Some special moment. It often goes with "都" to show an apparent discomfort or displeasure of the speaker.*

（7）都什么时候了,还那么大声地放音乐、跳舞。

（8）都什么时候了,还不做饭。

shíjiān 时间 →P416"时候"

用法 Usage:

名词 *n.*

1. 物质运动存在的一种客观形式,有物质运动、变化的顺序(过去、现在、将来)和持续性的表现。具有无限性和客观性,始终朝着一个方向流逝,一去不复返；光阴。*Time. It is an objective form of physical movement, including physical movement, the order of change (past, present, and future) and the continuous performance. With infinity and objectivity, it is always going in one direction, past and gone.*

(1) 时间就是金钱,时间就是生命。
(2) 写这篇文章要两天时间。

2. 钟表、日历上的某个准确的时刻。*A precise moment on a clock or calendar.*

(3) 快点儿出发,离飞机起飞的时间只有三个小时了。
(4) 现在的时间是九点三十分。

3. 从开始到结束的一个时段。*A period from the beginning to the end.*

(5) 现在是工作时间,不能打电话。
(6) 完成这部小说用了五年时间。

说明 Notes:

"时间"和"时候"都能表示时间里的某一段或某一点,有时可以通用。它们的区别是:*Both "时间" and "时候" can refer to a precise moment or point of time. They can be used interchangeably sometimes. Their differences are as follows:*

1."时间"着重指有起点有终点的某一段时间或某一点,界限很清楚。"时候"着重指时间里的某一点。"时候"有时也指有起点有终点的某一段时间,这时"时间"和"时候"可以通用,但两者对量词的使用要求不同。"段"的起止比较清楚,"个"的起止比较模糊。*"时间" has a clear boundary which focuses on a certain period or point with the starting point and an ending point, while "时候" focuses on a point in time. Yet "时候" sometimes refers to a certain period with a starting point and an ending point. In this case, "时间" and "时候" can be used interchangeably. However, the use of quantifiers is different. The beginning and ending of "段" is quite clear, while the beginning and ending of "个" is relatively vague.*

(7) 吃早饭那个时候你到哪儿去了?
(8) 晚上八点到九点那段时间你到哪儿去了?

"时间"的界限很清楚,常常用比较准确的时刻来表示某一段时间或某一点时间,并且可以直接跟在时间名词后面,组成时间短语。"的"可用可不用。"半天时间里、三个小时的时间、这三个月时间"中的"时间"不能用"时候"替代。*The boundary of "时间" is very clear, which is often used to express a certain period or a certain point of time. It can directly form a time phrase with a time noun. For example, the word "时间" in phrases such as "半天时间里,三个小时的时间,这三个月时间" can't be replaced by "时候." In the above formation, "的" is optional.*

"时候"常常用在动词或动词短语后面,用动作行为的内容来显示某个时间段或时间点,因此时间界线比较模糊,并且一定要用助词"的"。如:"吃饭的时候、上课的时候、睡觉的时候、讨论的时候、做作业的时候、打电话的时候"等。*"时候" often appears after a verb or a verb phrase. It shows a period or a time point with the content of an action. Therefore, the boundary of time is vague and should be followed by the auxiliary word "的." For example, "吃饭的时候,上课的时候,睡觉的时候,讨论的时候,做作业的时候,打电话的时候."*

2."时间"常与"利用、爱惜、掌握、浪费、花费、耽误、集中、省、费、抽、挤、用、拖"等动词搭配,可受"长、短"等形容词的修饰。"时候"不能与以上动词搭配,也不能受形容词"长、短"的修饰。"时候"常常与"当"构成固定的格式"当……时候",在句中常带动词或动词短语充当的定语,并且一定要用结构助词"的",常用作书面语。*"时间" is often used with such verbs as "利用,爱惜,掌握,浪费,花费,耽误,集中,省,费,抽,挤,用,拖," and it can be modified by adjectives such as "长" and "短." Yet "时候" cannot be used with the above verbs, nor can it be modified by "长" or "短." It is often used with "当" to form a fixed format "当…时候." In a sentence, it often takes a verb or a verb phrase as an attributive, and it must take the structural auxiliary word "的." It is often found in the written language.*

3. "时间"可以在判断句中做主语。"时候"不能。"时间" can be used as a subject in a judgmental sentence, but "时候" can't.

(9) 时间就是生命。

(10) *时候就是金钱。

4. 使用"时间""时候"时注意：More examples are given here to draw attention to the use of "时间" and "时候:"

(11) *他中学生时候不喜欢听古典音乐。

(12) 他上中学的时候不喜欢听古典音乐。

(13) *去年我想旅游的时间,没有钱,所以没有去。

(14) 去年我想旅游的时候,没有钱,所以没有去。

(15) 去年我想去旅游,可那个时候我没有钱,所以没有去。

shíkè 时刻 →P416"时候"

用法 Usage:

名词 n.

时间里短暂的某一段或某一点。Moment, a short period of time or a certain point of time.

(1) 国旗升起的时刻,运动员流下了激动的泪水。

(2) 比赛的最后时刻,他使出了全身的力量。

副词 ad.

表示每时每刻,经常。可重叠为"时时刻刻"。At every moment; constantly; always. It can be reduplicated as "时时刻刻."

(3) 他时刻提醒自己,开车要注意安全!

(4) 我心里会时时刻刻都想着你。

说明 Notes:

"时刻"和"时候"的区别是：The differences of "时刻" and "时候" are as follows:

1. 做名词用时,"时刻"是指特定的某一时间,所以"时刻"前面必定有修饰词语。"时候"是泛指时间里的某一点或某一段。When used as a noun, "时刻" refers to a particular time; therefore, there must be a modifier before "时刻." But "时候" generically refers to a point of time or a period.

2. "时候"只有名词用法,不能重叠。"时刻"还有副词用法,可以重叠为"时时刻刻"。"时候" can only be used as a noun and can't be reduplicated, while "时刻" can also be used as an adverb and can be reduplicated as "时时刻刻."

shíqī 时期 →P362"期间"

用法 Usage:

名词 n.

指较长的一段时间,多指具有某种特征的时间。A period of time. Usually it refers to a time with some special features.

(1) 我们正处于改革开放的大好时期。

(2) 唐朝是中国历史上比较繁荣的时期。

说明 Notes:

"时期"和"期间"都表示一段时间。它们的区别是：Both "时期" and "期间" denote a period of time. Their differences are as follows:

"时期"一般指用具体的修饰语表示出有某种特征的一段时间,如："战争时期、和平时期、经济发展时期、少年时期、老年时期、危险时期"等。"期间"专指有明显起止界限的一段时间,是从开始到结束的一段相对完整的时间,如："五一放假期间、高考期间、三年困难期间、恋爱期间"等。"时期" usually signifies with concrete descriptive words a period of time with its own special features such as "战争时期,和平时期,经济发展时期,少年时期,老年时期,危险时期." "期间," however, refers specially to a period of time with its beginning and end clearly defined: it is a fairly complete period of time from beginning to end, such as "五一放假期间,高考期间,三年困难期间,恋爱期间."

shíjiàn 实践 →P419"实现"、P419"实行"

用法 Usage:

动词 v.

1. 实行(某种思想、主张、观点等),履行

（承诺、诺言等）。*To put into practice a certain idea, proposal, opinion, etc.; to carry out a promise, engagement, etc.*

（1）二十年之后，他终于实践了自己的诺言。

（2）这种理论不错，但问题是如何实践？

2. 用具体行动改造世界和社会（跟"认识"相对）。可以重叠为"实践实践"。*To transform the world and society with practical actions (the opposite of "认识"). "实践" can be reduplicated as "实践实践."*

（3）大学生创业得勇于创新、勇于实践。

（4）多到社会上实践实践，一定有好处。

名词 *n.*

指人们利用自然、社会和改造自然、社会有意识的实际活动（与"理论"相对）。*Practice, referring to people's conscious practical activities that make use of nature or society, or that change nature or society (the opposite of "理论").*

（5）实践中积累起来的经验是非常宝贵的。

（6）我们会在教学实践中不断改进教材。

shíxiàn 实现 →P418"实践"、P419"实行"

用法 Usage：

动词 *v.*

使理想、目标、愿望、计划等成为现实。*To realize; to bring about; to turn an ideal, a goal, a wish, a plan, etc. into a reality.*

（1）经过多年的努力，他的理想终于实现了。

（2）实现这个计划需要多少资金？

shíxíng 实行 →P418"实践"、P419"实现"

用法 Usage：

动词 *v.*

用实际行动来实现。可带"着、了、过"。*To put into practice; to carry out. It can be followed by "着, 了, 过."*

（1）他们的办法，很难实行。

（2）实行改革开放政策以来，人民的生活有了很大的改变。

说明 Notes：

"实践""实现""实行"的区别是：*The differences between "实践," "实现," and "实行" are as follows:*

1. 在词义上，"实践"重在实行某种思想、主张、观点、承诺等的履行。"实现"强调理想等变成事实。"实行"则强调政策、计划等具体执行。*Semantically, "实践" emphasizes the implementation of some idea, proposal, opinion and the fulfillment of a promise. "实现" focuses on an ideal becoming a reality, while "实行" emphasizes the actual execution of a policy, a plan, and so on.*

2. 三个词可带的宾语有所不同。"实践"常带"诺言、主张、理论、计划"等。"实现"常带"理想、梦想、愿望、计划、目标"等。"实行"常带"政策、计划、纲领、制度、办法"等。即使有相同的宾语，如"计划"，但句子的语义不同。*The objects taken by the three words are different. "实践" is often followed by "诺言, 主张, 理论, 计划, etc." "实现" is often followed by "理想, 梦想, 愿望, 计划, 目标, etc." And "实行" is often followed by "政策, 计划, 纲领, 制度, 办法, etc." Even if they take the same object, say, "计划," their meanings might be different.*

（3）我们的计划必须实践。（着重理论必须进行社会实践的检验。*It emphasizes that the theory must be tested by social practice.*）

（4）我们的计划必须实现。（着重计划中的目标一定要达到。*It emphasizes that the goals in the plan must be achieved.*）

（5）我们的计划必须实行。（着重所订的计划一定要执行。*It emphasizes that the plan must be carried out.*）

3. "实现"与"实行"都可以带"得/不"构成可能补语，如："实现得/不了、实行得/不了"。"实践"不能。*Both "实现" and "实行" can be followed by "得/不" to form a potential complement such as "实现得/不了, 实行得/不*

了。" But "实践" cannot.

4."实践"还是名词。"实现"和"实行"不是名词。"实践" can also be used as a noun, while "实现" and "实行" cannot.

shíyàn 实验 →P422"试验"

用法 Usage:

名词 n.

指实验工作。Experiment.

(1) 同学们正在做物理实验。
(2) 实验报告明天会打印出来。

动词 v.

为检验某种理论或假设是否正确而在特定条件下进行某种操作或从事某种活动。To perform an operation or activity under a specific condition to test the correctness of a theory or a hypothesis.

(3) 他的结论是否正确要实验以后再说。
(4) 明天开始实验第二套方案。

shízài 实在

用法 Usage:

副词 ad.

1. 的确,确实。强调所陈述状况的程度,可与"非常、很、太、极了"等副词一起使用。Indeed; really. It is used to emphasize the extent of the state of what is being said and can go together with adverbs such as "非常、很、太、极了."

(1) 那孩子实在太可爱了。
(2) 他实在累极了,一头倒在沙发上就睡着了。

2. 实际上,其实。承接上文,表示下文才是真实情况或原因。Actually; as a matter of fact. It is used as a link between two parts: the first part showing a phenomenon and the second part revealing the truth.

(3) 学生们都说没有问题了,实在是想赶快下课。
(4) 他说菜都很好吃,实在只是客气话。

形容词 a.

真诚、不虚假。可以重叠为 AABB 形式。Sincere; honest. It can be reduplicated in the form of AABB.

(5) 这人很实在,不会说假话。
(6) 光说好话不行,得实实在在做点事才行。

说明 Notes:

在口语中,"实在"也读作"shízai",指人品忠厚老实,不虚假,也指做事儿不马虎。In colloquial language, "实在" can also be pronounced as "shízai," which means that someone is honest and upright in character, or meticulous and conscientious in doing things.

(7) 他为人很实在。
(8) 他做事儿实在,你就放心吧。

shǐ 使

用法 Usage:

动词 v.

1. 致使,让,叫。To make; to cause; to enable.

(1) 科技发展使我们的交流方式越来越方便。
(2) 他的话使我非常感动。

2. 使用。可重叠。To use; to employ. It can be reduplicated.

(3) 这种笔使惯了,不想换别的样式。
(4) 让我使使你的手机。

3. 支使,派遣。To have somebody do something; to dispatch.

(5) 这是个懒人,我可使不动他。
(6) 从小娇生惯养,自己不动手,使人使惯了。

shǐde 使得

用法 Usage:

动词 v.

1. 因某种原因而引起某种结果,常用"原因＋使得＋结果"的格式。(Of a certain factor) to cause a certain result. It is usually used in the pattern of "cause＋使得＋effect."

(1) 大雾使得飞机无法起飞。

(2) 痛苦使得他一夜白了头。

2. 可以使用。否定式为"使不得",可用"使得使不得"提问。*To be usable. Its negative form is "使不得." "使得使不得" can be adopted to ask a question.*

(3) 这手机还使得,不要丢。

(4) 这手机使不得了,买个新的吧。

(5) 这台洗衣机都十多年了,还使得使不得?

3. 可以,行得通。否定式为"使不得"。*To be workable. The negative form is "使不得."*

(6) 我觉得这个办法使得。

(7) 你不去可怎么使得?

shǐzhōng 始终 →P583 "一直"

用法 Usage:

名词 *n.*

从开始到终了的整个过程。*The whole process from beginning to end.*

(1) 做每件事都要有个始终,不能有头无尾。

(2) 困难总是伴随着生活的始终。

副词 *ad.*

表示行为、动作或状态从头到尾持续不变。*(Of a behavior, an action, or a state) lasting from beginning to end.*

(3) 这么多年他始终没有放弃自己的梦想。

(4) 他始终不知道是谁帮他交了学费。

说明 Notes:

"始终"用作副词时,在句子中要注意表达动词动作持续的时间段语义。*Pay attention to the span of time expressed by the verb when using "始终" as an adverb.*

1. 句子里要明确表达"始终"所强调的动作的持续性语义。*The sentence must clearly express the continuity emphasized by the action of the verb.*

(5) *他始终跑到家门口都没有休息。

(6) 从学校到家门口,他始终是跑步行进,没有休息。

(7) 他从学校一直跑到家门口都没有休息。

2. 表示时间段的数量词只能放在"始终"前面。*The numeral used to show the span of time must come before "始终."*

(8) *他昨天始终学了五个小时才去睡觉。

(9) 昨天晚上七点到十二点他始终在宿舍里学习。

(10) 他昨天晚上学了五个小时才睡觉。

shìchǎng 市场 →P401 "商场"

用法 Usage:

名词 *n.*

进行商品交易的场所或商品销售的区域。*Market, a place or an area where commodities are bought or sold.*

(1) 你去过这个城市最大的服装市场吗?

(2) 中国的市场经济正在慢慢地形成。

说明 Notes:

"商场"和"市场"的区别是: *The differences between "商场" and "市场" are as follows:*

"商场"主要是指买卖东西的大型综合商店,一般以零售为主。"市场"主要是指商品交易的场所,有时指一个大的区域,有时指专门一类货物商品的交易场所,可以零售,也可以批发。如:"义乌小商品市场、农贸市场、旧货市场、汽车市场、丝绸市场、服装市场、家电市场、人才市场、劳动力市场"等。*"商场" mainly refers to large and comprehensive stores that sell things, usually dealing with retailing. By contrast, "市场" refers to a place for commodity trading. In China, it sometimes refers to a large area or a trading location for a special kind of goods. It can be either retail or wholesale. For example, "义乌小商品市场,农贸市场,旧货市场,汽车市场,丝绸市场,服装市场,家电市场,人才市场,劳动力市场."*

shìde 似的

用法 Usage:

动词 *v.*

用在词或短语的后面,表示比喻,或说明跟

某人、物或情况相似。前面常用"像、好像、仿佛"等词搭配。Placed after a word or phrase to express a metaphor or to indicate that it is like a person, a thing, or a situation. Words such as "像,""好像" and "仿佛" often precede it.

1. 常常用在名词、代词或名词短语后面。有时,类比的事物并不具体地说出来,而用一个任指的疑问代词"什么"代替。"什么似的"一般用作补语,前面要加"得"。Often used after nouns, pronouns, or noun phrases. Sometimes, analogical things are not explicitly said. Instead, it is replaced by an interrogative pronoun "什么." "什么似的" is usually used as a complement and "得" should be put before it.

(1) 天空下着牛毛似的细雨。
(2) 他累得什么似的瘫在沙发里。

2. 用在动词、形容词或动词短语后面,说明情况相似,含有"好像是这样,但并非这样"的意思。Placed after verbs, adjectives, or verb phrases to show that somebody or something seems to be in a certain situation, but actually that is not the case.

(3) 他发疯似的叫了起来。
(4) 他很轻松似的把那个大箱子提了过来。

3. 用在主谓短语或更复杂的短语后面。Used after a subject-predicate phrase or a more complex phrase.

(5) 她什么事都要管我,好像我离了她就不能活了似的。
(6) 小学生冲出教室门,像条条河流归向大海似的跑向了操场。

4. "似的"用在单音节动词后面,为了使音节和谐,常常加一个"也"字。When "似的" follows a monosyllabic verb, "也" is often added in order to make the syllable sound more harmonious.

(7) 他飞也似的跑了过去。

说明 Notes:

1. "似的"用在词或短语之后组成助词结构,可以做定语(牛毛似的细雨)、状语(一阵风似的跑进)、谓语(他很痛苦似的)、补语(脏得像猪窝似的)等。"似的" is used after a word or a phrase to form an auxiliary-word structure. It can be used as an attributive (such as "牛毛似的细雨"), an adverbial (such as "一阵风似的跑进"), a predicate (such as "他很痛苦似的") or a complement (such as "脏得像猪窝似的").

2. 从语法作用看,"似的"能使名词动词化。一般名词是不做状语或补语的,但是加上"似的"就能充任状语或补语。From the perspective of grammatical function, "似的" can turn a noun into a verb. Generally, nouns cannot serve as an adverbial or complement. With "似的," however, they can.

(8) 你看他,胖得熊猫似的。
(9) 她云朵似的飘来飘去,停不下来。

shìyàn 试验 →P420"实验"

用法 Usage:
动词 v.

为了解或考察某事物的性能或某事的结果而在实验室或小范围内进行探索性的活动。To conduct an experiment, an exploratory activity in a laboratory or in a small area for understanding the performance of something or the result of something.

(1) 新的教学方法首先要在我们班进行试验。
(2) 海水能否种植水稻,他们已经试验了两年。

说明 Notes:

"试验"和"实验"的区别是:The differences between "试验" and "实验" are as follows:

"试验"的意思在于试探观察。"实验"的意思在于实际验证。The meaning of "试验" lies in exploratory observation, while "实验" emphasizes the actual verification.

(3) 我现在开始第一次试验。(对事物做第一次试探和观察 The first exploratory observation on something)

(4) 我现在开始第一次实验。(对假设的理论做第一次实验证明 The first actual verification of a hypothesis)

shì……de 是……的

用法 Usage:

1. 用于过去发生的事情,用来强调动作的时间、地点、方式等。否定形式在"是"前面加"不"。 To refer to something that happened in the past. It is used to emphasize the time, place or manner of an action. The negative form is to have "不" before "是."

(1) 他是/不是去年来上海的。(强调时间 Emphasizing the time)

(2) 他是在北京读的大学。(强调地点 Emphasizing the place)

(3) 他是坐船去韩国的。(强调方式 Emphasizing the manner)

2. 表示对描写或说明主语的情况加以肯定。 To affirm the description or the illustration of the subject.

(4) 他是会喝酒的。

(5) 这种观点我是不会支持的。(对"不会支持这种观点"这个说明的肯定 To affirm the description of "不会支持这种观点")

3. 表示领属、归类或质地。多数可以理解为"的"后面省略了一个跟前面相同的名词。 To indicate the possession, classification or quality of something. In most cases, it can be understood that the same noun which is supposed to repeat itself after "的" is omitted.

(6) 这本书是她的。(表示领属 Indicate the possession)

(7) 这几件衣服都是丝绸做的。(表示质地 Indicate the quality)

(8) 和我打招呼的同学都是北大的。(表示归类 Indicate the classification)

说明 Notes:

"是……的"表示领属、质地、归类的意思时,句子后面可以重复出现前面的名词,如:例(6)(7)(8)中"的"后面可以加"书、衣服、同学"。但实际使用时,后面的名词都不重复出现。 When "是…的" is used to refer to the possession, quality or classification of something, the noun can repeat itself after "的" as is shown in (6), (7) and (8). In other words, "的" can be followed by words such as "书,衣服,同学" respectively. However, in real communication, this would not happen.

shìfǒu 是否

用法 Usage:

副词 ad.

"否"即"不是","是否"即"是不是"。可用于疑问句、祈使句。 Whether or not; whether; if. "否" means "不是," and "是否" means "是不是." It can be used in interrogative sentences and imperative sentences.

(1) 他是否已经知道了这个秘密?

(2) 是否能请李教授来给我们讲讲课?

(3) 你必须自己判断现在的工作是否适合你!

说明 Notes:

"是否"和"是不是"的区别是: The differences between "是否" and "是不是" are as follows:

1. "是不是"是肯定和否定词组成的短语,具有及物动词的功能,后面可以接名词性成分,而"是否"为副词,后面不能接名词性成分。 "是不是" is a phrase consisting of affirmative and negative words, which has the function of a transitive verb, and can be followed by a nominal element. However, "是否" is an adverb and cannot be followed by any nominal elements.

(4) *我不知道打电话的是否王老师。

(5) 我不知道打电话的是不是王老师。

2. "是否"多用于书面语。"是不是"多用于口语。"是否" appears more in written language while "是不是" appears more in colloquial language.

shìdàng 适当 →P369"恰当"

用法 Usage:

形容词 a.

合适，恰当。Suitable; appropriate; proper.

（1）和别人讲话的时候，要保持适当的距离。

（2）政府每年都在适当增加老年人的社会福利。

说明 Notes:

"适当"和"恰当"都形容合适、妥当。可与"时间、时机、比喻、词句、人选、方式、方法"等名词和"安排、处理"等动词搭配。Both "适当" and "恰当" are adjectives which indicate something suitable and appropriate. They can be used with such nouns as "时间,实际,比喻,词句,人选,方式,方法," and verbs as "安排,处理."

它们的区别是：Their differences are as follows:

① 在词义上，"适当"着重于切合实际情况或客观要求。"恰当"着重于恰如其分，恰到好处，非常合适。词义比"适当"重。Semantically, "适当" focuses on the actual situation or objective requirement. However, "恰当" emphasizes something appropriate or just right; and semantically, it is stronger than "适当."

② "适当"做状语，与中心语之间可以不用"地"，如例(2)。"恰当"做状语，与中心语之间，一般要用"地"。When "适当" is used as an adverbial, "地" can be omitted between itself and the central word, as is shown in (2). But "地" is required when "恰当" is used as an adverbial.

（3）听说春节放假时间会适当延长。

（4）听说春节放假时间会恰当地延长。

③ "适当"可以与正反义对举的词语如"深浅、长短、大小、浓淡"等搭配。"恰当"一般不能。"适当" can pair with words of an opposite meaning such as "深浅,长短,大小,浓淡," etc. But "恰当" cannot be used this way.

（5）*这幅油画颜色深浅恰当。

（6）这幅油画颜色深浅适当。

shìhé 适合 →P193"合适"、P424"适应"

用法 Usage:

动词 v.

符合（某一方面的实际情况或客观要求），（人、物的特性或具有的性能）合宜。To suit (the actual situation or objective requirement of a certain aspect); (Of the characteristics or performances of a person or a thing) to be suitable.

（1）这种颜色并不适合你。

（2）听说海南很适合蜜月旅行。

说明 Notes:

"适合"和"合适"的区别在于："适合"是动词，可带宾语。"合适"是形容词，不能带宾语。The difference between "适合" and "合适" is: "适合" is a verb which can take an object while "合适" is an adjective which cannot take an object.

（3）*他合适这个工作。

（4）他适合这个工作。

shìyìng 适应 →P424"适合"

用法 Usage:

动词 v.

指（人、物）适合、顺应客观条件或客观需要，随着社会或者自然界客观条件的变化而做相应的改变。To suit; to adapt; to fit. Often it is used to describe people or animals or plants adapting to society or nature, that is, making changes in themselves to suit the objective condition or environment.

（1）这儿的气候我早就适应了。

(2) 这些动物是怎么适应沙漠环境的?

说明 Notes:

1. "适应"是及物动词,其主体常常是人或其他生物,对象多为"环境、条件、需要、方法、方式、发展、变化"等含有综合意义的抽象名词。"适应" is a transitive verb and its subject is often a person or other creatures. Its objects are always abstract nouns with a comprehensive meaning such as "环境,条件,需要,方法,方式,发展,变化."

2. "适应"和"适合"都是动词,都有表示合宜实际情况或客观要求的意义。Both "适应" and "适合" are verbs which indicate the adaptation to an actual situation or an objective requirement.

它们的区别是: The differences are as follows:

"适应"表现了主体与客观实际情况或客观要求的关系是可以改变的意思。主体可以发挥主观积极作用去顺应客观情况或客观要求,具有可以改变的动态过程。"适合"只是客观地叙述主体与客观实际、客观要求适合或不适合的情况,不含有改变的动态过程。"适应" shows that the relationship between the subject and the actual situation or the objective requirement can be changed. The subject can play an active role and adapt to the objective conditions or requirements. Therefore, "适应" is a dynamic process that involves changes. By contrast, "适合" is only an objective description of whether the subject and the environment suit each other. It does not indicate the dynamic process.

(3) *你是能够适合这里的生活环境的。

(4) 你是能够适应这里的生活环境的。(指现在暂时不习惯,但是以后会习惯的。It means that you're not used to it right now, but you'll get used to it later.)

(5) *我已经适合这里的气候了。

(6) 我已经适应这里的气候了。(指经过努力,已经从不习惯到习惯了。It means that I've gradually become adapted myself to the climate through my effort.)

shìyòng 适用

用法 Usage:

动词 v.

适合使用,适合应用。To suit; to apply to; to be suitable for use.

(1) 这种学习方法也适用于其他外语的学习。

(2) 这种成功的经验并不适用于所有的企业。

说明 Notes:

1. "适用"做谓语,一般不直接带宾语。如要带宾语,"适用"后面常带介词"于",如例(1)(2)。When "适用" is used as a predicate, it can't be followed by an object directly. If it needs to take an object, the preposition "于" must be added, as is shown in (1) and (2).

2. "适用"做谓语,前面如有介词"在"组成的介词短语,一般表示"适用"的范围或对象。When "适用" is used as a predicate and the prepositional structure with "在" is used before it, it generally represents the scope or object of "适用," as is shown in (3).

(3) 这套英语书太难,在小学英语教学中并不适用。

shōudào 收到 →P428"受到"

用法 Usage:

动词 v.

"收到"由动词"收"加上结果补语"到"构成,表示接收、获得。"收到" is composed of the verb "收" and the complement "到" which means "to receive or obtain."

1. 表示接收已经到达的东西,通常是别人邮寄或发送的,诸如邮件、包裹、快递或者电子邮件等。To receive something, usually mailed or sent by others, such as mail, parcel, express

delivery or email, text message.

（1）那个歌手收到了很多歌迷的来信。

（2）今天我收到妈妈给我寄的包裹了。

2. 表示信号等搜索到，接收到，常用于电子设备。To search and receive (the signal). It is often applied to electronic devices.

（3）我们村里能收到电视节目吗？

（4）国外也能收到中央电视台的节目。

3. 表示获得。宾语可以是"礼物、红包"等具体的事物，也可以是"效果、祝福"等抽象名词。To receive or get something as a gift. Its object can either be the concrete things such as "礼物" and "红包 (lucky money)" or the abstract things such as "效果,祝福."

（5）昨天生日晚会上你收到了什么生日礼物？

（6）新婚夫妇收到了大家的祝福。

说明 Notes：

"收到"可以在动词"收"和结果补语"到"之间加"得/不"，构成"可能补语"，即"收得到"和"收不到"。The structure of "收到" is "v. + 到." "得/不" can be put between the verb "收" and the complement "到" to form "收得到" and "收不到."

（7）你在国外也收得到春节晚会的节目吗？

（8）我的手机有时候收不到微信。

shōují 收集 →P440"搜集"

用法 Usage：

动词 v.

把分散各处的东西收拢、聚集在一起。To collect something or to gather things that are scattered around.

（1）我从小时候起就开始收集邮票。

（2）你把已经有的资料先收集到一起。

说明 Notes：

"收集"的宾语可以是"邮票、钱币、字画"等，或者是"材料、资料、证据、信息、意见"等类词，还可表示是把其他现有的任何实物，加以聚拢。The object of "收集" can be such words as "邮票，钱币，字画" or "材料，资料，证据，信息，意见." It can also refer to the gathering of any material objects.

shōushi 收拾

用法 Usage：

动词 v.

1. 整理、打扫。把脏、乱，没有秩序的地方或事物变得整齐、干净。可以重叠为"收拾收拾"。To tidy up; to clear away; to make the dirty and messy places or things neatly organized. It can be reduplicated as "收拾收拾."

（1）吃完饭，把桌子收拾干净。

（2）星期天我打算收拾收拾房间。

2. 修理。用于口语。To fix; to repair. It is used colloquially.

（3）你那辆自行车该拿去收拾一下了。

（4）这洗衣机怎么老坏呀，得收拾收拾了。

3. 惩罚，教训。用于口语。To punish; to teach (somebody) a lesson. It is used colloquially.

（5）这孩子这么不听话，得好好儿收拾收拾。

（6）你对我妹妹不好的话，小心我收拾你。

4. 消灭，杀死。用于口语。To wipe out; to kill. It is used colloquially.

（7）这帮强盗一定要收拾掉。

shǒuduàn 手段 →P427"手法"

用法 Usage：

名词 n.

1. 为达到某种目的，进行某项工作而采取的具体方法、措施。Specific means and measures taken to achieve a certain purpose.

（1）如今在网上买东西有很多支付手段。

（2）发展生产是脱离贫困的最好手段。

2. 指待人处事所用的不正当方法，多含贬义。Tricks; improper methods used to treat people (usually with a derogatory meaning).

(3) 想成功可以,但不要用那种损人的手段。
(4) 他是挺聪明的,可总喜欢耍手段。
3. 本领,技艺;能耐。Ability; skill; capacity.
(5) 陶艺师傅手段真高明。
(6) 没有点儿手段,这种铜壶真打不出来。

shǒufǎ 手法 →P426"手段"

用法 Usage:
名词 n.
1.(艺术作品或者文学作品的)表现技巧。(Of art works or literary works) techniques of expression.
(1) 这篇童话故事用了拟人的手法。
(2) 他用了传统的绘画手法。
2. 手段,指待人处事的不正当的方法。Means, referring to the improper way to treat people.
(3) 现在有一些公司用小恩小惠的手法欺骗客户。
(4) 他这种两面派手法,真让人瞧不起。

说明 Notes:
"手段"和"手法"都可以表示"待人处事的不正当的方式、方法",有时可互相替代。Both "手段" and "手法" can refer to improper ways or means of dealing with people or things. Sometimes they can be replaced by each other.
它们的区别是:Their differences are as follows:
1."手段"有一些固定搭配,如:"耍手段、不择手段"等。"手法"不能这样搭配。"手段" has some fixed collocations such as "耍手段,不择手段," while "手法" doesn't.
2."手法"有表示"艺术作品或文学作品的技巧"的意思,而"手段"没有。因此,例(1)(2)中的"手法"都不能用"手段"替代。"手法" can refer to the skills or techniques of a work of art or a work of literature, yet "手段" can't. Therefore, "手法" can't be replaced by "手段" in (1) and (2).

shòu 受

用法 Usage:
动词 v.
1. 接受,得到。To receive; to accept.
(1) 受了那么多年教育,这点道理我懂。
(2) 这次培训让年轻人去受一下教育吧。
2. 遭受、承受(到某种不好的情况)。To suffer; to undergo (some bad experience).
(3) 他小时候受过不少苦。
(4) 他受了伤,不能参加比赛了。
3. 忍受、经受(某种遭遇或不好的情况)。To endure; to tolerate (some bad experience or bad condition).
(5) 真受不了这么冷的天气。
(6) 他这种脾气,你受得了吗?
4. 适合。To suit; to be pleasant (to the eye or to the ear); to feel comfortable.
(7) 这小姑娘很受看。(表示看着舒服 Indicating that the girl is sightly)
(8) 你的话很受听。(听着入耳 Indicating that sb.'s words are pleasant to the ear)

说明 Notes:
1."受"带的宾语常为抽象名词,如:"影响、限制、教育、锻炼、欺骗、启发"等。The object of "受" is often an abstract noun such as "影响,限制,教育,锻炼,欺骗,启发."
2. 动词"受"后边可加结果补语"着、了、过、到"。The complement such as "着,了,过,到" can follow the verb "受."
3."受"与"得/不"搭配,可以构成可能补语"受得了、受不了"和疑问式"受得了受不了"。"受" can collocate with "得" or "不" to form a complement of potentiality such as "受得了,受不了" and the interrogative form such as "受得了受不了."

shòubuliǎo 受不了

用法 Usage:
1. 表示不能忍受某种遭遇或者不好的情

况。多做谓语。To be unable to bear or put up with some suffering or bad situation. It is usually used as the predicate.

（1）他的态度真让人受不了。

（2）我可受不了这种辛苦。

2."受不了"在形容词后面做补语，可构成"形容词＋得＋受不了"的格式，表示前边形容词所描述的状态或情况严重到不能忍受的程度。"受不了" is used as a complement after adjective in the form of "a.＋得＋受不了," indicating that the state or situation described by the adjective is so serious that it's completely unbearable.

（3）我冻得受不了了，咱们快回家吧。

（4）牙疼得实在让人受不了。

说明 Notes：

"受不了"是可能补语"受得了"的否定式。"受不了" is the negative form of the potential complement "受得了."

shòudào 受到 →P425"收到"

用法 Usage：

动词 v.

"受到"是动词"受"＋"到"（结果补语）构成的词语，表示遇到某种状况、某种遭遇等，所带宾语一般是抽象名词。"受到" is the combination of the verb "受" with the complement "到." It indicates that somebody has encountered a certain situation or suffering. The objects it takes are generally abstract nouns.

（1）他受到了很多人的帮助。

（2）因为常常迟到，他受到了老师的批评。

说明 Notes：

"受到"和"收到"都表示接受、得到某种东西。它们的区别是：Both "受到" and "收到" mean to get or receive something. Their differences are as follows：

1."收到"的对象一般指物质层面具体的事物。"受到"的对象一般指精神层面抽象的东西。The object of "收到" generally refers to something concrete on the material level while the object of "受到" generally refers to something abstract on the spiritual or emotional level.

2."收到"所带的宾语一般为"邮件、包裹、快递、微信、短信、礼物"等。"受到"所带的宾语一般为"教育、帮助、影响、批评、奖励、表扬"等。"收到" usually takes objects such as "邮件，包裹，快递，微信，短信，礼物，" while "受到" usually takes objects such as "教育，帮助，影响，批评，奖励，表扬."

shūfu 舒服 →P428"舒适"

用法 Usage：

形容词 a.

1. 身体或精神感到轻松、愉快。(Of one's) body or spirit) feeling well, relaxed and happy.

（1）爬山出了一身汗，洗完澡，真舒服！

（2）他被老师批评了几句，心里很不舒服。

2.（某事物、某行为）能使身体或精神感到轻松、愉快。(Something or some behaviors) making somebody feel relaxed and happy; comfortable.

（3）这张床看上去真舒服。

（4）他的话让人听了很舒服。

说明 Notes：

1."舒服"也有动词性用法，如："来，舒服一下。""来，舒服舒服！""舒服" can also be used as a verb. For example, "来，舒服一下." "来，舒服舒服！"

2."舒服"可以重叠。作为形容词可以重叠为"AABB"，作为动词可以重叠为"ABAB"。"舒服" can be reduplicated. When it is used as an adjective, it can be reduplicated as "AABB"; when it is used as a verb, it can be reduplicated as "ABAB."

（5）他回家后，舒舒服服地睡了一觉。

shūshì 舒适 →P428"舒服"

用法 Usage：

形容词 a.

给人以轻松愉快、舒服安逸的感觉。

Giving a pleasant, relaxed and comfortable feeling.

（1）她家的客厅又大又舒适。

（2）在我们公司,我的工作环境是舒适的。

说明 Notes:

"舒适"和"舒服"都有身心愉快的意思。Both "舒适" and "舒服" can refer to a pleasant and comfortable feeling.

它们的区别是：Their differences are as follows:

1."舒适"强调客观环境和条件适宜、生活环境和条件满意,使人感到安适愉快。"舒服"则更强调人在身体和心灵方面的主观感受。"舒适" emphasizes the objective pleasant environment or the appropriate conditions that make life easy and comfortable, while "舒服" emphasizes the subjective feeling about anything that constitutes one's life, material or spiritual.

2."舒服"使用范围较广,口语、书面语都常用。"舒适"多用于书面语。"舒服" is applied to both spoken language and written language, while "舒适" is more used in written language.

3."舒服"有"AABB"和"ABAB"两种重叠形式。"舒适"没有重叠式。"舒服" can be reduplicated in the form of "AABB" and "ABAB," but "舒适" can't be reduplicated.

shú 熟

用法 Usage:

形容词 a.

1.果实、蔬菜、庄稼等农作物完全长成,与"生"相对。(Of fruit, vegetable and crops) ripe; mature. It is opposite to "生 (raw)."

（1）西红柿熟了,一个个红通通的。

（2）苹果熟了,有的都掉下来了。

2.(食物)加热烧煮到可以食用的程度,与"生"相对。(Of food) cooked to a degree that is edible. It is opposite to "生 (uncooked)."

（3）牛肉只有七分熟,你喜欢吗?

（4）这种菜还是炒熟了好吃。

3.熟悉的,因常见或常用而知道得很清楚,与"生疏"相对。Familiar; well acquainted; well aware of something because of frequent encounter and use. It is opposite to "生疏 (unfamiliar)."

（5）我对这儿太熟了,因为我从小在这儿长大的。

（6）我和他还不太熟,见面也不知道说什么。

4.表示对某种技能掌握程度很高,熟练。Skilled; experienced, showing a high proficiency in a certain technique.

（7）课文已经背熟了,我来背。

（8）什么技术只要坚持练习就会熟能生巧。

5.程度深。(Of degree) deep; thorough.

（9）他睡得很熟,叫不醒。

（10）这个问题你必须深思熟虑,不要随便回答。

说明 Notes:

在口语里,表示第一、第二、第三义项时,北方人常常读为"shóu"。In colloquial language when "熟" is used as the first, second and third usages mentioned above, Northerners in China often pronounce it as "shóu."

shǔ 属

用法 Usage:

动词 v.

1.隶属。To be under the jurisdiction of; to be affiliated to.

（1）这个县属浙江省温州市。

（2）这是医科大学的附属医院。

2.归属。To belong to.

（3）婚后财产夫妻双方共有。

（4）胜利终属正义的人民。

3.是,符合。主要用于书面语。To be; to

be in accordance with. It is mainly used in written language.

(5) 他反映的情况属实。

(6) 有这种观点的人还属少数。

4. 用十二属相,记述生年时用。To belong to one of the twelve animals that make up the Chinese zodiac. It is used to record the year of one's birth.

(7) 我的生肖是猴,你属什么?

(8) 我属羊/我的属相是羊。

名词 n.

1. 表示类别,如"金属"等。The type or category of objects such as "金属."

2. 生物学科中把同科中又彼此相似的群叫做属,如"猫属、小麦属"等。Genus, which refers to the group from the same biological family that has similar characteristics such as "猫属,小麦属."

3. 家属,亲属,如"烈属、军属"等。Family members; dependents. For example, "烈属,军属."

说明 Notes:

"属"用来表示出生记年时是动词。When "属" is used to record the year of one's birth according to the twelve animals in the Chinese zodiac, it functions as a verb.

(9) *你的属是什么?

(10) 你属什么?

shùmǎ 数码

用法 Usage:

名词 n.

1. 表示数目的文字或符号。Word or symbol that represents a number.

(1) 每个商品上面都有数码条。

(2) 现在世界各国基本都用十进制的数码系统。

2. 指一系列信息数字化的技术。常与电子产品等搭配组成"数码相机、数码摄像机、数码印刷机、数码录音设备"等词组。The technology that digitizes data and information. It is usually used with electronic products to form phrases such as "数码相机,数码摄像机,数码印刷机,数码录音设备."

(3) 这款数码相机质量好、价格低。

(4) 听说这个周末电子商城的数码产品全部打折。

shuài 帅 →P279"酷"

用法 Usage:

形容词 a.

1. (长相)英俊,潇洒;(事物外观)漂亮,利落。可重叠为"帅帅的"。(Of one's appearance) handsome; (of the appearance of something) beautiful, neat. It can be reduplicated as "帅帅的."

(1) 他的太极拳打得好帅啊!

(2) 这孩子真是个小帅哥。

2. (行为、举止、气质等)潇洒。(Of one's manners and temperament) natural and unrestrained.

(3) 我觉得男人努力工作的样子最帅。

(4) 他的武打动作干净有力,真帅!

说明 Notes:

1. "帅"主要形容男性的长相英俊,气质迷人,举止潇洒,也可应用于打扮干练、举止动作精干的女性。"帅" is often used to describe a male who is handsome in appearance, charming in temperament, and unrestrained in manners. It can also refer to a female who is smart in dress and quick-witted in manner.

(5) 她在电影中有时帅气有时优雅,迷人极了。

2. "帅"还用作名词,表示将领,军队中最高的指挥员,如:"统帅,元帅,将帅,主帅"等。"帅" can also be used as a noun to refer to the general who is the commander-in-chief in the army, such as "统帅,元帅,将帅,主帅."

3. "帅"和"酷"都形容人的外表英俊潇洒,尤其用于男性。Both "帅" and "酷" can

describe the handsome appearance of a person, especially a male.

它们的区别是：Their differences are as follows:

① "酷"还有表示人的表情冷峻坚毅,有个性。"帅"没有这个词义。"酷" may also be used to describe a person who is cold but harshly persistent, while "帅" does not have this meaning.

② "帅"有名词用法。"酷"没有。"帅" can be used as a noun, but "酷" cannot.

shuàixiān 率先

用法 Usage:

副词 ad.

带头,首先。Taking the lead; being the first (to do something).

(1) 会议上,他率先发言,表达了自己的看法。

(2) 这个手机公司率先降了价。

说明 Notes:

"首先"和"率先"都表示最先做什么的意思。Both "首先" and "率先" can express the idea of being the first to do something.

它们的区别是：Their differences are as follows:

1. "首先"可以用作指示代词,表示"第一",用于列举事物,常与"其次、再次、然后、最后"等词语搭配使用。"率先"只是副词,不能用作代词。以下例句中的"首先"均不能用"率先"替换。"首先" can be used as a pronoun which means "first of all" in listing things. It often goes with such words as "其次,再次,然后,最后。" But "率先" can only be used as an adverb. Hence, "首先" in the following sentences cannot be replaced by "率先."

(3) 我在汉语大赛中取得了第一名。首先,我要感谢我的老师和同学。然后,想说说我学习汉语的体会。

(4) 毕业典礼的安排：首先,校长讲话。其次,学生代表发言。最后,授予学位证书。

2. "率先"强调领先做什么之后,别人也会相继做类似的行为。"首先"单纯强调最先要做什么时,不能用"率先"替代。"率先" implies that others will follow up when someone takes the lead in doing something. However, "首先" simply means doing something first; it cannot be replaced by "率先."

(5) 他首先到达了终点。(强调第一个到达。It emphasizes that he is the first one to arrive.)

(6) 他率先到达了终点。(强调第一个到后,后面别的人也会相继到达。It emphasizes that he is the first one to arrive, and others will follow him.)

(7) *要想结婚,率先得有个女朋友吧。

(8) 要想结婚,首先得有个女朋友吧。

shuìjiào 睡觉 →P432"睡眠"

用法 Usage:

动词 v.

1. 进入睡眠状态。在句子中主要做谓语,能带时量补语,不可以带宾语。To sleep. It mainly acts as the predicate in a sentence, and sometimes it can take a time complement. But it cannot take an object.

(1) 十二点了,快睡觉吧!

(2) 大家已经睡觉了,你们声音轻一点!

2. "睡觉"是个离合动词,中间可以插入别的成分。"睡觉" is a separable verb and can take other elements in the middle.

(3) 昨天晚上我睡了九个小时的觉,今天精神很好。

(4) 真想好好睡一觉!

说明 Notes:

1. "睡觉"后面不能直接带补语,如果有补语,要重复动词"睡"。"睡觉" cannot be followed by a complement directly. If there is a complement, the verb "睡" should be repeated.

(5) 这孩子睡觉睡得很好。

(6) 他睡觉睡得很晚。

2."睡觉"和"睡"的词义基本一样。在句子中,"睡"可以替换"睡觉",意思不变。如:"让他好好睡/睡觉,你别吵他。"*"睡觉" and "睡" basically bear the same meaning. They can replace each other. For example,"让他好好睡/睡觉,你别吵他."*

它们的区别是:*Their differences are as follows:*

① "睡"可以直接带补语。"睡觉"不能直接带补语。*"睡" can be followed by a complement directly, but "睡觉" can't.*

(7) *昨天晚上我睡觉得很好。

(8) 昨天晚上我睡得很好。

(9) 昨天晚上我睡觉睡得很好。

② "睡"可以带宾语,如"睡凉席、睡沙发、睡大床"等,表示"睡在哪儿"的意思。"睡觉"不能带宾语。*"睡" can be followed by an object, such as "睡凉席、睡沙发、睡大床," which indicates the place where someone sleeps. But "睡觉" can't be followed by an object.*

3. 运用时要注意以下例句所体现的语言点:*Please pay attention to the points shown in the following sentences:*

(10) *都睡觉了一天了,还不起床!

(11) 都睡了一天(觉)了,还不起床!

(12) *你睡觉得怎么样?

(13) 你(睡觉)睡得怎么样?

(14) *昨天晚上我喝了咖啡,所以不能睡觉。

(15) 昨天晚上我喝了咖啡,所以睡不着。

shuìmián 睡眠 →P431"睡觉"

用法 Usage:

名词 *n.*

一种与醒交替出现的技能状态,抑制过程在大脑皮层中逐渐扩散并达到大脑皮层下部各中枢的生理现象。*A state that appears alternately with wakefulness. It is a physiological phenomenon that the inhibition process diffuses gradually in the cerebral cortex and reaches the central part of it.*

(1) 睡眠时间短一点没关系,但睡眠质量要好。

(2) 长期睡眠不足,会影响健康。

说明 Notes:

"睡觉"跟"睡眠"的区别是:*The differences between "睡觉" and "睡眠" are as follows:*

1. "睡眠"是名词。"睡觉"是动词。*"睡眠" is a noun while "睡觉" is a verb.*

2. "睡眠"前面可以有定语,如"充足的睡眠、质量高的睡眠"等。可以做主语、宾语,如"睡眠很差、缺乏睡眠"等。可以充当定语,如"睡眠时间、睡眠状态、睡眠质量"等。"睡觉"不能。*There can be attributives before "睡眠," such as "充足的睡眠,质量高的睡眠." In addition, "睡眠" can be used as the subject or the object of a sentence, for example, "睡眠很差,缺乏睡眠." It can also be used as an attributive, such as "睡眠时间,睡眠状态,睡眠质量." But "睡觉" can't.*

shùn 顺 →P534"沿"

用法 Usage:

形容词 *a.*

1. 方向相同(与"逆"相对)。*Being in the same direction (opposite to "逆"); being orderly.*

(1) 祝你一路顺风!

(2) 你和我顺路,我带你回家。

2. 顺利,顺当。*Being smooth; without a hitch.*

(3) 今天办事不顺,真遗憾。

(4) 今天没有一个红灯,开车很顺。

动词 *v.*

1. 让方向相同,使得有顺序、有条理。可以重叠。*To turn something round; to put it in the same direction; to put something in order. It can be reduplicated.*

(5) 把船头顺过来,跟我们保持一个方向。

（6）文章的语句还要顺顺。

2. 顺从，依从。*To comply with somebody; to be obedient to somebody.*

（7）家长不能什么事儿都顺着孩子。

（8）他对父母真是百依百顺，从没说过一个"不"字。

3. 适合，如意，表示看起来心里很舒服。*To fit; to be agreeable; to look and feel comfortable.*

（9）我看他吃饭的样子很不顺眼。

（10）看你高兴的样子，最近很顺心吧。

介词 prep.

1. 依着、沿着某种方向或路线（做什么），后边一般不能跟抽象名词。*Following; going in a certain direction or along a certain route. It generally cannot be followed by abstract nouns.*

（11）顺着这条路一直往前走，就能看到医院。

（12）顺着河边走，要小心一点儿。

2. 表示顺便，或顺便做什么，一般与后面的单音节名词构成固定词语。*Doing something at one's convenience, usually used with the monosyllabic nouns to form a fixed term.*

（13）出去的时候请顺手关门。

（14）顺路去看看老王吧，听说他身体不好。

说明 Notes:

"顺"和后面单音节名词构成的"顺手"和"顺口"在不同语境下的语义并不相同。*"顺手" and "顺口," formed by "顺" plus a monosyllabic noun, bear different meanings in different contexts.*

注意以下句子：*Pay attention to the following sentences:*

"顺手"——

（15）这把刀使着最顺手。（表示工具等用起来便利、适用。*It indicates that the tool is convenient to use.*）

（16）刚开始他做得很顺手。（表示做事没有阻碍，很顺利。*It indicates that there is no hindrance in doing something.*）

（17）出去的时候请顺手关门。（表示随手、顺便做什么。*It indicates that you do something at your convenience.*）

"顺口"——

（18）这篇文章读起来很顺口。（表示读起来通顺、流畅。*It indicates that it is easy to read.*）

（19）他顺口说了一个让大家吃惊的秘密。（表示没有经过考虑就说出。*It indicates that someone speaks without much thinking.*）

shùnbiàn 顺便

用法 Usage:

副词 ad.

1. 表示趁做某件事的方便去做另一件事，在句子中做状语。*Conveniently, used as an adverbial in a sentence to indicate that one does something else at one's convenience.*

（1）你现在去超市吗？顺便帮我买瓶牛奶。

（2）我明天去上海办事儿，顺便和朋友见个面。

2. 表示在做完一件事情后的时间里说另一件事。这两件事情之间没有任何关系。*By the way; incidentally. It is used to indicate that someone talks about something else after completing one thing. The two things don't relate to each other.*

（3）今天的课到此结束。顺便提一下，明天早上九点在校门口集合，去参观博物馆。

（4）我的意见说完了。顺便说明一下，这是我个人的想法，大家不同意没关系。

说明 Notes:

1. 使用"顺便"一词，句子一般有两个部分：第一部分是（要）做的第一件事，这件事是主要的。第二个部分是（要）做的第二件事，这件事是次要的。这两件事，有的句子以两个分句的形式表现，有的句子第一件事出现在与"时"或"时候"组成的状语中。*A sentence with the word "顺便" can be divided into two parts: The first part is the primary one, which is*

something that needs to be done in the first place; the second part is the secondary which needs to be done in the second place. It can be expressed in the form of two clauses. Sometimes the first part appears as an adverbial along with "时" or "时候."

（5）你去图书馆借书，顺便帮我还一本书。
（6）你去图书馆还书时顺便也帮我还一本书。

2. 用"顺便"做句子，最重要的是句中要体现"趁做某件事的方便"这个语义。如：在例（5）和（6）中，方便的语义是"借书"和"还书"都在"图书馆"。"趁做某件事的方便"这个语义很明显。例（2）说去上海办事，顺便看朋友。从中可以意识到，朋友也在上海。"趁做某件事的方便"这个语义是"办事"和"看朋友"都在上海。这个语义有点隐性，但它是存在的。When "顺便" is used in a sentence, it expresses the idea of "at the convenience of doing something." As is shown in (5) and (6), the meaning of "convenience is that" "借书" and "还书" both happen in the library. Example (2) says "To visit one's friend while doing business in Shanghai." Obviously, one's friend is in Shanghai. Therefore, the meaning of "at the convenience of doing something" indicates that the two actions of "办事" and "看朋友" both happen in Shanghai. The meaning is hidden yet exists.

3. 用"顺便"做句子时，一定要注意"趁做某件事的方便"这个语义的存在。When "顺便" appears in a sentence, we should pay attention to the implication of "at the convenience of doing something."

（7）＊你去图书馆还书，顺便你喝茶。
（8）你去图书馆还书，顺便可以在图书馆的咖啡吧喝茶。
（9）＊我去商店，顺便买橘子了。
（10）我去商店买本子，顺便买几个橘子。
（11）我去商店买了本子，顺便也买了几个橘子。

4. "顺便"一般用在第二个句子的最前面。"顺便" usually appears at the beginning of the second sentence/clause.

5. "顺便"的第二个用法，常用比较固定的形式，如"顺便提一下，顺便说一下，顺便问一句"等提及第二件事，如例（3）（4）。For the second usage, "顺便" often appears in fixed patterns such as "顺便提一下，顺便说一下，顺便问一句." The second thing is then mentioned, as in (3) and (4).

shùnshǒu 顺手 →P446"随手"

用法 Usage:
形容词 a.

1. 做事顺利，没有遇到困难。Doing something smoothly, without encountering any difficulty.

（1）这次做护照、办签证都很顺手。
（2）在别人的厨房做饭有些不顺手。

2. 形容工具便利，适用。(Of tools) handy; convenient and easy to use.

（3）这支笔写字很顺手。
（4）吃面条，还是用筷子顺手。

副词 ad.

很容易地（一伸手就可以做成某事），随手，趁便。Conveniently (it is a breeze to have something done); without extra trouble.

（5）离开时他顺手关上了门。
（6）我经过餐桌时顺手拿了个苹果。

shuōbudìng 说不定

用法 Usage:
动词 v.

表示不能确切地说、确定地知道，还没有决定下来。一般在句中做谓语。Not to know for certain. It indicates that you cannot say for sure or that you cannot decide right now. It is usually used as the predicate in a sentence.

（1）下周的会议他到底参加不参加，还说不定。
（2）明天去还是后天去，还说不定。

副词 ad.

表示猜测,有"可能、恐怕、也许"的意思。做状语,在句中主要有以下几种位置: As a prediction, "说不定" bears the meaning of "可能,恐怕,也许." Its position in a sentence varies:

1. 用在主语之后、动词之前。Placed before the verb but after the subject.

(3) 别等了,他说不定已经走了。

(4) 妈妈说不定明天就到上海。

2. 用在句首,表示这句话是对某一事物的推测。Placed at the beginning of a sentence to indicate a prediction.

(5) 说不定,王老师也会来参加我们的晚会呢。

(6) 说不定他以后会成为最有名的歌手。

3. 有时用在推测内容之后,用"也"或"都"连接。Sometimes placed after the prediction, connected by "也" or "都."

(7) 到底是谁去很难说,你去也说不定。

(8) 你觉得这些老人是五六十岁,实际上已经七八十岁了都说不定。

说明 Notes:

1. "说不定"是惯用语。作为副词,表示猜测,句子末尾常带语气词"呢",如例(5)。"呢"用在句末有确认事实的语气作用,可加强对推测的事实的肯定,并且有稍许夸张的意味。"说不定" is a fixed expression. As an adverb, it is used to make a prediction and the interjection "呢" often appears at the end of the sentence, as in (5). "呢" is used at the end of the sentence to confirm the fact. This can enhance the affirmativeness of one's conjecture about fact and carry a slightly exaggerative tone.

2. "说不定"作为动词,着重于表示施事者本人对是否做某件事的决心与决定。一般句子中常有肯定与否定对举的词语,或由"到底、究竟"等副词组成的疑问句式,如例(1)(2)。"说不定"后面一般不带宾语。When "说不定" is used as a verb, it focuses on the agent's decision or determination about whether he will do something or not. There are often words that present a contrast between the affirmative and the negative. In interrogative sentences, it often goes with adverbial phrases such as "到底,究竟," as in (1) and (2). "说不定" usually doesn't have an object after it.

shuōfǎ 说法

用法 Usage:

名词 n.

1. 指说话或写文章时的措辞、叙说的方法等。Wording; the way in which a narration is made in speaking or writing.

(1) 你如果用请求的说法,他可能就同意了。

(2) 对一个人的批评有很多种说法。

2. 表示意见、见解。Viewpoint or idea.

(3) 对这件事情,每个人的说法都不同。

(4) 我不同意他们的说法。

3. 表示正当的理由、根据。Reasonable explanation or valid basis.

(5) 为什么你不同意?你得给我一个说法。

(6) 你要大家都相信你,你就要有个说法。

说明 Notes:

1. 汉语里有不少"动词+法"这样结构的词语,如:"用法、做法、写法、想法、吃法、洗法"等,它们的意思大致是"怎么用的、怎么做的、怎么写的、怎么想的、怎么吃的、怎么洗的"等。"说法"的意思是"怎么说的",包含两层意思:如果是指说话或写文章时的措辞,叙说的方法等,意思是"怎么组词造句的";如果是指表示意见、见解的,意思是指"怎么看待(这个问题)的"。There are phrases composed of "v.+法" in Chinese, such as "用法,做法,写法,想法,吃法,洗法." They bear a meaning similar to "怎么用的,怎么做的,怎么写的,怎么想的,怎么吃的,怎么洗的." As for "说法," it literally means "怎么说的," which has two implications. One is the wording or the way of narration in one's speech or article; it means "怎么组词造句的,"

the way in which words are chosen and sentences are made. The other is about the idea or viewpoint; it means "怎么看待(这个问题)的."

2. "说法"有另一个读音"shuōfǎ"是离合动词,佛教界指"讲解佛法"。 *Another way of pronunciation of* "说法" *is* "shuōfǎ," *which is a separable verb meaning* "讲解佛法 *(expounding Buddha dharma)" in Buddhism.*

shuōhuà 说话 →P228"讲话"、P455"谈话"

用法 Usage:

动词 *v.*

1. 用语言表达意思。 *To express one's idea in words.*

(1) 他就是不说话。

(2) 这小孩儿很晚才会说话。

2. 闲聊,聊天。 *To chat; to gossip.*

(3) 上课时请不要随意说话。

(4) 我们三班的同学在一起说话呢。

3. 指责,非议。 *To blame; to reproach.*

(5) 你在这儿抽烟,别人要说话的。

说明 Notes:

"说话"和"讲话"做动词用时,都是离合词。中间都可以插入其他词语。"讲话"和"说话"都有对别人行为动作指责、非议的意思。 "说话" *and* "讲话" *are separable verbs and so other words can be inserted into them. Both* "说话" *and* "讲话" *may carry the idea of blaming and reproaching others' behavior.*

它们的区别是: *Their differences are as follows:*

1. 在教室、会议等正式场合,请人说话时,常用"讲话",不用"说话"。 *On formal occasions such as in a meeting or in the classroom, we use* "讲话," *not* "说话," *when inviting someone to speak.*

(6) 下面请王老师给我们讲话。

2. "讲话"可以作名词用。"说话"一般不作名词用。 "讲话" *can be used as a noun, but* "说话" *cannot.*

(7) 我买了一本《现代汉语知识讲话》。

sīkǎo 思考 →P436"思索"

用法 Usage:

动词 *v.*

表示进行比较深刻、周到的思维活动的意思。能重叠使用。 *To consider; to think through. It refers to the process of thorough and profound thinking. It can be reduplicated.*

(1) 他喜欢闭着眼睛思考问题。

(2) 你好好地思考思考为什么会犯这个错误。

sīsuǒ 思索 →P436"思考"

用法 Usage:

动词 *v.*

表示思考探求的意思。 *To think deeply in exploration of something.*

(1) 怎样写好这篇论文,他苦苦思索了两个星期。

(2) 他思索了很久,还是想不出约她出来的理由。

说明 Notes:

"思考"和"思索"都表示深入地考虑,都多用于书面语。 *Both* "思考" *and* "思索" *mean* "*think about sth. carefully and deeply.*" *Both are often used in written language.*

它们的区别是: *Their differences are as follows:*

1. 在词义上,"思考"着重于深刻周到地对事物已有的方方面面进行考虑。"思索"着重于努力探求,求索、发现出原来没有的新东西,语义比"思考"更进一步。 *Semantically,* "思考" *emphasizes the idea of giving a thorough and deep consideration to something that exists. While* "思索" *focuses on probing or exploring something new. And so,* "思索" *carries a deeper meaning than* "思考."

2. "思考"可以重叠使用。"思索"一般不能重叠。"思考" can be reduplicated but "思索" can't.

3."思考"可以构成"思考题、思考能力、思考方式、思考方法",也可说"独立思考"。"思索"不能。相反,"思索"能构成"冥思苦索","思考"不能。"思考" can form phrases such as "思考题,思考能力,思考方式,思考方法." Also, one can say "独立思考," but "思索" can't. In contrast, "思索" can form the phrase "冥思苦索", but "思考" cannot.

sīwéi 思维 →P437"思想"

用法 Usage:

名词 n.

人类在表象、概念的基础上进行的分析、综合、判断、推理等认识活动的过程。The process of analysis, synthesis, judging, reasoning and other cognitive activities based on representation and concepts.

(1) 这个人的抽象思维能力非常强。
(2) 每个人的思维方式并不相同。

说明 Notes:

"思维"也可作动词用,表示进行思维活动。"思维" can be used as a verb which shows the activities of thinking.

(3) 他又在超前思维了。
(4) 对一个问题的研究要多方面思维,才能得出正确的结论。

sīxiǎng 思想 →P437"思维"

用法 Usage:

名词 n.

1. 客观存在反映在人的意识中经过思维活动而产生的结果。Thought, the result of an objective existence reflected in a person's consciousness through a series of thinking activities.

(1) 他专门研究孔子的教育思想。
(2) 现在人们的思想越来越开放了。

2. 念头,想法。An idea; a thought.

(3) 他早就有回家乡办农庄的思想了。

(4) 千万不要有不吃苦赚大钱的思想。

说明 Notes:

1. 思想是从社会实践中来的,其内容是由社会制度的性质和人们的物质生活条件所决定的。因此,"思想"只是一个结果,其内容是因人而异的。"思想" is obtained from social practice, its content determined by the nature of the social system and the living conditions of people. Hence, "思想" is a result, the content of which varies from person to person.

2."思维"和"思想"都表示人的大脑的活动。Both "思维" and "思想" can mean the process of brain activities.

它们的区别是：Their differences are as follows:

① 在词义上,"思维"是指大脑活动的整个过程。"思想"是指这个过程的结果。"思维" refers to the whole process of brain activity while "思想" is the result of that process.

② "思维"的适用范围有限,能搭配的词语有限,如:"思维方式、思维活动、思维混乱、思维停止、形象思维、抽象思维、逻辑思维"等。"思想"的运用范围很广,可搭配的词语非常丰富,如:"早期、晚期、封建、民主、爱国、政治、军事、理论、保守的、进步的、健康的"等形容词;"锻炼、改造、搞通、维持原状的、有(这种)、检查、解放、转变"等动词;"方法、工作、水平、基础、教育、动向、体系、问题"等名词或短语。"思维" can only be applied to a limited area in limited collocations, such as "思维方式,思维活动,思维混乱,思维停止,形象思维,抽象思维,逻辑思维". "思想" can be applied to a wide area with collocated words and phrases such as "早期,晚期,封建,民主,爱国,政治,军事,理论,保守的,进步的,健康的." It can also be applied to verbs such as "锻炼,改造,搞通,维持原状的,有(这种),检查,解放,转变," and to nouns such as "方法,工作,水平,基础,教育,动向,体系,问题."

sǐ 死

用法 Usage:

动词 v.

1. 失去生命,死亡(与"生、活"相对)。可带"了"。To lose one's life; to die (opposite to "生,活"). It can be followed by "了".

(1) 他种的三棵树死了两棵。

(2) 他很伤心,他爷爷刚死于车祸。

2. 比喻消失、消除,表示没有结果、没有出路等。可带名词宾语。To eliminate; to get rid of sth., the outcome of which is "no activity, no result or no way out." It can be followed by a noun as its object.

(3) 她已经结婚了,你就死了这条心吧。

(4) 电脑又死机了。

形容词 a.

1. 表示(生物)已失去生命的(与"生、活"相对)的。只修饰名词。Being dead (opposite to "生,活"). It can only modify nouns.

(5) 他们在树林里发现一只死猪。

(6) 水面上有很多死鱼。

2. 比喻不活动、不流通、不发展、不起作用。只修饰名词。(Figurative use) being inactive; ineffective; non-circulating; not developing. It can only modify nouns.

(7) 这是一座死火山。

(8) 这是条死胡同,走不出去的。

3. 比喻不可调和的。只修饰名词。(Figurative use) being irreconcilable. It can only modify nouns.

(9) 他们是死对头,平时谁也不理谁。

(10) 他是我的死敌,有他没我,有我没他。

4. 表示令人讨厌或气愤的。只用在名词前面。Being annoying and enraging. It can only be used before nouns.

(11) 这个死妹子,不知跑到哪儿去了。

(12) 这只死猫,除了鱼,其他什么都不吃。

5. 比喻不灵活,死板、固定。可做定语、谓语和状语。(Figurative use) being inflexible, rigid and fixed. It can be used as the attributive, predicate and adverbial.

(13) 学习不能靠死记硬背。

(14) 脑筋太死,做事就不灵活。

6. 不顾生命,拼死。只修饰单音节动词,做状语。Being desperate. It can only modify monosyllabic words as an adverbial.

(15) 比赛中,红队只是死守,不作进攻。

(16) 我们最后的一场比赛,只有死拼,必须打赢。

7. 坚决。多修饰否定式动词。Being determined and firm. It is often used to modify the verbs in the negative form.

(17) 他死不肯开门,我进不去。

(18) 孩子死不开口,我什么也问不出。

8. 非常,表示程度达到极点。Being extreme. It indicates an intense degree to the limit.

(19) 那是个死要面子的人。

(20) 他死拉着她的手,没让她掉下去。

9. 用在动词、形容词后面作补语。Used after the verbs or adjectives as a complement.

① 表示动作的结果是死亡。Indicating the result of the action is death.

(21) 因为没浇水,那些花都干死了。

(22) 三年前,那老人就病死了。

② 表示动作的结果是不流通、不活动、不更改、不灵活等。Indicating the result of the action is non-circulation, inaction, inflexibility or an unchanging state.

(23) 前面出交通事故了,这条路已经堵死了。

(24) 你别把话说得太死。

③ 表示动作的结果达到了极点。Indicating the result of the action is the extreme or the limit.

(25) 一口气爬到一千米高的山顶,把我累死了。

(26) 老师,饿死了,下课吧!

说明 Notes:

1. 动词"死"可以带结果补语,如"死掉了",

也可以带趋向补语,如"死去、死过去"等。*The verb "死" can be followed by a complement such as "死掉了" or a directional complement such as "死去,死过去."*

2. 动词"死"做补语时,有两种意思,在具体上下文中,比较容易区分。*When the verb "死" is used as a complement, it has two meanings and can be easily differentiated in the context.*

(27) 他是白天黑夜地干活,活活累死的。(因累而死 To die because of exhaustion)

(28) 一口气跑了五千米,累死我了。(累极了 To be extremely tired)

3. 习惯语"要死"是表示达到极点,用在"得"字句里作补语。*The idiom "要死" indicates the idea of reaching the extreme or the limit. It is used in a sentence with "得" as the complement.*

(29) 最近她忙得要死。

(30) 下午两点还没吃饭,我饿得要死了。

4. "该死"表示愤恨或厌恶,有时表示自责。可用作修饰语,也可以单用。*"该死" expresses a strong resentment and dislike, sometimes, a self-accusation. It can be used alone or as a modifier.*

(31) 该死的家伙,又把房间弄得那么脏。

(32) 真该死,我忘带钥匙了。

sìhū 似乎 →P144"仿佛"、P191"好像"

用法 Usage:
副词 *ad.*

仿佛,好像。表示揣测、可能,有时有商量的语气。*As if; seemingly. It indicates a conjecture and possibility, sometimes with a negotiable tone.*

(1) 他似乎并不喜欢我。

(2) 天上都是乌云,似乎要下雨了。

说明 Notes:

"似乎"与"仿佛""好像"的区别是:*"似乎,""仿佛" and "好像" differ in the following aspects:*

1. "似乎"不能用于打比方,不能与"一般""似的"相呼应。"好像"可以。*"似乎" cannot be used to make an analogy, nor can it echo with "一般" and "似的." But "好像" can.*

(3) *孩子们的脸红得似乎苹果似的。

(4) 孩子们的脸红得好像苹果似的。

2. "仿佛"有动词用法,常组成"相仿佛"的格式,表示人和事物相类似,可单独做谓语,常用于书面语。"似乎"和"好像"没有这种用法。*"仿佛" can be used as a verb; it often joins "相" to form the expression "相仿佛" to indicate the similarities between people and between things. It can also serve as the predicate, which often appears in written Chinese. Neither "好像" nor "似乎" can be used this way.*

(5) 姐弟俩的性格相仿佛,都喜欢安静。

sōng 松

用法 Usage:
形容词 *a.*

1. 松散,不紧密(与"紧"相对)。常与"系、扎、捆、绑"等动词搭配使用。*Loose; not tight (opposite to "紧"). It often collocates with verbs such as "系,扎,捆,绑."*

(1) 你的鞋带松了,系一下。

(2) 行李别绑得太松,要带着走远路呢。

2. 松散,不坚实。*Loose; not solid.*

(3) 这儿的土质很松。

(4) 怎么才能做出又松又软的蛋糕呢?

3. 宽缓,不紧张(与"紧"相对)。*Loose and relieved; not tight (opposite to "紧").*

(5) 这个老师给分数很松,大家都喜欢她。

(6) 加了工资,手头比以前松多了。

动词 *v.*

放开,使(什么)松开。*To let go; to let sth. loose.*

(7) 吃得太饱了,得松一松腰带才行。

(8) 考试结束了,终于可以松口气了。

sòng 送 →P440"送行"

用法 Usage:

动词 v.

1. 递交,传送。把东西运去或拿去给人。To submit; to deliver; to send or bring something to someone.

(1) 在网上买东西,让快递送货上门,多方便。

(2) 把妹妹的饭送到楼上去。

2. 赠送。To give as a present.

(3) 明天要送一份礼物给他过生日。

(4) 老师送了我两本书。

3. 陪着离去的人走一段路或到某处去。To accompany a departing person for some distance or to a certain place.

(5) 朋友会送我到上海虹桥机场。

(6) 我送你们到楼下。

sòngxíng 送行 →P440"送"

用法 Usage:

动词 v.

1. 到将要远行的人离开的地方与他告别,或看着他离开。To see sb. off; to go to the place where someone departs, say goodbye to him, and watch him leave.

(1) 孩子们含着眼泪,站在村口为老师送行。

(2) 我来中国留学时,爸爸妈妈到机场为我送行。

2. 向死者告别(含有死者将远行的意思)。To bid farewell to the deceased.

(3) 很多学生也为他送行,参加了他的遗体告别会。

3. 饯行(设宴为某人送行)。To give a farewell dinner.

(4) 我们就在食堂里会餐,为大家毕业离校送行。

(5) 今天晚上八点在西湖饭店,我为你送行。

说明 Notes:

1. "送行"后面一般不能直接跟宾语。"送行" can't be followed by an object directly.

(6) *昨天我送行了我的同屋。

(7) 昨天我为同屋送行了。

2. "送行"前面常常由"为"带出被送行的对象,如例(1)(2)(3)(4)等。"为" is usually used before "送行" to introduce the object that someone sees off, as is shown in (1), (2), (3) and (4).

3. "送行"与"送"都有送行告别的意思。Both "送行" and "送" express the idea of seeing somebody off.

它们的区别是:"送行"的意思侧重与将要远行的人告别。"送"的意思侧重送到什么地方离别。Their differences are as follows: "送行" emphasizes the idea of saying goodbye to people ready to make a long journey. But "送" focuses on the place where you bid farewell.

sōují 搜集 →P426"收集"

用法 Usage:

动词 v.

到处寻找和聚集(事物)。To collect; to find and gather sth. from all over.

(1) 他现在的兴趣是搜集文物古董。

(2) 为了写好这篇论文,他正在辛苦地搜集资料。

说明 Notes:

"收集"和"搜集"都有表示聚集的意思。Both "收集" and "搜集" can express the idea of collecting something.

它们的区别是:"收集"的意思着重把分散的东西收拢、聚集,对象是分散的事物。"搜集"着重指到处寻找或挑选,对象是不在一起而需要到处寻找才能得到的东西。Their differences are as follows: "收集" emphasizes the idea of gathering scattered things, therefore, its objects are scattered things. But "搜集" indicates collecting or selecting *something from all over. Its object is something that needs to be searched for everywhere.*

suàn 算 →P442"算是"

用法 Usage:

动词 v.

1. 计算。可带"着、了、过",可以重叠。*To calculate. It can be followed by "了,着,过." In addition, it can be reduplicated.*

(1) 数字的加减,他算得很快。

(2) 他算过了,一共花了一百多元。

2. 表示计算进去。*To include.*

(3) 算上我,我们班一共有六个俄罗斯人。

(4) 他去了但没吃,不能把他算进去。

3. 推算,推测。*To reckon; to guess.*

(5) 长大以后,她怎么样,你现在算得出来吗?

(6) 你算一下,还要多久才能干完?

4. 认作,当作。*To consider sb./sth. as.*

(7) 我算什么摄影家,只不过喜欢照相罢了。

(8) 这件事,算你做得对。

5. 算数,承认有效。后面的宾语只有"话、数"等少数名词。*To count; to carry weight. Its objects are limited to such nouns as "话" and "数."*

(9) 你一个人说了不算数,要大家讨论同意才行。

(10) 他是个说话算话的人。

6. 作罢,不再进行。后面常跟"了"。*To let it go; to give up. It's often followed by "了."*

(11) 算了,他不吃就不吃,你吃吧。

(12) 算了,他不想听,我们别说了。

7. 即使,表示让步。前面常加"就"。*To compromise. It bears the meaning of "even if." It's often preceded by "就."*

(13) 就算我们大家都不去,他也会去的。

(14) 父母就算不同意,他们还是要结婚的。

8. 表示比较起来最突出。*To indicate the most prominent person/thing.*

(15) 我们班里,算他的汉语学得最好。

(16) 我觉得水果中,算葡萄最好吃。

说明 Notes:

1. 在第一义项中,有时"算"也是收钱的意思。*In the first usage mentioned above, "算" sometimes means "to collect money."*

(17) 这家饭店只算菜钱,不收饭钱。

2. "算"表示比较起来最突出的意思时,句子中要有参照物,如:例(15)中,"他"的参照物是"我们班里的(同学)";例(16)中,"葡萄"的参照物是"(其他很多)水果"。*When "算" means the most prominent or outstanding person/thing, there should be a reference in a sentence. For instance, in (15), the reference of "他" is "我们班里(的同学)." In (16), the reference of "葡萄" is "(其他很多)水果."*

suànle 算了 →P101"得了"

用法 Usage:

"算了"在句子中可以:*"算了" may serve:*

1. 作为谓语,"算了"表示作罢、不再计较的意思。如果前边是表示否定,"算了"前面常有"就"修饰,表示承接上文,作出结论。在口语中,常为"(你)算了吧"形式,表示否定或作出决定的意思。不能重叠。*As the predicate in a sentence, meaning "come, come; let it be." If there is a negative before it, "算了" is a kind of connection leading to a conclusion. In oral Chinese, it often takes the form of "(你)算了吧" to signify a negative and come to a decision. But it cannot be repeated.*

(1) 你不想去就算了吧,我们去。

(2) 你就算了吧,别跟他吵了。

2. 用在句末,表示衡量、比较后,祈使、终止、劝说和建议的语气。*To indicate, at the end of a sentence, that the speaker has made an assessment and a comparison and is now offering some advice as to what to do, probably*

to "let it be."

(3) 这么讨厌那份工作,换别的工作算了。

(4) 算了,都是昨天的剩菜,不吃了。

3. 做句子中的独立成分,表示制止或同意,相当于"得了、行了",可以重叠为"算了算了"。常用于口语。As an independent element to signify a stop or "go-ahead." It is equivalent to "得了,行了," and can be reduplicated as "算了,算了." It is often used in colloquial language.

(5) 算了,算了,别再等他了。

(6) 算了,就让他去吧!

4. 与"还是"配合,在选择疑问句中强调后一项选择的疑问语气。To pair up with "还是" to emphasize the second choice in a selective question.

(7) 你是真想看电影呢,还是说说算了?

(8) 他是真想吃面条呢,还是为了让我简单做一点儿算了?

说明 Notes:

1. "得了"和"算了"都有动词"得""算"加"了"的用法。Both "得了" and "算了" can appear in the use of a verb "得" or "算" plus "了."

(9) A:他得第一名了吗?
　　B:得了。

(10) A:吃饭的钱算了吗?
　　B:算了。

2. "得了"和"算了"的用法基本相同。"得了" and "算了" are used in the same way. 它们的区别是:Their differences are as follows:

① 在否定句中,一般用"算了"。"得了"多用于肯定句。"算了" usually appears in a negative sentence while "得了" usually appears in a positive one.

② "算了"表示衡量、比较的意思比"得了"重。"算了" carries a heavier tone than "得了" in expressing an assessment and a comparison.

suànshì 算是 →P441"算"

用法 Usage:

副词 ad.

1. 算得上,表示虽然不太理想,不合条件,但大致上还勉强能过去。Meaning "although something is not ideal, it is not too bad." It expresses a grudging approval or agreement.

(1) 你这次口语考试算是及格了。

(2) 虽然只学了三个月,但也算是来中国留学过了。

2. 总算,表示某件事或某种愿望,经过长时间的努力,终于发生或实现。At last; it indicates that a thing or a desire is finally realized after protracted efforts.

(3) 我一直想自己写一本书,今天算是实现梦想了。

(4) 经过两年的努力,博士论文算是完成了!

3. 加强肯定语气,表示确实的语气。It's used to strengthen the definite tone or to express the certainty.

(5) 从今天起,我也算是外国留学生了。

(6) 他算是个聪明人,你的话他都能听懂。

动词 v.

表示认作、当作、应该说是、可以说是的意思。To be considered as; may claim to be.

(7) 我们算是朋友了,以后有什么困难就找我。

(8) 他们算是学习努力的学生。

说明 Notes:

1. 用"算是"造句要注意:When using "算是" in a sentence, the following points should be noticed:

① "算是"在句子中一般用在主语后面,动词或形容词前边。"算是" is often used after the subject but before the verb or adjective.

② "算是"作副词用时,经常隐含庆幸的意思,如例(1)(3)(5)等。When "算是" is used as an adverb, it has the implication of luck as in (1), (3) and (5).

③ "算是"作副词用,第一义项在使用时,

句子中必须表示出虽然不太理想、不合条件,但大体上还勉强说得过去的语义。When "算是" is used as an adverb, as is mentioned in the first usage above, there must be the idea that "though it is not ideal, it is not too bad" in the sentence.

(9) 我虽然在北京只待了两天,但也算是去过北京了。

句子中"只待了两天"表示了"不太理想"的语义。如果句子是：In this sentence, "只待了两天" indicates the meaning of "not ideal." It is not appropriate to express it as:

(10) *我虽然在北京只待过两个月,但也算是去过北京了。

对一个外地人来说,在一个地方待两个月时间已经不算短了,所以这个句子在逻辑上没有"不太理想、不合条件,但大体上还勉强说得过去"的语义,"算是"用在这里不合适。For an outlander, it's not a short time to stay in a place for two months. Therefore, this sentence doesn't bear the logical meaning of "not ideal but not too bad." That's why it's not proper to use "算是" in this sentence.

2. "算是"和"算"做副词时,用法差不多,可以互换。When "算是" and "算" are used as an adverb, they bear a similar meaning and can be used interchangeably.

它们的区别是："算"的动词用法较多。"算是"动词用法只有表示"认作、当作"一种用法。Their difference are as follows: "算" is more often used as a verb while "算是" can only mean "consider . . . as" when it is used as a verb.

(11) *好,算是你及格了。
(12) 好,算你及格了。

suī 虽 →P443"虽然"

用法 Usage:

连词 conj.

1. 意义和用法基本跟"虽然"相同,表示让步。用在转折复句的偏句里,表示先让一步,承认或肯定某一事,然后说出不受这一事实限制的另一事。正句里经常用"但是、可是、然而、而"等词语呼应。多用于书面语。"虽" has basically the same meaning and usage as "虽然," which indicates a concession. In the clause of a complex sentence of contrast, it implies that the concession is first made to admit or affirm something, and then it relates to another thing that is not restricted by the fact. In its main clause such words as "但是,可是,然而, and 而" are often used to echo the preceding content. It is more used in written language.

(1) 她的女儿年龄虽小,然而懂事得很。
(2) 事情虽小,但意义重大。

2. 纵然,即使。常用于书面语中的固定词组,如："虽死犹生、虽败犹荣"等。Even though; even if. It is often used in fixed phrases in written language, such as "虽死犹生,虽败犹荣."

suīrán 虽然 →P443"虽"

用法 Usage:

连词 conj.

表示让步,用在转折复句的偏句里,表示先让一步,承认或肯定某一事,然后说出不受这一事实限制的另一事。Though; although. It indicates a concession in the clause of a complex sentence of contrast. A concession is first made to admit or affirm something, and then it relates to another thing that is not restricted by the fact.

1. "虽然"用在前一分句(即偏句),可在主语前,也可在主语后。后一分句(即正句)经常用"但是、可是、不过、仍然、却、还是"等词语呼应。When "虽然" is used in the clause, it can be placed either before or after the subject. In the main clause, such words as "但是,可是,不过,仍然,却,还是" are often used to echo the preceding content.

（1）这件衣服虽然很漂亮，但是太贵了。

（2）她虽然不太想去，可还是去了。

2. "虽然"用在后一分句（偏句）主语前面，表示让步。前一分句（正句）不用"可是、但是"等词语呼应。多用于书面语。When "虽然" is used before the subject in the subordinate clause (after the main clause) indicating a concession, words such as "可是,但是" can't be used in the main clause. This usage is found more in written language.

（3）我们还是邀请王老师参加了毕业晚会，虽然我们都有些怕他。

（4）有病了就要找医生，虽然我们并不喜欢医院。

说明 Notes：

"虽然"和"虽"的用法基本相同。The usages of "虽然" and "虽" are basically the same.

它们的区别是：Their differences are as follows：

1. "虽然"用在复句的前一分句时，可以用在主语前后。用在复句的后一分句时，一般只能用在主语前面，如例（3）（4）。When "虽然" is used in the subordinate clause before the main clause, it can be placed either before or after the subject. However, when the subordinate clause comes after the main clause, it can only be placed before the subject, as seen in (3) and (4).

2. "虽"所在的偏句，一般只能放在正句的前面。"虽然"所在的偏句既可以放在正句的前面，也可以放在正句的后面。A clause with "虽" can only be placed before the main clause, while a clause with "虽然" can be placed either before or after the main clause.

3. "虽"一般只能用于书面语。"虽然"通用于口语和书面语。"虽" is generally used in the written language, while "虽然" can be used in both oral and written Chinese.

4. "虽"有"纵然、即使"意义的用法。"虽然"没有这种用法。"虽" can express the meaning of "纵然，即使，" while "虽然" doesn't bear this meaning.

suí 随 →P446"随着"

用法 Usage：

动词 v.

1. 表示跟随、跟从的意思。To follow; to go with.

（1）他已经随他大哥去南京了。

（2）你快快随我来！

2. 照着办，顺从别人的行为、习惯、风俗等。To comply with others' behaviors, habits and customs.

（3）客随主便，你去哪儿我就去哪儿。

（4）都说"入乡随俗"嘛，我们也用筷子吃饭吧。

3. 外貌、性格等相像，主要用于孩子和父母。(Of one's appearance or character) to take after somebody, usually referring to the kids and their parents.

（5）她长得随她母亲。

（6）我女儿性格特别开朗，这点儿随我爱人。

介词 prep.

1. 跟着，顺着，依着。可以引进动作、行为或事物变化所跟随、依附的对象，与后面的词语组成介词短语，用在主语后面。Following; complying with. It can be used to introduce the object that an action, behavior or change follows. Forming the prepositional phrase with the words behind it, it is used after the subject.

（7）我们随导游参观了古老又漂亮的故宫博物院。

（8）人们的能力只有随着科学技术的发展而提高，才能跟着社会前进。

2. 引进动作、行为或事物发展、变化的依据或凭借（表示一种条件），相当于"依据、根据"。In accordance with; on the basis of. It is used to introduce the basis or foundation (as a condition) that an action, behavior,

development or change depends on. It is similar to "依据,根据."

(9) 太阳花会随太阳光的方向转动花朵。

(10) 这次旅游一定要随旅游团的行程安排进行。

3. 引进动作、行为或事物的凭借,相当于"任、任凭",表示随便你怎么样。*At one's convenience; at one's discretion. It is used to introduce the basis that an action, behavior or something depends on. It is similar to "任,任凭," meaning "as you like."*

(11) 桌子上的东西随你喝、随你吃。

(12) 随你怎么想,反正我不喜欢他。

4. 顺便。*In passing.*

(13) 请随手关门!

副词 *ad.*

"随……随……"分别用在两个动词或动词性短语前面,表示前后两个动作、行为紧接着发生,意思相当于"随时……随时……",一般修饰单音节动词为多。*"随…随…" is used in front of two verbs or verbal phrases to indicate the two actions or two behaviors happen one after another, which is similar to "随时…随时…." It often modifies monosyllabic verbs.*

(14) 宿舍楼的服务员真好,有什么事总是随叫随到。

(15) 杭州下雪是随下随化的,所以杭州的雪景要在下雪的时候去看。

连词 *conj.*

表示在任何条件下(无条件)都是如此,相当于"任、任凭、不论、不管"等词语。后面常带"什么、怎么(样)"等疑问代词表示没有任何限制,在后一分句中常用"也、还、都、总"等词呼应。*It means that this is the case under any circumstances. Similar to "任,任凭,不论,不管," it is often followed by interrogative pronouns such as "什么,怎么(样)" to indicate no restrictions. Words such as "也,还,都,总" are used in the main clause to echo with it.*

(16) 随你买面包、买米饭、买什么,他就是不吃,真是没办法。

(17) 随你给他多少钱,他总是不够用。

suíbiàn 随便

用法 Usage:
动词 *v.*

离合动词。表示听任某人的方便(没关系,满不在乎的意思)。*To do as one pleases. Used as a separable verb, it means to do sth. at one's convenience.*

(1) 随便,你买什么,我就吃什么。

(2) 开车也行,坐公交车也行,随你的便。

形容词 *a.*

1. (言行)无拘束的,不加考虑的,不慎重的。可重叠为"随随便便"。*(One's words or behaviors) unrestrained, unconsidered, indiscreet. It can be reduplicated as "随随便便."*

(3) 对长辈说话可不能太随便了。

(4) 今天去公司面试,你不能随随便便地穿。

2. 不加以限制,没有明确的目的。*Having no restrictions; having no definite purpose.*

(5) 大家随便聊聊吧!

(6) 不买不要紧,随便看吧!

3. 不讲究,凑合。*Not paying attention to one's dress; being casual in dressing.*

(7) 我穿衣服很随便,不讲究。

(8) 时间来不及了,随便吃一点。

连词 *conj.*

任凭,无论。后面常跟"什么、怎么、怎么样"等词。*Despite; no matter what. It is often followed by such words as "什么,怎么,怎么样."*

(9) 随便什么书,他都爱看。

(10) 你对她好、对她不好,随便怎么样,她都不生气。

suíhòu 随后

用法 Usage:
副词 *ad.*

表示一种动作行为或情况跟着另一种动作

行为或情况发生。多用于动词之前,也可以用于主语之前。后面常跟"又、就、也、再、才"等词语搭配。*Soon after; soon afterwards. Referring to an action or a situation which happens following another action or situation, it is mostly used before a verb and before the subject, and usually followed by words such as "又,就,也,再,才."*

（1）你们先去吃吧,我随后就到。

（2）大家都说了自己的名字,随后老师也说了他的名字。

说明 Notes:

"随后"在实际使用中,可以在句中做定语。*"随后" can be used as an attributive in a sentence.*

（3）第一次创业失败了,随后的几年,他一直在找新的创业机会。

（4）他没有考上理想的大学,随后的一段时间,他心情很不好。

suíshí 随时

用法 Usage:

副词 ad.

1. 表示某种动作行为,经常保持着持续的状态,有"时时刻刻"的意思。*At any time. Referring to a certain action and behavior that maintains a continuous state, it has the same meaning as "时时刻刻."*

（1）他随时都带着汉语生词卡片,随时会拿出来学习。

（2）我们的咖啡店二十四小时营业,随时都可以让你喝上各种咖啡。

2. 表示在任何时间里,只要有需要,都可以进行某种相应的活动,有"无论何时"的意思。*It means that at any time, a certain activity can be done whenever necessary. It has the same meaning as "无论何时."*

（3）只要有问题,随时来问我。

（4）如电脑出现问题,可以随时与我们公司联系。

3. 表示某种情况经常出现,某种动作行为常常发生,有"经常、常常"的意思。*It means that a situation or a behavior will always happen. It has the same meaning as "经常,常常."*

（5）在街上随时都可以看到唱歌、拉琴的人。

（6）她是个善良的姑娘,随时可以看到她帮助别人的行为。

说明 Notes:

1. 表示任何时间、任何地方,可以用"随时随地"表达。*When it means at any time or at any place, it can be replaced by "随时随地."*

（7）她随时随地都带着她的弟弟。

（8）外出旅游,随时随地都要注意安全。

2. "随时"表示在任何时间里的意思时,可以在主语前后、助动词前后。*"随时" means at any time. It can be placed before or after the subject as well as the auxiliary verb.*

（9）出租车随时可以叫到。

（10）出租车可以随时叫到。

（11）有什么问题,你随时都可以来找我。

（12）有什么问题,随时你都可以来找我。

suíshǒu 随手 →P434"顺手"

用法 Usage:

副词 ad.

趁某种方便,顺便做某事,但一定是用手做的。*Doing sth. at one's convenience; doing sth. by the way. The action must be performed with hands.*

（1）他随手从桌子上拿起一张报纸,看了起来。

（2）他随手把垃圾扔进了垃圾筒里。

（3）他拿出手机一看,是广告信息,随手就删了。

说明 Notes:

"随手"与"顺手"都表示在做某件事时,顺便做另一件事。*Both "随手" and "顺手" indicate the idea that "when you do something, you do another thing at your convenience."*

它们的区别是：*Their differences are as follows:*

1. "随手"着重于做某件事之后,紧接着很自然地伸手做另一件事。"顺手"着重于做一件事时或做完以后,很容易地、顺便地、不费事地捎带着做另一件事。"随手" focuses on the idea that "after you do something you naturally do something else." While "顺手" focuses on the idea that "after you do something you do another thing at your convenience, easily and without taking too much trouble."

2."顺手"还有形容词用法,表示做事顺利的意思。"随手"没有这种用法。"顺手" can also be used as an adjective that means to do something smoothly. While "随手" can't be used in this way.

suízhe 随着 →P444"随"

用法 Usage:
介词 prep.

1.引进某种结果和现象产生、出现的原因和条件。"随着"常常用在句首。 Along with. Indicating the cause and conditions for some result or phenomenon, "随着," as a preposition, usually appears at the beginning of a sentence.

(1)随着科学技术的发展,人们的交流手段越来越多了。

(2)随着年龄的增长,我更能理解父母的辛苦了。

2.引进动作行为、某种情况或某种变化所跟随依附的对象,相当于"跟着、伴随着"。 Introducing an object followed by a certain behavior, situation or change. It equals "跟着,伴随着."

(3)随着一声响雷,大楼断电了,顿时一片黑暗。

(4)随着音乐声起,年轻人纷纷跳起舞来。

副词 ad.

表示某一动作、行为、情况伴随着或紧接着另一动作、行为、情况而产生,相当于"跟着、伴随着、接着",直接用在动词前面做状语。 It means that an action, behavior or situation is accompanied or followed by another action, behavior or situation. It equals "跟着,伴随着,接着," all of which can be used before a verb as an adverbial.

(5)运动员的身影随着一跳,就飞过了两米五的高度。

(6)随着一声叫喊,小姑娘就从床上掉到了地上。

说明 Notes:

1."随着"作为介词,用来引入变化的条件、原因时,后面短语中的动词一般应该含有能持续变化、动态的意义,如"发展、提高、增加、减少、改变、改善、扩大、扩张、加剧、加强、深入、延长、调整"等。没有这种含义的动词,一般不能在"随着"后面出现。 When "随着" is used as a preposition to refer to the condition or cause of a change, the verb in the phrase after "随着" should always carry a continuous and dynamic meaning, such as "发展,提高,增加,减少,改变,改善,扩大,扩张,加剧,加强,深入,延长,调整." Verbs without a dynamic and continuous meaning can't be used after "随着."

(7)＊随着来杭州留学,我越来越喜欢杭州了。

(8)随着对杭州了解的深入,我越来越喜欢杭州了。

2."随"和"随着"都作介词,引进跟随、依附的对象,表示"跟着"的意思。介词短语都在主语后面时,两个词可以互换。 Both "随" and "随着" can be used as a preposition to refer to the accompanying or following object. They have the same meaning as "跟着." When the prepositional structure is used behind the subject, the two words can be used interchangeably.

(9)大家随/随着我来。

它们的区别是: Their differences are as follows:

① "随"作介词有"顺着"的意思。"随着"没有。"随着"有"伴随着"的意思。"随"没有这种意思。 When "随" is used as a preposition, it can mean "to follow something," but "随着" can't. "随着" means "to be accompanied by something," while "随" doesn't.

(10) *我们家的老人，只有随着他的话去做，他才满意。

(11) 我们家的老人，只有随他的话去做，他才满意。

(12) *她随音乐跳起了舞。

(13) 她随着音乐跳起了舞。

② "随"和"随着"作介词，引进原因或条件时，"随"一般以成语或"随……而……"的结构形式用在主语之后，多用于书面语。"随着"的使用较随意。When "随" and "随着" are used as a preposition to introduce a cause or condition, "随" is often used in fixed phrases or the structure "随…而…" after the subject in written language while the usage of "随着" is rather casual.

(14) 人们的交流手段随科学技术的发展而越来越多。

(15) 人们的交流手段随着科学技术的发展而越来越多。

(16) 随着科学技术的发展，人们的交流手段越来越多。

3. "随"和"随着"都作副词，表示两个动作紧接着发生时，"随"一般以成语或"随……随……"结构形式出现，如"随叫随到"。"随着"没有这种限制。Both "随" and "随着" may serve as an adverb to indicate one action follows another immediately. In this use, "随" generally takes the structure of "随…随…," as in "随叫随到," while "随着" is not restricted by this rule.

4. "随"有连词用法。"随着"没有连词用法。"随" can serve as a conjunction, but "随着" cannot.

5. 注意句子中"随"作动词用，后面带"着"的形式跟介词"随着"的区别。Watch out for "随" serving as a verb and followed by "着." It is different from "随着" as a preposition.

(17) 您前边走，我后边随着。("随"的动词用法"随" used as a verb)

(18) 这样不仅帮助了别人，自己的能力也会随着提高。("随着"的副词用法"随着" used as an adverb)

sǔnhài 损害 →P401"伤害"、P448"损失"

用法 Usage:
动词 v.

指使利益、权利、事业、名誉或健康、身心等蒙受损失。(One's interests, rights, careers, reputation or health etc.) to suffer a loss or damage.

(1) 近距离看电视会损害视力。

(2) 父母经常吵架，会损害孩子的心理健康。

说明 Notes:

"损害"和"伤害"都表示受到损伤、危害。Both "损害 (harm, impair, damage)" and "伤害 (wound, harm, hurt)" indicate the harm and damage that have been experienced.

它们的区别是："损害"着重指因破坏而使蒙受损失，多用于抽象事物，如："健康、功能性、积极性、利益、事业、主权、独立"等。"伤害"着重使良好或正常的状态受创，多用于有生命的东西及人的思想感情、积极性、荣誉、威信等抽象事物。语意比"损害"重。They differ as follows: "损害" emphasizes the harm and damage resulting from destruction. Often it applies to abstract things such as health, functionality, enthusiasm, honor, prestige, interests, career, reputation, sovereignty, and independence. "伤害," however, stresses harm and damage done to a state that is good and normal. It applies mostly to things that have a life or abstract things such as people's ideas, enthusiasm, honor, and reputation. It usually means something more severe than "损害."

sǔnshī 损失 →P448"损害"

用法 Usage:
动词 v.

消耗或失去钱财、物品、人员等。To consume or lose money, goods or people, etc.

（1）这次投资损失了多少钱？
（2）火灾中损失了大量贵重物品。

名词 *n.*

消耗或失去的钱财、物品、人员等。*The money, goods or people that are consumed or lost.*

（3）这次投资，我的损失惨重。
（4）他的逝世是电影界的重大损失。

说明 Notes:

"损失"和"损害"的区别是：*The differences between "损失" and "损害" are as follows:*

1."损失"的对象可以是具体的，也可以是抽象的。"损害"的对象以抽象的为主。当"损害"的对象是健康时，一般是泛指，而且程度较轻。如果指使身体某部位或思想感情（包括自尊心、积极性等）受到损害，要用"伤害"。如果受到损害的对象是"团结、组织、规章、制度、条约"等，动词要用"破坏"。*The objects of "损失" can either be concrete or abstract; while the objects of "损害" are always abstract nouns. When the object is one's health, it expresses a general idea and its degree is relatively light. When its object turns out to be one's body, spirit or feeling (including one's self-respect and initiative etc.), "伤害" instead of "损害" should be adopted. When the objects are words such as "团结,组织,规章,制度,条约," the verb "破坏" is to be used.*

2."损失"有名词用法，可作句子的主语、宾语。"损害"一般没有名词用法。*"损失" can be used as a noun to function as the subject or the object of a sentence, but "损害" can't be used as a noun.*

3.用"损失"和"损害"造句时要加以注意。*Watch out for blunders when using "损失" and "损害."*

（5）*这次大火，学校宿舍损害了两层楼房。
（6）这次大火，学校损失了两层楼房。
（7）*鳄鱼常常会损害在水边饮水的羊和马。
（8）鳄鱼常常会伤害在水边饮水的羊和马。
（9）*你这样做，只会损失你自己的形象。
（10）你这样做，只会损害你自己的形象。

suǒ 所

用法 Usage:

名词 *n.*

表示机关或其他办事机构的名称。如："研究所、派出所、医务所"等。*The name of a department or some other agency, such as "研究所,派出所,医务所."*

助动词 *aux. v.*

"所"用在及物动词以前，使"所＋动"成为名词性短语。多用于书面语。*"所" is used before a transitive verb to form the nominal phrase "所＋v." It is always used in written language.*

主要句式有：*The main sentence structures are as follows:*

1.跟"为"或"被"合用。*To collocate with "为" or "被."*

① 表示被动。*To indicate a passive meaning.*

（1）我们被年轻美丽的汉语老师所吸引，上课非常专心。
（2）你们不要为他的甜言蜜语所欺骗。

② 只跟"为"合用，不表示被动。只是为协调音节和谐的结构助词。*"所" is used together with "为" to function as an auxiliary word to coordinate the harmonious syllables. It doesn't carry a passive meaning.*

（3）这一点为前人所未知。

2.用在做定语的主谓词组的动词前面，表示中心语是受事者。在一定的语言环境中，"所"修饰的中心语可以不出现。*Appearing before a verb as an attribute that is composed of a subject and a predicate, "所" indicates that the object is the center word. In certain contexts the head word modified by "所" may not appear in the sentence.*

（4）现在开始说一下大家所关心的考试问题。
（5）我所看到的(情况)，大概就是这些。

3.用在"是……的"格式中的名词、代词和动词之间,强调施事者和动作的关系。"所" is inserted between nouns, pronouns and verbs in the "是...的" pattern to emphasize the relation between the agent and the action.

(6) 物价问题,是人们所关注的。

(7) 这种高质量的商品,是年轻顾客所欢迎的。

4. "所"与一些动词一起,常作"有"或"无"的宾语。"有所"表示动作行为有一定程度的变化,"无所"中的"所"是任指,表示"什么"的意思。如:"有所变化、有所了解、有所发现、有所进步、无所作为、无所畏惧"等。"所" can be used together with some verbs to act as the object of "有" or "无." "有所" indicates that there is a certain degree of change in the action, while "所" in "无所" means something like "nothing whatever." For example, "有所变化,有所了解,有所发现,有所进步,无所作为 (to have accomplished nothing), 无所畏惧 (to have nothing to fear)."

5. 用在动词前面,组成固定结构。如"大失所望、众所周知、闻所未闻、所向无敌、为所欲为、大势所趋"等。"所" is used before verbs to form fixed phrases such as "大失所望,众所周知,闻所未闻,所向无敌,为所欲为,大势所趋."

说明 Notes:

用"所"造句时要注意:When "所" is used in a sentence, the following points should be noticed:

1. "所"跟"被、为"组成句子时,谓语动词一般都是双音节动词。When "所" is used with "被" and "为" to form a sentence, the predicate is always a disyllabic verb.

(8) 许多鱼还在幼小时就被人们所捕捉。

2. "所"后面的动词一定是及物动词。下面句子中"所"后面不是及物动词,因此不应该用"所"。The verb following "所" must be a transitive verb. Example (9) is wrong because the verb following "所" is an intransitive verb.

(9) *我们所休息的地方离这儿很近。

(10) 我们休息的地方离这儿很近。

3. "所"跟后面的动词之间不能加入其他成分。No elements can be inserted between "所" and the verb.

(11) *老师所向我们提的要求,我们都记住了。

(12) 老师向我们所提出的要求,我们都记住了。

4. "有/无+所+双音节动词"和由"所"组成的固定词组中"所"不能省略。"有+双音节动词"和"有+所+双音节动词"意思并不一样。如:"有所缓和",表示"有一定程度的缓和",不等于"有缓和"。In the pattern of "有/无+所+双音节动词" and the fixed phrase formed by "所," the word "所" can't be omitted. The meanings of "有+双音节动词" and "有+所+双音节动词" are different. For example, "有所缓和" means "to relax to a certain degree," and is not equal to "有缓和," which means "to have relaxation."

5. 在文言文里,"所"最早的用法就是把动词变成名词性的词语。如:"得"变成了"所得(到的东西)";"说"变成"所说(的话)"。在现代汉语里,"所"用在动词前面与动词构成体词结构的作用,由于结构助词"的"的使用,正逐渐弱化而形成可有可无的趋势。In ancient Chinese the earliest usage of "所" is to turn a verb into a noun phrase. For example, "得" has been transformed into "所得(到的东西)"; "说" has been changed into "所说(的话)." In modern Chinese, "所" is used before a verb to form the nominal structure. Due to the use of structural auxiliary word "的," the grammatical function of "所" in the structure is weakened and it becomes a dispensable trend.

(13) 他所说的不一定是对的。(他说的不一定是对的。What he said is not necessarily right.)

(14) 所花的还是妈妈的钱。(花的是妈妈的钱。What was spent was still mom's money.)

suǒwèi 所谓

用法 Usage:
形容词 a.

1. 一般所说的意思。多用于提出需要解释的词语或接着加以解释时。不能做谓语。So-called; what is generally said. It's mostly used to put forward words that require some explanation — right now or later. It can't be used as a predicate.

(1) 所谓网友,是指在网络上相识、相知,见面较少,甚至从没见面或只能在视频中才能见到的朋友。

(2) 所谓志愿者,联合国定义为"自愿进行社会公共利益服务而不获取任何利益、金钱、名利的活动者"。

2. 某些人所说的。含有不承认别人声称的意思,所引的部分常加引号。What some people say. It means that you do not approve of what someone has said. The quotation marks are often used for the quoted words.

(3) 要我代你做作业,这就是你所谓的"帮助"啊,那不行。

(4) 他们所谓的"朋友",其实是一起吃吃喝喝的朋友。

说明 Notes:

1. "所谓"和"所说的"意思一样,许多地方可以互换。"所谓"比较正式,通用于口语和书面语。"所说的"多用于口语。"所谓" and "所说的" have the same meaning and can be used interchangeably. "所谓" is relatively formal and can be used in both oral language and written language while "所说的" is usually used in oral language.

2. "所谓"的句子结构比较简单。一般为"所谓……,就是……",或者"……,这就是……所谓的……",如例(3)。The sentence of "所谓" is relatively simple. It is always used in the pattern "所谓...,就是..." or "...,这就是...所谓的...," as is shown in (3).

suǒyǐ 所以 →P586"因此"、P586"因而"

用法 Usage:
连词 conj.

在因果关系的语句中表示结果或者结论,主要句式有: So; therefore; hence. It is used to express a result or conclusion in a sentence about cause and effect. The main sentence structures are as follows:

1. 用在后一分句的开头,前一分句常常用"因为、由于"等词相呼应。Used at the beginning of the second clause, and words such as "因为" and "由于" are often used in the former clause to echo in meaning.

(1) 他因为学习努力,所以成绩非常好。

(2) 由于现代科技的快速发展,所以我们的生活越来越方便了。

2. 前一分句先说明原因,后一分句用"(就)是……所以……的原因"进一步解释和肯定这个原因产生的结果。The first clause explains the reason and the latter clause uses the pattern "(就)是...所以...的原因" for further explanation and affirming the result.

(3) 我和他是邻居,这就是我所以对他比较了解的原因。

(4) 想自己创业,这才是他所以离开公司的真正原因。

3. "所以"又可作为"之所以、其所以",用在前一分句,突出原因和理由,后一分句必用"是因为"相呼应。这一句式多用于书面。"所以" can also be expressed as "之所以" or "其所以," which is used in the former clause to emphasize the reason. "是因为" is always used in the latter clause to echo with the previous clause. It appears in written language.

(5) 她之所以得到那么多人的热爱,是因为她有一颗善良的心。

(6) 其所以选择哲学专业,是因为他受了父母的影响。

4. 单独成句,表示对前面所讲的原因的结论。To form a separate sentence, indicating the conclusion of the above-mentioned reason.

（7）A：听说你妈妈来中国了？
　　B：所以嘛，昨天我去上海浦东机场接妈妈了。

说明 Notes：

"所以"还有名词用法，表示实在的情况、缘由或者适宜的言行举止。仅限于在固定短语中做宾语，如"忘乎所以、忘其所以、不知所以"等。"所以" also has a nominal usage that expresses the real situation, reason or appropriate behavior. It can only be used as an object in fixed phrases such as "忘乎所以，忘其所以，不知所以."

suǒyǒu 所有 →P560"一切"

用法 Usage：

形容词 a.

全部的，一切的。与中心语之间"的"可加可不加。All; whole; entire. Sometimes the auxiliary word "的" may or may not be added between "所有" and the head word.

（1）所有人都喜欢他。
（2）我太喜欢这个歌手了，他的所有唱片我都收藏了。

动词 v.

领有。To claim ownership of something.

（3）这部分遗产归你所有。
（4）土地归国家所有。

名词 n.

领有的东西。常用在短语中，如："倾其所有、尽其所有"等。Things that somebody has or owns. It is usually used in phrases such as "倾其所有，尽其所有."

suǒzài 所在

用法 Usage：

名词 n.

1. 处所。多用于书面语。The location. It is usually used in written language.

（1）这就是你们教学实习的所在。
（2）环保是健康的所在，谁不想拥有呢！

2. 存在的地方。The place where something exists.

（3）条件太高，就是他找不到工作的原因所在。
（4）我是华裔，这是我学习汉语动力之所在。

3. 后面常跟名词，表示主语人物所属的、存在的地方。Often followed by a noun, indicating the place where the subject exists or belongs to.

（5）你的户口所在地是北京吗？
（6）要申请读博士的话，需要你所在学校教授的推荐信。
（7）你所在公司的待遇怎么样？

说明 Notes：

1. "所在"是书面语，非常口语化的语境一般不用。"所在" is always used in written language. It can't be used in a highly colloquial context.

（8）＊这是什么所在？
（9）这是什么地方？

2. "所在"一般要与其他词语一起做句子成分，表示什么范围的所在。不能单独使用。"所在" should always be used together with other words to indicate the scope of a problem. It cannot be used separately.

（10）＊睡眠不好的所在是什么？
（11）睡眠不好的问题所在是什么？
（12）＊大家都知道他每天迟到的所在原因。
（13）大家都知道他每天迟到的原因所在。

3. "所在"修饰名词做定语时，一定是指有人在的地方，如"所在公司、所在学校、所在部门、所在单位"等。When "所在" modifies a noun as an attributive, it must refer to the place where people are, such as "所在公司，所在学校，所在部门，所在单位."

tāshi 踏实

用法 Usage:

形容词 a.

1.（指工作或学习的态度）切实,不浮躁。可以重叠为"踏踏实实"。(Describing the attitude toward work or study) practical, down to earth. It can be reduplicated as "踏踏实实."

(1) 他这个人挺踏实的。

(2) 只有踏踏实实地学习,才能得到知识。

2.（指内心、情绪状态）安定,安稳。常与"心里、感到、觉得"等词语搭配使用,也可形容睡眠的情况。(Describing the emotional status) peaceful, steady. It often goes with words such as "心里,感到,觉得." It can also describe the quality of sleep.

(3) 跟着老王办事儿,我感到特别踏实。

(4) 天气太热,孩子昨晚睡得不太踏实。

tái 台

用法 Usage:

名词 n.

1.平而高的建筑物,便于在上面瞭望。如:"阳台、瞭望台、检阅台"等。Architecture with a high and flat top convenient for lookout, as in "阳台,瞭望台,检阅台."

2.公共场所室内外高出地面便于讲话或表演的设备(用砖砌或用幕布制成)。如:"舞台、讲台、主席台"等。An indoor or outdoor structure (established with bricks or wood) higher than the ground for speech or performance in public, as in "舞台,讲台,主席台."

3.某些做底座用的器物。如:"锅台、蜡烛台、磨台、炮台"等。Certain artifacts used as stands, as in "锅台,蜡烛台,磨台,炮台."

4.桌子或类似桌子的器物。如:"写字台、梳妆台、乒乓球台"等。Tables or artifacts like tables, as in "写字台,梳妆台,乒乓球台."

5.某些机构的名称。如:"天文台、电视台、广播台"等。Names of certain institutions, as in "天文台,电视台,广播台."

6.比喻官职或权力。Official position or power (used figuratively).

(1) 这个市长已经下台了。

(2) 她上台当市长五年了,现在还在台上。

táishang 台上

用法 Usage:

名词 n.

1."台"指高而平坦的建筑物,如:"戏台、舞台、演讲台、检阅台、主席台"等。"台上"则表示在台子的上面,与"台下"相对。"台" refers to an architecture with a high and flat top meant for lookout, as in "戏台,舞台,演讲台,检阅台,主席台." "台上" means on top of the structure, as opposed to "台下."

(1) 台上的那位歌手唱得真好!

(2) 俗话说:"台上一分钟,台下十年功"。

2.比喻在任的官职或权力。Incumbent official position or power (used figuratively).

(3) 他爸爸在台上的时候，我们一点都不知道那是他爸爸。

(4) 他虽然已经不是台上的县长，但老百姓还是很尊重他。

说明 Notes:

"台上一分钟，台下十年功"的意思是，在台上表演的时间只有短短的一分钟，可是为此需要付出很多年的时间反复练习。这句俗语最早用来表示戏曲表演艺术家们的艰苦付出，现在扩展到相关的其他领域。"台上一分钟，台下十年功" means that although the performance on stage may only last one minute, it often takes years of repeated practice. The idiom was first used to describe the hard work of traditional Chinese opera artists and was later used in other related fields.

tài 太

用法 Usage:

形容词 a.

1. 高；大。如："太空、太学"等。High or big, as in "太空, 太学."

2. 表示极端的。Indicating an extreme degree.

(1) 这是太古时代的鱼化石。

(2) 你强横太甚，别人不敢接近你的。

3. 辈分比自己的祖父母高一辈的；身份最高或辈分更高的，如："太姥爷、太姥姥、太爷爷、太奶奶；太老师、太夫人"等。Great-grand; more or most senior. It is used to refer to someone's grandparent's father or mother, as in "太姥爷, 太姥姥, 太爷爷, 太奶奶," or to respectfully refer to a senior, as in "太老师 (father of one's teacher or teacher of one's father), 太夫人 (someone else's mother)."

副词 ad.

表示程度很高或程度过分，可用在肯定句和否定句。句尾常带"了"，形成"太……了"的结构。Extremely, exceedingly, very; too. Indicating a high or extreme degree, it can be used in either a positive or a negative sentence. It forms the "太……了" structure with "了" used at the end of the sentence.

1. 用于肯定。表示赞叹，多用于感叹句，带有强烈的感情色彩。Indicating admiration, it is mostly used in exclamatory sentences with strong emotions.

(3) 你真是太好了！

(4) 这里的风景太美了。

2. 用于否定。表示程度过分，不如意或不满意。Used in a negative sentence to indicate an excessive degree and express dissatisfaction or discontent.

(5) 今天太热了，我不想出去。

(6) 这个房间太小了。

3. "太"用于否定句，有两种句式：Negative sentences with "太" have two forms as follows:

① "太＋不＋形容词/动词"。表示强烈的否定。"太＋不＋a./v.," indicating a denial with an emphatic tone.

(7) 你写汉字太不认真了。

(8) 她太不遵守交通规则了。

② "不＋太＋形容词/动词"。表示委婉的否定，意思跟"不大"相近。"不＋太＋a./v.," indicating a denial with a euphemistic tone, which is similar to "不大 (not very)" in meaning.

(9) 我觉得这件衣服不太好看。

(10) 我还不饿，不太想吃。

说明 Notes:

1. 只是一般的叙述或客观描述时，"太"不能直接用在形容词或动词前。"太" cannot be used directly before an adjective or a verb in an objective narration or description.

(11) *书店里有太多种汉语词典。

(12) 书店里有很多种汉语词典。

(13) *昨天上课，我太迟到了。

(14) 昨天上课，我迟到了很长时间。

2. 无论是肯定式还是否定，在比较句中，都不能用"太"。"太" cannot be used in

comparative sentences either in a positive or a negative form.

(15) *这本书比那本书太好了。
(16)这本书比那本书好多了。

tánhuà 谈话 →P228"讲话"、P436"说话"

用法 Usage:
动词 v.

1. 两个人或者两个以上的人在一起说话、对话。(Of two or more people) to converse; to talk.

(1) 他们在谈话,我听了一会儿,觉得没意思就回来了。
(2) 昨晚我们宿舍同学谈话谈到十二点。

2. 有话题、有目的地提出自己的看法、要求和意见等。常用"找、跟"引出交谈的对象,多用于上级对下级、长辈对晚辈、老师对学生等。句子中常有对谈话内容的说明。To offer one's opinion or to make a request on a specific topic or for a specific purpose. "找" or "跟" is often used to introduce the other party in the conversation. It is mostly used when a person senior or at a higher position asks to speak with another person who is junior or at a lower position, such as a boss to a staff member, a senior to a junior, or a teacher to a student. There is usually a description of the content of the conversation in the sentence.

(3) 听说经理找你谈话了,什么事儿?
(4) 老师又跟我谈了一次话,希望我不要退学。

名词 n.

用谈话的形式发表的意见。一般内容比较重要,含有庄重的色彩。The formal opinion expressed through a serious conversation.

(5) 报纸上发表了几个经济学家的谈话,你看了吗?
(6) 昨天电视上播送了市长的新春谈话。

说明 Notes:

"谈话"和"说话""讲话"都是离合动词,中间都可以插入其他词语。As separable verbs, "谈话," "说话," and "讲话" can have other words inserted between them.

它们的区别是:Their differences are as follows:

1. "讲话"和"说话"有对别人行为动作指责、非议的意思。"谈话"没有这个意思。"讲话" and "说话" can mean to criticize or disapprove someone else's behavior. "谈话" has no such meaning.

2. "讲话"和"说话"可以是说话方单方面的行为。"谈话"必须是两个人以上双方或几方的行为,在句子中必定出现谈话的对象。"讲话" and "说话" can indicate the behavior of the speaker alone. "谈话" must be between two or more people and the other party of the conversation has to be identified in the sentence.

(7) 他正在讲话,请你等半个小时。
(8) 他正在跟同学谈话,请你等一下。

3. 涉及两人以上的对话时,三者有时可以互相替换,表示"聊天儿、闲谈"的意思。更强调轻松、随意地闲谈、聊天儿的话,用"说话"更合适。如果表示比较正式地对话,说出自己的意见、要求、想法等,用"谈话"更合适。When describing a conversation between two or more people, sometimes the three expressions are interchangeable with the meaning like "聊天儿,闲谈." But "说话" is the most suitable to use with the emphasis on casual chat. "谈话" is a better choice for a more formal conversation to express one's opinion or request.

(9) 几个人站在街边谈/说/讲了一会儿话,就走了。
(10) 她和奶奶都靠在沙发上,看着电视,说着话。
(11) 老师又找玛丽谈话了,是因为迟到的事儿吗?

4. "谈话"和"讲话"有名词用法。"说话"没有名词用法。"谈话" and "讲话" can both be used as nouns, but "说话" cannot.

5. "讲话"与"谈话"的区别是：*The differences between "讲话" and "谈话" are as follows:*

① "讲话"是以讲演的形式发表意见。"谈话"是以对谈的形式发表意见。*When expressing an opinion, "讲话" takes the form of a speech whereas "谈话" takes the form of a conversation.*

② "讲话"没有"谈话"动词的第二种用法。*"讲话" does not have the second usage of "谈话" as a verb.*

(12) *今天下午老师要找我讲话。

(13) 今天下午老师要找我谈话。

tánlùn 谈论 →P456"讨论"、P584"议论"

用法 Usage：

动词 *v.*

用谈话的方式表示对人或事物的看法。*To express one's opinion about people or things in a conversation.*

(1) 他们在谈论什么？

(2) 关于写什么论文的问题，我们谈论了半天。

说明 Notes：

"谈论"也可用作名词。*"谈论" can also be used as a noun.*

(3) 他们的谈论，我不感兴趣。

tǎolùn 讨论 →P456"谈论"、P584"议论"

用法 Usage：

动词 *v.*

就某一问题交换意见并共同分析研究。可以重叠为"讨论讨论"。*To exchange ideas on a certain matter and analyze it together; to discuss. It can be reduplicated as "讨论讨论."*

(1) 今天我们讨论一下写毕业论文的问题。

(2) 关于班级活动的时间、地点，大家讨论讨论。

说明 Notes：

1. "讨论"可用作名词。*"讨论" can be used as a noun.*

(3) 老师请你参加关于教学实习问题的讨论。

(4) 明天的讨论时间还没定呢。

2. "谈论"和"讨论"都是动词，也都有名词用法。它们最基本的意思都是说出自己的意见。*"谈论" and "讨论" can both be used as a verb or a noun with the basic meaning of expressing one's opinion.*

它们的区别是：*Their differences are as follows:*

① "谈论"多以随意说话的方式，表示自己对人对事的看法，跟别人的意见没有关系。谈论内容非常广泛，有比较轻松的语言环境。*"谈论" expresses one's opinion on a person or a thing in the form of a free conversation and it has nothing to do with the view of other people. It covers a wide range of topics in a relatively easy and relaxed environment.*

② "讨论"着重于就某一问题彼此交换意见，各自强调自己的看法，也听取别人的意见。通过交流，取得大家认可的一致的结论。"讨论"多在比较正式的场合进行。*"讨论" emphasizes exchanging ideas or expressing one's view on a topic and it includes hearing views from other people. Through the exchange, a conclusion commonly recognized is reached. So "讨论" happens on a rather formal occasion.*

③ "讨论"可以重叠，"谈论"不能。*"讨论" can be reduplicated while "谈论" cannot.*

tè 特 →P457"特别"

用法 Usage：

副词 *ad.*

1. 非常，格外。*Extremely, exceptionally.*

(1) 这小姑娘特聪明。

(2) 这家饭馆儿的菜特好吃。

2. 特地，特意。表示专门为了做某事，带有书面色彩。*Specially, intentionally (carrying a literary tone).*

（3）您搬入新居，我们特来祝贺。

（4）我们学校特设了一家清真餐厅。

形容词 *a.*

超出一般的，不平常的，特殊的。不能单独做谓语。*Exceeding the normal; extraordinary; unusual. It cannot serve as a predicate alone.*

（5）这是特等舱的船票。

（6）你知道妈妈给孩子最大的特权是什么吗？

tèbié 特别 →P118"独特"、P456"特"、P458"特殊"、P593"尤其"

用法 Usage:

形容词 *a.*

不普通，与众不同。*Unusual; special.*

（1）他笑得很特别，有点儿奇怪。

（2）我没什么特别的爱好，就是喜欢做饭。

副词 *ad.*

1. 非常，格外。*Very; exceptionally.*

（3）今年夏天特别热。

（4）我特别喜欢这本书，已经看了好几遍了。

2. 特地，特意，着重（做某事）。*Intentionally; specifically; (doing something) on purpose.*

（5）今天老师特别表扬了小王。

（6）公司特别讨论了我提出的方案。

3. 尤其（从同类事物中提出某一事物加以说明或强调）。常说成"特别是"。*Especially. (to single out something from the same category for explanation or emphasis). It is often used as "特别是."*

（7）我很喜欢运动，特别是打羽毛球。

（8）这个城市打出租很难，特别是上下班时间。

说明 Notes:

1. "特"和"特别"的区别是：*The differences between "特" and "特别" are as follows:*

① "特"是单音节词，作形容词用时不能单独做谓语。"特别"是双音节词，作形容词用时可以单独做谓语。*As a monosyllabic adjective, "特" cannot stand alone as a predicate. But as a disyllabic adjective, "特别" can stand alone as a predicate.*

（9）*他的性格很特。

（10）他的性格很特别。

② "特"作副词用时，没有"尤其"的用法。"特别"有"尤其"的用法。*When used as an adverb, "特别" can mean "especially" but "特" cannot.*

③ "特"修饰形容词时，多用于口语；修饰动词时则多用于书面语。"特别"通用于口语和书面语。*When modifying adjectives, "特" is mostly used in spoken language. When modifying verbs, "特" is mostly used in written language. "特别" can be used both colloquially and in written language.*

2. "独特"和"特别"做形容词，都有不一般、不普通的意思。*"特别" and "独特" are both adjectives, meaning uncommon and not ordinary.*

（11）他对事物的看法很特别/独特。

它们的区别是：*Their differences are as follows:*

① "独特"侧重于独一无二，独有，其他人没有，词义使用范围较窄。"特别"侧重表示不普通，与同类、与平常的事物不相同。*"独特" emphasizes uniqueness, something others don't possess. It is applied to a more limited scope. "特别," by contrast, focuses on being uncommon, not the same as things of the same type, not the ordinary type.*

② "特别"用作形容词时，可以直接做定语，可受程度副词修饰。它还能用作副词，表示"特地、着重"的意思时，只能修饰动词，不能修饰形容词。"独特"只能作形容词用，没有副词用法。*As an adjective, "特别" can serve as an attribute and go with a degree adverb. Also, it can serve as an adverb. When it means "特地"*

or"着重，"it can only describe a verb, not an adjective. As for"独特，"it can only serve as an adjective, not as an adverb.

（12）＊他很喜欢音乐，独特是古典音乐。

（13）他很喜欢音乐，特别是古典音乐。

③ 词语搭配对象不完全相同。"独特"常与"构思、手法、风格、作用、标志"等搭配，而"特别"作形容词时可与一般的名词搭配，使用范围比较广。They collocate with different words and expressions."独特" goes with "构思，手法，风格，作用，标志。" "特别，" as an adjective, goes with ordinary nouns and covers a wider scope.

④ "特别"可以组成一些固定词组，如"特别快车、特别任务"等。"独特"不能。"特别" can be used to form specific expressions such as "特别快车，特别任务。" "独特" cannot be used in this way.

tèdì 特地 →P459"特意"

用法 Usage：
副词 ad.

表示专为某件事。Specially; for a specific purpose.

（1）我特地去上海看他，他却去外地出差了。

（2）每天要特地安排一个小时，让孩子自己看书。

tèdiǎn 特点 →P459"特征"

用法 Usage：
名词 n.

指人或事物具有独特的地方。Special characteristics of people or things.

（1）中国菜最大的特点是什么？

（2）每位老师都有自己上课的特点。

tèshū 特殊 →P457"特别"

用法 Usage：
形容词 a.

表示与众不同或程度超过一般。与"一般、平常、普通"等词语意思相对。Distinctive, with a degree higher than normal, as opposed to "一般，平常，普通."

（1）这种雨衣是用特殊的材料做成的。

（2）这是特殊情况，我们也是第一次遇到。

说明 Notes：

"特别"和"特殊"都形容人或物与同类的不同，或事物与平常的不同。"特别" and "特殊" both describe the differences between people (or things) and those of the same kind, as well as differences between ordinary things and special ones.

它们的区别是：Their differences are as follows：

1. "特别"着重在与众不同，不同于普通人、普通物，是个别的，有时含有"奇怪"的意思。多用来形容"式样、构造、结构、方法、脾气、会议、味道"等词语。"特别" emphasizes individual cases' being different from regular people or things. Sometimes it means "strange." It is often used to describe words such as "式样，构造，结构，方法，脾气，会议，味道."

"特殊"着重在与一般不同，不同于平常情况，异常的，词义比"特别"重。常用来形容"情况、环境、条件、材料、产品、规律、才能、本领、贡献、意义、地位、性格、教育、照顾、原因、关系、战斗、处理"等词语。"特殊" emphasizes being different from the normal situation with a heavier tone than "特别." It does not necessarily refer to individual cases. It is often used to describe words such as "情况，环境，条件，材料，产品，规律，才能，本领，贡献，意义，地位，性格，教育，照顾，原因，关系，战斗，处理."

2. "特别"多做谓语、定语、状语、补语，不能做宾语，可以受程度副词修饰，也可以带补语。"特殊"可以做谓语、定语、宾语、状语，不做补语，能受程度副词修饰，能带程度补语，多用于书面语。"特别" can serve as the predicate, attributive, adverbial or complement, but it cannot serve as the object. It can be modified by a degree adverb and

can be followed by a complement. "特殊" can serve as the predicate, attributive, object or adverbial, but it cannot serve as the complement. It can be modified by a degree adverb and can be followed by a degree complement. It is mostly used in written language.

（3）今天他穿得很特别/特别得很。
（4）*今天他穿得很特殊。
（5）我跟你们一样，没有半点特殊。（指待遇 Referring to the treatment one receives）
（6）*我跟你们一样，没有半点特别。

3."特别"有副词用法。"特殊"没有副词用法。"特别" can be used as an adverb, but "特殊" cannot.

tèyì 特意 →P458"特地"、P684"专门"

用法 Usage:

副词 ad.

表示为一个专门目的（而做某事）或由于重视（而做某事），特地。To do something for a special purpose or due to the importance attached to it.

（1）今天是好朋友的生日，我特意为她买了一个大蛋糕。
（2）妈妈特意准备了我最爱吃的菜。

说明 Notes:

"特地"和"特意"都是副词，都是指为某一目的而特别去做某件事。用法相同，一般可以互换。As an adverb, "特地" and "特意" both mean to do something for a special purpose. The two are usually interchangeable with the same usage.

它们的区别是："特地"着重出于为专门的目的而行动，重在行为动作本身。"特意"不仅有专门的目的，而且着重在出于主观意愿地为某人某事而采取行动。They differ as follows: "特地" emphasizes an action or behavior for a special purpose. "特意" emphasizes not only the special purpose, but also taking an action for someone or something out of a subjective will.

（3）我特地为你去买了一双旅游鞋。（着重在去买的动作 Emphasizing the action of buying）
（4）我特意为你去买了一双旅游鞋。（着重在购买者的心意 Emphasizing the buyer's good will）

tèzhēng 特征 →P458"特点"

用法 Usage:

名词 n.

指可以作为人或事物特点的征象或标志。Characteristics of people or things, often serving as a symbol or sign.

（1）中国南部的气候特征是温暖、湿润。
（2）亚洲人的外貌特征是黄皮肤、黑眼睛和黑头发。

说明 Notes:

"特点"和"特征"都指人或事物具有的独特的地方。"特点" and "特征" both refer to what is unique about people or things.

它们的区别是：Their differences are as follows:

1."特点"着重指出与同类事物相比，在性质、内容上的，或者形式、外表上的独具之处。可用于具体的人或事物，也可以用于抽象事物。可以是优点，也可以是缺点。"特点" emphasizes the uniqueness in nature, content, form or appearance as compared to other people or things in the same category. It can be used for specific people or things or abstract matters. It can be an advantage or a disadvantage.

（3）我很喜欢她开朗、乐观的性格特点。
（4）他写字有个特点，就是越写越小。

2."特征"着重指出人或事物外表或形式上的独特的表象，是显露于外的。多用于具体的人或事物，也可用于抽象事物。"特征" emphasizes the unique appearance or shape of people or things, which are observable from the outside. It is mostly used for specific people or things. It may also be used for abstract matters.

(5) 他写的字有个特征,每个字都是细细长长的。

(6) 志愿者的特征有志愿性、无偿性、公益性和组织性。

tí 提

用法 Usage:

动词 v.

1. 垂手拿着(有提把、绳套之类的东西)。 To grab (something with a handle or strap) with the arm hanging downward.

(1) 他提着一只塑料袋、一只篮子走过来。

2. 使(事物或位置)由下往上、由低往高移。 To raise a thing from a low position to a high one.

(2) 把你的右手再提高一下!

(3) 他由部门经理提到总经理了。

3. 把预定的期限往前挪。 To move the time for an event ahead.

(4) 讲座的时间提到星期二了。

4. 提出;举出;指出。 To offer (an idea or suggestion); to list; to point out.

(5) 我们向他提了意见。

(6) 大家提了他很多优点,也提了他一个缺点。

5. 谈(起、到);说(起、到)。 To mention; to talk about.

(7) 关于请假去旅游的事,他一句也没提到。

(8) 提起昨晚的事,我就觉得可笑。

6. 提取。 To withdraw (money); to accept the delivery of goods.

(9) 明天我得去银行提一笔钱,你跟我一起去好吗?

(10) 你去仓库提货,我去打开商店大门。

7. 汉字的一个笔画,也叫"挑"(tiāo)。如"提"的偏旁(扌)的第三个笔画就是"提"。 One stroke of Chinese characters, also called "挑" (tiǎo). For example, the third stroke of the radical "扌" in the character "提" is called "提."

8. 提议;推举。 To propose; to elect.

(11) 我提玛丽做我们的班长。

说明 Notes:

动词"提"后面带趋向动词"出"作补语,成为"提出",表示"举出、指出"的意思。"提"后面带"到"作补语,成为"提到",表示"提"这个动作有结果,如例(7)。 When the verb "提" is followed by the directional complement "出" to form "提出," it means "to offer (an idea or suggestion), to list, to point out." When it is followed by the complement "到" to form "提到," it indicates that the action of "提" has produced a result as in (7).

tíshì 提示 →P460"提醒"

用法 Usage:

动词 v.

提出对方想不到的、没有想到或应加注意的地方,使对方明白或注意。 To remind someone of something that is forgotten, neglected, or simply not thought of.

(1) 老师对我说:别紧张,如果忘了词儿,我在旁边提示你。

(2) 手机提示电量不足了。

tíxǐng 提醒 →P460"提示"

用法 Usage:

动词 v.

从旁指点、指出,促使对方注意别忘了要做的事儿。 To remind someone of something so that he/she will not forget it.

(1) 谢谢你提醒我,要不我真的忘了。

(2) 明天有个重要会议要参加,到时候你提醒我一下。

(3) 妈妈提醒了我好几次,我还是忘了。

说明 Notes:

1. "提醒"还可以说成"提个醒儿"。"提醒" can also be said as "提个醒儿."

（4）我给你提个醒儿，明天你要给妈妈打个电话。

2."提示"和"提醒"的区别是："提示"重在引导、启发要做的事情和怎么做。"提醒"重在指点对方别忘了原来定下要做的事情。The difference between "提示" and "提醒" lies in: "提示" emphasizes guiding someone as to what to do and how to do it while "提醒" focuses on reminding someone not to forget to do something as planned.

tǐhuì 体会 →P462"体验"

用法 Usage:

动词 v.

表示通过亲身接触，对事物有所感受、了解、认识。To understand something through hands-on experience.

（1）这篇文章的意义，需要细细体会。

（2）等你自己做了母亲，就能体会到做妈妈的感受了。

名词 n.

感受到、领会到的内容。The content experienced and understood.

（3）这两个月的实习中我有很多体会。

（4）同学们正在交流学习中的心得体会。

说明 Notes:

"体会"用作动词时，可加结果补语"到"，表示有效果。When "体会" is used as a verb, it can be followed by the resultant complement "到" to indicate the impact.

（5）自己做了妈妈，才体会到父母当年的辛苦。

（6）孩子们体会到了劳动的快乐。

tǐxiàn 体现 →P33"表现"

用法 Usage:

动词 v.

某种性质和现象在某一事物上具体表现出来。常带"了"。To show certain characteristics or a phenomenon through something. It is often followed by "了."

（1）这篇小说体现了作家热爱故乡的情感。

（2）长城体现了古代中国人的聪明才智。

名词 n.

指具体的表现。Specific manifestation.

（3）她的行为是真、善、美的最好体现。

（4）以善为本是他管理方法的突出体现。

说明 Notes:

"表现"和"体现"都有"显现、表露出来"的意思，后面都可以加"在"，表示从哪个方面表现出来。后面还可以加"出、了"，如"表现出、体现出、表现了、体现了"。"表现" and "体现" both mean "to show, to manifest." Both can be followed by "在" to indicate the outlet of the manifestation. Both can be followed by "出，了" as in "表现出,体现出,表现了,体现了."

它们的区别是：Their differences are as follows:

1. 在词义上，"表现"着重于某种作风、状态、思想、感情、态度等抽象的意义或事物，通过具体的语言、行为动作、现象或一定的形式表示、反映出来。宾语可以直接指人的名词。如"态度、样子、情绪、兴趣、品质"等。"体现"着重于某种抽象的精神、意愿等通过某种具体的事物来显示。宾语多是表示性质、概念等的抽象名词或名词性短语，如"本质、本色、作用、方针政策、优越性"等。Semantically, "表现" emphasizes something abstract such as style, status, thought, emotion, or attitude being reflected through a specific language, behavior, phenomenon or form. The object can be directly related to people, such as "态度,样子,情绪,兴趣,品质." "体现" emphasizes the abstract spirit or will reflected through certain concrete things. The object is often an abstract noun or noun phrase representing property or concept, such as "本质,本色,作用,方针政策,优越性."

（5）*她对中国文化体现出很大的兴趣。

（6）她对中国文化表现出很大的兴趣。

（7）*这种招聘方法表现了他们公司管理制度的特点。

（8）这种招聘方法体现了他们公司管理制度的特点。

2. 在语感上，"表现"比较直接地表露人或事物的行为作风、形态状况，让人直观地不用思索地感受到或觉察到。"体现"表示的意义则要求人们加以体会才能理解到的内在本质含义。"表现" directly reflects the behavior or style of people, or the shape or status of things, which can be felt intuitively without further thinking. "体现" reflects inherent essence that takes experience and further thinking to understand.

（9）在学习游泳这件事中，他表现得非常顽强。

（10）学习游泳这件事充分体现了他顽强的精神。

3. 在词性上，"体现"一般作为动词用。"表现"除了动词用法，还有名词用法。"体现" is usually used as a verb. "表现" can serve both as a verb and as a noun.

4. "表现"在语义上，还有故意显示自我、炫耀自己的意思。"体现"没有。"表现" can mean "to show off." "体现" has no such meaning.

5. "表现"可以带补语，如"表现得很勇敢"。"体现"不能。"表现" can be followed by a complement as in "表现得很勇敢。""体现" has no such usage.

tǐyàn 体验 →P460"体会"

用法 Usage:

动词 v.

通过实践来认识周围的事物；亲身经历；实地考察领会。To learn about the surroundings through hands-on experience or field trips.

（1）到西北高原可以体验完全不一样的生活。

（2）你先到工厂去体验一下吧。

名词 n.

通过实践获得的感受或认识；进行的考察。The experience or understanding acquired through practice; the investigation conducted.

（3）没有去农村的体验，他不可能写出反映农村生活的小说。

（4）把你的体验告诉我们吧。

说明 Notes:

"体会"和"体验"的区别是："体会"的词义重在通过对事物的亲身接触而产生的感受和认识。"体验"的词义则重在亲身去实践的过程。The difference between "体会" and "体验" is as follows: "体会" emphasizes the experience and understanding acquired through personal contact while "体验" focuses on the process of hands-on experience.

（5）看了少儿绘画展览，你体会到什么？

（6）很可惜，我小时候没有体验过绘画实践。

tì 替 →P87"代"、P88"代替"

用法 Usage:

动词 v.

代替，替换。后面可以带"着、了、过"，可以带补语，可以重叠。To substitute; to replace. It can be followed by "着，了，过，" or a complement and can be reduplicated.

（1）十号运动员受伤了，六号运动员替上。

（2）口语考试，谁也替不了你。

介词 prep.

为，给。For; on behalf of.

（3）我真不会喝酒，你替我喝了吧。

（4）下个星期我要出差，王老师替我上语法课。

说明 Notes:

1. "替"作介词用，后面一定带有表示对象的名词或代词，如例（4）。When "替" is used as a preposition, it must be followed by a noun or pronoun referencing the object as in (4).

2. 有时候"替"出现在相同句子里,可以有两种意思。到底是哪种意思,要看前后句子的语意决定。Sometimes the same sentence containing the word "替" allows two possible interpretations.

(5) 小王是他的好朋友,所以替他买词典。(小王买词典给他。Xiao Wang bought him a dictionary.)

(6) 小王家就在书店旁边,所以替他买词典。(小王代他买词典。Xian Wang bought a dictionary on his behalf.)

3. "替"和"代"做动词用,两个词的意思和用法基本相同。When used as verbs, "替" and "代" have similar meaning and usage.

它们的区别是:Their differences are as follows:

① "替"的口语色彩比"代"更浓。"替" is more colloquial than "代."

② "替"有介词用法。"代"没有。"替" can be used as a preposition but "代" cannot.

5. "替"和"代替"的意思、用法基本相同。"替" and "代替" have similar meaning and usage.

它们的区别是:Their differences are as follows:

① "替"是单音节,一般后面也带单音节词。"代替"是双音节,一般后面带双音节词语。As a monosyllabic word, "替" is generally followed by another monosyllabic word. "As a disyllabic word, "代替" is generally followed by another disyllabic word.

② "替"有介词用法。"代替"没有介词用法。"替" can be used as a preposition, but "代替" cannot.

tiānqì 天气 →P369"气候"

用法 Usage:

名词 n.

一定区域一定时间内大气中发生的各种气象变化,如温度、湿度、气压、降水、风、云等的情况。Various meteorological changes in the atmosphere at a certain location within a certain time, such as temperature, humidity, atmospheric pressure, precipitation, wind and cloud.

(1) 你每天都看天气预报吗?

(2) 今天天气真好,咱们去爬山吧。

说明 Notes:

"天气"和"气候"的区别是:The differences between "天气" and "气候" are as follows:

1. "天气"指一个地区较短时间内大气中发生的各种气象变化(如阴、晴、雨、雪或冷、暖、干、湿等)。"气候"指一个地区多年的天气特征和大气活动的全过程。"天气" refers to various meteorological changes in a region within a relatively short time (such as cloudy, sunny, rainy, snowy, or cold, warm, dry, wet, etc.). "气候" refers to the meteorological features and the entire process of the atmospheric activities of a region for years.

(3) *北京春天的天气怎么样?
(4) 北京春天的气候怎么样?
(5) *明天的气候预报你看了没有?
(6) 明天的天气预报你看了没有?
(7) *我们国家属于海洋性天气。
(8) 我们国家属于海洋性气候。

2. "气候"有比喻用法,"天气"没有比喻用法。"气候" can be used figuratively, but "天气" cannot.

(9) 这几个人成不了什么气候。(这几个人做不成什么大事。These guys won't make much of a difference.)

tiānrán 天然 →P693"自然"

用法 Usage:

名词 n.

自然存在的,自然产生的(区别于"人造"或

"人工"）。Naturally existing or produced (as opposed to "人造" or "人工").

（1）我们现在做饭用的全是天然气。

（2）山区的风景是天然的。

tiānxià 天下

用法 Usage:

名词 n.

1. 指中国或世界。China or the world.

（1）天下的母亲都是爱自己的儿女的。

（2）我们的朋友遍天下。

2. 指国家或国家的统治权。A country or the sovereignty of a country.

（3）千万别忘了这是人民的天下。

（4）老百姓就希望生活安定,天下太平。

说明 Notes:

1. 中国上古时代称中国为"天下",指天子统治的范围。In ancient China, "天下" referred to the territory under the sovereignty of the emperor.

2. "天下"常出现在一些俗语或者固定词组中。"天下" is often used in idioms or fixed expressions.

（5）天下乌鸦一般黑。（比喻所有地方的坏人都是一样的坏 A figurative sentence meaning that all villains are equally evil wherever they are）

（6）桃李满天下。（比喻老师所培养的学生非常多,遍布所有地方 A figurative sentence meaning that a teacher has nurtured many students who now spread out everywhere）

tiāo 挑

用法 Usage:

动词 v.

1. 选择,挑拣。To pick and choose.

（1）这些衣服都挺漂亮的,喜欢的话就挑几件吧。

（2）你要挑什么样的家政服务员,我给你介绍。

2. 挑剔。一般指故意找毛病、找出不好的地方。To nitpick (deliberately looking for problems).

（3）你别老挑我的毛病,你自己呢?

（4）老师总会在你的文章里挑出写得不够好的地方。

3. 用肩膀担起担子。To carry the load on one's shoulder.

（5）小和尚挑着水,走在山路上。

（6）这么重的担子,我挑不动。

4. 比喻承受工作重任。(Figuratively) to shoulder a heavy burden of work.

（7）他那么年轻,能挑起总经理工作的重担吗?

名词 n.

担子,挑子,挑儿。口语中常为儿化。Loads carried on a shoulder pole; a loaded carrying pole.

（8）这副挑儿太重,我挑不起。

说明 Notes:

"挑"的意思是"选择、挑拣"时,对象可以是人,也可以是物,如例(2)和(1)。"挑" means to pick and choose, the object of "挑" can be a person as in (2) or an object as in (1).

tiáojié 调节 →P465"调整"

用法 Usage:

动词 v.

对事物从数量上和程度上调整、控制,使适合要求。To adjust the amount or degree of something to meet the requirement(s).

（1）身体不好,首先要调节好自己的心态。

（2）电脑的页面太暗了,把亮度调节一下。

说明 Notes:

"调节"的对象一般是"温度、湿度、亮度、速度、气氛"或人的"精神状态、情绪、心态"等。The objects of "调节" are often "温度,湿度,亮度,速度,氛围" or people's "精神状态,情绪,心态."

tiáozhěng 调整 →P464"调节"

用法 Usage:

动词 v.

在原来的基础上,根据客观情况和要求,做些适当的改变,使正常或更好地发挥作用。可重叠为"调整调整"。 *To make proper adjustments according to the objective conditions or needs so as to perform better. It can be reduplicated as "调整调整."*

(1) 听说油价又要调整了。

(2) 你的睡眠时间需要调整调整。

说明 Notes:

1. "调整"的对象一般是"经济、计划、政策、机构、方案、结构、价格、工资、时间、人员、方向"等。 *The objects of "调整" can be "经济,计划,政策,机构,方案,结构,价格,工资,时间,人员,方向, etc."*

2. "调节"和"调整"的区别是: *The differences between "调节" and "调整" are as follows:*

① 在词义上,"调节"着重于节制,在一定数量或程度范围内调配。"调整"着重于重新整顿或配置,使原来混乱、不合理、不平衡等不符合要求的状况改变为适应客观情况或要求,以发挥更大的作用。 *Semantically, "调节" emphasizes the adjustment within a certain range of amount or degree. "调整," however, emphasizes reorganization or reconfiguration to change the originally chaotic, unreasonable or imbalanced situation to one that meets the needs of objective conditions and perform better.*

② "调整"改变的程度比"调节"深。"调节"只限于用在程度上、数量上的调配、调整。"调整"可以是程度上、数量上的调配,也可以是其他方面的重新整顿或整理,如"政策、方案"等。 *"调整" involves a higher degree of change than "调节." "调节" refers to adjustment in terms of degree or amount. In addition to these, "调整" can also refer to the reorganization of other things such as "政策,方案."*

tiǎo 挑

用法 Usage:

动词 v.

1. 用棍棒或竿子等的一头向上扯起。 *To pull up with one end of a stick or a pole.*

(1) 新郎高兴地挑开盖在新娘头上的红布。

(2) 小心一点儿,先用木棍儿把电线挑开。

2. 向外或向上的方向拨。 *To poke and shift outward or upward.*

(3) 请你找根针,帮我把手上的刺儿挑出来。

(4) 他把籽儿都挑出来,再给奶奶吃西瓜。

3. 比喻公开提出,常带补语"明",说成"挑明"。 *To put forward in public (figuratively); to bring something to light. It is often followed by a complement to form the phrase "挑明."*

(5) 我把话挑明了吧,你这次不能去国外留学。

(6) 虽然没有挑明,但谁都知道小王爱上那姑娘了。

4. 挑拨,挑动。 *To instigate, to provoke.*

(7) 他俩吵架,全是她挑起的。

(8) 他总是喜欢挑是非,让大家不团结。

tīngdào 听到 →P465"听见"

用法 Usage:

表示听见。 *To hear.*

(1) 我说的话,你们听到吗?

(2) 我们听不到你说的话。

tīngjiàn 听见 →P465"听到"

用法 Usage:

动词 v.

表示听到。 *To hear.*

(1) 我听见屋子里有人在说话。

(2) 很远的地方都能听见她的歌声。

说明 Notes:

"听到"和"听见"都是动补结构的动词,表示听到声音的意思。但是,它们在语义上有非常细微的区别:如果从主观能力上来说,一般用"听见",不用"听到"。"听到" and "听见" are both verb-complement structures meaning "to hear a sound or voice." The two have subtle differences in semantic meanings. "听见" rather than "听到" is usually used for subjective abilities.

（3）他出生还不到一个月,怎么能听见你说话呢？

（4）昨天晚上,你听见窗外的歌声了吗？

如果从客观条件上来说,一般用"听到",不用"听见"。"听到" rather than "听见" is usually used for objective conditions.

（5）坐在后面的同学也能听到老师讲的话。

（6）妈妈说的话你听到了吗？

tīngshuō 听说 →P258"据说"

用法 Usage:

动词 v.

1. 听别人说。To hear someone say something.

（1）我听说他感冒了。

2. 据说。多用作插入语。It is said (often serving as an insertion).

（2）听说,他去上海了。

3. 听和说,指语言学习的两种技能(有别于"读写")。To listen (to) and speak, two language skills, different from "读写 (to read and write)."

（3）学习外语,必须重视听说。

（4）他的汉语听说水平很高,但是读写能力较低。

说明 Notes:

"听说"和"据说"的区别是: The differences between "听说" and "据说" are as follows:

1."听说"的第三种用法,在句子中作为名词用法。

2."据说"只有"听说"的第一种、第二种用法,不能带宾语,不能带"了、过"。"据说" is used only in the first and second meanings of "听说," and it cannot take an object, nor can it be followed by "了" or "过."

tíngliú 停留 →P466"停止"

用法 Usage:

动词 v.

1. 停下来,暂时留在某处,不再继续前进。To stop moving forward and stay at a place temporarily.

（1）汽车不能在高速公路上停留。

（2）他在北京停留了一个星期。

2. 引申为停在某个阶段或水平上,不再向前发展或继续进行。To stop at a certain stage or level without further development (figuratively).

（3）你要努力做到,不能只停留在口头上。

（4）一个学期过去了,怎么你的口语还停留在原来的水平上？

说明 Notes:

"停留"表示停留在某处的意思时,后面常搭配表示时间(暂停的具体时间)的词语,如例（2）,或搭配表示处所(停留的地方)的词语,如例（1）（3）。When "停留" means to stop moving forward and stay at a place temporarily, it is often followed by a time word (the specific time for the pause) as in (2) or a location word (the place to stay) as in (1) and (3).

tíngzhǐ 停止 →P466"停留"

用法 Usage:

动词 v.

不再继续进行。可带宾语,但多为动词、小句宾语。可带"了、着、过",可带补语。To stop. It can be followed by an object but is mostly followed by a verb or a clause. It can be followed by "了,着,过," or a complement.

(1) 大家的笑声突然停止了。

(2) 老师一进来,大家立刻停止了讲话。

说明 Notes:

1. "停止"和"停留"意义不同。前者强调动作不再进行,后者强调暂时逗留。"停止" and "停留" have different meanings, with the former meaning "to stop" and the latter meaning "to stay temporarily."

(3) 他的呼吸已经停止了。

(4) 她在香港只停留了一天。

2. 使用"停止"时要注意：One should pay attention to the following rules when using "停止":

① 表示某一动作、活动,特别是自然现象,进行到最后阶段,不再继续时,一般不用"停止",而用"停"。"停" rather than "停止" should be used to describe that an action or activity, especially a natural phenomenon, has reached the final stage and stopped.

(5) *雨停止了。

(6) 雨停了。

② 表示关系中断,不用"停止"。"停止" is not used to describe the end of a relationship.

(7) *我来中国后,男朋友和我的关系停止了。

(8) 我来中国后,男朋友和我的关系断了。

tǐng 挺 →P170"怪"、P196"很"

用法 Usage:

副词 ad.

表示程度高,很。Very (indicating a high degree).

(1) 老师最近挺忙的。

(2) 这本书挺有意思。

动词 v.

1. 伸直(腰、脖子、身体等)。To straighten (one's waist, neck, body, etc.).

(3) 他走路时,胸部挺得高高的。

(4) 写汉字时要挺胸、挺腰,字才写得正。

2. 凸出(肚子)。To bulge out (the belly).

(5) 你挺着大肚子还挤公共汽车,小心一点儿。

(6) 怀孕到五个月的时候,肚子就挺出来了。

3. 勉强支撑。To endure with one's will.

(7) 累了就休息,别硬挺着。

(8) 他的肚子已经痛了三天,还挺着不去医院。

4. 支持。To support.

(9) 你去参加比赛,我们挺你。

形容词 a.

1. 表示直。Straight.

(10) 他的裤线很挺,好看!

2. 表示突出。Prominent.

(11) 他身高一米九,个儿挺挺的,一眼就能看到他。

说明 Notes:

1. "挺"和"很"的区别是：The differences between "挺" and "很" are as follows:

① "挺"比"很"的程度略低,多用于口语,常带有感情色彩。"挺" is at a lower degree than "很." It is often used colloquially to show emotions.

② "挺"有动词和形容词用法。"很"没有。"挺" can be used as a verb or an adjective. "很" has no such usage.

③ "很"可以用在动词后面做补语。"挺"不可以。"很" can follow a verb as a complement. "挺" has no such usage.

(12) 今天他高兴得很。

(13) *今天他高兴得挺。

2. "挺"和"怪"都可以作副词用,表示程度高的意思。它们的区别是：Both "挺" and "怪" may serve as a verb, meaning "a high degree." Their differences are as follows:

① "怪"能修饰的形容词、动词比"挺"少。如："对、坏、普遍、支持、说明(问题)、能够、愿意"等都能受"挺"的修饰,但是不能受"怪"的修饰。"怪" modifies fewer adjectives and verbs than "挺." Words such as "对,坏,普遍,支持,

说明(问题),能够,愿意" may be modified by "挺," but not by "怪."

②"怪"带动词、形容词,后面必须加"的",构成"怪……的"的结构。"挺"可以不用加"的"。 When followed by a verb or adjective, "怪" always has to go with "的" to form the pattern "怪...的." "挺" does not have to go with "的."

tōng 通

用法 Usage:
动词 v.

1. 用工具戳,使管道、炉灶等不堵塞。To poke with a tool to ensure that the pipe or the furnace is not clogged.

(1) 暖气炉的烟道堵塞了,要用棍子通一通。

(2) 下水道可能又堵了,找个东西通一下。

2. 连接,使没有阻碍,可以互相到达、来往。To connect for contact and communication.

(3) 现在中国的城市和农村都能自由通商。

(4) 我们两国什么时候才能自由通商呢?

3. 传达,通报,使别人知道"信息、情报"等。To deliver or circulate information or intelligence.

(5) 这事还没定下来,你们别去通风报信。

(6) 在资料收集上咱们得互通消息。

4. 了解;懂得。To know; to thoroughly understand.

(7) 老王通今博古,大家都喜欢听他讲故事。

(8) 我一门外语也不通。

形容词 a.

1. 没有阻碍,可以穿过。Being able to go through without blockage.

(9) 我们看到路边有个牌子,上写着"此路不通"。

(10) 山洞快打通了。

2. 比喻通畅。一般用作结果补语或可能补语。Clear, unobstructed (figuratively). It is used as a resultant or potential complement.

(11) 你们说的这个办法行得通。

(12) 想了一个晚上,他终于想通了。

3. 整个,全部。Whole, entire.

(13) 把文章先通读一遍再做作业。

(14) 我昨晚通宵没睡,一直在写毕业论文。

4. 普通;一般;通常。Ordinary, usual.

(15) 土豆是马铃薯的通称。

(16) 爱玩是孩子的通性。

5. 顺畅(一般指文章语句,多用于否定)。Clear and coherent (referring to sentences in an essay, mostly used in the negative form).

(17) 这个句子意思不通,要修改。

(18) 这篇文章读都读不通。

名词 n.

跟在名词后面,表示精通某一方面的人。Used after a noun, it refers to someone who is an expert in a certain field.

(19) 现在世界上中国通越来越多了。

(20) 他是电脑通,电脑上有什么问题,他都能解决。

说明 Notes:

1. "通"后面带动词或形容词是副词用法,表示整个、全部、十分的意思。When followed by a verb or an adjective, "通" is used as an adverb meaning wholly, entirely or completely.

(21) 孩子的两只小手冻得通红。

(22) 他们公司的股票我们通吃。(表示全部买进的意思 Meaning to buy all the shares)

2. "通"作名词用,也被认为是词缀的用法,如"万事通、中国通、手机通"等。When used as a noun, "通" may be considered a suffix, as in "万事通,中国通,手机通."

tōngcháng 通常 →P61"常常"、P415"时常"

用法 Usage:
形容词 a.

属性词。一般,平常。General; usual; normal.

(1) 通常情况下，我们公司六点下班。
(2) 面对这种问题，通常的方法有两种。

副词 ad.

表示事物或情况在一般、平常的条件下产生或发生。Indicating an event or a situation that occurs under normal conditions.

(3) 她七点半起床，通常不吃早饭就去上课。
(4) 通常，她一个星期跑步两次。

说明 Notes:

"通常"与"常常""时常"的区别是：The differences between "通常" and "常常，时常" are as follows:

1. "通常"做状语时，可以放在句首，并用逗号与主语断开。"常常""时常"一般都不可以。When used as an adverbial, "通常" can be placed at the beginning of a sentence and be separated from the subject by a comma. "常常" or "时常" is usually not used in this way.

(5) *常常/时常，她晚上都要喝一杯牛奶。
(6) 通常，她晚上都要喝一杯牛奶。

2. "通常"可用作形容词，做定语。"常常"和"时常"都不能。"通常" can be used as an adjective and serve as the attributive. "常常" and "时常" have no such usage.

(7) 这孩子通常的习惯是回家先做作业，做完作业再玩。

tōngguò 通过 →P244"经过"

用法 Usage:

动词 v.

1. 从一端或一侧到另一端或另一侧。可带"了、过"，可带处所宾语。To move from one side to the other; to pass through. It can be followed by "了、过" or a location object.

(1) 汽车半个小时就通过了跨海大桥。
(2) 前面堵车了，汽车不能通过。

2. 提案等经过法定人数的同意而成立。To pass a proposal with quorate votes; to adopt.

(3) 我的论文答辩五位老师全部通过。
(4) 全班同学举手通过选我当班长。

介词 prep.

引进动作的媒介或手段。"通过……"可用在主语前，有停顿。Introducing the medium or method of an action; by means of; by; through. "通过" can be used before the subject with a pause in the sentence.

(5) 通过这次参观，我对杭州的文化有了更深的了解。
(6) 通过玛丽介绍，我认识了一个中国朋友。

说明 Notes:

"经过"和"通过"的区别是："经过" and "通过" differ as follows:

1. 做介词时，"通过"的意义主要是用以引进作为媒介的人、事、方式、手段等。"经过"包含一定的实在意义，还有"经历……"的意思，所以，它引进的常是某个过程。When used as a preposition, "通过" introduces people, objects, or methods as the media. "经过" often introduces a certain process with a practical meaning. Sometimes its meaning is like "经历."

(7) 通过中国朋友的帮助，我的汉语口语提高了不少。（强调中国朋友的帮助。What is emphasized is the help of Chinese friends.）

(8) 经过中国朋友的帮助，我的汉语口语提高了不少。（强调中国朋友帮助的过程。What is emphasized is the process of the help from the Chinese friends.）

2. 做动词时，"通过"词义侧重畅通无阻地穿过某处。"经过"则既有"通过"的意思，又有"路过"的意思。在作为"通过"（时间）的意义时，"经过"后面不能直接跟"时间"作宾语，一般在"时间"前都要有修饰语。When used as a verb, "通过" emphasizes getting through without blockage. In addition to the meaning like "通过，" "经过" can also mean "to pass a place." When its meaning is like "通过，" "经过" cannot be directly followed by the word "时间" as the object. The word "时间" should be

preceded with a modifier.

(9) *我每天去学校要通过一家书店。

(10) 我每天去学校要经过一家书店。

(11) 通过一年多时间,他得到了汉语水平考试四级证书。

(12) 经过了一年多的时间,他得到了汉语水平考试四级证书。

3. "经过"常有时间上延续的意思,后面常带表示时段的词语。在这种情况下,一般不用"通过"。"经过" often indicates continuation in time. It is usually followed by a time word. "通过" has no such usage.

(13) 经过两年时间,他终于写成了这本书。

(14) *通过两年时间,他终于写成了这本书。

4. 表示议案等经过法定人数的同意而成立的意思时,只用"通过",不用"经过"。如:例(3)(4),句子中的"通过"都不能用"经过"替代。"通过" rather than "经过" is used for passing a proposal with quorate votes. As you can see, "通过" rather than "经过" is used in (3) and (4).

tōnghuà 通话

用法 Usage:

1. 通电话,在电话中交谈。To talk on the phone.

(1) 来中国留学以后,我每周都用微信和妈妈通话。

(2) 现在的手机可以视频通话。

2. 用彼此都懂的语言或者方言直接交谈。常用格式是"用……通话"。To talk directly in a language or dialect both sides can understand. It often takes the form of "用...通话."

(3) 她们俩用方言通话,我一点儿也听不懂。

(4) 咱们班的学生来自不同的国家,但互相可以用中文通话。

说明 Notes:

"通话"是离合动词,因此"通"和"话"中可插入动量词"次"等。Since "通话" is a separable verb, verbal measure words such as "次" can be inserted in between "通" and "话."

(5) 来中国留学以后,我每周都用微信和妈妈通一次话。

(6) 我们今天是第一次见面,之前只是在网上通过几次话。

tóng 同 →P166"跟"、P193"和"、P608"与"

用法 Usage:

形容词 a.

相同,一样,没有差异。一般不单独做谓语,常作定语修饰名词,名词以单音节居多。"同"和中心语之间不加"的"。Same; having no difference. It is often used as an attributive modifying a noun (often a monosyllabic noun) and usually not used alone as the predicate. "的" is not used between "同" and the center word.

(1) 她们俩是高中同班同学,所以关系特别好。

(2) 我们住同一个小区。

副词 ad.

共同,一起。Together.

(3) 他俩已经同居了两年,听说今年要结婚了。

(4) 我们俩同行了两站路就各自回家了。

介词 prep.

1. 引进共同施行某一动作行为的另一方,并表示在施行过程中,这一方起主导作用,二者的位置不能互换。在"同"后面常带有"一起、一齐、一块、一道"等词语搭配使用,表示动作行为是双方共同施行的。With, used to introduce the other party in an action that is to be co-conducted. The other party will take the leading role during the process. The positions of the two parties in the sentence are not interchangeable. "同" is often used with "一起,一齐,一块,一道," which indicates that the action is co-conducted by two parties.

(5) 这件事儿我要同妻子商量一下。

(6) 今天我同朋友一起喝喝咖啡、聊聊天儿,心情好多了。

2. 引进比较或比喻的事物。在"同……"后面常常有"相比、比较、似的"或"一样、相像、相似、不同、区别、差别、相反"等词语配合使用。意思相当于"跟"。As, used to introduce the other party for a comparison or analogy. The "同..." phrase is often followed with "相比, 比较, 似的" or "一样, 相像, 相似, 不同, 区别, 差别, 相反" with the meaning similar to "跟."

(7) 我同哥哥不一样,我喜欢运动,哥哥喜欢安静。

(8) 这儿的菜同我们老家的相比,太清淡了。

3. 引进动作行为的对象,意思相当于"跟、向、对"。With. Like "跟, 向, 对," it is used to introduce the recipient of an action or behavior.

(9) 大家不要走,王老师还有事儿要同我们商量。

(10) 王老师要我同他一起练习口语。

连词 conj.

表示并列关系。一般连接名词、代词、形容词或名词短语,不连接分句或句子。And; as well as; with. Indicating a parallel relationship, it often connects nouns, pronouns, adjectives or noun phrases. It is not used to connect clauses or sentences.

(11) 哥哥、弟弟同我都在这所大学学习汉语。

动词 v.

表示相同、一样。表示肯定时,必定带名词宾语。To be the same. When used in a positive sentence, it must be followed by a noun object.

(12) 冬天,北京和杭州的气候不同。

(13) 他们俩是同年、同月、同日出生的。

说明 Notes:

1. "同"作连词用时,要注意:When "同" is used as a conjunction, one should pay attention to the following rules:

① 连接的并列短语,一般只做主语,不做宾语。The parallel phrases connected by "同" usually serve as the subject rather than the object.

(14) *我要选修中国书法同中国绘画。

(15) 中国书法同中国绘画都是我喜欢的选修课。

(16) 我要选修中国书法和中国绘画。

② 如果"同"连接的并列短语做宾语后组成的小句,又充当了其他句子的主语,即成为兼语,则可以用"同"。"同" can be used to connect parallel phrases serving as the object if that object also serves as the subject in a pivotal sentence.

(17) 我八岁那年,妈妈带着我同妹妹去了东京。

2. "同"与"和"都可以做介词、连词用。"同" and "和" can both be used as prepositions or conjunctions.

它们的区别是:Their differences are as follows:

① "和"通用于口语、书面语,使用得很广泛,多用作连词。"同"流行于华中地区一带,带有方言色彩,在书面语中多用作介词。"和" can be used both colloquially and in written language with a wide range of usage. It is also often used as a conjunction. Carrying a dialectic tone, "同" is often used in central China. It is mostly used as a preposition in written language.

② "同"有副词用法。"和"没有。"同" can be used as an adverb, but "和" cannot.

3. "同"与"跟"都可以做介词、连词用。"同" and "跟" can both be used as prepositions or conjunctions.

它们的区别是:Their differences are as follows:

① "跟"多用于口语,在北方话中用得比较多。"跟" is mostly used colloquially in northern dialects.

② "跟"有名词用法。"同"没有。"跟" can be used as a noun, but "同" cannot.

③ "跟"没有形容词或副词用法。"跟" cannot be used as an adjective or adverb.

tóngshí 同时

用法 Usage:
连词 *conj.*

表示并列关系,常含有进一步说明的意味。相当于"并且",常用在第二分句开头,常与"也、还、又"配合使用。*At the same time. Indicating a parallel relationship, it often carries the meaning of further explanation. Like "并且," it is often used at the beginning of the second clause and used with "也, 还, 又."*

(1) 教授说我的论文不错,同时又指出了一些需要改进的地方。
(2) 他把自己的公司发展得非常好,同时,还很关注慈善事业。

名词 *n.*

在同一个时候。可放在动词前,也可以组成"……的同时"的格式。*At the same time. It can be used before a verb, and can also be used in the structure of "...的同时."*

(3) 小王能同时演奏三种乐器。
(4) 这部电视剧今天晚上同时在三个电视台播出。
(5) 在学习汉语的同时,我也了解了很多中国文化。

tóngyàng 同样 →P563"一样"

用法 Usage:
形容词 *a.*

相同,一样;没有区别。*Having no difference; being the same.*

(1) 她买了件跟姐姐同样的衣服。
(2) 同样一句话,我们说孩子不听,老师说他就听。

连词 *conj.*

连接并列的分句或句子,表示两者具有某种关联或一致性。"同样"后面一般有停顿。*Connecting parallel clauses or sentences to show the relationship or consistency between the two. There is often a pause after "同样."*

(3) 你对别人好,同样,别人也会对你好。
(4) 你不喜欢加班,同样,我也不喜欢。

说明 Notes:

"同样"在使用时要注意:*Pay attention to the following rules when using "同样:"*

1. "同样"用作形容词时,不能受程度副词"很、非常、特别"等的修饰。*When used as an adjective, "同样" cannot be modified by degree adverbs such as "很,非常,特别."*

(5) *她总喜欢穿跟姐姐很同样的衣服。

2. "同样"修饰动词时,一般不加"地"。*When "同样" modifies a verb, it is usually not followed by "地."*

(6) 男女职工,我们同样对待。

3. "同样"不能受"不"的修饰。否定式是"不同"或者"不一样"。*"同样" cannot be modified by "不." The negative form should be "不同" or "不一样."*

4. "同样"修饰名词时一般要加"的",如果名词前有数量词,则可以不用"的"。如:"同样的话/同样一句话"。*When describing a noun, "同样" is usually followed by "的," which can be omitted if there is a quantifier before the noun, as in "同样的话/同样一句话."*

tóngyì 同意 →P353"批准"、P616"允许"、P626"赞成"

用法 Usage:
动词 *v.*

对某种主张表示相同的意见,赞成,准许。*To agree to (with); to express approval of a certain idea or statement.*

(1) 我非常同意你的看法。
(2) 我不太同意现在就结婚。

说明 Notes:

"批准"和"同意"都表示对某些意见、建议或请求肯定的意思。*Both "批准" and "同意" show agreement to a certain idea, suggestion or request.*

它们的区别是:*Their differences are as*

follows:

1. 使用范围不同。"批准"必定用于上对下级,如"领导已经批准我们的教学实习计划"。"同意"不分上下级,既可以是上对下,也可以是同级之间、平辈之间,如同学之间、朋友之间等。They are applied to different scopes. "批准" is used when a boss or superior shows agreement with a subordinate. For instance, "领导已经批准我们的教学实习计划." "同意" doesn't differentiate the superior and the subordinate. It may be used by a superior toward a subordinate or by equals or people at the same level. For instance, it is applied to fellow students or friends.

2. 词语搭配不同。"同意"可以用在上对下,也可以用于同级之间,使用范围比较广,可以搭配的词语有"意见、建议、请求、方案、想法、看法、说法、他的话、我的观点"等词语。"批准"只用于上对下,使用范围相对狭窄,一般多与"建议、方案、请求、报告"等词语搭配,不能与"想法、看法、说法、意见、他的话、我的观点"等词语搭配。They go with different words. "同意" is applied to a superior toward a subordinate and to people at the same level. It has a fairly wide scope of application. Words to go with it include "意见、建议、请求、方案、想法、看法、说法、他的话、我的观点 etc." "批准" is applied only to a superior toward a subordinate. Its usage of application is rather narrow. Words to go with "批准" include "建议、方案、请求、报告, etc." But "批准" does not go with "想法、看法、说法、意见、他的话、我的观点, etc."

(3) ＊王老师批准我们的想法了。
(4) 王老师同意我们的想法了。

3. "同意"是心理动词,可以受程度副词的修饰。"批准"不能直接受程度副词的修饰。"同意" is a psychological verb, and it can be modified by degree adverbs. "批准" cannot.

(5) 全班同学都很同意你的看法。
(6) ＊老师很批准你的看法。

tòngkuài 痛快

用法 Usage:

形容词 a.

1.（心情、精神等）高兴,舒畅。(Describing the mood) happy, with ease of mind.

(1) 想说的话都说出来了,心里真痛快!
(2) 有什么不痛快的事儿都告诉我吧。

2. 兴趣得到极大地满足,尽兴。可以重叠为"痛痛快快"。To be fully satisfied with what one does. It can be reduplicated as "痛痛快快."

(3) 这次旅游玩得真痛快!
(4) 毕业啦,我们今晚痛痛快快地喝吧!

3. 形容人的行为或说话爽快,直截了当的。可以重叠。Describing someone's behavior or speech to be straightforward. It can be reduplicated.

(5) 我一说他就同意了,非常痛快!
(6) 有什么意见,痛痛快快地说出来吧。

说明 Notes:

1. "痛快"修饰动词,一定要带"地"。如例(4)(6)。When describing a verb, "痛快" must be followed by "地" as in (4) and (6).

2. "痛快"不能形容人的性格。"痛快" cannot be used to describe a person's personality.

(7) ＊他的性格很痛快。
(8) 他的性格很直爽。

tōu 偷 →P474"偷偷"

用法 Usage:

动词 v.

1. 窃取,趁别人不注意暗中拿走钱财、物品等据为己有。To steal.

(1) 我的手机被人偷走了。
(2) 偷电脑的人找到了吗?

2. 在很忙碌的情况下,抽出时间,挤出时间。To squeeze out some time in a busy period.

（3）最近忙死了，今天好不容易偷空儿去医院看了朋友。

（4）A：你这个大忙人，今天怎么有时间来喝茶？

B：忙里偷空嘛。

3. 背地里勾搭异性，通奸。To commit adultery.

（5）大家都说她偷汉子，那怎么可能？

（6）他偷人家媳妇的事儿，村民们都知道了。

副词 ad.

偷偷地，不使人觉察地。一般修饰单音节动词。Secretly. It usually modifies monosyllabic verbs.

（7）抓紧复习，别再偷偷玩手机了。

（8）你怎么又偷听别人说话！

说明 Notes：

1."偷"前面加"小"，成为名词"小偷"，表示偷东西的人。"小偷"means "a petty thief."

2."偷"做副词，修饰双音节和多音节词语时，常常为重叠形式，如例（7）。When used as an adverb, "偷" usually modifies disyllabic words. It is often reduplicated as in (7).

tōutōu 偷偷 →P473"偷"

用法 Usage：

副词 ad.

（行动）秘密地；不让别人察觉地。Secretly; behind one's back.

（1）老师在黑板上写字的时候，他偷偷吃了一大口面包。

（2）小姑娘一个人在房间偷偷地哭，不知道为什么。

说明 Notes：

1."偷偷"修饰动词时，"地"可加可不加，如例（2）和（1）。When describing a verb, "偷偷" can be used with or without "地" as in (2) and (1).

2."偷偷"口语中常用为儿化"偷偷儿"。"偷偷" is often used as "偷偷儿" in spoken language.

3."偷"和"偷偷"都有副词用法。"偷" and "偷偷" can both be used as adverbs.

它们的区别是：The differences between the two are as follows：

①"偷"多修饰单音节动词。"偷偷"多修饰双音节动词以上的词语或短语。"偷" often modifies monosyllabic verbs, whereas "偷偷" mostly modifies disyllabic verbs or phrases.

②"偷"有动词用法。"偷偷"没有。"偷" can be used as a verb, but "偷偷" cannot.

tóu 投

用法 Usage：

动词 v.

1. 向一定目标掷，扔，抛。To toss, throw or cast, usually with a purpose or direction.

（1）3号运动员那只球投得真漂亮！

（2）今年比赛，我投标枪。

2. 放进去，送进去。To put in; to send in.

（3）没有乘车卡的请投币！

（4）今天下午我们要投票选出班长。

3. 跳进去（专指自杀行为）。To jump into (to commit suicide).

（5）她那么年轻却投湖自杀了。

（6）那个小偷真是自投罗网。

4. 寄给人书信或稿件等。To mail letters or manuscripts.

（7）请把这封信投到街边的邮箱里。

（8）投给报社的文章，到现在还没有回音。

5. 迎合；契合。To cater to; to appeal to.

（9）送礼物要投其所好，不一定贵的就是最好的。

（10）他俩性格相投，像兄弟一样。

6. （光线、射线等）投射。To project light or rays.

（11）太阳光投进了小树林，小树林很好看。

（12）手机也可以把图片直接投到电脑上。

7. 找上去；参加进去。To look for (a

shelter); to join.

(13) 今晚在哪儿投宿？

(14) 那孩子很快就投到小朋友的圈子里玩开了。

tóurù 投入

说明 Usage:

动词 v.

1. 放进，进入某种阶段或状态。*To put into; to enter a stage or status.*

(1) 他们的研究成果已经投入生产了。

(2) 孩子每次都把零钱投入储蓄罐。

2. 参加（指人员、劳力参加某种行动）。*(Of people or labor force) to participate in a certain activity or event.*

(3) 所有的人都投入到地震后的救灾工作中了。

(4) 今天中小学生都投入到植树活动中去了。

3. 投放，将时间、金钱、精力、感情等用在事业、工作、感情生活中等。*To invest time, money or energy in a career, a project or one's emotional life.*

(5) 这幅画上，他投入了很多时间和精力。

(6) 公司在这个项目上投入了很多资金。

名词 n.

（在资金、时间、精力、感情等方面的）付出。*Investment in terms of money, time, energy, emotion, etc.*

(7) 他在学习上投入的时间精力并不多，可是学习成绩很好。

(8) 他觉得自己对事业上的投入太多，而对家庭的投入太少。

形容词 a.

形容做事聚精会神，全力以赴，一丝不苟。*Highly focused; fully occupied with.*

(9) 演员们的表演很投入，赢得了热烈的掌声。

(10) 她做什么事都很投入。

tòu 透

用法 Usage:

动词 v.

1. （液体、光线等）渗透，穿过，通过。*To permeate; to pass through.*

(1) 这种防风衣不透水，下雨天也可以穿。

(2) 太阳光都透过窗户晒到床上了，还不起床？

2. 暗地里告诉（信息、事情等）。*To secretly share (information) about something.*

(3) 你要是辞职先透个消息给我。

(4) 她结婚了？怎么一点儿消息都没透出来！

3. 显露出某种颜色、神色、情绪等，常带补语"出（来）"等。*To show one's mood through facial expression. It is often followed by a complement such as "出(来)."*

(5) 工作了一天，他脸上透出一些疲惫。

(6) 这孩子的小脸蛋儿白里透红，真可爱。

形容词 a.

1. 透彻，清楚（多用作结果补语或可能补语）。*Clear (often used as a resultant or potential complement).*

(7) 这个语法点，老师讲得很透，你还不懂吗？

(8) 我一点儿也猜不透她在想什么。

2. 表示彻底地、充分地，达到很深的程度（多用作结果补语）。*Thoroughly, fully, reaching a high degree (often used as a resultant complement).*

(9) 这西瓜还没熟透呢。

(10) 天已经黑透了，路上开车小心！

3. 表示程度极深（多用于贬义或消极义）。后面常带"了"。*Reaching a high degree (often with a negative or passive meaning). It is usually followed by "了."*

(11) 你这人坏透了。

(12) 房间这么脏，你真是懒透了。

tūchū 突出

用法 Usage:

形容词 a.

1. 凸起,隆起,鼓出来。Bulging; projecting.

(1) 年画上那位额头很突出的老人是"寿星"。

(2) 他活动太少,得了腰椎突出的毛病。

2. 与众不同;(成绩或成就)特别显著。Outstanding, with an exceptional grade or achievement.

(3) 她是个各方面成绩都很突出的学生。

(4) 这次汉语大赛中,大卫表现得很突出。

动词 v.

1. 更为明显,超过一般地显露。To be outstanding; to highlight.

(5) 你这篇作文没有突出主要内容。

(6) 这套邮票突出了书法艺术的美感。

2. 冲出。To break through.

(7) 他一个人突出对方球员的包围,三大步把球投进了篮筐。

tūrán 突然 →P199"忽然"

用法 Usage:

形容词 a.

形容情况发生得急促,而且出人意料。可以受"很、大、十分、非常、特别"等副词修饰。Describing an abrupt and/or unexpected happening. It can be modified by adverbs such as "很,大,十分,非常,特别."

(1) 小王的辞职有点儿突然。

(2) 他的病来得非常突然。

副词 ad.

在短促的时间里,(事情)出乎意料地发生。Suddenly; unexpectedly. It is used to describe the unexpected occurrence of something within a short time.

(3) 走着走着,突然,前面闯出来一条狗。

(4) 刚要睡下,他突然想起洗手间的灯还没关。

说明 Notes:

1. "突然"也常说成"突然间"或"突然之间"。经常用在主语之前,更强调事情发生的那一瞬间。"突然" can be used as "突然间" or "突然之间." It is often placed before the subject to emphasize the moment when something occurs unexpectedly.

(5) 突然之间,女朋友出现在了我的眼前,我真是太高兴了。

(6) 突然间,大雨直下,一下子街上没了人影。

2. "突然"和"忽然"的区别是: "突然" and "忽然" differ as follows:

① 从词性上看,"突然"除了有副词用法,还有形容词用法。"忽然"没有形容词用法。"突然" can be used as an adverb or an adjective. "忽然" cannot be used as an adjective.

(7) *这个消息来得很忽然。

(8) 这个消息来得很突然。

② 从语义上看,"突然"着重突如其来,让人想不到,语义较重。"忽然"着重时间短促,事情发生得迅速,语义较轻。"突然" emphasizes unexpectedness and carries a more serious tone. "忽然," however, emphasizes the abrupt occurrence of an event within a short time; it carries a less serious tone.

(9) 突然从前边开过来一辆车。

(10) 忽然从前边开过来一辆车。

tǔ 吐

用法 Usage:

动词 v.

1. 使东西从嘴里出来。To spit out.

(1) 请不要随地吐痰。

(2) 别把葡萄皮吐在地上。

2. 长出来,露出来,伸出来。常带趋向补语"出来"。To put out; to stick out; to stretch out. It is often followed by the directional complement "出来."

(3) 天太热了,小狗都吐出舌头来了。

(4) 春天来了,树枝儿吐出了嫩芽。

3. 说出来。To say something loud, often related to truth.

(5) 都说"酒后吐真言"啊。

(6) 怎么才能让你把真话吐出来？

tǔ 吐

用法 Usage:

动词 v.

1. 呕吐,(消化道或呼吸道里的东西)不由自主地从嘴里涌出。To vomit; to have something come out of the mouth from the digestive or respiratory tracts.

(1) 他喝醉酒了,吐了一身一地。

(2) 她的病有点重,已经吐血了。

2. 比喻被迫退出(侵吞的钱财)。To be forced to return (money pocketed).

(3) 一定要他把贪污的钱吐出来！

tuīdòng 推动 →P477"推进"

用法 Usage:

动词 v.

1. 加力于物体,使物体向前移动。To apply a force to an object and push it forward.

(1) 风推动沙石向湖边移动,湖面越来越小了。

(2) 这个雪球太大了,孩子们有点推不动了。

2. 使事物前进,使工作展开。To promote progress or development.

(3) 老板总有办法推动我们创新的积极性。

(4) 是什么力量推动着社会向前发展呢？

tuījìn 推进 →P477"推动"

用法 Usage:

动词 v.

1. 推动事业或工作,使发展前进。To promote the development of business or work.

(1) 科学家们的努力不断推进着科技事业的发展。

(2) 今年高铁的修建又向前推进了一万多米。

2. (指战线或作战的军队)向前进。(Of the battlefront or the soldiers in a battle) to move forward.

(3) 阵地已经推进到敌军城下了。

(4) 我军向敌方阵地推进了一百米。

说明 Notes:

"推进"和"推动"都是指使事物运动,前进。"推进" and "推动" both mean to push something forward.

它们的区别是：Their differences are as follows:

1. 在词义上,"推动"着重于用某种力量使事物由静止状态开始活动,或使发展缓慢的工作、事业等有所前进。"推进"着重于用某种力量使事物向前移动,或使前进中的事物加速前进。Semantically, "推动" emphasizes moving something from a static state or enabling work or career to progress faster. "推进" emphasizes applying a force to an object to move it forward or enabling it to move at an accelerated speed.

2. "推进"必定具有"前进"的含义。"推动"可以指前进,也可以指只动不进。"推进" definitely carries the meaning of "forward." "推动" also implies "forward," but it can also mean "moving without going forward."

3. "推动"是离合动词,可以插入词语,构成"推得动、推不动"。"推进"不能。Since "推动" is a separable verb, other words can be inserted between "推" and "动" to form words such as "推得动,推不动." "推进" has no such usage.

4. "推动"的对象除了事物外,还可以是人,表示使人进步、前进。"推进"多用于"社会、工作、事业"等抽象事物。有时用于"船、机器"等具体事物,但不用于人。The object of "推动" can be people as well as things, and so we can use "推动" to mean motivating people for progress. "推进," however, is mostly used for abstract things such as "社会,工作,事业." Sometimes it is applied to concrete objects such as "船,机器," but it is not applied to people.

5. "推进"有表示战线或军队作战向前进的意义。"推动"没有。"推进" can refer to the forward movement of the battlefront or the soldiers in a battle. "推动" has no such meaning.

W w

wàibian 外边 →P478"外部"、P479"外界"、P479"外面"、P480"外头"

用法 Usage:

名词 n.

1. 超出某一范围的地方（跟"里边"相对）。在口语中常读"外边儿"。*Outside, as opposed to "里边 (inside)"; out. It is usually pronounced as "外边儿."*

（1）大楼外边儿停着许多小车。

（2）下雨了，去外边儿要带雨伞。

2. 物体靠外的一边。*The outer edge of an object.*

（3）他坐在桌子里边儿，我坐在桌子外边儿。

3. 物体的表面。可受副词"最"的修饰。*The exterior of an object. It can be modified by the adverb "最."*

（4）把花纸包在最外边儿，一个漂亮的礼物就包好了。

4. 外地。*A place away from where one lives.*

（5）我奶奶每年要去外边旅游两次。

说明 Notes:

"外边"是方位名词，不能受数量词的修饰。*As a location noun, "外边" cannot be modified by numerals and measure words.*

wàibù 外部 →P478"外边"、P479"外面"、P480"外头"

用法 Usage:

名词 n.

1. 事物内部范围以外的地方。多用作定语。*Outside; external. It is often used as an attributive.*

（1）国家的内政不应该受到外部力量的干涉。

（2）每个人都要跟外部社会发生关系。

2. 物体的表面。一般用在有外部、内部结构的物体。*The exterior of an object. It is often used to describe an object with clear distinction between the interior and the exterior.*

（3）伤口外部一定要保持干净。

（4）这套房子外部的色彩很漂亮。

说明 Notes:

"外部"跟"外边"的区别是："外部"不是方位名词，而是指事物的结构内外。表示某一范围以外时，不是指地方，而是指部分。"外部"表示表面时，指的是事物的表面部分。不同于"外边"。*The difference between "外部" and "外边" lies in: "外部" is not a location noun. When used to describe an area that goes beyond a certain range, it does not refer to a place, but to the external part of an object. So it is different from "外边." The second usage refers to the surface area of an object.*

（5）*外部停着一辆汽车。

（6）外边停着一辆汽车。

（7）*房子正在进行外边装修。

（8）房子正在进行外部装修。（指外面部分 *Referring to the exterior of the house*）

wàijiè 外界 →P478"外边"、P479"外面"、P480"外头"

用法 Usage:

名词 *n.*

1. 某个物体以外的空间。*The space outside an object.*

(1) 声音要借助外界的物体才能传播。

(2) 飞机在高空飞行时,必须能承受住外界的气压。

2. 某个个体、集体以外的社会。*The external world; the society outside a collective or an individual.*

(3) 我们做的这件事,外界反映很好。

(4) 一个人的成长不可能不受外界事物的影响。

说明 Notes:

1. "外界"指某个事物以外的空间时,用法相同于"外面""外头""外边"。区别是,"外界"不表示方位。*When used to refer to the space outside an object, "外界" is similar to "外面," "外头" and "外边." The difference is that it does not indicate a location.*

(5) 最近,外界/外面/外边/外头有很多关于这方面的报道。

2. "外界"可指某个人、集体以外的社会。"外面""外头""外边"不能。

(6) 我们公司给工人加工资以后,外界的舆论反响很大。*"外界" can refer to the external world as opposed to an individual or a group. "外面," "外头," and "外边" have no such usage.*

wàilái 外来

用法 Usage:

形容词 *a.*

从外地或外族、外国来的,非本地固有的。*Coming from a different place, a different ethnic group, or a foreign country; not native.*

(1) 这社区居住着很多外来户。

(2) 汉语里有不少外来词,如"沙发、吉普、摩托"等。

(3) 改革开放以后,人们的思想也受到不少外来的影响。

说明 Notes:

"外来"能组成少量的名词词语,如"外来户、外来语、外来物种"等,但不是所有的名词都可以,如 *"外来工、外来人"等。*"外来" can be used with a limited number of nouns to form noun phrases such as "外来户, 外来语, 外来物种," but it cannot be used with most nouns. For example, it is incorrect to say "外来工" or "外来人."*

wàimiàn 外面 →P478"外边"、P480"外头"

用法 Usage:

名词 *n.*

1. 超出某一范围的地方,外边。*Outside; the area that goes beyond a certain range.*

(1) 公寓外面种了很多果树。

(2) 他外面穿了一件毛衣,不会受凉。

2. 指外地。*A place away from where one lives; a place out of town.*

(3) 退休后,我们常到外面旅游。

(4) 爸爸一直在外面打工。

3. 指社会上。*The society.*

(5) 你救了这个老人。知道外面是怎么夸你的吗?

说明 Notes:

1. 在口语中,"外面"常儿化为"外面儿"。*In colloquial usage, "外面" is often pronounced as "外面儿."*

2. "外面"读作"wàimiàn"时,表示"外表"的意思。*When pronounced as "wàimiàn," "外面" refers to the exterior of an object.*

(6) 墙外面的颜色不好看。

3. "外面"用作方位名词时,用法同"外边"。"外面"多用于书面及正式的表达。*When used as a location noun, the usage of "外面" is similar to "外边." "外面" is normally*

used in formal written language.

wàitou 外头 →P478"外边"、P479"外面"

用法 Usage:

名词 n.

外边,外面。常用于口语。Outside (often used colloquially).

(1) 外头有人叫你。
(2) 这个院子外头就是公园。

说明 Notes:

"外头"和"外边""外面"意思一样,只是"外头"多用于口语。"外头" has the same meaning as "外边" and "外面." The only difference is that "外头" is often used colloquially.

wánměi 完美 →P480"完善"

用法 Usage:

形容词 a.

完备美好。多形容结构、形式、语言、形象等。Perfect. It is often used to describe the structure, shape, language, image, etc.

(1) 这件衣服的颜色、款式和用料都很完美。
(2) 那姑娘的性格非常完美。

wánquán 完全 →P383"全部"、P481"完整"

用法 Usage:

形容词 a.

齐全,不缺少什么。可以重叠为"完完全全"。Complete, not in lack of anything (may be reduplicated as "完完全全").

(1) 他说的完全小学就是六年制的小学。
(2) 他把事情的经过完完全全地讲了一遍。

副词 ad.

全部,整个地。Totally; completely.

(3) 这点困难完全能克服。
(4) 我完全同意你说的话。

说明 Notes:

"完全"和"全部"都是副词,在表示"整个、整体"的词义上相近。在表示否定上,"不"和"没"都可以在"完全"和"全部"前后,表示不同的两种意思。"完全" and "全部" are both adverbs with a similar meaning of "totally, completely." For negation, both "不" and "没" can be used before or after "完全" and "全部," which indicate complete or partial negation respectively.

它们的区别是:Their differences are as follows:

1. 使用范畴不一样。"全部"着重于表示事物数量总和,着眼于所有的事物。"完全"着重于表示对事物的态度在程度上的百分之百,着眼于人的态度。The range of application of the two is different. "全部" emphasizes the inclusion of all the things. "完全" emphasizes the attitude of a person (or people) toward certain things.

2. 词语搭配不太一样。"完全"后面带的一般是表示态度或情状的动词或形容词,如"同意、赞成、反对"等或"了解、理解、明白、知道"等。"全部"后面带的一般是表示主动或被动的动作、行为的动词,表示情状的形容词,如"借、来、去、做"等或"红、干净、明白"等。The two are used with different words in sentences. "完全" is usually followed by verbs or adjectives describing an attitude or a state such as "同意,赞成,反对" or "了解,理解,明白,知道." "全部" is normally followed by verbs indicating an action or behavior (active or passive) such as "借,来,去,做," or adjectives describing a state such as "红,干净,明白."

wánshàn 完善 →P480"完美"

用法 Usage:

形容词 a.

完备而且良好,比较完美。Complete and refined; near perfection.

(1) 这个城市设备最完善的宾馆就是那家。
(2) 这种手机功能更加完善。

动词 v.

使得(某些事物,如"设备、设施、制度"等)

完备而美好。To perfect; to make things (such as "设备, 设施, 制度") complete and refined.

(3) 我们要不断完善公司的各项管理制度。

(4) 这个工厂的环保设施正在完善之中。

说明 Notes:

"完善"和"完美"都有齐全、良好的意思。"完善" and "完美" can both mean complete or refined.

它们的区别是：Their differences are as follow:

1. 在程度上，"完美"不但齐全，而且十分美好，比"完善"更进一步。In terms of the extent, "完美" is not only complete but also wonderful, which is even greater than "完善."

2. 在使用范围上，"完善"多用于事物。"完美"不但可以用于事物，也可以用于人。In terms of the range of application, "完善" is mostly used to describe things, whereas "完美" can be used to describe both things and people.

wánzhěng 完整 →P480"完全"

用法 Usage:

形容词 a.

指具有或保持着应有的各部分，没有破损或残缺。可以重叠。Keeping all components in good condition; having no damages or missing parts. It can be reduplicated.

(1) 故宫及其文物全都完完整整地保存下来了。

(2) 他把课文的内容概括得非常完整。

说明 Notes:

"完整"和"完全"都有表示齐全不缺的意思，有时两个词可以互换。"完整" and "完全" can both mean "complete with no parts missing." Sometimes the two are interchangeable.

(3) 这是一副完整/完全的恐龙骨骼化石。

它们的区别是：Their differences are as follows:

1. "完全"着重于各部分都齐全，什么也不缺少。"完整"着重于整体上完好，没有残缺。可构

成"比较完整、完整性"。"完全" emphasizes the complete range of individual parts; not anything is missing. "完整" emphasizes the whole thing or object being in fine condition; there is no damage at all.

2. "完全"有副词用法。"完整"没有副词用法。"完全" can be used as an adverb, but "完整" cannot.

wànwàn 万万 →P371"千万"

用法 Usage:

副词 ad.

绝对，无论如何。只用于否定句，表示极强烈的否定或禁止的语气，常与"不、没、不可、不能"等词语配合使用。Absolutely; no matter what. It is used only in negative sentences to indicate a very strong negation: forbidding someone to do something. Often it pairs with "不, 没, 不可, 不能."

(1) 万万没想到中国的变化那么大！

(2) 在陌生的地方，晚上，你一个人万万不可外出。

数词 num.

1. 表示一万个万，亿。与一到十组合使用。Going with 1 to 10, it means 10,000 × 10,000; 100 million.

(3) 1949年中国只有四万万人口，现在已经有十四亿了。

2. "万万"跟"千千"连用，表示数量大。When combined with "千千," it indicates a huge number.

(4) 春节前，火车站每天有千千万万个旅客在转车、乘车。

说明 Notes:

"万万"和"千万"都表示恳切请求、叮咛、劝阻的语气。用于祈使句或叙述句，表示祈使语气。Both "万万" and "千万" indicate a sincere pleading, request, or persuasion. They often appear in imperative sentences.

它们的区别是：Their differences are as

follows:

1. "千万"的词义着重于一定、务必。"万万"着重于绝对、无论如何,词义比"千万"重。"千万" emphasizes the idea of "be sure to." By contrast, "万万" means "absolutely, no matter what," carrying a greater sense of urgency.

2. "千万"做副词可以重叠为"千万千万",做数词可以重叠为"千千万万"。"万万"不能重叠。As an adverb, "千万" can be reduplicated as "千万千万." As a numeral, it can be reduplicated as "千千万万." But "万万" cannot be repeated.

3. "千万"可以用于否定句,也可以用于肯定句,还可以直接用于动词前面。"万万"只能用于否定句。"千万" can be used either in a negative or a positive sentence. It can also be placed directly before a verb. "万万" can only be used in negative sentences.

wànyī 万一 →P554"一旦"

用法 Usage:

名词 n.

1. 万分之一,表示极小的一部分。多做宾语。One in ten thousand; a tiny fraction of something. It is often used as an object.

(1) 这只是其财产之万一。

2. 万分之一,表示可能性极小的意外变化。一般用在"防、以防、备、以备、怕、只怕、就怕"等几个词语后面做宾语。Indicating a very low probability that something unexpected will happen. It is often used as an object following words such as "防、以防、备、以备、怕、只怕、就怕."

(2) 做每件事都要考虑周全,不怕一万,只怕万一。

(3) 外出旅游多带点儿钱,以防万一。

连词 conj.

1. 表示可能性极小的假设。连接分句,一般用在前一个分句,也可以跟其他表示假设的连词连用。Indicating a hypothesis with very low probability. Connecting clauses, "万一" is normally used in the first clause. It can also be used with other conjunctions indicating a hypothesis.

(4) 万一买不到飞机票,就得坐火车去了。

(5) 先打个电话给他。万一他不在家,你不是白跑了吗?

2. 在对话中常用"万一……呢"的格式提出问题。Used in the form of "万一…呢" to raise a question in a dialogue, meaning "what if."

(6) 万一他不愿意呢?

副词 ad.

表示发生的可能性极小,只用于不希望发生的事。Indicating a low probability of occurrence. It is only used for things that one tries to avoid.

(7) 万一你不习惯中国的饭菜,你就自己做饭吃。

(8) 多带点钱吧,万一你想买点什么。

说明 Notes:

1. "万一"作连词或副词时,表示可能性极小,一般用于不好的事情。When used as a conjunction or an adverb, "万一" indicates a low probability of occurrence. It is normally applied to unpleasant things.

(9) *这次考试万一考得好,我就能拿奖学金了。

(10) 只要这次考试考得好,我就能拿奖学金了。

2. 有时用"万一"只说出可能性极小的假设,而假设所产生的后果予以省略(不需要说出或不好说出),或者采用疑问句式,作为问题提出。Sometimes "万一" is used to introduce a hypothesis with a very low probability but the potential result is omitted (due to lack of need or awkwardness to mention). "万一" can also be used to raise a question.

(11) 带点钱去吧!路很远,万一有个什么……

(12) 一个人在国外生活,万一不习惯呢?

wǎng 往 →P63"朝"

用法 Usage:

介词 prep.

向。表示动作的方向,后面必带表示方向、处所的名词。Toward. Indicating the direction of an action, "往" must be followed with a direction or a location noun.

(1) 请大家往前走,别停下来!
(2) 一直往西走,看到第一栋高楼就是图书馆。

动词 v.

去。常用作书面语。To go. It is often used in written language.

(3) 朋友之间要常来常往。
(4) 他们俩走了。一个往学校,一个往书店。

说明 Notes:

1. "往"还可以用在很少数的几个形容词前,表示对数量的猜测或动作性质、程度的倾向性。"往" can be used before a limited number of adjectives to indicate an estimate of a certain number or of the nature or extent of an action.

(5) 这孩子这几年就往高里长。
(6) 那个西瓜往少里说也有10公斤重。

2. "往"与"朝"的区别是：The differences between "往" and "朝" are as follows:

① "往"与"朝"作介词用,都表示动作的方向。区别是,"往"的动作方向带有动态,表示向某方向活动的要用"往"。"朝"的动作是静态的,只表示动作方向的,只能用"朝"。When used as a preposition, "往" and "朝" both indicate the direction of an action. The difference is that "往" is used to describe a dynamic movement toward a certain direction, while "朝" mostly describes the direction of a static state.

(7) *学校有两个门。前门往南,后门往北。
(8) 学校有两个门。前门朝南,后门朝北。
(9) *这个包裹朝法国寄,那个包裹朝德国寄。
(10) 这个包裹往法国寄,那个包裹往德国寄。

② "朝"能表示动作针对的对象,"往"没有这个词义。"朝" can introduce the recipient of an action. "往" has no such meaning.

(11) *她往孩子招招手,孩子也高兴地招招手。
(12) 她朝孩子招招手,孩子也高兴地朝她招招手。

③ "往"可以用在动词后面,"朝"不可以用在动词后面。"往" can be used after a verb but "朝" cannot.

(13) *开朝北京的火车已经走了。
(14) 开往北京的火车已经走了。

④ "往"和"朝"都可以用作动词,但词义完全不一样。"往"的词义为"去"。"朝"的词义是人或物正对某个方向。Although "往" and "朝" can both be used as verbs, their meanings are completely different. "往" carries the meaning of going whereas "朝" simply means that a person or a thing faces a certain direction.

wǎngwǎng 往往 →P61"常常"

用法 Usage:

副词 ad.

表示动作、行为或某一状态在一般情况、条件下经常发生或存在。Often; frequently; usually. It means that under normal circumstances, an action or a behavior will happen, or a certain situation will exist.

(1) 有树的山往往有水。
(2) 他很聪明,往往提出一些别人想不到的问题。

说明 Notes:

1. "往往"不受否定副词的修饰。"往往" cannot be modified by a negative adverb.

2. "往往"也有"常常"的意思。"往往"

sometimes has the meaning similar to "常常."

它们的区别是：Their differences are as follows:

① "往往"表示在通常情况下一般怎样或可能怎样，带有规律性或推论性的性质。"常常"表示动作行为重复、次数多的意思，不一定有规律性。因此既可以用于客观描述，也可以表示主观意图。"往往" indicates what normally or possibly happens under normal circumstances. The emphasis is on a regular pattern or an inference. "常常" indicates the multiple repetition of an action or behavior, but not necessarily something regular. Therefore, "常常" can be used to make an objective description and a subjective desire.

② "往往"是对以前到现在情况的总结，有一定的规律性，不用于主观意愿。使用"往往"有时间范围要求，不能用于将来的事情。"常常"单纯指出现的数量多，可以表示主观愿望。在时间上，可以用于过去的事情、现在的事情，也可以用于将来的事情。"往往" introduces a conclusion of the situation with a regular pattern up until the present. It is not used to indicate any subjective wishes. "往往" has to be used within a certain range of time, including the future. Emphasizing the number of repetitions, "常常" can be used to indicate subjective wishes. It can be used with past, present and future occurrences.

（3）* 希望你们以后往往来玩儿。
（4）希望你们以后常常来玩儿。
（5）* 我往往去他们家玩儿。
（6）我常常去他们家玩儿。

③ 有些使用"往往"的句子中，一定要有表示与动作有关的情况、时间、条件、结果的语义。"常常"则不用。The use of "往往" requires that some words appear to indicate the situation, time, condition, or result related to an action. "常常" has no such limitation.

（7）我们常常去爬山。
（8）* 我们往往去爬山。
（9）周末，我们往往去爬山。
（10）我们是老同学，所以我们往往一起学习，一起吃饭。
（11）* 我们往往一起学习，一起吃饭。
（12）我们常常一起学习，一起吃饭。

wēixiǎn 危险 →P149"风险"

用法 Usage:
形容词 a.
有遭到灾难或失败的可能（跟"安全"相对）。Having the possibility of experiencing a calamity or failure (the opposite of "安全").
（1）这座山没有路，上山很危险。
（2）如果碰到狼群就非常危险。

名词 n.
遭到损害或失败的可能性。Experiencing a calamity or failure.
（3）她的病已经脱离了危险。
（4）沙漠上旅行，会有很多意想不到的危险。

说明 Notes:
"危险"和"风险"都表示有受到损害或失败的可能性。Both "危险" and "风险" signify the possibility of experiencing a calamity or failure.

它们的区别是：Their differences lie in:

1. "风险"侧重所指的事情未来结果的不确定性比较大。"危险"侧重所指的事情失败或者受到损害发生的概率可能性比较高。The use of "风险" indicates a fairly greater uncertainty of a future result, and "危险" focuses on the probability of experiencing a calamity or failure being fairly large.

2. "风险"多指在金融投资、理财或做某事中隐藏着的某种可能结果不好的事情，使用范围较小。"危险"可用于"危险期、危险区"，可用来指在生产过程、运动过程，或有关设施、有关场所中，人、财产或环境等有遭到损害或失败的可能，使用的范围比较大。"风险" is often used to indicate undesirable results involved in monetary

investment and financial management. Its scope of application is rather limited. "危险" may appear in "危险期" or "危险区," and is used to refer to the possible damage or failure that people, properties or the environment, etc. may suffer in the process of production or in sports activities, in facilities or places. Its scope of application is fairly wide.

wéi 为

用法 Usage:
动词 v.

1. 做,干。多用于固定结构,如:"事在人为、大有可为、敢作敢为、尽力而为、所作所为、为非作歹"等。To do; to labor. Mostly it is used in fixed expressions such as "事在人为,大有可为,敢作敢为,尽力而为,所作所为,为非作歹."

2. 充当,算作,作为。必带名词做宾语。To serve as; to be considered as; to be. It must be followed by an object.

(1) 我们选他为我们球队的队长。
(2) 我以她为榜样,常常向她学习。

3. 变成,变为。多带名词、形容词作宾语。To become. It is often followed by a noun or an adjective as its object.

(3) 现代人采用了科学技术,变废为宝,让环境更美好。
(4) 我们要化悲痛为力量,战胜地震灾害。

4. 是。必带名词、数量词作宾语。To be. It has to be followed by a noun, a numeral or a measure word as its object.

(5) 参加足球比赛的多为韩国和日本留学生。
(6) 本科专业的学历一般为四年。

5. 用在比较句中,表示"显得"的意思,"为"后面的形容词多为单音节。To appear (used in comparative sentences). The adjective following "为" is usually monosyllabic.

(7) 天在下雪,我看还是不去为好。
(8) 朋友之间还是友情为重。

介词 prep.

引进动作行为的施事者,相当于"被"。常与"所"构成"为……所……"的格式,加强动词的被动意义,多用于书面语。Similar to "被," "为" introduces the agent performing an action. The structure of "为...所..." is often used in written language to enhance the passive voice of the verb.

(9) 写汉字常常不为欧美学生(所)喜欢。
(10) 古人的智慧应该为今天所用。

说明 Notes:

1. "为……所……"的格式,"为"后面是名词,"所"后面是动词。一般来说,如果动词是多音节,"所"可用可不用,如果动词是单音节,必须用"所",如例(10)。In the structure of "为...所...," "为" is followed by a noun and "所" is followed by a verb. If the verb is monosyllabic, "所" must be used as in (10). If the verb is multisyllabic, the usage of "所" is optional.

2. "为"还可作为后缀,一是附在某些单音节形容词后面,构成副词性词语,修饰双音节形容词或动词,如:"广为宣传、深为感动、大为惊讶"等。二是附在某些表示程度的单音节副词后面,加强语气,修饰双音节形容词,如:"极为出色、颇为得意、更为深刻"等。Sometimes "为" can serve as a suffix. Following certain monosyllabic adjectives, it can form an adverbial structure to modify disyllabic adjectives or verbs such as "广为宣传,深为感动,大为惊讶." Following certain monosyllabic extent adverbs, it can also modify disyllabic adjectives and enhance the tone, as in "极为出色,颇为得意,更为深刻."

wéinán 为难 →P334"难为"

用法 Usage:
形容词 a.

感到难以应付,感到困难。Being embarrassed; feeling awkward or uneasy.

(1) 你们俩吵架,让我左右为难,说谁好呢?

(2) 这件事让我很为难, 我帮不了。

动词 v.

作对或刁难。To go against; to create obstacles for others.

(3) 我让他做最简单的工作, 根本没有为难他。

(4) 大家没有跟他为难, 只是开了一个玩笑。

说明 Notes:

1. "为难"用作动词时, 后面一般是表示人的代词或名词, 或者用介词引进表示人的代词或名词, 如例 (3) (4)。When used as a verb, "为难" is usually followed by a personal pronoun or noun, or preceded by a personal pronoun or noun introduced by a preposition as in (3) and (4).

2. "为难"和"难为"只有在做动词表示让人感到困难的意思时, 可以替换。"为难" and "难为" are mutually replaceable only when people feel embarrassed.

(5) 他不会喝酒, 你不要为难/难为他。

它们的区别是: Their differences are as follows:

① "难为"用作动词时, 后面一定要有宾语。"为难"可有可没有。"难为" has to be followed by an object when it serves as a verb. As for "为难," it may or may not be followed by an object.

(6) 我没有为难他/跟他为难, 只是请他唱一首歌而已。

(7) *我没有跟他难为, 只是请他唱一首歌而已。

② "为难"没有"难为"其他两种意思的用法。"为难" is not used in the other two meanings.

③ "为难"有形容词用法。"难为"没有。"为难" can be used as an adjective, but "难为" cannot.

wéibèi 违背 →P486 "违反"

用法 Usage:

动词 v.

违反, 不依从 (与"遵守"相对)。To violate; to disobey (as opposed to "comply with").

(1) 这家公司违背了合同。

(2) 他不愿违背自己的良心说假话。

wéifǎn 违反 →P486 "违背"

用法 Usage:

动词 v.

不符合 (法则、规定等)。To violate (laws, rules, etc.).

(1) 他违反了交通规则, 被罚了款。

(2) 你这样做要违反学校规定的。

说明 Notes:

"违背"和"违反"都表示不遵守、不依从。都可带名词作宾语, 如: "原理、原则、规律、制度"等。都可带"了、着、过", 都可带补语, 都不能重叠。"违背" and "违反" both mean "to violate," or "to disobey." They can both be followed by noun objects such as "原理, 原则, 规律, 制度." Also they can be followed by "了, 着, 过," or by a complement. Neither of them can be reduplicated.

它们的区别是: Their differences are as follows:

"违背"着重于背离, 不遵守, 不实行。对象除上述所及以外, 还常有"路线、法律、协议、合同、利益、事实、命令、诺言、意愿、良心、感情、道德标准"等。"违背" emphasizes deviation or disobedience. In addition to the aforementioned objects, it can also be used with "路线, 法律, 协议, 合同, 利益, 事实, 命令, 诺言, 意愿, 良心, 感情, 道德标准."

"违反"着重于完全不符合, 与之相反, 语义比"违背"重。对象除上以外, 还用于"规程、规则、纪律、程序、习惯"等, 使用范围比"违背"窄。"违反" carries a harsher tone than "违背": it means violating or doing the very opposite of the law or rule, etc. In addition to the aforementioned objects, "违反" can also be used with "规程, 规则, 纪律, 程序, 习惯." Its range of application is more limited than

"违背."

wéichí 维持 →P14"保持"

用法 Usage:

动词 v.

1. 使继续存在下去，保持。To ensure continuation; to sustain.

（1）我是用打工得来的钱维持生活的。

（2）病人现在只有靠药物维持生命了。

2. 维护，支持，保护。To maintain; to support; to protect.

（3）马路上有警察维持着交通秩序，行人非常安全。

说明 Notes:

"保持"和"维持"都有使事物的原貌或原状无变化地继续存在的意思。"保持" and "维持" can both mean to maintain the original appearance or state of things for continuation without change.

它们的区别是：Their differences are as follows:

1."保持"的语义着重于较长时间地持续保住原貌原状不变，被"保持"的常常是比较好的东西，在宾语前可以有褒义的修饰语。常用于人的活动、事物的状况、自然界的态势等，语义比较轻。与之搭配的名词常有"联系、距离、中立、水平、习惯、现状、沉默、传统、作风、本色、整洁"等。"保持" emphasizes maintaining the original appearance or state without change for a prolonged period of time. The recipient is usually something good and therefore can be preceded by a positive attributive. Carrying a mild tone, it is normally used with words indicating people's activities, the state of things, and natural states. It is often used with nouns such as "联系,距离,中立,水平,习惯,现状,沉默,传统,作风,本色,整洁."

（4）他保持着每天跑步运动的好习惯。

（5）我老家保持了每年两次庙会的传统风俗。

"维持"的语义着重于有一定限度地、需要付出一定的代价，有一定的条件，经过努力去维护，暂时地使不改变原貌和原状，有最低、勉强的语义，语义比较沉重。一般用于人的工作与生活的活动内容。与之搭配的名词常有"生活、生命、生计、局面、关系、秩序、原判"等。"维持" emphasizes a limited and temporary maintenance of the original appearance or state, which requires certain conditions and efforts and sometimes sacrifices. It carries a heavier tone indicating that even maintaining the minimum requires efforts. It is often used with nouns related to the activities of people's work and life such as "生活,生命,生计,局面,关系,秩序,原判."

（6）他那么一点工资维持一家四口的生活，很艰苦。

（7）为了孩子，他们俩还维持着关系，没有离婚。

2. 因为被"维持"的程度一般比较低，所以"维持"的宾语前一般没有褒义的修饰语。The object of "维持" is usually not modified by a positive adjective, since "维持" indicates a low level of maintenance.

（8）他们俩维持着关系。

（9）他们俩保持着友好的关系。

wéihù 维护 →P14"保护"

用法 Usage:

动词 v.

表示维持、保护，使原来的状况免于遭受破坏。宾语多为抽象事物名词。To maintain or protect the original state from damage. The object is usually an abstract noun.

（1）我们应维护消费者的利益。

（2）每个学生都有维护学校名誉的责任。

说明 Notes:

"维护"和"保护"都表示用心护卫，尽力照顾，使不受损失，不被破坏。"维护" and "保护" both mean to protect and take care of something with great efforts so that it does not get damaged or suffer from loss or extinction.

它们的区别是：Their differences are as follows:

1. "维护"着重于维持良好的状态,使免遭破坏,有庄重的色彩。"保护"着重于尽力妥善照顾、护卫,使不受损失或不遭破坏、伤害,有以较强的可靠的力量起保障作用的意味。Carrying a solemn tone, "维护" emphasizes protecting a state or situation from destruction. "保护" means taking care of and guarding something from loss or damage; it emphasizes providing security with a strong and reliable force.

2. "维护"的对象多为抽象事物,如"真理、制度、利益、权利、主权、威信、团结、统一、领土完整、世界和平、集体荣誉、个人名声"等,多用于书面语。"保护"的对象多指具体的人或事物,如"妇女儿童、大熊猫、原始森林、文物、庄稼、环境"等。也可以是抽象事物,如"生态平衡、合法利益、资源、积极性"等。使用范围较广,通用于口语和书面语。Often found in written language, "维护" is mostly used with abstract nouns such as "真理,制度,利益,权利,主权,威信,团结,统一,领土完整,世界和平,集体荣誉,个人名声." The recipients of "保护" are usually specific people or things, such as "妇女儿童,大熊猫,原始森林,文物,庄稼,环境." "保护" can also be used with abstract nouns such as "生态平衡,合法利益,资源,积极性." With a wider range of application, "保护" can be used in both colloquial and written language.

wèi 为

用法 Usage:
介词 prep.

1. 引进动作的受益者和有关的事物,相当于"替、给"。For. Introducing the beneficiary of an action, it is the same as "替" or "给."

(1) 妈妈为我们姐妹俩各做了一条连衣裙。
(2) 我可以为你去一趟邮局。

2. 引进动作行为的目的,相当于"为了"。常常与"而"配合使用。For; in order to. Introducing the purpose of an action or behavior, it is the same as "为了" and often used with "而."

(3) 为抓紧时间游玩几个风景点,他首先买了一张地图。
(4) 他打算今晚为明天的考试而开夜车。

3. 引进动作行为的原因,相当于"由于、因为"。常常与"而"配合使用。For, used to introduce the reason of an action or behavior. Like "由于" or "因为," it is often used with "而."

(5) 我们为祖国的强大而感到骄傲。
(6) 大家都为你能出国留学而感到高兴。

4. 引进动作行为的对象相当于"对、向"。常用于固定词组中,如:"不足为外人道(不值得或不必对别人说)、可与智者道,难为俗人言"等。To; toward. It is used to introduce the recipient of an action or behavior. Like "对" or "向," it often appears in fixed expressions such as "不足为外人道 (unnecessary or not worth mentioning to others)," "可与智者道,难为俗人言."

说明 Notes:

"为"也有动词用法,表示"帮助、卫护"的意思。现在已经用得不多。Although quite rare, "为" can be used as a verb meaning "to help" or "to guard."

(7) 你为人为到底,把这两件事都做了吧。

wèi 未

用法 Usage:
副词 ad.

古代沿用下来的常用语和书面语。用法有：Originating from archaism, "未" is often used in common expressions and written language as follows:

1. 表示情况还没有发生,否定动作、行为的发生,相当于"不曾、没、没有(跟'已'相对)"。*Not yet, used to negate the occurrence of an action or behavior. It is the same as "不曾," "没," or "没有" (as opposed to "已").*

(1) 他还是个未成年人。

(2) 他还未到学校报到。

2. 表示对情况的否定,相当于"不"(语气比"不"委婉)。"未"意思为"不"时,很少单用,多跟别的语素组成含有文言色彩的词。*Not. It is used to negate a situation. It is similar to "不" but with a milder tone. When meaning "不," "未" is seldom used alone, but rather form classical Chinese expressions with other morphemes.*

(3) 我打算即刻出发,未知君意如何?(不知道你的意思如何 *Not knowing your opinion*)

(4) 他的病刚好,还有点咳嗽,所以未去上课。

说明 Notes:

1. "未"还有助词用法,用在句末,表示疑问。如:"今晚来未?" *"未" can be used as an auxiliary word at the end of a sentence to introduce an inquiry such as "今晚来未?"*

2. "未"常用于成语。如:"未卜先知、前所未闻",相当于"没";"亡羊补牢,犹未为晚",相当于"不"。*Often found in idioms, "未" means "没" in phrases such as "未卜先知" and "前所未闻," or "不" in phrases such as "亡羊补牢,犹未为晚."*

3. "未"主要用于书面语或者固定结构。*"未" is mostly used in written language and fixed expressions.*

4. 副词"未"常修饰单音节动词。*As an adverb, "未" usually modifies monosyllabic words.*

wèibì 未必 →P40"不必"

用法 Usage:

副词 ad.

表示不能肯定或委婉的否定,相当于"不一定、不见得"。用在肯定式之前,表示否定,用在否定式之前,表示肯定。*Not likely; may not. It is used to indicate uncertainty or a euphemistic negation. Like "不一定" or "不见得," it carries a negative meaning when placed before a positive statement and a positive meaning when placed before a negative statement.*

(1) 今天他很忙,未必能来看你。

(2) 今天未必不下雪。

说明 Notes:

"未必"和"不必"的区别是:*The differences between "未必" and "不必" are as follows:*

1. 两者词形相近,都是表示否定的副词,但是意义完全不同。"未必"是一种委婉的否定方式。"不必"表示事理上或情理上不需要,相当于"不需要、没有必要"的意思。*Although both words are adverbs indicating negation, the meanings are completely different. "未必" introduces a euphemistic negation. "不必," however, simply means "unnecessary" based on logical or emotional judgment: it has the same meaning as "不需要" or "没有必要."*

(3) 老师未必来。(不一定来,有不来的可能 *May not come*)

(4) 老师不必来。(不需要来,没有必要来 *Need not come*)

2. "未必"后面可以带肯定式,也可以带否定式,带肯定式表示否定,带否定式表示肯定。"不必"后面只能带肯定式,表示否定。*"未必" can be followed by either a positive or a negative statement. It carries a negative meaning when used before a positive statement, and a positive meaning when used before a negative statement. "不必" can only be followed by a positive statement to indicate a negative meaning.*

(5) 他未必不愿意留在中国。(表示可能愿意留在中国 *May be willing to stay in China*)

(6) 他未必愿意留在中国。(表示可能不愿意留在中国 *May be reluctant to stay in China*)

（7）他不必留在中国。（表示不需要留在中国 Does not need to stay in China）

3. "未必"和"不必"都可以单独回答问题，但在省略句或单独回答问题时，语气不同，后面所用的语气词不同。Although "未必" and "不必" can both stand alone as a response, the tones are different in an elliptical sentence or a stand-alone response.

（8）A：我想她一定愿意跟你去。
　　B：未必吧！
（9）A：我来帮你一下。
　　B：不必了。

wèilái 未来 →P228"将来"

用法 Usage：
名词 n.

1. 表示现在以后的时间，将来。一般指距离现在比较远的时间。Future. It usually refers to the time far ahead of the present.

（1）未来的世界是年轻人的。
（2）我对未来充满了信心。

2. 表示现在以后就要或即将到来的时间（区别于"过去、现在"）。一般指距离现在半天、一天以上的时间。Time not far ahead (as opposed to "过去" or "现在"). It usually refers to half a day or one day from now.

（3）八号台风将在未来二十四小时之内到达东南沿海。
（4）在未来的一个月内，你有一次旅行的机会。

3. 借指希望。Hope.

（5）儿童是世界的未来。
（6）妈妈常说我是她的未来。

说明 Notes：

"未来"和"将来"都指今后的时间。在指距离现在较远的时间，用作定语、宾语时，两词可以通用。"未来" and "将来" can both refer to the future. The two words are interchangeable when used as attributives or objects to refer to the time far ahead of the present.

（7）将来/未来的成功就看现在的努力。
（8）孩子们都很懂事，她在他们的身上看到了美好的将来/未来。

它们的区别是：Their differences between are as follows:

1. "未来"具有庄重的色彩，多用于书面语。"将来"没有庄重色彩，口语、书面语都可以用。Often used in written language, "未来" carries a more solemn tone than "将来." "将来" can be used both in colloquial and written language.

2. "未来"含有以后的光景和希望的意思，如例(5)(6)。"将来"没有这个意思。"未来" can mean the hope in the future. See Examples (5) and (6). "将来" has no such meaning.

3. "将来"可以做状语。"未来"不能。"将来" can be used as an adverbial modifier but "未来" cannot.

（9）＊你的理想未来一定能实现。
（10）你的理想将来一定能实现。

wēnhé 温和 →P341"暖和"、P491"温暖"

用法 Usage：
形容词 a.

1. 形容气候不冷不热。(Of the climate) mild, warm (neither too cold nor too hot).

（1）这里的冬天气候也很温和，非常舒服。
（2）我喜欢温和的春天。

2. （性情、态度、言语等）不严厉，不粗暴，使人感到亲切。(About the temperament, attitude, or language) not harsh or rude; gentle; warm and sincere.

（3）这个老师对学生的态度很温和。
（4）她用温和的目光看着眼前的一群孩子。

说明 Notes：

"温和"跟"暖和"都形容温度适中，使人感到舒服。"温和" and "暖和" can both describe the moderate temperature that makes one feel comfortable.

它们的区别是：They differ as follows:

1. "暖和"的温度比"温和"高一点,侧重于没有冷意。"温和"侧重于温度宜人。*The temperature implied by "暖和" is slightly higher than that of "温和.""暖和" emphasizes not feeling cold, whereas "温和" emphasizes the pleasant temperature.*

2. "温和"可以形容性情、态度、言语等不严厉,不粗暴,使人感到亲切。"暖和"多形容环境、阳光、空气、被褥、衣服和身体等。*"温和" is often used to describe the temperament, attitude, or language as "not harsh or rude"; it makes one feel warm and sincere. "暖和" is normally used to describe the environment, sunshine, air, comforters, clothes, or body, etc.*

3. "暖和"还有动词用法,表示使暖和,可以重叠为"暖和暖和"。"温和"没有这个用法。*"暖和" can be used as a verb meaning "to keep warm." It can be reduplicated as "暖和暖和." "温和" has no such usage.*

wēnnuǎn 温暖 →P490"温和"

用法 Usage:

形容词 *a.*

1. 形容气候、环境不冷也不太热。*Mild; warm.*

（1）近几年冬天的天气越来越温暖了。

（2）找一个温暖的房间暖暖身体。

2. 比喻人际关系和谐、融洽而亲切。*(About interpersonal relationship) harmonious and cordial.*

（3）跟他在一起,你就觉得很温暖。

（4）我们班真是个让人感到温暖的集体。

动词 *v.*

使感到温暖。"温暖"后面一般要带宾语。*To make someone feel warm. It is usually followed by an object.*

（5）老师的关心温暖了全班同学的心。

（6）她治好了我爸爸的病,也温暖了我们全家。

说明 Notes:

"温和"和"温暖"作形容词用时都形容气候不冷不热。*When used as an adjective both "温和" and "温暖" can describe the mild temperature.*

它们的区别是:*Their differences are as follows:*

1. "温和"还能形容态度或性情,常跟"态度、脸色、谈吐"等词语搭配使用。"温暖"则表示一种心理感觉。*"温和" can be used to describe the attitude or temperament. It is often used with words such as "态度,脸色,谈吐.""温暖" emphasizes someone's feeling.*

2. "温暖"可以作动词,"温和"不能。*"温暖" can be used as a verb but "温和" cannot.*

wénhuà 文化 →P492"文明"

用法 Usage:

名词 *n.*

1. 特指人类在社会历史发展中所创造的物质财富和精神财富的总和。*Culture; the sum of the material and spiritual wealth created during the social and historical development of mankind.*

（1）五月,学院有很多中国文化讲座。

（2）每个民族都有自己的历史和文化。

2. 有时特指精神财富,如文学、艺术、科学、教育等。*Sometimes, it refers specially to spiritual wealth such as literature, art, science and education, etc.*

（3）学校里有个世界文化活动中心。

（4）学校里的文化生活是很丰富的。

3. 考古学上指同一个历史时期的不依分布地点为转移的遗迹、遗物的综合体。*An archaeological term to describe the sum of relics and legacies from the same historical period regardless of their locations.*

（5）良渚文化分布在杭州钱塘江流域。

（6）新石器文化开始于约七八千年前。

4. 指一般知识和运用文字的能力。*Literacy; general knowledge.*

(7) 他是中学教师，是我们村最有文化的人。

(8) 她是大学毕业生，文化水平很高。

wénmíng 文明 →P491"文化"

用法 Usage:

名词 *n.*

同"文化"一样，特指人类在社会历史发展中所创造的物质财富和精神财富的总和，有时专指精神财富，如文学、艺术、科学、教育等。Civilization. Like "文化," "文明" is used to refer to the sum of the material and spiritual wealth created during the social and historical development of mankind. Sometimes it is used specifically to refer to the spiritual wealth such as literature, art, science, education, etc.

(1) 我们要提高社会文明水平。

(2) 中华民族具有五千年的文明史。

形容词 *a.*

1. 指社会发展到较高阶段和具有较高文化状态的。Civilized. It is used to refer to the civilized stage of society.

(3) 中国是个文明古国。

(4) 随地扔垃圾是不文明的行为。

2. 指具有新的、现代色彩的（风俗、习惯、事物）。(Of customs and habits) modern.

(5) 父亲对我们孩子的态度很文明。

(6) 我的祖父母是文明结婚的。

说明 Notes:

"文化"和"文明"的区别是：The differences between "文化" and "文明" are as follows:

1. 一般"文化"着重特指文学、艺术、教育、科学等精神财富。"文明"着重指有高度文化，达到的昌盛开明、没有野蛮状态和非理性的行为，呈现出礼貌、文雅，有良好教养的人类社会的理想境界。"文化" is often used specifically to refer to the spiritual wealth such as literature, art, science, education, etc. "文明," by contrast, focuses on the ideal state of human society with a highly developed culture, good manners, upbringing, and elegance, as opposed to one with crude, uncivilized and irrational behaviors.

2. "文化"适用范围大，除了与"文明"相同的词语可搭配以外，"文化"还能与"传统、遗产、宝库、流派、生活、交流"等较多的词语搭配使用。"文明"适用范围小，可搭配使用的词语不多。除了与"文化"相同的词语搭配以外，"文明"前面还可受"精神、物质、社会"等少数词语的修饰。"文化" has a wider range of application than "文明." In addition to the words that can usually be used with "文明," "文化" can also be used with words such as "传统, 遗产, 宝库, 流派, 生活, 交流." "文明" may not be used with some of these words, but it can be modified by words such as "精神, 物质, 社会."

3. "文化"还有表示人运用文字的能力及掌握一般知识多少的词义。"文明"没有以上两种用法。"文化" can be used to refer to literacy or general knowledge. By contrast, "文明" has no such usage.

4. "文化"只是名词，"文明"还有形容词的意义和用法。"文化" can only serve as a noun, whereas "文明" can be used as an adjective as well.

(7) *这种行为很不文化。

(8) 这种行为很不文明。

wěndìng 稳定 →P3"安定"

用法 Usage:

形容词 *a.*

1. 表示社会形势、秩序、物价等平稳安定，没有变化。Stable. It is used to indicate stability and little or no change in the environmental situation, social order, prices of commodities, etc.

(1) 这几年的物价还比较稳定。

(2) 社会稳定、国泰民安是每个老百姓的愿望。

2. 表示某种情绪或者事情的状况（如病情）平稳，没有变化。Stable. It is used to indicate one's emotions or sickness or other things remaining unchanged.

（3）最近几天，他的病情比较稳定。

（4）受伤者的情绪已经稳定了。

动词 v.

表示使某事安定下来，不要有变化。To make stable and unchanged.

（5）你先到外面去稳定一下游客的情绪。

（6）今年我们要继续稳定物价、稳定市场。

说明 Notes:

1. "稳定"的动态感比较强，所以做谓语时，后面可以带趋向补语，如"稳定下来了、稳定起来了"。"稳定" carries a fairly strong sense of a dynamic action, and so, when it is used as a predicate, it can be followed by trend complements such as "稳定下来了，稳定起来了."

2. "稳定"用作动词时，后面可以带动量词或者不定量名词。"稳定" can be followed by a quantifier or an indefinite noun when it serves as a verb.

（7）你去稳定一下/他们的情绪。

（8）他们的情绪稳定一点儿了。

3. "安定"和"稳定"的区别是：The differences between "安定" and "稳定" are as follows:

① 在词义上，"安定"多为平面的状态描述，注重被描述事物面上的状况，不安定因素多为外界因素的骚扰。"稳定"侧重于上下、左右等多角度立体性的描述，注重事物本身的平稳性。Semantically, "安定" gives a horizontal sort of description of a state: the unstable factors come mostly from outside interference. "稳定," by contrast, tends to describe from different perspectives, up and down, left or right. It highlights the stability that exists in a thing itself.

② 在用法上，"安定"多形容变化频率比较缓慢、不多的事物状态，如"生活、形势"等。"稳定"多形容变化频率可能比较快和多的事物状况，如"物价、情绪"等。In terms of practical use, "安定" more often than not describes things that change slowly and not so often, such as "生活, 形势." By contrast, "稳定" often modifies things that change frequently such as "物价, 情绪."

③ "安定""稳定"都有动词用法。"稳定"的动词用法比"安定"的多得多。Both "安定" and "稳定" can serve as a verb, especially "稳定," which is used a lot more often.

④ "稳定"后面可以带趋向补语或数量词。"安定"一般不带。"稳定" may be followed by a trend complement or by a quantifier. But "安定" is usually not used this way.

wènhǎo 问好 →P493"问候"

用法 Usage:

动词 v.

询问安好，表示关切。To send greetings; to show care and concern.

（1）请向你父母问好！

（2）玛丽在信里问全班同学好。

wènhòu 问候 →P493"问好"

用法 Usage:

动词 v.

问好。To send greetings.

（1）我父母让我问候叔叔阿姨！

（2）中国朋友要我问候你们。

说明 Notes:

"问好"和"问候"都是动词。"问好" and "问候" are both verbs.

它们的区别是：Their differences are as follows:

1. "问好"不能直接带宾语，带宾语时，要采用"向……问好"或者"问……好"的格式。"问候"则可以直接带表示人的宾语。"问好" cannot be directly followed by an object. The object should be introduced by the structure of "向…问好" or "问…好.""问候" can be directly followed by an object introducing a person.

（3）我父母让我问候你们！
（4）我父母让我向叔叔阿姨问好！

2."问候"还可以用作"表示、表达、转达"等动词的宾语，"问好"不能。"问候" can serve as the object of certain verbs such as "表示,表达,转达.""问好" has no such usage.

（5）*我父母要我转达对你们的问好。
（6）我父母要我转达对你们的问候。

wúfǎ 无法

用法 Usage:

副词 ad.

没有办法。Unable to (do something); finding no solution.

（1）我无法买到明天的飞机票。
（2）他的话我无法相信。

说明 Notes:

1."无法"是副词，出现在谓语动词前，如"无法接受、无法回答、无法学习"等。As an adverb, "无法" is placed before a verb predicate such as "无法接受,无法回答,无法学习,无法想象."

2."无法"意思为"没有办法"，但是"无法"和"没有办法"两者用法不同。Although "无法" has the same meaning as "没有办法," the usage of the two is different.

① "办法"是"没有"的宾语。"没有办法"常跟别的动词一起组成连动式使用。"办法" is the object of "没有." "没有办法" is often used with another verb phrase to form a serial verb construction.

（3）四周都是高山，没有办法打电话。(连动谓语 Serial verbs predicate)
（4）四周都是高山，无法打电话。("无法"是状语。"无法" serves as the adverbial modifier.)

② "没有办法"可以单独使用。"无法"不能。"没有办法" can be used alone but "无法" cannot.

（5）A：你有办法借到这本书吗？
B：没有办法。/*无法。

wúlùn 无论 →P47"不管"、P494"无论如何"

用法 Usage:

连词 conj.

表示在任何条件下，结果或结论都不改变。用在有任指意义的疑问代词或有选择关系的并列成分的句子里，后边须有"都"或"也"等呼应。However; no matter what/how. It indicates that the result or the conclusion remains the same under all circumstances. When it appears in sentences with interrogative pronouns for general reference or parallel components for selection, "无论" corresponds with "都" or "也."

1."无论"引进的是一个分句。前后两个分句的主语相同时，主语可以在前一分句，也可以在后一分句。其格式为"无论＋什么/怎么/谁……＋VP，都……"。"无论" introduces a clause. When the two clauses have the same subject, the subject can be placed in either clause with the structure of "无论＋什么/怎么/谁…＋VP，都…."

（1）无论我们谁去，都必须告诉老师一下。
（2）无论有什么事，大家都愿意跟他商量。
（3）无论我怎么说，他都不听。

2."无论"引进的是短语，其格式为"无论A还是B，都……"。"无论" introduces a phrase with the structure of "无论A还是B，都…."

（4）无论你还是我，都不能迟到。
（5）明天无论天晴还是下雨，我们都要去参观博物馆。

说明 Notes:

1.在"无论……，都/也……"句式中，前一小句应该有表示任指的疑问代词，如"什么、怎么、怎么样、谁"等，或者有表示选择关系的并列成分，如例（5）。In the sentence structure of "无论…，都/也…," there must be either an interrogative pronoun for general reference such as "什么，怎么，怎么样，谁," or parallel components for selection in the first clause as in (5).

2. "无论"相同于"不论"。"无论" is the same as "不论."

3. "无论"和"不管"的区别是：The differences between "无论" and "不管" are as follows:

① "无论"多用于书面语。"不管"多用于口语。"无论" is mostly used in written language, while "不管" is often used colloquially.

② "无论"后可用"如何、是否、与否"等文言词语。"不管"后面不能用。"无论" can be followed by such classical Chinese words as "如何,是否,与否," while "不管" cannot.

wúlùnrúhé 无论如何 →P494"无论"

用法 Usage:

表示在任何条件下,结果始终不变,一定。No matter what; definitely. It indicates that the result remains the same under all circumstances.

(1) 今天无论如何你都得去医院看病。
(2) 今天我无论如何也要自己做饭吃。

说明 Notes:

1. "无论如何"是"无论"加上"如何"构成的固定词组,相当于"无论怎么样"。可位于主语前或主语后,谓语前常有"都"或"也"呼应。如例(1)(2)。A fixed expression with the same meaning as "无论怎么样," "无论如何" can be used either before or after the subject and corresponds with "都" or "也" before the predicate as in (1) and (2).

2. 在句子中,"无论"所在的分句是一种具体的行为动作或状况,另一分句则是不管这个行为动作或状况下不变的结果。Within the sentence, the clause with "无论" introduces a specific action or behavior, whereas the other clause indicates the unchanged result regardless of the action or behavior.

3. "无论"做句子,一般前后得由两个分句组成。"无论如何"一般只一个句子。"无论如何"总括了一切行为动作,所以后面不再带具体的行为动作,而直接跟不变的结果。There are usually two clauses in a sentence with "无论" but only one sentence with "无论如何." Summarizing all possible actions, "无论如何" is followed by the unchanged result rather than specific actions.

(3) 无论你去还是不去,我都去。
(4) 无论如何我都去。

wúsuǒwèi 无所谓 →P45"不在乎"、P317"没事儿"

用法 Usage:

动词 v.

1. 说不上,谈不上。表示还称不上某种名称。Not to deserve the name or title of.

(1) 我只是喜欢写毛笔字,无所谓书法家。
(2) 她跟我是高中同学,无所谓女朋友。

2. 表示不在乎,没有什么关系。相当于"没事儿、没关系、不在乎"。但侧重于"怎么样都可以"或"自有主张"。Not to care about; to have no relationship. Like "没事儿,没关系,不在乎," it emphasizes one's indifference or one's own opinion.

(3) 看什么电影,我无所谓。
(4) 房子大小无所谓,但是必须安静。

说明 Notes:

1. 表示"说不上、谈不上"的意思时,"无所谓"可以带宾语。如例(1)(2)。Meaning "not worthy of a name or a title," "无所谓" can be followed by an object as in (1) and (2).

2. 表示"不在乎,没有关系"的意思时,小句的主语可以是对举形式,或者前后两个小句的意义相对,或者句中有表示任指的疑问代词。如(3)(4)。When "无所谓" means "not caring about or having no relationship," the subject of the clause can appear in contrast. Alternatively, the two clauses may have

meanings that contradict each other, or there may be an interrogative pronoun for general reference in the sentence as in (3) and (4).

3. 不表示主观态度,只表示客观描述时,"无所谓"和"没关系、没什么、没事儿"可以互相替换。When used for objective descriptions rather than subjective attitudes, "无所谓" is interchangeable with "没事儿,没关系,不在乎."

(5) 这点小病无所谓/没关系/没什么/没事儿。

它们的区别是:Their differences are as follows:

① "无所谓"侧重指"不在乎",即主观上不关心,没有关系,因此可以说"无所谓的态度、无所谓的样子"。"没关系、没什么、没事儿"多指客观上不重要或没有影响,多见于"这点儿小病没关系/没什么/没事儿""这个小问题没关系/没什么/没事儿"等。Meaning "not caring about or with no relationship," "无所谓" emphasizes a person's indifference toward something. "没关系,没什么,没事儿," however, focuses on something being unimportant and therefore not consequential. And so we have "这点儿小病没关系/没什么/没事儿" and "这个小问题没关系/没什么/没事儿."

② "无所谓"可以带宾语。"没关系/没什么"不能。"无所谓" can be followed by an object, but "没关系/没什么" cannot be followed by an object.

4. "无所谓"与"不在乎"都有动词用法,区别是:"无所谓"有"说不上、说不到"的意思。"不在乎"没有。"无所谓" and "不在乎" both can be used as verbs. The difference is that "无所谓" has the meaning of "说不上" or "说不到," while "不在乎" does not.

wúyí 无疑

用法 Usage:
形容词 a.
毫无疑问,肯定。Certain; having no doubt.

(1) 她无疑是班上成绩最好的学生。
(2) 这些证据确凿无疑。

说明 Notes:

"无疑"一词用在动词前作状语,表示强调的语气。除了做状语,"无疑"不能单独使用,一般要与其他词语配合使用,如例(2)。"无疑" can be used as an adverbial before a verb to enhance the tone of the sentence. Except for such usage, "无疑" cannot be used alone. It has to be used with another word as in (2).

(3) *老师上课讲得很清楚,我无疑。
(4) 老师上课讲得很清楚,我没有疑问。

wùyè 物业

用法 Usage:
名词 n.

通常指建成并投入使用的各类房屋(如公寓、商品房、写字楼等)以及配套的服务、设备、设施、场地等。常可组成"物业管理、物业费、物业公司"等词语。Real estate; property. It is normally used to refer to constructions that have been completed and put to use (such as apartments, commercial houses, office buildings, etc.) and the supporting services, equipment, facilities, and space. It is often used in words such as "物业管理,物业费,物业公司."

(1) 我住的小区物业设施很完善。
(2) 我们小区的物业管理公司工作很负责。

wù 误

用法 Usage:
动词 v.

1. 耽误。常常带"了"。To delay (often followed by "了").

(1) 你明天五点必须起床,不然会误了上飞机。
(2) 因为洪水,火车被误了三个小时。

2. 因错误或耽误使人或事受到损失。To cause loss for people or things.

(3) 错误的教学方式会误人子弟的。

(4) 你这么做，误了别人，也误了自己。

形容词 *a.*

1. 不正确的。*Incorrect.*

(5) 老师把我误认为韩国同学了。

(6) 一个人如果总是误听误信，他一定会犯错误。

2. 不是故意的。*Unintentional.*

(7) 因为太匆忙，他误拿了同学的手机。

(8) 对不起，我误入了你的房间！

名词 *n.*

表示差错。*Errors.*

(9) 他说话口误很多。

(10) 在作文里，有些字错了，是笔误。

说明 Notes：

1. "误"后面带多音节名词的话，为使句子的音节和谐，一般"误"后面常常带"了"，如例(1)(2)(4)(8)。"了" is often inserted between "误" and the disyllabic word following it to make for a smooth connection between syllables as in (1), (2), (4) and (8).

(11) * 他起床很晚，误上课了。

(12) 他起床很晚，误了上课。

2. "误"动词用法，表示耽误事情，常常是与时间有关的具体事情。要根据具体的句子内容，强调用法上的逻辑性。When used as a verb, "误" introduces the thing that has been delayed, which is often a specific matter related to time. A logical explanation based on the context of the sentence should be provided.

(13) * 我的朋友因为妈妈不同意，误了他来中国留学。

(14) 我同学来不及买飞机票，所以误了昨天来中国的航班。

wùhuì 误会 →P497"误解"

用法 Usage：

动词 *v.*

误解对方的意思。*To misunderstand.*

(1) 请大家别误会了他做的这件事。

(2) 刚才我误会了你，请原谅！

名词 *n.*

对对方意思的误解。*Misunderstanding.*

(3) 这是你们之间的一个误会。

(4) 朋友之间有误会，互相说明白就是了。

wùjiě 误解 →P497"误会"

用法 Usage：

动词 *v.*

理解得不正确。*To misunderstand.*

(1) 你误解他了，他是喜欢你的。

(2) 大家千万别误解了题目的意思。

名词 *n.*

不正确的理解。*Misunderstanding.*

(3) 说吃土豆会发胖，这是一个误解。

(4) 你这是对我的误解，我说的话不是那个意思。

说明 Notes：

"误会"和"误解"的区别是：*The differences between "误会" and "误解" are as follows:*

1. 在词义上，"误会"侧重于对某一事物的错误感受和认识。"误解"侧重于对某一事物，尤其是对其意思的错误认识和理解。*In terms of the semantic meaning, "误会" emphasizes the erroneous recognition or experience of something, whereas "误解" emphasizes the wrong understanding of something, especially its meaning.*

2. 如果句子中的宾语是关于文章内容、句子或词语的意思的名词，一般多用"误解"，如例(2)(4)。*"误解" is normally used if the object of the sentence is a noun about the content of an article or about a sentence, or about the meaning of a word as in (2) and (4).*

xīwàng 希望 →P347"盼望"、P613"愿望"

用法 Usage:

动词 v.

心里想达到某种目的或出现某种情况。宾语常是句子或短语。To hope for certain conditions to occur or to achieve a certain goal. It often takes sentences or phrases as its objects.

(1) 他希望自己能在中国继续学习一年汉语。

(2) 我希望你能教我一下这个语法点的使用方法。

名词 n.

1. 表示实现某种愿望的可能性，常做动词"有""没/没有"的宾语。The possibility of realizing a desire, commonly used as an object of "有，""没/没有."

(3) 看来他通过 HSK 六级有希望了。

(4) 如果复习不好，考试想得优秀就没有希望。

2. 表示希望所寄托的对象。The object of one's hopes or desires.

(5) 孩子是父母亲的希望。

(6) 年轻人是这个社会的希望。

说明 Notes:

"希望"和"盼望"的区别是：The differences between "希望" and "盼望" are as follows:

1. "希望"是一般性的向往，语义比较轻。"盼望"的语气是急切的，含有等待性的向往，语义比较重。"希望" is a normal desire with a relatively light semantic connotation. "盼望" carries a more urgent tone with a heavier connotation and a sense of longing and awaiting.

2. "希望"可以对别人，也可以对自己。"盼望"多用于对某人或某事的热切期待。"希望" can refer to others or to oneself. "盼望," by contrast, refers to eager expectation on someone or something.

(7) 我希望明年能找到女朋友。

(8) ＊我盼望自己有更多的发明创造。

xīshēng 牺牲

用法 Usage:

动词 v.

1. 表示为了正义的目的而舍弃自己的生命。To give up one's life for a just cause.

(1) 为了抢救国家财产，他牺牲了自己年轻的生命。

(2) 这位军人在战场上光荣牺牲了。

2. 放弃或损害某些利益。To abandon or harm certain interests.

(3) 他牺牲了很多双休日为别人修理自行车。

(4) 为了学好汉语口语，玛丽牺牲了很多休息时间。

名词 n.

古代祭祀用的牲畜。Animals sacrificed for ritual usage.

(5) 古代祭祀用的牺牲主要有牛、羊、猪三牲。

说明 Notes:

1. "牺牲"也表示"死",但"牺牲"只有在为了国家或人民的利益等某一个正义的目的时死去,才能用"牺牲"一词。"牺牲" can also mean "死," but "牺牲" can only be used to describe death for the interests of a country or people or for some kind of righteous purpose.

2. "牺牲"词义比较严肃,前面修饰的词语一般有"英勇、壮烈"等,后面所带的宾语常有"生命、休息时间、个人利益"等。"牺牲" has a fairly serious implication, and is often preceded by modifiers such as "英勇,壮烈," or followed by objects such as "生命,休息时间,个人利益."

xǐ'ài 喜爱 →P499"喜欢"

用法 Usage:

动词 v.

对人或事物有好感或感兴趣。To have interest in or favorable impressions of a person or thing.

(1) 张老师特别喜爱游泳。
(2) 这孩子让人喜爱极了。

说明 Notes:

1. "喜爱"是心理动词,既可以带具体的表示人或事物的名词性宾语,也可以带动词性宾语,如"喜爱集邮、喜爱打球"等。"喜爱" is a verb describing a mental concept and can be used with either concrete noun objects expressing people or things with verb-type objects such as "喜爱集邮,喜爱打球."

2. 可以用副词修饰,如"很喜爱",也可以带程度补语,如"喜爱极了、喜爱得不得了"。This term can also be used as an adverb, for example: "很喜爱"; and can also take degree complements such as "喜爱极了,喜爱得不得了."

xǐhuan 喜欢 →P499"喜爱"

用法 Usage:

动词 v.

对人或事物有好感或感兴趣。To have interest in or favorable impressions of a person or thing.

(1) 孩子们都很喜欢《西游记》里的孙悟空。
(2) 女孩子最喜欢玩布娃娃。

说明 Notes:

"喜欢"与"喜爱"的区别是:The differences between "喜欢" and "喜爱" are as follows:

1. 在词义上,"喜爱"侧重于热爱的心理,"喜欢"侧重于高兴、愉快的心情。In terms of semantics, "喜爱" emphasizes feelings of love while "喜欢" emphasizes feelings of happiness.

2. "喜爱"的宾语多是具体的人或事物,多带名词性宾语。"喜欢"的宾语可以是具体的人或物,也可以是抽象的事物,能带名词性与非名词性宾语。"喜爱" is usually accompanied by concrete objects or people, often nominals. "喜欢" can be accompanied by either concrete or abstract objects that may or may not be nominals.

(3) 我喜欢安静,不喜欢热闹。

3. "喜欢"可以重叠为ABAB式"喜欢喜欢"。"喜爱"不可以。"喜欢" can be reduplicated with the ABAB structure as "喜欢喜欢" while "喜爱" cannot.

xìxīn 细心 →P516"小心"、P688"仔细"

用法 Usage:

形容词 a.

用心细密,周到。Careful and meticulous, attentive.

(1) 他做事很细心,你放心吧。
(2) 她非常细心地照顾每一个病人。

xià 下

用法 Usage:

动词 v.

1. 从高处到低处。如:"下山、下楼、下飞机、下火车、下船"等。To move from a high place to a low place such as "下山,下楼,下飞机,下火车,下船."

2. 雨、雪、霜、冰雹等降落。如:"下雪、下雨、下冰雹、下霜"等。*The falling of rain, snow, hail, etc. as in "下雪,下雨,下冰雹,下霜."*

(1) 昨晚的雨下得好大。

3. 到某处,去某处。*To go from one place to another.*

(2) 王主任天天下车间检查工作。

(3) 今天我们中餐下饭馆吧。

4. 进行(某种棋类游戏)。*To play (a game, e.g. in chess).*

(4) 咱们下两盘象棋如何?

(5) 张老师最爱下围棋。

5. 离开某个地方,退场。*To leave a place; to exit.*

(6) 我们下午五点下班。

(7) 现在球场上11号球员下,7号球员上。

6. 做出(某种结论、判断)等。*To make (a judgment, decision, verdict, etc.).*

(8) 现在就这么下结论还早了一点。

(9) 什么是"幸福",你能下个定义吗?

7. 发布,颁发,投递。后面常常跟"来"。*To issue, deliver, or award, often followed by "来."*

(10) 我们去教学实习的通知什么时候下来?

(11) 得到奖学金同学的名单已经下(来)了。

8. 使用。*To use.*

(12) 他下笔就写了两篇文章。

(13) 她下手很快,一会儿三个菜就做好了。

9. 趋向动词用法。用在动词后做补语,表示由高处到低处,或表示有空间能容纳、表示动作的完成或结果。*A directional verb used as a complement following another verb to indicate movement from a high area to a low area, to indicate that an area has space free to accommodate something, or to indicate the completion or result of a verb.*

(14) 你坐下,我再跟你说。

(15) 这个教室坐得下20个同学。

(16) 初级阶段打下扎实的基础,汉语就不难学。

名词 *n.*

1. 位置在低处的(跟"上"相对)。*A position at a lower area (the opposite of "上").*

(17) 他们刚刚从桥下走过。

(18) 山上风景迷人,山下景色也不错。

2. 时间或排序在后面的。*The latter part of a time period or sequence.*

(19) 这是下半年的学习计划。

(20) 下一次我们一起去海南旅游。

3. 属于一定情况、范围或条件的,常常与"在"组成"在……下"的短语格式。*Part of a fixed situation, scope, or condition, typically used with "在" to make the pattern "在…下."*

(21) 在大家的帮助下,我们顺利完成了任务。

(22) 在这种情况下,谁都有可能害怕。

4. 等级或品级低的。*A lower rank or grade.*

(23) 这些是下等货,所以价钱便宜。

(24) 学习成绩你在上、中、下的哪个等级?

5. 在两个的量中表示第二,在三个的量中表示第三。*The final volume in a set of two or three.*

(25) 看完上集看下集。

(26) 这套书有上、中、下三册,这是下册。

6. 用在数字后面,表示方位或方面。*Used after numbers to indicate direction, position, etc.*

(27) 他们两下里都同意自己解决那个矛盾。

(28) 我们往四下一看,一个人影也没有。

7. 表示正当某个时间或时节。*Indicating a certain time or season.*

(29) 年下是用钱的时候,你要不够用,就向我要。

(30) 时下都用手机的支付宝付钱了,我也得学会。

说明 Notes:

"下"的反义词是"上"。使用时很多情况两两相对,如:"上班、下班;上车、下车;上课、下课;上山、下山"等。但并不是完全相对,如:"上学"对应的是"放学",而不是"下学"。"下" and "上" *are typically used as opposites, as seen in* cases such as "上班,下班;上车,下车;上课,下课;上山,下山." However, this is not true for every case; for example, the opposite counterpart to "上学" is "放学," not "下学."

xiàhǎi 下海

用法 Usage:

动词 v.

1. 到海里去。To enter the sea.

(1) 下海要注意安全。

2. 渔民到海上捕鱼。(Of fishermen) to go out to sea to fish.

(2) 渔民下海捕鱼很辛苦。

(3) 初次下海,可能会头晕呕吐很难过。

3. 放弃原来的工作开始从事商业。To abandon one's original work to engage in a new trade.

(4) 叔叔十年前开始下海经商,现在生意做得很好。

(5) 改革开放后,有的老师离开学校下海了。

说明 Notes:

注意"下海"的第一、第二种用法,是"下"和"海"的短语结构。第三种用法,"下海"是一个具有隐喻性的动词短语。Note that in the first and second usages, "下海" is a verb-noun phrase composed of the verb "下" and the noun "海," while in the third usage "下海" is a fixed verbal phrase, used metaphorically to mean "to shift to a new trade."

xiàlái 下来

用法 Usage:

动词 v.

1. 由高处到低处来(说话人在低处)。To go from a high point to a low point (the speaker being at the low point).

(1) 妹妹从楼上下来了。

(2) 山上没有路,他们下得来吗?

2. 指领导到基层下面来,上级机关到下级机关来。(For a higher authority) to enter the sphere of influence at a lower-level department.

(3) 省里的工作小组明天下到我们学校来检查工作。

(4) 校长要下来参加我们学院的新年晚会。

3. 指谷物、蔬菜、水果等农作物成熟并收获。The ripening and harvesting of grains, vegetables, fruits, or other crops.

(5) 再等半个月,葡萄就下来了。

4. 用在时间词语后,表示一段时间结束。Used after time words to indicate the conclusion of a specified period of time.

(6) 一个学期下来,他竟然能去四班学中级汉语了。

5. 趋向动词,用在动词后面,表示人或事物随动作由高处向低处来。A directional verb used after another verb to indicate a person or object moving from a high position to a low one as a result of the action denoted by the verb.

(7) 老人们从山上走下来了。

(8) 请你把箱子从车上拿下来!

(9) 那么高,你跳得下来吗?

6. 用在动词后面,表示动作从过去继续到现在。Used after a verb to indicate that the verb has been carrying on from a point in the past until the present moment.

(10) 这些都是我外婆和妈妈传下来的民间故事。

(11) 汉语有点难学,但是你们都坚持下来了,真棒!

7. 用在动词后,表示动作的完成和结果。Used after a verb to indicate the verb's completion or result.

(12) 雨停下来了,我们走吧!

(13) 老师说的例句我给你记下来了。

8. 用在形容词后面,表示某种状态开始出现并继续发展。Used after an adjective to indicate that a condition has begun to emerge and is continuing to develop.

(14) 天色渐渐黑了下来。

(15) 看到老师走进教室,同学们就安静下来了。

说明 Notes:

1. 在"下来"的第一、第二种用法中,"下"是动词,"来"表示趋向。如果后面有宾语,宾语应该在"下"和"来"之间。In the first two usages of "下来," "下" is a verb and "来" indicates the direction. If followed by an object, the object should fall between "下" and "来."

(16) *妹妹下来楼了。

(17) 妹妹下楼来了。

2. "下来"用在动词后面作趋向补语时,如果动词后面有宾语,宾语也可以在"下"和"来"之间。When "下来" is used as a directional complement following a verb, the object can be placed between "下" and "来" if the verb is followed by an object.

(18) 他从楼上拿下来几个箱子。

(19) 他从楼上拿下几个箱子来。

3. "下来"和"下去"是表示动作方向相反的一对词语,除了方向相对,很多用法基本相似。"下来" and "下去" are a pair of phrases that are used to describe opposite directions, but otherwise they are fundamentally similar.

xiàqù 下去

用法 Usage:

动词 *v.*

1. 由高处到低处去(说话人在高处)。*To go from a higher point to a lower point (the speaker being at the higher point); to go down.*

(1) 妈妈下楼去了。

(2) 河水很急,你下得去下不去?

2. 指上级机关人员退出领导岗位或去下级机关、基层工作。*(Of higher-level personnel) to withdraw from authoritative or leadership posts or to return to lower-level positions and basic-level work.*

(3) 上级机关领导每人每月都要有一定的时间下基层去。

(4) 到了退休年龄,不管是谁都要从岗位上下去。

3. 演员离开前台到后台。*(Of performers) to exit the stage (and go backstage).*

(5) 那个歌星只唱了一首歌就下去了。

4. 食物已经吃下或消化;病情已经平复;情绪已经稳定。*Used to describe the conditions in which food has already been eaten or digested, an illness that has already been cured or healed, or for conditions that have already stabilized.*

(6) 一会儿时间,三个包子就下去了。

(7) 你放心吧,病人的体温正在下去。

5. 趋向动词。用在动词后做趋向补语,表示人或事物随动作由高处到低处或离开原地。*Used as a directional complement following another verb to indicate that a person or object has moved from a high place to a low place or has left its original position as a result of the action denoted by that verb.*

(8) 潮水退下去了。

(9) 马群从山岗上跑下去了。

6. 用在动词后,表示动作仍然继续进行。*(Used after a verb) to indicate that the action is still continuing.*

(10) 你别说下去了。

(11) 每天早晨读课文,你坚持下去的话,口语一定提高得很快。

7. 用在形容词后,表示某种状态已经存在并将继续发展(形容词多为表示消极意义)。*Used after an adjective to indicate that certain conditions already exist and are continuing to develop (frequently used with adjectives that have a negative connotation).*

(12) 他的身体一天天差下去了。

(13) 天气还会冷下去的。

说明 Notes:

1. 在"下去"的第一、第二种用法中,"下"是动词,"去"表示趋向。如果后面有宾语,宾语应该在"下"和"去"之间,如例(1)(3). In the first and second usages of "下去," "下" is a verb and "去" indicates the direction. If followed by an object, the object should fall between "下" and "去" as seen in (1) and (3).

2. "下去"用在动词后面作趋向补语时,如果动词后面有宾语,宾语也可以在"下"和"去"之间。When "下去" is used as a directional complement following a verb, the object can fall between "下" and "去" if the verb is followed by an object.

(14) 他从楼上拿下去了几个箱子。
(15) 他从楼上拿了几个箱子下去。

xiàzǎi 下载

用法 Usage:
动词 *v.*

从互联网或其他计算机上获取信息并装入、保存到某台计算机或其他电子装置上(跟"上传"相对)。*To download, the opposite of "上传 (upload)"; to receive information through the Internet or other computer-based source and install or save it onto another system.*

(1) 我昨天从网上下载了一部电影。
(2) 你发过来的文件我已经下载了。

xiān 先

用法 Usage:
副词 *ad.*

1. 表示时间或者次序在前(跟"后"相对)。*Indicates the beginning of a time or sequence (the opposite of "后").*

(1) 你先吃吧,我写完再吃。
(2) 大家先介绍一下自己吧。

2. 暂时,暂且,暂先。*Temporarily; for the moment.*

(3) 我们今天先学到这儿。
(4) 你先别去,最好先打电话问一下他在不在家。

3. "先"常与"是"合用,带有"先前、起初、本来"的意思。*"先" is often used together with "是" to express the meaning of "先前,起初,本来."*

(5) 今天先是天晴,后来又下了暴雨。
(6) 他先是低声地求她,接着又大声地发了脾气。

名词 *n.*

表示时间或次序在前的(跟"后"相对)。如:"有话在先、争先恐后"等。*The beginning of a time or sequence (the opposite of "后"), for example, "有话在先,争先恐后."*

说明 Notes:

1. "先"作副词用,意为"表示时间或者次序在先"时,常常是前面用了"先",后面用"然后、才、再、马上、而后"等呼应,如例(1)。有时,虽然只讲一件事,另一件事没说,但仍然表示出两件事发生的先后顺序。所讲的事发生在先,没讲的事发生在后,如例(2)。*When used as an adverb to indicate the beginning of a time or sequence, "先" is often used at the beginning of a phrase and followed by "然后、才、再、马上、而后, etc.," as seen in (1). Sometimes only one matter or occurrence will be described without explicitly mentioning a second, but the sequence of two occurrences happening in a specific order is still expressed. In such cases, the occurrence mentioned happens first and the omitted occurrence is understood as happening afterward, as seen in (2).*

2. 当意为"暂且、暂先"时,"先"字前后多半有否定词"别、不"等,如例(4)。*When expressing "as for the present moment," the phrases before and after "先" typically include a negation word such as "别" or "不," as seen in (4).*

3. "先"与"是"连用时,后面往往与"后来、接着"等词语呼应,如例(5)(6),表示事态前后的变化。*When "先" goes with "是," it is*

often followed by "后来,接着" or similar expressions, as seen in (5) and (6), which describe the changes of a situation over time.

4. "先"还有形容词用法,表示上一代的人或已经死去的人,如:"先人、先父先母(限于称自己已故的父母)"。"先" also has an adjectival usage which can be used to refer to individuals of the previous generation or individuals who have already passed away, for example, "先人," "先父先母 (these terms can only be used to refer to one's own late parents)."

xiānhòu 先后 →P371"前后"

用法 Usage:

名词 n.

指先和后。The succession of events.

(1) 要做的作业很多,就根据难易分个先后。
(2) 按照报名的先后顺序面试吧。

副词 ad.

前后相继。Successively; one after another.

(3) 合唱团先后在国内外演出,深受欢迎。
(4) 父母亲先后来信要求我尽快回国。

说明 Notes:

"先后"作副词用,要注意以下五个方面。When "先后" is used as an adverb, pay attention to the following five aspects.

1. "先后"常在动词谓语或动词短语前作状语。As an adverb, "先后" is often used before a verbal predicate or verb phrase in the form of an adverbial modifier.

2. "先后"可以用于同一主语的不同行为,如例(3),也可用于不同主语的同一行为,如例(4)。As an adverb, "先后" can be used with different actions of the same subject, as seen in (3), and can also be used with the same actions of different subjects, as seen in (4).

3. "先后"做副词用,常常有三种格式。As an adverb, "先后" is often used in three patterns.

① "先后+数量词+动词"。如:"先后两次发言、先后几次问我"。"先后+num.+v." For example, "先后两次发言,先后几次问我."

② "先后+动词+数量词"。如:"先后发言两次、先后问我几次"。"先后+v.+num." For example, "先后发言两次,先后问我几次."

③ "先后+动词1+数量词+名词+动词2"。如:"先后有三个人发言、先后请了三个同学帮忙"。"先后+v.1+num.+n.+v.2" For example, "先后有三个人发言,先后请了三个同学帮忙."

4. 强调"前后相继"这个意义时,"先后"还可以重叠成"先先后后"。When emphasizing the concept of a beginning-to-end succession, "先后" can be reduplicated as "先先后后."

5. "先后"和"前后"的区别是: Differences between "先后" and "前后" are as follows:

① "先后"可以用于时间,但不能用于空间;"前后"可以用于时间或空间。"先后" can be used to express time but cannot be used to express space or positioning, but "前后" can be used to express both.

(5) * 教室先后都种上了桃树和梅树。
(6) 教室前后都种上了桃树和梅树。
(7) 我春节前后要外出旅游。

② 指在一段时间里发生的事情顺序,用"先后",不能用"前后"。When expressing the order of occurrences in a time frame, use "先后", not "前后."

(8) * 在晚会上,她前后唱了歌跳了舞。
(9) 在晚会上,她先后唱了歌跳了舞。

③ 在不强调顺序的时候,"先后"和"前后"都可以用。When not emphasizing the timing of a sequence, either "先后" or "前后" can be used.

(10) 在三年时间里,她先后/前后生了两个小孩。

④ "前后"在表示某一时间的前或后时,"前后"是概数。"先后"不能用。When expressing the beginning or end of a certain time frame, "前后" can be used to express an approximation, whereas "先后" doesn't carry the same meaning.

(11) 他大约是1980年前后来到我们医院的。

xiānqián 先前 →P572"以前"

用法 Usage:

名词 n.

泛指以前或指某个时候以前。*A time in the past.*

(1) 先前我们是邻居。

(2) 他比先前高多了。

xiān 鲜

用法 Usage:

形容词 a.

1. 新鲜。*Fresh.*

(1) 我要鲜肉,不要咸肉。

(2) 每天喝一瓶鲜牛奶,有利于身体健康。

2. 鲜美。*Delicious.*

(3) 这个饭店做的菜真鲜!

3. 鲜明。*(Of color) bright; brilliant; distinctive.*

(4) 这件毛衣的红颜色很鲜。

4. 有时"鲜"也用作名词。*Sometimes "鲜" is also used as a noun.*

① 表示鲜美的事物,后面常带"儿"。*Referring to delicacy, often followed by "儿."*

(5) 刚采下来的苹果,大家来尝尝鲜儿吧!

② 特指鱼虾等水产食物。*Specifically referring to fish, shrimp and other seafood.*

(6) 我喜欢吃海鲜、河鲜。

说明 Notes:

"鲜"常与单音节词搭配,如"鲜奶、鲜菜、鲜花、鲜虾、海鲜、河鲜"等,多修饰具体事物。*"鲜" is often paired with monosyllabic words such as "鲜奶,鲜菜,鲜花,鲜虾,海鲜,河鲜" and typically it modifies concrete objects.*

xiānmíng 鲜明 →P326"明显"、P506"显明"

用法 Usage:

形容词 a.

1. (颜色、色彩、图案)明亮。*(Of color or pattern) bright.*

(1) 这幅画图案鲜明、清楚。

(2) 这件衣服的色彩鲜明,好看。

2. 清楚,分明,确定而不含糊。*Clear; definite; distinct; unambiguous.*

(3) 这篇文章主题鲜明,思路清晰。

(4) 在鲜明的对比之下,事情的结果很清楚了。

说明 Notes:

"鲜明"跟"明显"都是形容词。它们的区别是:*Both "鲜明" and "明显" are adjectives. Their differences are as follows:*

1. 在词义上,"鲜明"着重于分明而确定。"明显"侧重清楚地显露出来,容易让人看出或感觉到。*In terms of meaning, "鲜明" emphasizes clarity and definitiveness while "明显" expresses something that appears clearly and is therefore easy for people to see, feel, or notice.*

(5) 他的态度很鲜明。(很确定、很坚定 *Being firm and clear*)

(6) 他的态度很明显。(很容易看出来 *Being apparent*)

2. "鲜明"的反义词是"暗淡、含糊、暧昧",语义较重,经常形容"观点、立场、态度、主体、个性、倾向"等。"明显"的反义词是"模糊",语义较轻。除了能形容与"鲜明"搭配的抽象名词以外,还经常形容"颜色、优点、缺点、长处、短处、内容、问题、道理、事实、规律、标志、标记、错误"等名词,使用范围比较大。*Antonyms of "鲜明" include "暗淡,含糊,暧昧," all of which carry a relatively strong semantic tone and typically describe things such as "观点,立场,态度,主体,个性,倾向" while the opposite of "明显" is "模糊," which has a relatively light semantic tone. Aside from abstract nouns that*

can be described by "鲜明","明显" frequently modifies nouns such as "颜色,优点,缺点,长处,短处,内容,问题,道理,事实,规律,标志,标记,错误." It has a wider range of usages.

xiǎnchū 显出

用法 Usage:
动词 v.
　　表现出。To express or reveal.
　　(1) 这孩子从小就显出了特殊的才华。
　　(2) 他一身名牌,以显出他很有钱的样子。
说明 Notes:
　　"显出"做谓语,在后面一定有宾语。When "显出" is used as a predicate, it must be followed by an object.

xiǎnde 显得

用法 Usage:
动词 v.
　　表现出(某种情况、状态)。To show (a type of situation or state of affairs); to seem.
　　(1) 获得冠军的选手在领奖时显得十分激动。
　　(2) 节日的广场显得分外热闹。
说明 Notes:
　　1."显得"做谓语,一定要带上补语,如例(1)(2)。When "显得" is used as a predicate, it must be accompanied by a complement, as seen in (1) and (2).
　　2."显得"的补语,一般都是形容词。The complements that accompany "显得" are typically adjectives.

xiǎnmíng 显明 →P326"明显"、P505"鲜明"

用法 Usage:
形容词 a.
　　清楚,明白。Clear; evident.
　　(1) 他哥俩的性格形成了显明的对照。
　　(2) 助人为乐是他显明的性格特点。
说明 Notes:
　　1."鲜明"和"显明"都是形容词,都形容事物显而易见,不模糊。Both "鲜明" and "显明" are adjectives, meaning "clear and evident, not blurred."
　　它们的区别是：Their differences are as follows:
　　①"鲜明"着重于分明、确定,一点不含糊。"显明"着重指清楚、明白,语意较轻。"鲜明" emphasizes the idea of being clear-cut and well defined, "not blurred at all." "显明," meaning "clear and evident," is a little less emphatic.
　　②"鲜明"还可形容"颜色、色彩、图案"等鲜明、明亮。"显明"不能。"鲜明" can also be used to describe "颜色,色彩,图案" as being clear and bright, but "显明" cannot.
　　③"鲜明"是褒义词。"显明"是中性词。"鲜明" is a commendatory term while "显明" is a neutral one.
　　(3) *这次车祸,你的错误操作很鲜明。
　　(4) 这次车祸,你的错误操作显明得很。
　　2."显明"和"明显"都有清楚、明白的意思。Both "显明" and "明显" mean "clear and evident."
　　它们的区别是：Their differences are as follows:
　　① 在语义上,"明显"强调事物的形状清楚、明白地显露出来,强调对显露过程的要求。"显明"着重强调对显露结果的要求。Semantically, "明显" focuses on a thing becoming clear in shape and easy to discern: it emphasizes the process. "显明," however, lays the emphasis on the result.
　　②"明显"可做状语,直接修饰谓语,可带"地",也可不带"地"。"显明"一般做定语,不做状语。"明显" can serve as an adverbial to describe a predicate directly. It can go either with or without "地." However, "显明" usually serves as an attribute, not as an adverbial.
　　③"明显"可以与副词连用,单独提到句首。"显明"一般不能这样用。"明显" can go with an adverb and be placed at the beginning of

a sentence. "显明" *cannot be used this way.*

(5) *很显明,他们已经走了。

(6) 很明显,他们已经走了。

xiǎnrán 显然 →P326"明显"、P507"显著"

用法 Usage:

形容词 a.

很明显,容易让人看出或者感觉到。*Obvious and evident; easy for people to see, feel, or notice.*

(1) 这种做法显然是错的,你不能再这样错下去。

(2) 很显然,他对你是有意见的。

说明 Notes:

1. 使用"显然"时要注意：*When using "显然," take note of the following:*

① "显然"可以出现在句子主语的前面或者后面,充当状语,含有强调的语气,如：例(1)既可以说"这种做法显然是错误的",也可以说"显然这种做法是错误的"。"显然"做状语时很少带助词"地"。它也不能直接做定语。*"显然" can appear before or after the subject of a sentence, and can act as an adverbial modifier, and can be used for emphasizing a semantic tone, as seen in (1). One can either say "这种想法显然是错误的" or "显然这种想法是错误的." When functioning as an adverbial, "显然" rarely takes the particle "地." It cannot directly function as an attributive.*

② "显然"可以修饰句子,前面可以有程度副词"很"修饰,后面往往有停顿,这时句子表达的语气更重,如例(2)。*"显然" can modify a sentence, and can be preceded and modified by the degree adverb "很," and is often followed by a pause. In such cases, the semantic tone of the sentence is very strong, as seen in (2).*

2. "显然"和"明显"都表示容易看出或感觉到的意思。*"显然" and "明显" both express something that is easy to see or feel.*

它们的区别是：*Their differences are as follows:*

① 在词义上,"显然"着重于样子显而易见地非常清楚地显露出来,语义比"明显"重。"明显"着重于显露得十分清楚、明白。*In terms of meaning, "显然" emphasizes that something has been revealed obviously and clearly, and has a stronger semantic weight than "明显." "明显" emphasizes that something has been revealed fully and clearly in appearance and is understood.*

② 在词语搭配上,"明显"多用于抽象事物,如"特点、规律、意义、道理、原因、目的、结果"等词语,也可以搭配具体的事物,如"色彩、声音、表情"等,使用范围比"显然"广。"显然"只与抽象事物名词搭配使用。*In terms of compatible word groups, "明显" is often used to refer to abstract or conceptual nouns such as "特点,规律,意义,道理,原因,目的,结果." It can also be used with concrete nouns such as "色彩,声音,表情" and has a wider range of usage than "显然." "显然" can only be used with abstract nouns.*

③ "明显"可以受"不、比较、最、极其"等副词的修饰。"显然"除了"很"以外,不能受其他副词修饰。*"明显" can be modified by "不,比较,最,极其" and other adverbial modifiers. "显然" can only be used with "很" and cannot take any other adverbial modifiers.*

④ "明显"能做补语,做状语时可带结构助词"地"。"显然"一般不做补语,做状语时很少带助词"地"。*"明显" can be used as a complement, and when functioning as an adverbial it can take the auxiliary particle "地." "显然" typically cannot be used as a complement, and when functioning as an adverbial it rarely takes the auxiliary particle "地."*

xiǎnzhù 显著 →P326"明显"、P507"显然"

用法 Usage:

形容词 a.

非常明显。*Incredibly evident or obvious.*

（1）到中国来后，她的汉语口语水平有了显著的提高。

（2）这个城市最近几年，有了显著的变化。

说明 Notes：

1. 使用"显著"时要注意，"显著"一般只修饰抽象名词，如"显著的效果、显著的变化"等。When using "显著," take note that "显著" typically only modifies abstract nouns such as "显著的效果,显著的变化."

2. "显著"和"明显"的区别是：The differences between "显著" and "明显" are as follows:

① "显著"着重指事物的形态鲜明而突出地显露出来。"明显"着重指事物的形态清楚地显露出来，语义比"显著"轻。"显著" emphasizes that an object is distinctive in form and is outstanding and prominent in appearance. "明显" emphasizes that an object's form is clearly apparent, but has a lighter semantic weight than "显著."

（3）他的汉语口语有明显的进步。

（4）他的汉语口语有显著的进步。

② "明显"能受程度副词修饰，可以提到句首。"显著"一般不能。"明显" can be used with and modified by degree adverbs and can be placed at the beginning of a sentence, while "显著" typically cannot.

（5）＊很显著,他有了进步。

（6）很明显,他有了进步。

③ "显著"是褒义词。"明显"是中性词。"显著" is a commendatory term, while "明显" is a neutral term.

3. "显然"和"显著"的区别是：The differences between "显然" and "显著" are as follows:

① 在词义上，"显然"强调很容易、很清楚地看出事物情况。"显著"强调事物的情况、事物的结果突出地显露出来，词义比"显然"重。In terms of meaning, "显然" emphasizes that an object, situation, or condition is seen easily and clearly, while "显著" emphasizes that the result or consequence of an object, situation, or condition has come into the open, and has a heavier semantic weight than "显然."

② "显然"可以提到句首使用。"显著"一般不能。"显然" can be used to begin a sentence, while "显著" typically cannot.

（7）＊显著,在这件事情上,他是很努力的。

（8）显然,在这件事情上,他是很努力的。

③ "显著"可以直接修饰名词，如"显著成绩、显著贡献、显著效果、显著地位、显著特征"等。"显然"一般不可以。"显著" can directly modify a noun, as in "显著成绩,显著贡献,显著效果,显著地位,显著特征," but "显然" typically cannot.

xiāngbǐ 相比

用法 Usage：

动词 v.

互相对照比较。To compare (two people or two things).

（1）与玛丽相比,大山的汉语发音更地道。

（2）相比之下,黄队夺冠的可能性更大。

说明 Notes：

"相比"在使用时需要有两个或以上的对象进行比较。通常的用法是"与谁相比""谁与谁相比"。"相比" is used to compare two or more targets, and is typically used in the structure "与谁相比" or "谁与谁相比."

xiāngchǔ 相处

用法 Usage：

动词 v.

彼此在一起共同工作、学习和生活；彼此交往、互相对待。Working, studying, or living together with one another; associating closely with one another.

（1）夫妻相处是一门艺术。

（2）中国希望跟世界上爱好和平的国家友好相处。

(3) 你们俩先相处一下,再决定要不要成为男女朋友。

xiāngdāng 相当

用法 Usage:
副词 ad.

表示程度高。Fairly; pretty. It indicates a high degree, level, or extent.

(1) 这次你们搞的活动相当成功。
(2) 我买的这件羽绒衣相当暖和。

动词 v.

(两方面在数量、条件、价值等)差不多,配得上或者相抵。(Of two objects) to be relatively equal in quantity, conditions, value, etc.

(3) 这两个选手实力相当,比赛难以分出胜负。
(4) 这棵树有六七十米,相当于二十几层楼高。

形容词 a.

适合,合适。Assortative.

(5) 口语课还没找到相当的老师。
(6) 他已经找到了一个各种条件与他相当的女朋友。

说明 Notes:

1. "相当"作动词用时,有比较的意思。如果两个比较相像,一个在"相当"前面,一个在"相当"后面,"相当"常常与介词"于"连用,如例(4)。When used as a verb, "相当" expresses a comparison. If there are two similar objects or statements, one precedes "相当" and the other follows it. "相当" is often used with the preposition "于," as seen in (4).

2. "相当"做副词时,"相当"前面不能加"不",但是后面可以加。"相当不……"同样是强调程度。When acting as an adverb, "相当" cannot be preceded by "不," but can be followed by it as in "相当不…" which similarly emphasizes the degree.

(7) *我对他的印象不相当好。
(8) 我对他的印象相当不好。

xiāngfǎn 相反 →P139"反而"

用法 Usage:
形容词 a.

指事物的两个方面互相矛盾、互相对立或相互排斥。Contrary. It indicates that two aspects, sides, or fields are in conflict, oppose each other, or reject each other.

(1) 我的意见刚好和你相反。
(2) 他朝相反的方向走了。
(3) 小王提出了跟我们完全相反的意见。

连词 conj.

用在下文句子前或者句子中,做插入语,表示转折或递进。Rather than. It functions as an interjection when used in the beginning or middle of a sentence, indicating a shift or progressive increase.

(4) 这次失败不但没有吓倒他,相反,使他有了战胜困难的勇气。
(5) 这里的夏天不但不热,正好相反,海风很大,舒服极了。

说明 Notes:

1. "相反"作形容词用时,常用"跟/与/和……相反"的句式,如例(1)(3)。When "相反" is used as an adjective, it often follows the pattern "跟/与/和…相反" as seen in (1) and (3).

2. "相反"作连词用时,前面常常有"不但、不仅"等词相呼应,"不但、不仅"后面用表示否定的词语。"相反"前面可以加"正、正好、刚好、恰恰"等词语,如例(4)。When "相反" is used as a conjunction, it is often preceded by "不但,不仅" or other similar expressions, and "不但,不仅" is followed by a negative phrase or term. Other expressions such as "正,正好,刚好,恰恰" can be added to "相反," as seen in (4).

3. "相反"和"反而"在句子中都有表示转折递进的作用,如果转折递进的作用着重于违反常情、出乎意料时,"相反"和"反而"则可以互换。"相反" and "反而" can be added to a sentence to indicate a shift or progressive

increase. If the emphasis is on abnormality or an occurrence contrary to one's expectations, "相反" and "反而" can be used interchangeably.

(6) 爸爸不但没有批评我,反而/相反给了我很多奖励。

(7) 到了下午,不仅雨没停,反而/相反还飘起了雪花。

它们的区别是：Their differences are as follows:

① "相反"可以用在一件事情的矛盾或两个方面相对,带有辩证意义的句子中,起转折作用。"反而"不可以。如例(5)。"相反" can be used to compare two sides of an argument or to express the conflict between two things, and has an investigative connotation that brings about a shift. "反而" cannot be used in this way, as seen in (5).

(8) 做任何事,努力了,就有可能成功；相反,不努力,就什么也不会有。

(9) *做任何事,努力了,就有可能成功；反而,不努力,就什么也不会有。

② "相反"有形容词用法,可以做谓语和定语。"反而"是副词,不能做谓语和定语。所以,例(1)(2)(3)中,不能用"反而"。"相反" has an adjectival usage, and can also be used as a predicate or an attributive. "反而" is an adverb, and cannot be used as a predicate or attributive. Therefore, in (1), (2) and (3), "相反" cannot be replaced by "反而."

③ 使用"相反"和"反而"时,特别要注意下面的错句：When using "相反" and "反而", pay close attention to the following errors:

(10) *我的看法相反他的看法。

(11) 我的看法跟他的看法相反。

(12) *妈妈担心我来中国容易生病,我反而胖了。

(13) 妈妈担心我来中国容易生病,我不但没生病,反而还胖了。

xiānghù 相互 →P199 "互相"

用法 Usage:
副词 ad.

互相。Mutually.

(1) 朋友之间就应该相互了解,相互关心。
(2) 同学们要相互帮助,共同提高。

说明 Notes:

"相互"和"互相"都是副词,意思和用法基本相同,做状语时互相可以替换。都可以与"间、之间"组合成短语"互相/相互间、互相/相互之间"。"相互" and "互相" are both adverbs, and their meaning and usage are fundamentally similar. When used as an adverbial, they can be interchanged. They can both be combined with "间,之间" to form a phrase "互相/相互间," or "互相/相互之间."

它们的区别是：Their differences are as follows:

"相互"可以修饰少量名词,做定语,如"相互感情、相互关系"等。"互相"不可以。"相互" may be used to modify a few nouns, and can be used as an attributive, for example, "相互感情,相互关系." "互相" cannot be used this way.

(3) *他们互相关系很好。
(4) 他们相互关系很好。

xiāngsì 相似 →P295 "类似"、P511 "相同"

用法 Usage:
形容词 a.

相像。常由介词"和、跟、同、与"等引进比较对象,组成介词短语,做状语。Similar. Often paired with a preposition such as "和,跟,同,与" to introduce an object for comparison, and to compose a prepositional phrase by serving as an adverbial.

(1) 他俩的声音相似极了。
(2) 跟这种结构相似的房子还有吗?

说明 Notes:

"相似"和"类似"都表示相像。Both "相似"和"类似"mean "to be similar."

它们的区别是:Their differences are as follows:

1."相似"是形容词,既可以指事物个体,也可以指事物种类之间的相像。"类似"是动词,侧重指事物种类之间大致相像。"相似"相像的程度比"类似"高。"相似" is an adjective that can be used to describe not only the similarity between individual things, but also the similarity between groups of things. "类似" is a verb that focuses on an approximate similarity, but "相似" shows a similarity at a higher level.

2."类似"可以带宾语,可以组成"类似于……"的格式。"相似"不能带宾语,一般不能与"于"组合。"类似" can take an object to form "类似于…," but "相似" cannot.

xiāngtóng 相同 →P510"相似"

用法 Usage:
形容词 a.

彼此一致,没有区别。Identical to one another; having no differences.

(1) 这本书和那本书的内容完全相同。
(2) 她不喜欢穿跟别人相同的衣服。
(3) 我觉得这两个句子的意思并不相同。

说明 Notes:

"相似"和"相同"都是形容词,用法基本一样。"相似" and "相同" are both adjectives and have fundamentally similar usages.

它们的区别是:"相似"指两个事物基本相像,但还有点不同的地方。"相同"指两个事物完全一样。Their difference is as follows: "相似" indicates that two objects are fundamentally similar but still have some slight differences. "相同" indicates that two objects are completely identical.

xiāngxìn 相信 →P520"信任"

用法 Usage:
动词 v.

认为符合实际或正确而不怀疑。To believe; to have no doubts as to what is realistic or proper.

(1) 我们相信这个实验肯定能够成功。
(2) 你要相信自己一定能学好汉语。

xiǎng 想 →P540"要"

用法 Usage:
动词 v.

1. 思考,动脑筋。可重叠。做定语时必定带"的"。To consider or think over. It can be reduplicated and must go with "的" when used as an attributive.

(1) 我要好好儿想想今年暑假旅游的计划。
(2) 我正在想办法帮你呢。

2. 想念,惦记,盼望见到。带名词、代词宾语可受程度副词"很、可"等的修饰。To miss; to remember and worry about; to long to see. When used with a noun, pronoun, or object, it can be accompanied by a degree modifier such as "很" or "可."

(3) 最近,他很想家,很想妈妈。
(4) 你可想死我们了。(意思是我们非常想你。It means that we miss you very much.)

3. 推测,料想,估计。常带小句作宾语。不能用"想不想"提问,而应用"想没想"提问。否定式"没想"表示对已经发生的事没想到,后面常加"到",也表示没有想过。To infer; to presume; to estimate. It is often accompanied by short phrases as the object. In this usage, you can't use "想不想" to ask a question, but should use "想没想." The negative form "没想" expresses that one had not expected a past event to occur, and it is often followed by "到" to indicate that one had not given thought to the situation.

(5) 我想他今年不会出国留学了。
(6) 你想没想过他会做出什么决定?
(7) 我没想到他会做出这样的决定。

4. 回想,回忆。可重叠。To think back; to recall. It can be used in the reduplicated way.

(8) 他的名字?让我想一想。我会想起

来的。

(9) 想想已经过去的年代,比比现在,生活真是不一样了。

5. 记住,不要忘记。必定带"着",常用于祈使句。To remember; to bear in mind. It must be followed by "着," and is often used in imperative sentences.

(10) 你可要想着到了北京立刻就给我打电话。

(11) 他会想着给你写信的。

6. 希望,打算。作为助动词用,常做句子中第二个动词的状语。可受程度副词修饰。To hope, to plan. When used as an auxiliary verb, it is often the adverbial of the second verb in a sentence. It can also be modified by degree adverbs.

(12) 我星期天想去书店和银行。

(13) 我很想买一辆电动车。

说明 Notes:

使用"想"时要注意:When using "想," pay attention to the following aspects:

1. "想"表示"想念、惦记、盼望见到"的意思时,可以受"很、十分、非常"等程度副词的修饰,也可以带"极了、死了"等表示程度很高的补语,如例(3)(4)。When using "想" to express the meaning of "想念,惦记" or "盼望见到," it can be used with adverbial modifiers such as "很,十分,非常," and can also be used with "极了,死了" to indicate an extreme degree, as seen in (3) and (4).

2. "想"表示"回想、回忆"以前事情的意思时,常用重叠的方式"想想、想一想"或者带"着、了、过、起来、不起来、起了"等词语,或者带"想"的小句宾语,表示"想"的结果,如例(9)。When using "想" to express "回想,回忆" and discuss past events, it is often used in the reduplicated forms "想想,想一想" or accompanied by "着,了,过,起来,不起来,起来了," or other similar expressions. The clause attached to "想" expresses the result, as seen in (9).

3. "想"表示"预料、估计、推测"的意思时,不能用"想不想"提问,而用"想没想、有没有想"的词语提问。表示否定的意思常用"没+想"的形式,后面常常带"到"。When using "想" to express "预料,估计,推测," you cannot use "想不想" to ask any questions, but should use "想没想" or "有没有想." The negative form of this usage is typically "没+想" and is often followed by "到."

xiàng 向 →P63"朝"

用法 Usage:

介词 prep.

引进动作的方向、目标或对象。Introducing the direction of a verb, its goal or objective.

(1) 你要向南走五百米,才能到她家。

(2) 我们要向志愿者学习。

动词 v.

1. 面对着,特指脸或正面对着(与"背"相对)。To face, used to refer particularly to the face or the front side of something (the opposite of "背").

(3) 请你面向同学,回答他们的问题。

(4) 中国的房子建筑方向常常是坐北向南。

2. 偏袒。后面常常带"着"。To be partial to and side with, often followed by "着."

(5) 别因为她是你妹妹,你就向着她。

说明 Notes:

"向"和"朝"做介词表示引进动作方向或做动词表示面对着的意思时,可以互相替换,如"向/朝东、坐北向/朝南、请你的脸向/朝着我"等。When "向" and "朝" are used as a preposition to introduce the direction of a verb or are used as a verb to express facing something, they can be interchanged, as seen in "向/朝东,坐北向/朝南,请你的脸向/朝着我,etc."

它们的区别是:Their differences are as follows:

1. "向"可以引进动作对象。"朝"不能。"向" can introduce the object of a verb, while

"朝"cannot.

(6) *你朝谁借钱了？

(7) 你向谁借钱了？

2. "向"可以用在动词后面，表示动作目标。"朝"不可以。"向" can follow a verb to indicate the target of the verb, while "朝" cannot.

(8) *我们正在走朝更美好的将来。

(9) 我们正在走向更美好的将来。

3. 介词"向"可以引进抽象的名词对象。"朝"不可以。As a preposition, "向" can introduce an abstract noun object, while "朝" cannot.

(10) *我们要朝人民/群众负责。

(11) 我们要向人民/群众负责。

xiànglái 向来 →P77"从来"、P563"一向"、P583"一直"

用法 Usage:

副词 ad.

一向，从来。Continuously; all along.

(1) 阿里做事向来认真、踏实。

(2) 他们俩向来配合得很好，很多合作项目效果都不错。

说明 Notes:

"向来"和"从来"都表示行为、状态从过去到现在没什么改变的意思。"向来" and "从来" both can express that an activity or a situation has not changed for a period of time.

它们的区别是："向来"多用于肯定句。"从来"多用于否定句。Their difference is as follows: "向来" is mostly used in affirmative sentences while "从来" is mostly used in negative ones.

(3) *他从来住在上海，向来没住在杭州。

(4) 他向来住在上海，从来没住过杭州。

xiàngshàng 向上

用法 Usage:

动词 v.

朝着好的方向走，要求上进。To advance in the right direction; to make progress.

(1) 阿里积极向上，是个很求进步的好学生。

(2) 好好学习，天天向上。

说明 Notes:

注意区分"向＋上"与词语"向上"："向＋上"是向上面，朝上面，动宾短语。"向上"是不能拆分的一个词。Take care to differentiate between "向＋上" and the inseparable phrase "向上"："向＋上" is a verb-object phrase expressing moving in an upwards direction, while "向上" is a fixed phrase that cannot be separated into two components.

xiàng 像

用法 Usage:

动词 v.

1. 表示两个事物有某些共同点或形象上相同，能受程度副词的修饰。To resemble. It is used to indicate that two objects have a similar image or characteristics. It can be modified by degree adverbs.

(1) 他的鼻子和嘴长得很像他妈妈。

(2) 他说像，我看不像。

2. 表示例如、比如的意思。Such as.

(3) 中国的历史文化名城很多，像西安、北京、洛阳、南京、杭州等都是。

(4) 杭州的特产很丰富，像龙井茶叶、丝绸、扇子等都是很有名的。

3. "像"常跟"一样"组成"像……一样/一般＋形/动"的格式。可以用于比拟。"像" is often used with "一样" to form the structure "像…一样/一般＋a./v.，" which can be used to draw parallels.

(5) 这花儿像向日葵一样/一般跟着太阳转。

(6) 今天像昨天一样热，公园不去了，到图书馆去吧。

名词 n.

比照人物制成的形象。An object created in the image of an important person or figure.

(7) 天安门城楼上挂着毛主席像。

xiāofèi 消费 →P514"消耗"

用法 Usage:

动词 v.

为了生产或生活需要而消耗物质财富。To consume material objects in order to live or produce something.

(1) 人类每天要消费大量的粮食。

(2) 你们家就这样高消费啊!

xiāohào 消耗 →P514"消费"

用法 Usage:

动词 v.

指(精神、物质、力量等)因为使用而受损、逐渐减少。(Of energy, materials, strength, etc.) to be depleted as a result of being consumed.

(1) 这些实验消耗了他不少时间和钱财。

(2) 你不应该把宝贵的时间消耗在打游戏上。

说明 Notes:

"消费"和"消耗"的区别是：The differences between "消费" and "消耗" are as follows:

1. "消费"的意义侧重于把东西用掉，以满足生活、生产的需要。"消费"是中性词。"消耗"的意义侧重于一点点地用掉或逐渐减弱。"消耗"有时含有贬义，如"消耗"例(2)。The semantic meaning of "消费" places more weight on objects being used up in order to satisfy the needs of life or production, and it is a neutral term. "消耗" emphasizes the gradual weakening or depletion of something, and sometimes has a derogatory connotation, as seen in (2).

2. "消费"的主要对象多是具体的生活资料。"消耗"的对象还可指抽象的物力、财力、能力、精力等，也可以是人员等。The object of "消费" is typically a concrete material, while "消耗" can be used to refer to abstract objects such as financial resources, physical capability, energy, and can also be used to refer to people (i.e. personnel, staff).

3. "消费"可以加后缀构成合成词，如"消费者、消费品、消费热"等，或者前面加修饰词，构成"高消费、低消费、超前消费"等。"消耗"不能。"消费" can take a suffix and become a compound such as "消费者,消费品,消费热," or take a modifier such as in 构成"高消费,低消费,超前消费." But "消耗" cannot.

xiāomiè 消灭 →P514"消失"

用法 Usage:

动词 v.

灭亡,消失。To wipe out; to be destroyed; to disappear; to die out.

(1) 过去我们曾经想消灭蚊子苍蝇,但是消灭不了。

(2) 我总是消灭不掉房间里的蟑螂和老鼠。

xiāoshī 消失 →P514"消灭"

用法 Usage:

动词 v.

(人或事物)逐渐减少以至没有,不复存在。(Of people or objects) to be gradually reduced until there's nothing left and it no longer exists.

(1) 听到这个消息,妈妈脸上的笑容立刻消失了。

(2) 走出车站,他的背影很快就消失在人群之中。

说明 Notes:

"消灭"和"消失"都有表示不复存在的意思。"消灭" and "消失" both express something ceasing to exist.

它们的区别是：Their differences are as follows:

1. "消灭"侧重于某一事物不复存在的被动性,或者人和事物对某一事物不复存在的主观意图。"消失"侧重于事物本身慢慢地减少到最后不再存在。"消灭" emphasizes the passivity of an object ceasing to exist or a person's subjective

intention towards the object ceasing to exist. "消失" emphasizes that the object itself is slowly becoming scarce to the point that it finally no longer exists.

（3）改革就是为了消灭贫穷和落后。
（4）恐龙消失在6 500万年以前。

2."消灭"可以带宾语。"消失"后面不带宾语。"消灭" can take an object while "消失" cannot.

（5）*我一定要消失掉房间里的蚊子。
（6）我一定要消灭掉房间里的蚊子。

xiāoxi 消息 →P519"新闻"、P521"信息"

用法 Usage:

名词 n.

1.（在各种媒体上）关于人和事物情况的报道。News or reports about an object or situation (on some type of media).

（1）你知道关于游泳比赛的最新消息吗？
（2）今天的国际消息内容很丰富。

2.指人和事物的动向或变化的情况，音信。Information about the trends or changes in people and things.

（3）关于考试的情况，我们一点消息也没有。
（4）他回家以后就没了消息。

xiǎo 小

用法 Usage:

形容词 a.

1.在体积、面积、数量、力量、强度等方面不及一般的或不及比较的对象（跟"大"相对）。Inferior to or not as good as the target in terms of volume, area, quantity, power, intensity, etc. (the opposite of "大").

（1）你房间的音乐声小一点好吗？
（2）我的年龄比你小三岁。

2.排行最小的。Smaller or lower in rank or seniority.

（3）他是我的小弟弟。
（4）我是我家的小儿子。

3.（谦虚地）称自己或与自己有关的晚辈或事物。(Showing humbleness) used to refer to oneself, one's possessions, or the younger generation related to oneself.

（5）他们是我的小儿和小女。
（6）欢迎大家到我小店逛逛、看看。

前缀 prefix

1.加在名词性词根前，构成名词。如："小孩儿、小提琴、小米、小菜、小山、小河"等。Added to a word root that is a noun itself to form a new noun. For example, "小孩儿,小提琴,小米,小菜,小山,小河."

2.加在动词性词根前，构成名词。如："小说、小跑、小吃、小偷"等。Added to a word root that is a verb itself to form a noun. For example, "小说,小跑,小吃,小偷儿."

3.加在形容词词根前，构成名词。如："小寒、小暑、小便宜、小丑"等。Added to a word root that is an adjective itself to form a noun. For example, "小寒,小暑,小便宜,小丑."

4.加在姓氏前面，指年轻人（有时是昵称）。如："小王、小张、小周"等。Added to a surname to refer to young people (sometimes as a diminutive, nickname, or term of endearment). For example, "小王,小张,小周."

xiǎoqū 小区

用法 Usage:

名词 n.

在城市一定区域内建筑的、具有相对独立居住环境的成片居民住宅，配有成套的生活服务设施（商店、学校、医院等）的地方。An established place in a city that includes independent residences as well as facilities such as shops, schools, hospitals, etc.

（1）城西有很多高档小区，房价也很贵。
（2）对老百姓的生活来说，小区的安全最重要。

xiǎoshí 小时 →P678"钟头"

用法 Usage:

名词 n.

时间单位,一个平均太阳日的二十四分之一。A unit of time expressing one twenty-fourth of an average solar day; one hour.

（1）一天是二十四小时。
（2）她看了三个小时的电视。

说明 Notes:

"小时"前面可以直接加数词,如"一小时、五小时、八小时"等；也可以在数词后面加量词"个",如"一个小时、五个小时、八个小时"等。"小时" can be directly preceded by a number as seen in "一小时,五小时,八小时," etc., and can also be used with a number and the measure word "个," as seen in "一个小时,五个小时,八个小时," etc.

xiǎoxīn 小心 →P499"细心"

用法 Usage:

动词 v.

注意,留神,谨慎。To take note of; to take care; to be mindful of; to watch out for.

（1）下雨天,小心地滑。
（2）过马路要小心来往车辆。

形容词 a.

形容办事集中注意力,谨慎。Handling with care and attention.

（3）他做事一向很小心。
（4）这件事,你得小心一点儿做。

说明 Notes:

"细心"和"小心"都是形容词,表示做事时精神集中、很谨慎。"细心" and "小心" are both adjectives that describe carefully gathering one's attention to do something.

它们的区别是：Their differences are as follows:

1. 在词义上,"细心"主要指用心细密,没有疏忽。"小心"指做事谨慎,不出问题。In terms of meaning, "细心" mainly indicates doing something carefully and diligently without negligence or oversight, while "小心" indicates doing something with care to avoid problems.

2. "小心"可以独自成句,如"小心,别摔倒了"。"细心"得带上别的成分才可以独自成句,如"细心点儿,别再写错了"。"小心" can stand alone as a complete sentence, for example, "小心,别摔倒了。" But "细心" has to take some other word to make an independent sentence as in "细心点儿,别再写错了。"

xiàoguǒ 效果 →P516"效益"

用法 Usage:

名词 n.

事物或动作行为（某种力量、做法或因素）产生的有效结果。Effective results of doing something, taking an action, or allowing a certain force or factor to play its role.

（1）张老师的教学效果很好,学生很喜欢。
（2）每天定时散步对恢复健康很有效果。

xiàoyì 效益 →P516"效果"

用法 Usage:

名词 n.

效果和利益,用某种做法所获得的好处（多指物质方面）。Results and benefits; the advantages gained from utilizing a specific method of doing something (typically refers to material objects).

（1）这个工厂的经济效益很不错。
（2）应该充分提高经济效益,让老百姓过上更好的生活。

说明 Notes:

"效益"与"效果"都表示在行为动作以后取得的好结果。"效益" and "效果" both refer to the positive results obtained from a certain behavior or action.

它们的区别是：Their differences are as follows:

1. "效果"泛指好的结果（精神上的或物质上的）。"效益"侧重于物质、金钱上的利益。"效果" generally refers to good outcomes (either psychological or physical) while "效益" emphasizes benefit or profit in the form of material objects or money.

（3）你这次跟他谈话很有效果。他的情绪稳定多了。

（4）你这个技术革新提高了我们车间的经济效益。

2. "效果"是褒义词。"效益"是中性词。"效果" is a commendatory term while "效益" is a neutral term.

xiéshāng 协商 →P517"协调"

用法 Usage:
动词 v.

为了取得一致意见而共同商量。To negotiate; to discuss something with another party in order to come to a consensus.

（1）我们和他们经过协商，问题解决了。
（2）如果双方出现矛盾，最好还是协商解决。

说明 Notes:

"协商"一词常见搭配有"协商解决、协商会议、友好协商、政治协商、民主协商、参与协商"等。The word "协商" often appears in phrases such as "协商解决, 协商会议, 友好协商, 政治协商, 民主协商, 参与协商."

xiétiáo 协调 →P195"和谐"、P517"协商"

用法 Usage:
动词 v.

使某种关系、动作行为配合适当。To coordinate the behavior and conduct of different parties so that they are compatible.

（1）国家与国家之间的关系要互相协调，才能长久地和平共处。
（2）为了更好发展经济，我们要协调好供需关系。

形容词 a.

配合得适当。Appropriately compatible.

（3）这两种颜色搭配得很协调。
（4）这两位杂技演员动作协调，表演很精彩。

说明 Notes:

1. "协调"和"协商"的动词用法都指有关方面就产生的问题进行商量解决。The verb usages of "协调" and "协商" both indicate that the issues produced by the parties concerned have been resolved through discussion.

它们的区别是：Their differences are as follows:

① "协调"作动词用时，侧重通过商议、采取措施等，使双方关系和谐相处。"协商"则侧重双方为取得一致意见而进行具体商量。The verb usage of "协调" emphasizes that a harmonious relationship between two parties was produced through discussion or other measures. "协商" emphasizes that two parties have specifically undergone discussion in order to achieve a consensus.

② "协调"有形容词用法。"协商"没有。"协调" has an adjectival usage while "协商" does not.

2. "和谐"和"协调"都形容配合适当、步调一致，都能受程度副词的修饰。Both "和谐" and "协调" mean acting in cooperation and coordination, and both can be modified by a degree adverb.

它们的区别是：Their differences are as follows:

① "和谐"着重于事物内在彼此的融洽，相互之间没有矛盾，可用于修饰音调、颜色、线条、建筑物，或摆设的布局以及人的生活、行为举止等。"协调"着重于相互之间配合的适当、一致，多用于工作任务、上下左右工作关系、活动安排等。"和谐" focuses on harmony inherent in things: there is no conflict at all. It can be applied to tone, color, lines, buildings, or the lay-out of a decoration, and also to human relationships, their behaviors and manners. "协调," by contrast, focuses on the proper coordination between different parts. It is often applied to work and activity assignments, and to relationships with people on all sides.

②"和谐"常与"旋律、声音、色彩、节奏、情调、关系、气氛"等词语搭配。"协调"常与"动作、工作、安排、发展、配合"等词语搭配。"和谐" is often paired with "旋律,声音,色彩,节奏,情调,关系,气氛," while "协调" pairs more often with "动作,工作,安排,发展,配合."

xīnqíng 心情 →P381"情绪"

用法 Usage:

名词 n.

1. 内心的情感状态。One's mood or feelings; internal emotions.

(1) 人的身体健康与心情好坏很有关系。

(2) 这几天她心情不好,因为新买的电动车不见了。

2. 情趣、兴趣。Interest (in something).

(3) 我没有心情跟他们去滑冰。

(4) 作业没做好,我哪有心情看电影?

说明 Notes:

"心情"和"情绪"表示情趣或兴趣的意思时,可以替换。When "心情" and "情绪" are used to express interest in something, they can be interchanged.

(5) 这几天我没有心情/情绪跟你踢足球。

它们的区别是:Their differences are as follows:

1. "心情"侧重指情感状态。"情绪"侧重指整个心理、心境。"心情" emphasizes an emotional condition, while "情绪" refers to one's entire mental state or frame of mind.

2. "心情"前面可以加"没有",表示情绪不好或者没有兴趣。一般不加"有",但是如果有别的修饰语,可以加。"心情" can be negated with "没有" to indicate a bad mood or that one is not interested (in something), but "有" is not typically used on its own unless other modifiers are being used as well.

(6) *我有心情跟你玩游戏。

(7) 我没有心情跟你玩游戏。

(8) 今天我有好心情跟你玩游戏。

3. "情绪"前面可以加"有、没有",表示心情不高兴或者没有兴趣。"情绪" can be used with "有,没有" to express a negative emotion or disinterest in something.

(9) 他对你不让他参加今晚的活动很有情绪。

(10) 这孩子过一会儿就没有情绪了。

xīnténg 心疼

用法 Usage:

动词 v.

1. 疼爱。To love dearly.

(1) 爷爷奶奶最心疼小孙女。

(2) 每一个父母都心疼自己的儿女。

2. 舍不得,惋惜。To be reluctant to part with; to feel sorry (for/about something/someone).

(3) 一般老人都很心疼钱,平时出门连个出租车都舍不得坐。

(4) 老张的古董花瓶打破了,他心疼极了。

xīnkǔ 辛苦

用法 Usage:

形容词 a.

身心劳苦。可以重叠为"辛辛苦苦"。Toilsome for the body and mind. It can be reduplicated as "辛辛苦苦."

(1) 妈妈为我们辛苦地工作了一辈子,退休后该好好儿享受了。

(2) 哥哥辛辛苦苦地为我做了一个书架。

动词 v.

求别人去做某事时用的客气词语。A

polite expression used when asking others to do something.

（3）还得辛苦你帮我买一本词典,谢谢你了。

（4）辛苦你了,帮我拿了那么重的行李。

说明 Notes:

使用"辛苦"一词时,要注意跟"累"的区别: Be sure to take note of the differences between "辛苦" and "累":

1."辛苦"的词意侧重因不间断地劳动、工作带来的身体或精神上的劳苦。"累"侧重于体力上的劳苦。"辛苦"的含义比"累"重、丰富。所以两者有时不能换用。"辛苦" emphasizes a toilsome exhaustion of the body and mind brought on by uninterrupted work. "累" emphasizes a physical tiredness. "辛苦" has a much heavier and richer implication than "累." And so, they are not always interchangeable.

（5）*今天玩儿了很多地方,你一定辛苦了,早点休息吧。

（6）今天玩儿了很多地方,你一定累了,早点休息吧。

2."辛苦"多修饰表示工作和劳动等含有为他人利益服务的动作行为,一般不修饰学习、旅游等个人行为以后的身心劳累。如果修饰学习、旅游这类行为,则表示这个人的能力不够。"辛苦" mainly modifies actions or behaviors involved in work and physical labor that implies working for the benefit of others; it typically does not modify academic study, travel, or other similar behaviors, but can be used to express that an individual's ability is insufficient.

（7）*他学习很辛苦,所以成绩很好。

（8）他学习很努力,所以成绩很好。

（9）他学汉语学得很辛苦。

例（9）,句子意思是因为他的能力不够,所以学习很累。一般还是用"累"比较合适。As seen in (9), the meaning of the sentence is that the individual studies to the point of exhaustion due to their insufficient abilities. Still, it is often more suitable to use "累" in such a sentence.

xīnrén 新人

用法 Usage:

名词 n.

1. 具有新的道德品质的人。A person that possesses new moral principles.

（1）社会风气越来越好,不断涌现出新人新事。

2. 在某方面新出现的人物。New characters or persons emerging in some field.

（2）近几年出现了很多体育新人、文艺新人。

3. 指新娘和新郎。有时特指新娘。The bride and groom, sometimes specifically used to refer to the bride.

（3）这对新人在音乐声中来到了亲戚朋友面前。

4. 某个单位、团体等新来的人员。New personnel in a field, organization, group, etc.

（4）我们艺术团今年招聘了几个新人。

5. 指改过自新的人。An individual who has mended his way and make a fresh start; one who has turned over a new leaf in one's life.

（5）我相信他一定会改造成为一个新人。

说明 Notes:

"新人"指新娘和新郎的用法,与汉民族婚姻文化有关。类似的词语还有"新房、新床、新女婿、新媳妇"等。When "新人" is used to refer to the bride and groom, it is specifically related to the marriage culture of the Han nationality. Similar terms include "新房,新床,新女婿,新媳妇,etc."

xīnwén 新闻 →P515"消息"

用法 Usage:

名词 n.

1. 报社、通讯社、广播电台、电视台等传播媒体报道的消息。News broadcast through media

such as newspaper, radio, television, etc.

（1）每天晚上七点，我就看中央电视台的新闻节目。

（2）他是报社的新闻记者。

2. 泛指社会上最近发生的事情。Events that have occurred recently in society.

（3）天大的新闻！报纸上说，有个母亲竟生了九胞胎。

（4）我们班里的特大新闻：阿里得了全国汉语比赛第一名。

说明 Notes:

"新闻"和"消息"的区别是：The differences between "新闻" and "消息" are as follows:

1. "消息"一般指用语言文字通过电讯、简讯等形式做的报道。"新闻"内容可以是简短的，也可以是很长的，报道的形式不限于语言文字，还可以是图片、电视、电影等。"消息" is typically used to describe brief reports in a text-based format, while "新闻" can be short or long reports not limited to text but can also include images, television broadcasts, films, etc.

2. 作为口语词，"消息"指口头的或书面的音信。"新闻"则指社会上最近发生的新鲜事情。Colloquially, "消息" refers to oral or written news, while "新闻" refers to social events that have newly occurred.

xìn 信

用法 Usage:

名词 n.

1. 按照习惯的格式把要说的话写下来并给指定的对象看的文字；书信。如："一封信、证明信、公开信、介绍信"等。Letter or written message; words one wishes to communicate written down in accordance with the customary style, given to the targeted individuals to read. For example, "一封信、证明信、公开信、介绍信。"

2. 音信，信息。Mail; message; news.

（1）请你给我妈妈带个信，告诉她今天晚上我要加班。

（2）弟弟生病的事，谁也不能向家里报信。

3. 信用，承诺。Trustworthiness; keeping one's promise.

（3）一个人要守信，别人才会相信你。

（4）他从来不失信于人。

动词 v.

1. 相信，信任。To trust; to have confidence in.

（5）你喜欢的女孩子已经结婚了，信不信由你。

（6）你是好人，我信你。

2. 信奉。To believe in.

（7）在中国，很多人信佛教。

（8）我家老人信佛教，又信道教。

xìnrèn 信任 →P511"相信"

用法 Usage:

动词 v.

相信而敢于托付。To trust and be willing to entrust something to someone's care.

（1）小汪办事认真，大家都很信任她。

（2）夫妻之间应该互相信任、互相尊重。

说明 Notes:

"信任"和"相信"都有相信别人的意思。"信任" and "相信" both express the concept of trusting another individual.

它们的区别是：Their differences are as follows:

1. "相信"的词义层次是经过判断，认为是正确的，因而不怀疑。"信任"是因为相信，因此有所托付。"信任"的意思是在"相信"的基础上的，比"相信"的词义程度更为深入。"相信" means to consider someone correct and trustworthy on the basis of judgment. "信任" goes further and is ready to place things in his/her care.

2. "相信"的对象可以是人，也可以是事。"信任"的对象是人或者单位、组织等人组成的团体。The object of "相信" can be either a person or thing. The object of "信任" is a

person, organization, or other such group of people.

(3) 我相信他说的事情是真实的。

(4) *我信任他说的事情是真实的。

(5) 我相信组织一定会把那件事情调查清楚。（对组织会把事情调查清楚不怀疑。No doubt that the organization will figure things out.）

(6) 我信任组织一定会把那件事情调查清楚。（相信并托付组织把事情调查清楚。Trust the organization to figure things out.）

xìnxī 信息 →P515"消息"

用法 Usage:

名词 n.

1.（关于人或事物动向、变化的）音信，消息。News or information (regarding the changes in people, objects, trends, etc.)

(1) 他不给家里任何信息已经一年多了。

(2) 关于你找工作的事，有什么信息吗？

2. 信息论中用符号传达的报道。报道的内容是接受符号者事先不知道的。(In information theory) news transmitted or communicated through written medium. The information transmitted is previously unknown to the receiver of the news.

(3) 手机上一点信息也收不到。

(4) 屏幕上没有任何信息，是什么问题？

说明 Notes:

"信息"和"消息"在词义上都有表示人和事物动向、变化的音信。"信息" and "消息" both refer to news regarding the trends and changes of people and things.

它们的区别是：They differ as follows:

1. "消息"能表示传播媒体上报道的意思。"信息"不能。"消息" can be used to describe information broadcast through media outlets, while "信息" cannot.

(5) *信息报道，6号台风明天到达东南沿海。

(6) 消息报道，6号台风明天到达东南沿海。

2. "信息"是信息论方面的专业名词，"消息"不是。"信息" is a technical term used in the field of information theory while "消息" is not.

xíng 行

用法 Usage:

动词 v.

1. 走。To walk; to go.

(1) 这辆车日行千里，质量很好。

(2) 孔子说："三人行，必有我师焉。"

2. 做，办，实施。To do; to handle; to manage; to put into effect.

(3) 你的办法行不通。

(4) 他行医三十年了，很有经验。

3. 表示进行某项活动。多用于双音节动词前。To conduct a certain activity. Typically, it often appears before a disyllabic verb.

(5) 这次会议的举办时间和地点将另行通知。

(6) 公司将按管理条例要求即行整改。

4. 可以。To be all right; it's okay.

(7) 行，我们就这么办吧。

(8) 我们只要把问题搞清楚就行了。

形容词 a.

能干。Capable; competent.

(9) 连这么难的问题都解决了，你真行！

(10) 他会做很多菜，厨艺真行！

说明 Notes:

"行"是多音字。"行"（háng）是名词。表示："行" is a character with multiple pronunciations. When pronounced "háng," it is a noun, meaning:

1. 行列。Rows or columns.

(11) 湖边柳树成行，风景很美！

2. 行业。Trade, profession, industry.

(12) 他是个干一行爱一行的好员工。

3. 某些营业机构。Certain business organizations.

(13)明天你去不去银行取钱?

(14)今天我去车行看了看,感觉车价比较贵。

xíngdòng 行动 →P256"举动"、P522"行为"

用法 Usage:

动词 v.

1.行走,走动。To walk; to move about.

(1)他腿受伤之后,很少到外面行动。

(2)他现在还不能下床行动。

2.为了达到某个目的而进行的具体活动。To carry out specific activities in order to reach a certain goal.

(3)大家积极行动起来,把我们的教室布置得漂漂亮亮。

(4)小王经常单独行动,不跟班里同学一起活动。

名词 n.

具体的行为或举止。A specific action or behavior.

(5)他的实际行动说明了他是一个好哥哥。

(6)大家的决心都很大,今后就看你们的行动了。

说明 Notes:

"行动"和"举动"的区别是:The differences between "行动" and "举动" are as follows:

1."举动"一般指人的动作。"行动"除了人的动作,还指动物的动作,如"北极熊的行动迟缓"。"举动" usually refers to people's actions. "行动," however, refers not just to people's actions, but also to animal actions, as in "北极熊的行动缓慢 (polar bears move slowly)."

2."行动"有动词用法。"举动"没有。"行动" can be used as a verb, but "举动" cannot.

xíngwéi 行为 →P522"行动"

用法 Usage:

名词 n.

受思想支配而表现出来的活动。Behaviors or actions expressed as a result of ideology or thought.

(1)行为不良的人得不到他人的尊重。

(2)随地吐痰、乱扔垃圾等都是不文明的行为。

说明 Notes:

"行动"和"行为"都表示人表现出来的举止、动作。"行动" and "行为" both express actions and bearings displayed by people.

它们的区别是:They differ as follows:

1.作名词用时,"行动"指一般的举动或动作,使用范围广。"行为"侧重指能表现人的思想品德、精神风貌的举动或动作,只用于人。When used as a noun, "行动" refers to ordinary movements or actions, and has a wide scope of usage. "行为" specifically refers to actions that express an individual's ideologies or moral character, and can only be used to refer to people.

2."行动"使用范围广,所以修饰词语多,如"军事行动、秘密行动、集体行动、实际行动、马上行动、立刻行动、推迟行动、延缓行动"等。"行为"多指人的举动是否符合法律规定或道德标准,所以能修饰的词语一般是"高尚、模范、正义、犯罪、违法、合法"等词语。"行动" has a wider scope of usage, and thus can modify more words, for example, "军事行动,秘密行动,集体行动,实际行动,马上行动,立刻行动,推迟行动,延缓行动.""行为" mostly refers to whether or not an individual's actions are in accordance with laws or moral standards, and thus is typically used to modify words such as "高尚,模范,正义,犯罪,违法,合法."

3."行动"有动词用法。"行为"没有动词用法。"行动" can be used as a verb, but "行为" cannot.

4.使用时要注意"行动"和"行为"词义的区别。When using "行动" and "行为," pay attention to the differences in their semantic meaning.

(3) *半个小时过去了,他还没来,他的行为真慢。

(4) 半个小时过去了,他还没来,他的行动真慢。

xíngchéng 形成 →P701"组成"

用法 Usage:

动词 v.

通过发展变化而变成或构成(某种事物、情况或局面)。 *To form; to come into being; to turn into or become part of (an object, situation, or circumstance) through change and development.*

(1) 端午节的习俗形成于春秋战国以前。

(2) 阿里巴巴已经形成了一个巨大的网络销售系统。

说明 Notes:

"形成"是"成"用在动词后面组成的动补性词语。 *"形成" is a verb-complement phrase created by the addition of the suffix "成" to a verb.*

xíngtài 形态 →P524"形状"

用法 Usage:

名词 n.

1. 事物的外表形状或表现形式。 *The external appearance or manifestation of an object.*

(1) 这幅画中的人物形态很生动。

(2) 水的形态有固体、液体、气体三种。

2. 生物体外部的形状。 *An organism's external appearance.*

(3) 菊花的形态有很多种。

(4) 这是两种不同形态的病毒。

3. 词的内部形式变化,包括构词形式和词形变化形式。 *(Linguistics) the internal inflection of a word, including morphological form and configurative change.*

(5) 汉语的词汇是很少有形态变化的。

说明 Notes:

"形态"既可以指具体事物的外形,如"人物形态、水的形态、花的形态"等,也可以指抽象事物的形态,如"政治形态、经济形态、意识形态"等。 *"形态" can be used to refer to the outward appearance of physical objects, as in "人物形态,水的形态,花的形态, etc." It can also be used to refer to the form or pattern of abstract concepts such as "政治形态,经济形态,意识形态."*

xíngxiàng 形象

用法 Usage:

名词 n.

1. 能引起人的思想或感情活动的具体形状和姿态。 *An image; a specific form or bearing that is able to stir thoughts or emotions in an individual.*

(1) 这小伙子形象英俊、帅气,人见人爱。

(2) 在公共场所,需要时时注意自己的形象。

2. 文艺作品中创造出来的生动具体、激发人们思想感情的生活图景,通常指文学作品中人物的神情面貌或性格特征。 *Vivid scenes in literature or art that are able to arouse people's thoughts and emotions. Often it refers to distinctive features and expressions or traits, characters or dispositions of figures in literary works.*

(3)《西游记》中孙悟空的形象,中国人都喜欢。

(4) 在电影里,007这个人物形象给我很深的印象。

形容词 a.

指表达或描绘具体、生动。 *(Of expressions or descriptions) specific and vivid.*

(5) 这部小说的语言生动形象,很有吸引力。

(6) 老师把这个语法点解释得既形象又生动,我一听就懂。

说明 Notes:

"形象"侧重于生活中的人的具体外表或姿态,或者是文艺作品中人物的精神面貌、性格特征。"形象" emphasizes a person's specific appearance or attitude, or refers to the distinctive features, traits, and dispositions of figures in literary and artistic works.

xíngzhuàng 形状 →P523"形态"

用法 Usage:

名词 n.

物体或图形由外部的面或线条组合而呈现的外表,即物体的外貌、样子。The external appearance of an object or of the linear presentation of a figure or image.

(1) 这些窗的形状有的像苹果,有的像梨,还有的像葡萄,可爱又有趣。

(2) 这个建筑物的形状远看像一张风帆。

说明 Notes:

"形态"和"形状"的区别是:"形态" and "形状" differ as follows:

"形态"指事物不同的形状或生物体形式外部的样子,既可以指具体事物的外形,也可以指抽象事物的内形,如:"人物形态奇特、经济形态多样化"。"形状"只能指具体事物的外形或样子,如"树的形状、石头的形状、图案的形状"等,不指抽象事物的内形。"形态" refers to the different forms or shapes of objects or to the exterior appearance of an object or body. It can refer to the physical shape or the exterior of a concrete object or to the internal form of an abstract or intangible object, for example, "人物形态奇特,经济形态多样化。" "形状" can only refer to the external appearance of a concrete object, for example, "树的形状,石头的形状,图案的形状。" It cannot be used to refer to intangible or abstract objects or concepts.

xìngkuī 幸亏

用法 Usage:

副词 ad.

因某种有利条件或情况而侥幸避免不良后果。通用于口语和书面语,常与"才、不然、否则、要不"等词呼应使用。Fortunately. It is used to indicate that unfavorable results are avoided due to certain favorable conditions or factors. It is used both in colloquial speech and in written language, and often with words such as "才,不然,否则,要不。"

(1) 幸亏早起了一个小时,要不然我们肯定赶不上火车。

(2) 幸亏带了雨伞,否则今天那么大的雨,肯定要淋湿了。

说明 Notes:

1. "幸亏"在口语里也常说成"幸好"。In colloquial speech, "幸亏" is often said as "幸好."

2. "多亏""幸亏"构成的句子,一般有两个分句。"多亏""幸亏"一般用在句子开头,带"多亏""幸亏"的分句一般表示原因——因为有这样的帮助或有利条件,另一分句则表示在这个原因下产生的结果。"多亏" and "幸亏" are often used in two-part sentences; "多亏" or "幸亏" is typically placed at the beginning of the first clause, expressing a cause or reason, for instance, someone's help or a favorable condition, and the second clause expresses the result brought about by the cause or reason.

3. "幸亏"和"多亏"都表示因某种帮助而避免了不好的后果。"幸亏" and "多亏" both indicate that bad results are avoided due to some type of assistance or help.

它们的区别是:They differ as follows:

"多亏"多用于困难之时,亏得有某人的帮助而转危为安。"幸亏"则适用于各种情况,可以是亏得有某人帮忙,也可以是亏得有其他有利因素或人为的条件来渡过难关。"幸亏"的使用范围比"多亏"广。"多亏" is often used when one is able to pull through dire straits thanks to the assistance of another individual. "幸亏" can be used in various types of conditions, and can refer to turning a corner thanks to the friendly assistance of a person or other man-made conditions or favorable factors. "幸亏" has a wider scope of usage than "多亏."

（3）＊他们多亏带了棉衣，才没有受凉。

（4）他们幸亏带了棉衣，才没有受凉。

（5）幸亏/多亏你借给我棉衣，不然我会感冒的。

（6）＊多亏台风带来了风雨降了温，否则很多老人会热得受不了的。

（7）幸亏台风带来了风雨降了温，否则很多老人会热得受不了的。

xìnggé 性格 →P353"脾气"

用法 Usage:

名词 *n.*

在对人、对事的态度和行为方式上所表现出来的心理特点。*Character; psychological traits or characteristic features shown through one's actions or through one's attitude towards people or events.*

（1）她的性格很开朗，朋友们很喜欢她。

（2）一般男人都希望女孩有温和的性格。

说明 Notes:

"性格"和"脾气"在表示人的性情、性格时，用法基本相同。*When meaning a person's disposition or temperament, "性格" and "脾气" are quite similar.*

它们的区别是：*Their differences are as follows:*

1. 在词义上，"性格"包含的内容很广，有个人的品质、意志等。"脾气"主要与人的情绪有关，同时还特指易怒的性格。*In terms of meaning, "性格" includes a wider range of concepts, including a person's character, willpower, etc. "脾气" mainly has to do with a person's emotions, and also particularly refers to a temperament that is easily volatile.*

2. 词语搭配上，"性格""脾气"可以共同搭配"好、急躁、暴躁、粗暴、古怪、温和、温顺、随和"等。"性格"还能与"懦弱、刚强、耿直、乐观、坚强、内向、外向、温柔平和、多愁善感、坦诚、沉稳"等搭配，还可以组合成"民族性格、人物性格、培养孩子的性格、养成不好的性格"等等词语。"脾气"不能。*When it comes to pairing with other words, "性格" and "脾气" can both be used with words such as "好,急躁,暴躁,粗暴,古怪,温和,温顺,随和." "性格" can also be used with "懦弱,刚强,耿直,乐观,坚强,内向,外向,温柔平和,多愁善感,坦诚,沉稳," and can be formed into phrases such as "民族性格,人物性格,培养孩子的性格,养成不好的性格," while "脾气" cannot.*

3. "脾气"有专指发怒、急躁的情绪的意思。"性格"没有。*"脾气" specifically refers to a rash or irritable state of mind that is easily inflamed, while "性格" does not have this connotation.*

（3）你不要发脾气，有话可以好好说。

（4）＊你不要发性格，有话可以好好说。

xiōng 凶

用法 Usage:

形容词 *a.*

1. 不幸的，不好的（形容死亡、灾难等现象，跟"吉"相对）。*Unfortunate; bad. It is used to describe death, disaster, or other similar phenomena, and is the opposite of "吉."*

（1）我感到一种凶兆，最近可能会发生什么事。

2. 凶恶的。*Ferocious; fierce.*

（2）这个人的样子看起来很凶。

（3）你怎么可以对她那么凶？

3. （表示在程度上）厉害，过甚。*(Indicating degree) severe; formidable; excessive; exaggerated.*

（4）这个人骂人骂得真凶。

（5）这群人闹得很凶，大家都有点怕了。

名词 *n.*

1. 指杀害或伤害人的行为。*Acts that kill or harm people.*

（6）他们怎么能够行凶杀人？

2. 指行凶作恶的人。Criminals.

（7）那件杀人案的凶手已经抓到了。

说明 Notes:

"凶"一般不单独使用，而是用在词组中，如："凶事、凶信"；"很凶、那么凶、太凶、凶极了、凶得很"；"行凶、帮凶、元凶"等。或与"吉"组合，如："逢凶化吉、避凶趋吉"等。做形容词时，一般都需要有程度副词修饰。"凶" is typically not used alone, but rather in phrases such as "凶事，凶信，""很凶，那么凶，太凶，凶极了，凶得很，" or "行凶，帮凶，元凶." It is also combined with "吉" to make such phrases as "逢凶化吉，避凶趋吉." When used as an adjective, it is typically modified by a degree adverb.

xiūxián 休闲

用法 Usage:
动词 v.

1. 休息，过清闲的生活。To rest; to lead an idle life.

（1）想休闲，就去杭州。

（2）周末，大家可以到娱乐场所休闲一下。

2. 指土地一季或一年不种农作物。(In agriculture) to fallow arable land for a season or a year.

（3）那块地让它休闲一年。

说明 Notes:

日常生活中有"穿得很休闲、休闲衫"的用法，此处"休闲"是随意的意思，与"正式"相对。In everyday life, such expressions as "穿得很休闲，休闲衫" are often used, in which "休闲" refers to something casual, the opposite of "正式 (formal)."

xiūjiàn 修建 →P225"建设"、P225"建造"、P226"建筑"

用法 Usage:
动词 v.

按照具体的图纸要求建造、施工（土木工程）。"修建"的对象范围比较广，可以是道路、桥梁、水库、机场等敞开式的建筑物，也可以是宿舍、学校、厂房、博物馆等房屋类的建筑物。To build or construct (a civil engineering project) in accordance with a design or a drawing. It covers a fairly wide scope ranging from open-air projects such as a road, bridge, reservoir and airport to buildings such as a house, factory, dormitory, and museum.

（1）这里要修建一座大型的自然博物馆。

（2）我们山区也要修建铁路了。

（3）我们在那条河上已经修建了三座大桥。

说明 Notes:

1. "修建"与"建造"的用法基本相同。"修建" and "建造" are used basically in the same way.

2. "修建"与"建设"的对象不完全相同。"修建"的对象一般是具体的土木工程建筑物体。"建设"的对象除以上那些一样，还有如"国家、精神文明"等抽象名词。The targets of "修建" and "建设" are somewhat different. The targets of "修建" are usually concrete buildings of the civil engineering, while the targets of "建设" could be abstract objects such as "国家 (a country)，精神文明 (spiritual civilization)," apart from concrete buildings.

3. "修建"和"建筑"都有建造的意思，都是动词，可以用作谓语和定语，但是"修建"不能修饰人。如："建筑工人、建筑工程师"，不能用为"*修建工人、*修建工程师"。Both "修建" and "建设" carry the meaning of building. As a verb, both can serve as the predicate or an attribute in a sentence. But "修建" cannot be used to modify a person. One can say "建筑工人" or "建筑工程师，" but not "*修建工人" or "*修建工程师."

xūqiú 需求 →P526"需要"

用法 Usage:
名词 n.

因需要而产生的愿望、要求。A desire

based upon wants and needs.

（1）人们对电子产品的需求越来越大。

（2）当经济不发达的时候，人们对生活的需求不是很高。

xūyào 需要 →P526"需求"

用法 Usage：

动词 v.

应该有或必须有。Should or must have; to require.

（1）我们需要几台电脑。

（2）要学好汉语，需要多读、多说、多写、多练。

名词 n.

对事物的欲望或要求。Desires or requirements for things.

（3）你在上海有什么需要就告诉我。

（4）满足你们在生活上的需要就是我们的工作。

说明 Notes：

1."需要"作动词用时，要注意：When using "需要" as a verb, take note:

① 表示必须有，一定要得到的意思，前面可以有副词状语，后面可以带宾语。When expressing a requirement of something that must be obtained, it can be preceded by an adverbial modifier.

（5）我正需要这本书，你就给我送来了。

② 表示应该、必须的意思时，可以带动词、形容词作宾语。When expressing the meaning of "should" or "must," it can take a verb or adjective as its object.

（6）孩子长个儿了，需要补充各种营养。

③ 表示应该、必须的意思时，"需要"可以带主谓词组宾语，形成兼语句。(Linguistics) when expressing the meaning of "should" or "must," "需要" can take a subject-predicate word group as its object to form a pivotal sentence.

（7）老师需要我和你现在去他办公室。

2."需求"和"需要"用作名词时，都是指对事物(包括对精神)的要求。区别是："需要"有动词用法，"需求"没有。When used as a noun, "需求" and "需要" both express requirements for things (including mental ones). The difference between them is that "需要" has a verb usage while "需求" does not.

xuānbù 宣布 →P169"公布"

用法 Usage：

动词 v.

（用语言、文字）公开正式地告诉大家。To formally and openly announce to the public.

（1）上课的时候，老师宣布了得到奖学金同学的名单。

（2）他俩正式宣布他们要结婚了。

说明 Notes：

"宣布"和"公布"的区别是：The differences between "宣布" and "公布" are as follows:

1."宣布"侧重于正式地告诉大家。内容既可以是重大消息、事件，也可以是一般的消息（内容多带有约束性或强制性），如"宣布名单、宣布考试成绩、宣布结果、宣布规定"等。主要用于口头形式。"宣布" emphasizes formally announcing something to the public; it can be important news or large events or can be information of average occurrences (the content typically carries a binding or mandatory nature). For example, "宣布名单，宣布考试成绩，宣布结果，宣布规定." It is mainly used for oral announcements.

2."公布"侧重于当众宣布，让更多的人知道。多用于领导机关宣布"法令、法规政策、决议、指示、战报"等；或一般机关、团体、单位或个人告知某些具体事项，如"方案、名单、账目、成绩"等。通用于书面语和口语。"公布" emphasizes announcing something to an audience in order to make more people aware. It is often used in reference to leading organizations announcing "法令，法规政策，决议，指示，战报，etc."; or with average organizations, groups, professional units, or individuals informing others about a specific matter, such as "方案,名单,账目,成绩." It is used in both written and spoken language.

xuǎn 选 →P528"选择"

用法 Usage:

动词 v.

1. 挑选,挑拣。To choose; to select.

(1) 你可以在那堆衣服中选一件。

(2) 教学实习有两个地点,每个人只能选一个点。

2. 选举。To elect.

(3) 我们选他做我们班长。

(4) 学院要选五名同学组成学生会的委员会。

说明 Notes:

"选"还有名词用法,如"人选、作品选、散文选、小说选"等。"选" also has a noun usage, as seen in "人选,作品选,散文选,小说选, etc."

xuǎnzé 选择 →P528"选"

用法 Usage:

动词 v.

挑选。可以重叠使用。To choose. It can be reduplicated as "选择选择."

(1) 毕业以后,你会选择什么工作?

(2) 可以选择的城市很多,我要好好选择选择。

名词 n.

表示选择的过程或结果。可以做主语或用在"加以、进行、经过、做出"等动词后面做宾语。Describing the result or process of a selection. It can be used as the subject of a sentence or can follow verbs such as "加以,进行,经过,做出," and function as an object.

(3) 我的选择爸爸妈妈都很支持。

(4) 他终于做出了选择,去报考医学专业。

说明 Notes:

1. "选择"的对象可以是具体的,也可以是抽象的,如"选择苹果、选择工作、选择朋友、选择志愿、选择目标、选择机会"等。The target of "选择" can be either concrete or abstract, for example, "选择工作,选择专业,选择朋友,选择志愿,选择目标,选择机会."

2. "选择"和"选"都表示从若干选项中挑出好的。"选择" and "选" both mean to pick the best option from among several choices.

它们的区别是:They differ as follows:

① "选择"多用于比较庄重的场合,常用于书面语。"选"多用于比较随便的场合,挑选的对象多是具体的。"选择" is typically used when discussing more solemn or serious situations or in written language. "选" is typically used when discussing more casual or everyday situations, and the object of selection is usually specific.

② "选择"多与双音节词搭配使用。"选"多与单音节词搭配使用。"选择" is often used with disyllabic words. Since "选" is monosyllabic, it is more frequently used with monosyllabic words.

xuéwen 学问 →P663"知识"

用法 Usage:

名词 n.

1. 知识,学识。Knowledge.

(1) 这个人博览群书,很有学问。

(2) 生活中到处是学问。

2. 正确反映客观事物的系统知识。Accurately rendered systematic knowledge of objective things.

(3) 哲学是一门很深的学问,值得好好研究。

(4) 航天科学是门大学问。

xúnqiú 寻求 →P529"寻找"

用法 Usage:

动词 v.

寻找,追求。To seek; to pursue.

(1) 生活便是寻求新的知识。

(2) 这个科学家一生都在寻求真理。

xúnzhǎo 寻找 →P528"寻求"

用法 Usage:
动词 v.
为了要见到或得到所需要的人或事物而搜求。*To seek; to look for; to search.*

（1）昨晚他们一直在寻找那条宠物狗。

（2）生活的意义是什么？你得寻找一辈子。

说明 Notes:
"寻找"和"寻求"都有找事物、找人的意思。*"寻找" and "寻求" both describe the act of searching for something.*

它们的区别是：*Their differences are as follows:*

1."寻求"侧重于一种因主观愿望而刻苦追求的意思。"寻找"强调词义本身的意义，即"找"。*"寻求" emphasizes painstakingly searching for something due to a subjective desire. "寻找" emphasizes the act of searching.*

2."寻找"的宾语既可以指具体的东西，如例（1），也可以指抽象的东西，如例（2）。*"寻找" can be used to refer to physical objects as seen in (1), or abstract objects, as seen in (2).*

"寻求"的宾语多指比较抽象的对象，如"知识、理想、真理、办法、途径"等，一般不带具体的事物名词做宾语。*The objects taken by "寻求" are usually abstract, for example, "知识,理想,真理,办法,途径," and it typically does not take concrete nouns as its object.*

（3）*他寻求他的英汉词典好长时间了。

（4）他寻找他的英汉词典好长时间了。

yā 压 →P4"按"

用法 Usage:

动词 *v.*

1. 对物体施压力（多指从上向下）。*To apply pressure to an object (usually top-down).*

（1）请用书本把那些纸张压住，别让风吹散了。

（2）大箱子别压在小箱子上。

2. 抑制，使稳定，使平静。*To suppress; to stabilize; to calm down.*

（3）吃了那么多药，还是压不住咳嗽。

（4）你先把火压住，别骂人，问清楚情况再说。

3. 压制，用威力制服。*To repress.*

（5）你别拿那件事情压我。我没参与那件事。

（6）你别压他，让他先说。

4. 搁着不动。*To leave untouched.*

（7）我们的申请报告你别压着不管，请赶快讨论决定。

（8）他们俩打架的事情先压着吧。

5. 超越，胜过。多用于四字词语，如："技不压身，才不压人；艳压群芳；邪不压正"等。*To surpass, often used in four-character words such as "技不压身，才不压人；艳压群芳；邪不压正."*

说明 Notes:

"压"和"按"都有从上往下施力、搁下不动、抑制的意思。"压" and "按" both mean "to apply downward pressure," "to leave untouched," and "to suppress."

它们的区别是：*Their differences are as follows:*

1. "压"可以是人力，也可以是物体的重力对其他物体施加力量，如例（1）（2）。"按"只能是用手或手指向下用力。"压" *can refer to the pressure from people, or pressure from one object to another, as in (1) and (2).* "按" *can only refer to the downward pressure from one's hands or fingers.*

2. "按"有介词用法。"压"没有介词用法。"按" *can be used as a preposition, whereas* "压" *cannot.*

yālì 压力

用法 Usage:

名词 *n.*

1. 物体所承受的与表面垂直的作用力。*The force on an object perpendicular to its surface.*

（1）低空飞行时，飞机内外的压力基本上一致。

（2）空气压力低的时候，人体会感到难受。

2. 承受的负担。*Burden.*

（3）发展中的中国城市，承受的交通压力很大。

（4）他觉得在高班，学习压力很大。

3. 制服人的力量。*Pressure on people.*

（5）给他任何压力，他都不会改变自己的

想法。

(6) 在舆论的压力下,她只能离开了公司。

yáncháng 延长 →P531"延期"、P531"延伸"、P531"延续"

用法 Usage:

动词 v.

向长的方面发展(跟"缩短"相对)。*To extend, the opposite of "缩短 (shorten)."*

(1) 这条公路去年向前延长了一百公里。
(2) 我们的老师上课从来不延长时间。

说明 Notes:

"延长"的宾语一般为"长度、距离、时间"等名词。*The objects of "延长" are usually such nouns as "长度 (length), 距离 (distance), 时间 (time)."*

yánqī 延期 →P531"延长"

用法 Usage:

动词 v.

1. 推迟原来规定的日期。*To delay; to put off.*

(1) 去美国旅行的计划一定不会延期,你放心。
(2) 因为天气不好,我们只能延期交货了,对不起!

2. 延长使用期、有效期等。*To extend the period of validity.*

(3) 明天我要去办理签证延期手续。
(4) 你的签证还可以延期六个月。

说明 Notes:

"延期"和"延长"都有延长时间的意思。*"延期" and "延长" can both mean "to extend the time."*

它们的区别是:"延期"只能用在时间方面的延长。"延长"还可以用在距离和事物的长度上。*Their difference is as follows: "延期" can only refer to time, whereas "延长" can refer to distance or length of objects.*

yánshēn 延伸 →P531"延长"

用法 Usage:

动词 v.

(向某个方向)延长,伸展。*To extend, stretch (toward certain direction).*

(1) 天目山脉一直延伸到杭州西湖边的群山。
(2) 他又出钱把山里的公路延伸了两公里。

说明 Notes:

"延伸"和"延长"都有距离上向长发展的意思。*"延伸" and "延长" can both mean "to extend the distance."*

它们的区别是:"延伸"只能用于空间、距离方面的延长。"延长"还可以用在时间和事物的长度上。*Their difference is as follows: "延伸" can only refer to space and distance, whereas "延长" can refer to length of time or objects.*

yánxù 延续 →P531"延长"

用法 Usage:

动词 v.

持续,照原来的样子继续下去,延长下去。*To continue, or to extend.*

(1) 我们一定要把孝敬父母的优良传统延续下去。
(2) 城市建设讨论会又延续了两天才结束。

说明 Notes:

"延续"和"延长"表示时间向长方面发展时,可以互换。*"延续" and "延长" are interchangeable when referring to extension of time.*

它们的区别是:"延续"侧重继续时要保留原来的样子,"延续"的对象多为"会议、传统、作风、规定、规则"等。"延长"侧重事物向长的方面发展,可用在时间、距离、各种事物的长度等,使用的范围比较广泛。*Their difference is as follows: "延续" emphasizes maintaining the* original form in the continuation. It often takes objects such as "会议,传统,作风,规定,规则.""延长" emphasizes the extension in terms of length, which has a wider range of application compared to "延续."

yán 严 →P532"严格"

用法 Usage:

形容词 a.

1. 严密,紧密。Tight; secure.

(1) 放心吧,他的嘴很严,不会把你的事情说出去的。

(2) 一定要把瓶口盖严,出气的话,酒就不好喝了。

2. 严厉,严格。多与单音节词搭配使用。Strict. It is often used with monosyllabic words.

(3) 中国古代家庭对孩子的态度上,一般是严父慈母。

(4) 他对自己要求很严。

3. 程度深,厉害。修饰名词、形容词,表程度加深。Severe. It is used to modify nouns or adjectives to indicate a higher degree.

(5) 很多老人在严冬季节就去海南岛避寒。

(6) 在东北,严寒季节特别长,所以冬季农民就比较清闲。

yángé 严格 →P532"严"、P532"严厉"、P533"严肃"

用法 Usage:

形容词 a.

在遵守制度和掌握标准时认真、毫不放松。Being strict in abiding by rules and holding standards.

(1) 在生活上,父母对女孩儿要求很严格。

(2) 在严格的笔试和面试后,她终于被公司录用了。

动词 v.

认真、毫不放松地执行。To implement with stringent rules.

(3) 学校严格规章制度后,同学们上课不迟到了。

(4) 作为教师一定要严格教学纪律。

说明 Notes:

"严格"和"严"都有严厉、严格的意思。"严格" and "严" can both mean "strict" or "stringent."

它们的区别是：Their differences are as follows:

1. 在句子中,"严"多与单音节词搭配使用。"严格"则与双音节词语搭配使用。"严" is usually used with monosyllabic words, whereas "严格" is often used with disyllabic words.

(5) 学校对考试作弊的行为一向是严惩的。

(6) 学校对考试作弊的行为一向是严格处理的。

2. "严"还表示严密、紧密,程度深的意思。"严格"没有。"严" can mean "tight," "secure," or "with a high degree." "严格" has no such meaning.

3. "严格"有动词用法。"严"没有。"严格" can be used as a verb but "严" cannot.

yánlì 严厉 →P532"严格"、P533"严肃"

用法 Usage:

形容词 a.

(指人的行为或态度)严肃而厉害(与"宽厚"相对)。(Of someone's behavior or attitude) serious and strict, as opposed to "宽厚 (tolerant and generous)."

(1) 父母对我很严厉,对妹妹很宠爱。

(2) 妈妈严厉地对我说："好好学习,不准再玩游戏!"然后还收走了我的手机。

说明 Notes:

"严格"和"严厉"做形容词都表示要求严、不放松。As adjectives, "严格" and "严厉" both mean being strict with stringent rules.

它们的区别是：Their differences are as follows:

1."严格"侧重表示态度的认真。"严厉"侧重表示态度的严肃和手段的厉害。"严格" emphasizes a conscientious attitude, whereas "严厉" emphasizes a serious attitude and tough measures.

2."严格"可用于对自己，也对别人。"严厉"只用于对别人。"严格" can be applied both to oneself and to others. "严厉" is only applied to others.

3."严格"有动词用法。"严厉"没有。"严格" can be used as a verb but "严厉" cannot.

4."严格"常修饰"实行、执行、要求、按照、遵守、训练、管理、检查、区分"等动词，常与"纪律、标准、制度、规矩"等名词搭配使用，可构成"严格说来，严格来讲"等习惯用语。"严厉"常修饰"管教、责备、质问、打击、批评、处罚、处分、制裁"等动词，常与"目光、口气、表情、神情、态度、制度"等名词搭配使用，搭配时要用助词"的"。"严格" is often used with verbs such as "实行，执行，要求，按照，遵守，训练，管理，检查，区分," or nouns such as "纪律，标准，制度，规矩." It can be used in fixed expressions such as "严格来说，严格来讲。""严厉" is often used with verbs such as "管教，责备，质问，打击，批评，处罚，处分，制裁，" or nouns such as "目光，口气，表情，神情，态度，制度。" When describing a noun, "严厉" must be followed by "的."

yánsù 严肃 →P532"严厉"

用法 Usage:
形容词 a.

1.（指神情、气氛以及话题等）庄重，郑重，使人感到敬畏。(Of facial expression, atmosphere, or topics) solemn; formidable.

(1) 爸爸很严肃，很少跟我们开玩笑。

(2) 这是个严肃的问题，你要认真考虑回答我。

2.（指作风、态度等）认真严格。(Of style or attitude) serious; strict.

(3) 妈妈对工作很严肃认真，一回家对着我就严肃不起来。

(4) 你想有个家庭时，就要严肃认真地对待婚姻问题。

动词 v.

认真、郑重地执行。To execute conscientiously.

(5) 必须严肃交通法规，才能减少交通事故。

说明 Notes:

"严肃"和"严厉"做形容词都表示认真、郑重，令人敬畏，都可以形容人的态度。When used as adjectives, "严肃" and "严厉" can both mean solemn or formidable and can both describe attitudes.

它们的区别是：Their differences are as follows:

1."严肃"侧重于庄重、认真，让人敬畏，不敢随便，多形容人的神情和有关场合的气氛。"严厉"侧重于严肃而厉害，常常声色俱厉，让人望而生畏，语义比"严肃"重。多用于指人的神情、态度或行为，使用范围比"严肃"窄。"严肃" is often used to describe facial expression or atmosphere, emphasizing being solemn and formidable. Carrying a more serious tone than "严肃，""严厉" emphasizes being strict and even harsh. With a narrower range of application than "严肃，""严厉" is often used to describe facial expression, attitude, or behavior.

2."严肃"和"严厉"都可以形容人的态度，但即使修饰相同的名词或动词，"严厉"比"严肃"语义更重，因为"严厉"除了语气、神情让人感到害怕，有时还包括对人采取的手段等。"严肃" and "严厉" can both be used to describe attitudes. When used to describe the same noun or verb, "严厉" carries a more serious tone than "严肃." In addition to describing the formidable tone of voice or facial expression, "严厉" can also describe certain measures taken.

（6）父亲严肃地教训了儿子一顿。（主要指神情让人敬畏 Describing the formidable facial expression）

（7）父亲严厉地教训了儿子一顿。（除了神情以外,语言、语气,甚至手势都让人感到可怕。In addition to the facial expression, the language, the tone of voice, or even the gesture are all formidable.）

（8）＊教室里的气氛很严厉。

（9）教室里的气氛很严肃。

3."严肃"有动词用法。"严厉"没有动词用法。"严肃" can be used as a verb but "严厉" cannot.

4."严肃"和"严厉"有共同的反义词是"温和、和气",但它们也有各自不同的反义词: "严肃" and "严厉" have the same antonyms such as "温和" and "和气." They also have different antonyms:

说明人的性格很严肃,"严肃"的反义词是"活泼、幽默"。When describing a serious disposition, "严肃" has the antonyms of "活泼" and "幽默."

说明话题或气氛很严肃,"严肃"的反义词是"轻松"。When describing a serious topic or atmosphere, "严肃" has the antonym of "轻松."

说明对人的态度很严厉,"严厉"的反义词是"亲切"。When describing a strict attitude, "严厉" has the antonym of "亲切."

yányǔ 言语 →P609"语言"

用法 Usage:

名词 n.

言辞,说的话,指人们掌握和使用语言的活动。Speech; words (referring to people's command and use of language).

（1）因言语不和而发生争吵的事件常有发生。

（2）她言语温和,觉得她脾气很好。

yányu 言语 →P609"语言"

用法 Usage:

动词 v.

北京话中表示说话、回答、招呼、开口等意思。To speak, reply, greet, or talk (often used colloquially in Beijing dialect).

（1）你有什么事需要我帮忙,就言语一声。

（2）我问你话呢,你怎么不言语?

yán 沿 →P432"顺"

用法 Usage:

介词 prep.

顺着（江河、道路或物体的边）。Along (the edges of a river, road or object).

（1）老人每天沿/沿着河边走一个小时路。

（2）这个村每家每户都沿/沿着墙根儿种几棵水杉树,很漂亮。

动词 v.

1.依照以往的方法、规矩、式样等。To follow previous methods, rules or styles.

（3）以前,中医秘方传男不传女的家规世代相沿。

2.顺着衣物的边儿再缝上一道边儿。To sew an additional edge along the edge of the clothes.

（4）那件衬衣领子上沿着一条花边,很好看的。

名词 n.

边儿（多用在名词后面）。Edge (often used after a noun).

（5）桌沿儿还有点油,再擦一遍。

（6）炕沿儿坐着两个女孩子。

说明 Notes:

1."沿"作介词用时要注意：The usage of "沿" as a preposition follows these rules:

① 如果后面的名词性短语较长,"沿"后面要加"着",如例（1）（2）。If the noun phrase following "沿" is relatively long, "着" should be used after "沿" as seen in (1) and (2).

② 跟单音节名词组合,指处所时,用于"是"字句、"有"字句或其他描写句：When combined with a monosyllabic noun to refer to a location, "沿" is often used in existential sentences with "是" or "有," or sentences with descriptions.

（7）沿湖都是柳树和桃树。

（8）沿高墙有不少椅子供游客坐着休息。

2. "沿"和"顺"都有依着某种方向或路线（做什么）的介词用法。When used as prepositions, "沿" and "顺" can both mean "along with certain direction or route."

它们的区别是："沿"可带抽象意义的名词组成介词短语。"顺"的方向性比较明确和具体,所以不可以。The difference between the two is: "沿" can form prepositional phrases with abstract nouns, but "顺" cannot as it indicates clearer and more specific direction compared with "沿."

（9）*我们要继续顺着这条充满理想和希望的大道前进。

（10）我们要继续沿着这条充满理想和希望的大道前进。

yánfā 研发 →P535"研制"

用法 Usage:
动词 v.

研制开发。To develop through research.

（1）公司的科研人员都在研发新产品。

（2）世界上的科学家已经研发出激光注射方法。

yánzhì 研制 →P535"研发"

用法 Usage:
动词 v.

1.（中药）研磨制成。To produce (Chinese medicine) through grinding.

（1）中成药是由多味中药研制而成的。

2. 研究制造。To research and develop.

（2）这家公司近期研制出一种新型产品。

（3）我国自主研制了大型客机,并已投放市场。

说明 Notes:

"研发"和"研制"都指运用科学技术开发新产品的意思。"研发" and "研制" both refer to development of new products with technology.

它们的区别是："研发"侧重于"开发",可以与抽象名词"方法"搭配使用。"研制"侧重于"制造"。不能与抽象名词搭配使用。Their difference is as follows: "研发" emphasizes the development. It can be used with an abstract noun such as "方法." "研制" emphasizes the production. It cannot be used with any abstract nouns.

（4）*香港理工大学研制了5分钟可分辨"地沟油"的方法。

（5）香港理工大学研发了5分钟可分辨"地沟油"的方法。

yánsè 颜色 →P401"色彩"

用法 Usage:
名词 n.

1. 色彩。物体的光波通过视觉所产生的印象。Color, the impression of an object's light wave on a person's vision.

（1）彩虹是由七种颜色组成的。

2. 指脸上的表情。Facial expression.

（2）她站在门口,脸上现出羞愧的颜色,说："我迟到了。"

3. 指显示给人看的厉害的脸色或行动。What one shows by way of facial expression or behavior.

（3）还在玩游戏！当心你爸给你颜色看。

说明 Notes:

"颜色"和"色彩"都是名词,在表示色彩的意思时,两个词可以互换。Both "颜色" and "色彩" are nouns. The can replace each other when the meaning is color.

（4）白光经过分析发现有七种色彩/颜色。

除此之外,两个词的意义和用法没有相同的地方。Otherwise, the two words are different in meaning and usage.

yǎnguāng 眼光 →P329"目光"

用法 Usage:

名词 n.

1. 视线。Line of sight.

(1) 走进教室,同学们的眼光都看向了我。

(2) 他的眼光落到了墙上的一张照片上。

2. 观察鉴别事物的能力;眼力。Ability to observe and distinguish things.

(3) 男人和女人的眼光不同,各自的欣赏点也不同。

(4) 他的眼光真好,你看他买的一套西装多有气派。

3. 指观点、看法等。Point of view.

(5) 我们要用发展的眼光看问题。

(6) 书看得多,眼光自然跟常人不一样。

说明 Notes:

"眼光"和"目光"都有看东西的视线、观察事物能力的意思。"眼光" and "目光" can both mean the line of sight or the ability to observe things.

它们的区别是:Their differences are as follows:

1. "目光"观察事物侧重于预见事物的能力。"眼光"观察事物侧重于鉴别事物的能力,不但能用于对抽象事物的鉴别,也能用于对具体事物的选择。"目光" emphasizes the ability to predict. "眼光" emphasizes the ability to distinguish things. It can be used for distinguishing abstract things or selecting specific objects.

(7) 他是个很有经济眼光的人。

(8) 她很有眼光,选了一个那么有才能的丈夫。

上面句子中的"眼光"不能用"目光"替换。

2. "目光"多用于书面语,如"目光如鼠、目光短浅、目光远大"等,其中"目光"都不能用"眼光"替换。"目光" is usually used in written language, such as "目光如鼠,目光短浅,目光远大." It cannot be replaced with "眼光" in those phrases.

3. "眼光"有观点的意思。"目光"没有。"眼光" can mean "point of view" but "目光" cannot.

(9) *你不要再用老目光来看这座城市。

(10) 你不要再用老眼光来看这座城市。

4. "目光"有眼睛的神采的意思。"眼光"没有。"目光" can mean the look in one's eyes. "眼光" has no such usage.

(11) *姑娘们都被他那炯炯的眼光吸引住了。

(12) 姑娘们都被他那炯炯的目光吸引住了。

yǎnkàn 眼看 →P311"马上"

用法 Usage:

副词 ad.

马上。常与"就要……了、快要……了、要……了、快……了、到……了"等连用。Soon (often used with "就要…了,快要…了,要…了,快…了,到…了").

(1) 眼看就要高考了,你怎么还在玩游戏呢?

(2) 眼看天要下雨了,我们快走吧!

动词 v.

1. 指亲眼看到的正在发生的情况。没有否定式。"眼看"后面常带"着",必带小句做宾语。To witness what is happening. It has no negative form and is often followed by "着." "眼看" takes a clause as its object.

(3) 眼看着时间一天天过去,可爷爷的病一点都不见好。

(4) 眼看着风把一大块黑云吹过来,大雨就下来了。

2. 表示对眼前出现的不好的事情或情况没有办法,任凭其发生或发展而无能为力。必带"着",必带小句做宾语。To look on passively and be incapable of changing the current

situation; to watch helplessly. It has to be followed by "着" and a clause as its object.

（5）不能眼看着他什么也吃不下去，你得想办法呀！

（6）今年雨水多，不得不眼看着这些麦子烂在地里。

说明 Notes：

1."眼看"做副词时要注意，句中被修饰的动词的语义常常指向将来，如例（1）（2）。When "眼看" is used as an adverb, the verb being modified often refers to the future as seen in (1) and (2).

2."眼看"做动词要注意以下两点：When "眼看" is used as a verb, pay attention to the following two aspects:

① 在第一种用法中，做宾语的小句常常描述一种变化着的、正在进行着的一种动作或者某种状态，如例（3）（4）。In the first usage, the clause serving as the object often describes an ongoing or changing action or status as seen in (3) and (4).

② 在第二种用法中，句子由两个分句组成，一个分句必定表示正在进行或出现的不好的情况，常和"只好、不能、不得不、却"等词语连用，另一个分句表示无可奈何、消极的情状、态度或不可抵御的原因，如例（5）（6）。In the second usage, the sentence consists of two clauses. One clause indicates an ongoing situation that is undesirable. It often goes with words such as "只好, 不能, 不得不, 却." The other clause indicates the helpless and passive mood, attitude or an irresistible cause as seen in (5) and (6).

3."眼看"相当于"马上"的意思。"眼看" and "马上" can both mean "soon."

它们的区别是：Their differences are as follows:

① "眼看"只能用在表示动作要发生的那个句子前，客观地描述马上就要发生的情况，后面一个小句表示应该发生的动作还没发生。如例（1）（2）。"眼看" can only be used in a clause describing the action that is about to happen. The second clause indicates that what should have happened is yet to occur as seen in (1) and (2).

② "马上"可以用在表示主观动作行为的句子。"眼看"不能。"马上" can be used in sentences describing a subjective action or behavior but "眼看" cannot.

（7）"我马上就去"。

③ "眼看"不能用于祈使句。"马上"可以用于祈使句。"眼看" cannot be used in imperative sentences but "马上" can.

（8）＊快，让他们眼看出发！

（9）快，让他们马上出发！

（10）眼看他们就要出发了，怎么她还没来？

yǎnqián 眼前 →P322"面前"、P329"目前"

用法 Usage：

名词 n.

1. 眼睛前面，跟前。In front of one's eyes.

（1）我站在你眼前，你怎么都没看见？

（2）破旧的房屋不见了，眼前是一幢新建的楼房。

2. 表示时间，指"目前、现在"。Indicating time, it is similar to "目前 (at present)，现在 (now)."

（3）好好珍惜眼前的生活。

（4）我们要努力争取眼前的利益，也要想到将来的利益。

说明 Notes：

1."眼前"既能表示空间上近距离地方的意思，又能表示时间上较近、或距说话时间较近的意思，如例（1）（3）。"眼前" can refer to closeness in distance or time as seen in (1) and (3).

2."眼前"和"面前"都能表示空间上近距离地方的意思。区别是："眼前"还能表示较近的时间点。"面前"不能。"眼前" and "面前"

can both refer to closeness in distance. The difference between the two is that "眼前" can refer to closeness in time but "面前" cannot.

（5）*面前最重要的是快找到那个孩子。

（6）眼前最重要的是快找到那个孩子。

3."眼前"和"目前"都指说话的时候或最近的一段时间,相对的词语都可以是"将来",在一般句子中两个词语可以替换。"眼前" and "目前" can both refer to the time of speech or recently, as opposed to "将来." The two words are generally interchangeable.

它们的区别是：Their differences are as follows:

① 与"眼前"相对的词语是"长远"。与"目前"相对的词语是"以前"。The opposite of "眼前" is "长远." The opposite of "目前" is "以前."

② "眼前"除表示时间以外,还表示"跟前、眼睛面前"的空间。"目前"不能。In addition to time, "眼前" can refer to space with a meaning similar to that of "跟前,眼睛前面." "目前" has no such usage.

yǎnchū 演出

用法 Usage:
动词 v.

把戏剧、音乐、舞蹈等文艺节目演给观众欣赏。To perform drama, music, or dance for the audience.

（1）今天晚上这里要演出京剧《空城计》。

（2）中国的民族音乐节目在欧洲演出了十场。

说明 Notes:

"演出"有名词用法,表示演出的文艺节目内容。When used as a noun, "演出" refers to the program being presented.

（3）明天我有演出,没时间去看你。今天可以吗？

（4）昨天的演出节目很精彩。

yáng 洋

用法 Usage:
形容词 a.

1. 外国的（多指西洋的）。常与别的语素构成复合词,在句子中做定语,偶尔做状语。Foreign, mainly referring to Western. It is often combined with other morphemes to form compound words, and often used as an attributive and occasionally used as an adverbial.

（1）我们村里从没来过洋人。

（2）穿着洋服,坐着洋车,吸着洋烟,是旧社会有钱人的样子。

2. 现代化的,现代的（与"土"相对）。只出现在"洋气、洋办法、土洋结合"等少数词语中。Modernized, modern, as opposed to "土 (unmodernized, indigenous)." It is only used in a few set phrases such as "洋气,洋办法,土洋结合."

（3）那个姑娘穿得很洋气。

名词 n.

1. 覆盖地球表面、比海大的水域。Ocean.

（4）世界上有四大洋,它们是太平洋、大西洋、印度洋和北冰洋。

2. 外国（多指西洋）。Foreign countries, mainly referring to the West.

（5）我们要洋为中用,吸收西方先进的科学技术。

3. 洋钱,银圆。Silver coin.

（6）以前的银大洋现在是很值钱的。

说明 Notes:

1. "洋"后面带后缀"化",作为动词用。With the suffix "化," "洋" can be used as a verb.

（7）他出国才一年,生活上竟然完全洋化了。

2. 除了口语中,"洋"很少独立运用,常与别的语素组成复合词。"洋"是个社会、时代发展的词语。在20世纪初的时候,大量的外国产品进入中国,很多产品是中国以前没有的,如：

"洋火(火柴)、洋车(人力车)";有的是和中国不一样的,如:"洋学堂(教会学校)、洋服(西式服装)、洋烟"。人们就在这些产品的前面加了一个"洋"字,把外国人叫"洋人",把从国外运进来的废旧物品叫"洋垃圾"。随着时代的发展,中西文化交流的频繁,现在这些词语正在慢慢退化。Except for colloquial usage, "洋" is rarely used alone. It is often combined with other morphemes to form compound words. "洋" originated from the development of the society and the era. In the early 20th century, China imported large quantities of foreign products. Some were novelties such as "洋火" (matches) and "洋车" (rickshaw); some were different from those in China, such as "洋学堂" (mission schools), "洋服" (Western attire), "洋烟 (Western cigarette)." "洋" is added before these products to indicate the foreign origin. For example, foreigners are called "洋人," and waste from foreign countries are called "洋垃圾." With more cultural exchanges between China and Western countries in recent years, these words with "洋" are now less frequently used than before.

yǎng 养

用法 Usage:
动词 v.

1. 供给生活资料或生活费用,养活。To provide living expense or necessities.
(1) 全家七口人,全靠父亲一个人工作养家。
(2) 爷爷奶奶辛辛苦苦地养大了孙子孙女。

2. 饲养(动物),培植(花草)。To raise (animals or plants).
(3) 奶奶不喜欢养狗、养猫,就喜欢养花。
(4) 他不喜欢养花草,就喜欢种菜、种瓜果。

3. 生育,生殖。To procreate.
(5) 她已经养了两个孩子,看上去还那么年轻。
(6) 我家花猫还没养过小猫呢。

4. 培养。To develop.
(7) 你们要养成预习、练习、复习的好习惯。
(8) 好习惯坏习惯都是从小养成的。

5. 调养,使身心得到滋补或休息,以利恢复健康、增进精力。To nourish body and mind; to recuperate.
(9) 不要担心学习,你先养好脚上的伤。
(10) 你的病刚好,身体还得养一段时间。

6. 保养,维护。To maintain.
(11) 公路刚建好,路面还要养一段时间。

7. 蓄养(多指头发留着,不剪短)。To wear (one's hair long).
(12) 你的头发养得那么长,洗起来方便吗?

8. 扶植,扶助。To foster; to support.
(13) 以畅销书养学术著作的出版非常好。
(14) 以农养牧、以副养农是促进农业、牧业的好办法。

9. 领养(非亲生的、抚养性质的)。如:"养子、养女、养父、养母"等。To adopt (not related by blood), as in "养子,养女,养父,养母."

说明 Notes:

关于"养成"一词要注意以下几点:Here are a few things to note about the usage of "养成":

1. "养"做动词第四种用法,是"养"后面带补语"成",表示在一定的条件、环境下生成(某种习惯、性情、品行等)的意思,如例(7)(8)。When followed by the complement "成," "养" means to develop habits, characteristics, or dispositions under certain conditions as seen in (7) and (8).

2. "养成"常与"习惯、爱好、性格、品行、脾气、脾性、品德、作风、学风"等名词搭配使用。"养成" is often used with nouns such as "习惯,爱好,性格,品行,脾气,脾性,品德,作风,学风."

3. "养成"这个动词具有动作的持续性,表示是随着时间的推移逐渐出现结果的过程。常常受"慢慢、渐渐、从……开始、从小、长期、最后"等副词的修饰。*As a verb indicating continuity of actions,* "养成" *describes the gradual process leading to a result as time goes by. It is often modified by adverbs such as* "慢慢,渐渐,从...开始,从小,长期,最后."

(15) 从小学开始,他就养成了每天早上朗读的习惯。

(16) 在农村,他渐渐养成了不怕艰苦的性格。

yàopǐn 药品 →P540"药物"

用法 Usage:
名词 n.

药物和化学试剂的合称,多经过人工合成。*The general term for medicine and chemical reagent, often artificially synthesized.*

(1) 姐姐从北京买回来的药品是给奶奶治病的。

(2) 那家药品公司给灾区送去了一卡车的药物。

yàowù 药物 →P540"药品"

用法 Usage:
名词 n.

能防治疾病、病虫害等的物质,药的总称。*The general term for medicine or substance that treats illnesses or helps with pest control.*

(1) 通过药物治疗,他的体温终于正常了。

(2) 中药都是采用天然药物制成的。

说明 Notes:

"药品"和"药物"与词义比较抽象、概括性、可分类性强的词语搭配时,可以替换,如"化学药品/药物、放射性药品/药物、有毒药品/药物"等。"药品" *and* "药物" *are interchangeable when used with abstract words with characteristics of generality and classification such as* "化学药品/药物,放射性药品/药物,有毒药品/药物."

它们的区别是:*The differences are as follows:*

1. "药品"的词义一般指经过人工生产制成的药物,具有产品性质,富有各种实物形态。"药物"可有天然的和人工生产的,词义具有概括性、可分类性的特点,比较抽象。"药品" *often refers to artificially synthesized medicine with physical objects as products.* "药物" *can be natural or artificially synthesized. The lexical meaning is more abstract than* "药品" *with characteristics of generality and classification.*

2. "药物"多与词义比较抽象的词语搭配,如"天然药物、辅助药物、药物研究、药物治疗、药物的疗效"等。"药品"使用时,在句子中必定含有表示生产制造、产品形状、买卖等语义。所以"药品"和"药物"一般不能任意替换。"药物" *is often used with abstract nouns such as* "天然药物,辅助药物,药物研究,药物治疗,药物的疗效." "药品" *is used in sentences with meanings of production, shape of products or transactions related to medicine.* "药品" *and* "药物" *are generally not interchangeable.*

(3) * 绝大多数中药是天然药品。

(4) 绝大多数中药是天然药物。

(5) * 这几种药物都是华东制药厂生产的。

(6) 这几种药品都是华东制药厂生产的。

yào 要 →P511"想"

用法 Usage:
动词 v.

1. 希望得到或保持。可以直接带名词性宾语。*To hope to obtain or maintain. It can be directly followed by a noun as an object.*

(1) 我要一杯可乐,他要一杯咖啡。

(2) 他一直都想要一台笔记本电脑。

2. 向别人索取。可以带"了、过",可以直接带名词性宾语。*To ask for something from others. It can be followed by* "了,过," *and by a noun as an object.*

(3) 昨天我向姐姐要了一百块钱。

(4) 他向我要过你的手机号码。

3. 请求,要求。To request; to demand.

(5) 妈妈要孩子晚上八点前一定到家。

(6) 老师要我回答这个问题。

4. 需要。"要"的后面常带表示"时间、金钱"等名词的数量词。To need; to take. It is often followed by a quantifier modifying nouns such as "时间,金钱."

(7) 北京到上海坐火车只要六个小时。

(8) 一双鞋要一千多元,太贵了!

助动词 aux. v.

1. 应该,必须,相当于"得(děi)"。句中语义含有合情合理的意思。否定式为"不要"(也可以用"别"),多用于劝阻或禁止。前面可加"应该、必须、得(děi)"等。Must, should. It is similar to "得(děi)." The sentence with "要" in this context implies being reasonable. The negative form is "不要" or "别," which is often used for dissuasion or prohibition. It can be preceded by "应该,必须,得(děi)."

(9) 为了自己,我也得要好好学习。

(10) 你刚吃过饭,现在不要去跑步。

2. 表示做某事的意志,常指一种打算。"要"的前面可加"想、打算"。否定式为"不想、不愿意"不能说"不要"。To indicate the will for doing something, often related to a plan. It can be preceded by "想,打算." The negative form is "不想,不愿意," rather than "不要."

(11) 我要跟朋友一起去旅行。(否定 Negative form: 我不想跟朋友一起去旅行。)

(12) 我打算要参加玛丽的婚礼。

3. 将要。前面常用"快、就"等修饰,后面常有"了"。用于正反问句时,用"是不是要"格式。Shall; will; to be going to. It is often preceded by "快,就" and followed by "了." For the A-not-A type of questions, it takes the form of "是不是要."

(13) 天快要下雨了,我们走吧!

(14) 是不是要期末考试了?

4. 表示可能。否定式为"不会",不能说"不要"。用于正反问句时,用"是不是要"格式。Shall; will. It is used to indicate a possibility. The negative form is "不会" rather than "不要." For the A-not-A type of questions, it takes the form of "是不是要."

(15) 他大约要在中国待两年。

(16) 他不会在中国待两年。

(17) 他是不是要在中国待两年?

5. 表示估计,用在比较句中。"要"可以用在"比……"的前后,也可以用在"得"后面。用于正反问句时,用"是不是要"的格式。Might; must. Used in comparative sentences, "要" can either precede or follow "比…." It may also follow "得." For the A-not-A type of questions, it takes the form of "是不是要."

(18) 高铁要比汽车快得多。

(19) 高铁比汽车要快得多。

(20) 如果坐高铁,得要早一点。

(21) 坐飞机是不是要比坐高铁快得多?

连词 conj.

1. 表示假设,相当于"要是",多用于口语。"要"可以连接谓语或小句,可以直接带名词(代词),可以带"不是"。If; suppose; in case. It is used to indicate a hypothesis. Similar to "要是," it is often used colloquially, and can be followed by a predicate, a clause, a noun/pronoun, or "不是."

(22) 你明天要不去,我也不去了。

(23) 要能去巴黎看一场时装表演,那真太幸运了!

(24) 你老师要看到这样的作业,非让你重做不可!

(25) 要不是脚伤不能走路,我一定自己去。

2. 用在选择复句中,表示非此即彼。用于口语。"要(么)"后常常与"就"连用。表示这个意义时,"要么"用得多一些。Used in selective complex sentences, it means " either … or …" Used colloquially, it often takes the form of "要么" and is often used with "就."

(26) 要么就在家看电影,要么就出去逛街,你来决定。

(27) 她的业余生活很简单，要么看书，要么画画。

说明 Notes：

1. 使用"要"还要注意："要" has additional usages as follows:

①"要"做助动词时，表示做某件事的意志，一般不单独回答问题。When used as a verb, "要" shows one's will to do something. It usually does not stand alone as a response.

(28) A：你下周要去旅行吗？
　　　B：要去。

②"要"还有形容词用法，表示重要、简要的意思。When used as an adjective, "要" means important or concise.

(29) 大家快到我的宿舍来，我有要事相告。

(30) 下面我再把今天上课的要点重复一下。

③"要"还有一个读音是"yāo"，用于"要求、要挟、要功"等词语。"要" is pronounced as "yāo" in words such as "要求，要挟，要功."

2. "要"和"想"都可以用作助动词。"要" and "想" can both be auxiliary verbs.

它们的区别是：Their differences are as follows:

①"想"做助动词只有一个义项。"要"做助动词有五个义项。"想"和"要"只有在表示做某事的意愿时，意思才相近，但词义深浅程度不同。"想"着重表示一种愿望、一种打算。"要"着重表示做某件事的意志，是一种既定的要求。When used as an auxiliary verb, "想" has only one meaning whereas "要" has five meanings. The two words are only similar in meaning when indicating the will to do something, but the semantic degrees are different. "想" emphasizes a desire or a plan. "要" emphasizes one's resolution in doing something, which is an established requirement.

(31) 星期天我想去看电影。（表示一种想法，还没最后定下 A thought with no finalized plan）

(32) 星期天我要去看电影。（已经定下要看 With a finalized plan）

②"想"可受程度副词的修饰。"要"一般只受表示"意志坚定、决心不变"之意的副词如"非、偏、一定"等的修饰。能构成"非要……不可"的格式，表示坚定不变、不可动摇的决心。"想" can be modified by a degree adverb. "要" can only be modified by certain adverbs indicating a strong resolution such as "非，偏，一定." The fixed structure of "非要…不可" indicates an unshakable resolution.

(33) 他很想尝一下那家饭店的西餐。

(34) 他非要尝一下那家饭店的西餐不可。

③"想"和"要"做助动词的否定形式都是在前面加"不"，但是句子语义和使用范围有所不同。"不想"表示没有再做某件事的意愿。Although the negative form of "想" and "要" as auxiliary verbs is to add "不" in front, the meaning of the sentences and the range of application are different. "不想" indicates no inclination to do something.

"不要"则有三种语义和使用范围："不要" has three meanings and applications as follows:

一是常常用于"要什么、不要什么"带有选择意义的句子里。Used in sentences with selective words such as "要什么，不要什么."

(35) 他不要咖啡，要红茶。

二是"不要"相当于"别"，在第二人称或第三人称句子，表示禁止或劝阻的意思。Same as "别," it is used in second-person or third-person sentences to show prohibition or dissuasion.

(36) 你不要在家里抽烟！对孩子不好。

三是用于第一人称句子，如果否定原来的意愿，不能用"不要"，而是用"不想"进行否定。When negating in a first-person sentence, "不想" rather than "不要" is used.

(37) A：今天晚上我要去看电影。你要去看吗？
　　　B：今天晚上我不想看。

④"要"有形容词用法。"想"没有。"要"

can be used as an adjective but "想" cannot.

yàobù 要不 →P50"不然"、P543"要不然"

用法 Usage:

连词 conj.

1. 如果不这样,不然,否则。表示假设,引进表示结果或结论的小句,句中常有"就"。和"要不然"可以互换,多用于口语。*If not so; otherwise. Indicating a hypothesis, "要不" introduces a clause with a result or conclusion. It is often interchangeable with "就" and "要不然" in colloquial usage.*

(1) 快走吧,要不就迟到了!

(2) 赶快复习吧,要不/要不然 HSK 考试就通不过。

2. 要么,用在选择复句中,表示非此即彼。*Used in selective clauses, it means "either ... or."*

(3) 要不你去,要不我去,总之我们俩要有一个人去。

(4) 要不坐高铁,要不坐飞机,你决定吧。

说明 Notes:

"要不"和"不然"都可以连接假设关系的句子,引出如果不是这样,可能会产生与上文相反的结果;都可以连接选择关系的句子,表示对上文作假定性否定,下文作出另一选择,表示"如果不是这样,那就……"的意思,后一分句常用"就"呼应;"要不"和"不然"后面都可带"……的话",用来加强假设语气。*"要不" and "不然" can both link clauses with hypothetical relations, meaning that a result contrary to the hypothesis would otherwise emerge. Both words can link selective clauses, meaning "if not so, then." There is often "就" in the second clause to correspond with "要不" or "不然." Both words can be followed by "... 的话" to reinforce the hypothetical tone.*

(5) 你最好马上到医院检查一下,要不/不然真的发烧就麻烦了。

(6) 他上街可能去银行,要不/不然就是去书店。

它们的区别是:*Their differences are as follows:*

1. "要不"多用于口语。"不然"多用于书面语。"要不"的语气比"不然"委婉些。*"要不" is often used colloquially. "不然" is often used in written language. The tone of "要不" is more euphemistic than "不然."*

2. 表示选择关系时,"不然"前面可以加上"再"或"要",构成"再不然""要不然"的格式。"要不"不能这么用。*When indicating a selective relationship, "不然" can be preceded by "再" or "要" to form words such as "再不然" or "要不然." "要不" has no such usage.*

(7) 他上街可能去银行,再/要不然就是去书店。

3. "不然"除了连词的用法以外,还有形容词性用法,表示"不是这样"的意思,可做谓语。"要不"没有这一用法。*In addition to a conjunction, "不然" can also be used as an adjective meaning "not so," which can be used as a predicate. "要不" has no such usage.*

(8) 大家以为我很能喝酒,其实不然。

yàobùrán 要不然 →P543"要不"

用法 Usage:

连词 conj.

用法基本上与"要不"相同,多用于口语,其中"不"读轻声。*The usage of "要不然" is very similar to "要不." It is mostly used colloquially. "不" is pronounced with a neutral tone.*

(1) 你快去给她道个歉,要不然她真的生气了。

(2) 赶紧吃吧,要不然凉了,味道就不好了。

说明 Notes:

"要不然"和"要不"的区别是:*The differences between "要不然" and "要不" are as follows:*

1. "要不然"的假设语气比"要不"重。"要不然" carries a heavier hypothetical tone than

"要不."

2. "要不"还可以表示二者选一的选择关系。"要不然"不能。"要不" can indicate a selective relationship between the two. "要不然" has no such usage.

yàohǎo 要好

用法 Usage:

形容词 a.

1. 指感情融洽，亲密。Referring to a harmonious or close relationship.

(1) 他们两家很要好，经常带着孩子在一起玩儿。

(2) 她是我非常要好的一个朋友。

2. 努力求好，力求上进。Highly motivated for better performance.

(3) 这孩子很要好，每天学习都很自觉。

(4) 那是个不要好的人，不能向他学。

yàoshi 要是 →P398"如果"

用法 Usage:

连词 conj.

如果，如果是。连接表示假设关系的句子。多用于口语，常用在前面的分句，后面分句中常有副词"就"相呼应。可以构成"要是……的话"的格式。If; if so. Often used colloquially to connect clauses with a hypothetical relationship. "要是" or "要是...的话" is usually used in the first cause, and "就" is often used in the second clause.

(1) 要是明天不下雨，我们就去西湖。

(2) 她要是去的话，我就去。

说明 Notes:

1. 使用"要是"，要注意以下几点：When using "要是," one must pay attention to the following aspects:

① 在对话中，"要是"可以用在疑问句，句末常用"呢"。"要是" can be used in a question in a dialogue, which often ends with "呢."

(3) 要是他不愿意跟我一起去呢？

② 注意分清楚"要+是"跟连词"要是"的用法。"要+是"中的"要"，是"如果"的意思，"是"是这个句子的动词，后面一般带名词。"要是"后面一般带分句或句子。"要+是" and "要是" as a conjunction have different meanings and usage. The "要" in the "要+是" structure means "if." "是" is the verb of the sentence, which is usually followed by a noun. "要是" is usually followed by a clause or a sentence.

(4) 我要是律师，在法律上就可以给你很大帮助。

(5) 我要是学法律，以后在法律上可以给你很大帮助。

2. "要是"和"如果"的区别是：与"如果"相比，"要是"多用于口语；"要是"后面的内容，选定性比"如果"稍强。The difference between "要是" and "如果" is that, compared with "如果," "要是" is more often used colloquially.

yàosù 要素

用法 Usage:

名词 n.

构成事物的必要因素。Essential factor(s); key element(s).

(1) 语音四要素有音高、音长、音重和音色。

(2) 你知道一个人成功的要素是什么吗？

yě 也 →P116"都"

用法 Usage:

副词 ad.

1. 表示两件事相同。"也"可用在前后两个分句，或只用在后一个分句。Also; too; as well; either. Indicating that one is the same as the other, "也" can appear either in both clauses or only in the second clause.

(1) 你一个人来也可以，你们一起来也可以。

(2) 他妈妈是红头发，他也是红头发。

2. 表示做了好几件事，有行为动作累计的意味。As well as, indicating that several things are done with the accumulation of action.

句式有：The sentence structures are as follows:

① 主语相同,谓语不同。The same subject but different predicates.

(3) 周末,我们也学习,也看电视。

(4) 你学外语要练语法,也要练口语,也要练听力。

② 主语不同,谓语也不同。Different subjects and different predicates.

(5) 天亮了,我们也该走了。

(6) 他妈妈去上班了,他也去学校了。

③ 主语和谓语相同,宾语不同。宾语可以前置。The same subject and same predicate but different objects. The object can be placed before the subject.

(7) 英语我也会说,法语我也会说。

(8) 弟弟也会打篮球,也会打羽毛球。

④ 主语、谓语相同,状语不同。The same subject and same predicate but different adverbials.

(9) 上海他去年也去过,今年也去过。

(10) 我对这个城市也喜欢,也不喜欢。

3. 表示无论假设成立不成立,结果都一样。Indicating the same result will happen whether the hypothesis stands or not.

句式有：The sentence structures are as follows:

① "虽然(尽管、宁可、即使等)……也……",有时也可以不用连词。It is often used in structure such as "虽然(尽管、宁可、即使等)…也…." Sometimes the conjunction may be omitted.

(11) 即使妈妈不同意,我也要去。

(12) 你不说我也知道。

② "也"前面表示任指的指代词,有"无论……"的意思,"也"后面多数是否定式。"也" refers to the general reference word before it with the meaning of "regardless." It is usually followed by a negative form.

(13) 她说这个暑假就在家待着,哪儿也不去。

(14) 他最近身体不舒服,什么也不想吃。

③ "也"的前后重复同一动词,有"纵然"或"无论怎么"的意思,"也"后面的动词常带结果补语、趋向补语或其他附带成分。The same verb is used before and after "也," meaning "even if" or "regardless." The verb after "也" is often followed by other elements such as a resultative complement or directional complement.

(15) 这件衣服洗也洗不干净,丢掉算了。

(16) 他的胃病太严重,吃药也吃不好了。

④ "也"前面有某些副词,隐含"无论"的意思。Some adverbs before "也" imply the meaning of "regardless."

(17) 他永远也不会知道这件事的真实情况了。

(18) 反正我也是你最要好的朋友,你不帮我帮谁啊?

⑤ "再/最/顶多/至少……也……"。Often used in a structure such as "再/最/顶多/至少…也…."

(19) 他再怎么努力也没得过好成绩。

(20) 这个箱子顶多也就十斤,你怎么会拿不动?

4. 表示"甚至"。加强语气,相当于"连……也……"。前面可以是名词、数量词、数量词+名词,其中数词限于"一",多用于"否定句"。Even (to strengthen the tone). It is the same as "连…也…." And it can be preceded by a noun, a quantifier, or quantifier+noun. The numeral can only be "一." This structure is usually used in negative sentences.

(21) 这几天在公司连续加班,一次家也没回。

(22) 他学习非常努力,连一天假也没请过。

5. 表示委婉的语气。"也"后面常常带有其他副词。没有"也"字,语气就显得直率,甚至生硬。Indicating a euphemistic tone. "也" is

often followed by another adverb. Without "也," the tone of the sentence sounds direct or even rigid.

(23) 他的经济状况虽然不好,但也不像你说的这么穷吧!

(24) 你也太没礼貌了,快跟人家道歉。

说明 Notes:

1. 使用"也",要注意:When using "也," one must pay attention to the following aspects:

① "也"在古汉语中,也可作助动词,表示判断、解释的语气,如:"孔子,鲁国人也。"表示疑问或反诘的语气,如:"孔子,何许人也?"表示句中停顿,如:"听其言也,知其心。" In classic Chinese, "也" can be used as an auxiliary verb indicating judgment or explanation as in "孔子,鲁国人也。" Or an interrogative question as in "孔子,何许人也?" Or a pause in the sentence as in "听其言也,知其心."

② "也"在现代汉语中的助动词用法是作为结构助词。In modern Chinese, "也" is a structural word when used as an auxiliary verb.

(25) 阿里飞也似的冲过终点,得了第一名。

2. "也"前面是表示任指的指代词,句子含有"无论……"的意思时,"也"和"都"可以替换。"也"表示"甚至",加强语气,相当于"连……也……"时,"也"可以与"都"替换。"也" is preceded by a general reference word. With the meaning of "regardless," "也" and "都" are interchangeable. Meaning "even," "也" strengthens the tone. When it means the same as "连…也…," "也" and "都" are interchangeable.

它们的区别是:Their differences are as follows:

① "都"没有"也"的其他用法。"都" does not have other usages like "也."

② 在同一个句子里,"也"用在"都"的前面。Within the same sentence, "也" precedes "都."

(26) 我们不去,他们也都不去。

yěhǎo 也好

用法 Usage:
助词 aux.

1. 表示允许、赞成,也罢(语气较轻)的意思。To show permission, approval or the "so be it" attitude (with a lighter tone).

(1) 不跟他说也好,免得他担心。

(2) 也好,去西安能了解唐代的历史文化。

2. 连用两个(或更多),表示不以某种情况为条件,在任何情况下都是这样。前一分句中常与"无论、不管"呼应,后一句子中常与"也、都"呼应。The usage of two (or more) "也好" in one sentence indicates that the result stays the same regardless of conditions. "无论,不管" is often used in the first clause, and "也,都" is often used in the second clause.

(3) 无论你们来也好,他们来也好,我们都热烈欢迎,热情招待。

(4) 不管你吃也好,不吃也好,谁也不会再给你吃了。

说明 Notes:

1. 在对话中,"也好"可以单独使用,如例(2)。"也好" can stand alone in a conversation as in (2).

2. "也好"的助词用法与副词用法的区别是:"也好"副词用法是两个副词"也"和"好"的并用,相当于"也便于、也可以"的意思。The usage of "也好" as an auxiliary word is different from its usage as an adverb. When used as an adverb, "也好" is the combination of the adverbs "也" and "好," with the same meaning as "以便于,也可以."

(5) 给妈妈打个电话,也好让她知道我们在哪里,免得她担心。

yěxǔ 也许 →P273"可能"

用法 Usage:
副词 ad.

1. 表示估计,有可能,但不很肯定。Possibly

but not quite certain.

(1) 他也许会来,再等等看吧。

(2) 听他的口音,也许是浙江人。

2. 表示说话人有商量的意思,语气比较委婉。句中含有比较的意味。*With a euphemistic tone, the speaker is proposing a topic for discussion. The sentence implies a comparison.*

(3) 我们坐汽车去,也许更快一些。

(4) 你去说这件事,也许他会同意。

3. "也许"能单独回答问题,后面常带"吧",语气比较委婉。常用在口语。*"也许" can be a stand-alone response, which is often followed by "吧." Often used colloquially, it carries a euphemistic tone.*

(5) A：这次考试你能通过吗?

B：也许吧。

(6) A：你明天有时间跟我逛街吗?

B：也许。

说明 Notes:

"也许"和"可能"的副词用法基本相同。*The usage of "也许" and "可能" as adverbs is quite similar.*

它们的区别是：*Their differences are as follows:*

1. "可能"有形容词用法。"也许"只有副词用法。*"可能" can be used as an adjective, but "也许" can only be used as an adverb.*

2. "可能"可以加"性"成为名词,如"可能性"。"也许"不能。*"可能" can be followed by "性" to become a noun "可能性." "也许" has no such usage.*

yèyú 业余

用法 Usage:

形容词 *a.*

1. 工作时间以外的。*Spare-time (not during regular work hours); afterhours.*

(1) 你业余时间做些什么?

(2) 我要去业余学校补习一下英语。

2. 非专业的。*Amateur.*

(3) 她是个业余歌手,但是水平不错。

(4) 他只是个业余作家,本职工作是教师。

yèjiān 夜间 →P547"夜里"

用法 Usage:

名词 *n.*

与白天相对,一般指晚上九十点以后到天亮的一段时间。*Night (from 9-10 pm to sunrise).*

(1) 今天夜间到明天白天都有雨。

(2) 夜间比白天冷得多。

yèlǐ 夜里 →P547"夜间"

用法 Usage:

名词 *n.*

指天黑到天亮的一段时间。多用于口语。*From sunset to sunrise, often used colloquially.*

(1) 一直等到夜里十二点,她才回来。

(2) 半夜里远处传来一声声狗叫的声音。

说明 Notes:

"夜间"和"夜里"一般都指天黑以后,尤其指夜比较深的时候。*"夜间" and "夜里" generally refer to the time after dark, particularly late at night.*

它们的区别是：*Their differences are as follows:*

1. 在语义上,"夜间"着重强调"夜"的时间段。"夜里"着重强调对与白天相反的环境的陈述。*Semantically speaking, "夜间" emphasizes the time period at night, whereas "夜里" emphasizes the opposite of the daytime environment.*

2. "夜间"多用于书面语,说明性比较强。"夜里"适用范围广一些,多用于口语。*"夜间" is often used in written language with a strong sense of illustration. Mostly used colloquially, "夜里" has a wider range of application.*

3. "夜间"和"夜里"都不能受数量词"一个"的修饰。"夜间"除了少数表示日子的名词如"今天、明天、三号、六号"等以外,一般不受别的词语的修饰。"夜里"可受其他词语的修饰,也可受"长、深、半"等单音节词的修饰,如"长夜里、深夜里、半夜里、后半夜里"等。Neither "夜间" nor "夜里" may be modified by "一个." Except for a few nouns indicating dates such as "今天,明天,三号,六号,""夜间" is rarely modified by other words. "夜里" can be modified by other words as well as such monosyllabic words as "长,深,半," as in "长夜里,深夜里,后半夜里."

yèshì 夜市

用法 Usage:
名词 n.

1. 夜间做买卖的市场,营业的时间长短不一。Evening market with varied length of business hours.

(1) 在中国,很多城市都有夜市。
(2) 在夜市能买到很多便宜的东西。

2. 夜间的营业。Evening business.

(3) 他白天上班,晚上还要做夜市。
(4) 有时候夜市的收入比白天上班的还要高。

yèwǎn 夜晚

用法 Usage:
名词 n.

夜间,晚上(与"白天"相对),多用于书面语。多受形容词和表示季节、节日的名词修饰。Night (as opposed to daytime). Mostly used in written language, it is often modified by adjectives and nouns indicating seasons and festivals.

(1) 他经常在夜晚玩游戏,白天睡大觉。
(2) 中秋节的夜晚,月亮又圆又亮。

说明 Notes:

"夜晚"和"晚上"都表示一天中天黑的时间段,都可以受数量词"一个"的修饰,也都能受"今天、明天、昨天、那天、星期天"等表示日子的时间名词修饰。"夜晚" and "晚上" both refer to the time of the day when it is dark. Both of them can be modified by "一个" and nouns indicating dates such as "今天,明天,昨天,那天,星期天."

它们的区别是:Their differences are as follows:

1. "晚上"通常指太阳落了以后到深夜以前的时间,也泛指夜里。"夜晚"通常指从日落到日出这段时间。"晚上" usually refers to the time after the sun goes down until late at night, and also refers to night in general. "夜晚" usually refers to the period from sunset to dawn.

(3) 晚上我要去看一个朋友。
(4) 这注定是一个不平静的夜晚。

2. "晚上"可以受数词"一"的修饰。"夜晚"不可以。"晚上" can be modified by "一" but "夜晚" cannot.

(3) *昨天一夜晚都听见他的咳嗽声。
(4) 昨天一晚上都听见他的咳嗽声。

yī 一

用法 Usage:
数词 num.

1. 数目,最小的正整数。One, the smallest positive integer.

(1) 一加一等于二。

2. 最小的基数,用在量词前,如"一个、一块、一只"等。One, the smallest cardinal number, used before the measure word as in "一个,一块,一只."

3. "一"与后面的具体名词组成数量词修饰后面的名词,表示"整个,全,满"的意思。"一" can form a quantifier with the noun following it to describe the noun after this quantifier, which means "whole" or "full."

(2) 教室里坐了一屋子人。
(3) 他给我一箱子玩具。

4. "这+一+名词(指抽象事物)",表示强调突出。The "这+一+n." structure (referring to an abstract concept) indicates emphasis.

(4) 你说的这一问题非常重要。

(5) 这一办法很好。

5. 用在动词后面。When used after a verb.

① 表示动量。用在动词后,动量词前。Indicating momentum, it appears after a verb and before a word indicting momentum.

(6) 你的妈妈来电话了,要你回家一趟。

(7) 他打了我一拳,现在还痛呢。

② "动词＋一＋下"。表示动作是短暂的、不很费力的。The structure "v.＋一＋下" indicates a short and effortless action.

(8) 我来介绍一下,这是我的中国朋友。

(9) 下课以后你到我办公室来一下。

③ 用在两个重叠的单音节动词之间,表示动作行为是短暂的、不很费力的,或动作是尝试性的。Used between two reduplicated monosyllabic verbs, it indicates a short, effortless or tentative action.

(10) 你尝一尝,这饺子有一种特别的味道。

(11) 请看一看课文的内容!

6. 表示同一的意思,如"一视同仁、一码事、意见不一"等。The same, as in "一视同仁,一码事,意见不一."

副词 ad.

用在动词、形容词前。句式有：When used before a verb or an adjective, it has the following usages:

1. 表示动作变化是突然出现的。Indicating a sudden change in action.

(12) 他被突然一吓,病倒了。

(13) 他的眼前一亮,这不就是他要找的姑娘吗?

2. 表示动作是彻底的或变化是很大的,常出现在书面语的固定结构中。Often used in fixed expressions in written language, it refers to a complete action or a big change.

(14) 他们几个人一会儿工夫,就把桌子上的饭菜一扫而光。

(15) 经过改建,这条马路的面貌焕然一新。

3. 用在"值得"之后,常表示建议做某个动作。Used after "值得," it often indicates a suggestion for an action.

(16) 这电影不错,值得一看。

(17) 那件衣服的样式很气派,值得一买。

否定式用"不"。"不值得"可以略为"不值"。动词一般只用"提"。Negate with "不." "不值得" can be shortened as "不值." This structure usually takes the verb "提."

(18) 这个小问题,不值(得)一提。

4. "一＋形容词、动词/动补结构"出现在承接复句的第一分句,表示前面的动作完成或发生后,紧接着出现的情况或反应。常与副词"就、便"搭配使用。When the structure of "一＋a./v./v.＋complement" is used in the first clause, it means that as soon as the action is completed, the reaction or situation as a result immediately follows. It is often used with an adverb such as "就" and "便."

(19) 听她说完,我鼻子一酸,差点儿掉下泪来。

(20) 一打开窗,屋子里就吹进来一股凉风。

这类用法,也常用于"把"字句。This usage is also found in the "把" structure.

(21) 他们把门一锁,去看电影了。

(22) 他把手一招,大家都跑了过去。

"一＋动词"前面常用"这么",指示前面已经出现过的动作,起承接作用。Often preceded with "这么," the "一＋v." structure refers to an aforementioned action.

(23) 听他这么一介绍,我想起来他是谁了。

(24) 屋子这么一收拾,变得又整齐又干净。

5. "一＋动词/动补结构"出现在假设分句的第一分句,说明要是做了前一个动作,后面一定会出现什么结果。When the structure of "一＋v./v.＋complement" is used in the first clause of a hypothetical sentence, it means that the completion of the first action promises a certain result.

(25) 只要你一说,大家一定会同意。

(26) 如果一摔倒，他的腿一定骨折。

6. 一旦。表示有那么一天或忽然有一天。As soon as; once (something happens in the future).

(27) 一有去城里的汽车，我就打电话给你。

(28) 这些泥墙草房，一发大水肯定被冲走。

说明 Notes：

1. 关于"一"的读音："一" has different tones in different contexts.

① "一"单用或在一词一句末尾，读第一声，如："第一、十一、一一得一"等。"一" is pronounced in the first tone when it stands alone or when it is used at the end of a word or a sentence, as in "第一，十一，一一得一."

② 在第四声前读第二声，如："一半、一共、一下"等。It is pronounced in the second tone when it precedes a character pronounced in the fourth tone, as in "一半，一共，一下."

③ 在第一声、第二声、第三声前读第四声。如："一天、一年、一点、一场"等。It is pronounced in the fourth tone when it precedes a character pronounced in the first, second, or third tone, as in "一天，一年，一点，一场."

2. "一+动词/形容词"的用法："一"一般都用在句子的第一部分中，在语义上不完整，后面必定要跟后续句子。后续句子的主语可以与第一部分的主语相同，也可以不同。当主语相同时，后面句子的谓语动词应该是前面部分主语发出的。The usage of the "一 + v./a." structure follows the following rules: Usually used in the first clause, the structure with "一" is incomplete in terms of semantic meaning and therefore must be followed by another clause. The second clause can share the same subject as the first clause or carry a different subject. When the two clauses share one subject, the action in the second clause is completed by the same subject.

(29) 他把手一招，我们都跟了上去。

(30) 他把手一招，回头就走了。

yībǎshǒu 一把手

用法 Usage：

1. 在领导班子成员中的第一负责人（依次为二把手、三把手等）。The head of the leadership team (followed by "二把手，三把手").

(1) 他是我们公司的一把手。

2. 作为参加活动的重要一员。An important member of a program or project.

(2) 我们共同完成这个工程，你也算上一把手。

3. 能干的人，也说"一把好手"。A competent person (the same as "一把好手").

(3) 别看她是个小女孩，干起活来可是个一把手/好手呢。

说明 Notes：

在口语里，第一种用法中的"一"念为第一声。第二、第三用法中的"一"多念为第四声。In colloquial usage, "一" is pronounced in the first tone in the first example, and the fourth tone in the second and third examples above.

yī……jiù…… 一……就……

用法 Usage：

1. 前后连接两个不同的动词，前一个动作完成或情况出现后，紧接着发生另外一个动作或情况，表示两事时间上前后紧接着。两事可以是同一主语，也可以是不同的主语。Connecting two different verbs. As soon as one action or situation occurs, another action or situation follows. The two events can have the same subject or different subjects.

(1) 一到周末，我们就去附近的农村旅游。

(2) 这个句子老师一讲我们就明白了。

2. 前后连接两个不同的动词，表示如果有前一动作条件或原因，紧接着就会出现某种结果。前后可以是同一主语，也可以是不同的主语。Connecting two different verbs. If one action or situation occurs, a certain result will

follow. The two events can have the same subject or different subjects.

(3) 他不会喝酒,一喝酒就脸红。

(4) 我一感冒就要头疼、咳嗽。

3. 前后连接两个相同的动词,前后为同一个主语。后一动词常带结果补语、趋向补语或数量短语,表示动作一旦发生,就会出现某种结果,达到某种较高的程度,持续较长时间等。Connecting two identical verbs with the same subject. The second verb is often followed by a resultative complement, directional complement, or quantifier phrase. It means that once the situation occurs, a certain result will follow, which will usually reach a high degree or last a long time.

(5) 他一跑就跑出了100米的世界纪录。

(6) 我们一聊就聊到了吃午饭的时候。

4. "一……就……"的格式还可以用"一……就(是)……"的格式表示,"就(是)"后面常常是表示时间长度、事物数量的词语。"一…就…" sometimes can be used as "一…就(是)…" "就(是)" is often followed by a word indicating a length of time.

(7) 她在图书馆里一坐就是一天。

(8) 他们都喜欢喝啤酒,每个人一喝就是三四瓶。

说明 Notes:

1. "一……就……"使用时要求第一个动作完成后紧接着出现后面的动作或者结果,所以"一"后面的动词,必定有结果,否则就会出现错句。When "一…就…" is used, the second action or result immediately follows the first action. Therefore, the verb after "一" must have a result. Otherwise a grammatical error occurs.

(9) *妹妹的狗一不看妹妹就叫。

(10) 妹妹的狗一看不到妹妹就要叫。

(11) *今天晚上,我一吃晚饭就去教室。

(12) 今天晚上,我一吃完晚饭就去教室。

2. "一……就……"可以表示过去发生的情况,也可以表示现在或将来发生的情况。"一…就…" can refer to a past, present or future situation.

(13) 昨天我一接到妈妈的电话就到妹妹那儿去了。

(14) 我一接到妈妈的电话就到你这儿来了。有什么事吗?

(15) 明天你一接到妈妈的电话就到妹妹那儿去。

3. 本词条例句中"一"的具体读音,根据后面词语的声调进行变化。参见 P548"一"。The specific pronunciation of "一" in the example sentences changes according to the tone of the following words. See "一" on page 548.

yīliú 一流

用法 Usage:

名词 n.

同一类;一类。Of the same category or group.

(1) 他们是同一流的,都是爱好旅游的人。

(2) 他是属于新派一流的人物。

形容词 a.

第一等的。First-rate; top-rate.

(3) 他考上了全国的一流大学,这几天可高兴了。

(4) 她的英语口语水平是一流的。

说明 Notes:

"一流"的形容词用法,依次是"二流、三流"等。When used as an adjective, "二流,三流" follow "一流" based on the order of ranking.

(5) 她现在只是个三流演员。

yījiù 依旧 →P395"仍旧"、P553"依然"

用法 Usage:

动词 v.

依然,照旧,跟过去一样。To remain the same as before.

(1) 她是个舞蹈演员,虽然五十多岁了,但是身材依旧。

(2) 这里景物依旧，十几年都没什么变化。

副词 *ad.*

仍旧。Still.

(3) 虽然离婚了，他们俩依旧保持着联系。

(4) 下课后，别人都走了，只有他依旧坐在教室里。

说明 Notes：

"仍旧"和"依旧"都表示保持原样不变，或发生变化后，又恢复了原样。"仍旧" and "依旧" both mean to remain the same as before, or to resume the original form after a change has occurred.

它们的区别是：Their differences are as follows:

1. "仍旧"常用于表示转折关系的后一个分句中，句子前常有"但、但是、可"等与之呼应。"依旧"一般没有"但、但是、可"等与之呼应。如例(3)(4)。"仍旧" is often used in the second clause indicating a turn, which is usually preceded by a clause with words such as "但,但是,可." "依旧" is usually not used with these words as in (3) and (4).

2. "仍旧"通用于口语和书面语。"依旧"多用于书面语。"仍旧" can be used both colloquially or in written language. "依旧" is generally used in written language.

3. "依旧"还有形容词用法，形容事物保持原样不变。"仍旧"没有形容词用法。"依旧" can also be used as an adjective with the meaning of keeping the original form unchanged. "仍旧" cannot be used as an adjective.

yījù 依据 →P166"根据"、P554"依照"

用法 Usage：

动词 *v.*

以某种事物为依托或根据。To be based on.

(1) 你依据什么下这样的结论？

(2) 依据客观事实，才能做出正确判断。

名词 *n.*

作为论断前提或言行基础的事物。The basis of a conclusion or certain behavior.

(3) 以事实为依据，以法律为准绳。

(4) 你选这个论文题目的依据是什么？

介词 *prep.*

表示某种事物作为论断的前提或言行的基础。According to; in accordance with; on the basis of; judging by.

(5) 依据学生的建议，我们要增加两门选修课。

(6) 依据文物专家的鉴定，这是唐代的绘画。

说明 Notes：

"依据"和"根据"的用法基本相同。"依据" and "根据" have quite similar usage.

它们的区别是：Their differences are as follows:

1. 在语义上，"根据"强调不容置疑的事实前提和出发点。"依据"强调被依托的事物。In terms of the semantic meaning, "根据" emphasizes the unquestionable premise, whereas "依据" emphasizes the basis.

(7) 根据已有的实际病例，这种病是能够治好的。

(8) 依据科学记载，这种病是能够治好的。

2. "根据"通用于口语和书面语。"依据"多用于法令文件、科技、调查等方面的书面语。"根据" can be used both colloquially and in written language. "依据" is usually used in written language related to laws and regulations, technology or investigation.

yīkào 依靠 →P553"依赖"

用法 Usage：

动词 *v.*

指望（某种人或事物来达到一定的目的）。To depend on (someone or something to achieve certain objectives).

(1) 发展经济更多地要依靠创新。

(2) 她从小就很独立，从不依靠别人。

名词 n.

可以指望的人或东西。People or things to depend on.

（3）他从小就没有父母，社会和政府就是他成长的依靠。

（4）无论是物质还是精神，老人的依靠就是他的女儿。

yīlài 依赖 →P552"依靠"

用法 Usage:

动词 v.

1. 依靠某种人或事物而不能自立或自给。To be dependent on someone or something, not self-sufficient.

（1）自己的事情自己做，不要总依赖别人。

（2）她睡眠不好，必须依赖安眠药才能睡着。

2. 各个事物或现象互为条件而不可分离。(Of things or phenomena) to be dependent on each other.

（3）国家与国家之间的经济关系是相互依赖、互相支持的。

（4）农村和城市是互相依赖、互相促进的两大社会区域。

说明 Notes:

"依靠"和"依赖"的区别是：The differences between "依靠" and "依赖" are as follows:

1. "依靠"既可做动词，又可做名词。"依赖"只能做动词用。"依靠" can be used as a verb or a noun. "依赖" can only be used as a verb.

2. "依靠"的对象是别的人或事物，也可以是自身的力量。"依赖"的对象只能是别人或事物。The object of "依靠" can be someone or something else, or one's own power. The object of "依赖" can only be someone or something else.

3. "依赖"可以表示事物或现象互为条件而不可分离。"依靠"无此种用法。"依赖" can refer to things or phenomena being dependent on each other. "依靠" has no such usage.

yīrán 依然 →P395"仍然"、P551"依旧"

用法 Usage:

副词 ad.

表示动作行为、形状情况等保持不变或恢复到原来的样子，跟过去一样，依旧。Referring to the unchanged behavior or situation.

（1）三十年过去了，她依然年轻美丽。

（2）八十多岁的老人依然每天写作两个小时。

说明 Notes:

1. "依然"使用时有两种句式：一种是由两个分句组成，一个分句交代某种环境或条件，另一个分句表示在那样的环境和条件下，情况依然如此，如例（1）。另一种句式是只有一个句子，并不交代某种环境或条件，但可以体会到其中的语境条件，如例（2）。"依然" can be used in two sentence structures. The first one consists of two clauses, with one introducing a certain environment or condition and the other describing that the situation remains unchanged regardless of the environment or condition as in (1). The second sentence structure has only one sentence. It does not introduce the environment or condition, which can be inferred from the context as seen in (2).

2. "依然"和"依旧"的用法基本相同。The usage of "依然" and "依旧" is quite similar.

它们的区别是："依旧"与"依然"意思相同，但强调的重点不同。"依旧"强调照旧，岁月变化，仍然保持旧时模样。"依然"强调继续保持原来模样。Their differences are as follows: Although the two words have similar meaning, their emphases are different. "依旧" emphasizes the unchanged situation as time goes by. "依然" emphasizes the continuation of the situation.

3. "依然"和"仍然"都是副词，意思相同，但是"依然"书面语色彩较"仍然"强些。"依然"and"仍然"are adverbs with the same meaning. "依然" carries a stronger literary sense than "仍然."

yīzhào 依照 →P5"按照"、P552"依据"

用法 Usage:

动词 v.

依从，听从。以某事物为根据照着进行。后面必带名词宾语。To obey, to follow suit (has to be followed by a noun object).

（1）我们办事向来都是依照法律法规。

介词 prep.

按照。引进动作行为的根据或凭借，以某事物为标准照着进行。不能用在单音节名词前。To be based on. "依照" introduces the basis of an action or behavior. It cannot be used before a monosyllabic noun.

（2）依照辈分，你应该叫我"伯伯"。

（3）博物馆依照原件制作了复制品进行展出。

说明 Notes:

1. "依照"和"按照"的区别是：The differences between "依照" and "按照" are as follows:

①"依照"和"按照"组成的介词结构一般用在句首。在要求别人怎么做的祈使句中，一般不用"依照"，常常用"按照"。The prepositional structure with "依照" or "按照" is usually placed at the beginning of a sentence. Imperative sentences generally use "按照" rather than "依照."

②"依照"的宾语多为国家法律规定、政府军队文告等带有比较庄重色彩的内容。"按照"的宾语可以是上级的指示、决定、方针，也可以是方法、计划、情况、要求等具体内容。The objects of "依照" are usually national laws and regulations or government and military reports; they carry a sense of solemnity. The objects of "按照" can be instructions, decisions or policies from higher authorities, or specific content such as methods, plans, conditions or requirements.

③"依照"多用于书面语。"按照"使用的范围比较广，带有口语色彩，适用于各种语体。"依照" is usually used in written language. More often used colloquially, "按照" has a wider range of application and can be used in various styles of language.

2. "依照"和"依据"都有动词和介词用法。"依照" and "依据" can both be used as a verb or preposition.

它们的区别是：Their differences are as follows:

①"依照"的语义强调依从、按照已有的样本、情况和规定做另一件事情。"依据"强调某种是结论的前提，或某种语言行动的基础。"依照" emphasizes following the existing model, conditions or rules while working on something similar. "依据" emphasizes on the premise of a conclusion or the basis of an action or behavior.

（4）请你依照那个句子的结构，再造一个句子。

（5）依据你考试的情况，你可以到中级班学习。

②"依照"的对象可以是抽象事物，也可以是具体事物。"依据"的对象一般是抽象事物。The object of "依照" can be either abstract or concrete. The object of "依据" is usually abstract.

③"依据"有名词用法，可以做宾语。"依照"无此种用法。"依据" can be used as a noun and can serve as the object. "依照" has no such usage.

3. 注意以下句子：Pay attention to the following errors:

（6）*这个规定，我们可以依照。

（7）我们可以依据这个规定。

（8）*我们会依照钱买东西的。

（9）我们会依照钱数买东西的。

yídài 一代

用法 Usage:

名词 *n.*

1. 一个朝代。*A dynasty.*

(1) 唐朝,这一代创作的诗歌有五万多首。

(2) 成吉思汗是一代天骄,了不起的英雄。

2. 一个时代。*An era.*

(3) 改革开放这一代给年轻人创业提供了良好的条件。

3. 指同一辈分或同一时代的人。*People in the same generation or era.*

(4) 我和他是同一代出生的年轻人。

(5) 我们这一代人的生活跟你们是完全不一样的。

yídàn 一旦 →P482"万一"

用法 Usage:

名词 *n.*

一天之间,形容时间较短。*Within one day (describing a short span of time).*

(1) 发生那件事后,他在大家心中的形象就毁于一旦了。

副词 *ad.*

有一天(如果有一天或忽然有一天),表示不确定的时间。*Someday (if there is a day, or suddenly the day comes), indicating an uncertain time in the future.*

(2) 我们在一起学习了两年,一旦分开,怎么会不想念呢?

(3) 参加保险,一旦发生了意外,就会有所补偿。

说明 Notes:

"一旦"和"万一"的区别是:*The differences between "一旦" and "万一" are as follows:*

1. "一旦"和"万一"都有副词用法,可以互相替换,但是语义侧重点不一样。"一旦"侧重在发生事情时间的不确定性。"万一"侧重在事情发生的可能性。*"一旦" and "万一" can both be used as an adverb and can be interchangeable, but the two words have different semantic emphases. "一旦" emphasizes the uncertain time of a potential event. "万一" emphasizes the possibility of an event.*

2. "一旦"和"万一"都是名词,但词义完全不同。*When "一旦" and "万一" are used as a noun, they have completely different meanings.*

yídào 一道 →P581"一同"

用法 Usage:

副词 *ad.*

表示共同在一处,一起,一路,一同。有时写成"一道儿"。多用于南方人的口语中。*At the same place; on the same route; together. Sometimes it is written as "一道儿." It is often used colloquially in the south.*

(1) 我昨天是和王芳一道回家的。

(2) 他这个人很好,跟他一道工作很快乐。

(3) 今天下午我跟玛丽一道在图书馆。

说明 Notes:

"一道"如果表示一起去某地,表示两层意思:一是"一起"的意思,二是回家的路是相同的,一路,如例(1)。*When it means to go to a place together, "一道" has two meanings, "together" or "on the same route" as in (1).*

yídìng 一定 →P26"必定"、P277"肯定"

用法 Usage:

形容词 *a.*

1. 规定的,确定的。*Certain; regulatory.*

(1) 到国外留学要按照一定的规章制度办事。

(2) 支付宝付钱要按照一定的程序操作。

2. 固定不变,必然的。*Fixed.*

(3) 邮政编码与各行政区域之间有一定的联系。

(4) 学问的多少跟年龄大小没有一定的关系。

3. 特定的。*Specific.*

(5) 别着急,身体恢复要有一定的时间。
(6) 对外汉语老师都需要积累一定的文化知识。

4. 某种程度的,相当的。Substantial.

(7) 他在音乐上已经有了一定的成就。
(8) 这篇博士论文具有一定的学术水平。

副词 ad.

1. 表示意志和态度的坚决或确定,必定如此。含有"决心"的意思,多用于第一人称。用于第二、第三人称时,表示对人必须做到的要求、希望,或者推测。常用在动词或助动词"要、得"的前面。Indicating a firm attitude. Sometimes it means "resolution." It is often used in the first person. When used in the second or third person, it describes a request, hope or speculation of what someone else should/would do. It is often used before a verb or an auxiliary verb such as "要, 得."

(9) 我一定要努力学习,将来考个好大学。
(10) 明天的聚会,你一定得来啊!

2. 必然,确实无疑。表示对某种情况的确切估计或推断。一般不用于第一人称。如果用,"一定"后面要跟"能够、可以"等能愿动词。Definitely, undoubtedly. It is rarely used in the first person. When it is used in the first person, "一定" has to be followed by a modal verb such as "能够, 可以."

(11) 你在上海工作过两年,那你对上海一定很了解。
(12) 我一定能够在今天晚上完成这些作业。

说明 Notes:

1. "一定"的否定形式有以下几种:"一定" has the following negative forms:

① "不一定",表示不能作出肯定的判断,语义偏于否定。用于叮嘱、协商问题时,含有"可以不必"的意思。With a negative semantic meaning, "不一定" means that a judgment cannot be made for certain. When it is used in offering advice or discussing an issue, it can mean "don't have to."

(13) 她不一定去三班上课。
(14) 明天你没空就不一定到我家来了。

② "一定不"表示彻底否定。"一定不" indicates complete negation.

(15) 孩子一定不吃,就不要给他吃。

③ "一定别、一定不要、一定不能",用于祈使句,表示坚决禁止、劝阻的意思。"一定别,一定不要,一定不能" are used in imperative sentences, indicating firm forbiddance or dissuasion.

(16) 在教室里你一定别抽烟。
(17) 你一定不要把这件事告诉妈妈。
(18) 你一定不能再不吃药了。

2. "必定"与"一定"做副词都表示确实无疑和意志坚决的意思。When used as an adverb, "必定" and "一定" can both mean certainty and firm resolution.

它们的区别是:Their differences are as follows:

① "一定"着重于主观分析、估计、推断事物肯定会那样。书面色彩没有"必定"浓,常用于口语。"一定"肯定的语意比"必定"轻,但是主观意愿色彩比"必定"浓,所以在表示强烈主观意愿的句子中,只能用"一定",不能用"必定"。"一定" emphasizes subjective analysis or inference of the situation. Often used colloquially, it does not have a strong literary sense as "必定." "必定" shows a stronger sense of certainty than "一定," but "一定" has a stronger sense of subjectivity than "必定." Therefore, "一定" instead of "必定" should be used in sentences showing a strong subjective will.

(19) *我们必定要去西藏旅游。
(20) 我们一定要去西藏旅游。

② "一定"又是形容词,可以修饰名词。"必定"不能。"一定" can serve as an adjective modifying a noun. "必定" cannot.

(21) *我每天都有必定的口语练习时间。

(22) 我每天都有一定的口语练习时间。

③ "一定"可用于第二、第三人称,表示对他人的要求和叮嘱。"必定"没有这种用法。"一定" can be used in the second person or third person, indicating a request or advice for others. "必定" has no such usage.

④ "一定"有否定用法。"必定"没有否定用法。"一定" can be negated but "必定" cannot.

⑤ "一定"可以单独回答问题。"必定"一般不能。"一定" can stand alone as a response. "必定" generally cannot.

(23) A：你今天晚上一定来吗?
　　　B：一定！

3. "肯定"和"一定"都有副词用法,在表示必定,没有疑问的意思时,可以互用。Both "肯定" and "一定" can be used as an adverb. They may replace each other when they mean "certainly" and "undoubtedly."

它们的区别是：Their differences are as follows:

① 两个词表示的意思有所侧重,用"一定"表示说话人更强的主观意愿,用"肯定"表示更强的对事物确定的程度(与"否定"相对)。They indicate a different emphasis: While "一定" indicates a strong desire or inclination of the speaker, using "肯定" shows a higher certainty about the thing talked about. It is the opposite of "否定 (to negate)."

(24) 你的生日晚会,他肯定/一定会来。

(25) 去西安旅游,我肯定/一定参加。

② "肯定"和"一定"都有形容词用法,但是表示的意思不同。查看"肯定""一定"词条。Both can be used as an adjective, but their meanings are somewhat different. Refer to the entries of "肯定" and "一定."

③ "肯定"有动词用法。"一定"没有动词用法。"肯定" can be used as a verb, but "一定" cannot.

yígài 一概 →P559"一律"

用法 Usage:
副词 ad.

表示适用于全体和所有的,没有例外。Entirely; without exception.

(1) 来开后门的人,一概拒绝。

(2) 转基因有各种不同类别,不能一概而论。

说明 Notes:

"一概"后面不能只用单音节词。"一概" cannot go with monosyllabic words.

(3) *来开后门的人,一概不。

(4) 来开后门的人,一概不见。

yíhuìr 一会儿 →P561"一下"

用法 Usage:
数量词 quantifier

1. 表示很短的时间。放在动词或形容词的后面做时量补语。A very short time, used as a complement of duration after a verb or an adjective.

(1) 现在别叫他,他刚睡一会儿。

(2) 我跟他聊了一会儿。

2. 指在很短的时间内。放在动词前面,做时间状语,常与"就"连用。Within a very short time. As a time adverbial before the verb, it is often used with "就."

(3) 在这儿等着,我一会儿就回来。

(4) 他一会儿就去学校,你赶紧给他做点儿吃的。

3. 单独使用,表示在很短的时间内。用在句子主语前,有时和"工夫、时间"连用,有时前面可加"不",表示更短的时间。Within a very short time (used alone before the subject). It can be used with "工夫,时间." Sometimes it can be preceded by "不," indicating an even shorter time.

(5) 一会儿,他就把试卷做完了。

(6) 一会儿工夫/时间,火车已经到南京了。

(7) 不一会儿,他就睡着了。

副词 ad.

分别用在两个词或短语前,表示两种情况在短时间内交替出现。Used repeatedly before two words or phrases, it means that two situations alternate within a short time.

(8) 最近爷爷的身体一会儿好一会儿坏,你去看看吧。

(9) 她一会儿哭一会儿笑的,怎么啦?

说明 Notes:

1. "一会儿"用在动词后作时量补语,可以用"多长时间"来提问。When "一会儿" serves as a complement of duration after a verb, a question with "多长时间" may be asked.

(10) A:他们聊了多长时间了?
　　　B:他们才聊了一会儿时间。

2. "一会儿"用在动词前作时间状语,可以用"什么时候"来提问。When "一会儿" serves as a time adverbial before a verb, a question with "什么时候" may be asked.

(11) A:你什么时候回来?
　　　B:我一会儿就回来。

3. 数量词"一会儿"和"不一会儿"都表示时间短。"一会儿" and "不一会儿" can both mean a very short time.

它们的区别是:They differ as follows:

① "不一会儿"表示的时间更短,强调不需要多少时间。"不一会儿" represents an even shorter time and emphasizes the little time needed.

(12) 一会儿,她就把饭做好了。(时间短 A short time)

(13) 不一会儿,她就把饭做好了。(说话人强调时间很短 Even shorter time)

② "一会儿"可以表示从现在往后,将来的一小段时间。"不一会儿"不能,只表示已经过去的一小段时间。"一会儿" can refer to a short time period between now and the future. "不一会儿" can only refer to a short time period in the past.

(14) *不一会儿,我们上街去。

(15) 一会儿,我们上街去。

③ "一会儿"有时不一定指很短的时间。"不一会儿"只能表示很短的时间。"一会儿" does not necessarily mean a short time. "不一会儿" only means a short time.

(16) A:他睡了多长时间了?
　　　B:睡了一会儿了。/ *睡了不一会儿了。

(17) *他出去有不一会儿了,怎么还不回来?

(18) 他出去有一会儿了,怎么还不回来?

④ "一会儿"可以叠用成"一会儿……一会儿……"的格式,表示动作、情况不断地变化或交替出现。"不一会儿"没有这样的用法。"一会儿" can be reduplicated as "一会儿...一会儿...," indicating alternation or change of behavior or situation. "不一会儿" has no such usage.

yíkuàir 一块儿 →P580 "一起"

用法 Usage:

名词 n.

表示同一个处所,常与"在、到"连用,多用于口语。The same place. It is often used colloquially with "在, 到."

(1) 他们俩现在住在一块儿。

(2) 别跟她坐到一块儿。

副词 ad.

表示共同在一处,一同。相当于"一道、一起",用于几个不同个体在一处发出或接受相同的动作、行为或情况。几个不同个体词语前要用介词"跟、和"等连接。多用于口语。At the same place; together. Similar to "一道,一起," it indicates that several individuals initiate or receive the same action or behavior. The different individuals or objects need to be connected by prepositions such as "跟,和." It is mostly used colloquially.

(3) 明天我们一块儿去图书馆好吗?

(4) 我总是跟他一块儿吃饭。

(5) 妈妈把衣服、零食和我最喜欢的书一块儿寄了过来。

yílù 一路

用法 Usage:

名词 n.

1. 整个行程中,沿路。The whole journey; along the route.

(1) 祝你一路顺风!

(2) 这一路上的大树可真多。

2. 同一类。The same category.

(3) 分手吧,我们不是一路人。

(4) 阿里是性格开朗那一路的,玛丽是性格温和那一路的。

副词 ad.

1. 一起(来、去或走)。(Come, go, or walk) together.

(5) 别说了,我就要跟你一路去。

(6) 咱们是一路来的吧,怎么你不认识我了?

2. 一直,一个劲儿地。Continuously.

(7) 今天怎么搞的,股票一路下跌呢。

(8) 最近房价一路下降,快买房子啊!

说明 Notes:

"一路"做名词,后面带方位名词"上",组成短语"一路上",表示在路上这个范围内。如例(2)。When used as a noun, "一路" can be followed by the location noun "上" to form the phrase "一路上," which refers to the scope along the route as in (2).

yílǜ 一律 →P557"一概"

用法 Usage:

形容词 a.

一个样子,相同。Of the same (appearance); same; alike.

(1) 明天女同学一律红长裙,男同学一律黑西装。

(2) 你的回答为什么总是千篇一律"不知道",那怎么行?

副词 ad.

适用于全体,无例外。Without exception.

(3) 世界上的事,所有的国家是一律平等吗?

(4) 通知上说,明天七点上车,一律不得迟到。

说明 Notes:

"一律"和"一概"副词用法的区别是:When used as an adverb, "一律" and "一概" have the following differences:

1. 在通知或规定中,如果是指事物,"一律"和"一概"可以替换。When referring to objects in a notice or a regulation, the two are interchangeable.

(5) 那些货物的出口关税一律/一概免收。

2. 如果是指人,则常用"一律",不用"一概"。When referring to people, "一律" rather than "一概" is used.

(6) *不参加演出的同学一概凭票进入。

(7) 不参加演出的同学一律凭票进入。

3. "一律"还有形容词用法。"一概"没有。"一律" can be used as an adjective, but "一概" cannot.

yímiàn 一面 →P575"一边"、P577"一方面"

用法 Usage:

名词 n.

1. 常读"一面儿"。物体的几个面之一。One side of an object (often pronounced as "一面儿").

(1) 三面墙,有一面长满了绿色的植物。

(2) 木箱子的一面儿画着花儿。

2. 能力或事情的一个方面。One aspect of an event or one's ability.

(3) 他有独当一面的能力,可以让他负责这件事。

(4) 了解一个人,不能只听一面之词。

副词 ad.

1. 表示一个动作同另一个动作同时进行,有两种用法:When referring to two concurrent

actions, "一面" has two uses:

① 单用。"一面"相当于"一边"。常与"还"搭配使用。Used by itself, it is similar to "一边." It is often used with "还."

(5) 他吃着饭,还一面看着电视新闻。

(6) 聊着天儿,他一面还望着大门。

② 可以两个重复使用,也可以几个重复使用。相当于"一边……一边……"。"一面" can be repeated in one sentence, which is similar to "一边...一边...."

(7) 现在很多年轻人都是一面走路,一面看手机。

(8) 他一面吃饭,一面听音乐,还一面看手机。

2. 表示同一主体产生两种活动(或具备两种性质),这种活动一般没有具体的动作或动作性不强。相当于"一方面……一方面……"。Indicating that the same subject is engaged in two activities (or possesses two attributes). The activities are usually not specific actions. It is similar to "一方面...一方面...."

(9) 妈妈去世早。爸爸一面工作,一面要照顾他们兄妹俩。

(10) 我这次去欧洲,一面工作,一面旅游。

3. "一面……一面……"还可以连接两个意思相反的句子。"一面...一面..." can also link two sentences with opposite meanings.

(11) 他一面说要好好学习,一面又常常睡懒觉、旷课。

(12) 她一面说要回家,一面又坐着跟朋友不停地聊天。

yīqiè 一切 →P383"全部"、P452"所有"

用法 Usage:

代词 pron.

1. 全部,各种。All; all kinds.

(1) 只要努力,一切困难都是可以解决的。

(2) 院长说,要调动一切力量抢救他的生命。

2. 泛指全部事物。Generally referring to all things.

(3) 这个留学生对老北京的一切都很感兴趣。

(4) 我爱他的一切,不管是优点,还是缺点。

说明 Notes:

1. "一切"和"所有"都表示全部,都能修饰名词。Meaning "all," "一切" and "所有" can both modify nouns.

它们的区别是:They differ as follows:

① "所有"侧重指一定范围内某种事物的全部数量,"一切"必定指某种事物所包含的全部类别,范围比较广。"所有" emphasizes the total amount of something within a certain range. "一切" emphasizes every aspect encompassed by something, which has a wider range of application.

(5) 研究过程中,所有的困难我都会克服的。(指研究过程内的全部困难 All the difficulties within a certain range)

(6) 这个研究的一切困难我都会克服。(指现在的、将来的,有关这个研究的全部困难 All the difficulties at present and in the future)

② "所有"是形容词,只能做定语,"的"可带可不带。"一切"是代词,做定语时,一般不带"的",如例(1)。"一切"还可以做主语和宾语,如例(3)(4)。As an adjective, "所有" can only serve as an attributive. It can be followed by "的" or not. As a pronoun, when "一切" is used as an attributive, it is usually not followed by "的." "一切" can also serve as the subject or the object as seen in (3) and (4).

③ "一切"只能修饰可以分类的事物名词。"所有"没有这个限制,可以修饰任何事物的名词。"一切" can only modify nouns that can be categorized. "所有" has no such limitation and can modify various nouns.

(7) *一切篮球比赛他都喜欢看。

(8) 所有的篮球比赛他都喜欢看。

2."一切"和"全部"都表示所有的意思。区别是：Both meaning "all," "一切" and "全部" have the following differences:

① "全部"是名词,着重一个整体各个部分的总和。"一切"是代词,泛指所有的事物,范围较广。As a noun, "全部" emphasizes the sum of individual parts of an integral system. As a pronoun, "一切" generally refers to all things, which has a wider range of application.

(9) 公司要投入全部资金和人力搞这个项目。(指现在有的 Current resources)

(10) 公司要投入一切资金和人力搞这个项目。(包括将来可能有的 Current resources and potential ones in the future)

② "全部"有副词用法。"一切"没有。"全部" can be used as an adverb but "一切" cannot.

(11) *这些桌子一切都搬到楼上去。

(12) 这些桌子全部都搬到楼上去。

yíxià 一下 →P557"一会儿"、P562"一下子"

用法 Usage:

数量短语 quantitative phrase

"一下"是数量短语,口语中常作"一下(儿)"。"一下" is a phrase with a quantifier. It is often used as "一下儿" colloquially.

1. 用在动词后面,表示动作的次数。When it follows a verb, it refers to the number of times of the action.

(1) 他轻轻敲了一下(儿)门。

(2) 这个球又没进,他气得拍了一下(儿)自己的脑袋。

2. 用在动词或形容词后面,表示动作经历或状态持续的时间很短。When it follows a verb or an adjective, it may indicate a short duration of an action or state.

(3) 你等一下(儿),我马上就来。

(4) 今年的夏天比较凉快,只热了一下(儿)。

3. 用在动词后面,表示动作轻松随意,或带尝试意味。用在与别人商量或向对方提要求的句子时,语气比较委婉客气。When used after a verb, it may indicate a casual action or a trial of something new. It carries a euphemistic tone when it is used in a discussion with others or a request.

(5) 那本小说,我只翻了一下,还不知道故事最后的结果。

(6) 你尝一下(儿),味道好不好?

副词 ad.

1. 表示短暂的时间,也说"一下子"。In a minute; soon. Indicating a short time, it is the same as "一下子."

(7) 别着急,电一下(儿)就会来的。

(8) 他的脸一下(儿)红,一下(儿)白。发生什么事啦?

2. 表示突然,顿时。Suddenly; immediately.

(9) 听到有人开门,他一下(儿)跑到了门口。

(10) 我一下(儿)猜到了孩子会藏到哪儿。

说明 Notes:

1."一下(儿)"和"一会儿"都可以放在动词后面作补语。在表示动作持续的动词后面,两个词语都可以用,如例(3)(4)。"一下(儿)" and "一会儿" can both serve as a complement after a verb. Both words can be used after a verb to indicate the duration of an action as seen in (3) and (4).

它们的区别是：Their differences are as follows:

① "一下(儿)"着重表示动作的轻松、随意或尝试。"一会(儿)"着重表示动作持续的时间短,但从动作的整体量来说,比"一下儿"大。"一下(儿)" emphasizes the casualness, randomness or trial of an action. "一会儿" emphasizes the short duration of an action, which is still longer than the duration represented by "一下儿."

(11) 我听了一下(儿)他的课。

(12) 我听了一会儿他的课。

② "一下(儿)"是动量词,只能用在动词和

少数表示心理状态的形容词后,表示动作轻微或随意。因此,当有些动词本身带有"稍微"的意思,或者出于使用上的需要,使语气变得轻松或委婉而带的"一下(儿)",一般都不能换成"一会儿"。As a verbal measure word, "一下(儿)" can only be used after verbs or a few adjectives describing mental state to indicate subtleness or casualness of an action. "一会儿" cannot be used if the verb implies "slightly." When used to soften the tone, "一下(儿)" cannot be replaced by "一会儿."

(13) *我到楼下去拿一会儿报纸。

(14) 我到楼下去拿一下(儿)报纸。

2. "一下(儿)"和"一会儿"都有副词用法,都可以分别用在两个意义相反、相对的动词、形容词前面做状语,表示在短时间内交替出现的情况。"一下(儿)" and "一会儿" can both be used as an adverb. Both can be used as an adverbial before two verbs or adjectives with opposite or relative meanings to show alternate situations within a short time.

(15) 他一会儿/一下(儿)唱美声,一会儿/一下(儿)唱流行歌曲。

(16) 他的脸一会儿/一下(儿)红,一会儿/一下(儿)白。发生什么事啦?

它们的区别是:The differences between "一下(儿)" and "一会儿" are as follows:

① "一下(儿)"可以单独用在动词、形容词前面,表示动作或状况变化时间的短暂。"一会儿"一般不能。"一下(儿)" can be used directly before a verb or an adjective to indicate a short time within a change of action or situation. "一会儿" usually has no such usage.

(17) *一夜时间,他的头发一会儿全白了。

(18) 一夜时间,他的头发一下(儿)全白了。

② "一下(儿)"可以表示"突然"的意思,"一会儿"不能。"一下(儿)" can mean "suddenly" but "一会儿" cannot.

(19) *他一会儿明白了这句话的意思。

(20) 他一下(儿)明白了这句话的意思。

yíxiàzi 一下子 →P561"一下"

用法 Usage:

副词 ad.

"一下子"又作"一下"。"一下子" is similar to "一下."

1. 表示动作行为发生、完成得迅速,或事物情况出现、变化得突然。后边常跟"就"。有时"一下子"还可以放在主谓短语或整个句子的前面。多用于口语。Indicating the quick occurrence or fast completion of an action, or sudden occurrence or change of a situation. It is often followed by "就." It can be used colloquially before a subject-predicate phrase or at the beginning of a sentence.

(1) 我一下子就明白了他的意思。

(2) 一下子,我醒了过来。原来我做了一个梦。

2. 两个"一下子"连用,组成"一下子……一下子……"的格式,表示事物或情况在很短的时间内变化不定。The "一下子…一下子…" structure indicates sudden changes of an event or a situation within a short time.

(3) 这天一下子热得流汗,一下子又冷得穿毛衣。

(4) 他一下子说去,一下子又说不去,不知道他到底去不去。

说明 Notes:

1. "一下子"还可用作数量短语,表示"一次"的意思。"一下子" can be used as a quantitative phrase meaning "once."

① 用在有的动词后面,做动量补语。It can be used after certain verbs as a verbal complement.

(5) 咱们去深圳闯一下子,一定能挣点钱回来。

(6) 他敲了一下子,锁就敲开了。

② 用在句子前面或用在谓语前面。It can

be used before a clause or a predicate.

(7) 他只一下子就修好了电视机。

(8) 我已经掌握汉字组词的规律,这一下子就可以认识很多词语。

2. "一下子"和"一下(儿)"都是数量短语,都可用在动词后面作动量补语。As a quantitative phrase, "一下子" and "一下(儿)" can both serve as a verbal complement after a verb.

它们的区别是:Their differences are as follows:

① "一下子"语气比"一下(儿)"重,一般用在表示强烈动作的动词,或者比较重要的进行大胆尝试的,或者用于影响比较大的动作动词后面,如例(6)(7)。"一下(儿)"做动量词,着重强调动作是比较轻微的,是短时间的,往往用于比较随意、轻松的场合。Carrying a heavier tone than "一下(儿)," "一下子" is often used after verbs indicating a strong or important action with a bold attempt, or an action with a significant impact as seen in (6) and (7). "一下(儿)" emphasizes light actions with a short duration. It is often used in casual and relaxed contexts.

② "一下子"主要用在动词或形容词前作副词,表示动作或情况突然发生或出现。"一下(儿)"主要用于动词或形容词后面作动量补语。Mostly used as an adverb before a verb or an adjective, "一下子" indicates the sudden occurrence of an action or a situation. "一下(儿)" is mostly used as a verbal complement after a verb or an adjective.

3. 注意以下错句:Special attention should be paid to the following errors:

(9) *你休息一下子吧。

(10) *我打扫了一下子房间。

(11) *请你先等一下子。

以上错句中的"一下子"都应改为"一下(儿)"。In the above examples, "一下子" should be replaced by "一下(儿)."

yíxiàng 一向 →P513"向来"、P583"一直"

用法 Usage:

名词 n.

过去的一段时间。一般用于"前一向、这一向、那一向"等。A period of time from the past to the present. It is usually used to form the structure of "前一向/这一向/那一向, etc."

(1) 这一向爷爷的身体还不错。

(2) 他前一向常吃河鱼,但最近不怎么吃了。

副词 ad.

从过去到现在都是这样,没有改变。相当于"一直"。Without change from the past to the present, the same as "一直."

(3) 他做事一向很认真。

(4) 她一向喜欢穿蓝色或白色的连衣裙。

说明 Notes:

"一向"和"向来"做副词,意思基本相同,都可以用来说明行为、状态从过去到现在都是这样。When used as an adverb, "一向" and "向来" are quite similar in meaning. Both can be used to describe unchanged behavior or state from the past to the present.

它们的区别是:如果限定了时段,只能用"一向"。不能用"向来"。The difference between the two is that only "一向" can be used within a certain time period. "向来" cannot be used as such.

(5) *十岁以前,我向来住在外婆家。

(6) 十岁以前,我一向住在外婆家。

yíyàng 一样 →P471"同样"、P575"一般"

用法 Usage:

形容词 a.

同样,没有差别。The same, having no difference.

(1) 你们俩长得一样漂亮。

(2) 全家人跟你一样高兴。

助词 aux.

意义跟用法与"似的"基本相同。用在词或

短语后面,表示比喻,通过比较,说明情况相似。前面常用"像、好像"搭配使用。*Similar to "似的" in meaning and usage, it is used after a word or phrase to make a metaphor and indicate similarity through comparison. It is often used with "像,好像."*

(3) 天上的云就像羊群一样。

(4) 大家要努力学习,像阿里同学一样。

说明 Notes:

1."一样"可以受否定副词"不、没"的修饰,但不能受程度副词"很"的修饰。*"一样" can be modified by negative adverbs "不,没," but it cannot be modified by the degree adverb "很."*

2."一样"的形容词用法和助词用法,有时看上去差不多,其实不一样,请注意区别。*The usage as an adjective or an auxiliary word of "一样" is different, although they seem quite similar. Please watch out for their differences.*

3."一样"和"同样"都表示相同的意义,都可以做定语。*"一样" and "同样" can both mean "the same." Both can serve as attributives.*

它们的区别是:*Their differences are as follows:*

① "同样"不能做谓语和补语。"一样"可以。*"一样" can serve as a predicate or a complement but "同样" cannot.*

(5) *我们俩的分数同样。

(6) 我们俩的分数一样。

② "同样"前面不能用否定词"不、没"。"一样"可以。*"一样" can be preceded by negative words "不,没" but "同样" cannot.*

(7) *这两件衣服的颜色不同样。

(8) 这两件衣服的颜色不一样。

③ 形容词"一样"的否定形式是"不一样"。助词"一样"的否定形式是"不像……一样"。*The negative form of "一样" as an adjective is "不一样." The negative form of "一样" as an auxiliary word is "不像…一样."*

yízài 一再 →P620"再三"

用法 Usage:

副词 ad.

1. 表示动作行为在过去的时间里重复进行,相当于"一次又一次"。*Again and again; repeatedly Referring to a repeated action or behavior in the past, it is the same as "一次又一次."*

(1) 他一再地上班迟到。这次,老板一定要辞退他了。

(2) 在我上大学的四年中,王老师一再地被我们评为优秀老师。

2. 表示反复,含有强调的意味。相当于"再三"。*Repeatedly (with implied emphasis). It is the same as "再三."*

(3) 母亲一再叮嘱我要注意身体健康。

(4) 老师一再强调,作业明天必须交给他。

yíhàn 遗憾 →P274"可惜"

用法 Usage:

形容词 a.

1. 表示不符合心愿、不称心,感到惋惜。做谓语时,宾语多为小句。*Regretful; not as one wishes. When used as a predicate, its object is often a clause.*

(1) 我很遗憾你不能与我同班学习。

(2) 没有买到飞机票,这是很遗憾的事情。

2. 由于待人不周而表示歉意。常常单独使用,后面的句子多为表示遗憾的原因。*Expressing apology or regret to others. It often stands alone in a clause, with the following clause indicating the reason behind the regretful situation.*

(3) 非常遗憾,我要上班去了,不能与你们再聊天了。

(4) 很遗憾,没能带你们去看看黄鹤楼,下次来一定去。

3. 在外交上常用来表示不满和抗议。*With regret, often used to express dissatisfaction*

or protest in diplomatic situations.

(5) 对你方不友好的行为,我们深表遗憾。

名词 n.

遗恨。Regret.

(6) 没去见他最后一面成了我终生的遗憾。

说明 Notes:

"可惜"与"遗憾"都有表示惋惜的意思。当表示心中不满意、不称心时,"可惜"和"遗憾"可以互换。"可惜" and "遗憾" can both indicate regret or sympathy. The two are interchangeable when referring to dissatisfaction or discontent.

它们的区别是:Their differences are as follows:

1. 句子的语义重心有所不同。"可惜"侧重为失去那么好的事物或机会感到惋惜。"遗憾"侧重因没有这样的经历感到惋惜。The emphases of the two words are different. "可惜" focuses on feeling regret for the loss of a good thing or opportunity. "遗憾" emphasizes feeling regret for the lack of a certain experience.

(7) 你没买这本书很可惜,这本书很好。

(8) 你这本书也没看过,很遗憾。

2. "可惜"既可以对物质的损失感到惋惜,又可以因为心中不满意、不称心感到可惜。"遗憾"多用于精神上的不满意,心中的不愉快。一般不用于物质上的损失。"可惜" can be used to show regret for material loss as well as for dissatisfaction. "遗憾" is generally used to show psychological discontent rather than regret for material loss.

(9) *昨天刚买的词典,今天就撕破了两页,真遗憾!

(10) 昨天刚买的词典,今天就撕破了两页,真可惜!

3. "可惜"没有名词用法,也没有"遗憾"作为形容词的第二和第三义项的用法。"可惜" cannot be used as a noun and doesn't have the second or third meaning of "遗憾" as an adjective.

yǐ 已 →P565"已经"

用法 Usage:

副词 ad.

"已"在现代汉语中,意思和用法跟"已经"相同。In modern Chinese, the meaning and usage of "已" is the same as "已经."

(1) 这本词典,我早已买了。

(2) 我到中国已有两年了。

说明 Notes:

1. "已"在文言文中还有动词、介词用法。In classic Chinese, "已" can also be used as a verb or preposition.

2. 在现代汉语的固定词组中,还保留着"已"的动词用法,表示"停止"的意思,如"争论不已、学不可以已"等。"已" can still be used as a verb meaning "stop" in some fixed expressions in modern Chinese, such as "争论不已,学不可以已."

yǐjīng 已经 →P58"曾经"、P565"已"

用法 Usage:

副词 ad.

1. 表示动作、变化完成或达到某种程度。动词后或句末多有"了"呼应。Already. Indicating the completion (or reaching a certain extent) of an action or change, it is often used with "了" after the verb or at the end of the sentence.

(1) 他已经回家了。

(2) 天已经在下雨了。

2. 强调数量多、时间晚或时间长。修饰名词性成分时,后面必须带"了"。Already, emphasizing a large amount, a late or a long time. When used to modify a noun, it has to be followed by "了."

(3) 已经十点了,你怎么还不起床?

(4) 已经二十斤了,够了。

说明 Notes:

1. 使用"已经"要注意:When using "已

经，" one has to pay attention to the following aspects:

① 句子中"已经"和"了"的呼应。如果在单句中,用了"已经",没有用"了",单句的意义就会不够完整。"已经" should be used with "了" in a sentence. In a simple sentence, if "已经" is used without "了," then the meaning of the sentence is incomplete.

（5）＊晚饭他已经吃。

（6）晚饭他已经吃了。

② "已经"修饰形容词时,形容词后面必须带"了"和"起来、下来"等补语。When modified by "已经," the adjective has to be followed by "了" and a complement such as "起来,下来."

（7）天已经暖和起来了。

（8）他的心情已经平静下来了。

③ "已经"后面可以带"快、要、差不多"等副词,表示即将完成而还未完成。"已经" can be followed by adverbs such as "快,要,差不多," meaning to be completed soon.

（9）今天的作业我已经要做完了。

（10）现在已经差不多九点了,我要起床了。

2. "已经"和"已"意思、用法基本相同。The meaning and usage of "已经" and "已" are quite similar.

它们的区别是：Their differences are as follows:

① "已"多用于书面语。"已经"通用于口语和书面语。"已" is mostly used in written language, whereas "已经" can be used both colloquially and in written language.

② "已"多修饰单音节动词或形容词。"已经"多修饰双音节或多音节词语。"已" often modifies monosyllabic verbs or adjectives, whereas "已经" often modifies disyllabic or multisyllabic words.

（11）时间已晚,我要回家了。

（12）时间已经晚了,我要回家了。

③ "已"前面常常用"早、久"等单音节词修饰。"已经"前面一般不用。"已" is often preceded by a monosyllabic modifier such as "早、久." "已经" is generally not used as such.

（13）＊那件衣服我早已经不穿了。

（14）那件衣服我早已不穿了。

④ "已"修饰单音节动词、形容词时,句尾可不带"了"。"已经"必须要带"了"。When "已" modifies a monosyllabic verb or adjective, "了" can be omitted at the end of the sentence, whereas "已经" has to be used with "了."

（15）＊天已经冷,小心感冒。

（16）天已冷,小心感冒。

3. "已经"跟"曾经"都表示事情发生在过去。"已经" and "曾经" both refer to past occurrence.

它们的区别是：Their differences are as follows:

① "已经"着重事情的完成,完成事情的时间在不久以前,所表示的动作或情况可能还在继续。"曾经"着重表示从前有过某种情况,时间一般不是在最近,所表示的动作或情况一般现在已经结束。"已经" focuses on the completion of an action. The time of completion is in the recent past, and the action or the situation may still continue. "曾经" emphasizes a certain situation not in the recent past. The action or situation mentioned has usually ended.

（17）他已经学了三年汉语了。

（18）他曾经学过三年汉语。

② "已经"后的动词多与"了"搭配呼应。"曾经"后的动词多与"过"搭配呼应,如例（17）（18）。The verb after "已经" is usually used with "了," whereas the verb after "曾经" is often used with "过" as seen in (17) and (18).

③ "已经"可以修饰否定式。"曾经"一般不能。"已经" can modify negative words but "曾经" cannot.

（19）现在他已经不是足球运动员了。

（20）＊他曾经不是足球运动员。

（21）他以前不是足球运动员。

yǐ 以 →P568"以便"

用法 Usage:

介词 prep.

1. "以……"用在动词前面做状语。"以..." is used as an adverbial before the verb.

① 引进动作、行为、言语等赖以实现的依据、凭借，相当于"用、拿、按"的意思。With; by. It is used to introduce the condition for the completion of an action, behavior or speech, similar to "用,拿,按" in meaning.

（1）以他的健康情况,我想他可以活到九十岁。

（2）今天我以朋友的身份来劝你,别抽烟了。

② 表示方式、标准,相当于"按照、根据"的意思。"以"常常引出方式或标准,后面的句子表示在这个方式或标准下应该有的结果。According to, used to introduce methods or standards, similar to "按照,根据" in meaning. The second clause indicates the estimated result based on the method or standard introduced by "以."

（3）以每月八百元计算,我每年吃饭要花费近一万元。

（4）以每周读一本书的要求,我每年的业余时间要读五十四本书。

③ 表示原因,相当于"因为、由于"的意思。后面有时用"而"呼应。Because of, used to explain the reason, similar to "因为,由于." Sometimes it is used with "而" in the same sentence.

（5）龙井茶就是以这道泉水的美丽传说而出名的。

（6）他以善良而出名,大家都知道他。

2. "以……"用在单音节动词之后做补语。"以"的作用是用有关的情况、事物、感觉等对前面的动词起补充说明。这些情况、事物、感觉等在意念上受前面动词的支配。"给(予)……以"是最常见的格式。有时在单音节动词和"以"之间加"之"（多用于固定短语）。多用于书面语。"以..." is used as a complement after a monosyllabic verb, "以" provides additional explanation for the aforementioned verb with reference to a related situation, thing or emotion. The most common structure is "给(予)...以." Sometimes "之" is used between a monosyllabic verb and "以," which is mostly seen in fixed expressions in written language.

（7）每首歌唱完,歌迷们都报之以热烈的掌声。

（8）五乘以六等于三十。

3. "以"跟"为"搭配,构成"以……为……"的固定格式。这是从文言文沿用下来的。用法有三种：The "以...为..." structure from classic Chinese is still in use in modern Chinese. It can be used as follows:

① 相当于"拿……作为……"或"把……当作……"。"为"的宾语是名词或名词短语。Meaning "to take ... as ...," Similar to "拿...作为..." or "把...当作...," the object of "为" is a noun or a noun phrase.

（9）政府以人为本,制定了很多对老百姓有利的政策。

（10）这些孩子以孝顺父母为己任,对其他老人也很尊敬。

② 表示判断,含有"把……认作……"或"觉得……是……"的意思。"为"的宾语多是形容词。Indicating a judgment and meaning "to regard/think of ... as ...," similar to "把...认作..." or "觉得...是...." The object of "为" is often an adjective.

（11）他以读书为乐,一年要看差不多一百本书。

（12）你们不以千里为远,来中国学习汉语,我非常欢迎。

③ 含有"要算、要数"的意思。"为"的宾语多是形容词或描写性短语。Meaning "to consider ... as ...," similar to "要算,要数." The object of "为" is often an adjective or a descriptive phrase.

（13）他们班的成绩以他的为最高。

(14) 我们班同学的年龄以他为最小。

连词 conj.

表示目的关系。多连接分句,有时也连接动词短语。相当于"为了、以便"。*In order to; so as to. Indicating a purpose, it is often followed by a clause. Sometimes it can be followed by a verb phrase with the meaning similar to "为了,以便."*

(15) 她把房间收拾得干干净净,以迎接朋友的到来。

(16) 我们的超市必须货物齐全,以满足不同顾客的需求。

说明 Notes:

"以"是文言虚词,在现代汉语里仍然经常使用。此外,现代汉语中还有"动+以"组成的双音节动词,不必拆开解释,如"予以、借以、用以、难以、给以"等动词。这些动词后面的宾语常常也是动词性的,多为抽象意义,如"给以帮助、予以表扬、难以接受、用以说明、借以证明"等。*As a function word in classic Chinese, "以" is still widely used in modern Chinese. The disyllabic verbs in the form of "v.+以," such as "予以,借以,用以,难以,给以" can be understood as integral verbs. The objects of such verbs are often verbs with abstract meaning as in "给以帮助,予以表扬,难以接受,用以说明,借以证明."*

yǐbiàn 以便 →P567"以"

用法 Usage:

连词 conj.

也作"以便于"。用在第二个分句的开头,表示前面分句说的内容是为了容易实现后面分句所说的目的。前后两个分句主语相同时,后一小句不出现主语。多用于书面。*Like "以便于," "以便" is mostly used in written language. Placed at the beginning of the second clause, it means that what is mentioned in the first clause will help achieve the objective in the second clause. When the two clauses have the same subject, the subject is not repeated in the second clause.*

(1) 请把你的电话号码给我,以便我们今后联系。

(2) 你应该努力学习,以便将来能找个好工作。

说明 Notes:

"以"和"以便"作连词都表示目的关系。*When used as a conjunction, "以" and "以便" both indicate objectives.*

它们的区别是:*Their differences are as follows:*

1. 在语义上,"以"后面强调的是目的,因此常常连接的是主观意向较强的自主动词。"以便"的重点在于使目的容易实现,既可以连接自主动词,也可以连接非自主动词。*Semantically speaking, "以" focuses on the objective and is often followed by volitional verbs with a strong sense of subjectivity. "以便" emphasizes the smooth achievement of the objective. It can be followed by either volitional or non-volitional verbs.*

(3) *我们已经开始用这个方法,以便保证顺利完成任务。

(4) 我们已经开始用这个方法,以保证顺利完成任务。

(5) *出发的时间应早点通知,以大家做好准备。

(6) 出发的时间应早点通知,以便大家做好准备。

2. "以"所连接的前后两个分句的主语是同一个,一般主语不出现在第二句,如例(3)。"以便"连接的两个分句的主语可以不同,因此,"以便"后面常常带有主语的句子,如例(1)(5)。*The two clauses connected by "以" share the same subject, which is not repeated in the second clause as in (3). The two clauses connected by "以便" may have different subjects. Therefore, the clause after "以便" often has its own subject as in (1) and (5).*

yǐhòu 以后 →P198"后来"

用法 Usage:

名词 n.

时间名词。表示比现在或所说的某一时间晚的时间。用法有：As a time noun, it refers to a time later than the present or the time being discussed. The main usages are as follows:

1."名词(包括表示时间的数量词)＋以后"。"Noun (including a quantifier representing time)＋以后."

(1) 圣诞节以后,我要去一趟上海。

(2) 2018年以后,我就不在中国了。

2."动词/小句＋以后"。"Verb/Clause＋以后."

(3) 在北京分手以后,我们就没有见过面。

(4) 考试结束以后,我要去旅游。

3. 单独做状语。Used as an adverbial.

(5) 以后,我会在中国找工作。

(6) 这个语法点以后再讲。

4."很久＋以后",指比现在或某一时间晚得多的时间。"很久＋以后," referring to a time much later than the present or a certain time.

(7) 我回国很久以后才找到工作。

(8) 等到我结婚生孩子,那是很久以后的事情了。

5."不久＋以后",指比现在或某一时间不太晚的时间。"不久＋以后," referring to a time not much later than the present or a certain time.

(9) 他回国不久以后就在加拿大找了个工作。

(10) 他们结婚不久以后就有了孩子。

6. 习惯语"从此以后",其中"此"是指前文中指出的时间。Fixed expression "从此以后," with "此" referring to the aforementioned time.

(11) 去年她生了孩子,从此以后就没有工作过。

(12) 哥哥大学毕业了,从此以后家里的经济好起来了。

说明 Notes:

"以后"和"后来"都表示某个时间以后的时间。"以后" and "后来" both refer to the time after a certain time.

它们的区别是：Their differences are as follows:

1."以后"可以用在某个时间或某一事情的词语后面。"后来"不可以。"以后" can be used after words representing a certain time or event but "后来" cannot.

(13) *吃饭后来我们去看电影。

(14) 吃饭以后我们去看电影。

(15) *十八岁后来,我就可以喝酒了。

(16) 十八岁以后,我就可以喝酒了。

2."以后"可以指将来的时间。"后来"不可以,只指过去的时间。"以后" can refer to a future time, but "后来" can only refer to a past time.

(17) *今天我们先去银行,后来再去图书馆。

(18) 今天我们先去银行,以后再去图书馆。

(19) 那天我们先去了银行,后来因为时间来不及,没去图书馆。

yǐjí 以及

用法 Usage:

连词 conj.

表示并列关系。连接并列的名词、动词、介词短语和小句,多用于书面语。And. Indicating a parallel relationship, it is often used in written language to connect parallel nouns, verbs, prepositional phrases or clauses.

句式有：The main usages are as follows:

1. 所连接的成分在语义上有主次轻重的区别,前面的成分是主要的。The elements connected by "以及" have different weights in terms of the semantic meaning. The elements that come first are the primary ones.

(1) 这家商场卖电视机、洗衣机、空调、电冰箱以及电风扇、吹风机等小家电。

（2）一个学期要学的课有语法、口语、听力、写作以及文化选修课等。

2. 所连接的成分有时间、次序先后的区别。The elements connected by "以及" have differences in time sequence or order.

（3）今天的口语练习要你告诉我，你上午、下午以及晚上做了什么事情。

（4）请你说一下这件事情发生的原因、发展、结果以及你的感想。

3. 所连接的事物可以分为两类，"以及"前面往往是主要事物。The elements connected can be divided into two categories, of which the main element usually precedes "以及."

（5）今天的午餐有米饭、面条以及馄饨、包子。

（6）星期天我要做作业、运动以及打扫房间。

说明 Notes:

有时候用"以及"是为了避免同一个连词的重复使用。Sometimes "以及" is used to avoid repetition of the same conjunction.

（7）我们班里有四个法国学生和五个韩国学生以及五个日本学生。

yǐlái 以来 →P282"来"、P568"以后"

用法 Usage:

名词 n.

从过去某时到说话时（或特指的某一时间）为止的一段时间。与前面的时间词或表示时间意义的词语组成短语，在句中做状语。"以来"前面常用"从、自、自从"等介词。The time period from a certain time in the past (or a specific time) to the time indicated in the sentence. "以来" can form a phrase with the preceding time word to serve as the adverbial. It is often preceded by such prepositions as "从，自，自从."

（1）自从2016年以来，我就在父亲的公司工作。

（2）长期以来，他就在实验室搞研究，去年终于得到了很大的成果。

说明 Notes:

1. "以后"和"以来"都表示某个时间以后的时间。"以后" and "以来" both refer to the time after a certain time.

它们的区别是：Their differences are as follows:

① 在语义上，"以后"可以表示三个时间段，所表示的时间段终止点比较模糊。"以来"只表示从过去到现在（到说话时）一个时间段，所表示的时间段终止点比较清楚。"以后" can refer to three time periods with a vague end point of time. "以来" only refers to one time period from the past to the present (as indicated in the sentence), which has a clear end point of time.

（3）词典是到中国以后买的。（从过去到现在说话为止这段时间里 The time period from the past to the time indicated in the sentence）

（4）词典以后再买吧。（从现在到将来的这段时间里 The time period from the present to the future）

（5）词典到中国以后再买吧。（将来到中国以后的某段时间里 A certain time period after arriving in China）

（6）到中国以来，他只买了一本词典。（从过去到现在说话为止 From the past to the time indicated in the sentence）

所以，表示现在以后和将来以后的时间，"以后"都不能替换成"以来"。Therefore, "以后" cannot be replaced by "以来" when referring to the time after the present or the time in the future.

② "以来"可以受过去时间起点并不明确的时间词语的修饰，如"长期、多年、一段时间"等，表示从过去到现在较长的一段时间，后面的谓语表示的是已经出现或存在的情况。这类时间起点不明确的词语，一般不能修饰"以后"，但如果只表示将来的某个时间，后面的谓语所表

示的只是一种估计和预测,就可以修饰"以后"。"以来" can be modified by time words with a vague starting point in the past such as "长期,多年,一段时间," which refers to a relatively long period of time from the past to the present. The predicate indicates an existing situation. Such time words with a vague starting point in the past are usually not used to modify "以后." Words referring to a future time can modify "以后" when the predicate indicates an estimation or prediction.

(7) *长期以后,城市堵车的问题一直没有得到解决。

(8) 长期以来,城市堵车的问题一直没有得到解决。

(9) *多年以后,我一直坚持早上跑三千米。

(10) 多年以来,我一直坚持早上跑三千米。

(11) 多年以后,我可能会坚持早上跑三千米。

③ "以后"可以单独使用。"以来"不能单独使用,必须用在表示时间的词语后面。如例(6)(8)(10)。"以后" can be used alone, whereas "以来" has to follow a time word as seen in (6), (8) and (10).

2. "以来"和用在时间名词后的"来",都能用在表示时段性的时间词语后。前面一般不能用"从、自"等介词。Both "以来" and "来 + a time noun" can be used after a word indicating a period of time. Neither can go with prepositions such as "从, 自."

(12) 三天来/以来,他什么东西也没吃过。真急死人了!

两者的区别是:"以来"还可以用在表示时间意义的词语后面,并且前面可以用"从、自"等介词。"来"不可以这样用。Their difference is that "以来" can appear behind a word or expression indicating a time, and prepositions such as "从, 自" can appear before it. "来" cannot be used in this way.

(13) *自从冬天开始来,他一直感冒咳嗽。

(14) 自从冬天开始以来,他一直感冒咳嗽。

(15) *改革开放来,这个城市的变化非常大。

(16) 改革开放以来,这个城市的变化非常大。

yǐmiǎn 以免 →P321"免得"

用法 Usage:

连词 conj.

用在下半句的开头,表示上半句说的内容,目的为的是不至于产生下文所说的情况。*In order to avoid; so as not to. Used at the beginning of the second clause, "以免" means that the suggestion given in the first clause will help avoid the situation mentioned in the second clause.*

(1) 自行车在马路上不要乱放,以免影响行人走路。

(2) 不要轻易相信陌生人的电话,以免上当受骗。

说明 Notes:

"以免"和"免得"都表示要避免某种不希望发生的情况,一般都用在后一个分句的开头。*Generally used at the beginning of the second clause, "以免" and "免得" both mean avoiding the occurrence of an unpleasant situation.*

它们的区别是:Their differences are as follows:

1. 在语义上,"免得"着重避免发生不希望产生的情况。"以免"中的"以"着重指出不要因为前面分句中说的这种原因,使得产生不希望有的情况。"免得" *focuses on the avoidance of an unpleasant situation. The* "以" *in* "以免" *emphasizes the avoidance of an unpleasant situation due to the reason indicated in the first clause.*

2. "免得"连接的句子,前面分句的内容常常是告诉人们要怎么做。"以免"连接的句子,前面分句的内容常常是告诉人们不要怎么做。*The first clause in a sentence with* "免得" *usually provides a suggestion on what to do. The first clause in a sentence with* "以免"

usually provides a suggestion on what not to do.

（3）带一把雨伞吧，免得下雨淋湿了。
（4）别忘了带一把伞，以免下雨淋湿了。

yǐnèi 以内

用法 Usage:

名词 n.

方位词。在一定的界限之内（跟"以外"相对）。Locative noun. Within a certain range, within the limits of (as opposed to "以外").

（1）院子的篱笆以内种了十棵玫瑰花。
（2）五年以内我不会结婚。

说明 Notes:

1."以内"一般总是用在表示数量、范围的词语后面，不能单独使用，如例（1）（2）。"以内" usually follows words indicating an amount or range as in (1) and (2). It cannot be used alone.

2."以内"前面一般不能是单音节词，而要双音节以上的词语。

（3）*车以内有很大的烟味儿。
（4）车内有很大的烟味儿。
（5）*墙以内都是桃树。
（6）墙内都是桃树。
（7）围墙以内都是桃树。

yǐqián 以前 →P181"过去"、P504"先前"、P573"以往"

用法 Usage:

名词 n.

方位词。指比现在或所说某时间早的时期。Locative noun. Before; formerly. It refers to a time earlier than the present or the time indicated in the sentence.

用法有：Its usages are as follows:

1.在句子中表示时间，可做状语、定语。Indicating a time, it can be used as the adverbial or the attributive.

（1）以前我们这个小镇不通高铁。
（2）他是我以前中学的同学。
（3）你的性格跟以前不一样了。

2.用在名词或表示时间的数量词后面，表示时间。Used after a noun or a quantifier indicating a time.

（4）春节以前我去新疆旅游了。
（5）一年以前我就开始学汉语了。

3.用在动词或小句后，表示时间。Used after a verb or a clause to indicate a time.

（6）开会以前你先到我办公室来一下。
（7）你来我们学校以前就学过汉语吗？

4.用在"很久、很早"以后，表示过去很远的时间。Used after "很久,很早" to indicate a long time ago.

（8）很久很久以前这里是一片大海。
（9）很早以前我就认识李老师了。

5.用在"不久"以后，表示过去不远的时间。Used after "不久" to indicate a relatively short time ago.

（10）不久以前他来向我借过一本书。

说明 Notes:

1."以前"和"先前"都表示比现在或所说某时早的时候。Both "以前" and "先前" indicate a time earlier than now or a specified time.

它们的区别是："先前"没有"以前"的第二、三、四、五项的用法。Their difference is that "先前" doesn't have the 2nd, 3rd, 4th, and 5th usages of "以前."

2."以前"和做名词用的"过去"都表示现在以前的时间。它们的区别是：Both "以前" and "过去," when the latter means "以前," refer to a time in the past. Their differences are as follows:

①"以前"可以受名词性成分或动词性成分的修饰，如"八点以前、来中国以前、学汉语以前"。"过去"一般只受表示领属的名词性成分的修饰，如"他的过去、中国的过去"等。"以前" can be modified by a nominal or verbal element, such as "八点以前,来中国以前,学汉

语以前.""过去," however, is modified only by a nominal element indicating a sense of belonging such as "他的过去,中国的过去."

② "过去"常常与"现在"和"将来"并提,区别不同的时段。"以前"一般不与"现在""将来"并提。"过去" is often mentioned at the same time as "现在(now)" and "将来(in the future)" so as to distinguish different periods of time. "以前," however, is usually not used in this way.

yǐwài 以外

用法 Usage:
名词 n.
方位词。在一定的界限之外(与"以内"相对)。Locative noun. Outside a certain range (as opposed to "以内").

(1) 上课以外的时间你做些什么?
(2) 我只给你五十元,五十元以外的钱你自己付。

说明 Notes:
1. "以外"一般总是用在表示数量、范围的词语后面,不能单独使用,如例(1)(2)。"以外" usually follows words indicating an amount or range as in (1) and (2). It cannot be used alone.
2. "以外"前面一般不能是单音节词,而要双音节以上的词语。The words preceding "以外" are usually not monosyllabic words.

(3) *车以外的空气很新鲜。
(4) 车外的空气很新鲜。
(5) *墙以外都是桃树。
(6) 墙外都是桃树。
(7) 围墙以外都是桃树。

yǐwǎng 以往 →P572"以前"

用法 Usage:
名词 n.
以前,从前。Before; in the past.

(1) 我以往是六点起床,昨天有点累,今天起晚了。

(2) 父母退休以后,身体比以往好多了。

说明 Notes:
"以往"和"以前"都表示比现在早的时间。"以往"在句子中表示时间,做句子的状语、定语时,可以与"以前"替换。"以往" and "以前" both refer to a time earlier than the present. When used as an adverbial or attributive to indicate a time, "以往" is interchangeable with "以前."

(3) 以往/以前,星期天我都到图书馆看半天书。
(4) 爷爷八十五岁以后,身体比以往/以前差了。

它们的区别是:The differences between the two are as follows:

1. "以往"不能表示比所说时间早的时间。"以前"可以。"以前" can refer to the time earlier than the one indicated in the sentence but "以往" cannot.

(5) *明天上午十点以往,你们别给我打电话。
(6) 明天上午十点以前,你们别给我打电话。

2. "以往"不能用在"很早、很久、不久"等词语后面。"以前"可以。"以前" can be used after words such as "很早,很久,不久" but "以往" cannot.

yǐwéi 以为 →P393"认为"

用法 Usage:
动词 v.
认为,表示对人或事物做出某种论断,后面必带动词、形容词和小句做的宾语。当作出的判断与客观事实不符合时,"以为"前面可以加"很、满"等少数程度副词,后面必用另一小句指明事实真相。To think. Making a judgment about people or things, "以为" has to be followed by an object, which is often a clause with a verb or an adjective. When the judgment is different from the fact, "以为" can be preceded by a limited number of degree adverbs such as "很,满." The clause with "以为" has to

be followed by another clause indicating the fact.

（1）你别以为明天会下雨。

（2）我满以为这里的天气很热，没想到那么凉快。

（3）我以为八点上课，其实今天是九点才上课。

说明 Notes：

"以为"和"认为"都是动词，都表示对人或事物有某种看法、态度或做出判断。宾语多为动词短语或主谓短语。As a verb, "以为" and "认为" both mean making a certain judgment about people or things. The object is usually a verb phrase or subject-predicate phrase.

它们的区别是：Their differences are as follows:

1. 在语义上，"以为"着重于对事物的看法，属于推测、猜想、估计，强调主观、个人的认识，作出的判断常和客观事实相反，因此语气上不十分肯定。"认为"着重于经过认真思考后，对事物表明确定的看法，判断常常是在分析、理解、认识的基础上得出的，因此，"认为"的语气较为肯定。"以为" focuses on the assumption or estimate of a certain matter. The subjective and individual judgment is often contrary to the fact, and therefore carries an uncertain tone. "认为" emphasizes expressing a certain viewpoint after careful thinking. The judgment is often based on analysis and understanding and therefore carries a more certain tone.

2. "认为"的语气比较郑重，对象既可以是重大事物，也可以是一般事物。"以为"语气肯定时，可与"认为"互换，但语气不如"认为"郑重。对象多是一般事物。"认为" carries a more serious tone. The object can be something with or without any significance. When used in a positive tone, "以为" is interchangeable with "认为," but the tone is less serious. The object of "以为" is usually some ordinary matter.

（4）我以为/认为这种做法是不合适的。

（5）我以为你走错路了。（带有不肯定的语气 With an uncertain tone）

（6）我们认为抓教育是件大事。（语气比较肯定 With a certain tone）

3. "认为"的主语可以是个人或者某些人，也可以是集团、组织、会议、政党、国家等。"以为"的主语一般多为个人或某些人。The subject of "认为" can be an individual or some people, or a group, an organization, a meeting, a political party, a country, etc. The subject of "以为" is usually an individual or some people.

（7）中国历来认为，国家不分大小，都有自己的主权。

（8）学院领导认为，他是一个优秀的学生。

（9）我以为你不喜欢吃中国菜呢。

（10）大家都以为你不会去了，所以没有给你买票。

4. "以为"还可以表示判断、猜测是主观的、片面的，是与实际语义不符的。所以，"以为"前后两个句子之间多表示为对立的或者矛盾的意义关系。前一分句用"以为"指出不符合实际的，甚至是错误的推断，后一分句指出相反、相对的真实情况。在句子结构上，也有许多常用的搭配格式，如："还以为……，其实……""以为……，实际上……""满以为……，没想到……""本以为……，没料到"等。"认为"一般不表示这种语义，没有这种格式的句子。"以为" may indicate that the judgment is subjective, lopsided, or different from the fact. Therefore, the two clauses connected by "以为" often have contrasting or contradictory meanings. The first clause with "以为" indicates the judgment different from the fact or even erroneous, whereas the second clause provides the factual information contrasting or contradictory to the first clause. The two clauses often follow certain fixed structures such as "还以为..., 其实...," "以为..., 实际上...," "满以为..., 没想到," "本以为..., 没料到." "认为" has no such usage.

（11）我还以为他是东北人，其实他是在东北工作过的上海人。

(12) 我满以为这样做他会表扬我，没想到反而挨了批评。

(13) 我本以为这是在帮助他，没料到反给他添了麻烦。

5. 有时用"以为"的句子常常只用前一个单句，句子末尾多用"呢、的"。含有与之相反、相对意义的第二个分句，在语言环境清楚的情况下可以省略。这样的句子中一般也不能用"认为"。Sometimes "以为" can be used in a single sentence with "呢, 的" at the end of the sentence. The second clause with a contrasting or contradictory meaning may be omitted when the context is clear. "认为" is usually not used as such.

(14) 我以为你不想去了呢。（实际上你是想去的 Actually you want to go）

(15) 我以为他会反对的。（其实他同意了 Actually he agreed）

6. 用于被动句时，"认为"可以有"被/让……认为"的句式。"以为"只能有"让……以为"的句式。"认为" can be used in passive-voice structures such as "被/让...认为." "以为" can only be used in the structure of "让...以为."

(16) 我被他们认为是俄国人了。

(17) *我被他们以为我是俄国人了

(18) 我让他们以为我是俄国人了。

7. "以为"前面可以受程度副词"满、很"的修饰，如例(2)。"认为"不能。"以为" can be modified by degree adverbs "满, 很" as in (2), but "认为" cannot.

8. "以为"可以构成"自以为是、不以为然、信以为真、白以为得计"等词组。"认为"不能。"以为" can be used in phrases such as "自以为是, 不以为然, 信以为真, 自以为得计" but "认为" cannot.

yībān 一般 →P563 "一样"

用法 Usage:

形容词 a.

1. 一样，同样。Same.

(1) 高铁火车飞一般地快。

(2) 她们姐妹俩一般高。

2. 普通，平常（与"特殊"相对）。Normal; ordinary (as opposed to "特殊").

(3) 一个人每天一般应该有一个小时的运动时间。

(4) 这本汉英词典不一般。

3. 用在词或短语后面，表示比喻或说明情况相似，前面常与"像、好像、似"等词搭配使用，相当于"一样、似的"。有时"一般"可以略为"般"。Used after a word or a phrase, "一般" expresses a metaphor or similar situation. Similar to "一样, 似的," it is often used with "像, 好像, 似." "一般" may sometimes appear as "般."

(5) 他像爱护眼睛（一）般地爱护他的手机。

(6) 她如风一般地跑过我身边。

说明 Notes:

1. "一般"修饰的单音节形容词表示的意义一般是积极的，如例(2)。The monosyllabic adjective modified by "一般" is often positive in meaning as in (2).

2. "一样"和"一般"都表示相同的意义。区别是："一样"可以做谓语、定语，而"一般"则不能。"一样" and "一般" can both mean "the same." The difference is that "一样" can serve as the predicate or the attributive but "一般" cannot serve as the predicate.

(7) *你的手机跟他的手机一般。

(8) 你的手机跟他的手机一样。

(9) *爸爸和儿子有一般的脾气。

(10) 爸爸和儿子有一样的脾气。

yībānláishuō 一般来说

用法 Usage:

"一般"跟"来说"的搭配使用。表示在普通、平常（与"特殊"相对）的层面上，说明事物、道理的意思。插入语，常用于口语。Generally speaking. "一般来说" is used to describe or explain certain phenomena or things in general (as opposed to "特殊"). It is often used colloquially as a parenthesis.

(1) 一般来说,进城打工的农民都租房住。

(2) 中小学生一般来说都不能在学校里用手机。

yìbiān 一边 →P559"一面"

用法 Usage:

名词 n.

方位词。Locative noun.

1. 东西的一面,事情的一方面。常常儿化。One side of an object or one aspect of an issue, often followed by "儿."

(1) 你要在纸箱的一边(儿)写上你的名字。

(2) 事情的两方面总有一边(儿)是主要的,一边(儿)是次要的。

2. 旁边。By the side.

(3) 我们在打篮球,他坐在一边(儿)看书。

(4) 你不会下棋,就在一边(儿)看着学。

副词 ad.

1. 表示一个动作跟另一个动作同时进行,两个行为动作是同一主体发出,有时候前一个"一边"可以省略,有时候可以连用几个。At the same time when something is taking place. It is used to two simultaneous actions with the same subject. Sometimes the first "一边" can be omitted. Sometimes several "一边" can be used in one sentence.

(5) 她在洗衣服,还一边(儿)唱着歌。

(6) 妈妈说不能一边(儿)吃饭,一边(儿)看电视。

(7) 他一边(儿)学习,一边(儿)打工,一边(儿)还要照顾弟妹,很辛苦。

2. 两个动作、行为由不同主体发出,不能省略"一边"。While, used to refer to two simultaneous actions with different subjects. "一边" has to be used twice in the sentence.

(8) 中国朋友一边(儿)说怎么做,我一边(儿)跟着做,一会儿就学会包饺子了。

3. 连接两个意义上矛盾的内容。While, used to connect two contradictory actions.

(9) 他一边说要努力学习,一边不做作业,玩手机游戏。

说明 Notes:

1. "一边"和"一面"做名词,在表示物体、东西一面的意义上,用法相同。When used as a noun to refer to one side of an object or one aspect of an issue, "一边" and "一面" have the same usage.

(10) 箱子的一边儿/一面儿是黄色的。

2. "一边"和"一面"做副词,表示同一主体同时发出两个和几个动作、行为时,可以通用。区别是:"一边"可以表示两种动作、行为由不同的主体发出,而"一面"不能。When used as an adverb to describe two or more simultaneous actions or behaviors by the same subject, "一边" and "一面" have similar usage. The difference between the two is that "一边" can refer to two actions with different subjects but "一面" cannot.

(11) *妈妈一面说,我们一面做。我们很快就学会做饺子了。

(12) 妈妈一边说,我们一边做。我们很快就学会做饺子了。

3. "一边"和"一面"都可以叠用为"一边……一边……"和"一面……一面……",表示同一主体同时发出两个或几个动作、行为时,可以通用。区别是:"一边……一边……"可以表示两种动作、行为由不同的主体发出。"一面……一面……"不能。When reduplicated as "一边…一边…" and "一面…一面…" indicating two or more simultaneous actions or behaviors of the same subject, "一边" and "一面" have similar usage. The difference is that "一边…一边…" can refer to two simultaneous actions by different subjects but "一面…一面…" has no such usage.

(13) *玛丽一面在黑板上写,我们一面在座位上照着写。

(14) 玛丽一边在黑板上写,我们一边在座位上照着写。

yìdiǎnr 一点儿 →P582"一些"、P601"有(一)点儿"

用法 Usage:

数量词 *quantifier*

1. 表示量少而不确定。用法有：*A little, a bit. When indicating a small indefinite amount, "一点儿" has the following usages:*

① 在句中做主语、宾语、定语。可省略"一"。在上下文中，如果知道事物名词是什么，"一点儿"后面的名词可以省略。*Used as the subject, object, or attributive. "一" may be omitted. If the object is clear from the context, the noun may be omitted.*

(1) 她买了(一)点儿水果。
(2) 那(一)点儿馄饨不够吃的。
(3) 你再给我一点儿。

② 用在形容词后作补语，表示程度轻、数量略微增加或减少的意思。形容词后面一般要用"了"，表示有比较意义。*When used after an adjective as a complement, it refers to a low degree, slight increase or decrease of the amount. The adjective is usually followed by "了," which indicates a comparison.*

(4) 留学生宿舍的房间小了(一)点儿。
(5) 那个题目难了一点儿。

③ 重叠后可做状语。*Serving as an adverbial when reduplicated.*

(6) 小兔子一点儿一点儿地在长大。
(7) 现在他能一点儿一点儿地喝水了。

2. 与"(就)这么、(就)那么"连用，有强调少的作用。*When used with "(就)这么,(就)那么," it emphasizes a small amount.*

(8) 就那么点儿面包，怎么吃得饱？
(9) 这个月我就这么一点儿钱了。

3. 用在"不、没"的前面，表示完全否定。意思相当于"的确、确实"。有时"一点儿"和"不、没"之间可插入"也、都"等，强调语气。*When used before "不,没," it indicates a complete negation with a meaning similar to "的确,确实." Sometimes "也,都" can be inserted between "一点儿" and "不,没" to be more emphatic.*

(10) 这馒头一点儿也没坏，我吃吧。
(11) 他去上海我一点儿都不知道。

说明 Notes:

使用"一点儿"要注意：*Pay attention to the following aspects when using "一点儿."*

1. "一点儿"常用在"比"字句，但是不能用在递进式"比"字句中。*"一点儿" is often used in comparative sentences with "比," but it cannot be used in progressive comparative sentences.*

(12) 今天比昨天暖和一点儿。
(13) *天气一天比一天暖和一点儿。
(14) 天气一天比一天暖和。

2. 如形容词前已经受程度副词"很"等修饰，后面不能再带"一点儿"。*If the adjective is modified by a degree adverb such as "很," "一点儿" cannot be used after the adjective.*

(15) *他学习很努力一点儿。
(16) 他学习比以前努力一点儿了。

yìfāngmiàn 一方面 →P559"一面"

用法 Usage:

名词 *n.*

两种互相对立事物的一方或互相关联事物的一面。*One of the two opposite entities, or one aspect of a matter.*

(1) 这个问题责任不在我们这一方面，是在他们那一方面。
(2) 你说的只是情况的一方面，另一方面的情况呢？

连词 *conj.*

作为关联词语，常常叠用，有两个句式：*Often reduplicated as follows:*

1. 连接同一主体同时产生的两种活动或同一事物的两个方面。有时相当于"一面……一面……"。后一个"一方面"前常用指示代词"另"指示作用，后面常有副词"又、也、还"等呼应。有时候"一方面"可以用在主语前面。

Used to connect two simultaneous activities of the same subject or two aspects of a matter. Sometimes it is similar to "一面…一面…." The second "一方面" is often preceded by the demonstrative pronoun "另" and followed by such adverbs as "又,也,还." Sometimes "一方面" can appear before the subject.

(3) 我们一方面要刻苦学习,另一方面也要注意锻炼身体。

(4) 一方面你要对自己有信心,另一方面你还要有实干的行动。

2. 连接并列的两种互相关联的活动或事物。Used to connect two parallel activities or matters that are related.

(5) 我来中国,一方面是学汉语,另一方面是为了旅游。

(6) 你这次感冒,一方面是因为累了,另一方面是因为洗了冷水澡。

说明 Notes:

"一方面……(另)一方面……"和"一面……一面……"在句子中都起关联作用,当两者连接或表示同一主体同时产生两种活动(或作用),而这两种活动的动作性不太强时,可以通用。As a conjunction, "一方面…(另)一方面…" and "一面…一面…" are interchangeable when describing two simultaneous activities (or effects) of the same subject that are not very dynamic.

(7) 我们一方面/一面要努力学习,另一方面/一面也要注意身体锻炼。

它们的区别是:The differences between the two are as follows:

1. "一方面……(另)一方面……"连接动作性不强的两种活动或并存的两个方面的事物时,着重表示两种活动或并存的两个方面,时间上可有先后。"一面……一面……"着重表示同时进行的两种动作、行为,不能连接并存的两个方面的事物。When connecting two less dynamic activities or two aspects of the matter, "一方面…(另)一方面…" focuses on the chronological relationship between the two. "一面…一面…" is used to describe two simultaneous activities or behaviors. It cannot be used to connect two aspects of a matter.

(8) *我能得到奖学金一面是自己的努力,另一面是大家对我的帮助。

(9) 我能得到奖学金一方面是自己的努力,另一方面是大家对我的帮助。

2. "一方面……(另)一方面……"不能连接单纯的动词。"一面……一面……"可以。"一面…一面…" can connect two simple verbs or verb phrases but "一方面…(另)一方面…" cannot.

(10) *他一方面哭,一方面吃东西。

(11) 他一面哭,一面吃东西。

3. "一面……一面……"可以三四项连用。两个连用时,可以省略前一个"一面"。"一方面……(另)一方面……"一般只能连接两项,如果是多项,必须是两组两组,因为它连接的是事物的两个方面。"一面…一面…" can be used three or even four times in a sentence, and the first "一面" may be omitted. "一方面…(另)一方面…" usually connects only two things. Multiple things have to be described in pairs, as "一方面…(另)一方面…" connects two aspects of a matter.

(12) 她很快乐,常常一面唱歌,一面做饭,还一面洗衣服。

(13) 他做着作业,一面还听着音乐。

4. "一方面……(另)一方面……"可以用在主语前面。"一面……一面……"只能用在主语后面。"一方面…(另)一方面…" can be used before the subject. "一面…一面…" can only be used after the subject.

(14) 他没来考试,一方面是他生病了,另一方面是没有人通知他要考试。

(15) *一面他唱歌,一面他做作业。

5. 在后一个"一方面"前可以加指示代词"另"。"一面……一面……"不能。The second "一方面" can be preceded by the demonstrative pronoun "另." "一面…一面…" has no such usage.

yìkǒuqì 一口气 →P579"一连"

用法 Usage:

副词 ad.

表示迅速地、没有间歇地(做一个动作)。 Quickly, with no intermission (when performing an action).

(1) 他一口气吃下了四个包子。
(2) 她一口气跑了三千米。

说明 Notes:

"一口气"还是数量词加上名词,当名词用。"一口+气"表示呼吸的气息(多指微弱的、不愉快的等)。"一口气" can also be a noun phrase with a quantifier and a noun, "一口+气" which refers to the breath inhaled or exhaled (often weak and uncomfortable).

(3) 只要我还有一口气,就一定要完成这个科学实验。
(4) 他难受地叹了一口气说:她一句话也没说就离开了我。
(5) 让我喘一口气,喝杯水再说,好吗?

yìlián 一连 →P579"一口气"

用法 Usage:

副词 ad.

表示连续不断地。Continuously.

(1) 他一连喝了三杯水。
(2) 她一连三天没来上课,去旅游了吗?

说明 Notes:

"一口气"和"一连"用作副词都表示连续不断,句子中有表示主语(一般指人)一次性动作的数量词语时,两者可以互换。When used as an adverb, "一口气" and "一连" both mean "continuously." The two are interchangeable when there is a quantifier referring to a one-time action of the subject (usually people) in the sentence.

(3) 他一口气/一连背了十首唐诗。
(4) 我们一口气/一连爬了三座山。

它们的区别是:The differences between the two are as follows:

1. "一口气"修饰的动作是一次性的,发出动作的主体多是与人的体能有关的部分(如嘴、脚等)。"一连"修饰的动作有时不是一次性的,而是可以有间隔的连续几次或连续的一段的时间,发出的动作是主体的整体活动。"一口气" modifies a one-time action, which is often performed by a body part (such as the mouth or the feet). "一连" can sometimes modify actions that are repeated within a time frame rather than one-time actions. The action is performed by the subject as a whole.

(5) 我们一口气就爬上了十八楼。
(6) 他昨天一连给朋友打了五次电话。

2. "一连"可以修饰表示消极意义或产生消极结果的动词。"一口气"不能。"一连" can modify verbs that denotes an adverse situation or indicates a negative result but "一口气" cannot.

(7) *阿里一口气丢了两辆电动车。
(8) 阿里一连丢了两辆电动车。

yìqí 一齐 →P580"一起"

用法 Usage:

副词 ad.

表示同时。多用于书面语。Concurrently; in concerted efforts (mostly used in written language).

1. 表示几个个体同时发出或产生相同的动作、行为或情况。Indicating that several individuals perform the same action at the same time.

(1) 大家一齐拉住了他,说:"别往那儿走,那儿危险!"
(2) 表演一结束,观众们一齐热烈鼓掌并站了起来。

2. 表示几个个体同时接受相同的动作、行为或情况。Indicating that several individuals receive the same action or encounter the same situation at the same time.

(3) 今天下午我们一齐研究奖学金名单、教学实习等几个问题。
(4) 在同学们一齐帮助下,我的治病问题、学习问题都解决了。

yìqǐ 一起 →P558"一块儿"、P579"一齐"、P581"一同"

用法 Usage:

副词 ad.

表示共同在一处，意思相当于"一块儿"。句式有：At the same place, similar to "一块儿." It can be used as follows:

1. 表示几个主体在一处发出或产生相同的动作、行为或情况。几个不同个体词语之间要用介词"跟、和"等引出。Indicating that several subjects are engaged in the same action or involved in the same situation together. Prepositions such as "跟,和" should be used to link different subjects.

（1）你能跟我一起去银行吗？

（2）我现在不和父母一起生活。

2. 表示几个主体合在一处接受同样的动作、行为或情况。Indicating that several subjects receive the same action together.

（3）新年晚会全班同学一起唱中国民歌《茉莉花》。

（4）湖边的山、树、房子一起倒映在水面上，非常漂亮！

3. 方言中可以表示对数量的总括，相当于"一共、总共"。Indicating the total amount in some dialects, similar to "一共,总共."

（5）两个菜、一碗汤、一碗饭，一起多少钱啊？

（6）我们家四个人，一起有三台电脑、四部手机。

说明 Notes:

1."一起"还有名词用法，表示同一个处所。用于口语。常与"在、到"连用。"一起" can also be used as a noun referring to the same place. It is often used colloquially with "在,到."

（7）为了学习汉语，我们从世界各国走到一起来了。

（8）我希望能永远跟你在一起。

2."一起"和"一齐"一般不能互换，但是在动作、行为和情况是同处发生、同时发生的句子里，"一起"和"一齐"可以通用，但语义仍有侧重。"一起" and "一齐" are usually not interchangeable, with the exception when two actions or situations occur at the same place simultaneously.

它们的区别是：Their differences are as follows:

①"一起"着重于几个个体的动作行为在同一个空间发生。"一齐"着重于时间，强调几个个体的动作行为发生时间的统一性。"一起" emphasizes that the actions from different individuals occur at the same place. "一齐" focuses on the same time of various actions.

（9）星期五下午，五班同学一起去参观博物馆。（强调整体行为的空间统一性 Emphasizing the same place）

（10）星期五下午，五班同学一齐去参观博物馆。（强调整体行为时间的统一性 Emphasizing the same time）

（11）在宇宙间，太阳、地球和月亮永远是一起/一齐旋转的。

②"一起"还有名词用法和表示对数量的总括，如例（7）（5）。"一齐"没有这样的用法。"一起" can be used as a noun or referring to the total amount as in (7) and (5). "一齐" has no such usage.

3."一起"和"一块儿"都表示同一个空间，都有名词用法。"一起" and "一块儿" both can be used as a noun to refer to the same place.

它们的区别是："一块儿"多用于口语。"一起"通用于口语和书面语。Their difference is that "一块儿" is often used colloquially. "一起" can be used both colloquially and in written language.

yìshí 一时 →P625"暂时"

用法 Usage:

名词 n.

1. 表示一个时期。A period of time.

（1）唐朝也只是盛极一时的朝代。
（2）此一时彼一时，情况不一样了。

2. 表示短时间内。*Within a short time.*

（3）这种服装流行了一时就不再有人穿了。
（4）不要为了一时的快乐，不顾你的身体健康。

副词 ad.

1. 临时，暂时，偶然。后面多跟否定词语，表示短时间出现了某种情况或状态。"一时"多用在谓语前，有时也可以用在主语前。*Temporarily; occasionally. Often followed by negative words to indicate the occurrence of a certain situation or state within a short time.* "一时" *is often used in front of the predicate. Sometimes it can be used before the subject.*

（5）一时我想不起这个字怎么写了。
（6）你提出的问题一时还无法解决。

2. 重复使用，跟"时而"相同，表示情况在短时间内交替变化。*When reduplicated,* "一时" *is similar to* "时而," *indicating alternating changes of a situation within a short time.*

（7）他感到一时冷一时热，可能发烧了。
（8）车子一时停一时开，前面一定又堵车了。

说明 Notes:

1. "一时"作副词用，修饰的动词、形容词或短语大致有三类。*When used as an adverb,* "一时" *can modify three categories of verbs, adjectives or phrases.*

① 表示消极状态的动词、形容词。这些消极状态往往是动作者自己无法控制而出现的，如"糊涂、粗心、气愤、冲动、惊慌、忘了、愣住了"等动词或形容词。如果前面半句是表示原因的话，后面连接的多为消极性结果的半句。*Verbs or adjectives indicating a negative state of mind, which often cannot be controlled by the subject performing the action, such as* "糊涂，粗心，气愤，冲动，惊慌，忘了，愣住了." *If the first clause indicates the reason, the second clause usually shows the negative result.*

（9）我一时忘掉他叫什么名字了。

② 修饰动词的否定形式。这类否定形式或者是在动词前加"无法、不能"等否定词语，或者是可能补语的否定结构，如例（6）。*Negative form of verbs, which can be verbs preceded by negative words such as* "无法，不能" *or negative structures of potential complements as in (6).*

③ 句子常常分为前后两句，前一分句多表示原因，后一分句表示结果。"一时"用在后一分句的动词或形容词前面。*The sentence usually consists of two clauses, with the first one indicating the reason and the second one showing the result.* "一时" *is used in front of the verb or adjective in the second clause.*

（10）他才这么点年纪，一时还不会明白这些道理。
（11）同学们都来医院看我，感动得我一时流下了眼泪。

2. "一时"还可组成成语，如"红极一时、轰动一时、风靡一时"等。"一时" *can be used in set expressions such as* "红极一时，轰动一时，风靡一时."

yìtóng 一同 →P555"一道"、P580"一起"

用法 Usage:

副词 ad.

表示两个或两个以上的个体同时同地发出某种动作或产生某种现象、情况。*Together, used to indicate that two or more individuals are engaged in the same action or involved in the same situation simultaneously.*

（1）我跟她在国外一同留学了两年。
（2）学生们一同站起来向老师问好。

说明 Notes:

1. "一同"在句子中既表示空间，也表示时间。有时侧重于时间，相当于"一齐、同时"；有时侧重于空间，相当于"一起、一块"。"一同" *refers to both the location and the time. When it emphasizes the time, it is similar to* "一齐，同时." *When it emphasizes the location, it is similar to* "一起，一块."

（3）他终于和大家一同笑了起来。（侧重时间 Emphasizing the time）

（4）他醒过来首先看到的是老师和同学一同出现在他眼前。（侧重空间 Emphasizing the location）

2. "一同"和"一道"的区别是："一同"没有"一道"同路的意思。"一道"多用于南方地区。"一同" differs from "一道" as follows: "一同" does not have the meaning of taking the same route as "一道," and "一道" is often used in the south.

3. "一起"和"一同"的区别是："一起" differs from "一同" as follows:

① "一起"既用于口语，又用于书面语。"一同"多用于书面语。所以"一起"的使用频率比"一同"高。"一起" can be used both colloquially and in written language. "一同" is generally used in written language. Therefore, "一起" is more frequently used than "一同."

② "一起"有名词用法。"一同"只有副词用法。"一起" can be used as a noun, but "一同" can only be used as an adverb.

yìxiē 一些 →P577"一点儿"

用法 Usage:

数量词 quantifier

表示少量事物或形状。前面可用数词只能是"一"。但在口语里一般"一"省略不用。多用于书面语。A little, a few. Indicating a small amount or shape, "些" can only be preceded by the number "一," which is often omitted in colloquial usage. "一些" is often used in written language.

句式有：The sentence structures are as follows:

1. "一些＋名词"。"一些＋n."

（1）你给了她（一）些什么东西，她在房间里乐呢。

（2）我这里有一些面包和饼干，你可以拿去吃。

2. "有＋一些＋名词"，做主语、定语。"有＋一些＋n.," used as the subject or attributive.

（3）有一些小玩具就是让女孩子喜欢而买的。

（4）句子里有一些词语的意思我看不懂。

3. "动/形＋一些"。表示稍微,常和"稍微、略微"合用。"v./a.＋一些," often used with "稍微,略微" meaning "slightly."

（5）请你唱一些大家熟悉的歌！

（6）他比我稍微瘦一些。

说明 Notes:

"一些"和"一点儿"都指不定而又不多的数量或程度。"一些" and "一点儿" both indicate an indefinite small amount or degree.

它们的区别是：They differ as follows:

1. "一些"多用于书面语，一般不儿化。"一点儿"多用于口语,常常儿化。"一些" is usually used in written language and not followed by "儿." "一点" is often used colloquially with "儿."

2. "一些"着重指不多的若干数量，多用于可计数的人、具体事物或时间。"一点儿"着重指很少的数量或极低的程度。语意比"一些"轻。多用于不可计数的事物。指数量极少时,前面加"这、这么、那、那么"等指示代词,可以用于可计数的人、具体的事物或时间。Often used to count people, specific objects or time, "一些" emphasizes an amount that is not large. "一点儿" emphasizes a small amount or low degree with a lighter tone of voice than "一些." It is generally used to describe things that are not countable. When preceded by a demonstrative pronoun to indicate a small amount, "一点儿" can describe people, time or countable objects.

（7）*公园里一点人在跳舞，一点人在散步。

（8）公园里一些人在跳舞，一些人在散步。

（9）来了这么一点人，能帮什么忙？

3. 在句子中，"一些"表示的数量不一定很少。"一点儿"表示的一定是少量。"一些"

does not necessarily indicate a small amount, but "一点儿" definitely does.

（10）下课以后，你留一下，有一些事我要问你一下。(不止一件事 More than one thing)

（11）下课以后，你留一下，有一点儿事我要问你一下。(可能只有一件事 Possibly only one thing)

yìzhí 一直 →P421"始终"、P563"一向"

用法 Usage:

副词 ad.

1. 表示顺着一个方向不变。"一直"后或动词后常有表示方向的词。*Following the same direction with no change. "一直" or the verb is often followed by a direction word.*

（1）一直往前走，就是西湖。

（2）从窗口一直望西面，那座山就是香山。

2. 强调所指的范围。用在"到"前面，后面常有"都、全"呼应。*Emphasizing the scope. Often used before "到,""一直" usually corresponds with "都,全" in the sentence.*

（3）大教室的座位上、过道上，一直到门口，全是来听讲座的同学。

（4）学院从老师、同学一直到宿舍的服务员，都对我非常热情。

3. 表示动作连续不断或状态持续不变。*Indicating a continuous action or unchanged status.*

（5）毕业以后，我们一直没见过面。

（6）晚饭前他一直在做作业。

说明 Notes:

1. "一向"和"一直"的区别是："一向" *differs from "一直" as follows:*

① "一向"着重于强调保持不变，指动作行为或状态从过去到现在都很稳定，不改变。"一直"着重于连续性，不间断，指在某段时间内不间断地做某事。*"一向" emphasizes that the behavior or status remains stable and unchanged from the past to the present. "一直" emphasizes the continuity of doing something with no interruption within a certain period of time.*

（7）她的态度一向很好。

（8）我们做同屋以来，他一直对我很照顾。

② 在用"一直"的句子中，常常可以看到起止的时间，这是不间断做某事的时间范围，这种时间范围往往可长可短。表示时间短的，一般只用"一直"。用"一向"的句子中，可以有一个时段，但是不需要划定一个具体的起止时间。*A sentence with "一直" usually indicates the starting time and the range of time of an action or behavior, which can be either long or short. When indicating a short range of time, "一直" rather than "一向" is used. A sentence with "一向" may indicate a range of time but not necessarily a specific starting point.*

（9）从昨天起，他一直在实验室工作着。

（10）这几年，他一向住在北京，没回上海住过。

③ "一直"可以用于现在以前的时间，也可以用于现在以后的时间。"一向"没有这样的用法。*"一直" can be used for time in the past or the future. "一向" cannot be used as such.*

（11）我对中国书法很感兴趣，准备回国以后一直学下去。

2. 用"始终"的句子都可以用"一直"替换。*"始终" can always be replaced by "一直."*

（12）从初中开始，他一直/始终在学习外语。

它们的区别是：*They differ as follows:*

① "始终"着重强调动作行为完成的从开始到结束的整个过程。"一直"着重强调整个过程中动作行为的一致性，不改变。*"始终" is used to emphasize the whole process of an action or behavior — from the beginning to the end. "一直," by contrast, emphasizes the consistency of an action or behavior in the whole process. There is no change whatsoever.*

② "一直"后的动词可以带表示时间的词语。"始终"不可以。*"一直" can be followed by a word or expression indicating a time. "始*

(13) *昨天他始终学到晚上十二点。

(14) 昨天他一直学到晚上十二点。

③ "一直"可以指将来的时间。"始终"不可以。"一直" can be used to refer to a time in the future, but "始终" cannot.

(15) *在这个学校,我始终学到明年元旦。

(16) 在这个学校,我一直学到明年元旦。

④ 如果句子中有动作开始的时间词语,句子带有"会、将"等表示将来的词语,"一直"可以替换成"始终"。If there is a word indicating the beginning of a time, or if there is "会,将" to indicate a future time, "一直" can be replaced by "始终."

(17) 从现在开始,我会一直/始终记着你。

yìlùn 议论 →P456"谈论"、P456"讨论"

用法 Usage:

动词 v.

对人或事物的好坏、是非等表示自己的意见。Expressing one's opinion on certain people or matters.

(1) 在背后议论别人是个不好的习惯。

(2) 请几个人来议论议论这个问题,听听他们的意见。

(3) 关于论文的题目,你们议论得怎么样?

说明 Notes:

1. "谈论"和"议论"的区别是:"谈论" differs from "议论" as follows:

① "谈论"泛指对人或事物的描述、说明以及看法,多以随便谈话的方式在口头上进行。"谈论"只说自己的意见,跟别人的意见没有关系,用于比较轻松的语境。"议论"着重指对人或事物的好坏、是非等表示意见。"议论"表示自己的意见,跟别人的意见也没有关系,但它强调所说的意见主要是评价性的,比"谈论"更正式地说出自己的意见。Often in the form of casual conversation, "谈论" refers to descriptions, explanations of or viewpoints on certain people or matters. The speaker only expresses his/her own opinion, which has nothing to do with others' viewpoints. "谈论" is generally used in a casual context. "议论" emphasizes expressing one's opinion on certain people or matters. The speaker also expresses his/her own opinion unrelated to others' viewpoints, but the opinion expressed is mostly judgmental and more formal than "谈论."

② "议论"有名词用法,指写作手法的专门术语"议论"。"谈论"没有这个用法。"议论" can be used as a noun referring to a style of writing. "谈论" has no such usage.

(4) 写文章的方法有描述、说明、抒情和议论等。

2. "讨论"和"议论"都表示在一起各自发表自己的意见。"讨论" and "议论" both mean expressing individual viewpoints in a discussion.

它们的区别是:"讨论"着重于就某一问题交换意见或分析研究。多是在会议、课堂比较正式的场合,有人召集、主持。可以是两个人或两个以上的人在一起进行研究,交换意见。"议论"着重于对人或事物的好坏、是非等表示意见,也常常以随便谈话的方式,你一言我一语地在私下、背后等非正式场合里口头上进行。Their difference is as follows: "讨论" emphasizes exchanging ideas or analyzing certain matters by two or more people, often on formal occasions such as meetings and classes that are convened and hosted by someone. "议论" emphasizes expressing one's opinion on certain people or matters, often in casual conversations on private and informal occasions.

yìsi 意思

用法 Usage:

名词 n.

1. 指语言文字或其他信号所表达的意义、

思想内容。*Meaning or thoughts conveyed by language or other signals.*

(1) 这句话是什么意思?

(2) 他点了下头,意思是他同意了。

2. 表示意见、愿望。表示"愿望"时,前面常常加"有"。*Opinion or wish. When indicating a wish, it is often preceded by "有."*

(3) 我的意思是你不用去了。

(4) 你有意思认识一个中国朋友吗?

3. 某种趋势或苗头。*Certain trend.*

(5) 天有点儿要下雨的意思,我们回家吧。

(6) 他有点儿想跟你做朋友的意思。

4. 指情趣、趣味。*Interest.*

(7) 这种花儿像猴子的脸,真有意思!

(8) 他们的游戏很有意思。

5. 代表心意的礼物,或礼物表示的心意。常在送别人礼物时说。*A gift with a good wish, or the good wish contained in a gift (often used when giving a gift).*

(9) 这点小意思,你就收下吧!

(10) 这是你哥的意思,请收下吧!

动词 *v.*

指表示心意、感谢。常重叠使用或后面带有补语。*To show gratitude (often reduplicated or followed by a complement).*

(11) 他很热情地帮助我学汉语,我想送他点礼物意思意思。

(12) 他们俩结婚,我们应该意思一下。

yìwài 意外

用法 Usage:

名词 *n.*

指想不到的不幸事件。*Unexpected and unfortunate incidents.*

(1) 这里不能吸烟,以免发生意外。

(2) 他年纪大了,要有人照顾,以免发生什么意外。

形容词 *a.*

意料之外的,没有想到的。*Unexpected.*

(3) 他突然来到我家,我感到非常意外。

(4) 这个意外的消息让他高兴了好几天。

说明 Notes:

"意外"用作名词常常指不好的事情。使用时要注意,如例(1)(2)。*When used as a noun, "意外" usually refers to an unfortunate incident as in (1) and (2).*

yìwèizhe 意味着

用法 Usage:

动词 *v.*

1. 表示,标志着。*To indicate; to signify.*

(1) 科学的发展意味着人类社会的进步。

(2) 得到 HSK 五六级证书意味着可以在中国大学学习本科专业。

2. 含有某种意思,可以理解为。后面常跟着是什么意思的词语或小句。*To carry a certain meaning; to be interpreted as. It is often followed by a phrase or a clause indicating the meaning.*

(3) 她不跟你说话就意味着她在跟你生气了。

(4) 他来上课意味着他喜欢你的课。

说明 Notes:

"意味着"多用于书面语。用"意味着"的句子,其主语也多为动词或动词性小句,并且"意味着"后面要求带动词性宾语,如例(1)(2)(3)(4)。*"意味着" is generally used in written language. The subject of the sentence is often a verb or a verbal clause. "意味着" is usually followed by a verbal object as in (1), (2), (3) and (4).*

yīn 因

用法 Usage:

介词 *prep.*

1. 凭借,根据。*According to; based on.*

(1) 什么药治什么病也是因人而异的。

(2) 他们因陋就简,用雨布搭成临时休息处。

2. 由于,表示跟在后面的内容是原因。*Due to; as a result of (followed by the reason).*

（3）阿里今天因病请假，不能来上课。
（4）请大家注意，明天下午的会议因故改期。

连词 conj.

相当于"因为"，用在前一分句表示原因，后面常与"所以、就、才"等词语呼应。Like "因为," it is used in the first clause to indicate a reason, which often corresponds with "所以，就，才" in the second clause.

（5）这个湖面因水草太多，所以不能游泳。
（6）因治疗及时，她的病才好得那么快。

名词 n.

原因（跟"果"相对）。Reason (corresponding with "果" in the sentence).

（7）每件事情都会有前因后果。
（8）你这样做，外因是什么，内因又是什么？

动词 v.

沿袭，依照旧传统办理。To follow the tradition.

（9）划龙船是因循旧习，代代相传下来的风俗。

yīncǐ 因此 →P451"所以"、P586"因而"

用法 Usage:

连词 conj.

因为这个（原因、情况），用在后一个分句中表示结果。Therefore; as a result of this (reason, situation). Used in the second clause to show a result.

（1）我和他同班同学六年，因此对他比较了解。
（2）这里有山有水，风景因此很美。

说明 Notes:

"所以"和"因此"都是连词，都用在因果关系语句中，表示结果或结论。As a conjunction, "所以" and "因此" are both used in sentences with a causal relationship to indicate a result or conclusion.

它们的区别是：Their differences are as follows:

1."所以"可以和表示原因的"因为""由于"配合呼应。"因此"一般只能与表示原因的"由于"配合呼应。"所以" can be used with words indicating the reason such as "因为" or "由于." "因此" can only be used with "由于."

（3）*因为我没看到通知，因此我迟到了。
（4）因为我没看到通知，所以我迟到了。
（5）由于我没看到通知，因此我迟到了。

2."因此"只能用在表示因果关系的句子里，"所以"的其他用法都没有。"因此" can only be used in sentences with causal relationship. Except for this, it has no other usage as "所以" does.

yīn'ér 因而 →P76"从而"、P586"因此"

用法 Usage:

连词 conj.

相当于"因此"，表示因果关系，承接上文的前提、理由或原因，引出推论、判断、结论或结果。在表示原因或理由的分句中，有时用"由于"相呼应。Thus; as a result. Like "因此," it indicates a causal relationship. "因而" connects the premise or reason in the first clause and the judgment, conclusion or result in the second clause. Sometimes it corresponds with "由于" in the clause indicating the reason.

（1）由于增加了晚上的睡眠时间，因而白天的精神好多了。
（2）去西安旅游的名额满了。我没报上名，因而去不了。

说明 Notes:

1."因而"和"因此"的区别是：The differences between "因而" and "因此" are as follows:

①"因此"的"此"，主要用来指前面已经出现过的原因，当说话者强调由于前面的原因才造成了后面的结果时，一般用"因此"，"因此"着重于引出结果。"因而"着重于逻辑上的推导，所以两者有时不能互换。The "此" in "因此" refers to an aforementioned reason. "因此" is usually used to emphasize the result caused by that reason. "因而" emphasizes the logical reasoning. Sometimes the two are not interchangeable.

（3）她觉得汉语太难学,因此学别的专业了。（引出具体结果 Introducing the specific result）

（4）论文事实根据不足,没有分析,理论性不强,因而没有说服力。（因果推论 Logical reasoning）

② "因而"多连接分句,一般不能用于句号后,即不能连接段落。"因此"分句、句子都能连接。"因而" is generally used to connect clauses rather than paragraphs. Therefore, it cannot be used after the period. "因此" can be used to connect either clauses or sentences.

2. "从而"和"因而"都能连接分句,表示先有前事,才有后事。前后两事有连续相承的关系,区别是:连接前后分句的语用条件和表现出来的句子意义不同。Both "从而" and "因而" can connect clauses indicating that one thing happens in the first clause leading to another in the second, showing the relationship of one passing to the other. The difference is that the pragmatic condition and significance connecting the two clauses are distinct.

① 如果引出的是消极的、人们不愿意看到的结果,句子表达了强烈的因果关系,只能用"因而",不能用"从而"。If the result led by the first clause is negative or undesirable, and the sentence expresses a strong causality, only "因而" can be used.

（5）*他常常不做作业,从而受到了老师的批评。

（6）他常常不做作业,因而受到了老师的批评。

② "从而"可以用于表示目的的分句,前一分句是方法或要求,后一分句是要达到的目的。"因而"不能。"从而" can be used in the clause of purpose. In this case, the first clause expresses a method or request, while the latter expresses the purpose to reach. "因而" cannot be used in this way.

（7）*先复习当天上课的内容,充分理解知识点,因而更快更正确地完成当天的作业。

（8）先复习当天上课的内容,充分理解知识点,从而更快更正确地完成当天的作业。

yīnwèi 因为 →P595"由于"

用法 Usage:
连词 conj.

用于因果关系的复句中,表示原因或理由。Because, used in multiple clauses with a causal relationship to indicate the reason.

句式有: The sentence structures are as follows:

1. "因为"用在前面句子,后面句子开头常用"所以",句中常有"就、才"与之呼应。前后两个句子主语相同时"因为"可以在主语前,也可以在主语后。前后两个句子主语不同时,"因为"在主语前。Used in the first clause, "因为" often corresponds with "所以" at the beginning of the second clause and "就、才" in the sentence. When the two clauses have the same subject, "因为" can be used before or after the subject. When the two clauses have different subjects, "因为" should be used before the subject.

（1）因为要下雨,所以明天我不想出去玩了。

（2）他因为考上了大学,所以这几天特别高兴。

（3）因为哥哥考上了大学,所以这几天她很高兴。

2. "因为"用在后面的分句。"因为" can also be used in the second clause.

（4）玛丽非常想家,因为她是第一次离开家来那么远的地方。

（5）小李很想去西藏旅游,因为他爷爷曾经在那儿工作过。

介词 prep.

跟名词、代词或名词短语构成介词短语,表

示动作行为的原因或理由。在句中做状语。一般表示原因或理由的句子内容在前面,表示结果或结论的内容在后面。但也可以把表示原因或理由的内容放在后面,这时,需用判断词"是"。Forming a prepositional phrase with a noun, pronoun or noun phrase to serve as an adverbial, "因为" indicates the reason for an action or a behavior. The first clause usually indicates the reason and the second clause shows the result or conclusion. Sometimes when the reason is indicated later in the sentence, "因为" has to be preceded by "是."

(6) 她因为男朋友才一起来这儿学汉语。

(7) 我们俩成了朋友是因为他。

说明 Notes:

使用"因为"要注意:Pay attention to the following aspects when using "因为":

1. "因为"作介词用,构成的介宾短语可以放在主语前面,也可以放在主语后面。When "因为" is used as a preposition, the prepositional phrase with "因为" can be used before or after the subject.

(8) 因为天气关系,飞机不能按时起飞。

(9) 飞机因为天气关系不能按时起飞。

2. "因为"构成的介宾短语做状语时,在状语和中心语之间常常用"而、就"等词连接。When the prepositional phrase with "因为" serves as an adverbial, it is often connected to the center word by "而,就."

(10) 他不会因为脚痛而不去旅游。

(11) 我不能因为你反对就放弃留学的机会。

yīn 阴

用法 Usage:

形容词 a.

1. 中国气象部门规定,天空80%以上被云遮住,不见阳光或偶见阳光的天气称为"阴"。Overcast; cloudy. According to the criteria from the meteorological departments in China, the weather is described as "阴" when 80% of the sky is covered by grey cloud with no or little sunshine.

(1) 今天天气阴转晴。

(2) 天阴了,可能要下雨。

2. 凹进的(与突出的"阳"相对)。常用于印章的刻写、书帖的拓印时。Concave (as opposed to "阳" that means "convex"). Often used in inscription.

(3) 你的印章刻阴文还是刻阳文?

(4) 这本书帖的字是阴文。

3. 不露在外面的,暗藏的。Unexposed, hidden.

(5) 下水道在有的方言里叫阴沟。

名词 n.

1. 中国古代哲学认为存在于宇宙间的一切事物中的两大对立面之一(与"阳"相对)。如"阴面/阳面、阴历/阳历"等。One of the two opposite sides of all matters in the universe according to ancient Chinese philosophy, as opposed to "阳" in "阴面/阳面,阴历/阳历."

2. 指时间,光阴。Time.

(6) 寸阴寸金,时间是很宝贵的。

3. 不见阳光的地方。Shade.

(7) 我们去树阴/荫下,那儿比较凉快。

(8) 不对着太阳的那面是阴面。

yīng 应 →P152"该"、P589"应当"、P589"应该"

用法 Usage:

助动词 aux. v.

应该。多用于书面语。Should. It is often used in written language as an auxiliary verb.

(1) 人类应与大自然和谐相处。

(2) 老师在第一节课就应与学生讲清楚一个学期的教学计划。

说明 Notes:

1. 使用"应"要注意:"应"可以用肯定否定的形式提问,但是不能单独回答问题。When using "应," one has to note that "应" can be used in an A-not-A type of question but it cannot stand alone as a response.

(3) A：小王,我有点头痛,不知应不应该去医院?

B：应该。/＊应。

2."应"又读"yìng",作动词用。表示：When pronounced as "yìng," "应" is used as a verb with the following meanings:

① 回答,作出反应。To respond; to react.

(4) 你的朋友在叫你呢,你先应他一声。

② 受,满足要求。To accept; to meet the requirement.

(5) 他很热情,是个有求必应的好人。

③ 适应,应时。To adapt to.

(6) 这个设计师会应时设计出很多流行服装。

④ 采取措施对付,处理。To handle with proper measures.

(7) 星期天商店有很多顾客,我常常应接不暇。

3."应"和"该"做助动词时,意思相近。"应" and "该" are close in meaning when serving as an auxiliary verb.

它们的区别是：Their differences are as follows：

① "应"多用于书面语。"该"多用于口语。"应" appears more in written Chinese while "该" appears more in oral Chinese.

② "该"可以用在假设句的后一分句,表示情理上的推测。"应"不能。"该" may be used in the second clause of a suppositive sentence to make a logical supposition. "应" cannot be used this way.

(8) ＊假如他去而我没去,他应生气了。

(9) 假如他去而我没去,他该生气了。

③ "该"可以组成"该＋有＋多……"的格式。"应"不能。"该" may appear in the pattern "该＋有＋多…," but "应" cannot.

(10) ＊再过三年,这个城市的交通情况应有多大的变化啊！

(11) 再过三年,这个城市的交通情况该有多大的变化啊！

④ "该"前面可加"又"。"应"一般不能。"该" may be preceded by "又," but "应" cannot.

(12) ＊如果你再不穿毛衣,又应感冒了。

(13) 如果你再不穿毛衣,又该感冒了。

yīngdāng 应当 →P589"应该"

用法 Usage：

助动词 aux. v.

1.表示情理上必须如此,应该。可以单独回答问题。否定用"不应当"。Should; ought to (according to reason or logic). It can stand alone as a response. The negative form is "不应当."

(1) 自己的事情应当自己做。

(2) 快八点了,我们应当去上课了。

2.估计情况必然如此。Most likely.

(3) 我妈妈现在应当到了上海机场了。

(4) 明年九月你应当是个小学生了。

yīnggāi 应该 →P588"应"、P589"应当"

用法 Usage：

助动词 aux. v.

1.表示理所当然。可以单独回答问题。否定用"不应该"。"不应该"作谓语时前面可以加"很"。Certainly. It can stand alone as a response. The negative form is "不应该." When "不应该" serves as the predicate, it can be preceded by "很."

(1) 现在你应该做作业了。

(2) 你真的很不应该,到现在还在玩游戏。

2.估计情况必然如此。Most likely.

(3) 他是名牌大学毕业,又有实际工作经验,应该会找到一份好工作。

(4) 火车五点开,还有半个小时,应该来得及。

说明 Notes：

"应"和"应该""应当"的区别是：The differences among "应," "应该" and "应当" are as follows：

1."应"不能单独回答问题。"应该"和"应当"可以。"应" cannot stand alone as a response but "应该" and "应当" can.

2. "应"多用于书面语。"应该"和"应当"通用于口语和书面语。"应" is mostly used in written language. "应该" and "应当" can be used both colloquially and in written language.

3. "应该"和"应当"后面可以带小句,"应"不能。Both "应该" and "应当" can be followed by a clause but "应" cannot.

4. "应"能组成四字成语,如"理应如此、应有尽有"等。"应该"和"应当"不能。"应" can be used in four-character idioms such as "理应如此,应有尽有.""应该" and "应当" have no such usage.

5. "应该"或"不应该"做谓语,前面可以加副词"很"。"应当"一般不加。When "应该" or "不应该" serves as the predicate, the adverb "很" can come before them, but "应当" cannot be preceded by "很."

yìngyòng 应用 →P617"运用"

用法 Usage:

动词 v.

使用。To use; to put to use; to apply.

（1）在网络上支付这项技术已经应用得非常广泛。

（2）你可以应用这个方法做出很多新的句子。

形容词 a.

可以让人直接在生活或生产中运用的。Applicable in life or production; applied.

（3）我的研究项目是应用语言学。

（4）越来越多的人意识到,没有基础科学,应用科学就是无源之水。

yìng 硬

用法 Usage:

形容词 a.

1. 物体内部的组织紧密,受外力作用后不容易改变形状（跟"软"相对）,坚固。Hard; tough; firm. It is used to describe the dense texture of an object, the shape of which does not change easily when subject to an external force (as opposed to "软").

（1）这些家具都是硬木做的。

（2）这个面包已经硬了,还吃吗？

2. （性格）刚强,（意志）坚强。Strong; firm; tough. It is used to describe the firm character or will.

（3）那是个硬汉子,什么困难都难不倒他。

（4）妈妈不是个硬性子人,对人和蔼可亲,大家都喜欢她。

3. （能力）强,（质量）好。(Of ability) strong; (of quality) excellent.

（5）这款国产运动鞋质量确实过硬。

（6）在写毛笔字上,他有一手硬功夫。

4. 既定的,不能改变的,硬性的。多指规定的工作计划或任务。Fixed; unchangeable. It often refers to a work plan or task.

（7）1 500套运动衣裤,这是硬任务,十天必须完成！

（8）每天记20个生词是我学习外语的硬指标。

副词 ad.

1. 坚决地,执拗地（做某事）。Firmly; stubbornly.

（9）他的伤还没好,可是他硬要参加这次比赛。

（10）他硬要我吃下那几只辣椒。

2. 勉强地（做某事）。Managing with difficulty.

（11）他硬爬上了山,你看,他的脚又肿了。

（12）一个月300元生活费,他硬过了一年。

yōngyǒu 拥有 →P257"具有"

用法 Usage:

动词 v.

领有,具有（大量的土地、人口、财产等）。To own; to contain; to possess (lots of land, people or property).

（1）他家拥有三个农庄、六个葡萄园和两家酒厂。

（2）海南岛拥有丰富的风力资源。

说明 Notes:

"拥有"和"具有"都表示有、存在的意思。"拥有" and "具有" both mean to own or to exist.

它们的区别是:"拥有"的对象一般多指大量的、可宝贵的、很有价值的资源及财产。"具有"的对象多指意义、价值、作用等抽象概念。*Their difference is as follows: While the objects of "拥有" are often valuable resources or properties in large quantity, the objects of "具有" are often abstract concepts such as meaning, value, or function.*

(3) *他是个拥有浪漫主义情感的诗人。

(4) 他是个具有浪漫主义情感的诗人。

yòng 用

用法 Usage:

动词 *v.*

使用。可重叠,可带"着、了、过"。*To use. It can be reduplicated, and it can go with "着,了,过."*

句式有: *Its sentence structures are as follows:*

1. 表示使用所凭借的工具、方式或手段。*To use a tool or method.*

(1) 我会用手机,他还不太会用。

(2) 我用筷子吃饭,他用刀叉吃饭。

2. "用+来+动词","来"引出动词,表示事物的作用。*"用 + 来 + verb," with "来" introducing the verb to show the function of something.*

(3) 在饭店,手机可以用来支付饭钱。

(4) 风力可以用来发电。

3. "用+作/做+名词","用作/做"表示"当作……用"。*"用 + 作 + noun," with "用作" meaning "to be used as."*

(5) 这个餐厅有时也用作会场。

(6) 来的朋友很多,他把脸盆洗干净用作菜盘,装生菜色拉。

4. "用+在/于+名词性词语",表示事物所用的方面。*"用 + 在/于 + noun phrase" indicating the application of something.*

(7) 我要把时间和精力用在写论文上,找工作的问题以后再说。

(8) 这些钱要用于科学实验,不能乱花。

5. "用+以",表示"用这个来……"达到什么目的意思,多用于书面语。*"用 + 以" meaning to use something to achieve a goal (mostly used in written language).*

(9) 中国提出了"一带一路"倡议,用以促进参与国经济文化的发展。

(10) 每个公司都有广告,用以扩大影响,争取市场。

6. "用+开+了",表示广泛使用起来了的意思。*"用 + 开 + 了," meaning "to be used widely."*

(11) 这种牌子的手机很快就用开了。

说明 Notes:

"用"作动词可以带比较多的补语。除了上面所列以外,还有:"用上",表示"已经使用了……"的意思;"用得起",表示"有能力买来使用";"用起来",表示"开始用……"或"用的时候"等。"用"的具体语义则随着后面的补语不同而有所不同。*As a verb, "用" can be followed by various complements. In addition to the examples above, "用上" means "have already used…;" "用得起" means "can afford to buy something for use;" "用起来" means "to start using something" or "when using something." The specific meaning of "用" varies depending on the complement following it.*

yòngbuzháo 用不着

用法 Usage:

"用不着"是"用得着"的反义词。*"用不着" is the antonym of "用得着."*

1. 没有使用价值。*To have no value for use.*

(1) 这个旧手机已经用不着了。

(2) 这本词典里,有的解释现在已经用不着了。

2. 没有必要,不需要,不必。多用于口语。后面可带名词或形容词、动词性词语。*To be unnecessary; to have no need for. Often used colloquially, it can be followed by a noun, an adjective or a verb phrase.*

（3）你看,他们来了,我们用不着去找他们了。

（4）听说老师生病了,今天用不着上课了吗?

yòngchù 用处 →P592"用途"

用法 Usage:

名词 n.

用途,作用。句中一般有关于"是什么事物的用处"的提示。*Use; effect. There is usually a reference to what the use is for in the sentence.*

（1）学习外语时,词典有很大用处。

（2）现在手机的用处很广泛。

说明 Notes:

1. 和"用处"搭配使用的形容词有"广、广泛、狭窄、大、多、少"等,如例（2）。*Different adjectives can be used with "用处," such as "广,广泛,狭窄,大,多,少," as in (2).*

2. "用处"做宾语时,经常和动词"（没）有"搭配使用,如例（1）。*When used as an object, "用处" often follows the verb "(没)有," as in (1).*

yòngtú 用途 →P592"用处"

用法 Usage:

名词 n.

指物品应用的方面或范围。经常搭配使用的形容词有"多、少、广泛、狭窄"等。*Application (or range of application) of an object. It often goes with adjectives such as "多,少,广泛,狭窄."*

（1）说明书上清楚地写着这种产品的用途。

（2）现在手机的用途非常广泛。

说明 Notes:

"用处"和"用途"都指起作用的地方、应用的方面或范围。*"用处" and "用途" both refer to the application of an object or its range of application.*

它们的区别是：*Their differences are as follows:*

1. "用处"侧重指能起的某种作用或某种效用,使用的范围比较宽,可用于事物,也可用于人。"用途"侧重指应用的方面和范围,只用于物,不用于人。*"用处" focuses on a certain use or effect. The range of application is relatively wide, which can be applied to both objects or people. "用途" emphasizes the range of application of an object but not of people.*

（3）*这个人将来一定有很大的用途。

（4）这个人将来一定有很大的用处。

2. "用处"多用于口语。"用途"多用于书面语。*"用处" often appears colloquially, whereas "用途" is often used in written language.*

yōuliáng 优良 →P592"优秀"

用法 Usage:

形容词 a.

（品质、质量、成绩、作风等）十分好,很出色。*(Of the quality, grades, or style of work) excellent; superb; great.*

（1）这次考试你取得了优良的成绩。

（2）公司的科研小组又培育出了优良的玉米种子。

yōuxiù 优秀 →P592"优良"

用法 Usage:

形容词 a.

（品质、学问、成绩等）非常好,突出,出众,超出一般。*(Of a person's character, knowledge, performance) distinguished; superb; excellent.*

（1）这个学生各方面都很优秀,老师同学都很喜欢她。

（2）他每年都是公司的优秀员工。

说明 Notes:

"优良"和"优秀"都形容非常好,都可以形容成绩。*"优良" and "优秀" both mean "great"*

and can both describe grades or performance.

它们的区别是：Their differences are as follows:

1. "优良"着重于良好。除"成绩"外,还多形容"品种、质量、质地、传统、作风"等,不能形容人。"优秀"着重于非常出色,表示的程度比"优良"高。可形容"品行、品德、品质、作品、文化"等,可以用于事物,也可用于人,如"优秀人才、优秀文学家、优秀教师"等。"优良" focuses on being very good. In addition to "成绩," it can modify words such as "品种,质量,质地,传统,作风." It cannot be used to describe people. "优秀" emphasizes being exceptional with a higher degree than "优良." It can modify words such as "品行,品德,品质,作品,文化." It can be used to describe both things or people, as in "优秀人才,优秀文学家,优秀教师."

2. "优秀"可以受"很、非常"等程度副词的修饰。"优良"不能。"优秀" can be modified by degree adverbs such as "很,非常" but "优良" cannot.

yóuqí 尤其 →P457"特别"

用法 Usage:

副词 ad.

表示经过比较,下面所说的更进一步。相当于"更加"或"特别"的副词用法。Especially, indicating that compared with the subject mentioned in the first part of the sentence, the subject in the second part stands above the rest, or is more advanced. It is similar to "更加" or "特别" used as an adverb.

(1) 大家都喜欢唱歌,阿里尤其喜欢。

(2) 这几天天气很好,尤其是今天,蓝天白云,让人非常高兴!

说明 Notes:

1. 使用"尤其"要注意：Pay attention to the following aspects when using "尤其":

① "尤其"后面是名词时,常常可以用作"尤其是",如例(2)。When followed by a noun, "尤其" is often used as "尤其是" as in (2).

② "尤其"出现在句子中,一般有前后两个分句,前一分句表示总体情况,"尤其"常用在后一分句,表示比前面提到的更进一步、更突出。如果只有一个句子,"尤其"用在谓语前面,句中含有与总体情况比较更进一步的语义。"尤其" is generally used in a sentence with two clauses, with the first one introducing the general situation, and the second one with "尤其" indicating a higher degree compared with the general situation. If there is only one sentence without separate clauses, "尤其" is used before the predicate still indicating a higher degree compared with the general situation.

(3) 他尤其喜欢古典音乐。(总体情况是"他喜欢音乐"。The general situation is "他喜欢音乐.")

(4) 节日的西湖尤其热闹。(总体情况是"平时西湖也很热闹"。The general situation is "平时西湖也很热闹.")

③ "尤其"用在后一句子时,可以用在主语前,也可以用在主语后。When used in the second clause, "尤其" can be placed either before or after the subject.

(5) 这里经常下雨,春天尤其下得多/尤其是春天下得多。

2. "尤其"跟"特别"作副词都可以表示从总体情况中提出某人或某事物较其他人或事物更突出。两个词后面都可以加"是"。When used as an adverb, "尤其" and "特别" both emphasize a particular person or thing as compared with others in general. Both words can be followed by "是."

它们的区别是：Their differences are as follows:

① 在句子中,"尤其"着重指更加突出的意思,所指的对象一般总是包含在同类事物中的某一个或某一些。"特别"着重指与众不同的意思,所指的对象不限于同类事物中的某一个。使用范围较广。"尤其" focuses on the distinction, when the particular person(s) or thing(s) in question is/are included in the general population or group. "特别" emphasizes being different from others. The target is not limited to a particular person or thing. Therefore, "特别" has a wider range of usage than "尤其."

② "特别"通用于口语和书面语。"尤其"多用于书面语。"特别" can be used both colloquially and in written language. "尤其" is generally used in written language.

③ "特别"还有形容词用法。"尤其"没有。"特别" can also be used as an adjective but "尤其" cannot.

(6) *他是个很尤其的人。
(7) 他是个很特别的人。

yóu 由 →P75"从"、P688"自"

用法 Usage:

介词 prep.

1. 引进动作、行为的发出者。句子的主语是受事者。"由"后面的名词是施事，常跟表示人和团体的名词组成介词短语。这类介词短语后的谓语动词常是"负责、组织、解决、担任、承担、主持、办、解决"等动词，大多带有一定"责任、承担"的意义。By, used to introduce the performer of an action or behavior. The subject is the receiver of the action, and the word after "由" is the performer. It often forms a prepositional phrase with a noun representing people or groups. The verbs following such a prepositional phrase are often "负责、组织、解决、担任、承担、主持、办、解决"; they indicate a responsibility or duty.

(1) 签证的问题由留学生办公室的老师解答。
(2) 足球比赛什么时候进行由你决定。

2. 引进起点，相当于"从"。用法有：From, used to introduce a starting point. Similar to "从," it has the following usage:

① 表示处所起点或来源。"由"相当于"从、自"，跟处所词语组合。如果同时指出终点，后面往往有"到、至"呼应。Indicating the starting location or an origin. Similar to "从, 自," it is used with a location word. When the destination is also mentioned, it usually corresponds with "到, 至" in the latter part of the sentence.

(3) 由杭州到北京的火车现在开始检票了。
(4) 飞机明天早上七点由浦东机场起飞。

② 表示发展、变化、范围的起点。可以跟名词、形容词、动词组合。Indicating the starting point of a development, change or range. It can be used with a noun, adjective, or verb.

(5) 学了三个月汉语，我们已经由不会说到会说一点儿了。
(6) 游戏由你这儿开始到我这儿结束。
(7) 这种花的颜色由红慢慢变到白，很好看。

③ 表示时间起点。相当于"从"。跟时间词语组合。Indicating the starting time. Similar to "从," it is used with a time word.

(8) 由前年开始，他一直在中国的医院当大夫。

④ 表示经过的路线、场所。相当于"从"。跟处所词语组合。Indicating the route or location passed. Similar to "从," it is used with a location word.

(9) 参观中国山水画展览由东门入口。
(10) 去学校大门口由左边的小路走近多了。

⑤ 表示凭借、根据。相当于"依、根据"。跟名词组合。According to; based on. Similar to "依, 根据," it is used with a noun.

(11) 他的身体，由医生看来一定不是很健康。
(12) 你的发音由我听来已经很标准了。

3. 表示方式、原因或来源。"由"跟名词、动词组合成介词短语。表示原因时，相当于"由于"，后面常有"而"配合。Due to, used to indicate a method, reason, or origin. It forms a prepositional phrase with a noun or verb. Similar to "由于" when indicating the reason, it often corresponds with "而" in the latter part

of the sentence.

（13）这是由过马路不走行人道而造成的交通事故。

（14）他们两个人的误会由语言不通而产生。

4. 引进构成事物的成分、材料或方式等。 Introducing the ingredients or materials of a thing.

（15）人体是由细胞组成的。

（16）我们班二十个同学是由八个国家的学生组成的。

动词 v.

"由"用作动词，表示"听凭、听任、听从"的意思。后面必带名词性宾语或兼语。 When used as a verb, "由" must be followed by a nominal object or pivotal structure, with the same meaning as "听凭，听任，听从."

（17）这消息当然是真的，信不信由你。

（18）去哪个班学习由他自己决定。

说明 Notes:

1. 使用"由"要注意：Pay attention to the following aspects when using "由":

①"由"用作动词，重音在"由"上，用作介词，重音在后面的名词上。 When used as a verb, the accent falls on "由." When used as a preposition, the accent falls on the noun following "由."

②"由此"的意思表示"从这里"，习惯用语。可以承接上下文，进行推论。多用于书面语。常见的结构有"由此可见、由此可知、由此看来、由此得出"等。 As a fixed expression, "由此" means "from here." It is often used in written language to make a transition and introduce a conclusion. The common structures include "由此可见，由此可知，由此看来，由此得出."

2. "由"和"从"的区别是：The differences between "由" and "从" are as follows:

①"由"的文言意味比较重，多用于书面语。"从"通用于口语和书面语。 "由" is generally used in written language because it is carried over from classic Chinese. "从" can be used both colloquially and in written language.

②"由"有引进施动者、引进动作行为的原因、方式，表示事物的构成成分等用法。"从"没有这种用法。 "由" may introduce the performer, the reason or method of an action or behavior, or elements of a thing. "从" has no such usage.

③"从"有副词用法。"由"没有。 "从" can be used as an adverb but "由" cannot.

（19）我从没看过中国的京剧。

yóuyú 由于 →P587"因为"

用法 Usage:

介词 prep.

跟名词、代词或名词短语构成介词短语，表示原因或理由。它与句子后面的内容有因果关系，所以后面部分可以用关联副词"才、也、就"或连词"因而、所以、于是"等，进行直接或间接的呼应。 As a result of. It is used to form prepositional phrases with a noun, pronoun or noun phrase to show the reason. With a causal relationship in the sentence, it corresponds with adverbs such as "才，也，就" or conjunctions such as "因而，所以，于是" in the latter part of the sentence.

（1）由于劳动，人类才产生了语言。

（2）世界各国由于民族不同、历史发展经历不同等条件，所以形成的社会制度也不同。

如果表示原因、理由的内容放在句子后面，"由于"前面要加判断词"是"。 If the reason is placed in the latter part of the sentence, "由于" should be preceded by "是."

（3）今年的水果特别多是由于今年的天气特别好。

（4）家庭的产生是由于生产力的提高。

连词 conj.

表示原因或理由，相当于"因为"。用在因果复句的偏句里，表示结果或结论的句子开头用"所以、因此、因而"呼应，有时也可以用"才、就"等关联副词呼应。Because. It indicates a reason or excuse, similar to "因为." Used in a sentence with a causal relationship, it often corresponds with "所以，因此，" or "因而，" which appears at the beginning of a clause indicating a result or conclusion. Sometimes it can correspond with adverbs such as "才，就."

（5）由于坚持体育锻炼，因此他的身体很好。

（6）由于他跟大家都很友好，所以大家都愿意跟他交朋友。

说明 Notes：

1. 使用"由于"要注意：Pay attention to the following aspects when using "由于"：

①"由于"组成的介宾短语后面常带"的缘故"。The preposition-object phrase with "由于" is often followed by "的缘故."

（7）由于不习惯吃中国菜的缘故，他回国了。

（8）由于一班的汉语太容易的缘故，她去二班了。

②用"由于"构成的介词短语作状语时，在状语跟中心语之间，常用"才、而"等词语连接。When the preposition-object phrase with "由于" serves as an adverbial, words such as "才、而" are often used to connect the adverbial and the center word.

（9）恐龙是由于什么原因而消失的，科学家有很多种说法。

2. "由于"后面如果是名词、代词或名词性短语，组成介宾短语作状语，"由于"是介词用法，如例（1）（2）。"由于"后面如果是句子，"由于"是连词用法，如例（5）（6）。When the preposition-object phrase composed of "由于" and a noun, pronoun or noun phrase serves as an adverbial, "由于" is used as a preposition as in (1) and (2). When followed by a clause, "由于" is used as a conjunction as in (5) and (6).

3. "因为"和"由于"的区别是：The differences between "因为" and "由于" are as follows：

①"因为"通用于口语和书面语。"由于"多用于书面语。"因为" can be used both colloquially and in written language. "由于" is generally used in written language.

②"因为"不能跟"因此、因而"配合使用。"由于"可以。"因为" cannot be used with "因此，因而，" while "由于" can.

（10）由于大家的看法不一样，因此/因而没有做出最后的结论。

（11）*因为每个人的看法不一样，因此/因而没有做出最后的结论。

③"因为"可以用在后面的句子。"由于"不可以这样用。"因为" can be used in the second clause, while "由于" cannot.

（12）*他们累极了，由于他们连续爬了三座山。

（13）他们累极了，因为他们连续爬了三座山。

yóu 游

用法 Usage：

动词 v.

1. 人或动物在水里行动。(People or animals) to move in the water.

（1）快来看，那么多的金鱼在湖水里游来游去。

（2）他在长江里游泳游了三个小时。

2. 在各处从容地游览，闲逛。To tour and wander in different places leisurely.

（3）星期天下午我们坐船游了西湖。

（4）退休以后，我到处游山玩水，去了很多国家和城市。

形容词 a.

经常移动的，不固定的。Mobile; not fixed.

（5）大草原上牧民的生活是游动的。

（6）在大城市总会有一些一时找不到工作的无业游民。

名词 n.

江河的一段，如"上游、中游、下游"。A section of a river, such as "上游，中游，下游."

yóulǎn 游览 →P309"旅行"、P309"旅游"

用法 Usage:

动词 *v.*

从容地行走并观看,游玩、观赏(名胜、景点)。*To walk and look around at scenic spots; to go sightseeing.*

(1) 我在北京游览了长城、故宫和颐和园。

(2) 这次旅游我们去了三个城市,游览了十四个风景点。

说明 Notes:

1. "游览"后面带名词可以组成"游览车、游览区、游览胜地"等词语。*"游览" can be followed by a noun to form words such as "游览车,游览区,游览胜地."*

2. "旅行""旅游""游览"的区别是: *"旅行,""旅游" and "游览" differ as follows:*

① 在词义上,"旅行"的词义除了观光旅游的意思以外,还有出门在外办事的意思,着重于行程的流动,在三个词语中,"旅行"所包含的意思最广。"旅游"没有外出办事的意思,只是为了游览某地的风景、名胜而外出,词义着重在欣赏、游玩。"游览"的词义是在具体的景点从容地观看、游玩,如例(1)(2)。*In addition to sightseeing, "旅行" can refer to business trips. It emphasizes the mobile process. "旅行" has more meanings than the other two expressions. "旅游" only means to tour scenic spots and emphasizes sightseeing for pleasure. "游览" refers to visiting and sightseeing a particular scenic spot as in (1) and (2).*

② 在词语搭配上,虽然搭配的词语有时相同,但是搭配后的词语意思有所不同。如:"旅行车""旅游车""游览车"。旅行车中的旅客,不一定都是为了旅游的。旅游车中的旅客都是去旅游的,旅游车是为了送旅客去某地旅游的交通车。游览车是专门为旅客坐在车上观赏风景用的车。又如:可以说"旅游区、游览区",一般不说"旅行区";可以说"旅游胜地、游览胜地",不说"旅行胜地";可以说"旅行社、旅游社",不说"游览社"。*Although the three words can be used with the same noun to form new expressions, the meanings may be different, for example, "旅行车,旅游车,游览车." The passengers on "旅行车" may not do sightseeing, whereas the passengers on "旅游车" are all sitting in the vehicle to reach a scenic spot. "游览车" is for the passengers to enjoy the views while touring a scenic spot. One can say "旅游区,游览区" but not "旅行区.""旅游胜地,游览胜地" can be used but not "旅行胜地.""旅行社,旅游社" can be used but not "游览社."*

③ "旅行"和"旅游"可跟带数量词的名词短语搭配。一般不能跟表示具体风景、名胜地点的词语搭配。"游览"常常带表示具体风景、名胜地点的名词作宾语。*"旅行" and "旅游" can be used with a noun phrase with a quantifier. They are usually not used with proper nouns to refer to specific scenic spots. "游览" often takes a pronoun as an object to refer to a specific scenic spot.*

(3) 去年我旅行了一百多天。

(4) 我姑妈几乎每年都要出国旅游一次。

(5) *五一节,我旅行了长城。

(6) *五一节,我旅游了长城。

(7) 五一节,我游览了长城。

yǒu 有

用法 Usage:

动词 *v.*

1. 表示领有、拥有(跟"无、没"相对)。*To have, to own (as opposed to "无,没").*

(1) 我有两个姐姐。

(2) 你有没有足球比赛的票?

2. 表示存在。"有"后面是存在的事物。有时存在的事物可以在"有"前面。*To exist. The thing that exists often follows "有," but sometimes it can precede "有."*

(3) 我家门口有条河,河上有很多船。

(4) 椅子,那个教室有,可以去那儿搬。

3. 表示达到一定的数量或某种程度。句子有估量或比较的意思。"有"后面多有数量词。To reach a certain amount or degree. The sentence carries the meaning of an estimate or comparison. "有" is often followed by a quantifier.

(5) 这孩子有一米多高了,长得真快!

(6) 这个旅行箱有二十多公斤重。

4. 表示发生或出现。To occur or appear.

(7) 他有病了,今天不能来上班。

(8) 大家的口语有很大的进步。

5. 表示所领有的某种事物(常为抽象的)多、大、程度深。To show a large amount or a high degree of something one possesses (mostly something abstract).

(9) 他是个很有礼貌的孩子。

(10) 在教学上他很有学问,也很有经验。

6. 泛指,跟"某"的作用相近。Indicating a general reference, similar to "某."

(11) 有人说我家后面的山上有过老虎。

(12) 从前有座山,山上有座庙。

7. 用在"人、时候、地方"前面,表示全部的一部分,可以连用几个。When used before "人,时候,地方," it refers to a part of the whole entity. Sometimes "有" can be repeated.

(13) 我们班有人去北京,有人去西安,有人哪儿也不想去。

(14) 夏天这里很热,有时候气温高到40多摄氏度。

8. 用在某些动词前面组成套话,表示客气。To show politeness when used before certain verbs.

(15) 现在有请校长给我们讲话!

(16) 这件事有劳你多帮忙了。

9. 书面语,用在表示朝代的名词或形容词前面。Used before nouns indicating dynasties or certain adjectives in written language.

(17) 清代前面有唐、有宋、有元、有明,都是持续时间比较长的朝代。

(18) 公园里的菊花有红、有绿、有黄,还有白,很好看。

说明 Notes:

"有"发音为"yòu",表示整数以外再加零数,同"又"。如:"一有三分之一、三十有六"等。When pronounced as "yòu," it is similar to "又," meaning to add a fraction or fractional amount to the whole number, as in "一有三分之一,三十有六."

yǒudeshì 有的是

用法 Usage:

强调数量很多。语气较强,含有"不用担心没有或数量不够"的意思。To emphasize a large amount with a strong tone, which implies that one does not need to worry about the lack or the insufficient amount of something.

(1) 这种中草药山上有的是,一上山就能看到。

(2) 在蒙古大草原,牛奶、羊奶有的是,你就大口喝吧。

(3) 我们老家那里有的是山。

说明 Notes:

1. "有的是"是个习惯语,只用于口语。"有的是" is an idiom only used colloquially.

2. "有的是"强调数量多,含有夸张语气,一般作谓语。它所强调的对象可以放在前面做主语,如例(2),也可以放在后面作宾语,如例(3)。Emphasizing the large amount with a tone of exaggeration, "有的是" normally serves as the predicate. The target can be the subject as in (2) or the object as in (3).

3. 当强调的名词前面有表示确指的修饰语,如"这、那"时,名词一般放在"有的是"前做主语,如例(1)。When the target is preceded by a demonstrative pronoun such as "这" or "那," the noun usually goes before "有的是" as the subject, as in (1).

yǒuguān 有关 →P172"关于"

用法 Usage:

动词 v.

1. 表示有关系(跟"无关"相对)。常与介词"跟、和、同、与"等,构成"跟/和/同/与……有关"的格式。否定形式是"跟/和/同/与……无关"。"有关"一般用在句末作谓语,不能带宾语。*To be related to (as opposed to "无关"). It is often used with a preposition such as "跟,和,同,与" to form the structures of "跟/和/同/与…有关." The negative form is "跟/和/同/与…无关." "有关" is generally used at the end of the sentence as the predicate and cannot be followed by an object.*

(1) 她的身体那么好,跟她每天体育锻炼有关。

(2) 今年夏天那么热,同全球气候变暖有关。

2. 表示涉及,关系到。"有关"带名词或名词性词语组成"有关……"的动宾短语,表示"与……有关系"的意思,作句子的定语。*To involve. "有关" can form the verb-object phrase "有关…" with a noun or noun phrase to mean "to be related to," which serves as an attributive.*

(3) 他研究了历史上有关中医中药的人物和传说。

(4) 有关奖学金申请的通知公布了吗?

(5) 明天上午 8:30 开始停电,请有关单位做好准备。

(6) 今天课堂上,玛丽把她在西藏旅游的有关情况向大家作了介绍。

说明 Notes:

1. 使用"有关"要注意:*When using "有关," pay attention to the following aspects:*

① "有关"作动词第一义项的用法,所在的句子中一般都含有原因结果的意思,如例(1)(2)。*In the first usage of "有关" as a verb, the sentence usually indicates a causal relationship as in (1) and (2).*

② "有关"作动词第二个义项的用法,要强调指出"有关"必须同后面的中心语构成动宾短语再作句子的定语这一点。动宾短语与后面的中心语之间要有"的",如例(3)(4)。*In the second usage of "有关" as a verb, it's emphasized that "有关" must form a verb-object phrase with the center word that follows it to serve as an attributive of the sentence. "的" has to be used between the verb-object phrase and the center word as in (3) and (4).*

③ "有关"作形容词用法,"有关"直接修饰中心语,组成名词性短语,后面不加"的",如"有关部门、有关单位、有关学校、有关人士"等。*When used as an adjective, "有关" directly describes the center word and forms a noun phrase without "的," such as "有关部门,有关单位,有关学校,有关人士."*

④ "有关"组成的名词性短语可以做句子的主语,可以用于兼语短语作兼语,如例(5);可以用于"把"字句做介词短语,如例(6)。*The noun phrase with "有关" can be the subject, or a pivotal structure as in (5), or a prepositional phrase in a sentence with "把" as in (6).*

2. "有关"和"关于"都表示涉及的意思。*"有关" and "关于" can both mean "to involve."*

它们的区别是:*Their differences are as follows:*

① "有关"着重于指有关系的那一部分内容,不是全部。"关于"着重表示关涉到的范围的全部。因此有时看上去用法一样,但实际上语义有所不同。如:"有关加强纪律教育的问题"是指很多问题中关系到"加强纪律教育的"问题;"关于加强纪律教育的问题"是指"加强纪律教育"问题的全部范围。*"有关" focuses on the part that is related rather than the whole. "关于," by contrast, emphasizes the whole range that is related. Although sometimes the usage of the two seems the same, the semantic meanings are different. For example, "有关加*

强纪律教育的问题"means that many issues are related to "加强纪律教育." "关于加强纪律教育的问题" refers to the whole issue of "加强纪律教育."

②"有关"组成的是动宾短语,只能做句子的定语。"关于"组成的是介词短语,可以做定语、状语或用在判断词"是"的后面。The verb-object phrase with "有关" can only be an attributive. The prepositional phrase with "关于" can be an attributive, an adverbial or be used after "是."

③"有关"可以单独做定语,如"有关部门、有关单位、有关人员"等。"关于"不能,只能组成"关于……的"结构做定语。"有关" can be used as an attributive without "的," such as "有关部门,有关单位,有关人员." "关于" has to be used in the "关于...的" structure as an attributive.

yǒujìn 有劲

用法 Usage:

动词 v.

有力气(跟"没劲儿"相对)。用于口语常为"有劲儿"。 To be full of energy; to have strength (as opposed to "没劲儿"), often used as "有劲儿" colloquially.

(1) 他的手很有劲儿。

(2) 你有劲儿,请把这箱子搬到楼上去。

形容词 a.

指兴致很浓,有趣。Interesting; in good mood.

(3) 老朋友见面,喝酒聊天,越来越有劲儿。

(4) 今天玩儿得真有劲!

yǒukòngr 有空儿

用法 Usage:

"空(儿)"是没有被占用的时间。"有空儿"表示有时间(与"没空儿"相对)。常用于口语。"空(儿)" means free time. "有空儿" means "having free time" (as opposed to "没空儿"). It is often used colloquially.

(1) 你有空儿来我家玩儿。

(2) 明天下午你有空儿吗?我们上街去。

yǒumíng 有名 →P683"著名"

用法 Usage:

形容词 a.

表示(人或事物的)名字为大家所熟知,出名。Well-known; famous.

(1) 龙井茶是很有名的绿茶。

(2) 诺贝尔是全世界有名的科学家。

说明 Notes:

1. "有名"也可说成"有名气"。"有名" can also be used as "有名气."

2. "有名"在口语里,中间可以插入其他词语。In colloquial usage, other words may be inserted between "有" and "名."

(3) 现在他是我们这里有了名的企业家。

(4) 他有什么名气,只不过是个会唱歌跳舞的人罢了。

yǒushí 有时 →P600"有时候"

用法 Usage:

副词 ad.

表示不定的一部分时间,有时候。可以连续用。Sometimes; Indicating an indefinite time, it can be reduplicated in a sentence.

(1) 有时她不回来吃饭,我就自己做方便面。

(2) 江南的春天,有时冷,有时热,千万不要感冒。

yǒushíhou 有时候 →P600"有时"

用法 Usage:

副词 ad.

表示偶尔在某个时候(动作不是经常发生)。Sometimes (not occurring very often).

(1) 这孩子又聪明又调皮,有时候连他妈妈都不知怎么管他。

(2) 我们一般吃米饭,有时候也吃面。

说明 Notes:

"有时"和"有时候"意义、用法基本相同,在句子中常可替换。"有时" and "有时候" are similar in meaning and usage and are often interchangeable.

它们的区别是:They differ as follows:

1."有时候"修饰的动作一般不经常发生。"有时"动作发生的次数相对较多。所以当表示"偶尔"或比较难得时,多用"有时候"。The action described by "有时候" does not happen very often, whereas the action described by "有时" may happen more often. Therefore, "有时候" is often used to indicate "occasionally" or "rarely."

(3) 他一般都回家吃饭,有时候,他加班才在单位吃。

(4) 这里是缺水的地方,有时候下点儿雨,一到地上就不见了。

2."有时候"作状语可以放在主语前,并可用逗号同主语隔开,如例(3)。"有时"一般不这样用。When used as an adverbial, "有时候" can be placed before the subject and separated from the subject with a comma as in (3). "有时" is normally not used in this way.

3."有时"多用于书面语。"有时候"多用于口语。"有时" is usually used in written language, whereas "有时候" is mostly used colloquially.

yǒu(yì)diǎnr 有(一)点儿 →P577"一点儿"

用法 Usage:
副词 ad.

表示程度不高、稍微的意思。多用于不如意的事情。可用作"有点儿"。An adverb meaning "slightly," "有一点儿" means the same as "有点儿." It is often used for unpleasant things.

句式有:The sentence structures are as follows:

1."有点儿+形/动"。形容词多半是消极意义的或贬义的。"有点儿"后面的形容词前可以加"太",表示不满意。"有点儿+a./v." The adjective usually has a negative or derogatory meaning. The adjective can be preceded by "太" inferring unsatisfactory feelings.

(1) 我有点儿累,想睡觉了。
(2) 这件衬衫有点儿太大了。

2."有点儿+不+形/动"。形容词和动词多半是积极意义的或褒义的。"有点儿+不+a./v." The adjective or the verb usually carries a positive meaning.

(3) 妈妈认为我在学习上有点儿不主动、不自觉。
(4) 她真的有点儿不耐心。

3."有点儿"有时与"稍微"连用。Sometimes "有点儿" can be used with "稍微."

(5) 他学习汉语稍微有点儿吃力。
(6) 我稍微有点儿头疼。

4."有点儿+形/动+名"。"有点儿+a./v./n."

(7) 学生都有点儿怕老师。
(8) 我真有点儿不想吃米饭。

5."有点儿"可以单独回答问话。"有点儿" can stand alone as a response.

(9) A:你疼吗?
B:有点儿。

说明 Notes:

1. 使用"有点儿"要注意:Pay attention to the following aspects when using "有点儿":

① "有点儿"可以与被修饰的词语组成短语作状语。"有点儿" can form a phrase with the word that it modifies to serve as an adverbial.

(10) 那人有点儿担心地说:"不知道她到了没有?"
(11) 他有点儿难受地说:"那我们在这儿分手吧。"

② "有点儿"有时可以修饰可能补语的否定形式,表示出现了接近可能补语否定形式所表示的情况。有时,后面还可以带名词作宾语。

Sometimes "有点儿" can modify the negative form of a potential complement, showing the occurrence of a situation indicated by that complement. Sometimes "有点儿" can be followed by an object such as a noun.

(12) 电影院里太吵了,我有点儿受不了。

(13) 他痛得有点儿控制不住自己了。

③ "有点儿"着重修饰表示身体上的感觉和心理活动等状态的动词,其中以消极意义的居多,如"头疼、咳嗽、感冒、伤心、难过、灰心、失望、后悔、害怕、为难、紧张、烦、悲哀、痛苦、犹豫"等。一般不能修饰动作性很强、动作时间性很强或表示结论的动词,如"失败、成功、迟到"。"有点儿" mostly modifies verbs describing a physical or psychological status, often with a negative meaning, such as "头疼,咳嗽,感冒,伤心,难过,灰心,失望,后悔,害怕,为难,生气,紧张,烦,悲哀,痛苦,犹豫." It is usually not used to modify verbs with a strong sense of action or time or verbs indicating a conclusion such as "失败,成功,迟到."

(14) *我感到我有点儿迟到了。

④ 少数非消极意义的词语,如"高兴、激动、兴奋、明白"等,可以受"有点儿"的修饰。多用于表示变化的句子。A limited number of words with a positive meaning such as "高兴,激动,兴奋,明白" can be modified by "有点儿," which is mostly used in sentences indicating a change.

(15) 过了一会儿,她有点儿高兴了。

(16) 她现在有点儿明白是怎么回事了。

⑤ 副词"有点儿"在书面语中,"儿"可以省略,如:"有点难、有点冷"等。In written language, "儿" can be omitted in the adverb "有点儿," such as "有点难,有点冷."

2. "有(一)点儿"用在名词前面,是动词+量词"(一)点儿"的用法,"一点儿"是修饰后面的名词的。When "有(一)点儿" goes before a noun, it is used in the structure "verb + measure word + (一)点儿," where "一点儿" modifies the noun that follows it.

(17) 我有一点儿事。

(18) 事情还有一点儿希望。

3. "有点儿"和"一点儿"的区别是:The differences between "有点儿" and "一点儿" are as follows:

① "有点儿"是副词。"一点儿"是数量词。"有点儿" is an adverb. "一点儿" is a quantifier.

② "有点儿"和"一点儿"都跟形容词或心理动词发生关系,但是"有点儿"要用在形容词或心理动词前面。"一点儿"要用在形容词或心理动词后面。"有点儿" and "一点儿" both describe adjectives or verbs indicating mental activity. "有点儿" is used before those words, whereas "一点儿" is used after them.

(19) 这个房间小了(一)点儿。

(20) 这个房间有点儿小。

③ "一点儿"可以用在表示比较的"比"字句中。"有点儿"不能用在"比"字句中。"一点儿" can be used in comparative sentences with "比" but "有点儿" cannot.

(21) 这个房间比那个房间小一点儿。

(22) *这个房间比那个房间有点儿小。

④ "有点儿"多表示不如意的意思,所以修饰的形容词或动词多带有消极意义或贬义的。用在"有点儿+不+形/动"的格式中,形容词或动词多是表示积极意义或褒义的。"一点儿"对形容词或动词没有这个选择或限制。"有点儿" mostly modifies negative or derogatory adjectives or verbs. When used in the "有点儿+不+a./v." structure, the adjective or the verb usually carries an active or positive meaning. "一点儿" has no such restriction on adjectives or verbs that it modifies.

⑤ "有点儿"可以单独回答问题。一般"一点儿"前面要带动词,才能回答问题。"有点儿" can stand alone as a response. "一点儿" has to be preceded by a verb to make a response.

(23) A:你觉得难吗?

B：有点儿。

(24) A：你会说英语吗？

B：会一点儿。

4. 注意以下错句：*Pay attention to the following errors:*

(25) *我觉得他要吃药一点儿。

(26) 我觉得他要吃一点儿药。

(27) *这课课文一点儿难。

(28) 这课课文难了一点儿。

(29) 这课课文有点儿难。

yǒuxiē 有些

用法 Usage:

代词 pron.

有的，有一部分（指数量不大）。可以连用。*Some, a part of (not a large amount). It can be reduplicated.*

(1) 书架上有不少书，有些是中文书，有些是外文书。

(2) 公园里有很多人在锻炼，有些在打太极拳，有些在跑步。

副词 ad.

表示程度不太深，略微，稍微。多用在表示心理动词、形容词前面作状语。*Slightly. Indicating a low degree, it is often used as an adverbial before a verb or adjective related to mental activity.*

(3) 大家都安慰我，可我还是觉得有些难过。

(4) 你是不是有些喜欢她？那就去告诉她。

动词 v.

结构为"有｜些"，表示有一些。用在名词前面。"有＋些" *is used before a noun meaning "having some."*

(5) 我那里还有些牛奶，你想喝吗？

(6) 妈妈，我的头还有些痛。

说明 Notes:

1. 代词"有些"直接做主语时，一般在前面已经出现了表示"有些"所指范围的名词，否则就不能单独做主语。如例（1）。*When the* pronoun "有些" *serves as the subject, a noun representing the range of things including what goes after* "有些" *usually appears in the first clause before the clause with* "有些." *Otherwise,* "有些" *cannot serve as the subject as in (1).*

2. "有些"作动词用时，"有些"中的"些"，表示的数量大小或程度高低是相对的、不定的。有时前面也能受程度副词"很"的修饰，表示数量大、程度高。*When used as a verb, the* "些" *in* "有些" *indicates a relative or indefinite amount or degree. Sometimes* "有些" *can be preceded by degree adverbs such as* "很" *to show a large amount or a high degree.*

(7) 他在教学上很有些水平。

(8) 妈妈不再对我说"我对你很有些失望"这句话了。

yǒuyìsi 有意思

用法 Usage:

1. 有深意，耐人寻味。*Thought-provoking.*

(1) 他做的那几个动作很有意思。

(2) 这几句话很有意思，你好好想想。

2. 有趣。*Interesting.*

(3) 今天晚上演出的节目很有意思。

(4) 阿里讲话很有意思。

3. （对异性）产生爱慕之心。*To be affectionate (toward the opposite sex).*

(5) 她对你有意思，你没感觉？

(6) 你是不是对她有意思了？

说明 Notes:

在第一和第二义项用法中，"有意思"一般作形容词用。第三义项中，"有意思"作动词用。"有意思" *is usually an adjective in the first and second usage, and a verb in the third usage.*

yòu 又 →P184"还"、P618"再"

用法 Usage:

副词 ad.

1. 表示一个动作（或状态）重复发生，两个动作(或状态)相继发生或反复交替。Again, used to indicate the repetition of an action/status, or one action/status immediately following another, or two actions/statuses alternating repeatedly.

① 表示动作第二次出现。前后两个小句用同一个动词,主语可以相同,可以不同。有时候只用后面一个小句,暗含着以前有过这类事或该有这种事。Showing the second occurrence of an action. The two clauses take the same verb with the same subject or different subjects. Sometimes the first clause may be omitted, indicating a similar action that has happened or should have happened before.

（1）他昨天来过,今天又来了。
（2）我找了一遍,他又找了一遍,还是没找到。
（3）你不把衣服穿上,又该受凉了。

② 表示重复或反复多次。在一个句子内重复同一个动词。Indicating repetition. One verb is repeated within the same sentence.

（4）她把孩子的手洗了又洗。
（5）妈妈对我看了又看,最后说：你胖了。

③ "又"前后重复"一+量词",表示反复多次。"一 + measure word" is repeated before and after "又," which indicates repetitions.

（6）他一遍又一遍地读课文。
（7）一天又一天,他不知道等了多少天,才等来她的信。

④ 表示两个动作、行为或状态相继发生或出现。前后两小句的动词不同,"又"用在后面的句子里。Indicating one action, behavior, or status immediately occurs or appears after another. The two clauses take different verbs. "又" is used in the second clause.

（8）他刚洗完衣服,又去做饭了。
（9）她写完作业,又听录音了。

⑤ "又"用在两种动作、行为或状态之间,表示反复交替发生。Used between two actions, behaviors, or statuses, "又" indicates repeated alternations.

（10）他翻过来又翻过去,翻过去又翻过来,就是睡不着。
（11）他写了又擦掉,擦掉又写,不知道写了多少遍。

2. 表示几种动作、行为、情况或状态发生、出现或存在,累积在一起。不具有时间性。Indicating the accumulation of several actions, behaviors, situations or statuses, which involve no time.

① "又"用在后面几项。"又" is not used in the first clause.

（12）他是个聪明人,又很努力,不到两个月就会说汉语了。
（13）那天他没通知我,又是我最忙的一天,又没有车,所以我没有去。

② 每一项都用"又"。"又" is used in front of each verb.

（14）她又说又唱又跳,是个很活泼的孩子。
（15）他又能说又能写又能直接口头翻译,语言能力很强。

③ "又"前后重复同一形容词,表示程度高。如是单音节形容词,"又"前面加"而"(不加"而",只用于诗歌、歌词);如是双音节形容词,则可加可不加,一般不加。The same adjective repeated before and after "又" indicates a high degree. For monosyllabic adjectives, "又" should be preceded with "而" ("而" is not needed in poems or lyrics). For disyllabic adjectives, "而" is generally not added in front to "又," although occasionally it may be used.

（16）爸爸对我们的要求从小就是严而又严。
（17）小皮球圆又圆,一跳蹦得高又高。
（18）希望自己的一生顺利(而)又顺利,这是很难的。

④ "又"前后连接不同的形容词,"又"前面常加"而"。Different adjectives are used before and after "又." "又" is often preceded by "而."

(19) 那女孩子聪明而又漂亮,大家都很喜欢她。

(20) 他的汉语口语标准而又流利,学得真不错。

⑤ 构成"既……又……"的格式,"又"前后连接不同的形容词或动词。*In the pattern of "既…又…," "又" is preceded and followed by different adjectives or verbs.*

(21) 阿里的房间既干净又整齐。

(22) 他的学习既有远期目标,又有近期计划。

3. 表示语气。*Indicating a tone of voice.*

① 表示转折语气,常和"可以、但是、却、虽然"等词语搭配。*Indicating a turning tone, "又" is often used with "可以,但是,却,虽然."*

(23) 你们虽然怕冷,但是又不愿多穿衣服。开空调,其实对身体是不好的。

(24) 有的人心里有看法,却又不说出来。别人是很难明白的。

② 表示递进的语气。有时跟"不但、不仅"搭配。*Indicating a progressive tone. Sometimes "又" can be used with "不但,不仅."*

(25) 她不但要照顾一个卧床老人,又要给全家五个人做晚餐。

(26) 他不仅是我们班的好学生,又是全学院的好学生。

③ 加强反问语气或感叹语气,句中多用疑问代词。*Strengthening a rhetorical or exclamation tone. Interrogative pronouns are usually used in the sentence.*

(27) 下雨又有什么关系? 雨中的风景也很美。

(28) 这一点困难又算得了什么?

④ 加强否定语气。*Strengthening the negating tone.*

(29) 他又不会吃人,你怕他什么?

(30) 人家又不是故意的,算了算了。

4. 表示相加。如"一年又五个月、三小时又二十分、三又三分之一"等。*Indicating an addition, such as "一年又五个月、三小时又二十分、三又三分之一."*

5. 作"另、另外、再、再者"讲。常用于书信或文章额外补充的话前面,后面常用冒号或逗号。*Like "另,另外,再,再者," "又" is often used before an additional text in letters or articles and is usually followed by a comma or a colon.*

(31) 杭州西湖又名:金牛湖。

(32) 又:你要我买的书已经买了,明天给你寄出。

说明 Notes:

"又"和"还"都表示动作再一次出现。*While both "又" and "还" indicates the repetition of an action.*

它们的区别是:"又"主要表示动作已经完成。"还"主要表示动作还未完成。*Their difference is that "又" indicates the completion of an action, while "还" means the action is not yet completed.*

(33) 他昨天来过,今天又来了。

(34) 他昨天来过,明天还要来。

yú 于 →P622"在"

用法 Usage:

介词 *prep.*

"于"是文言虚词,但在现代汉语的书面语中仍大量使用。*A function word in classic Chinese, "于" still has a wide range of application in modern Chinese.*

1. 引进时间、处所、方位、范围等,相当于"在"。*Introducing a time, location, position or range, it is the same as "在."*

① 引进时间,可用在动词前或动词后。*Introducing a time, it can be used before or after the verb.*

(1) 鲁迅先生生于1881年,于1936年在上海逝世。

(2) 我们的老师毕业于1980年。

② 引进处所或方位,多用于动词后,个别

表示主语受事处所,则用在动词前。Introducing a location or position, it is often used after the verb. Occasionally, when indicating the location of the subject receiving an action, it is used before the verb.

(3) 很多外国朋友在中国的事业开始于上海。

(4) 这本书2016年于北京购买。

③ 引进范围,常与方位词搭配。可用于动词前或动词后。有时也用于句首。Introducing the range, it is often used with a noun of locality. It can be used before or after the verb. Sometimes it may be used at the beginning of the sentence.

(5) 于汉语学习之外,她最喜欢的事情就是做中国菜了。

(6) 这种方法不适用于外语学习。

2. 引进承受的一方,相当于"给、替、为"。一般只用在动词后面。Introducing the party receiving an action. Like "给, 替, 为," it is only used after the verb.

(7) 他们没想到最后竟败于留学生足球队。

(8) 老人是一位献身于科学与和平事业的杰出化学家。

3. 引进有关的人或事物,相当于"对、对于"。可用于动词前或动词后。Introducing the related people or things. Like "对, 对于," it can be used before or after the verb.

(9) 事情的结果于你是有利的。

(10) 他是个不满足于现状的人。

4. 引进来源、出处或起点,相当于"自、从、由"。多用在动词后。Introducing the origin or starting point. Like "自, 从, 由," it is used before the verb, but sometimes it can be used after the verb.

(11) 天才出于勤奋。

(12) 这条大江发源于中国西部的青藏高原。

5. 引进动作、行为涉及的对象,相当于"向"。用在动词或动宾短语后面。Introducing the party involved in an action or behavior. Like "向," it is used after a verb or a verb-object phrase.

(13) 你怎么总是事事求助于人呢?

(14) "问道于盲"的意思是向看不见东西的盲人问路。

6. 引进动作、行为的趋向或终点,相当于"到、至"。用在名词、动词或形容词前后。Introducing the direction or destination of an action or behavior. Like "到, 至," it appears before or after a noun, a verb, or an adjective.

(15) 春天到了,天气逐渐趋于暖和。

(16) 你记住报名时间不能晚于明天下午五点。

7. 引进相比的对象,表示比较。相当于"比"。用在形容词、动词或数量词后面。Introducing the target for comparison. The same as "比," it appears after an adjective, a verb, or a numeral.

(17) 中国的苦丁茶苦于纯咖啡。

(18) 在艺术方面,她的才华明显高于她哥哥。

8. 引进主动者,表示被动的意思,相当于"被……所……"。Introducing the party performing the action to show a passive voice. It is the same as "被…所…."

(19) 限于时间,我的话就讲到这里。

(20) 四班已经败于三班,现在就看我们班了。

9. 附着在动词、形容词(多为单音节,结合得比较紧密,有些可看作是一个词)后面,引进动作的方面、原因或目的等。意思比较虚,很难说出"于"相当于哪个词语的意思。如:"在于、属于、敢于"和"善于、忙于、便于、乐于、急于、至于、不至于"等。When used after a verb or an adjective (mostly monosyllabic words tightly connected to "于," the combination of which can be considered one word sometimes), it introduces the reason or purpose of an action. "于" may have different meanings in this context. It is hard to compare this usage to any other word. Sample words include "在于, 属于, 敢于"和"善于, 忙于, 便于, 乐于, 勇于, 急于."

yúshì 于是 →P586"因此"

用法 Usage:
连词 conj.

表示两事前后相承。有时候有"因此"的意思,表示后者是前者引起的。可以连接分句、句子或段落。可以用在主语后。Therefore. It is used to connect two succeeding events, indicating that the first event leads to the second. Sometimes similar to "因此," "于是" can connect clauses, sentences or paragraphs. It can be used after the subject.

(1) 他学了一年汉语,收获很大,于是决定在这儿再学习一年。

(2) 大家都说这儿的夏天很热,于是他决定今年暑假去北方旅游、度假。

说明 Notes:

1. 使用"于是"要注意:Pay attention to the following aspects when using "于是":

① "于是"也可以说成"于是乎"。Sometimes "于是" can be used as "于是乎."

② 如果表示结果或者结论的句子比较长,"于是"后面可以用逗号点开,停顿一下然后再跟上表示结果或者结论的句子。If the clause indicating a result or conclusion is quite long, a comma can be used after "于是" for a short pause.

(3) 他刚到不久,还不习惯这儿的生活。于是,作为他的好朋友,我要多多帮助他。

③ 连词"于是"是连接意义上紧密相承的两个句子,而不强调时间上紧密相承的句子。"于是" is used to connect two clauses closely related in meaning, rather than clauses describing events in succession.

(4) *下了课,于是我们就去打球。

(5) *经过不到一个星期的训练,于是他便参加了比赛。

以上两句是表示时间上的快,"于是"都应去掉,后面用上"就、便"即可。The two sentences above emphasize the immediate occurrence of the second event following the first event. So, "于是" should be deleted with "就" or "便" kept.

④ "于是"所连接的句子一般不用于经常性的、静态的叙述或描写。The clause with "于是" usually does not involve a routine and static narration or description.

(6) *我的汉语不太好,于是要好好学汉语。

(7) *他们准备放假后去旅行,于是不能很快回国。

以上两句,前面的分句是原因,所以"于是"应该改为"因此"。In the above two sentences, the first clauses both indicate the reason. "于是" should be replaced by "因此."

2. "于是"和"因此"的区别是:The differences between "于是" and "因此" are as follows:

① 由于"因"和"果"的顺序常常也是顺承的,所以"于是"有时也用在因果承接的句子中。但是,"于是"着重表示时间、顺序上的承接关系,"因此"着重表示因果关系。有的表示顺应次序的承接关系,"因此"就不能替换"于是",如例(8)。着重表示因果关系的句子,"于是"也不能替换"因此",如例(9)。Because the result usually follows the cause/reason, sometimes "于是" can be used in a sentence indicating a causal relationship. But "于是" focuses on the sequential relationship between two events, whereas "因此" emphasizes a causal relationship. "因此" should not be used if the sentence only indicates a sequential relationship without a causal relationship, as in (8). By contrast, if the sentence only indicates a causal relationship without a sequential relationship, "于是" should not be used, as in (9).

(8) 小孩哭得很厉害。阿姨说:"别哭了,我们去买橘子好吗?"孩子不哭了,说:"好。"于是阿姨抱起了孩子,锁好门后走下了楼梯。

(9) 没有复习就听写不出生词,因此听写前,我不能不复习生词。

② "因此"前面常常用"由于"表示原因,有

时也用"因为"搭配。"于是"前面一般不用"由于、因为"搭配。*In the clause before "因此," "由于" is often used to indicate a reason. Sometimes "因为" can be used with "因此" as well. "于是" is usually not used with "由于,因为."*

yúkuài 愉快 →P279"快乐"

用法 Usage:
形容词 *a.*

舒畅,高兴,心情轻松快乐。*Content; happy; light-hearted.*

(1) 这个星期天过得很愉快。
(2) 在幼儿园,他和同学们一起愉快地生活了三年。
(3) 这是个令人不愉快的消息。

说明 Notes:

"快乐"和"愉快"都表示高兴、喜悦的意思。*"快乐" and "愉快" can both mean happy or joyous.*

它们的区别是:*Their differences are as follows:*

1. "愉快"多用于人的心情。"快乐"除形容人的心情以外,还多用于气氛、场面。*"愉快" is applied to describe the mood one is in. "快乐," however, can also be used to describe an environment or atmosphere.*

2. "愉快"多用于书面语,"快乐"通用于口语和书面语。*"愉快" is mostly used in written language. "快乐" can be used both colloquially and in written language.*

3. "快乐"可以重叠成"快快乐乐"的形式。"愉快"没有重叠形式。*"快乐" can be reduplicated as "快快乐乐." "愉快" cannot be reduplicated as such.*

yǔ 与 →P166"跟"、P193"和"、P470"同"

用法 Usage:
介词 *prep.*

1. 引进另一施事者。*Introducing the second agent.*

(1) 昨天晚上我与他一起看了电影。
(2) 爷爷与爸爸对我说的话,我都记在了心里。

2. 引进动作行为涉及的对象,相当于"对、向、给"。*Introducing the target of an action or behavior. It is the same as "对,向,给."*

(3) 阿里与教室里的同学点了一下头。
(4) 我与老师打了招呼,她同意的。

3. 引进与某一事物相关的另一事物。*Introducing a second topic related to an aforementioned topic.*

(5) 他在这里生活得那么高兴,与你们的关心和帮助是分不开的。
(6) 今年的夏天那么热,与没台风有直接的关系。

4. 引进比较或比拟的对象。*Introducing an agent for comparison or analogy.*

(7) 年轻人的想法与我们的想法是完全不同了。
(8) 馒头已经与石头一样硬了,不能吃了。

连词 *conj.*

表示并列关系。只连接词或短语。常用在书名或标题中。多用于书面语。*Indicating a parallel relationship. It is often used in book titles in written language. It can only connect words or phrases.*

(9) 为什么爷爷与全家人的希望要寄托在我身上?
(10) 我给你买了一本《汉语教学与研究》。

说明 Notes:

"和、跟、同、与"可以做介词,也可以做连词。做连词时,都只能连接词或短语,不能连接分句或句子。*"和,跟,同,与" can all be used as a preposition or conjunction. When used as a conjunction, they can only connect words and phrases rather than clauses or sentences.*

它们的区别是:*Their differences are as follows:*

1. 做连词时,"和"通用于口语、书面语,使用得最广泛。"跟"多用于口语,在北方话中用得较多。"同"流行于华中一带,带有方言色彩,在书面语中多用为介词。"与"是古代汉语沿用下来的,多用于书面语。When used as a conjunction,"和" has the widest range of usage. It can be used both colloquially and in written language. "跟" is mostly used colloquially in northern dialects. "同" is widely used in dialects in central China. It is often used as a preposition in written language. Originating from classic Chinese, "与" is mostly used in written language.

2. 这四个词,现在使用的趋向是:"和、与"多作连词使用,"跟、同"多作介词使用。"和" and "与" are mostly used as a conjunction, whereas "跟" and "同" are mostly used as a preposition.

yǔyán 语言 →P534"言语(yányǔ)"、P534"言语(yányu)"

用法 Usage:

名词 n.

1. 人类所特有的用来表达意思、交流思想的工具,是一种特殊的社会现象,由语音、词汇和语法构成一定的系统。"语言"一般包括它的书面形式,但在与"文字"并举时只指口语。Language, the means by which people express themselves and communicate with each other. A special kind of social phenomenon, it is composed of phonetics, vocabulary, and grammar, which combine to make a system. Language generally includes the written form, but it refers just to oral language when it is mentioned at the same time as "writing (or characters)."

(1) 根据联合国调查,全世界约有7 000种语言。

(2) 联合国通用的语言有英语、法语、俄语、汉语、阿拉伯语、西班牙语6种。

2. 话语,是人们说出来或写出来的语言,是特定社会语境中人与人之间从事沟通的具体言语行为。Speech. It is the language spoken or uttered by people. It is the concrete verbal behavior when people communicate with each other in a specific society.

(3) 他的语言很让人感动。

(4) 孩子们天真的语言引起了大家欢乐的笑声。

说明 Notes:

"语言"的第二个意思跟"言语(yányǔ)、言语(yányu)"都有人与人从事交流言语行为的意思。The second meaning of "语言" is speech, which means the language behavior when people engage in communication. And "言语(yányǔ)" and "言语(yányu)" carry the same meaning.

它们的区别是:Their differences are as follows:

1. 使用场合有所不同。"言语(yányǔ)"着重指口头说出来的话语。"语言"词义科学性较强,多用于书面语。They are used on different occasions. While "言语(yányǔ)" lays emphasis on the oral words uttered by people, "语言" has more of a scientific nature: it appears more in the written form.

2. "言语(yányu)"用于口语,有表示说话、回答、招呼、开口等具体意思。"语言"没有。Appearing in oral communication, "言语(yányu)" carries the specific meanings of a talk, answer, greeting and starting to talk. "语言" doesn't carry these meanings.

(5) *你在屋里啊,回家怎么不语言一声。

(6) 你在屋里啊,回家怎么不言语一声。

yùbèi 预备 →P687"准备"

用法 Usage:

动词 v.

准备。To prepare.

(1) 双休日你预备到哪儿去玩?

(2) 明天的早饭,我给你预备好了。

yùdào 遇到 →P610"遇见"
用法 Usage:
碰上。*To run into; to encounter; to meet.*
(1) 今天在超市遇到了一个高中同学。
(2) 这事正好让我遇到了。
(3) 他遇到了麻烦。

yùjiàn 遇见 →P610"遇到"
用法 Usage:
与"遇到"用法相同,碰上。*To run into; to meet (similar to "遇到").*
(1) 今天在超市遇见了一个高中同学。
(2) 我正好遇见了她俩在书店买书。
说明 Notes:
"遇到"和"遇见"都表示意外地、事先没约定地见到。*"遇到" and "遇见" both mean "to run into someone or something accidentally."*
它们的区别是:*Their differences are as follows:*
"遇"后面的补语"到"跟"见"不同。"遇到"后面的对象除了人和具体的某件事外,还可以是"问题""麻烦"等。"遇见"的对象只是人和具体的事,一般不能是"问题""麻烦"等。*"遇" carries different meanings when it is followed by different complements "到" and "见." What follows "遇到" can be people or specific events or "问题,麻烦." What follows "遇见" can only be people or specific events but not "问题,麻烦."*
(3) 昨天我在街上遇到/遇见老同学了。
(4) 我遇到问题了。
(5) *我遇见问题了。

yuán 原
用法 Usage:
形容词 *a.*
1. 最初的,开始的。*Initial; beginning.*
(1) 老师的原话是怎么说的?
(2) 我们说的原人就是指猿人。
2. 原来的,本来的。*Original.*
(3) 你工作的原单位是哪里?
(4) 我原计划只学习一年汉语,现在我想再继续学一年。
3. 没加过工的(材料、物体)。*(Of material, object) raw.*
(5) 1月份的原油产量增加了3.6%。
(6) 我们村每亩土地能产原棉300多公斤。
动词 *v.*
原谅。*To forgive.*
(7) 你不知道这里的规矩,这次错误情有可原。
名词 *n.*
1. 宽广平坦的地方。*Wide and flat space.*
(8) 黄土高原和长江三角洲平原是完全不一样的地方。
2. 原来的状态,原状。*Original state or status.*
(9) 这个橡皮球很快就复原了。
(10) 你把我的雕塑还原到原来的头像!
副词 *ad.*
原来。用在动词前面。*Originally (used before a verb).*
(11) 这个班的学生原有二十五个,现在是二十二个。

yuánlái 原来 →P21"本来"、P611"原先"
用法 Usage:
形容词 *a.*
最初的,没有经过改变的。不能单独做谓语,修饰名词一定要加助词"的"。*Initial; unchanged. It cannot stand alone as a predicate. It has to be followed by "的" when modifying a noun.*
(1) 鲁迅原来的名字叫周树人。鲁迅是他的笔名。
(2) 我们的家还住在原来的湖边。
副词 *ad.*
1. 以前某一时期,当初。用在动词前面,含有现在已经有所改变的意思,所以在句子中常有以前和现在对比的词语和意思。*Originally; some time in the past. Used before a verb, it carries the meaning of a change. There are often words in the sentence comparing the past and the present in meaning.*

（3）我们家原来有七个人，姐姐出嫁后，现在只有六个人了。

（4）我原来不喜欢吃甜的，现在还可以。

2. 发现了以前不知道的情况，含有恍然大悟的意思。"原来"可用在主语前后。*So; it turns out to be. It is used to describe that someone discovers information that he/she was unaware of before. It can be used before or after the subject.*

（5）我以为是谁，原来是你啊！

（6）他到处找钥匙，后来发现钥匙原来就在他手中拿着。

说明 Notes:

"本来"和"原来"作副词都表示原先、先前的意思、做形容词都能修饰名词。*"本来" and "原来" both mean "originally" or "initially" when used as an adverb. They can both describe a noun when used as an adjective.*

它们的区别是：*Their differences are as follows:*

1. 在语义上，"本来"侧重于某种事实和状况原本如此，强调根本上的，有的甚至表示是本质的、本性的语义。"原来"侧重于某种事实和状况原先时候曾是这样的，一般含有现在有所改变的语义，强调起先的时间。*Semantically, "本来" focuses on fundamental facts or status. Sometimes it even carries the meaning of "essence." "原来" emphasizes how certain facts and the past status were; it carries the meaning of a change.*

比较下面句子可以体会：*Compare the following sentences:*

（7）我本来是不喜欢喝酒的人。（强调本性不喜欢。*Dislike drinking by nature.*）

（8）我原来是不喜欢喝酒的人。（强调以前不喜欢，现在可能有改变。*Did not like it before, but may have changed now.*）

2. "本来"有理应如此、理所当然的意思，"原来"没有。*"本来" can mean "go without saying." "原来" has no such a meaning.*

（9）他已经学过半年，他的汉语本来就应该比我们好。

（10）*他已经学过半年，他的汉语原来就应该比我们好。

3. "原来"有"没有改变的"意思，"本来"没有这个意思。*"原来" can mean "unchanged." "本来" has no such a meaning.*

（11）*我还要在本来的地方拍照。

（12）我还要在原来的地方拍照。

"原来"表示"没有改变的"意思时，在句子中须有一定的语用条件。一般在句子中，常常有副词"还"的配合使用，或者有前后两个分句。这两个分句一定含有原先和现在两个时间段的不同情况，在比较中体现"原来"这个词"没有改变的"意思。*When "原来" means "unchanged," certain pragmatic conditions have to be met. It is often used with the adverb "还." The sentence may consist of two clauses, which contain information about the past and the present and show what "unchanged" means through comparison.*

4. "原来"能表示从前不知道，后来恍然大悟的意思。"本来"没有这个用法。*"原来" can mean "discovering information that one was unaware of before." "本来" has no such meaning.*

（13）*我以为教室里没有人了呢，本来还有你在。

（14）我以为教室里没有人了呢，原来还有你在。

yuánxiān 原先 →P610"原来"

用法 Usage:

名词 *n.*

从前，起初，以前某一时期（含有现在已经有所变化的意思）。不能单独做谓语，修饰名词时要加"的"。 *Formerly; at a time in the past. It carries the meaning that some change has come to pass. It cannot stand alone as a predicate, and "的" has to be added when modifying nouns.*

（1）这里原先都是水稻田。

（2）原先我打算暑假回国，现在我想去旅游了。

（3）原先的计划不是这样的。

说明 Notes:

"原先"和"原来"都不能单独做谓语，修饰名词都要加"的"。*Neither "原先" nor "原来" can stand alone as a predicate. Both need to be followed by "的" when modifying nouns.*

它们的区别是： *They differ as follows:*

1. "原先"着重指早先、以前的时间。"原来"着重指过去、以前的情况。*"原先" emphasizes the time before, whereas "原来" emphasizes the situation before.*

（4）这是我原先住的房子。（着重时间 *Emphasizing time*）

（5）这是我原来住的房子。（着重原来的房子状态 *Emphasizing the original state of the house*）

2. "原先"多用于书面语。"原来"多用于口语。*"原先" is mostly used in written language. "原来" is often used colloquially.*

3. "原来"还有副词用法。"原先"没有副词用法。*"原来" can be used as an adverb but "原先" cannot.*

yuányīn 原因 →P296"理由"、P613"缘故"

用法 Usage:

名词 *n.*

造成某种结果或引起另一件事情发生的条件或根源。*Cause. It indicates the condition or origin of a certain result or the occurrence of a second event.*

（1）发生这样的事，原因是多方面的。

（2）他们找到了失败的原因。

说明 Notes:

"理由"与"原因"都表示事情或结果的根源。*"理由 (reason)" and "原因 (cause)" both refer to the origin of an event or a result.*

它们的区别是： *Their differences are as follows:*

1. "理由"着重指通过分析、研究而寻找出来的做某种事情或实现某种结果的道理，表示为什么要去做某件事情、为什么要取得这样结果的道理。"原因"着重指造成某种结果或发生某件事情的主、客观条件，是从某件事情或某种结果的外在方面寻找的缘由。要表示找出已经发生的事情或结果的根源时，只能用"原因"，不能用"理由"。*"理由" focuses on the reason for doing something or achieving a certain result; it is something that one has figured out through analysis and research. "原因" emphasizes the subjective and objective condition for a certain result or the occurrence of an event, which are extrinsic factors. When referring to the reason for a result of an event that has happened, "原因" rather than "理由" should be used.*

（3）*他突然咳嗽咳得那么厉害的理由是什么？

（4）他突然咳嗽咳得那么厉害的原因是什么？

2. 一般能修饰"原因"的名词，如"社会、主观、客观、具体"等词语都不能做定语，去修饰"理由"。*Nouns that can modify "原因", such as "社会,主观,客观,具体," cannot serve as an attributive and therefore cannot modify "理由."*

（5）*孩子们参加那么多校外辅导班的社会理由是什么？

（6）孩子们参加那么多校外辅导班的社会原因是什么？

yuánfèn 缘分

用法 Usage:

名词 *n.*

民间认为人与人之间命中注定的遇合的机

会,泛指人与人或人与事物之间发生联系的可能性。*Luck by which people are brought together. It is generally referenced as the possibilities of connections among people or between people and events.*

（1）我们班16个同学能在一起学习是很有缘分的,我们要珍惜。

（2）我跟烟酒没有缘分,一碰就要生病。

（3）他们俩还是有缘分,分手了两次,最后还是结婚了。

yuángù 缘故 →P612"原因"

用法 Usage:

名词 n.

也作"原故",原因。*Cause; reason. Also can be written as "原故."*

1. 常与"因为、由于"配合使用,形成"……是(因为/由于)……的缘故"的格式,作句子成分。*It is often used with "因为,由于" to form the structure of "…是（因为/由于）…的缘故."*

（1）也许是因为太高兴的缘故吧,奶奶都哭了。

（2）他到现在还没回家,不知道是什么缘故。

2. 可构成"无缘无故"的词组或介词词组作状语,常带"地"。*It can form phrases such as "无缘无故" or preposition-object phrases to serve as adverbials, which are often followed by "地."*

（3）你怎么能无缘无故地骂人呢?

（4）由于堵车的缘故,他到现在还没回来。

说明 Notes:

"原因"和"缘故"都指出造成某种结果或发生另一事情的条件或根源。凡是用"缘故"的地方。都可以换成"原因"。*Both "原因" and "缘故" indicate the condition or source of certain consequence or circumstance. In this sense, the two are interchangeable.*

（5）有的同学常常把"我"写成"找"。这是什么原因/缘故呢?

（6）不知道什么原因/缘故,她就是不要我抱她。

它们的区别是：*Their differences are as follows:*

1. 使用范围不同。"原因"词语色彩比较郑重,能用于重大事物,也用于一般事物。"缘故"不带郑重色彩,多用于一般事物,多用于口语。*The two words have different range of application. With a more serious tone, "原因" can be used for important events or ordinary matters. "缘故" is mostly used colloquially on ordinary matters.*

2. "原因"可用在具体因由前面,构成"……(的)原因是……"的格式,也可用在具体因由后面,构成"……是……(的)原因"。"缘故"一般多用在因由后面。*"原因" can be used before a reason as "…（的）原因是…" or after the reason as "…是…（的）原因." "缘故" is usually used after the reason.*

（7）她生病的原因是那天晚上吹了风、淋了雨。

（8）她生病是那天晚上吹了风、淋了雨的原因。

（9）*她生病的缘故是那天晚上吹了风、淋了雨。

（10）她生病是那天晚上吹了风、淋了雨的缘故。

3. "原因"所带的定语在内容上多是有待分析或说明的。"缘故"的定语多为有说明或解释的具体的因由。*The attributive describing "原因" often calls for further analysis or explanation. The attributive describing "缘故" often explains the specific reason for something.*

（11）发生这样的事情,有多方面的原因。

（12）由于堵车的缘故,大家的情绪都有点急躁。

4. "原因"可以用"社会、主观、客观、根本、主要、重要、具体"等名词、形容词作定语,可以与"寻找、找(出)、分析"等动词搭配使用。"缘故"一般不能。*Nouns or adjectives such as "社*

会,主观,客观,根本,主要,重要,具体"can be used as attributives with "原因.""原因"can also be used with verbs such as "寻找,找(出),分析.""缘故" usually has no such usage.

(13) *他的身体不好,有他自己的主观缘故,也有家庭的遗传缘故。

(14) 他的身体不好,有他自己的主观原因,也有家族的遗传原因。

yuànwàng 愿望 →P498"希望"

用法 Usage:

名词 n.

希望将来能达到某种目的或出现某种情况的想法。A wish for achieving a certain goal or the occurrence of a certain situation.

(1) 良好的愿望需要努力的行动。

(2) 我们是从团结的愿望出发来与你们交换意见的。

说明 Notes:

"希望"和"愿望"的区别是: The differences between "希望" and "愿望" are as follows:

1. "希望"作名词用时的意思和"愿望"不同。表示"实现某种愿望的可能性"的意思时,应该用"希望",不能用"愿望"。When used as a noun, "希望" and "愿望" have different meanings. To express the meaning of "the possibility of making a certain wish come true," "希望" rather than "愿望" should be used.

(3) *只要还有一丝愿望,就要全力抢救。

(4) 只要还有一丝希望,就要全力抢救。

2. "希望"还可以用作动词,受副词的修饰,常带非名词性宾语。"愿望"不能。"希望" can be used as a verb, which can be modified by an adverb and is often followed by an object that is not a noun. "愿望" has no such usage.

(5) *我很愿望去中国学习。

(6) 我很希望去中国学习。

(7) 我很希望去中国学习的愿望能早点实现。

yuē 约

用法 Usage:

动词 v.

1. 预先说定,共同商定。To agree on details of an upcoming appointment or event.

(1) 你约了大家一起去看画展了吗?

(2) 我们约个时间好好地聚一聚。

2. 邀请。To invite.

(3) 星期天我约了几个朋友去西湖划船。

(4) 妈妈,我约小王到家来吃饭,好吗?

副词 ad.

大概。只表示对数量和时间的估计。Approximately (used for an estimate of the amount and time).

(5) 今晚约八点时我会打电话给你。

(6) 那小孩约有七八岁,广场舞跳得好极了。

名词 n.

事先约定的事。共同商定双方必须要遵守的事项。An appointment that has been made; an agreement of all parties involved on ground rules to be followed.

(7) 我们有约在先,明天不见不散。

(8) 家务事谁来做,新婚夫妻常常会立约分工。

说明 Notes:

"约"是单音节词,在句中前后搭配的常常也是单音节词,如"约了、约个、约于、约有、有约"等。As a monosyllabic word, "约" is usually preceded or followed by monosyllabic words as in "约了,约个,约于,约有,有约."

yuēdìng 约定 →P615"约会"

用法 Usage:

动词 v.

经过商量而确定。To agree on something after a discussion.

(1) 我们约定好以后我们每个月见一次面。

(2) 关于同学会的时间大家约定一下。

名词 n.

经过商量所确定的内容。*The matter agreed on after a discussion.*

（3）这个约定大家一致同意了，就开始执行。

（4）你既然同意了这个约定，为什么不遵守？

yuēhuì 约会 →P614"约定"

用法 Usage：

名词 n.

预先约定的会晤。*An appointment that has been made.*

（1）星期六我已经有个约会，不能到你家去了。

（2）到了周末，她的约会特别多。

动词 v.

预先约定相会。*To make an appointment.*

（3）我们已经跟二班同学约会了。

说明 Notes：

"约会"跟"约定"都有动词用法。*"约会" and "约定" can both be used as verbs.*

它们的区别是："约会"是离合动词，后面不能再带宾语。"约定"后面可以带宾语。*Their difference is that "约会" is a separable verb and it cannot be followed by an object while "约定" can be followed by an object.*

（4）＊大家赶快约会一下明天集合的时间。

（5）大家赶快约定一下明天集合的时间。

yuè 越

用法 Usage：

动词 v.

1. 跨过（阻碍）。*To stride over (an obstacle).*

（1）听见开门的声音，那个小偷跳出窗口，越过矮墙逃了。

（2）这次旅游，他们在贵州翻山越岭很辛苦。

2. 不按照一般的次序，超过（范围），超出（次序）。*Not to follow the regular order; to act beyond one's authority.*

（3）越过老师向校长写信提意见，可以吗？

（4）他越过1 500米，直接参加了3 000米长跑比赛。

副词 ad.

重复使用，"越……越……"，表示程度随着事态的变化而变化。*Reduplicated as "越…越…" to show a change that comes with another change.*

（5）人的大脑是越用越聪明的。

（6）大家越唱越高兴，从下午一直唱到晚上。

yuèláiyuè…… 越来越…… →P396"日益"

用法 Usage：

表示程度随着时间的推移变化而发生变化。句子中只能是一个主语。*More and more. It indicates the progressive change as time moves on. The sentence can only have one subject.*

（1）现在手机的种类越来越多，功能越来越现代。

（2）我越来越喜欢吃中国菜了。

说明 Notes：

1. "越来越……"通用于口语和书面语。*"越来越…" can be used both colloquially and in written language.*

2. "越来越……"后面一般只能带形容词或心理动词，如例（2）。一般不带表示动作、行为的普通动词。*"越来越…" is usually followed by an adjective or a verb indicating a mental activity as in (2). It is usually not followed by regular verbs describing an action or behavior.*

（3）＊雨越来越下大了。

（4）雨越来越大了。

（5）＊我们越来越跑步快了。

（6）我们跑得越来越快了。

（7）＊这几年中国越来越发展了。

（8）这几年中国发展得越来越快了。

3. "越来越……"强调程度随时间的推移，

有所变化,这种变化已经出现,所以句末常加"了"。"越来越..." emphasizes the change of degree along with the time change, which keeps moving forward. Therefore, the sentence usually ends with "了."

(9) 她越来越漂亮了。

(10) 听了他的解释,我反而越来越糊涂了。

4. "日益"的意思跟"越来越……"相近,都表示程度随着时间的推移而增加。"日益" is close to "越来越... (more and more)" in meaning. Both indicate a higher degree with the passage of time.

它们的区别是:Their differences lie in:

① "日益"的时间推移是"一天比一天",时间要求比较严谨。"越来越……"推移的时间长度不定,比较松弛。"日益" refers to the increasing degree with each passing day. It is more strict in terms of time. "越来越..." is more relaxed in this regard; the passage of time may vary, sometimes long and sometimes short.

② "日益"多用于书面。"越来越……"多用于口语。"日益" is used more in written Chinese while "越来越..." is used more in oral Chinese.

(11) *我日益胖了。

(12) 我越来越胖了。

(13) *我们吵架了,我日益生气。

(14) 我们吵架了,我越来越生气。

yǔnxǔ 允许 →P397"容许"、P472"同意"

用法 Usage:

动词 v.

许可。To allow; to permit.

(1) 父母不允许我们喝酒。

(2) 时间已经不允许你再这么犹豫不决了。

说明 Notes:

1. "允许"和"容许"都表示许可的意思,施事者可以是人,也可以是事物。"允许"and "容许" both mean "to allow." The subject can be people or things.

它们的区别是:Their differences are as follows:

"允许"着重于应允、许可。多用于同意某种要求和做法,既可指被人允许,也可指被客观情况、时间和天气等条件的许可,表达的语气比较和缓。"容许"着重于容忍、许可。多用于容忍某种现象或情况的存在。施事者多为人、国家、机关、学校和工厂等企事业单位。表达的语气比较严厉。"允许" emphasizes giving consent or allowing. The subject can be people or objective conditions such as time or weather. The tone of voice is relatively mild. "容许" focuses on tolerating or allowing. It is mostly used to indicate tolerance of a certain phenomenon or situation. The subjects are usually people, the country, government offices, schools, factories, etc. The tone of voice is relatively harsh.

2. "允许"和"同意"的区别是:The differences between "允许" and "同意" are as follows:

两个词语的对象不太相同。"允许"的对象是某种要求或作法。"同意"的意思是对某种主张或看法表示相同的意见,它的对象是某种主张或看法。The targets of the two are different. The target of "允许" is a certain demand or method of work. "同意" means to agree on a certain proposal or perspective. Its target is usually a proposal or a perspective.

(3) *我允许他的看法。

(4) 我同意他的看法。

(5) *因为时间不同意,我们没去云南旅游。

(6) 因为时间不允许,我们没去云南旅游。

yùnqi 运气

用法 Usage:

名词 n.

1. 命运(指生死、贫富和一切遭遇,迷信的人认为这是生来注定的)。Destiny. People who are superstitious believe that all aspects of life such as life or death, poverty or wealth are pre-determined by fate.

(1) 这个人的运气不好,嫁了两个丈夫都死了。

(2) 你的运气真好,有这么孝顺的一对儿女!

2. 指偶然的好机会、好机遇。Good fortune or opportunity by chance.

(3) 听说你得到了一等奖,运气真好!

(4) 找工作有时也靠运气。

形容词 a.

幸运。Lucky.

(5) 你真运气,遇到了一位这么好的老师。

(6) 今天我好运气,找到了丢失的电动车。

说明 Notes:

1. "运气"还有一个读音是"yùnqì",作离合动词,意思是把力气贯注到身体的某个部位。When pronounced as "yùnqì," "运气" is used as a separable verb, meaning to focus one's vital energy on certain parts of the body.

(7) 打太极拳要注意运气。

(8) 气功师父运了一会儿气,一拳打碎了五块砖头。

2. "运气"是个口语词,常见的主谓搭配有"运气好、运气不好、运气不佳",动宾搭配常说"碰运气、有运气、靠运气、试试运气"等。"运气" is used colloquially. Common subject-predicate phrases include "运气好,运气不好,运气不佳." Common verb-object phrases include "碰运气,有运气,靠运气,试试运气."

3. 口语中还可以有"算你运气"的说法。"算你运气" may be used colloquially as well.

(9) 居然赶上了末班车,算你运气!

yùnyòng 运用 →P590"应用"

用法 Usage:

动词 v.

根据事物自身的特点加以利用,使用。To use something based on its characteristics; to put to use.

(1) 我们应该把学到的语法知识运用到口语中去。

(2) 科学家发现猴子具有运用工具的能力。

说明 Notes:

"运用"和"应用"都有使用的意思。"运用" and "应用" can both mean "to use."

它们的区别是:Their differences are as follows:

1. "运用"一般多用于抽象事物,宾语多为"方法、知识、技能、规律、观点、理论、权力"等抽象名词。"应用"所指的对象大多是"新技术、自动化设备、电脑、太阳能、煤炭"等较具体或范围较小的名词,如"电脑得到广泛应用、太阳能在生活中得到了应用"等,其中"应用"一般不能用"运用"去替换。"运用" is used for abstract things. The objects are mostly abstract nouns such as "方法,知识,原理,技能,智慧,规律,立场,观点,理论,权力." The targets of "应用" are often nouns that refer to something specific or with a small range, such as "新技术,自动化设备,电脑,太阳能,煤炭," as in "电脑得到广泛应用,太阳能在生活中得到了应用,应用了自动化设备." In such usage, "应用" cannot be replaced by "运用."

2. "应用"可以做定语。"运用"不做定语。如:"应用技术、应用科学、应用语言"等词语中的"应用"不能用"运用"替代。"应用" can serve as an attributive, such as "应用技术,应用科学,应用文," but "运用" cannot. Here, "应用" cannot be replaced by "运用."

zāihài 灾害 →P618"灾难"

用法 Usage:

名词 n.

因水、火、旱、涝、虫、雹等恶劣的自然现象或人为因素(如战争)所造成的祸害。Disasters caused either by natural calamities such as flood, fire, drought, waterlogging, insect pest and hail, or by the human factor such as a war.

(1) 这个地区每年都会发生几次洪水灾害。

(2) 我们应该尽可能预防各种自然灾害的发生。

zāinàn 灾难 →P618"灾害"

用法 Usage:

名词 n.

天灾人祸所造成的严重损害和痛苦。Severe damages or sufferings inflicted by natural or man-made disasters.

(1) 我们应该尽量防止航空灾难的发生。

(2) 我们不希望恐怖袭击灾难再次出现。

(3) 台风给沿海城市带来了很大的灾难。

说明 Notes:

"灾害"和"灾难"都有天灾人祸所造成的祸害的意思。"灾害" and "灾难" both mean the scourge caused by natural or man-made disasters.

它们的区别是：Their differences are as follows:

1. "灾害"着重指旱、涝、虫、雹、地震、飓风、海啸、战争等所造成的祸害,指祸害本身。"灾难"着重指灾害给人们所造成的损害和苦难。"灾害" focuses on the disaster itself caused by a drought, flood, insect pest, hail, earthquake, hurricane, tsunami or war. "灾难" focuses on the harms and sufferings the disaster inflicts on people.

2. 在句子中,"灾难"不能换成"灾害"。如：例(1)(2)(3)中的"灾难"都不能替换成"灾害"。In most sentences, "灾难" cannot be replaced by "灾害." See (1), (2) and (3) in "灾难."

zài 再 →P604"又"

用法 Usage:

副词 ad.

1. 表示同一个动作的重复或继续。Again; repeatedly. It is used to refer to the repetition or continuation of an action.

(1) 我没听清楚您说的话,请您再说一遍,好吗?

(2) 学习,学习,再学习。

2. 有时专指第二次。如："再次、再度、再婚、再生"等。Once more, specifically referring to a second occurrence, as in "再次,再度,再婚,再生."

(3) 那本书已经再版了。

(4) 医生一而再,再而三地告诉他不能吃冰冷食物。

3. 表示再继续,再出现。常用于书面语。如:"青春不再、盛会难再、良机难再"等。Again. It indicates that something is to continue or occur again. It is common in written language, such as "青春不再,盛会难再,良机难再."

说明 Notes:

1. 使用"再"要注意它与其他词语搭配时体现的语义。The meaning of "再" is worth our attention when it goes with other words.

① "再"多用于将要重复或继续的动作。"再" is often used with an action that is about to repeat or continue.

（5）太好吃了,请再来一碗！（动作重复 Action to be repeated）

（6）这里的风景太美了,再坐一会儿吧！（动作继续 Action to continue）

② "再"和"不"连用。"不再"表示动作不重复下去了。"再不"表示动作坚决不重复下去了。When "再" is combined with "不," "不再" suggests the action stops repeating; "再不" suggests the action shall never repeat itself.

（7）吃饱了,不再吃了。

（8）太饱了,我再（也）不吃了。

③ 表示程度加深,多用于形容词前。It indicates a deepened degree and is often used before an adjective.

（9）时间再晚,我也要回学校。

（10）我想买一条颜色再绿一点的裙子。

④ 表示如果动作重复或继续下去（就会怎么样）。It indicates that something will happen if an action continues or is repeated.

（11）我们再不走,就来不及上飞机了。

（12）你再不控制饮食,就会越来越胖了。

⑤ 表示即使重复或继续下去（也不会怎么样）。It indicates that something won't happen even if an action continues or is repeated.

（13）我们再怎么说,他都不会相信。

（14）你再洗十遍,这件衣服也洗不干净。

⑥ 表示一个动作将在另一个动作结束后出现,相当于"然后"。Similar to "然后," it suggests one action will occur when another action ends.

（15）我吃完饭再喝咖啡。

（16）我下了班再给你打电话。

⑦ 表示所说的范围有所扩大或补充,相当于"另外"。Similar to "另外," it suggests there is an expansion or supplement to what is being said.

（17）你是我的同屋,再说都是韩国人,怎么能不帮你？

（18）已经爬了两座山,再要爬山,我没有力气了。

⑧ 在肯定句和疑问句中"再"只能用在能愿动词后。在否定句中,"再"在能愿动词前后皆可。In affirmative and interrogative sentences, "再" can only follow a modal verb. In negative sentences, "再" can go either before and after a modal verb.

（19）*你再可以说一遍吗？

（20）你可以再说一遍吗？

（21）你不能再吃了。

（22）你再也不能吃了。

⑨ "再"和否定词"不、别"等连用时,句子后面一般常用"了",表示句子完整的意思和缓和的语气,如例（7）（8）（11）（18）等。When "再" goes with a negative word "不" or "别," "了" often appears at the end of a sentence so as to complete the meaning and mitigate the tone. See (7), (8), (11) and (18).

2. "再"与"又"都表示行为动作的重复或继续。"再" and "又" both suggest the repetition or continuation of an action.

它们的区别是：Their differences are as follows:

① "又"表示动作行为已经完成。"再"表示动作行为还没完成的将来式。"又" suggests an action has completed. "再" indicates a future tense and the action hasn't finished yet.

（23）他又喝了一瓶啤酒,已经喝了四瓶了。

(24) 他想再喝一瓶啤酒。

② "再"可以用在形容词前面。"又"不可以。"再" can be used before adjectives whereas "又" cannot.

(25) *照片贴得又高一点！
(26) 照片贴得再高一点！

zàisān 再三 →P564 "一再"

用法 Usage:
副词 ad.

表示动作、行为反复进行，并含有强调的意味，相当于"反复""一遍又一遍、一次又一次"。Over and over again; again and again; repeatedly. Indicating an action or behavior being repeated again and again in the past, it carries a sense of emphasis. It is equivalent to "反复 (repeatedly)," "一遍又一遍, 一次又一次."

(1) 经过再三修改，我才把论文交给了老师。
(2) 病人出院的时候，向医生再三道谢。

数词 num.

用在动词后面，表示多次。Placed after a verb, it means "a couple of times."

(3) 马克考虑再三，决定再学一年汉语。
(4) 她犹豫再三，最后还是没有玩过山车。

说明 Notes:

1. "再三"有数词和副词用法，一般区分方法是：用在动词后面做数量宾语，则是数词用法。用在动词前面做修饰语，则是副词用法。"再三" is used sometimes as a numerical and sometimes as an adverb. The way to distinguish the two is that it is a numerical if it is placed after a verb as its numerical object. It is an adverb if it is placed before a verb.

2. "一再"和"再三"都表示动作行为在过去一次又一次。Both "一再" and "再三" mean an action or behavior being repeated again and again in the past.

它们的区别是：Their differences are as follows:

① 作为副词，"一再"侧重修饰具有能发声的言语类动词，如"叮嘱、催促、强调、解释、道歉、要求"等；也可以修饰非言语类的动词，如"发生、失败、获奖、扩大、违背"等。它的使用范围比"再三"广。"再三"侧重修饰言语类表示思维性质的动词，如"考虑、思考、思索、思量、斟酌"等。很少跟其他动词搭配，如"破坏、打架、锻炼"等。As an adverb, "一再" tends to modify a kind of verbs that express a verbal activity such as "叮嘱, 催促, 强调, 解释, 道歉, 要求." Also it can modify verbs that do not belong to this type, such as "发生, 失败, 获奖, 扩大, 违背." It is applied to a wider scope than "再三." By contrast, "再三" tends to modify verbs of mental activity, especially verbs related to thinking, such as "考虑, 思考, 思索, 思量, 斟酌." It seldom goes with verbs not belonging to this type, such as "破坏, 打架, 锻炼."

② "再三"有时可以构成"再三＋动词＋一下"的格式。"一再"没有这样的用法。"再三" is sometimes used to make the pattern "再三＋v.＋一下."

(5) 关于安全问题，我要再三强调一下。
(6) 我再三提醒你一下，别忘了带护照。

③ "再三"有数词用法。"一再"没有。"再三" may be used as a numerical, but not "一再."

④ 一般情况下，"再三"还能表示动作行为在将来一次又一次反复出现的意思。"一再"不能这样用。In ordinary circumstances, "再三" may be used to refer to the repeated occurrence of an action or behavior to appear in the future. "一再" cannot be used in this way.

(7) *明天见到她以后，我会一再向她说明的。
(8) 明天见到她以后，我会再三向她说明的。

但某种动作或行为以前已经反复发生过，那么这一动作或行为如果在将来再反复发生，也可以受"一再"修饰。If an action or a behavior happened repeatedly in the past, it can be modified by "一再" if it may happen *repeatedly in the future.*

（9）昨天我回家，妈妈就再三问我你的事。明天你回去，她也会一再询问你的。

（10）上次我跟他谈，他就不承认作弊。下次你问他，他仍会一再否认的。

zàishuō 再说 →P36"并且"、P130"而且"

用法 Usage:

连词 conj.

表示在已经举出的理由以外，再补充一点理由或原因。连接分句，用于后一分句的开头，相当于"而且、并且"的意思。*Moreover; in addition; there is more to say apart from the listed reason or cause. Joining clauses, it is placed at the beginning of the second clause, similar to "而且,并且."*

（1）这本字典不错，再说也不贵，买一本吧。

（2）现在懂汉语找工作容易，再说我想去中国看看，所以打算去中国留学。

动词 v.

指某一件事先搁一段时间，以后再进行办理或考虑。常用在句末作谓语。*It means to put something off until some time later. It is usually placed at the end of a sentence as a predicate.*

（3）我最近没有时间跟你吃饭，以后再说吧。

（4）你别着急，找旅馆的事我们吃了饭再说。

说明 Notes:

1. 使用"再说"要注意：*When using "再说," the following points should be noted:*

①"再说"作连词用，要放在表示原因的第二分句的开头，如例（1）（2）。*As a conjunction, "再说" should be placed at the beginning of the second clause that indicates a reason. See (1) and (2).*

② 在第二分句中，"再说"常与"又、也"配合使用。*In the second clause, "再说" often goes with "又," or "也."*

2. "再说""并且""而且"做连词都有表示意思进一步的作用。*As a conjunction, "再说,""并且" and "而且" all carry the meaning of "in addition" or "moreover", similar to "此外 (besides)."*

"再说"着重表示说明进一步的理由或原因，句子中必定有因为这个理由或原因要去做或不做的事实。表示这个意思时，"再说"与"并且"和"而且"可以互相替换。*The focus of "再说" is on explaining a reason or cause further. The sentence must include a fact relevant to the reason or cause. In this case, "再说" can be replaced by "而且," or "并且."*

（5）他没有请我，再说/并且/而且我也不想去。

它们的区别是：*Their differences are as follows:*

①"并且"和"而且"能表示进一层的补充或说明。"再说"不能。*"并且" or "而且" suggests an additional explanation or supplement. "再说" has no such usage.*

（6）＊这里的人我认识很多，再说不少人还是我的同学。

（7）这里的人我认识很多，并且/而且不少人还是我的同学。

②"并且"和"而且"常与前面分句中的"不但"搭配呼应。"再说"不能与"不但"搭配使用。*"并且" or "而且" often echoes with "不但" that appears in the first clause, but "再说" cannot be used in this way.*

（8）＊他不但喜欢吃饺子，再说吃得还很多。

（9）他不但喜欢吃饺子，并且/而且吃得还很多。

③"再说"只能连接分句。"并且"和"而且"除了能连接分句以外，还能连接形容词、动词、副词。*"再说" can only connect clauses. "并且" and "而且" can not only connect clauses but also adjectives, verbs and adverbs.*

（10）＊她不但聪明，再说漂亮。

（11）她不但聪明，并且/而且漂亮。

④"再说"有动词用法,在口语中可以单独使用。"并且"和"而且"没有动词用法。As a verb, "再说" can be used independently in oral Chinese. Neither "并且" nor "而且" can be used as a verb.

(12) A：你打算什么时候去西安？
B：再说，再说。

zài 在 →P91"当"、P605"于"、P650"正在"

用法 Usage:

动词 v.

1. 表示人或事物存在的处所、位置。To be located in; to sit on. It refers to the location or place where people or things are.

(1) 我家在北京。
(2) 那本书在书架上，不在桌子上。

2. 存在，生存。"不在了"表示某人已经去世。To exist; to be living; to survive. "不在了" indicates someone is dead.

(3) 奶奶在的时候常给我讲故事，现在她不在了。
(4) 唐太宗在位二十三年。

3. 在于，决定于。To depend on; to lie in; to be determined by.

(5) 一个人聪明不聪明完全在自己。
(6) 牙齿不好，多半在平时不好好刷牙。

副词 ad.

表示动作持续不断，正在（进行中）。It indicates an action that is going on.

(7) 我出来的时候，同屋在做作业。
(8) 昨天这个时候，我还在吃饭呢。

介词 prep.

跟时间、处所、方位等词语组合，句式有：When "在" is combined with words indicating a time, location or direction, it appears in the following sentence structures:

1. 表示时间。Indicating a time.

①"在……"用在动词、形容词或主语前面，表示一般动作发生的时间。When used before a verb, an adjective or the subject, "在" indicates the time when an action occurs.

(9) 我是在去年回国的。
(10) 在小的时候她很可爱。

②"在……"用在动词后。单音节动词限于"死、生、定、处、放、派"等，双音节动词限于"出生、诞生、发生、出现、发现、布置、安排、确定、固定"等。When placed after a verb, there are certain limits: Monosyllabic verbs are limited to "死，生，定，处，放，派，etc." And disyllabic verbs are limited to "出生,诞生,发生,出现,发现,布置,安排,确定,固定，etc."

(11) 这个故事发生在抗日战争时期。
(12) 我生在1999年。

2. 表示处所。Indicating a location.

①"在……"用在动词、形容词或主语前，指动作发生或事物存在的处所。When used before a verb, an adjective or the subject, it indicates the location where an action occurs or something exists.

(13) 他喜欢在图书馆看书。
(14) 在中国的城市私家车已经很普遍。

②"在……"可以在动词前后，表示出生、居留或事情发生的处所、动作达到的处所。"在" can be placed either before or after a verb to indicate the place of birth, living or where something occurs or some action reaches.

(15) 我出生在上海/我在上海出生。
(16) 太阳光照在水面上亮闪闪的。

3. 表示范围。Indicating a scope.

构成"在……中、在……上、在……方面"等结构表示范围时，用在动词、形容词或主语前，其他情况用在动词后。In structures such as "在...中，在...上，在...方面，""在" indicates a scope, and it appears before a verb, an adjective or the subject. In other cases, it appears after a verb.

(17) 他在写汉字上还有一些问题。
(18) 在绘画方面,他很有才能。

4. 表示条件。Indicating a condition.

构成"在＋名词短语＋下"的格式，用在动词或主语前。In the structure "在 + noun

phrase＋下," it appears before a verb or a subject.

（19）他在朋友的帮助下，租到了一套满意的房子。

（20）在医生的抢救下，爷爷终于又活过来了。

5. 表示行为的主体。一般表示"对某人来＋动词"的意思。*It indicates the subject of an action, similar to the meaning of "对某人来＋verb."*

（21）中国的饭菜在他已经非常习惯了。（"对他来说"）

（22）在我看来，这不算困难。（"依我看来"）

说明 Notes：

1. 使用"在"要注意：*When using "在," be careful about the following points:*

① "在"作介词表示处所时，如果动词带宾语，宾语前要有数量词，否则要用"把"字句或宾语前置句。*When "在" indicates a location as a preposition, there should be a particle before the object if there is an object following the verb. Otherwise, either the "把" structure or an object-preposed sentence should be used.*

（23）＊请放笔在桌子上。

（24）请你在桌子上放一支笔。

（25）请你把笔放在桌子上。

（26）笔，请放在桌子上。

② 有时"在……"可在动词前，也可在动词后，但表示的意思不同。*"在" can be used before a verb or after it, but the meanings are different.*

（27）他在床上跳舞。（跳的动作发生在床上。*The action of jumping occurs on the bed.*）

（28）他从窗口跳在床上。（从别的地方跳到床上。*The action of jumping occurs from the open window.*）

③ 用在动词前，"在"与指示代词"这里、那里"组成的"在这里、在那里"，所表示的处所意义有时很不明显。句子主要表示"正在进行"的意思。*When used before a verb, the phrase "在这里"* or "在那里," which is the combination of "在" with the demonstrative pronoun "这里" or "那里," sometimes suggests a rather vague meaning of location. The sentence mainly indicates that something is in progress.*

（29）我在这里想星期天去哪儿呢。（主要表示正在想 *Suggesting one is currently in the process of thinking*）

（30）到中国以后，他时时刻刻地在那里找机会跟中国人说话。

④ "在"用在动词、形容词或主语前表示时间，有时可省略。*When "在" is used before a verb, an adjective or the subject indicating time, it can be omitted.*

（31）姐姐（在）前年结婚了。

（32）（在）三年的时间（里），他写了五篇小说。

⑤ "在"表示人或事物存在的处所、位置时，一般要带宾语，但如果处所是已知的，可不带宾语。一般用在对话中。*When "在" suggests a location or place where people or things stay or exist, it generally takes an object, but if the location is known, the object can be omitted. This use usually appears in a conversation.*

（33）A：张老师在家吗/张老师在吗？
　　　B：在，请进！

2. "在"与"当"做介词，都能表示时间和处所。如果后面带的是小句或动词短语构成的时间词组，"在"和"当"可以换用，如："在我回来的时候/当我回来的时候"。*When "在" or "当" serves as a preposition, they can both indicate a time and location. When followed by a time phrase composed of a clause or verb phrase, "在" and "当" are interchangeable, as in "在我回来的时候/当我回来的时候."*

它们的区别是：*Their differences are as follows:*

① 表示时间时，"当"不能跟单独的时间词组合。"在"可以。*When expressing a time,*

"当" cannot go with a sheer time word, but "在" can.

(34) *当昨晚六点,爷爷发病送了医院。
(35) 在昨晚六点,爷爷发病送了医院。

② 表示处所时,"当"只能跟少数名词组合,不能跟处所词、方位词组合。"在"正相反,只能跟处所词、方位词组合,不能跟名词组合。When expressing a location, "当" can only go with a few nouns instead of localizers or position words. By contrast, "在" can only go with localizers or position words instead of nouns.

(36) *大家有什么意见请在面讲。
(37) 大家有什么意见请当面讲。
(38) *大家有什么意见请当我面前讲。
(39) 大家有什么意见请在我面前讲。

3. "于"和"在"都是介词,都可以引进动作的时间、处所、方位等。Both "于" and "在" are prepositions capable of introducing the time, location, and direction of an action.

它们的区别是:Their differences are as follows:

① "于"是文言虚词,多用于书面语。"在"通用于口语和书面语。"于" is a function word in classic Chinese. It appears mostly in written Chinese. "在," however, appears both in oral and written Chinese.

② "在+处所名词"作状语比较常见。"于+处所名词"在动词前作状语则较少见。"在 + location noun" often serves as an adverbial, but "于 + location noun" rarely serves as an adverbial before a verb.

(40) *京剧讲座于第一大教室举行。
(41) 京剧讲座在第一大教室举行。

③ "于+处所名词"一般用于动词(大多为单音节动词,常见有"生、死、位、出、产、用、源、毕业")后面作补语,多数情况下"在+处所名词"不能替换。"于 + location noun" mostly serves as a complement after a verb (mostly monosyllabic verbs such as "生, 死, 位, 出, 产, 用, 源, 毕业"). In most cases, "在 + location nouns" cannot be replaced.

(42) 龙井茶产于/*在杭州。
(43) 他毕业于/*在北京大学。

一般来说,除了"他生/死于北京"可以说成"他生/死在北京"外,其他用"于"的句子多不能用"在"替换。"他生于/死于北京" can be rewritten as "他生/死在北京." But that is an exception. Generally speaking, other sentences using "于" cannot be replaced by "在."

④ "于"可以为动作或状态引出方向、方面、对象、原因等。"在"一般不能。"于" can introduce the direction, aspect, target or reason for an action or state, but "在" cannot.

(44) 他这半年忙于/*在找工作。
(45) 她很乐于/*在助人。
(46) 他决心从事于/*在教育事业。

zàihu 在乎

用法 Usage:

动词 v.

1. 指出事情的缘由或关键所在,在于。To lie in, indicating the reason or key point of a matter.

(1) 衣服不在乎它的好看,而在乎你穿这衣服合适不合适。
(2) 外语学得好不好在乎你用不用。

2. 放在心上,介意,在意。多用于否定句或问句。To bear in mind; to take to heart; to care about. It is often used in a negative sentence or a question.

(3) 只要把这件事做好,时间长一点不在乎。
(4) 他满不在乎地说,贵点就贵点。
(5) 别人对你态度不好,你会在乎吗?

zàiyú 在于

用法 Usage:

动词 v.

1. 指出事物的本质所在,正是,就是,或指出事物以什么为内容。必带宾语。To lie in;

to rest with; to be no other than. It points out the essence of a matter. It must take an object.

（1）你作业做不出的原因在于上课没认真听讲。

（2）人生的价值在于对别人的奉献。

2. 指出关键所在，决定于。必带宾语，主语常是选择性疑问小句。To depend on; to be decided by. It points out the key factor or essence of a matter. It must take an object, and the subject is often a selective interrogative clause.

（3）一年之计在于春，一日之计在于晨。

（4）能不能参加这次比赛在于他的脚伤能不能好。

zànshí 暂时 →P580"一时"

用法 Usage:

形容词 a.

1. 表示在短时间内，不长久。多形容名词，或用在"是……的"的短语中。Lasting only a short time; temporary. It usually modifies a noun, or is used in the phrase "是...的."

（1）这是暂时的问题，很快就会解决。

（2）堵车是暂时的现象，道路很快就畅通。

2. 表示某种动作行为或者某种情况持续的时间不长，短时间内。For the time being; for the moment. It suggests that a certain action or circumstance will not last long.

（3）您拨打的电话暂时无法接通。

（4）我刚到上海，暂时先住在朋友家。

3. 因为是短时间内的，因此有时含有"非正式的、非固定、临时性的"等意思。For the time being. It indicates that something is temporary, informal or non-fixed due to its short span.

（5）这件事情你暂时负责一下。

（6）总经理的工作暂时由你担当。

说明 Notes:

"一时"和"暂时"都表示动作是"短时间内"的意思。"一时" and "暂时" both indicate that an action will happen in a short time.

它们的区别是：The differences are as follows:

1. "一时"是副词，着重于在短时间内发生的情况。强调是短时间内无法完成的动作。"暂时"是名词用法或形容词用法，着重于情况持续是短时间内的，强调是短时间内的应变措施。"一时" is an adverb, which focuses on something lasting only for a short time, and it emphasizes that the action cannot be finished shortly. "暂时" is a noun or an adjective, which emphasizes the fact that the situation will continue only for a short period of time, and the action is a temporary, contingency measure.

2. "一时"作副词用的第一义项，表示在短时间出现某种情况时，"暂时"可以替换"一时"。相反，"一时"不能替换形容词用法的"暂时"。The first usage of "一时" as an adverb, which suggests that a certain situation will occur in a short time, is also applicable to "暂时." However, the adjective use of "暂时" is not applicable to "一时."

（7）他的情绪一时/暂时很难平静下来。

（8）*王老师生病了，他的课一时你代他上。

（9）王老师生病了，他的课暂时你代他上。

3. "一时"一般修饰表示消极状态的动词、形容词及其短语。"暂时"可以修饰的动词、形容词及其短语的范围比"一时"广泛。"一时" often modifies a verb, adjective or phrase that indicates a negative state. The verbs, adjectives and phrases that can be modified by "暂时" are broader in range than "一时."

4. "一时"修饰的一般是已经发生的或正在发生的动作行为或状态。"暂时"修饰的可以是已经发生的动作行为或状态，也可以是正在发生或者将要发生的动作行为或状态。"一时" often modifies an action or state that has already happened or is occurring. The action or state modified by "暂时" can be one that has

happened, is happening or is about to happen.

（10）这本书现在一时/暂时找不到，你过两天再来看看。

（11）＊这本书他看完以后一时放在你那里。

（12）这本书他看完以后暂时放在你那里。

zànchéng 赞成 →P472"同意"

用法 Usage:

动词 v.

喜欢并同意（某个计划、意见、建议、提案、看法或某人做某件事等，和"反对"意思相反）。To favor or agree with a plan, opinion, proposal, suggestion, or someone doing something, as opposed to "反对 (oppose)."

（1）我不赞成这个旅行计划。

（2）大家都赞成他当班长。

说明 Notes:

1."赞成"是动词，一般后面常带宾语，如"意见、提案、看法、建议"等。"赞成"也表示喜欢、赞赏的心理情绪，因此前面也可以用程度副词修饰，如"非常赞成、特别赞成、很赞成"等。"赞成" is a verb that usually takes an object, such as "意见，提案，看法，建议." It also indicates sentiments of affection or admiration, therefore it can be preceded by adverbs of degree, as in "非常赞成，特别赞成，很赞成."

2."赞成"和"同意"的区别是：The differences between "赞成" and "同意" are as follows:

①"赞成"表示相同的意见程度比"同意"高，并带有感情色彩，有拥护的意思。"赞成" indicates a higher degree of agreement than "同意." It carries an emotional color, meaning "support."

②"同意"多用于上级对下级。"赞成"没有这种限定，使用范围比较广。"同意" is often used by a superior when addressing a subordinate. "赞成" doesn't have this limit; it is applied to a fairly wide scope.

③"赞成"可以构成"赞成票"。"同意"不能。"赞成" can go with "票" to form "赞成票 (a vote of support)." But "同意" cannot.

zànzhù 赞助

用法 Usage:

动词 v.

帮助，支持（多指经济上帮助）。To sponsor; to help finance (a project or program).

（1）这部电影由几十家单位赞助拍摄而成。

（2）他赞助了十多个贫困大学生完成了学业。

（3）为了贫困地区的孩子能上学，他拉来了很多赞助。

zāodào 遭到 →P626"遭受"

用法 Usage:

动词 v.

遇到，受到（不幸、不利的事或不好的对待）。多与双音节词搭配。To encounter; to suffer from (something unfortunate, undesirable or simply bad treatment), often going with disyllabic words.

（1）出去旅行的时候，他们全家遭到了不幸。

（2）他的意见遭到了很多同学的反对。

说明 Notes:

"遭到"所带的不是名词性宾语，而是动词性宾语，如"遭到反对、遭到拒绝、遭到挫折、遭到歧视、遭到打击迫害、遭到冷遇、遭到讽刺"等等。What follows "遭到" is not a nominal object but a verbal object, as in "遭到反对，遭到拒绝，遭到挫折，遭到歧视，遭到打击迫害，遭到冷遇，遭到讽刺, etc."

zāoshòu 遭受 →P626"遭到"

用法 Usage:

动词 v.

受到（不幸、不利的事）。To suffer from (something unfortunate, undesirable).

（1）为了生下这个孩子，她遭受了很大的痛苦。

（2）这次地震中老百姓遭受的损失很大。

说明 Notes:

"遭到"和"遭受"都指遇到不好的事情。

"遭到"and"遭受"both mean someone encounters something bad.

它们的区别是：Their differences are as follows:

1."遭到"强调"遇到"的意思。"遭受"强调遇到不利的事后还要忍受这些事所带来的后果。因此，在有"忍受"的意思时，"遭受"和"遭到"不能互相替代。"遭到" focuses on the act of "encountering." "遭受" emphasizes the endurance of the consequences after encountering something bad. Therefore, when the sense of "忍受 (to endure)" is implied, "遭受" and "遭到" are not interchangeable.

（3）这次地震使四川人民遭到/遭受了巨大的损失。

（4）*森林在大火中遭受了极大的破坏。

（5）森林在大火中遭到了极大的破坏。

（6）*这个老人一直遭到晚年失子的精神痛苦。

（7）这个老人一直遭受着晚年失子的精神痛苦。

2."遭受"有"忍受"之意，可表示动作的持续，因此后面可加"着"。"遭到"的"到"已表示动作有结果，故后面不能加"着"。"遭受" has a meaning of "忍受," which indicates a continuation of an action, and it can be followed by "着." The word "到" in "遭到" signals the completion of an action, and it cannot be followed by "着."

（8）*他正遭到着病痛的折磨。

（9）他正遭受着病痛的折磨。

zāoyù 遭遇

用法 Usage:

动词 v.

碰到，遇上（对手、敌人、不幸的或不顺利的事等）。To encounter, to meet with (an opponent, enemy, or unfortunate or unsuccessful event, etc.).

（1）世界杯第一场比赛他们就遭遇了强手巴西队。

（2）前不久这个国家遭遇了严重的经济危机。

名词 n.

指遇到的不幸的情况或不幸的经历。An unfortunate event or experience one encounters.

（3）2008年，好多国家在金融危机中都有一样的遭遇。

（4）这部电影讲了一个女人的不幸遭遇。

zāo 糟

用法 Usage:

形容词 a.

1. 腐烂，腐朽，不结实。多指某些材料。Rotten; decayed; crumbled. It is often used to refer to certain materials.

（1）这是一堆糟木头，做不了桌子椅子。

（2）这块布已经糟掉，没有用了。

2. 指事情或情况不好，坏。Poor; bad. It can be used to describe almost anything and everything that has gone wrong.

（3）他的身体很糟，你们要多加关心。

（4）你把这件事情搞糟了，现在怎么办？

名词 n.

指制酒剩下的渣滓。Grain dregs after making wine.

（5）这些糟可以用来做糟鱼、糟肉。

说明 Notes:

"糟"用作形容词的第二个义项时，在口语中常常也作"糟糕"。As an adjective in its second meaning, "糟糕" is also often used colloquially.

（6）他的身体很糟糕，你们要多加关心。

（7）真糟糕，手机忘在家里了。

zǎo 早

用法 Usage:

名词 n.

早上，早晨。Morning.

（1）老人从早到晚都坐在门口看着街上来来往往的行人和车辆。

(2) 上班的日子,他每天都是早出晚归。

形容词 a.

1. 时间在先的,时间靠前的。Early in time.

(3) 早稻米没有晚稻米软、好吃。

(4) 吃完早饭,他去上学了。

2. 更早,较早,比一定的时间靠前。Earlier, relatively early, earlier than a designated time.

(5) 每次上课,他都早来一个小时。

(6) 你们学校有早恋的学生吗?

3. 问候的话,用于早晨见面时互相打招呼。如:"你早!""王老师早!" Word of greeting, used when greeting each other in the morning, as in:"你早!""王老师早!"

4. 直接用在动词前,表示假设。含有恨晚的意思。It is used directly before a verb as a hypothesis. It suggests a feeling of remorse for not having done something earlier.

(7) 这个问题你早说就解决了。

(8) 你早来半个小时就碰到他了。

副词 ad.

强调事情的发生已经离现在有一段时间,"早"常与"就"连用,表示很早以前就发生的。句末常用"了"。It emphasizes that something happened a fairly long time ago. In this use, "早" often goes with "就" to express that meaning, and the sentence often ends with "了."

(9) 他早就回国了。

(10) 这个消息我们早就知道了。

zǎowǎn 早晚

用法 Usage:

名词 n.

早上和晚上。一般用于在早上和晚上做同样的事情或发生同样的情况。Morning and night. It is generally used when the same thing is done or happens both in the morning and at night.

(1) 我们那儿早晚都很冷,但中午比较热。

(2) 大城市早晚都容易堵车。

(3) 这种药早晚各吃一粒。

副词 ad.

表示预料某事、某种情况或早或迟,总有一天一定会发生,只是时间不能确定。常跟"会、要、得"配合使用。Sooner or later. It indicates a prediction that something will happen (or some situation will appear). The only thing that is not certain is the exact time. It usually goes with "会,要,得."

(4) 他每天喝那么多酒,早晚得生病。

(5) 只要努力学习,早晚会通过汉语水平考试的。

说明 Notes:

1. 该词也可修饰名词,表示一定会发生的,如"早晚的事情,早晚的问题"。"早晚" can also modify a noun, indicating that something is bound to happen, as in "早晚的事情,早晚的问题。"

2. "早晚"可以重叠为"早早晚晚",多用于口语。"早晚" can be reduplicated as "早早晚晚," and is often used in spoken language.

(6) 开车那么快,早早晚晚要出事。

zǎoyǐ 早已

用法 Usage:

副词 ad.

早已经,早就。表示动作行为或者情况在说话之前很久就发生了,强调事情的发生离现在已经有较长的一段时间。句尾多用"了"呼应。Already; long ago. It means the action or situation took place long before the conversation, which emphasizes the long time between its occurrence and the current moment. The sentence often ends with "了."

(1) 这电影我早已看过了。

(2) 你给我寄来的咖啡我早已收到了。

说明 Notes:

1. "早已"可以用"早就"来替换,但"早就"的强调意味比"早已"强一些。"早已" can be replaced by "早就," but "早就" shows a

stronger emphasis than "早已."

2. 在北京话中,"早已"还有名词用法,表示从前、早先。In the Beijing dialect, "早已" can serve as a noun meaning early on or a long time ago.

（3）早已,父母批评孩子,孩子是不能回嘴的。

（4）那是早已的事了,我已经忘了。

zé 则

用法 Usage:

文言虚词,在现代汉语书面语中还经常使用。多用在复句或单句里,起关联作用。It is a function word in classic Chinese that is still in common use in written Chinese today. It serves as a connection in both complex and single sentences.

连词 conj.

1. 表示顺接关系。It serves to connect.

（1）冬去则春来,天气很快就暖和了。

（2）你别走了,既来之则安之。

2. 表示转折关系。It indicates a transition.

（3）这事情做起来不能快,你越想快则越容易出问题。

（4）这孩子的脾气是说他多了,他则更听不进。

3. 表示对比。It suggests a contrast.

（5）我俩性格不同,哥哥爱交朋友,我则喜欢一个人看书。

（6）你汉语口语很好,写汉字则差一点儿。

4. 表示因果。It means a cause and effect relationship.

（7）一般物体的特点是热则胀,冷则缩。

（8）小孩子都这样,高兴则笑,不高兴则哭。

5. 用在相同的两个词之间表示让步关系。It signifies a concession when it is sandwiched between two identical words.

（9）你提出的办法好则好,但是太费钱了。

（10）这间房大则大了一点,但太暗。

助词 aux.

一般附在一、二/再、三等后面,表示停顿,用于列举。It is generally used after words such as "一,二/再,三" to serve as a pause, which is used in enumeration.

（11）我这个寒假不回家,一则是时间太短,二则是我想参加书法练习班。

（12）他们一则力气小,再则肚子饿了,三则路走错了,所以得了最后一名。

名词 n.

1. 规范,榜样。Standard; norm; criterion; example.

（13）父母以身作则,孩子就会跟着做。

2. 规则,条文。Regulation; rule; law.

（14）学生就要遵守学校制定的各种规则。

说明 Notes:

"则"是书面语,一般不在口语中出现。"则" is not often used in spoken language.

zěnme 怎么 →P630"怎么样"

用法 Usage:

代词 pron.

1. "怎么+动",询问方式,动词不用否定式。当动词是单音节,主语是受事者时,有时句式为"怎么个+动+法"。The structure of "怎么+v." introduces a how-question. The verb cannot be in the negative form. When the verb is monosyllabic and the subject is the recipient of an action, the sentence structure can sometimes be "怎么个+v.+法."

（1）你每天怎么来学校?

（2）这个字怎么写?/这个字怎么个写法?

2. "怎么+动/形"。询问原因,相当于"为什么"。动词或形容词可以用否定式。有时"怎么"可以用在主语前。The structure of "怎么+v./a." introduces a why-question, equivalent to "为什么." The verb or adjective can be in the negative form. Sometimes "怎么" can appear before the subject.

（3）老板今天怎么这么累?

(4) 昨天怎么你没来上课？

3. "怎么+(一)+量+名"。询问性质、状态。量词多为"个、回"，名词多为"人、东西、事"。"怎么+(一)+particle+n." introduces a question about the state or nature of a thing. The particle is often "个" or "回," and the noun is often "人，""东西，" or "事."

(5) 大家都想知道他女朋友是怎么(一)个人？

(6) 这是怎么(一)回事？

4. 用于虚指。代替不知道或不必、不便说出来的方式、性质、状况等。It is used as an indefinite denotation. It usually stands for a manner, nature or state that is unknown or is inconvenient to mention.

(7) 他不知怎么就生病了。

(8) 他没说那件衣服怎么好、怎么漂亮，就让我们买。

5. 用于任指。It is used as a general denotation.

① "怎么(+动)+都/也"。强调在任何条件下情况都不会变。前面也可用"不论、无论、不管"等。The structure of "怎么(+v.)+都/也" emphasizes the fact that something remains unchanged under any conditions, and it can also be preceded by "不论,无论,不管," etc.

(9) 这种鱼无论怎么做都好吃。

(10) 这个汉字不管怎么写也写不好看。

② 前后两个"怎么"相呼应，构成"怎么+动+就/还+怎么+动"。前面的动作表示任意的情况，后面的动作由前面的动作、情况决定，表示条件关系。The structure of "怎么+v.+就/还+怎么+v." consists of two "怎么" echoing with each other. The former verb indicates an arbitrary situation, and the latter verb is dependent on the previous action or situation, which means a conditional relationship.

(11) 这件事你怎么说我就怎么说。

(12) 别紧张，你怎么想就怎么说吧。

(13) 很简单，上次怎么坐车，这次还怎么坐。

6. 用在反问句里，表示否定的语气。It is used in a rhetorical sentence to carry a negative tone.

(14) 孩子怎么会得癌症？

(15) 太阳这么大，怎么下雨了？

7. "不+怎么+动/形"。"怎么"表示一定的程度，但作用在于降低程度，轻于"很"，相当于"不太、不很"，语气比较婉转。In the structure of "不+怎么+v./a.," "怎么" indicates a certain extent, but its function is to reduce the extent. It is weaker than "很," equivalent to "不太,不很," with a relatively mild tone.

(16) 今年夏天这儿不怎么热。

(17) 我刚开始学汉语，还不怎么会说。

8. "怎么"用于句子开头，后面有停顿，表示出乎意料、惊讶。When "怎么" appears at the beginning of a sentence with a pause, it carries an unexpected and surprised tone.

(18) 怎么，你还没去过北京？

(19) 怎么，你不认识我了？

9. "怎么"直接做谓语，询问状况，句末用"了、啦"。When "怎么" is used as a predicate to question the situation, the sentence ends with "了" or "啦."

(20) 你怎么了？脸上那么多汗。

(21) 你爷爷的身体怎么啦？

zěnmeyàng 怎么样 →P629 "怎么"

用法 Usage:

代词 pron.

"怎么样"和"怎样"的用法基本相同。"怎么样" and "怎样" basically share the same usage.

1. "怎么样/怎样+的+名词"（如有"一+量词"时，"的"可以省略）。表示询问人或事物的性质。"怎么样/怎样+的+n." (when used with "一+quantifier," "的" can sometimes be omitted). It indicates an inquiry about the

nature of a person or thing.

(1) 你知道他是一个怎么样/怎样的人？

(2) 竹子是怎么样/怎样一种植物呢？

2."怎么样＋动"。询问方式。口语中用"怎么"或"怎样"较多。"怎么样＋v." asks a how-question. In spoken language, "怎么" or "怎样" is more often used.

(3) 你每天怎么样去公司？

(4) 这道菜是怎么样/怎么/怎样做的？

3. 用于虚指。代替不知道或不必、不便说出来的方式、性质、状况等。口语多用"怎么"。It is used as an indefinite denotation to stand for a manner, nature, or condition that is unknown, or is unnecessary or inconvenient to mention. In spoken language, "怎么" is more often used.

(5) 不知道怎么样/怎样一变，空箱子里出现了一个美女。

(6) 去过云南的同学都说那里怎么样、怎么样/怎样、怎样、怎么、怎么好。

4. 用于任指。口语多用"怎么"。It is used as a general denotation. In spoken language, "怎么" is more often used.

① "怎么样＋动/形＋都/也"。强调在任何条件下情况都不会变。前面也可用"不论、无论、不管"等。"怎么样＋v./a.＋都/也." It emphasizes that a situation will remain unchanged under any circumstances. It can also be preceded by "不论, 无论, 不管," etc.

(7) 这几个音，无论我怎么样/怎样/怎么练，都发不准。

(8) 不管旁边的声音怎么样/怎样/怎么闹，他都能一心一意地看书。

② 前后两个"怎么样/怎样"相呼应，表示条件关系。If there are two "怎么样/怎样" echoing in a sentence, they indicate a conditional relationship.

(9) 我怎么样/怎样写，你们就怎么样/怎样写。

(10) 我跟你一样，你怎么样/怎样，我就怎么样/怎样。

5. 询问状况或征求对方的意见。It serves as an inquiry about a condition or a request for advice.

(11) 我给你做的衣服怎么样/怎样？

(12) 你们在中国过得怎么样/怎样？

6. 用于否定或疑问句，代替某种不说出的动作或情况，是委婉的说法。一般用"怎么样"，有时也用"怎样"，但如果后面带宾语，"怎样"不能用。It is used in a negative or interrogative sentence to stand for an action or situation that is beyond description, and so it serves as a euphemism. In some areas, where "怎么样" is used, sometimes "怎样" is also used. But if there's an object following it, "怎样" cannot be used.

(13) 他唱歌唱得可不怎么样/怎样。

(14) 他就是不来，你能把他怎么样/怎样？

(15) *他就是不来，你也不能怎样他。

(16) 他就是不来，你也不能怎么样他。

说明 Notes:

"怎么样"和"怎么"的区别是：The differences between "怎么样" and "怎么" are as follows:

1."怎么"做状语时可以询问原因。"怎么样"不能。As an adverbial, "怎么" can be an inquiry about a reason, but "怎么样" cannot.

(17) *你昨天怎么样回来那么晚？

(18) 你昨天怎么回来那么晚？

2."怎么样"可以单独做谓语，询问情况。"怎么"不能。"怎么样" can serve as a predicate independently and ask about a situation, but "怎么" cannot.

(19) *无论以后我学得怎么，我都不会忘记你给我的帮助。

(20) 无论以后我学得怎么样/怎样，我都不会忘记你给我的帮助。

3."怎么"后面带"了、啦"表示问话人不知道出现什么新情况。"怎么样"后面带"了、啦"表示问话人已经知道情况，想了解进一步发展的新情况。If "怎么" is followed by "了,啦," it indicates that the speaker doesn't know any new circumstances. If "怎么样" is followed by "了,啦," then the speaker is already aware of the new circumstance and wants to keep up with the new development.

（21）你的文章怎么了？
（22）你的文章怎么样了？

4. "怎么样"可以做宾语,询问意愿、看法；还可以做补语,询问情况。"怎么"没有这种用法。"怎么样" can serve as an object to inquire about willingness or opinion, and it can also serve as a complement to inquire about a situation. "怎么" has no such usage.

（23）＊你觉得这个城市怎么？
（24）你觉得这个城市怎么样/怎样？
（25）＊你的作文写得怎么？
（26）你的作文写得怎么样/怎样？

5. "怎么样"做定语时,前后一般要有数量词。"怎么"做定语,后面必须要有数量词。As an attributive, "怎么样" is usually preceded or followed by a particle. When "怎么" serves as an attributive, it must be followed by a particle.

（27）＊他是一个怎么人？
（28）他是一个怎么样的人,你知道吗？
（29）他是怎么的一个人,你知道吗？
（30）＊这到底是怎么事？
（31）这到底是怎么一回事？

6. "怎么"可以构成"不＋怎么"的方式做状语,表示不太深的程度。"怎么样"一般没有这种用法。"怎么" can join with "不" to form "不＋怎么" as an adverbial to suggest a degree not so deep; "怎么样" generally doesn't have such a usage.

（32）流了那么多血,她好像也不怎么痛。（一般不用"怎么样"。Usually don't use "怎么样."）

7. "怎么"在句首单独使用,表示出乎意料、惊讶的意思。"怎么样"没有这种用法。If "怎么" is used independently at the beginning of a sentence, it suggests unexpectedness or a surprise. "怎么样" has no such usage.

（33）＊怎么样？你刚买的自行车丢了？
（34）怎么?! 你刚买的自行车丢了？

8. 从语义的角度讲,"怎么"多询问原因。"怎么样"多询问形状和意向。这是最大的区别。The fundamental difference between "怎么" and "怎么样" is that "怎么" usually inquires about a reason while "怎么样" often inquires about a shape or one's intention.

zēngjiā 增加 →P633"增进"、P633"增长"

用法 Usage:
动词 v.

表示在原来的基础上增多或加多（与"减少"相反）。搭配的词语可以是表示人或事物的具体名词,也可以是抽象名词,还可以是数量词。To increase or add to (as opposed to "减少"). It can go with concrete nouns that represent people or things, and also abstract nouns and quantifiers.

（1）这个学期增加了两门新课。
（2）今年我的工资增加了五万。
（3）公司今年又增加了投入。

说明 Notes:

1. "增加"可以用作名词。"增加" can be used as a noun.

（4）留学生人数的增加使学院老师的工作更忙了。

2. "增加"和"增多"都表示在原有基础上加多。"增加" and "增多" both suggest an increase over the original.

它们的区别是：They differ as follows:

① 词语的结构不同。"增加"是并列结构。"增多"是动补结构。The word structure is different: "增加" is a parallel structure and "增多" is a verb-complement structure.

② 因为结构不同,"增加"可以带宾语。"增多"不能。Due to the difference in structure, "增加" can take an object, but "增

多" cannot.

(5) 我们要节约用电用水,而且还要增加产量。

(6) *我们要节约用电用水,而且还要增多产量。

zēngjìn 增进 →P632"增加"

用法 Usage:

动词 v.

增强并促进。多与抽象事物名词搭配。还可以与少数形容词搭配。*To strengthen and improve; to promote. It usually goes with abstract nouns, and a few adjectives.*

(1) 我们应该互相帮助,增进团结。
(2) 经济发展增进了国家的繁荣和强大。

说明 Notes:

"增进"和"增加"的区别是：*The differences between "增加" and "增进" are as follows:*

1. 在词义上,"增进"着重于促进,常常有另一个动词表示经过某种行为、动作,对某一方面有所促进。"增加"着重于在数量上的加多。*In terms of meaning, "增进" emphasizes improvement, and there is often another verb to indicate that some improvement is already made thanks to a certain action or behavior. "增加" emphasizes the growth in amount or number.*

2. 在词语搭配上,与"增加"搭配的名词可以放在其后做宾语,也可以放在其前做主语,以放在后面居多。与"增进"搭配的词语一般都放在后面做宾语。*In terms of collocation, the noun that goes with "增加" can serve as the object after it or as the subject before it, the former case being more common. The noun that goes with "增进" is often used as the object after it.*

3. 在做句子成分上,"增进"一般做谓语。"增加"除了做谓语以外,还可以做主语、定语、宾语,如"人数的增加很快、增加的数量不多,争取有较大的增加"等。*As a sentence component, "增进" usually serves as the* predicate while "增加," apart from being the predicate, can also serve as the subject, attributive or object. For example, "人数的增加很快,增加的数量不多,争取有较大的增加."

4. "增加"既可以用于具体事物,也可以用于抽象事物,语义更着重于数量,所以"增加"可以带各种具体的数量词做宾语。"增进"一般只用于抽象事物,语义更着重于程度。*"增加" can be applied to both concrete and abstract things, and it emphasizes quantity semantically, therefore "增加" can take various concrete quantifiers as its object. "增进" is only applied to abstract things, with a semantic emphasis on degree.*

zēngzhǎng 增长 →P632"增加"

用法 Usage:

动词 v.

增加,提高。多与抽象事物名词或与表示比例的数字搭配,也可以与少数形容词搭配。也可以用作名词。*To increase; to rise; to raise. It usually goes with abstract nouns or numbers representing a proportion — or a few adjectives. It can also serve as a noun.*

(1) 旅游能让人增长各种知识。
(2) 这几年,我们公司的经济每年增长7%到8%。
(3) 对社会发展来说,人口的增长快也不好,慢也不好。

说明 Notes:

"增长"和"增加"的区别是：*The differences between "增长" and "增加" are as follows:*

1. "增加"着重于数量上的加多。"增长"着重于数量上的提高。*"增加" emphasizes the growth of quantity, and "增长" emphasizes the improvement of quantity.*

2. "增加"后面可以带部分形容词做宾语。"增长"后面一般不能带形容词做宾语。*"增加" can take certain adjectives as its object; "增长" normally cannot take any adjectives as its object.*

（4）*做个志愿者，一定会增长自己的善良和内心美。

（5）做个志愿者，一定会增加自己的善良和内心美。

3. "增加"后面可以带各种具体的数量词做宾语。"增长"除了百分比或倍数，不能带具体的数量词做宾语。"增加" can take various concrete quantifiers as its object; "增长" cannot take concrete quantifiers as its object except for percentages or multiples.

（6）*书法班的同学增长了五人。

（7）书法班的同学增加了五人。

zhǎnkāi 展开 →P264"开展"

用法 Usage:

动词 v.

1. 铺开，张开，伸展。表示把卷起来的东西舒展开来。To spread; to open; to extend. It means to spread something that is usually folded.

（1）鸟儿展开翅膀飞了起来。

（2）请大家把地图展开，找一下巴西在哪里。

2. 有领导、有组织、有规模地进行。一般指生产、活动等。To carry out activities — often on a large scale — in an organized way under some leadership. It usually refers to manufacturing and other activities.

（3）关于堵车这个话题，大家展开了讨论。

（4）节约用水、用电的活动要进一步展开。

说明 Notes:

"展开"和"开展"汉字的次序相反，词语中都有"展"，都有表示大规模进行某种活动的意思。"展开" and "开展" are two identical characters in a reversed order. Both mean carrying out a certain activity on a large scale.

它们的区别是：Their differences are as follows:

1. 词义上，"展开"侧重于"展"(伸展、铺开)。"开展"侧重于"开"(开始)。In terms of meaning, "展开" focuses on "展 (spread, extend)" whereas "开展" stresses "开 (start, initiate)."

2. "开展"做动词。后面一般都要有宾语或补语，而且宾语一般是双音节宾语。"展开"后面不一定要有宾语，如例（4）。As a verb, "开展" is usually followed by an object or a complement, and the object is often disyllabic. "展开" doesn't necessarily take an object, as in (4).

3. "开展"前面可以有"深入、继续、持久、进一步"等表示连续意义的词语做状语。"展开"着重于活动大规模铺开进行，用于活动开始发动阶段。不能带以上表示连续意义的词语做状语。"开展" can be preceded by words that suggest continuity such as "深入、继续、持久、进一步，" all of which serve as an adverbial. "展开" emphasizes the activity being carried out on a large scale, and is used at the beginning stage of an activity. It cannot go with the above-mentioned adverbials showing continuity.

4. "开展"还是"开始展出"的省略语。"展开"没有这个意思。"开展" is also the short form of "开始展出," but "展开" doesn't have such usage.

（5）两位从国外回来的油画家的作品将在这个画廊开展。

5. "展开"两字之间可以插入其他词语，构成"展得开、展不开"的词语。"开展"不可以。In between the two characters "展开，" some other words can be inserted such as "展得开，展不开，""展得开" means "being able to expand" while "展不开" means "being unable to expand." "开展" doesn't have such usage.

zhàn 占

用法 Usage:

动词 v.

1. 占领，占据。To occupy; to seize.

（1）你先去图书馆占座位，我吃完饭马上就去。

（2）桌子一人一张，他却独占了两张。

2. 处在某一种地位或属于某一种情况。To constitute; to be in a certain position or situation.

（3）我们班女同学占多数。

（4）这个国家平民思想占了统治地位，所以老百姓的收入都差不多。

说明 Notes：

"占"还有一个发音为"zhān"，名词用法，是"占卜（吉凶）、占卦"的意思。"占" has another pronunciation "zhān," which is used as a noun meaning fortune telling (about good or ill luck), and divination.

zhànlǐng 占领 →P635"占有"

用法 Usage：

动词 v.

1. 用武装力量取得（阵地或领土）。To capture with armed forces (battleground or territory).

（1）经过两天的战斗，政府军占领了那座城市。

（2）侵略者企图占领这个国家的领土。

2. 占有。用来比喻在商业、科技等方面取得或保持一定的控制范围。To occupy. It is used as a metaphor for having or maintaining a certain control over the fields of commerce, technology, etc.

（3）到去年，我们公司的手机占领了30%的销售市场。

（4）几十年来，电视剧一直占领着电视屏幕的影视舞台。

zhànyǒu 占有 →P635"占领"

用法 Usage：

动词 v.

1. 占据，据为己有。To occupy; to take something away as one's personal belonging.

（1）非法占有集体财产是一种犯罪行为。

（2）每一个人都不能占有另一个人。

2. 客观说明所拥有的数量。To possess, used to describe what one possesses or owns in an objective way.

（3）我们国家人均占有的土地面积很少。

（4）你们学校人均占有的图书量是多少？

3. 处在某种地位。To be in a certain position.

（5）在这次比赛中，我们队占有一定的优势。

（6）旅游业在这个城市占有非常重要的地位。

4. 掌握。To have; to own.

（7）科学研究必须占有大量材料。

（8）写这篇论文，你占有的资料已经足够了。

说明 Notes：

"占领"和"占有"都有表示依仗某种力量取得的意思。"占领" and "占有" both may mean occupy something by force.

它们的区别是：Their differences are as follows:

1."占领"着重于用武装力量或权势取得统治权。"占有"主要强调用权势或其他手段取得所有权、使用权、支配权等，语意比"占领"轻。"占领" focuses on gaining dominance by force or authoritative power; "占有" focuses on acquiring ownership, rights to use and control by power or other means, and so it is not so strong a word as "占领."

2."占领"的对象多是双方争夺的阵地、地方等，也可指别国的领土。现在又引申靠本身具有的实力取得并且控制某个领域范围或空间。"占有"的对象多是"土地、房屋、财产、人"等。使用范围比"占领"宽。The targets of "占领" are often territory or battleground that two sides contend for, and also the territory of other countries. Now it has made an extension to mean relying on one's own strength to gain control of a certain domain or space. By contrast, the objects of "占有" are mostly "土地，房屋，财产，人，etc.," and it is more extensively used than "占领."

3."占有"的第二、三、四种词义和用法是"占领"所没有的。"占领" doesn't have the second, third and fourth meanings and uses of "占有."

zhàndòu 战斗 →P636 "战争"

用法 Usage:

名词 n.

1. 指敌对双方进行的武装冲突。Armed conflict between two opposing parties.

（1）两支军队在山那边发生了激烈的战斗。

（2）他在那场战斗中受了伤。

2. 比喻指与比较大的困难、危险等进行的斗争。Fight, metaphorically referring to a battle with a greater obstacle, danger, etc.

（3）解放军与洪水进行了三天三夜的战斗。

（4）科学实验有时就像一场战斗,也是有危险的。

动词 v.

指敌对双方进行武装冲突。(Two opposing parties) to be engaged in armed conflicts.

（5）他们在大海上与海盗战斗了两天两夜。

（6）五十年前,我们跟敌人就战斗在那座大山上。

说明 Notes:

"战斗"的对象一般要用介词"和、跟、与"引入。The target of "战斗" is usually introduced by a preposition such as "和," "跟," or "与."

zhànzhēng 战争 →P636 "战斗"

用法 Usage:

名词 n.

指为了一定的政治目的,敌对双方进行的武装斗争。它常由不同的战斗组成。War, referring to the military fights between two opposing parties for some political aims. It is often composed of different battles.

（1）中国的抗日战争持续了十四年。

（2）历史上中东地区发生过很多次战争。

说明 Notes:

"战斗"和"战争"的区别是: The differences between "战斗" and "战争" are as follows:

1."战斗"指具体的一次武装冲突,是达到战争目的的主要手段。"战争"是指民族之间、国家之间、阶级之间、政治集团之间为了一定的政治目的而进行的具有一定规模的武装斗争,由许多战斗组成。因此"战争"既可以用于比较概括的规模性的武装冲突,也可以用于具体的某一场战斗,词义的范围比"战斗"大,持续的时间比"战斗"长。"战斗" refers to a specific armed conflict, a major approach to achieving the purpose of a war. "战争" refers to the armed struggle on a certain scale between nations, countries, classes or political groups for certain political purposes, and is composed of many battles. Hence "战争" can both refer to a generalized and large-scale armed struggle and a specific battle. It has a broader sense than "战斗," and it lasts longer than "战斗."

（3）我们要和平,不要战争。(不用"战斗" Not "战斗")

（4）战争破坏了这座城市。(不用"战斗" Not "战斗")

（5）南北战争是美国历史上最重要的一场战争。(不用"战斗" Not "战斗")

（6）那场战斗是在深夜里进行的。(不用"战争" Not "战争")

2."战争"只能做名词。"战斗"还有动词用法。"战争" can only serves as a noun. "战斗" can also be a verb.

3.词语搭配不同。"战斗"可受"激烈、壮烈、艰苦、紧张"等词语修饰,可做"打响、投入、投到"等动词的宾语。"战争"可受"正义、非正义、侵略、反侵略"等词语的修饰,可做"发动、爆发"等动词的宾语。The collocations are different. "战斗" can be modified by "激烈,壮烈,艰苦,紧张," etc., and can serve as an object for verbs such as "打响,投入,投到." "战争" can be modified by "正义,非正义,侵略,反侵略." It can serve as an object for a verb such as "发动," or "爆发."

zhāng 张

用法 Usage:

动词 v.

1. 使合拢的东西分开。To open; to spread what is folded.

(1) 我打开窗户,树上的小鸟张开翅膀就飞走了。

(2) 孩子不能成为衣来伸手,饭来张口的懒人。

2. 把弓箭的弦或琴瑟的弦绷紧。To tighten the string of a bow or a musical instrument.

(3) 年纪还小,你张不开这把大弓。

(4) 这把琴的弦张得太紧了。

3. 陈设,铺排。To furnish; to put in order.

(5) 商店里张灯结彩,迎接新年。

4. 看,望。To look around.

(6) 上课不要东张西望。

5. 商店开始营业。(Of a shop) to start doing business.

(7) 我的商店开张了,请你多多关照!

6. 扩大,夸张。多用于成语或固定词组,如"虚张声势、明目张胆"等。To expand; to exaggerate. It is often used in idioms or fixed phrases such as "虚张声势,明目张胆."

zhǎng 长

用法 Usage:

动词 v.

1. 生,产生。To form; to grow.

(1) 这面包长黑点了,不能吃。

(2) 山上长满了各种果树。

2. 生长,成长。To begin to grow; to develop.

(3) 几个月不见,这孩子又长高了。

(4) 春天,树叶长得很快。

3. 增进,增加,提高。To increase; to acquire; to enhance.

(5) 孩子到农村生活了一个星期,长了很多见识。

(6) 体育运动一个月后,他长了不少力气。

形容词 a.

1. 年纪较大(出生较早)。(Of birth order) elder.

(7) 他是我们班里最年长的。

(8) 我比他长三岁。

2. 同辈中排行第一。(Of the same generation) the eldest.

(9) 他是我们家的长子,是我的长兄。

3. 辈分高。(Of seniority) ranking high.

(10) 他们都是我的长辈。

名词 n.

1. 领导者。如:"部长、校长、市长、首长"等。Leader, such as "部长,校长,市长,首长."

2. 年龄大或辈分高的人。如:"兄长、师长(老师或师兄)"等。People older or higher in seniority, such as "兄长,师长 (teacher or senior fellow apprentice)."

说明 Notes:

"长"另有发音为"cháng",可用作:"长" has another pronunciation "cháng," which can be used as follows:

形容词 a.

1. 表示(时间或空间)两点之间的距离大。The long distance between two points (in terms of time or space).

(11) 山路又弯又长,汽车都开了两个小时。

(12) 要坐三个小时的汽车,时间太长了。

2. 擅长,对某事做得特别好。Being good at; proficient in doing something.

(13) 他长于毛笔书法,我长于钢笔书法。

名词 n.

1. 长度,两点之间的距离。Length, the distance between two points.

(14) 港珠澳海上大桥两端之长是55公里。

2. 专长，特长。Specialty; strength.

(15) 烹调是他的一技之长。

(16) 每个人都有长处短处，所以我们要互相取长补短。

zhǎngdà 长大

用法 Usage:

动词 v.

长成（生物体由小变大）。(Of a living organism) to grow from small to big; to grow up.

(1) 两个孩子已经长大成人，不用我操心了。

(2) 三年前，种在山上的小树都已经长大了。

说明 Notes:

"长大"是动词"长"带形容词"大"组成，在句子中多用作动词。类似的还有"长高、长胖"等。"长大" is the combination of the verb "长" with the adjective "大." It usually serves as the verb in a sentence. Similar words include "长高，长胖，etc."

zhǎngwò 掌握 →P9"把握"、P704"左右"

用法 Usage:

动词 v.

1.（在了解、理解事物的基础上）能充分支配或运用。To master; to know well enough to apply (based on one's knowledge and understanding of things).

(1) 公司要求每个职员都掌握一门外语。

(2) 老师通过考试来掌握学生的学习情况。

2. 主持。To preside over.

(3) 今天的讨论由同学自己掌握。

(4) 明天的会议你来掌握，行吗？

3. 控制。To control.

(5) 口语考试每个人十分钟，大家一定要掌握好时间。

(6) 红队总是掌握不住时机，浪费了很多次进球的机会。

4. 主宰。To dominate.

(7) 自己的命运要掌握在自己手里。

(8) 现在还有一些国家，女人的命运掌握在男人手里。

说明 Notes:

"掌握"和"把握"的区别是：The differences between "掌握" and "把握" are as follows:

1. 在词义上，"把握"指握住、控制住。"掌握"的词义更进一步，不仅能控制住，而且能充分运用。"把握" refers to " take hold and control." But "掌握" goes further. It not only means "to control" but also "to fully apply."

(9) *他在三年时间里把握了两门外语。

(10) 他在三年时间里掌握了两门外语。

2. "把握"的对象多为"时间、条件、时机"等。"掌握"的对象多为"技能、命运、原则、知识"等。The objects of "把握" are often "时间,条件,时机, etc." The objects of "掌握" are often "技能,命运,原则,知识, etc."

3. "把握"可作名词用。"掌握"不能。"把握" can serve as a noun while "掌握" cannot.

zhāo 招

用法 Usage:

动词 v.

1. 举手上下挥动，用手势叫人或致意。To raise one's hand and wave up and down to gesture or greet someone.

(1) 赶快向他们招招手，让他们知道我们在这里。

(2) 老人向服务员招了招手，服务员马上走到老人身边。

2. 用广告或通知等公开的方式使人来。To enroll; to recruit people by using advertisement or notice.

(3) 你们学校去年招了多少留学生？

(4) 那家饭店在招服务员，我想去。

3. 招引，引来（不好的事情）。To invite; to attract (something undesirable).

(5) 那块肉招苍蝇了，赶快把它放到冰箱里。

招 zhāo

(6) 树高招风啊！

4.（人或事物的特点）引起（爱憎等反应）。*(Of features of someone or something) to cause (reactions such as love, hate).*

(7) 这孩子真招人喜欢！

(8) 那么晚还高声唱歌，要招人骂了。

5.（言语、行动）招惹，触动。*(Of words or actions) to tease; to provoke.*

(9) 他正在生气呢，别招他！

(10) 谁招你啦，怎么又哭了？

6. 传染。*To infect.*

(11) 他离家两年，在外面招了一身病，现在回家来了。

(12) 这病不招人，不用害怕，好好休息一段时间就会好的。

7.（向审问者）承认罪行。*To confess (to the interrogator) one's crime or wrong-doing.*

(13) 这人胆小，警察还没问上几句就全招了。

(14) 你们是几个人抢银行的？老实招来！

名词 *n.*

借指办法、计策或手段。*(Figurative use) method, tactics or approach.*

(15) 一招不行，他又想了一招。

(16) 你来想办法解决这个问题吧，我没招儿了。

zhāodài 招待 →P233"接待"

用法 Usage:

动词 *v.*

对来宾或顾客表示欢迎并给以相应的待遇。*To extend welcome to a guest or a customer and treat him or her as such; to entertain.*

(1) 这个周末，我要在家里招待我的朋友。

(2) 除夕夜，学校举办了宴会，招待各国留学生。

说明 Notes:

"接待"和"招待"都有招待客人的意思，用法基本一样。*Both "接待" and "招待" mean treating a guest and they are used basically in the same way.*

它们的区别是：*Their differences are as follows:*

1. "接待"属于办事部门的迎来送往，是一般的迎接和对待，不必有过多、过高的礼节。"招待"对待来客或主顾除了讲求礼节之外，还常用酒席等去对待客人。*"接待" refers to the ordinary treatment of a guest including welcoming and seeing off. It does not require a lot of hospitality. "招待" often means more than that, such as hosting a dinner for him or her.*

2. 使用场合不同。"接待"常用于正式场合，一般说"接待外宾、接待代表团、接待来访人员"等，可以组成"接待室、接待站"等比较固定的词组。"招待"除了用于正式场合，也可用于非正式场合，如"招待客人、招待哥们"等。"招待"可以组成"招待会、招待所"等比较固定的词组。在固定词组里，"招待"跟"接待"都不能互相替换。*They are applied to different occasions: "接待" is used for formal occasions. We say, for instance, "接待外宾,接待代表团,接待来访人员." It can form fixed expressions such as "接待室,接待站." In addition to formal occasions, "招待" can also be applied to informal occasions, such as "招待客人,招待哥们." "招待" may be used to form fairly fixed expressions such as "招待会,招待所." In fixed expressions, "招待" and "接待" cannot be used to replace each other.*

3. "招待"可以带双宾语跟兼语短语。"接待"不能。"招待"作动词用，只能带名词性宾语。*"招待" can be followed by a double object or by an object + object complement. "接待" cannot be used in this way. And when "招待" is used as a verb, it can only be followed by a nominal object.*

(3) 昨晚他热情地招待我音乐会。

(4) 昨晚他热情地招待我去听了音乐会。

4. "招待"还有名词用法,可以组成"女招待、男招待"等词组。"接待"不能。"招待" may serve as a noun and form expressions such as "女招待,男招待." But "接待" cannot.

zhāohu 招呼

用法 Usage:

动词 v.

1. 呼唤。To call.

(1) 那边有人招呼你呢。

(2) 你快把楼上的同学招呼下来,我们开会了。

2. 问候。To greet.

(3) 他很友好,见面就招呼人。

(4) 大家一见面就互相打招呼:你早,你好!

3. 吩咐,关照,通知。To tell; to inform; to notify.

(5) 你去厨房招呼一声,快点做菜!

(6) 经理昨天就招呼大家,今天下午要开会。

4. 照料,伺候,接待,招呼。To take care of; to serve; to entertain; to greet.

(7) 老板一边招呼顾客,一边跟我们聊天。

(8) 那两个老人你们要多招呼一下。

zhāoshǒu 招手

用法 Usage:

动词 v.

举起手来左右上下摇动,表示叫人来或打招呼或回应示意。To beckon; to wave one's hands up and down, indicating calling someone, greeting or responding.

(1) 出租车看到前面路边有人招手就开了过去。(表示叫车 Calling a taxi)

(2) 那人在向你招手,你认识吗?(表示打招呼 Greeting)

(3) 他已经向你招手点头,表示知道了,我们走吧。(表示回应 Responding to a greeting)

zhāo 着

用法 Usage:

名词 n.

1. 下棋时,下一棋子或走一步。A move or a step (in chess).

(1) 你这着厉害,我得小心点。

(2) 好! 这是一步高着儿!

2. 计策,手段。Trick or means.

(3) 如果这办法还是不行,我也没着儿了。

动词 v.

1. (北京方言)表示同意,用于应答。(In Beijing dialect) to be all right, indicating approval as a response.

(4) 着! 我们不坐车,就走着去。

2. (北京方言)搁,放。(In Beijing dialect) to add; to put.

(5) 这菜太淡,再着点盐。

说明 Notes:

"着"是多音词。另见 P640"着 zháo"、P645"着 zhe"、P687"着 zhuó"。"着" is a polyphonic word. See also P640 "着 zháo," P645 "着 zhe," P687 "着 zhuó."

zháo 着

用法 Usage:

动词 v.

1. 接触,挨到。To touch; to sit next to.

(1) 四周都是山,前不着村,后不着店,今晚在哪儿过夜呢?

(2) 这大沙漠不着边儿,走到什么时候才是头啊?

2. 感受,受到。To be affected by; to suffer from.

(3) 别着凉,当心感冒!

3. 用在动词或形容词后(可带"了"、可插入"得、不"),表示达到了目的,产生了结果或影响。(When used after a verb or adjective) to be successful in attaining a goal, reaching a purpose, and producing an influence. It can go

with "了," or have "得" or "不" before it.

（4）那本词典我买着了。

（5）书架那么高，你够得着吗？

4.（北京话）睡着，多用于口语。*(Of Beijing dialect) to fall asleep, usually used in oral language.*

（6）他一躺下就着了，到现在还没醒。

5. 燃烧（跟"灭"相对）。*To be burning, as opposed to "灭 (to be out)."*

（7）炉子着了，先煮几个鸡蛋吧。

说明 Notes：

"着"是多音词。另见 P640"着 zhāo"、P645"着 zhe"、P687"着 zhuó"。*"着" is a polyphonic word. See also P640 "着 zhāo," P645 "着 zhe," P687 "着 zhuó."*

zháojí 着急 →P88"担心"

用法 Usage：

动词 v.

1. 发急，急躁不安。*To become irritable, impatient or restless.*

（1）别着急，离飞机起飞还有十分钟。

（2）火车都开走了，你着急有什么用？

2. 担心，放心不下。*To worry; to become anxious.*

（3）别着急，医生说，她的病没有生命危险。

（4）着什么急呢？他已经在路上了，马上就到家。

说明 Notes：

1. "着急"中间可以插入"什么"，组成"着什么急"，表示不用着急。*"着急" can be inserted with "什么," constituting "着什么急", which means not to worry.*

2. "着急"后面可以带补语"起来"，表示开始变得着急。*"着急" can take "起来" as a complement, which means starting to worry.*

（5）到了十二点妈妈还没回家，大家着急起来了。

3. "着急"前面可以用表示程度的副词修饰，如"非常、挺、特别"等。*"着急" can be modified by degree adverbs, such as "非常，挺，特别."*

4. "着急"和"担心"都有顾虑，放不下心的意思。*"着急" and "担心" both mean worry and concern.*

它们的区别是："担心"侧重人内心的担忧。"着急"侧重人外形担忧的状态。*The difference is that "担心" emphasizes one's inner concern, while "着急" focuses on one's anxious state.*

zhào 照 →P4"按"

用法 Usage：

动词 v.

1.（光线）照射。*(Of light) to illuminate.*

（1）灯光照在大楼上，非常漂亮。

（2）到了下午，太阳就照不到我的房间了。

2. 对着镜子或其他反光的东西看自己的影子，有反光作用的东西把人或物的形象反映出来。*To see one's image in the mirror or any other thing that reflects; to produce the image of someone or something cast in anything reflective.*

（3）我女儿特别爱照镜子。

（4）水面照出了岸边的树林。

3. 拍摄（相片）。*To shoot (pictures).*

（5）您能帮我们照张相吗？

（6）这张相片不清楚，照得不好。

名词 n.

1. 相片。*Photo.*

（7）明天我要回国了，送你一张我的小照，留个纪念。

2. 政府有关部门所发的执照、凭证。*Certificate and license issued by a government department.*

（8）你在这儿开店经营，有照吗？

介词 prep.

1. 按照，依照。可加"着"。*According to; in the light of. It can go with "着."*

(9) 照规定,狗不能坐火车。
(10) 你照着书上的生词写三遍。

2. 朝着,向着(某个目标行动)。可加"着"。Toward; in the direction of (a target). It can go with "着."

(11) 他照着苍蝇就打了过去。
(12) 你照着红绿灯的方向往前走一百米就到了。

副词 ad.
表示按原件或某种标准(做)。(Do something) according to the original copy or a certain standard.

(13) 课文上的生词,大家要照抄两遍。
(14) 这个通知要照发到每个人的手机里。

说明 Notes:
"照"和"按"都有表示按原件或某种标准(做)的意思。"照" and "按" both mean doing something according to the original copy or a certain standard.

它们的区别是:Their difference is as follows:

对时间、空间有所限定时,多用"按",如"按月完成、按社区划分"等。表示模仿或临摹,多用"照",如"照样子画、照着字帖写"等。"按" is used more often when there are restrictions on time and space, such as "按月完成,按社区划分." By contrast, "照" is used more often to indicate imitation or copying, such as "照样子画,照着字帖写."

zhàocháng 照常 →P642"照样"

用法 Usage:
副词 ad.
按照平常的情况(进行),情况继续不变。As usual; (like under normal conditions) giving the usual performance.

(1) 春节的时候,很多商店照常营业。
(2) 尽管身体不舒服,爸爸还是照常去公司上班。

动词 v.
跟平常一样。只做谓语,多与"一切"连用。不带宾语。To be as usual. It only serves as the predicate, and often goes with "一切." It does not take an object.

(3) 这个周末下午不休息,一切照常。
(4) 在中国圣诞节不放假,那几天工作、学习一切照常。

zhàoyàng 照样 →P642"照常"

用法 Usage:
副词 ad.
照旧,仍旧。表示动作行为或事物状态跟原来的一样,没有变化。(Something remains) in the same way; as usual. It indicates that an action, behavior or state remains the same as before.

(1) 虽然开了空调,但客厅太大,照样很冷。
(2) 人家做了总理,照样骑自行车上班。

动词 v.
按原有的样子或式样(做),照样子。中间可以插入其他词语,行动的结果一样。To do something after the previous pattern or model. Other words can be inserted between "照样," indicating the final result of the action will be the same.

(3) 你们看黑板上这个字,照着样写两遍。
(4) 照这件衬衣的样,你再做一件。

说明 Notes:
1. 副词"照样"和动词"照样"不同。动词"照样"的结构是离合动词、动宾式,中间可以插入其他成分,如例(3)。副词"照样"不能离合,中间不能插入其他成分。The adverb "照样" and the verb "照样" are different. The verb "照样" is a separable verb, a verb-object structure, which can be inserted with other words, as in (3). The adverb "照样" cannot be separated, and no other words can be inserted between them.

2. "照常"和"照样"都表示要按照原来的情况或样子。"照常" and "照样" both mean being the same as usual.

它们的区别是：The differences are as follows:

① "照常"强调情况或状态是跟平常一样。"照样"强调是跟过去已有的样式一样，对不作出改变有所不满。"照常" emphasizes that a situation or state will remain as usual. "照样" emphasizes that a situation remains the same because no change has been made. It indicates some dissatisfaction.

（5）虽然今天来的人不多，但老师照常上课。（强调跟平时一样上课 Having classes as usual）

（6）老师多次指出过他，可他照样迟到。（强调没改变 No change being made）

② 当主体的行为具有习惯性或常规性时，一般使用"照常"。"照常" is generally used when the action of the subject is habitual or routine.

（7）我跟上中学时一样，每天照常起床，准时上课。

（8）*我跟上中学时一样，每天照样起床，准时上课。

③ "照样"有动词用法。"照常"没有动词用法。"照样" has a verb usage, while "照常" doesn't.

zhèjiùshìshuō 这就是说 →P254"就是说"

用法 Usage：

"这"是代词，承前复指上文的短语、句子或段落。"就是说"位于"这"后，表示解释说明。合在一起为"这就是说"，表示对前面说过的话、陈述的情况的解释、说明或理解。在句子中用作插入语。"这就是说"与"就是说"用法相同，但更突出、强调说明的意思。"这" is a pronoun, an anaphora for a phrase, sentence or paragraph in the preceding text. Following "这" with "就是说" indicates an explanation or interpretation or understanding of what has previously been said or stated. It serves as a parenthesis in a sentence. "这就是说" is used in the way as "就是说，" but it highlights what is being explained.

（1）妈妈打电话说，她身体有些不好。这就是说/就是说，她希望我们能回家看看她。

（2）下雪天的西湖让她入迷了。这就是说/就是说，下雪天的西湖非常非常美！

zhème 这么 →P645"这样"

用法 Usage：

代词 pron.

"这么"是指示代词，能指示事物的性质、状态、程度、方式等。"这么" is a demonstrative pronoun that can indicate the shape, property, state, degree and method of things.

1. 指示程度。Indicating a degree.

① "有(像)……+这么+形/动"。"这么"前面有用来比较的事物。"有(像)...+这么+a./v." "这么" is preceded by things to compare.

（1）他有你这么胖。

（2）她的头发像你的这么长。

② "这么+形/动"。说话时常用手势比画，如果没有手势，"这么"就是虚指，带有夸张、使语言生动的作用。有时表示说话人的感叹。"这么 + a./v." When speaking, the speaker often uses gestures to make ideas clear. If not, "这么" is an indefinite denotation that indicates exaggeration and invigoration. Sometimes it suggests the speaker's exclamation.

（3）他的孩子有这么高。

（4）这儿的山水这么漂亮！

③ "这么+形/动+的+名"。"这么+a./v.+的+n."

（5）这么冷的天！

（6）这么好听的音乐！

"大、长、多"等单音节形容词之后，有时可以省略"的"。"的" can sometimes be omitted

after monosyllabic adjectives such as "大,长,多."

(7) 他这么大(的)年纪还没有退休。

(8) 这么短(的)时间,就见了三次面。

④ "这么"的强调作用适用于积极意义的形容词(大、高、多……),同样也适用于消极意义的形容词(小、低、少……)。如果是积极意义的形容词,而句子里有"只、就、才"等副词,那么"这么"加积极意义的形容词和加相应的消极意义的形容词,句子的意思没什么不同。The emphatic function of "这么" is applicable to both positive adjectives (such as "大,高,多") and negative adjectives (such as "小,低,少"). If the adjective is positive, and if there are adverbs such as "只,就,才" in the sentence, then it makes no difference in meaning from a corresponding negative adjective.

(9) 这间宿舍只有这么大/这间宿舍(只有)这么小。

(10) 苹果就这么多/苹果(就)这么少。

⑤ 否定式一般用"没(有)",只是对例(1)样句子的否定。否定动词时,一般只是否定表示心理活动的动词,并且是双音节动词。The negative form "没(有)" is only applied to sentences like (1). When negating a verb, it generally applies to verbs of mental activities, and only to the disyllabic.

(11) 考试没有你说得这么难。

(12) 他不是这么喜欢唱歌。

2. 指示方式。Indicating a way of doing things.

① "这么+动"。"这么+v."

(13) 你就这么画,先把苹果画好。

(14) 你就这么一直走,五分钟就到了。

② "这么+一+动"。"这么"是加强语气。"这么+一+v." In this structure, "这么" is used to strengthen the tone.

(15) 他这么一唱,就出名了。

(16) 他在空中这么一抓,就抓来一只兔子。

③ "动+这么+动量/时量"。"这么"强调动作达到的数量。"v.+这么+momentum/time." In this structure, "这么" emphasizes the number of times an action is done.

(17) 太极拳我就学了这么两次,就会打了。

(18) 她真聪明,这么看了一眼就记住了。

3. 指示数量。强调数量多或少。Indicating a number or a quantity. Its focus is on the amount being too big or too small.

(19) 都这么大的姑娘了,还不会做饭(强调年纪大 Emphasizing senior age)

(20) 就等了这么几分钟,他就没耐心了。(强调时间短 Emphasizing a short time)

4. 指示性质、状态。Indicating a state or nature.

(21) 面包这么硬,没有汤怎么吃?

(22) 他说得没错,他的房间就这么乱。

5. 代替某种动作或方式。这种用法时,多用为"这么着"。Standing for a certain action or manner. In this usage, "这么着" is used more often.

(23) 这么(着),好不好,你先去,我做完了作业再去。

(24) 这么着也可以,只要把这件事做好就行。

说明 Notes:

当"这么"与形容词、动词或形容词短语、动词短语组成简单句子时,句子常常会产生两种意思:表示程度和表示方式或动作,在口语中常为"这样"。到底是哪种意思,得看上下句子的语境决定。When a simple sentence is formed by "这么" plus an adjective, a verb, an adjective phrase or a verb phrase, the sentence may carry two possible meanings: one indicates a degree and the other an action or manner. The specific meaning is dependent on the context provided by the sentence. "这样" is often used in spoken language.

(25) 你穿这件衣服竟然这么合适!("这

么"表示程度,意思是:你穿非常合适。("这么" indicates a degree, meaning: "你穿非常合适。")

(26) 这么/这样放整齐,那么/那样放不整齐。("这么"表示"放"的一种样式。"这么" indicates a way of "放。")

zhèyàng 这样 →P643"这么"

用法 Usage:

代词 pron.

1. 指示性质、状态。需加"的"修饰名词,如果名词前面有"一+量词"时,"的"可以省略。 Indicating the shape and property of a thing. When modifying a noun, it takes "的." But "的" can be omitted if there's the structure "一+particle" before the noun.

(1) 对他来说,早饭不吃这样的事常常发生。

(2) 原来是这样(的)一件衣服。

2. 指示程度和方式。多用于书面语,口语多用为"这么"。 Indicating a degree and manner. This use is more common in written language. "这么" is used in spoken language.

(3) 你看,这个字写得很好。写毛笔字就要这样拿笔。

(4) 这件衣服这样大啊!

3. 代替某种动作或情况,可用作句子的各种成分。 Standing for a certain action or situation, it can function as different components in a sentence.

(5) 这样他不会去的。

(6) 他不喜欢这样的。

(7) 这样的事他是不会去做的。

说明 Notes:

"这么"和"这样"都是指示代词。"这么" and "这样" are both demonstrative pronouns.

它们的区别是: Their differences are as follows:

1. "这么"能够指示数量。"这样"不能指示数量。"这么" can indicate a quantity whereas "这样" cannot.

(8) 这么七八斤重的东西,你就拿不动了?

(9) *这样七八斤重的东西,你就拿不动了?

2. "这样"在客观的描述句中可以指示性状。"这么"一般不用。"这样" can indicate a shape or property in an objective description but "这么" cannot.

(10) 对他来说,这样胖,不算胖。

(11) *对他来说,这么胖,不算胖。

3. "这样"可以修饰名词。"这么"不能修饰名词。"这样" can modify a noun whereas "这么" cannot.

(12) *这么的妈妈真了不起!

(13) 这样的妈妈真了不起!

4. "这么"常用于口语。"这样"通用于口语和书面语。"这么" is often used orally while "这样" commonly appears both in written and spoken language.

zhe 着

用法 Usage:

助词 aux.

1. 用在动词后,表示动作的持续。 It is used after a verb to indicate the continuity of an action.

(1) 坐在树下看着书的那个人是我哥哥。

(2) 王老师正上着课呢,马上就下课了,请你等一下。

2. 用在动词或形容词后,表示状态的持续。 It is used after a verb or an adjective to indicate the continuity of a state.

(3) 窗台上、桌子上都放着花。

(4) 他红着脸对我说对不起。

3. 用在动词或表示程度的形容词后,表示祈使或提醒。 It is used after a verb or a degree adjective to indicate an imperative or to remind someone of something.

(5) 你得记着爷爷对你说的话。

(6) 下雨了,车慢着点儿开。

4. 用在连动句中,表示方式、手段、情态等。 It is used in a serial-verb construction to indicate a manner, method or mode.

(7) 老是躺着看书对眼睛不好。

(8) 他是坐着出租车去上海的。

5. 附在某些单音节动词后,使其变成介词。如"朝着、顺着、沿着、照着、跟着"等等。It is attached to some monosyllabic verbs to serve as a preposition, as in "朝着,顺着,沿着,照着,跟着," etc.

说明 Notes:

"着"是多音词。另见 P640"着 zhāo"、P640"着 zháo"、P687"着 zhuó"。"着" is a polyphonic word. See also P640 "着 zhāo," P640 "着 zháo," P687 "着 zhuó."

zhēnguì 珍贵 →P14"宝贵"

用法 Usage:

形容词 a.

宝贵。表示价值大、意义深刻的意思,强调稀少、难得、奇特。Precious, which indicates a great value or profound significance. The emphasis is on rarity, hard to come by and peculiar.

(1) 大熊猫是非常珍贵的动物。

(2) 这些五十年前的照片很珍贵。

说明 Notes:

"宝贵"和"珍贵"都表示"有价值,值得重视"的意思。"宝贵" and "珍贵" both indicate "有价值,值得重视 (something of high value and worthy of attention)."

它们的区别是:Their differences are as follows:

1. 它们在修饰具体的事物"资料"和"礼物"时,修饰的程度不同。"珍贵"的意思比"宝贵"重。When modifying a concrete object such as "资料" and "礼物," "珍贵" carries a stronger sense than "宝贵."

2. "宝贵"多指抽象事物,搭配的词语常有:"生命、感情、青春、财富、经验、意见、精神、遗产、品质"等。具体的事物词语则不多,有"资料、礼物"等。"珍贵"多形容动物、植物、工艺品、纪念物、文献资料、文物古董等比较具体的事物,词语搭配范围较广,也修饰抽象事物,如"珍贵的友谊、珍贵的友情",此处不能换用"宝贵"。"宝贵" often refers to abstract things such as "生命,感情,青春,财富,经验,意见,精神,遗产,品质." It also goes with a few concrete things such as "资料,礼物。""珍贵," however, often modifies animals, plants, handicrafts, monuments, documents, antiques and other concrete things in a wider range. It can also modify abstract things as in "珍贵的友谊,珍贵的友情," in which "珍贵" cannot be replaced by "宝贵."

zhēn 真 →P196"很"

用法 Usage:

形容词 a.

1. 表示跟客观事实一致,相当于"真实"(跟"假"相对)。Real, genuine, true, meaning "in full accord with the objective fact." It is equivalent to "真实" (as opposed to "假").

① 修饰名词时,一般不加"的"。When modifying a noun, it does not take "的."

(1) 这是一件真丝衬衫。

(2) 对你好,我是真心真意的。

② "真"可以跟助词"的"组成"的"字短语,指真实的事情(与"假的"相对),不能单独做谓语,多用在"是"后,组成"……是真的"结构。"真的," which is formed by "真" + "的," means "the real thing" (as opposed to "假的"). It cannot be used as a predicate alone, and it often follows "是" to form the structure of "…是真的."

(3) 桌子上摆的花儿是真的,不是假的。

③ "真"可以和语气词"的"结合,修饰形容词或动词,做状语或单用。强调说话人所说的是真实可信的。修饰整个句子时,可以用在主语前面,有停顿。"真" can go with the modal particle "的" to modify an adjective or verb, serving as an adverbial. Used independently, it emphasizes the truth and reliability of the speaker's words. When modifying a complete sentence, it can be placed before the subject with a pause.

（4）我真的很喜欢这个姑娘。

（5）真的,他不喜欢吃蛋糕,你不用买。

④ "真"可以重叠后做状语,强调说话人所说的是真实可信的。"真" can be reduplicated as an adverbial to emphasize the truth and reliability of the speaker's words.

（6）时间真真是过得快,一下子一个星期又过去了。

2. 表示清楚、真切、不模糊。Clear, real, and unambiguous.

① 一般用在"看、听、咬"等少数动词后做补语。It is generally used after a few verbs such as "看,听,咬" to serve as a complement.

（7）我看得很真,那个人确实是他妈妈。

（8）我就坐在他旁边,他说的话我听得很真,没有听错。

② "真"重叠后做补语,强调真切。"真真"后一般带"的"。When the reduplicated form of "真" serves as a complement, it emphasizes the truth. "真真" is often followed by "的."

（9）院长在报名单时,我听得真真的,我们班阿里得了奖学金。

（10）那个人从汽车下爬出来没有受伤,我看得真真的。

副词 ad.

表示对事物或情况的确认。相当于"实在、确实、的确"。加强句子的肯定语气,强调程度深,并带有说话者爱憎、好恶的感情色彩。在句中做状语。It indicates the confirmation of a thing or situation, equivalent to "实在,确实,的确." It strengthens the affirmative tone of the sentence as well as the depth of degree. Also it carries with it the speaker's sentiments of love, hate, likes or dislikes. It serves as an adverbial in a sentence.

（11）今天真冷! 我真不想去游泳了。

（12）他那个人真会开玩笑。

说明 Notes:

1. "真"和"真的"都可以做状语。Both "真" and "真的" can be used as adverbials.

要注意,用在陈述句中时,"真"和"真的"表达的意思有一点差别。"真"只强调程度,后面不能再带程度副词。In a narrative sentence, "真" and "真的" have a slight difference. "真" just emphasizes the degree and cannot be followed by other degree adverbs.

（13）听到她生病,不能再回校学习的消息,我真难受。

（14）* 听到她生病,不能再回校学习的消息,我真非常难受。

"真的"重在强调真实性,要求听话人相信他所说的是真实的语气,所以后面还可以带其他程度副词。"真的" emphasizes authenticity and a tone of request that the listener should believe in what is said, therefore it can be followed by other degree adverbs.

（15）听到她生病,不能再回校学习的消息,我真的非常难受。

2. "真"作副词用,不能修饰"副、单、低等、小型、无形、亲生、暂时"等不能做谓语的形容词。When "真" is used as an adverb, it cannot modify adjectives that cannot serve as a predicate such as "正,副,单,低等,小型,无形,亲生,暂时."

（16）* 这台电视机真小型。

（17）这台电视机真小。

3. "真"和"很"的区别是: The differences between "真" and "很" are as follows:

① "真"强调程度深,但常带有说话者比较强烈的、主观的感情色彩,有时句子后面还带有感叹词。"很"着重于对客观状态的陈述,感情色彩不太强烈。"真" emphasizes the depth of degree, usually with a relatively strong and subjective sentiment of the speaker. Sometimes the sentence ends with an interjection. "很" emphasizes the narration of an objective state where the emotion is less strong.

(18) 这个冬天真冷啊!
(19) 这个冬天很冷。

② 使用范围有所不同。"真"常在面对着某人、某地、某事物直接述说时用。"很"比较多的是用于事后陈述。*About the scope of application. "真" is used when the speaker faces someone, some place or something directly when he talks. "很," however, is more often used when the event is over.*

(20) 面对着广阔的大草原,大家都惊呼起来:"真美啊!"
(21) 去过新疆回来的同学都说新疆很美。

zhēng 争

用法 Usage:
动词 v.

1. 争夺,力求达到或得到。*To compete; to strive for.*

(1) 课堂上,大家争着举手发言。
(2) 100 米跑步,一定要分秒必争。

2. 争执,因意见不同而争论。*To argue or dispute due to different opinions.*

(3) 你们两人不用争了,谁对谁错,已经很清楚了。
(4) 他们只是争着玩玩,没有吵架。

zhēnglùn 争论 →P31"辩论"

用法 Usage:
动词 v.

观点不同的人各执一词,互相辩论。动作的发出必定在两个人以上。*(Of people holding different views or ideas) to argue back and forth. At least two people are usually involved in an argument.*

(1) 他们在争论什么问题,争论得那么激烈。
(2) 他又跟别人争论起来了。
(3) 关于要不要买房子的事情,她们又发生了争论。

说明 Notes:

"争论"和"辩论"都有彼此用自己一定的理由说明自己对事物或问题的看法。*Both "争论" and "辩论" carry the idea of explaining one's own view or idea on an issue through an argument.*

它们的区别是:*Their differences are as follows:*

1. "争论"重在"争"。争论双方各执己见,互不相让。"辩论"重在"辩",重在双方各自用一定的事实、理由证明自己的观点、看法的正确,指出对方的矛盾、问题。*"争论" focuses on "争 (contention)." Both sides stick to their own views, making no concession. "辩论," by contrast, focuses on "辩 (debate)," in which both sides enumerate facts or reasons to prove their own correctness and point out the contradictions or problems the other side faces.*

2. 相对比,"辩论"的过程逻辑性比较强。"争论"的过程逻辑性比较弱。*Comparatively, "辩论" tends to be a more logical process while "争论" tends to a less logical process.*

zhěng 整 →P649"整整"

用法 Usage:
形容词 a.

1. 完整,完全。全部在内,没有剩余或残缺。可直接修饰少数名词,如"整天、整晚、整套、整一年"等。*Complete; whole; having no remainders, surpluses or deformities. It can directly modify a few nouns, as in "整天,整晚,整套,整一年."*

(1) 这次旅行共花了三千元整。
(2) 你整晚都在看书,该休息了。

2. 整齐,有秩序。*Neat, in order.*

(3) 去公司面试,衣冠不整会影响你的形象。

(4) 操场上，各班同学整然有序地排着队，等待广播操比赛。

3. 与"是……的"结合用，表示强调作用。When combining with "是…的," it carries an emphatical meaning.

(5) 这些碗都有些破损，没有一只是整的。

动词 v.

1. 整理，整顿。To put in order; to rectify.

(6) 你把房间整一整，太乱了。

(7) 最近上课迟到的现象很严重，院长要严整学习纪律。

2. 修理。To repair.

(8) 现在很多女孩子都想整容。

(9) 那件衣服经过她的手，整旧如新了。

3. 使人遭受痛苦或不幸。To make someone suffer.

(10) 你得罪了老板，可能会挨整。

(11) 他很会整人，后来自己也被整了。

4. 搞，弄。方言常用。To make; to do. It is usually used in dialects.

(12) 衣服扣子掉了，请帮我整一下。

zhěnglǐ 整理 →P379"清理"

用法 Usage:

动词 v.

1. 使有条理，有秩序，收拾。To sort out; to straighten up; to put things in order.

(1) 你的房间太乱了，整理一下吧！

(2) 我要把桌子上的书啊、本子，好好地整理整理。

2. （对古籍）做点、校、加工等工作，使便于使用。To catalogue, check and proofread (classical works) so as to put … to better use.

(3) 他在博物馆整理古籍。

(4) 这些古籍书如果不整理，别人就看不懂。

说明 Notes:

1. "整理"可做"进行、加以、需要、开始、停止、继续、值得"等动词的宾语。"整理" may serve as an object to verbs such as "进行，加以，需要，开始，停止，继续，值得."

(5) 书架上的书籍进行整理了没有？

(6) 我已经开始整理这些资料了。

2. "整理"和"清理"都有通过处理使杂乱无章的事物变得有秩序、有条理的意思。表示这个意思时，"整理"和"清理"可以替换，如："整理/清理房间、整理/清理书桌、整理/清理衣柜"等。Both "整理" and "清理" mean to straighten things up so that they are not confusing. In that meaning, the two can replace each other. We say, for instance, "整理/清理房间，整理/清理书桌，整理/清理衣柜."

它们的区别是：Their differences are as follows:

① "清理"有清除无用东西的意思。"整理"没有这个意思。"清理" may carry the meaning of weeding out what is useless. "整理" doesn't carry that meaning.

(7) *把那堆杂物整理掉！

(8) 把那堆杂物清理掉！

② "整理"有做加工、修缮（文物、古籍书）等工作，便于别人使用的意思。"清理"没有这个含意。"整理" can be applied to cultural relics or classical works, meaning to repair or process for future use. "清理" doesn't have that meaning.

zhěngzhěng 整整 →P648"整"

用法 Usage:

副词 ad.

达到某个整数的。Fully (making an integer, with no fractions).

(1) 我来中国已经整整学了三年汉语了。

(2) 论文整整写了十万字，终于写完了。

说明 Notes:

1. "整整"多用于强调数量之大。"整整" is often used to emphasize that the amount is big.

2. "整整"用在动词前或用在数量词前，基本意思一样,但是强调重点有所不同。用在动词前,强调动作持续的时间。用在数量词前,直接强调所用的时间之久。"整整" basically keeps the same meaning when placed before a verb or a quantifier, but the emphases are somewhat different. When used before a verb, it emphasizes the duration of an action. When used before a quantifier, it emphasizes the length of time.

(3) 这个数学题,我整整做了三个小时才做出来。

(4) 这个数学题,我做了整整三个小时才做出来。

3. 副词"整整"和形容词"整"的区别是: The differences between the adverb "整整" and the adjective "整" are as follows:

① "整整"可以修饰谓语,强调数量大。"整"可以直接修饰名词,强调所指范围的全部,没有残缺或剩余。"整整" can modify a predicate to emphasize a large number. "整" can directly modify a noun to emphasize that all within the scope are included, without any remains or surpluses.

② "整"可以用在数量词后面。"整整"不能。"整" can be used after quantifiers, but "整整" cannot.

(5) 到今年年底,我在中国已经三年整了。

zhèng 正 →P652"正在"

用法 Usage:

形容词 a.

1. 符合标准方向,跟水平垂直(跟"歪、偏、斜"相对),常做动词的补语。Straight; upright; conforming to the standard direction; vertical to the horizon (as opposed to "歪,偏,斜"). Usually it serves as a complement to a verb.

(1) 这幅画挂得不正,歪了。

(2) 中国房屋的大门多数是对着正南方的。

2. 位置或时间在正中的(跟"偏、斜"相对)。(Of a position) situated in the middle or (of time) being exact (as opposed to "偏,斜").

(3) 这是故宫的正殿——太和殿。

(4) 太阳在头顶上就是正午时间了。

3. 正面(跟"反、反面"相对)。Obverse (as opposed to "反,反面").

(5) A4纸正反都可以用。

4. 正直。Upright.

(6) 他的为人很正,身上充满正气。

5 正当。Proper.

(7) 这笔钱会不会来路不正?

6. 合乎法则或规矩的。Conforming to laws or rules.

(8) 火车正点到站!

(9) 去年她才结婚,名正言顺地成了他的妻子。

7. 基本的,主要的(跟"副"相对)。Chief; major (as opposed to "副").

(10) 这位是正科长,那位是副科长。

(11) 这篇论文,正文有三万字。

8. 合乎法度,端正。Standardized; decent.

(12) 汉语书法中,正楷字不容易写好。

(13) 他是个正人君子,做什么事都很规矩。

9. 纯正不杂(多指色彩、味道)。(Of color, flavor) pure; unmixed.

(14) 这件衣服的绿色很正,真好看!

(15) 那碗菜的味道不正,不能吃了。

10. 物体或图形的各边、各角或所有半径都相等的。如:"正方形、正三角形、正圆形、正六面体"等。Regular, used to refer that the edges, angles and all semidiameters of an object are equal, as in "正方形,正三角形,正圆形,正六面体, etc."

11. 大于零的(相对于"负")。如"正数、正号、负负得正"等。Positive; plus (greater than zero, as opposed to "负"), as in "正数,正号,负负得正," etc.

12. 失去电子的(跟"负"相对)如"正电、正极、正离子"等。Positive, plus (loss of electrons, as opposed to "负"), as in "正电,正极,正离子," etc.

动词 v.

1. 使事物的位置正,使不歪斜。To straighten out; to put right.

(16) 你的帽子戴歪了,正一下!

(17) 墙上的画儿挂倒了,要正过来。

2. 改正,纠正(错误)。To rectify; to correct (errors).

(18) 今天语音课正音,首先要正四个声调。

副词 ad.

1. 恰好,刚好。Just, exactly.

(19) 这双鞋子我穿正好。

(20) 你来了,我正要找你!

2. 加强肯定的语气。Precisely. It is used to strengthen the positive tone.

(21) 正因为不按照笔画顺序写,所以写不好汉字。

(22) 正是为了他的孩子,他才这样辛苦地打两份工。

3. 表示动作的进行,状态的持续。Exactly. It indicates the progress of an action or the continuity of a state.

(23) 去年这个时候,我正跟丈夫旅游呢。

(24) 外面正下着雨呢。

zhèngdāng 正当 →P651"正好"

用法 Usage:

动词 v.

正处在(事情发生的某个时间或某个时期)。常跟"……的时候、……时刻、那时、这时"等一起连用。由它引导的词或短语一般做句子的时间状语。句子语义要求有两个动作,后一个动作是在前一个动作发生时发生的。Just when. It usually goes with "...的时候,...时刻,那时,这时," etc. The word or phrase following it often serves as an adverbial of time in the sentence. The meaning of the sentence requires two actions: the latter action happens just when the former is going on.

(1) 正当我发愁的时候,玛丽给我送来了钱。

(2) 正当大家谈得高兴的时候,老师进来了。

zhèngdàng 正当

用法 Usage:

形容词 a.

1. 符合法律要求或情理的。做状语时可以用重叠形式。Legitimate; rational. As an adverbial, it can be used in the reduplicated form.

(1) 你的要求是正当的,可以正正当当地向老师提出来。

(2) 他当时是正当防卫,不是故意杀人。

2. (形容人品、行为)端正,正派。(Of one's character) honest; upright; (of one's behavior) proper.

(3) 他为人正当,从不做虚假的事情。

(4) 那样办事不正当,我们不能那样做。

zhènghǎo 正好 →P651"正当"

用法 Usage:

副词 ad.

1. 表示数量不多不少,暗含"巧合"的意思。Exactly. It indicates just the right quantity or amount, implying "巧合 (coincidence)."

(1) 飞机到北京的时候正好是十点整。

(2) 我这里正好有三千元,你先拿去用吧。

2. 表示某个情况下,有一个条件刚好能满足要求。Indicating that one condition just meets the requirement under certain circumstances.

(3) 外边下雨了,我正好带了雨伞。

(4) 最近很想去旅行,正好下个月放假有时间出去。

形容词 a.

表示程度、数量、空间不多不少,和需要的一致。能做程度补语或谓语,也可以独立运用。Indicating that a degree, quantity, or space is just enough, being consistent with the requirement. It can be used as a degree complement or a predicate, and it can also be used independently.

（5）这件衣服你穿正好,很合身。

（6）这个手机一千元,你给了我一千。正好。

说明 Notes:

动词"正当"和副词"正好"都有表示两个动作同时进行的意思。Both the verb "正当" and the adverb "正好" can indicate two actions happening at the same time.

它们的区别是：Their differences are as follows:

1. "正好"表示两个动作之间有内在的呼应,常常是需要事情这样时,事情就这样发生了,而且发生的时间不早不晚,恰巧在需要的那一时刻发生,时段比较短,如例（3）（4）。"正当"所表示的两个动作之间没有内在的呼应,时段可长可短。"正好" indicates that there is an internal coherence between the two actions. It often happens coincidentally the moment it is required, neither early nor late, usually within a short span of time as in (3) and (4). "正当" indicates that the two actions do not have this internal coherence and the span of time can either be long or short.

2. 在句子中,"正当"所带的短语着重强调时间,作句子谓语的时间状语。"正好"所带的句子着重强调行为动作的发生,除了表示时间,还表示句子谓语的状态。In sentences, the phrase with "正当" emphasizes time, serving as a time adverbial of the predicate. The sentence with "正好" emphasizes the happening of an action, indicating time, and the state of the predicate as well.

（7）正当我要出门的时候,他来了。

（8）我刚要出门去找他,他正好来了。

3. "正好"还表示数量、体积不多不少,程度不高不低、碰上机会等。"正当"则没有这些意思。"正好" can also indicate that the quantity, volume or degree is just right; what's more, it can also mean the right opportunity.

"正当" does not have these meanings.

（9）*从这儿到那儿正当是十步。

（10）从这儿到那儿正好是十步。

zhèngzài 正在 →P622"在"、P650"正"

用法 Usage:

副词 ad.

表示动作在进行或状态在持续中。Indicating an action is going on or a state is continuing.

（1）生活正在变好,我们很有信心。

（2）老师正在上课,你下课再来吧!

说明 Notes:

"正""在""正在"都可以表示动作的进行和状态的持续。"正,""在" and "正在" all can indicate that an action is going on or a state is continuing.

它们的区别是：Their differences are as follows:

1. "正"着重指动作进行中的时间。"在"着重指状态。"正在"既指时间,又指动作进行的状态。"正" emphasizes the time when an action is happening, whereas "在" emphasizes the state. "正在" refers to both the time and state of an action.

（3）我正吃饭时,他来找我了。

（4）我在吃饭时,他来找我了。

（5）我正在吃饭时,他来找我了。

2. "正"后面不能用动词的单纯形式。"在"和"正在"可以。"正" cannot take the pure form of a verb, while "在" and "正在" can.

（6）*我们正学习。

（7）我们正/在/正在学习呢。

3. "在"后不能用介词"从"。"正"和"正在"可以。"在" cannot have the preposition "从" after it, while "正" and "正在" can.

（8）*妈妈在从楼上下来。

（9）妈妈正/正在从楼上下来。

4. "在"可以表示动作的反复进行或长期持续。"正"和"正在"不能。"在" can indicate that

an action happens repeatedly or continuously, while "正" and "正在" cannot.

(10) *我一直正/正在思考一个问题。

(11) 我一直在思考一个问题。

zhèngmíng 证明 →P653"证实"

用法 Usage:

动词 v.

用可靠的事实或材料来表明或断定人或事物的真实性。To prove; to show or assert the authenticity of someone or something by authentic facts and materials.

(1) 最近的天气变化证明了气象报告是比较正确的。

(2) 我可以证明姐姐昨天一直在家。

名词 n.

用以表明或推断人或事物真实性的事实或材料，一般指证明书或证明信。Facts or materials, usually certificates or testimonials, showing or deducing the authenticity of someone or something.

(3) 请三天病假需要医生的证明。

(4) 你要去办公室开个证明，才能延长签证。

zhèngshí 证实 →P653"证明"

用法 Usage:

动词 v.

证明其确实，确认其情况是真实的。作谓语时，宾语常是短语或小句。To prove the truth of; to confirm the authenticity of. When it is used as a predicate, its object is often a phrase or a clause.

(1) 每个农贸市场都可以证实当今农村经济的繁荣发展。

(2) 这段录像可以证实那天晚上他确实没在走廊上。

说明 Notes:

"证明"和"证实"都表示依据可靠的材料判断人或事物的真实性。Both "证明" and "证实" can indicate the deduction of the authenticity of someone or something by reliable materials.

它们的区别是：Their differences are as follows:

1. "证明"着重于根据可靠材料确定某种情况或说法（判断）是否正确，也指根据可靠的材料引出某种结论。"证实"着重于验证所说的对象的确实性，用于核实假想、预言、推断的正确，消息、传闻的确实，或情况、推论符合事实。"证明" emphasizes the correctness of a certain situation or statement deduced from authentic materials, and it can also refer to a certain conclusion drawn from reliable materials. "证实", by contrast, emphasizes the verification of the authenticity of the object mentioned, which is used to confirm whether a supposition, prediction, deduction is correct, whether a piece of news is authentic or just a rumor, or whether an inference conforms to the fact.

2. "证明"可用事实说明，也可以通过理论论证说明。通过分析论证才能说明的内在的抽象道理，一般用"证明"。"证实"主要通过事实说明，用于确认某一说法、消息的真实性。"证明" is to prove by facts or through theoretical argumentation. "证明" is generally used when internal abstract reasons can only be proved by analysis and argumentation. Yet "证实" is mainly to use facts to confirm the authenticity of a statement or a piece of news.

(3) 他用实际行动证明了自己的价值。

(4) 你的观点只能证明你和他的看法是相同的。

(5) 他要结婚的消息还无法证实。

3. "证明"的结果和对象可以相反。"证实"的结果和对象应该是统一的。当结果和对象都被肯定时，"证明"和"证实"可以替换。The result and object of "证明" can be contrary, whereas the result and object of "证实" should be consistent. When both result and object are affirmed, "证明" and "证实" are

interchangeable.

（6）＊所有的材料证实他的观点是错的。

（7）所有的材料证明他的观点是错的。

（8）试验证实/证明这种中药对胃病有一定的治疗效果。

zhī 之 →P103"的"

用法 Usage：

代词 pron.

代替人或事物，相当于"他、它"，多用作宾语。A replacement for someone or something. Equivalent to "他" or "它," it is often used as an object.

（1）哪儿有困难，他就去哪儿帮助，大家无不为之感动。

（2）无论什么困难，只有不断与之斗争，此外，没有其他办法。

助词 aux.

"之"作结构助词是古代汉语遗留下来的用法：The usage of "之" as a structural particle dates back to ancient Chinese.

1. 用在中心语和修饰成分之间，相当于结构助词"的"。"之"后面多为单音节词。Placed between the head word and its modifier, it is equivalent to the structural particle "的." In this case, "之" often goes with monosyllabic words.

句式有：The sentence patterns are as the follows：

① "之"常用在名词之前，表示修饰名词。"之" often appears before a noun to modify it.

（3）失败是成功之母。

（4）这是个博士之家，三个孩子都是博士生。

（5）这些建筑可称清代民居之代表。

② "之"常用在表示方位、时间或范围的词语"前、后、上、下、内、外、中"以及"间、际"等前面。如："之前、之后、之上、之下、之内、之外、之中、之间、之际"等。"之" is often used before words that indicate a direction, time or scope such as "前，后，上，下，内，外，中" and "间，际," as in "之前,之后,之上,之下,之内,之外,之中,之间,之际."

③ "之"后面如果是数词，"之"含有"中的"意思。When "之" is followed by a numeral, it has the meaning of "中的."

（6）他是我最喜欢的老师之一。

（7）我们班女同学正好是全班同学的百分之五十。

④ 在一个句子中，"之"和"的"并用，可以避免同一个结构助词的重复。有时还可以起划分层次的作用。"之" and "的" can be used together in a sentence to avoid the repetition of the same particle, which sometimes functions as a hierarchical division.

（8）杭州有休闲之都的美称。

2. 用在主谓短语之间，对"之"后面的词语起突出、强调的作用。Used between a subject and a predicate to highlight and emphasize the words after "之."

（9）郊区农民的生活水平提高之快，是他们自己也没想到的。

（10）阿里学习之认真、成绩之好是全学院有名的。

① 有时"之"后面还跟结构助词"所"连用。Sometimes "之" is followed by the structural particle "所."

（11）老师在教学上要教学生之所需、学生之所想。

（12）做领导的要想群众之所想，急群众之所急。

② "之"跟"所以"连用，插入主谓短语之间，作用相当于在谓语后面加上"的原因、的缘故"，"之"仍起突出、强调的作用。When "之" is followed by "所以" and inserted between the subject and the predicate, it is equivalent to "的原因,的缘故" after the predicate, where "之" is also used for highlight and emphasis.

（13）我之所以不让你去看电影，是因为你还在感冒。

(14) 他之所以来学汉语是因为他对中国文化感兴趣。

3. "之"用在副词"非常"后面,对"非常"所修饰的词语起突出、强调的作用。When "之" is used after the adverb "非常," it is used to highlight and emphasize the word modified by "非常."

(15) 诚信对做生意来说是非常之重要的。

(16) 打好基础对学任何知识都是非常之关键的。

4. "之"用在动词和补语之间,作用相当于结构助词"得"。When "之" is used between the verb and the complement, it is equivalent to the structural particle "得."

(17) 他的成绩来之不易。

(18) 同学们觉得他言之有理,就按照他说的去做了。

5. 虚用,跟其他词语结合用,不表示实际的意义,只是为了调节音节的和谐。When "之" is used as a function word with other phrases, it does not indicate any practical meaning. It is used only to achieve a harmonious rhythm.

(19) 久而久之,大家就习惯八点上课了。

(20) 这次汉语水平考试,你第一,他次之,我又次之。

说明 Notes:

"之"和"的"都能作为结构助词用。Both "之" and "的" can be structural particles.

它们的区别是:Their differences are as follows:

1. "之"是文言虚词遗留下来的用法。"的"是现代汉语的虚词。"之" is the function word from ancient Chinese, whereas "的" is the function word in modern Chinese.

2. "的"可以构成"的"字结构,如"教书的、穿红衣服的、黄头发的、卖苹果的"等。"之"没有这种用法。"的" can be used to form such structures as "教书的、穿红衣服的、黄头发的、卖苹果的," whereas "之" does not have this usage.

3. 从结构紧密上看,"的"跟修饰语的结合比较密切。"之"跟中心语的结合比较密切。Structurally, "的" is closer to the modifier, whereas "之" is closer to the headword.

(21) 这是我看的书,我写的字。

(22) 他是我最好的朋友之一。

4. 在下列情况中,只能用"之",不能用"的":Only "之" can be used in the following cases:

① 中心语是单音节词,修饰语是双音节以上的词或短语时。When the headword is monosyllabic and its modifier is disyllabic or multisyllabic.

(23) 我等了你三年之久。

(24) 狮子是百兽之王。

② 习惯使用的四字成语中。When used in some four-character idioms.

(25) 人应该有一技之长。

(26) 我不能只听你一面之词,还得听听他是怎么讲的。

③ "之"后面是数字时。When "之" is followed by a numeral.

(27) 孙子的年龄是爷爷的三分之一。

(28) 韩国留学生占全部留学生的百分之三十。

④ 固定格式"之所以"中的"之",可以不用,但是不能用"的"替代。"之" is optional in the set phrase "之所以", but it cannot be replaced by "的."

⑤ 表示方位、时间、范围的词语前面的"之",有时可以不用,有时可以用"以"替代(中、间、内、际等除外),但不能用"的"替代。"之" is optional when it is used before words indicating a direction, time or scope. Sometimes it can be replaced by "以," (excluding words such as "中、间、内、际") but it cannot be replaced by "的."

(29) *两山的间有一个小湖,我家就在那个湖边。

(30) 两山之间/两山间有一个小湖,我家就在那个湖边。

5. 在下列情况下,只能用"的",不能用"之": Only "的" can be used in the following cases:

① 表示领属关系的结构助词"的"不能用"之"替代。如:"我的书"不能说成"我之书"。When the structural particle "的" indicates subordination, it cannot be replaced by "之," for example, "我的书" cannot be expressed as "我之书."

② 修饰成分是单音节形容词,中心语前面的"的"不能用"之"替代。如:"红的花"不能说成"红之花"。When the modifier is a monosyllabic adjective, "的" before the headword cannot be replaced by "之," for example, "红的花" cannot be expressed as "红之花."

③ 并列的修饰成分中的"的"不能用"之"替代。When the modifiers are parallel, "的" cannot be replaced by "之."

(31) *大家都喜欢懂事之、聪明之、漂亮之孩子。

(32) 大家都喜欢懂事的、聪明的、漂亮的孩子。

zhījiān 之间 →P657"之内"、P658"之中"、P677"中间"

用法 Usage:
名词 n.

方位词。Locative noun.

1. 表示在两点(两个时间、两个地点、两个人物、两个数量)距离以内。不能单用,常与名词和数量词等构成方位短语后,做句子成分。Indicating the distance between two points (of time, location, people, quantity). It cannot be used alone, unless it forms a locative phrase with a noun or a quantifier as a sentence element.

(1) 妈妈打开了卧室和客厅之间的门。

(2) 上午八点到十一点之间,他没空儿。

(3) 同学之间应该互相帮助。

2. 用在表示心理活动、感觉的形容词或表示状态的固定短语之后,表示事件发生的背景或所处的状态。常用于书面语。Indicating the background or the state of an event when used after an adjective which shows a mental activity or feeling, or after a set phrase, which shows a state. It is used in written language.

(4) 紧张之间,她听不见任何别的声音。

(5) 欢声笑语之间,我好像又年轻了二十岁。

3. 用于少数双音节动词、副词和形容词如"眨眼、说话、忽然、猛然、突然"等之后,表示时间的短暂性、偶发性。Indicating transience and contingency when used after a few disyllabic verbs, adverbs or adjectives such as "眨眼,说话,忽然,猛然,突然."

(6) 说话之间,他就把一切事情都办好了。

(7) 突然之间,他感到头痛得非常厉害。

(8) 猛然之间,他想起了一个人。

说明 Notes:

使用"之间"时要注意:Pay attention to the following aspects when "之间" is used:

1. "之间"不能单用,除了第三个义项的用法,句子中都要有表示两点(或时间、或范围、或数量、或人物)意思的词语。As "之间" cannot be used by itself, there must be words showing the meaning of two points (of time, scope, quantity or people), except for the third usage mentioned above.

2. "之间"和名词、数量词组成的方位短语常与介词"在、到"搭配使用。Locative phrases formed by "之间" and a noun or a quantifier often go with a preposition such as "在,到."

(9) 事情发生在苏州到上海之间的高速公路上。

(10) 这个出口到那个出口之间有200米远。

3. 方位短语作补语时,一定要用"在"或

"到",如例(9)。When the locative phrase serves as a complement, "在" or "到" must be used, as in (9).

4. 方位短语作状语时,"在"可用可不用。如果状语提前在句子前面,一般不用"在"。When the locative phrase serves as an adverbial, "在" is optional. But if the adverbial is moved to the beginning of the sentence, "在" is not used.

(11) 忽然之间,所有问题都解决了。

5. 下面句子中的"在"都不用:"在" cannot be used in the following sentences:

(12) *杭州的天气在季节之间的变化是很明显的。

(13) *在同学之间应互相帮助。

(14) *在眨眼之间,他喝完了两瓶啤酒。

zhīnèi 之内 →P656"之间"、P658"之中"

用法 Usage:

名词 n.

方位词。表示不超过一定界限,多用于书面语。不能单用,一般与名词或数量词构成方位短语后作句子成分。Locative noun. Within certain limits, it is a locative noun used in written language. As it cannot be used by itself, it usually forms a locative phrase with a noun or quantifier to function as a sentence element.

1. 用在双音节以上的名词或名词短语之后(名词不能是单音节的),表示一定的处所、时间、范围等。Indicating a certain location, time, scope when used after disyllabic or multisyllabic nouns or phrases.

(1) 住在这个大楼之内的人都要遵守这个规则。

(2) 这篇作文要在三天之内交给老师。

2. 用在数量词之后,表示一定的距离、时间以及某些数量的范围。Indicating a certain distance, time, scope or quantity when used after a quantifier.

(3) 这件衬衣的价格在200元之内。

(4) 这个wifi在15米之内有效。

(5) 坐飞机只能带20公斤之内的行李。

说明 Notes:

1. 使用"之内"时要注意:Pay attention to the following aspects when "之内" is used:

① "之内"组成的方位短语要求范围有较强的限制性、封闭性。A locative phrase formed with "之内" requires a scope with strong restrictions and closure.

(6) *树林之内有很多小动物。(范围的限制性、封闭性不强 Weak restrictions and closure)

(7) 校园之内行车速度禁止超过25公里/小时。

② 由"之内"组成的方位短语,要求句子强调动作或事件有结果的意思,不重复动作行为的过程。A locative phrase formed with "之内" requires an emphasis on the result of an action or event, instead of the repetition of the process.

(8) *三天之内,他每时每刻都在担心远方的亲人。(强调动作行为重复的过程,前面不需要用"之内"。This sentence emphasizes the process of action repetition, so "之内" cannot be used.)

(9) 三天来,他每时每刻都在担心远方的亲人。

(10) 三天之内,你一定会接到朋友的电话。

③ 因为由"之内"组成的方位短语,要求句子表示比较封闭的范围,所以方位短语作补语的话,要求使用具有内敛意思的动词,如"控制、限制、减少、削减、降低、压"等。As a locative phrase formed with "之内" requires a scope with strong closure, verbs with restrained meaning such as "控制,限制,减少,削减,降低,压" must be used when it serves as a complement.

(11) 把电影票价格压到50元之内,才有人看。

(12) 把这项活动限制在初级班范围之内。

④ "之内"组成的方位短语书面语色彩较浓,多用于公文、应用文,如公告、通知、规章等。

A locative phrase formed with "之内" indicates a strong written language style, so it is often used in official documents and practical writings such as announcements, notices and regulations.

2. "之内"的用法与"以内"的用法基本相同。Usages of "之内" and "以内" are basically the same.

3. "之间"和"之内"的区别是："之间" differs from "之内" as follows:

① "之间"组成的方位短语可用于指人。"之内"组成的方位短语不能用于指人。表示人的名词与人称代词都不能用在"之内"前。A locative phrase formed with "之间" can apply to people but the one formed with "之内" cannot. Therefore, nouns referring to people and personal pronouns cannot be used before "之内."

（13）*朋友之内应该互相信任、互相帮助、互相关心。

（14）朋友之间应该互相信任、互相帮助、互相关心。

（15）*他们年轻人之内，用着很多新鲜的词儿。

（16）他们年轻人之间，用着很多新鲜的词儿。

② "之内"组成的方位短语，在意思上着重指群体的范围，不突出个体。"之间"突出群体中个体的差异。A locative phrase formed with "之内" highlights a group instead of individuals, whereas "之间" features the differences of individuals in a group.

（17）这几家公司之内一定有适合你的工作。（从一个整体中选择 Choosing a suitable job from what is offered by a group of companies）

（18）这几家公司之间最大的区别就是管理方法不一样。（突出个体的差异 Highlighting the differences of individuals）

zhīzhōng 之中 →P656"之间"、P657"之内"

用法 Usage:

名词 n.

方位词。表示在一定的范围、状态或背景中。不能单用，多用于书面语。一般要与双音节或双音节以上的词语结合成方位短语，作句子的成分。Within a certain scope. It is a locative noun indicating a state or background. It cannot be used by itself, and it's often used in written language. It generally forms a locative phrase with a disyllabic or multisyllabic word to function as a sentence element.

1. 用在表示处所、人员或状态名词、代词之后，可指处所、人员的范围或所处的状态、背景。Indicating the scope of a location and people, or the state and background when used after relevant nouns or pronouns.

（1）这几个朋友之中的任何一个都会帮助他。

（2）他们正处在欢乐之中。

（3）大山之中有一个小山村。

2. 用在部分表示状态的形容词和动词及其短语之后，指所处的状态。Indicating a state when used after some relevant adjectives, verbs and phrases.

（4）他正看着那些奔跑之中的人们。

（5）激动之中，他已经不知道该说些什么了。

3. 用在动作动词后表示一个动态的过程，用在状态动词后，表示状态的持续。常与介词"在、从"等配合。Indicating the dynamic process when used after an action verb, or the continuous state when used after a stative verb. It often goes with propositions such as "在, 从."

（6）我们要从调查之中找到答案。

（7）他还在昏迷之中。

说明 Notes:

1. 使用"之中"时要注意：Pay attention to the following points when using "之中":

① 与"之中"构成方位短语的词语都不能是单音节的。Locative phrases formed with "之中" cannot be monosyllabic words.

(8) *家之中父母的言行是孩子的榜样。

(9) 家庭之中父母的言行是孩子的榜样。

② "之中"所组成的短语做句子定语、宾语、主语时,不用带介词"在"等,如例(1)。When a phrase formed with "之中" serves as an attributive, object, or subject, it does not take the preposition "在," as in (1).

③ "之中"所组成的短语做补语时,前面一定要带"在"或"从"。When a phrase formed with "之中" serves as a complement, it must take the preposition "在" or "从."

(10) *现在她悲痛之中,这个消息不能跟她说。

(11) 现在她正在悲痛之中,这个消息不能跟她说。

2. "之间""之内""之中"都是方位名词,都不能独立使用,必须和非单音节词语结合使用,书面语色彩较浓。"之间,""之内" and "之中" are all locative nouns mainly used in written language, and they must be used with disyllabic or multisyllabic words.

它们的区别是：Their differences are as follows:

① "之间"和"之中"都可以跟名词、数量词、代词、形容词、动词等搭配使用。"之内"只能跟名词和数量词搭配使用。"之间" and "之中" can go with a noun, quantifier, pronoun, adjective, verb, whereas "之内" can only go with a noun or a quantifier.

② "之间"可以与副词如"猛然、忽然"合用。"之内"和"之中"都不能。"之间" can be used with adverbs such as "猛然,忽然," while "之内" and "之中" cannot.

③ 表示空间位置时,"之间"用于指两点的距离以内。"之内"用于指封闭的空间范围。"之中"用于相对开放的空间范围。When indicating spatial location, "之间" refers to the distance between two locations. "之内" refers to an enclosed space. "之中" refers to a relatively open space.

(12) 苏州、无锡在上海和南京之间。(表示距离,不能用"之内""之中"。Referring to distance, "之内" and "之中" cannot be used.)

(13) 大山之中有一座小山村。(大山不是一个完全封闭的空间,不能用"之内"。A mountain is not a completely enclosed space, so "之内" cannot be used.)

(14) 电视机机箱之内的温度不能太高。(机箱是比较封闭的空间。A TV cabinet is a comparatively enclosed space.)

④ 表示范围时,"之间"强调整体中个体差异的意思。"之中"和"之内"强调整体的意思。(详见"之内"条。) When indicating a scope, "之间" emphasizes individual differences within a group, whereas "之中" and "之内" emphasize the group. (Details can be found in the entry "之内.")

⑤ "之内"不能和表示人的名词和代词搭配使用(如果是"数量词+人"可以用"之内",仅限于做宾语和补语)。"之间"和"之中"可以。"之内" cannot go with a noun or pronoun of people (excluding its usage with "quantifier+人" only as an object or a complement), whereas "之间" and "之中" can.

(15) 这三个人之间的关系很复杂。(不用"之中"或"之内" Not "之中" or "之内")

(16) 在三个学生之中选择最合适的一个。(不用"之间"或"之内" Not "之间" or "之内")

(17) 第一名就在这三个人之中/之内产生。(不用"之间" Not "之间")

⑥ "之内"强调动作的结果。而"之间"和"之中"强调动作的过程或状态的持续。"之内" emphasizes the result of an action, whereas "之间" and "之中" emphasize the process of an action or the continuity of a state.

(18) 在这一个月之间/之中,他天天都要买菜烧饭。(不用"之内" Not "之内")

(19) 我一定能够在一个月之内完成。(不用"之间"或"之中" Not "之间" or "之中")

⑦ "之中"可以描述一种处于静态的状态,如例(13),也可以表示动态过程和持续状态,如例(16)。"之间"可以表示静态的状态,如例(12)。"之内"都不可以。"之中" can describe not only a static state as in (13) but also a dynamic process and continuous state as in (16). "之间" can indicate a static state as in (12). "之内" does not have these usages.

⑧ "之内"是三个词中界限意识最强的词。因此,在表示强制规定、执行某一事宜的界限时,多用"之内",故多见于公文通知等文体。Of the three, "之内" bears the strongest sense of limits, so when indicating administrative regulations and executive restrictions, "之内" is more often used and it is more frequently found in the writings such as official documents and notices.

(20) 按上级规定,所有人员必须在三小时之内离开这座大楼。(不用"之中"或"之间" Not "之中" or "之间")

zhīqián 之前 →P661"之上"

用法 Usage:

名词 n.

方位词。Locative noun.

1. 表示比现在或某个时间早的时间。Before or prior to the present or a certain time.

① 与名词或表示时间的数量词组成方位短语。一般做句子的时间状语。Forming a locative phrase with a noun or time quantifier, usually used as a time adverbial.

(1) 十点半之前我要上课,十一点我去看你。

(2) 去年九月之前,我在北京旅游。

② 与动词或主谓短语组成方位短语。Forming a locative phrase with a verb or subject-predicate phrase.

(3) 这是她回国之前留给我的电动车。

(4) 改革开放之前,他就自己开饭店了。

2. 与处所名词组成方位短语,表示在某个位置的前面,大多表示排列。书面语色彩较浓。Forming a locative phrase with a noun of locality to indicate being in front of a certain place, mostly used for positioning in written language.

(5) 我们宿舍之前,有一条马路。

(6) 我家的房子在一座小山之前,房子前面有一条小河。

3. 与"在+名词/代词"组成方位短语,表示某种顺序。Forming a locative phrase with "在+n./pron." to indicate a certain sequence.

(7) 他的成绩总在我之前。

(8) 在这个房客之前租房的是个美国人。

4. 与"在此"固定搭配成"在此之前"。Forming a set phrase with "在此."

(9) 他在此之前上课从来没有迟到过。

(10) 在此之前的事情他从来没说过。

说明 Notes:

使用"之前"时要注意:Pay attention to the following points when using "之前":

1. 一般情况下,"之前"不单独使用,多使用"以前"。如果在句子中单独出现"之前","之前"一般是指前文出现过的那个时空参照点,即前面的时间、空间,或是指在现在(说话时)之前。Generally, "之前" cannot be used by itself. ("以前" is used more often.) If it appears by itself, "之前" refers to the prior time-space reference point, namely, the above-mentioned time or space or the present (the time of speaking).

(11) 之前进来的人是我们的新老师。(前文出现的参照点可能是"小王进来以前"。The prior reference point might be "小王进来以前.")

(12) 之前的工作安排就说到这儿。(前文的参照点可能是"学期结束以前"。The prior reference point might be "学期结束以前.")

(13) 你突然到我家,之前为什么不给我一个电话?

2. 如果单独使用"之前","之前"不能与"在"搭配使用。If "之前" is used by itself, it cannot go with "在."

(14) *在之前,我们从来不认识。

(15) 之前,我们从来不认识。

zhīshàng 之上 →P660"之前"

用法 Usage:

名词 n.

方位词。Locative noun.

1. 与名词或名词短语组成方位短语,表示空间"在……的上面"的意思。常与"在"搭配使用。书面语色彩比较浓。Above. It forms a locative phrase with a noun or nominal phrase to indicate "在…的上面." It often goes with "在" in written language.

(1) 在雪线之上终年有雪的山才能叫雪山。

(2) 云层之下下着雨,云层之上却是万里晴空。

2. 与"在+名词/代词"组成方位短语,表示某个方面水平的高低。Forming a locative phrase with "在 + n./pron." to indicate one's level in a certain field.

(3) 他的口语水平在我之上。

说明 Notes:

1. 使用"之上"时要注意:"之上"跟名词组成方位短语,这个名词不能是单音节,如例(1)(2)。When "之上" is used with a noun to form a locative phrase, this noun cannot be a monosyllabic word as in (1) and (2).

2. "之上"和"之前"都可以表示具体的空间位置。Both "之上" and "之前" can indicate a specific spatial position.

它们的区别是:Their differences are as follows:

① 在词义上,"之前"着重表示具体时间的先后。"之上"着重表示具体空间位置的上下。Semantically, "之前" emphasizes the sequence of a specific time, whereas "之上" emphasizes the location of the spatial position.

(4) 之前,他来过几次电话。(不能用"之上" Not "之上")

(5) 四千米之上的山峰,你上不了。(不能用"之前" Not "之前")

② "之前"可以单独使用,做句子的定语、状语。"之上"不能,必定要构成方位短语才可用作句子的成分。"之前" can be used by itself, serving as an attribute or adverbial. "之上" cannot be used by itself unless it forms a locative phrase as a sentence element.

③ "之前"可以与时间短语、动词或小句组成方位短语。"之上"只能与名词或名词短语组成方位短语,并且使用时一般都要跟"在、于"搭配。"之前" can go with a time phrase, a verb or a clause to form a locative phrase, whereas "之上" can only go with a noun or a nominal phrase, and it is often used with "在,于."

④ "之前"和"之上"都有引申用法。"之前"多表示顺序的前后,常与"名次、排名"等词语搭配。"之上"多表示水平、程度的高低,常与"水平、技术、品质"等抽象名词搭配。Both "之前" and "之上" have extended meanings. "之前" indicates the sequence, and it often goes with words like "名次,排名." By contrast, "之上" indicates the level or the degree, and it often goes with abstract nouns like "水平,技术,品质."

(6) 他申请入学比我早,所以学号排在我之前。

(7) 我的英语水平在他之上。

⑤ "之上"的书面语色彩比"之前"重。"之上" is more formal in style than "之前."

zhīchí 支持 →P662"支援"

用法 Usage:

动词 v.

1. 同意别人的看法,给人以鼓励或帮助。补语常由"下去"充当。可以重叠。To support. It means to agree with someone and encourage or help him or her. "下去" often

serves as a complement. It can be used in the reduplicative form.

（1）父母支持我学汉语。

（2）他的建议很好，我们应该支持支持。

2. 勉强维持，尽力支撑。To have a hard time maintaining the current state; to do one's best to support.

（3）他肚子痛得支持不住了。

（4）要做两个大手术，你支持得了吗？

名词 n.

指对人的鼓励和帮助。Support; giving encouragement and help to someone.

（5）我的成功离不开大家的支持。

（6）在朋友的支持下，我开了一家咖啡馆。

说明 Notes：

"支持"作名词用，常做动词"得到、获得"的宾语。When "支持" is a noun, it often serves as the object of a verb like "得到" or "获得."

（7）他的建议获得了大家的支持。

zhīyuán 支援 →P661"支持"

用法 Usage：

动词 v.

用人力、物力、财力或其他实际行动去支持和帮助他人。可以重叠。To support; to assist someone with human, material and financial resources, or through other practical actions. It can be used in the reduplicative form.

（1）经济发达地区每年派技术人员支援西北地区的建设。

（2）他们的工作任务太重，我们去几个人支援支援。

名词 n.

用人力、物力、财力去支持和帮助的行动。The action of support and assistance through human, material and financial resources.

（3）哥哥给我的经济支援一直到我工作以后才停止。

（4）没有社会的支援，他是读不到大学毕业的。

说明 Notes：

"支持"和"支援"的区别是："支持" differs from "支援" in the following aspects:

1. "支持"着重在精神上同情和鼓励。"支援"着重在人力、物力、财力或其他实际行动给予援助。"支持" emphasizes psychological sympathy and encouragement, whereas "支援" focuses on assistance with human, materials and financial resources, or through other practical actions.

2. "支持"做谓语，不能带双宾语。"支援"做谓语，可带双宾语，或带其中的一个。When "支持" serves as a predicate, it cannot take a double object, but when "支援" serves as a predicate, it can take a double object or just one of them.

（5）*我们每年支持贫困地区小学三个老师。

（6）我们每年支援贫困地区小学三个老师。

zhīdào 知道 →P115"懂"、P306"了解"

用法 Usage：

动词 v.

表示对事实有了解，对道理有认识。常做谓语。可用在"是……的"格式中。可构成短语作定语。To know; to realize. It's often used as a predicate, followed by an object or a complement. It can be used in "是...的" structure to form a phrase and serve as an attribute.

（1）我知道他的名字，但是我们互相还不认识。

（2）我是知道这件事情的。

说明 Notes：

1. "懂"和"知道"的区别是："懂" differs from "知道" in the following aspects:

① 在表示知道某些事理意思的句子里，"懂"和"知道"可以互用。"懂" and "知道" are interchangeable when they indicate understanding something.

（3）我知道/懂对人要有礼貌的道理。

② 在了解某些事实意思的句子中，"懂"和"知道"不能互用。"懂" and "知道" are not interchangeable when they indicate knowing a fact.

（4）*我懂他的家住在哪里。

（5）我知道他的家住在哪里。

2. "了解"和"知道"的区别是："了解" differs from "知道" in the following aspects:

① "了解"的含义比"知道"更深刻、更广泛，除了有"知道"的意思以外，还有"理解、明白、懂得"等意思。"知道"没有"理解、明白、懂得"等的意思。"了解" covers a deeper and wider range of meanings than "知道." Apart from the meaning of "知道," "了解" can also mean "理解,明白,懂得." "知道" does not have these meanings.

（6）我知道这个人。（表示听说过这个人，具体怎么样不清楚。I have just heard of this person.）

（7）我了解这个人。（表示对这个人的情况，"我"非常清楚。I know a lot about this person.）

② "了解"是个有过程、动作有延续性的动词，可以做形式动词"进行"的宾语。"知道"不可以这样用。"了解" is a verb of process and continuity, which can serve as the object of the dummy verb "进行." "知道" cannot be used in this way.

（8）对那件事我们要进行了解后再决定怎么做。

③ "了解"可以做宾语，可以直接带补语。"知道"不能，要加"得"才能带补语。"了解" can serve as an object, and can take a complement directly, whereas "知道" has to take "得" before the complement.

（9）*我们要对这件事进行知道，而且一定要知道清楚。

（10）我们要对这件事进行了解，而且要了解清楚。

（11）对这件事，我们一定要知道得很清楚。

zhīshi 知识 →P528"学问"

用法 Usage:

名词 n.

1. 人们在社会实践中不断积累起来的认识和经验的总和。Knowledge; the total sum of knowledge and experience people acquire through continual accumulation in social practice.

（1）知识就是力量。

（2）他的历史知识比较丰富。

2. 指学术、文化或学问。Academic and cultural knowledge and learning.

（3）他是个知识分子，从来不骂人。

（4）这是个有知识、有文化的群体。

说明 Notes:

"知识"和"学问"都是名词，区别是：Both "知识" and "学问" are nouns. Their differences lie in:

1. "学问"侧重指程度上比"知识"更深入、更严谨的，并且有系统的知识。"知识"可以是一点，也可以是一个门类，在数量上，范围比较宽泛，在程度上可深可浅。"学问" is academically deeper and more strict and systematic than "知识." "知识" may be limited to a small amount or just one type. But it may also cover a pretty wide scope, and its degree may vary from deep to shallow.

2. "知识"一词可以组成"知识面、知识界、知识分子"等词语。"学问"不能。"知识" can combine with some other word to appear as "知识面，""知识界" and "知识分子，" but "学问" cannot.

zhí 直

用法 Usage:

形容词 a.

1. 不弯曲，不偏斜，成直线的（跟"曲"相对）。Straight, as opposed to "曲 (bent,

crooked)."

(1) 北方的杨树长得很直很高。

(2) 姐姐的头发又长又直,妹妹的又短又卷。

2. 从上到下的,与地面垂直的,从前到后的(与"横、弯"相对)。Vertical, as opposed to "横 (horizontal), 弯 (curved)."

(3) 千万只彩色气球直上万里蓝天,让人激动极了。

(4) 王字中的一竖,一定要写直。

3. 直爽,坦率。形容人的性格。(Of one's character) frank; straightforward.

(5) 她说话很直,有什么说什么,你别生气。

(6) 我太太是个心直口快的人。

副词 ad.

1. 用在动词前面,表示动作、行为不停顿、不间断地进行或频繁发生,含有"一个劲地、不停地、不断地"的意思。有时修饰动词短语,但主要修饰其中的动词。Continuously, indicating that an action or a behavior continues without stop or happens frequently, bearing the meaning of "一个劲地,不停地,不断地." Sometimes it can modify a verbal phrase, but the emphasis is mainly on the verb.

(7) 孩子掉了手里的冰淇淋,难过得直哭。

(8) 气温太低了,我全身冷得直发抖。

2. 表示立刻、马上,没有停留地做某事。Right away, indicating doing something immediately.

(9) 一做完工作,他就直奔机场。

3. 表示顺着一定的方向不变,不转折、不间断。相当于"直接、一直"。多用在单音节动词前作状语。Directly; straight. It is used to indicate following a certain direction without change, turn, or stop. An equivalent to "直接,一直," it often goes with a monosyllabic verb to function as an adverbial.

(10) 这架飞机直飞北京。

(11) 高铁从上海直达成都。

4. 表示动作、行为或情况、状态在一定的时间、范围内持续进行、发生或存在,相当于"一直"。为了表明时间、范围的起止点,在"直"的前后往往有"从、到"等介词配合使用。Indicating that an action, behavior, situation or state happens or exists continuously within a certain period of time or scope. It is equivalent to "一直." There is usually a preposition such as "从," or "到" before and after "直" to illustrate the starting and finishing points.

(12) 从幼儿园孩子直到大学生,都熟悉李白的《静夜思》这首诗。

(13) 从黑龙江直到云南、福建,都下了雪。

5. 表示达到或接近于某种程度或情况,相当于"简直",带有强调和夸张的语气,在句子中多修饰"想、像"等动词。Indicating being just, simply or indeed the case. Equivalent to "简直," it carries an emphatic and exaggerated tone and often modifies verbs like "想,像."

(14) 耳朵里有很大的声音,直像有人在里边打鼓!

(15) 听了这孩子讲的话,我直想哭!

动词 v.

挺直,伸直,使笔直。To straighten; to stretch.

(16) 坐了两个小时了,直直身子吧!

(17) 妈妈干了一天活,累得直不起腰来。

名词 n.

汉字的一个笔画,即"竖"。A stroke of the Chinese character "竖."

(18) 一横、一直,再一横。这是个"土"字。

说明 Notes:

1. "直"所修饰的动词,其动作往往是在较短时间内或在某个特定时间里不停顿地进行,动词的动作是直观、单纯的。动作进行的时间不长,不是经常性的。因此,如果句子表示动作经常反复发生而时间间隔比较长的意思,动词或动词短语前面就不宜用"直"。The verb modified by "直" indicates that the action usually happens continuously within a short period of time. The action of the verb is direct and simple, which does not last long, nor does

it happen frequently. Therefore, if an action happens repeatedly and frequently within a relatively long period of time, it is improper to use "直" before the verb or verbal phrase.

(19) *他直写汉字,怪不得汉字那么好。

(20) 他常常练习写汉字,怪不得汉字那么好。

(21) *我来中国以后,你直帮助我,我很感谢你。

(22) 我来中国以后,你常常帮助我,我很感谢你。

2."直"表示"不断地、不停地"的意思时与"一个劲儿"都形容某种动作与情状。区别是:"直+动词"描述的常常是一种结果性的动作、状态。句子中常有表示原因、理由的意思。"一个劲儿+动词"则没有这种限制。When indicating "不断地、不停地", both "直" and "一个劲儿" describe certain actions and situations. Their differences are: "直 + v." often describes a resultative action or state, by which some related reason can usually be found in the sentence; while "一个劲儿 + v." does not have this restriction.

(23) 他一个劲儿地笑,不知道为什么。

(24) *他直笑,不知道为什么。

(25) 他的故事讲得大家直笑。(表示结果性的动作或状态 Indicating a resultative action or state)

zhí 值 →P665"值得"

用法 Usage:

名词 n.

1.价值,价钱。Value; price.

(1) 最近黄金又升值了。

(2) 农民希望年年能提高农业产值。

2.数值,按数学程序运算出来的结果。Numerical value; the result made by mathematical calculation.

(3) 按这个数学程序算出来的值是多少?

动词 v.

1.货物和价值相当。To be worth.

(4) 这双皮鞋值500元钱吗?

(5) 我的手机已经值不了多少钱了。

2.有意义,有价值,值得。To be worthwhile; to be a real bargain; to deserve.

(6) 30块钱买两件衬衣,值!

(7) 虽然要1500元,但是从直升机上下来踏在冰川上,很值!

3.遇到、碰到(某个时间)。To happen to (at a certain time).

(8) 我到上海,正值上海举办国际电影节。

4.轮流担任一定时间内的工作。To be on duty (People take turns doing this).

(9) 明天我要值夜班。

(10) 今天谁值日?快把黑板擦干净!

zhíde 值得 →P665"值"

用法 Usage:

动词 v.

1.价格适宜,合算。To be worth.

(1) 这种手机那么便宜,值得买。

(2) 这本词典非常实用,买得很值得。

2.指这样去做有价值、有意义、有必要。(Something) to be worth doing; to be worthy of an action.

(3) 西安是值得一去的城市。

(4) 这个问题值得研究吗?

说明 Notes:

1.运用"值得"时要注意:When "值得" is used, pay attention to the following points:

① "值得"的否定式有"不值得、值不得"。The negative form of "值得" can be either "不值得" or "值不得."

(5) 跟不讲文明的人不值得生气。

(6) 是规定就要遵守,值不得跟他说那么多道理。

② "值得"可以带动词宾语。"值得" can take a verbal object.

(7) 这个电影值得看。

(8) 这本词典值得买。

③"值得"可以受程度副词的修饰。"值得" can be modified by a degree adverb.

(9) 上海是相当值得去的城市。

(10) 汉语是很值得学的语言。

2. "值"和"值得"只有在作动词用，表示有意义、有价值时，意思相同。"值" and "值得" are the same in meaning when they serve as a verb and mean being worth doing.

它们的区别是：Their differences are as follows:

①"值"的意思停留在对某件事评议、判断的层面上。"值得"除此以外，更重于去做某件事，如例(1)(3)(4)(7)(10)等。"值" focuses on the level of appraisal and judgement. "值得" emphasizes more the worthiness of doing something as in (1), (3), (4), (7) and (10).

②"值"是单音节词，前后一般只能带单音节词语，如"很值、值钱、值了"等。"值得"都可以，更多的是带双音节动词或动词短语。Being monosyllabic, "值" can only take another monosyllabic word before or after it as in "很值，值钱，值了." "值得" does not have this restriction, and in most cases, it takes a disyllabic verb or a verbal phrase.

zhǐ 只 →P175"光"、P88"单"

用法 Usage:
副词 ad.

表示除此之外没有别的，用来限定范围。Only; just; merely. It is used to set a limit to a range or scope.

1. 用在动词或动词短语前面，限制动作、行为所涉及的有关事物或范围，表示动词仅对于某个对象。"只"常常跟"不、没"对用。It is used before a verb or a verbal phrase to restrict something or a range of an action or behavior, indicating that the verb only refers to a certain object. In this case, "只" often goes with "不" or "没."

(1) 今天上午我只去过图书馆，没去过别的地方。

(2) 他只会说法语，不会说汉语。

2. "只"后面如果带有数量词语，只带与动作、行为有关的事物的数量。"只"用来限定宾语的数量，表示数量少或时间短。If there is a quantifier after "只," it must be related to the action or behavior. In this case, "只" is used to limit the number of the object, indicating a small quantity or a short time.

(3) 这本书我只看了一个晚上就看完了。

(4) 这个菜，他只吃了一口就不想再吃了。

3. 限制动作、行为本身以及动作、行为的可能性。句子中的动作、行为只有一个施事者或一个对象。"只"只修饰动词或动宾词组。It is used to limit an action or behavior itself, and the possibility of an action or behavior. There is only one doer or one object of the action or behavior in the sentence. In this case, "只" only modifies a verb or a verb-object phrase.

(5) 展览馆的展品大家只能看，不能动手。

(6) 老师只向我笑了笑，没有批评我。

4. 直接用在名词或名词短语前，限制人、事物有关的范围或数量，表示时间短或数量少。后面直接带有数量短语（可以理解为中间隐含一个动词如"有、是、要"等）。It is used directly before a noun or a noun phrase to limit the range or quantity relating to someone or something, indicating a short time or a small quantity. In this case, it is directly followed by a quantitative phrase (with an implicit verb such as "有，是，要" in between).

(7) 这次教学实习只安娜一人没去。

(8) 只半个小时，他们就会回来。

5. 用在名词或名词短语前，表示举出例子，说明整体或一般的情况，带有举例性质，句子前面部分是整体情况，后面部分是整体部分的其中之一，常有"就"搭配使用，相当于"光"。It is used before a noun or a noun phrase to give examples, illustrating the overall or general

situation. The former part of the sentence shows the overall situation, while the latter is a part of it. In this case, it often goes with "就," and is equivalent to "光."

(9) 我们班的欧美学生很多,只德国学生就有五个。

(10) 他有很多CD片,只古典音乐的就有五百多张。

说明 Notes:

一、运用副词"只"要注意:When the adverb "只" is used, pay attention to the following points:

1. "只"可用于"只……不/没/没有……"这一常见的格式,主要表示以下两种意思:"只" can be used in the common structure "只... 不/没/没有...," which mainly bears two meanings as follows:

① 表示主体仅发出某个动作或仅具有某种性状。"只……不/没/没有……"修饰的是并列的动词或动词短语。It indicates that the subject only takes one action or is only in one state. In this case, "只... 不/没/没有..." modifies the verbs or verbal phrases in parallels.

(11) 他这个人只说不做,我不喜欢这样的人。

(12) 他刚才只喝了咖啡,没吃蛋糕。

② 如果"只……不/没/没有……"所修饰的动词是相同的,"只"的作用在于限定动作的范围。If verbs modified by "只... 不/没/没有..." are the same, the function of "只" is to limit the range of the action.

(13) 你只给我买了笔,没给我买本子。

(14) 我只去杭州,不去苏州。

2. 当"只"直接用于名词短语之前时,必带数量词短语。When "只" is used directly before a nominal phrase, there must be a quantifier phrase.

(15) *昨天你给我的只是书。

(16) 昨天你给我的只是三本书。

二、副词"只"与"单"在表示限定动作、行为的范围方面用法相同,基本上可以互换。The adverbs "只" and "单" are basically interchangeable when both limit the range of an action or behavior.

它们的区别是:Their differences are as follows:

1. "单"可以重叠,说成"单单"。"只"不能重叠。"单" can be reduplicated as "单单," whereas "只" cannot.

2. "只"跟"是、有、要"等连用,形成固定格式,一般作连词用。"单"没有这种用法,但可以跟"是"组成"单是",仍然是副词。"只" can form a set phrase with words like "是, 有, 要" serving as a conjunction. "单" does not have this usage, but it can go with "是" as in "单是," which is an adverb in nature.

3. "只"可以直接修饰数量词或带有数量词的名词,如可以说"只三个月"。"单"不能。"只" can directly modify a quantifier or a noun with a quantifier, as in "只三个月," but "单" cannot.

三、"只"和"光"都能限定范围。区别是:"光"一般限定多项事物中的一项。"只"可以限定多项事物中的一项,也可以限定一项事物中的全部。Both "只" and "光" can limit a range. Their difference is: Generally, "光" limits one thing out of many, whereas "只" can not only limit one thing out of many but also the whole of one thing.

(17) *我光生词还没有写,其他作业都做好了。

(18) 我只生词还没有写,其他作业都做好了。

(19) 光/只一个生词我就写了十分钟。

zhǐbúguò 只不过

用法 Usage:

副词 ad.

限定范围或程度,含有往范围小里或程度轻里说的意味。Just. As an adverb, it limits a range or degree, with an implication of "small in range or low in degree."

(1) 以上只不过是我个人的看法。下面请大家谈谈。

(2) 没关系，只不过擦破了一点皮，不痛。

说明 Notes:

1. 多用于口语。*It is often used in spoken language.*

2. 常用在谓语前面。"只不过"后面常带动词短语或主谓短语。*It is often used before a predicate, taking with it a verbal phrase or a subject-predicate phrase.*

zhǐdé 只得 →P46"不得不"、P668"只好"

用法 Usage:

副词 *ad.*

表示由于条件的限制或情况的变化，迫不得已，只能如此。*Having no alternative but to; having no choice but to; due to the restriction of conditions or the change of situations.*

(1) 去北京的飞机票卖完了，我只得坐高铁去。

(2) 今天忘了带钱，只得明天再来买。

zhǐgù 只顾 →P668"只管"

用法 Usage:

动词 *v.*

只考虑，仅仅关心或照顾。*To be only concerned with; to consider ... only.*

(1) 人不能只顾自己，不顾别人。

(2) 你不能只顾学习，不顾身体。

副词 *ad.*

表示专一不变。*Being absorbed in; single-mindedly.*

(3) 你千万别只顾着看书，忘了时间！

(4) 他只顾着玩手机，把菜也烧糊了。

zhǐguǎn 只管 →P668"只顾"

用法 Usage:

副词 *ad.*

1. 尽管。*By all means.*

(1) 孩子由我照顾，你只管放心。

(2) 你只管去上班，家里的事我来做。

2. 只顾，表示动作行为专一不变。*Simply, just, indicating being engrossed in doing something.*

(3) 他从早到晚只管写写写，连饭也忘了吃。

(4) 你别只管往前走，孩子跟不上了。

说明 Notes:

1. 有时候，"只管"在句子里是两个词，如："会计的工作只管账，不管钱。"在本句中，"只"是副词，修饰动词"管"。*"只管" are two words in some sentences. For example,* "会计的工作只管账，不管钱。" *In this sentence,* "只" *is an adverb and it modifies the verb* "管."

2. "只顾"和"只管"作副词用，都表示动作行为专一不变的意思，用法基本相同。*When* "只顾" *and* "只管" *are adverbs, they both indicate being absorbed in doing something, in which case their usages are basically the same.*

它们的区别是：*Their differences are as follows:*

① "只顾"没有"尽管"的意思。"只管"有。*Unlike* "只管," "只顾" *does not have the meaning of* "尽管."

② "只管"没有动词用法。"只顾"有动词用法。*Unlike* "只顾," "只管" *cannot be used as a verb.*

zhǐhǎo 只好 →P46"不得不"、P668"只得"

用法 Usage:

副词 *ad.*

表示没有别的选择，只得。多用于口语。*Having no choice but to. It is often used in spoken language.*

(1) 下雨了，爬山不方便，我们只好以后再去了。

(2) 朋友没在宿舍，我只好给他留了个便条。

说明 Notes:

"不得不""只得""只好"都有"迫不得已、没有办法、只能这样"的意思。在句子中一般都做状语。*"不得不，""只得" and "只好" all indicate having no alternative or having no* choice. They generally serve as adverbials in a sentence.

它们的区别是：Their differences are as follows:

1. "不得不"的语意最重。"只得"多用于书面语。"不得不"和"只好"多用于口语。"不得不" bears the strongest sense in meaning. "只得" is often used in written language, whereas "不得不" and "只好" are mostly used in spoken language.

2. 用"不得不""只得""只好"造的句子，一般有两个分句。前一分句表示条件的限制或情况的改变，表示原因(也有在后一分句的)。后一分句即表示在这样的情况下，只能怎么做，表示结果。如例（1）（2）。There are usually two clauses in a sentence with "不得不," "只得," or "只好." The former clause shows the restriction of conditions or the change of a situation, which offers the reason (sometimes can be found in the latter clause). The latter shows there is no alternative under that circumstance. It indicates the result as in (1) and (2).

3. "只得"和"只好"可以替代"不得不"。但是"不得不"不能随意替代"只得"和"只好"，特别是"只好"。如：例（1）（2）两句，不能用"不得不"替代。"只得" and "只好" can replace "不得不," yet "不得不" cannot freely replace "只得" and "只好," especially "只好." For example, it is incorrect to use "不得不" in (1) and (2).

4. "不得不"强调直接地去做前面句子中规定的某一件事，侧重于受控制的、被动的、不是出于十分自愿的条件限制。"只得"和"只好"多侧重于因为客观情况的改变而改变原来的动作行为。这个动作行为可能只是时间的改变或方式、方法的改变，含有一种让步的意思。如例（1）句意是：原来就决定要去爬山，因为下雨了，所以只好改变时间，以后再去爬山，并不是改变爬山本身这件事，所以用"不得不"不妥。

例（2）并没有改变"朋友没在宿舍"本身行为，只是改变为"留个便条"的形式。用"不得不"也不妥。"不得不" emphasizes directly doing the thing specified in the former clause, under the condition of being controlled, passive and unwilling. "只得"和"只好" emphasize changing the original action because the objective situation has changed. It could be the change of time, manner or method, indicating a compromise. It is inappropriate to use "不得不" in Example (1). The sentence reads that the plan of climbing the mountain has not changed. What has changed is only the time of climbing because of the rain. In Example (2), the sentence reads that the situation "朋友没在宿舍" has not changed, what has changed is to leave a message instead. Therefore, it is also inappropriate to use "不得不."

5. "只得"和"只好"有时可以用在主语前面，"不得不"不能。"只得" and "只好" can sometimes be placed before the subject, while "不得不" cannot.

（3）别人都不在，只得/只好你去了。

zhǐshì 只是 →P42"不过"

用法 Usage:

副词 ad.

1. 表示限定范围，前后常有说明情况或进一步解释的词语。相当于"仅、仅仅、仅是、仅仅是、不过是"。有时候，句末用"罢了、而已"等词语呼应，表示语气更为缓和。Setting a limit to a range or scope. Either before or after "只是," one will find words clarifying the situation or offering an explanation. It is equivalent to "仅,仅仅,仅是,仅仅是,不过是." Sometimes, "罢了" or "而已" echoes with it at the end of the sentence to achieve a moderate tone.

（1）我和他只是认识，还不是好朋友。

（2）我没有生病，只是有点儿累罢了。

2. 强调在任何条件下情况都不变。相当

于"就是"。常用于否定句。*Indicating an emphasis on a situation that will not change under any circumstances, which is equivalent to "就是" and is often used in a negative sentence.*

(3) 我们谈天说地,非常热闹,她只是在旁边静静地听。

(4) 无论我们怎么问,他只是不开口。

连词 conj.

1. 用于后一分句,表示轻微的转折。全句意思重在前一小句,后一小句用"只是"补充修正上文的意思。相当于"不过",但转折的语气和程度比"不过"轻。*Showing a minor transition when "只是" is used in the second clause. In this case, the first clause bears the meaning of the sentence whereas the second one serves as a supplement of revision to the former through "只是." It is equivalent to "不过," but weaker as far as the transitional tone and degree are concerned.*

(5) 我是意大利人,只是小时候在西班牙住过几年。

(6) 我们老板对职员很好,只是有时候脾气急了点。

2. 解释原因,相当于"只因……"。*Explaining a reason, being equivalent to "只因…."*

(7) 他很爱自己的家,只是在外地工作,不能常常跟家人在一起。

(8) 她很喜欢你,只是不好意思对你说。

3. 表示条件关系。用"只是"在句子的前半部分引出必需的条件,句子的后半部分说出由这种条件所形成的结果或结论,后面常用"才"与前面的"只是"呼应。*Indicating a conditional relationship. "只是" is used to introduce a necessary condition in the first clause, whereas the second one introduces a consequent result or conclusion. What's more, in the second clause, "才" is often used to echo with "只是."*

(9) 她只是喜欢安静,才没来参加舞会。

(10) 只是在大家的帮助下,演出才能这样成功。

说明 Notes:

1. "只是"和"不过"都可以表示转折。*Both "只是" and "不过" can indicate a transition.*

它们的区别是:*Their differences are as follows:*

① "不过"只带轻微的转折意味。"只是"的转折意味比"不过"更轻。*The degree of transitional meaning is different. "不过" carries a weak sense of transition whereas "只是" shows an even weaker sense.*

② 句子中表示的意思有所不同。"只是"表示的转折只是对前面部分进行补充、修正或解释;"不过"有时也有补充或修正的作用,但还表示相对、相反的意思。如果有表示相对、相反的意思,不能用"只是"。*The meaning conveyed in the sentence is different. The transitional meaning by "只是" is just a supplement, revision or explanation to the former part. "不过" goes a step further: it may express something contradictory, in which case "只是" cannot be used.*

(11) 我早就想去看你了,只是/不过没有时间。

(12) *这件衣服看上去不怎么样,只是穿起来很舒服。

(13) 这件衣服看上去不怎么样,不过穿起来很舒服。

③ "只是"多用于口语。"不过"通用于口语和书面语。*"只是" is often used in spoken language whereas "不过" can be used in both written and spoken language.*

④ "不过"后面可以停顿。"只是"后面不能停顿。*There can be a pause after "不过," but there is no pause after "只是."*

(14) 这件衣服很好,只是我已经穿过了。

(15) 这件衣服很好,不过,是我穿过的。

⑤ "不过"没有连词"只是"第二、第三义项

的用法。如：例(7)(9)中的"只是"，都不能用"不过"替代。"不过" does not have the second and third usages under the entry of "只是" as a conjunction. For example, "只是" in (7) and (9) cannot be replaced by "不过."

2.注意副词"只是"跟副词"只"加上动词"是"的区别。副词"只是"后面还有并行动词。"只+是"中，"是"是句子的动词。There is a difference between the adverb "只是" and the combination of the adverb "只" and the verb "是." The adverb "只是" goes with a verb. In the structure of "只+是","是" is the verb of the sentence.

(16) 我只是希望你身体健康。

(17) 这只是我的一点想法。

zhǐyào 只要 →P671"只有"

用法 Usage:
连词 conj.

"只要"表示条件关系。用在偏句里提出充分的条件，然后在正句里说出由此条件产生或出现的结果或情况。正句里常有"就、便、总、还"等词与之呼应。As long as; provided. "只要" indicates a conditional relationship. It is used in a subordinate clause to introduce a necessary condition, which leads to a consequent result in the main clause. There are often such words as "就、便、总、还" in the main clause to echo with "只要."

(1) 只要手机上有支付宝，就可以到饭店吃饭。

(2) 只要到了冬天，他总会感冒。

说明 Notes:

1."只要"可以用在主语前，也可以用在主语后。有时也可以用在后一个分句。"只要" can be used either before or after a subject, and sometimes it can be used in the second clause.

(3) 只要你把病假证明给老师，他会同意你请假的。

(4) 你只要把病假证明给老师，他会同意你请假的。

(5) 老师会同意的，只要你把病假证明给他。

2.后一分句如果是反问句或"是……的"句，句中就不用"就""便"。If the second clause is a rhetorical question or a structure with "是…的,""就" or "便" is not used.

(6) 只要坚持少吃多运动，减肥会不成功吗？

(7) 你只要仔细一些，这几个字是不可能写错的。

3."只要"后面可带"是","只要是"有"凡是"的意思。"只要" can be followed by "是," and "只要是" bears the meaning of "凡是."

(8) 只要是去过中国的人，一定会说几句中国话。

(9) 只要是妈妈做的菜，我都爱吃。

4.注意副词"只要"与副词"只"修饰动词"要"的区别。Pay attention to the difference between the adverb "只要" and the combination of adverb "只" and verb "要."

(10) 只要是你学习上需要的东西，我都可以给你买。

(11) 她什么都不要，只要了一杯绿茶。

zhǐyǒu 只有 →P71"除非"、P668"只好"、P671"只要"

用法 Usage:
副词 ad.

表示在某种情况下非此不可的选择，相当于"只好、只得、不得不"。"只有"后面常常是动词短语。Meaning "have to or be forced to" under certain circumstances, it is equivalent to "只好,只得,不得不.""只有" is often followed by a verbal phrase.

(1) 买不到飞机票，我只有买火车票了。

(2) 末班车都开走了，看来我只有打的回家了。

连词 conj.

表示唯一的条件，非此不可。后面多用副

词"才"呼应,有时也用"还"。"只有"后面可以带名词、动词、介词短语、小句等。Indicating the only condition, having no choice but, it is often followed by the adverb "才" and sometimes "还." "只有" can go with a noun, verb, prepositional phrase, clause, etc.

(3) 中学生只有在周末回家,才能用手机。
(4) 只有你去请他,他才会来。
(5) 只有大家齐心协力,才能完成这项艰巨任务。

说明 Notes:

1. "只有"作连词用,一般用在前面表示条件的偏句中。后面正句中用"才"呼应。如果正句在前面,正句中就不必用"才",但一般得用"要、要想"等与"只有"呼应。When "只有" is a conjunction, it is often used in the former subordinate clause indicating a condition. There is "才" echoing with it in the latter main clause. If the main clause is placed at the beginning of the sentence, "要" or "要想" instead of "才" is used to echo with "只有."

(6) 要想很快会说汉语,只有每天开口练。
(7) 要到那座山上的庙里去,只有走这条路。

2. "只有"的副词用法要与副词"只"加上动词"有"的用法进行区别。The adverb usage of "只有" is to be differentiated from the combination of the adverb "只" and the verb "有."

(8) 我只有这本书,没有别的书。
(9) 你只有到新华书店,才能买到这本书。

3. "除非"和"只有"在表示唯一的条件的意思时,用法相同。"除非" and "只有" are used in the same way when they indicate the only condition.

它们的区别是:They differ as follows:

① "只有"是从正面提出某个唯一的条件。"除非"是从反面强调不能缺少某个唯一的条件,语气更加强调。"只有" recommends the only condition from the positive perspective while "除非" emphasizes from a negative perspective that a certain condition is absolutely necessary. Therefore, it carries an even stronger tone.

② "除非"可以用在"是"前面。"只有"不能用。"除非" can be placed before "是," but "只有" cannot.

(10) *只有是你才会记得我。
(11) 除非是你才会记得我。

③ "除非……,才……"也可以从假设的另一角度说成"除非……,不……"。"只有"不可以。"除非…, 才…" can make a recommendation from a hypothetical perspective by using "除非…, 不…." "只有" cannot be used this way.

(12) 除非你去,我才去。/除非你去,我不去。
(13) 只有你去,我才去。/ *只有你去,我不去。

④ "除非"后面可以有动词一正一反地使用,强调突出某种现象。"只有"不能这样用。"除非" can highlight a certain phenomenon by using the verb (positive + negative). Again, "只有" cannot be used this way.

(14) *只有他不唱,唱的话就没完没了。
(15) 除非他不唱,唱的话就没完没了。

4. 副词"只有"和"只好"的意义非常接近。The adverb "只有" and the adverb "只好" are very close in meaning.

它们的区别是:"只好"可以用在动词前,也可用在形容词前。"只有"一般只用在动词或动词短语前。Their difference is as follows: "只好" can be used either before a verb or before an adjective. "只有," by contrast, is generally placed before a verb or verbal phrase.

(16) *家里没米了,只有随便凑合着吃了。
(17) 家里没米了,只好随便凑合着吃了。

5. "只有"和"只要"作连词都可以表示条件关系。When "只有" and "只要" are conjunctions, they both can indicate a conditional relationship.

它们的区别是:"只要"着重于有充足的必要条件,但这个条件不是唯一的,别的条件也可能产生这个结果。正句中常常有"就、便、都、总、也"等副词与之呼应。"只有"则表示这个条件是唯一的,除了这个条件,任何其他条件都不能产生这一结果。正句中常常有"才、方"等副词与之呼应。Their difference is as follows: "只要" emphasizes a necessary condition, but it is not unique. There can be other conditions leading to the same result. Adverbs such as "就,便,都,总,也" are often used in the main clause in coordination with it. "只有," by contrast, indicates the only condition that will lead to such a result. The adverbs such as "才,方" are often used in the main clause in coordination with "只有."

(18) 只要天天锻炼,你的身体就会好起来的。

(19) 只有天天练习走路,你的小腿才会有力。

例(18)"只要"表示的不是唯一的、非此不可的条件,因为通过药物治疗、适当休息等方式也会使身体好起来的,但可能根据实际情况,"锻炼"是最重要的条件。例(19)"只有"表示唯一的、非此不可的条件,要想小腿有力,只有一个条件,那就是每天练习走路,否则不会产生这一结果。The condition introduced by "只要" in (18) is not the unique one, because medical treatment and proper rest can also help the recovery. "锻炼" might be the most important condition according to the real situation. In (19), "只有" indicates the only condition. That means if you want to restore the strength to your calf, practicing walking every day is the only condition for achieving the stated result.

6. 要注意用对正句中相呼应的关联词语。Attention should be paid to the right coordinating word in the main clause.

(20) *只要你愿意,他才会来帮你。

(21) 只要你愿意,他便/就会来帮你。

(22) *只有多听、多说,就能学好汉语。

(23) 只有多听、多说,才能学好汉语。

(24) *除非你去,我就去。

(25) 除非你去,我才去。

zhìshǎo 至少 →P368"起码"

用法 Usage:

副词 ad.

表示数量上的最低限度(与"至多"相对)、最小的可能。可用在动词或数量词前。用在主语前,需有停顿。At least, indicating the smallest amount (as opposed to "至多") and the least possibility. It can be used before a verb or a quantifier. It can also be used before a subject, usually with a pause after it.

(1) 每个月的生活费我至少得花两千元。

(2) 今天的温度至少有三十七度。

(3) 至少,我们住的酒店是安全的。

说明 Notes:

1. "至少"修饰动词时,动词后面必须带数量词短语或其他短语,否则句子意思不完整,如例(1)(2)。When "至少" modifies a verb, there must be a quantifier phrase or some other phrase after it, otherwise the meaning of the sentence is incomplete, as in (1) and (2).

(4) *今天的饺子我至少要吃。

(5) 今天的饺子我至少要吃三十只。

2. "至少"和"起码"都有表示最低限度、最小可能的意思。它们的区别是:Both "至少" and "起码" express the minimum degree or possibility. Their differences are as follows:

① "起码"是形容词,前面可以加程度副词"最、顶"。"至少"是副词,前面不能再加副词。"起码" is an adjective and it can be preceded by a degree adverb such as "最" or "顶"."至少" is an adverb, and so it cannot be preceded by any adverbs.

② "起码"多用于口语。"至少"通用于口语和书面语。"起码" appears mostly in oral Chinese, while "至少" is used both in oral Chinese and in written Chinese.

zhìyú 至于 →P172"关于"

用法 Usage:

动词 v.

表示达到某种程度,有"到……的地步"的意思(常用否定式"不至于",也常用于反问"何至于、哪至于"),后面多带动词性宾语。To go so far as to, indicating to a certain degree "到...的地步" (often used in the negative form "不至于" and the rhetorical question "何至于,哪至于"). It takes a verbal object in most cases.

(1) 这么一件小事,他不至于生气吧?

(2) 如果刚生病就去医院,哪至于现在这么严重?

介词 prep.

转换话题,引出另一件事。"至于"后面的名词、动词、小句等是引进的另一话题,后面常有停顿。As for; as to; as far as. It is used to change a topic, introducing another topic. In this case, the noun, verb or clause following "至于" is the new topic, after which there is often a pause.

(3) 他的理想很美好,至于能不能实现就不一定了。

(4) 上海是要去的,至于什么时候去,我再想想。

说明 Notes:

1. 运用"至于"要注意:When "至于" is used, pay attention to the following points:

① 承接上文或在对话中,"至于"用于否定时,可以单独作谓语。前面常有"我看",后面常有"吧"等,表示语气比较缓和。"至于" often appears in its negative form when it is used to carry on a previous topic or in a conversation. It can be used alone as a predicate, often with "我看" before it and "吧" after it, indicating a softened tone.

(5) 他忙是忙,要说一点儿时间都没有,我看不至于。

(6) A:你这个玩笑开大了,老王都生气了。
B:不至于吧。/至于吗?

② 习惯语"大而至于""小而至于"相当于"大到""小到"的意思。成对用于名词短语前,带有举例性质。When used in the idioms "大而至于" and "小而至于," the meanings are equivalent to "大到" and "小到." They often go in pairs before nominal phrases to give examples.

(7) 大而至于一个国家,小而至于一个单位,都要考虑群众的福利问题。

2. "至于"和介词"关于"的区别是:The differences between "至于" and the preposition "关于" are as follows:

① "关于"表示只涉及一个话题来说的意思。"至于"表示在原话题之外,提出另一话题的意思。"关于" is used when we talk about only one topic whereas "至于" introduces a new topic in addition to the original one.

(8) *这首歌很好听,关于作者是谁,我不太清楚。

(9) 这首歌很好听,至于作者是谁,我不太清楚。

② "关于"可以用于书名、文章名。"至于"不能。"关于" can be used in the title of a book or article, yet "至于" cannot.

(10) 今天下午的讲座,题目是《关于汉语语法特点》。

zhìdìng 制订 →P675"制定"

用法 Usage:

动词 v.

创制,拟订。多带名词性宾语。To formulate; to work out. It is often followed by a nominal object.

(1) 公司为客户制订了两个旅游方案。

(2) 每个学期开始,他一定会制订一个学习计划。

zhìdìng 制定 →P674"制订"

用法 Usage:

动词 v.

明确地定出(法律、规程、计划等)。多带名词性宾语。*To formulate; to lay down; to work out (law, regulation, plan, etc.). It is often followed by a nominal object.*

(1) 改革开放以来我国制定了许多新的法律。

(2) 既然学校制定了规章制度,每位师生都应严格遵守。

说明 Notes:

"制定"和"制订"都表示经过反复考虑或讨论而创制、拟定的意思。*Both "制定" and "制订" can mean the formulation of something (a plan, policy, rule, etc.) through careful consideration and repeated discussion.*

它们的区别是：*Their differences are as follows:*

1. "制定"着重于定出,使之确定下来成为定案,强调的是行为的结果。"制订"是表示从无到有地创制、拟订,强调的是制订行为本身。*"制定" indicates having something worked out and laid down. The emphasis is on the result of formulation, whereas "制订" indicates the whole process of planning and creating something from scratch. The emphasis is on the efforts involved in the formulation.*

2. "制定"和"制订"的搭配对象并无严格界限,使用"制订"的地方多可用"制定"去替换。但是,总体说来,"制定"多用于"重大的政策、法令、方针、路线、纲领"等,也可以是"学习计划、比赛规则、治疗方案"等。"制订"的对象可以是"方针、法律、总体方案"等,但偏重用于"具体的计划、办法、方案、措施、步骤、实施方案"等。"制定"通常比"制订"更为常用,范围更大。*About collocations, there is not a strict dividing line between "制定" and "制订." "制订" can be replaced by "制定" in most cases. But in general, "制定" often applies to "重大的政策,法令,方针,路线,纲领," and also "学习计划,比赛规则,治疗方案." The objects of "制订" can be "方针,法律,总体方案," but the particular stress is on "具体的计划,办法,方案,措施,步骤,实施方案." "制定" is more frequently and widely used than "制订."*

zhìzào 制造 →P675"制作"

用法 Usage:

动词 v.

1. 通过人的劳动使原材料成为可供使用的物品。*To make; to produce; to manufacture; to turn raw materials into usable goods through human labor.*

(1) 他们用塑料制造出许多日常用品。

(2) 这是中国制造的华为手机。

2. 人为地编出、引起某种气氛或不好的事情(含有贬义)。*To fabricate or create an atmosphere or something bad. It is used with a derogatory meaning.*

(3) 这个传言肯定是有人故意制造的。

(4) 他们故意制造混乱,企图从中获利。

zhìzuò 制作 →P675"制造"

用法 Usage:

动词 v.

制造。*To make; to manufacture.*

(1) 这个衣柜制作得十分精巧。

(2) 那件工艺品是手工制作的。

(3) 去年全国一共制作了五百部电视剧。

说明 Notes:

"制造"和"制作"都有"造"的意思,都可用于"是……的",如例(2)。*Both "制造" and "制作" have the meaning of "造," and can be used in the structure "是…的," as in (2).*

它们的区别是：*Their differences are as follows:*

1. "制造"多是大规模、成批地生产,其对象往往是大型的、比较复杂的器件。如"制造飞机、制造汽车、制造武器、制造机器、制造水泥、制造化肥"。"制作"多指小规模地、小型地生产,其对象多为个体,单一的物品。如"制作模型、制作家具、制作玩具、制作盆景、制作广告、制作电视剧"等。"制造" mainly refers to producing something in large quantities, and the products are often large and sophisticated such as "制造飞机,制造汽车,制造武器,制造机器,制造水泥,制造化肥," whereas "制作" mainly refers to producing something in small quantities and the products are mostly small and personalized goods such as "制作模型,制作家具,制作玩具,制作盆景,制作广告,制作电视剧."

2. "制造"可以带含有贬义的宾语,如"制造谣言、制造假象、制造麻烦"等。"制作"没有这一用法。The objects of "制造" can be derogatory, as in "制造谣言,制造假象,制造麻烦," but "制作" does not have this usage.

3. "制作"有时也可以作为抽象的名词宾语。"制造"没有这个用法。"制作" sometimes can be abstract nominal objects, whereas "制造" does not have this usage.

(4) 秦代的兵马俑是个精致而又伟大的制作。

4. "制作"的"作"不能写成"做"。The character "作" in "制作" cannot be written as "做."

zhōng 中 →P677"中间"

用法 Usage:

名词 n.

1. 方位名词。跟四周距离相等的位置,中心。A locative noun, it means the center of a location.

(1) 地震时震中所受破坏最大。

(2) 华中指的是长江中游湖北、湖南地区。

2. 在一定界限、一定范围以内,里面,内部。Inside; amidst; within a certain boundary or scope.

(3) 在我们山区,村中基本只有老人和孩子,年轻人都外出打工了。

(4) 足球比赛我们赢了,只是美中不足,比赛时天下雨了。

3. 过程中。In the process of.

(5) 他的身体还在恢复中。

(6) 在去西安的旅游中,他认识了两个中国朋友。

4. 位于两端之间的。In the middle of.

(7) 这条河的中游,河水特别深。

(8) 什么时候期中考试?

5. 等级、规模处于两端之间的。(Of rank, level, size) being medium.

(9) 中国的中学要学六年。

(10) 我们的老师中等个子,不胖不瘦。

6. 不偏不倚于任何一方或一端。Being neutral.

(11) 你俩一个说二元,一个说四元,来个折中,三元吧。

(12) 我中立,不帮你,也不帮他。

7. 为双方介绍、调解或作证的人。Intermediator; mediator.

(13) 我们应该请一个中人。

(14) 好,我来为你们做中。

8. 中国。如:"中医、中药、洋为中用、古今中外"等。China, as in "中医,中药,洋为中用,古今中外."

动词 v.

1. 适合于,适宜于。"中"的宾语仍然要动词充当。To be fit for; to be good for. Its object is always a verb.

(15) 这蛋糕中看不中吃。

(16) 人老了,不中用了。

2. (河南话)好,行,成。(In Henan dialect) all right; OK.

(17) 你看我这样写中不中?

(18) 你做的饭菜就是中!

zhōngjiān 中间 →P656"之间"、P676"中"

用法 Usage:

名词 n.

方位词。Locative noun.

1. 在事物两端之间或两个事物之间的位置。Between; intermediate.

（1）我们的村子在两座山中间。

（2）爸爸妈妈中间坐着他们的孩子。

2. 中心（跟四周距离相等的位置）。Center; middle.

（3）草地中间有一个喷泉。

（4）有一个小岛在湖中间。

3. 在一段时间内，里面。Within a period of time.

（5）我们上午上课，中间只休息半个小时。

（6）坐飞机的时候，我中间喝了两次水。

4. 在某个范围内，里面。Within a certain group.

（7）他在学生中间很有名。

（8）怎么教词语，老师中间有不同的意见。

5. 过程中。In the course of.

（9）说话中间就走到了湖边。

（10）实习中间会给你增加很多书本上没有的知识。

6. 处于两种对立状态之间的。如："中间人、中间状态、中间道路"等。Sandwiched between two opposing states or contradictory situations as in "中间人,中间状态,中间道路."

说明 Notes:

"中间""之间"和"中"的区别是："中间,""之间," and "中" differ as follows:

"中间"可以用于两点的距离以内，也可以用于某种事物的范围以内，如"两点中间、人群中间"。"之间"只能用于前者，不能用于后者，如可以说"两点之间"，不能说"人群之间"。"中"只能用于后者，不能用于前者，如可以说"人群中"，不能说"两点中"。"中间" can refer to the distance between two points or and within a certain range or scope as in "两点中间,人群中间.""之间" can only be used in the former situation such as "两点之间," but we cannot say "人群之间.""中" can only be used in the latter situation. For example, we can say "人群中," but not "两点中."

zhōngwén 中文 →P187"汉语"

用法 Usage:

名词 n.

1. 中国的语言文字，特指汉族的语言文字。The Chinese language, referring in particular to the language of the Han nationality.

（1）我已经学了三年中文。

（2）很多外国文学作品都已经翻译成了中文。

2. 中国的语言文学，特指汉语言文学。The Chinese language and literature, referring in particular to the language and literature of the Han nationality.

（3）我想到中文系读本科专业。

说明 Notes:

"中文"和"汉语"的区别是：The differences between "中文" and "汉语" are as follows:

"汉语"是中国汉族的语言，也是中国的通用语言，是世界上使用人数最多的一种语言，普通话是现代汉语的标准语。"中文"指中国语言，也指中国的文学。内容范围比"汉语"广泛。"汉语" refers to the language of the Han nationality in China, which is also the standard Chinese language spoken by more people than any other nationality in the world. Mandarin is the standard language of modern Chinese. "中文" refers to both Chinese language and Chinese literature, covering a wider range than "汉语."

zhōngyú 终于 →P97"到底"

用法 Usage:

副词 ad.

表示经过较长过程，最后出现某种情况和结果。Finally; eventually; in the end; at last.

It indicates the coming of the eventual situation or result after a long period of time.

1. 用在动词前面。"终于"后面至少要有两个音节的词语。Used before a verb, "终于" is followed by words of at least two syllables.

（1）我们等了他一个小时后,他终于来了。

（2）他终于买到了一双他能穿的鞋。

2. 用在表示状态变化的形容词或形容词短语的前面。Used before an adjective or an adjective phrase, it shows a change of state.

（3）妈妈的病终于好了,大家都很高兴。

（4）冬天快要过去了,天气终于暖和起来了。

说明 Notes:

1. "终于"有时可以用在句首（后面加逗号）。Followed by a comma, "终于" can sometimes be placed at the beginning of a sentence.

（5）终于,一个星期以后他醒了过来。

2. "终于"和"到底"的区别是："终于" differs from "到底" in the following aspects:

① "到底"修饰的动词或动词短语必须带"了"。"终于"可带可不带。The verb or verbal phrase modified by "到底" must be followed by "了" while it is optional for "终于."

（6）经过大家的努力,任务终于完成/完成了。

（7）*经过大家的努力,任务到底完成。

（8）经过大家的努力,任务到底完成了。

② "到底"可以用于问句,表示"究竟"的意思。"终于"不能。"到底" can be used in an interrogative sentence, meaning "究竟," but "终于" cannot.

（9）*你终于喝不喝？

（10）你到底喝不喝？

③ "到底"有"毕竟"的用法。"终于"没有。"到底" has the usage of "毕竟" while "终于" does not.

④ "终于"多用于书面语。"到底"多用于口语。"终于" is more used in written language while "到底" is more used in spoken language.

zhōngtóu 钟头 →P516"小时"

用法 Usage:

名词 n.

小时。多用于口语。Hour, often used in spoken language.

（1）下班后,她又加了三个多钟头的班。

（2）你已经玩了两个钟头游戏了,眼睛累了,别玩了。

说明 Notes:

"小时"和"钟头"做名词时可以通用,如"一个小时/钟头"。"小时" and "钟头" are interchangeable when they are nouns as in "一个小时/钟头".

它们的区别是：Their differences are as follows:

1. "钟头"口语色彩比较重一些。"钟头" is more colloquial.

2. "小时"还可以做量词用,如"一小时"。"钟头"不能。"小时" can serve as a particle as in "一小时," but "钟头" cannot.

（3）*星期一到星期五,每天上午上课三钟头。

（4）星期一到星期五,每天上午上课三小时/三个小时/三个钟头。

zhòngdà 重大 →P679"重要"

用法 Usage:

形容词 a.

重要而且影响大的。Important and influential.

（1）奥运会对运动员来说是一次重大的比赛。

（2）MH17航班失事是一起重大航空事故。

说明 Notes:

"重大"多修饰"课题、新闻、贡献、损失、意义、胜利、任务、事故"等抽象名词。"重大" is often used to modify abstract nouns such as "课题,新闻,贡献,损失,意义,胜利,任务,事故."

zhòngdiǎn 重点

用法 Usage:

名词 n.

同类事物或整体事物中重要的或主要的部分（跟"一般"相对）。*The essential or important part of the whole thing or of things of the same category (as opposed to "一般").*

（1）展开市场调查是我们公司三月份的工作重点。

（2）补语是汉语语法中的学习重点之一。

副词 ad.

有重点地，后面一定带有动词或动词短语。*Taking something as the focus, followed by a verb or verbal phrase.*

（3）这几年我们要重点发展西部地区的经济。

（4）老师要我们重点复习补语这个语法现象。

zhòngyào 重要 →P678"重大"、P681"主要"

用法 Usage:

形容词 a.

具有重大的、关键性的、值得特别重视的。*Important, crucial, being worthy of special attention.*

（1）公司领导常常把最重要的事交给我做。

（2）在发展经济的过程中，保护环境的工作显得特别重要。

说明 Notes:

1."重要"作定语时，如果后面修饰的是单音节词，一定要带"的"，如例（1），被修饰的是双音节词，"的"可带可不带。*As an attribute, "重要" must take "的" when it modifies a monosyllabic word as in (1). When it modifies a disyllabic word, "的" is optional.*

2."重大"和"重要"的区别是：*"重大" and "重要" differ as follows:*

"重大"的词义重在事情本身对别的事物的影响很大。"重要"的词义重于指出这件事在所有的事情中，是最关键、最需要重视的事情。*"重大" emphasizes the great influence of one thing over another, while "重要" emphasizes that one thing is the most crucial of all the issues.*

（3）这是个重大的问题。（是个重要并且对别的事物影响很大的。*This issue is important and has great influence over other issues.*）

（4）这是个重要的问题。（在许多问题中这是关键性的特别要重视的一个。*Of all the issues, this is the crucial one and worthy of special attention.*）

zhōu 周

用法 Usage:

名词 n.

1. 星期。*Week.*

（1）一个学期有十八周。

（2）这一周我们打算举办一次唱歌比赛。

2. 圈子，环形的路线。*Circle; circular route.*

（3）月亮绕地球一周要一个月时间。

（4）运动员入场常常要绕运动场一周。

3. 周围。*Circumference.*

（5）学校四周有很多小商店。

（6）中国周边有二十多个国家。

4. 时间的一轮。如："周年、周岁、周期"等。*Cycle, periodical duration, as in "周年, 周岁, 周期."*

5. 朝代。如："西周、东周、后周"等。*Dynasty, as in "西周, 东周, 后周."*

形容词 a.

1. 普遍，全。*Whole; all; entire.*

（7）一场大雨淋得我周身湿透。

（8）他用了整整一年时间，周游了五十多个国家。

2. 完备,周到,周密。*Considerate; thoughtful.*

（9）如果有招待不周的地方请多多原谅。

动词 *v.*

绕行一周。*To move in a circular course.*

（10）地球周而复始24小时，人类才有日夜交替的生活。

zhōudào 周到 →P680"周密"

用法 Usage:
形容词 *a.*

各个方面都照顾到，不疏忽。*Being considerate in all aspects; thoughtful.*

（1）他是个很仔细的人，考虑问题总是很周到。

（2）服务员十分周到地为客人服务。

zhōumì 周密 →P680"周到"

用法 Usage:
形容词 *a.*

周到细致（准确、完备、没有缺陷）。*Being careful and meticulous (accurate, complete, faultless).*

（1）计划订得很周密，没有问题。

（2）他们对四周的环境进行了周密的考察。

说明 Notes:

"周到"和"周密"的区别是：*The difference between "周到" and "周密" is as follows:*

"周到"多修饰"照顾、招待、考虑、服务、办事"等动词。"周密"强调周到而细密，没有任何缺失，多修饰"调查、计划、布置、准备"等。*"周到" often modifies such verbs as "照顾, 招待, 考虑, 服务, 办事," while "周密" often modifies words such as "调查, 计划, 布置, 准备," laying stress on being thoughtful, meticulous and faultless.*

zhúbù 逐步 →P680"逐渐"

用法 Usage:
副词 *ad.*

一步一步地（表示动作、行为有意识地循序渐进）。*Step by step; gradually. It is used to indicate that actions or behaviors proceed in an orderly way as planned.*

（1）交通拥堵的问题不可能一下子解决，只能逐步加以改善。

（2）中国正在逐步地实现现代化。

（3）大家的汉语水平正在逐步提高。

zhújiàn 逐渐 →P680"逐步"

用法 Usage:
副词 *ad.*

指行为状态的程度、数量等的变化缓慢有序地进行，渐渐。*Gradually, slowly in due order, often referring to the change in a behavior or state in terms of degree or quantity.*

（1）他的身体正在逐渐恢复，现在已经能下床了。

（2）傍晚，广场上的人逐渐多了起来。

说明 Notes:

"逐步"和"逐渐"都是副词，它们都表示程度或数量随时间的过去缓慢地增加或减少。*Both "逐步" and "逐渐" are adverbs indicating slow and gradual increase or decrease in degree or quantity with the passage of time.*

它们的区别是：*Their differences are as follows:*

1."逐步"着重表示人或事物的变化有明显的阶段性，是一步一步地变化，而且常用来表示人的有意识的动作行为。"逐渐"着重表示人或事物的变化是一种连续的、有序的、一点点渐变的过程，常常用来表示事物本身自然而然的变化。*"逐步" emphasizes the change of someone or something marked by obvious stages, and it often refers to the conscious actions of people. "逐渐," by contrast, emphasizes the successive, orderly and gradual change of someone or something and it often refers to the natural change of things.*

（3）为了解决交通拥挤的问题，市政府决定逐步地建设地铁。

（4）天色逐渐暗了下来，我们该回家了。

（5）孩子逐渐长大了，他们有了自己的生活。

一般来说，表示有意识、有步骤的变化用"逐步"。没有明显阶段性，是一种自然而然的延续变化，用"逐渐"。Generally speaking, "逐步" is used when referring to conscious and step-by-step changes, whereas "逐渐" is used when referring to natural and successive changes without obvious stages.

2. "逐步"用来修饰有意识、有步骤的阶段性变化的动作行为，因此只是表示性质状态的形容词一般不能受"逐步"修饰。"逐渐"则可以。As "逐步" modifies conscious and step-by-step periodic changes, adjectives that indicate the property or state of things cannot be modified by "逐步," but "逐渐" can modify these adjectives.

（6）＊天气逐步热起来了。
（7）天气逐渐热了起来。
（8）＊他逐步老了。
（9）他逐渐老了。

zhǔdòng 主动 →P690"自动"、P692"自觉"

用法 Usage:

形容词 a.

1. 不等外力推动而行动的，自觉地（跟"被动"相对）。做状语时后面一般不带"地"。Being active; on one's own initiative, without any external push (as opposed to "被动"). When used as an adverbial, it cannot take "地" after it.

（1）她在家总是主动帮妈妈做家里的事情。
（2）学生对学习感兴趣，就会主动积极地去学。

2. 能够造成有利局面，使事情按照自己的意图进行。Being able to create a favorable situation and make things develop according to one's intention.

（3）因为早有准备，比赛中他们一直处于主动地位。

（4）只有提高产品质量，才能让公司在竞争中更主动。

说明 Notes:

"主动"能与"性、权"组成"主动性、主动权"。表示通过努力，让事情按照自己的意愿进行的有利状态、有利条件。"主动" often goes with "性" and "权" to form "主动性" and "主动权，" meaning obtaining a favorable state and creating conditions through efforts, which enable things to develop according to one's intention.

（5）你应该掌握主动权，做好这件事。
（6）他在学习上主动性很强。

zhǔyào 主要 →P679"重要"

用法 Usage:

形容词 a.

有关事物中为主的，起决定性的。Main; decisive.

（1）游客很多，主要是欧洲游客。
（2）我们公司有四个主要负责人。

说明 Notes:

"主要"和"重要"的区别是：The differences between "主要" and "重要" are as follows:

1. "主要"着重于基本的、主体的或能起决定作用的意思，也指在两个或几个中为主的一个（与"次要"相对）。"重要"着重于具有重大意义、作用或影响的（与"一般"相对）。"主要" emphasizes being basic, main or decisive, and it also means being the primary (as opposed to "次要"). "重要" emphasizes being important and influential (as opposed to "一般").

2. "主要"是非谓语形容词，不能做谓语，多做定语、状语。"重要"是普通形容词，具有一般形容词的语法特征，可以做谓语。As a non-finite adjective, "主要" cannot serve as a predicate; it is more often used as an attribute or adverbial. As a common adjective, "重要" possesses all grammatical features of common

adjectives, so it can serve as a predicate.

（3）*保护环境越来越主要了。

（4）保护环境越来越重要了。

3. "主要"可以做状语。"重要"一般不能做状语，多做谓语和定语。"主要" can serve as an adverbial while "重要" cannot. "重要" often serves as a predicate or attribute.

（5）*今天上课，老师重要讲了新课的生词。

（6）今天上课，老师主要讲了新课的生词。

4. "重要"可以受程度副词或否定副词"不"的修饰。"主要"除了能受程度副词"最"的修饰外，不能受其他程度副词或否定副词"不"的修饰。"重要" can be modified by a degree adverb or the negative adverb "不，" but "主要" cannot — with the exception of the degree adverb "最."

5. "重要"可以构成"重要不重要"肯定否定式，"主要"不能。"重要" can be used to form the affirmative ＋ negative structure as "重要不重要，" while "主要" cannot be used in that way.

（7）*你觉得这个问题主要不主要？

（8）你觉得这个问题重要不重要？

zhǔfù 嘱咐 →P148"吩咐"

用法 Usage:

动词 v.

告诉对方记住应该怎样，不应该怎样。To tell the listener what to do and what not to do.

（1）妈妈再三嘱咐我，出门在外一定要注意安全。

（2）每个医生都会嘱咐感冒的病人要多喝开水多休息。

说明 Notes:

"吩咐"和"嘱咐"的区别是：The differences between "吩咐" and "嘱咐" are as follows:

1. "吩咐"着重于要求别人做什么，含"让、叫"的意思，多指长辈、上级的口头指派或命令，含有强制的色彩。"嘱咐"着重于告诉对方或让对方记住应该怎样，不应该怎样，是"告诉、叮嘱"的意思，没有命令的色彩，多用于书面语。"吩咐" emphasizes asking somebody to do something, often carrying the meaning of "让，叫." Usually, a superior or a senior family member uses it orally as a kind of command or request, which the listener is obliged to accomplish. "嘱咐" often appears in written Chinese and carries the meaning of "告诉，叮嘱." It is not a command, but is often used to tell the listener what to do, what not to do, and how to do it.

2. "吩咐"多用于对方听到后马上照做的场合，指派对方做的通常是非常具体的事情。"嘱咐"则一般不是马上就要做的事情，常常是要过一段时间再做或不能很快就能做完的事情，嘱咐的内容也可以是一些原则、精神，不是具体的事情。"吩咐" is primarily used for occasions where the listener does what he or she is asked to do — usually specific, day-to-day tasks. "嘱咐," however, usually does not involve things to be done immediately: they are things to be done sometime in the future. And usually they cannot be finished fast. Also, "嘱咐" often involves some principle or basic spirit.

3. "嘱咐"语气显得慎重，一般不带状语修饰语。"嘱咐"的语气恳切、温和，语重心长，前面常用"再三、反复、一再"等修饰语。"吩咐" carries a tone that is somewhat more serious; it does not go with an adverbial modifier. "嘱咐，" by contrast, carries a more sincere, kind, and earnest tone. It is often preceded by "再三、反复、一再" or other such expressions.

zhù 住 →P255"居住"

用法 Usage:

动词 v.

1. 居住，住宿。可带"着、了、过"，可直接带处所名词做宾语，可带"在"及补语。To live;

to stay. It can go with "着, 了, 过," and can be followed directly by nouns of places as objects. Furthermore, it can take "在" along with a complement.

（1）我朋友在我家住了一个星期。

（2）最近他一直住在奶奶家。

2. 停止。可带"了"，主语只限于风、雨、雷、雪等自然现象、声音的名词。*To stop. It can go with "了" and its subjects are confined to nouns of natural phenomena such as wind, rain, thunder, snow, and nouns of sounds.*

（3）早上雪住了，孩子们都到外面玩雪去了。

（4）半夜里邻居家的音乐声住了，我才睡着。

3. 让动作或行为停止，可带"了、过"，必须带宾语，宾语只限于"口、手、嘴"等少数单音节名词。*To bring an action or behavior to a halt. It can go with "了, 过" and its objects are confined to a few monosyllabic nouns such as "口, 手, 嘴."*

（5）住手！不许打人！

（6）你住口吧，别让妈妈生气了！

4. 用在动词后面作补语。*When used after a verb as a complement:*

① 表示停止或不让行进。可插入"得、不"。*Indicating a stop or halt, sometimes taking "得, 不" in between.*

（7）病人站不住了。

（8）那辆蓝色的电动车停住！

② 表示牢固、稳固。可插入"得、不"。*Indicating a steadiness or firmness, sometimes taking "得, 不" in between.*

（9）那么多生词他都记得住，真厉害！

（10）大家都被外面传来的歌声吸引住了。

③ 跟某些动词组合，构成固定短语，中间必有"得、不"，有些已经成为固定词语。*Forming set phrases with some verbs, taking "得, 不" in between.*

（11）是他对不住你，不是你对不住他。

（12）一个朋友靠得住还是靠不住，光凭嘴说，是没有用的。

说明 Notes：

"住"和"居住"的区别是：*The differences between "住" and "居住" are as follows:*

1. "居住"只能指较长时间的居住，不能指短时间居住。"住"可以是长时间居住，也可以指短时间居住。*"居住" only refers to long-term residence, while "住" can apply to both long-term and short-term residence.*

（13）我在上海住/居住了四年了。

（14）*我在上海只居住了一天。

（15）我在上海只住了一天。

（16）*昨晚我在朋友家居住的。

（17）昨晚我在朋友家住的。

2. "住"后面可以带人、处所或时间宾语，"居住"后面只能带时间宾语，如例（13）。*"住" can be followed by people or by a place or time as its object, while "居住" can only be followed by a time as its object as in (13).*

（18）*这样的房子能居住人吗？

（19）这样的房子能住人吗？

zhùmíng 著名 →P600 "有名"

用法 Usage：

形容词 *a.*

有名。*Famous; well-known.*

（1）听说作这个讲座的是一个著名的作家。

（2）这几首世界古典乐曲是很著名的。

说明 Notes：

"著名"和"有名"都表示名声在外，名字为大家所熟知。*Both "著名" and "有名" indicate a reputation, a name that is well-known.*

它们的区别是：*Their differences are as follows:*

1. "著名"着重于突出、显著，给人较深的印象。"有名"着重于有名气。"著名"的词义比"有名"重。*"著名" emphasizes being prominent and impressive, while "有名" emphasizes being well-known. "著名" is more famous than "有名."*

2."著名"是褒义词,修饰的名词都是突出的、显著的,为人们称道的人物、作品、事物、地方等,多用于积极意义方面。"有名"是中性词,可以指好的人或事物,也可以指坏人、坏事物。"著名" is a commendatory word, and the nouns it modifies are prominent, outstanding and commendable people, works, things or places. It is often used with a positive meaning. "有名" is a neutral word, referring to people or things, either good or bad.

zhuānmén 专门 →P459"特意"

用法 Usage:

副词 ad.

特地,特别。表示限定范围,把动作、行为集中施与某一目标或对象。修饰双音节动词或动词短语,多用于口语。*On purpose; specially. It indicates that an action or behavior is limited to a certain scope and done only to a certain target. It modifies disyllabic verbs or verbal phrases and is more used in spoken language.*

（1）老师专门给我辅导了两个小时。

（2）李阿姨专门负责留学生宿舍的清洁工作。

形容词 a.

有专长的,专业的。*Specialized; professional.*

（3）她受过专门的训练,所以钢琴弹得那么好。

（4）在计算机软件开发上,他是个专门人才。

说明 Notes:

"专门"和"特意"的词义、用法基本相同。在叙述句中,可以互相替代。*The meaning and usage of "专门" and "特意" are basically the same. They are interchangeable in declarative sentences.*

（5）他今天特意/专门给我送来了我们一起去西藏旅游时的相片。

它们的区别是：*Their differences are as follows:*

1."专门"多用于口语。"特意"多用于书面语。"专门" *is more used in spoken language while* "特意" *is more used in written language.*

2."专门"还有形容词用法。"特意"只有副词用法。"专门" *can also be an adjective whereas* "特意" *can only be an adverb.*

zhuǎn 转

用法 Usage:

动词 v.

1.旋动,改换方向、位置。*To turn; to change direction or position.*

（1）到路口,向右转。

（2）你把脸转过来,别背对着别人聊天。

2.改换形势、情况、状态等。后面常带形容词,组成"转……为……、由……转……"的结构。*To change a situation, condition, state, etc., often followed by an adjective to form the structure of* "转...为..." *or* "由...转...".

（3）天气渐渐转冷了,小心别感冒了。

（4）今天的天气由阴转晴了。

（5）手术以后,病人已经转危为安。

3.把一方的物品、信件、意见等,通过中间方传送到另一方。如:"转告、转播、转发、转车"等。*To forward, to transfer or pass on an article, letter or opinion to the other side through a medium or intermediary, as in* "转告,转播,转发,转车."

（6）我们房间的电话是88764390转9。

（7）我已经把邮件转给经理了。

说明 Notes:

"转"后面带的形容词或动词多为单音节词,如"转好、转暖、转晴"等。*Adjectives or verbs after* "转" *are largely monosyllabic words as in* "转好,转暖,转晴."

zhuǎnbiàn 转变 →P685"转化"

用法 Usage:

动词 v.

转换,变化,表示由一种情况变到另一种情况。*To transform or change from one state to* another.

（1）一个人要转变自己的思想是不容易的。

（2）他的学习态度慢慢地转变了。

说明 Notes:

"转变"可以做"有、开始"的宾语，一般指情况向积极方面或符合说话人愿望方面变化。"转变" can serve as an object of "有" or "开始." It usually indicates that a situation changes for the better or in agreement with the desire of the speaker.

zhuǎnhuà 转化 →P684"转变"

用法 Usage:

动词 v.

转变，改变。多指向相反方向变化。一般不带宾语。可以带补语"为、成"后再带宾语，表示转化的结果。To transform or convert, mainly towards the opposite direction. Generally, it does not take any objects. But it can take a complement such as "为" or "成," which is followed by an object showing the result of change.

（1）他的病情已经向好的方面转化了。

（2）在零度以上，冰就转化为水。

说明 Notes:

"转变"和"转化"的区别是：The differences between "转变" and "转化" are as follows:

1."转变"着重于"变"，即和以前有所不同，表示已经有一定或全部结果。"转化"着重于"化"的过程，即朝着与以前方向、状态相反的方面变化，还没有到最后的结果。"转变" emphasizes "变", that is, things are somewhat different from what they were in the past — with certain or all desirable results. "转化" emphasizes the process of "化," that is, changes are happening towards the opposite direction or state and no final results have been reported.

（3）他的思想转变了。（他的思想和以前不同了。His thought is different from what it was before.）

（4）他的思想转化了。（他的思想在向与以前相反的方面转变中，还没有最后的结果。His thought has begun to change towards a different direction, but no result has been achieved.）

"转化"是动态的，要表示结果，必定要用上"为、成"等补语。"转化" is dynamic. To indicate a result, it has to go with a complement such as "为" or "成."

2.语法上"转变"可以带宾语，如"转变立场、转变思想"等。"转化"却不可以。Grammatically, "转变" can take an object as in "转变立场，转变思想" while "转化" cannot.

3."转化"的词义范围比"转变"大。"转化" covers a wider range of meanings than that of "转变."

zhuāng 装

用法 Usage:

动词 v.

1.把东西放进容器内。To put something into a container.

（1）书包太小了，那么多书装不下。

（2）瓶子里装满了水。

2.把物品放到运输工具上（与"卸"相对）。To load something onto a transport vehicle (as opposed to "卸").

（3）快把箱子收拾好，要装车了。

（4）乘客已经上了飞机，但是行李还没装上飞机。

3.装配，安装。To install; to fix.

（5）新房子里电灯装好了吗？

（6）现在学校的教室里都装了无线网络和空调。

4.修饰，化妆，扮演。To decorate; to dress up; to act as.

（7）在电视剧里,他装成一个卖香烟的老头。

（8）她太年轻了,怎么也装不像奶奶。

5. 假装。To pretend.

（9）在学习上一定不要不懂装懂。

（10）他不想跟我打招呼,装着没看见就走过去了。

名词 n.

1. 包装的样子。A form of package or binding.

（11）你要买的啤酒是瓶装的还是罐装的?

（12）这套书有精装、平装两种。

2. 演员化妆时穿戴、涂抹的东西。Stage costume and makeup.

（13）她不想吃夜宵,还在后台慢慢下装呢。

3. 行装,装备。Luggage; traveling bag.

（14）孩子们很喜欢春游,都已经整装待发了。

zhuàngkuàng 状况 →P686"状态"

用法 Usage:

名词 n.

事物表现出来的现象和形式、状态。前面常有修饰语。一般不用"的"。A phenomenon, state or situation presented by things, often preceded by a modifier without "的."

（1）改革开放后中国的经济状况比过去好多了。

（2）他很想了解贫困地区老百姓的生活状况。

zhuàngtài 状态 →P686"状况"

用法 Usage:

名词 n.

人或事物表现出来的状况或情态。前面常有修饰语。一般不用"的"。A state or condition presented by someone or something, often preceded by a modifier without "的."

（1）她的精神状态一直很好。

（2）学习情绪影响到学习状态,最后要影响到学习效果。

说明 Notes:

"状况""状态"都可以表示事物所表现的某种样子、情形。Both "状况" and "状态" can indicate a certain state or situation presented by something.

它们的区别是：Their difference is as follows:

"状况"着重指事物表现出来的外表形态。"状态"着重指人或事物呈现出的外在和内在的具体情况本身。While "状况" emphasizes the external appearance of something, "状态" focuses on the specific condition both external and internal a person or thing presents.

zhǔn 准

用法 Usage:

动词 v.

准许,许可。多用于否定句式。To permit; to allow. It is often used in negative sentences.

（1）教室内上课时不准吃东西!

（2）老师准你到中级班上课了?

形容词 a.

准确,表示动作和标准一样。Accurate, showing that an action conforms to the standard.

（3）他的发音很准。

（4）这块表的时间不准了,已经慢了五分钟。

副词 ad.

一定,强调事实一定是这样。Definitely, emphasizing that "This is the fact."

（5）他今天没来上课,准是在宿舍睡觉。

（6）我对北京很熟悉,去那儿怎么走,听我的准没错。

名词 n.

标准,准则。常常儿化。Standard, norm, often going with the suffix "儿."

（7）说话要有个准儿,不能乱说。

(8) 做事情要有个准，没达到这个标准，等于没做。

说明 Notes:
"准"还用作词缀。用在名词前，表示程度上虽不完全够格，但仍可以作为某类事物对待。如"准妈妈、准爸爸、准北京人、准平原"等。"准" can also be used as an affix. When it is used before a noun, it expresses a quasi state of someone or something, though it is not actually in full degree, as in "准妈妈，准爸爸，准北京人，准平原."

zhǔnbèi 准备 →P609"预备"

用法 Usage:
动词 v.

1. 事先进行安排、筹划。To make preparations; to plan things ahead.

（1）早饭已经准备好了。

（2）为了给爷爷过生日，妈妈准备了很长时间。

2. 打算，考虑。To plan to do something; to consider doing something.

（3）我们准备去游览黄山。

（4）他们准备包饺子。

说明 Notes:
"预备"和"准备"都是事先安排、筹划的意思，可以互相替换。Both "预备" and "准备" mean planning ahead and therefore they can replace each other.

（5）晚饭我们已经准备/预备好了。

它们的区别是：Their differences lie in:

1. "准备"在句子中可以用作名词。"预备"不可以。"准备" can serve as a noun in a sentence, but "预备" cannot.

（6）*我们已经做好了预备。

（7）我们已经做好了准备。

2. "预备"可以组成"预备队员、预备干部、预备队"。"准备"不能。"预备" can join some other words to form expressions such as "预备队员, 预备干部, 预备队," but "准备" cannot.

zhǔnshí 准时 →P209"及时"

用法 Usage:
形容词 a.

不迟于也不早于规定的时间。Punctual; on time.

（1）高铁到达上海很准时，一分钟也不差。

（2）玛丽每天都准时到教室。

说明 Notes:
"准时"和"及时"都可用作形容词。Both "准时" and "及时" can serve as an adjective.

它们的区别是：Their differences are as follows:

1. "准时"的时间点是原来就规定的，要求施事者在规定的时间点不早不迟地到达。"及时"的时间点比较灵活，是施事者正赶上对方需要的时候到达。"准时" sets a point of time, requiring a person to start taking an action at exactly that time, neither early nor late. "及时" is more flexible about the time: he who takes the action is just required to arrive at a time that meets the needs of the other party.

（3）你来得真及时，我正想请人帮我抬一下箱子呢。

2. "及时"还有副词用法。"准时"没有。"及时" can be used as an adverb, but not "准时."

zhuó 着

用法 Usage:
动词 v.

1. 穿（衣）。To wear (clothes).

（1）小学生都有校服，着装整整齐齐。

（2）他是个富家子弟，一辈子吃着不用愁。

2. 贴近，接触，挨上。To get close to; to come into contact with; to touch.

（3）飞机准时安全地着地了，大家拍手欢呼起来。

（4）他不是个说话不着边际的人。

3. 把力量或注意力集中于某一方面。*To concentrate on.*

(5) 做事情不能总着眼于有多少钱可拿。

(6) 解决了拼音和书写的问题,现在我要着力于语法的练习了。

4. 使附着在别的物体上。*To apply to.*

(7) 那幅画,我要开始着色了。

(8) 他做事常常不着痕迹,是个很小心的人。

5. 派遣。*To send, to dispatch.*

(9) 他们很快就着人送来了我的签证。

说明 Notes:

"着"是多音词。另见P640"着 zhāo"、P640"着 zháo"、P645"着 zhe"。 *"着" is a polyphonic word. See also P640 "着 zhāo," P640 "着 zháo," P645 "着 zhe."*

zǐxì 仔细 →P499"细心"

用法 Usage:

形容词 *a.*

1. 细心。做谓语、状语等。*Careful. It serves as a predicate or an adverbial.*

(1) 他看书看得很仔细,所以看得不快。

(2) 做完作业要仔细地检查一遍。

2. 小心,当心。*Cautious; watchful.*

(3) 下雪天,路很滑,走路仔细点儿。

(4) 写汉字一定要仔细,多一点少一点就是不同的两个字。

说明 Notes:

"细心""仔细"都是形容词,表示做事时精神集中,注意到每一个细节的意思。在句子中可以做谓语、定语、状语、补语。*Both "细心" and "仔细" are adjectives, meaning that one focuses one's mind on what one is doing and on every detail. Both can serve in a sentence as the predicate, attribute, adverbial, or complement.*

它们的区别是:*Their differences are as follows:*

1. "细心"的反义词是"粗心",表示"用心细密、不疏忽"的意思时,可以和"仔细"互换。"仔细"的反义词是"马虎""粗略",词意侧重动作行为周密而认真,不放过细小的地方。*The antonym of "细心" is "粗心." It means doing things with care, not ignoring anything. It can be replaced by "仔细." The antonym of "仔细" is "马虎" or "粗略." Its meaning focuses on being careful, not ignoring the details.*

2. "仔细"可以重叠成"仔仔细细",修饰动词。"细心"不能。*"仔细" can be reduplicated as "仔仔细细" to modify a verb. But "细心" cannot.*

(5) 他又仔仔细细地找了一遍,终于找到了。

zì 自 →P76"从"、P593"由"、P690"自从"

用法 Usage:

代词 *pron.*

自己。多用于构词或固定结构,如"自以为是、自作聪明、自娱自乐"等。单用时做主语、宾语。*Oneself, often used to form words or set phrases such as "自以为是,自作聪明,自娱自乐." When used alone, it can serve as a subject or an object.*

(1) 她自说是打工者,可我觉得不像。

(2) 他自以为水平很高,但实际上并不是这样。

副词 *ad.*

自然,当然。表示情况的发生合乎情理。*Naturally, certainly, indicating that things happen reasonably.*

(3) 他这样做,自有他的道理。

(4) 他们十年不见了,自有说不完的话。

介词 *prep.*

表示"从、由"的意思。*Indicating the meaning of "从、由."*

1. 用在动词前面或后面,表示处所的起点,跟处所词语、方位词语组成介词短语,做句子状语或补语。*Used before or after a verb to show the starting point of a location. It goes with words of a location or position to form a prepositional phrase, serving as an adverbial or complement.*

(5) 这列火车自上海开往北京。

(6) 我们班的留学生大多来自韩国。

2. 与"而"组成固定格式"自……而……"，表示处所的范围。如："自上而下、自下而上、自左而右"等。*Going with "而" to form the fixed structure of "自…而…," indicating the range of a location as in "自上而下, 自远而近, 自下而上, 自左而右."*

(7) 一群人自远而近跑了过来。

(8) 我们自上而下坐船游了长江。

3. 表示时间的起点。与名词、动词或动词短语、小句组合。*Indicating a starting point of time, used with a noun, verb, verbal phrase or clause.*

(9) 自改革开放以来，中国的经济发展得非常快。

(10) 自今天起，我不说英语了，就说汉语。

说明 Notes:

1. 介词"自"只限于用在"来、寄、选、出、抄、录、摘、译、引、转引"等少数动词后面。*The preposition "自" is used only after a few verbs such as "来, 寄, 选, 出, 抄, 录, 摘, 译, 引, 转引."*

2. "自"作为代词和副词时，只用于书面语，作为介词时，口语用得也不多。*As a pronoun or adverb, "自" is used only in written language. As a preposition, it is not often used in spoken language.*

3. "自"跟"从"表示时间、地点或来源时，用法基本相同。*The uses of "自" and "从" are basically the same when they indicate a time, location or origin.*

它们的区别是：*Their differences are as follows:*

① "自"可以用在某些动词后面。"从"不能。*"自" can be used after some verbs whereas "从" cannot.*

(11) *他来从伦敦大学。

(12) 他来自伦敦大学。

(13) 他从伦敦大学来。

② "从"与处所名词组合，可以表示经过的地方。"自"不能。*"从," when combined with nouns of a location, can indicate the places you pass by, but "自" does not have this usage.*

(14) *她自我家经过的时候，进来看了我。

(15) 她从我家经过的时候，进来看了我。

③ "从"可以表示发展、变化、范围的起点。"自"不能。*"从" can mean the starting point of a development, change or range, but "自" cannot.*

(16) *自不懂到懂，自不理解到理解，都需要一个过程。

(17) 从不懂到懂，从不理解到理解，都需要一个过程。

④ "自"比"从"书面语色彩更重。*"自" is more used in written language.*

4. "自"跟"由"都能引进处所或时间的起点，表示由来或出处。文言意味都比较重。*Both "自" and "由" can introduce a starting point of a location or time to show where something starts. Both carry a flavor of classical Chinese.*

它们的区别是：*Their differences are as follows:*

① 表示由来或出处时，"由"多用于动词前面。"自"多用于动词后面。*Indicating where something is from, "由" is often used before a verb whereas "自" is often used after a verb.*

(18) 这个快递是由山东寄来的。

(19) 这个快递寄自山东。

② "由"可以表示发展、变化、范围的起点。"自"不能。*"由" can mean the starting point of a development, change or range, but "自" does not have this usage.*

(20) *自低级到高级，我们一般有二十四个班。

(21) 由低级到高级，我们一般有二十四个班。

③ "由"的其他义项和用法。"自"不能。

Other meanings and usages of "由" do not apply to "自."

zìcóng 自从 →P688"自"

用法 Usage:

介词 prep.

只指过去时间的起点。常和"以来、以后"组成固定格式。Since. Referring to a starting point of time in the past, it is often used with "以来" or "以后" to form fixed structures.

（1）自从学习第三册课本以来,我的汉语水平提高了很多。

（2）自从她离开以后,我们这儿就安静多了。

说明 Notes:

"自"和"自从"的区别是：The differences between "自" and "自从" are as follows:

1. "自"可表示过去的时间起点,也可表示现在或将来的时间起点。"自从"只能表示过去的时间起点,常常以某一件事或动作为起点,如例（1）（2）。The starting point of time expressed by "自" can be past, present or future. However, the starting point of time expressed by "自从" can only be in the past, often illustrated by a certain event or action as in (1) and (2).

2. "自"后面的宾语可以是单音节词,也可以是双音节词或短语。"自从"后面的宾语一般不能是单音节词,多是短语。The object after "自" can be either a monosyllabic word or a disyllabic word or a phrase, but the object after "自从" cannot be a monosyllabic word. In most cases, they are phrases.

3. "自"多用于书面语,而"自从"多用于口语。"自" is often used in written language, but "自从" is more used in spoken language.

4. "自从"没有"自"的其他义项和用法。Other meanings and usages of "自" do not apply to "自从."

zìdòng 自动 →P681"主动"

用法 Usage:

形容词 a.

1. 用在动词前面,表示出于自愿,主动。Voluntary; willing. It is used before a verb.

（1）他已经自动退出了高级汉语班,要求去中级班学习。

（2）这次志愿者活动大家自动报名参加。

2. 用在动词前面,表示动作、行为不凭借人为力量进行。Automatic; spontaneous. Appearing before a verb, it indicates that the action or behavior happens automatically, not relying on human forces.

（3）一连下了三天大雨,森林大火就自动熄灭了。

（4）草地上有很多自动浇水开关,定时给花草浇水。

3. 用在名词前面,形容不用人力而用机械装置自行操作的。Automatic. It is used before a noun, indicating the automatic operation of a mechanical device not relying on human forces.

（5）这是一台全自动洗衣机。

（6）现在已经有智能自动锅做中国菜了。

说明 Notes:

"主动"和"自动"都是形容词,都表示不靠外力推动而自己进行动作。Both "主动" and "自动" are adjectives, and both mean to carry on something without external forces.

它们的区别是：Their differences are as follows:

1. "主动"着重于自觉自愿,凭人的主观能动性去做,态度积极。"自动"着重于不被动,不是被强迫,积极的意思比"主动"轻。"主动" emphasizes the willingness, initiative and a positive attitude. "自动" emphasizes not being passive or not being forced. The positive meaning of "自动" is not as strong as "主动."

2. "主动"只用于人。"自动"可以用于人,也可用于物。"主动" can only apply to people,

whereas "自动" can apply to both people and things.

（7）她常常主动帮助别人。
（8）围观的人群渐渐自动离去。
（9）*大火烧了一天一夜后主动熄灭了。
（10）大火烧了一天一夜后自动熄灭了。

3."自动"还可表示不用人力而用机械装置直接操作。"主动"没有这一意义。"自动" can refer to the automatic operation by a mechanical device, without relying on human forces, but "主动" does not have this meaning.

（11）*这台主动洗碗机是他从国外带来的。
（12）这台自动洗碗机是他从国外带来的。

4."主动"可受"不"和程度副词的修饰。"自动"一般不能。"主动" can be modified by "不" and degree adverbs, but "自动" cannot.

（13）*他学习上很/不自动。
（14）他学习上很/不主动。

5."主动"可构成"主动性、主动权"等。"自动"一般不能。"主动" can form such words as "主动性,主动权," but "自动" cannot.

zìháo 自豪

用法 Usage:

形容词 a.

因为自己或与自己有关的集体或个人具有优良品质或取得伟大成就,内心感到豪迈、光荣。Proud; taking pride in oneself (or related individuals or affiliated institution) for excellent qualities or great achievements.

（1）我为我的祖国而自豪。
（2）妈妈为有我这样的儿子而感到自豪。

说明 Notes:

"自豪"和"骄傲"都是形容词,都有表示自豪的意思,有时常常连用。Both "自豪" and "骄傲" are adjectives and can mean being proud. Sometimes they are used together.

它们的区别是：Their differences are as follows:

1."自豪"侧重自感豪迈,充满豪情。让人自豪的多是重大事情。"骄傲"侧重感到确实了不起。引以骄傲的既可以是重大事情,也可以是一般事情。"自豪" emphasizes feeling pride in something significant. "骄傲" emphasizes feeling pride in something amazing, which can be either significant or ordinary.

（3）爷爷因为有一个聪明的孙子,感到非常骄傲。

2."骄傲"形容词用法中,词义为自以为是,看不起别人,是贬义词。"自豪"没有这个词义。The adjective usage of "骄傲" means "conceited, arrogant, looking down upon others," which is a derogatory term. "自豪" does not have this meaning.

（4）*自豪使人落后。
（5）骄傲使人落后。

zìjǐ 自己 →P694"自我"

用法 Usage:

代词 pron.

1.复指句子中已经出现的人(跟"别人"相对)。Oneself. A reflexive pronoun, it refers to the person who has appeared in a sentence (as opposed to "别人").

① 与人称代词或人名连用作主语、宾语,常表现为同位语的形式,有强调作用。Used with a pronoun or a name to serve as a subject or an object, often in the form of an apposition for emphasis.

（1）哥哥很难过,觉得他自己不能帮妹妹。
（2）爸爸自己也没有钱,怎么会给你钱？

② 单用。可做主语、宾语或修饰语。Used by itself, "自己" can serve as a subject, object, or modifier.

（3）我昨天在家,自己做了一个蛋糕。
（4）在国外,你要照顾好自己。

③ 用在名词前,表示属于说话者本人这方面的人、处所或单位。"的"可以不用。Used before a noun, "自己" indicates that people, places, or institutions are from the speaker's side. "的" can be omitted.

(5) 我从来不去外面过生日,就在自己家里过。

(6) 他是我们德国留学生自己的德国老师。

④ 用在动词前,有时也指事物。Used before a verb, "自己" sometimes refers to something.

(7) 不知道为什么,这扇门自己就开了。

(8) 大夫说,这颗牙自己会长出来的,你不用担心。

2. 泛指句中没出现的某个主体。Referring to a certain topic that has not been expressed in the sentence.

(9) 把困难留给自己,把方便留给别人。

(10) 自己的事情自己做。

说明 Notes:

1. "自己"在"自己人、自己兄弟"等固定结构中,表示"亲近的、亲密的、关系密切的"意思。"自己" means "亲近的,亲密的,关系密切的" in such set structures as "自己人,自己兄弟."

(11) 大家都是自己人,不用客气。

2. "自己"与"别人、人家、群众"等词相对,但又能与其组成同位语,如"人家自己会吃的、别人自己早去了、群众自己会教育自己的"。"自己" is opposite to words like "别人,人家,群众," yet it can go with them as an apposition as in "人家自己会吃的,别人自己早去了,群众自己会教育自己的."

zìjué 自觉 →P681"主动"

用法 Usage:
动词 v.

自己感觉到,自己觉得。相当于"感觉",常用于书面语。To be conscious of; to be aware of. Similar to "感觉," it is often used in written language.

(1) 他自觉自己学得很不错。

(2) 他自觉可以在这里开个韩国饭店,因为他学过韩国烹调。

形容词 a.

自己有所认识而觉悟。做状语时,后面一般不加"地"。Conscious; on one's initiative. When used as an adverbial, it usually does not take "地" after it.

(3) 她是个事事、处处都很自觉的学生。

(4) 大家都应该自觉遵守学校的纪律。

说明 Notes:

"主动"和"自觉"都可以用作形容词,有的句子"主动"和"自觉"可以替换。Both "主动" and "自觉" can be used as an adjective, and they are interchangeable in some cases.

它们的区别是:Their differences are as follows:

1. "主动"着重指出于自觉,强调人的主观能动性,自己积极地行动,不用外界、别人要求而已经有所行动,含义积极。"自觉"侧重于自己有所觉悟、有所认识,无须别人督促、监督。"主动"比"自觉"的范围更大、程度更进一步。"主动" emphasizes initiative out of self-consciousness, which means someone has already taken an action positively without being demanded by others. "自觉" emphasizes that someone is conscious and knowing and there is no need to urge or supervise him. "主动" is used in a wider range and carries a deeper degree than "自觉."

(5) 这孩子学习很主动。

(6) 这孩子学习很自觉。

2. "主动"所搭配的词语多能表示施事者主观意愿语义的动词,如"主动帮助、主动回答、主动提出、主动道歉、主动要求、主动表示、主动争取"等。"自觉"所搭配的词语一般多是表示客观要求这样或应该这样进行意思的动词,如"自觉遵守、自觉接受、自觉改正、自觉服从、自觉完成、自觉维护"等。Words going with "主动" are mainly verbs indicating the subjective intention of the doer, as in "主动帮助,主动回答,主动提出,主动道歉,主动要求,主动表示,主动争取." Words going with "自觉" are often verbs indicating objective requirements, as in "自觉遵守,自觉接受,自觉改正,自觉服从,自觉完成,自觉维护。"

3. "自觉"有动词的用法,"主动"只有形容词用法。"自觉" has the verb usage whereas "主动" can only be an adjective.

zìrán 自然 →P94"当然"、→P463"天然"

用法 Usage:

名词 n.

自然界。Nature; the natural world.

(1) 人类可以利用自然、改造自然,但是不能过分。

(2) 人类还没有完全认识自然。

形容词 a.

1. 不勉强,不呆板,不局促。Natural; feeling at ease; not feeling uncomfortable.

(3) 她是新同学,但是她对大家的态度很自然。

(4) 他脸上的表情很不自然,一定发生什么事了。

2. 自由发展的,不经人力干预的。Natural; free from affectation.

(5) 小孩子吵架,过一会儿自然就又和好了。

(6) 这点皮外伤过几天自然就好了。

副词 ad.

1. 表示事物按其内部规律发展变化,没有人为外力干预。Indicating that things will develop or change in accordance with their intrinsic laws without the interference of outside or human forces.

(7) 人体具有自然免疫的能力,所以不要轻易吃药。

(8) 船到桥头自然直。

2. 表示理所当然的,加强肯定的语气,相当于"当然"。Naturally, emphasizing the affirmative tone. It is similar to "当然。"

(9) 你把玻璃窗打破了,自然要赔偿。

(10) 你是学生,自然应该上课。

连词 conj.

连接分句或句子,表示追加说明或意思有转折。Naturally. Linking clauses or sentences, it indicates an additional explanation or a transition in meaning.

(11) 这本书我买到了,自然,是跑了四个书店才买到的。

(12) 这本书我买到了,自然,如果很贵,我是不会买的。

说明 Notes:

1. "自然"用作形容词时,一般修饰人的神态、表情、动作等。不修饰其他事物。When "自然" is an adjective, it is often used to modify a person's manner, expression, action rather than other things.

(13) *他虽然是外国人,却能说一口自然的北京话。

(14) 他虽然是外国人,却能说一口流利的北京话。

2. "自然"用作副词时,与"当然"一样,都表示在事理上和情理上必然如此、理所当然的意思,表示肯定语气。When "自然" is an adverb, it is similar to "当然。" It carries an affirmative tone and means that it is logical and reasonable for something to be what it is or something to happen.

它们的区别是：Their differences are as follows:

① "自然"着重于顺理成章、理应如此。语气比较缓和,语意比"当然"轻。句子中常常有表示顺理成章、理应如此的原因或条件的词语。"自然" emphasizes being a matter of course, with a relatively soft tone and a lighter semantic meaning than "当然。" One can find words that show the cause or condition that explains everything as a matter of course.

(15) 学习努力的人有了问题,自然会去请老师解答。

(16) 天冷了,自然会想到要多穿件衣服。

② "当然"着重当如此,不用怀疑的意思。可以单独回答问题。"当然" emphasizes being so rightly and undoubtedly. It can be used to answer a question by itself.

(17) 作为学生,学习当然是最重要的。
(18) 上口语课,当然应该让学生多说话。
(19) A:你是清华大学的学生?
　　B:当然,给你看我的学生证。

3. "自然"和"天然"都表示没有人为或外力干预而产生的。Both "自然" and "天然" indicate something produced through no interference of artificial or outside forces.

它们的区别是:Their differences are as follows:

① "天然"着重于是自然界天生的,强调指事物本身的来源,如"天然气、天然冰、天然磁铁"等。"自然"着重于指事物状态的形成过程,强调事物状态是本身自由发展而成的,如"自然村、自然经济、自然灾害、自然条件"等。以上两种例词中"天然"和"自然"都不可替换。"天然" focuses on something growing in the natural world: it is about the source of a thing such as "天然气,天然冰,天然磁铁." "自然," by contrast, emphasizes the process of formation of a thing: it is formed as a result of free development as in "自然村,自然经济,自然灾害,自然条件." No mutual replacement is permitted in the two groups of examples here.

② "天然"在句子中,一般只做定语。修饰对象是"景色"时,可以和"自然"替换,一般情况下,两个词不能互换。"天然" serves only as an attribute in a sentence. When "景色" is the target it describes, it can be replaced by "自然." Ordinarily, the two words cannot replace each other.

③ "自然"可以做定语、状语。"天然"不能做状语。"自然" can serve as an attribute and an adverbial, but "天然" cannot serve as an adverbial.

zìshēn 自身

用法 Usage:

名词 n.

自己(强调是自己本身,不是他人、他物)。多指代前面出现过的名词或代词。Self; oneself (emphasizing oneself instead of other people or other things). It often refers back to the noun or pronoun in the previous part.

(1) 两个警察不顾自身安危,冲进大火去救那个孩子。
(2) 大自然的发展有自身的规律。

zìwǒ 自我 →P691 "自己"

用法 Usage:

代词 pron.

自己,自身。Self; oneself.

1. 多用在双音节动词前面,表示这个动作是自己向自己进行的。Often used before a disyllabic verb to indicate an action done to oneself.

(1) 下面我们自我介绍一下,互相认识认识。
(2) 关于昨天的事情,我首先做一下自我批评。

2. 用在动词后面做宾语,表示自己本身正在进行的实际状况。Used after a verb as an object, it indicates an actual state that one is experiencing.

(3) 一个人要正确地认识自我,才会不断地取得进步。
(4) 人类在改造世界的同时也在不断地改造自我。

说明 Notes:

"自己"跟"自我"都可以指代人。Both "自己" and "自我" refer to oneself.

它们的区别是:Their differences are as follows:

1. 在词义上,"自己"着重自己本身,不是别人。"自我"着重自己对自己。Semantically, "自己" emphasizes oneself instead of other people, whereas "自我" emphasizes something done to oneself.

2. "自己"可以做主语。"自我"不能做主语。"自己" can serve as a subject while "自我" cannot.

3. "自己"可以与指代的名词、代词同位做句子的成分。"自我"不能。"自己" can serve as an apposition of the noun or pronoun referred to, serving as a constituent in a sentence while "自我" cannot.

（5）*老师，电影票我们自我买了。
（6）老师，电影票我们自己买了。

4. "自我"可以修饰"感觉、意识"等名词。"自己"不能。"自我" can modify such nouns as "感觉" and "意识," but "自己" cannot.

5. "自我"可以与"完善、欣赏、批评、表现、推荐、反省"等以人为对象的动词组成主谓短语，作句子的谓语或宾语，一般"自己"不这样用。"自我" can be used to form subject-predicate phrases with verbs which take people as objects, such as "完善,欣赏,批评,表现,推荐,反省." It serves as the predicate or object in the sentence. Generally "自己" does not have this usage.

（7）*他经常在镜子面前自己欣赏。
（8）他经常在镜子前面自我欣赏。
（9）他经常在镜子面前自己欣赏自己。

6. "自己"和"自我"都可作句子宾语。"自己"着重于人的具体的、物质性的"本身"，可以做"责备、折磨、要求、批评、检查、放松、相信、原谅、恨、靠"等动词的宾语。"自我"不能。"自我"着重于抽象的、精神上的意识，可以做"塑造、失去、剖析、创造"等动词的宾语，一般"自己"不能。Both "自己" and "自我" can be the object in a sentence. "自己" emphasizes one's specific and physical "本身," and can be the object of verbs such as "责备,折磨,要求,批评,检查,放松,相信,原谅,恨,靠." "自我" emphasizes one's abstract and spiritual awareness, and can be the object of verbs such as "塑造,失去,剖析,创造."

7. "自我"可以受"真实的、迷惘的、死去的、虚幻的"等词语的修饰。一般"自己"不能。"自我" can be modified by words like "真实的、迷惘的、死去的、虚幻的," while "自己" usually cannot.

zōnghé 综合 →P155"概括"

用法 Usage:
动词 v.

1. 把各种不同而互相关联的事物或现象组合在一起。To synthesize different but correlated things or phenomena.

（1）这是综合教材，包括了语法、口语、阅读等很多内容。
（2）这是个综合大学，什么专业都有。

2. 把分析过的对象或现象的各个独立而互相关联的部分、属性组合成一个统一的整体（与"分析"相对）。To combine independent but correlated parts and properties of the analyzed objects or phenomena into a comprehensive unity (as opposed to "分析").

（3）做研究，首先要学会分析和综合。
（4）我们把大家的意见综合了一下，一共有四个方面的问题。

说明 Notes:

"综合"和"概括"都有表示归纳汇集在一起的意思。Both "综合" and "概括" can mean to bring something together.

它们的区别是：Their differences are as follows:

1. "综合"着重于经过分析把事物或现象的各个部分、各个属性组合成一个统一的整体，是分析以后的汇总过程，词义含有包容性。"概括"着重于经过提炼把事物的共同特点或主要内容归结、总括在一起，是对原材料进行提炼的过程，词义含有筛选性。"综合" emphasizes combining the parts and properties of the analyzed things or phenomena into a comprehensive unity, which is a summarizing process after analysis. The meaning is inclusive. "概括" emphasizes combining the common features or main contents of things after selection, which is a process of raw material selection. The meaning is selective.

2. "综合"多用于独立而又相互关联的事物或现象。"概括"多用于本质、特点、性质、要点和人的品性等。"综合" often applies to independent but correlated things or phenomena, whereas "概括" mainly applies to things such as nature, feature, property, key points, and human character.

3. "综合"和"概括"都有形容词用法，但是词义不同。"综合"多用作定语。"概括"多用作状语或与"是……的"连用。Both "综合" and "概括" can be adjectives, but their meanings are different. "综合" is often used as an attribute, while "概括" is often used as an adverbial or used with "是…的."

zǒng 总 →P287"老"、P696"总是"

用法 Usage:

形容词 a.

1. 全部的，全面的，整体的。Total; overall; general.

(1) 同学们在学习上总的情况不错。
(2) 在要不要考试的问题上，大家总的认识是一致的。

2. 主要的，为首的，领导的。如："总店、总司令、总工会、总经理、总书记"等。Chief; head; general. For example, "总店,总司令,总工会,总经理,总书记."

副词 ad.

1. 表示推测或估计，含有"大概、大约、至少、起码"的意思，但语气比较肯定。At least. It indicates a speculation or estimation and carries the meaning of "大概,大约,至少,起码," but with a more affirmative tone.

(3) 他没来上课总有三四天了吧。
(4) 今天的气温总在三十度以上。

2. 表示持续不变，一直如此或经常如此，相当于"一直、一向、老是、经常、往往"等。如果"总"后面用上"也"，一般用在否定句中。Always; consistently; invariably. It is similar to "一直、一向、老是、经常、往往." When "总" is followed by "也," it is generally used in a negative sentence.

(5) 星期六晚上，酒吧的人总很多。
(6) 心情不好的时候，我总想家。
(7) 这几个字很难写，我总也写不好看。

3. 相当于"终归、终究、毕竟、一定"等词语的意思。After all; anyway; anyhow. It is similar to "终归,终究,毕竟,一定."

(8) 人只要活着，就总要碰到各种各样的问题。
(9) 不要着急，飞机票总会买到的。

动词 v.

汇集，总括。To assemble; to add up to.

(10) 这几笔钱总起来算一下，一共多少？

说明 Notes:

1. "总"和"老是"只有在表示持续不变，相当于"经常、一直、一向"时，意义相同，用法一样。"总"的其他用法，"老是"都没有。"总" and "老是" are similar in meaning and usage only when they indicate "invariably" and when they are equivalent to "经常,一直,一向." "老是" does not have the other usages of "总."

2. "总"和"老"都能表示持续不变的意思。"总" and "老" both indicate being invariable.

它们的区别是：Their differences are as follows:

① "老"有表示程度高的用法。"总"没有。"老" can indicate a high degree, yet "总" cannot.

(11) *大楼建得总高。
(12) 大楼建得老高。

② "总"有表示"推测、终究"两种用法。"老"没有。"总" can mean both "推测" and "终究", yet "老" cannot.

zǒngshì 总是 →P287"老"、P696"总"

用法 Usage:

副词 ad.

1. 表示持续不变，一直如此或经常如此，很少例外,相当于"一直、一向、老是、经常、往往"等。Invariably; always; all the time; having few exceptions. It is similar in meaning to "一直,一向,老是,经常,往往."

(1) 每天早上他总是到运动场跑步。
(2) 她对小孩儿总是那么耐心、那么热情。

2. 表示不管怎么样,最后必然如此的意思。相当于"终归、终究、毕竟、一定"。Eventually; no matter what happens. It is similar in meaning to words like "终归,终究,毕竟,一定."

(3) 不管怎么样,儿子总是要回家过春节的。
(4) 休息一下吧,再怎么忙也总是要吃饭睡觉吧。

说明 Notes:

1. "总"和"总是"表示持续不变、经常、一直的意思,用法基本相同。区别是:
"总"可以用在否定句,"总是"不能。When "总" and "总是" mean "invariably" or "always," their usages are basically the same. Their difference is that "总" can be used in a negative sentence, yet "总是" cannot.

(5) *他总是也不告诉我每天晚上在做什么。
(6) 他总也不告诉我每天晚上在做什么。

2. "老是"与"总是"的意义、用法相当。区别是:"老是"是口语词。"总是"通用于口语和书面语。"老是" and "总是" are similar in meaning and usage. They differ in that "老是" is more colloquial whereas "总是" can be used in both spoken and written language.

3. "老"与"总是"在表示动作或状态反复、持续、经常方面,用法相近。"老" and "总是" are used more or less the same way in expressing the repetition, continuity, or frequency of an action or behavior.

它们的区别是: Their differences are as follows:

① "老"可以表示程度,"总是"不能。"老" can be related to a degree, but "总是" cannot.

(7) *那个教室总是小的,没几个人能坐。
(8) 那个教室老小的,没几个人能坐。

② "总是"可以表示"终究、总归、一定、"等意思。"老"不能。"总是" may mean "eventually, finally, after all," but "老" cannot.

(9) *孩子老孩子,哭了一会儿就没事了。
(10) 孩子总是孩子,哭了一会儿就没事了。

zǒngsuàn 总算

用法 Usage:
副词 ad.

1. 表示经过相当长的时间或一定的努力以后,某种愿望终于实现。句末要带"了"。At long last, indicating a desire is finally reached after a long time or a lot of effort. "了" is used at the end of the sentence.

(1) 经过老师耐心的辅导,我总算懂了。
(2) 一连下了十多天的雨,今天总算晴了。

2. 表示虽然不太理想,但大体上还过得去,够得上。Indicating being reasonably good, though not ideal.

(3) 虽然才考了六十多分,但总算有进步了。
(4) 他的字写得总算不错了。

3. 含有侥幸的意思,表示碰上某种机遇,有"幸亏"的意思。Indicating a stroke of luck because of a favorable opportunity. It is similar to "幸亏."

(5) 总算在下雨之前回到了家,否则要淋湿了。
(6) 末班车总算赶上了,不然就回不了家了。

动词 v.

表示总括起来计算。To total up; to add up to.

(7) 我们家的收入总算起来比去年增加了百分之十。
(8) 总算今年的留学生人数,比去年多了五百名左右。

说明 Notes:

"总算"多用于口语。"总算" is often used in spoken language.

zǒngzhī 总之

用法 Usage:
连词 conj.

1. 总起来说。总结上文,表示下文是总结性的话。常用于句首,后面可以停顿,可以不停顿。In a word, indicating a summary with the concluding remarks after it. It is often used at the beginning of a sentence, and followed by a pause. Yet the pause is optional.

(1) 哥哥想去北京,妹妹想去西安,弟弟想出国。总之,大家的想法都不一样。

(2) 这个饭店有法国菜、印度菜、阿拉伯菜等等。总之,外国名菜这里都能吃到。

2. 由于某种原因,不能或不愿说出确切的情况,只说出概括性的结论,含有"反正"的意思。Anyway. It indicates that the speaker just makes the concluding remarks without going into the details. It is similar to "反正."

(3) 打球也好,游泳也好。总之,能锻炼身体的运动都可以。

(4) 无论你同意不同意,总之我要参加这个比赛。

说明 Notes:

"总之"是"总而言之"的省略形式。用"总而言之"时,后面必须有停顿。用"总之"时,停顿可有可没有。"总之" is abbreviated from "总而言之." When "总而言之" is used, there must be a pause after it. When "总之" is used, the pause is optional.

zǒu 走

用法 Usage:
动词 v.

1. 人或鸟兽的两脚交换向前移动,步行。可带"着、了、过"。可重叠。后面带"在、向",表示"走"的处所、方式或目标(多为抽象意义的目标)。(Of man, bird or animal) to walk or move on foot. It can be followed by "着, 了, 过," and can appear in a reduplicated form as "走走." When followed by "在" or "向," it refers to the location, manner or destination (often abstract in nature) of "走."

(1) 我从来没走过这样的路。

(2) 你们出去走走吧,附近景色不错的。

(3) 祝愿你走向美好的明天!

2. (按一定的规律)移动,挪动。可带"着、了、过"。可带少数名词宾语(多限于棋类活动用语)。(Following a certain rule) to move. It can go with "着, 了, 过," and can be followed by a few nominal objects (limited to use in chess games).

(4) 电子钟不走了,可能要换电池了。

(5) 这步棋走错了。他不应该走马,应该走炮。

3. 表示离开原来的地方,有的句子可以用"去"替代。可带"了"。可作补语。To leave. It can be replaced by "去" in some cases and followed by "了," serving as a complement.

(6) A:我要走了,你送送我吧!
    B:你要走/去了? 我开车送你去机场吧。

(7) 这封信快点儿寄走。

4. 表示通行或经过的处所。相当于"通行、经过"。To pass through. It is similar to "通行,经过."

(8) 我们走隧道去动物园吧。

(9) 现在申请护照只要走一次手续就可以了。

5. 指亲友之间来往,交往,走动。可带"了、过"。可重叠。(Between relatives and friends) to visit, call on. It can be followed by "了" or "过" and appear in a reduplicated form as "走走."

(10) 小时候,妈妈常常带她走亲戚。

(11) 朋友之间要互相多走走。

6. 漏出,泄漏。一般不能单独做谓语,须带宾语或补语。可带"了、过"。*To leak; to let out. It can be followed by "了,过," but it cannot serve as a predicate unless it takes an object or complement.*

（12）自行车车胎走气了，我要先去打气。

（13）我要回国的事，你们千万别走了风声（指消息 *Indicating leakage of the news*）。

7. 改变或失去原样。可带"了、过"。后面必带名词宾语（限于"样、味、调、形、题、神"等的儿化）。*To change or lose the original shape, flavor, color, etc. It can be followed by "了" or "过," and it must come before a noun object (limited to such words as "样, 味, 调, 形, 题, 神" ending with "儿").*

（14）这茶叶已经走味儿，不香了。

（15）他唱歌老走调儿。

8. 交上，碰上（好运气）。*To have good luck.*

（16）这几天他走了桃花运了。（指很多女孩子喜欢他。*It means that many girls like him.*）

（17）我从来没走过好运。

9. 跑，奔跑，奔逃，逃走。多用于文言书面语，或固定词语，如"飞沙走石、平原走马、不胫而走"等。*To run; to run away. It is often used in written language or set phrases such as "飞沙走石,平原走马,不胫而走."*

10. 委婉的说法，指人死。*(Of euphemistic use) to pass away.*

（18）老人昨天晚上安静地走了。

说明 Notes:

"走"可以带结果补语、趋向补语、可能补语等。*"走" can be followed by a resultative complement, directional complement, potential complement, etc.*

表示的意思列表如下：*Their meanings are listed in the following table:*

所带补语 Complement	表示的语义 Semantic meaning	例句 Examples
结果补语 Resultative complement	1. 表示走的样子有了变化。补语多由"成"充当。*Indicating the changed manner of walking. The complementary word is mostly "成."*	（1）他走成方步了。 （2）她走成S形了。
	2. 表示走的动作达到了某一处所或某一结果。补语多由"到、对、错、了"等词语充当。*Indicating that the action of walking has reached a location or a certain result. The complementary words are usually "到, 对, 错, 了," etc.*	（3）我们是走到火车站的。 （4）他还没走到家门口，就听到了家里孩子的歌声。 （5）我走错路了，所以来迟了。
趋向补语 Directional complement	1. 表示到达的处所或地位。补语多由"上"充当。*Indicating reaching a location or position. The complementary word is mostly "上."*	（6）他慢慢地沿着楼梯走上了顶楼。 （7）今年九月，他就要走上新的工作岗位了。 （8）他走上厂长这个职位以后，就更忙了。
	2. 表示走动作的继续状态。补语多由"下去"充当。*Indicating the continuous state of walking. The complementary word is mostly "下去."*	（9）你沿着这条路一直走下去，就到了。
	3. 表示走的动作离某一固定点近来或远去。补语常由"过去、过来"充当。*Indicating walking to or away from a certain point. The complementary word is usually "过去" or "过来."*	（10）他走过来对我说了几句话，就离开了。 （11）你走过去看就看得清楚了。

续 表

所带补语 Complement	表示的语义 Semantic meaning	例句 Examples
可能补语 Potential complement	1. 表示能不能离开。可能补语多由"成、开"充当。Indicating whether it is possible to leave. The complementary word is mostly "成" or "开."	(12) 下雨天,他们走得成吗? (13) 这么晚了,我们走不成了。 (14) 事情没做完。现在我还走不开。
	2. 表示有没有能力进行"走"的动作或"走"的动作达到一定的程度。补语多由"了、动"等充当。Indicating the ability or inability to walk or how far one can walk. The complementary word is often "了" or "动."	(15) 他那么大的年纪是走不动的。 (16) 他的脚伤了,走不了了。 (17) 一个下午是走不了五十里路的。
	3. 表示能不能胜过别人。Indicating if one is able to surpass the others.	(18) 说到走路,他可走不过我。 (19) 象棋,我走不过他。

zú 足

用法 Usage:

名词 n.

1. 脚,腿。Foot; leg.

(1) 他高兴得手舞足蹈。

(2) 你知道画蛇添足这个成语故事吗?

2. 指足球运动。Football.

(3) 全国女足比赛要在我们这个城市进行。

(4) 我们希望中国男足能早日进入世界足坛。

形容词 a.

充实,足够。Sufficient, enough.

(5) 这里的农民已经过上了丰衣足食的小康生活了。

(6) 我能有八级的汉语水平就心满意足了。

副词 ad.

1. 完全,充分,够得上某种数量或程度。Fully, as much as, in terms of quantity or degree.

(7) 这袋苹果足有十斤多。

(8) 做完这些作业,两个小时足够了。

2. 足以,值得。多用于否定式。Sufficiently; enough; often used in the negative form.

(9) 他说的话无足轻重,你不用担心。

(10) 一餐吃十个馒头,不足为奇。我能吃十五个呢。

zǔ'ài 阻碍 →P701"阻止"

用法 Usage:

动词 v.

阻挡去路,妨碍人或事物通过或发展。可带名词性、动词性宾语或兼语。To block the way; to hinder the movement or the development of someone or something. It can take a noun or a verb or a pivotal structure as its object.

(1) 快靠边,不要阻碍别人走路!

(2) 我每做一件事,他都要出来阻碍一下。

名词 n.

指阻碍前进的事物。Obstruction; obstacle; encumbrance.

(3) 要想做一件别人没有做过的事,阻碍是不会少的。

(4) 在人生的路上,一定会遇到各种各样的阻碍。

说明 Notes:

"阻碍"带的名词性宾语多表示人或事物所做的行为、动作,如"交通、发展"等。一般不带单纯的事物名词。The nominal object of "阻碍"often refers to the behavior or action of someone or something such as "交通,发展." It cannot take pure object nouns.

zǔzhǐ 阻止 →P700"阻碍"

用法 Usage:

动词 v.

使人或事物不能前进或停止行动。可带名词性、动词性宾语及兼语。可带"了、着、过"。To prevent things from moving forward; to stop an operation. It can take a noun, a verb or a concurrent structure as its object. It can go with "了,""着," or "过."

（1）谁也阻止不了孩子们发起的划船比赛。

（2）半夜三点了,他们还要去喝酒,要想办法阻止他们。

说明 Notes:

1."阻碍"和"阻止"都是直接使人或事物不能进行某种行为、动作或活动。一般不表示这个行为、动作"影响"另一个行为、动作的意思。Both "阻碍" and "阻止" mean to prevent someone or something from a certain behavior, action or activity. In general, they do not indicate that this behavior or action has an "impact" on another behavior or action.

（3）*你说话声音太大,阻碍/阻止我们做练习了。

（4）*建筑工地上发出的声音常常阻碍/阻止我们上课。

以上两句中的"阻碍/阻止"都应换为"影响"。"阻碍" and "阻止" in the above two examples should be replaced by "影响."

2."阻碍"和"阻止"都有表示妨碍别人行动的意思。Both "阻碍" and "阻止" can mean to prevent other people from taking an action.

它们的区别是：Their differences are as follows:

①"阻碍"着重于描述妨碍某种行为、动作的客观现实,一般都是指不利的情况对某事物的妨碍,句子多是客观情况的描述。"阻止"着重于表示要停止别人、别的事物发展的主观意图,对象多是他人的具体行动。行为的意图可以是善的,也可以是恶的。句子的主观意图强,如例（2）。"阻碍" emphasizes an objective reality that hinders a behavior or an action. Generally, it refers to the hindrance to things created by some unfavorable condition and the sentence often gives an objective description. "阻止" emphasizes the subjective intention of stopping someone or something from developing, and the object is largely some specific action of other people. The intention of the action might be good or evil. And the sentence reveals a strong will as in (2).

②"阻碍"有名词用法。"阻止"没有名词用法。"阻碍" can be used as a noun but "阻止" cannot.

zǔchéng 组成 →P522"形成"

用法 Usage:

动词 v.

（由部分或个体）组合成（整体）。To form; (A whole entity) to be composed of (individual parts).

（1）韩国学生和非洲学生组成了一支留学生足球队。

（2）中国是一个由五十六个民族组成的多民族国家。

说明 Notes:

"形成"和"组成"都是动词。Both "形成" and "组成" are verbs.

它们的区别是：Their differences are as follows:

1.在词义上,"形成"是指通过发展变化而成为具有某种特点的事物或出现某种情形、局面。这种特点或事物、情形、局面以前没有,是通过发展变化才产生的。"组成"侧重于指由本来已经存在的不同的个体、部分形成一种新的组织、整体等。Semantically, "形成" refers to the appearance or formation of a situation with its own features through development and change. "组成," by contrast, focuses on the composition of a new organization or entirety that is made up of different parts.

2. "形成"的主语或者宾语多是抽象的事物,如"局面、想法、理论、习惯、特色"等,"形成"前面可以加上"正在、逐渐、已经"等副词。此外,"形成+名词"还可以做"开始、提倡、鼓励"等动词的非名词性宾语。"组成"涉及的对象多为具体的人、事物或组织结构。The subject or object of "形成" is mostly something abstract such as "局面,想法,理论,习惯,特色." Preceding the term "形成" may be adverbs such as "正在,逐渐,已经." In addition, "形成+n." may serve as the non-noun object of verbs like "开始,提倡,鼓励." The target of "组成" is mostly concrete people, things or organizations.

3. "形成"后面有时加介词,构成"形成于"的格式;"组成"的格式为"由……组成"。"形成" is sometimes followed by a preposition to form the pattern of "形成于." "组成," by contrast, usually appears in the pattern of "由...组成."

zuì 最 →P113"顶"

用法 Usage:

名词 n.

表示居于首位的意思,没有能比得上的。如:"中华之最、世界之最"。First; best. For example, "中华之最,世界之最."

副词 ad.

1. 表示程度达到极点,超过所有同类的人或事物,多用在形容词、动词前面。(Of degree) indicating the extreme, surpassing all people or things of the same kind. It is often used before an adjective or a verb.

(1) 我们班这个德国学生最高。

(2) 她是我最好的朋友。

2. 表示估计或所能允许的最大限度,多用在形容词前面。(Of what is allowed or permitted) indicating the maximum. It often appears before an adjective.

(3) 飞机上可托运行李最重不能超过20公斤。

(4) 调查报告最晚明天要交到我手里。

3. 表示情绪、印象、态度评价等达到了极点,多用在动词(一般为心理动词)前面。(Of sentiment, impression, attitude or appraisal) indicating the utmost. It often appears before a verb (usu. a psych verb).

(5) 他最愿意带孩子们玩游戏。

(6) 她最喜欢别人送鲜花给她。

(7) 他是个最能帮助同学解决困难的人。

4. 表示方位的极限,用在某些方位词前面。(Of location) indicating the utmost within reach, used before locative words.

(8) 我的钱包在衣柜的最里边。

(9) 我坐在教室的最后面。

说明 Notes:

1. "最"前面不能出现"不",如"*不最多、*不最漂亮、*不最重要"。表示否定应为"不是最多、不是最漂亮、不是最重要"。"最" cannot be preceded by "不", as in "*不最多,*不最漂亮,*不最重要." The right version should be "不是最多,不是最漂亮,不是最重要."

2. "顶"和"最"作副词时,用法基本相同。When "顶" and "最" are adverbs, their usages are basically the same.

它们的区别是: Their differences are as follows:

① "顶"多用于口语。"最"通用于口语和书面语。"顶" is more used in spoken language whereas "最" is used in both spoken and written language.

② "最"能与形容词组合,直接修饰名词,如"最好办法、最高气温",能用在"先、后、前、本

质、新式"等形容词前面。"顶"没有这些用法。"最" can be used with an adjective to modify a noun directly as in "最好办法,最高气温." It can also be used before adjectives such as "先, 后, 前, 本质, 新式.""顶" does not have this usage.

③"顶"与某些形容词构成词组充当状语时,有一定的让步口气,因此,在完全没有让步意味的句子中,不能用"顶"。"顶" can be used with some adjectives to form phrases as adverbials. In this case, it carries a tone of concession. Therefore, "顶" cannot be used if there is no concessive meaning in a sentence.

(10) 你顶多只能吃三个馒头。
(11) *我们要顶大程度地发动同学参加运动会。
(12) 我们要最大限度地发动同学参加运动会。

zuìchū 最初 →P263"开始"

用法 Usage:

名词 n.

最早的时候,刚开始的时候。At the beginning; at the start.

(1) 最初这里是一片稻田,现在都盖起了楼房。
(2) 我最初看到她的时候,她还是个小姑娘。

说明 Notes:

"最初"和"开始"名词用法都表示事情、行动、现象的起初时间,用法基本相同。Both "最初" and "开始" mean the early time when a thing, action, or phenomenon began to appear. They are used more or less in the same way.

它们的区别是:Their differences are as follows:

1."开始"有动词用法,如"比赛开始了"。"最初"不能。"开始" can serve as a verb as in "比赛开始了," but "最初" cannot.

2."开始"可以做宾语,如"我们要争取有个良好的开始"。"最初"不能。"开始" can serve as an object as in "我们要争取有个良好的开始," but "最初" cannot.

zuìjìn 最近

用法 Usage:

名词 n.

指说话前后不久的日子。可用在主语前,也可用在主语后。Recently; lately. It is used to indicate a short time before or after one speaks. It can appear either before or after the subject.

(1) 最近我去了一趟上海。
(2) 我们班最近又来了两位新同学。

说明 Notes:

1."最近"还表示路程或距离最短的意思,是副词"最"和形容词"近"组成的短语。"最近" can also mean the shortest route or distance, which is formed by the adverb "最" and the adjective "近."

(3) 他家离学校最近。

2."最近"和"近来"都表示离说话不远的时间。Both "最近" and "近来" can mean not far from the time when one speaks.

它们的区别是:Their differences are as follows:

①"最近"可指说话前,也可指说话后的时间。"近来"只指说话前不久的时间。"最近" means a short time either before or after one speaks, whereas "近来" only means a short time before one speaks.

(4) *这京剧近来几天还会再演出。
(5) 这京剧最近几天还会再演出。

②"最近"可以作定语用。"近来"不可以。"最近" can be used as an attribute, but "近来" cannot.

(6) 最近的气温很低,老人要注意保暖。
(7) *近来的气温很低,老人要注意保暖。

③ 注意以下句子:More sentences for attention:

(8) *近来我有考试,不能出去旅游。

(9) 最近我有考试,不能出去旅游。
(10) *我近来有空就会去看他。
(11) 我最近有空就会去看他。

zūnjìng 尊敬 →P704"尊重"

用法 Usage:

动词 v.

重视而且恭敬地对待。可带名词性宾语(只指人称代词或指人的名词)。可受程度副词的修饰。To respect; to show high esteem for someone. It can be followed by nominal objects (only personal pronouns or nouns), and it can be modified by degree adverbs.

(1) 学生们很尊敬老师。
(2) 他们对父母、老人都非常尊敬。

形容词 a.

可尊敬的。一般用在对人的称呼上。如:"尊敬的女士们、先生们,尊敬的老师"等。Respected, generally used to address people as in "尊敬的女士们,先生们;尊敬的老师."

zūnzhòng 尊重 →P704"尊敬"

用法 Usage:

动词 v.

恭敬并重视。可带名词性宾语。可受程度副词的修饰。To respect and think highly of. It can be followed by a noun as its object and can be modified by a degree adverb.

(1) 我们要尊重科学、尊重人才、尊重发展的自然规律。
(2) 她对她的老师很尊重。
(3) 尊重别人的习惯、想法是有修养的表现。

说明 Notes:

"尊敬"和"尊重"都表示恭敬、敬重的意思。Both "尊敬" and "尊重" mean to respect.

它们的区别是: Their differences are as follows:

1. "尊敬"着重于恭敬。"尊重"着重于看重、重视。"尊重"使用范围比较大,表示的意义的程度比较深。"尊敬" emphasizes being respectful, whereas "尊重" emphasizes thinking highly of. "尊重" can be used in a wider range, and its meaning is deeper.

2. 适用对象上,"尊敬"着重于对人,特别用于下级对上级、晚辈对长辈,或对值得敬佩的人。"尊重"的对象可以是人,包括一切可以敬重的人,也可以是集体或抽象事物,如"事实、意见、权利、主权、人格、科学、知识、劳动、风俗、习惯"等,表示严肃对待的态度。In terms of objects, "尊敬" often applies to people, especially, subordinates vs. superiors, juniors vs. seniors, or us vs. admirable people. The objects of "尊重" can be people, including all admirable people, or abstract things such as "事实,意见,权利,主权,人格,科学,知识,劳动,风俗,习惯," showing a serious attitude.

3. "尊敬"没有"尊重"的表示庄重、重视的意思与用法。Different from "尊重," "尊敬" does not have the meaning of "thinking highly of."

(4) *我们很尊敬她的意见。
(5) 我们很尊重她的意见。

zuǒyòu 左右 →、P278"控制"、P371"前后"、P638"掌握"

用法 Usage:

名词 n.

1. 方位名词。多用于空间,指事物的左边和右边。Left and right. A locative noun related to space, it refers to the left and right sides of a thing.

(1) 左右邻居都知道楼里有个热心帮人的小伙子。
(2) 西湖白堤的左右两边种有柳树和桃树。

2. 用在数量词后面,表示比某一数量稍多或稍少。About; around; approximately. It follows a quantifier to indicate a little more or a little less.

(3) 这件衣服要三百元左右。

(4) 一个二十岁左右的年轻人走了过来。

3. 指随从在身边的人。*Entourage, attendants.*

(5) 经理让左右退出房间，他要单独跟这个人谈话。

(6) 他的左右都穿着黑衣服，戴着黑眼镜。

动词 *v.*

表示对人、对事物控制、支配的意思。*To control; to dominate.*

(7) 这样大的场面，那么多的人，我觉得他左右不了。

(8) 我们不能总是受他的左右。

说明 Notes:

1. "左右"分开，或与动词、名词连用，或与数量词连用，表示重复多次。*When "左右" is separated, or used with a verb, a noun, or a quantifier, it means repeating a number of times.*

(9) 他左思右想，还是没想出个办法来。

(10) 左也不是，右也不是，你到底要我怎么样？

(11) 我们左一张右一张地照，照了很多相片。

(12) 他左一趟右一趟地去你家，你都不在家。

2. "左右""上下""前后"都可以用在数字后面。*"左右," "上下," and "前后" can all be used after a numeral.*

它们的区别是：*Their differences are as follows:*

① 使用范围不同。"左右"和"上下"可以表示年龄的大小、重量的多少。"前后"不可以。*They apply to different categories, for example, "左右" and "上下" can refer to age and weight, meaning "about," but "前后" cannot.*

(13) *那位老人七十五岁前后。

(14) 那位老人七十五岁上下/左右。

(15) *这只小猪有四十斤前后了。

(16) 这只小猪有四十斤左右/上下了。

② "左右"和"前后"都可以表示时间，只是用法有所不同。"左右"可以用于时点或时段。"前后"只能用于时段。"上下"不能用于时点或时段。*Both "左右" and "前后" can mean time, yet their usages are different. "左右" can mean either a point or a period of time, whereas "前后" can only mean a period of time. "上下" cannot refer to time.*

(17) *我十五号上下回国。

(18) 我十五号左右/前后回国。

(19) *从东京到上海坐飞机只要两个小时前后/上下。

(20) 从东京到上海坐飞机只要两个小时左右。

3. "左右"跟"控制""掌握"都能表示对人、对事有把握的意思。*"左右," "控制," and "掌握" can all mean "to lord it over someone or dominate something."*

它们的区别是：*Their differences are as follows:*

① "左右"一般用于对人的把握，强调用某种力量对人或事物加以约束、限制，使听从支配。词义更接近于"控制"。*"左右" is generally used to mean lording it over people, emphasizing constraints and limitations by a certain force, and its meaning is close to "控制."*

② "左右"多用于口语。*"左右" is often used in spoken language.*

③ "左右"后面一般都带有宾语。*"左右" is often followed by an object.*

(21) *这件事/一群人他在背后左右。

(22) 他在背后左右着一群人/这件事。

④ "左右"没有"掌握"表示对人或事物客观规律控制的意思和用法。*"左右," unlike "掌握," cannot mean the mastery of objective laws.*

(23) *我们班有没有同学已经左右了这个动词的用法？

(24) 我们班有没有同学已经掌握了这个

动词的用法?

⑤ "左右"不能像"控制"那样能做具有得失意思动词的宾语。"左右," unlike "控制," cannot serve as the object of a verb with the meaning of gain and loss.

(25) *出租车失去了左右,冲下河去。

(26) 出租车失去了控制,冲下河去。

zuò 作 →P706"做"

用法 Usage:

动词 v.

1. 举行,进行。可带"了、过"。To do; to make. It can be followed by "了" or "过."

(1) 他来医院作过身体检查。

(2) 昨天下午王老师作了关于中国文化的讲座。

2. 写作,创作。宾语多表示思想文化方面的名词。To write; to compose. The objects are mainly nouns of ideology and culture.

(3) 他很有音乐才能,作曲写歌水平很高。

(4) 我不会用英语作报告。

3. 装出(某个样子)。To pretend (often meaning to present a false appearance).

(5) 他用手指在头上作了兔子的耳朵逗妹妹玩。

(6) 老师作了一个跑的动作,让大家说出"跑"这个动词。

4. 当作,作为。常与"用"连用。To regard as; to take for. It often goes with "用."

(7) 用龙井茶叶作礼物送给朋友是最好的办法。

(8) 这本护照已经作废了。

5. 起身,兴起。多用于固定词组,书面语。如"日出而作、兴风作浪、鼓声大作"等。To rise; to get up; to grow up. It is often used in set phrases in written language, as in "日出而作,兴风作浪,鼓声大作."

6. 发生,发作。多用于固定词组,书面语。如"令人作呕、周身作痛、胡作非为、为非作歹"等。To have; to feel; to show effect. It is often used in set phrases in written language, as in "令人作呕,周身作痛,胡作非为,为非作歹."

名词 n.

表示作品的意思。Writings; work.

(9) 这部小说是他的成名之作。

(10) 那幅画是世界名作之一。

zuòwéi 作为

用法 Usage:

名词 n.

1. 所作所为,行为举动。Conduct; behavior; achievement.

(1) 一个人的作为如何,取决于他的思想品德。

(2) 你的作为已经告诉我,你是一个怎么样的人。

2. 可以做的事。多指好的事情。Great deeds to accomplish. It often refers to things worth doing.

(3) 在这个 IT 平台上,你可以大有作为。

(4) 你们是一群有所作为的年轻人。

动词 v.

当作。To regard as; to take for.

(5) 我们带了面包和咖啡作为午饭。

(6) 我很难把这个专业作为自己的爱好。

介词 prep.

就人的某种身份,或事物的某种性质来说。常用在句首。As; in terms of a person's identity or status or a thing's property or nature.

(7) 作为一本教材,必须明确编写的目的和对象。

(8) 作为一名老师,帮助学生解决学习困难是你的工作。

zuò 做 →P161"干"、P163"搞"、P706"作"

用法 Usage:

动词 v.

1. 制作,制造。带一般具体实物的名词性宾语。可带"着、了、过",可重叠。*To make; to manufacture. It can be followed by nominal objects of concrete things, and can go with "着,了,过." It can appear in a reduplicated form as "做做."*

(1) 他做飞机模型,我做作业。

(2) 他八岁的时候就会做早饭了。

2. 从事或进行(一般指比较复杂的工作或活动)。*To do or engage in (usually referring to complicated work or activity).*

(3) 你做什么工作的?

(4) 他是搞科学研究的,一天到晚在做实验。

3. 写作,创作。宾语是常与思想文化有关的事情。*To write; to compose. The objects are mainly things relevant to ideology and culture.*

(5) 他还想用汉语做诗呢。

4. 举行庆祝或纪念活动。*To hold a celebration or commemorative activity.*

(6) 今天晚上我要给爸爸做八十大寿。

(7) 今天我们要给刚出生的宝宝做满月。

5. 充当,担任。可带"了、过",可重叠。可带名词性宾语和兼语。*To act as; to be. It can be followed by "了,过" and can appear in a reduplicated form as "做做." It can take a noun or a pivotal structure as its object.*

(8) 做母亲的一辈子都在为孩子操心。

(9) 那间办公室现在改做教室了。

6. 当作。*To be used as.*

(10) 我们大家都可以做您的儿女,给您养老。

(11) 竹子也可以做毛巾。

7. 结成(某种关系)。*To form a relationship.*

(12) 你可以做我的老师吗?

(13) 如果你愿意,就做我的女朋友吧。

8. 装出(某种样子)。*To pretend (often to present a false appearance).*

(14) 他仍然做出很高兴的样子跟别人玩儿。

(15) 你干吗伸舌头做鬼脸,我说错了吗?

说明 Notes:

1. "作"跟"做"都能表示从事某项活动,在表示充当或担任的意思中,可以通用。如"当作/做、叫做/作"等。表示写作、创作的意思时,也可以通用,如"作/做文章、作/做诗"等。*Both "作" and "做" mean engaging in an activity. They are interchangeable when they mean "acting as" as in "当作/做,叫做/作," or when they mean "writing or composing," as in "作/做文章,作/做诗."*

它们的区别是:*Their differences are as follows:*

① "作"着重用于举行、进行比较抽象的某种活动。宾语多是"报告、调查、研究、解释、说明、批评、斗争、总结"等双音节词,或书面语色彩比较浓的单音节词,如"词、曲、文、赋"和"恶、战、难"等。*"作" emphasizes holding or engaging in fairly abstract activities, and the objects are mainly disyllabic words such as "报告,调查,研究,解释,说明,批评,斗争,总结" or monosyllabic words, which are more formal in style, such as "词,曲,文,赋" or such words as "恶,战,难."*

"做"着重于从事某种工作或制造、制作某种具体的物品,一般都要用手劳作。宾语多是比较具体的"木工、值日、买卖、衣服、家具、练习、作业"等双音节词语和"鞋、饭、菜"等单音节词。*"做" emphasizes doing a job or manufacturing specific goods, which usually requires manual work. The objects are often specific disyllabic words such as "木工,值日,买卖,衣服,家具,练习,作业" and monosyllabic words like "鞋,饭,菜."*

② "做"能表示举行家庭的庆祝或纪念活动,如"做生日、做满月"。"作"一般不这样用。*"做" can indicate holding family celebrations or commemorative activities, as in "做生日,做满月," but "作" does not have this usage.*

③ "做"有表示"结成"某种关系的意思和用法。"作"没有这种用法。*"做" can indicate*

forming a relationship, but "作" cannot.

④"作"能表示"起身、兴起"的意思。"做"不能。"作" can mean "rise" and "grow up," but "做" cannot.

⑤"作"有名词用法。"做"没有。"作" can be a noun, but "做" cannot.

2."做"与"搞"都能替代少数具有具体意义的动词或比较复杂的抽象名词或词组。Both "做" and "搞" can be used to replace a verb with a specific meaning or a fairly complex abstract noun or a word group.

(16)他是搞/做生物方面研究的。

(17)你们先搞/做好市场调查,再制订有效的营销计划。

它们的区别是:Their differences are as follows:

① 在词义和词语搭配上,"搞"一般多用于有一定的计划,要动脑筋的动作行为,多表示大范围的第一层次意义的抽象词语,对象多为抽象事物,如"搞教育、搞艺术、搞农业"。但是"搞"也具有动词的替代性,所以也能表示一些具体的动词意义,对象也可以是很具体的事物。In terms of meaning and word collocation, "搞" is applied to an action that usually requires planning and thinking. Often, it expresses the first-level meaning of an abstract word in a large scope. Its targets are mostly abstract things such as "搞教育,搞艺术,搞农业." But "搞" may also replace a verb and so it can express the meaning of some specific verbs. Its targets may be very concrete things.

(18)请你帮我把自行车刹车搞一搞。(相当于"修理" Similar to "修理")

(19)我的衣服上有个小洞,请帮我搞一下。(相当于"修补" Similar to "修补")

"做"一般多用于指具体的、操作性强的动作行为,对象多为具体的事物。如"做饭、做练习、做卡片、做衣服、做句子"等。"做"也能带一些抽象名词,如"做学问、做报告、做研究工作、做思想工作、做群众工作、做买卖、做生意"等大多是与人有关系的抽象词语。"做" usually refers to actions and behaviors that are specific and operational. Its targets are usually concrete things such as "做饭,做练习,做卡片,做衣服,做句子." "做" may also go with some abstract nouns, such as "做学问,做报告,做研究工作,做思想工作,做群众工作,做买卖,做生意." They are mostly abstract nouns related to people.

(20)*我是做工业的,他是做农业的。

(21)我是搞工业的,他是搞农业的。

(22)*现在我去搞作业。

(23)现在我去做作业。

② 当宾语是具体的事物名词时,"搞"和"做"一般不能互相替代,因为句子的语义不同。When the object is the name of a concrete thing, "搞" and "做" cannot be used to replace each other because the meanings of the sentences are different.

(24)*手机坏了,你能帮我做做吗?

(25)手机坏了,你能帮我搞搞吗?

(26)你去搞点饭来。(想办法弄或买点饭来 Try to buy a meal)

(27)你去做点饭来。(自己动手做饭 Try to fix a meal)

3."做"与动词"干"在宾语是不具体的事情时可以替换。"做" and "干" are both verbs and they can replace each other if the object of the verb is not something specific or concrete.

(28)你下午干/做什么?

(29)我来干/做那件事。

它们的区别是:Their differences are as follows:

①"做"的宾语可以是一件具体的事情。"干"不能。The object of "做" can be something concrete, but "干" cannot.

(30)*你干作业,我来干饭吧。

(31)你做作业,我来做饭吧。

②"干"做动词,多用于口语,多用于问句。"做"通用于书面语和口语,什么句型都可用。

"干," serving as a verb, usually appears in oral Chinese. "做," however, appears in both written and oral Chinese, and in whatever sentence pattern.

③ "干"表示"担任（职务）"的词义时，一般用于军队的职务或比较低的行政职务。"做"没有这个限制。"干" carries the meaning of assuming a certain role in the army or a fairly low position in civil service. But "做" is not restricted in this respect.

（32）他在军队时，干过两年排长。

附录 量词的用法

bǎ 把

用法 Usage：

1. 用于有把手或能用手抓得起的器具。Applied to a device with a handle or one that can be grabbed with a hand, as in:

一把剪子　一把茶壶　一把扇子
一把椅子　一把火　　一把钥匙
一把尺子　一把刀　　一把伞

2. 表示能用手抓起来的数量，所抓的东西一般是细碎的、松散的。It is used to indicate the amount that can be held in a hand; what is held is usually loose or in fine scraps, as in:

一把米　　一把花儿　一把筷子
一把花生　一把钱　　一把瓜子

3. 用于某些抽象意思的名词。Applied to some abstract nouns, as in:

一把年纪　一把劲　一把力气

4. 用于能手。Meaning competent or a capable person, as in:

他干活儿是一把好手。
要完成这件事少不了他那把能手。

5. 用在动词后面，表示手的动作。Placed after a verb to indicate the action of one's hand, as in:

帮一把　　拉他一把　擦一把（脸/汗）
洗一把（脸/衣服）

说明 Notes：

1. "一把尺子"，"尺子"没有"把手"，着重于拿的时候手的动作。"A ruler (尺子)" doesn't have a hand. But why do we use "把" before it? We use "把" to emphasize the action of holding something in one's hand.

2. "一把火"是指下面有"把手"的火把数量。"一把火" is correct because it refers to the number of torches held in a hand.

bān 班

用法 Usage：

1. 用于人群。Applied to a group or crowd of people, as in:

南边走过来一班年轻姑娘。

2. 用于定时开行的交通运输工具。Applied to means of transport that starts operating regularly, as in:

下一班车　下一班飞机

bāo 包

用法 Usage：

用于计算用纸张、棉麻质地等的材料包起来成包的物品。It is used to count paper, cotton, and jute and other materials that are packed for transport, as in:

一包茶叶　一包大米　一包东西
一包饼干　一包香烟　一包白糖
一包棉花　一包书

说明 Notes：

"一包"与"一盒"有所区别。"包"的形状可以是无规则的。"盒"的形状一般是有规则的：长方形或正方形的。所以根据包装的形状，相同的东西可以有不同的量词，如"一包巧克力、一盒巧克力"。个别物品包装一样，但量词仍不同。如"一包香烟"和"一盒香烟"，南方人多用"包"。"一包" is different from "一盒." The shape of a "包" may be irregular, but that of a "盒" is regular. It could be rectangular or square or what. That is why "一包巧克力" and "一盒巧克力" are both correct: Different measure words are used to indicate different shapes of the package. Occasionally, the package might be the same in shape, but two different measure words are used, such as "一包香烟" and "一盒香烟." They mean the same, but Southerners tend to use "包" more.

bēi 杯

用法 Usage：

容器量词。用于用杯子装载的液体。*A measure word for a container, it is applied to liquids kept in cups, as in:*

一杯茶　　一杯酒　　一杯咖啡
一杯牛奶　一杯啤酒　再来一杯
再喝一杯　再倒一杯

bèi 辈

用法 Usage：

用于家族中的辈分。*Generation, as in:*

老一辈人　小一辈　　下一辈　孙辈
同辈　　　老少三辈　晚辈

bèizi 辈子

用法 Usage：

用于人的一生时间。*All one's life; lifetime. For example:*

这辈子　　下辈子　　半辈子

说明 Notes：

1. "一辈了"，表示一生。"二辈子"表示再一辈子。*"一辈子" means one's lifetime. "二辈子" means another lifetime.*

2. 用于计数就是"两辈子"。他家两辈子都是老师。*"两辈子" is used for counting. We say, for instance, "他家两辈子都是老师." It means that both the older generation (father and/or mother) and the younger generation (son and/or daughter) work as teachers.*

bèi 倍

用法 Usage：

"倍"是跟原数相等的数。某数的三倍就是用原数乘三。*"倍" means times or fold, a number equal to the original number. For instance, "某数的三倍" is three times as much as the original number.*

他的年龄是你的三倍。（如果你的年龄是二十岁，他的实际年龄就是六十岁。）*Another example: "他的年龄是你的三倍." If you are 20 years old, he would be 60 years of age.*

běn 本

用法 Usage：

用于书籍簿册。*It is used to talk about a book, a notebook or other such things, as in:*

一本书　　　一本日记　　一本杂志
一本练习本　一本小说　　一本字典
一本画报　　一本笔记本

说明 Notes：

为了在同一个词语或句子中不出现相同的字或音，"一本笔记本、一本练习本"常作为"一个练习本、一个笔记本"。*To avoid the repetition of the same word or same pronunciation in the same sentence, one might say "一个练习本，一个笔记本" instead of "一本笔记本，一本练习本."*

bǐ 笔

用法 Usage：

1. 用于钱款或与钱款有关的事。*It is used to talk about income, expenditure, or other things related to money, as in:*

一笔收入　一笔开支　一笔买卖
一笔生意　一笔交易　一笔财产
一笔债

2. 用于笔画。*It is used to talk about the number of strokes when writing a Chinese character, as in:*

"王"字有四笔。(Meaning, the character "王" has four strokes.)

这笔写得很好。(Meaning, "This stroke is well done.")

biàn 遍

用法 Usage：

"遍"做量词表示一个动作从开始到结束的整个过程，用于动作的全过程。As a measure word, "遍" indicates the whole process of an action from beginning to end. It is applied to the whole process, as in:

想一遍　说一遍　听一遍
复习一遍　预习一遍　学一遍
读一遍　问一遍　写一遍

bù 部

用法 Usage：

1. 用于内容、形式完整的书籍、影片等。Applied to a book or a film in its entirety, as in:

一部字典　一部影片　一部书
一部词典

2. 用于机器或车辆。Applied to a machine or a vehicle, as in:

一部机器　两部汽车(南方人口语常用 Often used by the southerners in spoken Chinese)

说明 Notes：

用于书时,常常是内容含量比较多的书籍。一般书的量词为"本"。When applied to books, "部" usually is large in volume. An ordinary book is referred to as "一本书."

cè 册

用法 Usage：

"册"原意指古代文字刻在竹简上,把竹简编连起来称为"册",从"册"的字形上也可见一斑。用于书籍。多用于书面语。In ancient China, Chinese characters were carved into bamboo slips. When they were combined, they were known as "册." Take a close look at the character, and you will be able to know more or less about its meaning. Today, "册" is still used to talk about books, but mostly in written Chinese, as in:

一册书　一册集邮本　课本有上下两册

说明 Notes：

"册"和"本"的区别如下：The differences between "册" and "本" are as follows:

1. "册"多用于书面语。"本"通用于口语和书面语。"册" appears more in written Chinese while "本" is used in both written and oral Chinese.

2. "本"可用于书籍和本子。"册"只用于书籍。"本" may refer to both books and notebooks, but "册" is applied only to books.

céng 层

用法 Usage：

1. 用于重叠、积累的东西。Applied to things that are placed one on top of another, as in:

两层玻璃窗　三层台阶　双层床
五层楼房　第一层　我住三层

2. 用于可以从物体表面揭开或抹去的东西。Applied to what can be opened or removed from the surface, as in:

湖上结了一层冰　桌子上有一层灰
一层土　　　　一层油

3. 用于可以分项分步的抽象事物。Applied to abstract things that can be itemized (in consideration), as in:

取消了一层顾虑　问题还得进一层考虑

cháng 场

用法 Usage：

次,用于涉及空间范围比较广或程度比较深的事物。The same as "次," applicable to things that cover a fairly large space or that go deeper than usual, as in:

一场大雨　一场大雪　一场战争
一场大病　一场大火　一场大哭
一场争论　一场灾难　一场梦

说明 Notes：

"场"另发音 chǎng，用于有场次或有场地的文娱体育活动。*Another pronunciation of "场" is chǎng. It is applied to recreational activities that are conducted in theaters or sports grounds — often in a serial, as in:*

一场电影　一场戏　　一场比赛
一场球赛　跳了一场舞

chéng 成

用法 Usage：

用于事物数量或性质的比例，把事物数量或性质定为十，十分之一为一成。*Used to talk about the ratio of a thing, both its amount and its quality. If the total is 10, then "一成" means one tenths, i.e. 10%, "二成" means two tenths, i.e. 20%, etc. etc. That is why we can say:*

三成新　　　　[*This (piece of furniture) is*] *30% new.*

九成金　　　　[*This (earring) is*] *90% gold.*

有八成希望　　[*This project or new idea*] *has 80% of a hope for success.*

chuàn 串

用法 Usage：

1. 用于能连贯起来的事物。*It is applied to things that can be strung up, as in:*

一串糖葫芦 (*a stick of sugar-coated haws*)
一串羊肉串儿 (*a shish kebab, mutton cubes roasted on a skewer*)
一串葡萄 (*a string of grapes*)
一串珍珠 (*a string of pearls*)

2. 引申用于连续发出的声音或思想。*It is applied to some sound or idea that is made or produced one after another, as in:*

一串笑声 (*a string of laughter*)
说了一大串话 (*a long string of words*)
一大串想法 (*a huge string of ideas*)

cì 次

用法 Usage：

1. 用于可以反复出现的事情。*It is applied to things that are repeated, as in:*

这次　　初次　　第一次　　第三次
上次　　下一次　有一次

2. 用于可能反复出现的事情。*It is applied to things that may repeat themselves, as in:*

一次事故　一次手术　一次战争
一次革命　一次改革　一次危机
一次试验

3. 用于可以重复的动作。*It is applied to a repeated action, as in:*

去一次　　来一次　　看一次
吃一次　　见一次面　听了一次课

dài 袋

用法 Usage：

1. 用于装在口袋里的东西。*It is applied to pocketable things, as in:*

一袋面粉　一袋大米　一袋粮食
一袋牛奶　一袋糖　　一袋盐

2. 用于水烟、旱烟、烟斗。*It is applied to shredded tobacco for a water pipe, tobacco for a long-stemmed Chinese pipe, or just an ordinary pipe, as in:*

一袋烟　抽了一袋烟

dào 道

用法 Usage：

1. 用于江河或某些长条形的东西，相当于"条"。*Like "条," it is used to describe a river or anything that resembles a long string, as in:*

一道河　　一道沟　　一道擦痕

一道缝儿　万道霞光

2.用于门、墙、关口等。形状也是长方形的。*It is applied to things rectangular in shape, such as a door, a wall or a mountain pass, as in:*

一道围墙　两道门　三道防线
一道篱笆

3.引申用于命令、题目等。*In an extended use, it is used to orders or questions in an examination, as in:*

一道命令　十道数学题　三道练习题

4.用于某些分程序的动作次数,相当于"次、遍"。*Applied to express the number of actions in a step-by-step procedure. It is similar to "次、遍," as in:*

办了四道/次手续　上了三道/遍漆
多了一道手续

5.用于用餐时,上饭菜的次数。*Course, applied to the number of dishes presented at a formal dinner, as in:*

一道汤　一道甜点心　四道菜
上了三道菜了

dī 滴

用法 Usage：

用于滴下的液体,液体一点也称一滴。*It is used to describe a liquid that may drip down. A drop of liquid is also called a drip, as in:*

一滴眼泪　一滴汗　一滴水　一滴血

说明 Notes：

可以重叠。如:"一滴滴水、一滴滴汗流下来"等。*It can be reduplicated, as in "一滴滴水,一滴滴汗流下来," etc.*

diǎn 点

用法 Usage：

1.用于少量的东西,前面数词限于"一、半",口语中数词常省去不用。*It is applied to things in a small amount, and it is preceded by two numerals only, namely, "一" and "半."*

It is omitted in oral Chinese if the numeral is long, as in:

吃一点饭　吃一点儿东西　尝点儿味道
喝点儿酒

2.用于有关事项。*It is applied to items related to ideas, suggestions, comments, etc. as in:*

一点意见　一点建议　三点体会
一点好处　三点错误　两点想法

说明 Notes：

可以重叠。如"一点点菜、有一点点甜、一点点想法"等。*It can be repeated as in "一点点菜,有一点点甜,一点点想法," etc.*

dǐng 顶

用法 Usage：

用于某些有顶的东西。*It is applied to describe things with a top, as in:*

一顶帽子　一顶帐子　一顶轿子

dòng 栋

用法 Usage：

用于计算房屋。一座房屋为一栋。*It is used to count the number of houses. One house is called "一栋," as in:*

住在三十二栋楼　两栋房子

dù 度

用法 Usage：

1.用于物质有关性质达到的程度。*It is used to describe the degree that is reached, as in:*

发烧到39度　室内温度有42度

2.计量单位名称。*The unit name in measuring, as in:*

180度　90度角　一天用电十度
经度　纬度　近视500度

3.用于行为、动作的次数,相当于"次"。*An equivalent of "次," it is used to count the number of action or behavior, as in:*

一年一度的春节　四年一度的奥运会
这个京剧曾两度公演。

duàn 段

用法 Usage：

1. 用于长条事物分成的若干部分。 *Sections of a thing that is long in shape, as in:*

　两段木头　一段马路　三段绳子
　一段管子

2. 用于时间、空间一定的距离。 *A certain distance in time or space, as in:*

　一段时间　一段路程　一段距离
　一段经历　一段历史

3. 用于以语言或音乐为形式的事物的一部分。 *A section of something that takes the form of language or music, as in:*

　一段故事　一段话　一段文章
　一段戏　一段音乐

duī 堆

用法 Usage：

用于成堆的事物或成群的人。 *People or things that are gathered or heaped together, as in:*

　一堆人　一堆土　一堆石头
　一堆东西　一堆书　一堆雪
　一堆衣服　一堆困难

duì 队

用法 Usage：

用于排成队列的人或动物。 *People or animals that are lined up, as in:*

　一队人马　一队骆驼
　空中飞过一队大雁。

duì 对　→P717 "副"、P727 "双"

用法 Usage：

用于按性别（异性）、左右、正反等配对的两个人、两个动物、两个具体的事物或抽象的事物等。 *Two persons, animals or concrete or abstract things that are paired together according to sex, left or right, positive or negative, etc.*

1. 按性别分，有： *Separated by sex:*

　一对夫妻　一对儿女　一对恋人
　一对鸳鸯等

2. 按左右分，有： *Separated by left or right:*

　一对花瓶　一对枕头　一对眼睛
　一对耳朵　一对蜡烛　一对翅膀

3. 按正反分，有： *Separated by positive or negative:*

　一对电极　一对矛盾

dūn 吨

用法 Usage：

质量或重量单位。 *Quality or weight unit, as in:*

一吨等于1 000千克。 *One ton is equal to 1,000 kilograms.*

过这座桥负重不能超过15吨。 *No vehicle is allowed to cross this bridge if it is over 15 tons.*

dùn 顿

用法 Usage：

用于吃饭、斥责、劝说、打骂等行为、动作的次数。 *The number of times of an action or behavior related to meal, scolding, persuasion, and beating, as in:*

　说了一顿　吵了一顿　批评了一顿
　打了一顿　骂一顿　一顿骂
　一顿打　一天三顿饭

duǒ 朵

用法 Usage：

用于花、云彩或类似形状东西的数量。 *The number of flowers, clouds and other things similar to them in shape, as in:*

　两朵玫瑰　一朵鲜花　一朵白云
　一朵云彩　一朵浪花

说明 Notes：

注意"一朵花""一枝花""一束花"在数量上的区别。Watch out for the difference between "一朵花，" "一枝花，" and "一束花":

"朵"着重于花的数量。"枝"着重于花枝的数量。"束"着重于很多花枝的集聚。"朵" emphasizes the number of flowers; "枝" focuses on the number of flower branches; and "束" means that many flower branches are bunched together.

fān 番

用法 Usage：

1. 相当于种类、样式。数词只限于"一"，常用于展开式的空间景象。一般后面带双音节词语。Similar to "kind" or "style," it is used to describe the scene of an opening space. It goes with only one numeral, that is, one, and it is followed by a word with two syllables, as in:

　　另有一番天地　一番风光　一番景色

2. 用于心思、言辞、过程所花的时间、精力的概数。数词限于"一、几"。It is used to describe the time and energy spent on contemplating, speech-making or doing a thing. It goes with two numerals, that is, "一" and "几," as in:

　　一番工夫　一番心思　一番口舌
　　一番好意

3. 用于费力较多、用力较大或过程较长的动作、行为次数，相当于"回、次、遍"。It is used to describe the number of times when one is engaged in strenuous work. It is an equivalent to "回,次,遍," as in:

　　打量一番　研究一番　解释一番
　　讨论一番　几番周折　三番五次地请求

4. 用于数量加了一倍。相当于"倍"，多用于工农业生产、经济方面的数字。Like "倍," it means times, fold. Often it is used to describe statistics in industry, agriculture, or other economic activities, as in:

　　翻了三番　产量多了一番

fēn 分

用法 Usage：

1. 表示计量单位名称：Unit name in measuring:

① 长度名称。如："一分（等于十厘米）"。Length, as in "一分" (equal to ten centimeters).

② 面积名称。如："十分（等于一亩）、三分土地"。Area or space, as in "十分 (equal to one mu of land), 三分土地."

③ 货币名称。如："十分（等于一角）"。currency, as in "十分 (equal to one jiao.)"

④ 时间名称。如："三十分（等于半小时）、一分（等于六十秒）"。Time, as in "三十分 (equal to half an hour), 一分 (equal to sixty seconds)."

⑤ 评定成绩。如："一百分、八十分"。Points scored in an examination, as in "一百分、八十分."

2. 表示事物、行为程度等级或成数，比例大小。Indicating the grade or ratio of a thing or a behavior, as in:

　　几分成绩　几分错误　九分把握
　　三分缺点

fèn 份

用法 Usage：

1. 整体中的一部分。Part of an entity, as in:

　　把礼物分成三份　你拿一份
　　得到了一份遗产

2. 用于不同部分搭配成组的东西。Something composed of different ingredients, as in:

　　一份饭菜　一份礼物　一份点心
　　一份快餐　一份人情

3. 用于报刊、文件、工资等。Used to talk about newspapers, documents, salaries, etc. as in:

一份报纸　一份杂志　一份文件
一份资料　一份工资

fēng 封

用法 Usage：

用于装封套封起来的东西，多指信件或电报等。*It usually refers to letters, telegrams, etc. that are kept in an envelope and then sealed, as in:*

一封信　一封电报　一封银子

fú 幅

用法 Usage：

1. 用于棉麻、丝绸、呢绒等织物。原为布、绸等纺织物的宽度。*Originally meaning the width of cloth or satin, it is now applied to fabrics woven out of cotton, jute, silk, wool, etc. as in:*

一幅布　一幅绸　两幅麻

2. 用于图画。因为中国古代的画轴大小及收藏形式像布帛一样。*Of pictures or maps. In ancient China, scroll paintings were of the same size as cloth and silk and are kept in the same way, as in:*

一幅画　一幅地图

3. 从图画引申，用于有人活动的景象或风光。*As an extension from paintings, it is used now to describe a sight or scene that features human activities, as in:*

一幅动人的场面　一幅丰收景象
一幅优美的山水风光

fù 副

用法 Usage：

1. 用于成对、成双的具体物品。两个主要部分常常是被有形无形地相连在一起。*Things in a pair. The two main parts are joined with each other tangibly or intangibly, as in:*

一副眼镜　一副耳环　一副耳机
一副对联　一副手铐　一副担子

2. 用于成套的具体物品。*Things in a set, as in:*

一副象棋　一副扑克牌　全副武装
一副麻将牌

3. 用于脸部表情。*Used to describe facial expressions, as in:*

一副笑容　一副表情　一副生气的样子
一副庄严的面孔

4. 用于嗓音。*Used to talk about human voice, as in:*

一副好嗓音

说明 Notes：

1. "幅"与"副"的区别："幅"与布帛、丝绸有关。"副"没有。*The difference between "幅" and "副" is that "幅" is related to cotton, silk or silk fabrics, but "副" has nothing to do with them.*

2. "对"和"副"的区别是：*The differences between "对" and "副" are as follows:*

① "副"着重用于成对成双的具体物品。使用范围比"对、双"小。*"副" focuses on concrete things in pairs; its scope of usage is smaller than that of "对" and "双."*

② "副"也可用于不止两个而是配套的具体事物或抽象事物。"对"和"双"不能替换。*"副" can be applied to concrete or abstract things more than two in number but put in a set. "对" and "双" cannot be replaced for each other.*

gè 个

用法 Usage：

"个"是应用最广的量词。主要用于没有专用量词的、结构相对比较完整的人或事物名词。有些名词除了专用量词之外也能用"个"。*"个" is a measure word in the most extensive use in Chinese. It is used primarily in the names for people and things that don't have special-purpose measure words to go with them and that are, comparatively speaking, complete* by themselves. And some nouns that do have special-purpose measure words to go with them may also take "个" as in:

1. 用于人。*Of person(s), such as:*
一个人　　两个小孩　　一个朋友
一个工人　一个农民　　一个演员
一个老师　一个留学生　一个医生

2. 用于人和动物的相对完整的器官,是器官的专用量词。*Of human or animal organs that are, comparatively speaking, quite complete by themselves, such as:*
一个脑子　一个鼻子　一个耳朵
一个舌头　一个肩膀　一个手指头

3. 用于完整的一个水果。*Of a complete fruit, such as:*
一个苹果　一个橘子　一个香蕉
一个桃　　一个梨

4. 用于星球。*Of a planet, such as:*
一个月亮　一个太阳　这个火星
那个土星

5. 用于湖、海等水域。*Of a lake, a sea or other areas covered by water, such as:*
一个湖　　一个海　　一个池塘

6. 用于相对完整的事件、动作。*Of an event or action that is basically complete by itself, such as:*
这个事件　做一个动作　洗个澡
敬个礼　　摔一个跟头　上了一个当

7. 用于日期、时间。*Of a date or time, such as:*
一个小时　两个月　　四个星期
一个春天　一个冬天　一个早上
一个中午　一个下午　一个晚上

8. 用于形状相对完整的食品。*Of a foodstuff whose shape is basically complete, as in:*
一个包子　一个面包　一个南瓜
一个饺子　一个蛋糕　一个鸡蛋
一个西红柿

9. 用于形状相对完整的用品。*Of any item whose shape is basically complete, as in:*
一个碗　　一个盘子　一个瓶子
一个枕头　一个盒子　一个窗户
一个灯泡　一个书包　一个箱子
一个袋子　一个柜子　一个信封

10. 用于机构、组织。*Of an institution or organization such as:*
一个政府　一个机关　一个办公室
一个医院　一个团体　一个组织
一个幼儿园　一个工厂　一个中学

11. 用于会议或有关会议的事项等。*Of a meeting or conference and their related items, as in:*
一个大会　一个讨论会　讨论三个问题

12. 用于理想、意愿等抽象事物。*Of abstract things expressing an idea, proposal, wish, etc., as in:*
一个理想　一个想法　一个主意
一个计划　一个建议　一个意见
一个惊喜　一个理由　一个道理
一个梦

13. 用于多在口头传颂的文章体裁等。*Of articles or stories that are passed on orally from generation to generation, as in:*
一个谜语　两个故事　一个笑话

14. 用于词句、语言的单位等。*Of words, sentences in language, as in:*
一个汉字　一个词　　一个句子
一个成语

15. 用于结构相对完整的建筑物等。*Of a building whose structure is complete by itself, as in:*
一个城市　　一个工厂　　一个学校
一个商店　　一个车站　　一个村子
一个教室　　一个体育馆　一个游泳池
一个飞机场

16. 用于动词和约数之间。*Placed between a verb and an approximate number, as in:*
走个六七十里　　喝个四五瓶啤酒
吃个五六个钟头　差个两三岁

17. 用于带宾语的动词后面,有时表示动量,有时表示随便、轻快之意。后面的名词如果是单音节,多为儿化,实际上是省略数词"一"。*Placed after a verb with a following object, it sometimes indicates a momentum and sometimes ease and briskness. If the following noun is a monosyllable word, it takes "儿" without the numeral "一," as in:*

见个面儿　　说个话儿　　照个相儿
娶个媳妇　　生个孩子　　写个字儿

18. 用于动词和补语之间,使补语略带宾语的性质(有时跟"得"连用,作用为引出补语)。*Placed between a verb and a complement, it turns the complement into a kind of object (Sometimes it goes with "得" to introduce the complement), as in:*

吃个饱　　玩儿个痛快　　说个清楚
笑得个不停　　扫得个干干净净

说明 Notes：

量词"个"和"没"或"有"连用,构成"没个""有个"的格式,用在少数形容词或动词前面,表示否定和肯定的意思。多用于否定句或肯定否定疑问句。*When the measure word "个" is used together with "没" or "有," it constitutes the structure of "没个" or "有个." And it is placed before a few adjectives and verbs to indicate a positive or negative meaning. This usage often appears in a negative sentence or an appositive-negative question, as in:*

你说起来有个完没个完？
这么便宜的东西,没个不买的。

gēn 根

用法 Usage：

1. 用于带根的蔬菜。*Used of a vegetable with roots, as in:*

一根胡萝卜　　一根小葱

2. 用于可数的头发或汗毛等。*Used of hair or fine hair on the human body, both of which are countable, as in:*

三四根头发　　一根汗毛　　几根胡须

3. 用于细长的、条形的东西。*Used of something thin and long, giving the appearance of a strip, as in:*

一根管子　　一根绳子　　一根头发
一根带子　　一根香蕉　　一根香肠
一根鱼骨头　　一根烟

gǔ 股

用法 Usage：

多用于具有动态的事物。*It is mostly used of a thing that is dynamic.*

1. 用于条状的东西。*Of something that takes the shape of a strip, as in:*

一股泉水　　一股暖流　　一股寒流
一股毛线　　一股绳子

2. 用于气体、气味、力气等。*Of gas, smell, or one's energy, as in:*

一股热气　　一股凉气　　一股冷气
一股香味　　一股烟　　一股劲儿

3. 用于成批的人。多指敌人或坏人。*Of people in a crowd, often the enemy or bad people, as in:*

一股土匪　　两股人马

4. 股份、股票的数量名称。*Of the amount of stocks and shares, as in:*

买了 3 000 股　　抛了 500 股
吃进 2 000 股

háng 行

用法 Usage：

用于排列整齐的人或物。*It is applied to people or things that are lined up.*

1. 用于成行的事物。*Things in a line, as in:*

一行字　　一行眼泪　　一行诗　　一行树
另起一行

2. 用于排列成行的人。*People lined up, as in:*

排成两行　　两行队伍

3. 排列成行的动物或植物。*Animals or*

plants that are lined up, as in:

一行白鹭　一行大雁　一行白菜
两行果树

hé 盒

用法 Usage：

容器量词。用于盒装，多儿化。*A measure word for containers, it is usually applied to boxes, and often goes with the Chinese character "儿," as in:*

一盒儿饼干　一盒儿茶叶　一盒儿豆腐
一盒儿粉笔　一盒儿香烟　一盒儿药
一盒儿巧克力

说明 Notes：

1. 凡是容器量词，都是名词作量词用，在后面的名词前可以加"的"表示强调。*All measure words for containers use a noun as the measure word. For emphasis, "的" is placed before the noun, as in:*

一盒儿的巧克力　一盒儿的茶叶

2. 容器量词都是名词充当的，所以它是列不完的量词类。*It is impossible to list all measure words for containers because they all use the name of the container as the measure word, as in:*

一大碗饺子　一大盘蛋糕
一罐头牛肉　一教室的留学生
一屋子人　一火车去西安旅游的人

huí 回

用法 Usage：

1. 用于事情的次数，相当于"件"。*Like "件," it is used to count the number of times something happens, as in:*

怎么一回事　没有那回事

2. 用于行为动作，相当于"次"。*Like "次," it is applied to a behavior or an action, as in:*

参观一回　参加一回　看一回
去一回　试一回　说一回

3. 用于小说、评书等，相当于"章"。章回小说的一章或说书的一个段落。*When used about a novel or what is done by a professional story-teller, it is equivalent to a chapter "章," as in:*

上一回　下一回　六十六回
且听下回分解

huǒ 伙

用法 Usage：

用于人群。*It is used as classifier for a group of people, as in:*

一伙年轻人　一伙商人

说明 Notes：

"伙"跟"群""帮"都可以用于人群。*Like "群" and "帮," "伙" can be applied to a crowd of people.*

"伙""群""帮"的区别是：*Their differences are as follows:*

1. "伙"一般用于口语，语气比较随便。多用于贬义词，如"一伙强盗"。*"伙" is usually used in oral Chinese, indicating an easy-going manner. Often, however, it is used as a derogatory word, such as "一伙强盗."*

2. "群"可以用于人，也可以用于动物。如"一群羊、一群牛"。*"群" can be applied to both people and animals "一群羊，一群牛."*

3. "帮"前面的数词限于"一"，可以加"大"，为"一大帮年轻人"。*Numerals before "帮" are limited to "一" only, and "大" could be added to say "一大帮年轻人."*

jià 架

用法 Usage：

1. 用于有支架的东西。*Something that has a support, as in:*

一架葡萄　三架屏风　两架衣服

2. 用于有机械器具。*Used of a mechanical device, as in:*

一架照相机　一架飞机　一架钢琴
一架梯子　一架望远镜

jiān 间

用法 Usage：

用于房间的数量，是计量房屋最小的单位。The name of a unit, it is used to count the number of rooms in a house, as in:

一间办公室　一间病房　一间厂房
一间教室　一间宿舍　一间屋子
一间厨房

jiàn 件

用法 Usage：

1. 用于衣类的数量，只用于上衣。The name of a unit, it is used to count the pieces of clothes for the upper part of a human body, as in:

一件衬衫　一件毛衣　一件大衣
一件雨衣　一件旗袍

2. 用于事情、案件、公文等的数量。The number of things, cases, and documents, etc. as in:

一件工作　一件大事　一件案子
一件公文

3. 用于结构比较复杂的个体器物。Individual devices that are rather complicated in structure, as in:

一件东西　一件行李　一件家具
一件礼物　一件玩具　一件包裹
一件文物　一件艺术品　一件乐器

说明 Notes：

不能说"一件裤子、一件箱子"，只能说"一条裤了、一只箱子"。Insteud of "一件裤于，一件箱子，" one has to say "一条裤子，一只箱子."

jié 节

用法 Usage：

原意为物体的分段或各段之间相连接的地方。借用于：Originally means the joint between different parts or sections of a thing, it is now applied to:

1. 自然分段的事物。Something that is naturally divided into sections, as in:

一节竹子　两节甘蔗　十节车厢
三节电池

2. 教学的课时数。Number of classes taught at school, as in:

一天八节课　上午四节课

3. 文章的段落，音乐的节拍。Different sections of an article or of the meter or tempo in music, as in:

课文有三节。　这首歌每小节三拍。

jiè 届

用法 Usage：

用于计量定期会议、毕业的班级、运动会及任职期限等。相当于"次、期"。An equivalent to "次" and "期," it is applied to regular meetings, graduating classes, sports meetings and the term of an official post, as in:

上届冠军　上届画展　三届毕业生
第28届奥运会　下一届政府
连任两届总统

jīn 斤

用法 Usage：

中国的重量单位。现行市制十市两等于一市斤。一市斤等于500克，相当于半公斤。A Chinese unit of weight, one jin is equal to 500 grams or half a kilogram. One jin is divided to 10 liang. For example:

买一斤苹果　一斤香蕉
一公斤等于两市斤。

jù 句

用法 Usage：

用于计量话语或诗文等语言的单位。Sentence. It is the basic unit of language in an article, a poem or what, as in:

一句话　一句诗　一句名言
一句歌词　一句玩笑话

juǎn 卷

用法 Usage:

原意是把纸张、布帛等软东西卷起来。用于成卷的东西。*Originally it meant to roll up paper, cotton or silk. As a noun now, it means something in a roll, as in:*

一卷中国画　一卷世界地图
一卷电线　　一卷设计图纸

说明 Notes:

"卷"另发音 juàn,用于书籍的册本或篇。*"卷" has another pronunciation, which is juàn. It now means the volume of a book (Volume 1, Volume 2, Volume 3, etc.) as in:*

这部书共有三卷：上卷、中卷和下卷。

kē 棵

用法 Usage:

用于植物。*Of a plant, as in:*

一棵草　一棵苗　一棵树　一棵大白菜

kē 颗

用法 Usage:

用于颗粒状的东西。*Of things that are small and roundish, as in:*

一颗汗珠　一颗珠子　一颗黄豆
一颗星　　一颗宝石　一颗心
一颗牙齿　一颗炮弹　一颗子弹
一颗人造卫星

kè 克

用法 Usage:

一、公制重量或质量单位。一克为公斤的千分之一。*Gram, the name of a unit for weight in the metric system. One gram is 1/1000 of a kilogram, as in:*

3 克黄金　一瓶水 550 克　1 000 克一袋

二、藏族传统计量单位。*A unit name for weight or area in the Tibetan system:*

1. 藏族传统重量单位,各地轻重不一。1 克约为 3 至 4 公斤/千克。*A unit of weight. One "克" varies from 3 to 4 kilograms in different parts of Xizang, as in:*

酥油 2 克（约 6—8 千克）
青稞 3 克（约 9—12 千克）

2. 藏族传统容量单位,各地大小不一,1 克约为 13 至 14 升。*A unit for the volume of a container in different parts of Xizang. One "克" varies from 13 to 14 liters, as in:*

1 克种子（约 13—14 千克）
2 克水（26—28 升）

3. 藏族土地面积单位,可以播种 1 克种子的耕地,面积约为 1 克地,1 藏克地大概和 1 市亩持平。*A unit for the area of a land in Xizang. An arable land where one "克" of seeds can be sowed is called a "克" of land. It is about 6.667 square meters.*

kè 刻

用法 Usage:

古代计时器漏壶中有立箭,箭上有刻度,一昼夜为一百刻。现在以钟表计时,十五分钟为一刻。*A quarter of an hour. In ancient times, however, a water clock or sand clock was used to mark the progress of time. In that clock there is a standing arrow whose graduation tells the march of time. One day and night is divided into 100 "刻." We say, for instance,*

说了三刻钟　不到一刻钟

说明 Notes:

用"刻"表示时间,一般常用为"一刻、三刻"。一般不说"二刻、两刻",而说为"半小时、三十分钟"。*When "刻" denotes a time, we usually say "一刻,三刻," not "二刻,两刻," for which we say "半小时,三十分钟."*

kǒu 口

用法 Usage:

1. 用于计算人口（数量不多的家庭人口或村子的人口）。*Used in counting the number of*

people, usually of a small family or village, as in:

五口人　四口之家

这个小山村只有六百多口人。

2. 用于猪的计量。 Used in counting the number of pigs, as in:

一口猪　六口猪

3. 用于计量有开口或有刃的器物。 Used in counting the number of devices with an opening or a blade or edge, as in:

一口钟　一口锅　一口井
一口水缸　一口宝剑　一口钢刀

4. 用于所说的话音, 数量仅限于"一"。 Used to describe a spoken language or dialect, it always goes with "一," as in:

一口上海话　一口伦敦英语
一口标准的普通话

5. 用于牙齿。 Used in talking about teeth, as in:

一口好牙　一口假牙

6. 用于口腔动作的次数。 Used in counting the number of the movement of a mouth, as in:

抽了一口烟　吸了两口气　喘了几口气
被狗咬了一口

7. 用于口腔吃、喝的动作次数。 Used in counting the number of times of action in eating or drinking, as in:

尝了一口　咬了一口　喝了一大口

kuài 块

用法 Usage：

1. 一般用于方形、长方形或其他块状的东西。 Usually it is applied to something solid or hard, in a square or rectangular shape, or without a particular shape, as in:

一块草地　一块黑板　一块招牌
一块玻璃　一块砖　一块蛋糕
一块西瓜　一块巧克力　一块糖
一块豆腐　一块肉　一块橡皮
一块金牌　一块手表　一块香皂

2. 用于某些薄型的、但是方形、长方形或其他片状的东西。 A piece of; something that is thin, but square, rectangular or without a particular shape, as in:

一块方围巾　一块毛巾　一块布
一块丝绸

3. 用于口语, 计量金币、银币或纸币, 用于纸币相当于"元"。 In oral Chinese, it is used to count gold or silver coins or paper notes. It is the same as "元" when talking about paper notes, as in:

五十块金币　三块银币　四十六块人民币
一百块美元

lèi 类

用法 Usage：

用于性质或特征相同或相似的人、事物的等级或种类。 It is used to talk about people or things that belong to the same category or have the same features, as in:

三类演员　同类物品
植物园有三万七千多类植物。

lì 粒

用法 Usage：

用于成颗粒状的细小东西, 相当于"颗"。 Like "颗," it is used to describe something that is small and roundish in shape, as in:

一粒米　一粒种子　一粒芝麻
一粒葡萄　一粒沙子　一粒药丸
一粒珠子　一粒子弹

说明 Notes：

"粒"与"颗"都用于细小的东西。"粒"更着重于体积的细小。"颗"着重于所计量的东西的完整形状。 Both "粒" and "颗" are applied to things that are small. Their difference is that "粒" emphasizes the thing being tiny while "颗" focuses on the thing being complete in shape.

liàng 辆

用法 Usage：

用于一般车辆（火车除外）。 It is used to

talk about all types of vehicles or means of transport except trains, as in:

一辆汽车　　一辆轿车　　一辆卡车
一辆摩托车　一辆坦克　　一辆自行车
一辆公共汽车

liè 列

用法 Usage：

用于成行列的事物。*It is used to talk about things that are lined up, as in:*

一列火车　一列货车　一列队伍
排成三列

mén 门

用法 Usage：

1. 用于计量科学技术、知识、课程等，可以儿化（从门类、种类引出）。*It is used to describe the number of branches of science, technology, knowledge, and curricula taught in school. Related to the classification of things being studied, it often goes with "儿." For example:*

一门功课　一门技术　一门科学
一门本领　一门（儿）知识
一门（儿）手艺　一门（儿）学问

2. 用于计量亲事、亲戚等（从一家一户一门引出）。*Used to talk about the number of relatives and marriages. (Every family has a house, which has a door, which is pronounced as "门.") For example:*

一门亲戚　一门亲事

3. 用于大炮的数量（从大炮的形状引出）。*When talking about the number of cannons (so used because of the shape of a cannon), as in:*

一门大炮　一门火箭炮

miàn 面

用法 Usage：

1. 用于表面扁平或能展开的物件。*Of something flat, smooth and/or stretchable,* as in:

一面鼓　　一面镜子　一面墙
一面红旗　十面彩旗

2. 用于见面的次数。*Of the number of meetings, as in:*

见了三面　去见他一面

3. 事物的一个表面。能独立使用，后面不需要名词。*Of the surface of a thing. It can be used independently: there is no need for a noun after it, as in:*

宝塔有四面十三层　书的两面都脏了

míng 名

用法 Usage：

1. 用于人数、名额，有一定的使用范围，不泛指，多指具有某种身份或某种职业的人。*Applied to the number of people and positions to be filled, "名" is limited in its scope of use. It cannot be extended without restrictions. In fact, it often applies to people in a certain position or profession, as in:*

一名代表　一名顾客　一名观众
一名教师　一名医生　一名警察
一名司机　一名工作人员
招聘十名管理人员　招收新生五十名

2. 用于名次。*Used to talk about ranking in an examination or competition, as in:*

考得第三名　得了第一名

说明 Notes：

1. 数量词"名"不能用于身份不明的人。如不能说"三名朋友、五名同学"。*"名," as a measure word, cannot be used to talk about someone whose identity is not clear. We cannot say, for instance, "三名朋友" or "五名同学."*

2. 不能重叠。如不能说"一名名留学生"，可以说"一个个留学生"。*"名" cannot be reduplicated. Instead of "一名名留学生," we should say "一个个留学生."*

mǔ 亩

用法 Usage：

市制土地面积单位。一亩等于十分(合六十平方丈)，约等于 6.667 公亩，约等于 666.7 平方米。*It is the unit name for the land area in the Chinese system. One mu（一亩）is approximately equal to 666.7 square meters, as in:*

我家有半亩蔬菜地、两亩水田。

pái 排

用法 Usage：

用于成行列的人或物，一般为左右排列。*It is used to describe people or things that are lined up. Usually they stand in two lines, left and right, as in:*

第一排老师　后面三排同学　有一排椅子
一排桌子　一排座位　一排房子
一排树　一排扣子

说明 Notes：

"排"和"行"都可以指"行列"。但"排"习惯上指横的行列。"行"习惯上指竖的行列。不能说"坐到前行来"，只能说"坐到前排来"。*Both "排" and "行" can mean lines ("行列"). But "排" usually means horizontal lines while "行" means vertical ones. Therefore, instead of "坐到前行来," one has to say "坐到前排来."*

pán 盘

用法 Usage：

1. 多用于圆形或有托盘的容器。*Primarily used to talk about a round container or one with a supporting plate, as in:*

四盘菜　三盘点心　一大盘水果

2. 用于计量盘绕起来的东西。*Something that is coiled up, as in:*

一盘磁带　一盘电线　一盘蚊香

3. 用于棋类比赛或某些球赛的次数。*Used to talk about the number of games of chess or ball in a competition, as in:*

下了一盘围棋　一盘象棋
打了一盘乒乓球　输了一盘
赢了一盘　和了一盘

pī 批

用法 Usage：

1. 用于大宗的货物。*Of large amounts of goods such as fruit, sea fish, etc. as in:*

一批产品　一批货物　一大批服装
一批水果　一批海鱼

2. 用于数量较多的书类、文件。*Of a fairly large number of books, documents, etc. as in:*

一批读物　一批公文　一批信件
一批绘画作品　一批文学作品

3. 用于在一起行动多数的人。*Of people engaged in the same kind of activity, as in:*

一批歌手　一批客人　一批学者
一批专家　一批美国朋友

pǐ 匹

用法 Usage：

1. 用于计量马、骡等牲畜。*Used in counting the number of domestic animals such as horses and donkeys, as in:*

一匹马　一匹骆驼　一匹骡子
一匹牲口

2. 用于计量整卷的绸缎、布匹等。古代四丈为一匹，现在为五十尺、一百尺不等。*Used in counting rolled silk, satin and cloth. In ancient China, "一匹" consists of four zhang "丈"; today it is 50 or 100 chi ("尺"). For instance:*

一匹丝绸　一匹棉布

说明 Notes：

"马"的量词只能用"匹"，骡或骆驼的量词还可以是"头"。*The horse ("马") has only one measure word, that is, "匹"; however, the camel or donkey has an additional measure word, that is, tou "头."*

piān 篇

用法 Usage：

用于文章的数量。*Used in counting the number of articles or essays, as in:*

一篇作文　一篇小说　一篇散文
一篇论文　一篇日记

piàn 片

用法 Usage：

1. 用于平而薄的东西。有时儿化。*Used to describe things thin and flat. It sometimes goes with "儿." For example:*

一片面包　一片儿肉　一片儿药
一片叶子　一片花瓣儿

2. 用于带平面的、范围较广的田野、景色、天象、水面等，数词只限于"一"。*Used to describe flat and extensive fields, waters, the sky and other scenes. There is only one measure word for it, and it is "一," as in:*

一片草地　一片稻田　一片森林
一片沙漠　一片平原　一片蓝天
一片晚霞　一片楼房　一片蓝色的海面

3. 用于景色、气象、声音、语言、心意等，数词只限于"一"。*Used to describe scenery, weather, voice, language, or one's intension or kindly feelings. Again, it has only one measure word, that is, "一." For example:*

一片嘈杂　一片混乱　一片空白
一片欢腾　一片笑语　一片议论
一片灯光　一片光明　一片阳光
一片红色　一片心意　一片真心
一片深情　一片忠诚　一片新气象

píng 瓶

用法 Usage：

用于计量瓶装的东西（容器量词），可以儿化。*A measure word for containers, it is applied to things kept in a bottle. It often goes with "儿." For example:*

一瓶果汁　一瓶牛奶　一瓶啤酒
一瓶胶水　一瓶香水　一瓶药水
一瓶咖啡　一瓶白糖　一瓶奶粉

qī 期

用法 Usage：

用于分时间阶段、分期事物或活动。*Used to describe things published or activities held regularly, as in:*

一期杂志　一期刊物　一期毕业生
一期学员　两期夏令营　一期培训

qún 群

用法 Usage：

1. 用于成群的人。*Used to describe people in a crowd, as in:*

一群孩子　一群人　一群学生

2. 用于聚集在一起的动物。*Used to describe animals or insects staying together, as in:*

一群鸽子　一群蜜蜂　一群鸭子
一群马　　一群牛　　一群牲口
一群野兽

3. 用于自然界的山脉、岛屿。*Used to describe mountains and islands, as in:*

一群火山　一群山脉　一群小岛

shēn 身

用法 Usage：

1. 用于成套的服装（包括上衣、裤子或裙子等），一般可以儿化。*Used to describe sets of clothes, including coats, trousers, skirts, etc. Often it goes with "儿." For instance:*

一身（儿）新衣服　一身西服
一身中式衣服　　一身套裙

2. 用于雕像、塑像、画像等。*Used to talk about sculptures and paintings, as in:*

塑了六身佛像　数一数有多少身画像

说明 Notes：

如果"身"后面是具体的服装名称，"一身"相当于"一套"。"一身" *is equivalent to "一*

套" if it is followed by the specific name of clothes, as in:

一身红衣裤　一身白衣裙

shēng 声

用法 Usage：

用于声音发出的次数，数词多用"一"。*It is used to count the number of times a voice is made. Often, it goes with the numeral "一." For instance:*

一声喊叫　一声号令　喊了两声
哭了几声　问了一声　告诉他一声

shǒu 首

用法 Usage：

用于诗、词、歌曲的数量。*It is used to count the number of poems, songs and other musical pieces, as in:*

一首诗　　一首歌　　一首曲子
一首交响乐　唐诗三百首　外国名歌一百首

shù 束

用法 Usage：

1. 用于计量捆起来的东西。*Used to describe things bundled up, as in:*

一束稻草　一束鲜花　一束黑头发

2. 用于聚在一起、细长的光线等。*Used to describe shafts of light that are thin and long but stay together, as in:*

一束太阳光　一束灯光　一束亮光

shuāng 双

用法 Usage：

用于成对的东西。*Things that come in pairs, as in:*

一双眼睛　一双手　　一双脚
一双鞋　　一双袜子　三双筷子
两双手套

说明 Notes：

"对"和"双"的区别是：*The differences between "对" and "双" are as follows:*

1. "对"用于按性别（异性）、左右、正反等配对的人、动物、具体的事物或抽象的事物，使用范围比较广。"双"着重用于左右对称的肢体、器官以及固定成双的物品。*"对" refers to people, animals, things concrete or abstract that are paired together according to sex (male or female), left or right, positive or negative. It covers a fairly large scope. "双" is mainly applied to arms, legs, organs being symmetric or things that always come in pairs, as in:*

一双眼睛　一双手　一双脚　一双鞋
一双袜子

2. 用"对"或"双"还受到语言区域性习惯使用的选择。如西北地区就有"一双男女"的用法。使用性物品可以用"对"，也可以用"双"，如"一双/对袜子、一双/对筷子"等。*Whether to use "对" or "双" is partly a choice of habit as far as the area where people speak the language is concerned. In northwest China, for instance, people would say "一双男女." For articles for daily use, "对" and "双" can both be used, as in "一双/对袜子，一双/对筷子."*

sōu 艘

用法 Usage：

用于船只、军舰的数量，多用于较大的船只。*Used in counting the number of ships or warships, both of which are large in size, as in:*

一艘海轮　一艘货轮　一艘军舰
一艘潜艇　一艘航空母舰

说明 Notes：

1. "艘"是船只的总称，后借用为量词。*"艘" is the general term for ships. It is now borrowed to serve as a measure word.*

2. "艘""只""条"都可以用于船的数量。"只"和"条"多用于小船的数量。*"艘," "只," and "条" could all be applied when talking about ships, but "只" and "条" are preferred when they are small in size.*

suì 岁

用法 Usage：

用于年龄的单位。The unit name for telling how old one is, as in:

三岁的孩子　老人已经七十岁了。

说明 Notes：

"岁"和"年"不同："年"是计量时间的，"岁"是计量年龄的。"岁" differs from "年" in that "年" is used to count the time while "岁" is used to tell how old one is.

suǒ 所

用法 Usage：

1. 用于计量房屋的单位。Used in counting the number of houses, as in:

一所别墅　一所房子　一所住宅

2. 用于计量学校、医院等单位。Used in counting the number of schools, hospitals, etc., as in:

一所机关　一所学校　一所医院
一所教堂　一所寺庙

tái 台

用法 Usage：

1. 用于舞台上正常标准、完整演出的戏剧或节目。Used to describe the formal performance of an opera or other items on stage, as in:

一台歌舞　一台话剧　一台节目
一台京剧　一台精彩的演出

2. 用于某些机器、设备。Used to talk about some machines and devices, as in:

一台冰箱　一台电脑　一台收音机
一台打字机　一台洗衣机　一台电视机
一台机器　一台发动机　一台拖拉机

说明 Notes：

1. "台"原意是高而平的建筑物。用为量词，被用的机器、设备相对有大与平的形状特点。The original meaning of "台" is a tall but flat building. As a measure word, it refers to machines or devices that are big and flat.

2. "台"用在演出上，是从舞台的角度着眼，表示一台完整的、按规定时间中有一定要求的节目演出。演出可以是只有一出完整的戏剧，也可以是折子戏等一些不同剧种的节目组成。When applied to stage performance, "台" refers to a complete item that must come up to certain standards within a certain period of time. But the performance could be either a full play or the collection of short items from different plays or even different genres of opera.

tān 摊

用法 Usage：

1. 用于成片的液体。Used to describe liquid that extends over a space, as in:

一摊水　一摊血　一摊油

2. 用于细软容易铺开的东西。Used to talk about things that are soft and thin, and can be stretched over a certain area, as in:

一摊细泥　一摊泥水

tàng 趟

用法 Usage：

1. 用于往返、来去的次数。相当于"次""回"。An equivalent of "次" or "回," it means the number of trips that are made, as in:

回去一趟　来一趟　还有一趟车
白跑一趟

2. 用于武术的一套或一段动作。Used to describe a whole set of martial arts (wushu) or just a section of it, as in:

耍一趟剑　练一趟拳

3. 用于条形或排列成行的东西。Things lined up in a strip of land or area, as in:

水果摊占了半趟街。　地上有两趟脚印。

说明 Notes：

"趟""次""回"都能用于交通工具来回或人行走的数量。"趟，""次，" and "回" can all

be used to describe the number of trips made by vehicles or pedestrians.

它们的区别是：They differ as follows:

1."趟""次""回"都能用于行走的数量。"趟"，"次" and "回" all may be used to describe the number of trips.

2."回"可以用于行走数量，不能用于交通工具的运行数量。"回" may be used to talk about the number of walks that are made, but it cannot be used to describe the number of trips made by trains or buses.

3.用于交通工具火车时，"次"指具体的车次。"趟"不是。When applied to the train as a means of transport, "次" specifically means the train number. "趟" doesn't carry that meaning.

tào 套

用法 Usage：

1.用于搭配成组的器具、衣类、书籍及其他东西。Used to talk about devices, clothes, books, etc. that are paired off, as in:

一套茶具　一套唱片　一套画片
一套邮票　一套课本　一套衣服
一套家具　一套沙发　一套房间
一套机器　一套设备

2.用于计量机构、制度、方法、能力、练习、试卷等。Used when measuring an institution, system, method, ability, or language, as in:

一套本领　一套方法　一套经验
一套机构　一套技术　一套管理制度
一套听说读写练习

3.跟指示词连用，表示褒义的或贬义的某种方法。Used either as a method of praise or criticism when it goes with a demonstrative pronoun, as in:

你这两套我们都熟悉了。
那一套程序不错。
没想到他还有那么一套。

tiáo 条

用法 Usage：

1.用于长条形的、细长的东西。Used in counting the number of things that are thin and long in shape, as in:

一条床单　一条裤子　一条领带
一条项链　一条香烟　一条道路
一条缝儿　一条大江　一条小河
一条大街

2.用于与人有关的事物。Used in counting the number of things related to human beings, as in:

一条腿　　一条心　　一条人命
一条好汉

3.用于某些外形细长的动物、植物。Used in counting the number of animals, insects or plants that are thin and long, as in:

一条虫子　一条鱼　　一条狗
一条狼　　一条黄瓜　一条长葫芦

4.用于分事项的事物。Used to talk about things that are itemized, as in:

一条新闻　一条广告　一条纪律
一条建议　两条标语　一条路线
一条命令　一条线索　一条出路
三条意见

tóu 头

用法 Usage：

1.用于比较大个的家畜和野兽。Used in counting the number large animals, domestic or wild, as in:

一头驴　　一头牛　　一头骡子
一头牲口　一头狮子　一头野兽

2.用于某些块茎蔬菜的数量。Used in counting the number of vegetables with a tuber, as in:

一头蒜　　一头洋葱

3.用于在头部的具体或抽象的东西。Used to talk about something related to the head, it can be either concrete or abstract, as in:

一头汗　　一头雾水

tuán 团

用法 Usage：

1. 用于成团的东西。*Used to talk about a ball-like thing that is circular in shape, as in:*

一团废纸　一团毛线　一团电线
一团白面

2. 用于某些抽象事物，数词只限于"一"。*Used to talk about abstract things, it has only one numeral, that is, "一" to describe it. For example:*

一团和气　一团漆黑　心里一团火
心里一团糟

wèi 位

用法 Usage：

1. 用于人（含敬意的）。*Showing respect when used to talk about people, as in:*

一位顾客　一位客人　一位经理
一位画家　一位老师　一位学者
一位教授　一位领导　一位专家

2. 用于计算数位。*Used to count the digit number, as in:*

多位数乘法　两位数加法　三位数
小数点以下三位

说明 Notes：

"位""名""个"都可以用于人。"位，""名，" and "个" *can all be used to talk about people.*

它们的区别是："位"表示尊敬。"名"多用于书面语。"个"多用语一般场合和口语。*Their difference is as follows: Their difference is that "位" shows respect, "名" is mostly used in written Chinese, and "个" is used for oral Chinese and ordinary occasions.*

xià 下

用法 Usage：

1. 用于动作的次数。*Used to describe the number of an action, as in:*

来一下　跳了一下　敲了三下门
打了他三下

2. 用在"两""几"后面，表示本领技能等。*Placed after "两" and "几," it indicates skills in doing a thing, as in:*

他做中国菜有两下。
他有几下中国功夫。

3. 用在动词后面，在不同的语境下，表示尝试，或者表示时间很短，或者表示事情动作很简单、很容易，数词限于"一"。*Placed after verbs, it means differently in different contexts: showing an attempt to do something, indicating time is very short, saying that the thing is simple and easy to do. Only one numeral, that is, "一," can go with it, as in:*

穿一下　　尝一下　　唱一下
听一下　　停一下　　来坐一下
我看一下　关一下门　去一下就可以了

说明 Notes：

"下"也作"下子"，用法相同。*"下" and "下子" mean the same thing and are used the same way.*

xiàng 项

用法 Usage：

用于分项目的事物。*Used to talk about itemized things, as in:*

一项任务　三项纪律　两项决定
各项条件

xiē 些

用法 Usage：

1. 用于人或事物不定量的数量。数词一般限于"一"。*Expressing an indefinite number of people and of things, it goes with only one numeral, that is, "一." For example:*

一些学生　一些朋友　一些问题
一些日子　一些事情

2. 用在形容词（有时带动词）后面，表示稍微的意思，描述事物的情况或形状。*Following an adjective, sometimes along with a verb, to mean "a little," it is used to describe a situation or the shape of a thing, as in:*

　　好一些了　容易一些　多吃一些　少穿些　快些洗　简单一些说

yàng 样

用法 Usage：

　　用于表示事物的种类。*It is used to mean different kinds of a thing (or things), as in:*

　　七样蔬菜　四样点心　各样水果
　　样样功课都很好

说明 Notes：

　　"样"与"种"都用于表示事物的种类。"样"多用于口头，在意义上偏重于外在式样的不同。"种"是表示动物、植物门类的科学术语，通用于口头与书面，在意义上偏重于内在质地、特性的不同。*Both "样" and "种" are used to mean different kinds of a thing (or things). Their difference is this: "样" is used more in oral Chinese, and it tends to focus on different appearances. However, as a scientific term in the classification of animals and plants, "种" focuses on the differences in the internal quality or special features. It is used both in written and oral Chinese nowadays.*

yè 页

用法 Usage：

　　用于书本、刊物中一张纸的一面。*Used to talk about one page of a sheet in a book or journal, as in:*

　　这篇文章有二十六页。
　　请翻到三十六页。

说明 Notes：

　　"打开新的一页"意思是推陈出新，从头做起，有个新的开始。所以不能说："*打开新的二页。""*打开新的三页。"*"打开新的一页 (Open a new page)" is an idiom meaning to weed through the old to bring forth the new, or simply, to make a new beginning. Therefore, we cannot say:"*打开新的二页，""*打开新的三页。"*

yuán 元

用法 Usage：

　　原指中国的本位货币金元、银元（也作圆），现在用为钱币的数量。*Originally it meant the standard unit of Chinese currency, that is, gold dollar and silver dollar (also written as "圆"); it is used to denote the amount of money today, as in:*

　　六元　一百元　二十万元

zhǎn 盏

用法 Usage：

　　用于灯的数量。*It is used to describe the number of lamps, as in:*

　　一盏台灯　五盏路灯　一盏 LED 灯

zhāng 张

用法 Usage：

　　1.用于可以延伸、展开成平面的东西。*Something that can be stretched out or extended to be a smooth surface, as in:*

　　一张纸　一张地图　两张画
　　两张照片　三张飞机票

　　2.用于床、桌子等有平面的家具。*Used to talk about furniture with a flat surface, as in:*

　　一张床　一张桌子　三张木板

　　3.用于人的脸和可以开合的嘴。*Describing a human face or a mouth that can open or close, as in:*

　　一张笑脸　那张哭脸真难看
　　家里有两张吃饭的嘴。

　　4.用于可以开合的东西。*Something that can open and close, as in:*

　　一张弓　一张渔网

zhāng 章

用法 Usage：

用于书籍、诗文、乐曲、法规的段落。 *Meaning a chapter or paragraph in a book, poem, law or rule or musical work, as in:*

这本书一共十六章。
这支乐曲有三章。
这首长诗分为四章。
约法三章。

zhèn 阵

用法 Usage：

1. 用于表示事情、动作经过的段落（多指突发的、持续时间比较短的）。 *Used to denote a period in the development of a thing or an action, usually referring to sudden events lasting a short period of time, as in:*

刮了一阵风　下了几阵雨　一阵剧痛
一阵掌声　　一阵欢呼

2. 用于动作持续的一小段时间。 *Used to describe an action that lasted a short period of time, as in:*

等了一阵　忙了一阵　哭了一阵
笑了一阵

zhī 支

用法 Usage：

1. 用于杆状的东西，相当于"枝"。 *An equivalent to "枝," it means something in the shape of a pole, as in:*

一支笔　一支箭　一支香烟　一支笛子

2. 用于歌曲或乐曲。相当于"首"。 *An equivalent to "首," it is used to talk about a song or a piece of music, as in:*

一支曲子　一支歌

3. 用于队伍和舰队。 *Meaning an armed force, a rescue team, a fire brigade, or a fleet, as in:*

一支军队　一支救助队　一支救火队
一支舰队

4. 用于分支的棉纱（粗细不同，支数多少不同）或毛线。 *Used to talk about cotton or wool yarn (whether crude or fine depends on the number of yarns). For example:*

一斤毛线有十支。
三十二支棉纱　六十支棉纱

5. 用于电灯的光度。 *Used to talk about the electrical lights giving out strong or weak light, as in:*

六十支光的灯泡
十二支光的 LED 很亮。

说明 Notes：

"支"和"首"都可以用于歌曲或乐曲。 *Both "支" 和 "首" can be used to talk about songs or other musical pieces.*

它们的区别是："支"着重于外形绵长的角度；"首"着重于歌曲或乐曲内容完整一体的角度。 *Their difference is that "支" focuses on the work being long in appearance while "首" emphasizes its content being complete.*

zhī 只

用法 Usage：

1. 用于动物（多指飞禽走兽和昆虫，或者是不能用匹、头、条等量词的动物）。 *Used to talk about the number of animals, mostly birds, insects and animals, but not those animals that cannot go with measure words such as "匹," "头," or "条." For example:*

一只鸡　两只小鸟　三只老虎
一只兔子　四只蝴蝶

2. 用于人或动物的某些器官。 *Used to talk about some organs found in human beings or animals, as in:*

两只手　两只耳朵　一只眼睛
一只脚趾

3. 用于某些用来装置东西的器具或某些成对用品中的一个。 *Used to talk about some devices to keep things or one of a pair of things*

that usually come in a set of two, as in:

一只箱子　一只口袋　一只书包

一只袜子　一只手套

4. 用于船只。*Used to talk about ships*, as in:

一只小船　一只游艇

zhī 枝

用法 Usage：

1. 用于杆状的东西。*Used to describe something in the shape of a pole*, as in:

一枝铅笔　两枝毛笔　三枝蜡烛

四枝枪　一枝箭

2. 用于带枝的花朵。*Used to describe flowers growing on the same branch*, as in:

三枝玫瑰花　一枝菊花

说明 Notes：

"支"和"枝"都可以用于杆状的东西。*Both "支" and "枝" can be used to talk about something in the shape of a pole.*

它们的区别是，"枝"没有"支"的其他意义和用法。*Their difference is that "枝" cannot be used in other meanings and usages of "支".*

zhǒng 种

用法 Usage：

1. 表示种类，用于人或任何事物内部一致而对外有区别的事物。*Meaning "kind" of a thing, it can be used to talk about anyone or anything that is the same inside but different in outside appearance*, as in:

两种人　十几种蔬菜　桃花有很多种

几十万种商品

2. 用于跟同类事物有所区别（多用于抽象事物）的经历、感受心情及其他。*Used to describe an experience or feeling(s) or other such things that are somewhat different from things of the same kind. Mostly it is used of abstract things*, as in:

一种痛苦的感受　一种难得的经历

一种特别的现象　一种情绪

zhū 株

用法 Usage：

用于树。*Used to talk about the number of trees*, as in:

几株桃树　三株柳树

说明 Notes：

"株"和"棵"都可以用于树。*Both "株" 和 "棵" can be used to talk about trees.*

它们的区别是："株"多用于书面语；"棵"多用于口语。*Their only difference is that "株" appears more in written Chinese while "棵" appears more in oral Chinese.*

zhuāng 桩

用法 Usage：

用于事情，相当于"件"。*Like "件," it is used to talk about the number of things*, as in:

一桩心事　一桩大事　一桩买卖

zhuàng 幢

用法 Usage：

用于房屋，多指楼房。*Used to talk about buildings, often with more than one story*, as in:

一幢高楼　两幢楼房　一幢花园别墅

zuò 座

用法 Usage：

用于较大或固定的自然景物或人工建筑。*It is used to describe fairly large or fixed natural scenery or artificial buildings*, as in:

一座山　一座高楼　一座水库

一座桥　一座灯塔　一座铜像

（共 109 个量词 *109 measure words in all*）

主要参考文献

1. 《汉语国际教育用音节汉字词汇等级划分》课题组编,《汉语国际教育用音节汉字词汇等级划分》(国家标准·应用解读本),北京:北京语言大学出版社,2010年。
2. 中国社会科学院语言研究所词典编辑室编,《现代汉语词典》(第7版),北京:商务印书馆,2016年。
3. 商务印书馆辞书研究中心编,《应用汉语词典》,北京:商务印书馆,2000年。
4. 朱丽云主编,《实用对外汉语重点难点词语教学词典》,北京:北京大学出版社,2009年(2016年6月第三次印刷)。

References

1. *The Graded Chinese Syllables, Characters and Words for the Application of Teaching Chinese to the Speakers of Other Languages (National Standard: Application and Interpretation)* (Beijing Language & Culture University Press, 2010)
2. *A Dictionary of Modern Chinese*, Seventh Edition, ed. The Editorial Department of Dictionary Editing of the China National Social Sciences Academy (The Commercial Press, 2016)
3. *A Dictionary of Applied Chinese*, ed. The Dictionary Research Center of the Commercial Press (The Commercial Press, 2000)
4. *A Practical Dictionary for the Teaching of Important and Difficult Words to Foreign Learners*, ed. Zhu Liyuan *et al* (The Peking University Press, 2009, reprinted in 2016)

图书在版编目(CIP)数据

汉英双解对外汉语常用重点难点词语实用词典/朱丽云,林珍珍,钱炜主编.—上海：复旦大学出版社,2024.6
ISBN 978-7-309-16087-1

Ⅰ.①汉… Ⅱ.①朱… ②林… ③钱… Ⅲ.①汉语-对外汉语教学-双解词典-汉、英 Ⅳ.①H195-61

中国版本图书馆 CIP 数据核字(2022)第 007751 号

汉英双解对外汉语常用重点难点词语实用词典
朱丽云　林珍珍　钱　炜　主编
责任编辑/曹珍芬

复旦大学出版社有限公司出版发行
上海市国权路 579 号　邮编：200433
网址：fupnet@fudanpress.com　http://www.fudanpress.com
门市零售：86-21-65102580　团体订购：86-21-65104505
出版部电话：86-21-65642845
江阴市机关印刷服务有限公司

开本 787 毫米×1092 毫米　1/16　印张 48.25　字数 1 235 千字
2024 年 6 月第 1 版
2024 年 6 月第 1 版第 1 次印刷

ISBN 978-7-309-16087-1/H・3146
定价：129.00 元

如有印装质量问题，请向复旦大学出版社有限公司出版部调换。
版权所有　侵权必究